Being and Nothingness

First published in French in 1943, Jean-Paul Sartre's *L'Être et le Néant* is one of the greatest philosophical works of the twentieth century. In it, Sartre offers nothing less than a brilliant and radical account of the human condition. The English philosopher and novelist Iris Murdoch wrote to a friend of "the excitement—I remember nothing like it since the days of discovering Keats and Shelley and Coleridge." This new translation, the first for over sixty years, makes this classic work of philosophy available to a new generation of readers.

What gives our lives significance, Sartre argues in *Being and Nothingness*, is not preestablished for us by God or nature but is something for which we ourselves are responsible. At the heart of this view are Sartre's radical conceptions of consciousness and freedom. Far from being an internal, passive container for our thoughts and experiences, human consciousness is constantly projecting itself into the outside world and imbuing it with meaning. Combining this with the unsettling view that human existence is characterized by radical freedom and the inescapability of choice, Sartre introduces us to a cast of ideas and characters that are part of philosophical legend: anguish; the "bad faith" of the memorable waiter in the café; sexual desire; and the "look" of the other, brought to life by Sartre's famous description of someone looking through a keyhole.

Above all, by arguing that we alone create our values and that human relationships are characterized by hopeless conflict, Sartre paints a stark and controversial picture of our moral universe and one that resonates strongly today.

This new translation includes an insightful Translator's Introduction, helpful discussion of key decisions, numerous explanatory footnotes, an index, and a Foreword by Richard Moran, Brian D. Young Professor of Philosophy, Harvard University, USA.

Jean-Paul Sartre (1905–1980) was one of the great philosophers of the twentieth century and a renowned novelist, dramatist, and political activist. As a teenager Sartre was drawn to philosophy after reading Henri Bergson's *Time and Free Will*. He passed the *agrégation* in philosophy at the École Normale Supérieure in Paris in 1929. His first novel *La Nausée*, which Sartre considered one of his best works, was published in 1938. Sartre served as a meteorologist in the French army before being captured by German troops in 1940, spending nine months as a prisoner of war. He continued to write during his captivity and, after his release, published his great trilogy of novels, Les Chemins de la Liberté. In 1964, Sartre was awarded the Nobel Prize in Literature but declined it. During the events of 1968 he was arrested for civil disobedience but swiftly released by President Charles de Gaulle, who allegedly said, "One does not arrest Voltaire." He died on April 15, 1980, in Paris, his funeral attracting an enormous crowd of up to 50,000 mourners. He is buried in the Cimetière du Montparnasse in Paris.

Translated by Sarah Richmond, University College London, UK.

"Sarah Richmond has now produced a meticulous, elegant translation."
—Jonathan Rée, *London Review of Books*

"Sarah Richmond's superb new translation . . . is supplemented by a wealth of explanatory and analytical material [and] a particularly detailed and insightful set of notes on the translation. . . . The first translation of *Being and Nothingness* was a major academic achievement that has influenced thought across a range of disciplines for more than sixty years. This new edition has the potential to be at least as influential over the coming decades."
—Jonathan Webber, *Mind*

"The publication of this excellent new English translation of *L'Être et le néant* is a welcome addition to the library of Sartre scholarship. . . . There is every chance that it will also attract nonspecialist readers to Sartre's early philosophy and will thus importantly contribute to keeping existentialist thought alive in a context and era chronically bereft of genuine philosophical enlightenment."
—Sam Coombes, *French Studies*

"Translating such a book is manifestly a labor of love—it was as much for Barnes as for Richmond, and generations of Anglophone Sartre scholars remain grateful to Barnes, even if, as I expect (and hope) it will, Richmond's careful, thoughtful, and thought-provoking translation becomes the standard one for use by students as well as professionals."
—Katherine J. Morris, *European Journal of Philosophy*

"Sarah Richmond's marvelously clear and thoughtful new translation brings Sartre's rich, infuriating, endlessly fertile masterpiece to a whole new English-language readership."
—Sarah Bakewell, author of *At the Existentialist Café*

"Sartre's philosophy will always be important. *Being and Nothingness* is not an easy read, but Sarah Richmond makes it accessible in English to the general reader. Her translation is exemplary in its clarity."
—Richard Eyre

Being and Nothingness

An Essay in
Phenomenological Ontology

Jean-Paul Sartre

Translated by Sarah Richmond

Washington Square Press/Atria
New York • London • Toronto • Sydney • New Delhi

Washington Square Press
An Imprint of Simon & Schuster, Inc.
1230 Avenue of the Americas
New York, NY 10020

First Washington Square Press/Atria Paperback edition September 2021

WASHINGTON SQUARE PRESS/ATRIA PAPERBACK and colophon are trademarks of Simon & Schuster, Inc.

For information about special discounts for bulk purchases, please contact Simon & Schuster Special Sales at 1-866-506-1949 or business@simonandschuster.com.

The Simon & Schuster Speakers Bureau can bring authors to your live event. For more information or to book an event, contact the Simon & Schuster Speakers Bureau at 1-866-248-3049 or visit our website at www.simonspeakers.com.

Manufactured in the United States of America

10 9 8 7 6 5 4 3 2 1

Library of Congress Cataloging-in-Publication Data has been applied for.

ISBN 978-1-9821-0544-0
ISBN 978-1-9821-0545-7 (pbk)
ISBN 978-1-9821-0546-4 (ebook)

CONTENTS

FOREWORD

Richard Moran

With this new translation by Sarah Richmond, Sartre's major work *L'Être et le Néant* is available to the English-speaking world as never before. Not only is the translation itself a great improvement in accuracy and readability on the Hazel Barnes version published in 1956 but the Translator's Introduction and Notes on the Translation illuminate this difficult text for both earlier readers of Sartre and those encountering this book for the first time. The inadequacies of the Barnes translation have been widely recognized for a long time, but it is always difficult to launch a new translation of a well-known work that is still selling, and in this case the scope of the task was especially daunting. The world of philosophy in English has reason to be grateful to Richmond and the people at Routledge for seeing this through.

*** *** ***

Jean-Paul Sartre was born in 1905 in Paris. He had already published a few short stories when he entered the École Normale Supérieure in 1924, where he met Simone de Beauvoir, who remained a companion for life and whose influence on *Being and Nothingness*, while difficult to determine, was no doubt considerable. Like most young French philosophers at the time, he was influenced by the work of Henri Bergson and by the neo-Kantianism represented by Léon Brunschvicg, but he had already conceived for himself the dream of a manner of writing that would be literary and philosophical at once. It was in 1932 that he had the famous meeting in a café with Raymond Aron, when Aron was back visiting Paris during the year he was spending at the Institut Français in Berlin, learning about the new philosophy called "phenomenology." As Beauvoir tells the story in The Prime of Life,

> We ordered the specialty of the house, apricot cocktails. Aron said, pointing to his glass: "You see, my dear fellow, if you were a phenom-enologist, you could talk about this cocktail glass and make philosophy out of it." Sartre turned pale with emotion at this. Here was just the thing he had been longing to achieve for years—to describe objects just as he saw and touched them, and extract philosophy from the process.[1]

Aron helped Sartre obtain a fellowship in Berlin for the following year, where he immersed himself in Husserl and Heidegger, and wrote his critique of Husserl, The Transcendence of the Ego, and the bulk of his first novel Nausea (published respectively in 1937 and 1938). Both works attracted considerable attention, but Sartre's budding fame was cut short by the German invasion of Poland in 1939 and the general mobilization in France. Sartre was called up and was captured by the Germans in 1940 and transferred to a prisoner-of-war camp in Trier. He does not describe his time there as having been harsh, and he seems to have spent most of his days teaching philosophy to fellow prisoners and working on the volumi-nous notebooks in which he sketched out the plan for his big book Being and Nothingness. After managing to get himself released in 1941, he returned to occupied Paris, where he sought unsuccessfully to form a resistance group independent of the Gaullists and the Communists. For the remain-der of the war he was by his own account an "intellectual resistant," and concentrated on finishing his magnum opus. It was published by Gallimard in 1943, at 722 pages weighing precisely one kilogram, which

---

1 Simone de Beauvoir (1962), The Prime of Life, trans. Peter Green (Harmondsworth: Penguin), p. 135.

(if Jean Paulhan is to be believed) helped with the initial sales, since the book was being used as a weight measure at home when the normal brass weights had been confiscated by the German authorities.

What sort of book is this, and what is its philosophical importance now? Any account of its importance and genuine brilliance has to come to grips with the several different forms of obstacle to its reception today, both those intrinsic to the book and those stemming from the contemporary intellectual context. Part of the problem is simply Sartre's own fame and the cultural saturation that was part of the reception of "existentialism" in France from the beginning. In the Paris of the 1950s something called "existentialism" was not merely a school of philosophy but an entire lifestyle, encompassing literature, music, film, and a succession of political stances. This broad influence was amplified by the fact that, in France as elsewhere, the postwar years were also the beginning of the first age of mass media and a new prominence of "youth culture" in European and American life. Sartre's own personality as *provocateur* and *intellectuel engagé* lent itself to this context. He was on television almost as soon as television came to France, and was perhaps the first major philosopher to have his own radio show. In the decades following the war in France he was rarely without an opinion or an opportunity for publishing it. And of course he threw himself into the various political crises of his day, creating a certain notoriety and gaining enemies among both the Catholic right and the Communist left in France. The result of this cultural saturation is that today everyone is entitled to an opinion about Sartrean existentialism, however minimal one's exposure to his writing may be. This presence as cultural reference is itself unusual for a philosopher and is an aspect of how his enduring fame is maintained even by his detractors. All philosophers wax and wane in their influence, and most can enjoy a posthumous existence in comfortable obscurity, but Sartre stands out among the notable twentieth-century philosophers for the extent to which he is still invoked for condescension, seen less as a philosopher than as a provocation to be put down both in intellectual circles and in the popular media.

Another obstacle is the sheer length and the style of *Being and Nothingness*. It can be an impossible and infuriating text; one can only dream wistfully of what a ruthless editor might have been able to do with its bulk. The tone is often abrupt and peremptory, with little or no explanation given to key philosophical terms, whether German or French. In a manner that we have become used to among certain philosophers, it is as though the presumed audience for the work could only be those for whom such things as the distinction between "the phenomenon of being and the being of the phenomenon" is always already quite familiar, and we are being invited to appreciate the unexpected spin the brilliant author is putting on these old ideas. It is extremely uneven as a piece of philosophical writing. Sometimes we do indeed get what look very much like arguments—powerful ones—and other times Sartre puts his powers of description to genuinely illuminating use, but too often we get bold declarations, invidious distinctions, and a fondness for paradoxical formulation that seems to know no bounds.

Sartre himself paid a price for the difficulty of access of *Being and Nothingness*, in the fact that readers who were curious but not prepared to take on the 722 pages of the original had available to them a much shorter Sartrean text—a pamphlet, really—called *Existentialism Is a Humanism*, something dashed off and never intended for publication in the first place. In October 1945, in the early months of the Liberation, Sartre was persuaded by a friend to give what was to be a small public lecture on the new philosophy at the Club Maintenant. It turned into a huge event, with an overflow crowd and people being carried out after having fainted from the heat and overcrowding. Sartre spoke without notes. To help pay for the rental of the hall and the damage to the premises, the organizer prevailed upon Sartre to agree to publish a version of his remarks for sale, which he agreed to. As a text it is full of crudities, misstatements, and willful exaggerations for effect, and soon became far and away the most famous and widely read piece he ever wrote. It is still commonly cited as representative of Sartrean existentialism by philosophers who should know better. A final obstacle to be mentioned is that so much of French thought since the 1960s and 1970s has proceeded from an assumed repudiation of Sartre. *Being and Nothingness* is, among other things, the last great expression of the "philosophy of the subject" that later French thought has expended so much energy in dismantling and decentering. Both structuralist (originally in the person of Claude Lévi-Strauss) and post-structuralist thinkers such as Michel Foucault, Jacques Derrida, and Jacques Lacan begin by repudiating the Cartesian starting point of so many of the reflections in *Being and Nothingness*, as well as Sartre's appropriation of phenomenology and early Heidegger.

All of this is further reason to welcome this new translation and the opportunity it gives readers in English to encounter this book with fresh eyes, for despite its flaws it is still one of the great and engaging texts of twentieth-century philosophy. It is a text to struggle with, yes, but when the writing is at its best it is rewarding and illuminating in ways that few major works of philosophy in the modern world can touch. Of course like any philosophical text it needs to be comprehended as a whole, but many of its famous sections (on bad faith, on the look of the Other, on various self-defeating strategies of love and desire, on freedom and responsibility, on the "existential psychoanalysis" of qualities) can be profitably read by themselves. Today it is easy to forget how daring this text is, and the different ways Sartre expanded the possible forms of philosophical writing. This new edition makes this available to a new generation of readers.

Different philosophers will have different reasons for engaging with *Being and Nothingness* today. From the perspective of the history of philosophy it may be read as a remarkably ambitious attempt to inherit the phenomenology of Husserl and the early work of Heidegger, in the context of a general metaphysical picture of the world and the place of human thought and action within it. Today one may be skeptical about the very idea of such a general metaphysical picture, and in particular the dualism of "being as such" and "nothingness," and yet still be impressed with the creative use to which it is put and how Sartre is able to begin from these bare categories to an analysis of the difference between the categories of ordinary objects ("being-in-itself") and the categories of human life ("being-for-itself"). Despite rumors to the contrary, the idea of "nothingness" here has little to do with despair or the contemplation of suicide. Rather, the idea of the negative is bound up with the most basic abilities to describe the world and pick out and discriminate objects themselves (Sartre never tires of alluding to Spinoza's formulation "*Omnis determinatio est negatio*"). At the same time the fundamental power of thought to negate, to assert difference, is also something that he seeks to derive from Husserl's basic thought about consciousness (itself an idea associated with Brentano): consciousness is pure relatedness to an object, which is to say something other than itself, something it is not. Consciousness just is this basic capacity for relatedness to the world and the distinguishing of itself from the world it is directed upon.

This assertion of difference is described as part of the "nihilating" action of consciousness, which enables Sartre to forge his unbreakable connection between consciousness (as "for-itself") and freedom, in action and in thought. For in the same way that a picture of the world as consisting purely of "positive reality" cannot account for the ability to grasp or even perceive the "negative" truth of, for instance, an object's being fragile (breakable but not broken), or different from another one, or no longer what it once was (not to mention Pierre's absence from the café), so understanding human action requires the "negative" modes of thought involved in being underway with an action not yet completed, and in the capacity to step back from or "posit one's freedom" with respect to one's currently constituted motives and one's past (one's "facticity"). The "stepping back" or "putting one's past out of play" is the same nihilating capacity of consciousness, the capacity to distinguish, hold oneself separate from the facticity of what the world has made of one so far, and raise the question for oneself of how one is to relate oneself to this positive reality from here on. It is along these lines that we can see that some of Sartre's most provocative formulations are no mere paradox-mongering: the human being "is what it is not" (in the sense that, as agent, I *am* my relation to my unrealized possibilities, the action I am embarked on but have not completed) and "is not what it is" (in the sense that in adopting the standpoint of freedom to my possibilities I posit my difference from my past and the facticities of my situation, which make up what I am so far).

Here as elsewhere Sartre's borrowings are as undeniable as the boldness and originality of his use of them. Are the notions of "negation," "nothingness," and "difference" being stretched here to do too many different kinds of work as we move from the more purely metaphysical structure of the world to the story of action and human subjectivity? No doubt that is a question one may and should press throughout the reading of Being and Nothingness, but what remains impressive is the richness and diversity of the phenomenon that Sartre manages in this way to bring into philosophical contact with each other, the new questions this orientation makes possible. The same vaulting ambition that takes him from the ancient Parmenidean problem of how there can be "thought about what is not," to the object-directedness of thought ("intentionality"), to a distinctive perspective on human freedom is also what helps us formulate new questions about how the appeal to freedom can be genuinely explanatory of human action, and how we should understand the relation between the intentionality of thought and the intentionality of action, and hence the understanding of action itself as a form of thought.

Being and Nothingness is not only about human freedom, it is a text that is plainly *obsessed* with the question of freedom and its meaning, and organizes all its many topics around it. In relation to freedom it is less concerned about solving the traditional problem of freedom and determinism and more concerned about understanding what is contained in the ordinary assumption of human freedom and the variety of ways it manifests itself. Part of Sartre's great originality here is in his drive to find the question of freedom not only in, say, the conditions for holding people accountable but virtually everywhere in human life, in the inescapability of some answer I give to how I relate myself to my past as well as my future, to the forms of intersubjectivity and what it is that is aimed at in seeking the desire or recognition of another person, in the conflicting demands of the first-person and third-person points of view in understanding oneself. What is sometimes criticized as the unboundedness of Sartre's conception of human freedom is a reflection of the fact that the place of freedom in his system is less that of a human capacity among others and more that of a principle of intelligibility of human affairs quite generally.

Sartre is of course a novelist and playwright as well as a philosopher, and part of the originality of Being and Nothingness as a piece of writing lies in the combination of an abstract and austere metaphysical picture with an essentially dramatic sense of the source of philosophical questions as they exhibit themselves in recognizable human situations. One of his great topics is that of the question of the forms of comprehensibility of human life, and of an individual human life taken as a whole (especially in his later books on Genet and Flaubert). He is properly and profitably struck by the contradictory demands we place on the comprehensibility of human life and action, and by the question of the priority of different forms of comprehensibility we demand of ourselves and others. The metaphysics of the in-itself and the for-itself, or the self-as-facticity and the self-as-transcendence, will have earned its philosophical keep if they are what bring into view and make available for thought what Sartre takes up in the sections of Being and Nothingness on bad faith, on the nature of shame and the self-consciousness that pertains to it, on the encounter with the Other through "the look," on the internal conflicts of love and desire.

Despite how long *Being and Nothingness* has been a looming presence on the philosophical scene, much of it is only recently getting the attention it deserves in the anglophone world. Sartre's long chapter on "The body" is one of the first extended philosophical meditations in the modern era on that meaning of one's identity with a certain living body, and is beginning to attract new attention today. And his reflections on the different forms of self-consciousness ("thetic" or "positional" versus "non-thetic" or "non-positional," as originally developed in his short work *The Transcendence of the Ego*) are entering into contemporary discussions on the nature of self-knowledge and the first-person point of view. In many ways, Sartre is as present on the scene as ever, but even in that presence we can see him still struggling with his fame, and his life and personality somehow continue to exert a fascination out of balance with attention to the works that are supposedly the reason for any special interest in the details of this man's life. With new biographies of Sartre appearing every few years, and words like "existential" being part of every pundit's vocabulary, this new translation makes this an opportune time to go back to the source and see what it's all about.

TRANSLATOR'S PREFACE TO THE US EDITION

Sarah Richmond

It's been more than three years since my translation of *Being and Nothingness* was first published, by Routledge, in the UK in the summer of 2018. I had hoped that North American readers might not have to wait so long, but a complicated situation involving rights ownership had first to be resolved. I'm delighted that the book is now available to a wider public.

A few revisions to the 2018 edition have been made. Spelling and punctuation have been Americanized. Sartre's imaginary character on p. 361, for example, now has a "flashlight" at his possible disposal, rather than a "torch," and a person who formerly walked on the "pavement" now finds himself on the "sidewalk." The new copyediting process has also allowed a number of typos from the original to be corrected, as well as a small number of errors that had come to my attention. I thank Peter Borland and Benjamin Holmes at Simon & Schuster for overseeing the production process.

Some further thanks are also due to the UK editors of the journal *Sartre Studies International*, John Gillespie and Katherine Morris, for publishing an excellent symposium on my translation in 2020 (volume 26, issue 1); and to the two contributing Sartre scholars, Matthew Eshleman and Adrian van den Hoven, for their careful and illuminating discussion, to which some of the recent corrections are owed. I gratefully acknowledge the helpful professional advice of my lawyer, Bernie Nyman, and the UK Society of Authors.

Last, a shout-out to Daniel Rothschild, my line manager in 2018, who generously marked the publication of this translation by organizing a celebratory, most happy event in the philosophy department at University College London.

Sarah Richmond
London
2021

NOTE ON ABBREVIATIONS

BN Jean-Paul Sartre, *Being and Nothingness* (unless otherwise stated, reference is to the present translation).

EN Jean-Paul Sartre (1943), *L'Être et le Néant* (Paris: Gallimard) (i.e., the original French text of *Being and Nothingness*).

EH Jean-Paul Sartre (1973), *Existentialism and Humanism*, trans. Philip Mairet (London: Methuen).

Note: The marginal pagination in the present translation corresponds to the pagination in the Gallimard Collection Tel edition of *L'Être et le Néant*, as published in 1976.

Footnotes: In the present translation, Sartre's notes have been labeled "Sartre's note" and those written by the translator labeled "TN" (Translator's Note).

Translator's Introduction

Sarah Richmond

L'Être et le Néant is widely and correctly regarded as Sartre's most important philosophical work, but it attracted little public attention when it first appeared in France in 1943. Perhaps we should not be surprised, as the Second World War was not yet over and the German Occupation was still in force in northern France. Today, the place of *Being and Nothingness* (hereafter BN)[1] within the canon of twentieth-century European philosophy is uncontested, and it is taught, read, and studied across the globe.

In this Introduction my primary aim is to describe BN's philosophical impact so far, focusing especially on France and the English-speaking world. As a great deal of Sartre criticism and exegesis is now available, I will only briefly survey the content of the text. Instead I offer an overview of its reception, to provide the reader with some background to my translation, produced three-quarters of a century later. For remarks about the practical task of translating it, challenges it has posed, and my reasons for some of my decisions, see the Notes on the Translation.

At the time of BN's first publication, Sartre had returned to teaching philosophy in the French secondary school system, after an uneventful stint of military service (his poor eyesight meant he was exempt from active combat) and a period spent in a German prisoner-of-war camp. Although

---

1 I will use EN only when the reference is necessarily to the French version of the text.

Sartre had published some impressive work in the 1930s, he was not yet well-known, and his reputation as a writer was owed primarily to his 1938 novel (*La Nausée*), some short stories and plays (*Les Mouches* was first staged in Paris in 1943), book reviews (mostly of fiction) published in various periodicals, and other journalism. A year later, after Pathé had commissioned him to write the screenplay for a feature film (*Typhus*, which was never made), Sartre believed he could earn a living as a full-time writer and gave up his teaching post. Not long after that—following his legendary public lecture (subsequently translated as EH) in which Sartre presented a simplified version of his philosophy to a packed audience in Paris in 1945—he became a national figure. By the 1960s Sartre's further writings, his association with Simone de Beauvoir, his appearances around the world, and his numerous political interventions had also made him an international figure, a "public intellectual" who is frequently described as the most famous philosopher of the twentieth century.

BN presents itself as a traditional, scholarly, and comprehensive work of philosophy. Sartre had not yet detached himself from the values of academia, and he adopts the persona of a distinguished professor who has the entire Western philosophical corpus at his fingertips. "Modern thought," he tells us in his opening sentence, has "[reduced] the existent to the series of appearances that manifest it." How, if at all, do statements of this highly abstract kind bear any relation to the doctrines and slogans that we associate with existentialist philosophy?

In fact, as readers are sometimes surprised to discover, the term "existentialist" is applied only retrospectively to the philosophy of BN, and it does not figure in the text. It does figure importantly in EH, where Sartre sums existentialism up quite simply in the famous claim that "existence comes before essence." To explain this claim, Sartre (an atheist) contrasts it with a religious conception, according to which we are created by God. Had God created us, Sartre argues, our essence *would* precede our existence, as it would be determined by God's intentions. But there is no such thing as human nature in a godless world, where "Man is nothing else but what he makes of himself." This contrast seems to suggest that existentialism is incompatible with religious belief, which would conflict with Sartre's acknowledgment in the same lecture that Christian existentialism also exists, but we will not pursue this here.

The French title of EH—*L'Existentialisme est un Humanisme*—asserts the thesis that Sartre will be defending for his audience (and, once it was published, for his readers). *Being and Nothingness* is rather more obscure, and its subtitle—*An Essay in Phenomenological Ontology*—is also unlikely to help anyone without a philosophical training. Ontology is the philosophical study of being—or of what exists, of what *is*—in the most general sense, and Sartre's fundamental claim is elegantly condensed within his title. In order to account for *being*, Sartre is saying, we need also to acknowledge *nothingness* (or non-being). The relationship between this ontological project and the better-known "existentialist" tenets that are associated with Sartre is in fact straightforward: the former provides the theoretical underpinnings for the latter. Nothingness explains why we humans are radically free, just as Sartre's account in BN of the interpersonal orientation he calls "being for the Other" explains why our interpersonal relationships are likely to be hellish.

The philosophy advanced in BN was of course attacked from the outset, in the first instance—and before it had been translated into any other languages—by Sartre's fellow French intellectuals. Indeed, just two years after the publication of EN in France, Sartre announces in EH his intention to defend existentialism against several "reproaches." Sartre is not too bothered by the censure of the "Christians," for whom atheistic existentialism is incompatible with morality: the points Sartre goes on to make in the lecture are supposed to refute that claim. He would have been more troubled by the attacks from the political left. In a discussion of EH that was organized specifically for Sartre to face his opponents, the Communist activist Pierre Naville raised several criticisms that have often been repeated since. (Indeed, only a year or so later, Herbert Marcuse's review of BN (Marcuse 1947) sounded a similar hostile Marxist note.) For Naville, Sartre's rejection of "human nature" was an illusion; rather than abolishing the idea, Sartre was regressively proposing an alternative to it, in the guise of human freedom. In more explicitly political terms, Naville also accused Sartre of "resurrecting liberalism" (Sartre 1973: 60).

The next most significant date in the history of BN is probably 1956, insofar as Sartre's international reputation as a philosopher depends— at least in the English-speaking world—on the first (and until now the only) English translation of EN, published in the US in that year. It was translated by Hazel Barnes (1915–2008), a Classics scholar at the University of Colorado, who took on the task because she admired Sartre's philosophy and wanted to make it available to the anglophone world. Barnes's own work was also important in acquainting English speakers with Sartre's existentialism: much of her academic output, in the form of books and essays, took the form of critical discussion of his philosophy. And that was not all: Barnes also presented a series of programs about philosophy on Ohio University radio in 1952, as well as a ten-episode television series about existentialism (broadcast nationally in the United States in the 1960s) entitled *Self-Encounter: A Study in Existentialism*. She even classified the memoir that she published in her eighties as a "venture in Existentialist autobiography" (Barnes 1997).

These details alone suffice to show how radically the relations between intellectuals—both within and outside academic institutions—and the wider public culture have changed since the middle of the twentieth century. Sartre and Barnes had different personalities and intellectual outlooks, but they both believed that philosophy should concern itself with contemporary human existence, and that it should correct our understanding of our existence in a way that would oblige us to live differently. And people were hungry for these ideas, willing to attend public lectures or to learn more from the radio, newspapers, and television. The philosophy of BN, with its emphasis on human freedom, agency, and responsibility, may also have held special appeal for a postwar public open to change and desiring a fresh start.

The early reception of EN in the English-speaking world also illustrates an intellectual cosmopolitanism within academic philosophy that is less common in today's more specialized and professional departments. In the postwar period, the gulf within philosophy that is still often thought to separate Sartre, as a Continental philosopher, from the anglophone analytical traditions was not yet evident.

Moreover, and especially in the UK, the profile of the philosophers who showed an interest in Sartre's work—in some cases, even before it had been translated—is remarkable. A. J. Ayer, who was a French speaker and had friends in Paris, published a two-part discussion of Sartre's work in the journal *Horizon* in 1945, quoting lengthy passages from it in French. Iris Murdoch's first book was a slim volume on Sartre, published in 1953: although she focuses mainly on his novels, she had also read EN (and other nonfiction by Sartre) in French, and her book pays particular attention to the way Sartre's philosophy influences his fiction. Later decades saw further contributions by other major British philosophers: Stuart Hampshire reviewed Barnes's translation in the *Observer* in 1957, while Alasdair MacIntyre wrote the entry on "Existentialism" for the *Encyclopedia of Philosophy* published in 1967. A few years later, MacIntyre also contributed to a collection of critical essays on Sartre edited by Mary Warnock (1971), another prominent Sartre scholar; this collection also included an excellent discussion by Hidé Ishiguro of Sartre's theory of the imagination which helped to establish Sartre as someone worthy of attention from analytical philosophers of mind.[2]

Two lines of thought about Sartre's philosophy, which jointly exhibit a marked ambivalence, are especially prominent in this first wave of anglophone critical discussion. On the one hand—and as the legacy of Logical Positivism's hostility to traditional metaphysics would lead one to expect—there is a dismissive attitude toward Sartre's ontological framework. In his review articles, Ayer was particularly harsh about Sartre's assertions in relation to le néant ("nothingness"), which he judged to be "literally nonsensical" (Ayer 1945: 19). (Although Ayer does not mention Rudolf Carnap, his criticism here bears a strong resemblance to Carnap's earlier criticism of Heidegger's concept of das Nichts, usually translated as "nothing"; nor is this a historical coincidence, as Heidegger's concept influenced Sartre's.)[3] Similarly, in his *Observer* review of BN, Hampshire mentions the malignant influences of Hegel and Heidegger, and asks whether the "sophistries of Hegelian logic" might conceal the banality of some of Sartre's observations—before conced-

---

2 Sartre's account of the imagination has also earned him a place within "analytical" aesthetics. See for example Hopkins (1998). Another, much bigger collection of papers appeared in the US a decade later: Schilpp (1981).

3 Isaiah Berlin, another influential figure in British philosophy at the time, was aware of Sartre's philosophy, although he never engaged with it in detail. (As Berlin was also centrally concerned with freedom, this was perhaps a missed opportunity.) In a letter written in 1955, Berlin reports: "I have been reading, of all people, the detestable Sartre. The novels are too slimy & dark, but he is a very clever man & his moral philosophy is what I think I 3/4 believe. What a fool I was to be deceived by Freddie's articles in *Horizon* at the end of the war which concentrated on Sartre's obscure logic & his attitudes to sex & "proved" it all bogus. It is not. It is most imaginative and bold and important" (Berlin 2009: 467).

ing, in Sartre's favor, that his criticism of "traditional theories of mind" is "at too many points convincing for his whole system to be ignored" (Hampshire 1957: 16).[4]

On the other hand, British commentators also noted the congruence between Sartre's phenomenological approach to philosophy in BN (sub-titled "An Essay in Phenomenological Ontology") and the empiricist tradition in British philosophy. Iris Murdoch was especially alert to this similarity: "It might even be argued that recent continental philosophers have been discovering, with immense fuss, what the English empiricists have known since Hume, whom Husserl himself claimed as an ancestor" (Murdoch 1967: 8).[5]

Sartre had studied the German philosopher Edmund Husserl (1859–1938) intensively in the 1930s: as he understood Husserl's phenomenological method, it directed philosophers to attend closely to humans' experience of the world, in order to describe "the phenomena" (the way the world *appears* to human consciousness) in rigorous detail. In an early paper about Husserl published in 1939, Sartre's excitement about this revolutionary method was palpable.[6] Along with two other German philosophers, Hegel and Heidegger, Husserl forms part of the trio—often referred to as the "three Hs"—with whom Sartre enters into dialogue at various points in BN, usually in order to argue for the advantages of his view over theirs. As a fellow novelist-philosopher, Iris Murdoch was well placed to understand the appeal for Sartre—indeed, for anyone with literary ambitions—of Husserl's descriptive philosophical methodology. The often-quoted and highly evocative vignettes in BN (Pierre in the café, the woman on the date, the hiker who gives in to fatigue) show Sartre taking full advantage of the opportunity to indulge in the detailed and stylish elaboration of fictional characters and scenarios which, he thought, the phenomenological method provided.

4 By "traditional theories of mind" Hampshire is referring to post-Cartesian conceptions. Sartre's relationship to Descartes is too complicated to discuss here.

5 Describing the reception of Sartre in the US, Ann Fulton suggests that a perceived affinity with empiricism—although in this case it was with William James's philosophy rather than Hume's—also helped to "legitimize" Sartre's philosophy there (Fulton 1999: 3).

6 Sartre's early paper about Husserl is available in translation as Sartre (1970). For a readable account of Husserl's phenomenology and its relation to Sartre's concerns, see Bakewell (2016).

And, some years later, when Murdoch came to downgrade her earlier opinion of Sartre, she produced a competing vignette of her own (featuring "M," a mother, and "D," her daughter-in-law) to illustrate her criticisms of Sartre (Murdoch 1970).

In America it took longer for serious interest in Sartre's philosophy to become established: with a few exceptions, most philosophical discussion postdated and depended on Barnes's translation.[7] This time lag seems also to have made it more difficult for Sartre's ideas to get an unprejudiced hearing: by the late 1950s Sartre was often presented outside France as a lightweight celebrity whose philosophy did not deserve to be taken seriously outside café society. Some of Sartre's critical articles about American society (written after a visit in 1945) had been translated into English in the 1950s; his increasingly vocal political criticisms of the West had also made him enemies.[8] Apparently Hazel Barnes herself, before she had read any of Sartre's philosophical work, had dismissed existentialism as a "fashionable philosophy of defeatism and despair" (Cannon 2008: 92).

The early reception of Sartre in the UK and the US was idiosyncratic in a number of ways. First, Sartre was often presented as a moral philosopher and, accordingly, criticized from that perspective. Both Murdoch and MacIntyre saw him this way, while, in the US, Marjorie Grene presented existentialism as a philosophy in which the central

7 The exceptions are interesting, however. Wilfrid Desan, who was born in Belgium and studied in Lille, was a native French speaker who apparently met Sartre during the Second World War. He moved to the US in 1948, gained a doctorate there, and spent his working life as a university professor of philosophy. His first book, published in 1954, was a critical study of EN and relied on the French text (Desan 1954). Marjorie Grene, an American who had spent time studying in Germany with Heidegger and Jaspers in the early 1930s, published various books and papers about existentialism. The Canadian-born Robert Denoon Cumming served as a US soldier in France in the Second World War and spent time as a student at the Sorbonne. Although his own work on Sartre (Cumming 1991–2001) was only published later, he introduced generations of students to contemporary European thought in his classes at Columbia University. Herbert Marcuse, who emigrated from Germany in 1932, was already developing his new interpretation of Marxism when he published his unfavorable review of EN (Marcuse 1947).

8 Beauvoir also had an international name by now as a controversial French intellectual. She visited America separately in 1947 and published her own ambivalent observations in France a year later (translated as Beauvoir 1999).

"virtue" was authenticity, a line of thought that was also taken up and criticized by Charles Taylor. Alvin Plantinga's hostile 1958 paper, "An Existentialist's Ethics," claimed Sartre's account of freedom was incompatible with any genuine morality and interpreted Sartre as a moral nihilist. From today's standpoint, and with the benefits of closer attention to BN as well as historical hindsight, this focus seems misguided. Sartre himself states explicitly at the end of BN (and in some important footnotes) that an adequate discussion of morality would have to appear in "a future work," but he never succeeded in fulfilling that promise, although we have some idea of the evolution of his moral thinking from the posthumously published *Notebooks for an Ethics* (Sartre 1992).[9] This moral perspective may have been encouraged to some extent by Barnes; although she was aware of Sartre's reticence in BN, her interest in Sartre was driven by her strong desire for a credible post-religious morality, a possibility she continued to explore in her academic writing. Many commentators also "read back" into BN the optimistic moral ideas that Sartre had sketched out in EH, erroneously conflating these two texts.

More generally, the categories used within analytical philosophy and the tacitly accepted boundaries of the discipline have shaped the approach of anglophone philosophers to BN. For example, it is probably because Freud is rarely included (outside France) within the philosophical curriculum that Sartre's conception of existentialist psychoanalysis has largely been ignored, while, on the other hand, his account of bad faith is seen as a contribution to the debate within the philosophy of mind about self-deception, and his account of shame is assessed with reference to the skeptical "problem of other minds."

In her introduction to the 1965 edition of her translation, Barnes complained that this "piecemeal" attention to BN hindered readers' understanding:

> One can no more understand Sartre's view of freedom, for instance, without considering his peculiar view of consciousness than one can judge Plato's doctrine that knowledge is recollection without relating

9 The *Notebooks'* many references to the desirability of a social revolution suggest that at least part of Sartre's reason for abandoning his work on morality was that political imperatives had come to seem more fundamental.

it to the theory of ideas. What critics usually fail to see is that Sartre is one of the very few twentieth century philosophers to present us with a total system.[10]

The predominantly ahistorical outlook of analytical philosophy has also inflected the study of Sartre. With a few exceptions, and in spite of Sartre's frequent references to the three Hs, most anglophone commentators have said little about Sartre's relations to these predecessors, or even about his place in the European post-Kantian tradition more broadly. Work still remains to be done exploring Sartre's relations not only to the three Hs but also to more shadowy figures behind the text, including Kierkegaard, Bergson, Leibniz, and the Stoics.[11]

It is perhaps especially surprising that so little attention was given to Sartre's relationship with Heidegger: after all, Heidegger was still alive when BN appeared and he predeceased Sartre by only four years.[12] In fact, Heidegger's influence pervades BN, although Sartre does not always acknowledge it. Heidegger's example may be responsible for BN's title (which can be seen as a response to Heidegger's most famous philosophical work, Being and Time), and is surely the reason for the mention of ontology in its subtitle. Heidegger's example must also have influenced Sartre's decision to make nothingness into a central philosophical concept. Sartre's focus on man's practical immersion in his everyday tasks, the choice of the activity of questioning as an investigative point of departure, and the redeployment of anguish within a new framework are also all indebted to Heidegger.[13]

Despite this debt, most of Sartre's reading of Heidegger appears to have been in French translation, and he relied heavily on a small anthology of extracts and essays translated by Henry Corbin and published in France

10 Barnes (1965: viii–ix).
11 The exceptions include the following: Aquila (1998), Baiasu (2011), Baldwin (1979), and Gardner (2005, 2009). More of this type of work has been published in France and Germany, where philosophy tends to be studied from a more historical perspective. See for example Hartmann (1966) and Simont (1998).
12 Various reasons may explain this neglect: in particular, I think Heidegger's writing style was a deterrent. It is difficult to imagine Ayer, Murdoch, Hampshire, or Berlin enjoying his dense and humorless prose.
13 Of course, Sartre also disagrees with Heidegger on many topics, including the significance of human death and the nature of our relations with others.

in 1938 (Heidegger 1938). Sartre borrowed the phrase "human-reality" (la réalité humaine) directly from Corbin (who had used it to translate Heidegger's term Dasein). This "monstrous translation," as Jacques Derrida famously described it a quarter of a century later (Derrida 1982b: 115), was subsequently held against Sartre. In conjunction with other evidence (including, importantly, EH), this usage was thought to warrant dismissal of BN as a philosophy resting on outdated and unacceptable humanist premises.

The "anti-humanist" criticism was one among several lines of attack within a broader critical backlash against Sartre that was at its height in the 1960s and 1970s, in both France and the English-speaking world. Feminist theory provided a different kind of opposition (about which more later).

Insofar as it involves Sartre, the so-called Humanism Debate begins in 1946 when Jean Beaufret (a French philosopher with an interest in German thought) wrote to Heidegger with the intention of reestablishing a dialogue between French and German philosophy after the disruption of the Second World War.[14] In EH, Sartre had cited Heidegger as a fellow existentialist, and Beaufret was effectively inviting Heidegger to respond. Heidegger's reply—published in an expanded version as the "Letter on Humanism" (Heidegger 1978b)—was disdainful. (It did not help that almost two decades had elapsed since the publication of Being and Time and Heidegger's philosophical focus had shifted.) Although Sartre is not extensively discussed in the "Letter," Heidegger makes it clear that, in his view, Sartre is one of the many Western philosophers who have misconceived the proper task of thought. Sartre's focus in EH on (free) human action is, Heidegger suggests, superficial: instead, we should develop our thinking in a way that "lets itself be claimed by Being so that it can say the truth of Being" (194). To do this, it is important to notice the resources of language and to reconceptualize our relationship with it. Indeed, the first page of the "Letter" contains one of Heidegger's most-quoted claims: "Language is the house of Being. In its home man dwells" (Heidegger 1978b: 193).

Why does Heidegger reject "humanism"—at least as it is normally conceived? Although the "Letter" pursues several relevant lines of thought, the central claim is that the way the human being is interpreted throughout the his-

---

14 See Baldwin (2007) for further discussion of this debate.

tory of humanism is insufficiently radical, and sets us on the wrong philosophical path. For example the Greek view that a human is essentially a "rational animal" helps itself uncritically to a conception of "life" and locates humans among other animals in a way that conceals our difference (which does not consist, for Heidegger, in "rationality"). Behind this criticism lies a more fundamental problem, namely that "every humanism is either grounded in a metaphysics or is itself made to be the ground of one. . . . Accordingly, every humanism is metaphysical" (Heidegger 1978b: 202).

Heidegger's critique of metaphysics is an immense topic; for our purposes, the key idea to retain is Heidegger's claim—which is taken up in Derrida's philosophy—that the Western philosophical tradition has repeatedly determined being in terms of *presence*. For Heidegger, humanism is complicit with this metaphysical tendency; in its Cartesian incarnation, for example, humans are characterized as thinking subjects to whom beings are made *present* (or "represented") as objects. Derrida elaborates the theme of the "metaphysics of presence" with particular reference to questions of linguistic meaning and reference (which had, by the late twentieth century, also become dominant in anglophone philosophy as well as in Continental Europe).

Had French thought taken a different path after Heidegger's anti-Sartrean intervention, the question of humanism might have been forgotten. But the massive impact of structuralism in virtually every branch of the human sciences in France in the 1960s resulted in a range of "antihumanist" theoretical proposals that were thought to be antithetical to Sartre's earlier philosophy, by authors who were often explicitly critical of Sartre. As its name suggests, structuralism's basic insight is that the production of meaning—where this is broadly understood to include linguistic meaning, the meaning of literary texts, and the meaning of social practices—depends on preexisting and socially shared structures or systems that determine and delimit the signifying possibilities available to the people who inhabit them. A host of famous French thinkers are associated with this paradigm, including Barthes, Foucault, Lévi-Strauss, Lacan, and Althusser.[15] Across these dif-

---

15 See Gutting (2001) for a helpful overview of many of these figures.

ferent fields of investigation, the structuralist model denies explanatory primacy to individual subjectivity, and emphasizes instead the often-quoted "decentering of the subject" and the "death of the author."[16] Sartre was portrayed as an advocate of the individualist humanism held by this body of work to be untenable.

Of course a case can be, and has been, made in Sartre's defense; champions have portrayed and promoted a "new Sartre." It should also be noted that many of the French theorists who distanced themselves from Sartre were separated from him by only a few years in age: Sartre's prominence in public life needed to be questioned if they were to displace him. A further question, which some have answered affirmatively, is whether Sartre's post-BN writings show him to be following a similar trajectory to the structuralist theorists in any case.[17]

The feminist attacks on Sartre were largely independent of this debate, and arose as part of the wider feminist *Zeitgeist* in the second half of the twentieth century.

One strand of feminist discussion has been biographically centered, insofar as it examines Sartre's relationship with Beauvoir and his intellectual debts to her through a feminist lens. In this context, the relevance of BN is exhausted by the light it throws on these wider questions (whether, for example, it reveals Beauvoir's influence). For this reason, I will merely remind the reader that Sartre dedicated BN *au Castor* and move on.[18]

The so-called second wave of feminism was at its height in the 1970s when two American scholars published an influential article, "Holes and Slime: Sexism in Sartre's Psychoanalysis" (Collins and Pierce 1976). Their purpose was to show that Sartre's examples in BN of the "psychoanalysis of things" manifest a sexism that contradicts BN's basic anti-essentialist standpoint. In the passages they cite from Barnes's translation, Sartre considers the significance of holes and slime.[19] "Slime," he tells us, has a nega-

---

16 Foucault's eloquent concluding paragraphs to *The Order of Things* are often quoted to the same effect. Foucault states that "man is an invention of recent date" and that, if "the fundamental arrangements of knowledge" were to crumble, "man would be erased, like a face drawn in sand at the edge of the sea" (Foucault 1970: 387).

17 See, for example, Caws (1992).

18 *Le Castor*, which is French for "beaver," was Sartre's nickname for Beauvoir. See Daigle and Golomb (2008) for the question of Beauvoir's influence.

19 Sartre's French term is *visqueux*, which (as I argue below) should be translated as "viscous" rather than "slimy."

tive ontological meaning, insofar as it signifies a threat to consciousness, or an inversion of its central characteristics (lucidity, freedom, etc.). Sartre describes the action of slime as "a moist and feminine sucking," which is also "the revenge of the In-itself. A sickly-sweet feminine revenge. . . ." Collins and Pierce's objections to Sartre's treatment of holes are less forceful, as Sartre mentions several types of hole (including non-corporeal ones). Nonetheless, his suggestion that the vagina is "a mouth and a voracious mouth which devours the penis" did not please them.

One response to these criticisms, voiced by Barnes and other critics, points out that these damning passages do not play an important role in BN; it would be absurd to take them to be "gendering" Sartre's ontology, i.e., to infer that the for-itself is implicitly male and the in-itself implicitly female throughout. According to this defense, we ought to distinguish the (incidental) sexism of Sartre's imagery from his central philosophical doctrines. As Barnes conceded, "A full investigation of the linguistic codes in Sartre's writing would reveal him to be a man comfortably ensconced in a world of male dominance" (Barnes 1990: 341). But, Sartre's supporters argued, we need to look beyond the regrettably sexist imagery and language in order to notice the emancipatory potential of Sartre's basic anti-essentialism.[20]

However, this defense of Sartre may not work in relation to another, more theoretically sophisticated line of feminist criticism. According to the French philosopher Michèle Le Dœuff (2007), a philosophical "imaginary," expressing a male outlook and male privilege, can be discerned within the Western philosophical canon as a whole and BN is no exception. As this orientation is largely unconscious and surfaces most often in imagery or examples that may *appear* to be incidental, we cannot dismiss these aspects of a text. One of Le Dœuff's most compelling analyses focuses on Sartre's depictions of women in his discussion of bad faith: not only the well-known woman on the date who tries not to notice her suitor's sexual ambitions but also the unfortunate women, featured in some case studies from Stekel and cited by Sartre, who claim not to enjoy sex with their husbands, although both Stekel and Sartre disagree (Le Dœuff 2007: 64–68). In her unconventional book, Le Dœuff also

---

20 Feminists have also found other elements in BN useful, e.g., its account of the objectifying effect of the Other's gaze. For a collection of feminist interpretations of Sartre, see Murphy (1999).

draws on a wide range of other materials, including Beauvoir's memoirs and letters from Sartre, arguing that the real-life consequence of their intellectual partnership was effectively that Beauvoir was deprived (or deprived herself) of the status of a philosopher.

Genevieve Lloyd's *The Man of Reason*, first published in 1984, also surveyed the Western philosophical canon from a feminist critical point of view, although through a slightly different lens (Lloyd 1993). Lloyd claims that the ideal of reason is repeatedly associated in philosophy with maleness; this association, moreover, is sometimes "inherited" by philosophers who may not consciously appreciate its workings. Lloyd argues that the idea of "transcendence" that Beauvoir took over from Sartre (and, via Sartre, from Hegel), and uses in *The Second Sex*, is contaminated in this way and therefore an unsuitable feminist ideal.

Le Dœuff's and Lloyd's books are insightful, and their remarks about BN deserve serious attention. Still, we should note that the ambition and generality of these surveys mean that Sartre is seen to instantiate a rule rather than an exception. In addition, these critics suggest that the bias they are documenting needs to be *unearthed*: it is not always obvious, and nor do the philosophers who exhibit it even necessarily intend it.

In this respect, these feminist interpretations of Western philosophy share some of the features of Derrida's deconstructionist approach to philosophy, published in France in several influential books and articles in the late 1960s and 1970s.[21] Some of these writings target the structuralism that was then so fashionable in France: because of their deflationary effect, Derrida is often described as a "post-structuralist." For Derrida there is something quixotic about the view that a signifying system can be mastered once its basic structures have been identified. Derrida's own writing focuses especially on the case of language: one of the features that makes his prose difficult to read (and even more difficult to translate) is the multiple "performances" of language eluding authorial control. Puns, ambiguities, and neologisms abound in Derrida's highly self-conscious texts.

---

21 Derrida continued to publish until his death in 2014, but the "classical" deconstructive texts appeared in the late 1960s and 1970s.

Derrida's ambitious and complicated project is difficult to sum up (in part because it deliberately resists presentation as a set of doctrines), but a few further remarks about his relationship to Sartre are called for. As we saw, Derrida blames Sartre for using the term "human-reality" and, more broadly, for perpetuating a naïvely "anthropological" or humanist reading of Heidegger's work (Derrida 1982b). Nonetheless, the effect of Derrida's wider analysis in this essay is ultimately to dilute Sartre's specific accountability for the persistence of humanism in recent philosophy by showing, for example, that despite Heidegger's stated intentions (in his "Letter" and elsewhere) there is a residual humanism in his thought too. As Derrida puts it:

> What must hold our interest . . . is the kind of profound justification, whose necessity is subterranean, which makes the Hegelian, Husserlian and Heideggerian critiques or *de-limitations* of metaphysical humanism appear to belong to the very sphere of that which they criticize or de-limit.
>
> (Derrida 1982b: 119)

How does BN stand in relation to these more recent developments in French philosophy? Although the phenomenon of language is occasionally discussed, it is not at the center of Sartre's concerns. Moreover, despite occasional instances of linguistic playfulness in the text, Sartre's style and tone exhibit a pre-Derridean confidence that language can be used to say what we mean that would not have been possible (or, at least, not without discussion) twenty-five years later. The same confidence emerges in some of Sartre's reflections on his own linguistic practice, as the following exchange, from an interview with Michel Contat in 1975, shows:

> Q: *Your philosophical manuscripts are written in long hand, with almost no crossings out or erasures, while your literary manuscripts are very much worked over, perfected. Why is there this difference?*
>
> A: The objectives are different: in philosophy, every sentence should have only one meaning. The work I did on *Les Mots*, for example, attempting to give multiple and superimposed meanings to each sentence, would be bad work in philosophy.
>
> (Sartre 1978b: 7)

But if Sartre's attitude toward language in BN is old-fashioned, the proponents of the "new Sartre" have shown that in other respects, and sympathetically read, BN is ahead of its time. The "humanist" criticisms voiced by Heidegger and the structuralists, for example, often draw on a simplifying interpretation of Sartre's "Cartesian" standpoint in BN that can easily be shown to be incomplete.[22] For Descartes, the *cogito* affords the subject indubitable first personal knowledge, while mind and body are two separate substances which are, respectively, immaterial and material. In Sartre's hands, all these elements are radically modified: the reflective standpoint of the *cogito* is shown to be epistemologically unreliable; consciousness is not a substance and, in addition, it has no contents. Moreover, Sartre's characterization of the for-itself as being-what-it-is-not and not-being-what-it-is "decenters" the Sartrean subject, and undermines the possibility of self-coincidence in a way that, arguably, keeps the "metaphysics of presence" at bay.[23]

Whatever its merits, the "new Sartre" exemplifies BN's relevance to later French thought, enlisting it in a dialogue with more recent philosophy. At the same time, academic philosophy in the English-speaking world, which typically resists European "fashion," has come to accept BN as a classic text that belongs in the post-Kantian tradition. I hope this new translation will help the reader to form her own view of it—for herself, responsibly and freely, as Sartre would have urged.

References

Aquila, Richard E. (1998), "Sartre's Other and the Field of Consciousness: A 'Husserlian' Reading," *European Journal of Philosophy* 6 (3): 253–276.

Ayer, A.J. (1945), "Novelist-Philosopher, Jean-Paul Sartre," *Horizon* 12 (67): 12–26 and 12 (68): 101–110.

Baiasu, Sorin (2011), *Kant and Sartre: Re-discovering Critical Ethics* (London: Palgrave Macmillan).

Bakewell, Sarah (2016), *At the Existentialist Café* (London: Vintage).

---

22 Heidegger's attack in particular can be seen to be limited by its reliance on EH rather than BN.

23 For fuller discussion, see Farrell Fox (2003) and Howells (1992b).

Baldwin, Thomas (1979), "The Original Choice in Sartre and Kant," *Proceedings of the Aristotelian Society* 80: 31–44.

Baldwin, Thomas (2007), "The Humanism Debate," in Leiter and Rosen (eds.) (2007): 671–710.

Barnes, Hazel (1965), "Translator's Introduction," in Sartre (1965): viii–xliii.

Barnes, Hazel (1990), "Sartre and Sexism," *Philosophy and Literature* 14 (2): 340–347.

Barnes, Hazel (1997), *The Story I Tell Myself* (Chicago: University of Chicago Press).

Beauvoir, Simone de (1999), *America Day by Day*, trans. Carol Cosman (Berkeley: University of California Press).

Berlin, Isaiah (2009), *Enlightening: Letters, 1946–60*, ed. H. Hardy and J. Holmes (London: Chatto & Windus).

Cannon, Betty (2008), "Hazel E. Barnes, 1915–2008: A Tribute and Farewell," *Sartre Studies International* 14 (2): 90–103.

Caws, Peter (1992), "Sartrean Structuralism?" in Howells (ed.) (1992a): 293–317.

Collins, Margery, and Pierce, Christine (1976), "Holes and Slime: Sexism in Sartre's Psychoanalysis," in Gould and Wartofsky (eds.) (1976): 112–127.

Cumming, Robert Denoon (1991–2001), *Phenomenology and Deconstruction* (4 vols.) (Chicago: Chicago University Press).

Daigle, Christine, and Golomb, Jacob (eds.) (2008), *Beauvoir and Sartre: The Riddle of Influence* (Bloomington: Indiana University Press).

Derrida, Jacques (1982a), *Margins of Philosophy*, trans. Alan Bass (Sussex: Harvester Press).

Derrida, Jacques (1982b), "The Ends of Man," in Derrida (1982a): 109–136.

Desan, Wilfrid (1954), *The Tragic Finale: An Essay on the Philosophy of Jean-Paul Sartre* (Cambridge, MA: Harvard University Press).

Edwards, Paul (ed.) (1967), *The Encyclopedia of Philosophy* (New York: Macmillan).

Farrell Fox, Nik (2003), *The New Sartre* (London: Continuum).

Foucault, Michel (1970), *The Order of Things* (London: Tavistock).

Fulton, Ann (1999), *Apostles of Sartre: Existentialism in America, 1945–1963* (Evanston, Ill.: Northwestern University Press).

Gardner, Sebastian (2005), "Sartre, Intersubjectivity, and German Idealism," *Journal of the History of Philosophy* 43 (3): 325–351.

Gardner, Sebastian (2009), *Sartre's Being and Nothingness* (London: Continuum).

Gould, Carol, and Wartofsky, Marx (eds.) (1976), *Women and Philosophy: Toward a Theory of Liberation* (New York: G. P. Putnam's Sons).

Gutting, Gary (2001), *French Philosophy in the Twentieth Century* (Cambridge: Cambridge University Press).

Hampshire, Stuart (1957), "Sartre the Philosopher," *The Observer* (London), May 12.

Hartmann, Klaus (1966), *Sartre's Ontology* (Evanston, Ill.: Northwestern University Press).

Heidegger, Martin (1938), *Qu'est-ce que la Métaphysique? Suivi d'Extraits sur l'Être et le Temps et d'une Conference sur Hölderlin*, trans. Henry Corbin (Paris: Gallimard).

Heidegger, Martin (1978a), *Basic Writings*, trans. David Krell (London: Routledge & Kegan Paul).

Heidegger, Martin (1978b), "Letter on Humanism," trans. David Krell, in Heidegger (1978a): 193–242.

Hopkins, Robert (1998), *Picture, Image and Experience* (Cambridge, UK: Cambridge University Press).

Howells, Christina (ed.) (1992a), *The Cambridge Companion to Sartre* (Cambridge, UK: Cambridge University Press).

Howells, Christina (1992b), "Sartre and the Deconstruction of the Subject," in Howells (ed.) (1992a): 318–352.

Le Dœuff, Michèle (2007), *Hipparchia's Choice*, trans. Trista Selous (New York: Columbia University Press).

Leiter, B., and Rosen, M. (eds) (2007), *The Oxford Handbook of Continental Philosophy* (Oxford: Oxford University Press).

Lloyd, Genevieve (1993), *The Man of Reason* (London: Routledge).

MacIntyre, Alasdair (1967), "Existentialism," in Edwards (ed.) (1967), Vol. 3: 147–154.

Marcuse, Herbert (1947), "Existentialism: Remarks on Jean-Paul Sartre's *L'Être et le Néant*," *Philosophy and Phenomenological Research* 8 (3): 309–336.

Murdoch, Iris (1967), *Sartre* (London: Fontana).

Murdoch, Iris (1970), *The Sovereignty of Good* (New York: Schocken Books).

Murphy, Julien (ed.) (1999), *Feminist Interpretations of Jean-Paul Sartre* (University Park: Pennsylvania University Press).

Plantinga, Alvin (1958), "An Existentialist's Ethics," *Review of Metaphysics* 12 (2): 235–256.

Sartre, Jean-Paul (1943), *L'Être et le Néant* (Paris: Gallimard).

Sartre, Jean-Paul (1965), *Being and Nothingness*, trans. and introduced by Hazel Barnes (New York: Washington Square Press).

Sartre, Jean-Paul (1970), "Intentionality: A Fundamental Idea of Husserl's Phenomenology," trans. Joseph Fell, *Journal of the British Society for Phenomenology* 1 (2): 4–5.

Sartre, Jean-Paul (1973), *Existentialism and Humanism*, trans. Philip Mairet (London: Methuen).

Sartre, Jean-Paul (1978a), *Sartre in the Seventies: Interviews and Essays*, trans. Paul Auster and Lydia Davis (London: Andre Deutsch).

Sartre, Jean-Paul (1978b), "Self-Portrait at Seventy," reprinted in Sartre (1978a): 4–92.

Sartre, Jean-Paul (1992), *Notebooks for an Ethics*, trans. David Pellauer (Chicago: University of Chicago Press).

Schilpp, P. A. (ed.) (1981), *The Philosophy of Jean-Paul Sartre* (La Salle, IL: Open Court).

Simont, Juliette (1998), *Jean-Paul Sartre: Un Demi-siècle de Liberté* (Brussels: De Boeck).

Warnock, Mary (ed.) (1971), *Sartre: A Collection of Critical Essays* (New York: Anchor Books).

NOTES ON THE TRANSLATION

Sarah Richmond

Frederick Olafson, an American philosopher, reviewed Barnes's translation of BN in 1958. He was unsympathetic to its content and also commented harshly on its style:

> The French text presents, notoriously, a thankless task; it is endlessly repetitive, full of ugly neologisms, and in places quite unintelligible. *Inevitably*, the English version shares these defects to a degree and readers are not likely to find it much easier going than the original.
>
> (Olafson 1958: 276, my emphasis)

When readers of this translation encounter stylistic infelicities, repetitions, and ramblings, I hope they will bear Olafson's sentences in mind. It is common for translators to dissociate themselves from the content of their translated text, but the despair I have sometimes felt has usually been in connection with BN's style. Where they seem legitimate, I have taken steps (detailed below) to mitigate stylistic defects, but in this respect the options available to a responsible translator are limited.

Punctuation is the main area where I have felt licensed to depart from Sartre's practice in order to make the text more readable. Written French often contains long sentences with multiple subordinate clauses that are often punctuated only by commas. Sartre uses such sentences throughout the text. Good English prose usually works differently: sentences tend to be shorter, and parentheses, colons, and semicolons (as well as commas) are used to order the meaning. It seems appropriate for a translator to take advantage, where she can, of these differences. In making some of Sartre's sentences shorter (by dividing one French sentence into two or more English ones) and/or punctuating them differently (with more semicolons and colons, and fewer commas), I do not think I have been unfaithful. In the same vein, I have not translated all the numerous instances of *en effet* ("indeed" or "in effect"); in the French, this phrase is often used more for emphasis than to add information, so where it seems unnecessary in the English, I have sometimes deleted it. Another phrase Sartre uses frequently is *c'est-à-dire*, which translates literally as "that is to say"; because it would badly clutter the English text if I translated each instance like that, I have often used the near-synonymous "i.e." instead.

As the rules for the use of quotation marks also differ between French and English (e.g., within dialogue, or to show that words are "mentioned" rather than "used"), I have also taken advantage of this difference and introduced quotation marks where that improves clarity.

Sartre likes to hyphenate phrases: it seems likely he got this habit from Heidegger. I have not felt entitled to interfere with this practice, despite the many cumbersome word strings that ensue: presumably (as in Heidegger's "Being-in-the-world") the hyphens are intended, at least in most instances, to emphasize the indissolubility of the terms they conjoin. This is true, for example, of *réalité-humaine*, which I translate as "human-reality." In other instances, the purpose of the hyphen is unclear. I have no idea why Sartre hyphenates "peopled-world" (*monde-peuplé*) at EN 601 or "human-will" (*volonté-humaine*) at EN 486. Sartre is also inconsistent in his use of hyphens, using the same phrase at different points in the text with or without them: although this is puzzling, I have not interfered. With some hyphenated phrases Sartre switches with apparent arbitrariness between one word order and its reverse, as, for example, in "Other-object" at EN 266 and "object-Other" at EN 296 (*objet-autrui* and *autrui-objet* respectively). I sometimes switch the order of the hyphenated words in translation: French and English follow different rules with respect to word order anyway, but there are also instances where I have switched the word order in the English, not because it is grammatically required but for the sake of a more euphonious phrase.

What are the main differences between Barnes's older translation and mine? Barnes's achievement was immense, especially when one bears in mind the limited technology at her disposal (no computers, Internet, etc.), and her translation of BN is far better than many other first English translations of French philosophical texts from the same period. Although some of Barnes's decisions were flawed, and she made a number of outright mistakes, these shortcomings alone might not warrant a new translation. Fortunately, and in part because of advances in technology and professional standards as well as the availability of recent philosophical scholarship and translations, I have also been able to enhance the text in a number of ways that I hope readers will find helpful.

Many of the writings to which Sartre refers—either directly or more allusively—were unavailable in English translation in the 1950s. To give just one example, Heidegger's *Being and Time* was first translated into English by John Macquarrie and Edward Robinson in 1962. This careful, thoroughly annotated translation has enabled me to find the source of many of Sartre's numerous Heidegger references in the published English version and to quote, or discuss, or direct the reader to the corresponding passages. In the same way, of course, I have been able to benefit from other reliable translations of other philosophical works, in particular those by Husserl and Hegel.

These English translations, in conjunction with additional critical discussion by anglophone scholars, have resulted in the existence of various "lexicons" associated with different European philosophers; this has allowed me, in some cases, to translate a French term into an English term from the relevant lexicon, and thus to maintain cross-textual consistency. In some instances this works well: I have followed most English translations of Bergson, for example, in rendering *élan* as "impulse" rather than the alternative terms offered by French–English dictionaries (e.g., "momentum"). But this accumulated history also creates complicated situations in which some advantages have to be sacrificed for others. Sartre's negative vocabulary offers an illustration: Sartre would have found the term *le néant* in Corbin's translation of Heidegger's "What Is Metaphysics?" where Corbin uses it to translate the German *das Nichts* (Heidegger 1938). Sartre was also familiar with Bergson's rejection of the idea of *le néant* in *L'Évolution Créatrice* (translated as Bergson 1911). Many English translations of Heidegger render *das Nichts* as "the Nothing," while Bergson's term le néant was for a long time rendered as "the Nought." Three different terms, then, are in circulation in English: nothingness, nothing, and the nought. Further complications arise when one tries to reproduce in English the connections between the words in this negative vocabulary. The intended assonance of Heidegger's controversial sentence Das Nichts nichtet has been reproduced, in a translation suggested by some Heidegger scholars, as "The nothing noths" (Inwood 1999). Sartre built a parallel assonance into his French text by inventing the verb néantiser. To reproduce this assonance in English, one could either translate néantiser by borrowing the verb "to noth" from Heidegger or make up a new verb along the same lines: "to nothingize," perhaps? However, néantir also closely resembles the existing French verb anéantir ("to annihilate"), and this connection speaks in favor of translating it into English as "nihilate." This was Barnes's solution, and after some reflection I have endorsed it.

The widespread use of Barnes's translation has of course "naturalized" some of her vocabulary, and where I disagree with her decision about a significant term, I have had to consider the cost to (some) readers of introducing a change. For example, Sartre frequently uses the noun surgissement and the related verb surgir to characterize the way the for-itself arises within the world. Surgir is not an unusual verb in everyday French, where it simply means "to arise," with an implication of abruptness that sometimes speaks in favor of a phrase such as "to suddenly appear" or "to crop up." The related noun is harder to translate: one option might be "sudden appearance," but that would blur the boundaries of the term "appearance" in BN, which is better confined, in my view, to instances where Sartre uses apparence or apparition (often with a phenomenological sense). The difficulties are clear; nonetheless, I think Barnes's choice of the term "upsurge" was eccentric. "Upsurge" is rarely used in English, and the first entry for it in most dictionaries defines it as an increase of something in its size or incidence: the word can be used, for example, in a phrase such as "a recent upsurge of crime." (Less commonly, the verb can be used intransitively to mean "to surge up," as in "the water upsurged": perhaps Barnes had this usage in mind.) I have decided to use the verb "to arise" instead and (where necessary) the noun "arising," as these are more faithful to the register used in the French.

The case for conservatism in relation to existing translations is sometimes strengthened by the weight of published commentary elsewhere:

even if I could think of an accurate way of translating *réalité-humaine* that did less violence to Heidegger's term *Dasein*, the "Humanism Debate" (discussed in my Introduction) has now made Sartre's and Corbin's decision into a significant event in the French reception of Heidegger. To reverse that decision would be rather like rewriting history, and in any case it is not the role of a translator to "correct" the author of her text.

Because many of the people to whom Sartre refers have since faded into obscurity, I have provided many identifying footnotes. In addition, where Sartre refers to passages or arguments in works by other philosophers, I have tried to reference these for the reader. Note that I have not provided explanatory footnotes for obvious names (e.g., Plato).

In the remainder of these notes I list some further elements of my translation, either to explain my decision or to provide further information, or both. I start with "parts of speech" and move on to various clusters of vocabulary.

Prepositions

Sartre frequently uses prepositions as if they were nouns (especially *l'au-delà* and *dehors*). I have often put quotation marks round the English equivalents, for example "the unconditioned 'beyond'" (EN 129) or "purely as an 'outside'" (EN 517), to make the grammatical structure clearer than it would otherwise be in English.

Pronouns

Il, elle, c'est: Several translation difficulties arise from the differences between the French and English pronoun systems. The following sets out my policy in relation to the main difficulties.

1. Often, once Sartre has used some noun in a sentence, he refers back to it with *il* or *elle*, where the gender of the pronoun in French helps the reader track the referent. (For example, having mentioned *une table*, Sartre may refer back to it with *elle*.) In these cases the English may be less clear, as the gender-neutral "it" may have more than one referent. To maintain clarity, I have sometimes repeated the noun in such cases.

2. Sartre's two modes of being—*pour-soi* and *en-soi*—are naturally trans-
    lated as "for-itself" and "in-itself"; a consistent description of the
    for-itself's doings will therefore refer to it with the impersonal pro-
    noun, "it." It needs to be remembered, however, that the for-itself
    is the mode of being of human consciousness, so it is exemplified by
    persons. In consequence, there are some contexts where the decision
    to translate with the pronoun "it" (rather than the personal pro-
    nouns "he" or "she") will cause strain. Where the phrase *pour-soi* is
    followed in close proximity by some characterization of an activity
    or attitude that clearly belongs to a person, I have therefore often
    switched (sometimes within the same sentence) from "itself" to
    "himself."

    For example, at EN 450 I have: "It may happen that the for-itself,
    having experienced these various avatars in the course of *its* histori-
    alization, decides—in full knowledge of the futility of *his* previous
    attempts—to pursue the other's death."

    Similarly, I have avoided using the pronoun "it" for the Other. At
    EN 281, for example, I translate Sartre's *autrui n'est pas pour soi comme il
    m'apparaît* as "the Other is not for himself as he appears to me."

    For greater clarity of reference, I also sometimes repeat the phrase
    "for-itself" within a sentence or paragraph.

3. Soi: Sartre sometimes uses this term (e.g., in the phrase *pour-soi*) such
    that it corresponds to the reflexive pronoun "itself" in English; at
    other times it is used as a noun to mean *the* self, or Ego. (Sartre also
    uses *le moi* in this sense: in some cases I signal whether the French
    has *moi* or *soi* by putting the French pronoun in square brackets in
    the text.)

    Sartre also uses the noun *soi* to refer to the unattainable self-coincidence
    that haunts the for-itself (e.g., at EN 126). Here, I have translated it as "the
    itself," sometimes putting "itself" within scare quotes to acknowledge
    the grammatical oddity. One advantage of "itself" is that it maintains the
    connection with the "for-itself" whose ideal it is; it also makes it clear
    that Sartre is not concerned in these instances with the kind of "self" pos-
    sessed by persons but rather with self-coincidence.

    For *conscience (de) soi*, see "Other words worthy of note" below.

4. Il: In line with French linguistic convention, Sartre often uses this
    masculine pronoun "universally" to refer to a man or a woman, and

(similarly) he uses l'*homme* to mean "man" in the general sense, i.e., humanity (male *and* female) in general. Of course, the corresponding terms can also be used like this in English. In both France and England, this practice has in recent decades been criticized for its implicit sexism, and many writers now use a more egalitarian alternative (e.g., "he or she," "they," etc.).

In relation to this political issue, it would clearly be an anachronistic imposition to alter Sartre's traditional use of the masculine pronoun (il); similarly, where he writes in the first-personal voice I have assumed that voice is male. In addition, once the topic of the Other is introduced (in Part Three), I have followed Sartre in referring to the Other as a "he."

Nonetheless, there are some contexts where, in my view, it is important to use female pronouns, as I explain in the next paragraph.

Gender pronouns in the context of interpersonal relations

In the sections in Part Three in which Sartre discusses love and sexual desire, the translation of the masculine pronoun il becomes particularly challenging. There is good reason to suppose that in Sartre's analysis of these relations he has a male-female (heterosexual) couple in mind. Sartre sometimes provides examples that make this explicit, and in any case any other supposition would have been unusual in the 1940s. (In addition, Sartre sometimes manifests—in BN and in other writings—the prejudiced attitudes of his time toward homosexuality.) Despite this implicit heterosexual assumption, Sartre continues to refer frequently, as French allows him to, to both members of the loving or sexual couple with the male pronoun. Thus, in speaking of the lover and his beloved, Sartre regularly refers to them as l'*amant* and l'*aimé* (not in the feminine form *aimée*) and uses the masculine pronoun il for each of them. Now, in French this usage is consistent with the belief that one member of the couple is female—the "universality" of il is sufficiently robust to allow that. But in English, if both members of a couple are referred to by "he," most people would conclude that they are both male (and, perhaps, that they are homosexual). For this reason, in sections I and II of Part Three, Chapter 3, I have often indicated that one partner in a couple is female by using the pronoun "she," even where this means translating Sartre's il as "she."

Note that my motive here is not political but to replicate in English the scenario I think Sartre has in mind. If it has the effect of increasing one's sense of female presence within the text, that is a happy but coincidental consequence. (From a political perspective, of course, the heteronormativity of the scenario may be regrettable.)[1]

In section III of the same chapter Sartre discusses groupings [nous]: here the relevant pronouns are "we" or "us." At this point I revert to using "he" throughout, as it is not clear that females are involved.

Neologisms and ungrammatical locutions

(NB: Although some of these words discussed here are now included in some French dictionaries, the earliest use given is most often Sartre's.)

chosifier, chosiste: Sartre invents this verb (and the corresponding adjective), using it to mean "to make into a thing [*une chose*]." As "thingify" is cumbersome in English and Sartre's verb is synonymous with the fairly ordinary English verb "to reify," I have often preferred the latter over the former. Where the idea of "thing" seems important, I signal it.

est été: In this ungrammatical locution, Sartre tampers with the correct way of saying that something "has been" in French (i.e., to use the verb *avoir* followed by *été*, the past participle of *être*), by replacing the main verb *avoir* by *être*. This generates a grammatically incorrect phrase equivalent to the English "is been." For example, at EN 57, Sartre writes *le néant* "*est été*," using scare quotes to acknowledge the oddness of the phrase. (Sartre also offers some reasons for using it in the same paragraph.) I cannot see any reason not to translate it literally, rendering the quoted phrase as "nothingness 'is been.'"

négatité is a noun coined by Sartre to refer to a particular instance of nothingness within the world. I do not think it is necessary to leave it in French (as Barnes did), when a mirror neologism—"negatity" (pl. "negatities")—can be used.

objectité can straightforwardly be translated as "objecthood."

---

1 With respect to the question of heteronormativity, some aspects of Sartre's *theoretical* account of human sexuality are interestingly ambiguous. His disagreement with biologically based theories leads him to deny the importance of physiological sexual difference and to claim that heterosexuality is not fundamental to sexual relations (EN 424), although a few pages later he also states that in our culture we do not often desire others "of the same sex" (EN 427).

Vocabulary relating to the mind: psychology, motivation, experience, perception

There is a cluster of issues that are worth noting in relation to the concept of the "mind" (or, as Sartre puts it, le psyche). From his earliest philosophical writing, Sartre engages in a polemical debate with empirical (or, as he often calls it, "positivist") psychology. In BN he regards it as a source of grave ontological misunderstanding and rejects a range of psychological common-places, including the existence of mental states, the passivity of the emo-tions, and the alleged differences between acts of "passion" and of reason. (Although Sartre often directs these arguments against psychologists, he also finds similar targets elsewhere; for example, he rejects Bergson's conception of the "deep-seated self" as well as Proust's analysis of jealousy.)

Sartre's account of our experience of the Other is also revisionary and also brought into line with his account of its ontological structure. He often describes our relations with the Other in negative and conflictual terms, as his discussion of shame shows. This is one reason for bringing out the negative connotation of the noun épreuve (discussed below).

Sartre rejects an account of motivation that was prominent in France in the first half of the twentieth century and often used by historians and biographers. The pair of terms mobiles and motifs (see below for discussion of their translation) is central to this account.

Sartre's attitude to the Gestalt theory of perception was more positive, and he relies on it at several points in BN. This theory was developed by the Czech psychologist Max Wertheimer (1880–1943) and others, and influenced many twentieth-century European thinkers. The German noun Gestalt translates as "form": accordingly, Gestalt theory emphasizes the role of structure within the perceptual field as a determinant of percep-tion. The organization of the perceptual field allows a specific "figure" to emerge against a "ground"; the same field, differently organized, may yield a different perception. (As these are the terms used in English trans-lations of Gestalt theory, I use them to translate Sartre's forme and fond.) In anglophone philosophy, the duck-rabbit discussed by Wittgenstein is one of the best-known Gestalt examples. Sartre also borrows the adjec-tive "hodological" from the psychologist Kurt Lewin (1890–1947), who was also associated with the Gestalt school. The Greek hodos means "path"; "hodological" space is therefore the space that we inhabit—lived space—in which our "pathways" are more or less difficult, according to our projects.

angoisse: I translate this as "anguish." Sartre inherits this word (via Corbin's translation) from Heidegger's *Angst*, which is usually translated into English as "anxiety." The term "anxiety" is also often used in English translation and discussion of Kierkegaard's philosophy, and within a broader theological tradition with which Heidegger engaged. These considerations weigh in favor of translating *angoisse* as "anxiety" (and this is compatible with the range of dictionary suggestions). On the other hand "anxiety" has a more medical sound in English, whereas "anguish" sounds more literary and, therefore, more Sartrean. In addition, several French dictionaries suggest that *angoisse* is a more severe form of affliction.

épreuve, éprouver: Sartre often uses the noun *épreuve* to characterize my experience of the Other (e.g., EN 403: *je suis épreuve d'autrui*). A choice has to be made between the many possible ways of translating this French term, which belongs to several semantic fields. It can mean "trial," as in a scientific trial or test, or an academic test, or the activity through which one "tries out" a horse or a car. It can also refer to the kind of challenge one might set someone—e.g., Hercules—to test their strength or courage. It can also mean "ordeal" or "hardship." At its most neutral, it might simply be translated as "experience." Because Sartre frequently emphasizes the asymmetrical and threatening aspects of our relation with the Other, I frequently translate *épreuve* into verbs that hint at these aspects (e.g., "I undergo the Other"); where a noun seems unavoidable, I sometimes use "ordeal." Where Sartre uses *éprouver* with a more neutral sense, I translate it as "to experience."

mobile(s) and *motif(s)*: Sartre sometimes uses the word *mobile* on its own; here it is unproblematically translated as "motive." Elsewhere, in the course of more extended discussions of motivation, Sartre uses the pair of terms *mobile(s)* and *motif(s)*, invoking a terminology that was familiar in French academic discourse in the twentieth century. The two terms are counterparts insofar as *mobile* refers to "subjective" (e.g., psychological) motivational forces, while *motif* refers to "objective" factors, i.e., *grounds* or *reasons* for action. Sartre discusses this familiar explanatory apparatus at length in Part Four. I translate *mobile* as "motive" and *motif* as "reason."

Barnes translated *motif* as "cause"; although she must have meant "cause" in the sense of "ground" (as in "cause for complaint"), this policy is potentially confusing, given Sartre's categorical denial of any causal relations within consciousness.

psyche, psychique: Sartre uses the term *psyche* to refer to the object studied by psychologists and presented to first-person reflection (EN 198): i.e., the "mind." This can usually be easily translated as the English equivalent "psyche." The corresponding adjective—"psychic"—is also available in English, but it is not ordinarily used in the way in which Sartre typically uses *psychique*, i.e., to mean "psychological" or "mental." If I were to use the word "psychic" in these contexts, the English would seem outlandish, and it might be difficult to keep the idea of paranormal (e.g., telepathic) phenomena at bay. In most instances, therefore, I translate *psychique* as "psychological."

Religious vocabulary

Given Sartre's atheism, the abundant use of religious vocabulary in BN may surprise some readers. However, for Sartre the concept of God is philosophically necessary, even if He does not exist. For helpful discussion of the relationship between theology and Sartre's philosophy, see Kirkpatrick (2017).

Apart from *ens causa sui* (discussed immediately below), the religious vocabulary does not cause difficulties in translation; the main purpose of this note is to draw it to the reader's attention. In some cases there is more room for doubt about whether a religious allusion is intended than in others. Examples of terms that (probably) import a religious allusion include "incarnation," "deliverance," "salvation," "emanation," "grace," and "passion."

ens causa sui: Sartre frequently uses this phrase, both in its original Latin, and translated into French as *cause de soi*. The reference of course is to God, or the Supreme Being, i.e., a being whose existence does not depend (causally or in any other way) on any other being. I have translated it as "[the being that] is its own cause" or, occasionally, "the self-caused."

Vocabulary from the three Hs

General note: Where Sartre uses a term in the German (sometimes without any translation), I usually explain it in a footnote on the same page.

The following notes explain how the French terms that Sartre takes from (translations of) these German philosophers correlate with those used by English translators and scholars. In many cases I also provide the original German term and offer a brief explanation of its meaning.

Hegel vocabulary

Sartre's footnote to EN 42 mentions a collection of extracts from Hegel's writing in French translation edited by Henri Lefebvre and published under the title *Morceaux Choisis* in 1938 (available in French as Hegel 1995). It turns out that Sartre took virtually every Hegel quotation he uses in BN from this anthology. In providing the sources of these quotations, Sartre follows Lefebvre in distinguishing (as is also customary in English) between Hegel's "lesser" (*Petite*) *Logic* and his "greater" (*Grande*) *Logic*. These are nicknames for Hegel's *Encyclopaedia Logic* and *Science of Logic*, respectively.

dépasser: In everyday French, this verb means "to go beyond," or "to overtake." However, it is also used in many French translations of Hegel to translate Hegel's German term *Aufhebung*, which is often translated into English as "to sublate." For this reason, where the context is clearly Hegelian, I use "to sublate."

poser: This verb is used by French translators of Hegel to render his verb *Setzen* (which many other German philosophers, including Husserl, also use). I follow most other translators by rendering it as "to posit." Sartre sometimes uses the noun *position* to mean the act of positing; here I translate it as "positing." Unlike "posit" in English, *poser* is also used in ordinary French, where it can mean "to put down" or "to pose" (e.g., a question). In these nontechnical contexts I have used everyday English vocabulary.

scission, scissiparité: The word "scission" also exists in English, although it is not commonly used: it means "split" or "division." French translators of Hegel use *scission* frequently to translate the German *Entzweiung*; English translations of Hegel sometimes use "sundering" or "division" for the corresponding term. I have stuck to "scission." Sartre appears to use the noun *scissiparité* interchangeably with *scission*: as "scissiparity" also exists in English, I have used it, mirroring Sartre's oscillation between the two terms.

Husserl vocabulary

As I have mentioned in my Introduction, Sartre discovered Husserl's work in the 1930s; he had read several of Husserl's texts in their original German before he wrote BN, as well as Emmanuel Levinas's early book on Husserl (translated into English as Levinas 1995). Readers should note that the correct interpretation of many of Husserl's concepts is contested (and there are questions about consistency across texts): the notes below provide no more than a rough idea.

Husserl's key methodological concept is the "phenomenological reduction." Sartre also sometimes refers to it with the Greek term ἐποχή (transliterated *epoché*), which Husserl also used. The basic idea is that, by effecting the phenomenological reduction, the philosophizing subject suspends or parenthesizes the "natural attitude" of everyday life, and reflects from the first personal point of view on the way the world *appears* (i.e., in *phenomena*) to consciousness. All presuppositions concerning the existence or non-existence of the things that appear are bracketed in this reflective exercise, which is supposed to deliver presuppositionless knowledge.

apprésenter: Husserl uses this verb for intentional objects that are mediately (i.e., indirectly) given to the subject. A central example would be other people's consciousness, which, for Husserl, is appresented in their bodies. I follow Husserl's English translators in rendering this verb as "to appresent."

en personne: Sartre sometimes uses this phrase, or "*présence en personne*," in scare quotes, perhaps to indicate its Husserlian origins. Husserl uses it to describe the direct way in which objects are given when they are actually there, as for example in ordinary sensory perception. "The spatial physical thing which we see is, with all its transcendence, still something perceived, given 'in person' in the manner peculiar to consciousness" (Husserl 1983: §43). I translate it as "in person."

hyle: Husserl borrows this term from the Greek word *hyle* for "matter." In Husserl's phenomenology the *hyle* in a mental act is its sensory matter, the brute "given."

intentionner: French translators use this verb to render Husserl's verb *meinen*, which is usually translated into English as "to intend," in the sense where this means the relation of consciousness to its (intentional) object. Sartre may have come across this verb in Levinas's writing on Husserl. I translate it as "to intend."

irréel: In ordinary usage, this French word can simply mean "unreal," but it is also used in philosophical contexts to translate Husserl's German adjective *irreal*. For this reason, if the context suggests that Sartre is using technical phenomenological vocabulary, I follow English translations of Husserl by using "irreal" for *irréel* (even though, of course, that is not an ordinary English word). In Husserl's phenomenology the term "irreal" is used to describe facts or objects (e.g., essences) that do not have spatial or temporal locations, as well as imagined objects.

nécessité de fait: Sartre uses this phrase frequently and tells us (at EN 21) that he borrows it from Husserl, who uses it to characterize consciousness. Husserl's point is that, although consciousness does not have any necessary existence, once it *does* exist, the non-being of its moments is inconceivable. Husserl scholars variously translate the phrase into English as "necessity of a fact," "factual necessity" and "*de facto* necessity." I use "factual necessity."

noème, noèse: In translations of Husserl, these French terms correspond to "noema" and "noesis" in English. (Husserl borrows the words from ancient Greek, where *noema* means "thought," "perception" or "idea.") The noema is, roughly, the content of a mental act, i.e., the way its referent is presented; the noesis is the correlative subjective process, for example the thinking of the thought or the perceiving of the perception.

objectivant, objectiver: The French adjective corresponds to Husserl's term *objektivierend*; in Husserl, it describes a basic feature of all mental acts, i.e., their having an object. English translations of Husserl render it as either "objectivating" or "objectifying." I use the latter, and I translate *objectiver* as "to objectify" throughout.

passéifier: Some dictionaries suggest that Sartre may have made this verb up. In any case he uses it to mean "to make/render past" and, while I have not been able to match it with Husserlian terminology, I would guess that he borrows the concept from Husserl. I translate it as my own neologistic verb "to pastify," although where that is ungainly I have sometimes translated it instead as "to make/render past."

poser: See entry above, in "Hegel vocabulary."

présentifier: French translators use this verb to translate Husserl's *vergegenwärtigen*. I have followed most English translators in using the neologistic verb "to presentify." Husserl uses this term to describe a way in which objects may be somehow "made present" to consciousness even though they are not perceptually given. For example, anticipation "presentifies" an object insofar as its presence is not thought to be actual but at some future date; recollection does the same thing but represents the object as having been in the past; another form of presentification is imagination, etc.

protension: French translators use this noun to translate Husserl's German noun Protention. I follow Husserl's English translators in rendering it as "protention." According to Husserl's account of temporal experience, protentions and retentions are counterpart non-independent elements of any conscious experience. Protentions "reach" forward, into the future, while retentions reach back into the immediate past.

remplir, remplissement: These terms correspond to Husserl's German erfüllen and Erfüllung; the usual English translations are "to fulfill" and "fulfillment." For Husserl, an act is "fulfilled" when evidence shows it to be as the subject took it to be. In the case of perception, for example, an intuition of a landscape is "fulfilled" by the sensory determinations that present it, as Husserl puts it, as being "there," "in person." Where an object is absent, a subject might intend it "emptily," i.e., without sensory fulfillment. (Thus I use "emptily" to render Sartre's adverbial phrase à vide.)

rétention: I translate this as "retention." See protension above for explanation.

thèse, thétique: A "thetic" act, for Husserl, is one that sets something forth, or posits it. For example, the object of a "doxic thesis" will be posited in some modality of belief.

Heidegger vocabulary

The reader should bear in mind that, as discussed earlier, Sartre's access to Heidegger is often mediated by Henry Corbin's French translations (Heidegger 1938), as well as by French commentaries, such as Alphonse De Waelhens's La Philosophie de Martin Heidegger (De Waelhens 1942) (where Sartre found the passage from Heidegger that he quotes in a footnote to EN 413).

dépasser: This verb is used in French translations of Heidegger as well as in translations of Hegel, although, confusingly, it does not usually render the same original German verb(s). In Heidegger's case, dépasser sometimes translates the German verb übersteigen (for which it is a good match, as both these verbs can simply mean "to go beyond" in ordinary language). English translations of Heidegger often use "to surpass" in these contexts.

Apart from Heideggerean contexts, Sartre frequently uses the verb *dépasser* in BN on his own account to characterize the relation of the for-itself to the objects in the world that it "goes beyond" in the pursuit of its ends (e.g., EN 638: *lorsque je dépasse mes objets vers un but*). Here I use the verb "to surpass," which avoids cumbersome prepositions and also harmonizes with the precedent set by Heidegger, which influences Sartre's use.

ek-stase: Sartre borrows this term (*Ekstase* in German) from Heidegger. Heidegger intends to exploit the Greek root meaning of the word (which is generally used to mean "displacement" or "removal"), i.e., "standing-outside." The hyphen in Sartre's French also emphasizes this etymology. In using *ecstasis* and *ecstases* (plural), I follow the English translation of Heidegger (1980) and therefore drop the hyphen.

en sursis: This expression is often used in French to mean "suspended" (e.g., in the judicial context of a suspended sentence), "pending," or "outstanding" (e.g., with reference to unpaid bills). It is highly probable that Sartre took it from Corbin's translations of Heidegger, where *en sursis* is used to translate the German noun *Ausstand* (something "outstanding," as in the financial sense just cited). The basic idea, then, in connection with human-reality, is that its life always stretches before it as something not yet "settled." For these reasons I translate the phrase as "suspended" or "pending."

être-dans-le-monde, être au milieu du monde: In *Being and Time* and other writings from the same period, Heidegger argues that our way of being in the world is wholly different from the way things—worldly objects—are in the world. The hyphens that he often uses—Being-in-the-world—emphasize the indissolubility of our connection to the world we inhabit, a world that "concerns" us. In contrast to this, the relation of worldly objects to the world that surrounds them is one of indifference; they are merely in the world *spatially*, and not *involved* in it (Heidegger 1980: §12). This merely spatial relation is rendered in some English translations as being *within* the world. I have translated the phrases with which Sartre makes the same distinction as "being in the world" and "being-in-the-midst-of-the-world" respectively. He is inconsistent in his use of hyphens.

facticité: This term is the French translation of the German word *Faktizität*, which appears frequently in Heidegger's philosophy, where it refers to the "fact-like" aspects of *Dasein*'s being. From the German, it is usually translated into English as "facticity"; as Sartre takes over the term from Heidegger, I translate it the same way.

historialiser, s'historialiser: This verb was coined by Corbin, in his translation of Heidegger, which is presumably Sartre's source (French dictionaries do not give earlier usages). It refers to *Dasein*'s basic constitutive capacity to "be historical." Although Macquarrie and Robinson (in Heidegger 1980: see §6) translate it into English as "to historize," I think it better to map Sartre's term more closely, and I translate it therefore as "to historialize," etc. (Sartre does not use it consistently, sometimes using *historiciser*— which I render as "to historicize"—instead.) Following Sartre, other French thinkers (e.g., Paul Ricoeur) have used this verb.

il y a (and grammatical variants): Sartre sometimes uses this ordinary French phrase (which means "there is" or "there are") with the intention of alluding to Heidegger's use of the roughly synonymous German phrase *es gibt*. In emphasizing this phrase, Heidegger wants to direct the reader's attention to two ideas: the idea of an event or happening (rather than a state); and (via the verb *geben*) the idea of *giving*, i.e., that Being is "given" to *Dasein*. At its first appearance and on occasional later ones (where I think signaling is helpful), I have inserted *il y a* in square brackets to remind the reader. Sartre frequently highlights this phrase himself (with italics, etc.): the reader should bear in mind the implicit allusion to Heidegger.

ipséité: Sartre would have found this term in Corbin's translations of Heidegger, where it translates Heidegger's *Selbstheit*, which is usually translated into English as "selfhood." Independently of his dialogue with Heidegger, Sartre also uses the word to characterize the for-itself's reflexive relationship to itself. The French *ipséité* builds on the Latin word *ipse* (itself) and is rare in French usage. As the Latinate term can be easily anglicized as "ipseity," I think that is how it should be translated.

on, l'on: Although the French term *on* is translated literally into the English "one," Sartre frequently uses it (implicitly or explicitly) to translate Heidegger's notion "*das Man*." This expression (which is also used in everyday German) is usually translated into English as "[the] they." The reader needs to keep in mind that here, as in Heidegger's usage, the sense of "they" at play is that vague, anonymous idea, as in "they say that the weather will improve."

possibiliser: Sartre would have found this verb in Corbin's translations of

Heidegger. Corbin uses it to translate Heidegger's German verb *ermöglichen*, which means "to make possible." As *possibiliser* is rare in French, and as Heidegger often italicizes the verb in German in order to emphasize its structure, I have used the neologism "to possibilize" in English. Sartre sometimes contrasts it with *probabiliser*, which I translate as "to probabilize."

possibilité, possible: Sartre seems to use the substantive *le possible* ("the possible") interchangeably with *la possibilité* ("possibility"). As "the possible" sounds terrible in English, and I cannot discern any difference in meaning between the two terms, as Sartre uses them, I considered the option of collapsing them into a single English noun "possibility." However, Sartre may have thought he was working with a real distinction (originating perhaps in Heidegger and/or Leibniz, both of whom are important background figures to discussions of "possibility" in the text). The conservative option seemed best.

projet, projeter, pro-jet, pro-jeter: I translate these respectively as "project" (noun), "to project" (verb), "pro-ject" (neologistic noun), and "to pro-ject" (neologistic verb). Sartre takes the hyphenated usage from Corbin, who seeks in turn to do justice to Heidegger's exploitation of the semantic resources of the German verb *entwerfen* (to design, sketch) and the noun *der Entwurf* (sketch, blueprint, etc.). Heidegger often connects these words with the similar-sounding verb *werfen* ("to throw") and its cognates (e.g., *geworfen*). Corbin's choice of *pro-jet*, etc., allowed him to retain this connection with the idea of "throwing" (*jeter*) in the French, a connection that is less obvious in the English.

réalité-humaine: As discussed earlier, Corbin used this phrase to translate Heidegger's term *Dasein*, and Sartre borrows it from Corbin. I translate it straightforwardly as "human-reality." English translators of Heidegger often leave *Dasein* untranslated.

ustensile, ustensilité, le complexe . . . des [réalités] ustensiles: Sartre borrows these terms from Corbin's translation of Heidegger. I translate *complexe d'ustensiles* as "structure of equipment" and the ungainly *ustensilité* as "equipmentality." I translate *ustensile* on its own as "implement."

Bergson vocabulary

Commentators have argued that the influence of the philosopher Henri Bergson (1859–1941) on BN is usually underestimated. As a student, Sartre had read a great deal of Bergson, whose influence on French philosophy only began to decline later in the twentieth century. There are passages in BN where Sartre is recognizably in dialogue with Bergson but does not explicitly say so. Of course, because Bergson's philosophy is written in French, it has not caused any additional translation difficulties. For the most part I retain the vocabulary used by Bergson's English translators.

durée, durer: I have followed Bergson's translators in rendering *durée*—Bergson's term for lived time—as "duration," and the verb *durer* as "to endure."

élan vital: This is one of Bergson's most famous concepts, usually translated as "vital impulse." It is possible that Sartre has it in mind when he uses the term *élan* in relation to the for-itself. For this reason I translate *élan* in these contexts as "impulse."

fantôme: Bergson often uses this adjective; following Bergson translators, I translate it as "phantom."

Negative vocabulary

néant: I have followed Barnes in translating this noun as "nothingness" (see discussion above). Although it is an unusual word in French and in English, it has been available in both these languages for many centuries. In French, it can be found in Descartes and Pascal. In English, it is used by John Donne in his poem "A Nocturnal upon St. Lucy's Day" (first published in 1633).

négatité: See the entry for this term under "Neologisms and ungrammatical locutions."

nier: This French verb corresponds to two different English verbs: "to deny" and "to negate." This can cause difficulty in some contexts, and especially in relation to Hegel's philosophy: the French *nier* manifests its proximity to the idea of negation (*négation* in French; *negieren* or *verneinen* in German), whereas the connection is far less obvious in the English verb "to deny." The use of "to negate" throughout, however, results in clumsy English sentences: for example, *pour nier de ce Pierre . . . qu'il soit là* (EN 61) will translate as "to negate, in relation to this Pierre . . . his being there," which leads us far from ordinary English. For this stylistic reason, I sometimes translate *nier* as "deny." The reader should bear in mind that "deny" and "negate" have a common ancestor in the Latin verb *negare*.

Words and metaphors for movement

Sartre repeatedly emphasizes the dynamic nature of the for-itself by characterizing it with various movement verbs. He often draws (metaphorically or quasi-metaphorically) on dynamic vocabulary whose literal use is to describe natural processes or events. Many of these verbs also convey the idea of upward movement. These verbs do not always translate easily into ordinary English, especially when Sartre uses the substantive form: we would not ordinarily say, for example, that the for-itself is a "bursting forth" or an "upheaval." It may be helpful for the reader to note the following examples of this kind of vocabulary.

jaillir, jaillissement: The verb *jaillir* is often used for movements of water—for example, in contexts where we might translate as "to spring up," "to gush," "to spurt," "to burst out," etc. I have often rendered this by "to burst forth."

surgir, surgissement: See my discussion above.

surrection: The relatively rare French term *surrection* is geological, referring to an upheaval or "uplift" of land, an area that has been elevated. I have translated it as "elevation" (e.g., EN 174).

Other words worthy of note

affecter, s'affecter: The verb *affecter* often straightforwardly means "to affect" (i.e., to have an effect on something), but its reflexive form *s'affecter* can be harder to translate. While it can mean "to affect oneself," Sartre often uses it with the preposition *de* in more abstract contexts, where the meaning is closer to "to assign" (e.g., a property to X) or "to endow" (e.g., X with a property). At EN 58, for example, Sartre writes that *l'homme . . . s'affecte lui-même de non-être à cette fin*: in cases like this I have often used "to assign."

apparence, apparition: Sartre uses both these words throughout BN. Although in many instances they appear to be interchangeable, there can be a difference in meaning in French. *Apparence* is more frequently used to mean "appearance" in the philosophical sense (as, for example, in the appearance/reality distinction); *apparition* means "appearance" in the sense of an *event*—for example, an unannounced appearance at a party, etc. If both these French terms are translated into English as "appearance," this distinction is of course hidden. However, Sartre does not explicitly indicate any intention to use these words with distinct senses in BN, and nor does he consistently use them with identifiably different meanings. In addition, "apparition" is a very unusual word in English and, used as a substantive, "[an] appearing" often sounds odd. I have therefore often used "appearance" for both these terms, using "appearing" instead only when it seems important to convey the event-like sense of *apparition*.

assumer: Sartre often uses this French verb in the sense in which it means "to take on/up" (e.g., a role or responsibility). Although the English verb "assume" can also be used in this sense (e.g., "to assume the leadership"), it is more frequently used in everyday English to mean "to presuppose." To avoid confusion in the English, I have used "assume" only sparingly in these contexts, varying it with "to take up" and "to accept."

l'autre, autrui, les autres: Sartre uses all of these terms to refer to another person or other people. Although in most cases the French term *autrui* (which, although it has no plural form, can refer to either one or more than one person) is synonymous with *l'autre* (or *les autres*), it has an old-fashioned and literary quality and is rarely used in everyday speech. The Littré dictionary suggests that *autrui* can have the sense of "this person here"; used with this sense, it may *oppose* the person spoken about (rather than people in general) to the speaker. Now, Sartre's account of inter-personal relations emphasizes the case in which one person stands in (asymmetric) opposition to another; one person looks, while the Other is looked at. For this reason I translate *autrui* as "*the* Other" (i.e., in the singular), capitalizing it in order to signal that it means another person. I translate *les autres* and *l'autre* slightly less strictly, using "others," "another" or sometimes "an other person" (leaving the o lowercase), where this makes the sense clearer. Sartre is not consistent in his terminology but I have avoided eliminating the difference (between *autrui* and alternative terms) from the translation.

conduite(s): I translate most occurrences of this everyday French word as "behavior," but I avoid the plural "behaviors," as it is less common in English. To handle Sartre's frequent use of *conduites* (plural), I sometimes use "forms of behavior" or a different synonymous noun.

conscience: This noun is used in French to mean both "consciousness" and "conscience" (e.g., moral conscience). In the first sense, the term appears throughout BN in various different contexts.

(i) Sartre uses *conscience* to refer to consciousness quite generally as a mode of being and

(ii) as in English, the same term can be used to apply to some *particular* consciousness, as in "my" or "his" consciousness. Neither (i) nor (ii) causes difficulty in translation.

(iii) In addition, *conscience* can be used in French, but not in English, to refer to particular conscious *events*, as for example at EN 311: *la notion même de conscience ne fait que renvoyer à mes consciences possibles*, where the latter half of this phrase means "to my possible acts of consciousness." Here I have sometimes inserted "[acts of]" into the translation, to make the meaning clearer.

(iv) Sartre sometimes uses the plural form [i.e., *consciences*] to refer, for example, to the coexisting "consciousnesses" of two or more people. Although this English plural ("consciousnesses") is clunky, I have not always been able to avoid it.

(v) The reader should note that the French phrase *avoir conscience de* translates as "to be conscious of." The translation will therefore replace French *avoir* ("to have") with "to be." I do not think this causes difficulty, but, as both verbs are charged with philosophical import in BN, it is worth pointing out.

conscience (de) soi: Sartre uses this phrase to describe the basic reflexivity of human consciousness. When he first introduces it (at EN 20), he explains that his reason for placing the preposition *de* in brackets is in order to emphasize the non-positionality of this mode of consciousness; in it, the "self" is not presented to the subject as a possible *object of knowledge*. Without any brackets, the French phrase *conscience de soi* means "self-consciousness" and, since that English phrase has no preposition, Barnes decided she could use it (see her footnote to Sartre 1965: liv). To my ear, however, "self-consciousness" may still suggest a "positional" attitude (in which the subject confronts his "self") of the kind Sartre wishes to avoid, and so I use phrases that retain Sartre's brackets. A further question about *soi* arises: Should *soi* be translated as "self" or as "itself?" Although the latter has some advantages (for example, it harmonizes with Sartre's view that there is no substantial "self" at the most basic level of first-personal experience), I think that to use it would be to over-interpret. Sartre's use of the phrase "prereflective *cogito*" (as well as "ipseity") registers that there is a self-like structure in consciousness (albeit not a substantial one) which, he argues, provides the ground of reflective self-consciousness.

dépasser: Sartre sometimes uses this verb in its everyday sense, to mean "to go beyond," "to reach beyond," "to exceed," "to outstrip," etc. Where the context is of this kind, I have chosen from this range of words, in a way that maximizes stylistic fluency. See above for uses of this verb in connection with Hegel and Heidegger.

engager, s'engager: This verb often means "to engage" or "to be/become engaged" in the physical sense in which we might say a cog was engaged in machinery. However, as in English, it can also be used to mean "to commit (oneself)" as well as "to enlist" (e.g., in the army). Given Sartre's emphasis on human responsibility and choice, the best translation in many contexts is "to commit," but the reader should bear in mind the range of meaning.

être (and phrases using this verb): As BN is a work of "phenomenological ontology" and heavily influenced by Heidegger, the verb "to be" and the (sometimes neologistic) uses that Sartre makes of it are extremely important. Two constructions that should be noted are the ungrammatical locution "*être été*" (discussed earlier) and *avoir à être*. This latter phrase is used by Sartre to indicate the future-oriented, dynamic and responsible aspects of the for-itself: rather than simply "being" something (e.g., myself) or some way, I have *it to be*. Although it can be quite simply translated into English as "to have to be," the reader needs to be careful in some instances not to read the phrase in the sense that involves the idea of *obligation*. If the for-itself "has X to be," it is not *obliged* to be X but chooses itself as being or aspiring to be X.

extériorité d'indifférence: This phrase, which translates literally but cumbersomely as "exteriority of indifference," occurs frequently in BN. Both the idea and the language are familiar in the German Idealist tradition, but less so in contemporary anglophone philosophy: Sartre would have found them in Hegel as well as Bergson. In both these philosophers, the adjectives "external" and "indifferent" are used to describe one form of relatedness, in contrast to another. Hegel, for example, holds that in mechanistic thinking an object consists of parts that are interrelated only "externally" and are "indifferent" to each other. This contrasts with objects that exhibit a genuine, intrinsic unity—for example, the soul, whose parts are not "indifferent" to each other.

I translate this phrase as "indifferent externality." Although "exteriority" is also available in English, "externality" has the advantage of establishing continuity with many English translations of Hegel and Bergson. (Note, however, that the second part of the title of Levinas's famous book *Totalité et Infini: Essai sur l'extériorité* has been translated into English as "An Essay on Exteriority" (Levinas 1969).)

manquer, le manque: The verb means "to miss [something]" or "to lack [something]"; the noun means "lack." Sartre uses these terms in some extremely complicated sentences to describe the relations in play where something is incomplete; the frequent repetition of m sounds is a feature of the original text.

The following sentence from (EN 122) includes the phrases built on *manquer* that Sartre uses most often in the text:

> *Un manque suppose une trinité: ce qui manque ou manquant, ce à quoi manque ce qui manque ou existant, et une totalité qui a été désagrégée par le manque et qui serait restaurée par la synthèse du manquant et de l'existant: c'est le manqué.*

I translate the phrase *ce qui manque* as "the missing item." The noun which follows—*le manquant*—can be used in French to refer to a missing thing (e.g., a missing person), and Sartre uses it here as a synonym for *ce qui manque*, but, as "missing" cannot be used that way in English, I have omitted this synonym from the corresponding English sentence (and for the second *manquant* of the quoted passage I have reused "the missing item"). I have translated *ce à quoi manque ce qui manque* as "that from which [the missing item] is missing," *le manque* as "the lack," and the final phrase *c'est le manqué* as "that which is missed." Sartre often puns by also using *manqué* in the way we sometimes use it in English (i.e., to mean "failed"); where it is not obvious, I have signaled this.

originel(le): Sartre uses this adjective frequently to mean "original," in the sense of "pertaining to the origin" (as in "original sin"). Because "original" in English is also often used to mean "inventive" or "new," I considered using "originary" instead, but this would undercut associations of "original" that one might want to keep: for example, Sartre's "original choice" has often been compared to a similar idea in Kant's philosophy. In the end I decided to stick to "original" for most instances, but the reader should bear Sartre's intended sense in mind.

positivité, positive: Although it is rare in English philosophy to find "positivity" used as a noun, the French term is well established. Sartre would have been familiar with it from the writings of Auguste Comte (1798–1857), who coined the term "positivism." For Comte, the sciences could be ranked in a hierarchy according to their degree of "positivity," or the extent to which the phenomena they studied could be demonstrated or measured. Sartre often uses "positivity" in opposition to "negativity," to refer to something unquestionably "real," capable of being affirmed. Because of this semi-technical context, I have translated the term as "positivity." I also use the related adjective "positive" in this sense.

réaliser, se réaliser, irréalisable: Sartre uses the verb quite often with the sense of "to make real." Although the English verb "to realize" can be used with that sense, using it to translate *réaliser* will sometimes produce English sentences that are easily misconstrued as meaning "to realize" in the more common, cognitive sense, i.e., to become aware of something. My policy has been to use "to actualize" most of the time, where the intended sense is "to make real." However, Sartre also uses the noun *irréalisable* to refer to something that *cannot* be made real. Here I translate *irréalisable* as "unrealizable" and, if Sartre uses the verb *réaliser* in the same context, I either translate the verb *in that context* as "to realize" or insert "to realize" in square brackets, to remind the reader of the connection to the unrealizable.

In addition, at EN 216 Sartre comments on the "double meaning" (ontological and gnostic) of the French verb *réaliser*: obviously, the verb needs to be translated here as "to realize."

reflet, reflétant, réflexion, réfléchi: This cluster of terms, already philosophically complicated in the text, presents additional difficulties in translation because the English fails to distinguish (by means of different spellings) between the types of "reflection" that Sartre is able to keep distinct by using two slightly different French verbs (*réfléchir* and *refléter*).

It will help if the reader keeps in mind Sartre's view that there is one basic form of "reflection" that is a permanent and necessary structure of consciousness. For this, Sartre uses the French verb *refléter*, which means "to reflect" in the sense of "to cast back an image/light," i.e., in the sense in which a mirror reflects. In this context Sartre often uses the hyphenated phrase *reflet-reflétant* to describe the back-and-forth play of reflections within consciousness. I translate this phrase as "reflection-reflecting." Sartre uses the different verb—*réfléchir*—to refer to a different type, or second level, of reflection—a cognitive act—in which consciousness takes itself as an object. According to Sartre, this kind of reflection is liable to distort what it reflects on; this is "complicit" reflection, which Sartre contrasts with "pure" reflection.

Because of the close connection in meaning (cognitive reflection can be seen to be a kind of "mirroring" of our minds), I do not think the answer would be to use two different verbs in English. In most cases the context makes it clear which type of reflection Sartre is talking about, but where I think it is possible that confusion may arise, I have provided a clarifying footnote.

regarder, le regard: For Sartre, the experience of *le regard* (usually translated as "the look") is fundamental to our experience of the Other. Shame is a paradigmatic instance of that experience, insofar precisely as it involves our being *looked at* by someone else.

Unfortunately, the effect of translating *le regard* as the noun "(the) look" is to produce some infelicitous English sentences. For example, *un regard à éviter* is better translated as "to avoid being seen" rather than by "a look to be avoided"; similarly, *son regard fixé à terre* translates well as "his gaze fixed to the ground," whereas "his look" in this sentence is terrible. However, the danger of these stylistically preferable alternatives is that they may distract from, or dilute the force of, "the look," which is almost a technical term in BN. I have compromised by sticking to "the look" most of the time, and using "gaze" occasionally in the interests of style.

tendance: Early translations of Freud into French often used the noun *tendance* ("tendency" in English) to translate the German term Trieb—which corresponds to "drive" in English. But this is not an ideal choice (at least not when *tendance* is translated again into English), because "tendency" sounds much weaker (and less instinctual) than "drive." Where Sartre is clearly in dialogue with Freud, therefore, I translate *tendance* as "drive," but elsewhere I sometimes use "tendency."

le visqueux, la viscosité: Hazel Barnes translated these terms as "slime" (adjective "slimy"); her aim, she tells us in a footnote, was to make the *figurative* meanings of the French and English terms correspond (Sartre 1965: 604). It is true that Sartre often uses *visqueux* figuratively and intends it to have unpleasant associations. On the other hand, some of these figurative uses are creative even in French, and in some instances "slimy" has, I think, an *overly* negative force. Moreover there are good reasons for translating *visqueux* straightforwardly as "viscous." Sartre's debt to Gaston Bachelard's "psychoanalysis of things" (an exploration of the psychological meaning of natural elements) is explicit, and this precedent is important. Both Bachelard and Sartre are concerned with the psychological significance of forms of materiality: the word "viscous," with its scientific or chemical register is, I think, best suited for this.

References

Bergson, Henri (1911), *Creative Evolution*, trans. Arthur Mitchell (New York: Henry Holt).

De Waelhens, Alphonse (1942), *La Philosophie de Martin Heidegger* (Louvain: Éditions de l'Institut Supérieur de Philosophie).

Hegel, G. W. F. (1995), *Morceaux Choisis*, trans. H. Lefebvre and N. Guterman (Paris: Gallimard Folio).

Heidegger, Martin (1938), *Qu'est-ce que la Métaphysique? Suivi d'Extraits sur l'Être et le Temps et d'une Conference sur Hölderlin*, trans. Henry Corbin (Paris: Gallimard).

Heidegger, Martin (1980), *Being and Time*, trans. J. Macquarrie and E. Robinson (Oxford: Blackwell).

Husserl, Edmund (1983), *Ideas Pertaining to a Pure Phenomenology and to a Phenomenological Philosophy*, First Book, trans. F. Kersten (The Hague: Martinus Nijhoff).

Inwood, Michael (1999), "Does the Nothing Noth?," in O'Hear (ed.) (1999): 271–290.

Kirkpatrick, Kate (2017), *Sartre and Theology* (London: Bloomsbury).

Levinas, Emmanuel (1969), *Totality and Infinity: An Essay on Exteriority*, trans. Alphonso Lingis (Pittsburgh: Duquesne University Press).

Levinas, Emmanuel (1995), *The Theory of Intuition in Husserl's Phenomenology*, trans. André Orianne (2nd edition) (Evanston, IL: Northwestern University Press).

O'Hear, Anthony (ed.) (1999), *German Philosophy since Kant* (Cambridge: Cambridge University Press).

Olafson, F. A. (1958), "Review of Being and Nothingness by Jean-Paul Sartre and Hazel E. Barnes," *Philosophical Review*, 67 (2): 276–280.

Sartre, Jean-Paul (1965), *Being and Nothingness*, trans. and introduced by Hazel Barnes (New York: Washington Square Press).

TRANSLATOR'S ACKNOWLEDGMENTS

Sarah Richmond

My thanks are due in the first instance to Tony Bruce at Routledge, who invited me to do this translation. He and Adam Johnson (also at Routledge) have been consistently encouraging and helpful. Their tactful inquiries about my progress on the project have enabled me to keep deadlines and promises in mind without becoming frozen by panic.

I am grateful to Luc Foisneau and Étienne Balibar, who have generously shared with me their expertise in French philosophy and their linguistic intuitions, and to Michèle Le Dœuff for helpful discussion of le visqueux. In the UK, I thank Mary Margaret McCabe for advice about terminology and sources for Aristotle and Plato, and Sebastian Gardner for the amazing helpline he has provided for numerous questions about Kant and post-Kantian German philosophy. Sebastian's solidarity, his sense of humor, and our lunches in the student caff have meant a lot to me. Armand D'Angour has answered my emails about ancient Greek and Latin words within seconds, providing translations, transliterations and Greek inscriptions on demand. Galen Strawson has been a valued correspondent for several years: his emails have encouraged me and I have also benefited from his excellent knowledge of French as well as his sense of English style. From Australia, Andrew Inkpin has sent many illuminating and informative messages about Heidegger, thereby saving me labor I would not have enjoyed. George di Giovanni has generously lent me his expertise as a Hegel translator and scholar, and helped me to locate several passages in Hegel. The text has also benefited from my correspondence with another experienced translator, Andrew Brown, with whom I have had several enjoyable face-to-face consultations in various Cambridge locations. Andrew put me in touch with Nick Walker, another UK-based translator, who has offered further useful thoughts. Jean-Pierre Boulé and Ben O'Donohoe, two former colleagues at *Sartre Studies International*, have also helpfully commented on a number of issues. Marcus Giaquinto has allowed me to pick his brains about mathematical terminology, while Henri Chabrol has advised about psychiatry. Tom Stern told me all I needed to know about Nietzsche's term *Hinterwelt*. Florence Caeymaex, Danièle Tort-Maloney, Jeanne Balibar, Antoine Amalric, and Pierre Amalric have also usefully commented.

Jonathan Wolff and José Zalabardo, who have served as heads of the Philosophy Department at UCL, have been sensitive line managers. They have been generous in awarding me research time as well as some funding for research assistance. This funding enabled me to delegate some tasks to two excellent research assistants, Alexandre Sayegh and Olivia Fairweather, whose help I also gratefully acknowledge. Jo Wolff also commented on a draft of the Translator's Introduction, as did Judith Barrett.

I would like to thank the two anonymous reviewers who wrote such positive reviews for my application for funding to the AHRC, and to record my disappointment in the AHRC for failing nonetheless to support it. I regret the immense amount of time I spent struggling with the AHRC's hideous electronic interface and with the many irrelevant questions they obliged me to answer. I am immensely grateful to the French government–funded CNRS (*Centre National de la Recherche Scientifique*) for maintaining the superb website for "textual and lexical resources," from which I have learned a great deal.

I am indebted to Dr. Maria Pozzi and Dr. Kate Kandasamy for their kind and expert support during a period of ill health. Their thoughtful advice was indispensable in helping me to keep going through a difficult time, and deeply appreciated.

A complete first draft of the translation was sent out for review to Ron Santoni, Jonathan Webber, Kate Kirkpatrick, and Curtis Sommerlatte, and I am grateful for their helpful feedback. Special thanks are due to

Curtis Sommerlatte for his painstaking and thoughtful scrutiny, which resulted in several important improvements. At a later stage I had the good fortune to work with Helen Moss, my copy editor; Helen's discriminating queries and her eagle eye led to the elimination of many typos and infelicities from the text. I would also like to thank Elizabeth Kent at Swales & Willis for all her help with production.

My parents, Theo Richmond and Lee Richmond, looked at passages of the translation as well as the Translator's Introduction, and offered helpful criticisms. As professional writers of English, they gave advice that has guided me in matters of register, style, and syntax. I must also thank them for their love and their unwavering interest in my activities.

Thanks also to Judith Barrett, who has been a brilliant friend ever since we were undergraduates together. My frequent phone calls and outings with her have significantly enhanced my well-being while I worked on this translation.

My greatest debt is to my spouse, Neil Vickers, and our two sons, Noah Vickers and Samuel Vickers. I cannot imagine three more wonderful family members, friends, and companions. I gratefully acknowledge their generous love, patience, and support. This translation would not have been possible without them, and I dedicate it to them.

Being and Nothingness

Au Castor

INTRODUCTION

In search of being[1]

I. THE IDEA OF THE PHENOMENON

By reducing the existent to the series of appearances that manifest it, modern thought has made considerable progress. The aim was to eliminate a number of troublesome dualisms from philosophy, and to replace them with the monism of the phenomenon. Has it succeeded?

In the first place, we have certainly got rid of the dualism that opposes an existent's inside to its outside. The existent no longer has an "outside," if by that we mean some skin at its surface that conceals the object's true nature from view. And if this "true nature" is, in turn, to be the thing's secret reality—something that we can anticipate or assume but that we can never reach, because it is "inside" the object in question—that does not exist either. The appearances that manifest the existent are neither internal nor external: they are all of equal worth, each of them refers to other appearances, and none of them has priority. Force, for example, is not a metaphysical *conatus* of some unknown

---

1 Translator's note (TN): Sartre's Introduction is entitled "A la recherche de l'être." I have been guided in my translation by the thought that Sartre probably intended to echo Proust's *A la Recherche du Temps Perdu*. Note that Proust is used as an example within BN's opening pages.

kind, concealed behind its effects (accelerations, deviations, etc.); it is the sum of these effects. Similarly, an electric current has no secret other side: it is nothing but the collection of physicochemical actions (electrolytic processes, the incandescence of a carbon filament, the movement of the galvanometer's needle, etc.) that manifest it. None of these actions is sufficient to reveal it. But it does not point to anything *behind* it; each action points to itself and to the total series. From this it obviously follows that the dualism of being and appearing no longer has a legitimate place in philosophy. An appearance refers to the total series of appearances, not to some hidden reality that siphons off all the existent's *being* for itself. And the appearance, for its part, is not an unstable manifestation of that being. For as long as we were still able to believe in noumenal realities, the appearance was presented as purely negative, as "that which is not being": it had no being other than that of illusion and error. But that being was itself borrowed, it was itself a sham, and the biggest problem facing us was how to maintain the appearance with enough cohesion and existence to stop it from being reabsorbed into non-phenomenal being. But once we have freed ourselves from what Nietzsche called "the illusion of backworlds"[2]—and if we no longer believe in any being-behind-appearance—the appearance becomes, on the contrary, full positivity. Its essence is an "appearing" that is no longer opposed to being but which is, on the contrary, its measure. For the being of an existent is precisely the way it *appears*. Thus we are led to the idea of the *phenomenon* as we encounter it, for example, in Husserl's or Heidegger's "Phenomenology": the phenomenon, or the absolute-relative. The phenomenon remains relative because its "appearing" necessarily implies someone to whom it appears. But it does not have the twofold relativity of Kant's *Erscheinung*.[3] It does not indicate behind its shoulder some true being, a being that is itself the absolute. It is what it is absolutely, because it is disclosed *as it is*. The phenomenon can be studied and described as such, because it is *absolutely indicative of itself*.

2 TN: Sartre is loosely quoting from a French translation of Nietzsche's *Thus Spake Zarathustra*. The French *arrière-mondes* is used to translate Nietzsche's German neologism *Hinterwelten*, which is often translated into English as "backworld." The idea is that of a world "beyond" or "behind" the world we experience.

3 TN: Kant's term *Erscheinung* is normally translated into English as "appearance."

At the same time, the duality of potentiality and actuality will collapse.[4] Everything is in actuality. Behind the act there is neither potentiality, nor "hexis,"[5] nor virtue.[6] The term "genius," for example—as it is used when we say that Proust "had" great genius or that he "was" a genius—should not be taken to mean a distinctive power to produce various writings, a power that is not exhausted in producing those writings. Proust's genius is neither his work considered in isolation nor the subjective power to produce it: it is his work, seen as the set of manifestations of his person. That is why we can, in the end, also reject the dualism of appearance and essence. Appearance does not hide essence but reveals it: it *is* the essence. The essence of an existent is no longer a power embedded deep inside it; it is the manifest law governing the succession of its appearances, the principle of the series. Duhem was right to oppose Poincaré's nominalism—which defined a physical reality (for example, an electrical power) as the *sum* of its various manifestations—with his own theory, according to which a concept is the *synthetic unity* of those manifestations.[7] Of course, nothing could be farther from nominalism than phenomenology. But ultimately, an essence, understood as the principle of a series, is no more than the connection between the appearances—which means it is itself an appearance. That explains how an intuition of essences (Husserl's *Wesenschau*, for example) is possible.[8] Thus phenomenal being manifests itself: it manifests its essence just as much as its existence, and it is nothing but the interconnected series of these manifestations.

Does this mean we have succeeded in eliminating *all* dualisms by reducing the existent to its manifestations? It seems rather that we have

13

---

4 TN: Sartre is referring to the distinction between *energeia* and *dunamis* in Aristotle's metaphysics. Both terms are variously translated in different English translations: I use "actuality" and "potentiality" for Sartre's *acte* and *puissance*.

5 TN: The ancient Greek term *hexis* is important in Aristotle's philosophy. Although it is agreed to be difficult to translate Aristotle's exact meaning, "habit" and "disposition" are both commonly used.

6 TN: Sartre uses the French word *vertu* here in its older sense, to mean a power or active principle—as it is used in English philosophy in the well-known example of "dormitive virtue."

7 TN: Pierre Duhem (1861–1916) was a French physicist and philosopher of science. Henri Poincaré (1854–1912) was a French mathematician, physicist, and philosopher of science.

8 TN: Husserl's English translators usually render *Wesenschau* as "intuition of essences."

converted them all into one new dualism: the finite and the infinite. For the existent cannot be reduced to a finite series of manifestations, as each of these is a relationship to a constantly changing subject. While an *object* may only be given through a single "*Abschattung*," the mere fact of being a *subject* implies the possibility of multiplying the points of view *on to* that "*Abschattung*."[9] This amounts to multiplying the "*Abschattung*" in question to infinity. Furthermore, if the series of appearances was finite, it would follow (absurdly) that the ones appearing first could not *reappear* or (even more absurdly) that they could all be given at the same time. We need to be quite clear that our theory of the phenomenon has replaced the thing's *reality* with the phenomenon's *objectivity*, and that it founds this latter by appealing to the infinite. The reality of this cup is that it *is* there, and that it *is not* me. We can express this by saying that the series of its appearances is connected by a *principle* that does not depend on my whim. But an appearance considered just as it is—without reference to the series to which it belongs—can only be an intuitive and subjective plenitude: the way in which the subject is affected. If a phenomenon is to show itself as *transcendent*, the subject himself must transcend the appearance toward the total series of which it is a member. He must grasp *redness*—i.e., the principle of the series—through his impression of red; the electric current through the electrolysis, etc. But if the object's transcendence is grounded in the necessity that any appearance can be transcended, it follows axiomatically that the series of appearances for any object is posited as infinite. Thus, a *finite* appearance indicates itself in its finitude, but at the same time, in order to be grasped as an appearance-of-that-which-appears, it demands to be surpassed toward the infinite. This new opposition, the "finite and the infinite" or, better still, "the infinite within the finite," replaces the dualism of being and appearing: what appears is in effect only an *aspect* of the object, and the object is entirely *within* this aspect and entirely outside it. Entirely *inside* insofar as it manifests itself in this aspect: it is indicated as the structure of the appearance, which is at the same time the principle of the series. Entirely *outside*, because the series itself never appears, and cannot appear. Thus, once again, the

9 TN: The term *Abschattung* refers in Husserl's phenomenology to the incomplete aspect of an object given in our perception of it—for example, to the one side of a six-sided die that we may be able to see. Kersten translates it as "adumbration" (Husserl 1983); it is sometimes translated as "profile."

outside is opposed to the inside, and the being-that-does-not-appear is opposed to its appearance. Similarly, a certain "power" returns to the phenomenon, inhabiting it and endowing it with its very transcendence: the power to be developed through a series of real or possible appear-   14 ances. Even if we reduce Proust's genius to the works he produced, it is still equivalent to the infinity of possible points of view that we can take up on Proust's work—its so-called inexhaustibility. But isn't this inexhaustibility, which implies a transcendence and an appeal to the infinite, a "hexis"—even at the very moment in which we apprehend it in the object? In the end, the essence is radically cut off from any individual appearance that manifests it, because it must be possible, as a matter of principle, for it to be manifested by a series of individual manifestations.

By replacing in this way a variety of oppositions with a single dualism that founds them all, have we gained or lost? Soon we shall see. For now, the primary consequence of the "theory of the phenomenon" is that the appearance does not refer to being in the way in which the phenomenon, in Kantian philosophy, refers to the noumenon. Because there is nothing behind the appearance, and it indicates nothing more than itself (and the total series of appearances), it cannot be *supported* by any being other than its own, and cannot therefore be the thin skin of nothingness separating subject-being from absolute-being. If the essence of appearance is an "appearing" that is no longer opposed to any *being*, there is a genuine problem of the *being of this appearing*. This is the problem with which we are concerned here, and it will be the point of departure for our investigations into being and nothingness.

II. THE PHENOMENON OF BEING AND THE BEING OF THE PHENOMENON

An appearance is not supported by some other, different, existent: it has its own *being*. The first being that we encounter in our ontological investigations is, therefore, the being of appearance. Is that being itself an appearance? So it seems, at first sight. A phenomenon is something that manifests itself, and being manifests itself in some way to all of us, since we can talk about it and have some understanding of it. Thus there must be a *phenomenon of being*, an appearing of being, that can be described as such. Being will be disclosed to us through some immediate means of access (boredom, nausea, etc.), and ontology will be the description of the phenomenon of being as it manifests itself, i.e., without intermediary. However, for any ontology, we need to ask a preliminary question: Is the phenomenon of being that we reach by these means identical to the being of the phenomena? Or: Is the being that is disclosed to me, that *appears* to me, the same in nature as the being of the existents that appear to me? Here there seems to be no problem: Husserl showed us how an eidetic reduction is always possible—in other words, how we can always surpass a concrete phenomenon toward its essence—and, for Heidegger, "human-reality" is ontico-ontological, which means it can always surpass the phenomenon toward its being.[10] But to move from a particular object to its essence is to move between two homogeneous items. Can the same be said of the movement from an existent to the phenomenon of being? In surpassing an existent toward the phenomenon of being, are we really surpassing it toward *its* being, as we might surpass a particular red toward *its* essence? Let us take a closer look.

In a particular object, we may always distinguish qualities such as color, smell, etc. And, on the basis of these, we can always establish the essence they imply—just as a sign implies its meaning. The "object–essence" pair is an organized whole: the essence is not *inside* the object; it is the object's meaning, the principle of the series of appearances which disclose it. But the object's being is neither one of its qualities, capable of being grasped among others, nor is it a meaning of the object. The object does not refer to being as it might refer to a meaning: it is not possible, for example, to define being as a *presence*, since *absence* also discloses being, since not being *there* is still a way of being. The object does not *possess* being, and its existence is not a participation in being or any other kind of relation. The only way to define its way of being is to say that it *is*; for the object does not conceal being but neither does it disclose it. It does not conceal it: it would be futile to set aside some of an existent's qualities, to try to find its being behind them; its being belongs to all of them equally. It does not disclose it: it would be futile to appeal to the object in order to apprehend its being. The existent is phenomenal; in other words, it designates itself as an

10 TN: Sartre probably has *Being and Time* in mind here (Heidegger 1980).

organized set of qualities. *Itself*, and not its being. Being is merely the condition of any disclosure: it is being-in-order-to-disclose, not being disclosed. What, then, does Heidegger mean when he speaks of a "surpassing toward the ontological?" Of course, I can surpass this table or this chair toward its being, and I can pose the question of the table-being or chair-being. But in that moment I look away from the table-phenomenon in order to fasten on the being-phenomenon, which is no longer the condition of all disclosure but which is itself something disclosed, an appearance which, as such, needs in its turn some being on whose foundation it could be disclosed.

If the being of phenomena cannot be resolved into a phenomenon of being, and if, however, we can only *say* anything about being by consulting this phenomenon of being, we must establish first and foremost the exact nature of the relationship that joins the phenomenon of being to the being of the phenomenon. This will be easier if we note that all our observations so far were directly inspired by the revealing intuition of the phenomenon of being. By considering being not as the condition of disclosure but rather as an appearance that can be fixed in concepts, we have understood in the first place that knowledge alone cannot account for being, i.e., that the being of the phenomenon cannot be reduced to the phenomenon of being. In brief, the phenomenon of being is "ontological" in the sense in which Saint Anselm's and Descartes's proof is called *ontological*. It is a call for being: it requires, insofar as it is a phenomenon, a transphenomenal foundation. The phenomenon of being requires the transphenomenality of being. That does not mean that being is hidden *behind* the phenomena (we saw that the phenomenon cannot mask being), nor that the phenomenon is an appearance that refers to a being distinct from it (the phenomenon has being *qua appearance*, i.e., it indicates itself on the foundation of being). The preceding considerations imply that, although the being of the phenomenon is coextensive with the phenomenon, it must escape the phenomenal condition in which existence is possible only to the extent that it is revealed, and consequently that it overflows and founds any knowledge we can have of it.

16

III. THE PREREFLECTIVE *COGITO* AND THE BEING OF THE *PERCIPERE*

One might be tempted to reply that all the difficulties mentioned so far stem from a particular conception of being, a kind of ontological realism that is wholly incompatible with the very idea of *appearance*. Indeed, the being of an appearance is proportionate to its *appearing*. And since we have limited reality to the phenomenal, we can say of the phenomenon that it *is* as it *appears*. Why not pursue this idea right to its limit and say that the being of an appearance is its appearing? That is simply a way of clothing Berkeley's venerable phrase "*Esse est percipi*" in new words. And effectively, that is just what Husserl does when, having carried out the phenomenological reduction,[11] he treats the noema as *irreal* and declares its "*esse*" to be a "*percipi*."[12]

Berkeley's famous formula seems unlikely to satisfy us. And essentially this is for two reasons: first, because of the nature of the *percipi*, and second, because of the nature of the *percipere*.

The nature of the "percipere"—If any metaphysics presupposes a theory of knowledge, it is equally true that any theory of knowledge presupposes a metaphysics. That means, among other things, that any idealism aiming to reduce being to our knowledge of it must first account in some way for the being of knowledge. If, on the contrary, you begin by positing the latter as a given—without any concern to found its being—and you go on to claim that "*esse est percipi*," the "perception-perceived" totality, deprived of any solid being to support it, will collapse into nothingness. Thus the being of knowledge cannot be measured by knowledge; it escapes the "*percipi*."[13] Thus the foundation-being of the *percipere* and of the *percipi* must itself escape the *percipi*: it must be transphenomenal. We are back where

17

---

11 TN: See my note on the phenomenological reduction in the section on Husserl vocabulary in Notes on the Translation.

12 TN: Husserl says this in §98 of *Ideas* (Husserl 1983). Berkeley's formula *Esse est percipi* means "To be is to be perceived." *Percipere*—in this section's title—is the infinitive form of "to perceive" in Latin. For the terms *noema*, *noesis*, and *irreal*, see the section on Husserl vocabulary in Notes on the Translation.

13 Sartre's note: It goes without saying that any attempt to replace the *percipere* by some other attitude of human-reality will be equally fruitless. If you allow that being is revealed to man in his "doing," you still need to establish the being of the doing, apart from the action.

we began. However, one might allow that the percipi refers to a being that escapes the laws of appearance while still maintaining that this transphenomenal being is the subject's being. The percipi would therefore direct us toward the percipiens—the known toward the knowledge—and this latter to the knowing being insofar as he is, and not insofar as he is known, i.e., to consciousness. Husserl understood this: for if in his view the noema is an irreal correlative of the noesis, whose ontological law is the percipi, he regards the noesis on the contrary as reality, whose chief characteristic is to offer itself up to the reflection that knows it as "having already been there first." For the law of being that governs the knowing subject is being-conscious. Consciousness is not a special kind of knowledge, called "inner sense" or "self-knowledge"; it is the subject's dimension of transphenomenal being.

Let us try to improve our understanding of this dimension of being. We said that consciousness is the knowing being insofar as he is, and not insofar as he is known. In consequence, we ought to abandon the primacy of knowledge if we want to found that knowledge itself. And, without doubt, consciousness can know and it can know itself. But it is, in itself, something other than knowledge turned back on itself.

As Husserl showed, all consciousness is consciousness of something.[14] In other words, there is no [act of] consciousness that does not posit a transcendent object or, if you prefer, consciousness has no "content." We need to give up these neutral "givens" that can constitute themselves, according to the chosen system of reference, into the "world" or the "psyche." A table is not in consciousness, not even as a representation. A table is in space, beside the window, etc. Indeed, the table's existence is a center of opacity for consciousness; an infinite process would be required to make an inventory of the total content of a thing. To introduce this opacity within consciousness would be to refer to infinity any inventory that consciousness might make of itself, to turn consciousness into a thing, and to reject the cogito. Philosophy's first course of action, therefore, should be to expel things from consciousness and to restore the true relationship between this latter and the world: namely, that consciousness is a positional consciousness of the world. All con-

14 TN: Husserl makes this point in many of his writings. See for example Husserl (1960: 72).

sciousness is positional in that it transcends itself to reach an object, and it is exhausted by just this act of positing. All that is intentional in my consciousness is directed outside, toward the table: all my judicative or practical activities, and all the affectivity of the moment, transcend themselves; they aim at the table, and are absorbed within it. Not every [act of] consciousness is a form of knowledge (for example, there are affective modes of consciousness), but every knowing consciousness can only be knowledge of its object.

Nonetheless, the necessary and sufficient condition for a knowing consciousness to be knowledge of its object is that it should be conscious of itself as being this knowledge. It is a necessary condition: if my consciousness were not conscious of being conscious of a table, it would thereby be conscious of the table without being conscious that it was so or, alternatively, it would be a consciousness that did not know itself, an unconscious consciousness—which is absurd. It is a sufficient condition: my being conscious of being conscious of the table suffices for me in fact to be conscious of it. It is not of course sufficient to enable me to claim that the table exists in itself—but rather that it exists for me.

What is this consciousness of consciousness? We are in the grip of the illusion of the primacy of knowledge to such an extent that we are willing to turn our consciousness of consciousness immediately into an *idea ideae*, as Spinoza does[15]—in other words, to turn it into a knowledge of knowledge. When Alain comes to express the evident fact that "to know is to be conscious of knowing," he translates it into these terms: "To know is to know that one knows." What is hereby defined is *reflection*, or the positional consciousness of consciousness or, better still, *knowledge of consciousness*. This is to be understood as an [act of] consciousness that is complete in itself and directed toward something that it is not—in other words, toward the reflected consciousness. It thus transcends itself and, like our positional consciousness of the world, its aiming at its object exhausts it. Only in this case its object is itself an [act of] consciousness.

This interpretation of the consciousness of consciousness does not seem acceptable. The reduction of consciousness to knowledge effectively imports the subject-object duality—which is typical of knowledge—within

---

15 TN: Spinoza advances this view of self-consciousness in Part Two of his *Ethics* (Spinoza 1985).

consciousness. But if we accept the law of the knowing-known dyad, a third term will become necessary for the knowing in its turn to become known, and we are placed in a dilemma. Either we stop at some term within the series: the known, the knowing that is known, the knowing of the knowing that is known, etc.—in which case the phenomenon in its totality collapses into the unknown (i.e., we always come up against a reflection that is not conscious of itself and is the final term)—or we declare an infinite regress (idea ideae ideae, etc.) to be necessary, which is absurd. In this way the necessity of ontologically founding knowledge is duplicated by a new necessity: that of founding it epistemologically. Surely we ought not to introduce the law of the dyad into consciousness? Consciousness of self is not a dyad. If we want to avoid an infinite regress, it must be an immediate and noncognitive relationship of self to self.

Moreover, reflective consciousness posits the reflected consciousness as its object: in the act of reflection, I bring judgments to bear on my reflected consciousness; I am ashamed of it, I am proud of it, I want it, I reject it, etc. The immediate consciousness that I have of perceiving does not allow me either to judge, or to want, or to be ashamed. It does not *know* my perception, or *posit* it: all that is intentional within my current [act of] consciousness is directed outward, toward the world. On the other hand, this spontaneous consciousness that I have of my perception is *constitutive* of my perceptual consciousness. In other words, any positional consciousness of an object is at the same time a non-positional consciousness of itself. If I count the cigarettes that are in this case, my impression is that of disclosing an objective property of this group of cigarettes: *they are twelve*. This property appears to my consciousness as a property existing in the world. I may well have no positional consciousness at all of counting them. I do not "know myself as counting." Proof of this can be seen in the fact that children who are capable of spontaneous addition are unable *to explain* afterward how they did it. The tests by Piaget which demonstrated this constitute an excellent refutation of Alain's formula: To know is to know that one knows. And yet, at the moment when these cigarettes disclose themselves to me as "twelve," I am non-thetically conscious of my adding activity.[16] Indeed, if I am questioned, if someone asks me "What are you doing?" I will

16 TN: . . . *une conscience non-thétique* . . . See note on *thèse* in the section on Husserl vocabulary in Notes on the Translation.

reply immediately "I am counting," and my reply does not aim only at the instantaneous [act of] consciousness that I can reach through reflection but also at those [acts of] consciousness that have passed by without being reflected on, which will forever remain *unreflected* in my immediate past. Thus, reflection lacks any kind of primacy in relation to reflected consciousness: it is not by means of the former that the latter is revealed to itself. On the contrary, nonreflective consciousness is what makes reflection possible: there is a prereflective *cogito*, which is the condition of the Cartesian *cogito*. At the same time, my non-thetic consciousness of counting is actually the condition of my activity of addition. How, if it were otherwise, could addition be the unifying theme of my [acts of] consciousness? In order for that theme to preside over the whole series of syntheses of unifications and of recognitions, it must be present to itself, not in the manner of a thing but as an operative intention that can exist only—to use an expression of Heidegger's—as a "revealing-revealed."[17] Thus, in order to count, it is necessary to be conscious of counting.

20

"Of course," it might be said, "but that is circular." Because isn't it necessary, for me to be able to be conscious of counting, that in fact I am counting? That is true. However, that does not lead to a circle—or, alternatively, it is the very nature of consciousness to exist "in a circle." We can express this in these terms: any conscious existence exists as the consciousness of existing. We can understand now why the most basic consciousness of consciousness is not positional: because it and the consciousness of which it is conscious are one and the same. In a single movement, consciousness determines itself as consciousness of perception, and as perception. The requirements of syntax here have obliged us until now to talk of "nonpositional consciousness of self." But we cannot go on using this expression, in which the phrase "*of self*" still evokes the idea of knowledge. (From now on we will put the "of" between brackets, to indicate that it answers only to a grammatical constraint.)[18]

---

17 TN: ...*comme "révélante-révelée"*...I have not been able to find this exact phrase in Heidegger; Sartre probably took it from Corbin's preface to his translations. Here Corbin says that the mode of being of human-reality is: "*d'être révélante et en même temps réalite-révélée*," using these phrases to translate Heidegger's *erschliessend* and *Erschlossenheit* (Heidegger 1938: 15).

18 TN: See my note on *conscience (de) soi* in Notes on the Translation.

We should not regard this consciousness (of) self as a new [act of] consciousness but as *the only possible mode of existence for any consciousness of something.* Just as an extended object is constrained to exist in three dimensions, so an intention, a pleasure, and a pain can exist only as immediately conscious (of) themselves. The being of an intention can only be consciousness; otherwise the intention would be a thing inside consciousness. We must not therefore take this to mean that some external cause (an organic disturbance, an unconscious drive, another "Erlebnis")[19] can determine the production of a psychological event—a pleasure, for example—and that the event whose material structure is hereby determined will in addition be compelled to produce itself as conscious (of) self. That would make non-thetic consciousness into a *quality* of positional consciousness (in the sense in which perception—as a positional consciousness of that table—might have the additional quality of consciousness (of) self), and would thereby lead us back to the illusion of the theoretical primacy of knowledge. In addition, it would turn the psychological event into a thing and *qualify* it as conscious, as I may qualify, for example, this blotting paper as pink. Pleasure cannot be distinguished—even logically—from the consciousness of pleasure. The consciousness (of) pleasure is constitutive of pleasure, as its very mode of existence, as the matter of which it is made, and not as a form that is subsequently imposed on some hedonic matter. Pleasure cannot exist "before" any consciousness of pleasure—not even in virtual form, or as a potentiality. A potential pleasure can exist only as a consciousness (of) its potentiality; there are no virtualities in consciousness that are not conscious of being virtual.

Conversely, as I showed earlier, we must avoid defining pleasure in terms of my consciousness of it. That would push us into an idealist view of consciousness that would lead us back—in a roundabout way—to the primacy of knowledge. We must not let pleasure disappear behind its consciousness (of) itself: it is not a representation but a concrete, full, and absolute event. Pleasure is *no more* a quality of consciousness (of) self than consciousness (of) self is a quality of pleasure. It is *no more* true that there is first a consciousness which *afterward* becomes affected by

19 TN: The term *Erlebnis* comes from Husserl, who uses it to mean "experience" in a broad sense. In deference to this broad sense, Kersten translates it as "mental process" (Husserl 1983). French translators, picking up the sense of *Leben* (to live), sometimes render it as *le vécu.*

"pleasure"—like water being dyed—than that there is first a pleasure (unconscious or psychological) which afterward receives the quality of being conscious, like a beam of light. There is one indivisible and indissoluble being—not a substance that supports its qualities as lesser beings but a being that is existence through and through. The pleasure is the being of the consciousness (of) self, and consciousness (of) self is the pleasure's law of being. Heidegger formulates this well when he writes (about "Dasein," to be exact, rather than consciousness) that "the 'how' (essentia) of this being must, if it is possible to speak of it at all, be conceived in terms of its being (existentia)."[20] This means that consciousness is not produced as a particular exemplar of an abstract possibility but that, in arising in the heart of being, it creates and maintains its essence, i.e., the synthetic arrangement of its possibilities.

This also means that the being of consciousness is opposite in type to the being revealed to us by the ontological proof: as consciousness is not possible before being but instead comprises—in its being—the source and condition of all possibility, its existence implies its essence. This is felicitously expressed by Husserl as its "factual necessity."[21] For there to be an essence of pleasure, there must first be the fact of some consciousness (of) this pleasure. And any attempt to invoke the alleged laws of consciousness, whose articulated sum would be said to constitute its essence, will be futile: a law is a transcendent object of consciousness; it is possible to have consciousness of a law but not a law of consciousness. For the same reasons, it is impossible to assign to consciousness any motivation other than itself. Otherwise we would need to conceive of consciousness, to the extent to which it is an effect, as not being conscious (of) itself. In some respect, consciousness would need to be without being conscious (of) being. We would succumb to that all-too-common illusion that makes consciousness into something half-unconscious, or passivity. But consciousness is consciousness through and through. It cannot therefore be limited by anything other than itself.

We must not conceive of this determination of consciousness by itself as a genesis, or a becoming, because that would require us to suppose that consciousness is prior to its own existence. Nor must we conceive of this

20 TN: Sartre is quoting from Being and Time (Heidegger 1980), §9.
21 TN: See my note on Husserl's "factual necessity" in Notes on the Translation.

self-creation as an act. In that case consciousness would be consciousness (of) itself as an act, which it isn't. Consciousness is a plenum of existence and this determining of itself by itself is an essential characteristic. We must be careful not to misuse the expression "cause of itself," which can lead one to suppose a progression, a relationship between a self-cause and a self-effect. It would be more accurate to say, quite simply, that consciousness exists *through* itself. And by this we do not mean that it is "drawn out of nothingness."[22] There could not be any "nothingness of consciousness" *before* consciousness.[23] "Before" consciousness we can conceive only of a plenum of being, no element of which could refer to an absent consciousness. For there to be a nothingness of consciousness, we would need a consciousness that has existed and is no longer, and a witness consciousness positing the nothingness of the first consciousness in the service of a synthesis of recognitions. Consciousness is prior to nothingness, and "derives from being."[24]

Perhaps these conclusions are difficult to accept. But, examined more carefully, they seem perfectly clear: the paradox is not that some existences exist through themselves but that there are any that do not. What is genuinely unthinkable is passive existence—in other words, an existence that can perpetuate itself without having enough power either to produce or to conserve itself. From this point of view, nothing could be more unintelligible than the principle of inertia. For if consciousness were indeed able to "come from" something else, where would it "come from?" Out of the limbo of the unconscious, or the physiological. But if we ask, in turn, how such a limbo can exist and how it derives its existence, we find ourselves led back to the concept of passive existence. In other words, we are absolutely unable to understand how these givens—which are not conscious and do not derive their existence from themselves—might nonetheless perpetuate this existence, and even find

---

22 TN: . . . *qu'elle se "tire du néant."* This phrase is often used in French to refer to the act of creation (as in God's creation of the world "out of nothing," for example).

23 TN: . . . *"néant de conscience"* . . . I am not sure why Sartre puts this phrase within quotation marks. Although it is tempting to translate it as "the *non-being* of consciousness" because that sounds better in English, I stick to "nothingness" for consistency.

24 Sartre's note: This does not at all imply that consciousness is the foundation of its being. On the contrary, as we will see later, the being of consciousness is fully contingent. We wish to point out merely that: 1. *nothing* is the cause of consciousness; 2. consciousness is the cause of its own way of being.

the power to produce a consciousness. We can see a clear symptom of this in the huge popularity of the proof "*a contingentia mundi*."[25]

Thus, by renouncing the primacy of knowledge, we have discovered the *being* of the knower and encountered the absolute—that same absolute that the seventeenth-century rationalists defined, and constituted logically, as an object of knowledge. But, precisely because we are concerned here with an absolute existence rather than knowledge, we escape the well-known objection, according to which a known absolute can no longer be absolute, because it becomes relative to the knowledge we have of it. For here the absolute is not the result of a logical construction in the field of knowledge but the subject of the most concrete experiences. And it is in no way *relative* to this experience, because it *is* this experience. It is therefore a non-substantial absolute. The ontological error of Cartesian rationalism was not to have seen that, if we define the absolute in terms of the primacy of existence over essence, we cannot conceive of it as a substance. There is nothing substantial about consciousness; it is a pure "appearance," where this means it exists only to the extent to which it appears. But it is precisely because consciousness is pure appearance, because it is a total void (since the entire world is outside it), because of this identity within it between its appearance and its existence, that it can be considered as the absolute.

IV. THE BEING OF THE *PERCIPI*

We appear to have reached the end of our investigation. Having reduced things to the combined totality of their appearances, we noted that these appearances called for a being that was no longer itself an appearance. The "*percipi*" directed us to a "*percipiens*," whose being was revealed to us as consciousness. Thus we have reached the ontological foundation of knowledge: the first being, to whom all other appearances appear; the absolute, in relation to which each phenomenon is relative. This being is not "the subject," in the Kantian sense of the term but subjectivity itself, in its self-immanence. In arriving here, we have escaped idealism,

---

25 TN: This Latin phrase means "from the world's contingency"; it often figures in a so-called "proof" of God's existence. The idea is that the contingent world requires a *ground* in necessity.

according to which being is measured by knowledge and is therefore subject to the law of duality. For idealism, all being is known, including thought itself: thought appears to itself only through its own products, such that we only ever grasp it as the meaning of thoughts that have occurred, and the philosopher in search of thought is obliged to consult the constituted sciences in order to derive thought from them as their condition of possibility. We have apprehended a being, on the contrary, that escapes and founds our knowledge, and we have laid hold of thought, not as it is given in representation, or as the meaning of thoughts that have been expressed, but directly, as it is—and this mode of apprehension is not a phenomenon of knowledge but the structure of being. We find ourselves here on the terrain of Husserlian phenomenology, even though Husserl himself was not always faithful to his primary intuition. Are we satisfied? We have found a transphenomenal being, but is that really the being to which the phenomenon of being points? Is it really the "being of the phenomenon?" In other words, is the being of consciousness sufficient to found the being of appearance *qua* appearance? We have robbed the phenomenon of its being, in order to give it to consciousness, and we expected consciousness subsequently to return it. Is consciousness able to do that? By examining the ontological requirements of the *percipi*, we will find out.

We should note at the outset that there is a being of the perceived thing *qua* perceived. Even if I wanted to reduce this table to a synthesis of subjective impressions, I would have to notice at least that it reveals itself *as a table* through that synthesis, of which it is the transcendent limit, the principle, and the goal. The table stands before our knowledge, and it cannot be assimilated to the knowledge we gain from it; otherwise it would be consciousness—i.e., pure immanence—and would dissolve *as* a table. On the same grounds, even if what separates the table from the synthesis of subjective impressions through which it is apprehended is purely a distinction within reason, at least the table cannot be this synthesis: that would be to reduce it to a synthetic activity of combination.[26] Insofar, then, as the known cannot be absorbed into our knowledge of it, we must recognize its *being*. This being, we are told, is the *percipi*. Let

24

26 TN: . . . *une activité synthétique de liaison.* Here I translate *liaison* as "combination" (which is normally used to translate Kant's *Verbindung* into English), as it is likely Sartre takes this phrase from Kant.

us acknowledge from the outset that we can no more reduce the being of the *percipi* to that of the *percipiens*—i.e., to consciousness—than we can reduce the table to the combination of representations. The most we can say is that it is *relative* to that being. But this *relativity* does not excuse us from the need to inspect the *percipi*'s being.

Now, the mode of the *percipi* is *passive*. If, then, the phenomenon's being resides in its *percipi*, its being will be *passivity*. The characteristic structures of *esse*, insofar as it can be reduced to *percipi*, turn out to be relativity and passivity. What is passivity? I am passive when I undergo a modification of which I am not the origin—that is to say, neither the foundation nor the creator. Thus my being supports a way of being of which it is not the source. Only, to be able to support something, I still need to exist, and my existence is in consequence always located beyond passivity. For example, "passively supporting" something is an attitude that I *uphold*, which engages my freedom just as much as "resolutely rejecting" it. If I am to be forever "the person who was offended," I must persevere in my being; in other words, I must assign existence to myself.[27] But, in so doing, I take up the offense on my own account in some way; I accept this offense, and I cease to be passive in relation to it. The result is this alternative: either I am not passive in my being—in which case I become the foundation of the ways I am affected, even if I was not at first their origin—or I am characterized by passivity in my very existence, and my being is received—in which case everything collapses into nothingness. Hence passivity is a doubly relative phenomenon: relative to the agent's activity, and to the patient's existence. From this it follows that passivity does not involve the very being of the passive existent: it is a relation between one being and another being, and not between a being and a nothingness. It is impossible for the *percipere* to *assign* the *perceptum* its being because, in order to be assigned anything, the *perceptum* would already need to be given in some way and thus to exist before receiving its being. We may think in terms of *creation*, on condition that the created being takes possession of itself, and separates itself from its creator in order immediately to close in on itself and take up its being: it is in this sense that a book exists *against* its author. But if the act of creation needs

25

---

27 TN: . . . *je m'affecte moi-même de l'existence.* See my note on *s'affecter* in Notes on the Translation.

to be continued indefinitely, if the created being is supported even in its minutest parts, if it has no proper independence, if it is in itself only nothingness, then the creature cannot be distinguished at all from its creator but is reabsorbed within him; what we have here is a false transcendence, and the creator cannot even have the illusion of leaving his subjectivity behind.[28]

Moreover, the passivity of the patient demands an equal passivity in the agent. This idea finds expression in the principle of action and reaction: it is because it is possible to crush my hand, to grasp it or to cut it that my hand can crush, cut, or grasp. How much passivity should we attribute to perception, to knowledge? They are entirely active, entirely spontaneous. It is precisely because it is pure spontaneity, because nothing can bite into it, that consciousness cannot act on anything. Hence, the doctrine of *esse est percipi* requires that consciousness, a pure spontaneity unable to act on anything, should bestow being on a transcendent nothingness while preserving the nothingness of its being—and this is absurd. Husserl attempted to ward off these objections by introducing passivity into the *noesis*: namely the *hyle*,[29] the pure flux of what is lived through, the materiality of the passive syntheses. But all he did was to add a further difficulty to those we have mentioned. In effect, he reintroduced those neutral "givens" whose impossibility we demonstrated earlier. Of course, these are not "contents" of consciousness, but that only adds to their unintelligibility. For the *hyle* cannot in fact belong to consciousness, or it would dissolve into translucency and be unable to provide the resistant impressional[30] base that we surpass toward the object. But if it does not belong to consciousness, what is the source of its being and its opacity? How can it retain at one and the same time the opaque resistance of things and the subjectivity of thought? Since it is not even perceived, and since consciousness transcends it toward its objects, its *esse* cannot derive from a *percipi*. But if we say that it derives its essence only from itself, we return to the insoluble problem of how consciousness can relate to any independent existents. And even if we were

26

---

28 Sartre's note: It is for this reason that the Cartesian doctrine of substance reaches its logical conclusion in Spinoza's thought.

29 TN: For *hyle*, see the section on Husserl vocabulary in Notes on the Translation.

30 TN: As *impressionel* is not an ordinary French word, I translate it with a parallel (made-up) adjective, "impressional."

to concede to Husserl that the noesis has a hyletic layer, we would still be unable to conceive how consciousness could transcend this subjective element toward objectivity. By endowing the *hyle* with the characteristics of a thing and the characteristics of consciousness, Husserl believed he could facilitate the passage from one to the other, but he succeeded only in creating a hybrid being that consciousness rejects and that cannot be part of the world.

But in addition, as we saw, the *percipi* implies that relativity governs the being of the *perceptum*. Is it conceivable that the being of the known should be relative to our knowledge of it? What could the relativity of its being mean, in the case of an existent, other than that the existent's being lies in something other than itself—in other words, *in an existent that it is not*? Admittedly, it is not inconceivable for a being to be external to itself, if we take this to mean that the being is *its own* externality. But that is not the case here. The perceived being stands before a consciousness that it cannot penetrate and that cannot make contact with it, and as it is cut off from consciousness, it exists cut off from its own existence. It is no use to claim, as Husserl did, that it is irreal: even if the status of what is perceived is irreal, it has to exist.

Thus, there is no case in which either of the two determinations of *relativity* and *passivity*—which concern ways of being—is applicable to being itself. The *esse* of the phenomenon cannot be its *percipi*. The transphenomenal being of consciousness cannot provide the foundation for the phenomenon's transphenomenal being. We can see the phenomenalists' mistake: having correctly reduced the object to the series of its combined appearances, they thought they had reduced its being to the succession of its ways of being. That is why they tried to explain being in terms of concepts which apply only to ways of being, because they refer to relations between a plurality of beings that already exist.

V. THE ONTOLOGICAL PROOF

We have not given being its due: we thought that our discovery of the transphenomenality of the being of consciousness excused us from the need to grant any transphenomenal being to the phenomenon. On the contrary, as we will see, the transphenomenality of consciousness actually requires the phenomenon's being to be transphenomenal. We can derive an "ontological proof," not from the reflective *cogito* but from the prereflective being of the *percipiens*. Let us try to set it out here.

All consciousness is consciousness of something. We can take this definition of consciousness in two quite distinct ways: we can take it to mean either that consciousness is constitutive of its object's being, or that consciousness is in its innermost nature related to a transcendent being. But the first interpretation of the phrase destroys itself: to be conscious of something is to confront a full and concrete presence that *is not* consciousness. Doubtless, one can be conscious of an absence. But that absence must necessarily appear against a ground of presence. Now, as we have seen, consciousness is a real subjectivity, and an impression is a subjective plenitude. But this subjectivity cannot step outside itself in order to posit a transcendent object by conferring upon it the plenitude of the impression. If, therefore, we want at any cost to make the phenomenon's being depend on consciousness, the object will need to distinguish itself from consciousness not through its *presence* but through its *absence*, not through its plenitude but through its nothingness. If being belongs to consciousness, the object must differ from consciousness not insofar as it is another being but insofar as it is a non-being. Here we have the recourse to the infinite that we discussed in the first section of this work. For Husserl, for example, the animation of the hyletic core by only those intentions which find their fulfillment[31] (*Erfüllung*) in that *hyle* is not sufficient to take us out of the domain of subjectivity. The genuinely objectifying intentions[32] are empty intentions—intentions that aim, beyond the present and subjective appearance, at the infinite totality of the series of appearances. Let us be clear, moreover, that these intentions aim at them as appearances that cannot ever be given all at the same time. The fact that it is necessarily impossible for the infinite number of terms in the series to stand before consciousness simultaneously, in conjunction with the fact that all but one of these terms is really absent, is the foundation of objectivity. If these impressions were present— even if their number were infinite—they would become merged into subjectivity; their absence is what gives them objective being. Thus, the

31 TN: . . . *trouver leur remplissement* . . . See my note on *remplir* in the section on Husserl vocabulary in Notes on the Translation.

32 TN: *Les intentions . . . objectivantes* . . . See my note on *objectiver* in the section on Husserl vocabulary in Notes on the Translation.

object's being is a pure non-being. It defines itself as a *lack*. It is elusive, something that, as a matter of principle, can never be given, that is delivered through successive, fleeting profiles. But how can non-being be the foundation of being? How can something that is subjectively absent and *expected* thereby become objective? I will grant that a great joy that I am hoping for, or a sorrow that I fear, may thereby acquire a kind of transcendence. But this transcendence within immanence does not take us out of the subjective. It is true that things are given through profiles—which means, quite simply, through appearances. But each of these is already on its own a *transcendent being*, and not a subjective impressional matter—a *plenitude of being*, not a lack—a *presence*, not an absence. It would be fruitless to attempt by sleight of hand to found the object's *reality* on the subjective impressional plenitude and its *objectivity* on non-being: we will never get objectivity out of the subjective, or transcendence out of immanence, or being out of non-being. But, it might be said, it is precisely as a transcendence that Husserl defines consciousness. Indeed: that is his postulate and his essential discovery. But once he makes of the *noema* something unreal, the correlative of the *noesis*, and whose *esse* is a *percipi*, he completely betrays his own principle.

Consciousness is consciousness of something: therefore transcendence is a constitutive structure of consciousness, which is to say that consciousness is born *bearing on* a being that it is not.[33] Let us call this the ontological proof. To this one might reply that a demand on the part of consciousness does not prove that this demand must be satisfied. But this objection is powerless in relation to an analysis of Husserl's intentionality, about whose essential character he was mistaken. To say that consciousness is conscious of something means that the entire being of consciousness is subsumed within this specific obligation: to be a revealing intuition of something, i.e., of a transcendent being. Pure subjectivity, if that is what is given first, will not only fail to transcend itself in order to posit anything objective but, in addition, any "pure" subjectivity will dissolve. Used properly, the term "subjectivity" refers to a consciousness (of) consciousness.

---

33 TN: ... *la conscience naît portée sur un être* ... No English verb has the combination of meanings of *portée sur* in this sentence. Although "directed upon" is the primary meaning, the verb *porter* also means "to carry"; perhaps Sartre's italics are to suggest the idea that consciousness is "carried" by its object.

28

But this consciousness (of being) consciousness must in some way be qualified, and it can only be qualified as a revealing intuition; otherwise it is nothing. Now, a revealing intuition implies something revealed. Absolute subjectivity can constitute itself only in relation to something revealed; immanence can define itself only in its grasp of something transcendent. This may sound like an echo of Kant's refutation of problematic idealism. But really we should be thinking of Descartes. We are at the level of being here, not of knowledge: it is not a matter of showing that the phenomena of inner sense imply the existence of objective and spatial phenomena but that consciousness implies in its being a non-conscious and transphenomenal being. In particular, it is pointless to reply that subjectivity does in fact imply objectivity, and that in constituting the objective domain it constitutes itself: we have seen that subjectivity lacks any power to constitute the objective. To say that consciousness is conscious of something is to say that it must produce itself as the revealed revelation of a being that it is not, and which is given as already existing when it is revealed.

In this way, having set out from pure appearance, we have arrived in the fullness of being. Consciousness is a being whose existence posits its essence and, inversely, it is conscious of a being whose essence implies its existence, i.e., a being whose appearance demands being. Being is everywhere. Admittedly, we could apply to consciousness the definition that Heidegger reserves for *Dasein*, and say that it is a being for whom, in its being, its being is in question[34]—but one would have to complete it and formulate it roughly like this: *Consciousness is a being for whom in its being there is a question of its being, insofar as this being implies a being other than itself.*

Naturally, this being is nothing other than the transphenomenal being of phenomena and not a noumenal being hiding behind them. Consciousness implies the being of this table, of this packet of tobacco, of the lamp, and, more generally, the being of the world. Consciousness requires simply that the being of that which *appears* does not exist only insofar as it appears. The transphenomenal being of that which is *for consciousness* is itself *in itself.*

29

---

34 TN: Heidegger characterizes *Dasein* like this in §4 of *Being and Time* (Heidegger 1980).

VI. BEING IN ITSELF

We are able now to provide some clarification of the *phenomenon of being* that we consulted in order to establish our preceding remarks. Consciousness is a revealed-revelation of existents, and these existents appear before consciousness on the foundation of their being. Nevertheless, it is characteristic of the being of an existent not to disclose *itself*, in person, to consciousness. An existent cannot be stripped of its being: being is the existent's ever-present foundation; it is in it everywhere, and it is nowhere; there is no being that is not the being of some way of being, and being can be grasped only through the way of being that manifests it and conceals it at the same time. However, consciousness can always surpass an existent, not toward its being but toward this being's *meaning*. That is what makes it possible to call consciousness "onticoontological," because a fundamental characteristic of its transcendence is to transcend the ontic toward the ontological. The meaning of the existent's being, insofar as it discloses itself to consciousness, is the phenomenon of being. This meaning itself has a being, on whose foundation it manifests itself. It is from this point of view that the well-known Scholastic argument can be understood, according to which there is a vicious circle in any proposition concerning being, since any judgment about being already implies being. But in fact there is no vicious circle, because it is not necessary to surpass the being of this meaning again, toward its meaning; the meaning of being is the same for the being of any phenomenon, including its own being. The phenomenon of being is not the same as being, as we have already noted. But it indicates being, and requires it—although, in truth, the ontological proof that we mentioned earlier does not apply *especially* or *uniquely* to it: there is *one* ontological proof, which applies to the whole domain of consciousness. But this proof is sufficient to justify everything we can learn from the phenomenon of being. The phenomenon of being, like any basic phenomenon, is disclosed immediately to consciousness. At every moment we have what Heidegger calls a "preontological understanding" of it, which means an understanding that has not been fixed in concepts or elucidated. What we should do now, therefore, is to examine this phenomenon and try by this means to determine the meaning of being. However, we must note that: (1) this elucidation of the meaning of being only applies to the being of the phenomenon. As the being of consciousness is radically different, its meaning will require its own distinctive elucidation based on the revealed-revelation of another type of being, being-for-itself, which we will define later, and which contrasts with the phenomenon's being-in-itself; (2) the elucidation of the meaning of being-in-itself that we will attempt here can only be provisional. The aspects that will be brought to light imply other meanings, which must be apprehended and determined at a later stage. The preceding reflections have in particular allowed us to distinguish two absolutely distinct regions of being: the being of the *prereflective cogito* and the being of the phenomenon. But although the concept of being is, therefore, characterized by its division into two incommunicable regions, we must still explain how these two regions can be placed under the same heading. That will require us to inspect these two types of being, and it is clear that we will not be able genuinely to apprehend the meaning of either of them until we have established their real relations with the notion of being in general, and the relations that link them. We have in fact established, by examining the non-positional consciousness (of) self, that the being of the phenomenon cannot in any case *act* on consciousness. Through that, we have ruled out a *realist* conception of the phenomenon's relations with consciousness. But we have also shown, by examining the spontaneity of the non-reflective *cogito*, that if subjectivity was given to consciousness first, it would not be possible for consciousness to step out of it; and neither would consciousness be able to act on transcendent being, or to include the elements of passivity necessary to constitute, without contradiction, a transcendent being on their basis. We have hereby ruled out the *idealist* solution to the problem. We seem to have closed every door, and to have condemned ourselves to seeing transcendent being and consciousness as two enclosed totalities with no possible communication between them. We will have to show that the problem allows of another solution, beyond realism and idealism.

However, some characteristics can be established immediately, because, for the most part, they show up for themselves in what we have just said.

A clear view of the phenomenon of being has often been clouded by a widespread prejudice that we will call "creationism." As it was supposed that God had given being to the world, being always appeared to be colored by a certain passivity. But a creation *ex nihilo* cannot explain how

31

being arises, because if being is conceived within a subjectivity—even a divine subjectivity—it remains an intrasubjective mode of being. Within such a subjectivity, objectivity could not even be *represented*, and, in consequence, it could not even be moved by its will to create something objective. Moreover, even if being could be placed all of a sudden outside subjectivity by means of the "fulguration" that Leibniz talks about, it could only affirm itself as being in spite of and against its creator; otherwise it would merge back into him. By removing any *"Selbstständigkeit"*[35]— as the Germans call it—from being, the theory of continuous creation makes it vanish into the divine subjectivity. If being exists in the face of God, it is because it provides its own support, because it does not retain the faintest trace of divine creation. In short, even if it had been created, being-in-itself could not be *explained* by creation because, beyond that creation, it takes up its own being. That is equivalent to saying that being is uncreated. But one should not conclude that being creates itself; that would require it to exist antecedently to itself. Being cannot be *causa sui* in the manner of consciousness. Being is itself. That implies that it is neither passivity nor activity. Each of these notions is *human*, and refers to human behavior, or instruments of human behavior. Activity occurs when a conscious being employs some means with a view to achieving some end. And we call the objects to which we apply our activity "passive" insofar as they do not spontaneously aim at the end for which we put them to use. In brief, man is active and the means he employs are said to be "passive." Taken to the absolute, these concepts lose all meaning. In particular, being is not active; for there to be any end or means, being is required. Still less can it be passive, for, to be passive, something must be. Being's consistence-in-itself is equally beyond the active and the passive. It is equally beyond both negation and affirmation. An affirmation is always the affirmation of something, which is to say that the act of affirming is distinct from the thing affirmed. But if we imagine an affirmation in which the affirming is filled up by what is affirmed, that affirmation could not be affirmed—because of the surfeit of plenitude and the noema's immediate inherence within the noesis. That is indeed what

35 TN: *Selbstständigkeit* is German for "independence." The philosophical use of this term that Sartre has in mind here is the idea of something's being capable of existing on its own, self-sufficiently.

being is if, to clarify our thinking, we define it in terms of consciousness: it is the noema within the noesis, i.e., a self-inherence without the
slightest distance. From this point of view, it would be wrong to call it
"immanence," because <u>immanence is,</u> after all, a relation between something and itself; it is <u>the smallest distance that it is possible for something
to have</u> in relation to itself. But being is not a relation to itself; it is <u>itself</u>.
It is an immanence that cannot be actualized, an affirmation that cannot
be affirmed, an activity that cannot act, because it has become thickened
by itself. It is as if a decompression of being were required to liberate
an affirmation of itself in the heart of being. Nor should we understand
being as *one* undifferentiated self-affirmation: the lack of differentiation
in the in-itself lies beyond an infinite number of self-affirmations, insofar as there are an infinite number of ways of affirming oneself. We can
sum up these first results by saying that *being is in itself.*

But if <u>being is in itself, that means it does not refer to itself, unlike
consciousness (of) self</u>: this *itself* is what it is. Indeed, we reach the point
at which the constant reflection that constitutes any "itself" merges into
identity. That is why being is ultimately beyond any *itself* and our initial
formulation cannot be more than an approximation, due to the necessities of language.[36] In fact being is opaque to itself precisely because it is
filled with itself. We can <u>express this better by saying that *being is what it is.*</u>
This formulation appears to be strictly analytical. In fact, a great distance
separates it from the principle of identity, regarded as the unconditional
principle of all analytical judgments. For a start, it refers to a particular
region of being, that of *being in itself.* We will see that the being of the for
itself is defined, on the contrary, as being what it is not and not being
what it is. We are dealing, therefore, with a principle that is regional
and, as such, synthetic. Moreover this formulation—being in itself is
what it is—needs to be contrasted with the one which designates the
being of consciousness: this latter, as in fact we will see, *has to be* what it
is. This informs us of the special sense that we need to give to the "is" in
the phrase "being is what it is." Once there are beings which have to be

36 TN: In this passage Sartre uses the same French word—*soi*—to mean "itself" (as in
   being-for-itself) *and* "self" (as in consciousness (of) self). The basic point being made
   is that we should not be misled by the term "itself" into thinking that being-in-itself
   relates to itself. See my note on *soi* in Notes on the Translation. Sartre discusses the misleading aspect of the term "itself" as it appears in the compound "in-itself" at EN 112.

what they are, the fact of being what one is is not in any way a purely axiomatic characteristic: it is a contingent principle of being in itself. In this sense, the principle of identity, the principle of analytical judgments, is also a regional synthetic principle of being. It refers to the opacity of being-in-itself. This opacity is not a function of our *position* in relation to the in-itself, such that we are obliged to *learn about* it and *observe* it because we are situated "outside." Being-in-itself has no *inside* that could be opposed to an *outside*, like a judgment, or law, or self-consciousness. The in-itself has no secret: it is *massive*. In a sense, we can call it a synthesis. But it is the most indissoluble of syntheses: the synthesis of self with self. From this it evidently follows that being is isolated in its being, and maintains no relationship with anything else. Transitions and becomings—anything that allows one to say that being is not yet what it will be, and that it is already what it is not—all of this is necessarily ruled out by being. Because being is the being of becoming, it is thereby beyond becom-

33   ing. It is what it is, which means that, on its own, it cannot even not be what it is not; indeed we saw that it does not include any negation. It is full positivity. Thus *alterity* is unknown to it: it never presents itself as *other* than some other being; it cannot sustain any relationship with the other. It is itself indefinitely, and exhausts itself in being it. From this point of view, as we will see later, it escapes temporality. It is, and when it collapses, one cannot even say that it is no longer. Or, at least, a consciousness, precisely because it is temporal, can become conscious of it as no longer being. But it does not itself exist as something missing from where it was: the full positivity of being re-forms itself where it collapsed. It was, and now other beings are: that is all.

Finally—this will be our third characteristic—being-in-itself *is*. In other words, being can neither be, nor be derived from, the possible, nor can it be equated with the necessary. Necessity concerns the connection between ideal propositions, not the connection between existents. A phenomenal existent can never, as an existent, be derived from another existent. That is called the *contingency* of being-in-itself. But neither can being-in-itself be derived from something *possible*. The possible is a structure of the *for-itself*, and so it belongs to the other region of being. Being-in-itself is never either possible or impossible; it is. Consciousness expresses this by saying—in anthropomorphic terms—that it is *de trop*, which is to say that it is absolutely unable to derive it from anything,

either from another being, or from something possible, or from a necessary law. Uncreated, without any reason for being or any relationship
with any other being, being-in-itself is *de trop* for eternity.

Being is. Being is itself. Being is what it is. These are the three features
that our provisional examination of the phenomenon of being enables
us to assign to the being of phenomena. For the moment it is impossible to continue our investigation further. An examination of the in-
itself—which is only ever what it is—will not enable us to establish and
explicate its relations with the for-itself. Thus, by taking "appearances"
as our point of departure, we have been gradually led to posit two types
of being—the in-itself and the for-itself—about which our information
is still only incomplete and superficial. A host of unanswered questions
still remain: What is the fundamental *meaning* of these two types of being?
What are the reasons for their both belonging to *being* in general? What is
the meaning of being, insofar as it includes within it these two radically
distinct regions of being? If both idealism and realism fail to explain the
relations that in fact unite these regions—which are in principle incommunicable—what other solution to this problem can we find? And how
can the being of the phenomenon be transphenomenal?

My purpose in writing this work has been to try to answer these
questions.

Part One

The problem of nothingness

Chapter 1

THE ORIGIN OF NEGATION

I. QUESTIONING[1]

Our investigation has taken us into the heart of being. But it has also reached a dead end because we have not been able to establish a connection between the two regions of being we have discovered. This is probably due to our choosing a perspective ill-suited to our inquiry. Descartes found himself confronting an analogous problem when he had to describe the relations between the soul and the body. He suggested then that we should seek a solution in the area where, as a matter of fact, the union of thinking substance with extended substance takes place, i.e., in the imagination. This is valuable advice. Of course, Descartes's concern was not the same as ours, and we do not conceive of the imagination as he did. But what we can learn is that we should not begin by separating the two terms in a relation, in order to try later to put them back together: a relation is a synthesis. It follows that the results of its analysis

---

1 TN: Sartre's section heading is "*L'interrogation*," but as "interrogation" in English suggests a formal activity (e.g., by the police), I translate it here as "Questioning." In this section, Sartre closely follows Heidegger's methodology in *Being and Time* (see especially Heidegger 1980: §2); as the term "question" (as substantive and as verb) centrally figures in English translations of Heidegger, this adds to the advantage of my choice. Elsewhere, I occasionally use "to interrogate," especially when *interroger* figures as a verb in the text.

cannot correspond to the *moments* of this synthesis. M. Laporte says that to abstract something is to consider it in an isolated state, when it is not made to exist in isolation.[2] In contrast, something concrete is a totality that can exist by itself, alone. Husserl takes the same view: redness, for him, is an abstraction, because color cannot exist without shape. A spatio-temporal and fully determinate "thing" is, on the other hand, concrete. From this point of view, consciousness is an abstraction, since it contains within it an ontological origin that reaches toward the in-itself and, reciprocally, the phenomenon is also an abstraction, since it has to "appear" to consciousness. The concrete entity can only be the synthetic totality, of which both consciousness and the phenomenon constitute mere moments. What is concrete is man in the world, with the specific union of man with the world that Heidegger, for example, names "being-in-the-world." To interrogate "experience," like Kant, with respect to its conditions of possibility, or to perform, like Husserl, a phenomenological reduction that reduces the world to the status of the noematic correlative of consciousness, is to begin deliberately from an abstraction. But we will no more succeed in reconstituting the concrete out of the sum or the organization of the elements abstracted from it than we will succeed, in Spinoza's system, in reaching the substance through the infinite sum of its modes. The relation of the regions of being is a primordial bursting forth, which forms part of the very structure of these beings. That is how we encounter it, from the moment we first inspect it. We need only open our eyes and interrogate, from a standpoint of naïveté, the totality that is man-in-the-world. The description of this totality will enable us to answer these two questions: 1. What is the synthetic relation that we are calling "being-in-the-world?" 2. What must man and the world be in order for this relation between them to be possible? In truth, each of these questions enters into the other, and we cannot hope to answer them separately. But each mode of human behavior, as the behavior of man in the world, can simultaneously deliver to us man, the world, and the relation that unites them—so long as we regard these modes of behavior as realities to be objectively apprehended, and not as subjective affections that are able to be disclosed only to the standpoint of reflection.

2 TN: Jean Laporte (1886–1948) was a French philosopher and historian of philosophy.

We will not confine ourselves to studying just one mode of behavior. On the contrary, we will try to describe several, and to penetrate, within each of them, the basic meaning of the "man-world" relation. But we ought to begin by choosing some initial mode of behavior to serve as a guiding thread in our investigation.

In fact, our investigation itself provides us with the behavior we are seeking: if I apprehend this man who I am, as he is at this moment in the world, I can see that his attitude toward being is interrogative. In the very moment in which I ask "Is there a mode of behavior that can reveal man's relation with the world?" I raise a question. I can consider this question objectively, since it makes little difference whether the questioner is me or the reader who is reading my words and raising the question alongside me. On the other hand, the question is not merely the objective set of words traced on this page: it is indifferent to the signs that express it. In short, it is a human attitude endowed with meaning. What does this attitude reveal?

In every question we confront a being that we interrogate. Every question presupposes, therefore, a being who questions and a being that is questioned. The question is not the most basic relation between man and being-in-itself; on the contrary, it stands within the limits of this relation and presupposes it. Moreover, we are questioning the being that we interrogate *with respect to* something. The thing *with respect to which* I interrogate being participates in being's transcendence: I interrogate being through its ways of being, or through its being. From this point of view, a question is a type of expectation: I wait for an answer from the interrogated being. In other words, against the ground of my pre-interrogative familiarity with being, I expect this being to disclose its being, or its way of being. The answer will be a Yes or a No. It is the existence of these two equally objective and contradictory possibilities which distinguishes as a matter of principle, a question from an affirmation or negation. Some questions appear not to admit of a negative answer—such as, for example, the one we raised earlier: "What does this attitude reveal?" But in fact we can see that it is always possible to answer this type of question with "Nothing" or "Nobody" or "Never." In this way, in the moment when I ask: "Is there a mode of behavior that can reveal man's relation with the world to me?" I allow *as a matter of principle* for the possibility of a negative answer, such as: "No; no such behavior exists." We accept, therefore, that

39

we may be confronted with the transcendent fact of the nonexistence of such a mode of behavior. It might be tempting to refuse to believe in the objective existence of a non-being: one could just say that the facts, in this case, direct me to my subjectivity; I learn from transcendent being that the sought-after behavior is a mere fiction. But, in the first place, to call this behavior a "mere fiction" is to conceal the negation without removing it. "Being a mere fiction" is equivalent here to "being no more than a fiction." Next, if you destroy the reality of the negation, you dissolve the reality of the answer. In fact it is being itself that gives me this answer and which, therefore, discloses the negation to me. Therefore the permanent and objective possibility of a negative answer does exist for the questioner. In relation to this possibility the questioner—by the very fact of asking a question—places himself in a state of non-determination: he *doesn't know* if the answer will be affirmative or negative. Thus the question is a bridge thrown between two non-beings: the non-being of knowledge in man, and the possibility of non-being in transcendent being. And finally, the question implies the existence of a truth. Through his very question, the questioner affirms that he is waiting for an objective response, in relation to which we can say: "It is like this, and not otherwise." In short, truth, in its capacity to differentiate being, introduces a third non-being as a determinant of the question: the non-being of limitation. This three-fold non-being conditions all questioning and, in particular, metaphysical questioning—i.e., *our* questioning.

We set off in search of being, and it seemed to us that our series of questions had led us into the heart of being. And yet a glance at the activity of questioning itself, just as we were approaching our goal, has suddenly revealed that we are surrounded by nothingness. Our questions about being are conditioned by the permanent possibility of non-being, outside us and within us. And non-being, again, circumscribes the answer: what being *is* necessarily detaches itself against the ground of what it *is not*. Whatever the answer, it will be possible to formulate it like this: "Being is *that* and, apart from that, *nothing.*"

In this way, a new component of reality has just appeared to us: non-being. This makes our problem more complicated, because we are no longer dealing only with the relations between human being and being in itself but also with being's relations with non-being, and those of human non-being with transcendent non-being. But let us take a closer look.

II. NEGATIONS

The objection will be raised that being-in-itself cannot supply negative answers. Did we not say, ourselves, that it lies equally beyond affirmation and negation? Moreover, ordinary experience, reduced to just what it is, does not seem to disclose any non-being. I think there are fifteen hundred-francs in my wallet and I find only thirteen hundred francs in it: that does not mean, we might be told, that experience has revealed the non-being of fifteen hundred francs but simply that I counted thirteen one-hundred-franc notes. The negation, strictly speaking, should be imputed to me: it appears only at the level of my act of judgment, through which I make a comparison between the result I anticipated and the result I obtained. In this way, negation is only a quality of judgment and what the questioner awaits is a judgment-answer. As for nothingness, it can be seen to originate in negative judgments, as a concept that establishes the transcendent unity of all such judgments, a propositional function of the type: "X is not." We can see where this theory is leading: we are made to observe that being-in-itself is full positivity and does not contain within itself any negation. In addition, those negative judgments, insofar as they are subjective acts, are wholly assimilated to affirmative judgments—without seeing that Kant, for example, distinguished the internal structure of a negative act of judgment from the structure of an affirmative: in both cases a synthesis of concepts takes place, only this synthesis, a full and concrete event within the life of the mind, operates, in one case, by means of the copula "is" and, in the other, by means of the copula "is not." Similarly, the manual operations of sorting (separation) and assembling (union) are two objective modes of behavior that possess the same *de facto* reality. Thus negation is said to be "at the other end of" the act of judgment, yet without thereby being "within" being. It is like something irreal squeezed between two full realities, neither of which lays claim to it: the being-in-itself that is interrogated with respect to negation refers us—since it is what it is—to our judgment; and the judgment, as something entirely positive and psychological, refers us to being, since the negation it formulates concerns being and is, in consequence, transcendent. Negation, incapable of existing by itself, the result of concrete psychological operations, and whose existence is maintained by these very operations, has the mode of existence of a noematic correlative, its *esse* consisting just in its *percipi*. And nothingness, as the conceptual unity of negative judgments, cannot have the slightest reality other than that conferred by the Stoics on their "*lekton*."[3] Can we accept this outlook?

We can put the question in these terms: Is negation, as the structure of a judicative proposition, the origin of nothingness or, on the contrary, is nothingness, as a structure of reality, the origin and foundation of negation? Thus, the problem of being has directed us to the problem of the question as a human attitude, and the problem of the question directs us to that of negation's being.

Evidently, non-being always appears within the limits of a human expectation. It is because I expect to find fifteen hundred francs that I find only thirteen hundred. It is because the physicist is expecting a particular verification of his hypothesis that nature can say "No" to him. It would be unproductive, therefore, to deny that negation appears against the basic ground of a relation between man and the world; the world does not reveal its non-beings to anyone who has not in the first place posited them as possibilities. But does that mean we should reduce these non-beings to pure subjectivity? Does it mean we should accord them the significance and the type of existence that belong to the Stoics' "*lekton*" or to Husserl's noema? We do not think so.

In the first place, it is not true that negation is merely a quality of judgment: a question is formulated by means of an interrogative judgment, but it is not a judgment; it is a prejudicative mode of behavior. I can question something with a look, with a gesture: by questioning being I take up a specific stance in relation to it—and this relation to being is a relation of being; a judgment is only an optional way of expressing it. Similarly, the questioner does not necessarily have to interrogate a *man* about being: this conception of the question, by making it an intersubjective phenomenon, peels it away from the being it adheres to, and leaves it hanging in the air purely as a modality of dialogue. On the contrary, we should conceive of a question within a dialogue as a particular kind within the category of "inter-

3 TN: The *lekton* in Stoic philosophy is the intelligible content of a thought. The concept roughly corresponds to the concept of a "proposition" in contemporary philosophy of language.

rogatives" and understand that what we are questioning is not first and foremost a thinking being. If my car has broken down, it is the carburetor, the spark plugs, etc., that I interrogate; if my watch stops, I can interrogate the watchmaker about the causes of its stopping, but the watchmaker will, in his turn, put his questions to the various mech-   42 anisms of the watch. What I expect from the carburetor, what the watchmaker expects from the cogs in the watch, is not a judgment: it is a disclosure of being, on the basis of which one can make a judgment. And if I expect a disclosure of being, it is because I am prepared at the same time for the eventuality of non-being. If I interrogate the carburetor, it is because I consider it possible that there is nothing in the carburetor. Thus my question includes, by its nature, a specific prejudicative understanding of non-being; it is, in itself, a relation of being with non-being, against the ground of an original transcendence, i.e., a relation of being with being.

If, moreover, the distinctive nature of questioning is obscured by the fact that questions are frequently asked by one man to other men, we should note that many non-judicative modes of behavior present, in its original undiluted form, this immediate understanding of non-being against the ground of being. If, for example, we consider destruction, we are obliged to acknowledge that it is an activity that can, of course, make use of judgment as an instrument but that cannot be defined as being solely, or even mainly, judicative. Yet it presents the same structure as interrogation. In one sense, of course, man is the only being through whom destruction can be brought about. A geological fold, or a storm, do not destroy anything—or, at least, they do not destroy directly; they merely alter the distribution of the mass of beings. After the storm there is no less than before. There is something else. And even this phrase is inappropriate, because in order to posit the disparity we need a witness, who can in some way retain the past and compare it to the present, in the form of a "no longer." In the absence of that witness, there is being, both before and after the storm: that is all. And if a cyclone should bring about the death of some particular living beings, this death can only be destruction if it is lived as such. For there to be destruction, there must first be a relation of man to being, i.e., transcendence, and, within the limits of this relationship, man must apprehend a being as destructible. For that, one being must be carved out in its limits within being, and this—as we saw in the case of truth—already involves nihilation. The being under consideration is *that one* and, apart from that, *nothing*. The artilleryman who is assigned his target takes care to point his cannon in a particular direction, *excluding* all the others. But that would still mean nothing if being had not been uncovered as *fragile*. And what is fragility, other than a particular probability of non-being, for a given being in some determinate set of circumstances? A being is fragile if it bears within its being a clear-cut possibility of non-being. But again, it is through man that fragility *arrives in* being, because the individuating limitation that we mentioned just now is a condition of fragility: *a* being is fragile, and not *all* being—which is beyond any possible destruction. Thus, the relation of individuating limitation that man maintains with *a* being, against the initial ground of his relation to being, brings fragility to this being as the appearance of a permanent possibility of non-being. But that is not all: in order for there to be destructibility, man must determine himself, either positively or negatively, as he confronts this possibility of non-being; he must take the necessary measures to bring it about (destruction in the strict sense) or, through a negation of non-being, to go on maintaining it at the level of a mere possibility (protective measures). Thus, it is man who renders towns destructible, precisely because he posits them as fragile and precious, and because he takes various measures to protect them. And it is because of this set of measures that an earthquake or a volcanic eruption can *destroy* these towns or human constructions. And the primary meaning of war, and its goal, are contained within man's slightest building. We must therefore acknowledge that destruction is an essentially human thing and that it is man who destroys his towns through the intermediary of earthquakes, or directly, and it is man who destroys his boats through the intermediary of cyclones, or directly. But at the same time we must allow that destruction presupposes a prejudicative understanding of nothingness as such, and a mode of behavior *in the face of* nothingness. In addition, although destruction arrives in being through man, it is an *objective fact* and not a thought. Fragility has impressed itself right into the being of this vase, and its destruction would be an irreversible and absolute event that I could only observe. There is a transphenomenality of non-being, as of being. Our examination of the behavior of "destruction" leads us therefore to the same results as our examination of questioning.

But if want to decide for certain, we need only consider a negative judgment in itself, and ask whether it makes non-being appear within being, or whether it confines itself to establishing some prior discovery. I am meeting Pierre at four o'clock. I arrive a quarter of an hour late: Pierre is always punctual; will he have waited for me? I look at the room, the customers, and I say, "He is not here." Is there an intuition of Pierre's absence or does negation only intervene alongside judgment? At first sight it seems absurd to talk here of "intuition," just because there cannot be an intuition of nothing, and Pierre's absence is this nothing. Yet popular consciousness bears witness to this intuition. Do we not say, for example, "I saw right away that he was not there?" In this case is the negation simply displaced? Let us take a closer look.

Certainly the café by itself, with its customers, its tables, its seats, its mirrors, its light, its smoke-filled atmosphere, and the sounds that fill it—of voices, saucers bumping against each other, footsteps—is a fullness of being. And all the particular intuitions I may have are fulfilled by these smells, these sounds, these colors, all of them phenomena that have a transphenomenal being. Similarly, Pierre's current presence in a place I do not know is also a plenitude of being. We seem to have found plenitude everywhere. But we must observe that in perception a figure is always constituted against a ground.[4] No object, or group of objects, is particularly earmarked to organize itself as either ground or figure: it all depends on the direction of my attention. When I enter the café to look for Pierre, a synthetic organization of all the objects in the café is formed, against which Pierre is given as having to appear. And this organization of the café as a ground is a first nihilation. Each element in the room—person, table, chair—tries to separate itself, to detach itself against the ground constituted by the totality of the other objects, and then collapses back into that undifferentiated ground, and is diluted within it. Because the ground is something that we only see "in addition"; it is the object of a purely marginal attention. So this first nihilation of all the figures—which appear and are swallowed up within the total equivalence of a

44

4 TN: For the figure/ground opposition, see my note on Gestalt psychology in Notes on the Translation.

ground—is the necessary condition for the appearance of the principal figure, in this case the person, Pierre. And this nihilation is given to my intuition; I am the witness of the successive dissolution of every object I look at, especially the faces, which detain me for a moment ("Could that be Pierre?") and immediately disperse, precisely because they "are not" Pierre's face. If, however, I were at last to encounter Pierre, my intuition would be fulfilled by a solid element; all at once I would become fascinated by his face and the whole café, in its inconspicuous presence, would organize itself around him. But in fact Pierre is not there. That does not mean that I discover his absence in some precise part of the building. In fact Pierre is absent from the whole café: his absence freezes the café in its evanescence; the café remains as ground; it continues to present itself to my merely marginal attention as an undifferentiated totality; it slides away, in pursuit of its nihilation. Only it makes itself the ground for a specific figure, it bears it everywhere in front of it, it presents me with it everywhere, and this figure, sliding constantly between my gaze and the real, solid objects of the café, is precisely a perpetual dissolution: it is Pierre, detaching himself as a nothingness against the ground of the nihilation of the café. What is given to intuition, therefore, is a flickering of nothingness: it is the nothingness of the ground, whose nihilation calls for, and requires, the appearance of the figure; and it is also the figure, a nothingness that slides in the guise of nothing across the surface of the ground. Therefore the foundation for the judgment "Pierre is not here" is clearly my intuitive apprehension of a double nihilation. And, of course, Pierre's absence presupposes an initial relation between me and this café; there are an infinite number of people without any relation to this café, for want of any genuine expectation that might register their absence. But, precisely, I was expecting to see Pierre, and my expectation has made Pierre's absence happen as a real event concerning this café. Now his absence is an objective fact that I have discovered, and it presents itself as a synthetic relation between Pierre and the room in which I am looking for him: Pierre, absent, haunts this café and is the condition of its nihilating organization as a ground. In contrast, the judgments that I might amuse myself by making next—such as "Wellington is not in this café," "Paul Valéry isn't here either," etc.— are purely abstract meanings, mere applications of the principle of negation, without any real basis or efficacy, and do not succeed in establishing any real relationship between the café, Wellington, or Valéry; here the relation "is not" is merely thought. That suffices to show that non-being does not come to things by means of a negative judgment: on the contrary, it is the negative judgment that is conditioned and supported by non-being.

How, moreover, could it be otherwise? How could we even conceive of the negative form of judgment if everything was a plenitude of being and positivity? We thought, for a moment, that negation might arise from the comparison established between an anticipated result and the result obtained. But let us look at this comparison; here is the first judgment, a concrete and positive mental act, recording a fact: "There are 1,300 francs in my wallet," and here is another, and this one also only records a fact and an affirmation: "I was expecting to find 1,500 francs." Here then are some real and objective facts, positive mental events, affirmative judgments. Where is there any space for negation? Should we believe that it is nothing but the pure and simple application of a category? And ought we to say that the mind possesses the not within it, as a form of sorting and separation? But in that case we would be removing the slightest suspicion of negativity from negation. If we allow that the category "not"—a category that exists in fact in the mind, as a positive concrete procedure for handling and systematizing our knowledge—is suddenly activated by the presence of certain affirmative judgments within us, and suddenly stamps with its seal certain thoughts that result from these judgments, we will—by means of these considerations—have scrupulously stripped negation of any negative function. Because negation is a refusal of existence. By its means, a being (or a way of being) is posited and then expelled into nothingness. If negation is a category, if it is only a stamp indifferently placed on various judgments, where do we get the sense that it can nihilate a being, that it can suddenly make something arise, and give it a name in order to expel it into non-being? If our previous judgments (like those we have used as examples) are records of fact, then negation must be like a free invention; it must separate us from this wall of positivity enclosing us. Negation must be an abrupt break 46 in continuity, an original and irreducible event, that cannot in any circumstances result from any earlier affirmations. But here we are in the sphere of consciousness. And consciousness cannot produce a negation, except in the form of consciousness of negation. No category can "inhabit" consciousness and reside there in the manner of a thing. The "not," as a sudden intuitive discovery, appears as the consciousness (of being) conscious of the "not." In brief, if there is being everywhere, it is not only nothingness that—as Bergson would have it—becomes inconceivable:[5] from being we can never derive negation. The necessary condition for the possibility of saying "not" is that non-being should be constantly present, within us and outside us—that nothingness should *haunt* being.

But where does nothingness come from? And if it is the most basic condition of questioning behavior and, more generally, of all philosophical or scientific investigation, what is the basic relation between human beings and nothingness? What is the most basic nihilating behavior?

III. THE DIALECTICAL CONCEPTION OF NOTHINGNESS

It is still too soon for us to claim to be able to extract the *meaning* of this nothingness, with which the activity of questioning has suddenly confronted us. But we are able now to provide a number of clarifications. In particular, it would be no bad thing to determine the relations between being and the non-being that haunts it. Indeed, we have noticed a degree of parallelism between human ways of behaving in relation to being and man's behavior in the face of nothingness, and this tempts us immediately to regard being and non-being as two complementary constituents of reality, like shadow and light. If we do that, we find ourselves dealing with two wholly contemporary notions, able in some way to come together in the production of existents, and which it would be fruitless to consider in isolation. Pure being and pure non-being would be two abstractions, whose combination alone would form the basis of concrete realities.

That is certainly Hegel's point of view. Indeed, he studies the relations

5 TN: Bergson gives his reductive argument against the idea of non-being—opposed here by Sartre—in Bergson (1911a).

of Being and Non-Being in his *Logic*, and he calls this logic "the system of pure thought-determinations."[6] And he clarifies his definition:[7]

> In the case of thought in the ordinary sense, we always represent to ourselves   47
> something that is not merely pure thought, for we intend by it something
> that is thought of, but which has an empirical content. In the *Logic*, thoughts
> are grasped in such a way that they have no content other than the one that
> belongs to thinking itself, and is brought forth by thinking.

Of course, these determinations are "what is most inward in things," but at the same time, when we consider them "in and for themselves," we deduce them from thought itself and we discover in them their truth. However, Hegel's logic aims to "make evident the incompleteness of the notions (that it) considers one by one, and the necessity, if we are to understand them, of rising to a more complete notion, which, in integrating them, sublates them."[8] Le Senne's remark about Hamelin's philosophy can be applied to Hegel: "Each of the lower terms depends on the higher term, as the abstract depends on the concrete that is necessary for its actualization."[9] The truly concrete, for Hegel, is the Existent with its essence; it is the Totality produced by the synthetic integration of all the abstract moments which, in demanding their complement, are sublated within it. In this sense, Being is an abstraction, the most abstract and impoverished, if we regard it in itself, i.e., by severing it from its sublation toward Essence. Indeed:

> Being stands in relation to Essence as the Immediate to the Mediate.
> Things simply are, but their Being consists in this: that they manifest
> their Essence. Being goes over into Essence; one can express it thus;

6 TN: Here and in the following sentence I use the published English translation of the French excerpt from Hegel; both are from Hegel (1991: §24).

7 Sartre's note: Introduction to the *Lesser Logic*, §XXIV, cited by Lefebvre, *Morceaux Choisis*. TN: The Lefebvre anthology is available in French as Hegel (1995).

8 Sartre's note: Laporte, *Le Problème de l'Abstraction*, p. 25 (Presses Universitaires, 1940). TN: The book by Laporte on which Sartre draws here has not been translated into English.

9 Sartre also takes this sentence from the Laporte text just cited on p. 24. The French philosopher René Le Senne (1882–1954) was a professor at the Sorbonne. Le Senne was influenced by the "dialectical idealism" of an earlier French philosopher, Octave Hamelin (1856–1907), also mentioned in this sentence.

> Being presupposes Essence. But although Essence, in comparison with Being, appears as that which is mediated, yet, notwithstanding, Essence is the true *Origin*. In essence, Being returns into its Ground; Being sublates itself in Essence.[10]

In this way, Being, cut off from the Essence that is its foundation, becomes "mere empty immediacy." And that is just how the *Phenomenology of Spirit* defines it, which presents pure Being "from the point of view of the truth" as the immediate. If the beginning of logic must be the immediate, we will be able to find our beginning in Being, as "the first beginning [which] cannot be anything mediated and further determined."[11]

But Being, thus determined, at once "passes over into" its opposite. "But this pure being," Hegel writes in the "lesser" *Logic*, "is the *pure abstraction*, and hence it is the *absolutely negative*, which, when taken immediately, is equally *nothing*."[12] Indeed, isn't nothingness simple self-identity, complete emptiness, the absence of any determinations or content? Therefore, pure being and pure nothingness are the same thing. Or rather, it is correct to say that they differ. But "because the distinction has here not yet determined itself, precisely because being and nothing are still the immediate—it is, as belonging to them, *what cannot be said*, what is merely *meant*."[13] In other words, and expressed in concrete terms, "nowhere on heaven or earth is there anything which does not contain both being and nothing in itself."[14]

It is still too soon to discuss Hegel's conception as it is: when we have all the results of our investigation, we will be able to take up a position in relation to it. We should simply point out that Hegel reduces being to a meaning of the existent. Being is surrounded by its essence, which

---

10 Sartre's note: *Esquisse de la Logique*, written by Hegel between 1808 and 1811, was the basis for his lessons in the Nuremberg Gymnasium. TN: Sartre found the text mentioned in this note in the Lefebvre anthology. The text was not published during Hegel's lifetime, but it is now available in English translation as "Logic (for the Middle Class)" (in Hegel 1986). I have used that translation; the passage Sartre quotes is on p. 76.

11 TN: I have quoted the corresponding English passage from Hegel (1991: §86).

12 TN: I have quoted the corresponding English passage from Hegel (1991: §87).

13 Sartre's note: Hegel, *Petite Logique*, E §88. TN: I quote the corresponding English passage from Hegel (1991: §87).

14 Sartre's note: Hegel, *Grande Logique*, chap. 1. TN: I quote the corresponding English passage from Hegel (2010: 61).

is its foundation and origin. Hegel's whole theory is based on the idea that a philosophical process is needed in order to reach—at the beginning of his Logic—the immediate from the mediated, and the abstract from the concrete which founds it. But we have already pointed out that being, in relation to the phenomenon, is not like the abstract in relation to the concrete. Being is not one "structure among others," a moment of the object: it is the very condition of all structures and all moments; it is the foundation on which the characteristics of the phenomenon will be made manifest. And similarly, we cannot allow that the being of things "consists in manifesting their essence."[15] If that were the case, there would need to be a being of that being. If moreover the being of things were "to consist" in their manifesting, it is difficult to see how Hegel could establish a pure moment of Being in which not even a trace of this initial structure can be found. It is true that pure being is fixed by the understanding, isolated by it and frozen in its actual determinations. But if its sublation toward essence constitutes being's main characteristic and if the understanding only "determines and holds the determination fixed,"[16] it is difficult to see why it does not determine being, precisely, as "consisting in manifesting." It might be said that for Hegel all determination is negation. But, on this view, the understanding limits itself to denying, in relation to its object, that it is *other* than it is. That is probably enough to prevent any dialectical process, but it will not be enough to make sublation disappear, to uproot it entirely. Insofar as being sublates itself *into something else*, it escapes the determinations of the understanding, but insofar as it sublates itself—i.e., insofar as it is, in the depths of its being, the origin of its own sublation—it must on the contrary appear as it *is* to the understanding that freezes it in its own determinations. To affirm that being is only what it is would at the very least leave being intact insofar as it *is* its sublation. That is the ambiguity of Hegel's notion of "sublation," which sometimes seems to be a surge from the depths of the being in view and at other times an external movement that carries it away. It is not enough to claim that the understanding finds in a being only what it is; it still needs to be explained how the being, which is what it is, can be *no more than that*; to be legitimate, such an

---

15 TN: Sartre found this in the Lefebvre anthology; it comes from the *Esquisse de la Logique*, §6. The corresponding English translation (slightly modified here) is at Hegel (1986: 76).
16 TN: I quote the corresponding English passage from Hegel (2010: 10).

explanation would need to consider the phenomenon of being as such, not the understanding's processes of negation.

But what we need to examine here is Hegel's claim that being and nothingness constitute two contraries whose difference, at the level of abstraction under consideration, is merely "meant."

To oppose being to nothingness as thesis to antithesis—as Hegel's understanding does—is to suppose them to be logically contemporaneous. In this way, the two contraries arise at the same time, like the two limiting terms of a logical series. But we must take care here to note that the contraries can enjoy this simultaneity only because they are equally positive (or equally negative). However, non-being is not the contrary of being but its contradictory. That implies that nothingness is logically subsequent to being, since being is posited first and then negated. Being and non-being cannot therefore be concepts with the same content because, on the contrary, non-being requires an irreducible intellectual process: notwithstanding being's primitive lack of differentiation, non-being is this same lack of differentiation *negated*. What enables Hegel to make being "pass over into" nothingness is his implicitly introducing negation into his very definition of being. This goes without saying, since a definition is negative, and since Hegel has told us—by taking up an expression from Spinoza—that *omnis determinatio est negatio*.[17] And doesn't he say: "If any . . . content were posited in [being] as distinct, or if it were posited by this determination or content as distinct from an other, it would therefore fail to hold fast to its purity. It is pure indeterminateness and emptiness. There is *nothing* to be intuited in it . . .?"[18] So he is the one who introduces this negation into being from outside—which he then rediscovers when he makes being pass over into non-being. But here there is a play on words in relation to the very notion of negation. Because if I negate, with respect to being, every determination and every content, I can do that only while affirming that at least being *is*. Thus, one can negate with respect to being as much as one likes, but one cannot make it *not be*, by virtue of the very fact that

17 TN: The Latin phrase means "every determination is negation." In fact this phrase does not appear in Spinoza's published writings but in a 1674 letter to Jarig Jelles. Arguably, the doctrine is implicit in Spinoza's *Ethics*.

18 TN: Sartre is quoting from Hegel's *Science of Logic*. I quote the corresponding English passage from Hegel (2010: 59).

one is negating its being this or that. Where being is absolute plenitude and entire positivity, negation cannot reach to being's core. However, non-being is a negation that aims at that core of plenary density itself. Non-being negates itself in its heart. When Hegel writes:[19] "[Being and nothing] are . . . empty abstractions, and . . . each of them is as empty as the other," he forgets that any void or emptiness must be empty of some-thing.[20] Now, being is empty of any determination other than its identity with itself, but non-being is empty *of being*. In brief, and against Hegel, what we need to remember is that being *is* and that nothingness *is not*.

Thus, even if being did not support any differentiated quality, noth-ingness would be logically subsequent to it, since it presupposes being in order to negate it, since the irreducible quality of "not" is superadded to that undifferentiated mass of being in order to deliver it. That does not only mean that we should refuse to place being and non-being on the same level but, in addition, that we should take care never to posit nothingness as a primordial abyss, out of which being comes. Our use of the notion of nothingness in its everyday guise always presupposes some preliminary specification of being. It is striking, in this respect, that language provides us with a nothingness of *things* ("*Nothing*") and a nothingness of human beings ("*Nobody*"). But in the majority of cases the specification is taken still further: we say, referring to a particular collection of objects: "*None* of them is to be touched," which is to say, very precisely, nothing *in this collection*. Similarly, someone who is ques-tioned about some quite specific events in private or public life may reply: "I know *nothing* about it," and this "nothing" comprises the set of facts about which he was questioned.[21] Even Socrates, with his famous phrase "I know that I know nothing,"[22] refers precisely by this "noth-

50

---

19 Sartre's note: *Petite Logique*, 2nd edn, E §87. TN: I quote the corresponding English pas-sage from Hegel (1991: §87).
20 Sartre's note: What makes this even stranger is that Hegel is the first to have noticed that "every negation is a determinate negation"—or, in other words, that it bears on a content.
21 TN: Sartre's examples of everyday locutions here cannot be translated in a way that both preserves Sartre's point and uses everyday English. I have slightly altered the examples where necessary in order to preserve Sartre's intended emphasis on the multiplicity of instances in which we talk about "nothing."
22 TN: Although this famous phrase is widely attributed to Plato's Socrates, it does not actually occur *verbatim* anywhere in Plato's works.

ing" to the totality of being, viewed as Truth. If, adopting for a moment the viewpoint of simple-minded cosmogonies, we tried to ask what "there was" before the world existed and replied "*nothing*," we would have to recognize that both these terms—"before" and "nothing"— work retrospectively. What *we*, lodged within being, are denying *today* is that there was any being before this being. The negation here emanates from a consciousness that turns back toward its origins. If we removed from this original void its property of being empty *of this world*, and of any structure that had taken on the form of a world, along with its property of *before*—which presupposes an *after* in relation to which I constitute it as "before"—the negation itself would vanish, making way for a total absence of determination that would be impossible to conceive— not even, and especially not, in terms of nothingness. In this way we can say, inverting Spinoza's formula, that all negation is determination. Therefore being is antecedent to nothingness and founds it. We must interpret this as meaning not only that being has logical priority over nothingness but also that, in concrete terms, it is from being that nothingness derives its efficacy. We expressed this by saying that *nothingness haunts being*. In other words, being can be conceived of without any need of nothingness, and that we can exhaustively explore the notion of being without finding in it the slightest trace of nothingness. But, on the contrary, the nothingness *that is not* can have only a borrowed existence: it takes its being from being; we can encounter its nothingness of being only within the limits of being, and being's total disappearance would not mean the accession of a reign of non-being but, on the contrary, the concomitant disappearance of nothingness; *there is non-being only on the surface of being.*

IV. THE PHENOMENOLOGICAL CONCEPTION OF NOTHINGNESS

It is true that we can conceive the complementarity of being and nothingness in another way. We can see both of them as two equally necessary components of reality, but without making being "pass over into" nothingness as Hegel does or insisting, as we were trying to do, that nothingness is logically subsequent: we can emphasize, on the contrary, the reciprocal forces of repulsion that being and non-being exert on each other, such that reality is in some way the tension that results from these antagonistic forces. Heidegger's thought is oriented toward this new conception.[23]

It takes no time to notice the progress that his theory of Nothingness represents in relation to Hegel's. First, being and non-being are no longer empty abstractions. In his major work Heidegger demonstrated the legitimacy of a questioning of being, where being no longer has the character of a Scholastic universal that it still retained in Hegel: there is a meaning of being that must be elucidated; there is a "preontological understanding" of being contained in all the ways in which "human-reality" behaves, i.e., in each of its projects. In the same way, the aporias that people habitually raise whenever a philosopher approaches the problem of Nothingness are shown to be unimportant: they are valid only insofar as they limit the use of our intellect, and they only show that this problem lies *outside the province* of the intellect. On the contrary, there are numerous attitudes of "human-reality" that imply an "understand-ing"[24] of nothingness: hatred, prohibition, regret, etc. There is even the permanent possibility that *Dasein* may find itself "faced" with nothing-ness, and encounter it as a phenomenon: that is anguish. Nonetheless, even though he establishes these possibilities of a concrete apprehen-sion of nothingness, Heidegger does not succumb to Hegel's mistake: he does not preserve any being for non-being, not even an abstract being; nothingness is not; it nihilates itself. It is maintained and conditioned by transcendence. As we know, Heidegger defines the being of human-reality as being-in-the-world. And the world is the synthetic structure of equipment, in which each part indicates another, in ever wider circles, such that man is acquainted by this structure with what he is.[25] This means at the same time that "human-reality" arises as *invested* by being,

---

23 Sartre's note: Heidegger, *Qu'est-ce que la Métaphysique?* (trans. Corbin, NRF, 1938). TN: Heidegger (1938a), available in English translation as Heidegger (1978c).

24 TN: . . . *une "compréhension" du néant* . . . I follow Heidegger's translators in using the word "understanding" rather than "comprehension." For the same reason I translate *entende-ment* in the previous sentence as "intellect," as Krell does in his translation of Heidegger (1978c).

25 TN: . . . *l'homme se fait annoncer . . . ce qu'il est.* Sartre uses this phrase frequently in the text, and borrows it from Corbin's translations of Heidegger (see Heidegger 1938b: 88). The basic idea here is that man makes sense of himself in terms of the world around him. As Sartre might put it, the world reflects back to man his "projects."

it "finds itself" (*sich befinden*) in being—and that it is human-reality that arranges this being by which it is besieged around itself in the form of a world. But human-reality can make being appear as a totality organized into a world only by surpassing it. For Heidegger, all determination is a surpassing, since it presupposes a step taken back, the taking up of a point of view. And *Dasein* brings about this surpassing of the world—the condition of the world's elevation as such[26]—*in relation to itself*. Indeed, the characteristic of ipseity (*Selbstheit*) is that man is always separated from what he is by the entire breadth of the being that he is not. He becomes acquainted with himself from the other side of the world, and he turns back from the horizon toward himself in order to internalize: man is "a being of distances."[27] It is with the movement of internalization—which traverses all of being—that being arises and is organized as a world, without there being any priority either of the movement over the world or of the world over the movement. But this appearance of the self beyond the world—in other words, beyond the totality of reality—is the emergence of human-reality in nothingness. It is only within nothingness that being can be surpassed. At the same time, the point of view from which being is organized into a world is beyond-the-world—which means, on one hand, that human-reality arises as the emergence of being within non-being and, on the other hand, that the world is "in suspense"[28] within nothingness. The discovery of this twofold and perpetual nihilation is anguish. And it is on the basis of this surpassing of the world that *Dasein* will actualize the world's contingency; in other words it will pose the question "Why is there something rather than nothing?" Therefore the world's contingency appears to human-reality, insofar as it has installed itself within nothingness in order to apprehend it.

Here, then, is nothingness encircling being on every side and at the

26 TN: . . . *condition de la surrection . . . du monde* . . . The relatively rare French term *surrection* is geological, referring to an upheaval or "uplift" of land. See my note on Sartre's many metaphors of upward movement in Notes on the Translation.

27 TN: . . . *l'homme est un "être des lointains."* Sartre is quoting from the final paragraph of Heidegger's *Vom Wesen des Grundes* (translated into English as Heidegger 1969), which had been published in French more than once in the 1930s. Corbin's translation has it in the singular: *un être du lointain.*

28 TN: Sartre is almost certainly alluding to Heidegger. Corbin, for example, translates Heidegger as saying *"Dans l'angoisse, nous 'flottons en suspens.'"*

same time expelled from being; here nothingness is given as the means by which the world acquires its contours as a world. Can we be satisfied by this solution?

Of course, we cannot deny that our apprehension of the world as the world is nihilating. As soon as the world appears as the world, it is given as being *no more than that*. Human-reality's emergence out of nothingness is the necessary counterpart to this apprehension. But how does human-reality have the power to emerge in this way from non-being? Heidegger is doubtless correct in insisting that negation derives its foundation from nothingness. But if nothingness can found negation, it is because it envelops within it, as its essential structure, the "*not*." In other words, nothingness does not found negation, either in the manner of an undifferentiated void, or as an instance of alterity that does not posit itself as alterity.[29] It is at the origin of negative judgment because it is itself negation. It can found negation as an *act* because it is negation as *being*. Nothingness cannot be nothingness without nihilating itself explicitly as the nothingness of the world; in other words, it must explicitly direct itself in its nihilation toward the world in order to constitute itself as the refusal of the world. Nothingness bears being in its heart. But how does the emergent being take account of this nihilating refusal? Transcendence, as "a project of itself, beyond . . . ," cannot found nothingness at all; on the contrary, it is nothingness that is at the very heart of transcendence, and conditions it. Now, Heidegger's philosophy is characterized by his use of positive terms for *Dasein*, all of which disguise implicit negations. *Dasein* is "outside itself, in the world," a "being of distances," "care," "its own possibilities," etc. This all amounts to saying that *Dasein* "is not" in itself, that it "is not" in immediate proximity to itself, and that it "surpasses" the world insofar as it posits itself as "not being in itself" and as "not being the world." In this sense Hegel is in the right, against Heidegger, when he asserts that "Spirit is the negative."[30] Only we can put the same question to each of them in almost the same form; to Hegel we must say "It is not enough to posit spirit as mediation and the negative; you need to show how the negative is the structure of spirit's being. What must spirit be, in order to be able to constitute itself as the negative?" And we can ask Heidegger: "If negation is the primary structure of transcendence, what

29 Sartre's note: In Hegel's parlance, "immediate alterity."
30 TN: . . . *c'est Hegel qui . . . déclare que l'Esprit est le négatif.* Hegel says that "spirit . . . is the negative" in the Preface to the first edition of the *Science of Logic* (Hegel 2010: 10).

must the primary structure of human-reality be, in order for it to be able to transcend the world?" In both cases we are shown a negating activity, without any concern to found this activity on a negative being. And furthermore Heidegger makes nothingness a sort of intentional correlate of transcendence, without seeing that he has already inserted it within transcendence itself as its primordial structure.

But, in addition, what is the point of claiming that nothingness founds negation if what follows is a theory of non-being that, *ex hypothesi*, severs nothingness from any actual negation? If I emerge out of nothingness *beyond* the world, how can this extraworldly nothingness found those little lakes of non-being that we encounter at each instant within being? I say that "Pierre is not there," that "I have no more money," etc. Is it really necessary, in order to found these everyday judgments, to surpass the world toward nothingness and then come right back to being? And how is this operation brought about? Not by making the world slide into nothingness but rather—while remaining within the limits of being—by simply withholding an attribute from a subject. But might it not be said that each withheld attribute, each negated being, is caught up within a single identical extraworldly nothingness, that non-being is like the totality of what is not, that the world is suspended within non-being, like the real within the possibles? In that case one would have to make each negation originate in a specific act of surpassing: the surpassing of being toward the other. But how could this surpassing be anything but, quite simply, Hegel's mediation? And haven't we already asked Hegel— in vain—for the nihilating foundation of mediation? And besides, even if the explanation worked for those simple, radical negations that deny of some particular object any sort of presence within being ("The Centaur *does not exist*," "*There is no* reason for him to be late," "The Ancient Greeks *did not practice* polygamy")—negations that might, at a stretch, contribute to the constitution of nothingness as a kind of geometric place of all failed projects, all inaccurate representations, all beings that have disappeared, or whose idea is made up—this interpretation of non-being would not work for a certain type of real particulars[31]—to tell the truth,

31 TN: . . . *un certain type de réalités* . . . Sartre's plural form (literally "realities") sounds odd in English; for clarity I have inserted the word "particulars." Sartre is referring here to negatities.

the most common—that include non-being in their being. How could we accept that part of them lies within the universe, while a wholly other part lies outside it, in extraworldly nothingness?

Take for example the notion of distance, which conditions the determination of a place, or the localization of a point. It is easy to see that it contains a negative moment: two points are distant when a specific length *separates* them. In other words, the length—a positive attribute of some segment of a line—enters in here as the negation of an absolute, undifferentiated proximity. Some might wish to reduce distance to being *no more than* the length of the segment of which the two points in question—A and B—are the limits. But surely they ought to see that in this case we have switched the direction of our attention and that, under cover of the same word, a different object has been given to intuition? The organized complex constituted by the segment with its two limiting terms can, in effect, deliver two different objects of knowledge. We can present the *segment* to ourselves as the immediate object of intuition; in that case, the segment will represent a full, concrete tension whose length is a positive attribute, and whose two points A and B appear only as a moment in the structure as a whole, i.e., only insofar as the segment itself implies them as its limits. In that case negation, expelled from the segment and its length, will take refuge in the two limits: to say that point B is the segment's limit amounts to saying that the segment *does not extend* beyond that point. Here the negation is a secondary structure of the object. If, on the contrary, we direct our attention to the two points A and B, they show up as immediate objects of intuition against the ground of space. The segment dissolves as a full, concrete object: it is grasped on the basis of the two points as the void, the negative, that separates them; the negation escapes from the points—which cease to be *limits*—to impregnate the actual length of the segment, in the capacity of *distance*. Thus the total figure, constituted by the segment and its two terms with the negation that is internal to its structure, allows us to apprehend it in two ways. Or rather, there are two figures and the condition of one of them appearing is the disintegration of the other, just as, in perception, we can constitute one object as the *figure* by repelling some other object to the point at which it becomes the *ground* and *vice versa*. In each case we find the same amount of negation, which at one moment is contained within the notion of the limits and at the next moment within the notion of distance, but which cannot in any case be eliminated. Might it be said that the idea of distance is psychological, and that it refers simply to the expanse we have to cross in order to go from point A to point B? We will reply that this "crossing" includes the same negation, since that notion expresses exactly the passive resistance of remoteness. We are happy to concede, with Heidegger, that human-reality is "de-distancing," i.e., it arises in the world as the being that creates distances and, at the same time, makes them dissolve (ent-fernend).[32] But this de-distancing, even if it is the necessary condition for "there to be" distance in general, contains distance within itself as the negative structure to be overcome.[33] We can try in vain to reduce distance to the simple result of a *measurement*: what we have seen in the course of the preceding description is that the two points, and the segment included between them, have the indissoluble unity of what the Germans call a "*Gestalt.*" Negation is the cement that brings this unity about. It defines precisely the immediate relationship connecting these two points, which presents them to intuition as the indissoluble unity of distance. If you claim the distance is reducible to the measurement of a length, you will only cover up this negation, because the negation is the measurement's *raison d'être*.

What we have just shown by examining *distance* might just as well have been pointed out by describing realities such as absence, alteration, alterity, repulsion, regret, absentmindedness, etc. There is an infinite number of realities that are not only objects of judgment but which are experienced, fought against, feared, etc., by human beings and which are inhabited in their internal structure by negation as a necessary condition of their existence. We will call them "negatities."[34] Kant glimpsed their importance when he talked about *limitative* concepts (the immortality of the soul), a sort of synthesis between the negative and the positive, in which negation is a condition of positivity. The negation's function varies according to the nature of the object in question: between the fully

---

32 TN: The French adjective *déséloignant* is a neologism used to translate Heidegger's complicated term *ent-fernend*. Here I follow Joan Stambaugh's practice in her translation of *Being and Time* (Heidegger 2010) and use "de-distancing."

33 TN: ... *pour "qu'il y ait"* ... The quotation marks signal that Sartre has in mind Heidegger's phrase *es gibt*, for which the French *il y a* is a good equivalent. See my note on Heidegger vocabulary in Notes on the Translation.

34 TN: The term *négatité* is Sartre's neologism. See my note in Notes on the Translation.

positive realities (which nonetheless retain negation as the condition of the sharpness of their contours, as that which fixes them as what they are) and those whose positivity is only an appearance concealing a hole of nothingness, all intermediaries are possible. In any case it becomes impossible to hurl these negations back into some extraworldly nothingness, as they are conditions of reality, dispersed throughout being and supported by being. Extraworldly nothingness can account for absolute negation; but we have just discovered a proliferation of intraworldly beings that possess as much reality and efficacy as other beings, but which enclose non-being within themselves. The explanation they require must remain within the limits of the real. Nothingness, if it is supported only by being, vanishes *as nothingness*, and we fall back into being. Nothingness can only nihilate itself on the ground of being: if nothingness can be given, it is neither before being nor after being; nor is it, in a general way, outside being; rather, it is right inside being, in its heart, like a worm.

V. THE ORIGIN OF NOTHINGNESS

At this point we should cast an eye behind us and take stock of the road we have traveled. First we raised the question of being. Then, turning back on this question itself and conceiving it as a type of human *behavior*, we interrogated it in its turn. We had then to acknowledge that, if negation did not exist, it would be impossible to raise any question at all—in particular the question of being. But this negation itself, brought into closer view, directed us to nothingness as its origin and foundation; for there to be negation in the world, and for us to be able in consequence to question ourselves about being, nothingness must in some way be given. We realized that we cannot conceive of nothingness *outside* being, nor as a complementary and abstract notion, nor as an infinite medium in which being might be suspended. Nothingness must be given in the heart of being if we are to be able to apprehend the distinctive type of real particulars designated by us as "negatities." But being-in-itself is not able to produce this intraworldly nothingness: the notion of being as full positivity does not contain nothingness as one of its structures. We cannot even say that it excludes it: it stands in no relation at all with it. Hence the question arises for us now with special urgency: if nothingness cannot be conceived of, either outside being or on the basis of being, and if

57

on the other hand it cannot (because it is non-being) derive from itself the necessary power to "nihilate itself," *where does nothingness come from?*

To get a firmer grip on the problem we must recognize in the first place that we cannot concede to nothingness the property of "nihilating itself." Although the verb "to nihilate itself" was conceived in order to remove even the slightest semblance of being from nothingness, we are obliged to acknowledge that only *being* can nihilate itself, because for something to nihilate itself it is necessary, in some way or other, for it to be. Now, nothingness *is not.* If we can talk about it, that is because it possesses only an appearance of being, a borrowed being, as we noted earlier. Nothingness is not, but "is been":[35] nothingness does not nihilate itself but "is nihilated." Nonetheless, it is true that some being must exist—and it cannot be the in-itself—with the property of nihilating nothingness, of supporting it with its being, of constantly underpinning it by its very existence, *a being through which nothingness comes to things.* But how must this being stand in relation to nothingness, in order for it to be the case that nothingness comes to things through it? We must observe first that the being we are envisaging cannot be passive in relation to nothingness: it cannot receive it; nothingness could only *come to* this being by means of some other being—which would send us on an infinite regress. But, on the other hand, the being through which nothingness comes to the world cannot *produce* nothingness while remaining indifferent to this production, like a Stoic cause that produces its effect without undergoing alteration itself. It is inconceivable that any fully positive being could sustain, and create outside itself, a transcendent nothingness of being—because there would be nothing in being through which it might sublate itself toward non-being. The being through which nothingness arrives in the world must nihilate nothingness in its being and, even then, it would still run the risk of establishing nothingness as something transcendent in the very heart of immanence, unless it were to nihilate nothingness in its being *with respect to its being.* The being through which nothingness arrives in the world is a being in which, in its being, the nothingness of its being is in question: *the being through which nothingness comes to the world must be its own nothingness.* And we must not construe this as an act of nihilation—which would in its turn require a foundation in

---

35 TN: ...*le néant "est été"* ...See my note on this ungrammatical phrase in Notes on the Translation.

being—but as an ontological characteristic of the being we are seeking. We have still to find out where—in which delicate and exquisite region of being—we will meet the being that is its own nothingness.

A fuller examination of the behavior that we took as our starting point will assist us in our search. We must return, therefore, to the activity of questioning. We saw, it will be recalled, that every question posits, in its essence, the possibility of a negative answer. In a question we interrogate a being about its being or about its way of being. And this being, or way of being, is concealed; the possibility always remains open for it to be disclosed as a nothingness. But it follows, from the very fact of our envisaging that an existent can always disclose itself as *nothing*, that every question presupposes that we have taken a nihilating step back in relation to the given, which becomes a mere *presentation*, oscillating between being and nothingness. What is important, therefore, is the permanent possibility through which any questioner is able to detach himself from the causal series that constitute being, and by which only being can be produced. Indeed, if we allowed that the question might be determined in the questioner by a universal determinism, it would cease not only to be intelligible but even to be conceivable. In point of fact, a real cause produces a real effect, and a being that is caused is wholly engaged by its cause within positivity: to the extent that it depends in its being on its cause, it cannot contain the slightest germ of nothingness within it; insofar as a questioner must be able to take a sort of nihilating step back in relation to the thing he is questioning, he escapes from the causal order of the world and extricates himself from the glue of being. In consequence, through a twofold movement of nihilation, he nihilates the thing he is questioning in relation to himself—by placing it in a *neutral* state, between being and non-being—and he also nihilates himself in relation to the questioned thing, by separating himself from being in order to draw out from himself the possibility of a non-being. In this way, any question introduces some measure of negatity[36] into the world: we see nothingness rendering the world iridescent, shimmering on things. But at the same time the question emanates from a questioner who motivates himself, in his being as questioning, by ungluing himself from being.

36 TN: Although the French text has *négatité* here, it seems likely that Sartre meant to write "negativity"; the latter is something that can come in "measures," whereas negatities are particulars.

It is therefore, by definition, a human process. Therefore man presents himself, at least in this case, as a being who makes nothingness open up within the world, insofar as he assigns non-being to himself to this end.

We can use these observations as a guiding thread to examine the negatities that we discussed earlier. They are transcendent realities, beyond any doubt; distance, for example, imposes itself on us as something we have to reckon with, that we must traverse with effort. Yet these realities have a very special nature: they all immediately underline an essential relation of human-reality with the world. They originate in a human being's act, or expectation, or project; all of them underline an aspect of being as it appears to a human being engaged within the world. And the relations of man with the world that these negatities point toward have nothing in common with the *a posteriori* relations that emerge from our empirical activity. Nor is it a matter of those relations of *equipmentality*[37] through which, according to Heidegger, "human-reality" discovers worldly objects. Rather, each negatity appears as one of the essential conditions of this relation of equipmentality. In order for the totality of being to order itself around us in the form of implements—in order for it to break up into differentiated co-referring structures that can be *used*— it is necessary that negation should arise, not as one thing among other things but as a categorial classification that governs the organization and division of the great masses of being into things. In this way, man's elevation in the middle of the being that "invests" him makes it happen that a world is disclosed. But the essential and primordial moment of this elevation is negation. Thus we have reached the first goal of this study: man is the being through whom nothingness comes into the world. But this question immediately provokes another: How must man be in his being, in order that nothingness can come to being through him?

Being can only engender being and, if this generative process encompasses man, nothing but being can come from him. If he must be able to interrogate this process—which is to say, to put it in question—he must be able to hold it up to view as a totality—that is, to place himself *outside being* and, in so doing, to weaken the structure of being's being. However, human-reality does not possess the ability to annihilate, even temporarily, the mass of being placed before it. What it can modify is its

---

37 TN: . . . *ces rapports d'ustensilité* . . . See my note on "equipmentality" in the section on Heidegger vocabulary in Notes on the Translation.

relation to that being. To disconnect some particular existent, for human-reality, is to disconnect itself in relation to it. In this case human-reality escapes the existent and cannot be acted on by it; it is out of reach, having withdrawn *beyond a nothingness*. Descartes, following the Stoics, gave a name to this possibility of human-reality, the possibility of secreting a nothingness that isolates it: it is *freedom*. But here freedom is only a word. If we wish to go further into the question, we cannot be content with this answer and we must go on to ask: What must human freedom be if nothingness must come to the world through it?

It is not yet possible for us to deal with the problem of freedom in its full extent.[38] In fact, the steps that we have taken so far show clearly that freedom is not a faculty of the human mind that can be contemplated and described in isolation. What we were trying to define was man's being insofar as he conditions the appearing of nothingness, and this being has appeared to us as freedom. In this way freedom, as the condition required for nothingness's nihilation, cannot be a *property* that belongs, along with others, to the essence of a human being. Moreover, we have already noted that, for man, the relation of existence to essence is not the same as for worldly things. Human freedom precedes man's essence and makes it possible; the human being's essence is in suspense   60 in his freedom. It is therefore impossible to distinguish freedom, in the sense in which we refer to it, from human-reality's *being*. Man does not exist first in order to be free *later*; rather, there is no difference between man's being and his *being-free*. At this point, therefore, we will not fully address a question that can be exhaustively considered only in the light of a rigorous elucidation of the human being; rather, we need to deal with freedom in connection with the problem of nothingness, and strictly to the extent that it conditions its appearing.

It is evident from the outset that human-reality can only separate itself from the world—through a question, methodical doubt, skeptical doubt, the ἐποχή, etc.—if by nature it is a self-separation. This was seen by Descartes, who founds doubt on freedom by claiming for us the possibility of suspending our judgments—and, after him, by Alain. It is in this sense, too, that Hegel affirms the freedom of spirit, to the extent that spirit is mediation, i.e., the Negative. And furthermore, one

---

38 Sartre's note: Cf. Part Four, Chapter 1.

of the directions taken by contemporary philosophy has been to discern in human consciousness a kind of escaping from itself: that is the meaning of Heidegger's transcendence; intentionality is also—in Husserl and Brentano—characterized in more than one respect by its self-separation. But we will not consider freedom as the internal structure of consciousness now: for the moment we lack the instruments and the technique that might enable us to succeed in this enterprise. What interests us at present is a temporal operation, since questioning is, like doubt, a way of behaving: it presupposes that the human being first rests within being, and then separates himself from it by taking a nihilating step back. What we are regarding here as the condition of nihilation is therefore a self-relation within a temporal process. We want simply to demonstrate that, if we assimilate consciousness to an indefinitely continued causal sequence, we transmute it into a plenitude of being and in so doing we return it to the unlimited totality of being—as we can see in the futile attempts to dissociate psychological determinism from universal determinism, and to constitute it as a separate series. The absent person's bedroom, the books he leafed through, the objects he touched, are only, in themselves, *books, objects*, i.e., they are full actualities: even the traces he has left can be interpreted as his traces only within a situation from which he is already posited as absent. Taken alone, the dog-eared book, with its worn pages, is not a book whose pages Pierre has turned or whose pages he is no longer turning: it is a volume with worn, folded pages. If we consider it as my perception's present and transcendent motivation, or even as the synthetic and rule-governed flux of my

61   sensory impressions, it can point no further than itself, or to objects that are present, to the light that illuminates it, the table that supports it. It would be pointless to invoke an association of contiguity, as Plato does in his *Phaedo*, that can make an image of the absent person appear in the margin of one's perception of the lyre, or the zither, that he touched. Such an image, if we consider it in itself and in the spirit of the classical theories, is a specific plenitude, a concrete and positive psychological fact. It follows that a judgment about it whose negativity faces two ways will be required: subjectively, in order to signify that the image *is not* a perception; and objectively, in order to deny in relation to this Pierre of whom I am forming an image that he *is there* at present. This is the famous problem of the characteristics of the true image that has preoccupied so

many psychologists, from Taine to Spaier.[39] We can see that association does not eliminate the problem: it pushes it back to the level of reflection. But, in any case, association demands a negation, which is to say at the least that consciousness has to take a nihilating step back from the image that it apprehends as a subjective phenomenon, in order to establish it, precisely, as being no more than a subjective phenomenon. Now I have tried to show elsewhere[40] that if we first present the image as a renascent perception, it is radically impossible to distinguish it *later* from our current perceptions. The image must contain within its very structure a nihilating thesis. It constitutes itself as an image by positing its object as existing *elsewhere* or as *not* existing. It carries within itself a twofold negation: it is in the first place a nihilation of the world (insofar as it is not the world that is presently providing, as an actual object of perception, the object aimed at in the image), and then a nihilation of the object of the image (insofar as it is posited as non-actual) and, at the same time, a nihilation of itself (insofar as it is not a full and concrete mental process). It would be futile to try to explain my apprehension of Pierre's absence in the bedroom by invoking Husserl's well-known "empty intentions" that are, in large part, constitutive of perception. Between the different perceptual intentions, there are indeed relations of *motivation* (but motivation is not causation), and some of these intentions are full—which is to say fulfilled by what they aim at—while others are empty. But, as the matter that is supposed to fulfill the empty intentions is, precisely, what *is not*, that matter cannot be what motivates them in their structure. And as the other intentions are fulfilled, they cannot motivate empty intentions, insofar as they are empty, either. Moreover these intentions are psychological in nature, and it would be a mistake to envisage them in the manner of things, i.e., as recipients that can in the first place be given and are—on a case-to-case basis—either empty or fulfilled, and which remain in their nature indifferent as to their state of emptiness or fulfillment. It seems that Husserl did not always escape this reifying illusion. To be empty, an intention must be conscious of itself as empty, and precisely as empty of the precise matter it aims at. An

39 TN: The French psychologist Hippolyte Taine (1828–1893) claimed that external perception was a "true hallucination."
40 Sartre's note: *L'Imagination* (Alcan, 1936). TN: Translated as Sartre (2012).

empty intention constitutes itself as empty to just that degree to which it posits its matter as inexistent or absent. In brief, an empty intention is consciousness of a negation that transcends itself toward an object that it posits as absent or nonexistent. Thus, whatever explanation we give of it, for Pierre's absence to be noted or felt, a negative moment is required in which consciousness, in the absence of any antecedent determination, constitutes itself as negation. In conceiving, on the basis of my perceptions of the bedroom that he lived in, the person who is no longer in the bedroom, I must necessarily perform an act of thought that cannot be determined or motivated by any antecedent state; in short, I must instantiate within myself a break with being. And as I make continual use of negatities to isolate and determine the existents—in other words, to think them—the succession of my "consciousnesses" constantly detaches each effect from its cause, since any nihilating process requires that its source should come only from itself. Insofar as my present state is a continuation of my previous state, any fissure through which negation might slip will be entirely blocked. Therefore any psychological process of nihilation implies a break between the immediate psychological past and the present. This break is, precisely, nothingness. It might be argued that at least the possibility remains of successive implication between the processes of nihilation. My noticing of Pierre's absence could still determine my regret at not seeing him; we have not excluded the possibility of a determinism of nihilations. But, in addition to the fact that the first nihilation in the series must necessarily be detached from the previous positive processes, what could a motivation of nothingness by nothingness possibly mean? A being can of course constantly nihilate itself, but to the extent that it nihilates itself it can no longer be the origin of any other phenomenon, not even of a second nihilation.

We still need to explain what this separation is, this disjoining of [acts of] consciousness that conditions every negation. If we examine the earlier state of consciousness, envisaging it as a motivation, it will be immediately obvious that nothing has entered in, sliding between that state and the present state. There has been no break in continuity within the flux of unfolding time: otherwise we would be back with the unacceptable conception of time as infinitely divisible, and of the temporal point, or instant, as the limit of division. Nor has any opaque element been suddenly intercalated, separating earlier from later, as a knife's blade can

separate a fruit into two. Nor has there been any *weakening* of the motivating power of the earlier state of consciousness: it remains what it is, and
loses nothing of its urgency. What separates earlier from later is precisely   63
nothing. And this nothing is insurmountable, just because it is nothing, for
in any obstacle to be surmounted something positive is given as needing to be surmounted. But in the case we are dealing with here, we will
seek in vain for any resistance to be broken or any obstacle to be surmounted. The earlier consciousness is always *there* (although modified
with "pastness"), it still maintains a relation of interpenetration with
the present consciousness, but, against the ground of this existential
relation, it is taken out of play, disconnected, bracketed—exactly as the
world is bracketed, in the outlook of someone practicing the phenomenological ἐποχή, both within and outside him. Thus, the condition of
human-reality's ability to negate all or part of the world is that it bears
nothingness within it as the *nothing* that separates its present from all of its
past. But that is not the whole of it—for, envisaged like this, the *nothing*
does not yet have the meaning of nothingness: it is a suspension of being
that remains without a name, that is not conscious of suspending being,
that comes from outside consciousness and has the effect of cutting it
into two, by reintroducing opacity within that absolute lucidity.[41] In
addition, such a nothing would in no way be negative. Nothingness, as
we saw earlier, is the foundation of negation because it holds negation
within it, because it is negation as being. Therefore the conscious being
must constitute himself in relation to his past as separated from that past
by a nothingness; he must be conscious of this breach in being, but not
as a phenomenon that he undergoes: as a structure of consciousness that
he is. Freedom is the human being putting his past out of play by secreting his own nothingness. We must be clear that this basic necessity of
being its own nothingness does not appear to consciousness intermit-
tently, on the occasion of particular negations: there is no moment of
psychological life in which negative or interrogative forms of behavior
do not appear, at least as secondary structures; and consciousness continually lives itself as the nihilation of its past being.

But here, it may well be surmised, an objection that we have frequently raised can be turned back against us: if the nihilating conscious-

41 Sartre's note: See Introduction, section III.

ness exists only as a consciousness of nihilation, it ought to be possible to define and to describe a constant mode of consciousness, present *as* consciousness, that is the consciousness of nihilation. Does this consciousness exist? Here, therefore, a new question arises for us: if freedom is the being of consciousness, consciousness must be as a consciousness of freedom. What form does this consciousness of freedom take? In freedom, the human being *is* its own past (as it is, also, its own future) in the form of nihilation. If our analyses have not led us astray, there must exist for the human being, insofar as he is conscious of being, some specific way of confronting his past and his future as *being* this past and this future and, at the same time, as not being them. We can provide an immediate response to this question: it is in anguish that man becomes conscious of his freedom or, alternatively, anguish is freedom's mode of being as consciousness of being; it is in anguish that freedom is, in its being, in question for itself.

Kierkegaard, in his description of anguish before sin, characterizes it as anguish in the face of freedom. But Heidegger—who, as we know, was greatly influenced by Kierkegaard[42]—considers anguish, on the contrary, as the apprehension of nothingness. To us, these two descriptions of anguish do not seem contradictory: on the contrary, each of them implies the other.

First, we must find in Kierkegaard's favor: anguish is distinguished from fear by the fact that fear is fear of beings in the world, and anguish is anguish before myself. Vertigo is anguish to the extent that I am frightened not of falling into the precipice but of throwing myself into it. A situation that provokes fear, insofar as it threatens to change my life and my being from outside, provokes anguish to the extent to which I mistrust my own reactions to this situation. The preparation of artillery that precedes an attack may provoke fear in the soldier undergoing the bombardment, but he will begin to feel anguish when he tries to foresee the behavior through which he will resist the bombardment, when

---

42 Sartre's note: J. Wahl, *Études Kierkegaardiennes*: Kierkegaard et Heidegger. TN: Sartre has misquoted the name of Wahl's essay; it was actually "Heidegger et Kierkegaard," first published in a French journal in 1932, then in a 1938 collection of Wahl's essays, *Études Kierkegaardiennes*. I have not been able to find it in English translation. The philosopher Jean Wahl (1888–1974) was teaching in Paris at the time Sartre wrote BN.

he wonders if he will be able to "hold out." Similarly, the mobilized soldier who joins his depot at the start of the war may, in some cases, fear death, but far more frequently he feels "fear of fear," which is to say anguish before himself. Most of the time, dangerous or threatening situations are multifaceted: they are apprehended with a feeling of fear, or a feeling of anguish, according to whether the situation is envisaged as acting upon the man, or the man as acting on the situation. The man who has just suffered "a hard knock," who has lost a large part of his resources in a financial crash, may fear the poverty that threatens. The next moment he will feel anguish as, nervously wringing his hands (a symbolic reaction to the action demanded of him, but which remains entirely indeterminate), he cries, "What am I going to do? But what am I going to do?" In this sense, fear and anguish each exclude the other, since fear is an unreflective apprehension of something transcendent, and anguish is a reflective apprehension of oneself; each is born from the other's destruction, and the typical process, in the case I have just given, is a constant transition from one to the other. But there are also situations in which anguish appears in its pure state without ever being preceded or followed by fear. If, for example, I have been promoted to a new rank and put in charge of some delicate and flattering mission, I may feel anguish at the thought that perhaps I will not be capable of accomplishing it, without feeling the slightest fear of the consequences of my possible failure.

What is the meaning of anguish, in the various examples I have just given? Let us return to the example of vertigo. Vertigo is introduced through fear: I am on a narrow path without a parapet that borders a chasm. The chasm presents itself to me as something *to be avoided*; it represents a danger of death. At the same time I can conceive of a number of causes, in accordance with universal determinism, that can transform this death threat into a reality: I may slip on a stone and fall into the abyss; the crumbly earth of the path may collapse under my tread. These various predictions present me to myself as a thing: I am passive in relation to these possibilities, which come to me from outside; insofar as I am *also* a worldly object, subject to the law of gravity, these possibilities are not *mine*. At this moment *fear* appears, in which I apprehend myself in this situation as one destructible transcendent item among others, as an object that does not contain within itself

65

the origin of its future disappearance. My reaction will be reflective in type: I will "pay attention" to the stones on the road, and I will stay as far away as I can from the path's edge. I actualize myself as resisting the threatening situation with all my strength, and I plan ahead for myself a number of future courses of action, whose purpose is to distance myself from the world's threats. These strategies are my possibilities.[43] I escape fear by the very fact of placing myself in a framework where my own possibilities are substituted for the transcendent probabilities in which human activity had no place. But these strategies, precisely because they are my possibilities, do not appear to me as being determined by external causes. Not only is it not absolutely certain that they will be effective but above all it is not absolutely certain that they will be upheld, for their existence is not self-sufficient: one might say, distorting Berkeley's phrase, that their "being is a being-upheld" and that their "possibility of being is no more than an ought-to-be-upheld."[44] Given this, the possibility of contradictory courses of action (not paying attention to the stones on the path; running; thinking about something else) and of contrary courses of action (setting off to throw myself into the chasm) is a necessary condition of their possibility.[45] The possible that I make into my concrete possible can only appear as my possible by detaching itself against the ground of the totality of logical possibilities that the situation allows. But these rejected possibles, in turn, have no being other than their "being-upheld"; I am the one who sustains them in being and, conversely, their present non-being is an "ought not to be upheld." No external cause will set them aside. I alone am the permanent source of their non-being, and I commit myself within them: to make my possible appear, I posit the other possibles—in order to nihilate them. That would not produce anguish if I were able to apprehend myself in my relations with these possibles as a cause producing its effects. In that case, the effect that was defined

66

---

43 TN: *Ces conduites sont mes possibilités* ... I translate *conduites* as "strategies" here, as it fits the sense well. See my note in Notes on the Translation.

44 Sartre's note: We will return to the subject of possibles in Part Two of this work. TN: Sartre is playing with Berkeley's phrase "to be is to be perceived."

45 TN: Here as elsewhere (see EN 49), Sartre uses an established logical distinction between "contradictory" and "contrary." As Sartre is drawing on a semi-technical distinction, I retain it.

as my possible would be strictly determined. But then it would cease to be *possible*; it would become merely forth-coming.[46] If, therefore, I wanted to avoid anguish and vertigo, it would be sufficient for me to be able to regard the motives (my instinct for self-preservation, my earlier fear, etc.) that make me reject the envisaged situation as *determining* my subsequent behavior,[47] in the way in which the presence of a given mass at a particular point determines the paths taken by other masses: it would require me to grasp within myself a strict psychological determinism. But I feel anguish just because my courses of action are only *possible* and this means precisely that, while they constitute a set of motives for resisting this situation, I grasp these motives at the same time as insufficiently effective. At the very moment when I apprehend myself as *horrified* of the chasm, I am conscious of this horror as *not being determining* in relation to my possible behavior. In one sense, my horror is a call for prudent behavior, it is in itself an initial sketch of this behavior, and—in another sense—it posits the subsequent developments of this behavior as only possible precisely because I do not grasp it as *causing* those subsequent developments but as a requirement, an appeal, etc., etc. Now, as we have seen, the consciousness of being is the being of consciousness. Here, therefore, we will not find some contemplative state that I might subsequently direct at an already constituted horror: it is the very being of horror to appear to itself as *not being a cause* of the behavior it calls for. In brief, to avoid fear, which abandons me to a strictly determined transcendent future, I take refuge in reflection—but this latter can offer me only an undetermined future. In other words, by constituting a specific course of action as *possible*, and precisely because it is my possible, I realize that *nothing* can oblige me to take this action. Yet I am situated over there, in the future; indeed it is the person who I will be in a moment, at the bend of the path, that I am striving toward with all my strength, and in this sense there is already a relation between my future being and my pre-

---

46 TN: . . . *il deviendrait . . . à-venir.* Sartre puns here by using the phrase *à-venir* ("to come"), a homophone with *avenir* ("future"). I have tried to match the pun by using the word "forth-coming." This pun appears again several times in the text; Sartre is imitating Heidegger's structurally similar pun *Zu-kunft.*

47 TN: . . . *ma conduite antérieure . . .* I have corrected what I assume to be a mistake in the French text—as "my *earlier* behavior" makes no sense here.

sent being. But, within this relation, a nothingness has slid: I *am* not the person who I will be. First, I am not he because I am separated from him by time and, in addition, because what I am is not the foundation of what I will be. Finally, I am not he because no current existent can determine strictly what I will be. As, however, I am already what I will be (otherwise I would have no interest in being any particular way), I *am the one who I will be in the mode of not being he.* It is through my horror that I am carried toward the future and, insofar as it constitutes the future as possible, my horror nihilates itself. It is precisely the consciousness of being one's own future, in the mode of not-being, that we call *anguish.* And the positive counterpart to the nihilation of my horror as a *reason*— whose effect is to reinforce my horror as a *state*—is that other courses of action (in particular the one that consists in my throwing myself into the chasm) appear as *my possible possibles.* If *nothing* constrains me to save my life, *nothing* prevents me from hurling myself into the abyss. The decisive behavior will emanate from a "me" that I am not yet, to exactly the extent to which the "me" that I am not yet does not depend on the "me" that I am. And my vertigo appears as my grasp of this dependence. I approach the chasm, and the person below it, whom I seek out with my gaze, is me. From that moment on, I am playing with my possibles. My eyes, scanning the abyss from top to bottom, rehearse my possible fall and symbolically actualize it; at the same time, the act of suicide, due to its becoming "my" possible "possible," reveals in its turn some possible reasons for adopting it (suicide would bring my anguish to an end). Fortunately these reasons, in their turn—by virtue simply of their being reasons for a possible—are presented as inefficacious and not as determining: they can no more *produce* my suicide than my horror of falling can *determine me* to avoid it. It is this counter-anguish that in general brings anguish to an end by transmuting it into indecision. That indecision, in its turn, calls for decision; suddenly, we move away from the edge of the chasm and continue on our way.

The example we have just analyzed has shown us what we might call "anguish in the face of the future." There is another kind: anguish in the face of the past. This is the anguish of the gambler who has freely and sincerely decided to stop playing and who, when he approaches the "green baize," suddenly sees his resolutions "dissolve." This phenomenon has often been described as if the mere sight of the gaming table brings out some tendency in us that enters into conflict with our earlier resolution, and ends up dragging us away in spite of it. Apart from the fact that such a description is couched in reifying language, and populates the mind with antagonistic forces (as, for example, in the moralistes'[48] well-known "struggle between reason and the passions"), it does not account for the facts. In reality—and we have the testimony of Dostoyevsky's letters—there is nothing in us that resembles an internal debate, as if we had to weigh up our reasons and motives for acting before deciding.[49] The earlier resolution to "stop playing" is still there and in most cases the gambler present at the gaming table will turn back to it, to seek its help: for he does not want to play; or rather, having made his resolution the night before, he still thinks of himself as no longer wanting to play; he believes his resolution might be effective. But what he grasps then, in anguish, is precisely the total inefficacy of his past resolution. It is there, of course, but frozen, inefficacious, surpassed, by virtue of the very fact that I am conscious of it. It is still part of me, to the extent that my identity with myself is constantly being actualized through the temporal flux, but, due to its being for my consciousness, it is no longer me. I escape it; it fails in the mission I had assigned to it. It is still there, and I am it in the mode of not-being. What the gambler grasps at this moment is again the constant break in determinism, the nothingness separating him from himself: I would have liked so much to stop playing; yesterday I even grasped the situation, in a synthetic apprehension (the threat of ruin, the despair of my loved ones), as prohibiting me from playing. It seemed to me that I had thereby constituted a real barrier between myself and the game, and suddenly now I realize that this synthetic apprehension is only the memory of an idea, the memory of a feeling. For it to help me again, I must reproduce it ex nihilo, and freely; it is only one of my possibles, just as the fact of playing is another, neither more nor less. This fear of destroying my family needs me to rediscover it, to re-create it as a lived fear; it stands behind me like a boneless ghost, and depends on me alone to lend it my flesh. I am

68

---

48 TN: I leave moralistes in French, as Sartre is referring to the group of French thinkers known by that term, which includes Pascal, La Bruyère, and La Rochefoucauld.

49 TN: ...peser des motifs et des mobiles...See the note on motifs and mobiles in the section on vocabulary relating to the mind in Notes on the Translation.

alone and naked before temptation, as I was last night and, after having patiently constructed barricades and walls, having locked myself into the magic circle of a resolution, I realize with anguish that *nothing* can prevent me from playing. And the anguish *is me*, since, by the mere fact of bearing myself in existence as consciousness of being, I make myself as *not being* this past of good resolutions *that I am*.

It would be pointless to object that the unique condition of this anguish is my ignorance of the underlying psychological determinism—that I am anxious for want of knowledge of the true and efficacious motives, in the shadows of my unconscious, that determine my action. We can reply by saying that, in the first place, we have not regarded anguish as a *proof* of human freedom: this latter presented itself as the necessary condition of questioning. We simply wanted to show that there is a specific way of being conscious of freedom, and this way of being conscious is anguish. In other words, our aim was to establish anguish in its essential structure as a consciousness of freedom. Now, from this point of view, the existence of psychological determinism would not invalidate the outcome of our description; anguish could be an unknowing ignorance of this determinism, in which case it does indeed grasp itself as freedom. Or, instead, one might claim that anguish is a consciousness of not knowing the true causes of our actions. In this case, the source of anguish would be our sense of the monstrous motives, lurking in the depths of our being, that might suddenly unleash sinful acts. But in that case we would appear to ourselves as *things in the world* and we ourselves would be our own transcendent situation. In that case anguish would dissolve to make way for *fear*, because the synthetic apprehension of something transcendent as fearful is fear.

We can characterize this freedom, disclosed to us in anguish, in terms of the existence of this *nothing* that insinuates itself between my motives and my act. It is not *because* I am free that my act escapes determination by my motives but, on the contrary, the structure of my motives as inefficacious is the condition of my freedom. And if we are asked what this *nothing* that founds freedom is, our reply will be that it cannot be described, since it *is not*, but that its meaning at least can be elicited, insofar as this nothing *is been* by the human being in his relations with himself. It corresponds to the fact that, necessarily, a motive can only appear as a motive as the correlative of one's consciousness of that motive. In short, as soon as we give up the hypothesis that there are any contents of consciousness, we are obliged to recognize that a motive is never *in* consciousness: it is only *for* consciousness. And owing to the very fact that a motive can arise only as an appearance, it constitutes itself as inefficacious. Of course, it does not have the externality of a spatio-temporal thing; it still belongs to subjectivity and is grasped as *mine*, but it is by nature a transcendence within immanence, and consciousness escapes it through its own positing of it, since now the task of bestowing upon it its meaning and its importance belongs to consciousness. In this way the *nothing* that separates the motive from consciousness can be characterized as a transcendence within immanence; it is in producing itself as something immanent that consciousness nihilates the nothing that makes it exist for itself as transcendent. But we can see that this nothingness, the condition of every transcendent negation, can be elucidated only on the basis of two other primordial nihilations: (1) consciousness *is not* its own motive insofar as it is *empty* of any content. This directs us to the nihilating structure of the prereflective *cogito*; (2) consciousness relates to its past and its future as to a self that it is in the mode of not-being. This directs us to a nihilating structure of temporality.

It is not yet possible for us to elucidate these two types of nihilation: at present we do not have the necessary techniques at our disposal. It will suffice to point out that a definitive explanation of negation cannot be provided without a description of consciousness (of) self and of temporality.

What we should note here is that the freedom manifested through anguish is characterized by a constantly renewed obligation to remake the *Me* by which the free being is designated. When we showed, just now, that my possibles are a source of anguish because it depends on *me* alone to maintain their existence, we did not mean to say that they derive from a *me*—a *me* that is, at least in this case, given from the outset, and passes from one state of consciousness to another within the flux of time. The gambler who must carry out anew his synthetic apperception of a *situation* able to prohibit him from playing must reinvent at the same time a *me* who is able to assess this situation, who is "in a situation." This "me," with its *a priori* and historical content, is man's essence. And anguish, as the manifestation of the freedom it confronts, signifies that man is always separated from his essence by a nothingness. Here we should repeat Hegel's phrase: *"Wesen ist was gewesen ist."*[50] Essence is what has been. A human being's essence is everything that can be indicated about him by the words "that *is.*" It is thereby the totality of features that can *explain* an act. But the act is always beyond this essence, and it is a human act only insofar as it goes beyond any explanation that we can give of it— precisely because everything about a man that can be designated by the phrase "that is" has, by virtue of this very fact, *been.* Man continually carries with him a prejudicative understanding of his essence, but, in consequence, he is separated from it by a nothingness. The essence of human-reality is everything it apprehends about itself as *having been.* And this is where anguish appears as an apprehension of oneself as existing in the perpetual mode of a separation from what is, or, better still, as making oneself exist as such. Indeed, we can never apprehend any *"Erlebnis"* as a living consequence of our own *nature.* This nature is constituted as our consciousness flows, but it always remains behind us, and it haunts us as the constant object of our retrospective understanding. It is insofar as this nature is a demand, without being a resource, that we apprehend it as a cause of anguish.

In anguish, freedom is the source of its own anguish, insofar as *nothing* either solicits or impedes that freedom. Still, it might be said, we have just defined freedom as a permanent structure of the human being: if anguish manifests freedom, it ought to be my permanent affective state. But it is on the contrary wholly exceptional. How can we explain the rarity of the phenomenon of anguish?

In the first place we should note that the most common situations in our lives—where we apprehend our possibles as such in and through our actively bringing those possibles about—do not manifest themselves to us through anguish because their very structure makes any anguished apprehension of them impossible. Anguish, in fact, implies that I recognize a possibility as my possibility; in other words, it constitutes itself when consciousness views itself as cut off from its essence by nothingness, or separated from the future by its very freedom. Put differently, a nihilating nothing deprives me of all excuses and, at the same time,

---

50 TN: This phrase translates into English, as Sartre tells us in the next sentence, as "Essence is what has been."

whatever I project as my future being is always nihilated and reduced to the level of mere possibility, because the future that I am remains beyond my reach. But we should note that we are dealing, in these various cases, with a temporal form in which I await myself in the future, in which I "arrange to meet myself in an hour, or a day, or a month, from now." Anguish is the misgiving that I will not attend that meeting, that I will no longer even want to attend it. But I can also find myself engaged in actions that, in the very moment of actualizing my possibilities, reveal them to me. It is in the act of lighting this cigarette that I learn about my concrete possibility of smoking or, alternatively, my desire to smoke. It is by means of the very act of pulling this sheet of paper and this pen toward me that I confer upon myself, as my most immediate possibility, the task of working on this book: there I am, engaged within it, and discovering it at the very moment at which I have already thrown myself into it. At this instant, of course, it remains my possibility, since at any moment I can turn aside from my work, push away my notebook, screw the lid onto my pen. But this possibility of interrupting my action is relegated to a secondary place, because the action revealed to me through my act has a tendency to crystallize into a transcendent and relatively independent shape. The consciousness of a man *in action* is unreflected consciousness. It is a consciousness of something, and the transcendent thing disclosed to it is of a distinctive kind: it is a *structure of requirement* that belongs to the world, within which various complex equipmental relations are correlatively discovered. In the act of forming the letters I am forming, the complete sentence—still unfinished—takes the shape of a passive requirement that it be formed. The sentence is the very meaning of the letters that I form, and its summons is not called into question, since, precisely, I cannot form the words without transcending them toward it, and I encounter it as the necessary condition of the meaning of the words I am forming. At the same time, and within the act's very framework, an indicative structure of implements shows and organizes itself (pen-ink-paper-lines-margin, etc.). We cannot grasp this structure in its own right; instead, it arises within the movement of transcendence that reveals to me, as a passive requirement, the sentence I am to write. In this way, within the quasi-generality of daily actions, I am committed, I have placed my bets and I discover my possibles as I actualize them— and in the very process of actualizing them—as requirements, matters of urgency, structures of equipment. And of course in any act of this type the possibility remains of calling the act into question, insofar as my act points toward more distant and more essential aims, along with its ultimate meanings and my essential possibilities. For example, the sentence I am writing is the meaning of the letters I am forming, but the sentence's meaning is the complete work I wish to produce. And this work is a possibility in relation to which I can feel anguish: it really is my possible, and I do not know if I will continue it tomorrow; tomorrow, my freedom may exercise its nihilating power in relation to it. Only this anguish implies the apprehension of the work as such as my possibility: I must confront it directly, and actualize my relation to it. The questions I must ask about it, therefore, are not only objective ones, of the following type: "Should this book be written?"—since these questions merely direct me to wider objective meanings, such as "Is this moment an opportune time to write it?"; "Doesn't it overlap with this other book?"; "Is its subject of sufficient interest?"; "Have I sufficiently thought it through?"; etc.—where all of these meanings remain transcendent, and are given as a host of requirements from the world. In order for my freedom to feel anguish in relation to the book I am writing, this book has to appear in its relationship to me: in other words, I must encounter, on the one hand, my *essence*, as *what I have been* (I have been "wanting to write this book," I conceived of it, I thought that it might be interesting to write it, and I have constituted myself in such a way that I can no longer be *understood* without taking account of the fact that the book *has been* my essential possible), and, on the other hand, the nothingness separating my freedom from that essence (*I have been* "wanting to write it" but *nothing*, not even what I have been, can force me to write it), and, last, the nothingness separating me from what I will be (I encounter the permanent possibility of abandoning it as the very condition of possibility of writing it and as the very meaning of my freedom). I have to grasp my freedom—in the very act through which I constitute the book as my possible—insofar as it may possibly destroy what I am, in the present and the future. In other words, I have to adopt the standpoint of reflection. As long as I remain at the level of the act, the book to be written is only the distant meaning presupposed by the act which reveals my possibles to me. It is only the act's implication, and it is not thematized and posited in itself; there is no "question" of it. I do not conceive of the book either

as necessary or as contingent; it is only the distant and permanent meaning on the basis of which I can understand what I am writing now and,
on this account, it is conceived of as *being*. In other words, it is only by
positing it as the *existing ground*, against which my present and existing
sentence emerges, that I can confer upon my sentence a determinate
meaning. Now, we are thrown into the world at every moment, and
committed within it. We act, therefore, before we have posited our possibles, and these possibles—which are revealed as having been actualized,
or as in the process of being actualized—direct us to meanings that can
be called into question only by some special action. The alarm clock that
rings in the morning refers to the possibility of going to my work, which
is my possibility. But to grasp the alarm clock's call as a call is to get up.   73
The act itself of getting up is therefore reassuring, because it avoids the
question: "Is work my possibility?" and in consequence it does not enable me to grasp the possibility of quietism, of a rejection of work and,
ultimately, a rejection of the world and of death.[51] In brief, insofar as I
grasp the meaning of the alarm bell by being already on my feet when it
sounds, this understanding protects me from the anguished intuition
that the person who confers on the alarm clock its requirement is me: it
is me, and me alone. In the same way, what we might refer to as "everyday morality" excludes any ethical anguish. Ethical anguish arises when
I consider myself in my original relation to values. These requirements,
in point of fact, stand in need of a foundation. But there is no circumstance in which this foundation could be *being*, because any value whose
ideal nature was founded on its being would thereby cease to be a value,
and would render my will heteronomous. Value derives its being from
the requirement it makes, not its requirement from its being. It cannot
therefore be given to some contemplative intuition, capable of grasping
it as *being* a value and, in so doing, of stripping it of any rights in relation
to my freedom. But, on the contrary, value can be disclosed only to an
active freedom, a freedom that makes it exist as a value by the mere fact
of recognizing it as such. It follows that my freedom is the unique foun-

---

51 TN: Here Sartre is probably referring to the Quietist orientation within Christianity,
influential in seventeenth-century France, according to which man's perfection consists in his self-annihilation and a withdrawal of his mind from worldly interests in
order to contemplate God.

dation of values and that *nothing*—absolutely nothing—can justify my adopting this system of values rather than that one. As the being through whom values exist, I am unjustifiable. And my freedom is beset by anguish at being the foundation—without foundation—of values. In addition, it is beset by anguish because, as values are essentially revealed to a freedom, they cannot be disclosed without at the same time being "called into question," since the possibility of reversing the system of values appears complementarily as my possibility. The anguish experienced in relation to values is a recognition of those values' ideality.

But usually my attitude toward values is profoundly reassuring. This is because I am, in effect, committed within a world of values. The anguished perception of values as being maintained in being by my freedom is a subsequent and mediated phenomenon. What is immediate is the world with its urgency and, in this world in which I am committed, my acts make values spring up like birds flying up from a tree:[52] it is through my indignation that I am given "baseness" as an anti-value, through my admiration that I am given "greatness" as a value. And, above all, my obedience—which is real—to a host of taboos reveals these taboos as existing in fact. It is not *after* their contemplation of moral values that the bourgeois who call themselves "decent people" become decent; rather they are thrown, from the moment they arrive in the world, into a pattern of behavior whose meaning is "decency." In this way decency acquires a being and is not called into question; values are strewn along my path like a thousand minor requirements, like the signs prohibiting me from walking on the grass.

74

Thus, in what we may call the "world of immediacy"—given to our unreflective consciousness—we do not appear to ourselves first, in order to be thrown *subsequently* into our undertakings. Rather, our being is immediately "in situation," which means it *arises* within our undertakings and knows itself in the first instance insofar as it reflects on them. We are therefore revealed to ourselves within a world populated by requirements, in the midst of plans that are "in progress": I am writing; I am going to smoke; I have an appointment this evening with Pierre; I

52 TN: ... *font lever des valeurs comme des perdrix* ... Sartre's metaphor—which I have slightly changed in the English—comes from shooting: the idea is that values spring up, like partridges flying up out of trees when the hunter fires his gun.

must not forget to reply to Simon; I have no right to conceal the truth any longer from Claude. In truth, the meaning of all these minor passive expectations on the part of reality, of all these banal and everyday values, derives from an initial project of myself, which is akin to my choice of myself within the world. But in fact this project of myself, aiming at a fundamental possibility which gives rise to the existence of values, appeals, expectations, and a world in general, only appears to me— from the other side of the world—as the abstract and logical meaning and significance of my initiatives. Apart from that, there are the concrete instances of alarm clocks, signposts, tax returns, policemen—all of them safeguards against anguish. But as soon as a distance separates me from my undertaking, as soon as I am directed back to myself because I have to await myself in the future, I suddenly encounter myself as the person who bestows meaning on the alarm clock, the person who prohibits himself—on the basis of a signpost—from walking on a flowerbed or a lawn, the person who lends the boss's order its urgency, the person who decides the interest of the book that he is writing, the person who, finally, makes values exist in order to determine his action in accordance with their requirements. I emerge alone and in anguish to confront the unique and basic project that constitutes my being; nihilated by my consciousness of my freedom, all barriers and safeguards crumble. I have no recourse, and I cannot have recourse, to any value to set against the fact that it is I who maintain values in being; nothing can insure me against myself, cut off from the world and from my essence by this nothingness that I am. I have to actualize the meaning of the world and of my essence: I decide it alone, without any justification or excuse.

Anguish is therefore freedom's reflective self-apprehension: in this sense it is a mediation, because—although it is immediately conscious of itself—it arises out of the negation of the calls made upon me by the world; it appears as soon as I disengage from the world in which I was committed, to apprehend myself as a consciousness with a preontological understanding of its essence, and a prejudicative sense of its possibles; it is opposed to the spirit of seriousness, which grasps values on the basis of the world and reassures us by conferring a reifying substance on values. In being "serious," I define myself on the basis of some object, setting aside as a priori impossible any plan that I am not in the process of pursuing, and grasping the meaning my freedom has given to the world   75 as if it came from the world, as if it constituted my obligations and my being. In anguish, I apprehend myself at the same time as being completely free, and as not being able to alter the world so that its meaning did not come from me.

However, it would be a mistake to think that all that is needed, in order to grasp oneself in a *pure* state of anguish, is to move to the reflective level and consider one's distant or immediate possibles. Every case of reflection gives birth to anguish, as a structure of reflective consciousness insofar as it considers its reflected consciousness; but I can still behave in various ways in relation to my own anguish and, in particular, there are various ways of fleeing from it. Indeed, everything happens as if one's immediate and essential response to anguish was to flee from it. Before being a theoretical conception, psychological determinism is in the first instance a course of action that aims to excuse or, alternatively, the foundation of every course of action that aims to excuse. In relation to anguish, it is a reflective strategy: it claims that there are antagonistic forces in us whose type of existence is comparable to that of things; it attempts to fill the holes that surround us, to reinstate the ties between past and present, present and future; it endows us with a *nature* that produces our acts, and it turns those acts themselves into transcendent entities; it confers an inertia and externality on our acts, thereby assigning their foundation to something outside themselves and rendering them— insofar as they make up a continual interplay of *excuses*—profoundly reassuring; it denies human-reality's transcendence, a transcendence that leads it to emerge, beyond its own essence, into anguish; at the same time, by reducing us to *only ever being what we are*, it reintroduces into us the absolute positivity of being-in-itself and, in so doing, it reintegrates us within being.

But this determinism, used as a reflective defense against anguish, is not given as a reflective intuition. It is powerless against the *evidence* of freedom, and it presents itself therefore as a belief in which we may take refuge, as the ideal term toward which we might flee from our anguish. That is shown, in the area of philosophy, by the fact that psychological determinists do not claim to base their thesis on the pure data of internal observation. They present it as a satisfying hypothesis whose value derives from its capacity to account for the facts—or as a postulate that is necessary for any psychology to be established. They accept that an immediate consciousness of freedom exists, which their opponents—who refer to it as the "proof based on the intuition of inner sense"—use against them. Only they make the debate turn on the *value* of this internal revelation. In this way, nobody disputes the intuition through which we apprehend ourselves as the first cause of our states and of our acts. The fact remains that any one of us is capable of trying to mediate anguish by raising himself above it and *judging* it as an illusion deriving from our ignorance of the real causes of our acts. The problem which arises in this case is the strength of our belief in this mediation. Does the act of judging our anguish disarm it? Clearly not. However, at this point a new phenomenon comes into being, a process of distraction in relation to anguish that presupposes within it, once again, a power of nihilation.

76

Since it is only a postulate or hypothesis, determinism alone cannot be the foundation for this distraction. It is a more concrete endeavor at flight, operating within reflection's own domain. It is in the first place an attempt to distract myself from the possibles that are contrary to my possible. When I constitute myself as understanding a possible as my possible, I must of course acknowledge its existence at the other end of my project and grasp it as myself, over there, awaiting me in the future, and separated from me by a nothingness. In this sense I apprehend myself as the first origin of my possible, and this is what we ordinarily mean by the "consciousness of freedom": it is this structure of consciousness, and it alone, that the advocates of free will have in mind when they talk about "the intuition of inner sense." But it may happen that I try at the same time to *distract* myself from the constitution of other possibles that contradict my possible. It is true that I cannot avoid positing their existence in the same movement that generates the chosen possible as mine; I cannot stop myself from constituting them as *living* possibles, i.e., as *possibles that may possibly become mine*. But I try to see them as if they possessed a transcendent and purely logical being—in short, as if they were things. If, from the standpoint of reflection, I consider the possibility of writing this book as my possibility, I conjure up—between this possibility and my consciousness—a nothingness of being that constitutes it as a possibility, and which I grasp, precisely, alongside the constant possibility that the possibility of not writing it is my possibility. But I try to behave in relation to this possibility of not writing it as if it were an observable object, and I immerse myself in what I wish to see there: I try to view it as something that only needs to be noted in passing, that does not concern me.

It needs to be an external possibility in relation to me, like movement in relation to that motionless ball. If I managed to do that, the possibles conflicting with my possible, constituted as logical entities, would lose their power: they would no longer threaten me because they would be *outside*, because they would surround my possible as if they were purely *conceivable* eventualities—which basically means conceivable by someone else, or as *the possibles of someone else who was in the same situation*. They belong to the objective situation in the manner of a transcendent structure, or— put differently, and in Heideggerean terminology—I *myself* will write this book but "*they*" may also not write it.[53] By these means I may hide from myself that these possibles are *myself* and immanent conditions of my possible's possibility. They will retain just enough being to preserve the gratuitous character of my possible—as the free possibility of a free being—but they have been stripped of their menacing character: they are *of no interest to me*, and the chosen possible appears, owing to its being chosen, as my only concrete possible. In consequence, the nothingness that separates me from that possible—and that, precisely, bestows upon it its possibility—will be filled in.

But my flight from anguish is not just an attempt at distraction from the future: it seeks at the same time to disarm the threat posed by the past. What I am trying to flee from here is my transcendence itself, inso- far as it maintains and surpasses my essence. I claim that I *am* my essence, in the mode of being of the in-itself. At the same time, however, I refuse to regard this essence itself as historically constituted and, therefore, as entailing my action in just the way in which a circle entails its proper- ties. I consider it—or at least I try to consider it—as the first beginning of my possible and I adamantly deny that it has any beginning in itself; I claim, therefore, that an act is free when it exactly reflects my essence. But in addition I try to relocate this freedom—which would worry me if it was a freedom *confronting* my Self[54]—inside my essence, i.e., inside my Self. It is a matter of imagining my Self as a small God inhabiting me and

---

53 TN: The terminology Sartre has in mind here is Heidegger's expression *das Man*, of which the French equivalent would be *l'on* (in literal English, "one"). See my note in the section on Heidegger vocabulary in Notes on the Translation.

54 TN: Sartre's use of *le Moi*, in conjunction with the argument here, makes it clear that his target is Bergson. To match English translations of Bergson, I translate *Moi* here as "Self" rather than "Me" or "Ego."

possessing my freedom as a metaphysical property. It is no longer my being that is free, insofar as it is; instead, what is free—at the heart of my consciousness—is my Self. This fiction is profoundly reassuring insofar as it pushes freedom into the depths of an opaque being: it is to the extent that my essence is not translucent, that it is something transcendent within immanence, that my freedom can become one of its properties. In brief, it is a matter of grasping my freedom within my Self as if it were the Other's freedom.[55] We can see the basic themes of this fiction: my Self becomes the origin of my acts in the way that someone else is the origin of his acts, and as an already constituted person. Of course, my Self lives and changes, and we can even concede that each of its acts plays a role in changing it. But these harmonious and continuous changes are conceived of biologically. They resemble the changes I may observe in Pierre, my friend, when I see him again after a separation. Bergson explicitly met these reassuring requirements when he devised his theory of the "deep-seated Self," structuring itself and enduring through time, a Self that is the constant contemporary of—and cannot be surpassed by—my consciousness, lying at the origin of our acts, not as a cataclysmic power but in the manner of a father begetting his children, so that the act, without flowing from the essence as its strict consequence, and without even being predictable, maintains a reassuring relation with it,   78 a family resemblance. Although the act moves beyond the essence, it moves along the same track; of course, it retains an element of irreducibility, but we can recognize ourselves in it and learn about ourselves, as a father can recognize and learn about himself in the son who continues his work.[56] Thus, by projecting freedom—which we grasp within ourselves—into a psychological object, the Self, Bergson helped to conceal our anguish, but at the expense of consciousness itself. In this way, what he constituted and described was not our freedom as it appears to itself: it is the Other's freedom.

Here, therefore, is the set of processes through which we try to hide our freedom from ourselves: in grasping our possible, we avoid thinking about other possibles and we turn these into possibles belonging to some undifferentiated Other. We do not want to see our possible as maintained

55 Sartre's note: See Part Three, Chapter 1.
56 TN: See Bergson (1960) for his account of the "deep-seated self" (le Moi profond) and its relation to freedom.

in being by a pure nihilating freedom; instead, we try to apprehend it as if it were generated by an already constituted object, which is nothing other than our Self, imagined and described as the Other's *person*.[57] We would like to hold on to the independence and responsibility conveyed by the earlier intuition but we are concerned to minimize anything it contains to do with original nihilation and we are prepared, moreover, to take refuge in a belief in determinism at any point if this freedom weighs on us, and if we need an excuse. Thus we flee from anguish by trying to grasp ourselves *from outside as an Other* or *as a thing*. There is nothing original about what we are accustomed to call "the revelation of inner sense" or "primary intuition" of our freedom: it is a process that is already constructed, with the clear intention of concealing our anguish, the genuine "immediate datum" of our freedom, from ourselves.[58]

Do we succeed, through these various constructions, in stifling or disguising our anguish? It is clear that we cannot eliminate it, since anguish is what we *are*. As for "masking it," apart from the fact that the very nature of consciousness and its translucency forbid us from taking this idea literally, we should note the particular type of behavior this phrase denotes: we can mask an external object because it exists independently of us; for the same reason we can divert our gaze or our attention away from it—that is, by focusing our eyes, quite simply, on some other object. At that point each reality involved—mine, and the object's—resumes its own life, and the accidental relation joining my consciousness to the thing disappears, without thereby changing either existence. But if I *am* the thing I want to mask, the question takes on an entirely different dimension: I cannot in effect will "not to see" some particular aspect of my being if I am fully aware of exactly the aspect that I want not to see. In other words, I am obliged to indicate it in my being, in order to be capable of turning away from it; better still, I am obliged constantly to think about it, in order to make sure I am not thinking about it. We must take this to mean not only that I must—necessarily—constantly carry along with me what I wish to flee from but

79

---

57 TN: . . . *la personne d'autrui*. "Person" is used here in its philosophical sense (implying psychological properties, agency, etc.). The translation sounds slightly odd: "personhood" sounds better but is less accurate.

58 TN: Sartre's expression *la véritable "donnée immediate" de notre liberté* alludes to the title of Bergson's influential work *Les Données Immédiates de la Conscience* (translated as Bergson 1960).

also that I have to aim at the object I am fleeing from in order to flee it; in other words, my anguish, my intentional aiming at anguish, and my flight from anguish toward reassuring myths must be given within the unity of a single consciousness. In brief, I flee in order not to know, but I cannot be unaware that I am fleeing, and a flight from anguish is just one way of becoming conscious of anguish. Thus, strictly speaking, it cannot be either masked or avoided. However, we cannot say that to flee from anguish and to be my anguish are quite the same thing: if I can be my anguish in order to flee from it, we have to presuppose an ability to decenter myself in relation to what I am, and to be anguish in the form of "not being it," and to make use of a nihilating power within anguish itself. This nihilating power nihilates anguish as I flee from it, and annihilates itself insofar as I *am it in order to flee it*. This is what we call *bad faith*. We are not, therefore, chasing our anguish out of consciousness, or constituting it as an unconscious psychological phenomenon; rather, I can—quite simply—adopt bad faith to grasp the anguish that I am, and this bad faith, whose purpose is to fill in the nothingness that I *am* in my relationship to myself, implies precisely the nothingness it eliminates.

Here we reach the conclusion of our initial description. Our examination of negation cannot take us any further. It has revealed the existence of a particular type of behavior—behavior in the face of non-being—that presupposes a special transcendence, requiring separate investigation. We find ourselves, therefore, in the presence of two human ecstases: the ecstasis through which we are thrown into being-in-itself, and the ecstasis that engages us in non-being.[59] Our initial problem, which was simply that of man's relations to being, seems in consequence to have become considerably more complicated; on the other hand, it is not impossible that, by pushing our analysis of transcendence toward non-being to its limit, we might obtain valuable information for our understanding of *any* transcendence. And furthermore, we cannot exclude the problem of nothingness from our inquiry: if, in confronting the in-itself, man *behaves*—and our philosophical questioning is a type of such behavior—it is because man *is not* that being. Therefore we return to non-being as a condition of our transcendence toward being. We need therefore to keep hold of the problem of nothingness, and not to let go of it before its elucidation is complete.

59 TN: See my note on *ek-stase* in Notes on the Translation.

But we have learned all that we can from our examination of questioning and of negation. It has led us to empirical freedom, as man's
nihilation within temporality and as the necessary condition of our transcendent apprehension of negatities. This empirical freedom itself remains
in need of foundation. It cannot be the first nihilation and the foundation of nihilation in general. It does play a role in constituting, within
immanence, transcendent items that condition all negative transcendents.
But the very fact that these transcendents of empirical freedom are constituted *as transcendent* within immanence shows us that these nihilations
must be secondary, and presuppose the existence of an original nothingness: they are only one stage within the analytic regression that leads us
from our transcendent *"negatities"* right up to the being that is its own
nothingness. Obviously we must locate the foundation of all negation in
a nihilation practiced *in the midst of immanence*; it is in absolute immanence,
in the pure subjectivity of the instantaneous *cogito*, that we may uncover
the original act through which man is his own nothingness in relation
to himself. What must consciousness be in its being, in order for man to
arise within the world in it, and on its basis, as the being that is its own
nothingness, and through whom nothingness arrives in the world?

At this point we seem to lack the instrument we need in order to
resolve this new problem: negation only directly engages with freedom.
We need to find, within freedom itself, a way of behaving that will enable
us to progress further. But we have already met this way of behaving—
which can lead us right up to the threshold of immanence while remaining sufficiently objective to allow us to objectively derive its conditions
of possibility. Didn't we point out, a short while ago, that in bad faith we
are-anguish-in-order-to-flee-it, within the unity of a single consciousness? If
bad faith is to be possible, therefore, it must be possible for us to encounter within the same consciousness the unity of being and not being, a
being-in-order-not-to-be. The next focus of our questioning, therefore,
must be bad faith. To be able to question anything, man must be able to
be his own nothingness, which means he can be at the origin of non-
being within being only if his own being is shot through, in itself and by
itself, by nothingness: in this way the transcendences of the past and the
future appear within the temporal being of human-reality. But bad faith
is instantaneous. What, then, must consciousness be, in the instantaneity
of the prereflective *cogito*, for man to be capable of bad faith?

Chapter 2

BAD FAITH

I. BAD FAITH AND LIES

The human being is not only the being through whom *negatities* are disclosed in the world; it is also the being that can adopt negative attitudes in relation to itself. In our Introduction we defined consciousness as "a being for whom in its being there is a question of its being, insofar as this being implies a being other than itself."[1] But now we have elucidated the activity of questioning we know that our formulation could also be expressed thus: "Consciousness is a being for whom in its being there is consciousness of the nothingness of its being." In the case of a prohibition or a veto, for example, the human being negates some future transcendence. But this negation is not a constative. My consciousness is not limited to merely envisaging a negatity. It constitutes itself, in its flesh, as the nihilation of a possibility projected by some other human-reality as its possibility. To do that, it must arise in the world as a No; and indeed it is as a "No" that the slave initially grasps his master, and as a "No" that the prisoner who is trying to escape grasps the sentry watching over him. There are even some men (guards, supervisors, jailers, etc.) whose social reality is uniquely that of a "No," who will live and

---

1 TN: Sartre here repeats *verbatim* his sentence from EN 29.

die without ever having been anything but a "No" on this earth. Others, who bear this "No" within their very subjectivity, are equally constituted in their human person as a constant negation: "No" is the meaning and function of Scheler's "man of resentment."[2] And there are subtler attitudes—such as irony—whose description would take us further into the intimacy of consciousness. In the case of irony, man annihilates, in the unity of a single act, what he advances; he makes you believe something in order not to be believed; he affirms in order to negate, and he negates in order to affirm; he creates a positive object whose being, however, is nothing more than its nothingness. These attitudes of negation in relation to oneself, therefore, enable us to raise a new question: What must man be in his being for it to be possible for him to negate himself? But we ought not to take the attitude of "self-negation" as a universal. The kinds of behavior we can classify under this heading are too diverse; we would run the risk of dealing only with their abstract form. We should choose and examine a specific attitude, essential to human-reality, and in which, at the same time, consciousness, instead of directing its negation outward, turns it against itself. It has seemed to us that this attitude must be *bad faith*.

Bad faith is often assimilated to lying. We may indifferently say that someone is exhibiting bad faith, or that he is lying to himself. Here we are willing to allow that bad faith consists in lying to oneself—on condition that "lying to oneself" is immediately distinguished from lying *tout court*. We can agree that lying is a negative attitude. But this negation does not bear on consciousness itself; it aims only at something transcendent. Indeed, the essence of the lie implies that the liar is fully aware of the truth he is disguising. We do not lie about something we do not know about; we do not lie in broadcasting a mistake of which one is oneself a victim; we do not lie when we get something wrong. The ideal of the liar is, then, a cynic in his consciousness who affirms the truth in itself and negates it in his words, while negating this negation for himself. Now, the targets of this doubly negative attitude are transcendent: the stated fact is transcendent, since it does not exist, and the first negation applies to a truth, i.e., to a specific transcendent type. As to the inner negation which I carry out correlatively to my

2 TN: Max Scheler (1874–1928) was a German phenomenologist. His famous essay on resentment is translated into English as Scheler (2003).

affirmation of the truth for myself, that is applied to words, i.e., to an event in the world. In addition, the liar's internal disposition is positive; it might be made the object of an affirmative judgment. The liar intends to deceive, and he does not seek to hide this intention or to mask the translucency of consciousness; on the contrary, when the need arises to decide on his secondary modes of behavior, he draws on this intention—it explicitly exercises a regulative control over all his attitudes. As to his advertised intention to tell the truth ("I do not want to deceive you," "That is true," "I swear to it," etc.), it is, of course, the object of an inner negation, but at the same time the liar does not recognize it as his intention. It is performed, rehearsed; it is the intention of the character he is playing in full sight of his interlocutor, but this character, precisely because he is not, is transcendent. In this way, a lie does not engage the internal structure of present consciousness: all its constitutive negations apply to objects that are, accordingly, expelled   83 from consciousness. A lie, therefore, requires no special ontological foundation and the explanations required for the existence of negation in general remain valid, without needing to be changed, in the case of deception. Doubtless what we have defined here is an ideal lie; it happens quite frequently, probably, that the liar is to a greater or lesser extent a victim of his lie, that he is half-persuaded by it; but these common and everyday forms of lie are also bastardized versions, which represent a halfway house between lying and bad faith. The lie is a behavior that involves transcendence.

But this is because the lie is an ordinary phenomenon within what Heidegger calls "Mitsein."[3] It presupposes my existence, the existence of another, my existence for another, and another's existence for me. Thus we have no difficulty in conceiving that the liar must undertake the project of his lie in full lucidity, that he must have at his disposal a full understanding of his lie, and of the truth he is altering. It is sufficient that a principle of opacity should mask his intentions to the other, sufficient that the other should be able to take the lie for the truth. Through the lie, consciousness affirms that it exists in its nature as hidden from the Other; it makes profitable use of the ontological duality between my own self and the Other's self.

3 TN: Heidegger uses the German term Mitsein (which translators render as "Being-with") to refer to the sociality of Dasein's existence.

The situation cannot be the same for bad faith, if this latter really is—as we have said—a lie *to oneself*. Of course, for the person exercising bad faith, it is still a matter of covering up an unpleasant truth or of presenting some pleasant error as the truth. In appearance therefore, bad faith has the structure of a lie. But what changes everything is that in bad faith it is from myself that I am concealing the truth. Thus the duality of deceiver and deceived is not present here. On the contrary, bad faith implies in its essence the unity of a *single* consciousness. That does not mean it cannot be conditioned by "*Mitsein*" (as, moreover, all the phenomena of human-reality are), but "*Mitsein*" can solicit bad faith only by presenting itself as a *situation* that bad faith is able to surpass: bad faith does not come to human-reality from outside. Bad faith is not undergone, nor does it infect us, nor is it a *state*. But consciousness itself takes on its bad faith. This requires an initial intention, and a project of bad faith; this project implies an understanding of bad faith as such, and a prereflective grasp (of) consciousness as performing its bad faith. From this it follows, first, that the person to whom one is lying and the person who is lying are one and the same person, which means that I must know—insofar as I am the deceiver—the truth that is hidden from me insofar as I am deceived. Better still, I must know this truth very precisely in order to hide it all the more carefully from myself—and this must not occur at two different moments within temporality (which might, at a stretch, reestablish an appearance of duality) but within the unitary structure of a single project. How, then, can the lie survive if its conditioning duality is abolished? To this difficulty, we can add another, deriving from consciousness's total translucency. A person who espouses bad faith must be conscious of his bad faith, because the being of consciousness is a consciousness of being. It seems, then, that I must be in good faith—at least insofar as I am conscious of my bad faith. But that would annihilate the entire psychological system. Nobody will dispute indeed that, if I deliberately and cynically attempt to lie to myself, I must completely fail in this undertaking: the lie recedes and collapses before our eyes; it is ruined, from behind, by the very consciousness of lying to myself that constitutes itself pitilessly before my project, as its very condition. The phenomenon in this case is *evanescent*, existing only in and through its self-definition. Of course, such phenomena are common and we will see in fact that "evanescence" belongs to bad faith—it is evident that bad faith oscillates constantly between good faith and cynicism. Nevertheless, if the existence of bad faith is highly precarious— if it belongs to the category of psychological structures that can be described as "metastable"—it is no less the case that it presents us with an autonomous and durable form of it: for a very large number of people it can even be the normal aspect of life. One can live in bad faith: this does not mean that there are no sudden awakenings of cynicism or good faith, but it implies a constant and distinctive style of life. We seem to be in an extremely difficult position, being able neither to reject nor to understand bad faith.

In order to escape these difficulties, many people blithely resort to the unconscious. In psychoanalytic interpretation, for example, the hypothesis of a censor will be used—conceived of as a demarcation line with its customs, passport services, currency control, etc.—to reestablish the duality between deceiver and deceived. Here the representative of *reality* is instinct or, alternatively, the primary drives and complexes of drives constituted by our individual history. An instinct is neither *true* nor *false*, because it does not exist *for itself*. It simply *is*, exactly like this table, which is neither true nor false *in itself* but simply *real*. As for the conscious symbolizations of instinct, they should be construed not as appearances but as real psychological facts. A phobia, a slip of the tongue, a dream—these really exist as concrete facts of consciousness, in the same way as the liar's words and attitudes are material ways of behaving, and really exist. Only the subject stands before these phenomena like a deceived person in relation to the behavior of his deceiver. He observes them in their reality, and he has to interpret them. There is a truth to the deceiver's behavior: if the deceived person could relate it to the deceiver's situation and to his lying project, they would become integral parts of the truth, accounted for as lying behavior. Similarly, there is a truth to symbolic actions: this is what the psychoanalyst uncovers when he links them to the patient's historical situation, to the unconscious complexes they express, to the barrier of censorship. Thus, the subject is wrong about the *meaning* of his behavior: he grasps it as it concretely exists but not in its truth, because he is unable to derive it from an initial situation and a psychological constitution that remain unknown to him. The fact is that, by means of his distinction between the "id" and the "ego," Freud split the totality of the psyche in two.[4] I *am* ego, but I am not *id*. My position in relation to my non-conscious psyche is in no way privileged. I *am* my own psychological phenomena insofar as I ascertain them in their conscious reality: for example, I am this drive to steal this or that book from this display, I am at one with it, I throw light on it, and I resolve to commit my theft in accordance with it. But I *am* not these psychological facts insofar as I passively undergo them and am obliged to hypothesize about their origin and their true meaning, just as an expert conjectures about the nature and essence of some external phenomenon: this theft, for example, which I may interpret as an impulse immediately dictated by the scarcity, the interest or the price of the volume I am about to steal, is in truth a process deriving from my need for punishment, which can be related more or less directly to an Oedipus complex. There is therefore a truth to the impulse to steal, to be reached only by means of hypotheses that are more or less probable. The criterion of this truth will be the extent of the psychological facts it can explain: from a more pragmatic point of view, it will also be the success of the psychiatric cure it enables. Finally, the discovery of this truth requires the assistance of the psychoanalyst, who appears as the mediator between my unconscious inclinations and my conscious life. The Other appears as the only person able to carry out a synthesis between the unconscious thesis and the conscious antithesis. I can only know myself through the mediation of the Other— which means that I am, in relation to my "id," in the position of the Other. If I have some notion of psychoanalysis, I can try, if circumstances are propitious, to psychoanalyze myself. But this attempt can succeed only if I mistrust any kind of intuition and apply to my own case—from outside— abstract schemas and rules I have learned. As for the results, whether they are gained by my own efforts or with the assistance of a technician, they will never enjoy the certainty conferred by intuition: they will merely have the ever-increasing probability of scientific hypotheses. The hypothesis of the Oedipus complex, like the atomic hypothesis, is nothing but an "experimental idea": as Peirce says, it cannot be distinguished from the set of experiments that it allows us to perform and the effects it enables us to predict. In this way, psychoanalysis substitutes the notion

86

---

4 TN: Although Sartre uses the French terms *ça* and *moi*, I have followed the convention in English of using the Latin words to translate Freud's terms for these parts of the mind.

of bad faith with the idea of a lie without a liar; it allows us to understand not how I am able to lie to myself but how I can *be lied to*, since it places me, in relation to myself, in the situation of the Other's relation to me; it replaces the duality of deceiver and deceived—an essential condition of the lie—with the duality of "id" and "ego," and it introduces into the depths of my subjectivity the intersubjective structure of *Mitsein*. Are these explanations satisfactory?

Examined more closely, psychoanalytic theory appears less simple than at first sight. It is not quite right to say that the "id" functions like a thing in relation to the psychoanalyst's hypothesis, because a thing is indifferent to the conjectures we make about it, and the "id," on the contrary, is *touched* by them as they approach nearer to the truth. Indeed, Freud draws attention to resistances when, at the end of the first period, the doctor approaches the truth. These resistances are instances of objective behavior, apprehended from an external point of view: the patient shows signs of suspicion, refuses to speak, gives far-fetched accounts of his dreams, and sometimes even removes himself completely from psychoanalytic treatment. We may nevertheless inquire which part of the patient can resist in this way. It cannot be the "Ego," understood as the totality of psychological facts in consciousness: the ego could hardly suspect the psychiatrist is reaching his goal, since its position in relation to the *meaning* of its own reactions is exactly that of the psychiatrist himself. The most that it can do is to objectively assess the degree of probability of the hypotheses that have been advanced—as a witness of the psychoanalysis might do—and, accordingly, the extent of the subjective facts they can explain. And if it seems to him that this probability verges on certainty, this ought not to cause him distress, since, most of the time, it is he who has committed himself, through a *conscious* decision, to the path of psychoanalytical therapy. Should we say that the patient is worried by the psychoanalyst's daily revelations, and tries to escape them, even while he acts in his own eyes as if he wishes to continue treatment? In that case we can no longer appeal to the unconscious to explain bad faith: it is out there, in full consciousness, with all its contradictions. In any case, that is not how the psychoanalyst intends to explain these resistances: in his view they are deep and hidden, and their source is distant; they are rooted in the very thing we are trying to elucidate.

However, it is equally impossible for the resistances to stem from the complex to be revealed. This complex, as such, will tend rather to collaborate with the psychoanalyst—since it seeks to express itself in clear consciousness, to trick the censor, and to get round it. The subject's refusal can be located only at the level of the censor. It alone is able to apprehend the psychoanalyst's questions or revelations as approaching, more or less closely, the drives in reality it is trying to repress—it alone, because it alone knows what it is repressing.

If in fact we reject the reifying language and mythology of psychoanalysis, we will see that, in order to pursue its activity discerningly, the censor must be acquainted with what it represses. Indeed, if we abandon all those metaphors that represent repression as a clash of blind forces, we will be obliged to acknowledge that the censor must *choose* and, in order to choose, it has to *represent itself*. How else could it happen, otherwise, that the censor allows permissible sexual drives through, and tolerates the clear expression in consciousness of needs (hunger, thirst, sleep)? And how can we explain its ability to *relax* its surveillance, or how the disguises of instinct can even *deceive* it? But it is not sufficient for the censor to discern the condemned drives; it has to apprehend them, further, as *to be repressed*—which implies, at the least, some representation on its part of its own activity. In brief, how could the censor discern the drives to be repressed without being conscious of discerning them? Can we conceive of knowledge as being ignorant of itself? "To know is to know that one knows," Alain said. We should say, instead: All knowing is conscious of knowing. Thus the patient's resistances imply, at the level of the censor: a representation of the repressed as such; an understanding of the goal toward which the psychoanalyst's questions are leading; and an act of synthetic combination, by means of which it compares the truth of the repressed complex to the psychoanalytic hypothesis directed on it. And these various operations imply in turn that the censor is conscious (of) itself. But what type of consciousness (of) itself can the censor have? It must be conscious (of) being conscious of the drive to be repressed, but precisely *in order not to be conscious of it.* What is there left to say, other than that the censor must be in bad faith? We have gained nothing from psychoanalysis, since, in order to eliminate bad faith, it installs between the unconscious and the conscious mind an autonomous consciousness in bad faith. The fact is that its attempt to establish a genuine duality— and even a trinity (*Id, Ego, Superego* expressing itself through the censor)— amounts to no more than a verbal terminology. The very essence of the reflexive idea of "hiding something from oneself" implies the unity of a single psyche and consequently a double activity in the heart of unity, tending on the one hand to maintain and to notice the thing to be hidden and, on the other, to push it away and to veil it; each of the two aspects of this activity complements the other, i.e., each implies the other in its being. In separating, by means of the censor, the conscious from the unconscious, psychoanalysis has not succeeded in dissociating the two phases of the act, because the *libido* is a blind conatus toward conscious expression, and the conscious phenomenon is a passive and rigged result: it has merely located this twofold activity of repulsion and attraction at the level of the censor. Moreover, in order to take account of the unity of the total phenomenon (the repression of the drive that disguises itself and "gets past" in symbolic form), we still need to establish some comprehensible connections between its different moments. How can the repressed drive "disguise itself" if it does not encompass: (1) the consciousness of being repressed; (2) the consciousness of having been driven back because it is what it is; and (3) a project of disguise? No mechanistic theory of condensation or transference can explain these changes effected in the drive by itself, because any description of the process of disguise implies a veiled appeal to finality. And similarly, how are we to take account of the pleasure or anguish accompanying the drive's symbolic and conscious satisfaction, if consciousness does not include—beyond the censor's reach—an obscure understanding of the goal to be reached, insofar as it is simultaneously desired and forbidden? Having rejected the conscious unity of the psyche, Freud is obliged to hint throughout at a magical unity linking phenomena together, across distances and through obstacles—as the primitive practice of participation brings together the person placed under a spell with the wax figure fashioned in his image. Through participation, the unconscious "Trieb"[5] takes on the characteristic of being "repressed" or "damned," which spreads through it, colors it, and magically provokes its symbolizations. And, similarly, the conscious phenomenon is entirely colored by its symbolic meaning, even though it cannot grasp this meaning by itself and in clear consciousness. But, in addition to its inferiority in principle, the explanation by magic does not abolish the coexistence—

88

5 TN: The German word *Trieb*, which features in Freud's writings, is translated as "drive."

at the unconscious stage, the stage of censorship, and the conscious stage—of two contradictory and complementary structures, each of which reciprocally implies and destroys the other. Bad faith has been hypostasized and "thingified,"[6] but it has not been avoided. This is what prompted the Viennese psychiatrist Stekel to disobey psychoanalytic doctrine and to write, in La Femme Frigide:[7] "Whenever I have been able to advance far enough in my investigations, I have observed that the kernel of the psychosis was conscious." And, moreover, the cases that he reports in his work testify to a pathological bad faith that Freudianism is unable to account for: the cases, for example, of women whose disappointment in marriage has made them frigid—which is to say that they manage to conceal from themselves the pleasure they receive from the sexual act. Note, in the first place, that for these women it is not a matter of hiding complexes from themselves that are deeply buried in semiphysiological darkness but rather of an objectively detectable activity that they cannot fail to register at the moment they perform it: frequently, indeed, the husband reveals to Stekel that his wife has shown objective signs of pleasure, and it is these signs that the wife, when questioned, fiercely endeavors to deny. What we have here is an activity of distraction. Similarly we learn from the confessions elicited by Stekel that these pathologically frigid women try to distract themselves in advance from the pleasure they fear; many of them, for example, at the moment of the sexual act, divert their thoughts toward their daily occupations and go through their household accounts. Who would want to speak here of the unconscious? However, if the frigid woman distracts her consciousness in this way from the pleasure she experiences, she does not do so cynically and in full agreement with herself: it is in order to prove to herself that she is frigid. The phenomenon here is clearly a case of bad faith, since the effort made to dissociate from the felt pleasure implies a recognition that the pleasure is felt, and implies it precisely in order to deny it. But we are no longer in the

---

6 TN: On a ... "chosifié" la mauvaise foi ... See my note on chosifier in Notes on the Translation. Here Sartre's scare quotes have led me to follow his emphasis on the novelty of the verb by using "thingify."

7 Sartre's note: NRF (1937). TN: Wilhelm Stekel (1868–1940) was an Austrian doctor and psychologist. Initially a follower of Freud, he came later to disagree with several aspects of Freud's theory. The English translation of the book quoted by Sartre is Stekel (1953).

territory of psychoanalysis. Thus the explanation in terms of the unconscious, by virtue, on the one hand, of severing the unity of the psyche,
cannot take account of the facts that, at first sight, seem to depend on that
unity. And, on the other hand, there are an infinite number of ways of
behaving in bad faith that explicitly contradict this type of explanation,
because their essence implies that they can appear only within the translucency of consciousness. We find ourselves back with the problem—
still intact—that we were trying to elude.

II. FORMS OF BAD FAITH[8]

If we wish to resolve this difficulty, we ought to take a closer look at the
forms of bad faith and attempt to describe them. This description may
allow us to delineate more sharply bad faith's conditions of possibility,
i.e., to answer the question from which we set out: "What must man be
in his being, if he must be capable of bad faith?"

Let us take, for example, this woman who has arrived at a first meeting. She knows full well the intentions entertained, in relation to her,
by the man speaking to her. She also knows that sooner or later she
will have to make a decision. But she does not want to feel its urgency:
she takes account only of the respectful and discreet aspects of her partner's attitude. She does not see his behavior as an attempt to make the
so-called opening moves; in other words, she does not want to see the   90
possibilities of development over time that his behavior presents; she
confines his activity to what it is in the present, and has no wish to read,
in the sentences he addresses to her, anything but their explicit meaning.
If he says "I admire you so much," she strips this sentence of its sexual
background: she attaches immediate meanings—envisaged as objective
properties—to her interlocutor's sayings and actions. The man speaking
to her appears to her as sincere and respectful, in the way a table is round
or square, or a wall-hanging blue or gray. And the properties she hereby
attaches to the person to whom she is listening are, therefore, frozen in
a thing-like permanence—which is nothing but the projection, into the
flow of time, of their strict present. The fact is that she is not aware of

8 TN: The French section heading is "*Les conduites de mauvaise foi*," but as I am avoiding the
plural "behaviors," I have settled here for "forms."

her wish: she keenly perceives the desire she inspires, but a crude, naked desire would humiliate and horrify her. However, she would find no charm in an attitude of respect that was nothing but respect. To satisfy her, she requires a feeling addressed to the whole of her *person*, i.e., to the whole of her freedom, and in recognition of her freedom. But, at the same time, this feeling must be entirely one of desire, i.e., it must address her body as an object. On this occasion, therefore, she refuses to see the desire for what it is, and does not even give it a name; she recognizes it only to the degree to which it is transcended—into admiration, esteem, respect—and entirely absorbed within the more elevated formations it produces, to the point where it no longer figures except as a sort of density and heat. But now he takes her hand. This action by her interlocutor threatens to change the situation by calling for an immediate decision: to leave her hand there is to consent, herself, to the flirtation; it commits her. To withdraw it is to disrupt the vague and unstable harmony that gave the moment its charm. The moment of decision needs to be deferred for as long as possible. We know what happens now: the young woman leaves her hand where it is but she *does not notice* she has left it there. She does not notice because it turns out by chance that she is, at that moment, pure spirit. She takes her interlocutor right up to the most elevated regions of sentimental speculation, she talks about life, her life, and she shows herself in her most essential aspect: as a person, a consciousness. And while she does this, the divorce of body from soul is accomplished: her hand rests there, inert between the hot hands of her partner, neither consenting nor resisting—a thing.

We will say that this woman is in bad faith. But we can see at once that she makes use of more than one method to maintain herself in this bad faith. She has disarmed her partner's actions by reducing them to being only what they are, i.e., to existing in the mode of the in-itself. But she allows herself to enjoy his desire, to the extent that she apprehends it as not being what it is, i.e., to the extent that she recognizes its transcendence. Finally, at the same time as she keenly senses her own body's presence— perhaps to the point of being aroused—she actualizes herself as *not being* her own body, and she contemplates it from a height as a passive object to which things might *happen*, but which can neither provoke them nor avoid them, because all its possibles lie outside it. What unites these various aspects of bad faith? It is a certain art of forming contradictory concepts, i.e., concepts in which an idea and the negation of that idea are united. The underlying concept generated in this way makes use of the twofold property of human beings, of being a *facticity* and a *transcendence*. These two aspects of human-reality are, in truth—and ought to be—capable of being validly coordinated. But bad faith does not want to coordinate them, or to resolve them by means of a synthesis. From its point of view, it is a matter of affirming their identity, even while preserving their differences. Facticity must be affirmed as *being* transcendence and transcendence as *being* facticity, in a way that allows us, at the moment we apprehend one of them, to find ourselves suddenly faced with the other. The prototypical formula of bad faith can be found in certain famous phrases that are modeled—in order to produce their effect—on the spirit of bad faith. We are familiar, for example, with this title of one of Jacques Chardonne's works: "Love Is Far More than Love."[9] Here we can see how love, as it is *present* in its facticity ("the contact of two skins," sensuality, egoism, Proustian workings of jealousy, Adlerian struggle of the sexes, etc.), is put together with love as *transcendence* (Mauriac's "river of fire," the call of the infinite, Plato's Eros, Lawrence's murmuring cosmic intuition, etc.). In this case we start out from facticity, to find ourselves suddenly—beyond the present and man's factual being, beyond the psychological—right at the heart of metaphysics. In contrast to this, this title of a play by Sarment: "I Am Too Big for Myself"[10]—which also displays the characteristics of bad faith—begins by throwing us straight into transcendence, in order to imprison us suddenly within the narrow limits of our *de facto* essence. We meet these structures again in the famous phrase: "He has become what he was," or in its equally famous counterpart: "Such as into Himself at last eternity changes him."[11] Of course, these various formulas only *appear* to be in bad faith; they were

9   TN: Jacques Chardonne (1884–1968) was a French novelist. The novel by him to which Sartre refers—*L'Amour, C'est Beaucoup Plus que l'Amour*—was published in 1937; no English translation exists.
10 TN: Jean Sarment (1897–1976) was a French actor and writer. The play by him to which Sartre refers—*Je Suis Trop Grand pour Moi*—was written in 1924; no English translation exists.
11 TN: ..."*Tel qu'en lui-même enfin l'éternité le change.*" Sartre is quoting the first line of a famous poem—"The Tomb of Edgar Poe"—by the French poet Stéphane Mallarmé (1842–1898). I have quoted the line from the English translation of this poem by Peter Manson.

explicitly conceived in this paradoxical form in order to make an impact, and to disconcert us mentally, with their enigma. But this appearance is precisely what concerns us. What matters here is that the formulas do not create any new or solidly structured notions; on the contrary, they are constructed in such a way as to remain in a state of continual disintegration, and to allow for a continual slippage from the naturalist present into transcendence, and back again. Indeed, we can see how bad faith makes use of these judgments, all of which aim to establish that I am not what I am. If I was only what I *am*, I would be able, for example, to think seriously about this reproach someone has made, to search myself scrupulously—and perhaps I would be obliged to admit its truth. But, precisely through my transcendence, I escape from everything that I am. I do not even have to discuss the legitimacy of the reproach, in the sense in which Suzanne says to Figaro: "To prove that I am right would be to grant that I could be wrong."[12] I am in a place where no reproach can reach me, because what I truly *am* is my transcendence; I abscond and I escape, leaving my rags behind in the preacher's hands. Only the ambiguity necessary for bad faith stems from the claim advanced here: that I *am* my transcendence in the mode of being of a thing. And it is only in this way, indeed, that I can feel myself escaping all these reproaches. It is in this sense that our young woman purifies desire of its humiliating aspects, wanting to consider only the pure transcendence that allows her to avoid even naming it. But conversely, "I am too big for myself"—by displaying a transcendence transformed into facticity—is the source of an infinity of excuses for our failures or our weaknesses. In the same way, the young coquette maintains her transcendence, to the extent to which the respect and esteem demonstrated in her admirer's behavior already belong in the order of the transcendent. But she stops this transcendence there, and thickens it with all the facticity of the present: the respect is nothing but respect; its frozen movement of surpassing is no longer surpassed toward anything.

But if this metastable concept of "transcendence-facticity" is one of bad faith's basic tools, it is not the only one of its type. A similar use can be made of another duplicity in human-reality, a duplicity that we can

---

12 TN: Sartre is referring to the characters in Beaumarchais's 1778 play *The Marriage of Figaro*.

roughly describe by saying that its being-for-itself implies a complementary being-for-the-Other. It is always possible to make any particular behavior of mine into the target of two converging points of view:
I look at it, and so does the Other. Now, to be precise, this behavior
will not present the same structure in each case. But as we will see later,
and as everyone senses, there is no difference between appearance and
being between these two aspects of my being—as if I were, in relation
to myself, my truth and the Other possessed only a deformed image of
me. The equal dignity in being of my being for the Other and my being
for myself allows for a constantly disintegrating synthesis and a constant
game of avoidance, in which the for-itself escapes to the for-the-Other,
and the for-the-Other escapes to the for-itself. We have also seen the use
our young woman was able to make of our being-in-the-midst-of-the-
world—i.e., of our inert presence as a passive object among other objects—
in order to unburden herself suddenly of the demands of her being-in-
the-world, i.e., of the being that makes the world happen, by projecting
itself beyond the world toward its own possibilities.[13] Finally, let us take   93
note of the confusional syntheses that play on the nihilating ambiguity
of the three temporal ecstases, affirming at the same time that I am what
I have been (the man who deliberately *stops* at one stage of his life and
refuses to take any further changes into account) and that I am not what I
have been (the man who, in the face of reproaches and resentment, completely dissociates himself from his past, insisting on his freedom and his
constant recreation). In all these concepts, whose role in the reasoning
process is merely transitive, and which—like the imaginary entities in
the calculations of physicists—are eliminated from the conclusion, we
can find the same structure: the idea is to constitute human-reality as a
being that is what it is not, and that is not what it is.

But what exactly is required in order for these concepts of disintegration to take on even an illusion of existence, so that they can appear
to consciousness for an instant, even if only within a process of evanescence? In this regard, a quick analysis of the idea of sincerity—the
antithesis of bad faith—will be most instructive. In effect, sincerity presents itself as a demand and in consequence it is not a *state*. Now, what

---

13 TN: For this distinction between ways of being in the world, see the section on
Heidegger vocabulary in Notes on the Translation.

is the ideal to be attained in this case? It is that man should be for himself only what he is—in brief, that he should fully and uniquely be what he is. But isn't that exactly our definition of the in-itself or, alternatively, the principle of identity? In positing the being of things as an ideal, must we not admit at the same time that this being does not belong to human-reality, and that the principle of identity—far from being a universal axiom—is no more than a synthetic principle, whose universality is merely regional? Thus, in order for the concepts of bad faith to be able to deceive us, even for a moment—for the candor of "the pure in heart" (Gide, Kessel)[14] to work as an ideal for human-reality—it must be the case that human-reality is not necessarily what it is, and that it can be what it is not. What does that mean?

If man is what he is, bad faith is forever impossible and candor ceases to be his ideal and becomes instead his being; but is it the case that man is what he is and, in general, how can one be what one is, when one's way of being is to be conscious of being? If candor or sincerity is a universal value, it follows that its maxim—"One should be what one is"—is not only a regulative principle for the judgments and concepts I may use to express what I am. It states not only an ideal for knowledge but an ideal for being: what it proposes, as the paradigm of being, is being's absolute self-adequation.[15] So we should make ourselves be what we are. But then what are we, if we are constantly obliged to make ourselves be what we are, if our mode of being is that of having to be what we are? Consider this café waiter. His movements are animated and intent, a bit too precise, a bit too quick; he approaches the customers with a bit too much animation; he leans forward a bit too attentively, his voice and his eyes expressing an interest in the customer's order that is a bit too solicitous. Finally, here he is, on his way back, and attempting in his attitude to imitate the inflexible exactitude of some kind of automaton while carrying his tray with the recklessness characteristic of a tightrope walker, holding

14　TN: Sartre alludes here to Les Coeurs Purs (translated into English as The Pure in Heart), a collection of three stories published in 1928 by the French author Joseph Kessel.

15　TN: The term "adequation" is less common in English philosophical writing than adéquation is in French, but I use it because Sartre's phrase is far from everyday French. Aquinas defines truth as adaequatio intellectus et rei, which means the "adequation of the intellect and thing."

it in a constantly unstable and constantly disrupted equilibrium, which he constantly restores with a light movement of his arm and hand. His behavior throughout strikes us as an act. He concentrates on his successive movements as if they were mechanisms, each one of them governing the others; his facial expression and even his voice seem to be mechanical; he adopts the pitiless nimbleness and rapidity of things. He is playing, amusing himself. But what, then, is he playing at? One does not need to watch him for long to realize: he is playing *at being* a café waiter. Nothing in this should surprise us: play is a type of research and investigation. The child plays with his body to explore it, to take stock of it; the café waiter plays with his condition in order to *actualize* it. This obligation is imposed in the same way on all shopkeepers: their condition is entirely ceremonial, and the public demands them to actualize it as a ceremony; there is the dance of the grocer, the tailor, the auctioneer, through which they try to persuade their customers that they are nothing more than a grocer, an auctioneer, a tailor. A grocer who dreams is offensive to the buyer, because he is no longer completely a grocer. Etiquette requires him to contain himself in his grocer's function, as the soldier standing to attention makes himself a soldier-thing, who looks straight ahead of him but sees nothing, whose gaze is no longer meant for seeing, because it is not the interest of the moment but the regulations that determine the spot he must focus on (eyes "fixed at a distance of ten paces"). We can see how many measures exist, to imprison man in what he is. It is as if we lived in the constant fear that he might escape from it, that he might burst out and suddenly elude his condition. But that is because, symmetrically, from the inside, the café waiter cannot immediately be a café waiter in the sense in which this inkwell is an inkwell, in which the glass is a glass. It is not that he is unable to form reflective judgments or concepts about his condition. He knows full well what it "means": the obligation to get up at five o'clock, to sweep the floor of the premises before the rooms are opened, to get the coffee machine going, etc. He knows the rights that come with it: the right to a tip, trade union rights, etc. But all these concepts and judgments refer to something transcendent. These are abstract possibilities, rights and duties, accorded to a "legal subject." And it is precisely this person that I *have to be* and that I am not. It is not that I don't want to be him, or that he is someone else. Rather, there is no common measure between his being and mine. For others

95

he is a "performance" and, for me, this means that I can be him only by performing him. But, precisely, if I represent him to myself, I am not him. I am separated from him, like an object from its subject: I am separated by nothing, but this nothing isolates me from him; I cannot be him; I can only play at being him, i.e., by imagining that I am him. And, through that very action, I imbue him with nothingness. Try as I might to carry out the tasks of a café waiter, I can be one only in a neutralized mode, in the way an actor is Hamlet, by mechanically making the typical gestures of my condition as I aim—through these gestures, and using them as an "analogon"— at being an imaginary café waiter.[16] What I am trying to actualize is a being-in-itself of the café waiter, as if it were not precisely in my power to confer upon the duties of my station their value and their urgency, as if it were not my own free choice to get up each morning at five o'clock, or to stay in bed, even if that gets me sacked. As if, by the very fact of maintaining this role in existence, I did not transcend it from all sides and did not constitute myself as being beyond my condition. However, there can be no doubt that in one sense I am a café waiter—otherwise would it not be equally possible to call myself a diplomat or a journalist? But if I am him, it cannot be in the mode of being in itself. I am the waiter in the mode of being what I am not. Moreover, this does not apply only to social roles: I am never any of my attitudes, any of my ways of behaving. A seductive speaker is someone who plays at speaking, because he cannot be a speaking being; the attentive pupil who wants to be attentive exhausts himself—his gaze riveted on his teacher, all ears—in playing the attentive pupil, to the point where he can no longer listen to anything. Constantly absent from my body and my actions, I am in spite of myself Valéry's "divine absence."[17] I cannot say either that I am here or that I am not, in the sense in which we might say "This box of matches is on the table": that would conflate my "being-in-the-world" with a "being-in-the-midst-of-the-world." Nor can I say that I am standing up, or that I am seated: that would conflate my body with the idiosyncratic totality in which it is just one structure. I escape from being on all sides—and yet I am.

16 Sartre's note: Cf. L'Imaginaire (NRF, 1940), Conclusion. TN: Translated as Sartre (2004b).
17 TN: The French poet Paul Valéry (1871–1945) uses the phrase "divine absence" in his poem "Fragments of the 'Narcissus,'" contained in English translation in Valéry (2007).

But here we have a mode of being that only concerns me: I am sad. Can we not say, about this sadness that I am, that I am it in the mode of being what I am? Yet what is this sadness, other than the intentional unity that gathers together and animates my behavior in its entirety? It is the meaning of this lifeless way I look out at the world, of my hunched shoulders, my lowered head, the limpness of my whole body. But surely I realize, in the very moment I act in these ways, that I am able not to act like that? Let a stranger suddenly appear, and I will raise my head, resume my lively and dynamic appearance: What remains of my sadness, other than the fact that I indulgently plan to return to it soon, after the visitor's departure? Moreover, isn't this sadness itself an *action*, a consciousness that imbues itself with sadness as it resorts to the use of magic in a pressing situation?[18] And even in this very example, isn't being sad, in the first instance, to make oneself sad? "So be it," one might say, "but even so, in adopting the *being* of sadness, haven't we *received* that being? Where it is received from, after all, hardly matters. The fact is that a consciousness that imbues itself with sadness *is* sad, precisely because of that." But this would misunderstand the nature of consciousness: being-sad is not some ready-made being that I can give to myself, in the way I might give this book to my friend. I do not have the power to *take on being*. If I make myself sad, I must make myself sad through the entire expanse of my sadness: I am unable to profit from any acquired momentum and, without needing to re-create or to carry it, to allow my sadness to spin itself out like an inert body that can pursue its movement beyond the initial impact: in consciousness, there is no inertia. If I make myself sad, it is because I *am* not sad: the being of my sadness eludes me, through and in my very act of adopting it. The being-in-itself of sadness constantly haunts my consciousness (of) being sad, but as a value that I cannot actualize, as a regulative meaning of my sadness, and not as its constitutive modality.

Might it be said that at least my consciousness *is*, whatever object or state it makes itself conscious of? But how can we distinguish my sadness from my consciousness (of) being sad? Are they not the same? It is true, in one way, that my consciousness *is*, if we take that to

18 Sartre's note: *Esquisse d'une Théorie des Émotions* (Hermann, Paris, 1939). TN: Translated as Sartre (1994).

mean that, for the Other, it forms part of the totality of being about which judgments can be made. But we must observe, as Husserl clearly saw, that my consciousness appears to the Other from the outset as an absence. It is the object whose constant presence is the *meaning* of all my attitudes and behavior—and that is always absent, because it is given to the Other's intuition as a constant question or, better still, as a constant freedom. When Pierre looks at me, I know without doubt that he is looking at me: his eyes—things in the world—are riveted on my body—a thing in the world; that is the objective fact of which I can say "It *is*." But it is also a fact that belongs to *the world*. The meaning of this look is not, and that is what bothers me. Whatever I do—smile, promise, threaten—nothing can *win* me the approval, the free judgment I am seeking. I know that it is always "beyond," and I can feel it in my very actions, which no longer maintain the *workmanlike* character they have in relation to things, which are—insofar as I relate them to the Other—no longer for me anything but mere *presentations*, waiting to be constituted as gracious or clumsy, sincere or insincere, etc., by an apprehension that is always beyond all my efforts to provoke it, and which they can never provoke unless of its own accord it lends them its strength—an apprehension that exists only insofar as it is provoked from outside, and which *is like its own mediation with the transcendent*. In this way, the objective fact of the being-in-itself of the Other's consciousness posits itself, only to dissolve into negativity and freedom: the Other's consciousness *is* as not being, the being-in-itself of its "now" and its "here" is to not be.

The Other's consciousness is what it is not.

And furthermore my own consciousness does not appear to me in its being like the Other's consciousness. My consciousness is, because it makes itself—since its being is a consciousness of being. But that means the making maintains the being: consciousness has its own being to be, and it is never maintained by being; it is consciousness that maintains being within subjectivity, which means once again that it is inhabited by being but without being it. *Consciousness is not what it is.*

In these conditions, what can the ideal of sincerity mean, other than a task that is impossible to accomplish and whose meaning contradicts the structure of my consciousness? "To be sincere," we said, "is to be what one is." This presupposes that I am not originally what I am. But here, of course, Kant's "You must, therefore you can"[19] is implicitly granted. I can *become* sincere—as my duty and my effort to be sincere imply. Now, precisely, we can see that the original structure of "not being what one is" makes it impossible from the outset to progress toward being in itself, or "being what one is." And this impossibility is not hidden from consciousness: on the contrary, it is the very fabric of consciousness; it is our constantly experienced unease; it is our inability even to recognize, or to constitute, ourselves as being what we are; it is the necessity that requires that, as soon as we posit ourselves—by means of a valid judgment, based on inner experience, or correctly inferred from *a priori* or empirical premises—as some specific being, we must surpass that being, through our very act of positing—and not toward another being but toward the void, toward a *nothing*. How then can we blame anyone for not being sincere, or rejoice in our own sincerity, when at the same time this sincerity appears to us impossible? How can we even make a start—in our speech, our confession, our soul-searching—at trying to be sincere, since this endeavor is essentially doomed to fail and since, at the very moment when we announce it, we have a prejudicative understanding of its futility? In examining myself, my goal is, in effect, to determine exactly what I am, in order to resolve that I will be it, without deviation— even if that sets me searching, thereafter, for the means by which I might be changed. But what does this aim amount to, other than that of constituting myself as a thing? Am I able to determine the set of reasons and motives that led me to perform this or that action? But that would already be to hypothesize a process of causal determinism, constituting the flux of my consciousness as if it were a succession of physical states. Will I discover—even if I am ashamed to admit to them—certain "tendencies" within me?[20] But in that case wouldn't I be forgetting that these tendencies are actualized with my cooperation, that they are not forces of nature, and that, by constantly deciding on their value, I lend them their efficacy? Will I bring some judgment to bear on my character, or my nature? But isn't that to conceal from myself, at that very moment,

98

---

19 TN: . . . *"tu dois, donc tu peux"* . . . This Kantian doctrine is normally expressed in English as "ought implies can."

20 TN: . . . *des "tendances"* . . . See my note on *tendance* in Notes on the Translation.

something that in any case I know: that I am hereby judging a past, from which my present by definition escapes? We can see proof of this insofar as the same man who—in sincerity—posits that he is just what, in fact, he was will be indignant at the Other's resentment, and will try to fend it off by claiming he is no longer able to be what he was. We are readily surprised and saddened that the penalties imposed by the courts weigh on a man who, in his renewed freedom, *is no longer* the culprit that he was. But at the same time we demand this man to recognize himself as *being* this culprit. What, therefore, is sincerity, other than a phenomenon, precisely, of bad faith? Indeed, have we not shown that bad faith is a matter of constituting human-reality as a being that is what it is not, and is not what it is?

It is common for a homosexual to feel intolerably guilty, and for that feeling to condition his entire existence. We can predict without difficulty that this man is in bad faith. And often, in fact, such a man—even while he admits to his homosexual weakness, even while he acknowledges, one at a time, each particular sin he has committed—will refuse with all his might to consider himself "a pederast."[21] His case is always "different," and particular: it involves games, accidents, mishaps; those mistakes are in the past; they can be explained by a particular conception of beauty that women are unable to instantiate; we should see them as the outcome of an anxious pursuit, rather than as manifestations of a deeply rooted drive, etc. Here we have, without doubt, a man whose bad faith borders on the comical as, while admitting to all the deeds ascribed to him, he refuses to draw the clear consequence. His friend— who is his harshest critic—therefore becomes irritated by this duplicity. The critic only demands one thing—and maybe then he would show some leniency: that the culprit should recognize his guilt, that the homosexual should straightforwardly declare—whether in a spirit of humility or assertion hardly matters—"*I am a pederast.*" Here we can ask: Who is in bad faith? The homosexual or the champion of sincerity? The homosexual acknowledges his misdemeanors, but he fights with all his strength against the crushing perspective from which his mistakes constitute for him a *destiny*. He does not want to let others regard him as

99

---

21 TN: I have used "pederast" in its old-fashioned use to mean (male) homosexual, to match Sartre's use of *pédéraste*, which is an outdated French term with the same meaning.

a thing: he understands, obscurely but powerfully, that a homosexual is not a homosexual in the way this table is a table, or this red-haired man is a redhead. It seems to him that he can escape from any mistake, the moment he posits and acknowledges it, or—even better—that psychological duration, by itself, washes him clean of every misdemeanor, constitutes an indeterminate future for him, and allows him to be born anew. Is he wrong? Is he not recognizing, by himself, the peculiar and irreducible character of human-reality? His attitude, therefore, contains an undeniable understanding of the truth. But at the same time he needs this continual renaissance, this constant escape, in order to live; to avoid the community's terrible judgment, he has constantly to place himself out of reach. In this way, he plays on the meaning of "*being.*" In fact he would be right, if he understood this sentence, "I am not a pederast," to mean: "I am not what I am." If he declared, in other words, that "to the extent to which a set of actions is defined as a pederast's behavior, and I have performed these actions, I am a pederast. To the extent that human-reality escapes any definition in terms of its behavior, I am not one." But he slides toward another meaning of "being." He means "not being" in the sense of "not being in itself." He asserts that he "is not a pederast" in the sense in which this table is not an inkwell. He is in bad faith.

But the champion of sincerity is not unaware of human-reality's transcendence and knows, when the need arises, how to assert it to his advantage. He even makes use of it, and posits it within his present demand: Doesn't he want the homosexual, in the name of sincerity—and therefore of freedom—to look back at himself and to recognize himself as a homosexual? Isn't he suggesting that such a confession would elicit his indulgence? What can this mean, other than that the man who recognizes himself as homosexual will no longer be the *same* as the homosexual he recognizes himself to be, and will escape into the domain of freedom and the good will?[22] He is therefore asking him to be what he is, in order no longer to be what he is. That is the true meaning of the saying "A fault confessed is half-redressed." He demands that the culprit constitute himself as a thing, precisely in order to stop treating him as a thing. And this contradiction is constitutive of what sincerity requires. Indeed,

22 TN: . . . *de la liberté et de la bonne volonté?* Sartre's reference to "the good will" here is presumably philosophical; he may be thinking of Kant's philosophy.

who could fail to see the offense caused to the Other, and the reassurance secured for me, in an utterance like "Bah! He's a pederast"—which erases with a single stroke an unnerving freedom, and aims to constitute henceforth all the Other's actions as if they were consequences that followed directly from his essence. Yet that is what the critic requires of his victim: that he constitute himself as a thing, and hand over his freedom to him like a fief, in order for the critic then to give it back to him, like a suzerain to his loyal subject. To the extent that the champion of sincerity wants to reassure himself (while he claims to be passing judgment), and to the extent that he demands of a freedom, insofar as it is freedom, to constitute itself as a thing, he is in bad faith. What we see here is only an episode in that fight to the death between consciousnesses that Hegel called "the master-slave relationship."[23] Consciousness is called on and required, in the name of its nature as consciousness, radically to destroy itself as a consciousness while it is made to hope, beyond this destruction, for a rebirth.

Be that as it may, one might say, but our man is using sincerity inappropriately, as a weapon against the Other. We should not be looking for sincerity in relations of "*Mitsein*" but in its pure form: in one's relations with oneself. But who could fail to see that objective sincerity is constituted in the same way? Who could fail to see that the sincere man, by the very act of sincerity, constitutes himself as a thing precisely in order to escape the condition of a thing? The man who admits that he is malicious has traded his troubling "freedom-to-do-wrong" for an inanimate character of malice: he *is* malicious; he adheres to himself; he is what he is. But at the same time he escapes from this thing, since he is the person contemplating it, and since it depends on him whether he maintains it in front of his eyes, or allows it to collapse into an infinity of individual acts. He makes his sincerity a *merit*, and a meritorious man is not malicious insofar as he is malicious but insofar as he exists beyond his malice.

At the same time, the malice is defused, since if it only exists deterministically it is nothing, and since, by acknowledging it, I posit my freedom in relation to it; my future is virgin, so everything is permitted. In this way, sincerity's essential structure does not differ from that of bad faith, since the sincere man constitutes himself as what he is in

23 TN: Hegel describes this "fight" in his *Phenomenology of Spirit* (Hegel 1977).

order not to be it. That explains the universally recognized truth that by dint of being sincere one can end up in bad faith. Stendhal would be such a case, Valéry said. Complete and constant sincerity as a constant attempt to adhere to oneself is, by its nature, a constant attempt to dissociate from oneself; the act through which one makes oneself into an object for oneself is itself an act of self-liberation. To keep constant account of what one is amounts to a constant disavowal of oneself; it is to take refuge in a sphere in which one is no longer anything but a pure and free act of looking. The goal of bad faith, we said, is to put oneself out of reach; it is an act of flight. We can see now that sincerity has to be defined in the same terms. What does this mean?

In fact, in the end, the goals of sincerity and bad faith are not that different. Of course, there is a type of sincerity—which is not our concern here—that bears on our past: I am sincere if I admit that I *had* this pleasure or that intention. We will see that, if this type of sincerity is possible, it is because man's being, as it slides into the past, becomes constituted as a being in itself. But our sole concern here is the type of sincerity that targets itself, in the immanence of the present. What is its goal? To admit to what I am, in order to make myself at last coincide with my being; in brief, to make it the case that I am, in the mode of the in-itself, what I am in the mode of "not being what I am." And its premise is that I am basically already, in the mode of the in-itself, what I have to be. Thus we encounter, in the depths of sincerity, an incessant play of mirrors and reflections, a constant transition from being that is what it is into being that is not what it is and—in the other direction—from being that is not what it is to being that is what it is. And what is the goal of bad faith? To make it the case that I am what I am, in the mode of "not being what one is," or that I am not what I am, in the mode of "being what one is." Here again we encounter the same play of mirrors. Indeed, in order for the intention to be sincere to exist, it is necessary that—from the outset and at the same time—I am and I am not what I am. Sincerity does not assign a particular quality or way of being to me but, in relation to the quality at issue, it aims to move me from one mode of being into another mode of being. And my nature prohibits me from achieving this second mode of being—the ideal of sincerity—and, at the very moment when I endeavor to achieve it, I understand—obscurely and prejudicatively—that I will not achieve it. But, similarly, for me to be able merely to conceive an intention to be in bad faith, I must, by my nature, escape in my being from my being. If I were sad or cowardly in the way this inkwell is an inkwell, the possibility of bad faith could not even be conceived. I would not only be unable to escape from my being but I would be unable even to imagine that I might escape from it. But if bad faith is possible, simply as a project, that is just because, in relation to my being, the distinction between being and not being is not all that clear. Bad faith is possible only because sincerity is conscious of missing its mark, by its nature. I can only try to grasp myself as "not being a coward"—when I "am" a coward—if my "being a coward" is "in question" in the very moment of its existence, and if it is itself *a* question, and if, in the very moment when I want to grasp it, it escapes from me on all sides, and is annihilated. The condition of my being able to attempt to be in bad faith is that in one sense I *am not* this coward who I do not want to be. But if I *was not* a coward, in the straightforward mode of not-being-what-one-is-not, I would be "in good faith" in declaring that I am not a coward. Thus it must be the case that, in addition, I am in some way that unreachable, evanescent coward who I am not. And we should not take this to mean that I must be "a bit" of a coward, in the sense in which "a bit" means "to a certain extent a coward—and to a certain extent not a coward." No: it is a complete coward, and a coward in all of its aspects, that I must be and, at the same time, not be.

102   Thus bad faith requires, in this case, that I am not what I am, i.e., that an imponderable difference separates being from non-being, in the mode of being that belongs to human-reality. But bad faith does not confine itself to refusing the qualities I possess, or to failing to see the being that I am. It also tries to constitute me as being what I am not. It apprehends me as being positively courageous, when I am not. And once again, that is possible only if I am what I am not, i.e., only if the non-being in me lacks being, even in its capacity as non-being. Of course, it is necessary that I should *not be* courageous; otherwise bad faith would not be *bad* faith. But in addition, my effort at bad faith must encompass an ontological understanding that, even in my everyday being, I am not really what I *am*, and that there is not such a difference between, for example, the being of "being-sad"—which I *am* in the mode of not being what I am—and the "not-being" of the not-being-courageous that I wish to conceal from myself. In addition, and above all, it is necessary for this very negation of being to be, itself, the object of a constant nihilation, and for the very

meaning of "not being" in human-reality to be constantly in question. If I *was not* courageous in the way in which an inkwell is not a table—which is to say, if I was isolated in my cowardice, stubbornly sticking to it, and incapable of relating it to its opposite—or if I was not capable of *determining* myself as cowardly—which is to say of negating any courage in relation to myself, and thereby escaping from my cowardice at the very moment in which I posit it—or if it was not necessarily *impossible* for me to coincide with my *not-being-courageous* (just as with my *being-cowardly*), any project of bad faith would be ruled out. Thus, in order for bad faith to be possible, it is necessary that sincerity itself should be in bad faith. The condition of possibility of bad faith is that human-reality, in its most proximate being, in the internal structure of the prereflective *cogito*, should be what it is not and not be what it is.

III. THE "FAITH" OF BAD FAITH

But so far we have only pointed out the conditions that make bad faith conceivable, the structures of being that make it possible to form the concepts used by bad faith. We cannot limit ourselves to these considerations: we have not yet distinguished bad faith from lying; the ambiguous concepts that we have described could, doubtless, be put to use by a liar to confound his interlocutor, even though their ambiguity,[24] being   103 founded in man's being and not on some empirical circumstance, can and ought to be apparent to everyone. Clearly, the real problem of bad faith arises from the fact that bad faith is *faith*. It cannot consist either in a cynical lie or in anything evident, if "evidence" means the possession of an object in intuition. But if we can give the name "belief" to the union of being with its object, where the object is either not given, or given indistinctly, then bad faith will count as belief, and the problem

---

24 TN: ... *les concepts amphiboliques ... encore que leur amphibolie* ... Sartre's term *amphibolique* is more precise in meaning than "ambiguous" (which translates as *ambigu*), but as there is no corresponding English term of comparable precision I use "ambiguous" here. As Littré explains, while *ambigu* applies to a word or sentence that has more than one meaning, *amphibolique* applies to a construction whose meaning is *uncertain*, as in cases when the grammar makes it possible to interpret a sentence in either of two ways. The French regard such sentences as linguistically deficient.

of bad faith is essentially a problem about belief. How can one believe, in bad faith, in concepts that have been deliberately forged for the purpose of persuading oneself? We must note that, in effect, the project of bad faith must itself be in bad faith: I am not in bad faith only when my endeavor is over, when I have constructed my ambiguous concepts and persuaded myself. To tell the truth, I have not persuaded myself: insofar as I ever could be persuaded, I always have been. And it was necessary, at the very moment when I was about to put myself in bad faith, for me to be in bad faith in relation to that inclination itself. To represent it to myself as bad faith would have been cynical; to sincerely believe it to be innocent would have been good faith. The decision to be in bad faith dares not speak its name; it believes, and it does not believe, that it is in bad faith. And, from the moment bad faith arises, that decision entirely determines one's subsequent attitude and, in a way, the *Weltanschauung* of bad faith. For bad faith does not retain the norms and criteria of truth that are accepted by the critical thinking of good faith. Effectively, and from the outset, bad faith determines the nature of truth. Alongside bad faith, a truth appears, a method of thinking, a type of being possessed by objects; and the ontological characteristic of this world of bad faith, in which the subject suddenly immerses himself, is that, in it, being is what it is not, and is not what it is. In consequence, a particular type of evidence appears: *non-persuasive* evidence. Bad faith apprehends facts that are evident, but it is resigned in advance not to be fulfilled by such evidence,[25] not to be persuaded and transformed into good faith. The person in bad faith becomes humble and modest: he is aware, he says, that faith is a decision and that after each intuition one is obliged to determine *what is and to will it*. Thus, in its basic project and from the moment it arises, bad faith determines the precise nature of its requirements: it becomes visible in its entirety in its resolution *not to ask for too much*, to consider itself satisfied when it is poorly persuaded, to force through, by means of a decision, its adherence to uncertain truths. This primary project of bad faith is a decision, in bad faith, about the nature of faith. This must be understood not as a reflective and voluntary decision but rather as a spontaneous determination of our being. One *puts oneself* into bad

---

25 TN: . . . *résignée à ne pas être remplie par ces évidences* . . . Although "fulfilled" sounds a little odd in this sentence, it is necessary in order to retain the Husserlian vocabulary used here.

faith as one goes to sleep, and being in bad faith is like dreaming. Once
this mode of being is actualized, it is as difficult to leave it as to wake   104
up: the fact is that bad faith—like being awake or dreaming—is a type
of being in the world that tends to perpetuate itself of its own accord,
even though its structure is metastable in kind. But bad faith is conscious
of its structure, and has taken precautions by deciding that a metastable structure is the structure of being, and that the structure of all our
convictions is non-persuasive. Still, if bad faith is faith, and if its own
negation forms part of its most basic project (I resolve to be poorly convinced in order to convince myself that I am what I am not), it must be
possible from the outset for there to be a type of faith willing its own
lack of conviction. What are the conditions of possibility of this type of
faith?

I believe that my friend Pierre has friendly feelings toward me. I
believe this in good faith. I believe it and I have no intuition attended by
evidence of these feelings, because such an object, by its nature, does not
lend itself to intuition. I believe it, which is to say I give in to my impulses
to trust, I decide to believe it and to stand by my decision, and, finally, I
behave as if I were certain of it—all within the synthetic unity of a single
attitude. What I define in these terms as good faith is what Hegel called
the immediate; it is "simple faith."[26] Hegel goes straight on to show that
the immediate calls for mediation, and that belief, by becoming belief for
itself, passes over into the state of non-belief. If I believe my friend Pierre
likes me, I will see his friendliness as the meaning of all his actions.
Belief is a distinctive consciousness of the meaning of Pierre's actions. But
if I know that I believe, belief appears as a purely subjective determination, without any external correlate. That is why the verb itself—"to
believe"—can refer, indifferently, to the unshakable assurance of a belief
("My God, I believe in you") and to its neutralized and strictly subjective
character ("Is Pierre my friend? I have no idea: I believe he is"). But the
nature of consciousness is such that, in it, the mediate and the immediate are one and the same being. To believe is to know one believes, and
to know one believes is to believe no longer. Thus, to believe—because
it is only to believe—is to believe no longer; and all this is within the

26 TN: . . . c'est la foi du charbonnier. The French expression Sartre uses here literally means
   "the coal-man's faith"; it is used in idiomatic French to denote simple or naïve faith—
   the faith of a simple man.

unity of a single non-thetic consciousness (of) self. Of course, we have stretched the description of the phenomenon here, by referring to it as *knowledge*: non-thetic consciousness is not *knowledge*. But, through its very translucency, it lies at the origin of all knowledge. In this way, one's non-thetic consciousness (of) believing is destructive of belief. But at the same time, the law of the prereflective *cogito* dictates that the being of believing must be a consciousness of believing. Thus, belief is a being that puts itself in question in its own being, and that can be actualized only in its destruction; it is a being that can become manifest to itself only by negating itself, a being for which to be is to appear, and to appear is to negate itself. To believe is not to believe. We can see why: the being of consciousness is to exist through itself, and so to make itself be, and, thereby, to surmount itself. In this sense, consciousness is constantly escaping from itself: belief turns into non-belief, the immediate into mediation, the absolute into the relative, and the relative into the absolute. The ideal of good faith (to believe what one believes) is—like the ideal of sincerity (to be what one is)—an ideal of being-in-itself. No belief is ever enough of a belief; we never believe in what we believe. And, in consequence, the basic project of bad faith merely makes use of this self-destruction of any conscious state. If every belief in good faith is an impossible belief, a place exists for every impossible belief. My incapacity to *believe* I am courageous will no longer discourage me, since, precisely, no belief can ever believe enough. I will define this impossible belief as my belief. Of course, I cannot hide from myself that I believe in order not to believe, and that I do not believe in *order to* believe. But bad faith's subtle and complete self-annihilation should not surprise me: it exists at the heart of all faith. What, then, does it involve? That at the moment when I wish to *believe* I am courageous, I *know* I am a coward? And this certainty is what will destroy my belief? But, in the first place, I *am* no more courageous than cowardly, if we are to understand these in terms of the mode of being of the in-itself. In the second place, I do not *know* I am courageous; such a view of myself could be accompanied only by *belief*, because it surpasses the pure certainty of reflection. In the third place, it is quite true that bad faith does not manage to believe what it wants to believe. But it is precisely in virtue of its accepting not to believe what it believes that it is bad faith. Good faith wants to flee from "not believing what one believes" into being; bad faith flees from being into "not believing what one believes." It has disarmed any belief in advance: the beliefs it wants to acquire and, at the same time, the beliefs from which it wants to escape. By willing this self-destruction on the part of belief—which science evades by moving toward evidence—it ruins any beliefs that might be opposed to it, which reveal themselves to be only belief. In this way we can better understand the basic phenomenon of bad faith.

There is no cynical lie in bad faith, or any knowing preparation of misleading concepts. But bad faith's most basic act is to flee from something it is impossible to flee from: to flee from what one is. Now, the very project of flight reveals to bad faith an internal disintegration at the heart of being—and this disintegration is what it wants to be. In fact, the two immediate attitudes that we can take up in relation to our being are both conditioned by the very nature of our being, and its immediate relation with the in-itself. Good faith seeks to flee from the internal disintegration of my being, in the direction of the in-itself that it ought to be, and is not. Bad faith seeks to flee from the in-itself into the internal disintegration of my being. But it denies this very disintegration, just as it denies its own bad faith. In fleeing, through "not-being-what-one-is," from the in-itself that I am not in the mode of being what one is not, bad faith—which disavows its own bad faith—aims at the in-itself that I am not in the mode of "not-being-what-one-is-not."[27] If bad faith is possible, that is because it threatens—immediately and permanently—every project made by human beings, and because consciousness harbors in its being the permanent risk of bad faith. And the source of that risk is that consciousness is what it is not and is not what it is, in its being and simultaneously. In the light of these observations, we can now begin an ontological study of consciousness, not as the totality of human being but as its instantaneous kernel.

106

27 Sartre's note: If it is a matter of indifference whether to be in good or bad faith, because bad faith takes hold of good faith and slides into its project even at its origin, that does not mean that we are unable radically to escape from bad faith. But that would require corrupted being to reclaim itself. We will call this "authenticity": its description does not belong here.

Part Two

Being-for-itself

Chapter 1

THE IMMEDIATE STRUCTURES
OF THE FOR-ITSELF

I. SELF-PRESENCE[1]

From negation, we were led to freedom, and from there to bad faith, and bad faith has led us to the being of consciousness, as its condition of possibility. We should then resume, in the light of the demands established in the preceding chapters, the description that we began in the Introduction to this book; we should return, in other words, to the field of the prereflective *cogito*. But the *cogito* only ever delivers what we ask it to deliver. Descartes inquired into its functional aspect: "I *doubt*, I *think*" and, wishing to move (without any guiding principle) from there to the dialectic of existence, he fell into the error of substantialism. Husserl, learning from this error, stayed timidly at the level of functional description. In so doing, he never advanced beyond the pure description of appearance as such; he locked himself up in the *cogito* and he deserves—despite his denials— to be called a phenomenalist rather than a phenomenologist; and his phenomenalism constantly comes close to a Kantian idealism. Heidegger, who wanted to avoid this descriptive phenomenalism—which leads to

---

1 TN: I translate Sartre's *présence à soi* as "self-presence" rather than the clunkier "presence to self." The reader should therefore bear in mind the element of "distance" (between the for-itself and itself) implied by Sartre's phrase.

a Megarian[2] and anti-dialectical isolation of essences—embarks on the existential analytic[3] directly, without going through the *cogito*. But if *Dasein* is stripped from the outset of its dimension of consciousness, it can never win it back. Heidegger endows human-reality with a self-understanding, defined as an "ecstatic pro-ject" of its own possibilities. And it is no part of our intention to deny this project's existence. But how should we conceive of an understanding that is not, in itself, conscious (of) being an understanding? If this ecstatic character of human-reality does not arise within a consciousness of *ecstasis*, it must collapse back into a blind and thing-like in-itself. In fact the *cogito* has to be our point of departure, but it is fair to say—in parody of a well-known expression—that it can lead anywhere, provided that you can get out of it.[4] The sole purpose of our earlier investigation (which focused on the conditions of possibility of various ways of behaving) was to put us in a position where we could inquire into the *cogito*'s being and to provide us with the dialectical instrument that might enable us to find a means, within the *cogito* itself, of escaping from instantaneity in order to approach the totality of being that constitutes human-reality. Let us return, then, to our description of non-thetic consciousness (of) self; let us examine its results and ask what it means, for consciousness, necessarily to be what it is not, and not to be what it is.

"The being of consciousness," we wrote in our Introduction, "is a being for whom in its being there is a question of its being."[5] That means the being of consciousness does not coincide with itself in the fullness of adequation. That adequation, which belongs to the in-itself, is expressed in this simple formula: being is what it is. In the in-itself there is not a single particle of being with any distance from itself. In the type of being hereby conceived, there is not even the slightest

2 TN: The Megarian school of philosophy was founded in the fourth century BC by Eucleides of Megara. Among their doctrines was a rejection of the evidence of the senses, from which perhaps Sartre derives the "isolation of essences" mentioned in this sentence.

3 TN: "Existential analytic" is Heidegger's phrase. He claims that fundamental ontology must begin with an "existential analytic" of *Dasein* (Heidegger 1980: §4).

4 TN: . . . *il mène à tout à condition d'en sortir.* This phrase was used by the writer and journalist Jules Jannin (1804–1874) to characterize journalism; it has been adapted numerous times in French.

5 TN: Sartre is quoting from his earlier discussion of Heidegger's formula at EN 29.

trace of duality; we can express this by saying that the in-itself has an infinite density of being. It is plenitude. We are able to characterize the principle of identity as "synthetic," not only because its scope is limited to a particular region but above all because it gathers within itself the infinity of density. "A is A" means: A exists in the form of infinite compression, in an infinite density. Identity is the limiting concept of unification.[6] It is not true that the in-itself requires any synthetic unification of its being: at its extreme limit, unity vanishes and passes over into identity. The identical is the ideal of the "one," and it is through human-reality that the "one" enters the world. The in-itself is full of itself and it is impossible to imagine a more complete plenitude, a more perfect adequation of any content to its container: there is not the slightest emptiness in being, not the slightest fissure through which nothingness might slip.

Consciousness is characterized, on the contrary, by its decompression of being. Indeed, it is impossible to define it as self-coincident. About this table here, I can say purely and simply that it is this table. But if I am talking about my belief, I cannot confine myself to saying that it is a belief: my belief is a consciousness (of) belief. It has often been said that the reflective gaze alters the fact of consciousness on which it is directed. Husserl himself admits that the fact of "being seen" brings about a complete modification in each "*Erlebnis*." But we believe that we have shown that the primary condition of any reflexivity is a pre-reflective *cogito*. Of course this *cogito* does not posit an object; it remains intra-conscious. But that does not make it any the less homologous with the reflective *cogito*, insofar as it instantiates the basic necessity, for unreflected consciousness, that it should be seen by itself. From the outset, therefore, it has this inescapable feature: it exists for a witness, even though this witness for whom consciousness exists is itself. In this way, by virtue solely of the fact that I grasp my belief as a belief, it *is no longer anything more than a belief*, which means it is no longer a belief; it is a troubled belief. In no case, therefore, can we take the ontological judgment "Belief is consciousness (of) belief" to be a judgment of identity: the

111

---

6 TN: The term *concept-limite* is used in French to render the German term *Grenzbegriff*. In Kantian philosophy it often means a concept that signals the limits of sense-experience. It is usually translated into English either as "boundary concept" or as "limiting concept," which is why I remove Sartre's hyphen.

subject and attribute are radically different, albeit within the indissoluble unity of the same being.

"So be it," someone might say, but you are obliged to say at the least that consciousness (of) belief is consciousness (of) belief. At this level, we rediscover identity and the in-itself; it was simply a matter of choosing the appropriate level at which to grasp our object. But that is not true: to claim that consciousness (of) belief is consciousness (of) belief is to dissociate consciousness from its belief, to remove the brackets, and to turn belief into an object for consciousness: it involves a sudden leap onto the plane of reflection. If consciousness (of) belief were only consciousness (of) belief, it would have to be conscious (of) itself as being a consciousness (of) belief. The belief would become merely a transcendent and noematic feature of consciousness; in confronting this belief, consciousness would be free to determine itself as it pleased; it would resemble the imperturbable gaze which consciousness, in Victor Cousin's account, casts over psychological phenomena, illuminating each of them in turn.[7] But Husserl's analysis of the method of doubt made this fact clear: only a reflective consciousness can dissociate itself from what reflected consciousness posits. It is only at the reflective level that an ἐποχή—a bracketing—can be attempted, and that we can refuse to "mitmachen," as Husserl put it.[8] Consciousness (of) belief, even though it irreparably modifies the belief, is not distinct from it: it *exists in order to* perform the act of faith. We have to acknowledge, therefore, that consciousness (of) belief is belief. In so doing, we can grasp this twofold structure of referral at its source: consciousness (of) belief is belief, and belief is consciousness (of) belief. In neither case can we say that consciousness is consciousness, or that belief is belief. Each of these terms refers us to the other and passes over into the other, and yet each term is different from the other. As we have seen, neither belief, nor pleasure, nor joy can exist *before* being conscious; consciousness is the measure of

---

7 TN: Sartre is referring to the method of "psychological observation" advocated by the French philosopher Victor Cousin (1792–1867) as a means to discovering the nature of consciousness and its elements.

8 TN: The Greek term in this sentence is usually transliterated as *epoché*. See my note in the section on Husserl vocabulary in Notes on the Translation. The German verb *mitmachen* means "to participate"; the idea here is that the reflective stance moves us out of our everyday "participative" attitude.

their being. But it is no less true that belief, because it can only exist as troubled, exists from the outset as escaping from itself, as shattering the unity of all the concepts in which we might wish to enclose it.

Thus belief and consciousness (of) belief are one and the same being,   112 whose characteristic is absolute immanence. But the moment we want to grasp this being it slips between our fingers and we find ourselves confronted with the outline of a duality, with a play of reflections, because consciousness is a reflection. But in fact, insofar as consciousness is reflection, it is also reflecting—and, if we attempt to grasp it as reflecting, it disappears and we find ourselves back with the reflection. This reflection-reflecting structure has disconcerted those philosophers who have sought to define it by resorting to the infinite, either by positing, as Spinoza does, an *idea-ideae* that calls for an *idea-ideae-ideae*, etc., or by defining self-return, as Hegel does, as the "true infinite."[9] But, in addition to freezing and obscuring the phenomenon, the introduction of the infinite into consciousness is no more than an explicative theory whose specific purpose is to reduce consciousness's being to that of the in-itself. If we accept it as it is given, the objective existence of the reflection-reflecting structure obliges us, on the contrary, to conceive of a mode of being different from the in-itself: not a unity that contains a duality, not a synthesis that surpasses and raises up the abstract moments of thesis and antithesis,[10] but a duality that *is* a unity, a reflection that *is* its own reflecting.[11] If we try to reach the total phenomenon—i.e., the unity of this duality, or consciousness (of) belief—we are referred immediately to one of its terms, and that term refers us in its turn to the unitary organization of the immanent. But if, on the contrary, we want to set out from the duality as such, and to posit consciousness and belief as a pair, we will arrive at Spinoza's *idea-ideae* and we miss the prereflective phenomenon that we wanted to investigate. The fact is that prereflective

---

9 TN: Spinoza discusses self-consciousness as the "idea of an idea" in his *Ethics* (Spinoza 1985).

10 TN: . . . *qui dépasse et lève les moments abstraits* . . . Sartre refers here to Hegel's concept of "sublation" (*Aufhebung*); see my note on *dépasser* in the section on Hegel vocabulary in Notes on the Translation. Hegel himself points out that the German verb *aufheben* can mean "to raise up."

11 TN: . . . *un reflet qui est sa propre réflexion*. The final word in this French sentence is commonly used to denote "reflection" as a cognitive activity. This is slightly less clear in the English.

consciousness is conscious (of) itself. And it is this very notion of *itself* that we need to study, for it defines the very being of consciousness.

To begin, we should note that the term "in-itself"—which we have borrowed from tradition to refer to transcendent being—is inaccurate. In fact, at the limit of self-coincidence, the "itself" vanishes, to make way for identical being. The *itself* cannot be a property of being-in-itself. It is in its nature *reflexive*,[12] as the syntax shows and in particular the logical rigor of the Latin syntax and the strict distinctions established in grammar between the uses of "*ejus*" and "*sui*." The term "*itself*" (or "himself") refers, but it refers precisely to the *subject*. It points to a relation of the subject with itself, and this relation is precisely a duality—but it is a special kind of duality, since it requires specific verbal symbols. But, on the other hand, "itself" does not designate being—either as a subject or as a complement. Indeed, if I consider the term "himself" in the phrase "he washes himself," for example, I will observe that it opens up a space that allows the subject himself to appear behind it.[13] It is not the subject—since the subject without a relation to himself would be condensed into the identity of the in-itself—but neither is it anything solidly articulated within reality, since it allows the subject to appear behind it. In fact, this *himself* cannot be grasped as a real existent: the subject cannot *be* himself because, as we have seen, where something coincides with itself, the "itself" disappears. But neither can he *not be* himself, since the "himself" points to the subject himself. The "himself" represents, therefore, an ideal distance, within the subject's immanence, in relation to himself, a way of *not being his own coincidence*, of escaping from identity even while positing it as unity—in short, a way of being in a constantly unstable equilibrium between identity as a state of absolute cohesion without any trace of diversity, and unity as the synthesis of a multiplicity. We may call this *self-presence*. The law of being of the for-itself as the ontological foundation of consciousness is to be itself in the form of self-presence.

113

12 TN: In this context—in which Sartre alludes to linguistic forms—*réfléchi* should be translated as "reflexive" (as in "reflexive pronouns"). It should be noted that the same word in French (*réfléchi*) is used for "reflected" *and* "reflexive."

13 TN: In this paragraph I have moved from "itself" to "himself," where Sartre uses the same French term—*soi*—for both. (See my discussion of pronouns in Notes on the Translation.) In this particular sentence I have changed Sartre's example to preserve his point: he uses *il s'ennuie*, whose reflexive structure vanishes in English translation ("he is bored"). Replacing the verb by "to wash oneself" provides the structure Sartre wants.

This self-presence has often been understood as a plenitude of existence, and a widely held prejudice among philosophers attributes to consciousness the highest dignity of being. But, in the light of a more thorough description of the notion of presence, this postulate cannot be maintained. In fact, any "*presence to*" implies a duality and thus at least a virtual separation. Being's self-presence implies a detachment on the part of being, in relation to itself. The coincidence of the identical is the true plenitude of being, precisely because this coincidence leaves no space for any negativity. Doubtless the principle of identity may call for the principle of non-contradiction, as Hegel saw. The being that is what it is must be able to be the being that is not what it is not. But in the first place this negation—like all negations—is brought to the surface of being by human-reality, as we have shown, and not through some dialectic that properly belongs to being itself. And further, this principle can only refer to being's relations with *exteriority*, since, precisely, it governs being's relations with what it is not. The principle we are considering here, therefore, is constitutive of *external relations* as they may appear to a human-reality present to being-in-itself and committed within the world; it does not concern being's internal relations; those relations, insofar as they can be said to posit alterity, do not exist. The principle of identity is the negation of any type of relation within being-in-itself. On the contrary, self-presence presupposes that an intangible fissure has slipped inside being. If it is present to itself, that is because it is not completely itself. Presence is an immediate degradation of coincidence, because it presupposes separation. But if we now ask *what* separates the subject from himself, we are forced to admit that it is *nothing*. Ordinarily, something which separates is a distance in space, an interval in time, a psychological disagreement, or simply the individuality of two co-present items: in short, it *qualifies* reality. But in the case we are concerned with here *nothing* can separate the consciousness (of) belief from the belief, since the belief is *nothing other* than the consciousness (of) belief. The introduction of an external and qualified element from outside the *cogito* into the unity of a prereflective *cogito* would break its unity and destroy its translucency; there would be something in consciousness that it was not conscious of, something that did not itself exist as consciousness. The separation that separates belief from itself cannot be grasped, or even conceived, on its own. If we try to reveal it, it vanishes: we find ourselves back with belief in the form

114

of pure immanence. But if, on the contrary, we want to grasp the belief as such, the fissure is there—it appears when we do not want to see it, and as soon as we try to contemplate it, it disappears. This fissure is therefore pure negativity. A distance, an interval of time, a psychological disagreement, can be grasped in themselves and, as such, they contain elements of positivity; it is merely their *function* that is negative. But the fissure within consciousness is nothing apart from what it negates, and it can have being only insofar as we cannot see it. This negative, which is both a nothingness of being and a nihilating power, is *nothingness*. In no other place can we grasp it in such unadulterated form. Everywhere else we are obliged, in one way or another, to endow it, as nothingness, with being-in-itself. But the nothingness that arises in the heart of consciousness *is not*. It *is been*. Belief, for example, is not a being that is contiguous with another being; it is *its own* self-presence, its own decompression of being. Otherwise the unity of the for-itself would collapse into the duality of two in-itselfs. Thus the for-itself must be its own nothingness. The being of consciousness, as consciousness, is to exist *at a distance from itself*, as self-presence, and this zero distance that being bears within its being is Nothingness. Thus, in order for an *itself* to exist, the unity of this being must involve its own nothingness, as a nihilation of the identical. For the nothingness that slides into belief is *its* nothingness, the nothingness of belief as in itself belief, as blind and full belief, as "simple faith."[14] The for-itself is the being that determines itself to exist, insofar as it is unable to coincide with itself.

We are able now to understand that our inquiry, without any guiding principle, into the prereflective *cogito* has not led us to find nothingness anywhere. We cannot find or *disclose* nothingness in the way we can find or disclose a being. Nothingness is always an *elsewhere*. It is the for-itself's obligation never to exist except in the form of an "elsewhere" in relation to itself, to exist as a being that is constantly qualified by its own inconsistency in being. This inconsistency, moreover, does not involve another being; it is only a constant referral from itself to itself, from the reflection to the reflecting, from the reflecting to the reflection. Nevertheless, this referral does not give rise to an infinite movement within the for-itself but is given in the unity of a single act: the infi-

---

14 TN: . . . *comme "foi du charbonnier."* Sartre uses this idiomatic expression again here.

nite movement appears only to the standpoint of reflection, which aims to grasp the phenomenon as a totality and which is referred from the reflection to the reflecting, from the reflecting to the reflection, without being able to stop. Thus, nothingness is this hole in being, this sliding of the in-itself toward the "itself" through which the for-itself constitutes itself. But this nothingness can "be been" only if its borrowed existence is correlative to a nihilating act of being. We may call this continual act through which the in-itself is degraded into self-presence the "onto-logical act." Nothingness is the putting into question of being by being: that, precisely, is consciousness, or the for-itself. It is an absolute event that is brought to being through being, and which—without having any being—is constantly maintained by being. Since being in itself is isolated within its being by complete positivity, no being can produce being, and nothing can happen to being through being—other than nothingness. Nothingness is being's distinctive possibility and its unique possibility. Even so, this original possibility can appear only in the absolute act of its actualization. As nothingness is the nothingness of being, it can only arrive within being through being itself. And, of course, it arrives in being through a particular being, which is human-reality. But this being is constituted as human-reality insofar as it is nothing but the original project of its own nothingness. Human-reality instantiates being insofar as it is, in its being and for its being, the unique foundation of the noth-ingness at the heart of being.

II. THE FOR-ITSELF'S FACTICITY

However, the for-itself is. It is, as some may say, even if its way of being is such that it is not what it is and it is what it is not. It is, because the project of sincerity, whatever stumbling-blocks it may run up against, can at least be conceived. It is, as an event: in the sense in which I can say that Philippe II *was*, or that my friend Pierre is, and exists. It is, inso-far as it appears in a condition that it has not chosen, insofar as Pierre is a French bourgeois in 1942, insofar as Schmitt *was* a worker in Berlin in 1870. It *is*, insofar as it is thrown into the world, abandoned in a "situ-ation"; it is, insofar as it is pure contingency, insofar as we can ask, in relation to it—just as for things in the world, for this wall, this tree, this cup—the basic question: "Why is this being such and not otherwise?"

115

It is, insofar as in it there is something of which it is not the foundation: its *presence to the world*.

Being's apprehension of itself as not being its own foundation lies within every *cogito*. In this respect, we should note that it is immediately encountered by Descartes's *reflective cogito*. Indeed, when Descartes wants to put his discovery to good use, he apprehends himself as an imperfect being, "since he doubts." But within this imperfect being he notes the presence of the idea of perfection. He recognizes, therefore, a disparity between the type of being he is able to conceive and the being that he is. This disparity or lack of being lies at the origin of the second proof of God's existence.[15] Indeed, if we set aside its scholastic terminology, what remains of this proof is a very clear sense that the being which possesses within it the idea of perfection cannot be its own foundation; otherwise it would have designed itself in conformity with that idea. In other terms: a being that was its own foundation would not tolerate the slightest mismatch between what it is and what it conceives, for it would build itself in conformity with its understanding of being and would be able to conceive only of what it is. Instead, this apprehension of being as a lack of being in the face of being is, from the outset, the *cogito*'s grasp of its own contingency. I think therefore I am. What am I? A being who is not his own foundation, and who, insofar as he is a being, might be other than he is, to the extent to which he does not explain his being. This is the primary intuition of our own contingency, cited by Heidegger as the primary motivation for our transition from inauthenticity to authenticity. It is uneasiness, the call of conscience ("*Ruf des Gewissens*"),[16] the feeling of guilt. In fact, Heidegger's description is overly influenced by his concern to provide an ontological foundation for an Ethics in which he claims to take no interest, and also to reconcile his humanism with the religious meaning of the transcendent. The intuition of our contingency should not be equated with a feeling of guilt. It remains no less true that, when we apprehend ourselves, we appear to ourselves with the character of an unjustifiable fact.

15 TN: Sartre is referring here to the second "proof" offered by Descartes in his *Principles* (Descartes 1983).

16 TN: Heidegger discusses the *Ruf des Gewissens* at Heidegger (1980: §54). It is usually translated as the "call of conscience."

But have we not—just now[17]—understood ourselves in terms of consciousness, i.e., as a "being that exists through itself?" How are we able to be—within the unity of a single arising into being—this being that exists through itself, as not being the foundation of its being? Or, to put it in other terms, how can the for-itself which—insofar as it *is*—is not its own being (in the sense in which it might be its own foundation) be the foundation—insofar as it is for-itself—of its own nothingness? The answer lies in the question.

If indeed being, as the nihilation of its own being, is the foundation of nothingness, that does not amount to saying it is the foundation of its being. In order for something to found its own being, it must exist at a distance from itself; that implies a specific nihilation of both the founded being and the founding being, and a duality that is a unity: we are back with the case of the for-itself. In brief, any endeavor to conceive the idea of a being that is the foundation of its being leads us, in spite of itself, to form the idea of a being that, contingent insofar as it is being-in-itself, is the foundation of its own nothingness. The act of causation through which God is *causa sui* is—like any reclamation by something of itself—a nihilating act, to the precise extent to which the most basic relation is necessarily a return to *itself*, a reflexivity. And this original necessity, in turn, appears on the foundation of a contingent being: the precise being which *is in order to* be its own cause. As for Leibniz's attempt to define the necessary on the basis of the possible—a definition that Kant took up—it is conceived from the point of view of knowledge, not from the point of view of being. As Leibniz conceives it, the movement from possibility to being (a necessary being is one whose possibility implies its existence) registers the movement from our ignorance to knowledge. Indeed, the possibility here can only be a possibility with respect to our thought, since it precedes existence. It is an external possibility, in relation to the being whose possibility it is, since being follows from it in the way a consequence follows from a principle. But, as we showed earlier, we can consider the notion of possibility under two aspects. We can, in effect, turn it into a subjective index (it is possible that Pierre is dead means I do not know Pierre's fate) and, in this case, it will be the witness, in the presence of the world, who determines what is possible: being's

117

---

17 Sartre's note: Cf. earlier in this work, Introduction, section III.

possibility lies outside it, in the pure act of looking that weighs up its chances of being; possibility may indeed be given *to us* before being, but it is given *to us*, and it is not the possibility of this being; if the marble rolling across the rug is diverted by a fold in the material, that is no part of the marble's possibility, and neither does the possibility of diversion belong to the rug; it can only be synthetically established by a witness, as an external relationship. But possibility may also appear to us as an ontological structure of reality: in that case it belongs to some beings as *their* possibility; it is the possibility that they *are*, a possibility that they have to be. In this case being maintains its own possibilities in their being, it is their foundation, and being's necessity cannot therefore be derived from its possibility. In brief, God—if he exists—is contingent.

Thus, the being of consciousness, insofar as this being is in itself in *order to* nihilate itself into the for-itself, remains contingent, i.e., consciousness does not have any capacity to give its being to itself, or to receive it from others. And furthermore, as the ontological proof—like the cosmological proof—fails to constitute any necessary being, we cannot seek the explanation and the foundation of my being, insofar as I am a being *like this*, in necessary being: the premises "Anything contingent must be founded in a necessary being. Now, I am contingent" show a desire for foundation, but not any explanatory connection to a real foundation. In fact they could account not for *this* contingency *here* at all but only for the abstract idea of contingency in general. And furthermore, they are concerned with value, not with fact.[18] But if being-in-itself is contingent, it becomes degraded into the for-itself by taking itself up. It is, in order to lose itself in the for-itself. In brief, being is and can only be. But the possibility that properly belongs to being—and which is revealed in the act of nihilation—is to be the foundation of itself as consciousness, through the sacrificial act that nihilates it; the for-itself is the in-itself losing itself as in-itself to found itself as consciousness. Thus consciousness owes its being-consciousness to itself, and it can implicate only itself insofar as it is its own nihilation: but *that which* annihilates itself to become consciousness—which cannot be described as the foundation of consciousness—is the

18 Sartre's note: Indeed, this piece of reasoning is based explicitly on the *requirements of* reason.

contingent in-itself. The in-itself cannot found anything; if it founds itself, that is by modifying itself to become the for-itself. It is its own foundation insofar as it is *already no longer* in-itself, and here we encounter the origin of every foundation. If being in-itself can be neither its own foundation nor the foundation of other beings, foundation in general enters into the world through the for-itself. The for-itself does not only, as nihilated in-itself, found itself but, along with the for-itself, foundation appears for the first time.

Still, this in-itself, swallowed up and nihilated in the absolute event that is the appearing of foundation, or the for-itself's arising, remains at the heart of the for-itself as its original contingency. Consciousness is its own foundation but it remains contingent that *there is* consciousness rather than the pure and simple in-itself, extending to infinity. The absolute event, or the for-itself, is contingent in its very being. If I articulate what is given in the prereflective *cogito* I will observe, of course, that the for-itself refers to itself. Whatever it is, it is in the mode of consciousness of being it. Thirst refers to the consciousness of thirst that it *is*, as if it were its foundation— and conversely. But, if it could be given, the "reflected-reflecting" totality would be contingent and in-itself. But I can never reach this totality, since I can say neither that my consciousness of thirst is consciousness of thirst, nor that my thirst is thirst. The totality is there as a nihilated totality, as the phenomenon's evanescent unity. If I grasp the phenomenon as a plurality, this plurality will indicate itself as a totalizing unity and it will thereby have the meaning of contingency. So I can ask: Why am I thirsty? Why am I conscious of that glass? Or conscious of this Self? But as soon as I consider this totality in itself, it nihilates itself before my eyes. It *is not*, it is in order not to be, and I am returned to the for-itself, apprehending it as it sketches out its duality as the foundation of itself: I am angry because I produce myself as a consciousness of this anger; remove this self-causation, constitutive of the for-itself's being, and you will cease to encounter anything, not even an "anger-in-itself," because it is in the nature of anger to exist as for-itself. Thus the for-itself is supported by a constant contingency that it takes up, and assimilates, without ever being able to get rid of it. We may call this constantly evanescent contingency of the in-itself—which haunts the for-itself and ties it to being-in-itself without ever allowing itself to be grasped—the for-itself's *facticity*. This facticity enables us to say that the for-itself *is*, that it *exists*, even though we

119

can never *actualize* our facticity, and we always apprehend it through the for-itself. We pointed out earlier that we can never be anything without playing at being it.[19] "If I am the café waiter," we wrote, "it can only be in the mode of *not being him.*" And that is true: if I were able *to be* a café waiter, I would constitute myself all at once as a contingent mass of identity. That is not how it is: that kind of being—contingent and in itself—will always escape me. But in order for me to freely bestow a meaning on the obligations attached to my condition, it must be the case that, within the for-itself as a perpetually evanescent totality, being-in-itself as the evanescent contingency of my *situation* is, in some sense, given. This becomes clear if we reflect on the fact that, although I have to *play at being* a café waiter in order to be one, it is also true that, however hard I try to play at being a diplomat or a sailor, I will not be one. This inapprehensible *fact* of my condition, this intangible difference that sets apart the play-acting that actualizes something from play-acting *tout court*, explains why the for-itself, even while it chooses the *meaning* of its situation and constitutes itself in situation as its own foundation, does *not choose* its position. It is the reason why I apprehend myself as being wholly responsible for my being, insofar as I am its foundation, and at the same time wholly unjustifiable. Without facticity, consciousness would be able to choose its attachments in the world, in the manner in which souls, in *The Republic*, can choose their condition: I could decide to be "born working-class" or "born bourgeois." But, on the other hand, my facticity cannot constitute me as *being* bourgeois or as *being* working-class. Strictly speaking, my facticity is not even the *resistance* of facts, since it is by taking it up within the infrastructure of my *prereflective cogito* that I endow it with its meaning and its resistance. My facticity is only an indication that I present to myself of the being I am obliged to keep company with, in order to be what I am. It is impossible to grasp it in its brute nakedness, because we only encounter it when we have already reclaimed and freely constructed it. The mere *fact* of "being there," at this table, in this room, is already the pure object of a limiting concept, and we can only make contact with it as such. And yet my "consciousness of being there" contains it, as its full contingency, as the nihilated in-itself against whose ground the for-itself produces itself as conscious of being there. In sounding the depths of its own consciousness of being there, the

120

---

19 Sartre's note: Part One, Chapter 2, section II: Forms of bad faith.

for-itself can discover in itself nothing but its *motivations*, which means it will be constantly referred back to itself and to its constant freedom (I am there in order to . . . , etc.). But the contingency that permeates these motivations— and just to the extent to which they entirely found themselves— is the for-itself's facticity. The relation between the for-itself—which, as for-itself, is its own foundation—and facticity can correctly be denominated a factual necessity. And Descartes and Husserl grasped that factual necessity, precisely, as the source of the *cogito*'s evidence. The for-itself is necessary, insofar as it founds itself. And that is why it can be the reflected object of an apodictic intuition: I cannot doubt that I am. But as it is possible that this for-itself, as such, could not be, it has all the contingency of a fact. Just as my nihilating freedom apprehends itself through anguish, so the for-itself is conscious of its facticity: it feels itself to be entirely gratuitous; it apprehends itself as being there *for nothing*, as being *de trop*.

We must not confuse facticity with that Cartesian substance whose attribute is thinking. Of course, that thinking substance exists only insofar as it thinks and, as a created thing, it shares in the contingency of the *ens creatum*. But it *is*. It retains the character of in-itself in its entirety, even though the for-itself is its attribute. This has been described as Descartes's substantialist illusion. For us, on the contrary, the appearance of the for-itself, or the absolute event, is the sign of an in-itself's endeavor to found *itself*: it corresponds to an attempt, on the part of being, to remove contingency from its being. But this attempt leads to the in-itself's nihilation, because the in-itself cannot found *itself* without introducing the *itself*—a reflexive and nihilating referral—into the absolute identity of its being and without, in consequence, becoming degraded into for-itself. The for-itself corresponds therefore to a destruction and decompression of the in-itself, and the in-itself nihilates itself and absorbs itself in its attempt to found itself. The in-itself is not therefore a substance, of which the for-itself is an attribute, a substance able to produce thought without being exhausted in that very act of production. It merely remains within the for-itself like a memory of being, as its unjustifiable *presence to the world*. Being-in-itself can found its nothingness but not its being; in its movement of decompression it nihilates itself into a for-itself that, as for-itself, becomes its own foundation—but its in-itself contingency remains untouched. It is what *remains* of the in-itself as facticity within the for-itself and it is the reason why the for-itself has only a factual necessity, why the for-itself is the foundation of its *consciousness-being* or *existence*, but cannot ever found its *presence*. In this way, consciousness cannot ever prevent itself from being, and yet it is completely responsible for its being.

III. THE FOR-ITSELF AND THE BEING OF VALUE

Any study of human-reality must begin with the *cogito*. But the standpoint of Descartes's "I think" conceives of temporality in terms of instants. Can we find, within the *cogito*, a way of transcending this instantaneity? If human-reality were limited to the being of the *I think*, its only truth would be the truth of an instant. And it is quite true that human-reality is, in Descartes's view, an instantaneous totality, since by itself it makes no claim on the future, and since it requires a continuous act of "creation" to pass from one instant to another. But can we even conceive of the truth of an instant? And doesn't the *cogito* engage in its own way the past and the future? Heidegger is so persuaded that Husserl's *I think* is a fascinating mirage[20] by which we may get trapped that he avoids completely any recourse to consciousness in his description of *Dasein*. His aim is to show *Dasein* in the immediate form of *care*,[21] i.e., as it escapes from itself in its project of itself toward the possibilities that it *is*. He calls this project of the self outside itself "understanding" (*Verstand*), which allows him to establish human-reality as being "revealing-revealed." But this attempt to *begin* by demonstrating *Dasein*'s escaping from itself encounters insurmountable difficulties in its turn: we cannot eliminate the dimension of consciousness first, not even if we then reestablish it later. An understanding can have meaning only if it is conscious of understanding. My possibility can exist as my possibility only if it is my consciousness that escapes from itself toward it. Otherwise the entire system of being and its possibilities collapses into the unconscious, i.e., the in-itself. At this point we find ourselves thrown back toward the *cogito*. That has to be our starting point. Can we expand it, without losing what

---

20 TN: . . . *un piège aux alouettes fascinant et engluant* . . . The French idiom used here invokes a "trap for larks" (in which a mirror or decoy is used). A corresponding English idiom might be "smoke and mirrors."

21 TN: Sartre's word *souci* is the standard French translation for Heidegger's term *Sorge* in *Being and Time*, which is in turn standardly translated into English as "care."

we have gained from it, i.e., the evidence of reflection? What has our description of the for-itself taught us?

In the first place, we have encountered a nihilation that is assigned, by the for-itself's being, to its being. And this revelation of nothingness did not seem to go beyond the boundaries of the *cogito*. But let us look more closely.

The for-itself cannot support its nihilation without determining itself as a *lack of being*. The nihilation, therefore, cannot coincide merely with the introduction of a void into consciousness. The in-itself has not been expelled from consciousness by any external being; instead, it is the for-itself that constantly determines itself *not to be* the in-itself. In other words, it can found itself only on the basis of, and against, the in-itself. Thus nihilation, as a nihilation of being, represents the original connection between the for-itself's being and the in-itself's being. The material and real in-itself lies wholly present at the heart of consciousness, as that which it determines itself not to be. The *cogito* ought to lead us necessarily to encounter this presence, complete and out of reach, of the in-itself. And, of course, the fact of this presence just is the for-itself's transcendence. But the origin of transcendence, conceived as the for-itself's original connection with the in-itself, is precisely nihilation. In this way we can glimpse a way of getting out of the *cogito*. And indeed we will see, later on, that the *cogito*'s innermost meaning is that, essentially, of an expulsion outside itself. But we are not yet ready to describe this characteristic of the for-itself. What our ontological description has made immediately apparent is that this being founds itself as a lack of being, i.e., it becomes determined in its being by a being that it is not.

However, there are many ways of not being, and some of them do not attain the inner nature of the being that is not what it is not. If, for example, I say of an inkwell that "it is not a bird," the inkwell and the bird remain untouched by the negation. The latter is an external relation that can be established only by a human-reality witness. By contrast, there is a type of negation that establishes an internal relation between what we negate and what our negation applies to.[22] Of all the internal negations, the one that

22 Sartre's note: Hegel's opposition belongs to this type of negation. But this opposition must itself be founded on a basic internal negation, i.e., on a lack. If, for example, the inessential becomes in its turn the essential, that is because it is felt as a lack within the essential.

penetrates most deeply into being—the one that constitutes *in its being* the being *to which* its negation applies with the being *that* it negates—is the *lack*. This lack does not belong to the nature of the in-itself, which is entirely positive. It appears within the world only when human-reality arises. Only within the human world can there be any lacks. A lack presupposes a trinity: the item that is missing; that from which it is missing, or the existent; and a totality that is broken apart by the lack, and which could be restored by the synthesis of the missing item with the existent: that which is *missed* [manqué].[23] For human-reality, the being that is delivered to intuition is always *that from which something is missing*, or the existent. For example, if I say that the moon is not full and that a quarter is missing from it, I make this judgment on the basis of a full intuition of a crescent moon. Thus, what is given to intuition is an in-itself that is neither complete nor incomplete in itself but which *is* quite simply what it *is*, without any relation to other beings. In order for this in-itself to be grasped as a crescent moon, a human-reality must surpass the given toward the project of the actualized totality—in this case, the full moon's disc—and then return toward the given in order to constitute it as a crescent moon, or, in other words, in order to actualize it in its being, on the basis of the totality that becomes its foundation. And in this same act of surpassing, the *missing item* will be posited as the item whose synthetic addition to the existent would reconstitute the synthetic totality of that which is missed [manqué]. In this sense the *missing item* shares a common nature with the existent: a reversal of the situation is sufficient for it to become the existent from which the missing item is missing, while the existent becomes the missing item. This missing item, as the complement of the existent, is determined in its being by the synthetic totality of that which is missed. Thus, *in the human world*, the incomplete being that is delivered to intuition as a missing item is constituted in its being by that which is missed [manqué], i.e., by what it is not. The full moon is what endows the crescent moon with its crescent being; what is not determines what is; it is characteristic of the existent's being—as the correlative to a human transcendence—to lead out of itself and right up to the being that it is not, which is its *meaning*.

123

---

23 TN: Sartre's stylistic effects in this sentence are not fully translatable into English. In particular "missed" does not fully capture Sartre's pun, where *manqué* means both "missed" and "failed." See my note on *manquer* in Notes on the Translation.

Human-reality, through which lacks can appear in the world, must itself be a lack. For it is only by means of a lack that a lack can come from being; the in-itself cannot be the occasion of a lack in the in-itself. In other terms, in order for being to be either a missing item or something missed, it is necessary that some being should make itself its own lack: only a being from which something is missing can surpass being toward that which is missed [*manqué*].

The existence of desire as a human fact suffices to prove that human-reality is a lack. How indeed can we explain desire if we try to see it as a psychological *state*, i.e., as a being whose nature is to be what it is? A being that is what it is (to the extent that we view it as being what it is) does not call for anything to make itself complete. An unfinished circle only calls to be finished insofar as it is surpassed by human transcendence. In itself it is complete as an open curve, and perfectly positive. A psychological state whose existence had the sufficiency of that curve could not in addition make the slightest "call" for anything else: it would be itself, without any relation to anything other than itself; in order to constitute it as hunger or thirst, an external transcendence would be required, surpassing it toward the totality of "assuaged hunger," as it surpasses the crescent moon toward the full moon. We cannot get out of this difficulty by making desire into a *conatus*, conceived on the model of a physical force. That is because, once again, even if we concede that it has causal efficacy, no *conatus* can possess, in itself, the qualities of an appetite in relation to another state. As a *producer* of acts, the *conatus* cannot be identified with desire as something that *calls* for some state. No recourse to psychophysiological parallelism can enable us to escape these difficulties: thirst as an organic phenomenon, as a "physiological" need for water, does not exist. An organism deprived of water presents certain positive phenomena—for example, a certain coagulating thickening of the liquid blood—which in their turn provoke other phenomena. Taken together, these amount to a positive state of the organism, referring only to itself; similarly, we cannot regard the thickening of a solution whose water evaporates as a desire, on the part of the solution, for water. If we assume an exact correspondence between the mental and the physiological, that correspondence can be established only on the basis of an ontological identity—as Spinoza saw. In consequence, the being of psychological thirst must be the being in itself of a *state* and we are directed,

124

once again, to the transcendence of a witness. But then the thirst will be a desire for that transcendence, and not for itself: it will be a desire in the eyes of the Other. If desire must be able to relate to itself as a desire, it must itself be transcendence; i.e., it must be in the desire's nature to escape from itself toward the desired object. In other terms, it must be a lack—but not an object-lack, or a lack that is suffered, created by an act of surpassing that it is not: it must be its own lack of. . . . Desire is a lack of being, and is haunted in its innermost being by the being that it desires. In this way, desire testifies to the existence of a lack in human-reality's being. But if human-reality is a lack, then it is through human-reality that the trinity of the existent, the missing item, and the missed [manqué] arises within being. What are the three terms in this trinity, in point of fact?

In this case, the element that plays the role of the existent is given to the *cogito* as the immediacy of the desire; for example, it is this for-itself, which we have grasped as not being what it is and being what it is not. But what kind of being belongs to that which is missed [manqué]?

To answer this question, we need to return to the idea of the lack, and to determine more precisely the connection between an existent and the item that is missing from it. This connection cannot be mere contiguity. If the missing item is so profoundly present—in its very absence—at the heart of the existent, that is because the existent and the missing item are apprehended and surpassed all at once, within the unity of a single totality. And something can only constitute itself as a lack by surpassing itself toward a large, disaggregated form. In this way the lack makes its appearance against the ground of a totality. Moreover, it does not matter whether this totality was originally given, and has now been broken up ("the arms of the Venus de Milo *are missing* . . ."), or whether it has not yet ever been actualized ("What is missing in his case is courage"). What matters is only that the missing item and the existent should be given or apprehended as needing to be annihilated within the unity of the missed [manquée] totality. Any missing item is missing from . . . for . . . And what is given within the basic event of arising is the for, conceived either as not yet being or as no longer being: as an absence toward which the truncated existent, which is constituted by that very means as truncated, surpasses itself or is surpassed. What is the for that characterizes human-reality?

The for-itself, as the foundation of itself, is where negation arises. It founds itself insofar as it negates of itself a certain being or way of being. As we know, what it negates or nihilates is being-in-itself. But not just any being-in-itself: human-reality is first and foremost its own nothingness. What it negates or nihilates of itself, as for-itself, can only be itself.[24] And, as it is constituted in its meaning by this nihilation and by this presence within it—as the nihilated—of what it nihilates, human-reality's meaning consists in the missed [manqué] itself-as-being-in-itself. Insofar as human-reality, in its basic relation to itself, is not what it is, its relation to itself is not basic, and can derive its meaning only from an earlier relation: the null relation, or identity. What allows us to grasp the for-itself as not being what it is is an "itself" that is able to be what it is; the relation that is negated in the definition of the for-itself—and which, as such, must first be postulated—is a relation, given as constantly absent, of the for-itself to itself, in the mode of identity. The meaning of that subtle trouble through which thirst escapes from itself and (insofar as it is consciousness of thirst) is not thirst is a thirst that is able to be thirst, which haunts it. What is missing from the for-itself is the "itself"—or its own self as in-itself.

Nonetheless, we should not confuse this missed in-itself with the in-itself of facticity. Facticity's in-itself, in its failure to found itself, is swallowed up into the for-itself's pure presence to the world. The missed in-itself, on the contrary, is pure absence. In addition, the failure of the founding act will have made the for-itself arise out of the in-itself, as the foundation of its own nothingness. But the meaning of the missed [manqué] founding act remains as something transcendent. The for-itself is, in its being, a failure because it is only its own foundation insofar as it is nothingness. In truth, this failure is its very being, but it can have meaning only if it apprehends itself as a failure in the presence of the being that it has failed to be, i.e., the being that could be the foundation of its being and no longer the foundation only of its nothingness, the being that is able to be its own foundation as self-coincidence. The cogito refers, in its nature, to what it misses,

---

24 TN: . . . ce ne peut être que soi. In this passage I use "itself" to express what I take to be Sartre's core idea (using occasional variants or additional words where these are needed to communicate additional meaning). See my note on soi in Notes on the Translation.

and to what is missing from it, because—as Descartes clearly saw— it is a *cogito* haunted by being. And such is the origin of transcendence: human-reality is its own surpassing toward what it misses; it surpasses itself toward the particular being that it would be if it were what it is. Human-reality is not something that can exist first, in order to find itself, afterward, missing this or that item: it exists from the outset as a lack, and in an immediate synthetic link with its missing item. In this way, the pure event through which human-reality arises in the form of presence to the world is its apprehension of itself as being *its own lack*. Human-reality grasps itself in its arrival within existence as an incomplete being. It grasps itself as being insofar as it is not, in the presence of the particular totality that is what it is, and that it misses, and that it is in the form of not being it. Human-reality is a constant surpassing toward a self-coincidence that is never given. If the *cogito extends* toward being, that is because it surpasses itself toward being, through its very elevation, by qualifying itself in its being as the being from which the self-coincidence needed to be what it is is missing. The *cogito* is inseparably linked to being-in-itself, not like a thought in relation to its object (which would make the in-itself relative) but like something missing in relation to the thing that determines what it is missing. In this sense, Descartes's second proof is rigorous: imperfect being surpasses itself toward perfect being: the being that is the foundation only of its nothingness surpasses itself toward the being that is the foundation of its being. But the being toward which human-reality surpasses itself is not a transcendent God: it lies at its own heart; it is only itself, in the form of a totality.

In fact, this totality is not the pure and simple contingent in-itself of something transcendent. If the being toward which consciousness surpasses itself were grasped as pure in-itself, it would coincide with the annihilation of consciousness. But what consciousness surpasses itself toward is not its annihilation; it does not wish to lose itself, at the limit of its surpassing, within the in-itself of identity. The for-itself claims being-in-itself for the for-itself as such.

Thus this constantly absent being which haunts the for-itself is itself— but frozen into in-itself. It is the impossible synthesis of the for-itself and the in-itself: able to be its own foundation, not as a nothingness but as being, and able to retain within it the necessary translucency of consciousness, at the same time as the self-coincidence of being in itself. It will preserve, within it, the self-return that conditions every necessity and foundation. But this self-return will occur without any distance; it will not in any way be a self-presence but, instead, a self-identity. In short, this being will be exactly the *itself*, whose existence—as we have shown—can only be a constantly evanescent relation, but it will be that "itself" as a substantial being. Thus human-reality arises as such, in the presence of its own totality or its own itself, as the lack of this totality. And it is in the nature of this totality that it cannot be given, since, in it, the incompatible characteristics of the in-itself and the for-itself are gathered together. And let nobody reproach us for freely inventing a being of this kind: when the being and the absolute absence of this totality are hypostasized—through an additional movement of mediation—as a transcendence beyond the world, it goes by the name of God. And isn't God both a being who is what he is, insofar as he is entire positivity and the foundation of the world—and, at the same time, a being who is not what he is and who is what he is not, insofar as he is conscious of himself, and is his own necessary foundation? Human-reality suffers in its being because it arises in being as constantly haunted by a totality that it is, without being able to be it, just because it could never attain the in-itself without losing itself as for-itself. It is therefore in its nature an unhappy consciousness, without   127 any possibility of surpassing its state of unhappiness.

But what exactly is this being, in its being, toward which the unhappy consciousness surpasses itself? Should we say that it does not exist? The contradictions in it that we have brought to light show only that it cannot be *actualized* [or *realized*]. And nothing can defeat this self-evident truth: consciousness can exist only as *committed* within this being, which surrounds it from all sides and permeates it with its ghostly presence—this being that consciousness is, and which, however, is not it. Should we say this being is *relative* to consciousness? That would be to confuse it with the object of a *thesis*.[25] This being is not posited by consciousness, and in front of it: there is no consciousness of this being, since it haunts our non-thetic consciousness (of) self. It marks consciousness as the meaning of its being, and it is no more conscious of it than it is conscious

---

25 TN: . . . *l'objet d'une thèse*. By "thesis," Sartre means a thetic act of consciousness, in which an object is explicitly posited – as contrasted, as the text goes on to explain, with the "non-thetic" consciousness exemplified in the prereflective *cogito*.

of itself. However, it cannot escape from consciousness either: rather, insofar as it brings itself to being as the consciousness (of) being, it is there. And it is precisely not consciousness that confers this meaning on this being, as it does with this inkwell or this pencil: rather, without this being that it is in the form of not being it, consciousness would not be consciousness, i.e., a lack; on the contrary, it is from it that consciousness derives for itself its own significance as consciousness. It arises at the same time as consciousness, in its heart and, at the same time, outside it. It is absolute transcendence within absolute immanence; it has no priority over consciousness and nor does consciousness have any priority over it: they *make a couple*. Doubtless it could not exist without the for-itself, but nor could the for-itself exist without it. Consciousness maintains itself in relation to this being in the mode of *being* this being—because this being is consciousness itself—but as a being that it cannot be. It is consciousness itself, at the heart of itself and out of reach, unrealizable and like an absence, and its nature is to contain its own contradiction within itself; its relation to the for-itself is a complete immanence that ends up as a complete transcendence.

We should not conceive of this being, moreover, as being present to consciousness with only the abstract characteristics we have established in our investigation. A concrete consciousness arises in situation and is a particular and individualized consciousness of this situation and (of) itself in situation. The "itself" is present to this concrete consciousness and every concrete characteristic of consciousness has its correlative within the totality of the itself. The "itself" is individual, and it haunts the for-itself as its individual completion. A feeling, for example, is a feeling in the presence of a norm, i.e., a feeling that is of the same type, but one that can be what it is. This norm, or this totality of the affective self, is directly present as a lack that is *suffered* in the very heart of suffering. We suffer, and we suffer through not suffering enough. The suffering that we talk about is never quite the suffering that we feel. What we call the "greatest" or "best" or "true" suffering—a suffering that moves us—is the suffering we can read on others' faces or, better still, on portraits, on a statue's face, on a tragic mask. This suffering has *being*. It presents itself to us as an objective and compact whole, which did not need our arrival in order to be, and which overflows our consciousness of it: it is there, in the midst of the world, and it persists, impenetrable and dense, like

128

this tree or this stone; in short, it is what it is; we can talk about it as "that suffering there," the suffering expressed by this rictus, or this frown. It is supported and presented by the physiognomy but not created by it. Upon it, the suffering, which is beyond passivity and activity, beyond negation and affirmation, has been placed: it is. And yet it can be only in the form of self-consciousness. We are fully aware that this mask does not express the unconscious grimace of somebody sleeping, or the rictus of somebody dead: it refers us to possibles, to a situation in the world. The suffering is a conscious relationship to these possibles, to this situation, but made solid, and cast in the bronze of being, and it is as such that it fascinates us; it is like a degraded approximation of the suffering-in-itself that haunts our own suffering. The suffering that I feel, on the contrary, is never suffering enough, because it nihilates itself as in itself, in the very act through which it founds itself. It escapes itself as suffering toward my consciousness of suffering. I can never be *surprised* by it, because it is only to the exact degree in which I feel it. Its translucency deprives it of any depth. I cannot observe it, as I observe the statue's suffering, since I make it and I know it. If I must suffer, I would like my suffering to take hold of me and overflow me like a storm: but, on the contrary, I am obliged in my free spontaneity to raise it into existence. I would like to be it and at the same time to undergo it, but this huge and opaque suffering, which would transport me out of myself, continually brushes past me with its wing and I am unable to take hold of it; I can find only *myself*, my complaining, moaning self, the self who must, in order to actualize this suffering that I am, relentlessly put on the performance of suffering. I wring my hands, or I shout, in order that beings in themselves—sounds and gestures—might race throughout the world, ridden by the suffering in itself that I am unable to be. Every groan, every facial expression of the suffering person, aims to sculpt an in itself statue out of suffering. But this statue can exist only through others, and only for others. My suffering suffers from being what it is not, from not being what it is; just as it is on the point of catching up with itself it escapes from itself, and is separated from itself by nothing, by this nothingness of which it is itself the foundation. My suffering chatters, because it is not enough—but its ideal is silence. It is the silence of a statue, of the overburdened man who lowers his head and conceals his face without saying anything. But it is *for me* that this silent man does not speak. Within himself, he chatters

129   inexhaustibly, because the words of his inner speech are like first drafts of the "itself" of his suffering. It is in my eyes that his suffering "crushes" him: in himself he feels himself responsible for this pain that he wants, while he does not want it, and does not want, while he wants it—a pain that is haunted by that constant absence of the motionless and mute suffering that is *itself*, the concrete and unattainable totality of the suffering for-itself, the *for* of human-reality in its suffering.[26] As we can see, this suffering-itself, which attends my suffering, is never *posited* by the latter. And my actual suffering is not an *endeavor* to attain the "itself." But it can only *be* suffering as a consciousness (of) *not being enough* suffering, in the presence of that complete and absent suffering.

We are able now to determine the being of the "itself" more clearly: it is value. In fact value has that twofold character—which moralists have barely begun to explain—of being unconditionally, and not being. In effect, value possesses being, insofar as it is value; but, precisely insofar as it is encountered in reality, this normative existent has no being. Its being is to be value, i.e., not to be being. Thus value's being, insofar as it is value, is the being of something that has no being. Value seems, therefore, to elude us: if we take it as being, we run the risk of completely failing to recognize its unreality and, like the sociologists, turning it into a factual requirement among other facts. In this case, the contingency of being kills the value. But, conversely, if we look only at the ideality of values, we will deprive them of their being and, without any being, they collapse. Of course, as Scheler showed, I can manage to intuit values on the basis of concrete examples: I can grasp nobility in a noble action.[27] But, apprehended in this way, value is not given as existing at the same level of being as the act that it renders valuable—in the way, for example, that the essence of "red" is related to a particular instance of red. It is given as lying beyond the actions we consider—for example, as the limit to the infinite progression of all noble actions. Value is beyond being. However, if we are not to be led astray by words, we must acknowledge

---

26 TN: . . . *en souffrance*. There is an untranslatable pun here, as the French expression *en souffrance* is also used to characterize something (e.g., a payment or delivery) that is overdue, or outstanding.

27 TN: Sartre has already alluded to Scheler in Part One. The phenomenological account of values to which Sartre refers here is available in translation as Scheler (1973).

at the least that this being that lies beyond being does in some way possess being. These considerations enable us to recognize that value arrives in the world through human-reality. Now, the meaning of value is to be that toward which some being surpasses its being: any action that is valued separates itself from its being toward. . . . As value, always and everywhere, lies beyond every act of surpassing, it may be regarded as the unconditioned unity of all the surpassings of being. And it thereby forms a pair with the being that surpasses its being from the outset, and through which surpassing enters being, i.e., with human-reality. And we can also see that value, as the unconditioned "beyond" of all surpassings, must be the original "beyond" of just that being which does the surpassing, because only in that way can it be the original "beyond" of 130 every possible surpassing. Indeed, if every act of surpassing must be able to be surpassed, the being that surpasses must *a priori* be surpassed, just *insofar as* it is the very source of all surpassing; thus value in its origin—or the supreme value—is the "beyond" and the *for* of transcendence. It is the "beyond" that surpasses and founds all my acts of surpassing, but toward which I can never surpass myself, precisely because my acts of surpassing presuppose it. It is what is *missed* [*manqué*] by every lack, not what is missing from it. Value is the "itself" insofar as it haunts the for-itself at its heart, as that for which it is. The supreme value toward which consciousness surpasses itself at every moment through its very being is the absolute being of the "itself," with its attributes of identity, purity, permanence, etc., and insofar as it is the foundation of itself. This allows us to understand how value can, at the same time, be and not be. It is like the meaning and the "beyond" of every act of surpassing; it is like the absent in-itself that haunts being for itself. But as soon as we examine it, we can see that value itself surpasses this being-in-itself, since that in-itself *is given to it*. It is beyond its own being, since—as its being enjoys self-coincidence—it immediately surpasses that being, with its permanence, its purity, its consistency, its identity, and its silence, as it lays claim to these qualities in its capacity as self-presence. And reciprocally, if we start out by considering it as self-presence, this presence becomes immediately solidified and frozen into in-itself. And furthermore, value is in its own being the missed totality toward which a being makes itself be. It arises for any being not insofar as that being is, in its full contingency, what it is but insofar as it is the foundation of its own nihilation.

In this sense, value haunts being insofar as it founds itself and not insofar as it is: it haunts *freedom*. So value's relation to the for-itself is quite
distinctive: it is the being that the for-itself has to be, insofar as it is the
foundation of its nothingness of being. And if the for-itself has this being
to be, that is not because it is in the grip of some external constraint;
nor is it because value—like Aristotle's prime mover—exerts a *de facto*
attraction over it; nor is it in virtue of some character it receives from
its being; rather, it is because it makes itself be in its being as having to
be this being. In brief, the *itself*, the for-itself, and their relationship are
at one and the same time held within the limits of an unconditioned
freedom—in the sense in which *nothing* can make value exist, other than
the freedom that simultaneously makes me exist myself—and within the
boundaries of concrete facticity insofar as the for-itself, as the foundation
of its nothingness, cannot be the foundation of its being. *Being-for-value*,
therefore, is characterized by a complete contingency which thereafter
affects morality in its entirety, penetrating it and relativizing it—and at
the same time by a free and absolute necessity.[28]

¹³¹ (marginal: 131)

Value, as it first arises, is not *posited* by the for-itself: it is consubstantial
with it—to such an extent that no consciousness exists without being
haunted by *its* value and, in its broad sense, "human-reality" includes the
for-itself and value. If value haunts the for-itself without being posited
by it, that is because it is not the object of a thesis: for that, the for-itself
would have to be a posited object in relation to itself, since value and the
for-itself can arise only within the consubstantial unity of a pair. Thus the

---

28 Sartre's note: It is perhaps tempting to translate into Hegelian terms the trinity we are
examining, and to make the in-itself into the thesis, the for-itself into the antithesis,
and the in-itself-for-itself—or Value—the synthesis. But we should note here that, if
the in-itself is *missing* from for-itself, the for-itself is not missing from the in-itself. The
opposition is not therefore reciprocal. In brief, the for-itself remains inessential and
contingent in relation to the in-itself, and this inessential character is what we referred
to earlier as "facticity." In addition, although the synthesis or Value does indeed return
to the thesis and therefore involves a self-return, it is an unrealizable totality, and so
the for-itself is not a moment that can be surpassed. As such, its nature is much closer
to Kierkegaard's "ambiguous" realities. In addition, we find here a twofold structure of
unilateral oppositions: in one sense, the in-itself is missing from the for-itself, and the
for-itself is not missing from the in-itself – but, in another sense, what is missing from
the for-itself is its possible (or the missing for-itself), while the for-itself, again, is not
missing from the possible.

for-itself, as a non-thetic consciousness (of) self, does not exist *confronting* value, in the sense in which, for Leibniz, the monad exists "alone, before God."[29] Value is not therefore known at this stage, since knowledge posits its object and confronts consciousness with it. Value is given only alongside the non-thetic translucency of the for-itself, which makes itself be as conscious of being; it is everywhere and nowhere, at the heart of the nihilating "reflection-reflected" relation, present and out of reach, lived simply as the concrete meaning of this lack that constitutes my present being. In order for value to become the object of a thesis, the for-itself that it haunts must appear before the reflective gaze. Indeed, reflective consciousness posits the reflected *Erlebnis* in its nature as a lack, and at the same time it brings value to light, as the unreachable meaning of what has been missed [*manqué*]. Thus reflective consciousness can properly be said to be a moral consciousness, since it cannot arise without at the same time disclosing values. It goes without saying that I remain free, in my reflective consciousness, to direct my attention toward these values or to overlook them—exactly as it is up to me whether to look more closely at my pen or at my packet of tobacco on this table. But whether or not these values become the object of detailed attention, they *are*.

We should not conclude from this, however, that value can appear only to the reflective point of view, and that we analogically project the values of our for-itself into the transcendent world. If the object of intuition is a phenomenon belonging to human-reality, but a transcendent one, it is immediately disclosed with its value, because the Other's for-itself is not a hidden phenomenon that might present itself only as the conclusion to an argument by analogy. It is manifested from the outset to my for-itself and—as we will see—its presence as for-the-Other is a necessary condition of the constitution of the for-itself as such. And value is given as the for-the-Other arises, just as it is given—although in a different mode of being—in the for-itself's arising. But we cannot discuss the way values are encountered objectively in the world until we have elucidated the nature of the for-the-Other. We will defer our examination of this question, therefore, to Part Three of this work.

132

---

29 TN: Although the sentence suggests this quote comes from Leibniz, I have not been able to find it there verbatim. However, it is consonant with Leibniz's claims about how to conceive our relationship to God.

IV. THE FOR-ITSELF AND THE BEING OF POSSIBLES[30]

We have seen that human-reality is a lack and that, as a for-itself, it lacks a certain self-coincidence. In concrete terms, some particular and concrete reality is missing from each individual for-itself (Erlebnis), whose synthetic assimilation would transform it into itself. It is missing some . . . for . . . as the dented disc of the moon is missing some of what is required for it to be complete, and to be transformed into a full moon. In this way, the missing item arises in the process of transcendence and is determined in a return to the existent, from the standpoint of what has been missed [manqué]. Defined in this way, the missing item is transcendent in relation to the existent, and its complement. Its nature, therefore, is the same: the item that the moon's crescent is missing, in order for it to be the moon, is precisely a part of the moon; the item missing from the obtuse angle ABC, in order to make two right angles, is the angle CBD. What is missing therefore from the for-itself, in order for it to become inte-grated within the "itself," is some for-itself. But a stranger's for-itself—in other words, a for-itself that I am not—would not work here. In fact, since the ideal that has appeared is that of self-coincidence, the for-itself that is missing is a for-itself that I am. But, on the other hand, if I were that for-itself in the mode of identity, the whole structure would become in-itself. I am the missing for-itself in the mode of having to be the for-itself that I am not, in order to identify myself with it in the unity of the "itself." In this way the for-itself's initial relation of transcendence is constantly drafting something like a project of identification, in which the for-itself is identified with an absent for-itself that it is and that is missing from it. What is given in the case of each for-itself as its own missing item—and which is strictly determined as missing from this precise for-itself, and none other—is the for-itself's possible. The possible arises from the depths of the for-itself's nihilation. It is not thematically conceived afterward as a means of uniting with the "itself." But the for-itself's arising as the nihilation of the in-itself, and as a decompression of being, gives rise to the possible as one aspect of this decompression of being, i.e., as a way of being at a distance from the "itself" that we are. Thus the for-itself cannot appear without being haunted by value, and projected toward its

133

---

30 TN: . . . l'être des possibles. See my note on possible in Notes on the Translation.

own possibles. However, the moment the *cogito* directs us toward its possibles, it chases us out of the instant and toward what it is, in the mode of not-being it.

But to understand more fully how human-reality is, and at the same is not, its own possibilities, we must return to this notion of the *possible* and try to elucidate it.

We can say the same about the possible as about value; we have the greatest difficulty understanding its being, because it presents itself as preceding the being whose pure possibility it is, and yet—at least as a possible—it surely must have being. Do we not say: "It is possible that he will come?" We are willing, after Leibniz, to describe as "possible" any event that is not engaged within an existing causal series (such that we can determine it with certainty), and that does not contain any contradiction, either with itself or with the system we are dealing with. Defined in this way, the possible is only possible with respect to knowledge, since we are incapable of affirming, or denying, the possible at hand. It follows that there are two attitudes which we can adopt in relation to the possible: we can take the view, like Spinoza, that it exists only from the standpoint of our ignorance, and that, when our ignorance vanishes, the possible vanishes. In this case, the possible is only a subjective stage on our path to perfect knowledge: its only reality is that of a psychological mode; it possesses concrete being insofar as it is a confused or truncated thought, but not as a property of the world. But it is also permissible to make the infinite number of possibles, as Leibniz does, the object of thoughts in a divine understanding, which confers on them a kind of absolute reality; here, the power to actualize the best system within the possibles is reserved for the divine will. In this case, although the sequence of the monad's perceptions is strictly determined, and an all-knowing being is able—on the basis of the very formulation of his substance—to establish Adam's decision with certainty, it is not absurd to say "It is possible that Adam will not pick the apple." That means only that there exists, as a thought in the divine understanding, some other system of compossibles in which Adam appears as not having eaten the fruit of the tree of Knowledge.[31] But is this account so different from Spinoza's? In fact, the possible's reality is exclusively that of divine thought, which

---

31 TN: "Compossible" is an adjective used by Leibniz to mean individuals that are capable of existing alongside each other, i.e., in the same possible world.

means its being is that of a thought that has not been actualized. Of course the idea of subjectivity is taken to its limit here, because we are 134   talking about a divine consciousness, not mine; and if we have taken care to merge subjectivity and finitude together from the outset, subjectivity will disappear once the understanding becomes infinite. It remains no less true that the possible is a thought that is *only a thought*. Leibniz himself seems to have wanted to bestow on his possibles an autonomy and a kind of weight of their own, since in many of the metaphysical fragments published by Couturat[32] we are shown the possibles organizing themselves into systems of compossibles and the fullest, richest system tending toward its own actualization. But this is only the outline of a doctrine, and Leibniz did not develop it—probably because it could not be developed: to give the possibles a tendency toward being means either that the possible already consists of full being and has the same type of being as being (in the sense in which we can give the bud a tendency to become a flower) or that the possible at the heart of the divine understanding is already an idea-force and that the system organizing the maximum number of idea-forces automatically triggers the divine will. But in this latter case we do not leave subjectivity. If, therefore, we define the possible as non-contradictory, it can have being only as the thought of some being prior to the real world, or prior to any pure knowledge of the world as it is. In both cases, the possible ceases to have the nature of a possible, and is absorbed into the subjective being of a representation.

But this being-represented of the possible cannot explain the possible's nature, since, on the contrary, it destroys it. In our everyday way of using it, we do not grasp the possible in any way as an aspect of our ignorance, or as a non-contradictory structure that belongs to some unactualized world in the margins of our world here. The possible appears to us as a property of beings. It is after I have glanced at the sky that I decree: "It is possible that it will rain," and here I do not understand "possible" to mean "not in contradiction with the present state of

---

32 TN: Louis Couturat (1868–1914) was a French philosopher, author of an influential book about Leibniz, *La Logique de Leibniz*. The collection of previously unpublished writings by Leibniz which Couturat edited, and to which Sartre refers here, is *Opuscules et Fragments Inédits de Leibniz* (Paris, 1903).

the sky." This possibility belongs to the sky like a threat, it represents a surpassing of the clouds that I perceive toward the rain, and this surpassing is borne by the clouds themselves—which does not mean that it will be actualized but simply that the structure of the cloud's being is transcendence toward the rain. Here the possibility is given as belonging to a particular being, of which it is a *power*, as can be seen quite clearly in the fact that we may equally say, about a friend we are waiting for: "It is possible he will come" or "He *may come*." Thus the possible cannot be reduced to a subjective reality. Nor does it precede the real or the true. Rather it is a concrete property of realities which already exist. For the rain to be possible, there must be clouds in the sky. The attempt to eliminate being in order to establish the possible in its pure state is absurd: the frequently quoted procession, advancing from non-being to being and passing through the possible, does not correspond to reality. Certainly, a possible state is not yet; but it is the possible state of a specific existent that supports through its being the possibility and the non-being of its future state.

There is an evident risk that these remarks will lead us to Aristotle's "potentiality." And we will be thrown from Charybdis onto Scylla if, by avoiding a purely *logical* conception of the possible, we fall back into a *magical* conception. Being-in-itself can neither "be as a potentiality" nor "have potentialities." In itself, it is what it is, in the absolute plenitude of its identity. The cloud is not "rain as a potentiality"; it is, in itself, a particular quantity of water vapor that is—at a given temperature and pressure—strictly what it is. The in-itself is in actuality.[33] But we can understand quite clearly how the scientific viewpoint, in its attempt to dehumanize the world, regarded possibles as potentialities and eliminated them by turning them into mere subjective outcomes of our logical calculation, and of our ignorance. The first part of the scientific approach is correct: the possible arrives in the world through human-reality. These clouds can change into rain only if I surpass them toward the rain, just as the moon's dented disc is only missing a crescent if I surpass it toward the full moon. But, after that, was it really necessary to turn the possible into a mere given of our psychological subjectivity? Just as there can be

135

---

33 TN: *L'en-soi est en acte*. The last two words belong to Aristotelian terminology, and are most often translated into English as "in actuality."

a lack in the world only if the lack arrives in the world through a being that is its own lack, so too can there be no possibility in the world unless it arrives through a being that is, in relation to itself, its own possibility. But the essence of possibility is, precisely, its non-coincidence with the mere *thought* of possibilities. In point of fact, if possibility is not given from the outset as an objective structure of beings, or of a particular being, thought—however we conceive of it—will not be able to contain the possible within it, as its thought content. Indeed, if we reflect on the possibles that lie at the heart of the divine understanding, as the content of divine thought, we will see that they become pure and simple *concrete representations.* Let us allow purely hypothetically—and even though we are unable to understand how a being that is entirely positive could acquire this negative power—that God has the power of negation, in other words that he can make negative judgments about his representations: even so, we will remain unable to grasp how he could transform these representations into *possibles.* At the most, the effect of the negation would be to constitute them as "lacking correspondence in reality." But to say that the Centaur does not exist is not at all to say that he is possible. Neither affirmation nor negation can confer the character of possibility on a representation. And, in response to the suggestion that a synthesis of negation and affirmation might produce this character, we can point out that a synthesis is not a sum, and that this synthesis has to be accounted for as an organic totality endowed with its own meaning, and not on the basis of the elements it synthesizes. Similarly, the subjective and negative act of noticing our ignorance about the relation to reality of one of our ideas could not, on its own, account for that representation's character of possibility: it could only place us in a state of indifference in relation to it, but it could not confer that *right* over reality which is the possible's fundamental structure. And, in response to the further claim that various tendencies incline me to prefer this outcome or that, we can say that, far from being explained by these tendencies, my transcendence is, on the contrary, presupposed by them: as we have seen, they must already exist as a lack. And further, if the possible is not in some way given, these tendencies may induce us to *wish* that my representation adequately corresponds to reality, but they cannot confer on me a right over reality. In brief, any apprehension of a possible as such presupposes an original surpassing. Any attempt to establish the possible on the basis of a subjectivity construed as being what it is—i.e., as closed in upon itself—is necessarily doomed to fail.

But if it is true that the possible is an option on being, and if it is true that the possible can arrive in the world only through a being that is its own possibility, it follows that human-reality must necessarily be its being in the form of an option on its being. Possibility is in play when, rather than being purely and simply what I am, I am as the Right to be what I am. But this right itself separates me from what I have the right to be. The right to property appears only when someone contests my property, when, in fact, it is in some aspect already no longer mine: my tranquil enjoyment of what I possess is straightforwardly a fact, and not a right. For there to be a possible, therefore, human-reality must, insofar as it is itself, be something other than itself. The possible is that element of the for-itself whose nature it is to escape from the for-itself, insofar as it is for-itself. The possible is a new aspect of the nihilation of the in-itself into for-itself.

If the possible can arrive in the world only through a being that is its own possibility, that is because the in-itself—whose nature is to be what it is—cannot "have" any possibles. Its relation to a possibility can only be established externally, by a being who is placed before the possibilities themselves. The possibility of being stopped by a fold in the carpet belongs neither to the rolling marble nor to the carpet: it can arise only within a system in which the marble and the carpet are organized by a being who has an understanding of the possibles. But this understanding cannot come from *outside*, from the in-itself, and it cannot be limited to being only a thought, as a subjective mode of consciousness: it must coincide with the objective structure of the being who understands possibles. To understand possibility as possibility, or to be one's own possibilities: these amount to one and the same necessity for the being in whom, in its being, there is a question of its being. But to be one's own possibility—i.e., to define oneself through it—is precisely to define   137
oneself through the part of oneself that one is not; it is to define oneself as an escaping-from-oneself toward. . . . In brief, the moment I want to account for my immediate being insofar, quite simply, as it is what it is not and is not what it is, I am thrown back outside it, toward a meaning that is unreachable and which cannot in any way be identified with an immanent subjective representation. In grasping himself through the

cogito in the form of *doubt*, Descartes cannot hope to define this doubt as "methodic doubt"—or even just as doubt—if he limits himself to what the pure instantaneous viewpoint is able to grasp. Doubt can be understood only on the basis of the constantly open possibility that a piece of evidence will "remove" it; it can be grasped as doubt only insofar as it refers to possibilities of the ἐποχή that are not yet actualized but remain open. There is no fact of consciousness that can properly be said to be *this* consciousness—even if, like Husserl and somewhat artificially, we endow the internal structure of this consciousness with protentions[34] which, as they do not have in their being any means of surpassing the consciousness to whose structure they belong, will pitifully cave in on themselves and resemble flies who bang their noses against a window without being able to pass through the pane. As soon as we want to define a consciousness as doubt, or perception, or thirst, etc., we are directed to the nothingness of what is not yet. My consciousness (of) reading is not a consciousness (of) reading this letter, or this word or sentence, or even this paragraph—but the consciousness (of) reading *this book*, which in turn refers me to all the pages that are not yet read, and all the pages that are already read, and which, by definition, separates consciousness from itself. A consciousness that was conscious only of what it is would be obliged to spell each word out.

In concrete terms, each *for-itself* is the lack of a certain self-coincidence. In other words, it is haunted by the presence of that with which it would have to coincide, in order to be *itself*. But as this coincidence in itself is also a coincidence with itself, what is missing from the for-itself, as the being whose assimilation would make it "itself," is more for-itself. We have seen that the for-itself is "self-presence": what self-presence lacks can be missing from it only as self-presence. The decisive relation between the for-itself and its possible is a nihilating slackening of the link involved in self-presence: this slackening reaches all the way to the transcendent, since the self-presence that is missing from the for-itself is a self-presence that *is not*. Thus the for-itself, insofar as it is not *itself*, is a self-presence from which a certain self-presence is missing—and it is as lacking that presence that it is self-presence. All consciousness is missing

34 TN: For *protension*, see my note in the section on Husserl vocabulary in Notes on the Translation.

some . . . for. But we must be clear that the lack does not come to it from outside, as the lack of the moon's crescent comes to the moon. The lack of for-itself is a lack that it is. It is the draft of a self-presence, as something missing from the for-itself, that constitutes the for-itself's being   138 as the foundation of its own nothingness. The possible is an absence that constitutes consciousness, insofar as it makes itself. A thirst—for example—insofar as it makes itself thirst, is never enough of a thirst: it is haunted by the presence of the "itself," or thirst-itself. But, insofar as this concrete value haunts it, the thirst calls itself into question in its being, as missing a certain for-itself that would actualize it as a *satisfied thirst*, and would confer upon it being-in-itself. This missing for-itself is the Possible. It is not quite correct to say that a thirst aims at its own annihilation as thirst: no consciousness ever aims at its elimination, as such. However—as we noted earlier—thirst is a lack. As such, it wants *to be satisfied*, but the aim to satisfy this thirst, which might be achieved by the synthetic assimilation, in an act of coincidence, of the for-itself-desire (or thirst) with the for-itself-replete (or the act of drinking), does not aim at eliminating the thirst. On the contrary, it aims at a thirst that has passed over into the plenitude of being, a thirst that takes hold of and incorporates the state of fullness, as Aristotle's form takes hold of and transforms matter; it becomes eternal thirst. The man who drinks to get rid of his thirst adopts a reflective point of view, which arises much later—like that of the man who goes to brothels to get rid of his sexual desire. In their unreflected and naïve state, thirst and sexual desire seek to take pleasure in themselves: they seek the self-coincidence of satisfaction, in which thirst comes to know itself as thirst at the very moment when it is satiated by the act of drinking and when, precisely by becoming satiated, the thirst loses the character of a lack, even while making itself be thirst, in and through its satiety. Thus Epicurus was right and, at the same time, he was wrong: on its own desire is, indeed, a void.[35] But no unreflected project aims merely to eliminate this void. Desire tends by itself to

35 TN: Epicurus is the ancient Greek philosopher best known for his view that death should not be feared. An important aspect of his view concerns the proper attitude that humans should take up toward their various desires. My translation of *remplir* as "to replenish" in the preceding sentence has been influenced by the reference in this passage to Epicurus: Epicurus's translators often use "replenishment."

perpetuate itself; man stands by his desires fiercely. What desire wants to be is a void that has been filled in—but that informs its fullness, as a cast informs the bronze that was poured into it. The possible that belongs to the consciousness of thirst is the consciousness of drinking. Besides,[36] we know that it is impossible for the *itself* to coincide with itself, because the for-itself that is attained by actualizing a possible will make itself be as for-itself—i.e., within a different horizon of possibles. Hence there is the constant disappointment that accompanies one's state of repletion, the well-known "Is that all it is?"—which does not target the concrete pleasure of satisfaction but the evanescence of self-coincidence. And here we can glimpse the origin of temporality, since thirst is—at the same time as it is *not*—its possible. This nothingness separating human-reality from itself lies at time's source. But we will return to that. What we must note is that the for-itself is separated from the self-presence that is missing from it and which is its own possibility; it is separated, in one sense, by *nothing* and, in another sense, by the totality of the existent in the world, insofar as the missing for-itself or possible is for-itself in the form of *presence to* a specific worldly state. In this sense, the being beyond which the for-itself projects its coincidence with itself is the world, or the infinite distance in being, beyond which man will be reunited with his possible. Let us call the for-itself's relation to the possible that it is the "*circuit of ipseity*"[37]—and the totality of being, insofar as it is traversed by the circuit of ipseity, the "*world*."

139

We are able now to clarify the possible's mode of being. The possible is that which the for-itself is missing *some* of . . . *for* being itself. In consequence, we should not say that, as a possible, the possible *is*—unless what we mean by "is" is the being of an existent who "*is been*" insofar as it is not been or, alternatively, the appearance, at a distance, of what I am. The possible does not exist merely as a representation—not even a negated one—but as a real lack of being which, as a lack, is beyond being. It has the being of a lack and, as a lack, being is missing from it. The possible is not; the possible possibilizes itself[38] and, to the precise extent to which the for-itself makes itself be, it determines, by schemati-

36 TN: I assume there is a mistake in the French, which says *de reste*, and that *du reste*—which I translate as "besides"—was intended.

37 TN: See my note on *ipséité* in Notes on the Translation.

38 TN: See my note on *possibiliser* in Notes on the Translation.

cally outlining it, the site of a nothingness that the for-itself is, beyond itself. Naturally it is not in the first instance posited thematically: it is merely outlined beyond the world, and it gives my present perception its meaning, insofar as my perception grasps the world within the circuit of ipseity. But neither is it unknown or unconscious: it sketches out the limits of my non-thetic consciousness (of) self as a non-thetic consciousness. An unreflected consciousness (of) thirst is an apprehension of the glass of water as desirable, in which the self is not centripetally posited as the goal of the desire. Instead, the possible state of repletion appears as the non-positional correlate of my non-thetic consciousness (of) self, at the horizon of the glass-in-the-midst-of-the-world.

V. MY SELF AND THE CIRCUIT OF IPSEITY

I tried to show, in an article in *Recherches Philosophiques*, that the Ego does not belong to the domain of the for-itself.[39] We do not need to return to that. Let us merely note the reason for the Ego's transcendence: as the unifying pole of the "*Erlebnisse*," the Ego is in-itself, not for-itself.[40] If it were "of consciousness," it would be its own foundation of itself, within the translucency of the immediate. But in that case it would be what it was not, and would not be what it was—which is not the mode of being of the "I." In fact, my consciousness of my "I" can never exhaust it, and neither does it bring it into existence: the "I" is always given   140 as *having been* there first and, at the same time, as possessing depths that will gradually be disclosed. In this way, the Ego appears to consciousness as a transcendent in-itself, as an existent of the human world and not as [something] of consciousness.[41] But it would be a mistake to conclude that the for-itself is purely and simply an "impersonal" contemplation. It is simply that, far from the Ego being the personalizing pole of a

---

39 TN: The article Sartre refers to is published as *The Transcendence of the Ego* (Sartre 2004a), which was indeed first published in the journal *Recherches Philosophiques*, for 1936–37.

40 TN: In addition to the term *Erlebnisse*, the concept of a "unifying pole" belongs to Husserl's work.

41 TN: . . . *non comme de la conscience*. Sartre means this phrase (which appears twice in this paragraph) to have a double meaning: something may either be "of" consciousness by being made out of it, or by belonging to it. I try to convey this with the additional word in square brackets.

consciousness that would, without it, remain at the impersonal stage, it is consciousness, on the contrary that, in its fundamental ipseity, enables the Ego to appear in certain conditions as the transcendent phenomenon of that ipseity. In fact, as we have seen, it is not possible to say, of the in-itself, that it is *itself*. It *is*, quite simply. And similarly, we should say of the "I"—which is quite incorrectly regarded as an inhabitant of consciousness—that it is the "Me" of consciousness, but not that it is its own *self* or *itself*.[42] Thus, by hypostasizing the for-itself's reflected-being into an in-itself, we freeze and destroy the movement of reflection on the self: consciousness will refer purely to the Ego as its *self*, but the Ego will no longer refer to anything; the relation of reflection has been transformed into a simple centripetal relation whose center, moreover, is an opaque node. We have shown, on the contrary that, by definition, no *self* or *itself* can inhabit consciousness.[43] It is, if you like, *the reason* for the infinite movement through which the reflection refers to the reflecting, and this latter to the reflection; it is by definition an ideal, a limit. And what makes it arise as a limit is the nihilating reality of being's presence to being, as a type of being within the unity of being. In this way, consciousness, from the moment it arises, makes itself *personal* through the pure nihilating movement of reflection: for it is not the possession of an Ego—which is only the *sign* of a personality—that confers personal existence on a being but rather the fact of existing for oneself as self-presence. But, in addition, this first reflective movement leads to a second movement, to ipseity. Within ipseity, my possible casts its reflection onto my consciousness and defines it as what it is. Ipseity represents a degree of nihilation that goes further than the pure self-presence of the prereflective *cogito*, insofar as the possible that I am is not a presence to the for-itself (in the way that the reflection relates to the reflecting) but is a *presence-absence*. But this underlines the existence of *referral* as the structure of the for-itself's being even more clearly. The for-itself is itself *over there*, out of reach, in the distance of its possibilities. And this free necessity to be over there what one is, in the form of a lack, is what constitutes ipseity, or the

42 TN: . . . *son propre soi*. Here I give both ways of translating *soi*, as Sartre seems to exploit both.

43 TN: Here again Sartre may be exploiting both meanings of *soi*: "self" (as in Ego) and "itself" (as in for-itself). See my note on *soi* in Notes on the Translation.

second essential aspect of a person. And how indeed should we define a person, other than as a free relationship to himself? As for the world—i.e., the totality of beings as they exist within the circuit of ipseity—it cannot be anything but what human-reality surpasses toward itself or, to borrow Heidegger's definition: "That on the basis of which human-reality becomes acquainted with what it is."[44] In effect, the possible that is my possible is a possible for-itself and, as such, it is present to the in-itself as consciousness of the in-itself. In confronting the world, what I seek is to coincide with a for-itself that I am, which is a consciousness of the world. But this possible, which is non-thetically present-absent to my present consciousness, is not present like an object of positional consciousness—otherwise it would be reflected. The satisfied thirst that haunts my current thirst is not a consciousness (of) self as a satisfied thirst: it is a thetic consciousness of the glass-being-drunk-from and a non-positional consciousness (of) self. It is therefore transcended toward the glass of which it is conscious and, as the correlative of this possible non-thetic consciousness, the glass-drunk-from haunts the full glass as its possible and constitutes it as a glass for drinking from. Thus the world, in its nature, is mine insofar as it is the in-itself correlative of nothingness; in other words, the correlative of the necessary obstacle, beyond which I rediscover myself as what I am in the form of "having it to be." Without the world there would be no ipseity, and no person; without ipseity, and without the person, there would be no world. But the world's belonging to the person is never posited at the level of the prereflective cogito. It would be absurd to say that the world, insofar as it is known, is known as mine. And yet this "mine-ness" of the world is a fugitive and ever present structure that I live. The world (is) mine because it is haunted by possibles, of which the possible [acts of] consciousness (of) self that I am are conscious, and it is these possibles as such that give the world its unity and its meaning as a world.[45]

Our examination of negative forms of behavior and of bad faith has allowed us to make a start on the ontological study of the cogito, and

---

44 Sartre's note: We will see in Part Two, Chapter 3, the ways in which this definition—which we are provisionally adopting—is inadequate and erroneous.

45 TN: I follow the French text in placing the first "is" in this sentence in brackets and italics.

the *cogito*'s being has appeared to us as being-for-itself. Before our eyes, this being has transcended itself, toward value and toward its possibles; we have not been able to contain it within the substantialist limits of instantaneity that belong to Descartes's *cogito*. But, precisely for that reason, we cannot be content with the results we have just obtained: if the *cogito* rejects instantaneity, and if it transcends itself toward its possibles, a temporal surpassing is required. It is "in time" that the for-itself is its own possibles in the mode of "not being"; it is in time that my possibles appear at the horizon of the world which they make into "mine." If, therefore, human-reality grasps itself as temporal, and if the meaning of its transcendence is its temporality, we cannot hope to elucidate the for-itself's being until we have described and established the meaning of the Temporal. It is only then that we will be able to turn to the problem that concerns us: the problem of consciousness's original relation to being.

Chapter 2

TEMPORALITY

I. PHENOMENOLOGY OF THE THREE TEMPORAL DIMENSIONS

Temporality is obviously an organized structure, and we should not conceive of the three so-called elements of time (past, present, and future) as a collection of "data" whose sum we are obliged to work out—for example, as an infinite series of "nows," of which some are not yet, and others are no longer—but rather as structured moments within an original synthesis. Otherwise we will encounter this paradox at the outset: the past is no longer, the future is not yet and, with respect to the instantaneous present, everyone knows that it has no being at all, and lies at the limit of an infinite division, as a dimensionless point. In that way the entire series is annihilated and doubly so, since the future "now," for example, is a nothingness insofar as it is future and it will be actualized as a nothingness when it passes into the state of a present "now." The only possible method for studying temporality is to approach it as a totality that dominates its secondary structures, and confers their meaning on them. We must never lose sight of this. However, we cannot launch ourselves into an examination of the meaning of Time without a prior elucidation, through a preontological and phenomenological description, of the meaning of these three dimensions, which remains all too often obscure. However, we must regard this phenomenological description as a provisional piece of work, whose aim is only to allow us access to an intuition of global temporality. And, in particular, we must allow each of the dimensions we consider to appear *against the ground* of the temporal totality, while keeping constantly before our memory the dimension's "*Unselbstständigkeit*."[1]

143   ## (A) The past

Any theory of memory presupposes something about the being of the past. These presuppositions, which have never been elucidated, have obscured the problem of memory and, more generally, of temporality. We must, therefore, raise the question once and for all: What is *the being* of a past being? Common sense oscillates between two equally vague conceptions: the past, it is said, no longer exists. From this point of view, it seems, we want to attribute being only to the present. This ontological assumption gave rise to the notorious theory of brain traces: since the past is no longer, and since it has collapsed into nothingness, if a memory continues to exist it must be in the capacity of a *present* modification of our being—for example, as a trace that is presently imprinted on a group of brain cells. On this account, everything—the body, the present perception, and the past—is present in the form of a trace that is present in the body. And everything is *in actuality*: because the trace's existence is not virtual, *insofar as* it is a memory; it is an entirely *actual* trace. If a memory is revived, it is in the present, and at the conclusion of a process occurring in the present, i.e., as a disruption of the protoplasmic equilibrium of the cellular group being investigated. Psychophysiological parallelism, which is instantaneous and extratemporal, is at hand to explain how this physiological process is the correlative of a phenomenon that is strictly psychological but equally present: the appearance of the memory-image in consciousness. The more recent concept of the *engram* achieves nothing further—other than adorning the theory with a pseudo-scientific terminology. But if everything is present, how are we to explain the memory's *pastness*,

---

1 TN: The German word *Unselbstständigkeit* arises frequently in philosophical texts, and roughly translates as "dependence." It is of course the opposite of *Selbstständigkeit*, used earlier in the text.

i.e., the fact that, in its intention, a memory-consciousness transcends the present to aim at the event, there where it *was*? We have shown elsewhere that we will be unable to distinguish a perception from an image, if we start out by making the latter a renascent perception.[2] Here we encounter the same impossibility. But in addition we have deprived ourselves of the means of distinguishing a memory from an image: neither the "weakness" of the memory, nor its pallor, nor its incompleteness, nor its contradictions with what is given in perception, can distinguish it from an image-fiction, since it presents the same characteristics; and these characteristics, moreover, being *present* qualities of the memory, cannot take us out of the present in order to direct us toward the past. It is futile to invoke—as Claparède does—the memory's participation in the self or its "me-ness"[3] or—as James does—its "intimacy."[4] Either these characteristics are merely manifestations of a present atmosphere surrounding the memory, in which case they remain present and refer to the present, or they already relate to the past as such, but then they presuppose what we need to explain. Some people believed we could easily get rid of the problem by equating recognition with a first attempt at localization, and the latter to a group of intellectual operations facilitated by the existence of "social frameworks of memory."[5] It is beyond doubt that these operations exist, and they should be made the subject of a psychological study. But if the relation to the past is not in some way given, these operations cannot create it. In brief, if we begin by turning man into an islander, shut up in the instantaneous islet of his present, and if all his modes of being, the moment they appear, are essentially bound to a perpetual present, we will have radically deprived ourselves of any means of understanding man's original relation to the past. We will not succeed in constituting the dimension of the "past" out of elements borrowed exclusively from

144

2 Sartre's note: *L'Imagination* (Alcan, 1936). TN: Translated into English as Sartre (2012).
3 TN: Édouard Claparède (1873–1940) was a Swiss psychologist. In keeping with English translations of Claparède, I translate moïté here as "me-ness." Claparède's view was that a feeling of me-ness was necessary for any image or experience to become a memory. Sartre mentions his work in both his earlier texts on the imagination.
4 TN: By James, Sartre is of course referring to the American psychologist William James.
5 TN: Sartre is alluding to the theory of the French sociologist Maurice Halbwachs (1877–1945), who emphasized the social aspect to personal memory.

the present any more than the "geneticists" succeeded in constituting extension out of non-extended elements.[6]

Moreover, popular consciousness finds it so hard to deny any real existence to the past that, at the same time as allowing this first thesis, it also allows another equally imprecise conception, according to which the past has a sort of honorary existence. For an event to be past is, quite simply, for it to have entered retirement, to have lost its efficiency without losing its being. Bergson's philosophy took up this idea: in turning to the past, an event does not cease to be; it ceases to act, quite simply, but it remains "in its place," at its date, for eternity. We hereby restore being to the past, and rightly so: we even claim that duration is an interpenetrating multiplicity, and that the past continually organizes itself with the present.[7] But, even so, we have still not properly accounted for this organization and interpenetration: we have not explained how the past can "be reborn" and can haunt us or, to be concise, how it can exist for us. If it is unconscious, as Bergson would have it, and if the unconscious is inactive, how can it insert itself into the fabric of our present consciousness? Does it have a power of its own? But is this power present, then, since it acts on the present? How can it emanate from the past as such? Should we reverse the question—like Husserl—and point to the play of "retentions" within our present consciousness, retentions that hook on to erstwhile [acts of] consciousness, maintaining them at their date and preventing them from vanishing?[8] But if Husserl's *cogito* is given in the first instance as instantaneous, we will have no means of getting outside it. We saw, in the last chapter, how protentions bump up in vain against the windowpanes of the present, without being able to break them. The same thing happens with retentions. Throughout his philosophical career, Husserl was haunted by the idea of transcendence and surpassing. But the philosophical instruments at his disposal—and in particular his idealist conception of existence—deprived him of the means of accounting for this transcendence: his intentionality is only a

14

---

6 TN: According to the psychological doctrine known in France as *génétisme*, our capacity to perceive spatial relations in the world is not innate but acquired.

7 TN: Bergson's *Time and Free Will* provides an early statement of his account of duration as an "interpenetrating multiplicity" (Bergson 1960).

8 TN: For *rétention*, see my note in the section on Husserl vocabulary in Notes on the Translation.

caricature of it. In reality, Husserl's consciousness is unable to transcend itself: either toward the world, or toward the future, or toward the past.

Thus we have gained nothing by conceding being to the past because, according to the terms of this concession, it is obliged to be for us as if it had no being. Whether the past *is*, as Bergson and Husserl would have it, or whether it *is no longer*, as Descartes wants to say, is hardly of importance if we have begun by cutting the bridges between it and our present.

If we give the present, as "presence to the world," a privileged status, we are effectively adopting the perspective of intraworldly being to confront the problem of the past. We imagine that we exist first as contemporaries of this chair or this table, and temporal meaning is pointed out to us by the world. Now, if we place ourselves in the midst of the world, we lose all possibility of distinguishing between what *is no longer* and what *is not*. Yet—it might be said—at least something that is no longer has been, whereas something that is not has no connection with being of any kind. That is true. But, as we have seen, we may describe the law that applies to the being of an intraworldly instant in these simple words: "Being is"—and these words designate a massive plenitude of positivity, in which nothing of what *is not* can be represented in any way whatsoever, not even by a trace, or a void, or a reminder, or a "hysteresis." Being that is exhausts itself entirely in being; it has nothing to do with what is not, or with what is no longer. No negation, whether it be radical or in the milder form of "no . . . longer," can find any place within this absolute density. Given that, the past may well exist in its way: all bridges have been broken. Being has not even "forgotten" its past: that would still be a kind of connection. The past has slipped away from it like a dream.

If we can treat Descartes's and Bergson's conceptions alike, dismissing both of them, it is because each of them is vulnerable to the same reproach. Whether it is a question of destroying the past, or of preserving for it the type of existence of the Lares spirits,[9] these authors envisaged its fate *separately*, isolating it from the present: and, however they conceived of consciousness, they endowed it with the existence of the in-itself;

9 TN: In Ancient Rome the Lares deities were domestic gods, believed to guard over the household. The family Lar was often represented by a small statue, placed in a shrine.

they understood it as being what it was. We have no reason to marvel, after this, at the fact that they fail to connect the past to the present, since conceived in this way the present is going to reject the past with all its strength. If they had thought about the phenomenon of time in its totality, they would have seen that "my" past is in the first place *mine*, which is to say that it exists as a function of a specific being that I *am*. The past is not *nothing*, nor is it the present; rather, its nature is to be connected, from its very source, to a specific present and a specific future. The "me-ness" that Claparède talked of is not some subjective nuance that breaks into our memory: it is an ontological relation that unites the past with the present. My past never appears in the isolation of its "pastness": it would be absurd even to think it could *exist* like that; it is, from the outset, the past of *this* present. This is what we need to elucidate first.

146

I write that Paul, in 1920, was a student at the École Polytechnique. *Who* is the person who "was?" Paul, obviously—but which Paul? The young man in 1920? But the only tense of the verb "to be" that is appropriate for Paul—considered in 1920, and insofar as we attribute to him the property of being a Polytechnique student—is the present. We ought to have said of him, as he was then: "he is." If the Paul who was a student at the Polytechnique is now in the past, any relation with the present is severed: the man who supported that property—the subject—has remained back there, with that attribute, in 1920. If we want an act of recollection to remain possible, we will be obliged, on this hypothesis, to allow that a recognitional synthesis could reach out from the present in order to maintain contact with the past. It is impossible to conceive of such a synthesis other than as an original mode of being. Without a hypothesis of this sort, we will be obliged to abandon the past in its superb isolation. Moreover, what could such a split within the personality mean? Of course Proust allows for a plurality of successive "Mes," but if we take this conception literally, we will fall back into the insurmountable difficulties encountered by the associationists in their time. Perhaps the hypothesis of permanence within change will be suggested: the person who was a Polytechnique student is the same Paul who existed in 1920, and who exists now. It is of him that, having said "he *is* a Polytechnique student," we can now say "he *is* a former Polytechnique student." But this appeal to permanence will not get us out of trouble: if nothing takes up the flow of "nows" in the other direction to constitute the time series and, within this series, some permanent characteristics, permanence will be nothing more than a specific instantaneous content, without any breadth, of each individual "now." For something permanent there must be a past and, in addition, something or someone who *was* this past: rather than helping us to constitute time, permanence presupposes it, so that permanence can be disclosed within it, and, alongside it, change. We come back, therefore, to the point we glimpsed earlier: if the existential persistence of being in the form of my past does not arise originally from my current present, and if yesterday's past does not take the shape of a transcendence behind today's present, we have lost any hope of connecting the past to the present. If therefore I say, about Paul, that he *has been* a Polytechnique student or that he *was* one,[10] I am saying it about this Paul who *is* in the present, and about whom I can also say that he *is* in his forties. The person who *was* at the Polytechnique is not the adolescent. About that person, while he was there, we should say: he *is*. It is the man in his forties who *was* the student. To tell the truth, the man aged thirty *was* also that student. But who would that man aged thirty be, in his turn, without the man in his forties who was once him? And as for the man in his forties, it is at the full height of his present that he "*was*" the Polytechnique student. And, in the end, it is the "*Erlebnis*"—in its very being—whose mission it is to be a man in his forties, a man aged thirty, and an adolescent, in the mode of *having-been* him. Today we say that this "*Erlebnis*" *is*: in their time we also said, about the man in his forties and the adolescent, that they *are*; today they form part of the past, and the past itself *is*, in the sense in which at present it *is* Paul's past, or the past of this "*Erlebnis*." Thus the beings that are designated by the particular forms of the perfect tense all really exist, although in various modes of being, but one of them *is* and, at the same time, *was an other*: the past is characterized as the past of something or someone; we *have* a past. It is this implement, this society, and this man which *have* their past. There is not first a universal past, which subsequently becomes particularized into concrete pasts. But, on the contrary, what we find from the first instance is *various* pasts. And the real problem—which we will approach in the following

147

---

10 TN: *Si donc je dis de Paul qu'il fut ou qu'il était élève de Polytechnique* . . . Since each of these two different tenses of *être* translates into English as "was," I have altered Sartre's sentence in order to make the same point.

chapter—will be how to understand the process through which these individual pasts can be united, in order to form the past.

It will be objected, perhaps, that we have made things easy for ourselves by choosing an example where the subject who "was" still exists in the present. Other cases may be cited. For example, I can say of Pierre, who is dead, that "he liked music." In this case both the subject and the attribute are in the past. And there is no current Pierre to be the starting point from which this past-being could arise. We agree about this. We can even agree about it to the extent of recognizing that a taste for music has never been *past* for Pierre. Pierre has always been the contemporary of this taste, which was *his* taste; his living personality has not survived him, and neither has he survived it. It follows that, in this instance, what is past is Pierre-liking-music. And I can raise the question that I raised just now: *Of whom* is this past-Pierre the past? It cannot be in relation to a universal Present which purely affirms being; it is, therefore, the past of my actuality. And as a matter of fact Pierre has been for-me and I have been for-him. As we will see, Pierre's existence has affected me right to the core: while he was alive it formed part of a present "in-the-world, for-me and for-the-Other" that was my present—a present that I have been. In this way, concrete objects that have disappeared are in the past, insofar as they form part of some survivor's concrete past. "The terrible thing about Death," says Malraux, "is that it transforms life into Destiny."[11] We should take this to mean that death reduces our for-itself-for-the-Other to the state of a mere being-for-the-Other. Today I am the only one responsible, in my freedom, for the being of Pierre who is dead. And those dead people who have not been rescued and carried aboard by some survivor's concrete past are not in the *past*; rather, they—and their pasts—have been annihilated.

148   There are therefore beings that "have" pasts. We alluded just now, as if there were no difference between them, to an instrument, a society, and a man. Were we right? Can we attribute an original past to all finite existents, or only to specific categories within them? To determine

11 TN: André Malraux (1901–1976) was an influential French novelist. Sartre slightly misquotes a sentence from Malraux's 1937 novel *L'Espoir* (translated into English as Malraux 1970). It should read as: *La tragédie de la mort est en ceci qu'elle transforme la vie en destin* ("The tragedy of death lies in the fact that it transforms life into destiny").

this, it will help to examine more closely the quite distinctive notion of "having" a past. It is not possible "to have" a past in the way in which one might "have" a car or a racing stable. In other words, the past cannot be possessed by a being in the present whose relation to it remains strictly external—in the way in which, for example, I remain external to my fountain pen. In brief, in the sense in which "possession" normally expresses an *external* relation between possessor and possessed, this term is inadequate. External relations would conceal an impassable gulf between past and present, which would be two *de facto* givens, without any real communication. Even an absolute interpenetration of the present by the past, in the way Bergson conceives of it, will not resolve the difficulty, because this interpenetration, which is how the past is organized with the present, basically comes from the past and is no more than a relation of *habitation*. It may well enable us to conceive of the past as being in the present, but we have deprived ourselves of any way of presenting this immanence other than by analogy with a stone at the bottom of a river. The past may well haunt the present, but it cannot be the present; it is the present that *is* its past. If therefore we study the relations of the past with the present by taking the past as our starting point, we will never be able to establish *internal* relations between them. In consequence, an in-itself—whose present is what it is—cannot "have" any past. The examples cited by Chevalier in support of his thesis and, in particular, the facts of hysteresis do not succeed in establishing that some matter's past can act on its present state.[12] There is not a single one, in fact, that cannot be interpreted using the ordinary terms of mechanistic determinism. One of these two nails, Chevalier tells us, has just been made and has never been used; the other has been twisted, and then straightened, by the blows of a hammer: they appear to be exactly the same. However, at the first blow one of them sinks straight into the partition and the other becomes twisted again: the action of the past. From our perspective, to see this as the action of the past requires some bad faith. It is easy to substitute, for this unintelligible explanation of the being characterized by density, the only possible explanation: outwardly, these two nails have a similar appearance, but their present

12 TN: I have had difficulty in tracking down this scientist or his work, but Sartre is
    probably referring to one H. Chevalier, who worked on magnetism at the turn of the
    twentieth century.

molecular structures are markedly different. And the present molecular state is at each instant strictly the effect of the previous molecular state, which does not show, in the eyes of an expert, that there is a "passage" from one instant to another and that the past is permanent but merely that there is an irreversible connection between the contents of two instants of physical time. To present the remanent magnetization of a piece of soft iron as proof of this permanence of the past is not to prove

149   anything more serious: what we see here, in effect, is a phenomenon that survives its cause, and not a cause that subsists as a cause in its past state. Long after the stone that pierced the water has reached the bottom of the pond, the concentric waves are still traveling across its surface: to explain this phenomenon, we do not appeal to any kind of action of the past: the mechanism is almost visible. The facts of hysteresis or remanence do not seem to necessitate a different type of explanation. Indeed, it is quite clear that the phrase "to have a past"—which, when we apply it to matter, allows us to envisage a mode of possession in which the possessor may be passive, and which is not as such shocking—ought to be replaced by that of being one's own past. There is a past only for a present that cannot exist without being its past "over there," behind it. In other words, the only beings that have a past are those beings for whom there is a question, in their being, of their past being—beings that have their past to be. These observations allow us to deny a priori any past to the in-itself (which does not mean, moreover, that we ought to confine it to the present). We will not settle the question of the past of living things. We will merely point out that, if we are required—as is far from certain— to attribute a past to life, this could only be subsequent to some proof that life's being is such that it involves a past. In short, one would first have to prove that living matter is something other than a physicochemical system. The attempt to go in the opposite direction—which is what Chevalier does—and which consists in presenting the greater urgency of the past as constituting life's originality, is a completely meaningless ὕστερον πρότερον.[13] The existence of a past is evident only for human-reality, because it has been established that it has to be what it is. The past

---

13 TN: Sartre gives this phrase in Greek. Transliterated, it says Hýsteron próteron and means "the latter one first" (i.e., "the wrong way round").

arrives in the world through the for-itself, because its "I am" takes the form of an "I am *myself*."[14]

What therefore is the meaning of "was?" First we can see that it is a transitive. If I say "Paul is tired," we can perhaps contest the copula's ontological validity; we might perhaps wish to see it only as a sign of inherence. But when we say "Paul *was* tired," the essential meaning of the word "was" stares us in the face: Paul in the present is currently responsible for having had this fatigue in the past. If he were not maintaining this fatigue with his being, his state would not even amount to something forgotten; rather, there would be a "no-longer-being," strictly identical to a "not-being." The fatigue would be *lost*. The present being is therefore the foundation of its own past; and the "was" manifests this characteristic of being a foundation. But we should not take this to mean that it founds its past indifferently, and without being profoundly modified by it: "was" means that the present being has to be in its being the foundation of its past by itself *being* this past. What does this mean? How is the present able *to be* the past?

The crux of the question lies obviously in the term "was," which, acting   150
as an intermediary between the present and the past, is itself neither wholly present nor wholly past. Indeed it cannot be either one or the other, since, in that case, the tense that is supposed to denote its being would contain it. The term "was" designates, therefore, the ontological leap from the present into the past and represents an original synthesis of these two modes of temporality. How should we understand this synthesis?

I see first that the term "was" is a mode of being. In this sense I *am* my past. I do not have it but I am it: what I am told in connection with an action I performed yesterday, or a mood that I had, does not leave me indifferent: I am wounded or flattered, I rear up or I let it be said, I am affected right to the core. I do not dissociate myself from my past. Of course, in the long run, I may attempt such a dissociation; I may assert that "I am no longer what I was," and cite some change or some progress. But that is a second reaction, and presents itself as such. In denying any solidarity of being with my past, in relation to this or that particular point, I am affirming it for the whole of my life. Ultimately, at the infinitesimal

14 TN: . . . "*Je me suis*." The reflexive way in which Sartre makes this point cannot be preserved in translation.

instant of my death, I will no longer be anything but my past. It alone will define me. That is what Sophocles means to express when, in *The Trachiniae*, he makes Deïanira say: "An old saying goes: 'You can never know for sure whether a mortal's life has been good or bad until his death.'"[15] It is also the meaning of the sentence from Malraux that we quoted earlier: "Death changes life into destiny.'[16] Finally, it is what strikes the believer when he realizes with terror, at the moment of his death, that the bets are placed and he has only one card left to play. Death reunites us with ourselves, as eternity has changed us into ourselves.[17] At the moment of death we *are*, which means we are helpless before the Other's judgments: it is possible to decide what we are in truth; we no longer have any chance of escaping the total sum that an all-knowing intelligence might calculate. And if we repent at the eleventh hour, our repentance is wholly an attempt to crack open all the being that has slowly taken shape and solidified *on us*; it is a final recoil in order to disso-ciate ourselves from what we *are*. In vain: death freezes our recoil, along with the rest; it merely becomes combined with what has preceded it, as one factor among others, as one particular determination that can be understood only on the basis of the totality. Through death, the for-itself changes for eternity into in-itself, to the extent to which it has entirely slipped into the past. Thus the past is the ever-increasing totality of the in-itself that we are. However, as long as we are not dead, the mode in which we are this in-itself is not that of identity. We *have it to be*. Usually resentment comes to an end with death, because the man has united with his past; he *is* it, yet without thereby being responsible for it. While he is living, he is the object of my resentment, which means I blame him for his past not only insofar as he *is* it but insofar as in each moment he takes up that past again and maintains it in being, insofar as he is *responsible* for it. It is not true that resentment freezes a man into what he was; if it did, it would survive his death. Resentment is directed toward a liv-

15 TN: This play by Sophocles is also sometimes translated with the English title *The Women of Trachis*. I do not know if Sartre was quoting from a published version or from mem-ory. I have quoted Deïanira's line from David Raeburn's translation (Sophocles 2008).

16 TN: Sartre quotes this at EN 147.

17 TN: Sartre is alluding here to the first line of the famous poem "The Tomb of Edgar Poe" published by Stéphane Mallarmé in French in 1887. The line is often translated into English as "As to Himself at last eternity changes him" (Mallarmé 1996: 71).

ing person who is in his being freely what he was. I am my past and, if I were not my past, it would no longer exist—either for me or for anyone. It would no longer have any relation to the present. This certainly does not mean the past would have no being but only that its being would be undetectable. I am the one through whom my past arrives in this world. But we must be sure to understand that I do not give my past its being. In other words, it does not exist in the capacity of "my" representation. It is not because I "represent" my past that it exists. Rather, it is because I am my past that it enters the world, and it is on the basis of its being-in-the-world that I can, by means of a specific psychological process, represent it to myself. The past is what I have to be, yet it differs by nature from my possibles. A possible—which is also something that I have to be—remains, as my concrete possible, something whose opposite is equally possible—although to a lesser degree. The past, on the contrary, is without any possibility of any kind, something that has used its possibilities up. What I have to be no longer depends in any way on my being-able-to-be; it is already in itself all that it can be. I have to be the past that I am without any possibility of not being it. I accept responsibility for it entirely, as if I could change it; and yet I cannot be anything other than it. We will see later that we always retain the possibility of changing the past's meaning, insofar as the past is an ex-present that has had a future. But I am unable either to eliminate from or to add to the content of the past as such. In other words, the past that I was is what it is; it is an in-itself, like the things in the world. And the relation of being that I have to maintain with the past is a type of in-itself relation, i.e., a relation of identification with itself.

But, on the other hand, I am not my past. Since I was it, I am not it. The Other's resentment still surprises and outrages me: How is it possible to hate the person that I was, in the person that I am? Ancient wisdom placed great emphasis on this fact: I am unable to state anything about myself without it becoming false once I have stated it. Hegel did not scorn the use of this argument. Whatever I do, whatever I say, at the moment in which I will to be it, I have already been doing it, or been saying it. But let us look at this aphorism more closely: it amounts to saying that any judgment that I make about myself is already false when I make it, which is to say I have become something else. But how should we understand something else? If we take it to mean a mode of human-reality possessing the same existential type as that whose present existence we are denying, it amounts to the claim that we have made a mistake in attributing the predicate to the subject, and that it remained possible to attribute another predicate: we should simply have aimed at it in the immediate future. In the same way, a hunter who targets a bird *where he sees* it misses it—because the bird is no longer still at that place when the projectile reaches it. He will hit it, on the contrary, if he aims slightly ahead, at a point which the flying creature has not yet reached. If the bird is no longer at this place it is because it *is already* at another; in any case it *is* somewhere. But, as we will see, this Eleatic conception of movement is profoundly mistaken: if we really can say that the arrow *is* in AB, then movement becomes a succession of unmoving items. Similarly, if we conceive that there was an infinitesimal instant, which no longer exists, in which I was what I am no longer, we constitute me out of a series of frozen states that succeed each other like a magic lantern's images. If I *am* not it, it is not because of a slight interval between the judicative thought and being, because of a time-lag between judgment and fact; it is because in my immediate being, in the presence of my present, I *am* necessarily not it. In brief, it is not because of some change—a becoming, conceived as a passing over into heterogeneity within being's homogeneity—that I *am* not what I was; but, on the contrary, it is because my being is, necessarily, heterogeneous in relation to my ways of being. To explain the world in terms of becoming, conceived as a synthesis of being and non-being, is easily done. But has anyone considered that no being that becomes could be such a synthesis unless it were, in relation to itself, an act that founded its own nothingness? If I am already no longer what I was, I must still have it to be, in the unity of a nihilating synthesis that I myself maintain in being; otherwise I would have no relation of any kind with what I am no longer, and my full positivity would exclude the non-being that is essential to becoming. Becoming cannot be *given*, as an immediate mode of being's being, because, if we conceive of such a being, the being and non-being at its heart could only be juxtaposed, and no imposed or *external* structure can make one of them merge with the other. Being's connection with non-being can only be internal: non-being must arise within being as being; being must show up within non-being, and this cannot be a fact, or a natural law, but rather the emergence of the being that is its own nothingness of being. If therefore I *am* not my own past, this cannot be in the original mode of becoming but rather insofar as I *have it to be in order not to be it*, and I *have to not be it in order to be it*. This should illuminate the nature of the mode "was" for us: if I am not what I was, it is not because I have already changed—which would presuppose that time is already given—it is because I am, in relation to my being, in the mode of an internal connection with "*not-being.*"

Thus it is insofar as I *am* my past that I am able to not be it; my necessarily being my past is even the only possible foundation for the fact that I am not it. Otherwise, in each instant, I would neither be it nor not be it, other than in the eyes of a strictly external witness who, moreover, would himself have to be his past in the mode of *not-being.*

These observations allow us to understand what is incorrect in the skepticism that began with Heraclitus, and whose main point is only that I am no longer what I say I am. Of course, if we consider everything I can be said to be, I am not that. But the assertion that "I am *already* no longer that" says it badly, because, if we take "that" to mean "being in itself," I have never been that; and on the other hand it does not follow, either, that it would be an error for me to say I am that, since clearly I have to be that in order not to be that; that is what I am in the mode of "*was.*"

Thus, everything that we can say that I *am*—in the sense of being in itself, with full and compact density (he is quick-tempered, he is a civil servant, he is discontented)—is always *my past.* It is in the past that I am what I am. But, from another angle, this heavy fullness of being is behind me; there is an absolute distance that cuts it off from me and plants it out of my reach, out of contact, where it cannot adhere to me. If I was or if I have been happy, it is because I am not happy. But that does not mean that I *am* unhappy: merely that I can only *be* happy in the past. It is not *because* I have a past that I carry my being behind me in this way: rather, the past is precisely *only* this ontological structure that obliges me to be what I am *from-behind.* That is the meaning of "was." By definition, the existence of the for-itself obliges it to accept its being, and it cannot be anything but for itself. But, precisely, it can accept its being only by reclaiming that being—which places it *at a distance* from that being. Even as I assert that I *am* in the mode of the in-itself, I escape this assertion, because in its very nature it implies a negation. Thus the for-itself is always beyond what it is, by virtue of being it for-itself, and by virtue of having it to be. But, at the same time, what remains behind it really is its being, and not another being. In this way we can understand the meaning of "was," which simply describes the for-itself's type of being, i.e., the for-itself's relation to its being. The past is the in-itself that I am, insofar as I have *surpassed* it.[18]

It remains for us to study the particular way the for-itself "was" its own past. Now, we know that the for-itself appears in the original act through which the in-itself nihilates itself in order to found itself. The for-itself is its own foundation insofar as it makes itself the failure of the in-itself, in order to be its own failure. But it does not thereby manage to deliver itself from the in-itself. The surpassed in-itself remains and haunts it, as its original contingency. The for-itself can never make contact with it, or grasp itself as *being* this or that, but neither can it prevent itself from being, at a distance from itself, what it is. This contingency, this heaviness that belongs to the for-itself at a distance, a heaviness that it never *is* but that it has to be as a heaviness that is surpassed, and preserved in its very surpassing, is *facticity*, but it is also the past. "Facticity" and "the past" are two words to refer to one and the same thing. In fact the Past, like Facticity, is the in-itself's invulnerable contingency—what I have to be, without any possibility of not being it. It is the inevitability of a factual necessity: inevitable not *qua* necessity but *qua* fact. It is the *de facto* being that cannot determine the content of my motivations but whose contingency penetrates them, because they can neither remove it nor change it; rather, and on the contrary, my motivations must necessarily carry it along with them—in order to modify it—and they preserve it, in order to flee from it; it is what they have to be, even as they try to not be it, and it is the basis on which they make themselves what they are. It is what explains how, in each instant, I *am not* a diplomat and sailor, and that I am a teacher—even though I can only perform this being, without ever being able to join it. If I cannot return to the past, that is not because some magical power places it out of reach but simply because it is in-itself and I am for-myself; the past is what I am without being able to live it. The past is substance. In this sense, Descartes's *cogito* ought to be reformulated as: "I think, therefore I was." What misleads us is the apparent homogeneity of the past and the present. For this shame that I

154

---

18 TN: *Le passé c'est l'en-soi que je suis en tant que dépassé.* Sartre uses the same pun elsewhere in the text.

experienced yesterday was—when I felt it—for-itself. We believe therefore that it remains for-itself today and, from that, we wrongly conclude
that, if I cannot return to it, that is because it *is no longer*. But, to arrive at
the truth, we need to reverse this relationship: there is an absolute heterogeneity between past and present, and if I cannot enter the past, that
is because it *is*. And the only way I could be it would be by being, myself,
in-itself, in order to lose myself within it through an identification with
it: and that is essentially denied to me. In fact, the shame I felt yesterday—
which was shame for itself—is still shame in the present and, on the
basis of its essence, it might still be described as for-itself. But in its being
it *is no longer* for itself, because its form is no longer a reflection-reflecting.
Describable as for-itself, it quite simply *is*. The past presents itself as for-
itself that has *become* in-itself. This shame, while I live it, is not what it
is. Now that I *was* it, I can say: it *was* a feeling of shame. It has become
what it was, behind me, with the permanence and the constancy of the
in-itself; it is eternally at its date, and it has the total self-belonging of
the in-itself. In a sense, therefore, the past which is for-itself and in-itself
at the same time *resembles* the value, or the "itself," which we described
in the previous chapter; in the same way, it represents a certain synthesis
of the being that is what it is not and is not what it is, with the being that
is what it is. It is in this sense that we can talk about the past's evanescent
value. That is why memory presents us with the being that we were
with a fullness of being that bestows on it a kind of poetry. By becoming frozen in the past, the pain that we *had* does not cease to present the
meaning of a for-itself, and yet it exists within itself, with the silent fixity
of someone else's pain, of a statue's pain. It no longer needs to appear   155
before itself to make itself exist. It is, and its character as a for-itself—far
from being the mode of being of its being—becomes on the contrary
simply a way of being, a quality. It is because they have contemplated
the psyche *in the past* that psychologists have claimed consciousness was
a quality that it might or might not possess, without modifying it in its
being. The past psyche is first, and it is for-itself afterward, in the way in
which Pierre is blond, or this tree is an oak.

But precisely because of that, the past that *resembles* value *is not* value. In
the case of value, the for-itself becomes itself by surpassing and founding its being; the itself reclaims the in-itself; by virtue of this, the contingency of being gives way to necessity. The past, on the contrary, is in

the first instance in itself. The for-itself is maintained in being by the in-itself, such that its *raison d'être* is no longer to be for-itself; it has become in-itself and accordingly it appears to us in its pure contingency. There is no *reason* why our past should be this or that way: it appears, in the totality of its series, as a pure fact that we have to admit as a fact, as something gratuitous. To sum up, it is an inversion of value, the for-itself reclaimed by the in-itself, thickened by the in-itself to the point at which it can no longer exist as a reflection for the reflecting, or as a reflecting for the reflection, but merely as an in-itself sign of the reflecting-reflection pair. That is why the past can, at the extreme, be the object aimed at by a for-itself who wills to make value *real* and to flee from the anguish produced by the permanent absence of any "itself." But in its essence it is radically distinct from value: it is the indicative from which precisely no imperative can be inferred, the distinctive fact of each for-itself, the contingent and unalterable fact that I *was*.

Thus the past is a for-itself seized back and drowned by the in-itself. How can that happen? We have described the meaning of *to-be-past* in the case of an event, and the meaning of *to have a past* for a human-reality. We have seen that the past is an ontological law of the for-itself, which means that, with respect to everything a for-itself may be, it must be it over there, behind itself, and out of reach. In this sense, we can accept Hegel's phrase: "*Wesen ist was gewesen ist.*'[19] My essence is in the past; that is the law of its being. But we have not explained why a concrete event of the for-itself *becomes* past. How does a for-itself that *was* its past become the past that a new for-itself has to be? To pass over into the past involves a modification of being. What is this modification? To understand it, we must first of all grasp the *present* for-itself's relation to being. Thus, as we were able to foresee, the study of the past directs us to the study of the present.

(B) The present

Unlike the past, which is in-itself, the present is for-itself. What is its being? The present has its own antinomy: on the one hand, we readily describe it in terms of *being*: what is present is opposed to the future,

---

19 TN: Sartre has already quoted this expression from Hegel at EN 70.

which is not yet, and also to the past, which is no longer. But, on the other hand, a strict analysis that aimed to rid the present of everything it is not—i.e., its immediate past and future—would in fact find nothing more than an infinitesimal instant, which is to say, as Husserl observes in his *Phenomenology of Internal Time-Consciousness*,[20] the ideal term of an infinitely pursued division: a nothingness. Thus, as on every occasion when we approach the study of human-reality from a new point of view, we find ourselves back with this indissoluble pair: Being and Nothingness.

What is the primary meaning of the present? Clearly, what distinguishes anything existing in the present from any other existence is its character of *presence*. When the register is called, the soldier or the pupil replies "Present!" in the sense of "*adsum*." And the opposite of *present* can be *absent*, just as much as *past*. Thus the meaning of *present* is "presence to . . ." We ought therefore to ask *to what* is the present a presence? And *who* is present? These questions will doubtless lead us now to elucidate the very being of the present.

My present is being present. Present to what? To this table, to this bedroom, to Paris, to the world—in short, to being-in-itself. But, inversely, is being-in-itself present *to me*, and to the rest of being-in-itself? If so, the present would be a reciprocal relation between presences. But, as we can easily see, it is nothing of the kind. Presence to . . . is an internal relation between the present being and the beings to which it is present. In no case can it be a matter of a mere external relation of contiguity. Presence to . . . means existence outside itself, alongside . . . Anything that can be present to . . . must be in its being such as to have within it a relationship of being with other beings. I can be present to this chair only if I am unified with it in an ontological relation of synthesis, only if I am over there, in the being of this chair as *not being* this chair. A being that is present to . . . cannot therefore repose "*in-itself*"; the in-itself cannot be present, any more than it can be past; it *is*, quite simply. There can be no question of any one in-itself existing in some kind of simultaneity alongside another in-itself—other than from the point of view of a being who was co-present to the two in-itselfs, and who had its own capacity for presence. Therefore the present can only be the for-itself's presence to being-in-itself. And this presence cannot be the outcome

20 TN: This work is translated into English as Husserl (1991).

of some accident, of concomitance: on the contrary, any concomitance presupposes it, and presence must be an ontological structure of the

157 for-itself. This table must be present to this chair in a world haunted by human-reality in the form of a presence. In other words, we cannot conceive of a type of existent that exists first as for-itself in order *afterward* to be present to being. Rather, the for-itself makes itself present to being in making itself be for-itself, and it ceases to be presence when it ceases to be for-itself. The for-itself's presence to being defines it.

To which being does the for-itself make itself a presence? The answer is clear: the for-itself is present to being-in-itself as a whole. Or rather the for-itself's presence makes it the case that there is a totality of being-in-itself. Indeed, by this very mode of presence to being in its capacity of being, any possibility of the for-itself being *more present* to some favored being than to other beings is set aside. Even if the facticity of the for-itself's existence means it is *there*—rather than elsewhere—to be *there* is not to be *present*. *Being-there* only determines the perspective from which the presence to the totality of the in-itself takes place. The for-itself thereby brings it about that the beings are *for* one same presence. The beings are disclosed as co-present in a world in which the for-itself unites them with its own blood through the complete ecstatic sacrifice of itself that we know as "presence." "Before" the for-itself's sacrifice it would have been impossible to say any beings existed—either together or separately. But the for-itself is the being through whom the present enters the world; effectively, worldly beings are co-present insofar as the same for-itself is present to them all at the same time. Thus what we ordinarily describe as "present," in the case of in-itself beings, is to be clearly distinguished from their being, even though it is *nothing more*: it is merely their co-presence insofar as a for-itself is present to them.

We know now *who is present* and *to what* the present is present. But what is *presence?*

We have seen that it cannot be the pure coexistence of two existents, conceived as a mere relation of externality, because a third term would be required, in order to establish this coexistence. This third term exists in the case of things' coexistence in the midst of the world: what establishes their coexistence is the for-itself, as it makes itself co-present to all of them. But in the case of the for-itself's presence to being-in-itself, there can be no third term. No witness—not even God—can *establish* this presence; even the

for-itself cannot know it unless it *already is*. Nonetheless, it cannot have the in-itself's mode of being. In other words, the for-itself is originarily presence to being insofar as it is its own witness of coexistence, in relation to itself. How should we understand this? We know that the for-itself is the being whose existence takes the form of witnessing its own being. Now the for-itself is present to being if it is intentionally directed outside itself on to that being. And it has to stick as closely to being as possible, short of identification. We will see in the following chapter that this adherence is realist, by virtue of the for-itself's being born to itself in an original con-   158
nection with being: it bears witness to itself of itself as *not being* that being. And it is thereby outside itself—on being and in being—as not being this being. Moreover, we can infer this from the very meaning of presence: our presence to any being implies that we are linked to that being by an internal connection; otherwise no link between the present and being would be possible. But this internal connection is negative: it denies, with respect to a present being, that it is that being to which it is present. Otherwise the internal connection would disappear into a straightforward identification. Thus the for-itself's presence to being implies that the for-itself bears witness to itself, in the presence of being, as not being that being: presence to being is the for-itself's presence, insofar as it is not. That is because the negation does not bear on a difference in a way of being—which might distinguish the for-itself from being—but on a difference in being. We can express this concisely by saying that the present *is not*.

What does this non-being of the present and of the for-itself mean? To grasp this we must return to the for-itself, to its mode of existing, and briefly sketch a description of its ontological relationship to being. We can never say of the for-itself as such that it *is*, in the sense in which, for example, we can say: "It *is* nine o'clock," which is to say in the sense of being's total self-adequation, which posits and eliminates the "itself," and offers the outward appearance of passivity. For this reason, the for-itself exists as an appearance, paired with a witness of a reflection, and the reflection refers to a reflecting, without there being any object whose reflection could be the reflection. The for-itself does not have being because its being is always at a distance: over there, in the reflecting, if you are considering the appearance, which is an appearance or reflection only for the reflecting; over there, in the reflection, if you are considering the reflecting which, in itself, is purely the function of reflecting *this* reflection. But in addition, the for-itself, taken by itself, is not being—because it explicitly makes itself be for-itself as not being being. It is consciousness of . . . as the inner negation of . . . The basic structure of intentionality and of ipseity is negation, as an internal relation of the for-itself to a thing; the for-itself is constituted outside itself, on the basis of the thing, as the negation of that thing; in this way, its first relationship with being in itself is negation; it "is" in the mode of the for-itself, i.e., as an existent which, insofar as it is revealed to itself as not being being, is dispersed. It doubly escapes being, through its inner disintegration and through its explicit negation. And the present is precisely this negation of being, this escape from being insofar as being is there, as what we escape from. The for-itself is present to being in the form of flight; the present is a constant flight in the face of being. Thus we have clarified the primary meaning of the present: the present is not; the present instant comes from a reifying and actualizing conception of the for-itself; this conception leads to the practice of denoting the for-itself by means of what is, and of what it is

159   present to—for example, by this hand on the dial. In this sense, it would be absurd to say that, for the for-itself, it is nine o'clock; rather, the for-itself can be present to a hand that points at nine o'clock. What we incorrectly refer to as "the present" is the being to which the present is presence. It is impossible to grasp the present in the form of an instant, because the instant would have to be the moment at which the present is. Yet the present is not; it is presentified in the form of flight.[21]

But the present is not only the for-itself's presentifying non-being. As for-itself, it has its being outside, in front of and behind itself. Behind it, it was its past; and in front of it, it will be its future. It is the flight out of co-present being and away from the being that it was, toward the being that it will be. As present, it is not what it is (past) and it is what it is not (future). We are hereby directed to the Future.

(C) The future

Let us note first that the in-itself cannot be the future, and nor can it contain any part of the future. When I look at this crescent moon, the full moon is in the future only "within the world" that is disclosed to

---

21 TN: . . . il se présentifie . . . For [se] présentifier, see the section on Husserl vocabulary in Notes on the Translation.

human-reality: it is through human-reality that the future arrives in the world. In itself, this quarter of the moon is what it is. Nothing is in it as potentiality. It is in actuality. As a phenomenon of being-in-itself's original temporality, therefore, there is no future—any more than there is a past. If the in-itself's future existed, it would exist *in-itself*, cut off from being like the past. Even were we to accept, as Laplace does,[22] a complete determinism that would enable us *to predict* a future state, this future circumstance would still need to be profiled against an antecedent disclosure of the future as such, a being-to-come of the world— otherwise time must be an illusion and chronology disguises a strictly logical order of deducibility. If the future can be seen in profile at the world's horizon, that can only be by means of a being that *is* its own future, i.e., which is "forth-coming" to itself, whose being is constituted by a coming-to-itself of its being.[23] Here, again, we encounter ecstatic structures that are analogous to those we described for the past. Only a being who has to be its being, rather than merely being it, can have a future.

But what exactly is it to be one's future? And which type of being possesses a future? We must, from the outset, abandon the idea that the future exists in the form of *representation*. First of all, it is rare for the future to be "represented." And when it is—as Heidegger says—it is thematized and it ceases to be my future in order to become the indifferent object of my representation. And further, even if the future were represented, it could not be the "content" of my representation because that content, if there was one, would have to be present. Might it be said that a "futurizing" intention can animate this present content? That would make no sense. If such an intention even existed, it would be necessary for it to be present itself—in which case the problem of the future is impossible to solve—or, otherwise, for it to transcend the present into the future, and in that case the intention's being is "to come" [and] we are obliged to recognize that the being of the future differs from the mere *percipi*.[24] If moreover the for-itself was confined within the present, how could it represent the future? How could it know it or foresee it? No manufactured idea can provide an

160

---

22 TN: Pierre-Simon Laplace (1749–1827), a French astronomer and mathematician, is often said to be the first person to formulate causal determinism.

23 TN: . . . *qui est son propre avenir . . . qui est à-venir* . . . Sartre repeats the pun used earlier.

24 TN: As the sentence in the French text is ungrammatical, the suggested "[and]" is mine.

equivalent of it. If at first we have confined the present within the present, it goes without saying that it will never get out of it. It is no use to describe it as "pregnant with the future."[25] Either this expression means nothing, or it designates an actual, efficient power of the present, or it points to the law of the for-itself's being, as being future in relation to itself and—in this last case—it only highlights what we need to describe and explain. The for-itself can neither be "pregnant with the future," nor an "awaiting of the future," nor "knowledge of the future," except against the ground of an original and prejudicative relation of the self to itself: we cannot conceive of the for-itself possessing the slightest possibility of any thematic prediction—not even of the determined states of the scientific universe—unless it is the being that, on the basis of its future, returns to itself, the being that makes itself exist as having its being outside itself, in the future. Let us take a simple example: this position which I keenly take up on the court has meaning only through the movement I will make next, with my racket, to send the ball back over the net. But I am obeying neither my "clear representation" of the future movement, nor my "firm resolution" to accomplish it. Representations and acts of will are idols invented by psychologists. It is my future movement which, without even being thematically presented, turns backward to the positions I adopt, in order to illuminate, to connect and to modify them. From the outset I am, all at the same time, over there and on this court, as a lack in myself, and returning the ball, and the intermediate positions I adopt are only means for bringing me closer to this future state in order to merge within it, each of whose full meaning is given only through this future state. There is not a moment of my consciousness that is not similarly defined by an internal relation to a future; whether I write, I smoke, I drink, or I rest, the meaning of my [acts of] consciousness is always at a distance, over there, outside. In this sense Heidegger is right to say *Dasein* is "always infinitely more than what it would be if we limited it to its pure present."[26] Better still, such limitation is impossible, because we would thereby make the present into an in-itself. It was, therefore, correct to claim that finality is

---

25 TN: Sartre quotes Leibniz's description of the present as "pregnant with the future" from §22 of the *Monadology* (Leibniz 2014: 18). The other phrases in quotation marks a few lines later are harder to place. The "awaiting" phrase probably alludes to Heidegger.

26 TN: I have been unable to find this quotation in Heidegger.

causality in reverse, which is to say the efficient power of a future state. But we forget too often to take this sentence literally.

We should not understand the future as a "now" that is not yet. We would fall back into the in-itself and, above all, we would be obliged to envisage time as a given and static container. The future is *what I have to be* insofar as I cannot not be it. Recall that the for-itself, confronted with being, presentifies itself as not being that being, and as having been its being in the past. This presence is flight. What we have here is not a delayed presence, resting now alongside being, but rather an escape out of being and toward . . . And it is a twofold flight, because, in fleeing from the being that it is not, presence flees from the being that it was. *What* does it flee toward? Let us not forget that the for-itself, insofar as it presentifies itself to being in order to flee from it, is a lack. The Possible is *what* is missing from the for-itself for it to be itself or, alternatively, the appearance—at a distance—of what I am. From this we can grasp the meaning of the flight involved in presence: it is a flight toward *its being*, which is to say toward the "itself" that it would become by coinciding with what is missing from it. The future is the lack that, as a lack, separates it from the in-itself of presence. If nothing were missing from it, it would fall back within being and would lose even its *presence to being*, in order to acquire in exchange the isolation of complete identity. The lack, as such, allows it to be presence; it is because it is outside itself, and directed toward a missing item beyond the world, that it is able to be outside itself, as presence to an in-itself that it is not. The future is the determining being that the for-itself has to be, beyond being. There is a future because the for-itself has its being to be—rather than straightforwardly being it. As for the being that the for-itself has to be, it cannot be in the same way as the co-present in-itselfs, or it would be without having to be been; we must not, therefore, picture it as a completely defined state, from which only presence is missing, in the way in which, for Kant, existence adds nothing more to the object of a concept. But neither can it not exist; otherwise the for-itself would only be a *given*. It is what the for-itself makes itself be, as it constantly grasps itself for itself as incomplete in relation to it. It is what haunts the reflecting-reflection pair from a distance, and explains why the reflecting grasps the reflection (and *vice versa*) as a Not-yet. But this missing item must, precisely, arise alongside the for-itself that is missing something in the unity of a single event, or there would be nothing in relation to which the for-itself could grasp itself as not-yet. The future was revealed to the for-itself as what the for-itself is not yet, insofar as the for-itself constitutes itself non-thetically for itself—within the perspective of this revelation—as a not-yet, and insofar as it makes itself be as a project of itself out of the present toward what it is not yet. And, of course, there can be no future without this revelation. And this revelation itself demands to be revealed to itself, which is to say that it demands the for-itself's revelation to itself; otherwise the whole structure—Revelation, revealed—would fall into the unconscious, i.e., into the in-itself. Thus only a being that is what it reveals to itself—i.e., whose being is in question for itself—can have a future.

162   But conversely, such a being can be for itself only within the perspective of a not-yet, because it grasps itself as a nothingness, i.e., as a being whose complement of being is at a distance from it. "At a distance"— or, in other words, beyond being. In this way, the future is all that the for-itself is, beyond being.

What does "beyond" mean? To grasp this, we must note that the future has one of the for-itself's essential characteristics: it is (future) presence to being. And it is the presence of this for-itself here—of the for-itself whose future it is. When I say "I will be happy," it is this present for-itself that will be happy; it is the current "Erlebnis," with all that it *was*, dragging it behind it. And it will be happy as presence to being, i.e., as the for-itself's future presence to a co-future being. So what is given to me as the meaning of the present for-itself is, in the ordinary case, co-future being, insofar as that will be disclosed to the future for-itself as what the for-itself will be present to. This is because the for-itself is thetically conscious of the world in the form of presence, and not thetically conscious of itself. Thus what is usually disclosed to consciousness is the *future world*, without consciousness noticing that it is the world as it will appear to a consciousness, the world as it is posited in the future, by the presence of a for-itself to come. This world has meaning as a future world only insofar as I am present to it as *another who I will be*, in another position physically, affectively, socially, etc. However, he lies at the other end of my present for-itself, and beyond being-in-itself, and that is why we tend to present the future in the first place as a state of the world, and to have ourselves appear subsequently against this worldly ground. If I am writing, I am conscious of the words as written, or as having to be written. The words alone seem to be the future awaiting me. But the mere fact that they appear as *to be written* implies that my writing, as my non-thetic consciousness (of) self, is the possibility that I am. In this way the future, as a for-itself's future presence to a being, drags the in-itself into the future with it. This being, to which it will be present, is the meaning of the in-itself that is co-present to the present for-itself, just as the future is the meaning of the for-itself. The future is presence to a co-future being because the for-itself can exist only outside itself, alongside being, and the future is a future for-itself. But in this way, through this future, a future arrives in the world,[27] which means the for-itself is its meaning as presence to a being that is beyond being. Through the for-itself a "beyond" to being is disclosed, alongside which it has to be what it is. I must, according to the famous phrase, "become what I was,"[28] but I must become it within a world that has itself *become*, and within a world that has become *on the basis of* what it is. In other words, I give the world its particular possibilities on the basis of the state in which I grasp it: determinism appears against the ground of the futurizing project of myself. In this way, we can distinguish the future from the imaginary—where I am, equally, what I am not, and where, equally, I find my meaning in a being that I have to be, but where this for-itself that I have to be emerges from the depths of the world's nihilation, *beside* the world of being.

163

But the future is not solely the for-itself's presence to a being situated beyond being. It is something awaiting the for-itself that I am. This something is myself: when I say that I will be happy, it is clearly understood that it is my present self, dragging its past after it, who will be happy. Thus the future is myself insofar as I await myself as present to a being beyond being. I project myself toward the future in order to merge with what is missing from me, i.e., with that which, synthetically added to the present, would make it the case that I am what I am. Thus, what the for-itself has to be, in the form of presence to being beyond being, is its own

---

27 TN: Sartre uses the two synonymous terms for "future" available in French (but not in English) to differentiate the future of the for-itself (futur) from the future (avenir) of the world: *Mais ainsi, par le futur, un avenir arrive au monde.*

28 TN: In fact the more common expression exhorts one to "become who one is." This is the phrase famously used, for example, in the title of Nietzsche's *Ecce Homo* (Nietzsche 2009).

possibility. The future is the ideal point at which the infinite and sudden compression of facticity (Past), of the for-itself (Present) and of its possible (Future) will finally allow the *Itself* to arise as the in itself existence of the for-itself. And the for-itself's project toward the future that it *is* is a project toward the in-itself. In this sense, the for-itself has its future to be, because it can only be the foundation of what it is by being ahead of itself and beyond being: the for-itself is, in its very nature, obliged to be "a hollow that is always future."[29] So it will never have *become*, in the present, what it had to be, in the future. The present for-itself's future falls— as a future—entirely into the past, along with this for-itself itself. It will be a specific for-itself's past future, or the future perfect.[30] This future is not *actualized*. What is actualized is a for-itself *designated* as the future, and constituting itself in connection with this future. For example, my final position on the court determined—from the depths of the future—all my intermediate positions, and in the end it was joined by a final position identical to what it had been in the future, as the meaning of my movements. But this "joining" is, precisely, purely ideal, and not a real operation: the future does not allow us to join it; it slides into the past as a former future, and the present for-itself is disclosed in all its facticity as the foundation of its own nothingness and, once again, as lacking a new future. Hence comes that ontological disappointment that awaits the for-itself each time it reaches a future: "How wonderful the Republic was, under the Empire!"[31] Even if my present is strictly identical in content to the future beyond being toward which I was projecting myself, it is not *this* present that I was projecting myself toward, because I was projecting myself toward the future as the future, i.e., as the point at which I would join up with my being, as the place where the *Itself* would arise.

We are in a better position, now, to question the future about its being, since this future that I have to be is simply the *possibility* of my presence to

---

29 TN: . . . *devoir être* "*un creux toujours futur.*" Sartre puts the phrase within quotation marks because he is citing it from Paul Valéry's poem "Le Cimetière Marin." There are various English translations of this famous poem; the rather literal translation I have provided here seems to map Sartre's intended meaning.

30 TN: Sartre is referring to the grammatical tense.

31 TN: "*Que la République était belle sous l'Empire!*" The French historian Alphonse Aulard (1849– 1928) famously said this in 1885, expressing his disappointment with the current regime.

being beyond being. In this sense, the future is thoroughly opposed to the past. It is true that the past is, in effect, the being that I am outside myself— but it is the being that I am without any possibility of not being it. That is what we called being one's past *behind* oneself. The future that I have to be, on the contrary, is in its being such that I only *can* be it, because my freedom eats away at its being from below. In consequence, the future constitutes the meaning of my present for-itself, as the project of its possibility, but it does not at all predetermine my for-itself to come, since the for-itself is forever abandoned in that nihilating obligation to be the foundation of its nothingness. The future only drafts in advance the framework in which the for-itself will make itself be as a presentifying flight to being, and toward another future. The future is what I would be if I were not free, and what I can *have to be* only because I am free. At the same time as it appears at the horizon, in order to acquaint me with what I am, on the basis of what I will be ("What are you doing?" "I *am* in the middle of nailing this carpet, of hanging this picture on the wall"), its nature as a future present-for-itself disarms it, since the mode in which the for-itself will be will be that of determining itself to be, and since the future—once it has become a past future, as the preliminary draft of this for-itself—can only request it, in its capacity as past, to be what it makes itself be. In brief, I am my future within the constant perspective of the possibility of not being it. Hence comes that anguish, described earlier, which stems from my not sufficiently being this future that I have to be, and which gives my present its meaning: because I am a being whose meaning is always problematic. The for-itself may wish to be chained to its possible—as if to the being that lies outside itself but which, at least, lies *surely* outside itself—but in vain: the for-itself can only ever be its future problematically, because it is separated from it by the nothingness that it is. In brief, the for-itself is free, and its freedom sets its own limit to itself. To be free is to be condemned to be free. Thus the future, insofar as it is future, has no being. It is not *in itself* and nor does it have the for-itself's mode of being either, since it is the for-itself's *meaning*. The future is not; it *possibilizes* itself. The future is the continual possibilization of possibles, as the present for-itself's meaning, insofar as this meaning is problematic and—as such—radically escapes the present for-itself.

The future, thus described, does not correspond to a homogeneous and chronologically ordered succession of instants to come. Of course,

164

my possibles lie within a hierarchy. But this hierarchy does not corre-spond to the order of universal temporality, as it becomes established on the basis of original temporality. I *am* an infinity of possibilities, because the for-itself's meaning is complex and cannot be contained within a for-mula. But one possibility may do more to determine the meaning of the present for-itself than another one, which is closer in universal time. For example, this possibility of going at two o'clock to see a friend whom I have not seen for two years really is a possible that I *am*. But the pos-sibles that are closer—possibilities of going there by taxi, bus, metro, on foot—remain at present undetermined. I *am not* any of these possibilities. Thus, within the series of my possibilities, there are holes. At the level of knowledge, these holes will be filled in by the constitution of a homoge-neous time without any lacunae and, at the level of action, by my will, i.e., through my rational and thematizing choice, in accordance with my possibles, of possibilities that are not and never will be my possibilities, and that I will actualize in the mode of complete indifference *in order to join up* with a possible that I am.

165

II. THE ONTOLOGY OF TEMPORALITY

(A) Static temporality

Our phenomenological description of the three temporal ecstases ought now to allow us to address temporality, as a totalizing structure within which the secondary ecstatic structures are organized. But this new study must be carried out from two different points of view.

Temporality is often thought to be indefinable. Yet everyone will admit that it is above all a succession. And we can define the succes-sion, in turn, as an order, whose ordering principle is the before-after relation. A multiplicity ordered in terms of "before" and "after": such is temporal multiplicity. We can begin, therefore, by considering the constitution and the requirements of the terms "*before*" and "*after*." Let us call this the temporal "*static*," since these notions of "before" and "after" may be considered strictly in their ordinal aspect, and indepen-dently of any change in the literal sense. But time is not only a fixed order for a determinate multiplicity: if we observe temporality more carefully, we will note the *fact* of succession—i.e., the fact that a particu-lar "after" *becomes* a "before," that the present *becomes* the past, and that the future becomes the future perfect. This is what we should examine in second place, calling it the temporal "*Dynamic.*" Doubtless, the secret of the static constitution of time should be sought within the temporal dynamic. But it is preferable to separate out the difficulties. Indeed, in one sense, we can say that the temporal static may be considered on its own, as a particular formal structure of temporality—what Kant calls the *order* of time—and that the dynamic corresponds to the material flowing or—in accordance with Kant's terminology—the *course* of time.[32] It will be profitable, therefore, to consider this order, and this course, successively.

166

The "before-after" order is defined in the first place by its irreversibility. We call a series "successive" if its terms can only be considered one by one, and in only one direction. But many people have wanted to see the *before* and the *after* as forms of separation—precisely because the terms of the series are disclosed *one by one*, and because each of them excludes the others. And indeed time really does separate me, for example, from the actualization of my desires. If I am obliged to wait for their actualization, that is because it is situated *after* other events. Without the succession of "afters" I could be what I want to be *straightaway*, and there would no longer be any distance between me and myself, or any separation between an action and a dream. It is essentially this separating power of time that has been emphasized by novelists and poets, as well as a related idea (which, in fact, belongs to the temporal dynamic): that any "now" is destined to become an "erstwhile." Time eats away at things, and hollows out; it separates, and flees. And, still in its capacity as something that separates—by separating man from his affliction, or from the object of his affliction—time heals.

"Leave all to time," says the king to Don Rodrigo.[33] More generally, what strikes us especially is the necessity, to which all being is subject, of being split into an infinite dispersion of successive *afters*. Even *permanent* things, even this table, which remains invariable while I change, must extend and refract its being within the dispersion of time. Time sepa-

32 TN: . . . *au cours du temps* . . . Sartre must have Kant's *Critique of Pure Reason* (Kant 1998) in mind, but the generality of his allusion precludes identification of any specific passage.

33 TN: "*Laisse faire le temps*" . . . Sartre is quoting from Corneille's play *Le Cid*, Act V, Scene 7. I quote from the English translation by John C. Lapp (Corneille 2012).

rates me from myself, from what I have been, from what I want to be, from what I want to do, from things, and from the Other. And we choose time as a practical measure of distance: we are half an hour away from this town, an hour away from this other one, it will take three days to finish this work, etc. It follows from these premises that a temporal outlook on man and the world must collapse into the fragmentation of before and after. The unit of this fragmentation—the temporal atom—will be the instant, whose place is before some determinate instants and after other instants, without including either the "before" or the "after" within its own form. The instant cannot be split and, since temporality is a succession, it is timeless;[34] but the world collapses into an infinite dust of instants, and poses the problem (for Descartes, for example) of knowing how there can be any transition from one instant to another: because the instants are juxtaposed, i.e., separated by nothing, and yet there is no communication between them. Similarly, Proust wonders how his "Me" is able to pass from one instant to another; he wonders how, for example, after a night of sleep, he can rediscover precisely his "Me" from the night before, rather than any other. And the empiricists, more radically, having denied any permanence to the Self, tried in vain to establish an appearance of transversal unity running through the instants of psychological life. Thus, when we consider in isolation temporality's power to dissolve, we are forced to admit that the fact of having existed at any given instant does not constitute the right to exist at the following instant, nor even a mortgage or an option on the future. And now the problem is to explain how there can be a world, i.e., instances of interconnected changes, and of permanence within time.

167

However, temporality is not solely, or even in the first place, separation. To appreciate this, we need only consider the notion of "before" and "after" more precisely. We said that A is after B. We have thereby established between A and B an explicit relation of order, which presupposes therefore their unification within that very order. If there were no other relation between A and B than this one, that would at least still be

---

34 TN: L'instant est ... intemporel ... The French adjectives intemporel and atemporel are synonymous, but, as Sartre uses both, I translate the former as "timeless" and the latter as "atemporal."

enough to assure their connection, for the relation allows us to move in thought from one to the other, and to unite them within a judgment of succession. If therefore time is separation, it is at least a separation of a special type: a division, which reunites. So be it—one might say—but this unifying relation is an external relation *par excellence.* When the associationists wanted to establish that impressions within the mind were bound with each other only by purely external connections, were they not ultimately reducing all associative connections to the before-after relation, conceived in terms of mere "contiguity?"

Without doubt. But didn't Kant show that a unity of experience was required and thereby the unification of the temporal manifold, in order for the slightest empirical associative connection even to be conceivable? Let us consider the theory of associationism more closely. Accompanying it is a monist conception of being, as being everywhere being-in-itself. Every impression in the mind is, in itself, what it is, isolated in its present plenitude; no trace of the future is involved, no lack. Hume, when he issues his famous challenge, was concerned to establish this law, which he claims to derive from experience: we may inspect an impression, strong or weak, as we wish, but we will never find anything in it but itself, so that any connection between an antecedent and a consequent, however constant it may be, remains unintelligible. Let us suppose, therefore, some temporal content A, existing as a being in itself, and a later temporal content B, existing in the same way, i.e., in the self-belonging of identity. We must note from the outset that this self-identity obliges each of them to exist without any separation at all from itself—not even temporal separation—and hence to exist in eternity or in the instant: these amount to the same thing, since the instant, not being internally defined by the "before-after" connection, is timeless. Given these conditions, we can ask: How can state A come *before* state B? It will be of no use to reply that it is not the *states* that are earlier or later but rather the *instants* that contain them, because these instants are, *ex hypothesi,* *in itself,* like the states. Now, A's anteriority in relation to B presupposes in A's very nature (as an instant or a state) an incompleteness which points toward B. If A is earlier than B, it is because A is able to acquire this determination *in* B. If not, it will be impossible for B, isolated within its instant, to confer upon A—isolated within its own—the slightest specific quality, either as it arises or in its annihila-

168

tion. In brief, if A is to be earlier than B, it must in its very being be *in* B, as its future. And conversely, if B is to be later than A, it must lag behind itself, in A, which confers its meaning of posteriority upon it. If therefore we concede being in itself *a priori* to A and B, it is impossible to establish the slightest connection of succession between them. Such a connection would in effect be a purely external relation and, as such, we would have to accept its remaining up in the air, deprived of any substrate, and unable to bite either on A or on B, within a sort of time-less nothingness.

There remains the possibility that this before-after relation can exist only for a witness who establishes it. Only, if this witness can be in A and in B *at the same time*, it is because he is himself temporal, and then the problem arises again, in relation to him. Or else, on the contrary, he can transcend time by means of the gift of temporal ubiquity, which is equivalent to timelessness. This solution was settled on, in the same way, by Descartes and Kant: for them, the temporal unity within which the synthetic before-after relation is disclosed is conferred upon the multiplicity of instants by a being which itself escapes from temporal-ity. Both of them set out by assuming that time is the form of division, a time which itself dissolves into pure multiplicity. As the unity of time cannot be provided by time itself, they burden an extratemporal being with this task: God, and his continuous creation, in Descartes; the *I think*, and its forms of synthetic unity, in Kant. Only, in Descartes's case, what unifies time is its material content, which is maintained in exis-tence through a constant creation *ex nihilo*, while in Kant's case—on the contrary—the concepts of pure understanding are applied to the form of time. In any case, something *timeless* (God, or the *I think*) is respon-sible for providing *timeless* beings (the instants) with their temporal-ity. Temporality becomes a mere external and abstract relation between timeless substances: the aim is to reconstruct it entirely out of a-temporal materials. Evidently, no reconstruction like this, made from the outset against time, can subsequently lead us to the temporal. Either we are—implicitly and surreptitiously—temporalizing the timeless or else, if we scrupulously protect its timelessness, time will become a pure human illusion, a dream. Indeed, if time is *real*, then God has to "wait until the sugar melts"; he must be over there, in the future, and yesterday, in the past, in order to work the connection between moments, because it is necessary for him to go and find them where they are.[35] In this way, God's pseudo-timelessness masks other concepts, that of temporal infinity and temporal ubiquity. But these can have meaning only for a synthetic form of self-separation—which no longer corresponds in any way to being in itself. If, on the contrary, we make God's omniscience, for example, rest on his extratemporality, he will not need to wait for the sugar to melt to *see* that it will melt. But, in that case, the necessity of waiting—and, in consequence, temporality—can only represent an illusion resulting from human finitude, and the chronological order becomes nothing but the confused perception of a logical and eternal order. The argument can be applied without modification to Kant's "I think." And it would be pointless to object that, in Kant's view, time has a unity as such, since it arises from timelessness as an *a priori* form— because our problem is not so much that of accounting for time's total unity as it arises but rather the intratemporal connections of "before" and "after." Should we invoke a virtual temporality, which the unification actualizes? But this virtual succession is even less comprehensible than the real succession we talked about earlier. What kind of succession awaits its unification in order to become a succession? To whom, or to what, does it belong? And yet, if that succession was not already given somewhere, how could something timeless secrete it, without losing all its timelessness within it? How could succession even emanate from timelessness without shattering it? Moreover, the very idea of unification used here is absolutely incomprehensible. In effect, we are presupposing two in-itselfs, isolated in their place and at their time. How can they be unified? Is this unification *real*? In that case, either we are just engaging in empty talk—and the unification has no purchase on two in-itselfs, isolated in their respective identities and completeness—or we have to constitute a unity of a new type, which is precisely ecstatic unity: each state will be outside itself, over there, in order to be *before* or *after* the other. Only that will require us to shatter their being, to decompress it: in short, to temporalize it, and not merely bring them closer.

35 TN: With this expression Sartre is probably alluding to Bergson's remark in *Creative Evolution*, chapter 1. As the English translation puts it: "If I want to mix a glass of sugar and water, I must . . . wait until the sugar melts. This little fact is big with meaning" (Bergson 1911a: 9).

Now, how could the timeless unity of the I think, as a mere faculty of thought, be able to operate this decompression in being? Should we say the unification is virtual, i.e., that a type of unity has been projected beyond the impressions, somewhat like Husserl's noema? But how can a timeless being, having to unify timeless elements, conceive of the kind of unification that belongs to succession? And if—as we would need to agree in that case—the esse of time is a percipi, how will the percipitur[36] be constituted? In short, how could a being with an a-temporal structure apprehend any in-itselfs—isolated in their timelessness—as temporal, or enable them to be intended as such? Thus, insofar as it is at the same time a form of separation and a form of synthesis, temporality will not permit us either to derive it from something timeless or to impose it from outside on timeless things.

170   Leibniz, reacting against Descartes, and Bergson, reacting against Kant, wanted in turn to view temporality as nothing more than a pure relation of immanence and cohesion. Leibniz regards the problem of the transition from one instant to the other and its solution—continuous creation—as a false problem with a pointless solution: according to him, Descartes forgot time's continuity. In asserting time's continuity, we deny ourselves any conception of it as formed out of instants and, if there are no longer any instants, there is no longer any before-after relation between the instants. Time is a vast, continuous flowing, to which it is impossible to assign elements whose existence is antecedent and in-itself.

But this is to forget that the before-after is also a form that separates. If time is a given continuity with an undeniable tendency toward separation, we can raise Descartes's question in a different form: What is the source of continuity's cohesive power? Of course, there are no initial elements that are juxtaposed within the continuous. But that is precisely because it is from the outset a unification. As Kant says, it is because I draw a straight line that the straight line, actualized within the unity of a single act, is something other than an infinite line of dots. Who, therefore, draws time? In short, this continuity is a fact that must be accounted for; it cannot be a solution. We should recall moreover Poincaré's famous

36 TN: . . . comment se constitue le percipitur . . . The Latin percipitur literally means "it is perceived." Sartre therefore is asking "How is what is perceived constituted?"

definition: a series a, b, c, he says, is continuous when $a = b$, $b = c$, $a \div c$.[37]
This is an excellent definition, just because it allows us to anticipate a
type of being that is what it is not, and is not what it is: by virtue of
an axiom, $a = c$; by virtue of the continuity itself, $a \div c$. Thus a is, and
is not, equivalent to c. And b, which is equal to a and equal to c, differs
from itself, insofar as a is not equal to c. But as long as we consider it
from the perspective of the in-itself, this ingenious definition remains
a mere flight of fancy. And if it provides us with a type of being that is
and—at the same time—is not, it does not provide us with its principles, or its foundation. Everything remains to be done. In the study of
temporality in particular, we can appreciate how useful continuity is,
by intercalating between an instant a and an instant c—however close
they may be—an intermediate b such that, as in the formula $a = b$, $b = c$,
$a \div c$, b is at the same time indiscernible from a and indiscernible from
c, which are absolutely discernible from each other. This will actualize
the before-after relation, and provide an element able to come before
itself—insofar as it is indiscernible from a and from c. Splendid! But how
can such a being exist? What is the source of its ecstatic nature? How is it
that the splitting that we can see beginning within it never comes to an
end? Why does it not explode into two terms, of which one merges with
a and the other with c? How can we fail to see that its unity poses a problem? Perhaps a more thorough examination of this being's conditions
of possibility would have taught us that only the for-itself could exist in
that way, in the ecstatic unity of itself. But it is precisely this examination   171
that has not been attempted, and Leibniz's temporal cohesion hides in its
depths the cohesion of absolute immanence which belongs to logic, i.e.,
identity. But if the chronological order is continuous, then, precisely, it
cannot be symbolized by the order of identity, because continuity is not
compatible with identity.

In the same way, Bergson, with his duration as a melodic organization
and interpenetrating multiplicity, does not seem to see that an organization of multiplicity presupposes some organizing act. He is right, against
Descartes, to eliminate the instant; but Kant is right to oppose him, by

37 TN: Jules Henri Poincaré (1854–1912) was a French mathematician, physicist, and
    philosopher of science. The French text uses a division sign here between a and c, but
    I think there must have been a mistake transcribing the manuscript. The "does not
    equal" symbol ($\neq$) makes far more sense of the text.

asserting that no synthesis is *given*. This Bergsonian past, adhering to the present and even penetrating it, is hardly more than a figure of rhetoric. And this is clearly displayed by the difficulties encountered by Bergson with his theory of memory. For if the past, as he asserts, lacks agency, it can only remain behind; it can never return to penetrate the present in the form of a memory, unless some present being has taken on the additional task of existing ecstatically in the past. And of course, in Bergson's theory, it is definitely one single being that endures. But that is just what makes us feel in need of ontological clarifications, because we do not know if, in the end, it is being that endures, or duration that is being. And if duration is being, then we must be told the ontological structure of duration; and if, on the contrary, it is being that endures, we must be shown what, in its being, enables it to endure.

What may we conclude, at the end of this discussion? In the first place, this: temporality is a force that dissolves, but it does so within an act of unification; it is not so much a real multiplicity—which could not subsequently receive any unity and could not, in consequence, even exist in the form of multiplicity—as a quasi-multiplicity, the first draft of a dissociation within unity. We must not try to envisage either of these two aspects on its own: if we start by positing temporal unity, we are at risk of no longer even being able to understand anything about the irreversible succession as the *meaning* of this unity; but if we regard the disaggregating succession as time's primordial character, we are at risk of no longer even being able to understand that there is *one* time. If therefore there is no priority, either of unity over multiplicity or of multiplicity over unity, we must conceive of temporality as a unity that multiplies *itself*, which means temporality can be only a relation of being within that same being. We cannot envisage it as a container whose being is *given*, because that would mean giving up forever any understanding of how this being in-itself can fragment itself into multiplicity, or how the in-itself of the most minimal containers—or instants—can be gathered into the unity of *one* time. Temporality *is not*. Only a being with a specific structure of being can, in the unity of its being, be temporal. "Before" and "after" are intelligible, we noted, only as an internal relation. It is over there, in the "after," that the before becomes determined as "before" and conversely. In brief, the "before" is intelligible only as being what is *before* itself. In other words, temporality can only designate

172

the mode of being of a being that is, itself, outside itself. Temporality must have the structure of ipseity. In effect, it is only because the itself is itself over there, and outside itself, in its being, that it can be before or after itself—and, in general, that there can be any before and an after. Temporality can exist only as the internal structure of a being that has its being to be, i.e., as the for-itself's internal structure. It is not that the for-itself has any ontological priority over temporality. Rather, temporality is the for-itself's being insofar as the for-itself has it ecstatically to be. Temporality is not; rather the for-itself, in existing, temporalizes itself.

Conversely, our phenomenological study of the Past, the Present, and the Future allows us to show that the for-itself cannot be, unless its form is temporal.

In arising within being as the nihilation of the in-itself, the for-itself constitutes itself in every possible dimension of nihilation at the same time. From whichever angle we consider it, it is the being that is only held together by a thread or, more precisely, the being that, in being, makes every possible dimension of its nihilation exist. In the Ancient world, the term "diaspora" referred to the profound cohesion and dispersion of the Jewish people. We can make use of this word to refer to the for-itself's mode of being: it is diasporic. Being-in-itself has only one dimension of being, but the appearance of nothingness, as that which is *been*, at the heart of being complicates the existential structure, by causing the onto-logical mirage of the Itself to appear. We will see later that reflection, transcendence and being-in-the-world, and being-for-the-Other repre-sent several dimensions of nihilation or, alternatively, several original relations of being with itself. Nothingness, therefore, introduces a quasi-multiplicity within being. This quasi-multiplicity is the foundation of every multiplicity within the world, because multiplicity presupposes an initial unity, within which the multiplicity takes shape. In this sense it is not true, as Meyerson claims, that diversity is a scandal and that reality is to be held responsible for this scandal.[38] The in-itself is not diverse, it is not a multiplicity, and, in order for it to take on multiplicity as a charac-

---

38 TN: Émile Meyerson (1859–1933) was a Polish-born chemist and philosopher of sci-ence, who moved to France aged 22 and died there. Meyerson claimed that the goal of scientific reason was to explain experience through identification. The diversity discovered in reality shows its recalcitrance to reason.

teristic of its being-in-the-midst-of-the-world, it is necessary for a being to arise that is simultaneously present to each in-itself isolated in its identity. It is through human-reality that multiplicity comes to the world; the quasi-multiplicity within being-for-itself enables number to be disclosed within the world. But what do these multiple, or quasi-multiple, dimensions of the for-itself mean? They are its various relations to its being. When one is, quite simply, what one is, there is only one way of being

173   one's being. But as soon as one is no longer one's being, various ways of being it—even while not being it—simultaneously arise. If we confine ourselves to the primary ecstases—those which show the original meaning of the nihilation and, at the same time, represent the *least* nihilation— the for-itself can and must at the same time: (1) not be what it is; (2) be what it is not; (3) within the unity of a constant referral, be what it is not and not be what it is. Here we encounter three ecstatic dimensions, where the meaning of "ecstasis" is distance from itself. It is impossible to conceive of a consciousness that does not exist in these three dimensions. And if the *cogito* encounters one of them first, that does not mean that it is the first but merely that it is more easily disclosed. But, taken alone, it is an "*unselbstständig*"[39] that immediately allows the other dimensions to be seen. The for-itself is a being that must exist in all its dimensions at the same time. Here *distance*—understood as distance from itself— is nothing real, nothing that might in some general way *be*, as in itself: it is merely the nothing, the nothingness that "*is been*" as separation. Each dimension is one way of projecting ourselves, in vain, toward the Itself, of being what one is beyond a nothingness; each dimension is a different way of being this wilting of being, or this frustration of being, that the for-itself has to be. Let us consider each of them separately.

In the first dimension, the for-itself has its being to be behind it, as what it is without being its foundation. Its being is there, up against it, but separated from it by a nothingness—the nothingness of facticity. The for-itself as the foundation of its nothingness—and, as such, necessary—is separated from its original contingency insofar as it is unable either to remove it or to merge into it. It is for itself, but its mode is irremediable

---

39 TN: This is the adjectival counterpart to the German noun Sartre has used earlier: it is used to characterize something as not being capable of existing on its own, or independently.

and gratuitous. Its being is for itself, but it is not for this being—precisely because such reciprocity in the reflection-reflecting would make the original contingency of what *is* disappear. Precisely because the for-itself grasps itself in the form of being, it is at a distance—as if the reflection-reflecting activity had leaked into the in-itself, where the reflecting was no longer made to exist by the reflecting, nor the reflecting by the reflection. In consequence, the being that the for-itself has to be is given as something to which we can never return, precisely because the for-itself cannot found it in the mode of reflection-reflecting but insofar as it can only found the connection between this being and itself. The for-itself does not found the being of this being but merely the fact that this being can be *given*. This is a matter of unconditional necessity: whichever for-itself we consider, it *is* in some way; it is, since we can name it, since we can assert or deny that it has various features. But insofar as it is for-itself, it is never what it is. What it is lies behind it, as constantly *surpassed*. And this surpassed facticity is exactly what we call "the past." The past is, therefore, a necessary structure of the for-itself, because the for-itself can exist only as a nihilating surpassing, and this surpassing implies a surpassed. It is therefore impossible, at any moment in which we consider a for-itself, to grasp it as not-yet-having a past. We should not believe that the for-itself exists first, and arises in the world with the absolute newness of a being without any past, in order to constitute its past afterward, bit by bit. But, regardless of the for-itself's elevation in the world, it enters the world in the ecstatic unity of a relation with its past: there is no absolute beginning that, without having a past, becomes a past; rather, as the for-itself, insofar as it is for-itself, has to be its past, it enters the world with a past. These remarks allow us to consider the problem of birth in a rather new light. In effect, it strikes us as scandalous that consciousness should at some moment "appear," and should come "to inhabit" the embryo or, in short, that there should be one moment in which the living thing, as it develops, lacks any consciousness and another moment in which a consciousness without any past becomes imprisoned within it. But the scandal is over once it appears that there can be no consciousness without a past. That does not mean, however, that any consciousness presupposes some earlier consciousness, frozen into the in-itself. This relation between the present for-itself and the for-itself that has *become* in-itself conceals the primitive relation of pastness, which is a relation of the for-itself to

174

the pure in-itself. In point of fact, it is as the nihilation of the in-itself that the for-itself arises, and it is through this absolute event that the past is constituted as such, as the for-itself's original and nihilating relation to the in-itself. The for-itself's being is originally constituted by this relation to a being that *is not* consciousness, existing within the complete night of identity,[40] that the for-itself is, however, obliged to be, outside itself, behind itself. With this being—to which the for-itself cannot in any case be *brought back*, and in relation to which the for-itself is represented as absolutely new—the for-itself feels a deep solidarity of being, which shows up in the word "before": the in-itself is what the for-itself was *before*. In consequence, it makes perfect sense that our past does not appear to us as if it were limited by a clean line, with no smudges—which is what would happen if consciousness were able to spring up in the world *before* having a past—but that, on the contrary, it becomes lost within a progressive darkening, all the way back into shadows that, however, *we* still are; we can appreciate the ontological meaning of our shocking solidarity with the fetus, a solidarity that we are able neither to deny nor to understand. Because, after all, this fetus *was* me: it represents the *de facto* limit of my memory, but not the *de jure* limit of my past. There is a metaphysical problem about birth, to the extent that I can be concerned to know how I came to be born *from that* embryo—and perhaps that problem is insoluble. But there is no ontological problem: we do not have to ask ourselves how a consciousness can be born, because consciousness can appear to itself only as the nihilation of in-itself, i.e., as *having already been born*. As an ecstatic relation to the in-itself that it is not, and as the *a priori* constitution of pastness, birth is a law that governs the for-itself's being. To be for-itself is *to be born*. But there is no need, thereafter, to raise metaphysical questions about the in-itself from which the for-itself is born such as: "How was there an in-itself *before* the for-itself's birth?," "How is the for-itself born from *this* in-itself, rather than from that other one?," etc. None of these questions takes any account of the fact that it is through the for-itself that the past in general can exist. If a *before* exists, it is because

---

40 TN: Sartre may be alluding here to Hegel's famous sentence in *Phenomenology of Spirit* in which Hegel criticizes a view of absolute knowledge based on immediate intuition, arguing that its dissolution of all differentiation in what we know leaves us in "the night in which all cows are black" (Hegel 1977: 9).

the for-itself has arisen within the world, and it is on the basis of the for-itself that it can be established. To the extent to which the in-itself is made co-present to the for-itself a *world* appears, replacing the isolated instances of in-itself. And, in this world, designation becomes possible, and we can say: *this* object *here, that* object *there.* In this sense, insofar as the for-itself, in arising to being, makes a world of co-presences exist, it also makes its "before" appear as co-present to some in-itselfs in a world or—alternatively—in a state of the world that has passed. So, in one sense, the for-itself appears as being born from the world, because the in-itself from which it is born lies in the midst of the world, as a past co-present among past co-presents: a for-itself who was not there before is born, and arises in the world, and on the basis of the world. But, in another sense, the for-itself is what allows a "before" to exist quite generally and, within this "before," some co-presents that are united within the unity of a past world in such a way that we can *designate* one or the other of them by saying: "*this* object." Universal time does not exist first, in which a for-itself that does not as yet possess any past might suddenly appear. But it is on the basis of *birth*—as an original and *a priori* law of being of the for-itself—that a world with a universal time is disclosed, within which we can designate a moment at which the for-itself was not yet there, and a moment at which it appears, beings *from which* it was not born and a being *from which* it was born. Birth is where the absolute relation of pastness arises, as the for-itself's ecstatic being in the in-itself. Through it, a Past of the World appears. We will return to this. For now it will suffice to note that consciousness or the for-itself is a being that arises in being beyond something irreparable that it is—and that this irreparable element, insofar as it lies behind the for-itself, in the midst of the world, is the past. The past as the irreparable being that I have to be, without any possibility of not being it, does not lie within the "reflection-reflecting" unity of the "*Erlebnis*": it is outside. However, it is not what I am conscious of either—in the sense, for example, in which the perceived chair is what I am perceptually conscious of. In the case of my perception of the chair, a thesis is involved, i.e., an apprehension and affirmation of the chair as the in-itself that my consciousness is not. What my consciousness has to be, in the for-itself's mode of being, is not-being-the-chair. This is because, as we will see, its "not-being-the-chair" takes the form of a consciousness (of) not-being, i.e., an appearance of not-being, for a witness who is   176 there only to testify to this non-being. The negation is therefore explicit and constitutes the connection of being between the perceived object and the for-itself. The for-itself is nothing more than this translucent *nothing*, as the negation of the perceived thing. But although the past is *outside*, the connection here is not of the same type, because the for-itself is given as being the past. There cannot, therefore, be any *thesis* of the past, because we can only posit what we are not. Thus, in perceiving an object, the for-itself accepts for itself its not being the object, whereas, in disclosing the past, the for-itself accepts its *being* the past, and is separated from it only by its nature as a for-itself, incapable of being anything. Thus there is no *thesis* of the past, and yet the past is not immanent in relation to the for-itself. It haunts the for-itself at the very moment when the for-itself accepts itself as not being this or that particular thing. What the for-itself *looks* at is not the object. The for-itself's gaze, translucent in itself, is directed beyond the thing, and toward the future. The past, as a thing that one *is* without positing it, as something that haunts the for-itself without being noticed, lies behind it, and outside its thematic field, which lies before it, as what it illuminates. The past is "posited against" the for-itself, and accepted as what it has to be, without being able to be affirmed, or denied, or thematized, or absorbed by it. Of course, it is not true that the past cannot ever be the object of a thesis for me, or even that it is not often thematized. But in that case it is the object of an explicit investigation, where the for-itself affirms itself as not being this past that it posits. The past is no longer *behind*; it does not cease to be past, but I myself cease *to be* it: in my primary mode I was my past without knowing it (but not without being conscious of it); in the secondary mode I know my past, but without any longer being it. How is it possible—one might ask—for me to be conscious of my past other than in the mode of a thesis? Yet the past is constantly *there*: it is the very meaning of the object I look at and have already seen, of the familiar faces that surround me; it is the beginning of this movement presently being pursued, a movement I would be unable to describe as circular had I not myself been the witness, in the past, of its beginning; it is the origin and springboard of all my actions, and the constantly given breadth of the world that allows me to orient and locate myself; it is myself insofar as I live myself as a person (the Ego is also structured by what is to come); in short, it is my contingent and gratuitous connection to the world and to myself, insofar as I continually live these, as utterly abandoned. The psychologists call this *knowledge*. But in addition to the fact that, even by using this term, they "psychologize" it, they deprive themselves of any means of accounting for it. For our knowledge is everywhere, and conditions everything, even memory: in short, knowledge is presupposed by intellectual memory, and what is their "knowledge"—if we take that to mean some present fact—other than an intellectual memory? This supple, pervasive, and changing knowledge, which forms the texture of all our thoughts and is composed—without any image, words, or thesis—of a thousand empty indications, a thousand designations discernible behind us, is my concrete past insofar as I was it, insofar as it is the irreparable background-depth of all my thoughts and all my feelings.

177

In its second dimension of nihilation, the for-itself grasps itself as a certain lack. It is this lack and it is also the *missing item*, because it has to be what it is. To drink, or to be drinking: that means to have never finished drinking, or to have still to be drinking, beyond the drinking that I am. And when "I have finished drinking," I *have drunk*: the whole structure slides into the past. In currently drinking I am, therefore, this drinking that I have to be and that I am not; any designation of myself will escape from me into the past, if it has to be heavy and full, if it must have the density of something identical. If it makes contact with me in the present, it is because it stretches itself into the Not-yet, because it designates me as an incomplete totality that is unable to make itself complete. The for-itself's nihilating freedom eats into this Not-yet. It is not only being-at-a-distance; it is a dwindling of being. Here the for-itself—which was, in the first dimension of nihilation, in front of itself—is behind itself. In front of or behind itself: never *itself*. That is the very meaning of the two ecstases, the Past, the Future, and that is why value in itself is, in its nature, self-repose—timelessness! The eternity that man seeks is not the infinity of duration, that futile chasing after itself for which I myself am responsible: it is self-repose, the atemporality of absolute self-coincidence.

Finally, in the third dimension, the for-itself—dispersed within the constant play of the reflected-reflecting—escapes from itself, in the unity of a single flight. Here being is everywhere and nowhere: wherever we try to grasp it, it stands before us; it has escaped. This back-and-forth within the for-itself is *Presence* to being.

Present, past, and future *at the same time*, and dispersing its being in three dimensions, the for-itself is, by the mere fact of nihilating itself, temporal. None of these dimensions has ontological priority over the others, and none of them can exist without the other two. Nonetheless, the emphasis should still be placed on the present ecstasis—unlike Heidegger, who emphasizes the future ecstasis—because it is as a revelation to itself that the for-itself is its past, as what it has to-be-for-itself in a nihilating surpassing, and it is as a revelation to itself that it is a lack and haunted by its future, i.e., by what it is for itself over there, at a distance. The present is not ontologically "prior" to the past and the future—it is just as conditioned by them as it conditions them—but it is the cavity of non-being that is indispensable to the total synthetic form of temporality. Thus temporality is not a universal time that contains all beings, and human-realities in particular. Nor is it a law of development imposing itself on being from outside. Nor is it being; rather, it is the internal structure of the being that is its own nihilation, i.e., the mode of being that belongs to being-for-itself. The for-itself is the being that has to be its being in the diasporic form of temporality.

178

(B) The temporal dynamic

The fact that the for-itself arises necessarily in conformity with the three dimensions of temporality teaches us nothing about the problem of duration, which comes under the temporal dynamic. At first sight, the problem appears twofold: Why does the for-itself undergo this modification of its being, through which it becomes past? And why does a new for-itself arise ex nihilo in order to become the present of that past?

This problem was concealed for a long time by a conception of human being as in-itself. It is the crux of Kant's refutation of Berkeley's idealism, and it is a favorite argument in Leibniz that, by itself, change implies permanence. Given that, if we assume that a certain atemporal permanence remains through time, temporality is reduced to being no more than the measure and order of change. Without change there would be no temporality, since time can have no purchase on the permanent and identical. If, moreover, change itself is presented—as in Leibniz—as the logical analysis of a relation of consequences to premises, i.e., as the development of a permanent subject's attributes, then there is no real temporality anymore.

But this conception is based on many mistakes. First of all, the subsistence of some permanent element *alongside* something changing cannot enable any change to be constituted as such—apart from in the eyes of a witness, who would himself be the unity of something changing with something that remains. In brief, the change's *unity* with the permanent is necessary for the constitution of a change as such. But this term itself, "unity," which Leibniz and Kant misused, does not mean much here. What do we mean by this unity of disparate elements? Is their attachment merely external? In that case, it has no meaning. It has to be a unity of *being*. But this unity of being amounts to the requirement that the permanent should *be* what changes, which makes it essentially ecstatic and, in addition, destroys the *in-itself* character of both permanence and change. And let nobody say that permanence and change are construed, here, as phenomena and have only a *relative* being: the in-itself cannot be opposed to the phenomena, like the noumenon. According to the very terms of our definition, a phenomenon is in itself when it is what it is—even if it is in relation to a subject or another phenomenon. And, moreover, the appearing of a *relation*, which determines some phenomena in relation to others, presupposes that an ecstatic being—able to be what it is not—has already arisen, in order to found the "elsewhere" and relatedness.

The appeal to permanence in order to found change is, moreover, utterly useless. The idea is to show that any absolute change is, strictly speaking, no longer a change, since *nothing* remains that is changing—or in relation to which there could be change. But in fact it suffices that what is changing should *be* its former state, in the mode of the past, for permanence to become redundant. In such a case, the change may be absolute, and we may be dealing with a metamorphosis that affects the being in its entirety: the change will nonetheless be constituted, in relation to an earlier state that it will be in the past, in the mode of "*was.*" With this link to the past as a replacement for the pseudo-necessity of permanence, we may—and should—consider the problem of duration in relation to absolute changes. Moreover, there is no other kind, not even "in the world." Up to a certain threshold, they are nonexistent; once this threshold is passed, change extends to the complete form, as the Gestaltists' experiments have shown.

But in addition, when we are dealing with human-reality, what is necessary is pure and absolute change, which moreover is

179

perfectly able to be a change while *nothing* changes—and which is duration itself. Even if, for example, we allowed that a for-itself could be an absolutely empty presence to a permanent in-itself—as this for-itself's simple consciousness—the very existence of that consciousness would imply temporality, since it would have to be, without changing, what it is, in the form of "having been it." In that case there would be no eternity but rather the constant necessity for the present for-itself to become the past of a new present, and this would be on account of consciousness's very being. And if we are told that this constant recovering of the present into the past by means of a new present implies an internal change in the for-itself, we may reply that it is the for-itself's temporality that, in this case, is the foundation of the change, and the change does not found the temporality. Nothing therefore can conceal these problems from us, which appear at first to be insoluble: Why does the present *become* the past? What is this new present which then springs up? Where does it come from, and why does it arise? And we should note—as our hypothesis of an "empty" consciousness shows—that the necessity in question here is not that anything permanent must cascade from instant to instant, even while materially remaining something permanent, but rather that being, of whatever kind, must metamorphose itself in its entirety and all at once, in form and content, to sink into the past and to produce itself at the same time, *ex nihilo*, in the direction of the future.

180   But are there two problems? Let us look more closely: the present cannot *pass* except by becoming the "*before*" of a for-itself that thereby constitutes itself as "after." There is therefore just one phenomenon: the arising of a new present that "pastifies" the present that it *was* and, in the wake of the pastification of a present, the appearing of a for-itself for whom that present will become the past.[41] The phenomenon of temporal becoming is a global modification, since a past of nothing would no longer be a past and since any present must necessarily be the present of this past. This metamorphosis, moreover, does not extend only to the pure present: the past perfect and the future are equally affected. The past

---

41 TN: . . . *passéification d'un présent* . . . See my note on *passéifier* in the section on Husserl vocabulary in Notes on the Translation.

of the present that has undergone its pastification becomes the past of a past—or the pluperfect.[42] In relation to it, the present's heterogeneity with the past is immediately eliminated, since what had been distinguished from the past as the present has become the past. In the course of its metamorphosis, the present remains the present of this past, but it becomes the past present of this past. That means, in the first instance, that it is homogeneous with the series of the past which reaches back from it right up to the moment of birth and, second, that it is no longer its past in the form of having it to be but in the mode of having had it to be. The connection between the past and pluperfect is a connection in the mode of the in-itself and it appears upon the foundation of the present for-itself. That is what maintains the series of the past and the pluperfects, welded into a single block.

On the other hand, although the future is equally affected by the metamorphosis it does not cease to be the future—which means it remains outside the for-itself, in front of it, beyond being—but it becomes the future of a past, or the future perfect. It can maintain two kinds of relation with the new present, depending on whether it is the immediate future or the distant future. In the first case, the present is given as *being* this future in relation to the past: "Here it is, what I was waiting for." It is the present of its past in the mode of that past's future perfect. But at the same time as being for-itself as that past's future, it actualizes itself as for-itself and therefore as not being what the future promised to be. A split comes about: the present becomes the future perfect of the past even as it denies its being *that* future. And the primitive future is not actualized at all: without having ceased to be the future in relation to the past, it is no longer the future in relation to the present. It becomes the present's unrealizable co-present, and preserves a total *ideality*: "So, is that what I was waiting for?" It remains a future that is ideally co-present to the present, as the unactualized future of this present's past.

In the case where the future is more remote, it remains as future in relation to the new present but, unless the present is itself constituted as the lack of *this* future, it loses its character of possibility. In this case the future perfect becomes a possible to which the new present is indifferent;

---

42 TN: In these sentences Sartre uses the names of grammatical tenses to describe forms of the temporal past.

181   it is not *its* possible. In this sense it no longer possibilizes itself but, in its capacity as possible, it takes on being-in-itself. It becomes a *given* possible, i.e., an in itself possible of a for-itself that has become in-itself. Yesterday, it was possible—in the form of my possible—that I would leave next Monday to go to the country. Today, this possible is no longer my possible; it remains the object of my contemplation, thematized as the possible, and still in the future, *that I have been*. But its only connection with my present is that I have to be this present that has become a past—whose possible, beyond my present, it has not ceased to be—in the mode of "was." But on the foundation of my present, the future and the past present have become solidified into in-itself. In this way the future, in the course of the temporal process, passes into in-itself without ever losing its character as the future. As long as the present has not affected it, it becomes simply the *given* future. When the present reaches it, it acquires the character of *ideality*; but this ideality is an *in itself* ideality, because it is presented as the *given* lack of a *given* past, and not as the missing item that a present for-itself has to be in the mode of *not being*. When the future is surpassed, it remains forever as the future perfect, in the margin of the series of pasts: the future perfect of this past that has become pluperfect; the future ideal that is given as co-present to a present that has become past.

What remains to be studied is the present for-itself's metamorphosis into the past alongside the interrelated arising of a new present. It would be a mistake to believe the abolition of a previous present involves the arising of a present *in-itself*, able to preserve an *image* of the present that has disappeared. In a sense, we should almost reverse the terms to get to the truth, since the pastification of the ex-present is a transition to the in-itself, while the appearance of a new present is the nihilation of this in-itself. The present is not a new in-itself: it is what is not, and what is beyond being; it is that about which we can only say "it is" in the past; the past is not abolished and it has become what it was; the past is the being of the present. Finally, as we have sufficiently emphasized, the relation of the present to the past is a relation of being, not of representation.

So the primary feature to strike us is the way the for-itself is seized back by being, as if it no longer had the strength to maintain its own nothingness. The deep fissure that the for-itself has to be gets filled in, and the nothingness that must "be been" ceases so to be, and is expelled, to the extent to which the pastified being-for-itself becomes a *quality* of the in-itself. If I have felt this sadness, in the past, it exists no longer in the way in which I felt it: this sadness no longer has exactly that degree of being that an appearance that makes itself its own witness can have; it is, because it has been; its being comes to it almost as an external necessity. The past is a backward fatality: the for-itself makes itself what it wants, but it cannot escape the necessity that a new for-itself will be, irremediably, what it wanted to be. The past, therefore, is a for-itself that has ceased to be a transcending presence to the in-itself. As itself in itself, it has fallen into the midst of the world. I am what I have to be as presence to the world that I am not; but I was what I *was* in the midst of the world, in the manner of things, as an intraworldly existent. Nonetheless, this world in which the for-itself has to be what it was cannot be the same as the one to which it is currently present. In this way, the for-itself's past is constituted as a past presence to a past state of the world. Even if the world has not varied in any way while the for-itself "was passing" from the present to the past, it is at least grasped as having undergone the same formal change that we described earlier within being-for-itself. This change is no longer anything but a reflection of the true internal change in consciousness. In other words, the for-itself, falling into the past as an ex-presence to being that has become in-itself, becomes a being "in the midst of the world"—and the world is *retained* in the dimension of the past as that in the midst of which the past for-itself is in itself. Like the mermaid whose human body ends in a fish's tail, the extraworldly for-itself ends, behind itself, in *a thing in the world*. I am quick-tempered, or melancholic, I have the Oedipus complex or the inferiority complex forever—but in the past, in the form of "was," in the midst of the world, in the way that I am a civil servant, or one-armed, or proletarian. In the past the world hems me in and I become lost within a universal determinism, but I radically transcend my past toward my future, to just the extent to which I "was" that past.

A for-itself that has expressed all its nothingness, seized back by the in-itself and diluting itself into the world: such is the past that I have to be; such is the for-itself's avatar. But this avatar is produced in connection with the appearing of a for-itself that nihilates itself as presence to the world, and that has its transcended past to be. What is the meaning of this arising of the for-itself? We must be careful not to regard it as the appearance of a new being. It is as if the present were a constant hole in being which, the moment it is filled in, constantly reappears: as if the present were in constant flight from the threat of becoming bogged down in "in itself," a threat that continues until the in-itself's final victory, which drags it into a past that is no longer any for-itself's past. This victory is death, because death puts a radical stop to temporality, by pastifying the entire system or, alternatively, by the in-itself's seizing back of the human totality.

How can we *explain* this dynamic character of temporality? If the latter is not—as we hope to have shown—a contingent quality added to the for-itself's being, we ought to be able to show that its dynamic is an essential structure of the for-itself, conceived as the being that has its own nothingness to be. We seem to be back where we started.

But the truth is that there is no problem. If we thought we had encountered one, that is because, in spite of our efforts to formulate the for-itself as such, we have not been able to stop ourselves freezing it into in-itself. In fact, if we take the in-itself as our point of departure, the appearance of change becomes a problem: if the in-itself is what it is, how can it no longer be it? But if, on the contrary, we start from an adequate understanding of the for-itself, what needs explaining will no longer be change: instead, it would be permanence, if it were able to exist. Indeed, if we consider our description of the *order* of time—aside from anything that might result from its course—it becomes clear that, once temporality is reduced to its order, it immediately becomes an *in-itself* temporality. The ecstatic character of temporal being can make no difference, since that character is now located in the past—not as the for-itself's constitution but as a quality supported by the in-itself. And if we envisage a future, just insofar as it is straightforwardly a future of a for-itself, which is the for-itself of a specific past, and if we think change poses a new problem in relation to the description of temporality as such, we will be conferring upon the future, conceived as *this* future, an instantaneous immobility, and making the for-itself into a frozen quality, a quality that can be designated; in the end, the entire structure becomes a *made* totality; the future and the past confine the for-itself and constitute its given limits. The whole structure, as a temporality that *is*, lies petrified around a solid core—which is the for-itself's present instant—and the real problem now is to explain how, from this instant, another instant can arise, with its retinue of past and future. We have escaped from the theory of instants—to the extent to which we regard the instant as the only in-itself reality, limited by a future nothingness and a past nothingness—but we have fallen back into it by implicitly conceding a succession of temporal totalities, each of which is centered around an instant. In brief, we have given the instant some ecstatic dimensions but, as we have not thereby eliminated it, we are supporting the temporal totality by the timeless; time, if it *is*, becomes a dream once again.

But change naturally belongs to the for-itself, insofar as this for-itself is a spontaneity. A spontaneity about which we are able to say "it is," or simply "*this* spontaneity," ought to generate its own definition, i.e., it will be the foundation not only of its nothingness of being but also of its being and, simultaneously, that being will seize it back, in order to freeze it into the given. A spontaneity that posits itself as spontaneity is immediately obliged to reject what it posits, or its being will become an acquisition, and it will be by dint of this acquisition that it perpetuates itself in being. And this rejection is itself an acquisition that has to be rejected, on pain of getting bogged down within an inert prolongation of its existence. It might be said that these notions of prolongation and acquisition already presuppose temporality—and that is true. But that is because spontaneity itself constitutes what it acquires by rejecting it, and what it rejects by acquiring it—because unless it temporalizes itself it cannot be. Its distinctive nature means it does not profit from the acquisition it constitutes in actualizing itself as a spontaneity. It is impossible to conceive of spontaneity in any other way, unless we contract it into an instant and by that very means freeze it into in-itself, i.e., unless we suppose that time is transcendent. It is futile to object that we are unable to think about anything outside the form of temporality and that—since we temporalize being in order, a moment later, to derive time from it—our view begs the question: it is futile to remind us of the passages in the *Critique* where Kant shows that a timeless spontaneity is inconceivable but not contradictory. It seems to us, on the contrary, that a spontaneity that did not escape from itself, and did not escape from that very act of escaping—of which we could say "it *is* thus," and confine it within an immutable name—would precisely be a contradiction, and would in the end amount to a particular affirmative essence, an eternal subject that is never a predicate. And it is precisely its character as spontaneity which constitutes even this irreversibility of its escapes, since, the moment it appears, it is precisely in order to reject itself and the "assertion-rejection" sequence cannot be reversed. In effect, the assertion itself ends up as a rejection, without ever attaining the plenitude of affirmation: otherwise

184

it would exhaust itself within an instantaneous in-itself, and it is only insofar as it is *rejected* that it passes over into being, within the totality of its achievement. The combined series of "assertion-rejections," moreover, has ontological priority over *change*, because change is merely the relation of the material contents in the series. And we have shown such an irreversibility of temporalization to be necessary to the entirely empty and *a priori* form of a spontaneity.

We have presented our thesis by using the concept of spontaneity, which we thought would be more familiar to our readers. But we are able now to redeploy these ideas within the perspective of the for-itself, and using our own terminology. A for-itself that did not endure would remain, of course, the negation of the transcendent in-itself and the nihilation of its own being, in the form of a "reflection-reflecting." But this nihilation would become a *given*, which is to say it would acquire the contingency of the in-itself, and the for-itself would cease to be the foundation of its own nothingness: it would no longer be anything, as having it to be; rather, within the nihilating unity of the reflection-reflecting dyad, it *would be*. The for-itself's flight is a rejection of contingency, through the very act that constitutes it as being the foundation of its nothingness. But what this flight constitutes as contingency is precisely what it flees from: the for-itself it flees from remains on the spot. It cannot annihilate itself, since I *am* it, but neither can it be in the form of the foundation of its own nothingness, since it can be only in fleeing: it is *achieved*. Naturally, what is true of the for-itself as presence to . . . is also true of the totality of temporalization. This totality *is not* ever completed: it is a totality that rejects and flees from itself; it separates from itself, in the unity of a single event of arising; it is an elusive totality that, at the moment it is given, already lies beyond this gift of itself.

The time of consciousness, therefore, is human-reality temporalizing itself as a totality that is its own unfinished task; it is a nothingness, sliding into a totality like a detotalizing enzyme. This totality is simultaneously chasing after, and rejecting itself; it is unable to find any final term within itself for its surpassing, because it is its own surpassing, and surpasses itself toward itself; such a totality cannot, in any case, exist within the limits of an instant. There is never an instant in which we can assert that the for-itself is—precisely because the for-itself never is. On the contrary, temporality temporalizes itself entirely as a rejection of the instant.

185

III. ORIGINAL TEMPORALITY AND PSYCHOLOGICAL TEMPORALITY: REFLECTION

The for-itself endures in the form of a non-thetic consciousness (of) enduring. But I am able to "feel time passing" and to apprehend myself as a unity of succession. In this case I am conscious of enduring. This consciousness is thetic and closely resembles knowledge, just as the duration being temporalized before my eyes comes close to being an object of consciousness. What kind of relation exists between original temporality and this psychological temporality that I encounter as soon as I apprehend myself "in the course of enduring?" This problem leads us immediately to another problem, because to be conscious of duration is to be conscious of a consciousness that endures; in consequence, to ask about the nature and entitlements of this thetic consciousness of duration amounts to asking about the nature and entitlements of reflection. Indeed, it is to reflection that temporality appears in the form of psychological duration and all the processes of psychological duration belong to a consciousness that is reflected on. Before we ask, therefore, how any psychological duration is able to be constituted as an immanent object of reflection, we ought to try to answer this preliminary question: How is reflection possible for a being that can be only in the past? Descartes and Husserl present reflection as an advantageous type of intuition, because it grasps consciousness in a present and instantaneous act of immanence. Can its certainty be preserved, if the being to be known is *past* in relation to it? And as our entire ontology is founded in a reflective experience, is it not at risk of losing all its authority?[43] And incidentally, must the object of reflective [acts of] consciousness really be past being? As for reflection itself, if that is for-itself, must it be limited to an instantaneous existence and certainty? We can decide this only by returning to the phenomenon of reflection, in order to determine its structure.

186

43 TN: . . . *perdre tous ses droits?* I translate *droits* (literally "rights") as "authority," which seems to me to be the closest semantic equivalent in ordinary English. Note that this loses a potentially significant connection (in the original text) with ideas of "right," "law," and "entitlement."

Reflection is the for-itself as conscious of itself. As the for-itself is already a non-thetic consciousness (of) self, we are used to representing reflection as a new consciousness, suddenly appearing, targeting the reflected consciousness and living in symbiosis with it. Spinoza's old *idea ideae* may be recognized here.

But, in addition to the difficulty of explaining how reflective consciousness arises *ex nihilo*, it is completely impossible to account for its absolute unity with reflected consciousness, a unity which alone can render the authority and certainty of reflective intuition conceivable. We cannot define here the *esse* of what is reflected on as a *percipi*, since its being is, precisely, such that it does not need to be perceived in order to exist. And its primary relation with reflection cannot be the relation that unites a representation with a thinking subject. In short, if the known existent must have the same dignity of being as the knowing existent, we will have to adopt the perspective of naïve realism to describe the relation between these two existents. But in that case, precisely, we will encounter realism's major difficulty: How can two isolated and independent wholes—possessing the sufficiency of being that Germans call *"Selbstständigkeit"*—sustain any relations with each other and, in particular, the type of internal relations that go by the name of "knowledge?" If we conceive of reflection first as an autonomous consciousness, we will *never* be able to reunite it subsequently with the reflected consciousness. They will always add up to two and, if by some miracle the reflective consciousness was able to be conscious of the reflected consciousness, this connection between the two consciousnesses could only be *external*; at most, we might envisage that the reflection, isolated in itself, possesses something like an image of the consciousness it reflects on, and we would fall back into idealism. Reflective knowledge, and the *cogito* in particular, would lose their certainty and would obtain nothing in return other than a specific probability that would, moreover, be difficult to define. We should allow, therefore, that a connection of being joins reflection to what it reflects on, and that reflective consciousness is the consciousness it reflects on.

But, on the other hand, there can be no question here of a complete identification of the reflective with the reflected: that would immediately eliminate the phenomenon of reflection, and allow only the phantom duality of the "reflection-reflecting" to remain. Here we encounter, once

187

again, the type of being that defines the for-itself: reflection requires, if
it is to be apodictic evidence, that the reflective should *be* what it reflects
on. But, to the extent to which it is *knowledge*, it is necessary that the
reflected consciousness should be an *object* for reflective consciousness,
which implies a separation from it. Thus it is necessary at the same time
for the reflective consciousness to be, and not to be, what it reflects on.
We have already come across this ontological structure at the heart of the
for-itself. But there it did not have quite the same meaning. In effect, it
presupposed a radical "*Unselbstständigkeit*" in the two terms, "reflected and
reflecting," of the nascent duality, i.e., an inability to posit themselves
separately, such that the duality remained constantly evanescent and
such that each term, in positing itself for the other, *became* the other. But
the case of reflection is rather different, since the "reflection-reflecting"
that is reflected on exists for a reflective "reflection-reflecting." In other
words, what is reflected on is an *appearance* for the reflective consciousness without however thereby ceasing to be a witness (of) itself, and
the reflective consciousness *witnesses* what it reflects on, without thereby
ceasing to be an appearance in relation to itself. It is even *insofar as* it is
reflected in itself that what is reflected on can be an appearance for reflective consciousness, and the reflective consciousness can be a witness only
insofar as it is conscious (of) being one, i.e., only to the precise extent
to which this witness that it is is a reflection for a reflecting that it also
is. The reflective consciousness and the consciousness it reflects on each
tend, therefore, toward "*Selbstständigkeit*" and the *nothing* that separates them
divides them more deeply than the nothingness of the for-itself separates
the reflection from the reflecting.[44] Only, we should note: (1) that the
reflection that takes the form of a witness can have its being as a witness
only in and through the appearance, which is to say that its reflexivity
profoundly affects it in its being and, this being so, it can never attain the
"*Selbstständigkeit*" it aims at, since it derives its being from its function, and

---

44 TN: This is one of the passages where Sartre's account, involving both a "first-level"
(and inescapable) reflection within the for-itself, and a second-level (optional) reflection as a cognitive act, makes clear English translation difficult, as the same English
word—"reflection"—appears at both levels. In this sentence, Sartre begins by talking
about the cognitive act, but the "reflection" and "reflecting" at the end of the sentence
refer to the first-level structure. See my note on *réfléchir*, etc., in Notes on the Translation.

its function from the for-itself it reflects on; (2) that what is reflected on is profoundly altered by reflection, because it is a consciousness (of) self as a reflected-on consciousness of this or that transcendent phenomenon. It knows itself to be looked at: to use a sensory image, we can find no better comparison for it than a man bent over a table who is writing and who knows, even while he is writing, that he is being observed by someone standing behind him. What is reflected on is therefore already, in a way, conscious (of) itself as having an *outside* or, rather, the beginnings of an *outside*, which is to say that it makes itself an object for . . . so that its meaning as something reflected on is inseparable from the reflective, and exists over there, at a distance from itself, in the consciousness reflecting on it. In this sense, it does not possess any more *"Selbstständigkeit"* than the reflective consciousness itself. Husserl tells us that what we reflect on "is given as having been there before the reflection." But we should not be misled by this: the *"Selbstständigkeit"* that characterizes unreflected consciousness—insofar as it is unreflected in relation to any possible reflection—does not pass over into the phenomenon of reflection, precisely because the phenomenon loses its unreflected character. For a consciousness, to become reflected is to undergo a deep modification in its being and precisely to lose the *"Selbstständigkeit"* it possessed insofar as it was the "reflected-reflecting" quasi-totality. At any rate, to the extent that a nothingness separates reflective consciousness from what it reflects on, this nothingness—which cannot derive its being from itself—must "be been." We should take this to mean that only a unitary structure of being can be its own nothingness, in the form of *having it to be*. In fact, neither reflective consciousness nor what it reflects on is able to establish this separating nothingness. But reflection is, just like the unreflected for-itself, *a being*, not an addition of being—*a being that has its own nothingness to be*; it is not the appearing of a new consciousness, directed on the for-itself, but a modification in its internal structure, actualized in itself by the for-itself; in brief, it is the for-itself itself that makes itself exist in the reflective-reflected-on mode, rather than simply being in the reflected-reflecting mode, where this new mode of being, moreover, allows the reflected-reflecting mode to subsist as the primary internal structure. The person who reflects on me is not some kind of pure, timeless gaze: it is myself, an enduring me, who is committed within the circuit of my ipseity, in danger within the world, and with my historicity. Only the for-itself that I am lives this historicity, this being in the world, and this circuit of ipseity in the mode of a reflective splitting into two.

As we have seen, reflective consciousness is separated from what it reflects on by a nothingness. In this way, the phenomenon of reflection is a nihilation of the for-itself that does not come to it from outside but that it *has to be*. Where does this more pronounced nihilation come from? What can its motivation be?

In the for-itself's arising as presence to being, there is an original dispersion: the for-itself loses itself outside, alongside the in-itself, and within the three temporal ecstases. It is outside itself and, in its innermost being, this being-for-itself is ecstatic, since it has to seek its being elsewhere—in the reflecting, if it makes itself reflected, or in the reflected, if it posits itself as reflecting. The arising of the for-itself confirms the failure of the in-itself, which was unable to be its own foundation. Reflection remains a permanent possibility for the for-itself, as an attempt to reclaim being. Through reflection, the for-itself that gets lost outside itself attempts to internalize itself within its being; this is a second attempt to found itself, which involves its *being for itself what it is*. If indeed the reflection-reflecting quasi-duality was gathered into a totality for a witness identical to itself, it would be in its own eyes what it is. In short, the goal is to overcome the being that flees from itself by being what it is in the mode of not being, and which, in being its own flowing away, flows by; it is to overcome the being that slips through its own fingers, and make of it something *given*, a given that, finally, *is what it is*. The goal is to gather within the unity of a gaze this incomplete totality,   189 which is not complete only because it is, in relation to itself, its own incompleteness; it is to escape from the sphere of the constant referral that has, in relation to itself, its referral to be, and—precisely because one has escaped through this referral's net—to *make that referral be* as something *seen*, i.e., as a referral that is what it is. But at the same time it is necessary that this being that reclaims and founds itself as a given—i.e., which confers being's contingency upon itself, in order to come to its rescue by founding it—should itself be what it reclaims and founds, what it rescues from ecstatic dispersal. The motivation of reflection consists in a twofold and simultaneous attempt at objectification and internalization. To be, in relation to oneself, an object-in-itself within the absolute unity of internalization: that is what reflection-being has to be.

This attempt to be, in relation to oneself, one's own foundation, to reclaim and to dominate one's own flight within interiority, in order finally *to be* this flight—rather than temporalizing it as a flight that flees from itself—must end in failure; and reflection is precisely this failure. In point of fact, the being who gets lost is *itself* the being who has to reclaim it, and it is obliged to be this reclamation in the mode of being that belongs to it, i.e., in the mode of the for-itself, and therefore of flight. It is *insofar as it is for-itself* that the for-itself will attempt to be what it is or, alternatively, it will be *for itself* what it is-for-itself. Thus reflection, or the endeavor to reclaim the for-itself by turning back on itself, leads to the for-itself's appearing for the for-itself. The being that wishes to found something within being is itself the foundation only of its own nothingness. The structure remains, therefore, nihilated in-itself. And at the same time, being's turning back on itself can only make a *distance* appear between its turning back and what it turns back to. This turning back on itself is a self-separation, in order to turn back. And this turning back makes the nothingness of reflection appear, because the for-itself's structural necessity requires that it can be retrieved in its being only by a being that itself exists in the form of the for-itself. Thus, the being that operates this recovery must be constituted in the mode of the for-itself, and the being to be reclaimed must exist as for-itself. And these two beings must be the *same being*, but precisely, insofar as that being reclaims *itself*, it brings into existence an absolute distance between itself and itself, within the unity of being. This phenomenon of reflection is a permanent possibility for the for-itself, because a reflective scissiparity lies as a potentiality within the for-itself that is reflected on: indeed, it suffices for the reflecting for-itself to posit itself as a witness of the reflection for it, and for the reflection-for-itself to posit itself for it as the reflection of this reflecting.[45] Thus reflection, as an attempt at the retrieval of a for-itself by a for-itself that (in the mode of not-being) it is, is an intermediate stage of nihilation between the pure and simple existence of the for-itself and

45 TN: . . . *le pour-soi reflétant se pose . . . comme témoin du reflet et . . . le pour-soi reflétant se pose . . . comme reflet de ce reflétant.* I quote to make it clear that the "reflecting" and "reflection" in this sentence are at the most basic level of being of the for-itself.

existence *for the Other* as an act of retrieval of a for-itself by a for-itself   190
that it is not, in the mode of not-being.[46]

Can we limit the authority and scope of reflection, as we have just
described it, by appealing to the fact that the for-itself temporalizes
itself? We do not think so.

If we want to grasp the reflective phenomenon in its relation to temporality, we need to distinguish between two kinds of reflection: reflection can be pure or impure. Pure reflection, which is the simple presence
of the reflective for-itself to the for-itself it reflects on, is the original
form of reflection and, at the same time, its ideal form: impure reflection
appears on the foundation of pure reflection and, in addition, the latter
is never *given* from the outset; it has to be won through a sort of *catharsis*. Impure or complicit reflection, which we will discuss later, includes
pure reflection but goes beyond it, because it presses its claims further.[47]

What are the entitlements and authority of pure reflection with respect
to evidence? Reflective consciousness is evidently what it reflects on. If
we left that behind, we would have no means of legitimizing reflection.
But reflective consciousness *is* what it reflects on in full immanence, even
though it has the form of "not-being-in-itself." This is shown clearly by
the fact that what we reflect on is not quite an object but a *quasi-object* for
reflection. In effect the consciousness that we reflect on is not yet delivered up to reflection as an "outside," i.e., as a being on which we might
"take up a point of view," in relation to which we can take a step back,
or increase or diminish the distance separating us from it. For the consciousness we reflect on to be "seen from outside" and for our reflection
to be able to orient itself in relation to it, it would be necessary for our
reflective consciousness to not be what it reflects on, in the mode of not
being what it is not; this scissiparity can be actualized only in existence

46 Sartre's note: Here we rediscover that "division of the self-identical" which for Hegel
   is distinctive of consciousness. But, rather than leading to a higher integration, as it
   does in *Phenomenology of Spirit*, this scission only hollows out more deeply and more
   irremediably the nothingness that separates consciousness from itself. Consciousness
   is Hegelian—but that is its greatest illusion. TN: The passage Sartre has in mind is at
   Hegel (1977: 100–101).
47 TN: *La réflexion impure . . . complice . . .* Barnes translated *réflexion complice* as "accessory reflection," presumably because *complice* can have the (legal) sense of a "partner in crime." I
   think the ordinary English adjective "complicit" is closer to the intended meaning.

for the Other. Reflection is knowledge; that is beyond doubt; it possesses a positional character, and it affirms the consciousness it reflects on. But, as we will soon see, every affirmation is conditioned by a negation: to affirm this object is simultaneously to deny that I am this object. To know something is to make oneself other. Now, precisely, a reflective consciousness is not quite able to make itself other than what it reflects on, since it is-in-order-to-be what it reflects on. Its affirmation is stopped midway, because its negation is not entirely actualized. It does not therefore completely detach itself from what it reflects on, and cannot embrace it "from some point of view." Its knowledge is totalizing: it is a lightning intuition without any contrasts, or any point of departure, or any point of

191 arrival. Everything is given at once, in a kind of absolute proximity. What we ordinarily call "knowing" presupposes contrasts, levels, an order, a hierarchy. Even mathematical essences are revealed to us with an orientation in relation to other truths, to specific consequences; they are never disclosed with all their characteristics at the same time. But the reflection that delivers up to us what it reflects on—not as something given but as the being that we have to be—without any distinction or point of view, is a knowledge that overflows itself and is inexplicable. At the same time, it never surprises itself; it teaches us nothing, and only posits. In the case of knowledge of a transcendent object, the object is effectively disclosed—and the disclosed object may disappoint or astonish us. But reflective disclosure posits a being that was already a disclosure in its being. The reflection confines itself to making this disclosure exist for itself; the disclosed being is not revealed as something given but with the character of having "already been disclosed." Rather than being knowledge, reflection is recognition. It implies a prereflective understanding of what it aims to retrieve as the original motivation for that retrieval.

But if reflective consciousness is what it reflects on—if this unity of being founds and limits the authority of reflection—we ought to add that what we reflect on is itself its past and its future. There is no doubt, therefore, that reflective consciousness, even though it is constantly overflowed by the totality of what it reflects on (and that it is, in the mode of not being it), extends the authority of apodicticity to the very totality that it is. Thus we should not limit Descartes's reflective conquest, the cogito, to the infinitesimal instant. We can reach this conclusion, moreover, from the fact that thinking is an act that commits the past, and is sketched out in advance by the future. "I doubt, therefore I am," said Descartes. But what would remain of methodic doubt if we were able to limit it to the instant? A suspension of judgment, perhaps. But a suspension of judgment is not doubt but only a necessary structure of doubt. For there to be doubt, it is necessary for this suspension to be motivated by an insufficiency of reasons either to assert or to deny—which refers to the past—and that it should be deliberately maintained until new elements intervene—which is already a project of the future. Doubt appears against the ground of a preontological understanding of knowing, and of requirements concerning truth. This understanding and these requirements, which give doubt all its meaning, commit the totality of human-reality and its being in the world: they presuppose the existence of an object of knowledge and of doubt, i.e., a transcendent permanence within universal time; doubt therefore is a conduct that involves combination, and represents one of human-reality's modes of being in the world.[48] To discover oneself as doubting is already to be: ahead of oneself, in the future that contains the goal, the ending, and the meaning of this doubt; and behind oneself, in the past that contains the constitutive motivations of the doubt and its phases; and outside oneself, in the world, as a presence to the object one is doubting. The same points will apply to any reflective observation: I am reading; I am dreaming; I am perceiving; I am acting. Either they must lead us to withhold apodictic evidence from reflection—in which case the original knowledge that I have of myself collapses into probability, and my very existence is only a probability, because my being-in-the-instant is not a being—or else we will have to extend the authority of reflection to the human totality: to the past, to the future, to presence, and to the object. Now, if our findings are correct, reflection is a for-itself seeking to reclaim itself as a totality that is constantly in a state of incompleteness. It affirms the disclosure of the being that is, in relation to itself, its own disclosure. And as the for-itself temporalizes itself, the consequences are: (1) that reflection, as a mode of being of the for-itself, must be in the form of temporalization and that it is, itself, its past and its future; (2) that, by virtue of its nature, its authority and certainty extend as far as the possibilities

192

---

48 TN: ... une conduite liée ... This phrase is difficult to translate: the idea is that doubt is not contained within an instant, it is an activity, and so it involves the "combination" (in the Kantian sense) of several elements over time.

that I *am* and to the past that I *was*. Reflective consciousness does not grasp what it reflects on as an instant, but neither is it instantaneous itself. This does not mean that reflective consciousness knows, with its future, the future that it reflects on, or that, with its past, it knows the past of the consciousness that it knows. On the contrary, it is through the future and the past that the reflective consciousness and what it reflects on are distinguished in the unity of their being. The reflective consciousness's future is, in effect, the set of distinctive possibilities that the reflective consciousness has to be, as reflective. As such, it cannot include any consciousness of the future that it reflects on. The same remarks apply to the reflective past, even though this latter will be founded, ultimately, in the past of the original for-itself. But if it draws its meaning from its future and its past, reflection is already—insofar as it is a fleeing presence to a flight—ecstatically extended throughout this flight. In other words, the for-itself that makes itself exist in the mode of a reflective split into two derives its meaning, as for-itself, from its possibilities and from its future; in this sense, reflection is a diasporic phenomenon; but, as *self-presence*, it is a presence that is present to all its ecstatic dimensions. We still need to explain—it might be said—how this supposedly apodictic reflection is able to make so many mistakes, precisely in relation to that past which we accord it the right to know. Our answer will be that it makes no mistakes at all, to exactly the degree to which it grasps the past as something haunting the present in a non-thematic form. As we have shown, when I say "I am reading," "I am doubting," "I am hoping," etc., I overflow in great measure my present, toward my past. And I cannot go wrong, in any of these cases. The apodicticity of reflection is not in doubt, to the extent to which it grasps the past exactly as it is for the reflected consciousness that has it to be. If, on the other hand, I am able to make a great many mistakes when, in the mode of reflection, I remember my past feelings or ideas, that is because I am at the level of memory: in that moment I *am* no longer my past, but I thematize it. We are no longer dealing, therefore, with an act of reflection.

193

Thus reflection is a consciousness of the three ecstatic dimensions. It is a non-thetic consciousness (of) flowing, and a thetic consciousness of duration. For it, the past and the present of what it reflects on begin to exist as *quasi-outsides*, in the sense that they are not only held within the unity of a for-itself that exhausts their being by having it to be but also for a for-itself that is separated from them by a nothingness, for a for-itself that—although it exists with them within the unity of a being—does not have their being to be. And in addition, through reflection, the flowing tends toward being, like an "outside" sketched out within immanence. But pure reflection still encounters temporality only in its original non-substantiality, in its refusal to be in-itself: it encounters possibles *insofar as they are possibles*, made lighter by the for-itself's freedom; it discloses the present as transcending and, if the past appears to it as in-itself, it remains on the foundation of presence. And finally, reflection encounters the for-itself in its detotalized totality, as the incomparable individuality that it *is itself* in the mode of having it to be; it encounters it as the "reflected-on" *par excellence*, the being that only ever exists as *itself* and that is this "itself," therefore, at a distance from itself, in the future, in the past, in the world. Reflection, therefore, grasps temporality insofar as it is disclosed as the unique and incomparable mode of being of an ipseity, i.e., as historicity.

But the psychological duration that we are acquainted with and use daily is the opposite of historicity, insofar as it consists in successions of organized temporal figures. In point of fact, it is the concrete weave of psychological units in a flow. This joy, for example, is an organized form appearing in the wake of some sadness and, earlier on, there was the humiliation I experienced yesterday. Between these units in the flow—qualities, states, and acts—the relations of "before" and "after" are usually established, and we can even make use of these units to *date* events. In this way, the reflective consciousness of man-within-the-world finds itself, in its daily existence, confronted with psychological objects that are what they are, appearing on the continuous texture of our temporality like designs and motifs on a tapestry, and succeeding each other in the manner of things in the world, within universal time—i.e., by replacing each other without maintaining any relations with each other apart from purely external relations of succession. We talk about a joy that I *have* or that I *had*,[49] and we call it my joy, as if I were its support and it stood out against me in the way in which Spinoza's finite modes stand out against

---

49 TN: *On parle d'une joie que j'ai* . . . It sounds a little strange to say in English "I have joy," but it is easy to think of similar expressions, to make Sartre's point just as effectively. Think for example of the phrase "I have great delight in announcing . . ." I have not changed the example, because Sartre uses "joy" so often in the text.

the attribute's ground. We even say that I *feel* this joy, as if it came to imprint itself like a seal on the fabric of my temporalization or, better still, as if the presence within me of these feelings, ideas, and states was a kind of *visitation*.[50] This psychological duration constituted by the concrete flow of autonomous structures—or, in other words, by the succession of psychological *facts*, of *facts* of consciousness—cannot be called an illusion: indeed, their reality provides the object of psychology; in practical terms, it is at the level of psychological fact that concrete relations between men—demands, jealousies, resentments, suggestions, battles, stratagems, etc.—are established. However, we cannot conceive of the unreflected for-itself—which historializes itself as it arises[51]—as *itself being* these qualities, states and acts. Its unity of being would collapse into a multiplicity of existents, each external to the other; the ontological problem of temporality would reappear and, this time, we would have removed any means of resolving it because, even if it is possible for the for-itself to be its own past, it would be absurd to require my joy to be the sadness that preceded it, even in the mode of "not-being." The psychologists offer a degraded representation of this ecstatic existence when they assert that psychological facts are relative to each other, and that we apprehend the thunderclap that we hear after a long silence as a "thunderclap-after-a-long-silence." That is all well and good, but by removing from it any ontological foundation they have made it impossible for themselves to explain this relativity within succession. In fact, if we apprehend the for-itself in its historicity, psychological duration vanishes; states, qualities, and acts disappear, to make way for being-for-itself as such, which exists only as the unique individuality whose historializing process is indivisible. That individuality is what flows by and calls to itself from the depths of the future and is weighed down by the past that it was; it is what historializes its ipseity, and we know that—in its primary or unreflected mode—it is conscious of the world, and not conscious of itself. Thus, qualities and states cannot be beings within its being (in the sense in which the flowing unit of "joy" might be a "content" or a "fact" of consciousness);

---

50 TN: The French *visitation*, like the English "visitation," is used in Christian writings to refer specifically to the arrival of some *divine* being. Sartre may intend this ambiguity.

51 TN: . . . *qui s'historialise dans son surgissement* . . . For *historialiser*, see the section on Heidegger vocabulary in Notes on the Translation.

all that exists of it is internal non-positional nuances of color, nuances which are nothing other than itself, insofar as it is a for-itself, and that cannot be apprehended outside it.

We find ourselves therefore in the presence of two temporalities: original temporality, of which we *are* the temporalization; and psychological temporality, which exists at the same time both as something incompatible with our being's mode of being, and as an intersubjective reality, an object of science, a goal of human actions (in the sense, for example, in which I do everything I can to "make myself loved" by Anny, to make her "*feel love for me*"). This psychological temporality, which is obviously *derived*, cannot be a direct product of original temporality; nothing is constituted by the latter apart from itself. As for psychological temporality, it is incapable of constituting *itself*, because it is only a successive order of facts. Moreover, psychological temporality cannot appear to the unreflected for-itself, which is a pure ecstatic presence to the world: it is to reflection that it is disclosed, and by which it must be constituted. But how is it possible for reflection to do this, if it is purely and simply the uncovering of the historicity that it is?

At this point we need to distinguish pure reflection from impure or constituting reflection, because it is impure reflection that constitutes the succession of psychological facts, or *psychè*. And, in daily life, impure or constituting reflection is given first, even though it incorporates pure reflection within it as its original structure. But this latter can be attained only after a modification, effected by itself, in the form of a *catharsis*. This is not the place to describe the motivation for, and structure of, this *catharsis*. What matters to us is to describe impure reflection insofar as it constitutes and discloses psychological temporality.

Reflection, as we have seen, is a type of being in which the for-itself is, for the purpose of being what it is in relation to itself.[52] Reflection does not therefore capriciously arise within being's pure indifference but is produced within the perspective of a "*for the purpose of*." Indeed, we have seen just here that the for-itself is the being that is, in its being, the foundation

195

52 TN: . . . *pour être à lui-même ce qu'il est*. Although I would normally translate *pour* in this sentence as "in order to," Sartre intends to connect this (purposive) sense of *pour* with the *pour-soi* ("for-itself") mode of being. To capture this connection in the English, I use the phrase "for the purpose of," which allows me to use (and repeat) the word "for."

of any "for." The meaning of reflection, therefore, is its being-for. In particular, reflective consciousness involves a self-nihilation in what it reflects on for the purpose of retrieving itself. In this sense, reflective consciousness, insofar as it has what it reflects on to be, escapes from the for-itself that it is *qua* reflective in the form of "having it to be." But if it did that only for the purpose of being the reflected-on that it has to be, it would, in escaping from the for-itself, rediscover it; everywhere, and no matter how it affects itself, the for-itself is condemned to being-for-itself. In effect, that is exactly what pure reflection discovers. But impure reflection, as the first (but not the *original*) spontaneous movement of reflection, is-for-[the-purpose-of-]being[53] what it reflects on in the form of in-itself. Its motivation lies within itself, in a twofold movement—which we have described—of internalization and objectification: to grasp what it reflects on as in-itself, in order to make itself be this in-itself it grasps. Impure reflection, therefore, only grasps what it reflects on as such within a circuit of ipseity, where it stands in immediate relation with an in-itself that it has to be. But on the other hand, this in-itself that reflective consciousness has to be is what it *reflects on* insofar as the reflective consciousness attempts to apprehend it as being in-itself. In consequence, there are three forms within impure reflection: the reflective consciousness; what it reflects on; and an in-itself that the reflective has to be, insofar as this in-itself will be what it reflects on—which is nothing but the *in-order-to* of the phenomenon of reflection. This in-itself is sketched out in advance, behind the reflected-for-itself, by a movement of reflection that traverses what it reflects on, in order to reclaim and to found it; it is like a projection of the reflected-for-itself into the in-itself, as its meaning; its being is not to be but *to-be-been*, like nothingness. It is what is reflected as a pure object for reflective consciousness. From the moment reflection takes up a point of view on its reflecting, and thereby moves away from that lightning and dimensionless intuition in which what is reflected on is given to reflective consciousness without any point of view, and as soon as it posits itself as *not being* what it reflects on and as determining *what that is*, reflection brings into view—behind what it reflects on—an in-itself that can be determined and qualified. This transcendent in-itself— or the shadow cast into being by what is reflected on—is what reflective

196

---

53 TN: . . . *est-pour-être* . . . The emphasis of for and the inserted square brackets are mine: again, I am trying to reproduce the pattern in Sartre's use of *pour*.

consciousness *has to be*, insofar as it is what the reflected *is*. We should not confuse it in any way with the *value* of what we reflect on—which is given to reflection in its totalizing and undifferentiated intuition—nor with the *value* that haunts reflective consciousness as a non-thetic absence, and as the *in-order-to* of reflective consciousness, insofar as it is non-positionally conscious (of) itself. It is the necessary object of any reflection; for it to arise, it suffices that reflection should regard what it reflects on as an object; it is just that decision, through which reflective consciousness determines itself to consider what it reflects on as an object, that makes the in-itself appear as the transcendent objectification of what it reflects on. And the act through which reflection determines itself to take what it reflects on as an object is, in itself: (1) a positing of reflective consciousness as *not being* what it reflects on; (2) the adoption of a point of view in relation to what is reflected on. In reality, moreover, these two moments amount to just one, since the concrete negation that reflective consciousness makes itself be in relation to what it reflects on is manifested precisely *in and through* the fact of taking up a point of view. The act of objectification is, we can see, a direct prolongation of the reflective splitting into two, since this split comes about through a deepening of the nothingness that separates the reflection from the reflecting.[54] The objectification takes up the reflective movement as not being what it reflects on *in order that* what is reflected on should appear to reflective consciousness as an object. Only this reflection is in bad faith, because if it appears to sever the link that joins reflective consciousness to what it reflects on, if it seems to assert that reflective consciousness *is not* what it reflects on in the mode of not being what it is not—whereas, in reflection as it originally arises, reflective consciousness is not what it reflects on in the mode of not being what it is—it does so *in order to* subsequently resume the assertion of identity and to assert, in relation to this in-itself, that "I am it." In brief, reflection is in bad faith insofar as it is constituted as disclosing *the object that I myself am*. But, in the second place, this more radical nihilation is not a real and metaphysical event: the real event, the third process of nihilation, is the for-the-Other. Impure reflection is an abortive effort on the

---

54 TN: . . . *ce dédoublement se fait par approfondissement du néant qui sépare le reflet du reflétant.* This is another instance where the English makes it more difficult to recognize the switch in focus, in this last part of Sartre's sentence, to the "first-level" reflection that is a permanent structure of the for-itself.

part of the for-itself *to be another* by *remaining itself*. The transcendent object that has appeared behind the reflected for-itself is the only being about which the reflective consciousness can say, in this sense, that it *is not it*. But it is a shadow of being. It is been, and reflective consciousness has it to be, in order to not be it. It is this shadow of being, the necessary and constant correlative of impure reflection, that the psychologist studies as the so-called *psychological fact*. The psychological fact is, therefore, the shadow of what is reflected on, insofar as reflective consciousness has it ecstatically to be, in the mode of not-being. Thus, reflection is impure when it presents itself as an "intuition of the for-itself in the in-itself"; what is disclosed to it is not the temporal and insubstantial historicity of what it reflects on but— beyond what it reflects on—the actual substantiality of organized forms within the flow. The unity of these virtual beings is called *psychological life*, or the *psychè*, a virtual and transcendent in-itself that subtends the for-itself's temporalization. Pure reflection is only ever a quasi-knowledge, but the only thing of which reflective knowledge is possible is the *Psychè*. Naturally, in every psychological object we will rediscover the characteristics of what is really reflected on, but degraded into in-itself. A brief and *a priori* description of the *psychè* will enable us to understand this.

(1) By "*psychè*" we mean the *Ego*, its states, its qualities, and its acts. The *Ego*, in the twofold grammatical form of the "I" and the "Me," represents our person insofar as it is a transcendent psychological unity. We have described it elsewhere.[55] It is as an Ego that we are subjects *de facto* and subjects *de jure*, active and passive, voluntary agents, possible objects of an evaluative judgment, or a judgment of responsibility.

The *Ego*'s qualities represent the set of virtualities, latencies, and potentialities that constitute our character and our habits (in the Greek sense of ἕξις). It is a "quality" to be quick-tempered, hardworking, jealous, ambitious, sensuous, etc. But we should also recognize qualities of another kind, originating in our history, to which we may refer as *habits*: I may be *aged, weary, embittered, diminished*, or *making progress*; I may appear to myself as "having grown in confidence since my success" or, on the contrary, as "having gradually developed the tastes, habits, and sexuality of a patient" (after a long illness).

55 TN: Sartre is referring implicitly to his earlier short book *The Transcendence of the Ego* (Sartre 2004a).

In opposition to these qualities, which exist "in potentiality," *states* are given as existing in actuality. Hatred, love, and jealousy are states. An illness—insofar as the patient grasps it as a psychophysiological reality—is a state. In the same way, a number of characteristics that become attached to my person from outside may, insofar as I live them, become states: absence (in relation to some particular person), exile, dishonor and triumph are states. We can see what distinguishes a quality from a state: after yesterday's anger, my "irritability" lives on as a simple, latent disposition to get angry. On the contrary, after Pierre's action and the resentment I felt in relation to it, my hatred survives as an *actual* reality, even though my thoughts are presently occupied by another object. In addition, a quality is an acquired or innate mental disposition that helps to *qualify* my person. A state, on the contrary, is far more accidental and contingent: it is *something that happens to me*. However, there are also instances that fall between states and qualities: for example, even though Pozzo di Borgo's hatred for Napoleon did exist in fact, and represented a contingent, affective relationship between Pozzo and Napoleon I, it was constitutive of Pozzo's *person*.[56]   198

We should understand *acts* as all of a person's synthetic activity, i.e., every ordering of means in view of ends—not insofar as the for-itself is its own possibilities but insofar as the act represents a transcendent psychological synthesis that the for-itself is obliged to live. For example, the boxer's training is an act, because it overflows and maintains the for-itself which, moreover, is actualized in and through this training. The same goes for the scholar's quest, the artist's work, the politician's election campaign. In all cases the act, as a psychological being, represents a transcendent existence and the objective face of the for-itself's relation with the world.

(2) The term "Psychological" applies exclusively to a special category of cognitive acts: the acts of the reflective for-itself. At the unreflective level, the for-itself is its own possibilities in a non-thetic mode and, as its possibilities are possible presences to the world beyond the world's given state, what is thetically, but not thematically, revealed through them is a state of the world that is synthetically connected to its given

---

56 TN: Carlo Andrea Pozzo di Borgo (1768–1842) was a Corsican nobleman who entered the Russian diplomatic service and was active in opposing Napoleonic interests.

state. In consequence, the changes to be made to the world are thetically given, within the things that are present, as objective potentialities to be actualized by using our body as the instrument of their actualization. In this way, an angry man may see in his interlocutor's face the objective quality of asking for a punch. That allows us to describe someone's face as "needing a slap" or "asking to be attacked," etc.[57] Here our body merely resembles a medium in a trance.[58] Through it, a specific potentiality of things is to be actualized (a drink-to-be-drunk, aid-to-be-brought, a harmful-animal-to-be-wiped-out, etc.); the reflection that arises in these circumstances grasps the for-itself's ontological relation to its possibles, but as an *object*. In this way, the *act* arises as a virtual object of reflective consciousness. It is therefore impossible for me to be conscious at the same time, and at the same level, of Pierre and of my friendly feelings toward him: these two existences are always separated by a dimension of for-itself. And this for-itself is, itself, a hidden reality: in the case of unreflected consciousness, it exists, but non-thetically, and it is hidden by the worldly object and its potentialities. And in the case where reflection arises, the for-itself is surpassed toward the virtual object that the reflective consciousness has to be. Only a *pure* reflective consciousness can disclose the reflected for-itself in its reality. We will refer to the organized totality of these existents, which constantly accompany impure reflection and are the natural object of *psychological* investigation, as the "*psychè.*"

(3) Although they are virtual, these objects are not abstractions: reflective consciousness does not aim at them emptily; instead, they are given as the concrete in-itself that reflective consciousness has to be, beyond what it reflects on. We will refer to the immediate presence "in person" to reflective consciousness of hatred, exile, or methodic doubt as "*evidence.*"[59] To be convinced that this presence exists, we need only remind ourselves of cases in our personal experience when we have tried to remember a love that has died, or a certain intellectual atmosphere, lived through in

199

---

57 TN: D'où l'expression de *"tête à gifles,"* de *"menton qui attire les coups"* ... As these phrases do not have close English equivalents, I have had to approximate.

58 TN: Sartre means "medium" in the sense of a psychic (a person who allows absent voices to speak to them).

59 TN: Sartre borrows the phrase "in person" from Husserl. See my note on *en personne* in the section on Husserl vocabulary in Notes on the Translation.

our past. In these different cases we had a distinct consciousness of aiming at these different objects *emptily*. We may have been able to form specific concepts of them, or to attempt a literary description, but we knew they were not there. Similarly, there are periods of intermittence within a living love, in which we *know* we are in love but we do not *feel* it. Proust described these "intermittences of the heart" very well. In contrast, it is possible to grasp a love fully, to contemplate it. But for that, a specific mode of being of the reflected for-itself is required: it is *through* my liking him in the moment—which has been reflected on by my reflective consciousness—that I am able to apprehend my friendly feelings for Pierre. In short, the only way of presentifying these qualities, states, or acts is by apprehending them through a reflected consciousness, whose shadow they cast into the in-itself, in which they are objectified.

But this possibility of presentifying a love demonstrates, better than any argument, the psyche's transcendence. When I suddenly discover my love, when I *see* it, I also grasp it as standing *before* consciousness. I am able to take up points of view on it, to judge it; I am not committed within it like reflective consciousness in relation to what it reflects on. By virtue of this very fact, I apprehend it as *not being* akin to the for-itself. It is infinitely heavier, more opaque, more solid than that absolute transparency. That is why the *evidence* with which psychological facts are given to intuition in impure reflection is not apodictic. Indeed there is a gap between the reflected for-itself's future—which is constantly eaten into and made lighter by my freedom—and my love's dense and threatening future, which is the source of its meaning precisely as *love*. If I did not in fact grasp, within the psychological object, that its future as love was settled, would it still be love? Would it not descend to the level of whim? And doesn't even a whim commit the future, to the extent that it is given as having to remain a whim, and never to change into love? In this way, the for-itself's constantly nihilated future precludes any in itself determination of the for-itself as a for-itself who loves or hates; and the projected shadow of the reflected for-itself naturally possesses a future that has become degraded into in-itself, and that fuses with it to determine its meaning. But, correlatively with the continual nihilation of the reflected futures, the psychological structure that includes its future remains only *probable*. And by that we should not understand some external quality deriving from its relation to my knowledge and which is 200 able to be transformed—should the occasion arise—into certainty, but an ontological characteristic.

(4) The psychological object, as the shadow cast by the reflected for-itself, possesses the characteristics of consciousness in degraded form. In particular, whereas the for-itself makes itself exist in the diasporic unity of a detotalized totality, it appears as a complete and probable totality. In other words, the psyche, which is apprehended through the three ecstatic dimensions of temporality, appears as being constituted through the synthesis of a Past, a Present, and a Future. A love, or an undertaking, is the organized unity of these three dimensions. It is not enough to say, in effect, that a love "has" a future, as if the future were external to the object it characterizes: rather, the future is part of the organized form of the flow that is "love," because its being in the future is what gives love its meaning as love. But because it is in-itself, the psyche's present cannot be flight, nor can its future be pure possibility. In these forms of flow there is an essential priority of the past—i.e., what the for-itself *was*—that already presupposes the for-itself's transformation into in-itself. The reflective consciousness projects a psyche with three temporal dimensions, but it constitutes these three dimensions solely out of what it reflects on *was*. The future already *is*: How else could my love be love? Only it is not yet *given*: it is a "now" that has not yet been disclosed. Therefore it loses its character as a *possibility-that-I-have-to-be*: my love and my joy *do not have their future to be*; they *are* it, in the tranquil indifference of juxtaposition, just as this fountain pen is at the same time its nib and, over there, its cap. Similarly, the present is grasped in its real quality of *being-there*. Only this being-there is constituted into a having-been-there. The present is already entirely constituted, and armed from head to toe; it is a "now" that the instant brings and takes away, like a ready-made suit; it is a card that is taken out of the game, and then put back. The "now," in its transition from the future to the present, and from the present to the past, does not undergo any modification, since in any case—whether it is future or not—it is already in the past. The naïve recourse of psychologists to the unconscious, in order to distinguish the three "nows" of the psyche, illustrates this well: the now that is present to consciousness is called the "*present*." The past or future "nows" have exactly the same characteristics but are waiting in limbo in the unconscious, and if we examine them in this undifferentiated environment,

we will be unable to tell the past from the future: a memory surviving within the unconscious is a past "now" and, at the same time, a future "now" insofar as it awaits its evocation. In this way, the psyche's form is not to be: it is already made; it is already entirely past, present, and future, in the mode of "has been." Nothing remains for the "nows" that compose it but to undergo, one at a time, the baptism of consciousness, before they return to the past.

Consequently, two contradictory modalities of being coexist within   201
the form of the psyche, since it is already made and appears in the cohesive unity of an organism and—at the same time—it can exist only through a succession of "nows," of which each one tends toward its own isolation in the in-itself. This joy, for example, moves from one instant to the other because its future already exists as the final culmination and given meaning of its development—not as what it has to be but as what it already "has been," in the future.

In point of fact, the psyche's inner cohesion is nothing but the for-itself's unity of being, hypostasized within the in-itself. A hatred has no parts: it is not a sum of ways of behaving and [acts of] consciousness; instead it is given, through ways of behaving and [acts of] consciousness, as the temporal unity, without any parts, of their appearances. But here the for-itself's unity of being is explained by the ecstatic character of its being: it has to be, fully spontaneously, what it will be. The psyche, on the contrary, "is-been," which means it is incapable of determining itself by itself to exist. It is maintained before reflective consciousness by a kind of inertia, and psychologists have often emphasized its "pathological" character. It is in this sense that Descartes is able to talk of the "passions of the soul"; it is this inertia that makes it possible to grasp the psyche in relation to existents in the world, even though it is not on the same plane of being as those existents.[60] A love is given as having been "provoked" by the loved object. The result is that the psychological form's total cohesion becomes unintelligible, because it does not have this cohesion to be, because it is not its own synthesis, because its unity has the character of something given. To the extent to which a hatred is a given succession of ready-made and inert "nows," we can find within it the seeds of infinite divisibility. And yet this

---

60 TN: The Passions of the Soul is a treatise by Descartes, written in 1649 and translated as Descartes (1989).

divisibility is concealed and denied, insofar as the psyche is an objectification of the for-itself's ontological unity. Hence there is a kind of *magical* cohesion between the hatred's successive "nows," which are given as *parts* only in order subsequently to negate their externality. This ambiguity is exposed by Bergson's theory of an enduring consciousness as a "multiplicity of interpenetration." What Bergson arrives at here is the psyche, and not consciousness conceived as the for-itself. Indeed, what can "interpenetration" mean? Not the absence, as a matter of principle, of any divisibility. For there to be interpenetration, there must be interpenetrating parts. But these parts, which by rights ought to sink back into isolation, flow into each other through a magical cohesion that is wholly unexplained, and this total fusion has hitherto defied analysis. Bergson has no intention of founding this property of the psyche on any absolute structure of the for-itself: he registers it as something given; it is a mere "intuition" that reveals the psyche to him as an internalized multiplicity. Its character of inertia, as a passive *datum*, is further accentuated by its existing without *being for* a consciousness, thetic or not. It is, without any consciousness (of) being, since, in the natural attitude, man misconceives it entirely, and a recourse to intuition is required to grasp it. In the same way, an object of the world may exist without being seen, and disclose itself later, when we have forged the necessary instruments to detect it. For Bergson, the characteristics of psychological duration are a pure contingent fact of experience: they are that way because that is how we encounter them, and that is all there is to be said. Psychological temporality, therefore, is an inert *datum*, quite similar to Bergson's duration, which *undergoes* its inner cohesion without creating it, and is constantly temporalized without temporalizing *itself*, and whose irrational and magical *de facto* interpenetration of elements that *are* not united by any ecstatic relation of being can be compared only to the magical action of a spell working across a distance, and conceals a multiplicity of ready-made "nows." And these characteristics do not have their source in a mistake of psychologists or a lack of knowledge; they are constitutive of psychological temporality, a hypostasis of original temporality. The psyche's absolute unity is the projection of the for-itself's ontological and ecstatic unity. But as this projection is made into the in-itself—that is what it is in the proximity without distance of identity—the ecstatic unity is fragmented into an infinity of "nows" that are what they are and which, precisely for that reason, tend to become isolated in their in-itself-identity.

Thus psychological temporality, participating at the same time in the in-itself and the for-itself, harbors a contradiction that is not overcome. And we ought not to be surprised: as a product of impure reflection, it will naturally *"be been"* what it is not, and not be what it *"is-been."*

An examination of the relations which psychological forms maintain with each other within psychological time will render this still more apparent. We should note, first, that the connections between our feelings—for example, within a complex psychological form—are genuinely subject to interpenetration. We all know those feelings of friendship that are "nuanced" by envy, those hatreds that are, despite everything, "penetrated" by esteem, those amorous friendships that novelists have often described. In addition, we unquestionably grasp a friendship nuanced by envy like a cup of coffee that contains a cloud of milk. And this comparison is probably crude. However, it is clear that a loving friendship is not given as a mere specification of the genus of friendship, in the way in which an isosceles triangle is a specification of the genus of triangle. The friendship presents itself as being entirely penetrated by the love in its entirety—and yet it is not love, nor does it "turn into" love; otherwise it would lose its autonomy as friendship. But an inert and in-itself object is constituted that our language finds it difficult to name, in which the in-itself and autonomous love is magically extended throughout the friendship, in the way in which, in the Stoic doctrine of σύγχυσις, the leg extends throughout the sea.[61]   203

But psychological processes also imply the action across a distance of earlier forms on later forms. We cannot conceive of this action at a distance on the model of simple causality that we find, for example, in classical mechanics, where the wholly inert existence of a moving body, contained within an instant, is assumed. Nor can we conceive of it on the model of physical causality, in the manner of Stuart Mill, which is defined by the constant and unconditioned succession of two states, each of which, in its own being, excludes the other.[62] Insofar as the psyche is an objectification of the for-itself, it possesses a degraded spontaneity

---

61 TN: This Greek term is transliterated as *sugchusis*. Literally meaning "pouring together," it refers to a state of fusion of elements that are thoroughly blended together.

62 TN: Sartre is referring to the British philosopher John Stuart Mill (1806–1873), and the account of laws of causation developed in Mill's *System of Logic*, published in 1843 and included in Mill (1963–91).

that we apprehend as an internal and given quality of its form and which is, moreover, inseparable from its cohesive force. It cannot therefore be given as strictly the product of some earlier form. But, on the other hand, this spontaneity cannot determine itself in existence, since we grasp it only as one determination among others of a given existent. It follows that the earlier form has to give birth—across a distance—to a form of the same kind, which spontaneously structures itself as a form in a flow. Here we do not have a being that *has* its future and its past *to be* but only successions of forms that are past, present, and future; each of these, however, exists in the mode of "having-been-it" and influences the others across a distance. This influence will become manifest either through penetration or through motivation. In the first case, reflective consciousness apprehends as a single object two psychological objects that were at first given separately. The result is either a new psychological object, in which each characteristic is the synthesis of two others, or an object that is in itself unintelligible, which is given as simultaneously being entirely one of these two and also entirely the other, without there being any alteration in either of them. In motivation, on the contrary, each of the two objects remains in its place. But a psychological object, as a structured form and a multiplicity of interpenetration, can act only in its entirety, and all at once, on an entirely different object. The consequence is a total action by one on the other, occurring across a distance and by means of a magical influence. For example, my humiliation yesterday is what motivates entirely my mood this morning, etc. What demonstrates— better than any analysis—the wholly magical and irrational character of this action across a distance is the futile attempts made by intellectualist psychologists to reduce it (while remaining at the level of psychology) to a causality that intellectual analysis might make intelligible. Thus Proust constantly tries to find, through his intellectualist dissection of psychological states within their temporal succession, connections of rational causality between these states. But once he has performed these analyses, all he is able to offer us is this kind of result:

> For once Swann could picture her [Odette] to himself without revulsion, could see once again the friendliness in her smile, once *the desire to tear her away from every rival was no longer imposed by jealousy upon his love*, that love *became once again*, more than anything, a taste for the

204

sensations which Odette's person gave him, for the pleasure he took in admiring as a spectacle, or in examining as a phenomenon, the dawn of one of her glances, the formation of one of her smiles, the emission of a particular vocal cadence. And this pleasure, different from any other, *had in the end created in him a need of her* which she alone by her presence or her letters could assuage. . . . And so, *through the chemical action of his malady*, after he had *created jealousy out of his love*, he began again *to manufacture tenderness* and pity for Odette.[63]

Obviously, this text is about the psyche. In it, we can see feelings that are inherently separated and individualized, and which act upon each other. But Proust tries to clarify these actions and to classify them, hoping thereby to make intelligible the alternatives that Swann is obliged to experience. He does not confine himself to describing what he has been able to observe himself (the transition, through "oscillations," from hateful jealousy to tender love); he wants to explain these observations.

What are the results of this analysis? Does it eliminate the psyche's unintelligibility? On the contrary, we can see without difficulty that this rather arbitrary reduction of the major psychological forms into simpler elements demonstrates the magical irrationality of the relations maintained between the psychological objects. How can jealousy "impose upon" love the "desire to tear her away from every rival?" And, once this desire is added to the love (the image here is still of a cloud of milk "added" to the coffee), how does that prevent it from *becoming once again* "a taste for the sensations which Odette's person gave him?" And how can pleasure *create* a need? And as for love, how does it *manufacture* the jealousy that, in its turn, imposes on him the desire to tear Odette away from every rival? And how, once he is freed from that desire, can he once again *manufacture* tenderness? Here Proust is attempting to constitute a symbolic "chemistry," but the chemical images he employs are able only to conceal motivations and actions that are irrational. The idea is to lead us into a mechanistic interpretation of the psyche that, without being any

---

63 Sartre's note: *Du Côté de chez Swann*, 37th edition, II, p. 82, my emphasis. TN: I have taken the English passage which corresponds to the French quoted (and emphasized at parts) by Sartre from *Swann's Way*, in the translation by C. K. Scott Moncrieff and Terence Kilmartin, and revised by D. J. Enright (Proust 2005: 366).

more intelligible, completely distorts its nature. And yet it is impossible to avoid showing us bizarre and almost human relations (creating, fabricating, adding) between the states, which allow us almost to suppose that these psychological objects are animate agents. In Proust's descriptions, we see the limits of intellectualist analysis appearing in every moment: its dissections and classifications can be carried out only on the surface, and against a ground of complete irrationality. We must give up any attempt to reduce the irrationality of psychological causality: that causality is the

205   magical degradation of an ecstatic for-itself that is its being at a distance from itself, into an in-itself that is what it is, at its place. The action through influence, working magically across a distance, is the necessary result of this loosening of the connections within being. The psychologist ought to describe these irrational connections and to regard them as a primary given of the psychological world.

In this way, reflective consciousness is constituted as a consciousness of duration and, in consequence, psychological duration appears to consciousness. This psychological temporality, as the projection of original temporality into the in-itself, is a virtual being whose phantom flowing endlessly accompanies the for-itself's ecstatic temporalization, insofar as reflection grasps this latter. But if the for-itself remains at the unreflected level, or if impure reflection is purified, it disappears completely. Psychological temporality resembles original temporality in that it appears as a mode of being of concrete objects, not as a preestablished framework or rule. Psychological time is no more than the combined set of temporal objects. But its essential difference from original temporality is that it *is*, whereas the latter temporalizes itself. As such, it can be constituted only out of the past, and the future can only be a past that is to come after the present past, i.e., the empty "before-after" form has become hypostasized, and orders the relations between objects that are equally past. At the same time, this psychological duration, unable to be through itself, must constantly *be been*. This temporality, constantly oscillating between the multiplicity of juxtaposition and the absolute cohesion of the ecstatic for-itself, is composed out of "nows" that have been, and which remain at the place assigned to them, but which influence each other across a distance in their totality; that is what makes it quite similar to the magical duration of Bergsonian philosophy. As soon as one takes up the standpoint of impure reflection—the kind of reflection that

seeks to determine the being that I am—an entire world appears, to populate this temporality. This world—a virtual presence, and the probable
object of my reflective intention—is the psychological world, or *psychè*.
In one sense, its existence is purely ideal; in another sense, it *is*—since it
is-been, since it is disclosed to consciousness: it is "my shadow," what is
disclosed to me when I want *to see myself*. And furthermore, as it may be
the basis on which the for-itself determines itself to be what it has to be
(I will not go to this or that person's house "because of" the antipathy I
feel in relation to him, I decide on this or that action by taking my hatred
or my love into account, I refuse to discuss politics because I know my
irritable temperament, and do not want to risk becoming angry), this
phantom world exists as the for-itself's *real situation*. And with this transcendent world, which takes up residence in the infinite becoming of
antihistorical indifference, the temporality that we refer to as "internal"
or "qualitative"—which is an objectification of original temporality into   206
in-itself—is constituted, precisely, as a virtual unity of being. Here we
find the first draft of an "outside"; the for-itself sees itself almost conferring an "outside" on itself, in its own eyes: but this "outside" is purely
virtual. Later on we will see how being-for-the-Other *actualizes* the first
draft of this "outside."

Chapter 3

TRANSCENDENCE

To arrive at as complete a description of the for-itself as we can, we chose the investigation of negative forms of behavior as our guiding thread. As we saw, it is the permanent possibility of non-being, outside us and within us, that conditions the questions we are able to ask, and the answers we can give them. But our primary aim was not only to disclose the for-itself's negative structures. In our Introduction, we encountered a problem, and that problem is what we wished to resolve: what is human-reality's original relation to the being of phenomena, or being-in-itself? And we have been obliged to reject, in our Introduction and thereafter, the realist solution and the idealist solution. It seemed to us that transcendent being could not act in any way upon consciousness and, at the same time, that consciousness could not "construct" anything transcendent by objectifying elements borrowed from its subjectivity. Subsequently, we came to understand that the original relationship to being could not be the kind of external relation that joins two primitively isolated substances. "The relation of the regions of being is a primordial bursting forth," we said, "which forms part of the very structure of these beings."[1] What showed

---

1 TN: Sartre is repeating *verbatim* this sentence from EN 38, above.

itself to be concrete was the synthetic totality, of which consciousness and the phenomenon only constitute articulations. But if, in one sense, consciousness considered in isolation is an abstraction, and if the phenomena—and even the phenomenon of being—are similarly abstract, insofar as they cannot exist as phenomena without *appearing* to a consciousness, we cannot regard the being of phenomena, as in-itself that is what it is, as an abstraction. To be, it needs nothing but itself; it refers only to itself. Our description of the for-itself, on the other hand, showed it to be, on the contrary, as far removed as possible from a substance and from the in-itself: we saw that the for-itself is its own nihilation, and that only within the ontological unity of its ecstases is it possible for it to be. If, therefore, the for-itself's relation to the in-itself must from the outset constitute the very being that enters into relation, we should take this to mean not that it constitutes the in-itself but, instead, the for-itself. It is within the for-itself alone that we must seek the key to that relation to being, for example, that goes by the name "knowledge." The for-itself is responsible in its being for its relation with the in-itself or, alternatively, it produces itself from the very beginning on the foundation of a relation to the in-itself. This we had already foreseen when we defined consciousness as "a being for whom in its being there is a question of its being, insofar as this being implies a being other than itself."[2] But since we formulated that definition we have acquired new knowledge. In particular, we have grasped the for-itself's innermost meaning, as the foundation of its own nothingness. Is now not the time for us to make use of this knowledge to determine and to explicate this ecstatic relation of the for-itself to the in-itself, on whose foundation it is possible for *knowledge* and *action* in general to appear? Do we not have what we need to answer our initial question? In order to be a non-thetic consciousness (of) self, consciousness must be thetically conscious of something, as we noted. Now, so far, we have studied the for-itself as the original mode of being of any non-thetic consciousness (of) self. Were we not led, in doing just that, to describe the for-itself specifically in its relations to the in-itself, insofar as these are constitutive of its being? Are we not now able

208

2 TN: Sartre is once again referring to his revision of Heidegger's formula, first discussed at EN 29.

to find an answer to questions of this type: given that the in-itself is what it is, how and why is it the case that the for-itself has, in its being, to be knowledge of the in-itself? And what is knowledge in general?

I. KNOWLEDGE AS A TYPE OF RELATION BETWEEN THE FOR-ITSELF AND THE IN-ITSELF

The only kind of knowledge is intuitive. Deduction and discourse, which are incorrectly labeled as "knowledge," are only instruments leading to intuition. When we reach the intuition, the means that were used to reach it are set aside; in cases where we cannot reach it, reasoning and discourse are left in the position of signposts that point toward an intuition that is out of reach. Finally, if an intuition has been reached but is not a present mode of my consciousness, the maxims that I employ persist, as the results of operations that I carried out earlier, like Descartes's "memories of ideas."[3] And if we ask what intuition is, Husserl will reply (in agreement with most philosophers) that it is the presence of the "thing" (Sache) in person to consciousness. Knowledge, therefore, has the type of being that we described in the previous chapter under the heading of "presence to . . ." But we established that the in-itself cannot by itself ever be a *presence*. In point of fact, being-present is an ecstatic mode of being of the for-itself. We are obliged therefore to reverse the terms of our definition: intuition is the presence of consciousness to the thing. What we need to come back to now, therefore, is the nature and the meaning of this for-itself's presence to being.

In our Introduction—by making use of a non-elucidated concept of "consciousness"—we established the necessity for consciousness to be conscious of something. In fact it is through whatever it is conscious of that consciousness can distinguish itself with its own eyes, and be a consciousness (of) self. A consciousness that was not conscious of something would not be conscious (of) anything. But now we have elucidated the ontological meaning of consciousness, or the for-itself. We are able therefore to present the problem in more exact terms and to ask:

209

3 TN: . . . "*souvenirs d'idées*." I have not been able to track down this phrase in Descartes.

What might this necessity—that consciousness should be-conscious of something—mean, if we consider it at the level of ontology, i.e., within the perspective of being-for-itself? We know that the for-itself is the foundation of its own nothingness in the form of the phantom dyad: reflection-reflecting. The reflecting exists only in order to reflect the reflection, and the reflection is only a reflection insofar as it refers back to the reflecting. In this way each of the two nascent terms of the dyad points toward the other, and the being of each one is engaged within the other's being. But if the reflecting is nothing but a reflecting of this reflection, and if the reflection can be characterized only by its "being-in-order-to be reflected in this reflecting," the two terms of the quasi-dyad, bracing their two nothingnesses against each other, are jointly annihilated. The reflecting has to reflect *something* if the whole is not to collapse into nothingness. But if, on the other hand, the reflection was *something*—independently of its being-in-order-to-be-reflected—we would have to qualify it not as a reflection but as in-itself. That would introduce opacity within the "reflection-reflecting" system and, in particular, it would bring the nascent scissiparity to completion. For, within the for-itself, the reflection *is also* the reflecting. But once the reflection is qualified, it becomes separated from the reflecting and its appearance is separated from its reality; the *cogito* becomes impossible. The reflection can only be "something to be reflected" and at the same time *nothing* if it becomes qualified by something other than itself or, alternatively, if it is reflected as a relation to an "outside" that it is not. What defines the reflection for the reflecting is always *that to which it is presence*. Even an instance of joy, apprehended at the unreflected level, is nothing but a "reflected" presence to a laughing and open world, full of happy perspectives. But the preceding sentences allow us already to anticipate that *not-being* is an essential structure of presence. Presence includes a radical negation, as presence to something that we are not. What is present to me is not me. We should note, moreover, that this "not-being" is implied *a priori* by any theory of knowledge. It is impossible to construct the notion of an object if there is not, from the beginning, a negative relation by which the object is designated as that which *is not* consciousness. The phrase "not-self," which was fashionable at one time, conveyed this well—even though it was impossible to discern the slightest concern, in the people using it, to provide any foundation for this original "not" that characterized the external world.[4] In fact, neither the combination of representations, nor the necessity of certain subjective structures, nor the irreversibility of time, nor the recourse to the infinite can serve to constitute the object as such—i.e., to serve as a foundation for a further negation that delineates the not-self, and opposes it to the self as such—unless that negation, precisely, is given first and is the *a priori* foundation of all experience. In advance of any comparison, or any construction, a thing has to be present to consciousness as *not being* consciousness. The original relation of presence, as the foundation of knowledge, is negative. But as it is through the for-itself that negation comes into the world, and as a thing is what it is in the absolute indifference of identity, what posits itself as not being the for-itself cannot be a thing. The negation comes from the for-itself itself. We should not conceive of this negation on the model of a judgment, bearing on the thing itself and denying, in relation to that thing, its identity with the for-itself: that type of negation could be conceived only if the for-itself were a ready-made substance and, even in that case, it could only emerge from a third person establishing, from outside, a negative relation between two beings. Instead, it is the for-itself that constitutes itself, through original negation, as *not being* the thing. So the definition of consciousness we gave a short time ago can be expressed, from the for-itself's perspective, as follows: "The for-itself is a being for whom its being is in question in its being insofar as this being is essentially a specific way of *not being* a being that it posits at the same time as other than itself." Knowledge appears therefore as a mode of being. Knowing is neither a relation that is subsequently established between two beings, nor an activity of one of these two beings, nor is it a quality, a property or a virtue. It is the for-itself's very being insofar as it is presence to . . . , i.e., insofar as the for-itself has its being to be, in making itself not be a specific being to which it is present. That implies that the for-itself can exist only in the mode of a reflection that gets reflected as not being a specific being. The "something" that has to qualify what is reflected—in order to prevent the "reflection-reflecting" pair from collapsing into

211

---

4 TN: Sartre probably has in mind the opposition of the Self and not-Self (or the I and not-I) in German Idealist philosophy. Both Hegel and Fichte refer to the "not-I." I have translated *non-moi* as "not-self" here.

nothingness—is pure negation. The reflected becomes qualified *outside*, alongside some specific being, as *not being* that being; that is precisely what "to be conscious of something" means.

But we should clarify what we mean by this original negation. We need, in fact, to distinguish between two types of negation: external negation and internal negation. The former appears as a purely external connection between two beings, established by a witness. For example, when I say "The cup is not the inkwell," it is quite clear that the foundation of this negation lies neither in the cup nor in the inkwell.[5] Each of these objects is what it is, and that's all that is to be said. The negation is like an ideal and categorical connection that I establish between them, without modifying them in any respect, without enriching or impoverishing them with the slightest quality; they are not in the least touched by this negative synthesis. As it serves neither to enrich them nor to constitute them, it remains strictly external. But if we consider sentences such as "I am not rich" or "I am not handsome" we will already be able to guess the meaning of the other type of negation. Uttered with a certain melancholy, these phrases mean not only that I am withholding from myself some particular quality but that the refusal itself comes to influence, in its internal structure, the positive being to whom it has been refused. When I say "I am not handsome," I do not confine myself to denying that some particular property applies to me, taken as a concrete whole—such that this property passes into nothingness, leaving the positive totality of my being intact (as when I say "The vase is not white; it is gray," "The inkwell is not on the table; it is on the mantelpiece"). What I mean is that "not being beautiful" is a particular negative property of my being, which characterizes me from inside, and also that—*qua* negativity— "not being beautiful" is a real quality of myself, and this negative quality explains my melancholy, for example, just as effectively as my lack of worldly success. By "internal negation" we mean a relation between two beings, where the one that we deny in relation to the other qualifies the other, at the heart of its essence, precisely by its absence. In this case the negation becomes an essential connection of being, since at least one of the beings on which it bears is such that it indicates the other, and

5 TN: The French text has "table" instead of the second instance of "cup." Assuming this is a mistake, I have corrected it in the English.

bears the other in its heart as an absence. It is clear, however, that this type of negation cannot apply to being-in-itself. It belongs by its nature to the for-itself. Only the for-itself can be determined in its being by a being that it is not. And if internal negation can appear within the world—as when we describe a pearl as a fake, or a fruit as unripe, or an egg as not being fresh, etc.—it is through the for-itself that it enters the world, like all negation in general. If, therefore, knowing appertains only to the for-itself, it is because it is characteristic only of the for-itself to appear to itself as not being the thing that it knows. And as appearance and being are just one and the same here—since the for-itself has the being of its appearance—we are obliged to conceive of the for-itself as including, within its being, the being of the object that it is not, insofar as it is in question in its being as not being *that* being.

We must dissociate ourselves at this point from an illusion that can be formulated in these terms: in order to constitute oneself as *not being* this or that being, we must first in some way or other have some knowledge of that being, because I am unable to judge how I differ from a being about which I know nothing. Certainly, in our empirical existence we are unable to know how we differ from someone Japanese or English, from a worker or a sovereign, before we have any notion of these various beings. But these empirical distinctions cannot provide our starting point here, because we are preparing to study an ontological relation that is required to make all our experience possible, and our aim is to establish how it is possible in general for an object to exist for consciousness. It cannot be the case, therefore, that I have an experience of the object—as an object which is not me—before I constitute it as an object. But, on the contrary, what makes all experience possible is the object's *a priori* arising for the subject or—since the for-itself's original fact is its arising—an original arising of the for-itself as presence to the object that it is not. We need therefore to reverse the terms in our earlier formulation: the fundamental relation through which the for-itself has to be, as not being this particular being to which it is present, is the foundation of all knowledge of this being. But if we want to make this initial relation comprehensible, we need a better description of it.

Part of the statement of the intellectualist illusion that we criticized in the last paragraph remains true: it is not possible for me to determine myself not to be some object that is from the outset cut off from any connection with me. I am not able to deny that I am *that* being, *at a distance* from that being. If I conceive of a being that is entirely closed in on itself, that being by itself will quite simply be what it is and, in consequence, there will be no space in it either for a negation, or for knowledge. In fact, it is on the basis of the being that it is not that any being is able to *become acquainted with* what it is not. In other words, the for-itself, in the case of internal negation, appears to itself as not being what it is not over there, in and on the being that it is not. In this sense, internal negation is a concrete ontological connection. What we have here is not an instance of empirical negation, in which the qualities that are negated are distinguished primarily by their absence, or even their non-being. In internal negation, the for-itself is crushed against what it negates. The negated qualities are precisely what is most present to the for-itself; it is from them that the for-itself draws its negative power, and constantly renews it. In this sense, we must regard them as a constitutive factor of the for-itself's being, because it is obliged to be over there, outside itself, against them: it has to be *them*, in order to negate its being them. In short, the origin-term[6] of internal negation is the in-itself, the thing that *is there*; and outside it there is nothing, apart from an emptiness, a nothingness that is only distinguished from the thing by a pure negation, whose content is provided precisely by *this* thing. The difficulty encountered by materialism in deriving our knowledge of an object stems from the fact that it tries to produce one substance on the basis of another substance. But this difficulty will not stand in our way, because we are claiming that, outside the in-itself, there is *nothing*—other than a reflection of that nothing which is itself polarized and defined by the in-itself insofar as it is precisely the nothingness of *this* in-itself, the individualized nothing which is nothing because it *is not* the in-itself. Thus, within this ecstatic relation, through which internal negation and knowledge are constituted, the concrete pole in its plenitude is the in-itself in person, and the for-itself is nothing apart from the void within which the in-itself stands out. The for-itself is outside itself in the in-itself, since it comes to be defined by what it is not: the primary connection of the in-itself to the for-itself is therefore a

213

6 TN: ... *le terme-origine* ... The phrase that I translate (literally) as "origin-term" is also unusual in French. Sartre may have a mathematical series in mind, and be referring to the first term, from which the rest of the series is generated.

connection of being. But this connection is neither a *lack* nor an *absence*. In fact, in the case of absence I am effectively determined by a being that I am not and which does not exist, or does not exist there, which means I am determined by something like a cavity, in the midst of what we may call my empirical plenitude. In knowledge, on the contrary, construed as an ontological connection of being, the being that I am not represents the in-itself's absolute plenitude. And, in contrast, I am the nothingness, the absence that determines itself to exist on the basis of that plenum. So, in this type of being that we call "knowing," the only *being* that we can encounter and which is constantly *there* is the *known*. The knowing is not; we cannot get hold of it. It is nothing but that which makes it the case that the known involves a *being-there*, a presence—because, by itself, the known is neither present nor absent; it simply is. But this presence of the known is a presence to *nothing*, because the knowing is purely a reflection of a non-being; it appears therefore, through the total translucency of the knowing, as an *absolute* presence. Cases of *fascination* can furnish examples—psychological and empirical—of this original relation. Indeed, in such cases, where the immediate fact of knowledge is represented, the knowing is absolutely nothing but a pure negation: in no place can it be found, or retrieved; *it is not*; the only property it is able to support is, precisely, that of *not being* this fascinating object. In the state of fascination, nothing continues to exist apart from a giant object, in a deserted world. And yet the fascinated intuition is not in any way a *fusion* with the object. This is because it is a condition of fascination that the object should detach itself in absolute relief against an empty ground, i.e., that I should be, precisely, the immediate negation of the object, and nothing but that. We meet this pure negation again in the pantheistic intuitions that Rousseau occasionally describes as concrete psychological events in his history. At

these points he declares that he "melted into" the universe, that suddenly the only thing found to be present was the world, as an absolute presence and unconditioned totality. And of course we can understand this total and deserted presence of the world, its pure "being-there"; we can readily acknowledge that in this exceptional moment there was nothing other than the world. But that does not mean we should concede, as Rousseau would have it, that consciousness has become fused with the world. Such a fusion would imply that the for-itself had solidified into the in-itself and, thereby, the disappearance of the world and the in-itself as presence.

It is true that, in a pantheistic intuition, there is nothing more than the world—apart from whatever makes it the case that the in-itself is present as the world (i.e., a pure negation that is non-thetically conscious (of) itself as negation). And, precisely because knowledge is not *absence* but *presence*, there is *nothing* separating the knowing from the known. Intuition is often defined as the immediate presence of the known to the knowing, but only rarely has anyone reflected on the requirements of the notion of the *immediate*. The immediate is the absence of anything which mediates, which goes without saying—otherwise what is known would be the mediator, and not the mediated. But if we are unable to posit any intermediary, we are obliged at the same time to reject both continuity and discontinuity as the type of presence of the knowing to the known. Indeed, we cannot allow any continuity between the knowing and the known, because that would require some intermediate term that is at the same time knowing and known, which would destroy the autonomy of the knowing in relation to the known, by committing the being of the knowing within the being of the known. In that case the structure of the object disappears, since the object requires to be absolutely negated, *qua* the for-itself's being, by the for-itself. But neither can we regard the for-itself's original relation to the in-itself as a relation of *discontinuity*. Of course, the separation between two discontinuous elements is a void, i.e., a *nothing*, but it is a nothing that has been *actualized* or *realized*, and therefore *in-itself*. As such, this substantialized nothing is a non-conductive density; it destroys the immediacy of presence, because it has become *something*, insofar as it is nothing. The for-itself's presence to the in-itself, which we cannot describe either in terms of continuity or in terms of discontinuity, is purely a *negated identity*. To get a better grasp of this, we can use a comparison: when two curves are at a tangent to each other, they display a type of presence without any intermediary. But it is also the case that, for the entire length of their tangent, the eye apprehends only *one single line*. Even if we were to cover up the two curves—so that all we could see was the AB length at which they are co-tangent—it would be impossible to distinguish them. This is because what separates them is in fact *nothing*: there is neither continuity nor discontinuity but pure identity. And should we suddenly uncover the two figures, we will once again apprehend them, throughout their length, as being two—not because of a sudden *de facto* separation that has suddenly been actualized between them, but

215   because each of the two movements through which we *draw* the two
curves, in order to perceive them, includes a negation as its constituting act. Thus, what separates the two curves even where they are tangent is *nothing*, not even a distance: it is a pure negativity, as the
counterpart to a constituting synthesis. This image will allow us to
grasp more clearly the relation of immediacy that, from the outset,
joins the knowing to the known. In the ordinary case, in fact, a negation bears on a "something" that preexists the negation and constitutes
its matter: if, for example, I say that the inkwell is not the table, the
table and the inkwell are objects that are already constituted, whose
being in itself will be what supports the negative judgment. But in the
case of the "knowing-known" relation, there is nothing, on the side of
the knowing, that could support the negation: "there is not" any difference, or any distinguishing principle, to separate *in-itself* the knowing from the known. Rather, within the complete lack of distinction in
being, there is nothing but a negation—which does not even exist—a
negation that *has to be*, and does not even posit itself as a negation. So,
in the end, the knowledge and the knowing itself are nothing, other
than the fact that "there is" being, that being in itself *is given* and stands
out in relief against the ground of this nothing. In this sense, we can
call knowledge the "pure solitude of the known." This suffices to show
that the basic phenomenon of knowledge *adds* nothing to being, and
creates nothing. Being is not enriched through it, because knowledge
is pure negativity. It only makes it the case *that there is* being. But this fact
"that there is" being is not an internal determination of being—which
is what it is—but of negativity. In this sense, every disclosure of a
positive characteristic of being is the counterpart of an ontological
determination of the for-itself in its being as pure negativity. For example, as we will see later on, the disclosure of being's spatiality is just
one and the same thing as the for-itself's non-positional apprehension
of itself as *non-extended*. And the for-itself's non-extended character is not
some mysterious positive property of mentality, concealed beneath a
negative description: it is by nature an ecstatic relation, because it is
through and within the extension of the transcendent in-itself that the
for-itself becomes acquainted with and realizes or actualizes its own
non-extension. The for-itself cannot in the first place be non-extended,
in order subsequently to enter into relation with some extended being

because, no matter how we think about it, the concept of non-extension cannot by itself have any meaning: it is nothing but the negation of extension. If by some miracle it were possible to eliminate extension from the disclosed determinations of the in-itself, the for-itself would not remain *a-spatial*; it would be neither extended nor non-extended, and it would become impossible to characterize it in relation to extension in any way. Extension, in this case, is a transcendent determination that the for-itself has to apprehend to the exact degree to which it negates itself as extended. That is why the best term to use, to signify this internal relation of knowing and being, is the verb we were using just now: "*to realize*," with its double meaning, ontological and gnostic.[7] I realize a project insofar as I give it being, but I also *realize* my situation, insofar as I live it, insofar as I make it be with my being, and I "realize" the enormity of a catastrophe, the difficulty of an enterprise. To know is *to realize* in the two senses of this verb. It is to make it the case that there is being, by having the reflected negation of this being to be: the *real* is a *realization*. We can give the name "transcendence" to this internal and realizing negation which discloses the in-itself by determining the for-itself in its being.

II. ON DETERMINATION AS NEGATION

To which being is the for-itself present? Let us note straightaway that the question is badly put: being is what it is, and it cannot bear by itself the determination "this one," in answer to the question "which one?" In short, a question can have meaning only if it is raised within a world. In consequence, the for-itself cannot be present to this one rather than that one, since its presence is what makes it the case that there is [il y a] a "this one" rather than a "that one." Yet our examples have shown us a for-itself concretely negating its being that particular being. But that is because, in describing the relationship of knowledge, we were concerned first and foremost to bring its structure of negativity to light. So, by virtue of its being disclosed by means of examples, this negativity was already secondary. The negativity of original transcendence is not determined on the basis of a this; rather, it makes it the case that a this exists. The for-itself's

7 TN: See my note on *réaliser* in Notes on the Translation.

original presence is *presence* to being. Should we say, then, that it is presence to *all* of being? But then we would fall back into our previous error, because totality can come to being only through the for-itself. Indeed, any totality presupposes an internal relation of being between the terms of a quasi-multiplicity, in the same way as a multiplicity presupposes, in order to be that multiplicity, a totalizing internal relation between its elements; in this sense, addition itself is a synthetic act. Totality can come to beings only through a being that has its own totality to be in their presence. This is precisely the case for the for-itself, a detotalized totality that temporalizes itself within a constant incompleteness. It is the for-itself in its presence to being that makes it the case that *all being* exists. Indeed, we should be quite clear that we can only refer to *this* being right here as "this" against the ground of the presence of *all* being. It does not follow

217 that, in order to exist, *one* being needs *all* of being, but rather that the for-itself actualizes itself as an actualizing presence to this being against the original ground of an actualizing presence to *everything*. But, conversely, as the totality is an internal ontological relation of the "*thises*," it can be disclosed only in and through the particular "*thises*." So the for-itself actualizes itself as an actualizing presence to all of being, insofar as it is an actualizing presence to the "*thises*"—and to the particular "*thises*," insofar as it is an actualizing presence to all of being. In other words, the for-itself's presence to the *world* can be actualized only through its presence to one or to several particular things; and, conversely, its presence to a particular thing can be actualized only against the ground of a presence to the world. Perception can be articulated only against the ontological ground of a presence to the world, and the world is concretely disclosed as the ground of each particular perception. It remains for us to explain how, in arising to being, the for-itself can make it the case that there is an *all*, and that there are "*thises*."

The for-itself's presence to being *as a totality* stems from the fact that the for-itself has to be—in the mode of being what it is not and not being what it is—its own totality as a detotalized totality. Indeed, insofar as the for-itself makes itself be, in the unity of a single movement of arising, as *everything* that is not being, being stands before it as *everything* that it is not. The original negation is, in effect, a radical negation. The for-itself placed before being as its own totality, in being itself the whole of negation, is the negation of the whole. In this way, the completed totality—or the world—is disclosed as constitutive of the being of the incomplete totality through which the being of the totality arises in being. It is through the *world* that the for-itself becomes acquainted with itself as a detotalized totality; in other words, through its very arising, the for-itself is the disclosure of being as a totality, insofar as the for-itself has, in detotalized mode, its own totality to be. Thus the for-itself's very meaning is outside, within being, but it is through the for-itself that the meaning of being appears. This totalization of being *adds nothing* to being: it is nothing but the way that being is disclosed as not being the for-itself, the way in which *there is* being; it appears *outside the for-itself*, escaping any attempt to reach it, as that which determines the for-itself in its being. But the act of disclosing being as a totality does not impinge on being, any more than my act of counting two cups on the table impinges on either cup in its existence or in its nature. But nor is it purely a subjective modification of the for-itself, since, on the contrary, it is through the for-itself that any subjectivity is possible. But if the for-itself is obliged to be the nothingness through which "there is" being, there can only be being, originally, as a totality. In this way, therefore, knowledge is *the world*; to use Heidegger's language, it is the world and, outside that, *nothing*.[8] However, it is not originally within this "nothing" that human-reality emerges. This *nothing* is human-reality itself, as the radical negation through which the world is disclosed. And certainly, the mere apprehension of the world as a totality makes a nothingness appear *on the world's side*, maintaining this totality and surrounding it. It is even this nothingness—as the absolute nothing that is left outside the totality—that determines the totality as such: it is for just this reason that the totalization adds nothing to being, since it is merely the result of nothingness appearing as the limit of being. But this nothingness *is not* anything, other than human-reality grasping itself as excluded from being and as constantly beyond being, in commerce with nothing. To say that human-reality is that through which being is disclosed as a totality, or that human-reality is what makes it the case that "there is" nothing outside being, amounts to the same thing. This nothing, as the possibility of there being a "beyond" to the world, insofar as (1) this possibility discloses being as the world, and (2) human-reality has this possibility to be, constitutes, with our original presence to being, the circuit of ipseity.

218

8 TN: Sartre is probably alluding to Heidegger (1978c) here, as earlier in the text.

But human-reality only makes itself the incomplete totality of negations to the extent that it overflows some particular negation—a negation that it has to be as its current presence to being. Indeed, if human-reality was purely conscious (of) being one syncretic, undifferentiated negation, it would not be able to determine itself and could not therefore be the concrete totality—albeit detotalized—of its determinations. It is a totality only insofar as it escapes, through all its other negations, the concrete negation that it presently is: its being can only *be* its own totality to the extent that it is a surpassing of the partial structure that it is toward the whole that it has to be. Otherwise it would simply be what it is, and could not in any way be considered either as a totality or as a non-totality. Therefore, just as any partial negative structure has to appear against the ground of the undifferentiated negations that I am—and of which it forms part—being-in-itself acquaints me with a specific concrete reality that I have not to be. The being that I presently *am not*, insofar as it appears against the ground of the totality of being, is the *this*. This—i.e., what I presently am not, insofar as I have nothing in being to be—is what is disclosed against the undifferentiated ground of being, in order to acquaint me with the concrete negation that I have to be, against the totalizing ground of my negations. This original relation between the whole and the *this* is at the source of the relation, illuminated by *Gestalttheorie*, between the ground and the figure. The *this* always appears against a ground—i.e., against the undifferentiated totality of being—insofar as the for-itself is its radical and syncretic negation. But it may always become diluted within this undifferentiated totality when another *this* arises. But the appearance of the *this*, or the figure against the ground, as the correlative of the appearance of my own concrete negation against the syncretic ground of a radical negation, implies that I am, and at the same time that I am not, this totalizing negation—or, alternatively, that I am it, in the mode of "not being," and that I am not it, in the mode of being it. Indeed, it is only thus that the present negation can appear against the ground of the radical negation that it is. Otherwise, it would be entirely cut off from it—or else it would become merged into it. The appearance of the *this* against the *whole* is correlative to a specific way that the for-itself has of being the negation of itself. There is a *this* because I am not yet my future negations, and I am no longer my past negations. The disclosure of the this presupposes that "the emphasis is placed" on some specific negation, with the others receding into the syncretic disappearance of the ground, which is to say that the for-itself can exist only as a negation that is constituted on the withdrawal of radical negativity in its totality. The for-itself is not the world, spatiality, permanence, matter—in brief, the in-itself in general—but its way of not-being-these is to have not to be this table, this glass, this bedroom, against the total ground of negativity. Therefore the this presupposes a negation of negation—but a negation that has the radical negation it is negating to be, and does not cease to be attached to it by an ontological thread but remains ready to merge into it through the arising of another this. In this sense, the this is disclosed as a this by the "withdrawal into the ground of the world" of all the other thises; its determination—which is at the origin of all determinations—is a negation. We should be clear that this negation—seen from the side of the this—is wholly ideal. It adds nothing to being, and subtracts nothing from it. The being that is regarded as this is what it is, and does not stop being it; it does not become. As such, it cannot be outside itself within the whole, as a structure of the whole, and neither can it be outside itself within the whole, in order to negate, in relation to itself, its identity with the whole. Negation can arrive at the this only through a being that has to be presence to the whole of being and, at the same time, to the this—i.e., an ecstatic being. And as it leaves the this intact as a being-in-itself, as it does not perform any real synthesis of all the thises as a totality, the constitutive negation of the this is a negation whose type is external; the relation of the this to the whole is a relation of externality. Thus we see determination appearing as an external negation that is correlative to the internal, radical, and ecstatic negation that I am. This explains the ambiguous character of the world, which is disclosed at the same time as a synthetic totality and as a purely additive collection of all the thises. Indeed, to the extent that the world is a totality disclosed as what the for-itself has radically to be its own nothingness against, the world presents itself as an undifferentiated syncretism. But insofar as this radical nihilation is always beyond some concrete and present nihilation, the world appears to be always on the point of opening up like a box, in order to allow one or several thises to appear that already were, within the ground's lack of differentiation, what they

220   are now, as a differentiated figure. In this way, if we move progressively closer to a landscape that was introduced to us as various large masses, we will see objects appear that are given as having already been there, as elements within a discontinuous collection of *thises*; and in this way, in the experiments of *Gestalttheorie*, the continuous ground, once it is apprehended as a figure, bursts into a multiplicity of discontinuous elements. Thus the world, as the correlative of a detotalized totality, appears as an evanescent totality, in the sense that it is never a real synthesis but rather an ideal limitation—by means of nothing—of a collection of *thises*. In this way the *continuous*, as a formal quality of the ground, allows the discontinuous to appear as a type of external relation between the *this* and the totality. This constant evanescence of the totality into a collection, and of the continuous into the discontinuous, is precisely what we refer to as "space." Indeed, space cannot be a *being*. It is a moving relation between beings that have no relation. It is the total independence of the in-itselfs, insofar as that is disclosed to a being who is present to "all" of the in-itself as the independence *of each of them in relation to the others*; it is the unique way in which beings are able to be revealed, to the being through whom relations arrive in the world, as having no relation: i.e., as pure externality. And as this externality cannot belong to any of the *thises* under consideration and as, moreover, insofar as it is a purely local negativity it is destructive of itself, it is unable either to be by itself or to "be been." The spatializing being is the for-itself, insofar as it is co-present to the whole and to the *this*; space is not the world but the instability of the world that we grasp as a totality, insofar as it can always break up into an external multiplicity. Space is neither the ground nor the figure but the ground's ideality insofar as it can always break up into figures; it is neither the continuous nor the discontinuous but the constant passage from the continuous to the discontinuous. The existence of space proves that the for-itself, in making it the case that *there is* being, adds *nothing* to being; it is the ideality of synthesis. In this sense, to the extent that it derives its origin from the world, space is the totality—but at the same time it is *nothing*, insofar as it results in the proliferation of the *thises*. Space does not allow itself to be grasped in a concrete intuition, because it is not; rather, it is continuously spatialized. Space depends on temporality and appears within temporality, insofar as it can enter the world only through a

being whose mode of being is temporalization, because it is the way in which that being ecstatically loses itself in order to actualize being. The spatial property of the this is not synthetically added to the this but is only its "place," i.e., its external relation with the ground, insofar as this relation may collapse into a multiplicity of external relations with other thises, when the ground itself breaks up into a multiplicity of figures. In this sense it is pointless to conceive of space as a form imposed by the a priori structure of our sensibility on phenomena: space cannot be a form because it is nothing; on the contrary, it marks the fact that nothing, apart from negation (and even here as a type of external relation that leaves what it joins intact), can arrive in the in-itself through the for-itself. As for the for-itself, if it is not space, that is precisely because it apprehends itself as not being being-in-itself, insofar as the in-itself is disclosed to it in the mode of externality known to us as "extension." It is precisely insofar as the for-itself negates externality in relation to itself—by grasping itself as ecstatic—that it spatializes space. This is because the for-itself's relation to the in-itself is not juxtaposition, or indifferent externality: its relation to the in-itself, as the foundation of all relations, is internal negation, and it is through the for-itself, on the contrary, that being-in-itself comes into its relation of indifferent externality with other beings existing within a world. When indifferent externality is hypostasized into a substance that exists in and through itself—which can happen only at a lower stage of knowledge—it becomes the object of a particular branch of study, called "geometry," and becomes a mere specification of the abstract theory of multiplicities.

What remains to be determined is the type of being possessed by external negation, insofar as it enters the world through the for-itself. We know that external negation does not belong to the this: this newspaper does not deny, in relation to itself, that it is the table against which it stands out; otherwise it would be ecstatically outside itself, in the table it negates, and its relation to the table would be an internal negation; the newspaper would thereby cease to be in-itself, and would become for-itself. The determinative relation of the this cannot therefore belong either to the this or to the that: it surrounds them without touching them, without conferring on them the slightest new character; it leaves them as what they are. In this sense, we are obliged to modify

221

Spinoza's famous formulation, described by Hegel as infinite in its riches—"*Omnis determinatio est negatio*"[9]—and to assert instead that any negation that does not belong to the being who has its own determinations to be is an ideal negation. Moreover, it is inconceivable that it could be otherwise. Even if, in the style of a critical-empiricist psychologism, we were to regard things as purely subjective contents, it would be impossible to conceive how the subject could actualize any internal synthetic negations between these contents without *being them*, within a radical ecstatic immanence that would remove all hope of any passage to objectivity. *A fortiori*, we are unable to imagine the for-itself operating any synthetic and deforming negations between transcendent items that it is not. In this sense, the external negation constitutive of the *this* cannot appear as an *objective* feature of the thing, if what we mean by "objective" is something that belongs by its nature to the in-itself or something that, in some way or other, *really* constitutes the object as it is. But this should not lead us to conclude that external negation has a subjective existence, as a pure mode of the for-itself's being. The for-itself's type of existence is pure internal negation; the existence within it of any external negation would nullify its very existence. In consequence, external negation cannot be a way of arranging and classifying phenomena insofar as they are only subjective phantasms, and nor can it "subjectivize" being, insofar as the disclosure of being is constitutive of the for-itself. Its very externality requires it, therefore, to remain "in the air," as *external* to the for-itself as it is to the in-itself. But, on the other hand, precisely because this negation is external, it cannot exist through itself; it rejects all supports, and is "*unselbstständig*" by nature—and yet it is unable to form a relation to any substance. It is a *nothing*. Evidently, it is because the inkwell is not the table—and nor is it the pipe or the glass, etc.—that we are able to grasp it as the inkwell. And yet, if I say "the inkwell is not the table," what I *think* is *nothing*. Thus, any determination is a *nothing*, which belongs as an internal structure neither to the thing nor to consciousness, but whose being is *to-be-cited* by the for-itself through a system of internal negations within which the in-itself is disclosed in its indifference to everything that it is not. Insofar as the for-itself is acquainted through the in-itself with what it

222

9 TN: Sartre has already quoted this phrase at EN 49.

is not, in the mode of internal negation, the in-itself's indifference—as an indifference that the for-itself has not to be—is revealed within the world as determination.

III. QUALITY AND QUANTITY, POTENTIALITY AND EQUIPMENTALITY

Quality is nothing other than the being of the this, when we consider it outside any external relation to the world or to other thises. All too often, it has been conceived of as a purely subjective determination, so that its quality-being becomes confused with the subjectivity of the psyche. Then the problem appears primarily to be that of explaining the constitution of an object-pole, conceived of as the transcendent unity of qualities. We have shown that this problem is insoluble. A quality cannot be objectified if it is subjective. Even if we suppose ourselves to have projected the unity of an object-pole beyond its qualities, each quality will be directly given, at most, as the subjective effect of the action of things upon us. But the lemon's yellow is not a subjective mode of apprehension of the lemon: it is the lemon. And nor is it true that the object-X appears as the empty form that holds the disparate qualities together. In fact, the lemon extends throughout its qualities, and each one of these qualities extends throughout each of the others. It is the lemon's acidity that is yellow, and the lemon's yellowness that is acidic; we eat the color of a cake, and the taste of that cake is the instrument that discloses its form and its color to what we may call our "alimentary intuition." Conversely, if I plunge my finger into a jar of jam, the jam's sticky coldness is a revelation of its sweet taste to my fingers. The fluidity, the warmth, the bluish color, the undulating mobility of the water of a swimming pool are given all at once, each through the others; this complete interpenetration is what we mean by "this." The experiments of the painters—Cézanne's in particular— provide an excellent illustration: it is not true, as Husserl thinks, that some synthetic necessity unconditionally joins something's color to its form. Instead, the form is color and light; if the painter varies any one of these factors, the others will also vary, not because they are bound by some law or other but because they are fundamentally just one and the same being. In this sense, each quality of being is all of being: it is the presence of its absolute contingency, the irreducibility of its indifference;

223

the apprehension of a quality adds nothing to being, other than the fact that *there is being like this*. In this sense, a quality is not an external aspect of being, because being, lacking any "inside," cannot have any "outside." Only, in order for there to be any quality, it is necessary that *there is* being for a nothingness that, by its nature, *is not* being. However, being is not quality *in itself*—although it is nothing more or less than it. Rather, any quality is *being in its entirety*, disclosing itself within the limits of the "there is." It is not being's *outside* but the whole of being, insofar as there can be no being for being, but only for something that makes itself not be that being. The for-itself's relation to quality is an ontological relation. The intuition of a quality is not a passive contemplation of something given, and the mind is not an in-itself that, in the course of such contemplation, remains what it is—i.e., remains in the mode of indifference in relation to the contemplated *this*. But, through the quality, the for-itself becomes acquainted with what it is not. To perceive the red as the color of this notebook is to reflect oneself as the internal negation of this quality. In other words, the apprehension of the quality is not, as Husserl would have it, a "fulfillment" (*Erfüllung*) but the informing of a void as the determinate void of this quality. In this sense, quality is a presence that is constantly out of reach. Descriptions of knowledge have all too often been given in terms of food. There is still too much pre-logical thinking in epistemological philosophy and we have not yet rid ourselves of that primitive illusion (of which we must, later, give an account) according to which to know something is to eat it, i.e., to ingest the known object, to be filled by it (*Erfüllung*) and to digest it ("assimilation").[10] We can give a better account of the original phenomenon of perception by emphasizing the fact that quality stands in relation to us in a relation of absolute proximity—it "*is there*," it haunts us—without either giving or withholding itself, but we must add that this proximity implies a distance. Quality is immediately out of our reach and, by definition, it points us out to ourselves as a void. Its contemplation can only increase our thirst for being, just as the sight of the foods that were out of his reach increased Tantalus's hunger. A quality is an indication of what we are not, and of

224

---

10 TN: Sartre's 1939 article about Husserl, "*Une idée fondamentale de la phénoménologie de Husserl: L'intentionnalité*" (translated as Sartre 1970), focused on just this "digestive" model of knowledge.

the mode of being that is withheld from us. To perceive whiteness is to be conscious of the impossibility, as a matter of principle, of the for-itself's existing as a color—i.e., of its being what it is. In the same vein, it is not only that we cannot distinguish being from its qualities but also that any apprehension of a quality is the apprehension of a *this*; no matter what it is, the quality is disclosed to us as a being. The scent that I suddenly inhale, with my eyes closed, even before I have related it to an aromatic object, is already a *scent-being* and not a subjective impression; the morning light that strikes my eyes, through my closed eyelids, is already a light-being. One only needs to reflect that quality *is*, for this to appear obvious. As a being that is what it is, a quality can certainly *appear* to a subjectivity, but it cannot insert itself within the fabric of that subjectivity—which is what it is not, and is not what it is. To say that any quality is a quality-being is in no way to endow it with some mysterious support, analogous to a substance; it is simply to point out that its mode of being is radically different from the "for-itself" mode of being. We are wholly unable, indeed, to apprehend the being of whiteness, or of acidity, as ecstatic. If, now, we ask how it is possible for a *this* to possess "some" qualities, our reply will be that in fact the *this* is liberated as a totality against the ground of the world, and it is given as an undifferentiated unity. It is the for-itself that is able to negate itself from various points of view as it confronts the *this*, and to disclose quality as a new *this*, against the ground of the thing. To each negating act through which the for-itself's freedom spontaneously constitutes its being, there corresponds a complete disclosure of being "through a profile." This profile is nothing but a relation of the thing to the for-itself, actualized by the for-itself itself. It is the absolute determination of negativity: because it is not enough for the for-itself, through a primordial negation, not to *be* being, nor for it not to be *this* being; for its determination as a nothingness of being to be complete, it is also necessary that the for-itself should actualize itself as a specific, irreplaceable way of not being *this* being; and this absolute determination, which determines the quality as a profile of the *this*, belongs to the for-itself's freedom; it *is not*; it exists as something "to be." Anyone can see this for himself, by considering how the disclosure of *one* quality of a thing always appears as a gratuitous fact apprehended *through* a freedom; I cannot make it the case that this peel is not green, but it is I who make it the case that I grasp it as a green-that-is-coarse, or as a coarseness-that-is-green. Only here the figure-ground relation is quite different from the relation of the this to the world. This is because the figure, rather than appearing against an undifferentiated ground, is entirely penetrated by the ground; the figure retains the ground within itself as its own undifferentiated density. If I apprehend the peel as green, its "luminosity-coarseness" will be disclosed as that green's undifferentiated internal ground and plenitude of being. No abstraction is involved here—in the sense in which abstraction separates out what is joined—because the being still appears in its entirety in its profile. But the being's actualization is a condition of abstraction, because to abstract is not to apprehend some quality "in the air" but a this-quality, in which the lack of differentiation within its internal ground approaches an absolute equilibrium. The abstract "green" does not lose its density of being—otherwise it would no longer be anything more than a subjective mode of the for-itself—but the luminosity, the shape, the coarseness, etc., that are given through it merge into the nihilating equilibrium of a pure and simple massivity. Nonetheless, abstraction is a phenomenon of presence to being, since an abstract being retains its transcendence. But it can be actualized only as a presence to being beyond being: it is a surpassing. This presence of being can be actualized only at the level of possibility, and insofar as the for-itself has its own possibilities to be. An abstraction is disclosed as the meaning that a quality has to be, in its capacity as co-present to the presence of a for-itself still to come. In this way the abstract "green" is the forth-coming-meaning of the concrete this, insofar as it is revealed to me through its green-luminous-coarse profile. It is this profile's own possibility, insofar as that is revealed through the possibilities that I am, i.e., insofar as it is been. But this directs us toward equipmentality and worldly temporality, to which we will return. For now, it will suffice to say that the abstract haunts the concrete like a possibility frozen into the in-itself that the concrete has to be. No matter what our perception is, as an original contact with being, the abstract is always there but it is to come; and it is in the future, and with the future, that I grasp it.[11] It is the correlative of my present and concrete negation's own possibility, as the possibility of being nothing more than this negation. The abstract is the meaning of the this, insofar as it reveals itself to the future through my

11 TN: As earlier in the text, Sartre puns in this passage on à venir and avenir.

225

possibility of freezing the negation that I have to be into the in-itself. Should someone remind us here of the classical aporias of abstraction, we will reply that these aporias arise from the assumption that the constitution of the this and the act of abstraction are distinct. It is clear that, if the this does not bring its own abstract features with it, it will not be possible subsequently to derive them from it. Rather, the abstraction operates in the very constitution of the this as a this, as the disclosure of the profile to my future. The for-itself is not "an abstractor" because it is able to effect some psychological operation of abstraction but because it arises, as presence to being, with a future, i.e., as what is beyond being. In-itself, being is neither concrete nor abstract, neither present nor future: it is what it is. However, abstraction does not enrich being; it only reveals a nothingness of being beyond being. But we challenge anyone to formulate the classical objections to abstraction without implicitly deriving them from a way of considering a being as a this.

226

The original relation between the thises cannot be interaction, or causality, or even that they arise against the same ground of the world. Indeed, if we assume that the for-itself is present to a this, the other thises will exist "in the world" at the same time, but they will be undifferentiated: they constitute the ground against which the envisaged this will stand out in relief. In order for a relation of any kind to be established between a this and another this, it is necessary for the second this to be disclosed, by arising from the ground of the world on the occasion of some explicit negation that the for-itself has to be. But, at the same time, each this needs to stand at a distance from the other one, as not being the other one, through a negation whose type is purely external. Thus the relation of this one to that one is an external negation. That one appears as not being this one. And this external negation is disclosed to the for-itself as something transcendent; it is outside, and it is in-itself. How should this be understood?

The appearance of this-one-that-one can in the first place come about only as a totality. The first relation here is the unity of a totality that can be disintegrated; the for-itself determines itself en bloc not to be "this-one-that-one" against the ground of the world.[12] The "this-one-that-one" is my bedroom in its entirety, insofar as I am present to it. This

12 TN: As the phrase en bloc is also used in English, I have left it in French.

concrete negation does not disappear when the concrete whole disintegrates into this one *and* that one. On the contrary, it is the very condition of its disintegration. But against this ground of presence, and through this ground of presence, being allows its indifferent externality to appear: it is disclosed to me insofar as the negation that I am is a unity-multiplicity, instead of an undifferentiated totality. My negative arising to being is fragmented into independent negations, whose only connection is that of being negations that I have to be—which means they derive their internal unity from me, and not from being. I am present to this table, and to these chairs, and as such I synthetically constitute myself as a polyvalent negation, but, insofar as it is a negation of being, this purely internal negation is permeated by zones of nothingness: it nihilates itself as a negation; it is a detotalized negation. The indifference of being appears through these grooves of nothingness that I have to be as my own nothingness of negation. But I am to actualize this indifference, through this nothingness of negation that I have to be, not insofar as I am originally present to *this* but insofar as I am also present to *that*. It is in and through my presence to the table that I actualize the indifference of the chair—the chair that I will also presently have not to be—as an absence of any launchpad, a pause in my momentum toward not-being, a break in the circuit. *That one* appears beside this one, within a totalizing disclosure, as something that I am unable to make use of in determining myself not to be *this one*. The cleavage, therefore, comes from being, but *there is* a cleavage and separation only through the for-

227   itself's presence to all being. The negation of the unity of negations—insofar as it discloses being's indifference, and grasps the indifference of *this one* through *that one*, and of *that one* through *this one*—discloses the original relation between the *thises* as an external negation. A *this one* is not that one. This external negation within the unity of a totality that can disintegrate is expressed by the word "and." "This one is not that one" can be rewritten as "this one *and* that one." External negation has the two-fold character of being-in-itself and of being purely ideal. It is in-itself by dint of not belonging in any way to the for-itself; it is even through the absolute internality of its own negation (since in aesthetic intuition I apprehend an imaginary object) that the for-itself uncovers being's indifference as externality. This is not a negation, moreover, that being has to be: it does not belong to any of the envisaged *thises*; it straightforwardly

is; it is what it is. But at the same time it is not in any way a feature of the this; it is not one of its qualities. It is even completely independent of the thises, precisely because it belongs neither to one nor to the other. For being's indifference is nothing: we cannot think it, or even perceive it. It signifies quite simply that the annihilation or variations in that one cannot engage the thises in any way; in this sense, it is only an in-itself nothingness separating the thises, and this nothingness is the only way in which consciousness can actualize the cohesion of identity that is characteristic of being. This ideal and in-itself nothingness is quantity. In effect, quantity is pure externality: it does not depend at all on the terms that are added together; it only asserts their independence. To count is to make an ideal discrimination, within a totality that can disintegrate and is already given. The number that we obtain through the addition does not belong to any of the counted thises, nor to the disintegrable totality, insofar as that is disclosed as a totality. It is not by virtue of apprehending them from the outset as a "group in conversation" that I may count these three men talking in front of me, and the fact of counting them as three leaves the concrete unity of their group perfectly intact. Being "a group of three" is not a concrete property of the group. But neither is it a property of its members. We cannot say of any one of them that he is three, or even that he is the third, because the quality of being third is only a reflection of the freedom of the for-itself doing the counting; any one of them might be third, and none of them is. The relation of quantity is therefore a relation that is in-itself, but purely negative: a relation of externality. And it is precisely because it belongs neither to things nor to totalities that it becomes isolated, and stands out against the surface of the world like a reflection of nothingness on being. As a pure relation of externality between the thises, it is itself external to the thises and, in conclusion, external to itself. It is being's elusive indifference—only able to appear if there is being and which, although it belongs to being, can only   228
come to being from a for-itself, insofar as this indifference can be disclosed only through an infinite externalization of an external relation that must be external to being, and to itself. In this way, space and quantity are only one and the same type of negation. Solely by virtue of the disclosure of the this and the that as having no relation to me—I who am my own relation—space and quantity enter into the world, because both of these are relations between things that have no relation (or, equivalently,

a nothingness of relation that is grasped as a relation by the being that is its own relation). Through this fact itself, we can see that what we, along with Husserl, refer to as "*categories*" (unity-multiplicity; relation of the whole to the part; more and less; around; beside; following; first, second, etc.; one, two, three, etc.; inside and outside, etc.) are only ideal mixtures of things, in which they are left entirely intact, without being enriched or impoverished even by an *iota*, and they only point out the infinite diversity of ways in which the for-itself's freedom can actualize the indifference of being.[13]

We have discussed the problem of the for-itself's original relation to being as if the for-itself were a simple instantaneous consciousness, as might be revealed to the Cartesian *cogito*. In fact, we have already encountered the for-itself's escaping from itself, insofar as that is a necessary condition of the appearance of any *thises* and abstractions. But the for-itself's ecstatic character was still only implicit. If we have had to proceed like this for the clarity of our exposition, we ought not to conclude from it that being is disclosed to a being that is in the first place a presence, in order to constitute itself subsequently as a future. Rather, being-in-itself is disclosed to a being that arises as forth-coming in relation to itself. Therefore, the negation that the for-itself makes itself be in the presence of being has an ecstatic future dimension: it is insofar as I am not what I am (an ecstatic relation to my own possibilities) that I have not to be being-in-itself as the disclosing actualization of the *this*. Therefore, I am present to the *this* within the incompleteness of a detotalized totality. What consequence does this have for the disclosure of the *this*?

Insofar as I am always beyond what I am, and forth-coming in relation to myself, the *this* to which I am present appears to me to be something I surpass toward myself. The perceived is in the first place what I surpass: within the circuit of ipseity, it is like a conductor—and it appears within the limits of that circuit. To the extent that I become the negation of the *this*, I flee from this negation toward a complementary negation, whose fusion with the first one should make apparent the in-itself that I am. And this possible negation has a connection of being with the first one; it is not anonymous but precisely the negation which is

13 TN: Husserl discusses categories in several of his philosophical writings. Sartre is probably thinking of *Logical Investigations* (Husserl 2001).

complementary to my presence to the thing. But as the for-itself constitutes itself, as presence, as a non-positional consciousness (of) self, it
becomes acquainted from outside itself, through being, with what it is
not; it recuperates its being on-the-outside in the mode of "reflection-
reflecting." The complementary negation that it is as its own possibility   229
is therefore a presence-negation, which means that the for-itself has it to
be, as a non-thetic consciousness (of) self, and as a thetic consciousness
of being-beyond-being. And the being-beyond-being is not connected
to the present this by any old external relation but rather by a precise
connection of complementarity, which stands as the exact correlative of
the relation of the for-itself and its future. And in the first place the this is
disclosed within the negation of a being who makes itself not be this—
not simply as a presence but as a negation which is forth-coming in relation to itself, which is its own possibility beyond its present. And this
possibility, haunting pure presence as its out-of-reach meaning and as
what is missing from it in order for it to be in itself, is in the first instance
like a projection of the present negation, in the shape of a commitment.
Indeed, any negation that did not have the meaning of a commitment—
beyond itself, in the future, as a possibility coming toward it, and in
whose direction it flees from itself—would lose all its meaning as a negation. What is negated by the for-itself is negated "with the dimension
of the future," whether it is a matter of an external negation—"this one
is not that one," "this chair is not a table"—or of an internal negation,
directed on itself. To say "this one is not that one" is to posit the externality of the this in relation to the that—either for now and the future, or
strictly within the "now"—but in that case the negation has a provisional
character, which constitutes the future as pure externality in relation to
the present determination, "this one and that one." In both cases, the
meaning comes to the negation on the basis of the future; all negation
is ecstatic. Insofar as the for-itself negates itself in the future, the this of
which it makes itself the negation is disclosed as coming toward it from
the future. The possibility that consciousness non-thetically is—as a consciousness (of) being able not to be this—is disclosed as the potentiality of
the this to be what it is. An object's first potentiality, as the correlative of
commitment, an ontological structure of negation, is permanence, which
constantly comes toward it from the depth of the future. The disclosure
of the table as a table requires a permanence of the table, which comes to

it from the future and which is not a purely observed *given* but a potenti-ality. This permanence, moreover, does not come toward the table from a future situated within the temporal infinite: infinite time does not yet exist; the table is not disclosed as having the possibility of being a table indefinitely. The time that is in question here is neither finite nor infi-nite; potentiality merely makes the dimension of the future appear.

But negation's forth-coming meaning is to be what is missing from the for-itself's negation in order for it to become a negation in *itself*. In this sense the negation, in the future, makes the present negation more precise. It is in the future that the exact meaning of what I have not to be is disclosed, as the correlative of the exact negation that I have to be. The polymorphous negation of the *this*, in which the green is formed out of a "daylight-coarseness" totality, only acquires its meaning if what it has to be is a negation of the green, i.e., of a green-being whose ground tends toward the equilibrium of an absence of any differentiation: in short, the absent-meaning of my polymorphous negation is a narrower negation—of a green that is more purely green, against an undifferenti-ated ground. In this way, the pure green comes, from the depth of the future, to the "green-daylight-coarseness" as its meaning. Here we are in a position to grasp the meaning of what we referred to as *abstraction*. The existent does not *possess* its essence as some present quality. The existent is even a negation of the essence: the green *is never* green. But the existent's essence comes to it from the depth of the future, like a meaning that is never given and which always haunts it. It is the pure correlative of my negation's pure ideality. In this sense, no operation of abstraction ever occurs—if we mean by that some psychological and affirmative act of selection, on the part of a constituted mind. Far from it being the case that we abstract specific qualities on the basis of things, we ought on the contrary to see that abstraction—as an original mode of being of the for-itself—is necessary for there to be things in general, and a world. The abstract is a structure of the world that is necessary for something concrete to arise, and the concrete is only concrete to the extent that it moves in the direction of its abstraction, and becomes acquainted, through that abstraction, with what it is: the for-itself is, in its being, disclosing-abstracting. From this standpoint we can see that permanence and abstraction are just one and the same. If the table, as a table, has the potentiality of permanence, the table has that potentiality to the extent

that it has being a table to be. For any *this*, permanence is the pure possibility of conforming to its essence.

We saw, in Part Two of this work, that the relation between the possible that I am and the present I am fleeing from is that of a missing item
to that from which it is missing.[14] The ideal fusion—in the shape of an
unrealizable totality—of the missing item with what that missing item
is missing from, haunts the for-itself and constitutes it in its very being
as a nothingness of being. That, as we said, is the in-itself-for-itself—or
value. But, at the unreflective level, the for-itself does not apprehend
this value thetically: it is only a condition of being. If our deductions
are correct, this constant indication of an unrealizable fusion should
not appear as a structure of unreflected consciousness but as a transcendent indication of an ideal structure of the object. This structure can
easily be disclosed: as the correlative of the indication of a fusion of the
polymorphous negation with the abstract negation that is its meaning,
a transcendent and ideal indication must be disclosed—the indication
of a fusion of the existing *this* with its forth-coming essence. And this
fusion must be such that the abstract is what founds the concrete and, at
the same time, the concrete founds the abstract: in other terms, the concrete "flesh and bones" existence must *be* the essence; the essence must
be produced as a total concretion, which is to say with the full richness
of something concrete, without, however, our being able to find within
it anything other than itself in its complete purity. Or, alternatively, the   231
form must be in relation to itself—and completely—its own matter. And
conversely, the matter must be produced as absolute form. This impossible and constantly indicated fusion of essence and existence belongs
neither to the present nor to the future; rather, it indicates the fusion
of past, present, and future and it presents itself as a synthesis of the
temporal totality that is *to be performed*. It is value, as transcendence: we
refer to that as "*beauty*." Beauty represents therefore an ideal state of the
world, correlative to an ideal realization of the for-itself, in which the
essence and existence of things are disclosed as identical to a being who,
within this disclosure itself, might merge with itself into the absolute
unity of the in-itself. It is precisely because the beautiful is not only a

---

14 This sentence sounds odd, because it is in Part Two. Sartre presumably means to refer
to an earlier passage within Part Two (probably in Chapter 1).

transcendent synthesis to be performed but can be realized only within and through a totalization of ourselves—that is precisely why we *want* the beautiful, and why we apprehend the universe as *lacking* the beautiful, to the extent to which we apprehend ourselves as a lack. But the beautiful is no more a potentiality of things than the in-itself-for-itself is a possibility that belongs to the for-itself. It haunts the world as an unrealizable. And to the extent that man *realizes* the beautiful within the world,[15] he realizes it in the mode of the imaginary. This means that, in aesthetic intuition, I apprehend an imaginary object through an imaginary realization of myself as a totality that is in-itself and for-itself. Ordinarily the beautiful, in the form of value, is not made thematically explicit as value-out-of-reach-of-the-world. It is implicitly apprehended in things, as an absence; it is implicitly disclosed through the world's *imperfection*.

These original potentialities are not the only ones to characterize the *this*. Indeed, to the extent that the for-itself has, beyond its present, its being to be, it discloses a "beyond" of the qualified being, which comes from the depth of being to the *this*. Insofar as the for-itself is beyond the crescent, alongside a being-beyond-being consisting in the future full moon, the full moon becomes the crescent moon's potentiality; insofar as the for-itself is beyond the bud, alongside the flower, the flower is the bud's potentiality. The disclosure of these new potentialities implies an original relation to the past. It is in the past that the link between the crescent moon and the moon, between the bud and the flower, has been gradually uncovered. And the for-itself's past is a body of knowledge for the for-itself. But this knowledge does not remain as an inert given. Doubtless, it lies behind the for-itself—unknowable as such, and out of reach. But, within the ecstatic unity of its being, it is on the basis of this past that the for-itself becomes acquainted with what it is in the future. My knowledge about the moon escapes me as something thematically known. But I am it and my way of being it is—at least in some cases—to make what I am no longer come to me, in the form of what I am not yet. I am this negation of the *this*—the *this* I have been—in a twofold way: in the mode of no-longer-being, and of not-yet-being. I am beyond the crescent moon as the possibility of a radical negation of the moon as a

232

---

15 TN: ... *l'homme réalise le beau* ... Here I translate *réaliser* as "to realize" because of its connection to the "unrealizable" mentioned in the preceding sentence. See my note on *réaliser* in Notes on the Translation.

full disc and, correlatively to my turning back from my future negation toward my present, the full moon returns toward the crescent in order to determine it as a this in the shape of a negation: it is what is missing from it, and what it is made to be—as a crescent—by what it lacks. Thus, within the unity of a single ontological negation, I attribute the dimension of the future to the crescent insofar as it is a crescent—in the form of permanence, and essence—and I constitute it as a crescent moon by my determining movement back to it, from what it is missing. In this way the range of potentialities is constituted, extending from permanence all the way to *powers*. Human-reality, by surpassing itself toward its own possibility of negation, makes itself be that through which the negation involved in surpassing arrives in the world. It is through human-reality that *lack* comes to things, in the form of "power," "incompleteness," "suspension,"[16] and "potentiality."

Nonetheless, the lack's transcendent being cannot have the nature of the ecstatic lack within immanence. Let us take a closer look. The in-itself does not have its own potentiality to be in the mode of the not-yet. The disclosure of the in-itself is, from the outset, a disclosure of the identity of indifference. The in-itself is what it is without any ecstatic dispersion of its being. It does not therefore have its permanence, or its essence, or what is missing from it, *to be*—in the way that I have my future to be. My arising in the world makes potentialities arise, correlatively. But these potentialities are frozen even as they arise: *externality* eats into them. Here we meet again that twofold aspect of the transcendent which, in its very ambiguity, has given birth to space: a totality that becomes dispersed into relations of externality. Potentiality returns to the this, from the depth of the future, in order to determine it, but the relation of the this as in-itself to its potentiality is a relation of externality. The moon's crescent is determined as *lacking*, or as *deprived of* something—in relation to the full moon. But at the same time it is disclosed as fully being what it is, this concrete sign in the sky, in need of nothing in order to be what it is. The same goes for this bud, or for this match, which is what it is, whose match-being meaning remains external to it—which *may* of course burst into flame but which, at present, is this stick of white wood with a black tip. Even though the potentialities of the this are strictly connected to it, they

---

16 TN: . . . *sous forme de* . . . *"sursis"* . . . See my note on *en sursis* in the section on Heidegger vocabulary in Notes on the Translation.

present themselves as in-itselfs, and they are in a state of indifference in relation to it. This inkwell may be broken, thrown against the marble of the fireplace where it will smash. But this potentiality is entirely cut off from it, because it is only the transcendent correlative of my possibility of throwing it against the marble of the fireplace. In itself it is neither breakable nor unbreakable: it is. That does not mean I am able to consider a this apart from any potentiality at all: rather, and merely because I am my own future, the this is disclosed as endowed with potentialities; to apprehend the match as a stick of white wood with a black tip is not to strip it of all potentiality but simply to confer new potentialities on it (a new permanence, a new essence). In order for the this to be entirely dispossessed of its potentialities, it would be necessary for me to be a pure present, which is inconceivable. Only the this has various potentialities that are equivalent, i.e., in a state of equivalence in relation to it. For this reason: the this does not have these to be. In addition, my possibles are not; rather, they possibilize themselves, because my freedom eats into them from the inside. In other words, whatever my possible may be, its opposite is equally possible. I might break this inkwell, but I can just as well put it away in a drawer; I may target the full moon, beyond the crescent—but I can just as well lay claim to the crescent's permanence as such. In consequence, the inkwell is endowed with possibles that are equivalent: to be put away in a drawer, to be broken. This crescent moon may be an open curve in the sky, or a disc that is still outstanding. We may call these potentialities—which return to the this without having been been by it, and without it having them to be—its "probabilities," to mark their existing in the in-itself's mode of being. My possibles are not; they possibilize themselves. But probables do not "probabilize" themselves; as probable, they are in itself. In this sense, the inkwell is, but its being-an-inkwell is a probable, because the inkwell's "having-to-be-an-inkwell" is a pure appearance that merges immediately into a relation of externality. These potentialities or probabilities, which are being's meaning—beyond being—precisely because they are in-itself beyond being, are nothings. The inkwell's essence is been as the correlative of the for-itself's possible negation, but it is not the inkwell, and it is not being: insofar as it is in itself, it is a hypostasized, reified negation, which is to say that it is precisely a nothing; it belongs to the sleeve of nothingness that surrounds and determines the world. The for-itself reveals the inkwell as an inkwell. But this revelation occurs beyond the inkwell's being, in this future which is not: all of being's potentialities, ranging from permanence right up to a qualified potentiality, are defined as what being *is not yet*, without it ever being the case that it truly *has them to be*. Here again, knowledge neither adds nor takes anything away from being; it does not adorn it with any new quality. Knowledge makes it the case that there is being, by surpassing it toward a nothingness that maintains only negative relations of externality with it: this pure nothingness which characterizes potentiality also stands out in the procedures of the sciences which, aiming to establish relations that are straightforwardly external, radically eliminate anything potential, i.e., essence and powers. But, on the other hand, its necessity as a signifying structure of perception appears with sufficient clarity to excuse us from insisting on it: indeed, scientific knowledge can neither overcome nor eliminate the potentializing structure of perception; on the contrary, it presupposes it.

234

We have tried to show how the for-itself's presence to being discloses it as a *thing*. And, for the sake of clarity in our exposition, we have had to demonstrate the thing's various structures successively: the *this* and spatiality, permanence, essence, and potentialities. It goes without saying, however, that this successive exposition does not correspond to any real priority of some of these moments over others: in arising, the for-itself makes the thing disclose itself, with the totality of its structures. Besides, there is not a single one of them that does not imply all of the others: the *this* does not even have a logical priority over its essence; on the contrary, it presupposes it and, conversely, any essence is an essence of "this." In the same way, the *this* as quality-being can appear only against the ground of the world, but the world is a collection of *thises*; and the world's disintegrating relation to the *thises*, and of the *thises* to the world, is spatiality. Here, therefore, we find no substantial form, no principle of unity to stand *behind* the phenomenon's modes of appearing: everything is given at once, without any primacy. For the same reasons, it would be a mistake to conceive of the *representational* as having any kind of primacy. Our descriptions have led us, in fact, to emphasize the *thing in the world*, and we might be tempted by this to believe that the world and the thing are disclosed in a kind of contemplative intuition: only subsequently would objects be placed in relation to each other, in a practical order of equipmentality. We can avoid such a mistake if we bear fully in mind that the world appears within the circuit of ipseity. The world is what separates the for-itself from itself or—to use an expression from Heidegger—it is on the world's basis that human-reality becomes acquainted with what it is.[17] This project of the for-itself toward itself, which constitutes ipseity, is in no way a contemplative repose. It is a lack, as we have said, but not a *given* lack: it is a lack that has its own lack to be, in relation to itself. Indeed, we need fully to appreciate that any *noted* lack—or any in-itself lack—will vanish into externality: we showed this in the foregoing pages. But a being that constitutes itself as a lack can only determine in relation to *that* thing, over there, what it lacks and what it *is*—by means, in short, of constantly separating itself from itself toward the itself that it has to be. In other words, the lack can only be, in relation to itself, its own lack as *a lack that is refused*: the only properly internal connection between that from which . . . is missing, and what is missing from it, is refusal. Indeed, to the extent to which the being from which . . . is missing is not what is missing from it, we can grasp a negation within it. But if this negation is not to vanish into pure externality—and, with it, all possibility of negation in general—its foundation will lie in the necessity, for the being from which . . . is missing, *to be* what is missing from it. In this way, the foundation of negation is a negation of negation. But this foundation-negation is no more a *given* than the lack of which it is an essential moment: it is as having to be. The for-itself makes itself be its own lack, in the phantom unity of the "reflection-reflecting," i.e., it projects itself toward that lack as it refuses it. It is only as a lack *to be eliminated* that the lack can be an internal lack for the for-itself, and the for-itself can only actualize its own lack by having it to be, i.e., by being a project toward its elimination. In this way, the for-itself's relation to its future is never static or given; instead, the future comes to the for-itself's present to determine it at its heart, insofar as the for-itself is already over there, in the future, as its elimination. The for-itself can only be a lack *here* if it is an elimination of the lack *over there*: but it has this elimination to be, in the mode of not-being. It is this original relation that allows us subsequently to note some particular lacks as lacks that are *suffered* or *endured*. This relation, in general, is the foundation of affectivity: this is

17 TN: Sartre has already mentioned Heidegger's account of the world in these terms earlier in the text (e.g., at EN 141).

also what we may try to explain psychologically by installing those idols and phantoms within the psyche known as *drives* or *appetites*. These drives, or forces, which are violently inserted within the psyche, are not comprehensible in themselves, because the psychologist presents them as in itself existents—which means that their very character as *force* is contradicted by their inner repose of indifference, and that their unity is dispersed into a pure relation of externality. We can grasp them only in the capacity of a projection into the in-itself of an immanent relation of being between the for-itself and itself, and this ontological relation is, precisely, the *lack*.

But this lack cannot be thetically grasped and known by unreflective consciousness (any more than it can appear to impure and complicit reflection, which apprehends it as a psychological object, i.e., as a drive or a feeling). It is accessible only to purifying reflection, with which we are not concerning ourselves here. At the level therefore of consciousness of the world, the lack can appear to itself only as a projection, with a transcendent and ideal character. Indeed, if what is missing from the for-itself is an ideal presence to a being-beyond-being, we grasp that being-beyond-being from the outset as missing-from-being. Thus the world is disclosed as haunted by absences to be actualized, and each *this* appears with a retinue of absences indicating and determining it. These absences are basically no different from potentialities. Only we have a better grasp of their meaning. In this way, the absences indicate the *this* as a *this* and, conversely, the *this* points toward the absences. As each absence is being-beyond-being—i.e., absent in-itself—each *this* points toward another state of its being, or toward other beings. But, of course, this organization into referring structures is frozen and petrified into in-itself, since here we are dealing with the in-itself; all these mute and petrified references, falling back into indifference and isolation at the very moment in which they arise, resemble the stony smile and empty eyes of a statue. So the absences appearing behind things do not appear as absences *to be presentified* by things. Nor can we say that they are disclosed as having to be actualized *by me*, since my ego is a transcendent structure of the psyche that only appears to reflective consciousness.[18] They are

236

---

18 TN: . . . *comme à réaliser par moi, puisque le moi est une structure transcendante* . . . I have translated Sartre's *moi* as "me" in the first instance, and "ego" in the second, as Sartre is clearly reiterating the central claim of his earlier essay *The Transcendence of the Ego* (Sartre 2004a).

pure demands, raising themselves in the midst of the circuit of ipseity as "voids to be filled." Only their character as "voids to be filled by the for-itself" manifests itself to unreflected consciousness by a direct, personal urgency that is *lived* as such, without being either connected to a *someone* or thematized. It is precisely in and through our living them as requirements that what we called (in another chapter) their "ipseity" is revealed. They are *tasks*; and this world is a world of *tasks*. In relation to these tasks, their indicated *this* is, at the same time, the "*this* of these tasks"— i.e., the unique in-itself determined by them, and indicated as being able to *fulfill* them—and something that can in no way have these tasks *to be*, since it is in the absolute unity of identity. We will call this connection within isolation, this relation of inertia within the dynamic, the "relation of means to end." It is a degraded-being-for, pounded by externality, and whose transcendent ideality can be conceived of only as the correlative of the being-for that the for-itself has to be. And the thing—insofar as it rests within the calm beatitude of indifference and yet at the same time points, beyond itself, toward tasks to fulfill through which it is acquainted with what it has to be—is the instrument, or implement. The original relation of things with each other—the relation that appears on the foundation of the quantitative relation of the *thises*—is, therefore, the relation of *equipmentality*. And this equipmentality is not subsequent, or subordinated, to the structures that were previously pointed out: in one sense, it presupposes them, and in another sense they presuppose it. A thing is not first a thing, in order later to be an implement; it is not first an implement, in order later to be disclosed as a thing: it is an implement-thing. Nonetheless, it is true that it will be discovered, in the scholar's subsequent inquiry, as purely a *thing*, i.e., as stripped of all equipmentality. But that is because the scholar is concerned only to establish pure relations of externality; moreover, the result of this scientific inquiry is that the thing itself, stripped of all instrumentality, ends up evaporating into absolute externality. We can see the extent to which Heidegger's formula needs to be corrected: of course the world appears within the circuit of ipseity, but, as the circuit is non-thetic, the annunciation of what I am cannot itself be thetic. To be in the world is not to escape out of the world toward oneself but to escape out of the world toward a "beyond" of the world that is the future world. What the world announces to me is uniquely "worldly." It remains the case that, if the equipment's infinite referral never refers to a for-itself

237

that I am, the equipmental totality is the exact correlative of my possibilities. And as I *am* my possibilities, the order of equipment in the world is the image, projected into the in-itself, of my possibilities, i.e., the image of what I am. But I can never decipher this worldly image: I adapt to it in and through action; in order for me to be an object for myself, the scissiparity of reflection is required. It is not therefore through inauthenticity that human-reality becomes lost in the world; rather, being-in-the-world is, for human-reality, radically to lose itself within the world through the very disclosure that makes it the case that there is a world; it is to be endlessly referred, from one implement to another, without even the possibility of a "What is the point?"—without any recourse, other than the revolution of reflection. It will not help to object that the chain of "For whats?" must depend on some "For whose sakes?" (*Worumwillen*).[19] Of course, that "*Worumwillen*" refers us to a structure of being that we have not yet elucidated: being for-the-Other. And the "for whom" constantly appears behind our instruments. But this "*for whom*"—whose constitution is different from "for what"—does not break the chain. It is simply a link and, seen from the perspective of instrumentality, it does not enable us to escape the in-itself. Of course, these work clothes are for the worker. But that is so the worker can repair the roofing without getting dirty. And why should we not get dirty? In order not to spend the largest part of our salary on buying clothes. Because, in point of fact, this salary is allocated to the worker as the minimum amount of money that will allow him to provide for his keep, and he "keeps himself," precisely, in order to be able to use the power of his labor to repair roofs. And why must he repair the roof? In order for it not to rain in the office, where the employees are doing the accounts, etc. This does not mean we must always apprehend the Other as an instrument of some particular type but merely that, when we consider the Other on the basis of the world, we do not thereby escape from the infinite referral of equipmental structures.

19 TN: Heidegger uses the phrase *Worumwillen*, in *Being and Time*, where it is translated into English as "for-the-sake-of-which." The idea is that, in inquiring about what some equipment is for, we will end up mentioning *Dasein*, the user (Heidegger 1980: §18). To build the bridge to Heidegger's text, in this sentence I translate Sartre's *pour qui* as "For whose sake?"

Thus, to the extent to which the for-itself is its own lack in the shape of refusal, being is disclosed to it, as the correlative of its impulse toward itself, against the ground of the world as implement-thing, and the world arises as the undifferentiated ground of referring structures of equipment. The set of these references lacks any meaning, but that is in the sense in which—at this level—there is not even any possibility of raising the problem of meaning. We work in order to live, and we live in order to work. The question of the meaning of the "work-life" totality—"Why am I working, I who am living?" "Why am I living, if it is in order to 238   work?"—can be raised only at the level of reflection, since it implies a discovery of the for-itself by itself.

What remains to be explained is why equipmentality, as the correlative of the pure negation that I am, is able to arise in the world. How is it that I am not a sterile and endlessly repeated negation of a this, qua pure this? How is it possible for this negation to disclose a plurality of tasks that are my image, if I am nothing but the pure nothingness that I have to be? To answer this question, we must remember that the for-itself is not purely and simply a future that comes toward the present. It also has its past, in the form of "was," to be. And the ecstatic implication of the three temporal dimensions is such that, if the for-itself is a being that is acquainted, through its future, with the meaning of what it was, it is— in the same movement of arising—also a being that has its "will be" to be, within the perspective of a specific "was" from which it flees. In this sense, we must always seek the meaning of a temporal dimension elsewhere, in another dimension: we named this the "diaspora," because the unity of diasporic being is not a pure belonging-together that is given; it is the necessity of actualizing the diaspora by becoming conditioned—over there, and outside—within the unity of itself. Therefore the negation that I am and which discloses the this has therefore to be in the mode of "was." This pure negation—which, as a simple presence, is not—has its being behind it, as its past, or facticity. As such, we must acknowledge that it can never be a negation without roots. But it is, on the contrary, a qualified negation— if we understand this to mean that it drags its qualification behind it, as the being that it has not to be in the form of "was." Negation arises as a nonthetic negation of the past, in the mode of an internal determination, insofar as it becomes a thetic negation of a this. And it arises within the unity of a twofold "being for," since negation is produced in existence—in the reflection-reflecting mode—as a negation of a *this*, in order to escape from the past that it is, and it escapes from the past in order to extricate itself from the *this* by fleeing from it in its being, toward the future. We called this the for-itself's point of view on the world. This point of view, which can be equated with facticity, is an ecstatic qualification of negation as the original relation to the in-itself. But, on the other hand—as we have seen—whatever the for-itself is, it is what it is in the mode of "was," as an ecstatic belonging to the world. I do not rediscover my presence in the future, since the future delivers the world to me as the correlative of a forth-coming consciousness; rather, my being appears to me in the past, albeit non-thematically, within the framework of being-in-itself—i.e., it appears in relief, in the midst of the world. Of course, this being is still consciousness of . . . , i.e., for-itself; but it is a for-itself that has frozen into in-itself and, in consequence, it is a fallen consciousness of the world, in the midst of the world. The meaning of realism, naturalism, and materialism lies in the past: these three philosophies all describe the past as if it were present. The for-itself is therefore a twofold flight from the world: it escapes its own being-in-the-midst-of-the-world as presence to the world from which it flees. The flight's free and final term is the possible. The for-itself cannot flee toward something transcendent that it is not but only toward a transcendent that it is. This is what removes any possibility of there being an end to this constant flight. If I may use an image that is somewhat demotic—but helps to capture my thought—I would remind the reader of the donkey pulling a cart behind him, trying to catch a carrot that someone has fixed to the end of a stick, which is in turn attached to the shafts. Every attempt made by the donkey to catch the carrot has the effect of moving the harnessed cart forward in its entirety—along with the carrot itself, which remains always at the same distance from the donkey. In this way, we run after a possible that is brought into view precisely by our running—a possible that is nothing other than our running, and which by that very fact is determined as being out of reach. We are running toward ourselves and we are, in consequence, the being that cannot ever be reunited with itself. In one sense, our running lacks any meaning, since its final term is never given but invented and projected even as we run toward it. And, in another sense, we cannot withhold from it the meaning that it rejects, since, despite everything, the possible is the for-itself's meaning. Instead, our flight has—and has not—meaning.

239

Now, in this very flight from the past that I am, toward the future that I am, the future is prefigured in relation to the past at the same time as it endows the past with all its meaning. The future is the past, surpassed as the given in-itself toward an in-itself that could be its own foundation, i.e., an in-itself that would be, insofar as I would have it to be. My possible is the free reclamation of my past—insofar as this reclamation may salvage my past, by founding it. I flee from the being without any foundation that I was, toward the founding act that I can be only in the mode of *"would be."* In this way, the possible is the lack that the for-itself makes itself be; i.e., it is what is missing from the present negation, insofar as it is a *qualified* negation (which means a negation whose quality lies outside itself, in the past). As such, it is itself qualified. But it is not qualified in the manner of something *given*, which could be its own quality in the mode of the in-itself, but rather as an indication of the reclamation that might found the ecstatic qualification that the for-itself *was*. In this way, thirst is three-dimensional: it is a present flight from a state of emptiness that the for-itself was. And it is this flight itself which confers on the *given* state its character as a void or lack: in the past, the lack could not be a lack, because the given can only "lack" something if it is surpassed toward . . . by a being that is its own transcendence. But this flight is a flight toward . . . and this "toward" is what gives it its meaning. As such, it is itself a *lack that makes itself*—which is to say it is, at the same time, the constitution in the past of the given as a lack or a potentiality, and a free reclamation of the given by a for-itself making itself a lack in the form of a reflection-reflecting, i.e., as consciousness of the lack. And *that toward which* the lack flees, insofar as it becomes conditioned in its being-a-lack by what is missing from it, is the possibility that it should be a thirst that is no longer a lack, i.e., the possibility of repletion-thirst. The possible points toward repletion, and value—as the phantom-being that surrounds the for-itself and penetrates it throughout—points toward a thirst that might simultaneously be *given*—in the way that "it was"—and reclaimed—as the play of the reflection-reflecting ecstatically constitutes it. What we have here, as we can see, is a plenitude that determines itself as thirst. The ecstatic past-present relation provides the sketch of this plenitude with the structure of "thirst" as its meaning—and the possible that I am must provide its actual density, its body of plenitude, as repletion. In this way, my presence to being, which determines it as a this, is a negation of the this, insofar as I am also a lack qualified in relation to this. And to the extent to which my possible is a possible presence to being-beyond-being, the qualification of my possible discloses a being-beyond-being—as the being to which my co-presence will be co-presence—that is strictly connected to a forthcoming repletion. Thus absence is disclosed within the world as a being to be actualized, insofar as this being is the correlative of the possible-being that is missing from me. The glass of water appears as having-to-be-drunk, i.e., as the correlative of a thirst that is apprehended non-thetically, and in its very being, as having to be satisfied. But these descriptions, which all imply a relation to the world's future, will become clearer if we turn now to show how, on the foundation of original negation, world-time—or universal time—is disclosed to consciousness.

IV. WORLD-TIME[20]

Universal time enters the world through the for-itself. The in-itself does not have temporality at its disposal precisely because it is in-itself, and because temporality is the unitary mode of being of a being that is constantly for itself at a distance from itself. The for-itself, on the contrary, is temporality, but it is not a consciousness of temporality, except when it puts itself into the "reflective-reflected" relationship. In the unreflective mode it discovers temporality on being, which is to say outside. Universal temporality is objective.

(A) The past   241

The this does not appear as a present that will thereafter become past and which, hitherto, was in the future. As soon as I perceive it, this inkwell already exists in three temporal dimensions. Insofar as I apprehend it as something permanent—that is, as its essence—it is already in the

---

20 TN: Heidegger uses the term Weltzeit in his seminal discussion of time (see Heidegger 1980: §82), translated into English as "world-time" (sometimes without the hyphen) and into French as le temps du monde. As Heidegger's account of time is so central to the discussion to which Sartre is contributing, I have preserved the (implicit) allusion to Heidegger in my translation of the phrase—le temps du monde—used by Sartre to give this section its title.

future, even though I am not present to it in my current presence but as forth-coming-to-myself. And by the same token I can only apprehend it as having already been there, in the world, insofar as I was already there, myself, as present. In this sense, no "synthesis of recognition"[21] exists, if we take that to mean a progressive operation of identification which, through its successive ordering of the "nows," confers on the perceived thing its *duration*. Instead, the explosion of the for-itself's temporality extends alongside the entirety of the in-itself it discloses, as if it ran the length of an immense and monotonous wall, whose end was out of sight. I am this original negation that I have to be, in the mode of "not-yet" and "already," alongside the being that is what it is. If, therefore, we suppose that consciousness arises within an immobile world alongside one, and just one, being, that is unchangeably what it is, this being will be disclosed with an unchangeable past and future that do not require any "operation" of synthesis, and which are not distinct from that very disclosure. An *operation* would be necessary only if the for-itself had to retain and, at the same time, to constitute its own past. But from the simple fact that it is its own past, as well as its own future, it follows that the disclosure of the in-itself can only be temporalized. The *this* is disclosed temporally, not because it is refracted through an *a priori* form of inner sense but because it is disclosed to a disclosing whose very being is temporalization. Nonetheless, the atemporality of being is *represented* in its disclosure itself: insofar as we apprehend the *this* through and within a temporality that temporalizes itself, it appears from the outset as temporal; but, insofar as it is what it is, it refuses *to be* its own temporality, and only *reflects* time. In addition, it reflects back the internal ecstatic relation—which is at the source of temporality—as a pure objective relation of externality. Therefore permanence, as a compromise between timeless unity and the ecstatic unity of temporalization, appears purely as a sliding-by of in-itself instants, small nothingnesses that are separated from each other and reunited by a relation of simple externality, at the surface of a being that preserves an atemporal unchangeability. It is not therefore true that the atemporality of being escapes us: it is, on the contrary, *given in time*; it founds the way of being of universal time.

21 TN: The quotation marks around this phrase suggest Sartre has some author in mind; it may be Bergson, who invokes the role of recognition in perception in *Matter and Memory* (Bergson 1911b).

Therefore, insofar as the for-itself "was" what it is, the implement or thing appears to it as having *already* been there. The for-itself can be presence to the this only as a presence that *was*: every perception is, in itself and without any "operation," a recognition. Now, what gets revealed, through the ecstatic unity of the past and the present, is one identical being. That being is not apprehended as being *the same* in the past and at present but as being it.[22] Temporality is only an organ of sight. And yet the this was *already* the "it" that it is. In this way, it appears as having a past. Only it refuses *to be* this past; it merely *has* it. Insofar as it is apprehended objectively, therefore, temporality is a pure phantasm, because it is given neither as the for-itself's temporality, nor as the temporality that the in-itself has to be. At the same time, since the transcendent past is—*qua* transcendent—in-itself, it cannot be what the present has to be; it is isolated in a phantom *Selbstständigkeit*. And as each moment of the past is a "having-been-present," this isolation continues, right inside the past. So the immutable this is disclosed through an infinite flickering and fragmentation of phantom in-itselfs. That is how this glass or this table is revealed to me: they do not endure; they *are*; and time flows over them. Of course, it might be objected that I do not *see* them changing. But that introduces, irrelevantly, a scientific perspective. That perspective has no justification, and actually our perception contradicts it: the pipe, the pencil, all of those beings that are delivered in their entirety within each of their "profiles," and whose permanence is wholly indifferent to the multiplicity of profiles, are also, although they are disclosed within temporality, transcendent in relation to any temporality. The "thing" exists all at one go, as a "form," i.e., as a whole that is not affected by any of the superficial and parasitic variations we can see in it. Each this is disclosed with a law of being that determines its *threshold*, which means the degree of change at which it would simply cease to be what it is, in order to be no longer. And this law of being by which "permanence" is expressed is immediately disclosed as a structure of its essence; it determines a limit-potentiality of the this—the limit at which it disappears from the world. We will return to this. Thus the for-itself apprehends temporality *on* being, as a pure reflection playing on being's surface, without any possibility of changing it. A scholar

---

22 TN: . . . *mais comme étant lui.* Here I have rendered *lui* as "it."

may use the term "homogeneity" to fix in a concept this absolute and phantom negativity of time.[23] But the transcendent grasp of the ecstatic unity of the temporalizing for-itself on the in-itself occurs as the apprehension of an empty form of temporal unity, without any being that founds this unity by *being* it. In this way, therefore, at the level of the present-past, that curious unity of absolute dispersion which is external temporality appears—in which each before and after is an "in-itself" isolated from the others by its indifferent externality, and yet in which these instants are gathered together within the unity of being of a single being, that common being—or Time—being nothing other than the dispersion itself, conceived in terms of necessity and substantiality. This contradictory nature can appear only on the twofold foundation of the for-itself and the in-itself. On that basis, scientific thinking—insofar as it aims to hypostasize the relation of externality—conceives of the in-itself (that is, thinks it emptily) not as something transcendent that we aim at through time but as a content that passes from instant to instant or, better still, as a multiplicity of contents each of which is external to the others and absolutely *similar* to them.

Our attempt to describe universal temporality has, so far, adopted the hypothesis that nothing can come from being, apart from its timeless immutability. But *some thing* does, precisely, come from being, which we will call—for want of anything better—"abolitions" and "apparitions."[24] These abolitions and apparitions ought to be the subject of a purely metaphysical clarification, not an ontological one, because we cannot conceive of their necessity on the basis either of the for-itself's structures of being, or of those of the in-itself: their existence is that of a contingent and metaphysical fact. We cannot know precisely what comes from being in the phenomenon of apparition, since that phenomenon already concerns a temporalized *this*. However, experience teaches us that various *thises* arise and are annihilated and, as we know now that perception discloses the in-itself and, outside the in-itself, *nothing*, we cannot regard the in-itself as the foundation of these aris-

---

23 TN: The "scholar" to whom Sartre refers must be Bergson, who describes time's "homogenization" in space in Bergson (1960).

24 TN: Here I translate *apparition* as "apparition," as in this context Sartre clearly means to refer to *events*.

ings and annihilations. In addition, we can see clearly that the principle of identity, as the in-itself's law of being, requires that any abolition and apparition should be completely external to the in-itself that has appeared or been abolished—otherwise the in-itself would at the same time be and not be. An abolition cannot be the degradation of being that consists in an *end*. Only the for-itself can know such degradations because it is, in relation to itself, its own end. As a quasi-affirmation in which the affirming is thickened by what it affirms, being exists without internal finitude, in the distinctive tension of its "self-affir-mation." Its "up-until-now" is completely external to it. In this way, an abolition does not imply the necessity of an *after*—which can be manifest only in a world, and for a for-itself—but of a *quasi-after*. We may express this quasi-after like this: being-in-itself is unable to effect any mediation between itself and its nothingness. Similarly, apparitions are not *adventures* of some being that appears. We will find the self-anteriority presupposed by any adventure only in the for-itself, whose apparition and its end are internal adventures. Being is what it is. It is, without "setting itself to be," without childhood, or youth: what has appeared is not its own innovation; it is being from the outset, without any relation to a "before" that it has to be in the mode of *not-being* it, and in which it would have to be as a pure absence. Here again we encounter a quasi-succession, i.e., the complete externality of what has appeared in rela-tion to its nothingness. But in order for this absolute externality to be given in the form of "there is," there must already be a world, i.e., the   244 arising of a for-itself. The in-itself's absolute externality in relation to the in-itself ensures that the sheer nothingness that is the quasi-before of an apparition or the quasi-after of an abolition cannot even form part of the plenitude of being. It is only within the unity of a world, and against the ground of the world, that a *this* that *was not* can appear, and that the relation-of-an-absence-of-relation instantiated by externality can be disclosed; the nothingness of being that consists in anteriority in relation to something that has appeared and that "was not" can enter into a world only retrospectively, through a for-itself that is its own nothingness and its own anteriority. In this way, the arising and the annihilation of a *this* are ambiguous phenomena: here again, what the for-itself brings into being is a pure nothingness, a not-yet-being and a being-no-longer. Their foundation is neither the being in question nor the world as a totality that we apprehend *before* or *afterward*. But on the other hand, as the movement of arising is disclosed in the world by a for-itself that is its own "before" and "after," an apparition is given from the outset as an adventure; we grasp the *this* that has appeared as already being there in the world, as its own absence, insofar as we were ourselves already present to a world from which it was absent. Thus a thing can arise from its own nothingness. What is involved here is not a conceptual way of seeing, belonging to the intellect, but a primary structure of perception. The *Gestalttheorie* experiments show clearly that a pure apparition is always apprehended as dynamically arising; what has appeared *comes running* into being, from the depths of nothingness. At the same time, we find here the origin of the "principle of causality." The paradigmatic example of causality is not the negation of what has appeared as such, as Meyerson would have it; nor is it our assigning of a permanent external connection between two phenomena. Primarily, causality is an apprehension of what has appeared before it appears—as being already there in its own nothingness, in order to prepare its apparition. Causality is simply the primary apprehension of the temporality of what has appeared as an ecstatic mode of being. But the event's *adventurous* character, like the ecstatic constitution of an apparition, disintegrates within the act of perception itself: the "before" and "after" are frozen within its in-itself-nothingness, and what has appeared is frozen in its indifferent identity; the non-being, in the previous instant, of what has appeared is disclosed as the indifferent plenitude of the being in existence at this instant; the relation of causality disintegrates into a pure relation of externality between some *thises* which preceded what appeared, and the thing that appeared itself. In this way the ambiguity of an apparition and a disappearance stems from the fact that they are given, like the world, like space, like potentiality and equipmentality, like universal time itself, in the guise of totalities that are constantly disintegrating.

Such, therefore, is the world's past, made up of instants that are homogeneous and connected to each other by a pure relation of externality. Through its past, as we have noted already, the for-itself merges into the in-itself. In the past the for-itself that has become in-itself shows itself as a being in the midst of the world: it *is*; it has lost its transcendence. And its being is thereby pastified *within* time: between the past of the for-itself and the past of the world that was co-present to it, there is no difference other than that the for-itself has its own past to be. In this way there is only *one* past, which is being's past, or the *objective* past within which I was. My past is a past within the world, a belonging to the totality of past being that I am, and that I flee. In other words, for one of the dimensions of time there is a coincidence between the ecstatic temporality that I have to be and world-time, as pure given nothingness. It is through the past that I belong to universal temporality; it is through the present and the future that I escape from it.

(B) The present

The for-itself's present is a presence to being and, as such, it is not. But it is a disclosure of being. The being that appears to the presence is given as *being in the present*. That is the reason why the present is given antinomically: as not being, when it is lived, and as being the unique measure of being, insofar as it is disclosed as being what it is in the present. It is not that being does not overflow the present, but this overabundance of being can be grasped only through the organ of apprehension that is the past, i.e., as what no longer is. This book on my table, therefore, *is* in the present and it *was* (identical with itself) in the past. In this way the present is disclosed through original temporality as universal being, and at the same time it is nothing—nothing more than being; it is purely a sliding alongside the length of being, purely a nothingness.

The foregoing remarks might seem to suggest that nothing comes from being in the present, apart from its being. That would be to forget that being is disclosed to the for-itself either as motionless or as moving, and that the two notions of movement and rest stand in a dialectical relation. Now, we cannot derive movement ontologically, either from the nature of the for-itself, or from its fundamental relation to the in-itself, or from anything that we can discern from the outset within the phenomenon of being. A world without movement is conceivable. Of course, it is not possible to envisage the possibility of a world without change—other than as a purely formal possibility—but change is not movement. A change is an alteration in a quality of a *this*; as we have seen, it comes about as a whole, through the arising or disintegration

246 of a form. Movement, on the contrary, presupposes the permanence of quiddity. If a *this* had at the same time to be translated from one place to another and, during this translation,[25] to undergo a radical alteration in its being, that alteration would negate the movement, since *nothing* moving would remain. A movement is purely a change in place of a *this* that remains otherwise unaltered—as the principle of the homogeneity of space clearly shows. Movement therefore—which cannot be derived from any essential characteristic of the existents in presence, which was denied by Eleatic ontology, and which required, in Descartes's ontology, the well-known recourse to a "fillip"[26]—has exactly the value of a fact; it participates in the entire contingency of being and must be accepted as something given. Of course, as we will soon see, for "there to be" movement, a for-itself is necessary, which makes it especially difficult to allocate exactly what, in pure movement, comes from being. But in any case it is beyond doubt that the for-itself, here as elsewhere, *adds nothing* to being; here, as elsewhere, it is the pure Nothing, against whose ground a movement detaches itself. But if we are prohibited, by movement's very nature, from attempting any *deduction* of it, it is at least possible, and even necessary, to provide a *description*. How, therefore, should the *meaning* of movement be conceived?

We believe that movement is simply an *affection* of being, because any moving body is found, *after* its movement, to be as it previously was. So obvious has it seemed that movement is added on to being without modifying it that it is often claimed as a principle that the translation of a figure does not deform it; and it is certain, as we have seen, that the quiddity of the *this* remains unaltered. Nothing typifies this conception better than the resistance encountered by a theory such as Fitzgerald's "contraction" theory,[27] or Einstein's "variations in mass," because they

25 TN: I use "to translate," even though it sounds a little odd, to match Sartre's French verb *translater*, which is normally only used in mathematical contexts.
26 TN: Sartre is alluding to Pascal's criticism of Descartes, at §77 of his *Pensées* (translated as Pascal 1995): "I cannot forgive Descartes. In all his philosophy he would have been quite willing to dispense with God. But he had to make Him give a fillip to set the world in motion; beyond this he has no further need of God."
27 TN: Sartre is alluding to the "contraction hypothesis" advanced by the Irish physicist George Francis Fitzgerald (1851–1901).

seemed especially to attack what a moving body's being consists in. From this, the principle of the relativity of movement obviously follows—which makes perfect sense if movement is an external characteristic of being and if it is not determined by any internal structural change. In that case, movement becomes a relation between being and its surroundings that is so *external* that to say that a being is moving and its surroundings at rest is equivalent to saying that the surroundings are moving and the being under consideration is at rest. From this point of view, movement appears neither as a being nor as a mode of being but as a relation from which all substance has been stripped.

But the fact that a moving body remains identical to itself at the points of departure and arrival—that is, in the two stases that frame the movement—does not in any way prejudice the question of what it was while it was moving. One might as well say that the water boiling in an autoclave undergoes no change while it is boiling, because it presents the same characteristics when it is cold, and when it has been cooled. Nor should we allow the fact that we can assign different successive positions to a moving body while it is moving, and that it appears to be the same in each position, to detain us—for these positions define the space that is crossed, not the movement itself. On the contrary, it is this mathematical tendency to treat a moving body as if it were a body at rest that could be displaced along a line without ceasing to be at rest that lies at the origin of the Eleatic aporias.

So we must regard the claim that being—whether it be moving or at rest—remains unchanged in its being, as a mere postulate that we cannot accept without criticism. To subject it to such criticism, let us return to the Eleatics' arguments, and especially the argument about the arrow. We are told that an arrow, in passing through the position AB, "is" exactly as an arrow at rest would be, with the extremity of its tip at A and the extremity of its tail at B. That seems obvious if we accept that movement is superadded to being and that, in consequence, nothing can show us whether some being is moving or at rest. In brief, if movement is an accident of being, movement and rest are indiscernible. The arguments that are usually opposed to the most famous Eleatic aporia—that of Achilles and the Tortoise—carry no weight here. What use is it to object that the Eleatics relied on the infinite divisibility of space without taking equal account of the infinite divisibility of time? The question here is not about *position*, or an instant, but about *being*. We will come closer to conceiving the problem correctly if we answer the Eleatics by saying that they were not talking about movement but rather about the space that subtends movement. But this is to limit ourselves to pointing out the question without solving it. What, in fact, must the being of a moving body be in order for its quiddity to remain unaltered and for it nonetheless to be, in its being, distinct from a being at rest?

If we try to clarify our resistance to Zeno's arguments, we will note that it has at its origin a specific and natural conception of movement: we accept that the arrow "passes" in AB, but it seems to us that *to pass* in a place cannot be equivalent to *staying there*, i.e., to *being there*. But in general we are seriously confused, because we judge that the moving body only *passes* in AB (in other words, that it never *is* there) and at the same time we continue to suppose that, in itself, it *is*. So, at the same time, it will be in itself, and it will not be in AB. That is the origin of the Eleatics' aporia: How could the arrow *not be* in AB, since, in AB, it *is*? In other words, in order to avoid the Eleatic aporia, we have to give up the generally accepted premise, according to which a moving body retains its being-in-itself. To merely pass, in AB, is to-be-in-passage. What is it, to pass? It is to be in a place and, at the same time, to not be there. There is no moment at which we can say that the being in passage *is* here, unless we suddenly stop it; but neither can we say that it is not, or that it is not *there*, or that it is *elsewhere*. Its relation to its place is not a relation of *occupation*. But we saw earlier that the *place* of a *this* at rest was its external relation to the ground, insofar as this relation may collapse into a multiplicity of external relations with other *thises* when the ground itself disintegrates into a multiplicity of figures.[28] The foundation of space is therefore the reciprocal externality that enters into being through the for-itself, and whose origin is that being is what it is. In brief, it is the being which defines its place by revealing itself to a for-itself as indifferent to the other beings. And this indifference is nothing but its very identity, its want of ecstatic reality, insofar as it is apprehended by a for-itself that is already present to other *thises*. By virtue solely of the fact, therefore, that the *this* is what it is, it *occupies* a place, and it *is* at a site—which is to say that the for-itself sets it into the relation with the other *thises* of *having no relations*

28 Sartre's note: Chapter 3, section II.

with them. Space is a nothingness of relation,[29] apprehended as a relation by the being that is its own relation. The fact that something *passes* in some place, rather than being there, can therefore be interpreted only in terms of being. In other words, a being,[30] having founded a place, no longer suffices to found its place: it only sketches it out; the for-itself is unable to establish its relations of externality with other thises because it is necessary for it to establish these on the basis of a this that is. These relations, however, cannot be annihilated, because the being on whose basis they get established is not a pure nothingness. It is just that, in the very "now" in which they are established, it is already external to them; i.e., new relations are *already* being disclosed, simultaneously with their disclosure, whose foundation is the extant this, and whose relation with the earlier relations is one of externality. But this continuous externality of the spatial relations that define a being's place can only be founded in the fact that the this under consideration is external to itself. And indeed, to say that the this "passes" in a place is to convey that, while it is still there, it is there no longer; in other words, its relation to itself is not an ecstatic relation of being but purely a relation of externality. Thus, a "place" may exist, to the extent to which some this is disclosed as external to the other thises. And in this place there can be a *passage*, or transition, to the extent to which the being is no longer defined by this externality but is, on the contrary, external to it. In this way movement is the being of a being that is external to itself. In the case of movement, the only metaphysical question to be raised is the question of self-externality. How should we understand this?

In moving, *nothing* about a being changes, when it passes from A to B. Therefore its quality, insofar as that represents the being disclosed to the for-itself as this, is not transformed into another quality. Movement can in no way be assimilated to becoming; it does not alter a quality in its *essence*, any more than it *actualizes* it. The quality remains exactly what it is; what changes is its way of being. This red ball, rolling along the billiard table,

249

29 TN: *L'espace est le néant de rapport* ... This might be expressed in more ordinary English as "Space is a null-relation," but, as Sartre uses *néant* (which is also odd in French), I retain "nothingness."
30 TN: ... *ne peut donc s'interpréter qu'en termes d'être* ... *le lieu étant fondé par l'être, l'être n'est plus assez* ... I quote here to indicate Sartre's switch in reference from "being" in the abstract, in the preceding sentence, to some particular being in this sentence.

does not cease *to be* red but it is no longer this red that it is in the same way as when it was at rest: it remains suspended between abolition and permanence. In fact, insofar as, by being already at B, it is external to what it was in A, its redness has been annihilated—but insofar as it is beyond B, in C, it is external to that same annihilation. In this way it escapes from being through its abolition, and it escapes abolition through its being. Therefore we encounter within the world a category of *thises* whose peculiarity is never to be—yet without thereby being nothingnesses. The only relation that the for-itself is able to apprehend from the outset in these *thises* is the relation of self-externality. For, as externality is *nothing*, it is necessary, in order for there to be any "self-externality," for there to be some being that is its own relation to itself. In brief, it is impossible to define purely in terms of the in-itself anything that is revealed to the for-itself as self-externality. Such an externality can be encountered only by a being that is already, *over there*, what it is *here*—in other words, by a consciousness. That self-externality, which appears as a sheer sickness in being—in other words, as the impossibility of certain *thises* being at the same time themselves and their own nothingness—must be registered by something resembling a *nothing within the world*, i.e., something like a substantivized nothing. In fact, since self-externality is not at all ecstatic, the relation that a moving body has to itself is purely a relation of indifference, and can be encountered only by a witness. It is an abolition unable to accomplish itself, and an apparition unable to accomplish itself. This nothing—which measures and exhibits self-externality—is the *trajectory*, as the constitution of externality within the unity of a single being. A trajectory is a line that draws itself, i.e., a synthetic unity suddenly appearing in space, an illusion that immediately collapses into the infinite multiplicity of externality. When the *this* is at rest, space *is*; when it is moving, space *generates itself*, or *becomes*. A trajectory can never *be*, because it is *nothing*: it vanishes immediately into pure relations of externality between various places, i.e., into the simple externality of indifference, or spatiality. And movement *is not* any more than that; it is the least-being of a being that does not manage fully either to abolish itself or to be; it is indifferent externality, arising right in the heart of the in-itself. This pure vacillation in being is a contingent adventure of the being.[31] The for-itself can grasp it only through the

---

31 TN: . . . *aventure contingente de l'être*. As earlier, Sartre means a *particular* being—or entity— here, e.g., some moving thing.

ecstasis of time, and in an ecstatic and permanent identification of the
moving body with itself. No operation is presupposed by this identification, nor, in particular, any "synthesis of recognition"; rather, for the for-
itself, it is nothing other than the ecstatic unity of being of the past with
the present. In this way *temporal* identification of the moving body with
itself—through the constant positing of its own externality—allows its
trajectory to be disclosed; i.e., it makes space arise in the form of an evanescent becoming. Through movement, space is generated within time;
the movement draws the line, like a contour of self-externality. The line
vanishes at the same time as the movement, and this phantom temporal
unity of space continually merges into timeless space, i.e., into the pure
multiplicity of dispersion that is without becoming.

The for-itself is, in the present, a presence to being. But the eternal
identity of the permanent prevents us from grasping this presence as
something reflected in things because, within permanence, nothing dif-
ferentiates what is from what was. Without movement, therefore, the
present dimension of universal time would elude us. It is movement that
determines universal time as the pure present. That is because, in the first
place, it reveals itself as a *present* vacillation: already, in the past, it is nothing more than an evanescent line, a trail that erases itself; in the future,
it is not at all, because it cannot be its own project; it is like the constant
progression of a crack in the wall. Moreover, its being has the instant's
elusive ambiguity, because we can say neither that it is, nor that it is not;
in addition, it barely appears before it is already surpassed, and external
to itself. It is therefore the perfect symbol of the for-itself's present: the
self-externality of the being that can neither be, nor not be, sends back
to the for-itself the image—projected onto the plane of the in-itself—of
a being that has to be what it is not, and not to be what it is. The difference lies entirely in what separates self-externality—in which being
is not in order to be its own externality but which, on the contrary, "is
being" through an ecstatic witness's identification—from the pure temporalizing ecstasis in which being has to be what it is not. Through some
moving thing, the for-itself becomes acquainted with its present; it is its
own present in simultaneity with the current movement; it is movement
that performs the task of *actualizing* universal time, insofar as the for-itself
is acquainted with its own present by the present of the moving body.
This actualization highlights the instants' reciprocal externality, as the
present of the moving body is defined—owing to the very nature of

movement—as something external to its own past, and as an externality in relation to that externality. Time's infinite division is founded in this absolute externality.

(C) The future

The original future is the possibility of this presence that I have to be, beyond the real, to an in-itself beyond the real in-itself. My future brings with it, as a future co-presence, the draft of a future world and, as we have seen, it is that future world that is disclosed to the for-itself that I will be, and not the for-itself's own possibilities (which can be known only from the standpoint of reflection). Since my possibles—as the meaning of what I am—also arise as a "beyond" of the in-itself to which I am present, the future of the in-itself that is revealed to my future is directly and closely connected with the reality to which I am present. It is the present in-itself, but changed—because my future is nothing more than the possibilities of my presence to an in-itself that I will have changed. Thus the world's future is disclosed to my future. It is made out of the range of potentialities, starting from the simple permanence and pure essence of a thing, and extending all the way to powers. As soon as I determine a thing's essence, whether I apprehend it as a table or an inkwell, I am already over there, in the future. That is, first, because its essence can only be something co-present to my later possibility of being-nothing-but-this-negation and, next, because its permanence and its very equipmentality as a table or inkwell refer us to the future. We have sufficiently developed these points in the previous sections to make any further emphasis unnecessary. The only thing we would like to note is that, as soon as anything appears as an implement-thing, some of its structures and properties will be lodged from the outset in the future. From the moment the world and its thises appear, there is a universal future. Only we noted earlier that every future "state" of the world remains foreign to it, in the full, reciprocal externality of indifference. There are some futures of the world that are defined by chances, and become autonomous "probables"; they do not make themselves probable but they are as "probables," as already constituted "nows" whose content is clearly determined but not yet actualized. These futures belong to every this, or set of thises, but outside them. What, then, is the universal future? We must regard it as the abstract frame for that hierarchy of equivalences constituted by the *futures*: as a container of reciprocal externalities that is, itself, external; as the sum of the in-itself that is, itself, in itself. In other words, whichever "probable" carries the day, there is and there will be one future but, in consequence, this future—which is indifferent and external to the present, and composed of "nows," each of which is indifferent to the other, and joined through the substantivized before-after relation (insofar as this relation, emptied of its ecstatic character, no longer means anything more than an external negation)—is a series of empty containers joined together by the unity of their dispersion. So sometimes the future appears as a crisis and a threat, insofar as I place the future of a *this* closely beside its present through the project of my own possibilities beyond the co-present; and sometimes this threat breaks up into pure externality and I no longer apprehend the future other than purely as a formal container, indifferent to whatever fills it and homogeneous to space, as simply a law of externality; and, finally, sometimes it shows itself as an in-itself nothingness, insofar as it is pure dispersion beyond being.

Thus the temporal dimensions through which the timeless *this* is given to us—in its very a-temporality—take on new qualities when they appear on the object: being-in-itself, objectivity, indifferent externality, absolute dispersion. Time, insofar as it is encountered by an ecstatic self-temporalizing temporality, is always a self-transcendence, and refers from "before" to "after" and from "after" to "before." But, insofar as Time is grasped on the in-itself, this self-transcendence is not what Time has *to be*; it is been, within Time. Time's cohesion is a pure phantom, an objective reflection of the for-itself's ecstatic project toward itself and of human-reality's cohesion within movement. But if we consider time by itself, this cohesion has *no raison d'être*; it collapses immediately into an absolute multiplicity of instants which, considered separately, lose their temporal nature entirely and are straightforwardly reducible to the total a-temporality of the *this*. In this way, time is a pure in-itself nothingness, which can seem to have a *being* only through the very act in which the for-itself passes through it, in order to make use of it. Further, this being is that of a distinctive figure, detached against time's undifferentiated ground—which we may call a *lapse* of time. Indeed, our primary apprehension of objective time is *practical*: it is in *being* my possibilities, beyond co-present being, that I encounter objective time as the correlative, in

252

the world, of the nothingness that separates me from my possible. From this point of view, time appears as a finite and structured form, within an indefinite dispersion; a *lapse* of time is time that is compressed within an absolute decompression, and it is the project of ourselves toward our possibles that brings the compression about. Of course, this compressed time is a form of dispersion and separation, because it expresses within the world the distance that separates me from myself. But on the other hand, as I only ever project myself toward a possible through an ordered series of dependent possibles that are what I have to be, in order to be . . . , and as their non-thematic and non-positional disclosure is given in the non-positional disclosure of the major possible toward which I am projecting myself, time is disclosed to me as an objective temporal form, as a spacing out of "probables": this objective form, or *lapse*, is akin to the *trajectory* of my act.

In this way time appears through *trajectories*. But, just as spatial trajectories will decompress and collapse into pure static spatiality, so does a temporal trajectory collapse, the moment it is not simply lived as something objectively underpinning[32] our awaiting of ourselves. In fact the "probables" that I encounter naturally tend to isolate themselves into *in itself probables* and to occupy a strictly separated fraction of objective time; the *lapse* of time vanishes, and time is revealed as a shimmering of nothingness at the surface of a strictly a-temporal being.

253   V. KNOWLEDGE

This rapid sketch of the world's disclosure to the for-itself allows us to conclude. We can concede, to idealism, that the for-itself's being is knowledge of being, but we will add that there is a being to that knowledge. The for-itself's being is identical with the being of knowledge, but that is not because knowledge is the measure of being but because the for-itself becomes acquainted with what it is by the in-itself—or, in other words, because it is, in its being, a relation to being. Knowledge is nothing other than the presence of being to the for-itself, and the for-itself is only the

---

32 TN: I assume that the original text—*ce qui sous-entend objectivement*—contains a mistake, and that Sartre intended to use the verb *sous-tendre*, which he uses elsewhere, to mean "to underpin."

nothing that actualizes this presence. In this way, knowledge is, in essence, an ecstatic being and it thereby merges into the for-itself's ecstatic being. The for-itself does not exist in order subsequently to know; nor can we say that it only is insofar as it knows (or is known), as that would make being disappear into an ordered infinity of particular instances of knowledge. Rather, there is the absolute arising of the for-itself in the midst of being and beyond being, on the basis of the being that it is not, and as the negation of that being and the nihilation of itself—and knowledge is that initial and absolute event. In brief, through a radical reversal of the idealist position, knowledge is absorbed into being: it is neither an attribute, nor a function, nor an accident of being; but *there is* only being. From this point of view it appears necessary to abandon the idealist position entirely and, in particular, it becomes possible to envisage the for-itself's relation to the in-itself as a fundamental ontological relation; we will even be able, at the end of this book, to regard this articulation of the for-itself in relation to the in-itself as the constantly moving sketch of a quasi-totality to which we can give the name *Being*. From the point of view of this totality, the for-itself's arising is not only the event that is absolute for the for-itself; it is also *something that happens to the in-itself*, the in-itself's only possible adventure. It is just as if the for-itself, through its very nihilation, constituted itself as a "consciousness of . . . ," i.e., as if it escaped, through its very transcendence, that law of the in-itself by which any affirmation is thickened by what it affirms. The for-itself, through its negation of itself, becomes an affirmation of the in-itself. The intentional affirmation is like the reverse side of the internal negation; there can be an affirmation only through a being that is its own nothingness, and only of a being that is not the being that affirms. But then, within the quasi-totality of Being, the affirmation *happens to* the in-itself; the in-itself's adventure is *to be* affirmed. The in-itself could not effect this affirmation as an affirmation of itself without destroying its being-in-itself; what happens to the in-itself is the affirmation's actualization by the for-itself; it is like a passive ecstasis of the in-itself that leaves it unchanged and yet which occurs within it, and on its basis. It is as if there were a passion of the for-itself, which loses itself in order for the "world" affirmation to happen to the in-itself. And, certainly, this affirmation exists only for the for-itself; it is the for-itself itself, and disappears when it does. But it is not *in* the for-itself, because it is the ecstasis itself, and, if the for-itself is one of its terms (the affirming),

254

the other term—the in-itself—is *really* present to it; it is outside, on being, that there is a world to be disclosed.

To the realist, on the other hand, we will concede that what is present to the knowing consciousness is being itself, and that the for-itself adds *nothing* to the in-itself, other than the very fact that *there is* [*il y ait*] an in-itself, i.e., the affirmative negation. Indeed, the task we have set ourselves is to show that the world and the implement-thing, space, quantity, and universal time are pure substantivized nothingnesses, and change nothing about the pure being that is revealed through them. In this sense, everything is given, present to me without distance and in the entirety of its reality: *nothing* of what I see comes from me; there is *nothing* apart from what I see or what I am able to see. Being is around me everywhere, and it seems that I can touch it, and grasp it; *representation*, as a psychological event, is a pure philosophers' invention. But this being that "invests" me from all sides and from which I am separated by *nothing* is separated from me by precisely *nothing*; and, because it is nothingness, this nothing is impassable. "There is" being because I am a negation of being; and worldhood, spatiality, quantity, equipmentality, and temporality arrive in being only because I am a negation of being. They add nothing to being: they are purely nihilated conditions of the "there is"; they only actualize the "*there is.*" But these conditions—which *are nothing*—separate me from being more radically than any prismatic distortions, through which I might still hope to be able to uncover it. To say "there is being" is to say nothing—and yet it effects a complete metamorphosis, because *there is* being only for a for-itself. It is not through some quality of its own that being is *relative* to the for-itself, nor is it through its being, and we hereby escape Kantian relativism; rather, it is through its "there is," since in its internal negation the for-itself affirms that which cannot affirm itself, and knows being *as it is*, where that "as it is" cannot belong to being. In this sense, the for-itself is at the same time an immediate presence to being and slides, like an infinite distance, between being and itself. The fact is that knowledge's ideal is "being-what-we-know," and its original structure is "not-being-what-we-know." Worldhood, spatiality, etc., only express this not-being. Thus, I find myself everywhere—between being and myself—as the nothing that *is not* being. The world is human. We can see the highly distinctive position of consciousness: being is everywhere, against me and around me, weighing on me and besieging me, and I am constantly referred from being to being: that table there is being, and nothing more; that rock, that tree, that landscape, are being and, other than that, nothing. I want to grasp that being and I no longer find anything but myself. That is because knowledge, which is intermediate between being and non-being, directs me to absolute being when I want it to be subjective and, when I believe I am grasping the absolute, it directs me to myself. The very meaning of knowledge is what it is not and is not what it is, for, to know being as it is, it would be necessary to be that being, but there is only an "as it is," because I am not the being that I know and, if I were to become it, the "as it is" would vanish and I would no longer be able even to think it. What we have here is neither a skepticism—which would presuppose, precisely, that the "*as it is*" belongs to being—nor a relativism. Knowledge places us in the presence of the absolute and there is a truth to knowledge. But this truth, although it delivers us nothing more and nothing less than the absolute, remains strictly human.

It may seem surprising that we have discussed the problem of knowledge without raising the question of the body and the senses, or even addressing it once. It is no part of our intention to fail to recognize, or to neglect, the body's role. But what matters before anything else, in ontology just as everywhere else, is to observe a strict order in one's discussion. Now the body, whatever its function may be, appears in the first place as something *known*. We cannot therefore relate knowledge back to it, or discuss it, before we have defined knowledge; nor can we, in any way or by any means, derive knowledge in its fundamental structure from it. In addition, the body—our body—has as its distinctive characteristic the fact that it is essentially *known by the Other*: what I know is the body of others, and my *knowledge* of my body essentially comes from the way in which others see it. In this way the nature of *my* body directs me to the existence of the Other, and to my being-for-the Other. With it, I encounter another mode of existence for human-reality, which is as fundamental as being-for-itself, and which I will call "being-for-the-Other." If I want to describe man's relation with being exhaustively, it will be necessary now to turn to the study of this new structure of my being: my for-the-Other. For human-reality is obliged to be, in its being, and in one and the same arising, for-itself-for-the-Other.

Part Three

Being-for-the-Other

Chapter 1

THE OTHER'S EXISTENCE

I. THE PROBLEM

We have described human-reality on the basis of its forms of negative behavior and the *cogito*. By following this guiding thread we discovered that human-reality was-for-itself. Is that the *whole* of what it is? Without abandoning our standpoint of reflective description, we can encounter modes of consciousness that seem, even while they remain in themselves strictly for-itself, to point to a radically different type of ontological structure. This ontological structure is *mine*, which is to say that my concerns are on my account and yet this concern "for myself" reveals to me a being that is my being without being-for-myself.

For example, let us consider shame. It involves a mode of consciousness whose structure is identical to all the structures we have previously described. It is a non-positional consciousness (of) self as shame and, as such, it is an example of what the Germans call *Erlebnis*; it is accessible to reflection. In addition, its structure is intentional; it is an ashamed apprehension of something, and that something is *me*. I am ashamed of what I *am*. Shame therefore brings about an intimate relation between me and myself: through shame I have discovered an aspect of my being. And yet, although some complex and derivative forms of shame can appear at the level of reflection, shame is not in the first instance a phenomenon of reflection. In effect, whatever results one might be able to obtain alone through the religious *practice* of shame, shame in its primary structure is shame *before somebody*. I have just made some clumsy or vulgar gesture: this gesture sticks to me; I neither judge it nor blame it; I simply live it; I actualize it in the mode of the for-itself. But now, all of a sudden I raise my head: somebody was there, and has seen me. All at once I realize the vulgarity of my gesture in its entirety, and I am ashamed. It is evident that my shame is not reflective, because the Other's presence to my consciousness—even in the role of a catalyst—is incompatible with the attitude of reflection; within the field of my reflection the only consciousness that I can encounter is mine. Now, the Other is the indispensable intermediary between me and myself: I am ashamed of myself *as I appear* to the Other. And merely by appearing the Other enables me to pass judgment on myself as I might pass judgment on an object, for it is as an object that I appear to the Other. However, this object that has appeared to the Other is not an idle image in some other's mind. Such an image could, in effect, be entirely imputed to the Other, and it could not "touch" me. I might feel irritation or anger in relation to it, as if I were placed before a bad portrait of myself, attributing to me an ugliness or a baseness of expression that is not mine; but it would not be able to reach me at my core; inherently, shame is *recognition*. I recognize that I *am* as the Other sees me. There is no question, however, of any comparison between what I am for myself and what I am for the Other—as if I could find within myself, in the mode of being of the for-itself, an equivalent of what I am for the Other. In the first place, we do not encounter such a comparison as a particular psychological operation within ourselves: shame is an immediate shudder that runs through me from head to toe, without any discursive preparation. And next, that comparison is impossible: I am unable to place what I am in the intimacy of the for-itself—without distance, or detachment, or perspective—in relation to the being, unjustifiable and in itself, that I am for the Other. There is no yardstick or table of correspondences here. Moreover, the very notion of *vulgarity* implies an inter-monadic relation. One cannot be vulgar all alone. Thus the Other has not only shown me what I was; he has constituted me in a new type of being, obliging me to support new qualifications. This being was not in me as a potentiality before the Other appeared, because within the for-itself there could have been no place for it; and, even if we wanted to attribute to me a body that was entirely constituted *before* it existed for others, we could not accommodate my vulgarity or my clumsiness as potentialities within it because they are meanings and, as such, they surpass my body and refer us to a witness disposed to understand them and, at the same time, to the totality of my human-reality. But this new being that appears for the Other does not reside in the Other; I am responsible for it, as we can see clearly in the method of education that consists in making children "ashamed" of what they are. In this way shame is shame *of myself before the Other;* these two structures are inseparable. But, by the same token, I need the Other in order to fully grasp all the structures of my being; my for-itself refers to my for-the-Other. If, therefore, we want to grasp the relation of being between man and being-in-itself in its totality, we cannot rest content with the descriptions that we sketched out in the preceding chapters of this work. We are obliged to answer two quite differently formidable questions: in the first place, the question of the Other's existence, and then the question of my relation of *being* to the Other's being.

261

II. THE REEF OF SOLIPSISM

It is strange that realists have never really worried about the problem of Others. To the extent that, for the realist, "everything" is "given," it probably seems to him that he is given the Other. What, indeed, in the midst of the real, could be more real than the Other? Here is a thinking substance with the same essence as me, which cannot disappear into secondary qualities and primary qualities, and whose essential structures I can find in myself. Nonetheless, to the extent that realism attempts to account for knowledge by means of the world's acting on a thinking substance, it has not been concerned to establish any immediate and reciprocal action of the thinking substances between themselves. It is through the intermediary of the world that they communicate; between the Other's consciousness and mine, my body as a worldly thing and the Other's body are necessary intermediaries. The Other's soul is therefore separated from mine by all the distance that separates in the first instance my soul from my body, then my body from the Other's body, and finally the Other's body from his soul. And if it is uncertain whether the for-itself's relation to the body is a relation of externality (we will be discussing this problem later), it is at least evident that the relation of my body with the Other's body is a relation of pure indifferent externality. If souls are separated by their bodies, they are distinct in the way that this inkwell is distinct from this book, which means it is impossible to conceive of any immediate presence of the one to the other. And even if we were to allow that my soul was immediately present to the Other's body, I would still fall short, by the entire breadth of a body, of reaching through to his soul. If therefore realism founds its certainty on the spatio-temporal thing's presence "in person" to my consciousness, it cannot lay claim to the same evidence for the reality of the Other's soul, since, by its own admission, that soul is not given in person to mine: it is an absence, a meaning; the body points toward it without delivering it up. In brief, in a philosophy founded on intuition, there is no intuition of the Other's soul. Now, if we are not playing with words, this means that realism makes no room for the intuition of an Other: it does not help to say that at least we are given the other's body, and that this body is a certain presence of the Other, or of a part of the Other: it is true that the body belongs, as one of its structures, to the totality that we are calling "human-reality." But it is a man's body, precisely, only insofar as it exists within the indissoluble unity of that totality, just as an organ is a living organ only within the totality of an organism. By delivering the body to us not as contained within the human totality but apart from it, like a stone or a tree, or a piece of wax, the position of realism has killed the body as definitively as the physiologist's scalpel does, when it separates a piece of flesh from the totality of the living thing. It is not the Other's body that is present to the realist's intuition: it is a body—a body that, doubtless, has a particular ἕξις and particular aspects, but which belongs nevertheless within the large family of bodies. If it is true, for a spiritualist realism, that the soul is easier to know than the body, it will be easier to know the body than the Other's soul.

In truth, the realist does not greatly concern himself with this problem: that is because he holds the Other's existence to be certain. That is why the realist, positivist psychology of the nineteenth century, which took my fellow man's existence as granted, is exclusively concerned to establish the means by which I can know this existence, and to decipher on the body the traces of a consciousness that is foreign to me. The body, it is said, is an object whose ἕξις calls for a particular interpretation. The hypothesis that best accounts for its ways of behaving is that of a consciousness that is analogous to mine, whose various emotions it reflects. What remains to be explained is *how* we form this hypothesis: sometimes we will be told that it is through an analogy with what I know about myself, at other times that we learn from experience how to decipher, for example, the sudden coloring of a face as a promise of blows and of furious shouts. It will be readily acknowledged that these methods can only give us a knowledge of the Other that is *probable*; it will remain always probable that the Other is only a body. If animals are machines, why shouldn't the man whom I see walking down the street be one? Why shouldn't the behaviorists' radical hypothesis be correct? What I apprehend on this face is nothing but the effect of certain muscular contractions, and these in their turn are only the effect of a nerve impulse whose path is known to me. Why should we not reduce the set of these reactions to some simple or conditioned reflexes? But the majority of psychologists remain convinced of the Other's existence as a totalizing reality with the same structure as their own. For them, the Other's existence is certain and the knowledge that we have of it is probable. We can see the sophistry of realism. In fact we ought to reverse the terms of this claim and acknowledge that, if the Other is accessible to us only through the knowledge that we have of him, and if this knowledge is only conjectural, the Other's existence is only conjectural and the task of critical reflection will be to determine its exact degree of probability. Thus, through a curious reversal, by having posited the reality of the external world, the realist is obliged to slide into idealism when he considers the Other's existence. If the body is a real object, acting really on the thinking substance, the Other becomes a mere representation, whose *esse* is a mere *percipi*, i.e., whose existence is measured by the knowledge that we have of it. The more modern theories of *Einfühlung*, *sympathy*, and *forms* only improve the description of our means of presentifying the Other, but they do not place the debate on its true terrain: whether the Other is in the first instance *sensed*, or whether he appears in our experience as a singular form prior to any habit and in the absence of any analogical inference, it remains no less the case that the signifying and sensed object and the expressive form direct us purely and simply toward a human totality whose existence remains purely and simply conjectural.

If realism returns us in this way to idealism, would it not be more prudent to place ourselves immediately within the perspective of critical idealism? Since the Other is "my representation," would it not be better to investigate this representation within a system that reduces the set of objects to a connected group of representations, and which measures every existence by the knowledge that I have of it?

Yet someone like Kant will be of little help to us: concerned as he was to establish universal laws of subjectivity, the same for everyone, he did not in fact address the question of *persons*. The subject is only the essence that is common to those persons; it will no more allow us to determine their multiplicity than man's essence, for Spinoza, allows us to determine the multiplicity of concrete men. At first sight it seems therefore that Kant placed the problem of the Other among those that were not relevant to his critique. But let us take a closer look: the Other is given, as such, within our experience; the Other is an object, a particular object. Kant took up the point of view of the pure subject in order to determine the conditions of possibility not just for an object in general but for various categories of object: the physical object, the mathematical object, the object that is beautiful or ugly, and the one that presents teleological characteristics. From this point of view, his work has been reproached for its lacunae, and some have wanted, for example, to establish—in the Dilthey tradition—the conditions of possibility for the historical object, i.e., to attempt a critique of historical reason. Similarly, if it is true that the Other represents a particular type of object disclosed to our experience, it is necessary, even within the perspective of a strict Kantianism, to ask how knowledge of the Other is possible, i.e., to establish the conditions of possibility for the experience of others.

It would really be a great mistake to assimilate the problem of the Other to the problem of noumenal realities. Of course, if *Others* exist, and if they are similar to me, the question of their intelligible existence can arise in relation to them, as the question of my noumenal existence can arise for me; and also, of course, the same answer will apply in relation to them and to me: this noumenal existence may only be thought but not conceived.[1] But in my everyday experience, when I aim at the Other, what I am aiming at is not at all a noumenal reality—any more than I apprehend or aim at my intelligible reality when I gain empirical knowledge of my emotions or my thoughts. The Other is a phenomenon which refers to other phenomena: to an anger-phenomenon which he experiences toward me, to a series of thoughts which appear to him as phenomena of his inner sense; what I aim at in the Other is nothing more than what I might find in myself. Only these phenomena are radically distinct from all others.

In the first place, the Other's appearing within my experience is manifested by the presence of structured forms—such as facial and other expressions, actions and ways of behaving. These structured forms point toward an organizing unity that is situated by definition outside our experience. It is the Other's anger, insofar as it belongs to his inner sense and insofar as it is by its nature denied to my apperception, that is the meaning and perhaps the cause of the series of phenomena that I apprehend in my experience under the heading "expression," facial or otherwise. The Other, as the synthetic unity of his experiences, and, equally, as will and as passion, comes to organize my experience. What is involved is not the straightforward action of an unknowable noumenon on my sensibility but the constitution, within the field of my experience, by a being that is not me, of combined groups of phenomena. And these phenomena, in contrast to all the others, do not point toward possible experiences but toward experiences that are, by definition, outside my experience and which belong to a system that is inaccessible to me. But, on the other hand, the condition of possibility for any experience is that the subject should organize his impressions into a combined system. In this way we can find in things "only what we have put there." The other cannot therefore appear to us, on pain of contradiction, as organizing our experience: the phenomenon would be overdetermined. Can we still make use of causality here? This question is a good example of the ambiguous character of the other within Kantian philosophy. In effect, the only things that causality can combine together are phenomena. But

---

1 TN: ...*pensée, mais non conçue*. Although "think" and "conceive" seem very close in meaning, Sartre may be thinking here of Kant's distinction between being able to "think" something and to "know" it, i.e., to fully "conceive" it.

265   the anger felt by the other is, precisely, a phenomenon, and the furious expression that I perceive is another. Can there be a causal link between them? That would be consistent with their phenomenal nature; and in that sense I do not hold myself back from regarding the red of Paul's face as the effect of his anger; that forms part of the assertions I habitually make. But, on the other hand, causality makes sense only if it connects the phenomena of *one same* experience, and contributes to constituting that experience. Can it be used as a bridge between two radically separated experiences? Here we should note that, in using it in that capacity, I would strip it of its nature as an *ideal* unification of empirical appearances: Kant's causality is a unification of the moments of my time, in the form of irreversibility. How could we allow that it unified my time and the other's? What temporal relation could we establish between the decision to express oneself—as a phenomenon that appeared within the weave of the Other's experience—and its expression, a phenomenon in my experience? Simultaneity? Succession? But how could an instant of my time be in a relation of simultaneity or succession with an instant of the Other's time? Even if a preestablished harmony—which would in any case be incomprehensible within the Kantian perspective—were able to make the two times in question correspond, instant to instant, we would still be left with no less than *two* times without relation, since, for each of them, the unifying synthesis of moments is an act of the subject. The universality of time, in Kant's thought, is only the universality of a concept; it implies only that each temporality has to possess a determinate structure, and that the conditions of possibility for a temporal experience apply to every temporality. But this identity of temporal essence does not rule out an incommunicable diversity of times, any more than the identity of man's essence rules out an incommunicable diversity of human consciousnesses. In this way, since the relation between consciousnesses is by its nature unthinkable, the concept of the Other cannot *constitute* our experience; it needs to be ranked, along with the teleological concepts, among the *regulative* concepts. The Other therefore belongs to the category of "as-ifs"; it is an *a priori* hypothesis that has no justification other than the unity that it enables to be brought about within our experience, and which it is impossible to think without contradiction. Indeed, if it is possible to conceive— purely as an instance of knowledge—of an intelligible reality acting on

our sensibility, it is nevertheless not even thinkable that a phenomenon, whose reality is strictly relative to its appearing within the Other's experience, might really act upon a phenomenon of my experience. And even if we were to allow that the action of an intelligible reality might operate at the same time on my experience and on the Other's (such that the intelligible reality would be affecting the Other to just the extent that it was affecting me), it would remain no less radically impossible to establish, or even to postulate, a parallelism and a table of correspondences between two systems spontaneously constituting themselves.[2]

266

But, on the other hand, is the status of a regulative concept really appropriate for the concept of the Other? What is at issue is not, in fact, to establish a stronger unity between the phenomena of my experience by means of a purely formal concept which would simply enable discoveries of detail within the objects that appear to me. What is at issue is not a kind of a priori hypothesis that does not reach beyond the field of my experience, and which conduces to new investigations within the very limits of that field. The perception of the Other-object directs me to a coherent system of representations, and that system is not mine. Consequently, the Other is not, within my experience, a phenomenon that points toward my experience but rather one that refers in principle to phenomena that are situated outside any possible experience for me. And, to be sure, the concept of the Other enables discoveries and predictions within my system of representations, a narrowing in the weave of phenomena: thanks to the hypothesis of others, I am able to predict this movement on the basis of this expression. But this concept does not present itself in the manner of those scientific notions (like imaginary numbers, for example) which come up in the course of a physical calculation, as instruments, without being present in the empirical description of the problem, and in order to be eliminated from the results. The concept of the Other is not purely instrumental: rather than its existing for use in the unification of phenomena, we ought on the contrary to say that various categories of phenomena seem only to exist for it. The existence of a system of meanings and experiences that are radically distinct from

2 Sartre's note: Even if we were to escape Kant's metaphysics of nature, and the table of principles he drew up, it would be possible to conceive of radically different systems of physics on the basis of those principles.

mine is the fixed framework toward which diverse series of phenomena are *pointing*, even as they flow. And this framework, which is by definition external to my experience, is gradually fulfilled. That *Other*, whose relation to myself cannot be apprehended, and who is never given, is gradually constituted by us as a concrete object: he is not the instrument of which I make use to predict an event within my experience; rather, it is the events in my experience that are used to constitute the Other as Other, i.e., as a system of representations that is beyond reach as a concrete and knowable object. What I constantly aim at *through* my experiences is the Other's feelings, the Other's ideas, the Other's acts of will, the Other's character. That is because the Other is not, in point of fact, only the one whom I see but the one *who sees me*. I aim at the Other insofar as he is a connected system of experiences out of reach, within which I

267   figure as one object among others. But, to the extent to which I endeavor to determine the concrete nature of this system of representations, and the place that I occupy within it as an object, I radically transcend the field of my experience. I concern myself with a series of phenomena which can never, as a matter of principle, be accessible to my intuition and, in consequence, I exceed the entitlements of my knowledge; I try to connect experiences that will never be my experiences with each other and, in consequence, this work of construction and unification can in no way serve to unify my own experience; to the extent that the Other is an absence, he escapes from *nature*. We cannot therefore characterize the Other as a regulative concept. And doubtless some ideas—like the World, for example—also escape my experience as a matter of principle, but at least they relate to it, and have meaning only through it. The Other, on the contrary, is presented as in some sense the radical negation of my experience, since he is the one for whom I am not a subject but an object. As a subject of knowledge, therefore, I endeavor to determine as an object the subject who negates my character as a subject, and who is himself determining me as an object.

In this way, within the perspective of idealism, the *other* cannot be regarded either as a constitutive concept or as a regulative concept of my knowledge. He is conceived as real and yet I am unable to grasp his real relation with me; I construct him as an object, and yet he is not given through intuition; I posit him as a *subject* and yet it is as the object of my thoughts that I consider him. For the idealist, therefore, only two solutions remain: either to entirely get rid of the concept of the other, and prove that he is unnecessary to the constitution of my experience; or to affirm the Other's real existence, which amounts to positing a real and extra-empirical communication between consciousnesses.

The first solution is known under the name of solipsism. But if it is formulated, in keeping with its designation, as the affirmation of my ontological *solitude*, it is a pure metaphysical hypothesis, utterly unjustified and gratuitous, because it amounts only to saying that outside myself *nothing* exists; strictly, therefore, it goes beyond the field of my experience. But if it is introduced more modestly, as a refusal to leave the solid ground of experience, as a positive attempt not to make use of the concept of the Other, it is wholly logical, it remains at the level of critical positivism and—although it is in conflict with the most fundamental inclinations of our being—it draws its justification from the contradictions in the notion of *others*, as the idealist perspective regards it. A psychology that aspires to be exact and objective—such as Watson's "behaviorism"[3]—is ultimately only adopting solipsism as a working hypothesis. This does not involve any denial, within the field of my experience, of the presence of objects that we might designate as "mental entities," but only that a kind of ἐπ□□ή be operated with respect to the existence of systems of representations organized by a subject, and situated outside my experience.

268

Confronted with this solution, Kant and the majority of post-Kantians continue to affirm the Other's existence. But, in order to justify their affirmation, they can appeal only to good sense, or to our deep inclinations. As we know, Schopenhauer calls the solipsist "a madman locked up in an impregnable blockhouse."[4] What an admission of helplessness. The fact is that, by positing the Other's existence, one is abruptly bursting apart the framework of idealism, and falling back into a metaphysical realism. In the first place, by positing a plurality of closed systems that can communicate only through their outsides, we are implicitly

3 TN: Sartre is referring to the American psychologist John B. Watson (1878–1958), who is usually regarded as the founder of behaviorism.
4 TN: Sartre is thinking of the passage in Schopenhauer (2008: 124) where he writes, "As a serious conviction, on the other hand, it [theoretical egoism] could be found only in a madhouse; as such, what is then needed in response to it is not so much a proof as a cure."

reestablishing the notion of substance. Of course these systems, since they are mere systems of representation, are non-substantial. But their reciprocal externality is an *in itself externality*: it is, without being known; we do not even grasp its effects with certainty, since the solipsist's hypothesis remains always possible. We are confined to positing this in-itself nothingness as an absolute fact: rather than being relative to our knowledge of the Other, it is, on the contrary, what conditions that knowledge. Therefore, even if consciousnesses are only pure conceptual connections of phenomena, even if the principle of their existence is the *"percipere"* and the *"percipi,"* it remains no less the case that the *multiplicity* of these relational systems is an in-itself multiplicity and that it transforms them immediately into in-itself systems. But in addition, if I posit, as the correlative to my experience of the Other's anger, a subjective experience of anger in another system, I am reinstating the system of the true image, which Kant took such pains to get rid of. Of course, what we have here is a relation of concordance between two phenomena—the anger that is perceived in the movements and facial expressions, and the anger that is apprehended as a phenomenal reality of inner sense—and not a relation between a phenomenon and a thing in itself. But it remains no less the case that the criterion of truth here is the conformity of thought to its object, and not the representations' agreement with each other. In fact, precisely because any recourse to the noumenon here is set aside, the phenomenon of the experienced anger is, in relation to that of the observed anger, like that of something *real and objective* to its image. The problem really is the problem of adequate representation, since there is something *real*, and a mode of apprehension of this reality.[5] If it were a question of my own anger, I could regard its subjective manifestations and its physiological and objectively discernible manifestations as two series of effects of a single cause, without one of these series representing the anger's *truth* or the *reality*, while the other represented only its effect or its image. But if one of the series of phenomena resides in the Other, and the other in me, the first functions as the reality of the other, and the realist schema of truth is the only one that can apply here.

269

5 TN: ... *comme le réel objectif* ... I have slightly altered the sentence, as Sartre's use of "*le réel*" as a substantive sounds so odd in English ("an objective real").

Thus we abandoned the realist way of posing the problem only because it necessarily led to idealism; we deliberately placed ourselves within the idealist perspective and have gained nothing from it because, conversely, to the extent that it rejects the solipsist hypothesis, it leads to a dogmatic and completely unjustified realism. Let us see if we can understand this sudden inversion of the doctrines, and if we may be able to draw some instruction from this paradox, which may help us to pose the problem correctly.

At the origin of the problem of the Other's existence there is a fundamental presupposition: that the Other is indeed the other, which is to say the me that is not me; here, therefore, we are apprehending a negation as a constitutive structure of Other-being. The presupposition common to idealism and to realism is that the constituting negation is a negation of externality. The Other is the one who is not me, and who I am not. This not indicates a nothingness as a given element of separation between the Other and myself. Between the Other and myself, there is a nothingness of separation. The origin of this nothingness derives neither from me, nor from the Other, nor from a reciprocal relation between the Other and myself; rather, on the contrary, it is in its origin the foundation of any relation between the Other and myself, as the initial absence of any relation. For the fact is that the occasion of the Other's empirically appearing to me is the perception of a body, and this body is an in-itself external to my body; the relation that joins and separates these two bodies is spatial in type, as a relationship between things that are not related to each other, as pure externality insofar as it is given. The realist who believes he apprehends the Other through his body considers therefore that he is separated from the Other as one body from another body, which means that the ontological meaning of the negation contained in the judgment "I am not Paul" is of the same type as that of the negation contained in the judgment "The table is not the chair." In this way, as the separation of the consciousnesses is attributable to the bodies, there is something like an original space between the different consciousnesses, which is to say a nothingness that is, precisely, given, a distance that is absolute and passively undergone. Of course, idealism reduces my body and the Other's body to objective systems of representation. For Schopenhauer, my body is nothing other than the "immediate object." But we do not thereby eliminate the absolute distance between the consciousnesses. As a complete system of representations—in other words, each monad—can be limited only by itself, it cannot maintain any relation with anything other than itself. The knowing subject can neither limit nor become limited by another subject. It is isolated through its positive plenitude and, in consequence, a *spatial* separation is preserved, as the very type of externality, between itself and another, similarly isolated, system. In this way it is still *space* that implicitly separates my consciousness from that of the Other. And, we ought also to add, the idealist resorts, without being aware of it, to a "third man" in order to get this external negation to appear. For, as we have seen, every external relation, insofar as it is not constituted by its terms themselves, requires a witness to posit it. Thus, for the idealist and for the realist, a conclusion is imposed: by virtue of the Other's being revealed to us within a spatial world, there is a space—real or ideal—that separates us from the Other.

This presupposition brings in its wake a serious consequence: if in fact I am obliged to be, in relation to the Other, in the mode of indifferent externality, I will not be able to be any more affected in my being by the Other's arising or by his abolition than an in-itself is by the appearing or disappearing of another in-itself. In consequence, from the moment that the Other becomes unable to act on my being through his being, the only way in which he can be revealed to me is by appearing as an *object* to my knowledge. But we must understand that as meaning that I have to constitute the Other as the unification imposed by my spontaneity on a diverse set of impressions, which means I am the one who constitutes the Other within the field of his experience. The Other can only therefore be an *image* for me, even if, moreover, the entire theory of knowledge that I have constructed aims to reject this notion of the image; and only a witness who is external at the same time to myself and to the Other will be able to compare the image to the model, and to decide if it is true. Moreover, for this witness to have authority, he must not in his turn stand in a relation of externality to me and to the Other; otherwise he would only be able to know us through images. It would be necessary for him, within the ecstatic unity of his being, to be at one and the same time *here*, with me, as the internal negation of myself—and *over there*, with the Other, as the internal negation of the Other. In this way, the recourse to God that we find in Leibniz is quite simply a recourse to an internal negation. This is what the theological notion of *creation* conceals: God is, and at the same time is not, myself and the Other, since he creates us. Indeed, it is fitting that he should *be* myself, in order to apprehend my reality without intermediary and in apodictic evidence, and that he should not be me, in order to retain his impartiality as a witness, and to be able to be, and to not be, over there, the Other. The image of creation is the most adequate one here, because in the creative act I can see right to the depths of what I am creating—because what I am creating is me— and yet what I am creating is opposed to me, by closing in on itself in an affirmation of objectivity. In this way, the spatializing presupposition does not leave us any choice: we must have recourse to God, or fall into a probabilistic position which leaves the door open for solipsism. But this conception of a God who is his creatures lands us in a new difficulty: the one that is manifested by the problem of substances in post-Cartesian thought. If God is me and if he is the Other, what will guarantee my own existence? If creation must be *continuous*, I remain constantly suspended between a distinct existence and a pantheistic fusion within the Creative Being. If creation is an original act, and if I have closed in on myself against God, nothing any longer guarantees my existence to God, because he is no longer joined to me by anything but a relation of externality, like the sculptor to the completed statue, and henceforth he can know me only through images. In these conditions, the notion of God, even while it reveals the negation of interiority as being the only possible connection between consciousnesses, makes all its insufficiency apparent: God is neither necessary nor sufficient as the guarantor of the Other's existence; in addition, the existence of God as intermediary between me and the Other already supposes the presence, in a connection of interiority, of an Other to myself, since God, being endowed with the essential qualities of a Spirit, appears as the quintessence of the Other, and since he must be able to be in a connection of interiority with myself for a real foundation of the Other's existence to have validity for me. It seems therefore that a positive theory of the existence of the Other ought to be able to avoid solipsism and at the same time do without any recourse to God, if it envisages my original relation to the Other as a negation of interiority, i.e., as a negation that posits the original distinction of the Other and myself to exactly the extent to which it determines me by the Other, and determines the Other by me. Can we consider the question from this perspective?

271

III. HUSSERL, HEGEL, HEIDEGGER

The philosophy of the nineteenth and twentieth centuries appears to have understood that we cannot escape solipsism if we set out by conceiving myself and the Other in terms of two separate substances: indeed, we must take any union of these substances to be impossible. For that reason, an examination of these modern theories reveals an attempt to apprehend, at the heart of any instance of consciousness, a fundamental and transcendent connection to the Other that is constitutive of each consciousness even as it arises. But if we appear to have abandoned the premise of external negation, its essential consequence has been retained—in other words, the claim that my fundamental connection to the Other is brought about through *knowledge*.

272   Indeed, when Husserl concerns himself with refuting solipsism in the *Cartesian Meditations* and in *Formal and Transcendental Logic*, he believes that, by showing that the recourse to the Other is an indispensable condition of the constitution of a world, he has succeeded. Without entering into the detail of the doctrine, we will confine ourselves to pointing out its mainspring: for Husserl, the world as it is revealed to consciousness is inter-monadic. The Other is present within it not only as this concrete and empirical appearance but as a permanent condition of its unity and its richness. Whether I consider—in solitude or in company—this table, or tree, or this section of the wall, the Other is always there as a layer of constitutive meanings that belong to the very object I am considering; he is there, in short, as the true guarantor of its objectivity. And as my psychophysical self is contemporary with the world, forms part of the world, and falls, along with the world, within the scope of the phenomenological reduction, the Other appears as necessary even for the constitution of this self. If I am to doubt the existence of my friend Pierre—or of others in general—insofar as this existence is by definition outside my experience, I will be obliged also to doubt my concrete being, my empirical reality as a teacher with this inclination, these habits, this character. There is no privilege for my self: my empirical Ego and the Other's empirical Ego appear within the world at the same time; and the meaning of "the Other" in general is just as necessary to the constitution of one of these "Egos" as it is to the other. In this way, each object, rather than being constituted (as it is for Kant) by a mere relation to a *subject*,

appears within my concrete experience as universal; it is given from the outset as possessing systems of references to an indefinite plurality of consciousnesses; the Other is disclosed to me with the table, with the wall—as a constant referent of the object in question—just as much as he is on the occasion of particular appearances of Pierre or of Paul.

Of course, in relation to the classical doctrines, these views amount to progress. It is incontestable that the implement-thing refers us, from the moment it is disclosed, to a plurality of for-itselfs. We will return to this. It is evident too that the meaning of "the Other" cannot come from experience, or from an argument from analogy made on the occasion of experience: rather, and quite to the contrary, it is in the light of the concept of the Other that experience is interpreted. Does that mean that the concept of the Other is *a priori*? We will try, in what follows, to determine this. But, despite these incontestable advantages, Husserl's theory does not seem to be markedly different from Kant's. The point is that, if my empirical Ego is no more sure than the Other's, Husserl has retained the transcendental subject, which is radically distinct from it, and which is extremely similar to the Kantian subject. Now, what needs to be demonstrated is not the parallelism between the empirical "Egos," which nobody is calling into doubt, but the parallelism between the transcendental subjects. In fact, the Other is *never* the empirical character whom I encounter in my experience: he is the transcendental subject to whom this character refers by his very nature. Thus the real problem is that of the connection of transcendental subjects beyond experience. If the reply to this is that the transcendental subject refers from the outset to other subjects, *in order to constitute* the noematic totality, we can easily respond by saying that it is as *meanings* that it refers to them. Here the Other will be like an additional category, which allows a world to be constituted, and not a real being, existing beyond that world. And, doubtless, the "category" of the Other implies, in its very meaning, a reference from the other side of the world to a subject, but this reference can only be hypothetical, and its value is purely that of the content of a unifying concept; its validity is within and for the world, its authority is limited to the world, and the Other is by his nature outside the world. Moreover, Husserl has deprived himself even of the possibility of understanding what the Other's extraworldly *being* could mean, since he defines *being* as the mere indication of an infinite series of operations to be effected. There could be no better way of mak-

273

ing knowledge the measure of being. Now, even if we allow that knowledge is generally the measure of being, the Other's being is measured in its reality through the knowledge that the Other has of himself, and not through the knowledge I gain of him. What needs to be reached by me is the Other, not insofar as I acquire knowledge of him but insofar as he acquires knowledge of himself, which is impossible: that would actually imply an identification of my interiority with the Other's. What we come back to here, therefore, is that distinction in principle between the Other and myself, which is derived not from the externality of our bodies but from the simple fact that each of us exists as interiority, and that a legitimate knowledge of interiority can be gained only within interiority, which rules out as a matter of principle any *knowledge* of the Other as he knows himself, i.e., as he is. Husserl understood this, moreover, since he defines "the Other" as he is disclosed to our concrete experience as an *absence*. But how—at least in Husserl's philosophy—can there be a full intuition of an absence? The Other is the object of empty intentions; the Other denies himself to us as a matter of principle and flees. The only reality that therefore remains is that of my intention: the Other, to the extent that he appears concretely within my experience, is the empty noema that corresponds to my aiming toward the Other; to the extent to which he appears as a transcendental concept, he is a set of operations in the unification and constitution of my experience. Husserl replies to the solipsist that the Other's existence is just as certain as the existence of the world, including my psychophysical existence within the world; but the solipsist does not disagree—"It is just as certain," he will say, "but not more." The world's existence, he will add, is measured by the knowledge I have of it; it cannot be otherwise for the Other's existence.

274   I once believed that I could escape solipsism by denying Husserl the existence of his transcendental "Ego."[6] At the time it seemed to me that, since I was emptying it of its subject, nothing would be left in my consciousness that could be privileged in relation to the Other. But in fact, even though I remain persuaded that the hypothesis of the transcendental subject is useless and harmful, abandoning it does not advance the ques-

6 Sartre's note: "The Transcendence of the Ego," in *Recherches Philosophiques* (1937). TN: Sartre's reference is to the journal where the text was originally published. It is translated into English as Sartre (2004a).

tion of the Other's existence by a single step. Even if, outside the empirical Ego, there was *nothing other* than the consciousness of that Ego—that is, a transcendental field without a subject—it would remain no less true that my assertion of the Other postulates and demands the existence, beyond the world, of a similar transcendental field and in consequence that, here too, the only way of escaping solipsism will be by proving that my transcendental consciousness is, in its very being, affected by the extraworldly existence of other consciousnesses of the same type. Thus, by having reduced being to a series of meanings, the only connection that Husserl was able to establish between my being and the Other's is that of *knowledge*; he cannot therefore, any more than Kant could, escape solipsism.

If, without observing the rules of chronological succession, we follow those of a kind of timeless dialectic, the solution that Hegel provides to the problem—in the first volume of the *Phenomenology of Spirit*—may seem to us to show significant progress in relation to that proposed by Husserl. Now it is no longer for the constitution of the world and of my empirical "ego" that the Other's appearing is indispensable but for my consciousness's existence itself, as self-consciousness. As self-consciousness, in fact, the Ego intuits itself. The equivalence of "Ego = Ego" or "I = I" is just what expresses this fact. In the first place, this self-consciousness is a pure identity with itself, pure existence for itself. It has certainty of itself, but this certainty still lacks truth. In point of fact, this certainty could be true only to the extent to which its own existence for itself could appear to it as an independent object. In this way, self-consciousness at first takes the form of a syncretic relation, without truth, between a subject and an object that has not yet been objectified, which is that subject itself. As it is impelled to actualize its concept by becoming conscious of itself in every respect, it aims to make itself valid externally, by endowing itself with objectivity and manifest existence: it is a matter of explicating the "I am I" and producing itself as an object, in order to attain the final stage of the development—a stage that is, naturally, in another sense, the first motor of consciousness's becoming—which is the general self-consciousness that recognizes itself in other self-consciousnesses and which is identical with them, and with itself. The intermediary is the other. The other appears with myself, since self-consciousness is identical with itself through the exclusion of every other. Thus the primary fact is the plurality of consciousnesses, and this plurality is actualized in the form of a double and reciprocal relation of exclusion. Here we are in the presence of that link of internal negation which we demanded earlier. No external or in itself nothingness separates my consciousness from the Other's consciousness; rather, it is through the very fact of being me that I exclude the other: the other excludes me by being himself, and he is what I exclude by being me. Each consciousness bears directly on the other, in a reciprocal imbrication of their being. This enables us, at the same time, to determine the way in which the other appears to me: he is what is other than me; therefore he is given as an inessential object, with a character of negativity. But this other is also a self-consciousness. As such he appears to me as an ordinary object, immersed in the being of life. And, equally, that is how I appear to the other: as a concrete, sensuous and immediate existence. Here the terrain occupied by Hegel is not that of the univocal relation from me (as apprehended through the *cogito*) to the other but that of the reciprocal relation that he defines as the "beholding of oneself in another."[7] Indeed, it is only insofar as each one is opposed to the other that he can be absolutely for itself; each one affirms against the other, and in relation to the other, his right to be as an individual. Thus the *cogito* itself cannot be a point of departure for philosophy; in fact it can arise only as a consequence of my appearing for myself in the form of individuality, and this appearing is conditioned by the other's recognition. It is not at all on the basis of the *cogito* that the problem of the other arises; on the contrary, it is the other's existence that makes the *cogito* possible as the abstract moment in which the ego apprehends itself as an object. In this way the "moment" that Hegel calls "being for the other" is a necessary stage in the development of self-consciousness; the path of internality passes through the other. But the other is of interest to me only to the extent to which he is another Ego, an Ego-object for my Ego, and, conversely, to the extent to which he reflects my Ego, i.e., insofar as I am an object for him. Through the necessity that means I can be an object for myself only over there, within the other, I am obliged to obtain the *recognition* of my being from the other. But if my consciousness for *itself* has to be mediated in relation to itself through another consciousness, its being-for-itself—and in consequence

---

7 TN: Sartre would have found this quotation in Lefebvre's anthology. I quote from the English translation, at Hegel (1986: 62, §31).

its being in general—depends on the other. As I appear to the other, so I am. In addition, since the other is as he appears to me and since my being depends on the other, the way in which I appear to myself—i.e., the moment in which my consciousness of myself develops—depends on the way in which the other appears to me. The value of the other's recognition of me depends on the value of the recognition by me of the other. In this sense, to the extent to which the other intuits me as bound to a body and immersed in life, I am myself *only an other*. In order to make the other recognize me, I have to risk my own life. To risk one's life, in fact, is to show oneself as not being bound to the objective form, or to any determinate existence. But at the same time I pursue the other's *death*. In other words, I want to become mediated by another who must be only other—i.e., by a dependent consciousness whose essential character is that of existing only for another. That will be brought about in the very moment in which I risk my life because, in the struggle against the other, I have abstracted from my sensuous being by *risking* it; the other, on the contrary, prefers life to freedom, thereby showing that he has not been able to posit himself as not being bound to the objective form. He remains therefore bound to external things in general; he appears to me and appears to himself as *inessential*. He is *the Slave* and I am *the Master*; for him, I am the one who is the essence. In this way the famous "Master-Slave" relation appears, which was to influence Marx so profoundly. We do not need to enter into its details. It will suffice for us to note that the Slave is the Master's truth, but this unilateral and unequal recognition is insufficient, because the truth of his self-certainty is, for the Master, an inessential consciousness; he is not therefore certain of *being for itself* as truth. For this truth to be attained, what is required is a "moment in which what the master does to the other he also does to himself, and what the slave does to himself he also does to the other."[8] At this moment the general self-consciousness will appear, which recognizes itself in other self-consciousnesses and is identical to them and to itself.

Thus Hegel's brilliant intuition here is to make me depend on the

276

---

8 Sartre's note: *Phénoménologie de l'Esprit*, p. 148 (Edition Lasson). TN: Sartre found this passage in the Lefebvre anthology. The corresponding passage in the English translation is Hegel (1977: 116, §191) (which I have altered slightly in the text to match Sartre's French—for example, by using "Master" and "Slave" rather than "Lord" and "Bondsman").

other in my being. I am, he says, a being for itself which is only for itself through an other. It is therefore in my heart that the Other penetrates me. I cannot put him in doubt without doubting myself, since "self-consciousness is . . . only real insofar as it knows its echo (and reflection) in another."[9] And as doubt itself implies a consciousness that exists for itself, the Other's existence conditions my attempt at doubting it, to the same degree that, for Descartes, my existence conditions methodical doubt. In this way, solipsism appears to be decisively taken out of action. By moving from Husserl to Hegel we have made enormous progress: first, the negation that constitutes the Other is direct, internal, and reciprocal; next, it takes on and bites into each consciousness in the very depths of its being; the problem is posed at the level of inner being, that of the universal and transcendental I; it is in my essential being that I depend on the Other's essential being, and my being for myself does not need to be opposed to my being for the Other; far from it, being-for-the-Other appears as a necessary condition of my being for myself.

277

And yet, despite its scope, despite the rich and deep insights at the level of detail with which the theory of the Master and Slave is teeming, can we be satisfied by it?

To be sure, Hegel has raised the question of the being of consciousnesses. What he examines is being-for-itself and being-for-the-Other, and he presents each consciousness as including the other's *reality*. But it is no less clear that this ontological problem remains formulated throughout in terms of knowledge. The mainspring of the struggle of consciousnesses is the attempt each of them makes to transform its self-certainty into truth. And we know that this truth can be attained only insofar as my consciousness becomes an *object* for the other, at the same time as the other becomes an *object* for mine. Thus Hegel replies to the question raised by idealism—how is the other able to be an object for me?—by remaining on idealism's own territory: if there is an Ego in truth for whom the *other* is an object, that is because there is an *other* for whom the Ego is an object. Here the measure of being is still knowledge, and Hegel does not even conceive that there might be a being-for-the-

---

9 Sartre's note: *Propedeutik*, p. 20 (first edition of the complete works). TN: Sartre found this quotation in the Lefebvre anthology. The corresponding passage in the English translation is at Hegel (1986: 63, §39) (from which I depart slightly to match Sartre's French).

Other that was not ultimately reducible to an "object-being." Therefore the universal self-consciousness that tries to emerge through all of these dialectical stages is, by his own admission, tantamount to a pure empty form: the "I am I." "This proposition of Self-Consciousness," he writes, "is devoid of all contents."[10] And elsewhere: "[It is] the movement of absolute abstraction which consists in sublating all immediate existence and which leads to the purely negative being of self-identical consciousness."[11] Universal self-consciousness, itself the final term of this dialectical conflict, has not become enriched in the midst of its transformations: on the contrary, it has been entirely stripped bare; it is nothing more than "I know that another knows me as myself." Doubtless that is because, for absolute idealism, being and knowledge are identical. But where will this assimilation lead us?

In the first place, this "I am I"—a pure universal formula of identity—has nothing in common with the concrete consciousness we tried to describe in our Introduction. We established there that the being of consciousness (of) self could not be defined in terms of knowledge. Knowledge begins with reflection, but the reflection-reflecting play is not a subject-object dyad, not even implicitly, and it does not depend in its being on any transcendent consciousness; rather, its mode of being is precisely to be in question for itself. Then we showed, in Chapter 1 of Part Two, that the relation of the reflection to the reflecting was in no way a relation of identity, and could not be reduced to Hegel's "Ego = Ego" or "I am I." The reflection produces itself as not being the reflection; what we have here is a being that nihilates itself in its being, and which tries in vain to merge into itself as itself. If it is true that this description is the only one that allows us to understand the original fact of consciousness, we will judge Hegel as having failed to take account of that abstract duplication of the Ego which he presents as the equivalent of self-consciousness. Finally, we succeeded in ridding the pure unreflected consciousness of the transcendental I that was obscuring it, and we showed that ipseity—

278

---

10 Sartre's note: *Propedeutik*, p. 20 (first edition of the complete works). TN: The counterpart English translation is at Hegel (1986: 59, §23).

11 TN: Sartre does not provide a reference for this quotation, which comes from *Phenomenology of Spirit* and is included in *Morceaux Choisis*. The corresponding English translation is at Hegel (1977: 113, §186). I have departed from it where necessary to match Sartre's French.

the foundation of personal existence—was entirely different from an Ego, or an Ego's reference to itself. Therefore there could be no question of defining consciousness in terms of transcendental egology. In brief, consciousness is a concrete and *sui generis* being, not an abstract and unjustifiable relation of identity; it is ipseity, and not the site of an opaque and pointless Ego; its being allows transcendental reflection to reach it and there is a *truth* of consciousness that does not depend on the Other, but consciousness's very *being*, as independent of knowledge, preexists its truth. In this domain, as in naïve realism, it is being that is the measure of truth, because the truth of a reflective intuition is measured by its conformity to being: consciousness *was there* before being known. If therefore consciousness affirms itself in the face of the Other, it is because it lays claim to the recognition of its being, and not of an abstract truth. It is difficult to conceive, in fact, that the ardent and perilous struggle of the master and the slave could have as its only outcome the recognition of so impoverished and abstract a formulation as "I am I." Moreover that struggle itself would involve a deception, since the end that was finally attained would be universal self-consciousness, the "intuition of the self existing through the self." Here, as everywhere, we need to oppose Hegel with Kierkegaard, who represents the claims of the individual as such. What the individual claims is his achievement as an individual, the recognition of his concrete being and not the objective explication of a universal structure. Doubtless the *rights* that I claim from the Other posit the universality of the *self* [*soi*]; the respectability of persons demands the recognition of my person as universal. But it is my concrete and individual being that takes shape within this universal and fulfills it, and the rights that I claim are for that being-*there*: here, the particular supports and founds the universal; in this case, the universal can have no meaning unless it exists *for the purpose of* the individual.

Here again, this assimilation of being to knowledge will result in a large number of errors or impossibilities. We will summarize them here under *two headings*. In other words, we will level against Hegel a twofold accusation of optimism.

In the first place, it seems to us that Hegel sins through his epistemological optimism. Indeed it seems to him that it is possible for the *truth* of self-consciousness to appear, which is to say that an objective agreement

279

can be achieved between consciousnesses under the so-called recognition of me by the Other and of the Other by me. This recognition can
be simultaneous and reciprocal: "I know that the Other knows me as
myself"—it produces the universality of self-consciousness in truth. But
the correct formulation of the problem of the Other makes this transition
to the universal impossible. If in point of fact the Other is to return my
"self" to me, it is necessary, at least at the end of the dialectical evolution,
that there should be a commensurability between what I am for him,
what he is for me, what I am for myself, and what he is for himself. Of
course, this homogeneity does not exist at the outset, as Hegel agrees:
the Master-Slave relation is not reciprocal. But he claims that it must be
possible for reciprocity to be established. In effect, what happens is that
at the beginning he introduces a confusion—so deft that it appears to be
voluntary—between *objecthood* and life. The other, he says, appears to me
as an object. Now, this object is *Me* within the other. And when Hegel
wants to give a better definition of this objecthood, he discerns three
elements within it:

> This apprehension of oneself in the other is: 1. the abstract moment of
> self-sameness. 2. But each has also the determination of appearing to
> the other as an external object, and, insofar as an immediate, sensuous,
> and concrete existence. 3. Each exists absolutely for itself and as an
> individual insofar as opposed to the other.[12]

We can see that the abstract moment of self-identity is given in the
knowledge of the other. It is given along with two other moments of
the total structure. But the curious thing in a philosopher of Synthesis is
that Hegel did not ask himself whether these three elements might not
each react against the other in such a way as to constitute a new form,
which would be resistant to analysis. He clarifies his point of view in
Phenomenology of Spirit by asserting that the other appears at first as inessential (that is the point of the third moment, quoted above) and as a
"consciousness immersed in the being of life." But this is a matter of pure
coexistence between the abstract moment and life. It suffices therefore

12 Sartre's note: *Propedeutik*, p. 18. TN: The corresponding passage in English translation is
    Hegel (1986: 61, §31).

for me or the other to risk our life for us to bring about, in the very act of offering ourselves to danger, an analytical separation between life and consciousness:

> What the other is for consciousness, each one is itself for the other; each in its own self through its own activity, and through the activity of the other, achieves this pure abstraction of being for itself. . . . To present itself as the pure abstraction of self-consciousness consists in showing itself as the pure negation of its objective form, in showing that it is not bound to any specific existence . . . in showing that it is not bound to life.[13]

And of course Hegel will say later on that, through the experience of risk, and of the danger of death, self-consciousness learns that life is as essential to it as pure self-consciousness; but that is from another point of view, and it remains no less the case that I can always separate, in the other, the pure truth of self-consciousness from its life. In this way the slave apprehends the master's self-consciousness; he is its truth even while, as we have seen, this truth is not yet adequate.

But does it amount to the same thing to say that the Other appears to me as a matter of principle as an object, or to say that he appears to me as bound to some particular existence, as immersed in life? If at this point we stay at the level of pure logical hypotheses, we will observe right at the start that it is quite possible for the Other to be given to a consciousness in the form of an object, without that object being specifically bound to that contingent object which we know as a living body. In fact our experience only presents us with conscious and living individuals, but as a matter of principle we need to take note that the Other is an object for me because he is the Other, and not because he appears on the occasion of a body-object: otherwise we would fall back into the spatializing illusion that we discussed earlier. In this way, what is essential to the Other as Other is objectivity, and not life. Moreover, Hegel started out from that logical observation. But if it is true that the connection of a consciousness to life

---

13 Sartre's note: *Phenomenology of Spirit.* Ibid. TN: The corresponding passage in English translation is Hegel (1977: 113, §§186–187). I have made slight changes to the translation to match Sartre's French.

does not deform the "abstract moment of self-consciousness" in its nature, which remains there, immersed, and always liable to be discovered, does the same thing apply to objectivity? In other words, since we know that a consciousness is before being known, isn't a known consciousness completely modified just by virtue of being known? Does a consciousness that appears as an object for a consciousness continue to be a consciousness? It is easy to answer this question: the being of self-consciousness is such that in its being its being is in question; therefore, it is pure interiority. It constantly refers to an *itself* that it has to be. Its being is defined by this: that it is this being in the mode of being what it is not, and of not being what it is. Its being is, therefore, a radical exclusion of all objectivity: I am the one who cannot be an object for myself, and who cannot even conceive for himself of existence in the form of an object (other than at the level of the reflective splitting into two—but we saw that reflection is the drama of the being who cannot be an object for himself). And this is not because of any lack of distance, or an intellectual preclusion, or a limit that is imposed on my knowledge but because objectivity demands an explicit negation: the object is what I make myself not be, whereas what I am, myself, is the one who I make myself be. I am myself everywhere, I cannot escape myself, I reapprehend myself from behind, and even if I could attempt to make myself an object, I would already be myself, at the heart of this object that I am, and from the very center of that object I would have to be the subject who was looking at it. That is, moreover, what Hegel foresaw when he said that the Other's existence is necessary for me to be an object for myself. But by postulating that self-consciousness expresses itself through the "I is I"—i.e., by assimilating it to self-knowledge—he missed the consequences to be drawn from these first observations, since he introduced into consciousness itself something like an object in potentiality which the Other would need only to draw out, without modifying it. But if to be an object is precisely *to-not-be-myself*, the fact of being an object for a consciousness radically modifies consciousness, not in what it is for itself but in its appearing to the Other. The Other's consciousness is that which I am able merely to contemplate and which therefore appears to me as purely given, rather than being that which has myself to be. It is something that is delivered to me within universal time—i.e., in the original dispersion of moments—rather than appearing to me within the unity of its own temporalization. For the only consciousness that can appear to me in its

281

own temporalization is *mine*, and it can do that only by renouncing all objectivity. In brief, the *for-itself* is unknowable as for-itself by the Other. The object that I apprehend by the name "Other" appears to me in a form that is radically *other*: the Other is not *for himself* as he appears to me; I do not appear to myself as I am *for the Other*; I am no more able to apprehend myself for myself as I am for the Other than I am able to apprehend what the Other is for himself on the basis of the Other-object which appears to me. How therefore could we establish a universal concept that subsumes, under "self-consciousness," my *consciousness* for myself and (of) myself and my *knowledge* of the Other? But that is not all: according to Hegel, the other is an object and I apprehend myself as an object in the other. Now, one of these claims destroys the other: for it to be possible for me to appear to myself as an object in the other, I would have to apprehend the other as a subject, i.e., to apprehend him in his interiority. But insofar as the other appears to me as an object, my objectivity for him cannot appear to me: of course I can apprehend that the other-object *relates himself to me* through intentions and actions but, just because he is an object, the Other-mirror becomes obscure and no longer reflects anything because these intentions and these actions are things in the world, apprehended in World-Time, observed and contemplated, and whose meaning is an object for me. Thus I am able to appear to myself only as a transcendent quality to which the Other's actions and intentions refer but, precisely, as the Other's objectivity destroys my objectivity for him, it is as an internal subject that I apprehend myself, as that to which these intentions and these acts relate. And we must be careful to understand this apprehension of myself by myself purely in terms of consciousness and not of knowledge: in having to be what I am in the form of an ecstatic consciousness (of) myself, I apprehend the Other as an object that indicates me. In this way Hegel's optimism ends in failure: between the Other-object and me-subject there is no commensurability, any more than between my consciousness (of) self and my consciousness of the other. I cannot know myself in the Other if the Other is at first an object for me, nor can I apprehend the Other in his true being, i.e., in his subjectivity. No universal knowledge can be derived from the relation of consciousnesses. Let us describe that as their ontological separation.

But there is another, more fundamental form of optimism in Hegel, which we may suitably call his ontological optimism. For him, the truth is in effect the truth of the Whole.[14] And, in order to consider the problem of the other, he locates himself in the perspective of truth, i.e., of the Whole. In this way, when Hegel's monism considers the relation of consciousnesses, it does not locate itself within any particular consciousness. Even though the Whole is to be actualized, it is already there as the truth of all that is true. When Hegel writes, therefore, that every consciousness, being identical with itself, is other than the other, he has established himself within the whole, outside the consciousnesses, and is considering them from the point of view of the Absolute. For the consciousnesses[15] are moments of the whole, moments that are, by themselves, "unselbstständig," and the whole is what mediates between the consciousnesses. This generates an ontological optimism parallel to the epistemological optimism; the plurality can and must be sublated toward the totality. But, if Hegel can affirm the reality of this sublation, it is because he has already given it to himself from the outset. In fact, he has forgotten his own consciousness; he is the Whole and, in this respect, if he resolves the problem of the consciousnesses so easily, that is because the question never posed a genuine problem for him. In fact, he does not raise the question of the relations between his own consciousness and the Other's but, abstracting entirely from his own, he investigates purely and simply the relationship between Others' consciousnesses, i.e., the relationship between consciousnesses that are already objects for him and whose nature, according to him, is precisely to be a specific type of object (the subject-object) and which, from the totalizing standpoint at which he places himself, are strictly equivalent to each other, without any one of them being separated from the others by some particular prerogative. But if Hegel forgets himself, we cannot forget Hegel and so we are directed back to the *cogito*. If in fact, as we have established, the being of my consciousness is strictly irreducible to knowledge, then I cannot transcend my being toward a reciprocal and universal relation from which I could see, at the same time, my being and the being of others as equivalents. On the contrary, I must establish

14 TN: Sartre is paraphrasing Hegel's famous claim that "the True is the whole" (Hegel 1977: 11, §20).

15 TN: ... *les consciences* ... By emphasizing *les*, I take it that Sartre is emphasizing that the article is in the plural (which gets lost in the English "the").

myself *in my being*, and raise the problem of the Other on the basis of my being. In brief, the only reliable point of departure is the interiority of the *cogito*. And we must take this to mean that each person must be able, by setting out from his own interiority, to find the Other's being as a transcendence that conditions the very being of this interiority, which necessarily implies that the multiplicity of consciousnesses cannot as a matter of principle be surpassed, because, while I can, of course, transcend myself *toward* a Whole, I cannot establish myself within that Whole in order to contemplate myself and to contemplate the Other. No logical or epistemological optimism is able to end the scandal of the plurality of consciousnesses. If Hegel believed that it could, that is because he never grasped the nature of that peculiar dimension of being, consciousness (of) self. The task that an ontology can set itself is to describe this scandal and to found it in the very nature of being: it lacks the power, however, to surpass it. It is possible—and this will become clearer soon— that we can refute solipsism and show that the Other's existence is evident for us and certain. But even if we were to make the Other's existence participate in the apodictic certainty of the *cogito*—i.e., of my own existence—we would not for all that have "surpassed" the Other toward some inter-monadic totality. The dispersion and struggle of consciousnesses will remain what they are: we will have simply discovered their foundation, and their true domain.

What have we gained from this lengthy critique? Simply this: if it must be possible to refute solipsism, my relation to the Other is, first and fundamentally, a relation of being to being, and not of knowledge to knowledge. Indeed, we have seen the failure of Husserl, who, on this particular front, measures being by knowledge, and the failure of Hegel, who identifies knowledge and being. But, equally, we have recognized that Hegel, even though his vision was clouded by the postulate of absolute idealism, saw how to locate the debate at its true level. It seems that Heidegger, in *Being and Time*, has profited from the meditations of his precursors and has profoundly absorbed this twofold necessity: (1) the relation of "human-realities" must be a relation of being; (2) this relation must make "human-realities" depend on each other in their essential being. At least his theory is a response to these two requirements. With his brusque and slightly barbaric way of cutting through Gordian knots—rather than trying to untie them—Heidegger answers the question he has raised with a pure and simple *definition*. He has discovered various moments (which are, moreover, inseparable, other than by abstraction) within the "being-in-the-world" that characterizes human-reality. These moments are "world," "being-in" and "being." He described the *world* as "that through which human-reality becomes acquainted with what it is"; "being-in" was defined by him as "*Befindlichkeit*" and "*Verstand*";[16] what remains to be talked about is *being*, i.e., the mode in which human-reality is its being-in-the-world. That, he tells us, is "*Mit-Sein*," i.e., "being-with . . . ." Thus the characteristic of human-reality's being is that it is its being *with* others. This is not a matter of chance: I do not exist first, such that subsequently some contingency makes me *encounter* the Other; what is in question here is an essential structure of my being. But this structure is not established from outside and from a totalizing point of view, as it is in Hegel. To be sure, Heidegger does not set out from the *cogito*, in the Cartesian sense of the self-discovery of consciousness; instead, the human-reality that is disclosed to him, and whose structures he seeks to determine through concepts, is his own. "*Dasein ist je meines*,"[17] he writes. It is by explicating my own preontological understanding of myself that I grasp being-with-the-Other as an essential characteristic of my being. In short, I discover the transcendent relation to the Other as constituting my own being, just as I discovered being-in-the-world to be the measure of my human-reality. Thereafter the problem of the Other is only a pseudo-problem: the Other is no longer first some particular existence that I encounter in the world (and who cannot be indispensable to my own existence, since I existed before I encountered him); he is the ex-centric term that contributes to the constitution of my being. The examination of my being, insofar as I am thrown by it out of myself, toward structures which at the same time escape me and define me—this examination is what originally discloses the Other to me. Let us note, in addition, that the type of connection to the Other has changed: with realism, idealism, Husserl, and Hegel, the type of relation between consciousnesses was *being-for*: the Other appeared

---

16 TN: Sartre has already referred to Heidegger's definition of the world earlier in the text (at EN 141). The German word *Befindlichkeit* means "state of mind," and *Verstand* means "understanding." Both terms are translated that way in Heidegger (1980).

17 TN: This German phrase means "*Dasein* is in each case mine"; it appears in Heidegger (1980: §9).

to me, and even constituted me, insofar as he was for me, or I was for him; the problem was the mutual recognition of consciousnesses placed before each other, each of which appeared to the others *within the world* and confronting each other. *Being-with* has an entirely different meaning: *with* does not designate the reciprocal relation of recognition and of struggle that might result from the appearance *in the midst* of the world of a human-reality other than mine. Rather, it expresses a kind of ontological solidarity for the exploitation of this world. The other is not originally connected to me as an ontic reality, appearing in the midst of the world, among "implements," as a particular type of object: in that case, he would already be degraded and the relation that might join him to me could never become reciprocal. The other is not an *object*. He remains, in his connection to me, a human-reality; the being through which he determines me in my being is his pure being, apprehended as "being-in-the-world"—and we know that "in" has to be understood in the sense of "*colo*," "*habito*," and not in the sense of "*insum*";[18] to-be-in-the-world is to haunt the world, not to be glued down within it—and it is in my "being-in-the-world" that he determines me. Our relation is not a *frontal* opposition; rather, it is an interdependence *alongside*: insofar as I make it the case that a world exists as a structure of equipment, of which I make use for the purposes of my human-reality, I come to be determined in my being by a being who makes it the case that the same world exists as a structure of equipment for the purposes of his reality. And, moreover, we must not understand this *being-with* as a pure collaterality, passively received by my being. To be, for Heidegger, is to be one's own possibilities, to make oneself be. What I make myself be is, therefore, a mode of being. And this truth means even that I am responsible for my being for the Other insofar as I actualize it freely, in authenticity or inauthenticity. It is as wholly free and through an original choice that, for example, I actualize my *being-with* in the form of the "they."[19] And if we are asked how my *being-with* can exist for-me, the reply should be that I become acquainted through the world with what I am. In particular, when I am in the mode

285

18 TN: Heidegger discusses the meanings of "in" in relation to these Latin words, with the exception of *insum* (which may be Sartre's mistake), in Heidegger (1980: §12).

19 TN: ... *sous la forme du "on."* As earlier in the text, I follow Heidegger's translators in rendering *das Man* as "the they."

of inauthenticity—of the "they"—the world sends back to me something like an impersonal reflection of my inauthentic possibilities in the guise of implements and structures of equipment that belong to "everyone," and which belong to me insofar as I am "everyone:" ready-made clothes, public transport, parks, gardens, public places, shelters that are built so that anyone can shelter there, etc. In this way I become acquainted with myself as anyone by the referential structure of equipment, which refers to me as a "Worumwillen,"[20] and the inauthentic state—which is my ordinary state for as long as I have not effected any conversion to authenticity—reveals my being-with to me, not as the relation of one unique personality with other equally unique personalities, not as the mutual connection between the "most irreplaceable of beings,"[21] but as a complete interchangeability in the terms of the relation. The terms still lack determinacy: I am not opposed to the other, because I am not me; we have the social unity of the "they." To raise the problem at the level of the incommunicability of individual subjects was to commit a ὕστερον πρότερον,[22] to turn the world on its head. Authenticity and individuality have to be won: I will be my own authenticity only if, under the influence of the call of conscience (Ruf des Gewissens), I throw myself toward death, as toward my ownmost possibility, with resolute-decision (Entschlossenheit). At that moment I am disclosed to myself in authenticity, and I raise others, too, along with me, in the direction of authenticity.

The empirical image that symbolizes Heidegger's intuition best is not that of the struggle; it is the image of the team. The other's original relation with my consciousness is not the you and me, it is the we, and Heidegger's being-with is not the clear and distinct positing of one individual confronting another, it is not knowledge; it is the muted existence of the team-member in common with his team, that existence of which the rhythm of the oars or the regular movements of the cox

---

20 TN: Heidegger's translators render Worumwillen as "for-the-sake-of-which." Sartre has already used this term, at EN 237.

21 TN: The phrase quoted by Sartre is from a well-known passage at the end of André Gide's prose poem, published in French in 1897, Les Nourritures Terrestres: "Ce qu'un autre aurait aussi bien fait que toi, ne le fais pas. Ce qu'un autre aurait aussi bien dit que toi, ne le dis pas, – aussi bien écrit que toi, ne l'écris pas. Ne t'attache en toi qu'à ce que tu sens qui n'est nulle part ailleurs qu'en toi-même, et crée de toi, impatiemment ou patiemment, ah! le plus irremplaçable des êtres." Translated as Gide (1949).

22 TN: Sartre has already used this Greek phrase earlier in the text (see Part Two, Chapter 2, note 13).

will make the oarsmen aware, and which will be manifested to them by their common goal to be attained, the boat or the skiff to be overtaken, and the entire world (spectators, the performance, etc.) outlined at the horizon. It is against the common ground of this coexistence that I will stand out through the sudden disclosure of my being-toward-death, within an absolute "solitude in common," while at the same time I elevate the others, right up to this solitude.

286

This time we have really been given what we were asking for: a being that implies the Other's being in its being. And yet we cannot consider ourselves satisfied. First of all, Heidegger's theory offers us more of an indication of the solution to be found, rather than that solution itself. Even if we were to admit without reservation this substitution of "being-with" for "being-for," it would remain for us a mere assertion without foundation. Doubtless we encounter certain empirical states of our being—in particular, what the Germans denote by their untranslatable term Stimmung[23]—that seem to reveal a coexistence of consciousnesses rather than a relation of opposition. But this coexistence is precisely what needs to be explained. Why does it become the unique foundation of our being, why is it the fundamental type of our relation with others, and why did Heidegger believe he was entitled to pass from this empirical and ontic observation of being-with to posit coexistence as the ontological structure of my "being-in-the-world?" And which kind of being has this coexistence? To what extent has the negation that makes of the Other an other, and constitutes him as inessential, been maintained? If we eliminate it entirely, will we not fall into monism? And if we have to preserve it as an essential structure of our relation to the Other, what modification will it be necessary for it to undergo, for it to lose the character of opposition that it had in being-for-the-Other and for it to acquire this character of a binding connection that is the very structure of being-with? And how do we move from that to some concrete experience of the Other within the world (as when I see from my window a passerby walking

---

23 TN: The German term Stimmung is usually translated as "mood." The untranslatability mentioned by Sartre here is Heidegger's achievement. Because Heidegger argues that Stimmung should not be conceived as a psychological phenomenon, and connects it with the verb stimmen ("to attune"), Stambaugh suggests (in her translation of Heidegger 2010) that the metaphorical "attunement" works well.

down the street)? Of course it is tempting to conceive of myself as delin-
eating myself—through the impulse of my freedom, through the choice
of my unique possibilities—against the undifferentiated ground of the
human; and perhaps this conception contains a substantial part of the
truth. But, at least in this form, it raises considerable objections.

In the first place, the ontological point of view converges here with
the abstract point of view of the Kantian subject. To say that through its
ontological structure the human-reality—even if it is my human-reality—
'is-with," is to say that it is-with by its nature, i.e., essentially and
universally. Even if that claim were proved, it would not enable us to
explain concrete being-with; in other words, the ontological coexistence
that appears as the structure of my "being-in-the-world" cannot in any
way serve as the foundation of an ontic being-with such as, for example,
the coexistence that appears in my friendship with Pierre or in the couple
that I form with Anny. What would need to be shown, in fact, is that   287
"being-with-Pierre" or "being-with-Anny" is a constitutive structure
of my concrete-being. But that is impossible, from the standpoint that
Heidegger has taken up. In point of fact, viewed at the ontological level,
the other in the "with" relation cannot be any more concretely determined than the human-reality that is directly in view and of which he
is the alter ego; it is an abstract term and thereby unselbstständig, and does
not at all have within it the power to become this other, Pierre or Anny.
Thus, the "Mitsein" relation cannot help us at all to resolve the psychological and concrete problem of our recognition of the Other. There are
two incommunicable planes and two problems, which demand separate
solutions. That, we will be told, is only one aspect of the difficulty that
Heidegger experiences generally, in passing from the ontological level
to the ontic level, from "being-in-the-world" in general to my relation
with this particular implement, from my being-toward-death—which
makes my death into my most essential possibility—to this "ontic" death
that I will have through my encounter with this or that external existent.
But in all other cases this difficulty can just about be concealed, since,
for example, it is human-reality that makes it the case that a world exists
where a threat of death which concerns it can be hidden: better still, if
the world is, it is because it is "mortal," in the sense in which we say that
a wound is "mortal." But, in the context of the problem of the Other,
the impossibility of passing from one level to the other explodes. For if,

indeed, through the ecstatic arising of its being-in-the-world, human-reality makes it the case that a world exists, we cannot say, in the same way, that its *being-with* makes another human-reality arise. Of course, I am the being through whom "there is" (*es gibt*) being. Might it be said that I am the being through whom "there is" another human-reality? If we take that to mean that I am the being for whom there is another human-reality *for me*, that is a straightforward truism. If we mean that I am the being through whom *there are* others in general, we fall back into solipsism. In point of fact, this human-reality "with whom" I am is itself "in-the-world-with-me"; it is the free founding of a world (How does it come about that it is *mine*? From *being-with*, we cannot infer the identity of the worlds "in which" the human-realities are), and it is its own possibilities. This human-reality is therefore *for itself*, without waiting for me to make its being exist in the form of "there is." In this way, I may constitute a world as "mortal," but not a human-reality as a concrete being that is its own possibilities. My *being-with*, apprehended on the basis of "my" being, can be regarded only as a pure demand, founded in my being, and which does not constitute the least proof of the Other's existence, the least bridge between me and the other.

Better still, far from facilitating a specific and ontic relation from me to Pierre, this ontological relation from me to an abstract Other—by virtue of the very fact that it defines my relation in general to the Other—makes any concrete connection between my being and a particular Other given in my experience radically impossible. If in fact my relation with the Other is *a priori*, it exhausts any possibility of a relation with the Other. Empirical and contingent relations will not be able to be specifications, or particular cases, of it: a law can have specifications in only two circumstances; either the law is inductively derived from empirical and particular facts, and that is not the case here; or else it is *a priori* and unifies experience, like Kantian concepts. But in that case, precisely, its scope is only within the limits of experience: I find in things only what I have put into them. Now, the establishment of a relation between two concrete "beings-in-the-world" cannot belong to my experience; it escapes therefore the domain of *being-with*. But, precisely because the law *constitutes* its own domain, it excludes *a priori* any real fact that it has not constructed. A time that existed as the *a priori* form of my sensibility would exclude me *a priori* from any connection with a noumenal time that possessed the characteristics of a being. In this way the existence of a being-with that is ontological and, in consequence, *a priori* renders any ontic connection with a concrete human-reality, arising *for-itself* as an absolute transcendence, impossible. *Being-with*, conceived as a structure of my being, isolates me as inexorably as the arguments for solipsism. The fact is that Heidegger's *transcendence* is a concept in bad faith: of course it aims to move beyond idealism and, to the extent to which the latter presents us with a subjectivity at rest in itself, contemplating its own images, it manages to do that. But the idealism that is hereby left behind is only an adulterated form of idealism, a kind of empirico-critical psychologism. Without doubt Heidegger's human-reality "exists outside itself." But, in Heidegger's doctrine, it is precisely this existence outside itself that defines the *self*. It bears no resemblance to Plato's ek-stasis, in which existence is really an aliena-tion, an existence in an other,[24] or to Malebranche's vision in God,[25] or to our own conception of ecstasis and internal negation. Heidegger does not escape idealism: his flight from oneself, as an *a priori* structure of one's being, is no less isolating than Kant's reflection on the *a priori* conditions of our experience: indeed, what human-reality finds, at the unattainable end of this flight from itself, is still itself; the flight out-side oneself is a flight toward the self, and the world appears purely as the distance from self to self. It would be pointless, in consequence, to try to find in *Sein und Zeit* the simultaneous overcoming of any idealism or any realism. And the difficulties that idealism encounters generally when it comes to founding the existence of concrete beings who resem-ble ourselves and who, as such, escape our experience—beings who do not in their very constitution fall under our *a priori*—still arise in the   289 face of Heidegger's attempt to take "human-reality" out of its solitude. He seems to escape them because some of the time he takes "outside-

24 TN: Sartre does not provide enough detail here to identify one particular passage in Plato, who talks in several dialogues about various forms of "alienation" (by which he means madness). As for the term *ek-stasis*, Hazel Barnes hints in her translation that Sartre may in fact have been thinking of Neo-Platonic writings (Sartre 1992: 249).

25 TN: The French philosopher Nicolas Malebranche (1638–1715) argues that "we see all things in God" (Malebranche 1997: 230). This doctrine is also known as "Vision in God" in English.

oneself" to be "outside-oneself-toward-oneself" and at other times to be "outside-oneself-in-the-Other." But the second understanding of "outside-oneself," which he cunningly slips into the course of his reasoning, is strictly incompatible with the first: right in the midst of its ecstases, human-reality remains alone. That is because—and here is the new insight to be drawn from our critical examination of Heidegger's doctrines—the nature of the Other's existence is that of a contingent and irreducible fact. We *encounter* the other; we do not constitute him. And if this fact has nonetheless to appear to us under the aspect of necessity, it will not be the necessity that belongs to the "conditions of possibility of our experience" or, alternatively, ontological necessity: the necessity of the Other's existence must, if it exists, be a "contingent necessity," i.e., of just that type of *factual necessity* with which the *cogito* impresses itself on us. If the Other must be able to be given to us, it is through a direct apprehension which leaves the encounter with its character of facticity— just as the *cogito* itself leaves my own thinking with the entirety of its facticity—and which nonetheless participates in the apodicticity of the *cogito* itself, i.e., in its indubitability.

This lengthy exposition of doctrine will not have been in vain, therefore, if it enables us to clarify the necessary and sufficient conditions for a theory of the Other's existence to be valid.

(1) Such a theory must not supply a new *proof* of the Other's existence, an argument against solipsism that is better than the others. If indeed solipsism is to be rejected, it can only be because it is impossible or, alternatively, because nobody is truly a solipsist. The Other's existence may always be called into doubt, unless we are specifically doubting the Other only in words, and abstractly, in the same way that I am able to write that "I am doubting my own existence," though I am unable even to think it. In brief, the Other's existence must not be a *probability*. In fact probability can only concern objects that appear within our experience, or whose new effects are able to appear within our experience. There is probability only if in each moment its confirmation or disconfirmation is possible. If the Other is as a matter of principle and in his "for-itself" outside my experience, the probability of his existence as *another self* can never be either confirmed or disconfirmed, and nor can it increase or decrease, or even be measured: therefore it loses its very character of probability and becomes a novelist's mere conjecture. In the same way,

M. Lalande has succeeded in showing[26] that a hypothesis about the existence of living beings on the planet Mars will remain purely a conjecture, and without any "chance" of being true or false, as long as we do not have at our disposal any instruments or scientific theories that allow facts which confirm or disconfirm this hypothesis to appear to us. But the Other's structure is such that, as a matter of principle, no new experience will ever be able to be conceived, and no new theory will ever arrive to confirm or disconfirm the hypothesis of his existence, nor will any instrument come along to reveal new facts that would prompt me to assert or to reject that hypothesis. If therefore the Other is not immediately present to me, and if his existence is not as assured as my own, any conjecture about him is completely lacking in meaning. But, precisely, I do not conjecture the Other's existence: I assert it. A theory of the Other's existence must therefore simply question me in my being, illuminate and clarify the meaning of that assertion, and above all, far from inventing a proof, explicate the very foundation of that certainty. In other words, Descartes did not prove his existence. Because in fact I have always known that I existed, I have never ceased to practice the *cogito*. Similarly, my resistance to solipsism—a resistance that is as lively as that which an attempt to doubt the *cogito* would arouse—proves that I have always known that the Other existed, that I have always had a complete *understanding*, albeit implicit, of his existence, that this "preontological" *understanding* includes an intelligence about the Other's nature and his relation of being with my being that is more assured and more profound than any theory that has ever been constructed outside it. If the Other's existence is not a vain conjecture or pure fiction, it is because there is something like a *cogito* that applies to it. It is this *cogito* that we need to bring to light, by explicating its structures and determining its scope and its entitlements.

(2) But, on the other hand, Hegel's failure showed us that the only possible starting point was the Cartesian *cogito*. Moreover, that alone can establish us in the territory of that *factual necessity* that belongs to the Other's existence. Thus, what we were calling—for want of a better

---

26 Sartre's note: *Les Théories de l'Induction et de l'Expérimentation*. TN: Pierre André Lalande (1867–1963) was a French philosopher, who taught at the ENS and the Sorbonne. The book to which Sartre refers was published in 1929.

term—the *cogito* of the Other's existence merges with my own *cogito*. The *cogito*, examined once again, must throw me outside it onto the Other, as it threw me outside it onto the in-itself; and it must do that, not by revealing to me an *a priori* structure of myself that would point toward an equally *a priori* Other but by disclosing to me the concrete and indubitable presence of *this or that* concrete Other, as it had already revealed to me my incomparable, concrete, contingent, yet necessary existence. Thus it is the for-itself that we must ask to deliver to us the for-the-Other, and we must ask absolute immanence to throw us into absolute transcendence: in the depths of myself it is not *reasons to believe* in the Other that I must find but the Other himself, as not being me.

291

(3) And what the *cogito* must reveal to us is not an Other-object. It ought to have occurred to us long ago to reflect that to talk about an *object* is to talk about something *probable*. If the Other is an object for me, he refers me to probability. But probability is founded solely on the congruence *ad infinitum* of our representations. The Other, being neither a representation, nor a system of representations, nor a necessary unity of our representations, cannot be *probable*; he cannot be an object first. If therefore he is *for us*, that can be neither as a constitutive factor in our knowledge of the world nor as a constitutive factor in our knowledge of the self but insofar as he "interests" our being[27]—and that will be not insofar as he contributes *a priori* to constituting it but insofar as he interests it concretely and "ontically," in the empirical circumstances of our facticity.

(4) If it is a matter of attempting for the Other, in some way, what Descartes attempted to do for God with the extraordinary "proof through the idea of the perfect," which is animated entirely by the intuition of transcendence, we will be obliged to reject, in our apprehension of the Other as the Other, a certain kind of negation, which we have called "external negation." The Other must appear to the *cogito* as *not being me*. This negation may be conceived in two ways: either it is a pure, external negation and it will separate the Other from myself like a substance

---

27 TN: ... *mais en tant qu'il "intéresse" notre être* ... Sartre puns on the French verb *intéresser*; the scare quotes bring to the fore, I think, a range of meanings such as "to have an interest [i.e., stake] in something" or something's "being in one's interest." Translated into English, the sentence does this less successfully.

from another substance—and in this case any grasp of the Other is by definition impossible—or it will be an internal negation, which means a synthetic and active connection of two terms, each of which constitutes itself by negating itself from the other. This negative relation will therefore be reciprocal and it will feature a twofold interiority. That implies, first, that the multiplicity of "Others" cannot be a *collection* but a *totality* (on this point we agree with Hegel, since each Other finds his being in the other); but it also means that this Totality is such that it is impossible, as a matter of principle, to take up "the viewpoint of the whole." We saw, in point of fact, that it is not possible to extract any abstract concept of consciousness from the comparison of my being-for-myself with my objecthood for the Other. In addition, this totality—like that of the for-itself—is a detotalized totality because, since existence-for-the-Other is a radical refusal of the Other, no totalizing and unifying synthesis of the "Others" is possible.

By setting out from these various observations, we will try, in our turn, to address the question of the Other.

IV. THE LOOK[28]

This woman whom I see coming toward me, this man passing in the street, this beggar whom I hear from my window singing are objects for me: that is beyond doubt. Thus it is true that one, at least, of the modalities of the Other's presence to me is objecthood. But we have seen that, if this relation of objecthood is the Other's fundamental relation to myself, the Other's existence remains purely conjectural. Now, it is not only conjectural but *probable* that this voice I am hearing is that of a man, and not a song on the gramophone; it is infinitely *probable* that the passerby whom I see is a man, and not a sophisticated robot. In other words, my apprehension of the Other as an object, without going beyond the limits of probability and just because of that probability, essentially refers to a fundamental grasp of the Other, in which the Other is no longer disclosed to me as an object but as a "presence in person." In brief, in order for the Other to be a probable object,

---

28 TN: See my note on *regarder* in Notes on the Translation.

and not a dream of an object, his objecthood must refer not to an original solitude out of my reach but to a fundamental connection in which the Other is manifested in some other way than through the knowledge I gain of him. The classical theories were right to hold that every perceived human organism *refers* to something, and that what it refers to is the foundation and the guarantee of its probability. But their mistake is to think that this reference points to a separate existence, a consciousness that lies behind its perceptible manifestations, in the way that the noumenon lies behind Kant's *Empfindung*.[29] Whether or not this consciousness exists in a separate state, that is not what the face that I see refers to; it is not the truth of the probable object that I perceive. The *de facto* reference to a twinned arising in which the other is present to me—in short, to a "being-in-a-couple-with-the-other"—is given outside knowledge strictly speaking, even if we conceive of it as an obscure and ineffable instance of the intuitive type. In other words, we have generally considered the problem of the Other as if the primary relation through which the Other is disclosed is objecthood, i.e., as if the Other first revealed himself (directly or indirectly) to our perception. But, as this perception *refers*, by its very nature, to something other than itself, and as it cannot refer either to an infinite series of appearances of the same type—as in the idealist account of the perception of a table or chair—or to an isolated entity that is situated by definition out of my reach, its essence must be to refer to a primary relation between my consciousness and that of the Other, in which the Other must be directly given to me as a subject, although in a connection with me, and which is the fundamental relation, the very type of my being-for-the-Other.

Nonetheless, what we are directed to here cannot be some mystical experience, or something ineffable. The Other appears to us within everyday reality, and his probability refers to everyday reality. The problem, therefore, becomes more specific: Is there in everyday reality an original relation to the Other that is constantly within our sights, and which can in consequence be disclosed to me, without any reference to some religious or mystical unknowable? In order to find out, we need to examine more closely this banal appearance of the Other within the field

29 TN: Kant's German term *Empfindung* is usually translated as "sensation."

of my perception: since *that appearance* is what refers to this fundamental relation, it must be capable of revealing to us, at least as a reality that we aim at, the relation to which it refers.

I am in a park. Not far from me I see a lawn and, along this lawn, some chairs. A man is passing by, close to the chairs. I see this man; I apprehend him as an object and, at the same time, as a man. What does this mean? What do I mean when I assert, in relation to this object, that it *is a man?*

If I were to think that it was nothing but a doll, I would apply to it the categories that I ordinarily use to group spatio-temporal "things." In that case I might apprehend him as being "beside" the chairs, at 2.20 meters from the lawn, as exerting a specific pressure on the ground, etc. His relation with the other objects would be of a purely additive type, such that I could eliminate him without any significant modification of the relations between the other objects. In brief, no new relation would appear *through him* between these things in my universe: grouped and synthesized *on my side* into instrumental structures, they would break apart *on his side* into multiplicities of indifferent relations. To perceive him as *a man, on the contrary,* is to grasp a non-additive relation between the chair and him; it is to register an organization *without distance* of the things in my universe around that special object. Of course, the lawn remains 2.20 meters away from him but it is also connected to him, *as the lawn,* in a relation that transcends and contains the distance at the same time. The two terms of the distance are not indifferent, interchangeable, and reciprocally related; rather, the distance *unfolds away* from the man I can see and reaches *right up* to the grass, as a univocal relation that synthetically arises. We are dealing here with a relation *without parts* that is given all at once, and within which a spatiality that is not my spatiality unfolds because, rather than being a grouping of objects *toward me,* we have an orientation *that flees me.* Of course, this relation without distance and without parts is in no sense the original relation of the Other to me that I was looking for: in the first place, it involves only the man and the things in the world. And further, it is still an object of knowledge; I might express it, for example, by saying that this man *sees* the grass or that, in spite of the sign prohibiting it, he is about to walk on the lawn, etc. And finally, it retains a character of pure probability: in the first place, it is *probable* that this object is a man; further, even if it were

294

certain that he is one, it remains merely probable that he *sees* the grass in the same moment as I see it: he might be dreaming of some enterprise without being fully conscious of his surroundings, he might be blind, etc. Nonetheless, this new relation between the man-object and the grass-object has a particular character. It is given to me in its entirety, since it is there, in the world, as an object that I am able to know (and it really is an objective relation that I express when I say "Pierre glanced at his watch," "Jeanne looked through the window," etc.), and at the same time it escapes me entirely: to the extent to which the man-object is the fundamental term in this relation, to the extent to which this relation *leads toward him*, it escapes me, and I am unable to place myself at the center; the distance that unfolds between the grass and the man, through the synthetic arising of this primary relation, is a negation of the distance that I establish—as external negation, in its purest type— between these two objects. It appears as a pure *disintegration* of the relations that I apprehend between the objects in my universe. And I am not the one who brings this disintegration about; it appears to me as a relation that I aim at across the distances that I originally establish between things. It is like a backdrop to things that necessarily escapes me, and which is conferred upon them from outside. The appearance among the objects in my universe of an element of disintegration of that universe is, therefore, what I mean by the appearance of *a* man in my universe. The Other is in the first instance the permanent flight of things toward a term that I apprehend at the same time as an object at a specific distance from me, and which escapes me insofar as it unfolds its own distances around it. But this disaggregation gradually spreads; if a relation without distance, and which creates distance, exists between the grass and the Other, there necessarily exists another one between the Other and the statue that stands on its pedestal *in the middle* of the grass, and between the Other and the tall chestnut trees that border the path; around the Other, an entire space is grouped, and this space is made with *my space*; it is a regrouping, at which I am present, and which escapes me, of all the objects that populate my universe. This regrouping does not stop there: the lawn is something qualified; it is *this* green lawn, which exists for the Other, such that just this quality of the object— its deep, harsh green—is directly related to this man; this green turns toward the Other a face that escapes me. I grasp *the relation* of the green to the Other as an objective relation, but I am unable to grasp the green *as* it appears to the Other. Thus, all of a sudden, an object has appeared that has stolen the world from me. Everything is in place, everything still exists for me, but now an invisible and frozen flight toward a new object penetrates everything. The Other's appearing in the world corresponds, therefore, to a frozen sliding away of the universe in its entirety, to a decentering of the world that undermines the centralization I simultaneously impose.

But the *Other* remains an object *for me.* He belongs to my distances: the man is there, twenty steps away from me, and he turns his back *to me.* As such, he is once again 2.20 meters away from the grass, six meters away from the statue; the disintegration of my universe is thereby contained within the limits of that universe itself. It is not a matter of the world fleeing toward nothingness or somewhere outside itself; rather, it seems as if it has been pierced, in the middle of its being, by a drainage hole and as if it is constantly flowing out through that hole. The universe, the flowing away, and the drainage hole, all these are retrieved once again, seized back, and frozen into an object; it is all there *for me,* as a partial structure of the world, even though what is at issue here is in fact the universe's total disintegration. Often, moreover, I am able to contain these disintegrations within tighter limits: here, for example, is a man who is reading as he walks. The disintegration of the universe that he represents is purely virtual: he has ears that hear nothing, eyes that see nothing but his book. Between his book and him I grasp a relation that is undeniable, and without distance, of the same type as the relation that connected the walking man, earlier on, to the lawn. But, this time, the figure has closed in on itself: an object is there in full, to be grasped. In the midst of the world I can say "reading-man," just as I might say "cold stone" or "fine rain"; I grasp a closed "*Gestalt,*" of which *reading* forms the essential quality and which, apart from that, blind and dumb, lets itself be known and perceived purely and simply as a spatio-temporal thing whose relation with the rest of the world seems to be pure indifferent externality. Only that very quality of "reading-man"—as the relation between the man and the book—is a small, particular crack in my universe; at the heart of this solid and visible figure, there is a particular emptying out; it is massive only in appearance, and its true sense is to be, in the midst of my universe, ten steps away from me, at the heart of this massivity, a leak[30] that is sealed over and remains strictly local.

None of this, therefore, removes us in any way from the territory in which the Other is an *object*. At the most, we are handling a specific type of objectivity, which is quite similar to the kind that Husserl designated as *absence*, even though he did not point out that the Other is not defined as the absence of a consciousness in relation to the body I can see but by the absence of the world that I perceive, right at the heart of my perceiving of this world. At this level the Other is a worldly object that we can define in terms of the world. But this relation of flight, and of the world's absence in relation to me, is only probable. If that is what defines the Other's objectivity, what is the original presence of the Other to which it refers? Now we are able to reply: if the object-Other is defined in connection with the world, as the object who *sees* what I see, it must be possible to sum up my fundamental connection with the subject-Other through the constant possibility of my *being seen* by the Other. It is in and through the revelation of my object-being for the Other that I must be able to apprehend the presence of his subject-being. For, just as the Other is for the subject-me a probable object, so—in the same way—I can only discover myself in the process of becoming a probable object for a subject who is certain. This revelation cannot follow from the fact that my universe is an object for the Other-object, as if the Other's gaze, having wandered over the grass and the surrounding objects, came, by following a particular path, to rest on me. I have emphasized that I cannot be an object for an object: what is required is a radical conversion of the Other, through which he escapes objectivity. I cannot therefore consider the look that the Other directs at me as one of the possible manifestations of his objective being: the Other cannot look at me in the way that he looks at the lawn. And, moreover, my objectivity cannot itself follow for me from the world's objectivity, since I am precisely the one through whom there is a world; in consequence, and as a matter of principle, I cannot be an object for myself. Thus this relation, which I describe as "being-seen-by-the-Other," is far from being one of the relations—among others—to which

---

30 TN: ... *une fuite rigoureusement colmatée* ... Although as a rule I translate *fuir* as "to flee" and *fuite* as "flight," I think that the hydraulic imagery used here (e.g., drainage hole, etc.) makes "leak" the better translation.

the word "man" can refer; rather, it represents an irreducible fact that cannot be deduced either from the essence of the object-Other or from my subject-being. But on the contrary, if the concept of the object-Other is to have a meaning, it can acquire it only through the conversion and the degradation of that original relation. In brief, what my apprehension of the Other in the world as being probably a man refers to is my constant possibility of being-seen-by-him, i.e., the constant possibility that the object seen by me will be substituted by a subject who sees me. "Being-seen-by-the-Other" is the truth of "seeing-the-Other." In this way, the notion of the Other cannot in any circumstance target a solitary and extraworldly consciousness that I am unable even to think: man is defined in relation to the world, and in relation to myself; he is the object in the world that determines an internal flowing away of the universe, an internal hemorrhage; he is the subject whom I encounter in that flight of myself toward objectification. But the original relation between myself and the Other is not only an absent truth, aimed at through the concrete presence of an object in my universe: it is also a concrete and everyday relation, experienced by me in every instant; at every instant the Other is looking at me. It is easy therefore for us to undertake, with concrete examples, the description of this fundamental connection that must provide the basis of any theory of the Other; if the Other is, as a matter of principle, the one who looks at me, we ought to be able to explicate the meaning of the Other's look.

297

Any look directed at me manifests itself in connection with the coming into view of a sensible figure within our perceptual field but—contrary to what one might think—it is not connected to any figure in particular. Doubtless, a look is manifested most often by the convergence of two eyeballs toward me. But it can show itself just as well in a rustling of branches, a sound of steps followed by silence, a half-open shutter, a slight movement of a curtain. In the course of a coup de main,[31] what the men crawling in the bushes apprehend as a look to be avoided[32] is not two

---

31 TN: As the French phrase coup de main is used in English, in military contexts, and there is no corresponding English phrase, I have left it untranslated. It refers to a military operation that depends on catching the enemy by surprise and direct assault. It seems likely that Sartre is thinking of tactics used by the French Resistance in the Second World War.

32 TN: The expression éviter le regard is used in French in contexts where one is avoiding exposure, attention, or scrutiny. If I did not have to include the word "look," a smoother English translation here might be "the risk of being seen."

eyes but an entire white farm standing out against the sky at the top of a hill. It goes without saying that the object constituted in this way is still manifesting the look only as something probable. It is merely probable that, behind the bush that has just moved, someone is lying in ambush and watching me. But we will not allow this probability to detain us now; we will return to it. What matters first is to define the look in itself. Now, the bush and the farm are not the look; they only represent the *eye*, because the eye is not grasped in the first instance as a visual sensory organ but as the look's support. They never refer, therefore, to the eyes made of flesh of the person watching, lying in wait behind the curtain, behind a window of the farm: taken in themselves, they are already eyes. On the other hand, the look is neither one quality among others of the object that functions as the eye, nor the total figure of that object, nor some "worldly" relation established between that object and me. Quite on the contrary, rather than perceiving the look in the objects that are manifesting it, my apprehension of a look that is directed at me appears against a background destruction of the eyes that "are looking at me." If I apprehend the look, I cease to perceive the eyes: they are there, they remain within my perceptual field as pure *presentations*, but I do not make use of them; they are neutralized, taken out of play, and they are no longer the object of any thesis;[33] they remain in that state of "disconnection" that characterizes the world in relation to a consciousness that has effected the phenomenological reduction prescribed by Husserl. We can never judge eyes that are looking at you to be beautiful or ugly, or notice their color. The Other's look conceals his eyes; it seems to arrive *before them*. This illusion stems from the fact that the eyes, as objects of my perception, remain at a precise distance that is unfolded from me to them—in brief, I am present to the eyes without distance, but they are distant from the place at which I "find myself"—while the look rests upon me without distance and at the same time holds me at a distance; i.e., its immediate presence to me unfolds a distance that separates me from it. I cannot therefore direct my attention to someone's gaze without my perception decomposing and moving into the background. The process here is analogous to what I have tried to demonstrate elsewhere,

---

33 TN: *... objets d'une thèse ...* See my note on *thèse* in the section on Husserl vocabulary in Notes on the Translation.

in relation to the imaginary:[34] what I said then is that we are unable to perceive and to imagine at the same time; it must be either one or the other. Here I am disposed to say: we cannot perceive the world and apprehend at the same time a look that is directed on us; it must be either one or the other. That is because to perceive is to be looking, and to grasp a look is not to apprehend a look-object within the world (unless the look is not directed at us) but to become conscious of being-looked-at. The look manifested by the eyes—whatever their nature—refers me purely to myself. What I grasp immediately when I hear the branches breaking behind me is not that someone is there but that I am vulnerable, that I have a body that can be hurt, that I am occupying a place and that I cannot in any circumstance escape from the space in which I am, defenseless—in short, that I am seen. Thus the look is in the first place an intermediary by which I am referred to myself. What is the nature of this intermediary? What is the meaning for me of being seen?

Let us imagine that, through jealousy, curiosity, or vice, I have come to stick my ear against a door or to look through a keyhole. I am alone and non-thetically conscious (of) myself. That means in the first place that there is no me inhabiting my consciousness. There is nothing, therefore, to which I can relate my actions in order to characterize them. They are in no way known, but I am them and for that simple reason they carry within themselves their complete justification. I am a pure consciousness of things, and the things, caught within the circuit of my ipseity, offer me their potentialities as a response to my non-thetic consciousness (of) my own possibilities. Thus, behind this door, a spectacle is proposed as "to be seen," a conversation as "to be heard." The door and the keyhole are instruments and obstacles at the same time: they are presented as "to be handled with caution"; the keyhole is given as "to be looked through from close by and a little to the side," etc. Henceforth "I do what I have to do"; no transcendent view confers upon my acts the character of something given, to which a judgment might be applied: my consciousness sticks to my actions; it is my actions; they are governed only by the ends to be attained and the instruments to be employed. My stance, for example, has no "outside"; it is purely what connects the instrument (the keyhole) with the end to be attained (the spectacle

34 Sartre's note: L'Imaginaire (NRF, 1940). TN: This text is translated as Sartre (2004b).

to be seen), purely a way of losing myself in the world, of allowing things to soak me up—like ink by a piece of blotting paper—so that an equipment-structure, oriented toward an end, stands out synthetically against the ground of the world. The order reverses the order of causality: it is the end to be attained that organizes all its preceding moments; the end justifies the means; the means do not exist for themselves and outside the end. The totality, moreover, exists only in relation to a free project of my possibilities: it is precisely my jealousy—as a possibility that I *am*—that organizes this equipmental structure as it transcends it toward itself. But I *am* this jealousy; I do not know it. I could learn of it from the worldly equipmental structure only if I were contemplating it rather than creating it. It is this totality in the world with its twofold and inverse determination—there is only a spectacle *to be seen* behind the door because I am jealous, but my jealousy is nothing but the simple objective fact that *there is a spectacle to be seen* behind the door—which we will refer to as the *situation*. This situation reflects back to me my facticity and, at the same time, my freedom: with respect to some specific objective structure in the world that surrounds me, it returns my freedom to me in the shape of tasks that are freely to be done; there is no constraint here, since my freedom eats into my possibles and, correlatively, the world's potentialities are only indicated and proposed. I cannot therefore define myself truly as *being* in situation: first, because I do not have a positional consciousness of myself; next, because I am my own nothingness. In this sense, and because I am what I am not and I am not what I am, I cannot even define myself as truly *being* in the process of listening at doors;[35] I escape from this provisional definition of myself through the entirety of my transcendence; that, we saw, is the origin of bad faith. In this way, I am not only unable to know myself but my very being escapes me, even though I *am* this very escaping from my being and I am not completely anything; nothing is *there* but a pure nothingness that surrounds and brings out a specific objective structure that is delineated within the world, a real system, an ordering of means in view of an end.

And now I hear footsteps in the corridor: someone is looking at me. What does this mean? That all of a sudden I am touched in my being, and that

---

35 TN: ... *comme étant vraiment en train d'écouter* ... Here the need to find an English sentence that uses Sartre's emphasized participle *being* causes some awkwardness.

essential modifications appear within my structures—modifications that I am able to apprehend and conceptually fix through the reflective *cogito*.

In the first place, I exist now for my unreflected consciousness as my self [moi]. In fact, this sudden entrance of the self [moi] is what has been most frequently described: the claim has been that I see myself because someone sees me. In this form, it is not entirely correct. But let us take a closer look: while we were considering the for-itself in its solitude, we were able to maintain that the unreflected consciousness could not be inhabited by a self: my self could only be given, as an object, to reflective consciousness. But now we see the self coming to haunt unreflected consciousness. Now, unreflected consciousness is a consciousness *of* the world. For it, therefore, the self exists at the same level as worldly objects; but now this role—the role of presentifying the self—which we had assigned only to reflective consciousness, belongs to unreflected consciousness. However, reflective consciousness takes the self directly   300 as an object. Unreflected consciousness does not apprehend the *person* directly, and as its object; the person is present to consciousness *insofar as he is an object for the Other*. In other words, I am suddenly conscious of myself insofar as I escape from myself, not insofar as I am the foundation of my own nothingness but insofar as I have my foundation outside myself. For myself, I am no more than a pure reference to the Other. Nonetheless, we should not take this to mean that the object is the Other and that the *ego* that is present to my consciousness is a secondary structure, or a meaning of the Other-object; here, the Other is not an object and, as we have shown, he cannot be an object without my self simultaneously ceasing to be an object-for-the-Other and disappearing. Thus I do not aim at the Other as an object, nor at my *ego* as an object for myself; I cannot even direct an empty intention toward this *ego*, as if it were an object presently out of my reach; in effect, it is separated from me by a nothingness that I am unable to bridge, since I apprehend it *insofar as it is not for me* and since it exists as a matter of principle for the *other*. I do not aim at it therefore insofar as it might one day be given to me but, on the contrary, insofar as it necessarily flees from me and will never belong to me. And yet I *am* it, I do not push it away as a foreign image, but it is present to me as a self that I *am* without *knowing* it, for it is in shame (and, in other cases, pride) that I discover it. It is shame or pride that reveals the Other's look to me, and myself at the furthest point of his gaze; they make me *live*, and not *know*, the situation of being looked at. Now, as we noted at the beginning of this chapter, shame is shame of *oneself*; it is the *recognition* that I really *am* this object that is looked at and judged by the Other. I can be ashamed of my freedom only insofar as it escapes me to become a *given* object. In this way, the connection between my unreflected consciousness and my looked-at-*ego* is not originally a connection of knowing but of being. Beyond any knowledge I can possibly have, I am this self that is known by an other. And I am this self that I am within a world that the Other has alienated from me, because the Other's look encompasses my being, and correlatively the walls, the door, the keyhole—all these implement-things—turn toward the other a face that necessarily escapes me. In this way I am my *ego* for the Other in the midst of a world that is flowing away toward the other. But, earlier, we were able to describe the flowing away of my world toward the object-Other as an internal hemorrhage: because the very fact that I was freezing that Other, toward whom this world was bleeding, into an object of my world meant, effectively, that the bleeding was caught and confined; in this way, not a drop of blood was lost, and everything was retrieved, encircled, and confined—albeit within a being that I was unable to penetrate. Here, on the contrary, the flight is without end, and loses itself outside; the world flows away out of the world, and I flow away out of myself; the Other's look makes me be, beyond my being in the world, in the midst of a world that is *this one* and, at the same time,

301   beyond this world. What kind of relations am I able to maintain with this being that I am, that is disclosed to me by shame?

In the first place, it is a relation of being. I *am* this being. Not for an instant would I dream of denying it; my shame is an admission. I might, later on, make use of bad faith in order to conceal it from me, but bad faith is also an admission, since it is an effort to flee from the being that I am. But I am not this being that I am either in the mode of "having it to be" or in the mode of "was:" I do not found it in its being; I cannot directly produce it, but neither is it some close, indirect effect of my actions, as in the case where my shadow on the ground, or my reflection in the mirror, moves according to the moves I am making. This being that I am retains a certain indeterminacy, a certain unpredictability. And these new characteristics do not stem solely from the fact that I cannot know the Other; they also originate, above all, in the fact that the Other is free—or, to be precise, and reversing our terms, the Other's freedom is revealed to me through the disturbing indeterminacy of the being that I am for him. This being, therefore, is not my possible; it is not always in question at the heart of my freedom. On the contrary, it is the limit of my freedom, its "hidden side" in the sense in which we talk about "the hidden side of the cards"; it is given to me as a burden that I carry, without ever being able to turn back toward it in order to know it, without even being able to sense its weight; if it can be compared with my shadow, it will be a shadow that is projected onto some moving and unpredictable material, such that no system of cross-references could allow us to calculate the distortions resulting from these movements. And yet it really is a question of my being, and not my being's image. It is a question of my being as it is inscribed in and through the Other's freedom. It is as though I had a dimension of being from which I was separated by a radical nothingness, and this nothingness is the Other's freedom; the Other has to make my being-for-him be, insofar as he has his being to be; in this way, each of my free undertakings commits me within a new setting, in which the very fabric of my being is the other's unpredictable freedom. And yet, through my shame itself, I lay claim to this freedom of another as my own, and I affirm a profound unity of consciousnesses: not that harmony of monads that has sometimes been taken as a guarantee of objectivity but a unity of being, since I accept, and I want others to confer on me, a being that I recognize.

But shame reveals to me that this being is what I *am*—not in the mode of *was*, or "having to be," but *in-itself*. On my own, I am unable to actualize my "being-seated"; at the most we can say that I am it and I am not it at the same time. It suffices that the Other should look at me, to make me what I am. Not what I am for myself, of course—I will never succeed in actualizing this being-seated that I apprehend in the Other's look, and I will always remain a consciousness—but for the other. Once again, the for-itself's nihilating movement of escape is frozen, and once again the in-itself re-forms itself on the for-itself. But, once again, the metamorphosis operates at a distance: for the other I *am seated* in the way in which this inkwell *is on* the table; for the other I am *leaning* toward the keyhole in the way in which this tree *is bent* by the wind. Thus I have been stripped, for the other, of my transcendence. That is because for anyone who witnesses it—i.e., for anyone who is determined as 302 *not being* this transcendence—it effectively becomes a transcendence that is purely observed, a given-transcendence, which means it acquires a nature solely by virtue of the fact that the other—not through some distortion or some refraction that is imposed on it by his categories but through his very being—confers upon it an outside. If there is an other, however or whoever he may be, and whatever relations he has with me, and even if he does not act on me in any way other than through the pure arising of his being, I have an outside, and I have a *nature.* My original fall is the Other's existence, and shame—like pride— is my apprehension of myself as a nature, even though this nature itself escapes me and is unknowable as such. Strictly speaking, I do not feel myself losing my freedom, in order to become a *thing;* instead, my freedom is over there, outside the freedom that I live, like a given attribute of this being that I am for the other. I apprehend the other's look at the very center of my *act,* as the solidification and alienation of my own possibilities. In point of fact, through fear, and through my anxious or sensible expectations, I feel that these possibilities that I *am*—and that are the condition of my transcendence—are being giving elsewhere to an other as having to be transcended in their turn by his own possibili- ties. And the other, *qua* look, is no more than that: my transcendence transcended. And doubtless I *am* still my possibilities, in the mode of my non-thetic consciousness (of) those possibilities, but at the same time the look alienates me from them. Up until then, I apprehended these possibilities thetically, on and in the world, as the potentiality of implements; the dark corner, in the corridor, transmitted back to me the possibility of hiding as a simple potential quality of its shadows, like an invitation from its darkness; this object's quality or equipmentality belonged only to it, and was given as an objective and ideal property, marking out its genuine belonging to the structure that we have called the *situation.* But, with the Other's look, a new organization of structures comes to be superimposed on the first. To grasp myself as seen is, in effect, to grasp myself as seen *in the world,* and on the basis of the world. The look does not carve me out from the universe, it comes to find me within my situation, and all that it grasps of me is indissoluble relations with implements: if I am seen as seated I must be seen as "seated-on-a- chair," if I am grasped as stooping, it is as "stooping-over-the-keyhole," etc. But, in consequence, the alienation of myself that is *being-seen* implies

303

the alienation of the world I am organizing. I am seen as seated on this chair insofar as I do not see it, insofar as it is impossible for me to see it, insofar as it escapes me in order to become organized, with other relations and other distances, in the midst of other objects (which, similarly, have a hidden side) into a new, and reoriented, structure. Thus it is that I—who, insofar as I am my possibles, am what I am not, and am not what I am—I am someone. And what I am—and what necessarily escapes me—is what I am *in the midst of the world*, and insofar as it escapes me. In consequence, my relation to the object or to the object's potentiality disintegrates beneath the Other's look and appears to me within the world as my possibility of using the object, insofar as this possibility necessarily escapes me, i.e., insofar as the other surpasses it toward his own possibilities. For example, the potentiality of the dark corner becomes a given possibility of hiding in the corner, simply by virtue of the fact that the other can surpass it toward his possibility of using his flashlight to light up the corner. This possibility is there, and I grasp it—but as something absent, as *within the other*—through my anguish and through my decision to abandon this hiding place which is "*unsafe.*" In this way, my possibilities are present to my unreflected consciousness insofar as the other is *watching me*. If I see his demeanor, prepared for anything, his hand in his pocket where he has a weapon, his finger poised on the electric bell ready to alert the guardhouse "at my slightest move," I learn of my possibilities from outside and through him, at the same time as I am them—rather as we learn what we are thinking objectively, through our very speech, at the same time as we are thinking it *in order to* mold it into speech. This drive to run away, by which I am pulled and mastered and which I *am*, is something I can read in this watchful look, and in that other look: the weapon trained on me. I learn of it from the other, insofar as he has foreseen it and already provided for it. I learn of it from him insofar as he surpasses and disarms it. However, I do not grasp this surpassing itself but merely the death of my possibility. It is a subtle death: for my possibility of hiding still remains my possibility; insofar as I *am* it, it is still alive; and the dark corner does not stop signaling its potentiality to me, sending it back to me. But if equipmentality can be defined as the state of "being able to be surpassed toward . . . ," then my possibility itself becomes part of it. My possibility of hiding in the corner becomes something that the Other may surpass, toward his possibility of unmasking me, identifying me, and apprehending me. For the Other it is at the same time an obstacle and a means, like all implements. It is an obstacle because it will oblige him to take various new actions (to walk toward me, to switch on his flashlight). And it is a means because, once I am uncovered in the impasse, I am "caught." In other words, any action that I take against the Other can, as a matter of principle, be an instrument for the Other to use against me. And, precisely, I do not apprehend the Other with a clear vision of what he might make of my action but in fear, a fear that lives all my possibilities in ambivalence. The Other is the hidden death of my possibilities, insofar as I live this death as hidden in the midst of the world. The connection between my possibility and the implement is now nothing more than that between two instruments that are arranged one outside the other, in view of an end that escapes me. The obscurity of the dark spot and my possibility of hiding there are at the same time surpassed by the Other when—before I have been able to make any move to take refuge in it— he lights up the corner with his lantern. Thus, in the sudden jolt that shakes me when I grasp the Other's look, there is this: that suddenly I see a subtle alienation of all my possibilities, which are arranged far away from me, in the midst of the world, alongside the world's objects.

But two important consequences result from this. The first is that my possibility becomes, outside me, a probability. Insofar as the Other apprehends my possibility as it is eaten into by a freedom that he is not—a freedom whose witness he becomes and whose effects he calculates—it is a pure indeterminacy within the possibles at play; and that is exactly how I sense it to be. And later, when we liaise directly with the Other through language, and gradually learn what he thinks of us, this can be, at the same time, a source of fascination and of horror: "I swear that I will do it!" "You may well be right. That is what you say, and I'd like to believe you; it is possible, indeed, that you will do it." The very meaning of this dialogue implies that, from the outset, the Other is positioned before my freedom as if before some given, indeterminate property, and confronts my possibles as if they were my probables. In fact, and from the outset, I feel myself to be over there, for the Other, and this phantom-outline of my being reaches me right at my heart, because—through shame, rage, and fear—I do not cease to accept myself as such. And I accept myself blindly, since I do not know what I am accepting: I am it, quite simply.

On the other hand, the implement-possibility structure of myself in relation to the implement appears to me as surpassed, and organized into a world, by the Other. With the Other's look the "situation" escapes me—or, to use a common expression which nonetheless conveys our thought well: *I am no longer master of the situation*. Or, more exactly, I remain its master, but it has a real dimension through which it escapes me, through which unforeseen reversals make it *be* otherwise than it appears to me. Of course it can happen that, while I am quite alone, I perform some action whose consequences are the exact opposite of what I foresee and desire: I tug gently at a plank, in order to bring this fragile vase closer. But this movement has the effect of knocking over a small bronze statue, which smashes the vase into a thousand pieces. Only there is nothing here that I could not have foreseen if I had been more attentive, if I had noticed the way the objects were arranged, etc.: *nothing that escapes me as a matter of principle*. When the other appears, on the contrary, he makes an aspect appear within the situation that I did not want, of which I am not the master, and which escapes me as a matter of principle—because it is *for the other*. This is what Gide felicitously named "the devil's share." It is the *reverse side*, unpredictable and yet real. It is to this unpredictability that Kafka applies his descriptive skills in *The Trial* and *The Castle*: in one sense, everything that K. and the land surveyor do belongs to them as their own and, insofar as they act on the world, the results are strictly in conformity with their predictions: they are actions that succeed.[36] But at the same time the truth of these actions constantly escapes them; they necessarily have a meaning that is their *true meaning*, and which neither K. nor the land surveyor will ever know. And doubtless Kafka is trying here to capture a divine transcendence; it is for a divinity that human action becomes constituted as truth. But here God is the concept of the Other pushed to its limit. We will return to this. This painful and elusive atmosphere of the *Trial*, this ignorance that is nonetheless lived out as ignorance, this complete opacity that can be sensed only through a complete translucency, is nothing but the description of our being-in-the-midst-of-the-world-for-the-Other. In this way, therefore, the situation, in and through its surpassing for the Other, becomes frozen and organized

305

36 TN: K. and the land surveyor are central characters in Kafka's novels *The Trial* (Kafka 1994) and *The Castle* (Kafka 2009), respectively.

around me as a *figure*, in the sense in which the Gestalt theorists use this term: in it there is a given synthesis in which I am an essential structure, and this synthesis possesses at the same time an ecstatic cohesion and an in-itself character. My connection with these people whom I can see talking is given all at once, outside me, as an unknowable substrate of the connection that I myself establish. In particular, my own *look*— or my connection without distance to these people—is stripped of its transcendence, by virtue of the very fact that it is a *looked-at-look*. In point of fact the people whom I *see* are frozen by me into objects; I am, in relation to them, like the Other in relation to them; in looking at them, I take the measure of my power. But if the Other sees them and he sees me, my gaze loses its power: it cannot transform these people into objects *for the Other*, since they are already objects he is looking at. My looking merely manifests a relation in the midst of the world between the me-object and the object-looked-at, rather like the attraction exerted on each other by two masses across a distance. Arranged around this look are, on the one hand, its objects—now the distance from me to the things I am looking at *exists*, but it is closed in, circumscribed, and constricted by my look; the objects-distance structure is like a ground against which my look stands out like a "this" against the ground of the world—and, on the other hand, my postures, which are given as a series of means for "maintaining" my look. In this sense I constitute an organized whole that *is* the look: I am a look-object, i.e., a structure of equipment that is endowed with internal finality, and which can itself be placed into a means-end relation in order to actualize a presence to some other object, across a distance. But the distance *is given to me*. Insofar as I am looked at, I do not unfold distance but confine myself to *crossing* it. The Other's look confers spatiality on me. To grasp oneself as looked at is to grasp oneself as spatialized-spatializing.

But the Other's look is not only grasped as spatializing: it is also *temporalizing*. The appearance of the Other's look is manifested for me by an "*Erlebnis*" that I could not, by definition, have acquired on my own: simultaneity. A world for just one for-itself could not include simultaneity but only co-presences, because the for-itself loses itself outside itself throughout the world, and connects all beings solely through the unity of its presence. Now, simultaneity presupposes a temporal connection between two existents that are not connected by any other relation. Two existents, each of which exerts a reciprocal action on the other, are not simultaneous, precisely because they belong to the same system. Simultaneity, therefore, does not belong to worldly existents; it presupposes the co-presence to the world of two presents that can be viewed as *presences-to*. Pierre's presence *to* the world is simultaneous *with* my presence. In this sense, the primary phenomenon of simultaneity is that this glass is for Paul *at the same time* as it is for me. That presupposes therefore a foundation of all simultaneity, which must necessarily be the presence of an Other who temporalizes himself beside my own temporalization. But, precisely, insofar as the Other temporalizes *himself*, he temporalizes *me* with him: insofar as he launches himself into his own time, I appear to him within universal time. The *Other's look*, to the extent that I grasp it, comes to give my time a new dimension. As a present that the Other grasps as my present, my presence has an outside; this presence that is presentified *for me* becomes alienated for me into a present to which the Other makes himself present; I am thrown into the universal present, insofar as the Other makes himself be a presence to me. But the universal present in which I take up my place is a pure alienation of my universal present; physical time flows away toward a pure and free temporalization that I am not; what is outlined, at the horizon of this simultaneity that I live, is an absolute temporalization from which I am separated by a nothingness.

As a spatio-temporal worldly object, as an essential structure of a spatio-temporal situation within the world, I am offered to the Other's assessment. I grasp that, too, through the pure exercise of the *cogito*: to be looked at is to grasp oneself as the unknown object of unknowable assessments and, in particular, evaluative assessments. But, to be precise, at the same time as I recognize—through shame or pride—the validity of these assessments, I do not cease to take them for what they are: a free surpassing of the given toward possibilities. A judgment is the transcendental act of a free being. In this way, being seen constitutes me as a defenseless being for a freedom that is not my freedom. It is in this sense that we may regard ourselves as "slaves," insofar as we appear to the Other. But this slavery is not the result—historical, and capable of being overcome— of a *life*, in the abstract form of consciousness. I am a slave to the extent to which I am dependent in my being at the heart of a freedom that is not mine, and which is the very condition of my being. Insofar as I am the object of values that enter in to qualify me—without my being able either to act upon this qualification or even to know it—I am enslaved. By the same token, insofar as I am the instrument of possibilities that are not my possibilities, whose pure presence I can only glimpse beyond my being, and which negate my transcendence in order to constitute me as a means, toward ends of which I am ignorant, I am *in danger*. And this danger is not an accident but the permanent structure of my being-for-the-Other.

Now we have reached the end of this description. First we must take note—before we can make use of it to explore the Other—that it has been produced *entirely at the level of the cogito*. We have only explicated the meaning of those subjective reactions to the Other's look that comprise fear (the feeling of being in danger before the Other's freedom), pride or shame (the feeling of being in the end what I am, but elsewhere, over there for the Other), and the recognition of my slavery (the feeling of the alienation of all my possibilities). In addition, this explication is in no way a conceptual determination of items of (more or less obscure) *knowledge*. Let anyone consult their own experience: there is no person in existence who has never been surprised one day in an attitude that is culpable, or simply ridiculous. The sudden modification that we then experience is not in any way elicited by the incursion of an item of knowledge. Rather, it is in itself a sudden solidification and stratification of myself, which leaves my possibilities and my structures "for-me" intact, but which suddenly pushes me into a new dimension of existence: the dimension of the *unrevealed*. In this way, I grasp the appearing of the look as the arising of an ecstatic relation of being, of which one of the terms is myself—as a for-itself that is what it is not, and is not what it is—and whose other term is me again, but outside my reach, outside my action, outside my knowledge. And this term, precisely because it is connected with the infinite possibilities of a free Other, is in itself an infinite and inexhaustible synthesis of unrevealed properties. Through the Other's look I live myself as frozen in the midst of the world, in danger, and irremediable. But I do not know either *who* I am or *what* my place is within the world, or which face the world I am in is turning toward the Other.

Henceforth we can clarify the meaning of this arising of the Other, in and through his look. The Other is not in any way given to us as an object. The objectification of the Other would be the collapse of his look-being. Moreover, as we saw, the Other's look even means the disappearance of the Other's *eyes* as objects that manifest the look. The Other cannot even be an object that I emptily aim at, at the horizon of my being for the Other. As we will see, the objectification of the Other is a defense of my being which, precisely, liberates me from my being for the Other by conferring on the Other a being for me. In the phenomenon of the look, the Other is by definition something that cannot be an object. At the same time, we can see that he cannot be a *term* in the relation between me and myself through which I arise for myself as *unrevealed*. Nor can the Other be what I direct my *attention* to: if, when the Other's look arose, I were to *pay attention* to the look or to the Other, these would have to take the form of *objects*, because attention is an intentional directedness toward objects. But it would be wrong to conclude from this that the Other is some abstract condition, a conceptual structure of the ecstatic relation: in fact, there is no object here able to be genuinely thought, of which the Other might be a universal and formal structure. To be sure, the Other is the condition of my unrevealed-being. But he is its concrete and individual condition. He is not committed within my being in the midst of the world as one of its integral parts, precisely because it is he who transcends this world in whose midst I am, as unrevealed; as such, he cannot therefore be either an object or a formal and constitutive element of an object. He cannot appear to me, as we saw, as a unifying or regulative category of my experience, because he comes to me by means of an encounter. What, therefore, is he?

In the first place, he is the being toward whom I do not turn my attention. He is the one looking at me, and whom I am not yet looking at; the one who delivers me to myself as *unrevealed*, but without revealing himself; the one who is present to me insofar as he aims at me, and not insofar as he is aimed at: he is the concrete and unreachable pole of my flight, of the alienation of my possibles, and of the flowing away of the world toward another world that is *the same* as this one and yet cut off from it. But he cannot be distinct from that alienation itself and from that flowing away; he is its meaning and direction, and he haunts this flowing away, not as a *real* or *categorial* element but as a presence that becomes frozen and worldly if I attempt to "presentify" it and which is never more present, or more urgent, than when I am not watching out for him. If, for example, I am entirely caught up in my shame, the Other is the immense and invisible presence that supports this shame, encompassing it from all sides, the medium that supports my unrevealed-being.

Let us see how the Other is manifested as *unrevealable* through my lived experience of the unrevealed.

In the first place, the *Other's look*, as the necessary condition of my objectivity, is the destruction of all objectivity for me. The Other's look reaches me through the world and is not only a transformation of myself but a complete metamorphosis of the world. I am looked at in a world that is looked at. In particular, the Other's look—which is a looking-look, not a looked-at-look—negates my distance to objects and unfolds its own distances. This look of the Other is immediately given as the way in which distance enters the world, at the heart of a presence without distance. I step back; I am deprived of my presence without distance to my world, and provided with a distance to the Other. Here I am, fifteen steps away from the door, and six meters from the window. But the Other comes to get me, to constitute me at a certain distance from him. To constitute me as being six meters away from him, the Other must be present to me without distance. In this way, within my very experience of my distance from things and from the Other, I feel the Other's presence without distance to me. Anyone can recognize, in this abstract description, that immediate and burning presence of the Other's look that has so often filled us with shame. In other words, insofar as I experience myself as looked at, a transmundane presence of the Other is actualized for me: it is not insofar as he is "in the midst" of my world that the Other looks at me but insofar as he comes in the entirety of his transcendence toward the world and toward me, insofar as he is separated from me not by any distance, or any real or ideal worldly object, or by any worldly body but solely by his nature as the Other. Thus the appearing of the Other's look is not an appearance *in the world*—either in "mine" or in "the Other's"—and the relation that joins me to the Other cannot be a relation of externality within the world; rather, through the Other's look, I concretely experience that there is something beyond the world. The Other is present to me without any intermediary as a transcendence *that is not my own*. But this presence is not reciprocal: it would require the entire density of the world for me to be present to the Other. An omnipresent and elusive transcendence, resting upon me, insofar as I am my unrevealed-being, without intermediary and separated from me by the infinity of being, insofar as this look plunges me into a world which, with its distances and implements, is complete: such is the Other's look, when I first experience him as a look.

But, in addition, by freezing my possibilities, the Other reveals to me that it is impossible for me to be an object unless it is for another freedom. I cannot be an object for myself, because I am what I am: with only its own resources, the reflective effort to split into two leads to failure; I am always seized back by myself. And when I naïvely postulate that it is possible that—without realizing it—I am an objective being, I implicitly presuppose, in that very claim, the Other's existence: for how could I be an object, other than for a subject? Thus the Other is for me in the first instance the being for whom I am an object, i.e., the being through whom I gain my objecthood. If it must merely be possible for me to conceive any one of my properties in the objective mode, the Other is already given. And he is given not as a being in my universe but as a pure subject. Thus this pure subject whom I am unable, by definition, to know—i.e., to posit as an object—is always there, out of reach and without distance, when I try to grasp myself as an object. And when I undergo the look, in my experience of my unrevealed objecthood, I experience directly and with my being the Other's elusive subjectivity.

310

By the same token, I experience his infinite freedom. That is because it is for and through a freedom—and only for and through it—that my possibles can be limited and frozen. A material obstacle could not freeze my possibilities, and is only an opportunity for me to project myself toward other possibles; it could not confer on them an *outside*. It is not the same thing to stay at home because it is raining or because you have been forbidden to go out. In the first case I determine myself, through a consideration of the consequences of my actions, to remain; I surpass the obstacle "rain" toward myself and I make it into an instrument. In the second case, it is my possibilities themselves—of going out or of remaining—that are presented to me as surpassed and frozen, and which a freedom is at the same time predicting and preventing. If it often happens that we will do something quite happily and naturally but would be annoyed if someone else were to command us to do it, our behavior is not perverse. For orders and prohibitions require us to undergo the Other's freedom, through our own slavery. In this way, in the look, the death of my possibilities makes me experience the Other's freedom; it is only brought about at the heart of that freedom, and I am myself, inaccessible to myself and yet myself, thrown and abandoned within the Other's freedom. In connection with this experience, my belonging to universal time can appear to me only as contained and actualized by an autonomous temporalization; only a for-itself that temporalizes itself is able to throw me into time.

Thus, through his look, I experience the Other concretely as a free and conscious subject who makes it the case that there is a world by temporalizing himself toward his own possibilities. And the presence of this subject without an intermediary is the necessary condition for any thought I might attempt to form about myself. The Other is this "myself" from which nothing separates me, absolutely nothing—unless it is his pure and total freedom, i.e., this indeterminacy of himself that only he has to be, for and through himself.

We know enough now to try to explain the unshakable resistance that good sense has always opposed to solipsistic reasoning. In fact, that resistance is founded on the fact that the Other is given to me as a concrete and evident presence that I can in no way derive from myself and which cannot in any way be placed in doubt, be made the object of a phenomenological reduction, or any other "ἐποχή."

If someone looks at me, then, I am conscious of being an object. But this consciousness can be brought about only in and through the Other's existence. About that, Hegel was right. Only this other consciousness and this other freedom are never given to me, because if they were, they would be known—and therefore objects—and I would cease to be an object. Nor can I derive their concept or representation from my own depths. This is because, first, I do not "conceive" or "represent" them to myself: expressions of that kind would return us again to the "knowing" that has by definition been ruled out of play. But, in addition, any concrete experience of freedom that I am able to effect by myself is an experience of my freedom, and any concrete apprehension of consciousness is a consciousness (of) my consciousness; the very notion of consciousness refers only to my possible [acts of] consciousness. Indeed, we established in the Introduction that the existence of freedom and consciousness precedes and conditions their essence; these essences, in consequence, can only subsume particular exemplifications of my consciousness or my freedom. In the third place, the freedom and consciousness of the Other cannot be categories that serve to unify my representations. Of course, as Husserl showed, the ontological structure of "my" world demands that it be at the same time a world for the Other. But, to the extent to which the Other confers a particular type of objectivity on the objects of my world, it is because he is already in that world, as an object. If it is correct that Pierre, reading in front of me, bestows a particular type of objectivity on the side of the book that is turned toward him, that objectivity is given to a side that I am, as a matter of principle, able to see (even though it escapes me, as we saw, precisely insofar as it is read), which belongs to the world in which I am and which, in consequence, is bound, beyond the distance and through a magical connection, to the Pierre-object. In these conditions, the concept of the Other may in fact be fixed as an empty form, and constantly used to reinforce the objectivity of the world that is mine. But the Other's presence in his looking-look cannot help to reinforce the world; on the contrary, it unworlds it because it actually makes it the case that the world escapes me.[37] When it is *relative*, and an escaping toward the Other-object, the world's escaping from me reinforces objectivity; when it is *absolute*, and operating in the direction of a freedom that is not my own, the escaping of the world—and of myself—from me is a dissolution of my knowledge; the world disintegrates, in order to reintegrate itself as a world over there, but this disintegration is not given to me; I cannot know it, or even merely think it. The presence to me of the Other-look is not, therefore, an item of knowledge; neither is it a projection of my being, or a form of unification or category. It is, and I am unable to derive it from myself.

At the same time I cannot make it fall under the phenomenological ἐποχή. The goal of this latter is, in effect, to place the world within parentheses in order to uncover transcendental consciousness in its absolute reality. Whether or not this operation is possible in general is not something that we intend to talk about here. But, in the case that does concern us, it cannot put the Other out of play because, precisely insofar as he is a looking-look, he does not belong to the world. I am ashamed of myself *before* the Other, we said. The consequence of the phenomenological reduction must be to take the object of shame out of play, in order to throw the shame itself into sharper relief, within its absolute subjectivity. But the Other is not shame's *object*: its objects are my act, or my situation within the world. Strictly speaking, it is these alone that it is possible to

312

37 TN: ... *elle le démondanise au contraire* ... I have matched Sartre's neologistic *démondaniser* with the neologistic verb "to unworld."

"reduce." The Other is not even an objective condition of my shame. And yet he is something like its very being. Shame is the revelation of the Other, not in the way in which a consciousness reveals an object but in the way in which one moment of consciousness laterally implies another moment as its motivation. Were we, through the *cogito*, to have reached pure consciousness, and were this consciousness to be only a consciousness (of being) shame, the Other's consciousness would still haunt it as an elusive presence and would thereby escape any reduction. This is enough to show us that it is not within the world that we must first seek the Other but on the side of consciousness, as a consciousness in which and through which our consciousness makes itself be what it is. Just as my consciousness—apprehended through the *cogito*—bears witness indubitably to itself and to its own existence, there are some particular [acts of] consciousness—for example "shame-consciousness"—that bear witness to the *cogito* both of themselves and of the Other's existence, indubitably.

But—it might be asked—isn't the Other's look simply the *meaning* of my objectivity-for-me? With that we would fall back into solipsism: in integrating myself as an object within the concrete system of my representations, the meaning of this objectification would be projected outside myself and hypostasized as *the Other*.

But here we must note that:

(1) My objecthood for me is not in any way an explication of Hegel's "*Ich bin Ich*."[38] There is no question here of a formal identity, and my object-being or being-for-the-Other is radically different from my being-for-myself. Indeed, as we pointed out in Part One, the notion of *objecthood* requires an explicit negation. The object is what is not my consciousness and, in consequence, something that does not have the characteristics of consciousness, since the only existent that has the characteristics of consciousness for me is the consciousness that is *mine*. Thus the me-object-for-me is a me which *is not* me, i.e., a me that does not have the characteristics of consciousness. It is a *degraded* consciousness: objectification is a radical metamorphosis and, even if I were able to see myself clearly and distinctly as an object, what I would see would not

---

38 TN: The German phrase means "I am I"; Sartre has discussed Hegel's use of this equation in the previous section.

be an adequate representation of what I am in myself and for myself, of this "incomparable monster, to be preferred to everything" that Malraux talks about,[39] but the apprehension of my being-outside-myself, for the other, i.e., the objective apprehension of my other-being, which is radically different from my being-for-myself and does not link up to it. I could not grasp myself as *wicked*, for example, by referring to what I am for myself, because I am not, nor can I be, wicked for myself. That is because, first, I *am* not wicked for myself, any more than I "am" a civil servant or a doctor. In fact, I am in the mode of not being what I am and of being what I am not. To qualify me as "wicked" is, on the contrary, to characterize me as an *in-itself*. And next, because if I were *to be* wicked for myself, I would have to be that in the mode of *having it to be*, i.e., I would have to grasp myself and to will myself as wicked. But that would mean that I had to be disclosed to myself as willing something that appears to me as the opposite of my Good and precisely because it was Evil, or the opposite of my Good. It would be necessary therefore for me explicitly to want the opposite of what I want, within the same moment and within the same relation, i.e., for me to hate myself precisely to the extent that I am myself. And in order to actualize fully this essence of wickedness in the territory of the for-itself, it would be necessary for me to accept myself as wicked, i.e., to approve of myself through the same action that makes me blame myself. This suffices to show us that this notion of wickedness can in no way derive its origin from me insofar as I am myself. And even if I try to push to its extreme limits the ecstasis or self-separation that constitutes me for-myself, if I am left with my own resources I will never succeed in conferring wickedness upon myself, nor even in conceiving it for myself. For I *am* my self-separating, and I *am* my own nothingness; to make all objectivity disappear, it suffices that, between me and myself, I should be my own intermediary. It is not that I must *be* this nothingness that separates me from the object-me, since there must be a *presentation* to me of the object that I am. In this way I cannot confer any quality on myself without the mediation of an objectifying power that does not lie within my own power and that I am unable either to feign or to forge.

39 TN: ... *ce "monstre incomparable et préférable à tout"*... Sartre is alluding to a passage (about human egoism) in Malraux's novel *La Condition Humaine*, published in France in 1933 and translated as Malraux (1990).

Of course, this has been said: for a long time we have been saying that the Other teaches me who I am. But the same people who put that thesis forward were asserting, on the other hand, that I derive the concept of the Other from myself, through reflection on my own powers, or through a projection or analogy. They remained therefore in a vicious circle, from which they were unable to get out. In fact, the Other cannot be the meaning of my objectivity; he is its concrete and transcendent condition. In fact, these qualities—"wicked," "jealous," "nice," or "unpleasant"—are not mere dreams; when I make use of them to qualify the Other, I am aware that I want to reach him in his being. And yet I am unable to live them as my own realities: if the Other confers them on me, they are not rejected by what I am for-myself; when the Other offers me a description of my character, I do not "recognize" myself and yet I know that "it's me." I immediately accept this stranger with whom I am presented, without his ceasing to be a stranger. For he is not a simple unification of my subjective representations, nor is he a "Me" that I am, in the sense of "*Ich bin Ich*"; nor is he a hollow image that the Other forms of me, and for which he would alone bear the responsibility. This "me" which is incomparable to the me that I have to be is still me, but metamorphosed within a new medium, and adapted to that medium; it is a being, my being, but with entirely new dimensions of being and modalities; it is a me that is separated from me by an unbridgeable nothingness, because I *am* this me, but I am not this nothingness that separates me from myself. It is the me who I am through a final ecstasis that transcends all *my ecstases*, because it is not the ecstasis that I have to be. My being-for-the-Other is a fall toward objectivity, through an absolute void. And as this fall is an *alienation*, I cannot make myself be for myself as an object, because in no circumstance can I alienate myself from myself.

(2) Moreover, the Other does not constitute me as an object for myself but *for him*. In other words, he is not used as a regulative or constitutive concept for instances of *knowledge* that I can have of myself. The Other's presence therefore does not make the object-me "appear:" I grasp nothing but an escaping away from myself toward . . . Even when language has revealed to me that the Other regards me as wicked or as jealous, I will never have a concrete intuition of my wickedness or my jealousy. They will only ever be fleeting notions, whose very nature will be to escape me: I will not grasp my wickedness but, in relation to this or that

action, I will escape from myself; I will feel my alienation and my flowing away toward a being that I am able to think only emptily as wicked and yet that I will feel myself to be, and that I will live at a distance, through shame or fear.

Thus my me-object is neither knowledge nor a unity of knowledge but unease, a lived separation from the for-itself's ecstatic unity, a limit that I cannot reach and yet that I am. And the other through whom this self of mine arrives at me is neither knowledge nor a category but the fact of the presence of a foreign freedom. In fact, my separating from myself and the arising of the Other's freedom are one and the same; I can only feel them and live them together, and I cannot even try to conceive of one without the other. The fact of the Other is incontestable and reaches right to my heart. I actualize it through my *unease*; by virtue of it, I am constantly *in danger* in a world that is *this* world and yet which I am able only to sense; and the Other does not appear to me as a being who is   315 constituted first in order to encounter me subsequently but as a being who arises in an original relation of being with me, and whose indubitability and *factual necessity* are those of my consciousness.

However, numerous difficulties remain. In particular, through shame we confer on the Other an indubitable presence. Now, as we have seen, it is only *probable* that the Other is looking at me. It is certain that this farm that, at the summit of the hill, *seems* to be looking at the soldiers of the irregular military is occupied by the enemy;[40] but it is not certain that the enemy soldiers are at this moment watching through its windows. It is not certain that this man, whose steps I can hear behind me, is looking at me; his face may be turned in another direction, his gaze fixed on the ground or on a book; and in the end, quite generally, I cannot be sure that the eyes that are fixed on me are eyes; they might only be "made," "in the likeness of" real eyes. In short, because I am able constantly to believe myself to be looked at when I am not, doesn't the look in its turn become *probable*? And will all our certainty of the Other's existence hereby reassume a purely hypothetical character?

We may express the difficulty in these terms: on the occasion of certain appearances within the world that seem to me to manifest a look,

---

40 TN: . . . *les soldats du corps franc* . . . As before, Sartre is thinking of the Resistance fighters in the French Occupation.

I grasp in myself a certain "being-looked-at" with its own structures, directing me to the Other's real existence. But it is possible that I am mistaken: perhaps the worldly objects that I took to be eyes were not eyes; perhaps it was only the wind making the bush behind me shake; in brief, perhaps these concrete objects were not *really* manifesting a look. In that case, what becomes of my certainty that I am *being looked at*? My shame was in effect *shame before somebody*: but there is nobody there. Does it not thereby become *shame before nobody*, which is to say—since someone was posited as being there, when there was nobody—a *false* shame?

This difficulty will not detain us for long, and we would not even have mentioned it if it did not offer the advantage of furthering the progress of our investigation and highlighting more distinctly the nature of our being-for-the-Other. In fact it confuses two distinct orders of knowledge and two incomparable types of being. We have always known that the object-in-the-world can be only probable. That stems from its very character as an object. It is probable that the passerby is a man; and if he turns his eyes toward me, although I immediately experience, with certainty, my *being-looked-at*, I cannot transfer this certainty into my experience of the object-Other. In effect, it only discloses the subject-Other, a transcendent presence to the world and the real condition of my object-being. In any event, it is therefore impossible to transfer my certainty of the subject-Other on to the object-Other who was the occasion of this certainty and, conversely, to disconfirm the evidence of the subject-Other's appearance, on the basis of the probability that is constitutive of the object-Other. Better still, the *look*, as we have shown, appears on the ground of the destruction of the object manifesting it. If this fat and ugly passerby who is approaching me, and skipping, suddenly looks at me, that is the end of his ugliness and obesity and skipping: throughout the time in which I feel myself to be looked at he is a pure freedom, mediating between myself and me. Being-looked-at cannot therefore *depend on* the object which manifests the look. And since my shame, as an "*Erlebnis*" that can be grasped reflectively, testifies to the Other to the same degree as to itself, I am not going to put it in question on the occasion of a worldly object that can, as a matter of principle, be revoked by doubt. I might as well doubt my own existence because the perceptions that I have of my own body (when, for example, I see my hand) are subject to error. If therefore, *being-looked-at*, considered in its purest form, is not linked to the Other's body any more than my consciousness of being a consciousness, when the *cogito* is purely actualized, is linked to my own body, we must consider the appearance of certain objects within the field of my experience, and in particular the convergence of the Other's eyes in my direction, as a pure *monition*, as the pure occasion for the realization of my being-looked-at, in the way in which, for Plato, the contradictions of the sensible world are the occasion for bringing about a philosophical conversion. In brief, what is certain is that I *am looked at*; what is only probable is that the look is connected to this or that intramundane presence. Moreover, nothing in that should surprise us, since, as we saw, it is never *eyes* that are looking at us; it is the Other as a subject. But, we may be told, it remains the case that I may discover that I was mistaken: there I am, bent over the keyhole; suddenly I hear some steps. A shudder of shame runs through me: someone has seen me. I stand up, and I scan with my eyes the deserted corridor: it was a false alarm. I take a breath. Here, do we not have an experience that is its own destruction?

Let us take a closer look. Is it my objective-being for the Other that has been revealed as an error? Not at all. The existence of the Other is so far from being placed in doubt that this false alarm may easily have as a consequence that I abandon my enterprise. If on the contrary I persevere, I will feel my heart beating and I will watch out for the slightest noise, the slightest creaking of the steps in the staircase. Far from the Other having disappeared with my first alert, now he is present everywhere, beneath me, above me, in the neighboring bedrooms, and I continue to feel my being-for-the-Other profoundly. It is even possible that my shame does not disappear: it is with a red face, now, that I lean over toward the keyhole; I do not cease to *undergo* my being-for-the-Other;[41] my possibilities do not cease to "die," nor do the distances stop unfolding toward me from the staircase where someone "might" be, from that dark corner where a human presence "might" be hiding. Better still, if I start at the slightest sound, if each creak announces a look to me, that is because I am already in the state of being-looked-at. In brief, what therefore was it that misleadingly appeared and was then destroyed during the false alert? It is not the subject-Other, or his presence to me: it is the Other's *facticity*,

317

41 TN: ...*je ne cesse plus d'éprouver mon être-pour-autrui* ... See my discussion of *éprouver* in the section on vocabulary relating to the mind in Notes on the Translation.

i.e., the contingent connection between the Other and an object-being within my world. Thus it is not the Other himself who is doubtful; it is the Other's *being-there*, which is to say this historical and concrete event that we can express by the words "There is someone in that bedroom."

These observations will enable us to go further. The Other's presence in the world cannot follow analytically, in effect, from the Other-subject's presence to me, because this original presence is transcendent, which is to say being-beyond-the-world. I believed that the Other was present in the room, but I was mistaken: he was not there; he was "absent." What, then, is *absence*?

If we take the word *absence* in its empirical and everyday usage, it is clear that I will not use it to refer to just any kind of "not-being-there." In the first place, if I do not find my packet of tobacco in its usual place, I do not say that it is *absent* from that place, even though I might assert that "it should be there." That is because, even though it may sometimes be carefully assigned to it, the place for a material object or an instrument does not follow from its *nature*. This latter may just about confer on it a location, but it is through me that an instrument's *place* is actualized. Human-reality is the being through whom a *place* comes to objects. And it is human-reality, alone, insofar as it is its own possibilities, that is able from the outset to take up a place. But, on the other hand, I would not say either that the Aga Khan or the Sultan of Morocco is absent from this apartment here—but rather that Pierre, who usually lives there, has been absent from it for a quarter of an hour. In brief, absence is defined as a mode of being of human-reality in relation to locations and to places that it has itself determined through its presence. Absence is not a nothingness of connection with a place but, on the contrary, I determine Pierre in relation to some determinate place by declaring that he is absent from it. And finally I do not talk about Pierre's absence in relation to a natural place, even if he often passes through it. But, on the contrary, I might deplore his absence from some picnic that "takes place" in some region where he has never been. Pierre's absence is defined in relation to a place at which he ought to determine himself to be, but that place itself is not delimited as a place by its site, or even by solitary relations between that place and Pierre himself, but by the presence of other human-realities. It is in relation to *other men* that Pierre is absent. Absence is a concrete mode of Pierre's being in relation to Thérèse: it is a connection of being between human-realities, and not between human-reality and the world. It is through his relation to Thérèse that Pierre is absent *from this location*. Absence therefore is a connection of being between two or several human-realities that necessitates the fundamental presence of each of these realities for the others, and which, moreover, is only one of the particular ways of instantiating that presence. To be absent, for Pierre in relation to Thérèse, is a particular way of being present to her. In fact absence is significant only if all Pierre's relations with Thérèse remain intact: he loves her, he is her husband, he provides for her keep, etc. In particular, absence presupposes the conservation of Pierre's *concrete* existence: death is not an absence. From this it follows that Pierre's *distance* from Thérèse does nothing to change the fundamental fact of their reciprocal presence. In fact, if we consider this presence from Pierre's point of view, we can see that it means *either* that Thérèse is existing in the midst of the world as an Other-object *or* that he feels himself to exist for Thérèse as for an *Other-subject*. In the first case the distance is a contingent fact and means nothing in relation to the fundamental fact that it is Pierre through whom "there is" a world in the form of a Totality, and that Pierre is present without distance to this world, as the one through whom distance exists. In the second case, wherever Pierre is, he feels himself to exist for Thérèse without distance: she is *at a distance* from him to the extent to which she separates him from her, and unfolds a distance between herself and him; the entire world separates him from her. But, insofar as he is an object in the world that she brings into being, he is without any distance to her. In either case, in consequence, their separation cannot modify these essential relations. Whether the distance is small or great, between Pierre-object and Thérèse-subject, between Thérèse-object and Pierre-subject, there lies the infinite breadth of a world; between Pierre-subject and Thérèse-object, between Thérèse-subject and Pierre-object, there is no distance at all. In this way the empirical concepts of "absence" and "presence" are two specifications of a fundamental presence, of Pierre to Thérèse and of Thérèse to Pierre; all they do is express that presence in one way or another, and only through it do they have any meaning. In London, in India, in America, on a desert island, Pierre is present to Thérèse, who has remained in Paris; he will only cease to be present to her at his death. That is because a being is not *situated* through his relation with places, by his degree of longitude and his degree of latitude: he is situated within a human space, between "the

Guermantes way" and "Swann's way," and what allows that "hodological" space in which he is situated to unfold is the immediate presence of
Swann or of the Duchess of Guermantes.[42] Now, this presence takes place
within transcendence; it is the presence to me, within transcendence, of
my cousin from Morocco that enables me to unfold, between myself and
him, this path that situates-me-in-the-world and which we might call
"the road to Morocco." In fact, this road is no more than the distance
between the object-Other that I am able to *perceive* in its connection with
my "being-for" (and) the subject-Other who is present to me without
distance.[43] In this way I am *situated* by the infinite diversity of the roads that
lead me to objects of my world in correlation with the immediate presence
of transcendent subjects. And as the world with all of its beings is given to
me all at once, these roads represent only the set of instrumental complexes that enable some Other-object—already implicitly and really contained within it—to appear as a "this" against the ground of the world.
But these remarks can be generalized: it is not only Pierre, René, and
Lucien who are absent or present in relation to me against the ground of
an original presence, because it is not they alone who contribute to situate
me. I am also situated as a European in relation to Asians or to Negroes, as
an old man in relation to young people, as a magistrate in relation to
offenders, as a bourgeois in relation to workers, etc. In brief, it is in relation to every living man that the entirety of human-reality is present or
absent against the ground of an original presence. And this original presence can only have meaning as a being-looked-at or as a looking-being—
in other words, according to whether the Other is an object for me or I
myself am an object-for-the-Other. Being-for-the-Other is a constant fact
of my human reality and I grasp it, with its *factual* necessity, in the slightest
thought that I form about myself. Wherever I go, whatever I do, I am only
changing my distances to the object-Other, only following roads toward

---

42 TN: ... *un être n'est pas situé par son rapport* ... Although Sartre's use of *un être* ("a being")
in this sentence hypothetically includes non-human beings, I think the intended reference is limited to humans and so I use the pronoun "he" rather than "it." Sartre's
allusions to the *côté de Guermantes* and the *côté de Swann* are of course to Proust's *À la Recherche
du Temps Perdu*. For "hodological," see the section on vocabulary relating to the mind in
Notes on the Translation.

43 TN: Sartre puts the brackets round *et* in this sentence, presumably to remind the reader
that the Other as subject and as object are in one sense the same person.

the Other. To move away, to come closer, or to discover this particular Other-object is only to enact empirical variations on the fundamental theme of my being-for-the-Other. The Other is present to me everywhere, as that through which I become an object. Given that, I may well be mistaken about the empirical presence of an Other-object that I have just met on my way. I may well believe it is Anny who is coming toward me on the path, and discover that it is an unknown person: Anny's fundamental presence to me is not thereby modified. I may well believe that a man is watching me in the shadows, and discover that it is a tree trunk which I took to be a human being: my fundamental presence to all men, the presence to me of all men, is not thereby altered, because the appearing of some man as an object within the field of my experience is not what teaches me that *there are* men. My certainty of the Other's existence is independent of these experiences and it is the former, on the contrary, that makes them possible. What appears to me then, and what I can be wrong about, is not the Other, nor the real and concrete connection between the Other and me, but rather a *this* by which an object-man *might* be represented—just as, also, it might not represent him. What is only probable is the Other's distance and his real proximity, which is to say that his character as an object and his belonging to the world that I bring to dis-   320
closure are not doubtful, insofar as I make it the case, merely by arising, that an Other appears. Only this objectivity is founded within the world under the description "the Other within the world somewhere:" as something that appears, the object-Other is certain, and the correlative of my taking up of my subjectivity; but it is never certain that the Other is *this* object. And, similarly, the fundamental fact—my being-an-object for a subject—is supported by evidence of the same type as the evidence of reflection, but not the fact that, in this precise moment and for one particular Other, I stand out as a *this* against the ground of the world, rather than remaining drowned within some ground's lack of distinction. That I exist now as an object for a German, whoever he is: that is indubitable. But do I exist in my capacity as a European, a Frenchman, or a Parisian within these undifferentiated groupings, or in my capacity as *this* Parisian, around whom the Parisian population and the French collectivity are suddenly organized in order to provide him with a ground? On this point I will be able to obtain knowledge that is only probable—even though it may be infinitely probable.

We are able now to grasp the nature of the look: in every look an object-Other appears within my perceptual field as a concrete and probable presence and, on the occasion of various attitudes of this Other, I determine myself to grasp—through shame, anguish, etc.—my "being-looked-at." This "being-looked-at" is presented as the pure probability that I am presently the concrete this—a probability that can derive its meaning, and its very nature as probable, only from a fundamental certainty that the Other is always present to me insofar as I am always for the Other. The experience of my condition as a man, as an object for all other living men, thrown into the arena before millions of eyes—and escaping millions of times from myself—is concretely actualized by me on the occasion of an object's arising within my universe, if this object indicates to me that I am probably an object now as a differentiated this for some consciousness. That is the totality of the phenomenon that we are calling "the look." Each look makes us concretely experience—and within the indubitable certainty of the cogito—that we exist for all living men, i.e., that there are (some) consciousnesses for whom I exist. We put "some" in brackets in order to highlight that the subject-Other who is present to me in this look is not given in the plural form, any more than he is, moreover, given as a single item (except in his concrete relation to one particular object-Other). In point of fact, plurality only belongs to objects; it arrives in being through the appearance of an enworlding for-itself.[44] Being-looked-at, by making (some) subjects arise for us, puts us in the presence of a reality that is not numbered. On the contrary, from the moment I am looking, the people who are looking at me—the other consciousnesses—become isolated within a multiplicity. If, on the other hand, by turning away from the look in the circumstance of some particular experience, I try to think the human presence, in its infinite lack of distinction, emptily and to unify it under the concept of the infinite subject who is never an object, I will obtain a purely formal notion, which refers to an infinite series of mystical experiences of the Other's presence: the notion of God as the omnipresent and infinite subject for whom I exist. But both of these two objectifications, the concrete objectification that is

321

44 TN: ... par l'apparition d'un pour-soi mondifiant. I borrow the neologistic "to enworld," used in English translations of Heidegger, for Sartre's neologistic mondifier. The idea is that the for-itself brings with it and actualizes its own world.

countable, and the abstract and unifying objectification, miss the reality that is undergone, i.e., the Other's pre-numerical presence. The following observation—which anyone can make—will render these remarks more concrete: if we find ourselves appearing "in public" in order to perform a role or to give a lecture, we do not lose sight of the fact that we are looked at, and we carry out the series of actions that we have come to perform *in the presence* of the look; or, better, we try to constitute a being and a set of objects for this look. But we do not enumerate the look. For as long as we are speaking, and attending only to the ideas that we want to develop, the Other's presence remains undifferentiated. It would be a mistake to unify it under the categories "*the class*," "*the audience*," etc.: we are not in fact conscious of a concrete and individuated being with a collective consciousness; those are images that we might use later to express our experience and largely to betray it. But neither do we grasp a plural look. Rather, we find ourselves dealing with an intangible, fleeting, and omnipresent reality, which actualizes our non-revealed Me before us, and collaborates with us in producing this Me that escapes me. If, on the contrary, I want to check that my idea has been clearly understood, and if I look in my turn at the audience, I will suddenly see *some* heads and *some* eyes appearing. In becoming objectified, the pre-numerical reality of the Other has become decomposed and pluralized. But the look has also disappeared. It is for this pre-numerical and concrete reality, rather than for some inauthentic condition of human-reality, that we ought to reserve the term "*they*."[45] Constantly, wherever I am, *they* are looking at me. The *they* is never grasped as an object; it immediately disintegrates.

Thus the look has set us on the path to our *being-for-the-Other* and revealed to us the indubitable existence of this Other, for whom we are. But it cannot take us any further: what we are obliged to investigate next is the fundamental relation between Me and the Other, as we have encountered it or—alternatively—our task now is to explicate and to determine thematically everything included within the limits of this original relation and to ask ourselves what the *being* of this being-for-the-Other is.

---

45 TN: . . . *qu'il convient de réserver le mot de "on."* As explained in Notes on the Translation, as Sartre is borrowing Heidegger's concept of *das Man*, "they"—and not "one"—is the best translation.

A consideration—implicit in our earlier remarks—that will help us in this task is that being-for-the-Other is not an ontological structure of the for-itself: we cannot expect, in fact, to derive being-for-the-Other from being-for-itself, in the way we can derive a consequence from a principle; nor, conversely, can we derive being-for-itself from being-for-the-Other. Doubtless, it is a requirement of our human-reality that it be simultaneously for-itself and for-the-Other, but our present investigation does not aim to constitute an anthropology. It would not perhaps be impossible to conceive of a for-itself who was wholly free of any for-the-Other and able to exist without even suspecting the possibility of being an object. Only this for-itself would not be "man." What the *cogito* reveals to us here is simply a *factual* necessity: it happens—and this is indubitable—that our being, in connection with its being-for-itself, is also for the Other; the being that is revealed to reflective consciousness is for-itself-for-the-Other; the Cartesian *cogito* only asserts the absolute truth of a *fact*, the fact of my existence; likewise, the slightly expanded *cogito* that we have been using here reveals as a fact the Other's existence to us, and my existence for the Other. That is all we can say. Therefore my being-for-the-Other, like the arising into being of my consciousness, has the character of an absolute event. As this event is at the same time a historialization—because I temporalize myself as a presence to the Other—and the condition of any history, we will call it an "ante-historical historialization." And it is in this capacity, as an ante-historical temporalization of simultaneity, that we are considering it here. By "ante-historical" we do not mean that it exists in some time that is anterior to history—that would make no sense—but that it forms part of that original temporalization which historializes itself as it makes history possible. It is as a fact—as a primary and a constant fact—and not as an essential necessity that we are studying our being-for-the-Other.

We saw earlier the difference between the two types of negation: internal and external negation. In particular, we noted that the foundation for any knowledge of a determinate being is the original relation through which the for-itself, even as it arises, has to be as not being *this* being. The negation that the for-itself hereby actualizes is an internal negation; the for-itself actualizes it in the fullness of its freedom; better, it *is* this negation, insofar as it chooses itself as finitude. But it connects it indissolubly to the being that it is not, and we were able to say

that the for-itself includes, within its being, the being of the object that
it is not, insofar as it is in question in its being as not being this being.
These observations can be applied without any essential change to the
for-itself's first relation with the Other. If there is an Other in general, it
is necessary above all that I should be the one who is not the other, and
it is in this negation itself—operated by me, and in relation to me—that I
make myself be and that the Other arises as the Other. This negation that
constitutes my being—and which, as Hegel says, makes me appear as the
Same in the face of the Other—constitutes me in the domain of non-thetic
ipseity as "Myself." We should not take this to mean that some me comes
to inhabit our consciousness but rather that my ipseity is reinforced by
arising as the negation of another ipseity, and that this reinforcement is
positively grasped as the ipseity's continuous choice by itself of itself as
the same ipseity, and as this ipseity itself. A for-itself that had its "itself" to be
without being its self is conceivable. Only the for-itself that I am has to be
what it is in the form of a refusal of the other, i.e., as its self.[46] In this way,
by using expressions that we apply to our knowledge of the Non-me
in general, we are able to say that the for-itself, as its self, includes the
Other's being within its being insofar as it is in question in its being as
not being the Other. In other words, in order for it to be possible for
consciousness not to be the Other and, therefore, in order for it to be
possible for "there to be" an Other without this "not being"—which is
the condition of the "itself"—being purely and simply an object remarked
by a "third man" witness, it is necessary that it should have to be this
not-being itself, and spontaneously; it is necessary that it should detach
itself freely from the Other, and separate itself from him, by choosing
itself as a nothingness that is simply other than the other and is thereby
reunited with itself within "its self." And this very separation that is the
for-itself's being makes it the case that there is an Other. That does not
mean that it gives being to the other but simply that it gives him "other-
being," or the essential condition of the "there is." And it goes without
saying that, for the for-itself, the mode of being-what-is-not-the-Other is

323

46 TN: . . . le pour-soi que je suis a à être ce qu'il est . . . comme soi-même. This passage causes difficulty
in relation to Sartre's pronouns. Note that I translate soi-même as "its self" to differentiate it from soi, which I translate as "itself."

entirely penetrated by Nothingness: the for-itself is that which is not the Other in the nihilating mode of its reflection-reflecting; my not-being-the-Other is never *given* but constantly chosen in a perpetual resurrection; consciousness can only *not be* the Other insofar as it is conscious (of) its self as not being the Other. In this way, internal negation—here, as in the case of presence to the world—is a unitary connection of being: it is necessary that the Other be everywhere present to consciousness and even that he should penetrate it in its entirety, in order for consciousness to escape—precisely by *being nothing*—from this Other in whom there is a risk of becoming stuck. If consciousness suddenly *were* something, the distinction between oneself and the Other would disappear within a complete lack of differentiation.

Only this description has to include an essential addition, which will radically modify its impact. When consciousness was effectively actualized as not being such and such a *this* in the world, the negative relation was not reciprocal: the envisaged *this* did not make itself as not being consciousness; consciousness determined itself in it and through it—as not being it—but its relation to it remained that of pure indifferent externality because, effectively, it retained its nature as *in-itself*. And it is as *in-itself* that consciousness revealed it, in the very negation through which the for-itself was making itself be, by denying in relation to itself that it was in-itself. But when it is a question of the Other, on the contrary, the negative internal relation is a reciprocal relation. The being that consciousness has not to be is defined as a being who has not to be this consciousness. This is because, at the moment when a *this* was perceived within the world, consciousness was in fact differentiated from the *this* not only by its own individuality but also by its mode of being. It was *for-itself*, in the face of the *In-itself*. In contrast, in the case of the Other's arising, consciousness does not differ at all in relation to its mode of being from the other: the other is what consciousness is; it is for-itself and consciousness; it refers to possibles that are its possibles; it is itself through its exclusion of the other; there can be no question of its opposing itself to the other purely by some numerical determination. There are not *two* consciousnesses, or *several* consciousnesses, here: enumeration would effectively presuppose an external witness, and consists in a straightforward observation of externality. There can be an other for the for-itself only in a spontaneous and pre-numerical negation. The other exists for consciousness only as a *oneself* that is *refused*.[47] But precisely because the other is a oneself [or himself], he can be a himself that is refused for me and through me only insofar as he is *himself the one who refuses me*.[48] I can neither grasp nor conceive of a consciousness that does not grasp me. The only consciousness that can exist without in any way apprehending me or refusing me—and that it is possible for me to conceive—is not a consciousness isolated somewhere outside the world but my own. In this way, the other that I recognize in order to refuse to be him is above all the *one for whom my for-itself is*. The one who I make myself not be, in effect, is not only not me by virtue of my denying that he is me; instead, the being whom I make myself not be is, precisely, a being who makes himself not be me. Only this double destruction is in a sense destructive of itself: either, in fact, I make myself not be some specific being and, in that case, he is an object for me and I lose my objecthood for him; in this case the other ceases to be the me-other, i.e., the subject who makes me be an object by refusing to be me; or else this being really is the other and makes himself not be me—but in this case I become an object for him, and he loses his own objecthood. Thus, from the outset, the other is a Not-me-not-object. Whatever the subsequent processes in the dialectic of the Other may be, if the other is first of all to be the other, he is the one who, as a matter of principle, cannot be revealed in just that event of arising through which I deny that I am him. In this sense, my fundamental negation cannot be direct, because there is nothing for it to bear upon. In the end, what I refuse to be can be nothing but that refusal to be me through which the other makes me an object; or, alternatively, I refuse my refused Me; I determine myself as myself by my refusal of the refused-Me; I posit this refused Me as an alienated-Me in the very moment of arising through which I separate myself from the Other. But, just by so doing, I recognize and affirm not only the Other but the existence of my Me-for-the-Other—because, in effect, I cannot *not be* the Other unless I accept my object-being for the Other. The disappearance

---

47 TN: . . . *comme soi-même refusé*. I think "oneself" rather than "himself" better captures the intended meaning here.

48 TN: . . . *en tant qu'il est soi-même qui me refuse*. Further difficulties with pronouns arise in this paragraph – in this sentence, I switch in the translation of *soi-même* from "oneself" to "himself," signaling this switch with the square brackets.

of the alienated Me would bring the Other's disappearance in its wake, through the collapse of my Me-self.[49] I escape from the Other by leaving my alienated Me between his hands. But as I choose myself as this separation from the Other, I take up this alienated Me and recognize it as mine. My separating from the Other—i.e., my Me-self—is in its essential structure the acceptance as *mine* of this Me that the Other refuses; it is even *no more than that*. Thus this alienated and refused Me is at the same time my connection to the Other and the symbol of our absolute separation. In fact, to the extent to which I am the one who makes it the case that *there is* an Other, through the affirmation of my ipseity, the object-Me is mine and I lay claim to it because the separation between the Other and myself is never given and I am constantly responsible for it in my being. But insofar as the Other is co-responsible for our original separation, this Me escapes from me, since it is what the Other makes himself not be. In this way I lay claim, as being *mine* and for me, to a me which escapes me, and as I make myself not be the Other, insofar as the Other is a spontaneity identical to my own, it is precisely as a Me-that-escapes-from-me that I lay claim to this object-Me. This object-Me is a Me *that I am* just to the extent to which it escapes me, and I would on the contrary refuse it as being mine, if it were possible for it to coincide with myself, in pure ipseity. Thus my being-for-the-Other, which is to say my object-Me, is not an image cut off from me and vegetating within a foreign consciousness: it is a being that is perfectly real, my being as the condition of my ipseity in the face of the Other, and of the Other's ipseity in the face of me. It is my *being-outside*: not a being that is undergone, and that has itself come from outside, but an outside that is taken up and recognized as my outside. In effect it is only possible for me to negate the Other in relation to me insofar as the Other is himself a *subject*. If I could refuse the Other immediately, as a pure object—i.e., as an existent in the midst of the world—it would not be the *Other* that I was refusing but instead an object that would, as a matter of principle, have nothing in common with

---

49 TN: ... *par effondrement du Moi-même*. It is not possible to match the surplus meaning Sartre is exploiting in *Moi-même*: his intention is to emphasize the *Moi* ("Me") component within the word *moi-même* (which is ordinarily straightforwardly translated as "myself" in English). To honor the oddity introduced by Sartre's upper-case "M," I am translating *Moi-même* as "(my) Me-self," with the cost that the English sounds even odder than the French.

subjectivity; I would remain without any defense against a complete assimilation of myself with the Other, for want of staying on my guard within the Other's true domain, subjectivity, which is also my domain. I can hold the Other at a distance only by accepting a limit to my subjectivity. But this limit cannot come from me, nor can it be thought by me, because I cannot limit myself; otherwise I would be a finite totality. On the other hand, and in accordance with Spinoza's terms, thought can be limited only by thought. Consciousness can be limited only by consciousness. The limit between two consciousnesses, insofar as it is produced by the limiting consciousness and taken up by the limited consciousness: that is what delivers my object-Me. And we must understand this in both senses of the word "limit." From the side of what limits me, I grasp the limit as the content that contains me and surrounds me, the sleeve of emptiness that exempts me as a totality, by taking me out of play; from the side that is limited, the limit relates to any phenomena of ipseity in the way a mathematical limit relates to the series that approaches it without ever reaching it; all of the being that I have to be is, in relation to its limit, like a curve that is the asymptote to a straight line. In this way I am a detotalized and indefinite totality, contained within a finite totality that surrounds it at a distance and that I am, outside myself, without ever being able to actualize it or even to reach it. A good image of my efforts to apprehend *myself* and of their futility is provided by that sphere, discussed by Poincaré, whose temperature decreases from its center to its surface: living creatures attempt to get through to the surface of this sphere, setting out from its center, but the lowering of the temperature induces in them a continuous process of increasing contraction; as they approach their goal they tend toward an infinite flatness and are thereby separated from it by an infinite distance. However, this unreachable limit that is my object-Me is not ideal: it is a real being. This being is not *in-itself* because it is not produced in pure indifferent externality; but neither is it *for-itself* because it is not the being that, in nihilating myself, I have to be. It is precisely my *being-for-the-Other*, the being that is pulled between two negations whose origins are opposed and which face in different directions, since the Other *is not* this Me of whom he has an intuition and, as for me, *I do not have an intuition* of this Me that I am. Yet this Me, produced by one and taken up by the other, derives its absolute reality from the fact that it is the only possible separation between two beings that are fundamentally identical with respect to their mode of

326

being, and of which each is immediately present to the other, since—as it is consciousness alone that is able to limit consciousness—any middle term between them is inconceivable.

It is on the basis of this subject-Other's presence to me, in and through the objecthood that I have accepted, that we will be able to understand the Other's objectification as the second moment in my relation to the Other. In effect, the Other's presence beyond my unrevealed limit can serve to motivate me to seize myself back as a free ipseity. To the extent that I negate myself as the Other and that the Other is manifested first, he is able to be manifested only as the Other, which is to say as a subject beyond my limit, i.e., as that which limits me. In effect, nothing apart from the Other can limit me. He appears therefore as that which, in his full freedom and in his free projection toward his possibles, takes me out of play and strips me of my transcendence by refusing "to do or to make [faire] anything with me" (in the sense of the German: mit-machen).[50] Thus I am obliged to grasp first, and solely, the one of the two negations for which I am not responsible, the one that does not come to me from me. But, in my very apprehension of this negation, a consciousness (of) me as myself arises, which means I am able to become explicitly conscious (of) myself insofar as I am also responsible for a negation of the Other that is my own possibility. That is the explication of the second negation, the one that goes from me to the Other. To tell the truth, it was already there, but concealed by the other, since it was disappearing in order to make the other appear. But the other is, precisely, the motivation for the new negation to appear: because if there is an other who takes me out of play by positing my transcendence as something purely contemplated, that is because, in taking up my limit, I separate myself from the Other. And my consciousness (of) this separation or my consciousness (of being) the same in relation to the other is a consciousness (of) my free spontaneity. Through this very act of separating from him—which puts the other in possession of my limit—I have already taken him out of play. Insofar therefore as I become conscious (of) myself as one of my free possibilities and I project myself toward myself in order to actualize this ipseity, I find

50 TN: ... en refusant de "faire avec" (au sens de l'allemand: mit-machen). Here Sartre uses faire avec to mirror the components of the quoted German term mit-machen "to make" and "with"). I have had to approximate.

myself responsible, now, for the Other's existence: it is I who make it the case, just by affirming my free spontaneity, that *there is* an Other and not merely an infinite referral of consciousness to itself. The Other therefore finds himself put out of play—as what it is up to me not to be—and, in consequence, his transcendence is no longer a transcendence that *transcends me* toward himself; it is a transcendence that is purely contemplated, a circuit of ipseity that is merely *given*. And as I cannot actualize the two negations at the same time, the new negation, even though it was motivated by the first one, conceals it in its turn: the Other appears to me as a degraded presence. In fact, the other and I are co-responsible for each other's existence, but the two negations needed for this are such that I am unable to experience either one of them without its immediately concealing the other. In this way the Other now becomes what I limit, in my very projection toward not-being-the-Other. Naturally, we have to conceive of the motivation for this transition as affective in type. For example, nothing would prevent me from remaining fascinated by this Unrevealed with its beyond, were it not that I was actualizing precisely this Unrevealed in my fear, in shame, or in pride. And the affective character of these motivations, precisely, explains the empirical contingency of these changes in viewpoint. But these feelings themselves are nothing more than our way of experiencing affectively our being-for-the-Other. Fear, in fact, implies that I appear to myself as threatened in my capacity as a presence in the midst of the world, and not in my capacity as a for-itself who makes it the case that there is a world. It is the object that I am that is in danger in the world and which, as such, because of its indissoluble unity of being with the being that I have to be, is able to drag with it the ruin of the for-itself that I have to be, along with its own. Fear is therefore the discovery of my object-being on the occasion of the appearance of another object within my perceptual field. It directs us to the origin of all fear, which is the fearful discovery of my pure and simple objecthood, insofar as it is surpassed and transcended by possibles that are not my possibles. It is by throwing myself toward my own possibles that I will escape from fear, to the extent to which I will regard my objecthood as inessential. That is possible only if I grasp myself insofar as I am responsible for the Other's being. The Other becomes in that case *what I make myself not to be*, and his possibilities are possibilities that I refuse, and that I can merely contemplate, therefore dead-possibilities. In so doing, I surpass my present possibilities, insofar as I consider them as always being able to be surpassed by the Other's possibilities, but I also surpass the Other's possibilities, by considering them from the point of view of the only quality that he has that is not his own possibility—his very character as the Other, insofar as I make it the case that there is an Other—and by considering them as possibilities of surpassing me that I can always surpass toward new possibilities. Thus, in the same move, I have reconquered my being-for-itself through my consciousness (of) myself as a constant center of infinite possibilities, and I have transformed the Other's possibilities into dead-possibilities by modifying them all with the character of "not-lived-by-me," i.e., of being simply given.

Shame, similarly, is only the original feeling of having my being outside, committed within another being and, as such, without any defense, illuminated by the absolute light that emanates from a pure subject: it is the consciousness of being irremediably what I always was, "suspended," i.e., in the mode of "not-yet" or "already-more-than." Pure shame is not the feeling of being this or that reprehensible object but, in general, of being an object, i.e., of recognizing myself in that degraded, dependent, and frozen being that I am for the Other. Shame is the feeling of an original fall, not in virtue of my having committed this or that misdeed but merely by virtue of having "fallen" into the world, in the midst of things, and of needing the Other's mediation to be what I am. Modesty and, in particular, the fear of being surprised in a state of nakedness are only a symbolic specification of original shame: here the body symbolizes our defenseless objecthood. To get dressed is to disguise one's objecthood; it is to retrieve the right to see without being seen, which is to be a pure subject. That is why the biblical symbol of the fall, after the original sin, is the fact that Adam and Eve "know that they are naked." The reaction to shame will consist precisely in apprehending as an object the one who was apprehending my own objecthood. In effect, from the moment the Other appears to me as an object his subjectivity becomes a mere property of the object in question. It becomes degraded and defined as "a set of objective properties that are necessarily hidden from me." The object-Other "has" a subjectivity in the way in which that empty box has "an inside." And I thereby retrieve myself: because I cannot be an object for an object. I do not deny that the Other retains, through his "inside," a connection with me, but the consciousness that he has of me, as an object-consciousness, appears to me as something purely internal, without efficacy: it is one property among the others of this "inside," something comparable to an impressionable film in the dark chamber of a camera. Insofar as I make it the case that there is an Other, I grasp myself as the free source of the knowledge that the Other has of me, and the Other appears to me as *affected* in his being by this knowledge that he has of my being insofar as I 329 have *affected* him with the character of the Other. This knowledge acquires then a *subjective* character, in the new meaning of "relative"; i.e., it remains in the subject-object as a quality that is *relative* to the Other-being that I have assigned to him. It no longer *touches* me: it is an image *in him of me*. In this way subjectivity has become degraded into interiority, free consciousness into a mere absence of principles, possibilities into properties, and the knowledge through which the Other reaches me in my being into a pure *image* of me in the Other's "consciousness." Shame motivates the reaction that surpasses it and eliminates it insofar as it includes within it an implicit and unthematized understanding of the possibility-of-being-an-object of the subject for whom I am an object. And this implicit understanding is nothing other than the consciousness (of) my "being-myself," i.e., of my reinforced ipseity. In effect, in the structure expressed by "I am ashamed of myself," the shame presupposes a me-object for the other, but also an ipseity that is ashamed, which the "I" in the formula imperfectly expresses. Thus shame is the unitary apprehension of three dimensions: "*I am ashamed of myself before the Other.*"

Should one of these dimensions disappear, the shame disappears as well. If, however, I conceive of the "they" subject before whom I am ashamed insofar as he is unable to become an object without becoming scattered into a plurality of the Other—if I posit him as the absolute unity of the subject that can in no way become an object—I thereby posit the eternity of my object-being and I perpetuate my shame. That is shame before God, i.e., the recognition of my objecthood before a subject who can never become an object; by the same token I actualize my objecthood in the absolute and I hypostasize it; God's position is accompanied by a reification of my objecthood. Better still, I posit my object-being-for-God as more real than my for-itself; I exist alienated and I learn from my outside what I have to be. That is the origin of fear before God. Black masses, profanations of the Host, satanic associations, etc., are so many efforts to confer the character of an object on the absolute Subject. In willing Evil for the sake of Evil, I attempt to contemplate the divine transcendence—whose distinctive possibility is Good—as a transcendence that is purely given, and that I transcend toward Evil. In that case I "make God suffer," I "irritate" him, etc. These endeavors, which imply the absolute recognition of God as the subject who cannot be an object, carry their contradiction within them and are in a state of constant failure.

As for pride, it does not exclude original shame. It is built even in the territory of fundamental shame, or the shame of being an object. It is an ambiguous feeling: in pride I recognize the Other as the subject through whom objecthood arrives in my being, but in addition I recognize myself as responsible for my objecthood; I place the emphasis on my responsibility, and I accept it. In a sense, therefore, pride is in the first instance resignation: in order to be proud of being that, it is necessary for me first to be resigned to being only that. It is a matter therefore of an initial reaction to shame and it is already a reaction of flight and bad faith because, without ceasing to regard the Other as a subject, I try to apprehend myself as affecting the Other through my objecthood. In brief, there are two authentic attitudes: the one through which I recognize the Other as the subject through whom I come to objecthood—that is shame; and the one through which I apprehend myself as the free project through which the Other comes to Other-being—that is pride, or the affirmation of my freedom in the face of the object-Other. But pride—or vanity—is a feeling that lacks equilibrium and is in bad faith: in the case of vanity, I try to act upon the Other insofar as I am an object: I aim to make use of this beauty or strength or intelligence that he confers on me insofar as he constitutes me as an object in order to assign to him, by reversing the direction of flow, a passive feeling of admiration or love. But in addition I demand that this feeling, as what sanctions my object-being, should be felt by the Other insofar as he is a subject, i.e., as a freedom. In fact, that is the only way of conferring absolute objectivity upon my strength or my beauty. Thus the feeling that I demand from the Other bears within itself its own contradiction, since I have to assign it to the Other insofar as he is free. It is experienced in the mode of bad faith, and its internal development leads it to disintegrate. In effect, in order to take possession of my object-being that I accept, I try to retrieve it as an object; and, as the Other is the key to it, I try to seize hold of the Other so that he will deliver to me the secret of my being. Thus vanity propels me to seize hold of the Other and

330

to constitute him as an object, in order to excavate into the heart of this object and discover my own objecthood in it. But that is to kill the goose with the golden eggs. In constituting the Other as an object, I constitute myself as an image at the heart of the object-Other. Hence the disillusion of vanity: in this image that I wanted to grasp, in order to retrieve it and to merge it into my being, I *no longer recognize* myself; whether I like it or not, I must impute it to the Other as one of his subjective properties; freed in spite of myself of my objecthood I remain alone in the face of the object-Other, in my unsayable ipseity that I have to be without ever being able to be relieved of my function.

Shame, fear, and pride are therefore my original reactions, they are merely the various ways in which I recognize the Other as a subject out of reach, and they include within themselves an understanding of my ipseity which can and does provide me with the motivation to constitute the Other into an object.

This object-Other that suddenly appears to me does not remain a pure objective abstraction. He arises before me with his specific meanings. He is not only the object whose freedom is a *property*, as a transcended transcendence. He is also "angry" or "joyful" or "attentive," "friendly" or "unfriendly," "greedy," "bad-tempered," etc. That is because, in grasping myself as myself, I make it the case that the object-Other exists in the midst of the world. I recognize his transcendence, but I recognize it not as a transcending transcendence but as a transcended transcendence. It appears therefore as a surpassing of implements toward certain ends, to exactly the extent to which I surpass, in a unitary project of myself, these ends, these implements, and this surpassing by the Other of the implements toward the ends. In fact I never apprehend myself abstractly as the pure possibility of being myself but, instead, I live my ipseity in its concrete projection toward this or that end: I exist only as *committed* and it is only as such that I am conscious (of) being. In this capacity I grasp the object-Other only within a concrete and *committed* surpassing of his transcendence. But, conversely, the Other's commitment, which is his mode of being, appears to me insofar as it is transcended by my transcendence as a *real* commitment, as a *rootedness*. In brief, insofar as I exist *for-myself*, my "commitment" within a situation has to be understood in the sense in which we say "I am committed toward somebody," "I am committed to returning this money," etc. And it is this commitment or engagement

331

that characterizes the subject-Other, since it is another myself.[51] But, when I grasp the Other as an object, this objectified engagement is degraded and becomes an engagement-object, in the sense in which we say "The knife is deeply engaged within the wound" or "The army was engaged within a narrow pass." It has to be understood indeed that the being-in-the-midst-of-the-world which comes to the Other through me is a real being. It is not purely a subjective necessity that makes me know him as an existent in the midst of the world. And yet, on the other hand, the Other has not got lost by himself in this world. Rather I make him get lost in the midst of the world that is mine, by virtue solely of the fact that he is for me the one that I have to not be, which is to say by virtue solely of the fact that I maintain him outside me as a reality that is purely contemplated and surpassed toward my own ends. Thus objectivity is not the pure refraction, through my consciousness, of the Other: it comes to the Other through me as a real qualification; I make it the case that the Other is in the midst of the world. What I grasp therefore as real characteristics of the Other is a being-in-situation: in effect I organize him, in the midst of the world, insofar as he organizes the world toward himself; I grasp him as the objective unity of implements and of obstacles. We explained in Part Two of this work[52] that the totality of implements is the exact correlative to my possibilities. As I am my possibilities, the order of implements within the world is the image, projected into the in-itself, of my possibilities, i.e., the image of what I am. But I can never decipher this worldly image; I adapt to it in and through my action. The Other, insofar as he is a subject, finds himself similarly committed within his image. But insofar as I grasp him as an object, on the contrary, it is this worldly image that leaps into sight: the Other becomes the instrument who is defined by his relation with all the other instruments, an ordering of my implements which is enclosed within the order that I impose on these implements. To grasp the Other is to grasp this enclosed-order and to

332

---

51 TN: . . . c'est cet engagement . . . In this passage Sartre slides from using the verb engager in the sense of "to commit" to using it in the more physical sense of "to engage" (as a knife is engaged in a wound). To accommodate this shift in sense, I have used both words in this sentence, i.e., "commitment or engagement." See my note on engager in Notes on the Translation.

52 Sartre's note: Part Two, Chapter 3, section III.

relate it to a central absence or "interiority"; it is to define this absence as a frozen flowing away of the objects in my world toward a determinate object in my universe. And the meaning of this flowing away is provided by these objects themselves: it is through the arrangement of the hammer and the nails, of the chisel and the marble, insofar as I surpass this arrangement without being its foundation, that the meaning of this intraworldly hemorrhage is defined. In this way the world announces the Other to me in his totality, and as a totality. Of course, the announcement remains ambiguous. But that is because I grasp the ordering of the world toward the Other as an undifferentiated totality, against whose ground some explicit structures appear. If I were able to explicate all the structures of equipment insofar as they are turned toward the Other—i.e., if I could grasp not only the place that the hammer and the nails occupy within this structure of equipment but also the street, the town, the nation, etc.—I would have explicitly and completely defined the being of the Other as an object. If I am mistaken about one of the Other's intentions, that is absolutely not because I am relating his action to a subjectivity that is out of reach: there is no common measure between this subjectivity, in and by itself, and the movement, because it is a transcendence for itself, a transcendence that cannot be surpassed. But that is because I organize the entire world around this action differently from the way it is in fact organized. Thus, by virtue solely of the fact that the Other appears as an object, he is given to me as a matter of principle as a totality; he extends throughout the whole world as a worldly power of synthetically organizing this world. Only I am no more able to explicate this synthetic organization than I am able to explicate the world itself insofar as it is my world. And the difference between the subject-Other—i.e., the Other as he is for-himself—and the object-Other is not at all a difference of the whole to the part, or of the hidden to the revealed, because the object-Other is necessarily a whole that is coextensive with the subjective totality; nothing is hidden and, insofar as the objects refer to other objects, I can indefinitely increase my knowledge of the Other, by explicating indefinitely his relations to the other implements in the world; and the ideal of knowledge of the Other remains the exhaustive explication of the meaning of the world's flowing away. The difference in principle between the object-Other and the subject-Other stems uniquely from this fact, that the subject-Other can in no way be known or even conceived as such: there is no problem of knowledge of the subject-Other, and the objects in the world do not refer to his subjectivity; they refer-only to his objecthood within the world, as the meaning—surpassed toward my ipseity—of the intraworldly flowing away. In this way, I experience the Other's presence to me as the maker of my objecthood as a subject-totality; and, if I turn back toward this presence in order to grasp it, I apprehend the Other once again as a totality: an object-totality that is coextensive with the totality of the world. And this apprehension comes about all at once: it is on the basis of the world in its entirety that I approach the object-Other. But these are only ever particular relations, which stand out in relief as *figures* against the world's ground. Around this man, unknown to me, and who is reading in the metro, the world in its entirety is present. And it is not only his body—as an object in the world—that defines him in his being: it is his identity card, the direction of the metro train that he has boarded, and the ring he is wearing on his finger. These do not function as *signs* of what he is—that notion of the sign effectively returns us to a subjectivity that I am unable even to conceive and within which, to be exact, there is strictly speaking nothing of him, since he is what he is not and he is not what he is—but as real characteristics of his being. However, if I *know* that he *is* in the midst of the world (in France, in Paris, and doing some reading), I can only, for want of seeing his identity card, *suppose* that he is a foreigner (which means: suppose him to be subject to inspection, that he figures on such and such a list in the Prefecture, that it is necessary to speak to him in Dutch, or in Italian, in order to obtain this or that action from him, that the international post travels toward him by this or that route taken by the letters, which carry this or that stamp, etc.). However, this identity card is necessarily given to me in the midst of the world. It doesn't escape me—from the moment it was created, it began to exist for me. Only it exists implicitly, like each point of the circle that I see as a completed figure, and, to make it appear as an explicit *this* against the ground of the universe, it would be necessary to change the present totality of my relations to the world. In the same way, the anger of the object-Other—as it is manifested to me through his shouting, his foot stamping, and his threatening gestures—is not the sign of a subjective and hidden anger: it refers to nothing, only to other gestures and other shouting. It defines the Other; it *is* the Other. Of course I may be wrong, and take what is only a feigned

333

irritation to be a true fit of anger. But I can go wrong only in relation to other movements and other actions that can be objectively grasped: I go wrong if I grasp the hand's movement as a *real* intention to strike. In other words, I go wrong if I interpret it in terms of a movement that can be objectively discerned, and which will not occur. In brief, anger that is objectively apprehended is an arrangement of the world around an intraworldly presence-absence. Does this mean the behaviorists were right? Definitely not: because if the behaviorists interpret man on the basis of his situation, they have lost sight of his principal characteristic, which is transcendence-transcended. The Other is in fact the object that 334 cannot be limited to itself, an object that can be understood only in terms of its end. And, doubtless, the hammer and the saw are not understood differently. Both of them are grasped through their function, i.e., through their end. But that is just because they are already human. I can understand them only insofar as they refer me to an implement-organization whose center is the Other, insofar as they form part of a structure that is entirely transcended toward an end that I transcend in my turn. If therefore the Other can be compared to a machine, it is insofar as the machine, as a human fact, already presents the trace of a transcended-transcendence, insofar as the looms, in a spinning mill, can be explained only through the fabrics that they produce; the behaviorist point of view has to be reversed and, moreover, this reversal will leave the Other's objectivity intact, because what is objective in the first instance—whether we call it "meaning," in the style of the French and English psychologists, "intention," in the style of phenomenologists, "transcendence," like Heidegger, or "figure," like the Gestaltists—is the fact that the Other cannot be defined other than through a totalizing organization of the world, and that he is the key to this organization. If therefore, in order to define him, I move back from the world to the Other, that is not because the world will make me understand the Other but rather because the Other-object is nothing but an autonomous and intraworldly center of reference in my world. In this way, the objective fear that we can apprehend when we perceive the object-Other is not the set of physiological manifestations of disarray that we can see, or that we can measure with the blood pressure gauge or the stethoscope: fear is the flight, the fainting. And these phenomena themselves are not delivered to us purely as a series of *movements* but as a transcended-transcendence: the flight or the fainting is not only this distraught running across the brambles, or this heavy fall onto the stones of the path; it is a total upheaval in the implement-organization whose center was the Other. A moment ago, this soldier in flight had the enemy-Other at the end of his rifle. The distance from the enemy to him was measured by the trajectory of his bullet, and it was possible for me, as well, to grasp and to transcend this distance as a distance that was organized around the "soldier" center. But now he throws his rifle into the ditch and runs away. Immediately, the presence of the enemy surrounds him and presses in on him; the enemy, who had been held at a distance by the bullets' trajectory, leaps on him, in the very instant in which the trajectory collapses; at the same time, this hinterland that he was defending and which he had been leaning against like a wall suddenly turns round, opens up into a fan and becomes what is in front of him, the welcoming horizon in whose direction he takes refuge. I take note of all of that objectively, and what I apprehend as *fear* is precisely *that*. Fear is nothing but a magical behavior, which aims to eliminate by incantation the terrifying objects that we are unable to hold at a distance.[53] And it is precisely through its results that we apprehend fear, for it is given to us as a new type of intraworldly hemorrhage of the world: the transition of the world into a type of magical existence.

However, we must take note that the Other is only a qualified object for me to the extent that I can be that for him. He will become objectified therefore as a non-individualized piece of the "they," or as "absent," represented purely by his letters and his tales, or as *this-person-here*, present in fact, depending on whether I have myself been for him an element of the "they," or an "absent friend," or a concrete *this-person-here*. What decides in each case the type of objectification of the Other and his qualities is at the same time my situation in the world and his situation, i.e., the equipmental structures which we have each organized and the different *thises* that appear to each of us against the ground of the world. All this leads us back, naturally, to facticity. It is my facticity and the Other's facticity that decide whether the Other can *see* me, and if I can see *that* Other. But the problem of facticity is outside the scope of this general exposition: we will consider it in the course of the next chapter.

335

---

53 Sartre's note: Cf. my *Esquisse d'une Théorie Phénoménologique des Émotions*. TN: Sartre gets the title of his book slightly wrong; it is translated into English as Sartre (1994).

Thus, in my being-an-object-for-the-Other, I experience the Other's presence as a quasi-totality of subjects, and against the ground of this totality I am able to experience more particularly the presence of a concrete subject, without always being able to specify it as this Other. My defensive reaction to my objecthood will summon the Other before me in the capacity of this or that object. In this capacity he will appear to me as a "this one," which is to say that his subjective quasi-totality is degraded and becomes an object-totality coextensive to the totality of the world. This totality is revealed to me without reference to the Other's subjectivity: the relation between the subject-Other and the object-Other is not comparable at all to the one that we are accustomed to establishing, for example, between the object of physics and the object of perception. The object-Other is revealed to me for what he is; he refers only to himself. Only the object-Other is as he appears to me, on the level of objecthood in general and in his object-being; it is not even conceivable that I could relate some piece of knowledge that I have of him to his subjectivity, such as I experience it on the occasion of the look. The object-Other is only an object, but my apprehension of him includes the understanding that I will always be able, as a matter of principle, to have a different *experience* of him by placing myself at another level of being; this understanding is constituted, on the one hand, by the *knowledge* of my past experience, which is moreover, as we have seen, the pure past (out of reach, and as what I have to be) of this experience and, on the other hand, by an implicit apprehension of the dialectic of the other: the other is presently what I am making myself not to be. But, even though for the instant I have got rid of him, and escape him, there remains around him the permanent possibility that he will *make* himself other. However, this possibility, which is sensed with a kind of discomfort and constraint that is what distinguishes my attitude in the face of the object-Other, is strictly speaking inconceivable: in the first place because I am unable to conceive of a possibility that is not my possibility, or to apprehend a transcendence except by transcending it, i.e., by grasping it as a transcended transcendence; then, because this possibility that I sense is not the object-Other's possibility; the object-Other's possibilities are dead-possibilities, which refer to other objective aspects of the Other; as the distinctive possibility of grasping myself as an object is the possibility of the subject-Other, it is not actually for me anybody's possibility: it is the absolute possibility—which draws its source only from itself—of a

336

subject-Other's arising, against the ground of the object-Other's complete annihilation, which I will experience through my objectivity-for-him. Thus the object-other is an explosive instrument that I handle with apprehension, because I sense the constant possibility around him that they will make it explode and that, with this explosion, I will suddenly experience outside me the world's flight and the alienation of my being. My constant concern therefore is to contain the Other within his objectivity, and my relations with the object-Other are essentially made up of ruses whose intention is to make him remain as an object. But a look from the Other suffices to make all these artifices collapse and for me to experience once again the Other's transfiguration. In this way I am sent back from transfiguration into degradation, and from degradation to transfiguration without ever being able to form a view of these two modes of the Other's being together—because each one of them is sufficient to itself and refers only to itself—or to hold firmly to one of them—because each one has its own instability, and collapses in order that the Other will arise on its ruins. It is only the dead who are able constantly to be objects without ever becoming subjects, because to die is not to lose one's objectivity in the midst of the world—all of the dead are there, in the world, around us—but to lose any possibility of being revealed as a subject to an Other.

At this level of our investigation, once we have elucidated the essential structures of being-for-the-Other, we are tempted, evidently, to raise the metaphysical question: "Why are there Others?" As we have seen, the existence of others is not in effect a consequence that flows from the for-itself's ontological structure. It is of course a primordial event, but of a *metaphysical* order, which is to say that it has to do with the contingency of being. It is essentially in relation to these metaphysical existences that the question of the "why" arises.

Besides, we know that the answer to the "why" can direct us only to an original contingency, but we still need to prove that the metaphysical phenomenon that we are examining is irreducibly contingent. In this sense, it seems to us that it ought to be possible to define "ontology" as the explication of the structures of being of the existent, taken as a totality, and we will define "metaphysics" instead as the putting into question of the existence of the existent. That is why, in virtue of the existent's absolute contingency, we are assured that any metaphysics must end with a "that is," i.e., by a direct intuition of this contingency.

337

Is it possible to raise the question of the existence of others? Is this question an irreducible fact or ought it to be derived from a fundamental contingency? These are the preliminary questions that we can raise in turn to the metaphysician who raises questions about the existence of others.

Let us examine the possibility of the metaphysical question more closely. What appears to us first is that being-for-the-Other represents the for-itself's third ecstasis. The first ecstasis is in fact the for-itself's three-dimensional project toward a being that it has to be in the mode of not-being. It represents the first fissure, the nihilation that the for-itself has itself to be, the for-itself's separation from everything that is, insofar as this separating is constitutive of its being. The second ecstasis—or the reflective ecstasis—is a separation from that very separation. The reflective scissiparity corresponds to a futile effort to take up a point of view on the nihilation that the for-itself has to be, in order that this nihilation, as a phenomenon that is simply given, should be a nihilation *that is*. But at the same time the reflection wants to retrieve this separating which it is attempting to contemplate as a pure given by affirming, in relation to itself, that it *is* this nihilation that is. The contradiction is flagrant: in order to be able to grasp my transcendence, it would be necessary for me to transcend it. But, precisely, my own transcendence is able only to transcend; I *am* it, and cannot make use of it in order to constitute it as a transcended transcendence; I am condemned constantly to be my own nihilation. In brief, the reflection *is* the reflected. However, the nihilation of reflection is more extreme than that of the pure for-itself as simple consciousness (of) self. In effect, in the consciousness (of) self, the incapacity of the two terms of the reflected-reflecting duality to present themselves separately was such that the duality remained constantly evanescent, so that each term, in positing itself for the other, *became* the other. But in the case of reflection the process is different, since the reflected "reflection-reflecting" exists for a reflective "reflection-reflecting."[54] The reflected and the reflecting therefore each reach toward independence,

---

54 TN: ... le "reflet-reflétant" réfléchi existe pour un "reflet-reflétant" réflexif. I quote to show the difference between the levels of reflection in play in this sentence (which is concealed in translation).

and the nothing that separates them tends to divide them more deeply than the nothingness that the for-itself has to be separates the reflection from the reflecting. However, neither the reflective nor the reflected is able to secrete this separating nothingness; otherwise the reflection would be an autonomous for-itself, entering in to target what is reflected, which would presuppose an external negation as the precondition of an internal negation. There can be no reflection unless it is entirely a *being*, a being that has to be its own nothingness. Thus the reflective ecstasis is located on the path toward a more radical ecstasis: being-for-the-Other. The ultimate term of the nihilation, the ideal pole, ought in fact to be an external negation (i.e., an in-itself scissiparity) or a spatial, indifferent externality. In relation to this external negation, the three ecstases are ranked in the order that we have just set out, but they can in no way attain it; it remains necessarily ideal. In effect, the for-itself cannot on its own actualize, in relation to some being, a negation that is in itself, without ceasing by the same token to be-for-itself. The constitutive negation of being-for-the-Other is therefore an *internal negation*; it is a nihilation that the for-itself has to be, just like the reflective nihilation. But here the scissiparity attacks the negation itself: it is no longer only the negation that splits the being into two—the reflected and the reflecting—and, in its turn, splits the reflected-reflecting pair into the (reflected-reflecting) reflected and the (reflected-reflecting) reflecting. Rather, the negation splits into two internal and opposite negations, each of which is an internal negation and yet is separated from the other by an elusive external negation. In effect, since each negation is consumed in denying, in relation to one for-itself, that it is the other, and is entirely committed within this being that it has to be, it has no more of itself available with which to deny, in relation to itself, that it is the opposite negation. Here, all of a sudden, the *given* appears, not as the result of an identity of being-in-itself but as a kind of phantom externality that neither of the two negations has to be, and yet which separates them. In truth, we could already find the beginning of the negative inversion in reflective being. In effect, the reflective, as witness, is profoundly affected in its being by its reflexivity and consequently, insofar as it makes itself reflective, it aims not to be the reflected. But, inversely, the reflected is a consciousness (of) self as the reflected consciousness of this or that transcendent phenomenon. What we said about it was that it knows itself to be looked at. In this sense, it aims on its part to not be the reflective, since every consciousness is defined by its negativity. But this tendency toward a twofold schism was reclaimed and stifled by the fact that, in spite of everything, the reflective had the reflected to be, and the reflected had the reflective to be. The twofold negation remained evanescent. In the case of the third ecstasis, it is as if we are in the presence of a more extreme reflective scissiparity. The consequences may surprise us: on the one hand, since the negations are effected internally, neither the Other nor I myself is able to approach each other from the outside. It is necessary for there to be an "Other-me" *being*, which has the reciprocal scissiparity of the for-the-Other to be, just as the "reflective-reflected" totality is a being that has its own nothingness to be, which is to say that my ipseity and that of the Other are structures within one same totality of being. Thus Hegel appears to be right: it is the viewpoint of the totality that is the viewpoint of being, the *true* point of view. Everything happens as if my ipseity in the face of the Other's was produced and maintained by a totality that could press its own nihilation to the extreme; being for the Other appears to be the prolongation of the pure scissiparity of reflection. In this sense, everything happens as if we—the others and myself—were registering the futile effort of a totality of the for-itself to seize itself back and to envelop what it *has to be* in the pure and simple mode of the in-itself: this endeavor to seize hold of itself as an object, taken here to the limit—i.e., far beyond the reflective scission—would bring about the opposite result to the end toward which this totality projects itself: through its endeavor to be a consciousness of itself [*soi*], the for-itself-totality would constitute itself in the face of the "itself" [*soi*] as a consciousness-itself that has not to be the itself [*soi*] of which it is conscious; and conversely, in order *to be*, the object-itself would have to experience itself as *been* by and for a consciousness that it has not to be, if it wants to be.[55] In this way the schism of the for-itself is born; and this dichotomous division will repeat itself to infinity, to constitute the consciousnesses as the smithereens of a radical explosion. "There would be" *some others*, in consequence of a failure

339

---

55 TN: As Sartre is referring in this passage to the impossible self-coincidence at which consciousness aims, I think *soi* needs to be translated as "itself" rather than "self," but I insert the French term to remind the reader of the ambiguity in the French. See my note on *soi* in the section on pronouns in Notes on the Translation.

that is the opposite of the failure of reflection. If, in effect, I do not manage to apprehend myself as an object in reflection but only as a quasi-object, it is because I am the object that I want to apprehend; I have the nothingness that separates me from myself to be; I cannot escape my ipseity, nor can I take up a point of view on myself; in this way, I do not manage to actualize myself as being, or to grasp myself in the form "there is"; my retrieval fails because the retrieving part stands in relation to itself as what is retrieved. In the case of being-for-the-Other, on the contrary, the scissiparity is taken further; the reflected (reflection-reflecting) is radically distinguished from the reflecting (reflection-reflecting) and by that very fact it can be an object for it. But this time the retrieval fails because what is retrieved is not what does the retrieving. Thus the totality that is not what it is, while being what it is not, through a radical endeavor to separate itself from itself, produces its being everywhere as an "else-where:" the flickering being-in-itself of a broken totality, always else-where, always at a distance, never in itself, yet always maintained in being by this totality's constant explosion; such is the being of others, and the being of myself as other.

But on the other hand, simultaneously with my negation of myself, the Other denies in relation to himself that he is me. These two negations are equally indispensable to being-for-the-Other, and there is no synthesis that can bring them together. That is not because an external nothingness has separated them at the origin but rather because the in-itself would seize each one back in relation to the other, by virtue solely of the fact that each one is not the other, without having to not be it. Here there is something like a limit to the for-itself which comes from the for-itself itself but which, insofar as it is a limit, is independent of the for-itself: we rediscover something like facticity and we are unable to conceive how the totality that we were discussing earlier can have produced in its being, right at the heart of the most radical movement of separation, a nothingness that it has in no way to be. It seems in effect that it has slipped within this totality in order to break it, as non-being, in Leucippus's atomism, slides within Parmenides's totality of being in order to make it explode into atoms.[56] It represents therefore the nega-

340

56 TN: Leucippus (fifth century BC) was an ancient Greek philosopher, sometimes said to have been the first to introduce the theory of atomism.

tion of every synthetic totality on whose basis one might claim to understand the plurality of consciousnesses. Doubtless it is elusive, since it is
produced neither by the other nor by myself, nor by an intermediary,
for we have established that the consciousnesses experience each other
without intermediary. Doubtless, no matter where we direct our gaze,
we will encounter as an object of description only a pure and simple
internal negation. And yet it is there, in the irreducible fact of there
being a *duality* of negations. It is certainly not the *foundation* of the multiplicity of consciousnesses, because if it preexisted this multiplicity it
would make any *being-for* the Other impossible; we must on the contrary
conceive it as the expression of this multiplicity: it appears with it. But as
there is *nothing* that is able to found it, neither a particular consciousness,
nor a totality exploding into consciousnesses, it appears as pure and
irreducible contingency, *as the fact that my denying the Other in relation to myself
does not suffice to make the Other exist, but it is necessary in addition for the Other to deny
me in relation to himself simultaneously with my own negation.* That is the facticity of
being-for-the-Other.

Thus we arrive at this contradictory conclusion: being-for-the-Other
can only be if it *is been* by a totality that loses itself in order for it to arise:
this might lead us to postulate the existence and passion of *spirit*.[57] But, on
the other hand, this being-for-the-Other can exist only if it brings with
it an elusive external non-being, which no totality, not even *spirit*, is able
to produce or to found. In one sense, the existence of a plurality of consciousnesses cannot be a basic fact, and it directs us to an original fact of
a self-separation which is the fact of spirit; in this way, the metaphysical
question "Why are there *some* consciousnesses?" receives a reply. But, in
another sense, the facticity of this plurality seems to be irreducible, and
if we consider spirit on the basis of the *fact* of the plurality, it vanishes;
the metaphysical question no longer has meaning, we have encountered
fundamental contingency, and we can reply to it only by saying: "That is
how it is." In this way the original ecstasis is deepened: we seem unable
to give nothingness its due. The for-itself has appeared to us as a being
that exists insofar as it is not what it is and it is what it is not. The ecstatic
totality of spirit is not simply a detotalized totality, but it appears to us
as a broken being about which we are unable to say either that it exists

57 TN: ...*l'esprit*. Sartre's italics here probably signal an allusion to Hegel's term *Geist*.

or that it does not exist. Thus our description has enabled us to satisfy
341 the preliminary conditions that we placed on any theory of the Other's
existence: the multiplicity of consciousnesses appears to us as a *synthesis*
and not as a *collection*; but it is a synthesis whose totality is inconceivable.

Does that amount to saying that this antinomic character of the totality
is itself irreducible? Or will we be able to make it disappear, from some
higher point of view? Ought we to posit that spirit is *the being that is and is
not*, as we have posited that the for-itself is what it is not and is not what it
is? The question has no meaning. It would presuppose in effect that it is
possible for us to *take up a point of view* on the totality, i.e., to consider it from
outside. But that is impossible, since, precisely, I exist as myself on the
foundation of this totality, and to the extent that I am committed within
it. No consciousness, not even God's, is able "to see the reverse side," i.e.,
to grasp the totality as such. For, if God is a consciousness, he is included
in the totality. And if by his nature he is a being *beyond consciousness*—
i.e., an in-itself that could be its own foundation—the totality can appear
to him only as an *object*, in which case its internal disaggregation, *qua*
the subjective endeavor to seize back the self, is missing, or as a *subject*,
and, in this case, as he *is not* this subject, he is able only to experience it
without knowing it. In this way it is impossible to conceive of any point
of view on the totality: the totality has no "outside," and even the question of the meaning of its "reverse side" lacks meaning. We can go no
further.

Here we have reached the end of this exposition. We have learned that
the Other's existence is experienced with evidence, in and through the
fact of my objectivity. And we have also seen that my reaction to my own
alienation for the Other is conveyed through the apprehension of the
Other as an object. In short, the Other can exist for us in two forms: if I
experience him with evidence, I fail to know him; if I know him, if I act
on him, I reach only his object-being and his probable existence in the
midst of the world: no synthesis of these two forms is possible. But we
cannot stop here: this object that the Other is for me and this object that
I am for the Other are manifested as *bodies*. What therefore is my body?
What is the Other's body?

Chapter 2

THE BODY

The problem of the body and its relations to consciousness is often obscured by the fact that we posit the body right from the start as a certain thing, possessed of its own laws and capable of being defined from the outside, while we reach consciousness through the type of inner intuition that is distinctive to it. If, in effect, after having apprehended "my" consciousness in its absolute interiority, and through a series of reflective acts, I try to join it to a certain living object, constituted by a nervous system, a brain, some glands, some digestive, respiratory, and circulatory organs, whose very matter lends itself to being chemically analyzed into atoms of hydrogen, carbon, nitrogen, phosphorus, etc., I will encounter insurmountable difficulties: but these difficulties stem from the fact that I am not trying to join my consciousness to my body but to the body of *others*. In effect, the body whose description I have just sketched is not *my* body, as it is *for me*. I have never seen and never will see my brain, or my endocrine glands. But, quite simply, because I who am a man have seen men's corpses dissected, and because I have read physiological tracts, I conclude that my body is constituted exactly like all those I have been shown on a dissection table or whose representation in color I have looked at in books. Of course, I will be told that the doctors who have treated me, the surgeons who have operated on me, have been able to experience directly this body that I do not know myself. I do not deny this, and I am not claiming that I lack a brain, a heart, or a stomach. But, before anything else, it is important to choose the order of our elements of knowledge: to start out from the experiences that doctors have had of my body is to start out from my body in the midst of the world, and as it is for the Other. My body as it is for me does not appear to me in the midst of the world. Of course, I have myself been able to see on a screen, in the course of an X-ray, the image of my vertebrae, but I was precisely outside, in the midst of the world: I was apprehending an entirely constituted object, as a this among other thises, and it is only through a process of reasoning that I could lead it back to being mine: it was far more my property than my being.

It is true that I can see and touch my legs and my hands. And nothing stops me from conceiving of some sensory arrangement such that a living being could see one of his eyes, while the eye that was being seen directed its own gaze upon the world. But we need to note that, in this case again, I am the other in relation to my eye: I apprehend it as a sensory organ constituted in such and such a way within the world, but I cannot "see it seeing," which is to say I cannot apprehend it insofar as it reveals an aspect of the world to me. Either it is a thing among things, or it is that through which things are disclosed to me. But it cannot be both at the same time. Similarly, I can see my hand touching objects, but I do not know it, in its act of touching them. That is the reason why, necessarily, Maine de Biran's famous "sensation of effort" does not really exist. For my hand reveals to me the resistance of objects, their hardness or their softness, but it does not reveal itself. In this way, I see my hand no differently from the way I see this inkwell. I unfold a distance from me to it, and this distance becomes integrated with the distances that I establish between all the worldly objects. When a doctor takes my bad leg and examines it, while I, semi-upright in my bed, watch him do this, there is no difference of kind between the visual perception that I have of the doctor's body and the one I have of my own leg. Better still, they differ only to the extent that they are different structures within a single global perception; and there is no difference in kind between the perception that the doctor has of my leg and the one I myself am presently having of it. Of course, when I touch my leg with my finger, I feel that my leg is being touched. But this phenomenon of double sensation is not essential: the cold, or a morphine injection, can make it disappear; that

suffices to show that we are dealing with two essentially different orders
of reality. To touch and to be touched, to feel that one is touching and
to feel that one is touched, these are two species of phenomena that, try
as one might, cannot be joined together in the so-called double sensation. In fact they are radically distinct, and they exist on two incommunicable levels. Moreover, when I touch my leg, or I see it, I surpass it
toward my own possibilities; it is, for example, in order to put on my
trousers, or to redo the dressing around my wound. And of course I am
able at the same time to arrange my leg in such a way as to allow me to
"work" on it more comfortably. But that in no way changes the fact that
I transcend it toward the pure possibility of "getting better" and that,
in consequence, I am present to it without it *being me*, and without me
being it. And what I am in this way bringing to be is the "leg" thing; it is   344
not the leg as *the possibility that I am* of walking, of running, or of playing
football. Thus, to the extent to which my body indicates my possibilities
in the world, to see it or to touch it is to transform these possibilities
that are mine into dead-possibilities. This metamorphosis necessarily has
to bring in its wake a complete *blindness* in relation to what the body is
as a living possibility of running, of dancing, etc. And, of course, the
discovery of my body as an object really is a revelation of its body. But
the being that is in this way revealed to me is its *being-for-the-Other*. That
this confusion leads to absurdities can be clearly seen in relation to the
famous problem of "inverted vision." We know the question raised by
physiologists: "How are we able to turn the objects that are painted on
our retinas upside down the right way up?" And we also know the philosophers' reply: "There is no problem. An object is the right way up,
or upside down, in relation to the rest of the universe. To perceive the
whole universe upside down has no meaning, because it would have to
be upside down in relation to something." But what interests us especially is the origin of this false problem: which is the wish to connect
my consciousness of objects to the *other's* body. Here is the candle, the
crystal which provides the lens, the inverted image on the retinal screen.
But here, precisely, the retina enters into a physical system: it is a *screen*,
and only that, while the crystal is a *lens*, and only a lens; both of these are
homogeneous in their being with the candle that completes the system.
In order to study the problem of vision, therefore, we have deliberately
chosen the physical point of view, which is to say the point of view

from outside, of externality; we have considered a dead eye in the midst of the visible world, to give an account of this world's visibility. How, after that, can we be astonished that consciousness, which is absolute interiority, refuses to allow itself to be connected with this object? The relations that I establish between an Other's body and the external object are *really* existing relations, but they have as their being the being of the for-the-Other; they presuppose an intraworldly center of flowing away of which knowledge is a *magical* property, of the "action at a distance" type. Right from the start, these relations are placed within the perspective of the object-other. If then we wish to reflect on the nature of the body, we have to establish an order in our reflections that conforms to the order of being: we cannot continue to confuse the ontological levels, and we must successively examine the body insofar as it is being-for-itself, and insofar as it is being-for-the-Other; and, in order to avoid absurdities of the "inverted vision" genre, we will fully embrace the idea that each of these two aspects of the body, being at two different and incommunicable levels of being, is irreducible to the other. It is in its entirety that being-for-itself has to be body, and in its entirety that it has to be consciousness: it cannot be *joined* to a body. Similarly, being-
345 for-the-Other is in its entirety body; here there are no "psychological phenomena" to be joined to the body; there is nothing *behind* the body. Rather, the body is in its entirety "psychological." It is these two modes of being of the body that we are going to investigate now.

I. THE BODY AS BEING-FOR-ITSELF: FACTICITY

It seems at first sight that our preceding observations are in conflict with the findings of the Cartesian *cogito*. "The soul is easier to know than the body," said Descartes.[1] And by that he intended to draw a radical distinction between the facts of thought that are accessible to reflection, and the facts about the body, whose knowledge has to be guaranteed by divine goodness. And, indeed, it seems at first that reflection does only disclose

---

1 TN: Sartre is probably thinking of the title of Descartes's Second Meditation: "Of the Nature of the Human Mind; and That It Is More Easily Known than the Body" (Descartes 1996: 16).

pure facts of consciousness to us. Of course we will encounter phenomena at this level that appear to include within themselves some connection with the body: "physical" pain, discomfort, pleasure, etc. But these
phenomena are not any the less *pure facts of consciousness*. There is a tendency
therefore to make them into *signs*, affections of consciousness *on the occasion* of the body, without realizing that in so doing we have irremediably
chased the body out of consciousness and that no connection will any
longer be able to reunite this body, which is already the body-for-the-
Other, and the consciousness that, it is claimed, is its manifestation.

We should not therefore set out from that point but from our first
relation to the in-itself: from our being-in-the-world. We know that
there is not, on the one hand, a for-itself and, on the other, a world, as
two closed wholes, whose means of communication it is necessary afterward to seek. Rather, the for-itself is by itself a relation to the world; in
denying, in relation to itself, that it is being, it makes it the case that there
is a world and, in surpassing this negation toward its own possibilities, it
discloses the *thises* as implement-things.

But when we say that the for-itself is in-the-world, and that consciousness is conscious *of* the world, we must be careful not to understand this as meaning that the world exists facing consciousness as an
indefinite multiplicity of reciprocal relations, on which it is able to look
down without any perspective and to contemplate without any point of
view. *For me*, this glass is to the left of the carafe, and slightly behind it;
for Pierre, it is to the right, and slightly in front. We cannot even conceive
that a consciousness might look down on the world in such a way that
the glass is given to it as being *at the same time* to the right and to the left of
the carafe, in front of it and behind it. And that is not in consequence of a
strict application of the principle of identity but because this fusion of 346
right and left, of front and back, would bring about the complete disappearance of the *thises* within a primitive indistinction. Similarly, if the leg
of the table is hiding some arabesques on the carpet from my view, that
is not because of some finitude or imperfection of my visual organs but
because a carpet that was neither hidden by the table, nor under it, nor
above it, nor beside it, would no longer have any relation of any kind
with it, and would no longer belong to the "world" in which *there is* the
table: the in-itself that shows itself in the guise of the *this* would return
to its indifferent identity; space itself, as a pure relation of externality,

would vanish. The constitution of space as a multiplicity of reciprocal relations can, in fact, only be applied from the abstract point of view of science: it cannot be lived, nor is it possible even to represent it; the triangle that I draw on the board to help me with my abstract reasoning is, insofar as it is on the board, necessarily to the right of the circle, at a tangent to one of its sides. And I endeavor to surpass the concrete characteristics of the figure drawn in chalk by taking no more account of its orientation in relation to me than of the breadth of the lines or the imperfection of my drawing.

Thus, by virtue solely of the fact that there is a world, this world cannot exist without a univocal orientation in relation to me. Idealism correctly insisted on the fact that relations make the world. But, as it situated itself in the domain of Newtonian science, it conceived of these relations as relations of reciprocity. In this way it was able to achieve only abstract concepts of pure externality, action and reaction, etc., and for just that reason it missed the world, and only managed to explicate the limit-concept of absolute objectivity. All in all, this concept came down to that of the "desert world," or a "world without men," which is to say a contradiction, since it is through human-reality that there is a world. Thus, when it is taken to its conclusion, the concept of objectivity—which aimed to replace the in-itself of dogmatic truth by a pure relation of reciprocal concordance between representations—is itself destroyed. Scientific progress, moreover, has led to the rejection of this notion of absolute objectivity. What Broglie, for example, came to describe as an "experiment" is a system of univocal relations from which the observer is not excluded.[2] And if microphysics is obliged to reintegrate the observer at the heart of the scientific system, it is not as a pure subjectivity—that notion would have no more meaning than the notion of pure objectivity— but as an original relation to the world, as a place, as that toward which all the relations under consideration are oriented. That is why, for example, Heisenberg's principle of indeterminacy[3] cannot be regarded

2 TN: Louis-Victor-Pierre-Raymond de Broglie (1892–1987) was a French physicist who made important contributions to quantum theory.
3 TN: Werner Heisenberg (1901–1976) was a German theoretical physicist who made advances in quantum mechanics. The principle to which Sartre refers is often known as Heisenberg's "uncertainty principle."

either as a disconfirmation or as a confirmation of the determinist thesis. Only, rather than being a pure connection between things, it includes within it man's original relation to things, and his place within the world. This shows up clearly, for example, in the fact that we cannot increase the proportional quantities of the dimensions of moving bodies without changing their relations of velocity. If I examine the movement of one body toward another with the naked eye, and then through the microscope, it will seem to me to be a hundred times faster in the second case because, although the moving body has not come any closer to the body toward which it is moving, it has covered in the same time a space that is a hundred times bigger. In this way, the notion of velocity no longer means anything unless it is in relation to some given dimensions of moving bodies. But it is we ourselves who decide on these dimensions through our very arising in the world, and we have to decide on them; otherwise they would not *be* at all. In this way they are not relative to the knowledge we gain of them but to our initial commitment at the heart of the world. This is what the theory of relativity expresses perfectly: there is no experience through which an observer placed within a system can determine whether the system is at rest or moving. But this relativity is not a "relativism:" it does not concern *knowledge*; better still, it implies the dogmatic postulate according to which knowledge delivers us *what is*. The relativity of modern science targets *being*. Man and the world *are* relative beings, and relation is the principle of their being. It follows that the primary relation goes from human-reality to the world: to arise, for me, is to unfold my distances to things and in so doing to make it the case that there are things. But, in consequence, things are precisely "things-which-exist-at-a-distance-from-me." In this way the world sends back to me this univocal relation that is my being and through which I make it the case that it is revealed. The point of view of pure knowledge is contradictory: the only point of view is that of *committed* knowledge, or, in other words, knowledge and action are only two abstract sides of an original concrete relation. The real space of the world is the space that Lewin describes as "hodological." Pure knowledge would in effect be knowledge without any point of view, and therefore a knowledge of the world that was necessarily situated outside the world. But that has no meaning: the knowing being would only be knowledge, as he would be defined by his object, and his object would disappear within the complete lack of distinction of reciprocal relations. Thus knowledge can only be something that arises for someone engaged within a determinate point of view that he *is*. To be, for human-reality, is *to-be-there*; which is to say "there, on that chair," "there, by the table," "there, at the summit of this mountain, with these dimensions, this orientation, etc." That is an ontological necessity.

Still, we need to be quite clear. In fact, this necessity appears between two contingencies: on the one hand, if it is indeed necessary for me to be in the form of being-there, it is wholly contingent that I should *be*, because I am not the foundation of my being; on the other hand, if it is necessary for me to be committed within this or that point of view, it is contingent that it should precisely be in this one, to the exclusion of all others. It is this twofold contingency, encircling a necessity, that we have called the for-itself's *facticity*. We described it in Part Two. We showed there that the in-itself, nihilated and engulfed in the absolute event of the appearance of the foundation, or the for-itself's arising, remains at the heart of the for-itself as its original contingency. Thus the for-itself is maintained by a constant contingency that it takes up on its own account and assimilates, without ever being able to eliminate it. There is no place where the for-itself can find it within itself, no place where it can seize hold of it and know it, not even through the reflective *cogito*, because it is always surpassing it toward its own possibilities, and the for-itself only encounters in itself the nothingness that it has to be. And yet this contingency never ceases to haunt it, and that is what makes me grasp myself at the same time as wholly responsible for my being and wholly unjustifiable. But the world sends back to me the image of this unjustifiability in the form of the synthetic unity of its univocal relations to me. It is absolutely necessary that the world appears to me *in order*. And, in this sense, this order *is me*; it is that image of me that we described in the last chapter of Part Two. But that it should be *this* order is completely contingent. In this way it appears as the necessary and unjustifiable disposition of the totality of beings. This absolutely necessary and wholly unjustifiable order of things in the world, this order which is myself insofar as my arising makes it necessarily exist, and which escapes me insofar as I am neither the foundation of my being nor the foundation of some *particular* being, is the body as it is at the level of the for-itself. In this sense, we can define the body as *the contingent form taken by the necessity*

of my contingency. It is nothing other than the for-itself; it is not an in-itself
in the for-itself because in that case it would freeze everything. But it is
the fact that the for-itself is not its own foundation, insofar as this fact is
expressed through the necessity of existing as a contingent being, committed among contingent beings. As such, the body cannot be distinguished from the for-itself's situation, since, for the for-itself, to exist and
to be situated are one and the same; and, on the other hand, it is identified with the world in its entirety, insofar as the world is the for-itself's
total situation and the measure of its existence. But a situation is not a
pure contingent given: quite on the contrary, it reveals itself only to the
extent to which the for-itself surpasses it toward itself. In consequence,
the body-for-itself is never a given that I am able to know: it is there,
everywhere, as what is surpassed, and it exists only insofar as I escape it
in nihilating myself; it is what I nihilate. It is the in-itself surpassed by
the nihilating for-itself and seizing back the for-itself in this very surpassing. It is the fact that I am my own motivation without being my own
foundation, the fact that I am nothing unless I have to be what I am, and   349
yet—insofar as what I have to be is what I am—I am without having
to be. In a sense, therefore, the body is a necessary characteristic of the
for-itself. It is not true that it is the product of a Demiurge's arbitrary
decision, nor that the union of body and soul is the contingent association of two radically distinct substances; but, on the contrary, it follows
necessarily from the for-itself's nature that it should be a body, i.e., that
its nihilating escaping from being comes about in the form of a commitment within the world. And yet, in another sense, the body manifests
my contingency, and is even nothing but this contingency: the Cartesian
rationalists were right to be struck by this characteristic; in effect, it represents the individuation of my commitment within the world. And
Plato was not wrong, either, to present the body as *what individuates the soul*.
Only it would be fruitless to suppose that the soul *is* the body, insofar as
the for-itself is its own individuation.

We will be better able to grasp the significance of these observations if
we try to apply them to the problem of sensory knowledge.

The problem of sensory knowledge was posed on the occasion of the
appearance in the midst of the world of certain objects that we know as
the *senses*. First we observed that the Other had eyes and, after that, techni-
cians who were dissecting corpses learned the structure of these objects;

they distinguished the cornea from the crystalline lens, and the lens from the retina. They established that the crystalline object was to be classified within a family of particular objects—lenses—and that the laws of geometric optics concerning lenses could be applied to the object of their study. More precise dissections, carried out as surgical instruments were being improved, taught us that a group of nerves led out from the retina and terminated in the brain. Under the microscope, we examined the nerves of corpses and determined their exact route, their point of departure, and their point of arrival. The set of these items of knowledge concerned, therefore, a certain spatial object called "the eye:" they implied the existence of space and of the world, and they implied, in addition, that we are able to *see* this eye, or to touch it, which is to say that we ourselves possess a sensory point of view on things. Finally, all our technical knowledge (the art of making scalpels, lancets) and our scientific knowledge (e.g., the geometric optics that makes it possible to construct and make use of microscopes) is interposed between our knowledge of the eye and the eye itself. In short, between myself and the eye that I am dissecting, the entire world—such as I make it appear just through my arising—is interposed. After that, a more thorough investigation allowed us to establish the existence of various nerve endings at the periphery

350   of our body. We have even succeeded in acting on some of these nerve endings separately, and to perform experiments on living subjects. We found ourselves then to be in the presence of two worldly objects: on the one hand, the stimulant; on the other, the sensory corpuscle, or the free nerve ending, that we are stimulating. The stimulant was a physico-chemical object, an electric current, a mechanical or chemical agent, whose properties we knew precisely and whose intensity or duration we were able to vary in a determinate way. We were dealing therefore with two worldly objects, and their intraworldly relation could be observed through our own senses, or through the medium of instruments. Once again, the knowledge of this relation presupposed an entire system of scientific and technical knowledge, in short the existence of a world, and our original arising within this world. In addition, our empirical information allowed us to conceive of a relation between the "interior" of the object-other and the collection of these objective findings. In effect, we learned that by acting on certain senses we were able "to cause a modification" in the other's consciousness. We learned that *through language*, i.e.,

through the other's signifying and objective reactions. A physical object (the stimulant), a physiological object (the sense), a psychological object (the other), objective manifestations of meaning (language): these are the terms in the objective relation that we wanted to establish. None of them was able to lead us out of the world of objects. I have also on occasion acted as a subject in investigations carried out by physiologists or psychologists.[4] If I offered myself to some experiment of this type, I found myself suddenly in a laboratory and perceiving a screen that was more or less brightly lit, or else I experienced small electric shocks, or else I was brushed by an object that I was unable to determine very precisely but whose global presence in the midst of the world, and against me, I was able to grasp. Not for an instant was I isolated from the world; all these events happened for me in a laboratory, in the center of Paris, in the south building of the Sorbonne; and I remained in the presence of the Other, and the point itself of the experiment required that I should be able to communicate with him through language. From time to time the experimenter asked me if the screen appeared to me to be more or less brightly lit, if the pressure that was exerted on my hand seemed to be more or less strong, and I answered—which is to say that I gave objective information about things that were appearing in the midst of my world. Perhaps one inept experimenter asked me if "my sensation of light was more or less strong, more or less intense." This sentence would have had no meaning for me—since I was in the midst of objects, in the process of observing these objects—had I not been taught long ago to call the objective light, such as it appeared to me in the world at a given instant, a "sensation of light." I replied therefore that the sensation of light was, for example, less intense, but what I meant by that was that the screen was, in my opinion, less brightly lit. And this "in my opinion" did not correspond to anything real—because I was apprehending the screen in fact as less brightly lit—other than to an endeavor not to confuse the world's objectivity for me with a stricter objectivity, the result of experimental measurements and of the agreement of minds with each other. What

351

4 TN: *Il nous est arrivé . . . de servir aux recherches* . . . Throughout this paragraph Sartre uses the plural pronoun *nous*, but I assume (as elsewhere in the text) that we should understand it as "I."

I was not in any case able to know was a specific object that the experimenter was observing during this time and which was my visual organ, or certain tactile nerve endings. The result obtained, therefore, at the end of the experiment could only be to establish a relation between two series of objects: those that were revealed to me during the experiment and those that were revealed during the same time to the experimenter. The illumination of the screen belonged to my world; my eyes, as objective organs, belonged to the experimenter's world. The connection between these two series was claimed therefore to be like a bridge between two worlds; in no case could it be a table of correspondences between the subjective and the objective.

Why, indeed, would we call the collection of luminous, or heavy, or scented objects, as they appeared to me in this laboratory, in Paris, one day in February, etc., "subjectivity?" And if in spite of everything we were to regard this collection as subjective, why should we confer objectivity on the system of objects that were simultaneously revealed to the experimenter, in this same laboratory, on this same day in February? There are not two weights here, or two measures: nowhere will we encounter something that is given as purely *sensed*, as lived for me without objectification. Here as always I am conscious of the world and, against the ground of the world, of certain transcendent objects; as always, I surpass what is revealed to me toward the possibility that I have to be—for example, toward the possibility of answering the experimenter correctly and enabling the experiment to succeed. Of course, these comparisons may provide certain objective results: for example, I can observe that the tepid water seems cold to me when I plunge my hand in it after having plunged it into hot water. But this observation, which is pompously named "the law of relativity of sensations," does not concern sensations in any way. What we have here really is a quality of the object that is revealed to me: the tepid water *is* cold when I plunge my heated hand into it. Only, a comparison of this objective quality of water with an equally objective piece of information—the one I am given by the thermometer—reveals a contradiction to me. This contradiction motivates on my part a free choice of the true objectivity. The objectivity that I have not chosen is what I will call "subjectivity." As for the *reasons* for the "relativity of sensations," further investigation will reveal them to me in certain objective and synthetic structures that I will call *figures* (Gestalt).

352

The Müller-Lyer illusion, the relativity of the senses, etc., are so many names given to objective laws concerning the structures of these figures. These laws do not inform us about *appearances* but concern synthetic structures. I only intervene here to the extent to which my arising within the world engenders the *establishing of a relation* of each of the objects with each other. As such, they are revealed as *figures*. Scientific objectivity consists in considering the structures separately, in isolating them from the whole: thereafter, they appear with different characteristics. But there is no case in which we leave an existing world. We could show in the same way that the so-called threshold of sensation, or the specificity of the senses, comes down to pure determinations of objects as such.

However, the claim has been that this objective relation of the stimulant to the sensory organ is itself surpassed toward a relation between the *objective* (stimulant–sensory organ) and the subjective (pure sensation), this subjective being defined by the action that the stimulant exerts on us, through the intermediary of the sensory organ. The sensory organ appears to us to be affected by the stimulant: the protoplasmic and physico-chemical changes which indeed appear in the sensory organ are not produced by this organ itself: they come to it *from outside*. At least, that is what we assert, in order to remain faithful to the principle of inertia which constitutes nature in its entirety as externality. When therefore we establish a correlation between the objective system—the stimulant–sensory organ, which we are currently perceiving, and the subjective system which is for us the set of internal properties of the object-other—we are forced to admit that the new modality that has just appeared within this subjectivity, in connection with the stimulation of the sense, is also, itself, produced by something other than itself. If in fact it brought itself about spontaneously, that would immediately sever any connection it had with the stimulated organ or, alternatively, the relation that we would be able to establish between them would be *any relation whatsoever*. We conceive therefore of an objective unity corresponding to the smallest and the shortest of the perceptible stimulations and we call that "sensation." We endow this unity with *inertia*, which is to say that it will be pure externality, since, as it is conceived on the basis of the *this*, it participates in the externality of the in-itself. This externality, projected into the heart of the sensation, affects it almost in its very existence: the principle of its being and the occasion of its existence are outside it. It is therefore *external* to itself. At the same time, its *raison d'être* is not located in some "internal" fact that has the same nature as it but in a real object, the stimulant, and in the change that affects another real object, the sensory organ. And yet, as it remains inconceivable that a certain being, existing at a certain level of being and incapable of maintaining itself on its own in being, should be determined to exist by an existent that occupies a radically distinct level of being, I conceive of a medium that is homogeneous with it, and itself also constituted in externality, in order to maintain the sensation and to supply it with being. To this medium I give the name "mind," or sometimes even "consciousness." But I conceive of this consciousness as the *other's* consciousness, i.e., as an object. Nonetheless, as the relations that I wish to establish between the sensation and the sensory organ have to be universal, I postulate that the consciousness conceived in this way must also be my consciousness, not *for the other* but *in itself.* In this way I have determined a kind of internal space, within which certain figures called "sensations" are formed, on the occasion of external stimulations. As this space is pure passivity, I assert that it *undergoes* its sensations. But by that I do not mean only that it is the internal medium that serves as their matrix. Now I am inspired by a biological vision of the world, which I borrow from my objective conception of the sensory organ in question, and I claim that this internal space *lives* its sensation. In this way "life" is a magical connection that I establish between a passive medium and a passive mode of this medium. The mind does not produce its own sensations and, in consequence, they remain *external* to it; but, on the other hand, it appropriates them by living them. In effect, the unity of the "lived" and the "living" is no longer a spatial juxtaposition, or a relation between what is contained and its container: it is a magical inherence. The mind *is* its own sensations, even while it remains distinct from them. Therefore the sensation becomes a particular type of object: inert, passive, and simply lived through. We are thereby obliged to endow it with absolute subjectivity. But we must be clear about this word "subjectivity." Here it does not mean belonging to a subject, which is to say to an ipseity which spontaneously motivates itself. The psychologist's "subjectivity" is wholly different in kind: it manifests, on the contrary, inertia and the absence of all transcendence. What is subjective is something unable to get out of itself. And, precisely, to the extent to which a sensation, as pure externality, can only be an impression in the mind, and to the extent to which it is only itself, only that figure that a flurry has formed in psychological space, it is not transcendence but purely and simply what is undergone, the mere determination of our receptivity: it is subjectivity because it is in no way *presentative* or *representative*. The object-other's subjectivity is purely and simply a closed casket. The sensation is in the casket.

Such is the notion of *sensation*. We can see its absurdity. In the first place, it is purely invented. It corresponds to nothing that I experience in myself or in the Other. We have only ever grasped the objective universe; all our personal determinations presuppose the world, and arise as relations to the world. As for sensation, it presupposes that man is already in the world, since he has sensory organs at his disposal, and it appears in him as a pure cessation of his relations with the world. At the same time, this pure "subjectivity" presents itself as the necessary base on which he will have to reconstruct all those transcendent relations that its apparition has just caused to disappear. Thus we encounter these three moments of thought: (1) In order to establish the sensation, it is necessary to start out from a certain realism: we regard our perception of the Other, of the Other's senses and of the instruments of induction as valid. (2) But, at the level of the sensation, all this realism disappears: the sensation, as a pure modification that is undergone, can provide us with information only about ourselves; it is "lived." (3) And yet that is what I present as the base for my knowledge of the external world. This base cannot be the foundation of a *real* contact with things: it does not enable us to conceive of an intentional structure of the mind. We are obliged to use the term "objectivity" not for an immediate connection with being but for certain conjunctions of sensations that present more permanence or more regularity or which accord better with the set of our representations. In particular, that is the way in which we are obliged to define our perception of the Other, the Other's sensory organs, and the instruments of induction: we are dealing with subjective formations with a particular coherence, and that is all. There can be no question at this level of explaining my sensation in terms of the sensory organ, such as I perceive it in the Other or myself but, quite to the contrary, it is the sensory organ that I explain as a certain association of my sensations. We can see the inevitable circle. I use my perception of the Other's senses as the foundation for an explanation of some sensations and, in particular, of my

sensations; but, conversely, my sensations, conceived in this way, constitute the only *reality* of my perception of the Other's senses. And within
this circle the same object—the Other's sensory organ—has neither the
same nature nor the same truth in each of its appearances. It is in the first
place *reality* and, precisely because it is reality, it founds a doctrine which
contradicts it. In *appearance* the structure of the classical theory of sensation
is exactly that of the Cynic argument of the Liar, in which it is precisely
because the Cretan is telling the truth that he finds himself lying. But, in
addition, as we have just seen, a sensation is pure subjectivity. How can
it be claimed that we construct an object out of subjectivity? No synthetic
grouping is able to confer an objective quality on what is as a matter of
principle lived through. If there must be perception of objects in the
world, then it is necessary for us to be, from the very moment of our
arising, in the presence of the world and of objects. Sensation, a notion
that is a hybrid between subjective and objective, conceived on the basis
of an object, and afterward applied to a subject, of whose bastard existence we are unable to say whether it is *de facto* or *de jure*—such a sensation
is a pure psychologist's fantasy, and must be pointedly rejected from any
serious theory about the relations of consciousness and the world.

355   But if sensation is only a word, what becomes of the senses? It will
probably be acknowledged that we never encounter in ourselves this
phantom and rigorously subjective impression that is sensation; it will
be admitted that I only ever grasp *the* green of this notebook, or this
foliage, and never the sensation of green or even the "quasi-green"
that Husserl posits as the hyletic matter that is animated by intention
into a green-object; others will declare themselves convinced without
difficulty that if we assume that the phenomenological reduction is
possible—which remains to be proved—it will confront us with objects
that have been placed within parentheses, as the pure correlatives of
positional acts, and not with impressional residues. But the fact remains
that the senses remain. I *see* the green; I *touch* this polished and cold
marble. An accident may deprive me of an entire sense: I may lose my
sight, or become deaf, etc. What, then, is a sense that does not give us
any sensation?

The answer is easy. Let us note first that the *sense* is everywhere, and
everywhere it eludes us. This inkwell, on the table, is immediately given to
me in the shape of a thing and yet it is given to me *through sight*. Its presence,

therefore, is a visible presence and I am conscious that it is present to me as visible, which is to say I am conscious (of) seeing it. But even while sight is *knowledge* of the inkwell, sight eludes any knowledge: we do not have knowledge of sight. Even reflection will not give us this knowledge. My reflective consciousness will indeed give me knowledge of my reflective consciousness of the inkpot, but not knowledge of a sensory activity. It is in this sense that we should take Auguste Comte's famous claim: "The eye cannot see itself."[5] We can allow that another organic structure, a contingent arrangement of our visual apparatus, might allow a third eye to *see* our two eyes while they were seeing. Can I not see and touch my hand while it is touching? But in that case I would be taking up the other's viewpoint on my sense, and I would be seeing object-eyes; I cannot see the seeing eye, and I cannot touch the hand insofar as it is touching. In this way a sense, insofar as it is-for-me, eludes me: it is not the infinite collection of my sensations, since I only ever encounter objects in the world; on the other hand, if I take up a reflective view of my consciousness, I will encounter my consciousness of this or that thing-in-the-world, and not my visual or tactile sense; finally, if I am able to see or to touch my sensory organs, I have a revelation of pure objects in the world, and not of a disclosing or constructive activity. And yet the sense is there: *there is* [il y a] sight, touch, hearing.

But if, on the other hand, I consider the system of *seen* objects as they appear to me, I observe that they are not presented to me in just any order: they are *oriented*. Since, then, a sense cannot be defined either by an act that can be grasped or by a succession of states that are lived through, it remains for us to try to define it through its objects. If sight is not the sum of visual sensations, could it not be the system of objects that are seen? In this case we must return to this idea of *orientation* that we pointed to a moment ago, and try to grasp its meaning. 356

First of all, let us note that it is a constitutive structure of a thing. An object appears against the ground of the world and manifests itself in a relation of externality with other *thises* that have appeared. In this way, its disclosure implies the complementary constitution of an undifferentiated

5 TN: Auguste Comte (1798–1857) was a French philosopher, best known for his doctrine of positivism. I have not been able to find the sentence Sartre quotes.

ground, which is the total perceptual field, or world. The formal structure of this relation between the figure and the ground is therefore necessary; in brief, the existence of a visual or tactile or auditory field is a necessity: silence, for example, is the acoustic field of undifferentiated noises, against which the particular sound that we are considering stands out. But the material connection of some *this* in particular to the ground is at the same time chosen and given. It is chosen insofar as the for-itself's arising is the explicit and internal negation of a *particular this* against the ground of the world: I *look at* the cup or the inkwell. It is given such that my choice is made on the basis of an original distribution of *thises*, which manifests the very facticity of my arising. It is necessary that the book appears to me to the right or the left of the table. But it is contingent that it should appear precisely to the left and, in fact, I am free to look at *the book* on the table or *the table* supporting the book. *Sense* is the name that we are giving to this contingency, between the necessity and the freedom of my choice. It implies that the object *always appears to me all at once in its entirety*—what I see is the *cube*, the *inkwell*, the *cup*—but that this appearance always takes place within a particular perspective that expresses its relations to the ground of the world, and to the other *thises*. What I hear is always *the note of the violin*. But it is necessary that I hear it *through a door*, or *through the open window*, or in the concert hall: otherwise the object would no longer be in the midst of the world and would no longer manifest itself to an existent-arising-within-the-world. But, on the other hand, if it is quite true that it is not possible for all the *thises* to appear *at the same time* on the ground of the world, and that the appearance of some of them causes some of the others to fuse into the ground, and if it is true that each *this* can only manifest itself in just one way *at a time*, even though there are an infinite number of ways in which it can appear, we ought not to suppose these rules of appearance to be subjective and psychological: they are strictly objective, and follow from the nature of things. If the inkwell is hiding a portion of the table from me, that is not due to the nature of my senses but to the nature of the inkwell and the light. If the object looks smaller as it moves away, we should not explain that by some illusion on the part of the observer but by the strictly external laws of perspective. In this way, through these objective laws, a strictly objective center of reference is defined: it is the eye, for example, insofar as it is the point, on a diagram of perspective, toward which all the objective lines come to converge.

357

Thus the perceptual field refers to a center that is objectively defined by this reference, and situated in the field itself that is oriented around it. Only we do not see this center as a structure of the perceptual field in question: *we are it*. Thus the order of objects in the world constantly sends back to us the image of an object that cannot, as a matter of principle, be an object *for us*, because it is what we have to be. Thus the structure of the world implies that we cannot *see* without *being visible*. The intraworldly references can only be to objects in the world, and the seen world is constantly defining a visible object, to which its perspectives and arrangements refer back. This object appears in the midst of the world at the same time as the world: whatever the grouping of objects, it is always given in addition, since it is defined by these objects' orientation. Without this object there would be no orientation, as every orientation would be equivalent: it is the contingent arising of one orientation within the infinite possibility of orienting the world; it is *this* orientation, raised to the absolute. But this object only exists for us at this level as an abstract indication: it is what everything points out to me, and what I cannot as a matter of principle take hold of, since it is what I *am*. Indeed, what I am necessarily cannot be an object for me insofar as I am it. The object that is indicated by worldly things, and which they enclose within their circle, is for itself and, as a matter of principle, a non-object. Rather, the arising of my being, in unfolding distances from the *starting-point of a center*, determines, through the very act of this unfolding, an object which is itself insofar as it is indicated by the world, and which however cannot be intuited by me as an object because I am it; it is me, in my presence to myself as the being that is its own nothingness. In this way my being-in-the-world, solely by virtue of its *actualizing* a world, is indicated to itself as a being-in-the-midst-of-the-world by the world that it actualizes, and it could not be otherwise, because there is no other way to enter into contact with the world other than *being of the world*. It would be impossible for me to actualize a world without me in it, and which would be a pure object of contemplation from above. But, on the contrary, I have to lose myself within the world in order for the world to exist and for me to be able to transcend it. In this way, to say that I have entered the world, "come to the world," or that there is a world in which I have a body comes to one and the same thing. In this sense, my body is everywhere upon the world: it is just as much over there, in the fact that the lamppost conceals the shrub that is growing on the sidewalk, as in the fact that the attic, up there, is above the windows of the sixth floor, or in the fact that the passing car is moving from right to left behind the lorry, or that the woman crossing the road seems smaller than the man who is seated on the terrace outside the café. My body is coextensive with the world, spread right through things, and at the same time it is concentrated in this single point that all those things are indicating, and that I am without being able to know it. This should enable us to understand what the senses are.

358

A sense is not given *before* sensory objects; is it not in fact capable of appearing to the Other as an object? Nor is it given *after* them: in that case we would have to suppose a world of incommunicable images, mere copies of reality, without being able to conceive of the mechanism of their appearance. The senses are contemporaneous with the objects: they are even things in person, such as they are disclosed to us in perspective. They merely represent an objective rule of this disclosure. In this way, sight does not *produce* visual sensations, and nor is it *affected* by light rays; rather, it is the collection of all visible objects insofar as their objective and reciprocal relations all refer to specific magnitudes that are chosen—and undergone at the same time—as measures, and to a specific center of perspective. From this point of view, a sense cannot in any way be assimilated to subjectivity. All the variations that it is possible to record within a perceptual field are in effect *objective* variations. In particular, the fact that one can eliminate vision by "closing one's eyelids" is an external fact that is not connected with the subjectivity of apperception. The eyelid is in fact an object perceived among other objects, and which conceals the other objects from me by virtue of its objective relation with them: *to no longer see* the other objects in my room because I have closed my eyes is *to see* the screen of my eyelid; similarly, if I put my gloves on a tablecloth, *to no longer see* this design on the cloth is precisely *to see my gloves*. Similarly, the *accidents* that affect a sense always belong to the region of objects: "I see yellow" because I have jaundice or because I am wearing yellow glasses. In both cases the reason for the phenomenon does not lie in a subjective modification of the sense, or even an organic alteration, but an objective relation between worldly objects: in both cases we are seeing "through" something, and the truth of our vision is objective. If, finally, in some way or other the visual center of reference is destroyed (the destruction only being able to come from the world's

development, in accordance with its own laws, which is to say that it expresses in a particular way my facticity), the visible objects are not annihilated at the same time. They continue to exist *for me*, but they exist without any center of reference as a *visible totality*, without the appearance of any particular *this*, i.e., in the absolute reciprocity of their relations. Thus it is the for-itself's arising in the world which in one stroke makes the world exist as the totality of things, and the senses as the objective way in which the things' qualities are presented. What is fundamental is   359
my relation to the world, and this relation defines at the same time the world and the senses, depending on the point of view that one occupies. Blindness, color blindness, and myopia represent in the first place *the way in which there is* a world for me, which is to say that they define my visual sense insofar as this latter is the facticity of my arising. That is why my sense can be objectively known and defined by me, but *emptily*, on the basis of the world: all that is needed is that my rationalizing and universalizing thought should prolong into the abstract the indications that things are giving to me about my sense, and that it should *reconstitute* the sense on the basis of these signals, as the historian reconstitutes a historical character in accordance with the remains that indicate him. But in this case I have reconstructed the world on the terrain of pure rationality in abstracting myself through thought from the world: I look down on the world without being attached to it, I take up an attitude of absolute objectivity, and the sense becomes one object among objects, a *relative* center of reference which, itself, presupposes coordinates. But, precisely by so doing, I establish in thought the world's absolute relativity, which is to say that I posit the absolute equivalence of every center of reference. I destroy the world's mundanity, without even realizing. In this way the world, by constantly indicating to me the sense that I am, and by inviting me to reconstitute it, encourages me to eliminate the personal equation that I am by restoring to the world the worldly center of reference in relation to which the world is arranged. But by the same token I escape—through abstract thought—the sense that I am, which is to say that I sever my links with the world, I place myself in a state of merely looking down on it, and the world vanishes within the absolute equivalence of its infinite possible relations. In effect, a sense is our being-in-the-world insofar as we have it to be, in the form of being-in-the-midst-of-the-world.

We can generalize these observations; they may be applied to my *body* in its entirety, insofar as it is the total center of reference indicated by things. In particular, our body is not only what has for a long time been known as "the seat of the five senses"; it is also the instrument and the goal of our actions. It is even impossible to distinguish "sensation" from "action," even according to the terms of classical psychology: this is what we were showing when we pointed out that reality is presented to us neither as a *thing* nor as an *implement* but as an implement-thing. That is why, for our investigation of the body insofar as it is the center of action, we can take as our guiding thread the reasoning that we have used to disclose the true nature of the senses.

Indeed, the moment that we formulate the problem of action, we are at risk of falling into a confusion with serious consequences. When I pick up this fountain pen and plunge it into the inkwell, I am acting. But if I am looking at Pierre, who in the same instant is bringing a chair closer to the table, I also observe that he is acting. Here, therefore, there is a clear risk that we will commit the error that we denounced in relation to the senses, i.e., that we will interpret my action, as it *is-for-me* on the basis of the other's action. For in fact the only action that I am able *to know* in the actual time in which it is taking place is Pierre's action. I see his movement and I determine his goal at the same time: he is bringing a chair closer to the table *in order to* be able to sit near this table and to write the letter that he told me he wanted to write. In this way I am able to grasp all the intermediate positions of the chair, and of the body which is moving it, as instrumental organizations: they are means in order to reach a goal that is pursued. Here, therefore, the other's body appears to me as an instrument in the midst of other instruments: not only as a tool for making tools but, in addition, as *a tool for handling tools*, in brief as a tool-machine. If therefore I interpret the role of my body in relation to my action in the light of my knowledge of the other's body, I will come to regard myself as having at my disposal a certain instrument of which I can make use as I wish and which, in its turn, arranges the other instruments in accordance with a certain end that I am pursuing. This brings us back to the classic distinction between the mind and the body: the mind uses the tool that is the body. The parallelism with the theory of sensation is complete: as we saw, this theory set out from my knowledge of the other's sense and goes on to endow me with senses that exactly resemble the sensory organs that I perceived on the other. We also saw the difficulty that such a theory immediately encounters, which is that here I am perceiving the world—and in particular the Other's sensory organ—through my own sense, a distorting organ, a refractive environment, which can inform me only about its own affections. In this way the theory's consequences ruin the objectivity of the very principle that was used to establish it. The theory of action, which has an analogous structure, encounters analogous difficulties. If in fact I set out from the Other's body, I grasp it as an instrument, and insofar as I can make use of it myself as an instrument: I am able in effect to *utilize* it in order to reach ends that I would be unable to reach on my own; I *command* its acts, through orders or through prayers; I am also able to bring them about through my own acts, while at the same time I am obliged to take precautions in relation to a tool that is particularly dangerous and delicate to handle. I have in relation to it the complex attitude of a worker in relation to his tool-machine when he directs its movements and, simultaneously, avoids being hit by it. And, once again, in order to make use of the Other's body to maximally serve my interests, I need an instrument that is my own body, just as, in order to perceive the Other's sensory organs, I need other sensory organs, which are my own ones. If therefore I conceive of my body in the image of the Other's body, it is an instrument in the world that I am obliged to handle delicately and which is like the key to the handling of other tools. But my relations themselves to this special instrument can only be technical ones, and, in order to handle this instrument, I need an instrument, which places us in an infinite regress. In this way, therefore, if I conceive of my sensory organs as those of the other, they require a sensory organ in order to perceive them—and if I grasp my body as an instrument that resembles the other's body, it calls for an instrument in order to handle it—and, if we refuse to conceive of this infinite regress, then we will be forced to accept that paradox of a physical instrument being *handled* by a mind, which, as we know, pushes us into inextricable aporia. Let us see if instead we can try, in this case as in the other, to restore to the body its nature-for-us. Objects are disclosed to us within a structure of equipment in which they occupy a determinate *place*. This place is not defined by pure spatial coordinates but in relation to axes whose reference is practical. "The glass *is on the tray*:" that means we must take care not to knock the glass over if we move the tray. The packet of

361

tobacco is on the fireplace: that means you have to cross a distance of three meters if you want to go from the pipe to the tobacco, avoiding certain obstacles, small tables, armchairs, etc., which are arranged between the fireplace and the table. In this sense, there is no distinction at all between perception and the practical organization of existents into a world. Each implement refers to other implements: to the ones that are its keys, and to those of which it is the key. But these references would not be grasped by a purely contemplative consciousness: for such a consciousness, the hammer would not refer to the nails but would be next to them; even the phrase "next to" loses all its meaning if it fails to sketch out a path that goes from the hammer to the nail, and which must be taken. The space that is originally disclosed to me is hodological space: it is crisscrossed by paths and by routes; it is instrumental and the site of tools. In this way the world, from the moment that my for-itself arises, is disclosed as indicating actions that are to be done, these acts referring to other acts, and those acts to others, and so on. However, it should be noted that if, from this point of view, perception and action are indiscernible, action is nonetheless presented as a specific efficacy of the future, surpassing and transcending what is purely and simply perceived. What is perceived, as what my for-itself is present to, is disclosed to me as co-present; it is an immediate contact, a present adherence, brushing up against me. But, as such, it offers itself up without my being able to grasp it in the present. The perceived thing is full of promise, and provocative, and every property that it promises to reveal to me, every tacitly consented act of abandonment, every meaningful reference to other objects, commits the future. Thus I am in the presence of things that are only promises, beyond an ineffable presence that I am unable to possess, and which is the things' pure "being-there," which is to say my own, my facticity, my body. The cup is there, on the saucer; it is given to me in the present with its base which is there, which everything points to, but which I do not see. And if I wish to see it—i.e., to make it explicit, to make it "appear-against-the-ground-of-the-cup"—I will have to take hold of the cup by its handle, and turn it over: the base of the cup is at the end of my projects, and to say that the cup's other structures point to it as an indispensable element of the cup is equivalent to saying that they point it out to me as the action that will best appropriate the cup in its meaning to me. In this way the world, as the correlative of the possibilities that I am, appears from the moment I arise as the enormous outline of all my possible actions. Perception naturally surpasses itself toward action; better still, it can be disclosed only in and through projects of action. The world is disclosed as a "hollow that is always in the future," because we are always future in relation to ourselves.

However, we must note that this world's future that is disclosed to us in this way is strictly objective. The instrument-things point to other instruments or to objective ways of making use of them: the nail is "to be driven in" in such and such a way, the hammer "to be picked up by the handle," the cup "to be picked up by its handle," etc. All these properties of things are immediately disclosed, and Latin gerundives express them perfectly. Of course they are correlative to the non-thetic projects that we are, but they are revealed only as structures of the world: potentialities, absences, equipmentality. In this way the world appears to me as objectively articulated; it never refers to a creative subjectivity but to the infinite structures of equipment.

Nevertheless, as each instrument refers to another instrument, and this latter to another, all of them end up by pointing to an instrument which is like the key to them all. This center of reference is necessary; otherwise, as all instrumentalities would become equivalent, the world would vanish through the complete lack of differentiation of its gerundives. Carthage is "*delenda*" for the Romans, but "*servanda*" for the Carthaginians.[6] Without any relation to these centers, it is nothing; it returns to the indifference of the in-itself, because the two gerundives are annihilated. However, we need to be clear that the key is never given to me but only "indicated as a hollow." What I grasp objectively in action is a world of instruments, of which each one is hooked on to the other, and of which each one, insofar as it is grasped in the very action through which I adapt to it and surpass it, refers to another instrument which ought to enable me to use it. In this sense, the nail refers to the hammer and the hammer refers to the hand and to the arm that use it. But it is only to the extent that I get the Other to plant nails that the hand and the arm become in their turn instruments that I am using, and that I surpass

---

6 TN: The Latin gerundives mean "to be destroyed" and "to be preserved," respectively. Cato the Elder is said to have ended his speeches with "Carthage must be destroyed."

363   toward their potentiality. In this case the Other's hand refers me to the instrument that will allow me to use this hand (threats, promises, salary, etc.). The first term is present everywhere but it is only *indicated*: I do not grasp my hand in the act of writing but only the fountain pen which writes; in other words, I am using the fountain pen to trace the letters, but not my *hand* to hold the fountain pen. In relation to my hand, I do not have the same utilizing attitude as in relation to the fountain pen; I *am* my hand. In other words, my hand is where the references lead, and where they come to a stop. In this sense it is the unknowable and unusable term that is indicated by the last instrument in the series: "book to be written—characters to be traced on the paper—fountain pen," and, at the same time, the orientation of the series in its entirety; the printed book itself refers to it. But I can only grasp it—at least insofar as it is active—as the constant evanescent reference of the entire series. In this way, in a duel with swords, or with sticks, it is the stick that I am following with my eyes, and which I handle; in the act of writing, it is the tip of the pen that I am looking at, in a synthetic connection with the line or the grid that is traced on the sheet of paper. But my hand has vanished; it has become lost in the complex system of equipment, in order for this system to exist. It is simply its meaning and its orientation.

Thus we seem to find ourselves faced with a twofold contradictory necessity: as it is possible to use—and even to grasp—each instrument only through the medium of another instrument, the universe is an objective, indeterminate reference from tool to tool. In this sense the world's structure implies that we can only insert ourselves within the field of equipmentality by being ourselves an implement, that we cannot *act* without *being acted on*. On the other hand, however, a structure of equipment can only be disclosed by determining one cardinal meaning of this structure, and this determination is itself practical and active—to plant a nail, to sow some seeds. In this case, the structure's very existence refers immediately to a center. In this way, this center is at the same time a tool that is objectively defined by the instrumental field that refers to it, and the tool that we are unable to *utilize* because we would be referred *ad infinitum*. We do not employ this instrument; we *are* it. It is not given to us in any way other than through the equipmental order of the world, through hodological space, through the univocal or reciprocal relations between machines, but it cannot be *given* to my action: I do not have to adapt to it, or to adapt some other tool to it; rather, it just is my adaptation to tools, the adaptation that I am. That is why, if we put to one side the analogical reconstruction of my body on the basis of the Other's body, there remain two ways of grasping the body. Either it is known, and objectively defined on the basis of the world, but emptily: for that, it suffices that rationalizing thought should reconstitute the instrument that I am on the basis of the indications given by the implements that I am using—but in that case the fundamental tool becomes a relative center of reference which itself presupposes other tools in order to use it and, by the same token, the world's instrumentality disappears because, in order to be disclosed, it requires a reference to an absolute center of instrumentality; the world of action becomes the world of classical science that is acted on, while consciousness looks down on a universe of externality and can no longer in any way enter into the world. Or, instead, the body is concretely given and in full, as just the way in which things are arranged, insofar as the for-itself surpasses it toward a new arrangement; in this case it is present in every action, even though it is invisible—because action reveals the hammer and the nails, the brake and the change of gear, not the foot which puts on the brake or the hand which is hammering—it is lived, and not known. That is what explains why the well-known "sensation of effort" with which Maine de Biran tried to answer Hume's challenge is a psychological myth.[7] We never have the sensation of our effort, but nor do we have the peripheral, muscular, skeletal, tendinous, or cutaneous sensations which have been proposed in its stead: we perceive the resistance of things. What I perceive when I want to carry this glass to my mouth is not my effort but its heaviness, i.e., its resistance to entering into a structure of equipment that I have brought to appear within the world. Bachelard[8] is right to reproach phenomenology for taking insufficient account of what he calls objects' "coefficient of adversity." That is correct, and it applies to Heidegger's transcendence as much as to Husserl's intentionality. But we have fully to understand that equipmentality comes first: it is in relation to an original structure of equipment that things

7 TN: The French philosopher Maine de Biran (1766–1824) argued that effort ought to be the central concept for psychology.
8 Sartre's note: Bachelard, L'Eau et les Rêves (Editions José Corti, 1942). TN: Translated into English as Bachelard (1983).

reveal their resistances and their adversity. The screw is revealed as too big to be screwed into the nut, the support as too fragile to support the weight that I want to support, the stone as too heavy to be raised right up to the ridge of the wall, etc. Other objects appear as threatening for an equipment-structure that has already been established: the storm and hail for the harvest, the phylloxera for the vine, the fire for the house. In this way, gradually and through the structures of equipment that are already established, their threat will extend right up to the center of reference that all these implements are indicating and it, in its turn, will indicate the threat through them. In this sense every *means* is at the same time favorable and adverse, but within the limits of the fundamental project that is actualized by the for-itself's arising in the world. Thus my body is in the first place indicated by the equipment-structures, and secondarily by the vehicles of destruction. I live my endangered body in relation to threatening machines, just as much as in relation to docile instruments. It is everywhere: the bomb that destroys my house also opens on to my body, insofar as the house was already an indication of my body. For my body is always extended through the tool that it utilizes: my body is at the end of the stick on which I am leaning, against the ground; it is at the end of the telescope which shows me the stars; it is on the chair, in the entire house, because it is my adaptation to these tools.

365

Thus, as we conclude our descriptions, sensation and action have become united, and amount to one and the same thing. We have abandoned the idea of first endowing ourselves with a body in order to examine *afterward* the way in which we apprehend or change the world through it. Rather, on the contrary, we have provided, as the foundation for the disclosure of the body as such, our original relation with the world, i.e., our very arising in the midst of being. Far from its being the case that our body is for us what is first and discloses things to us, it is implement-things which, in their original appearance, indicate our body to us. The body is not a screen between things and us: it manifests only the individuality and contingency of our original relation with implement-things. In this sense we have defined a sense, and a sensory organ in general, as our being-in-the-world insofar as we have that to be in the form of being-in-the-midst-of-the-world. Similarly, we can define action as our being-in-the-world, insofar as we have that to be in the form of being-an-instrument-in-the-midst-of-the-world. But if I am in the midst of the world, it is because I have made it the case that there is a world by transcending being toward myself; and if I am an instrument of the world, it is because I have made it the case that there are in general instruments through the project of myself toward my possibles. It is only in a world that there can be a body, and an initial relation is indispensable for this world to exist. In one sense the body is what I immediately am; in another sense I am separated from it by the world's infinite breadth; it is given to me by the world's surge backward, toward my facticity, and the condition of this constant backward surge is a constant surpassing.

We are able now to clarify our body's nature-for-us. The preceding remarks have allowed us, in effect, to conclude that the body is what is constantly surpassed. Indeed, the body, as the sensory center of reference, is that beyond which I am, insofar as I am immediately present to the glass, or the table, or the distant tree I perceive. In effect, perception can only come about at the very place where the object is perceived, and without distance. But at the same time it unfolds distances, and that in relation to which the perceived object indicates its distance, as an absolute property of its being, is the body. Similarly, as the instrumental center of the structures of equipment, the body can only be what is surpassed: it is what I surpass toward a new combination of structures and what I will constantly have to surpass, no matter which instrumental combination I will have arrived at, because every combination, as soon as my surpassing freezes it in its being, points to the body as the center of reference of its frozen immobility. In this way the body, being what is surpassed, is the Past. It is the immediate presence of "sensible" things to the for-itself, insofar as this presence indicates a center of reference and is already surpassed, either toward the appearance of a new this, or toward a new combination of implement-things. In every project of the for-itself, in every perception, the body is there; it is the immediate Past insofar as it still shows up in the Present that flees from it. Consequently, it is at the same time a point of view and a point of departure: a point of view and a point of departure that I am and that I surpass at the same time toward what I have to be. But this constantly surpassed point of view, which is constantly reborn at the heart of the surpassing—this point of departure that I never cease to cross and which is myself, remaining behind me—is the necessity of my contingency. And it is doubly necessary. That is because,

366

first, it is the continual seizing back of the for-itself by the in-itself and the ontological fact that the for-itself can only be as the being that is not its own foundation: to have a body is to be the foundation of one's own nothingness, and not to be the foundation of one's being; I *am* my body to the extent to which I *am*; I *am* not it to the extent to which I am not what I am; it is through my nihilation that I escape from it. But I do not thereby make of it an object, because it is constantly from what I *am* that I am escaping. And the body is also necessary as the obstacle that is to be surpassed in order to be within the world, i.e., the obstacle that I am to myself. In this sense, it is not different from the world's absolute order, that order that I introduce into being by surpassing it, toward a being-that-is-to-come, toward the being-that-is-beyond-being. We can clearly grasp the unity of these two necessities: to-be-for-oneself is to surpass the world and, in surpassing it, to make it the case that there is a world. But to surpass the world is precisely not to look down on it: it is to be committed within it in order to emerge out of it, to make oneself neces- sarily *this* surpassing perspective. In this sense, finitude is the necessary condition of the for-itself's original project. The necessary condition for me to be—beyond a world that I bring to being—what I am not, and for me to not be what I am, is that, at the heart of the infinite pursuit that I am, there is constantly an elusive given. I am unable either to grasp or to know this given that I am without having it to be—apart from in the mode of not-being—because it is everywhere reclaimed and surpassed, used for my projects, taken on. But on the other hand everything points it out to me; its outline is hollowed out by the entirety of the transcen- dent, through its very transcendence, without my being ever able to turn back toward what it points out, since I *am* the being that is pointed out. In particular, we should not understand the given that is pointed out as a pure center of reference of a static ordering of implement-things; rather, on the contrary, their dynamic ordering—whether or not it depends on my action—refers to it according to rules and, just by so doing, the center of reference is defined in its changing as much as in its identity. It could not be otherwise, since it is by denying, in relation to myself, that I am being that I bring the world to being, and since it is on the basis of my past—which is to say by projecting myself beyond my own being—that I am able to deny, in relation to myself, that I am this being or that one. From this point of view, the body—i.e., this elusive

367

given—is a necessary condition of my action: if in fact the ends that I am pursuing could be attained through a purely arbitrary wish, if it were enough to wish for something in order to obtain it, and if the use of implements were not determined by definite rules, I would never be able to distinguish within me a desire from a volition, or a dream from an act, or the possible from the real. No pro-ject of myself would be possible, since in order to actualize something it would suffice to conceive of it; in consequence, my being-for-itself would be annihilated in the lack of distinction between the present and the future. A phenomenology of action will show, in effect, that an act presupposes a break in continuity between its mere conception and its actualization, which is to say between a universal and abstract thought—"It is necessary for the car's carburetor *not to be clogged*"—and a technical and concrete thought that is directed on *this* carburetor as it appears to me with its absolute dimensions and its absolute position. The condition for this technical thought, which cannot be distinguished from the action it directs, is my finitude, my contingency—in a word, my facticity. Now, I am *de facto* precisely insofar as I have a past, and this immediate past refers me back to the first in-itself, from whose nihilation I arose through my *birth*. In this way, the body as facticity is the past insofar as it originally refers back to a *birth*, which is to say to the first nihilation that makes me arise from the in-itself that I am *de facto*, without having it to be. My birth, the past, contingency, the necessity of a point of view, the *de facto* condition of any possible action on the world: such is the *body*, as it is *for me*. It is not therefore in any way a contingent addition to my mind but, on the contrary, a permanent structure of my being and the permanent condition of possibility of my consciousness as a consciousness of the world and as a transcending project toward my future. From this point of view we have to acknowledge at the same time that it is wholly contingent and absurd that I should be disabled, the son of a civil servant or a worker, irritable and lazy and yet that it is necessary that I should be *that*, or something else, French or German or English, etc., proletarian or bourgeois, or an aristocrat, etc., disabled or puny or strong, irritable or obliging in character, precisely because I cannot *look down* on the world without the world disappearing. *My birth*, insofar as it conditions the way in which objects are disclosed to me (items that are luxuries or basic necessities are more or less *accessible*, certain social realities appear to me as *forbidden*, there

368   are barriers and obstacles within my hodological space), my race, insofar as it is pointed out by the Other's attitude toward me (they are revealed as contemptuous or admiring, as trusting or distrusting me), my class, insofar as it is revealed through the disclosure of the social community to which I belong and insofar as the places that I frequent refer to it, my nationality, my physiological structure, insofar as instruments imply it by the very manner in which they are revealed as resistant or compliant and through their very coefficient of adversity, my character, my past, insofar as everything that I have lived through is pointed out, by the world itself, as my point of view on the world: all of that, insofar as I surpass it in the synthetic unity of my being-in-the-world, is my body, as the necessary condition of the existence of a world, and as the contingent actualization of that condition. We can now grasp in its full clarity the definition that we gave earlier of the body in its being-for-us: the body is the contingent form taken by the necessity of my contingency. We are never able to grasp this contingency as such, insofar as our body is for us, because we are a choice and, for us, to be is to choose ourselves. Even this disability that I suffer is something that, by the very fact of living it, I have taken up; I surpass it toward my own projects, I make of it the necessary obstacle for my being, and I cannot be disabled without choosing myself as disabled, which is to say choosing the way in which I constitute my disability (as "intolerable," "humiliating," "to be concealed," "to reveal to everyone," "an object of pride," "the justification for my failures," etc.). But this elusive body is precisely the necessity of there being a choice, i.e., the necessity of my not being everything all at once. In this sense my finitude is a condition of my freedom, for there is no freedom without choice and, just as the body conditions consciousness as a pure consciousness of the world, it also makes it possible, even in its freedom.

We need still to conceive what the body is for me because, precisely because it is elusive, it does not belong to the world's objects, which is to say those objects that I know and use; and yet, from another angle, since I cannot be anything without being conscious of what I am, it has to be given in some way to my consciousness. In one sense, of course, it is what all the implements that I grasp are pointing toward, and I apprehend it without knowing it in just those indications that I perceive in the implements. But if we were to limit ourselves to this observation we would not be able to distinguish, for example, between the body and the telescope through which an astronomer looks at the planets. In effect, if we are defining the body as the contingent point of view on the world, we must acknowledge that the notion of a point of view presupposes a twofold relation: a relation to the things on which it is a point of view, and a relation with the observer for whom it is a point of view. When we are dealing with the body-point-of-view, this second relation is radically different from the first; when it is a point of view within the world (through a lorgnette, from a belvedere, through a magnifying glass) which is an objective instrument, distinct from the body, the relations are not really distinct. A walker who contemplates a panorama from a belvedere can see the belvedere as well as the panorama: he can see the trees between the belvedere's columns, the belvedere's roof hides the sky from him, etc. However, the "distance" between him and the belvedere is by definition smaller than that between his eyes and the panorama. And the point of view can come up closer to the body, to the point where it has almost merged into it, as we can see for example in the case of glasses, opera-glasses, monocles, etc., which become, so to speak, a supplementary sensory organ. In the end (and if we conceive of an absolute point of view), the distance between it and the person for whom it is a point of view disappears. In other words, it becomes impossible to take a step back in order to "gain perspective" and to constitute a new point of view on one's point of view. That is exactly what, as we have seen, characterizes the body. It is the instrument that I am unable to use by means of another instrument, the point of view on which I can no longer take a point of view. Indeed, at this hill's summit—which I describe, precisely, as a "lovely point of view"—I am, in the very instant in which I look at the valley, taking up a point of view, and this point of view on the point of view is my body. But I cannot take a point of view on my body without an infinite regress. From this it follows, however, that my body cannot be transcendent and known for me; my spontaneous and unreflective consciousness is no longer a consciousness of the body. Rather, we should say, by using the verb "to exist" transitively, that it exists its body. Thus the relation between the body-point-of-view and things is an objective relation, and the relation between consciousness and the body is an existential relation. How should we understand this latter relation?

It is evident, in the first place, that consciousness can exist its body only as consciousness. In this way, my body is a conscious structure of

369

my consciousness. But, precisely because it is the point of view on which there can be no point of view, there is no consciousness of the body at the level of the unreflective consciousness. The body, therefore, belongs among the structures of non-thetic consciousness (of) self. Can we, however, straightforwardly identify it with that non-thetic consciousness? That is not possible either, because the non-thetic consciousness is a consciousness (of) self insofar as it is a free project toward a possibility that is its own, i.e., insofar as it is the foundation of its own nothingness. Non-positional consciousness is conscious (of) the body as what it surmounts and nihilates in making itself consciousness, which is to say as something that it is without having it to be, and *over which it passes* in order to be what it has to be. In brief, consciousness (of) the body is lateral and retrospective; the body is what is *neglected*, "*passed over in silence*," and yet it is what consciousness *is*; it is even nothing but the body; the rest is nothingness and silence. We may compare the consciousness of the body to the consciousness of a *sign*. The sign, moreover, belongs with the body; it is one of the body's essential structures. Now, a consciousness of the sign exists; otherwise we would not be able to understand its meaning. But a sign is *surpassed toward its meaning*, neglected in favor of its sense; it is never grasped for itself; the gaze is constantly directed beyond it. As consciousness of the body is a lateral and retrospective consciousness of what it is without having it to be—i.e., a consciousness of its elusive contingency, of that on the basis of which it makes itself a choice—it is a non-thetic consciousness of the way it *is affected*. Consciousness of the body is inseparable from original affectivity. Still, we need to properly grasp the meaning of this affectivity, and, in order to do that, a distinction is necessary. Affectivity, such as it is revealed to us by introspection, is in effect already an affectivity that has been *constituted*; it is consciousness of the world. Every hatred is a hatred of somebody; every anger is an apprehension of someone as odious or unjust or at fault; to like somebody is to "find him likable," etc. In these different examples, a transcendent "intention"[9] is directed toward the world and apprehends it as such. Already, therefore, there is a surpassing, an internal negation; we are in the domain of transcendence and of choice. But Scheler

___

9 TN: Sartre is using the term "intention" here as Husserl and his disciples use it, i.e., to refer to an act of an intentionally directed consciousness.

rightly pointed out that we must distinguish this "intention" from pure affective qualities. If, for example, I have a "headache," I can discover within me an intentional affectivity directed toward my pain in order to "suffer" it, to accept it with resignation or to reject it, to give it value (as unfair, or deserved, or purifying, or humiliating, etc.), or to flee from it. Here it is the intention itself that is affection; it is a pure act that is already a project, purely a consciousness of something. We cannot consider that to be consciousness (of) the body.

But, precisely, this intention cannot be all that affectivity is. Since it is a surpassing, it presupposes something that is surpassed. Proof of that, moreover, is the existence of what Baldwin unhappily called "abstract emotions."[10] In effect, this author established that we are able to affectively bring about in ourselves certain emotions without concretely experiencing them. If, for example, someone tells me about some painful event that has cast a shadow over Pierre's life, I will exclaim "How he must have suffered!" I do not know this suffering and yet I do not actually feel it. Baldwin calls these intermediaries between pure knowledge and true affection "abstract." But the mechanism for such an abstraction remains quite obscure. Who abstracts? If, according to M. Laporte's definition, to abstract something is to think separately structures that are unable to exist separated, we are obliged either to identify abstract emotions with pure abstract concepts of emotions, or to acknowledge that these abstractions are unable to exist as such, as real modalities of consciousness.[11] In fact, the professed "abstract emotions" are empty intentions, pure projects of emotion. In other words, we direct ourselves toward pain and shame, and reach out toward them; consciousness transcends itself, but emptily. The pain is there, objective and transcendent, but it lacks concrete existence. It would be better to refer to these meanings that lack matter as affective images: they are undeniably important for artistic creation and psychological understanding. But what matters here, what separates them from real shame, is the absence of anything "lived through." Pure affective qualities exist, therefore, which

10 TN: James Mark Baldwin (1861–1934) was an American philosopher and psychologist who moved to Paris in later life. His developmental psychology was an important influence on Piaget.

11 TN: Sartre refers to this idea of Laporte's earlier as well, at EN 37.

are surpassed and transcended by affective projects. We should not turn these—as Scheler did—into some kind of "*hyle*" that is carried away by the flux of consciousness: what is in question here is simply the way in which consciousness *exists* its contingency; it is the very texture of consciousness insofar as it surpasses this texture toward its own possibilities; it is the manner in which consciousness *exists*—spontaneously and in its non-thetic mode—what it *constitutes* thetically, but implicitly, as its point of view on the world. It might be pure pain, but it might also be one's mood, as the non-thetic, affective tone, the purely pleasant or purely unpleasant—in general terms, everything that we include under the term "*coenesthetic.*" This "*coenesthetic*" rarely appears without being surpassed toward the world by a for-itself's transcendent project; as such, it is extremely difficult to study it in isolation. However, there are certain favorable experiences in which we can grasp it in its purity, in particular the experience of what we call "physical" pain. We will therefore turn to this experience in order to conceptually establish the structures of consciousness (of the) body.

My eyes are hurting, but this evening I have to finish reading a philosophical work. I read. The book is the object of my consciousness and, through the book, the truths it signifies. The body is in no way grasped for itself, but it is a point of view and a point of departure: one after the other, the words slide before me; I *make them slide*; those at the foot of the page that I have not yet seen still belong to a relative ground, or "page-ground," which is organized against the "book-ground" and against the absolute ground, or the ground of the world; but, from the ground of their indistinctness, the words call to me; they already have the character of a "*friable totality*"; they are given as "to be made to slide beneath my eyes." In all of that, the body is only given *implicitly*: the movement of my eyes appears only in the observer's view. For myself, all that I grasp thetically is these words, frozen in their arising, one after the other. Through my own temporalization, however, the succession of words within objective time is given and known. Their immobile movement is given through a "movement" of my consciousness; and, for me, this "movement" of consciousness—which is purely a metaphor, which refers to a temporal progression—is the movement of my eyes; it is impossible for me to distinguish my eyes' movement from the synthetic progression of my [acts of] consciousness without recourse to

372

the Other's viewpoint. And yet, in the very moment in which I am reading, my eyes *are hurting*. We should note, first, that this pain may itself be
indicated by objects in the world, i.e., by the book I am reading: it may be
more difficult to drag the words away from the undifferentiated ground
that they constitute; they may tremble or flicker; their meaning may be
yielded ineptly; the sentence that I have just read may present itself twice,
or three times, as "not understood," as "needing to be reread." But these
signs themselves may be absent—for example, when "I am absorbed" by
my reading and "I forget" my pain (which does not at all mean that it
has disappeared, since, if I make myself conscious of it in a further *reflective* act, it will be given as having already been there); and in any case,
that is not what matters to us; what we are trying to grasp is the manner in which consciousness *exists* its pain. But, before anything else, we
might ask, how does the pain present itself as pain *in the eyes*? Do we not
find there an intentional reference to a transcendent object, to my body,
precisely insofar as it exists outside, within the world? It is incontestable
that the pain contains information about itself: it is impossible to confuse
a pain in the eyes with a pain in one's finger or stomach. However, the
pain is wholly lacking in intentionality. We must be clear: if the pain is
given as pain "in the eyes," there is no mysterious "local sign" here, and
not any knowledge either. Only the pain *is precisely the eyes*, insofar as consciousness "exists them." And, as such, it distinguishes itself from any
other pain through its very existence, not through a criterion or anything
added on. Of course the denomination "pain *in the eyes*" presupposes an
entire constitutive labor, which remains for us to describe. But, from the
standpoint we occupy now, we do not yet have to consider it, because
it has not yet been undertaken: we are not considering the pain from a
reflective point of view; it is not being related to a body-for-the-Other.
It is eye-pain or sight-pain, and is not distinguished from the way in
which I apprehend the transcendent words. We have called it "pain in
the eyes," for clarity in our exposition, but it is not named within consciousness, because it is not *known*. It simply distinguishes itself, ineffably
and through its very being, from other possible pains.

This pain, however, does not exist anywhere among the actual objects
of the universe. It is not to the right or the left of the book, or within
my object-body (the one that the Other sees, which I am able to touch
partially and to see partially), or in my point-of-view-body insofar as   373

the world implicitly points that out. Nor ought we to say that the pain is "superimposed" or, like a harmonic, "added on" to the things I can see. Those are images that have no meaning. It is not therefore in space. But nor does it belong to objective time: it temporalizes itself, and it is in and through that temporalization that world-time can appear. What, then, is this pain? It is simply consciousness's translucent matter, its *being-there*, its attachment to the world; in short, it is the contingency that belongs to the act of reading. It exists beyond any attention or knowledge, since it slides within every act of attention and act of knowledge, since it is that act itself, insofar as it is without being the foundation of its being.

And yet, even at this level of pure being, the pain can only be non-thetically existed by consciousness, as the contingent attachment to the world, if it is surpassed. The painful consciousness is an internal negation of the world, but at the same time it exists its pain—i.e., itself—as a separation from itself. It is not possible for us to reach pure pain, as what is simply lived: it belongs to the category of undefinables and indescribables, which are what they are. Rather, the painful consciousness is a project toward a further consciousness which would be empty of any pain, i.e., a consciousness whose texture, and being-there, would not be painful. This *lateral* movement of escape, this self-separation that characterizes a painful consciousness, does not thereby constitute the pain as a psychological object; it is a non-thetic project of the for-itself. We learn of it only through the world; it is given, for example, in the way in which the book appears to me as "needing to be read at a faster pace," whose words squeeze up against each other in an infernal, frozen circle, whose universe in its entirety is struck by *disquiet*. Moreover—and this is what characterizes bodily existence—we re-encounter the ineffable from which we want to flee within this very act of separation: it will come to constitute the [acts of] consciousness that surpass it; it is in fact the contingency and being of the flight that aims to flee from it. Nowhere else can we come so close to this nihilation of the in-itself by the for-itself, and to the in-itself's seizing back of the for-itself that fuels this very nihilation.

Granted, one might say. But you have made things too easy for yourself by choosing a case where the pain is precisely a pain in the functioning organ, a pain in the eye while it is looking, in the hand while it is grasping. For, of course, I can suffer from a wound in my finger while

I am reading. In this case, it will be difficult to maintain that my pain is the very contingency of my "act of reading."

Let us first take note that, however absorbed I may be by my reading, I do not thereby cease to bring the world to being; better still, my reading is an act that implies in its very nature the existence of the world as a necessary ground. That does not mean at all that I have a lesser consciousness of the world but that I am conscious of it *as the ground*. I do not lose sight of the colors or the movements surrounding me, or cease to hear the sounds—it is simply that they become lost within the undifferentiated totality that serves as the ground of my reading. Correlatively, the world does not cease to point out my body as the total point of view on the worldly totality but it is the world as ground that points it out. In this way, my body does not cease *to be existed* as a totality to the extent to which it is the total contingency of my consciousness. It is at the same time what the totality of the world as ground points to, and the totality that I exist affectively, in connection with the objective apprehension of the world. But, to the extent to which a particular *this* detaches itself as a figure against the ground of the world, it points correlatively toward a functional specification of the bodily totality and, by the same token, my consciousness exists a bodily figure, which stands out against the body-totality that it exists. The book is read and to the extent to which I exist and I surpass the contingency of vision—or, alternatively, of reading— my eyes appear as the figure, against the ground of bodily totality. Of course, at this level of existence, my eyes are not the sensory organ seen by the Other but only the actual texture of my consciousness of seeing, insofar as this consciousness is a structure of my wider consciousness of the world. Indeed, to be conscious is always to be conscious of the world, and in this way the world and the body are always present, albeit in different ways, to my consciousness. But this total consciousness of the world is conscious of the world as the ground for this or that particular *this* and so, just as consciousness becomes specified in its very act of nihilation, a particular structure of the body is present against the total ground of embodiment. In the very moment in which I am reading, I do not therefore cease to be a body, seated in such an armchair, three meters away from the window, in given conditions of temperature and atmospheric pressure. And this pain in my forefinger is not something that I stop *existing*, just as I exist my body in general.

Only I exist it insofar as it vanishes within the ground of embodiment, as a subordinate structure within the bodily totality. It is neither absent nor unconscious; it simply forms part of that existence without distance that positional consciousness has for itself. If, a moment later, I turn the pages of the book, the pain in my forefinger will—without thereby becoming an object of knowledge—change its position to a contingency that is existed as a figure, against a new organization of my body as the total ground of contingency. Besides, these remarks correspond to this empirical observation: that it is easier to "distract oneself" from a pain in one's forefinger or lower back while one is reading than from a pain in one's eyes. That is because the pain in my eyes is *precisely my reading*, and in each instant the words I am reading direct me toward it, whereas the pain in my forefinger or lower back, as an apprehension of the world as ground, gets lost itself as a partial structure within the body as the fundamental apprehension of the ground of the world.

But now, suddenly, I stop reading and am absorbed, at present, in *grasping* my pain. In other words, I direct a reflective consciousness on to my present consciousness, or vision-consciousness. In this way, the current texture of my reflected consciousness—and in particular my pain—is apprehended and *posited* by my reflective consciousness. Here we must remember what we said about reflection: it is a totalizing grasp without any point of view, a knowing that bursts its own bounds and which tends to objectify itself, to project what is known across a distance, in order to contemplate and to think it. Reflection's primary move is therefore to transcend the pure quality of conscious pain toward a *pain-object*. Thus, if we stick to what we have called "complicit" reflection, reflection tends to make pain into something *psychological*. This psychological object, apprehended through pain, is an *ache*.[12] This object has all the characteristics of pain, but it is passive and transcendent. It is a reality that has its own time, which is neither the time of the external universe nor that of con-

12 TN: *Cet objet . . . appréhendé à travers la douleur, c'est le* mal. In French the expression *avoir mal* is used to mean "to have a pain (or ache)," or in instances where in English we would say something *hurts*. On its own, *le mal* also means "evil," and possibly Sartre intends a pun here. As Sartre is describing the creation of a psychological *object*, it seems important to translate *le mal* as a noun, and obviously it needs to be some noun other than "pain" (which I use, contrastively, to translate *douleur*). "Ache" seems to be the term that works best.

sciousness: psychological time. It can therefore bear various assessments and determinations. As such, it is distinct from consciousness itself, and appears through it; it remains permanent while consciousness evolves, and this permanence itself is a condition of the ache's opacity and passivity. But on the other hand this ache, insofar as it is grasped through consciousness, has all the characteristics of unity, interiority, and spontaneity of consciousness, but degraded. This degradation endows it with psychological individuality. This means, in the first place, that it is absolutely cohesive and has no parts. In addition, it has its own duration, since it is outside consciousness and possesses a past and a future. But this duration, which is only a projection of the original temporalization, is an interpenetrating multiplicity. This ache is "penetrating," or "caressing," etc. And these features aim only to render the way this ache is profiled within duration: they are melodic qualities. A pain that presents itself through stabs followed by pauses is not apprehended through reflection as a pure alternation of painful and non-painful instances of consciousness: for the reflection that structures it, the brief moments of respite form part of the ache, as the silences form part of a melody. The whole constitutes the *rhythm* and the *pace* of the ache. But at the same time as it is a passive object, the ache, insofar as it is seen through an absolute spontaneity that is consciousness, is a projection of this spontaneity into the in-itself. As a passive spontaneity it is magical: it is given as perpetuating itself, as mastering entirely its temporal form. It appears and disappears in a different way from spatio-temporal objects: if I can no longer see the table, it is because I have turned my head; but if I no longer feel my ache, it is because it "has gone." What occurs here in fact is a phenomenon that is analogous to what the form-psychologists[13] call the "stroboscopic illusion." In disappointing the projects of the reflective for-itself, the disappearance of the ache is given as a movement of withdrawal, almost as something willed. There is an animism to the ache: it presents itself like a living being that has its form, its own duration, and its habits. The ill have a kind of intimacy with it: when it appears, it is not as a new phenomenon; it is, the ill person will say, "my afternoon attack." In this way, reflection does not link together the moments of a

376

---

13 TN: ... *les psychologues de la forme* ... Sartre refers here to the Gestalt psychologists. See my note in the section on vocabulary relating to the mind in Notes on the Translation.

single attack but, throughout an entire day, it links the attacks to each other. Nonetheless, this recognitional synthesis has a special character: it does not aim to constitute an object that would remain existing even while it was not given to consciousness (in the manner of a hatred that remains "dozing," or stays "in the unconscious"). In fact, when the ache goes away it disappears for good; "*nothing remains of it*." But the curious consequence that follows is that, when it reappears, it arises—in its very passivity—through a kind of spontaneous generation. For example, we can faintly detect it "starting"; now it is "coming back"; "there it is." In this way, the first pains are not, any more than the others, apprehended in themselves as the simple and naked texture of reflected consciousness: they are the "signs" of the ache, or even the ache itself, which emerges slowly, like a locomotive slowly starting up. But, on the other hand, it must be recognized that I constitute the ache *with* my pain. That does not mean that I grasp the ache as the cause of my pain but, rather, that each particular pain works like a note in a melody: it is at the same time the melody in its entirety and one "beat"[14] within the melody. Through each pain I can grasp the ache in its entirety, and yet it transcends them all, because it is the synthetic totality of all pains, the theme that is developed by and through them. But the ache's material does not resemble that of a melody: first, it is purely lived through; there is no distance between the reflected consciousness and the pain, or between the reflective consciousness and the reflected consciousness. In consequence, the ache is transcendent but without distance. As a synthetic totality, it is outside my consciousness and already at the point of being *elsewhere* but, from another angle, it is inside it; it penetrates within it, through all its serrations, through all of its notes, which *are my consciousness*.

At this level, what has become of *the body?* Let us note that, with the reflective projection, there has been a kind of scission: for unreflected consciousness, the pain *was* the body; for reflective consciousness, the ache is distinct from the body, has its own shape, and comes and goes. At the reflective level at which we are positioned—i.e., before the for-the-Other intervenes—the body is not explicitly and thematically given to consciousness. The reflective consciousness is a consciousness of the

377

---

14 TN: ... *un "temps" de la mélodie*. In musical contexts, the French noun *temps* refers to what the "time-signature" denotes, e.g., 4/4 or 6/8 time.

ache. Only, if the ache has a form that is distinctively its own, and a melodic rhythm that confers on it a transcendent individuality, it adheres through its matter to the for-itself, since it is disclosed through my pain and as the unity of all of my pains of the same type. It is *mine*, insofar as I give its matter to it. I grasp it as being sustained and nourished by a specific passive environment, whose passivity is the exact projection into the in-itself of the contingent facticity of my pains, and which is my passivity. This medium is not grasped for itself, except in the way that a statue's matter is grasped when I perceive its form, and yet it is there: it is *the passivity on which the ache gnaws* and which magically gives it new strength, as the earth did to Antaeus.[15] It is my body at a new level of existence, i.e., as the pure noematic correlative of a reflective consciousness. Let us call this the *psychological body*. It is not yet in any way known, because the reflection that seeks to grasp the painful consciousness is not yet cognitive. It is affectivity, as it originally arises. It does grasp the ache as an object, but as an affective object. We turn toward our pain in the first instance to hate it, to patiently endure it, to apprehend it as unbearable, sometimes to love it, or to be glad of it (if it is a sign of liberation or of recovery), to evaluate it in some way. And, of course, what we are evaluating is the ache or, rather, that is what arises as the necessary correlative of the evaluation. Therefore the ache is not known, it is *suffered* and, in the same way, the body is disclosed through the ache, and is equally suffered by consciousness. For the body as it is given to reflection to be enriched with cognitive structures, a recourse to the *other* is required; we cannot discuss that now, because we would need first to have illuminated the structures of the body-for-the-other. However, we can note right now that this psychological body, as the projection—at the level of the in-itself—of consciousness's internal texture, provides the implicit matter of all psychological phenomena. Just as the original body was existed by each instance of consciousness as its own contingency, so is the psychological body *suffered* as the contingency of hate or of love, of actions and qualities, but this contingency has a new character: insofar as consciousness existed it, it was the in-itself's seizing back of consciousness;

15 TN: In Greek mythology, Antaeus is the son of Poseidon and the Earth goddess Gaea. He compelled all strangers passing through the country to wrestle with him. Whenever Antaeus touched the Earth (his mother), his strength was renewed, so that even if he was thrown to the ground he won the fight.

insofar as it is suffered in the ache, or the hatred, or the undertaking, it is *projected into* the in-itself by reflection. In consequence, it represents the tendency of every psychological object, beyond its magical cohesion, to become fragmented into externality; it represents, beyond the magical relations that join psychological objects to each other, the tendency of each one of them to become isolated within an indifferent insularity: it is like an implicit space, therefore, which subtends the melodic duration of the psyche. Insofar as the body is the contingent and indifferent matter of all our psychological events, the body determines a *psychological space*. This space has neither top nor bottom, right nor left; it is still without parts, insofar as the psyche's magical cohesion enters in, and fights the fragmentation of indifference. That does not make it any less a real characteristic of the *psyche*: it is not that the psyche is *joined* to a body but, beneath its melodic organization, the body is its substance and its constant condition of possibility. It is what appears the moment we name the psyche; it is what lies at the basis of the mechanistic and chemical metaphors that we use in order to classify and to explain psychological events; it is what we aim at and inform in the images (imaginative acts of consciousness) that we produce to aim at and presentify absent feelings; it is, finally, what motivates and to some extent justifies psychological theories such as the theory of the unconscious, and problems such as the preservation of memories.

It goes without saying that we have chosen physical pain as an example, and that there are a thousand other ways, which are themselves contingent, of existing our contingency. In particular, whenever any pain, any pleasure, or any precise displeasure is "existed" by consciousness, the for-itself does not cease to project itself beyond a contingency that is pure and, so to speak, unqualified. Consciousness does not cease "to have" a body. Coenesthetic affectivity is, then, the pure non-positional apprehension of a colorless contingency, a pure apprehension of oneself as a *de facto* existence. This constant apprehension by my for-itself of a *dull* and distanceless taste that accompanies me even in my efforts to escape from it, and which is *my* taste, is what I have described elsewhere under the name of *Nausea*. A discreet and insurmountable nausea constantly reveals my body to my consciousness: it may happen that we seek out pleasure or physical pain in order to escape from it, but the moment that the pain and pleasure are existed by consciousness they manifest in their turn its facticity and its contingency, and it is against the ground of nausea that they are disclosed. Far from our having to understand this term "nausea" as a metaphor drawn from our physiological disgust, it is, on the contrary, on its foundation that all concrete and empirical instances of nausea, leading us to vomit (nausea at the sight of rotten meat, fresh blood, excrement, etc.), are produced.

II. THE BODY-FOR-THE-OTHER

We have just described the being of my body for-me. At this ontological level my body is as we have described it, and it is only that. We will seek in vain in it for the traces of a physiological organ or of an anatomical and spatial constitution. Either it is the center of reference that is emptily aimed at by the world's implement-objects, or it is the contingency that the for-itself exists; more accurately, these two modes of being are complementary. But the body knows the same avatars as the for-itself does: it has other levels of existence. It also exists for the Other. It will be within this new ontological perspective that we are obliged to study it now. Whether we study the way in which my body appears to the Other or the way in which the Other's body appears to me amounts to the same thing. Indeed, we have established that the structures of my being-for-the-Other are identical to those of the Other's being for me. For reasons of convenience, therefore, it is on the basis of these latter structures that we will establish the nature of the body-for-the-Other (which is to say, the Other's body).

In the preceding chapter we showed that it is not the body that first manifests the Other to me. If in fact the fundamental relation between my being and that of the Other could be reduced to the relation of my body to the other's body, it would be a pure relation of externality. But unless it is an internal negation, my connection with the Other is inconceivable. I must apprehend the Other in the first instance as that for which I exist as an object; in a second moment of ante-historical historialization, my seizing back of my ipseity makes the Other appear as an object; the appearing of the Other's body is not therefore the first encounter but it is, on the contrary, only an episode in my relations with the Other and, more particularly, in what we have called the Other's objectification; or, alternatively, the Other exists for me first, and I apprehend him in his body *afterward*; for me, the Other's body is a secondary structure.

In the fundamental phenomenon of the objectification of the other, the Other appears to me as a transcended transcendence. In other words, by virtue solely of my projecting myself toward my possibilities, I surpass and transcend his transcendence; it is out of play, an object-transcendence. I apprehend this transcendence in the world and (from the outset), as a specific arrangement of the implement-things in my world, insofar as they indicate *in addition* a secondary center of reference that is in the midst of the world and which is not me. These indications are not, in contrast to the indications that indicate me, constitutive of the indicating thing; they are lateral properties of the object. As we saw, the Other cannot be a concept that is constitutive of the world. Therefore, they all have an original contingence, and the character of an *event*. But the center of reference that they indicate really is *the other*, as a transcendence that is merely contemplated or transcended. It really is to the Other that I am directed by the secondary arrangement of the objects, as the organizer or the beneficiary of this arrangement—in short, to an instrument who arranges the implements in view of an end that he himself produces. But, in its turn, I surpass and I utilize this end; it is in the midst of the world and I can make use of it for my own ends. In this way, the Other is first indicated by things as an instrument. I too am indicated by things as an instrument, and I am a body precisely insofar as I become indicated by things. It is therefore the Other as a body who is indicated by things, through their lateral and secondary arrangements. Indeed, I do not even know any implements that do not refer secondarily to the other's body. But, earlier on, I was unable to take up any point of view on my body insofar as it was designated by things. My body is, in effect, the point of view on which I cannot take up any point of view, the instrument of which I cannot make use by means of any instrument. When I tried, through universalizing thought, to think it emptily, purely as an instrument in the midst of the world, the immediate result was the collapse of the world as such. On the contrary, by virtue solely of the fact that *I am not the other*, his body appears to me from the outset as a point of view on which I can take a point of view, as an instrument that I can utilize with other instruments. It is indicated by the sweep of implement-things, but in its turn it indicates other objects, and in the end it is integrated within my world, and what it indicates is *my body*. In this way, the Other's body is radically different from my body-for-me: it is the tool that I am not, and of which I make use (or which resists me, which comes to the same thing). It is presented to me from the outset with a specific objective coefficient of utility and adversity. The Other's body, therefore, is the Other himself as a transcendence-instrument. The same remarks can be applied to the Other's body as a synthetic system of sensory organs. We do not *discover*, in and through the Other's body, the Other's possibility of knowing us. That possibility is fundamentally disclosed in and through my *object-being* for the Other; in other words, it is the essential structure of our original relation to the Other. And within this original relation, the flight of my world toward the Other is equally given. By seizing back my ipseity, I transcend the Other's transcendence insofar as this transcendence is the permanent possibility of apprehending me as an object. It hereby becomes a transcendence that is purely given, and surpassed toward my own goals, a transcendence that simply "is-there," and the knowledge that the Other has of me and of the world becomes a knowledge-object, which means it is a property given to the Other, a property that I in turn can *know*. Strictly speaking, this knowledge that I gain of him remains empty, insofar as I can never know *the act of knowing*: as pure transcendence, that act can only be grasped by itself, in the form of nonthetic consciousness or by means of the reflection that stems from it. What I can know is only his knowledge as *being-there* or, alternatively, the *being-there of the knowledge*. In this way, the sensory organ's relativity, which was disclosed to me through universalizing reason but which I was unable—in the case of my own sense—to think without bringing about the collapse of the world, is what I apprehend *first* when I apprehend the object-Other, and I apprehend it *without danger*, since, as the Other is part of my universe, its relativity cannot bring about this universe's collapse. This sense that belongs to the Other is *a sense that is known as knowing*. We can see, at the same time, how to explain the error of the psychologists—who define *my sense* by means of the Other's sense and bestow on the sensory organ as it is for me a relativity that belongs to its being-for-the-Other— and how this error can become a truth if, once we have determined the true ordering of being and knowing, we reposition it at its level of being. In this way, the objects in my world indicate laterally an object-center-of-reference that is the Other. But this center, in turn, appears to

381

me from a point of view without any point of view that is mine, and which is my body or my contingency. In short, to use an expression that is inapt but familiar, I know the Other through my senses.[16] Just as the Other is the instrument of which I make use, by means of the instrument that I am, so too is he the system of sensory organs that is revealed to my sensory knowledge; in other words, he is a facticity appearing to a facticity. Thus it is possible to carry out, in its true place within the order of knowing and of being, a study of the Other's sensory organs as they are known sensorily by me. And this study will take maximal account of the function of these sensory organs, which is to know. But this knowledge, in turn, will be a pure object for me, which gives rise, for example, to the false problem of "inverted vision." In point of fact, from the outset, the Other's sensory organ is in no way an instrument of knowledge for the Other; it is merely the Other's knowledge, his pure act of knowing, insofar as this knowledge exists in the mode of an object within my universe.

Nonetheless, as yet we have defined the Other's body only insofar as it is laterally indicated by the implement-things in my universe. Strictly speaking, that does not provide us with his being-there "in flesh and blood." Of course, the Other's body is present everywhere, in just those indications of him that are given by the implement-things, insofar as they reveal themselves as being used by him, and known by him. This sitting room in which I am waiting for the master of the house reveals to me, in its totality, its owner's body: this armchair is the armchair-where-he-sits; this desk is the desk-at-which-he-writes; this window is the window through which the light-that-illuminates-the-objects-that-he-sees comes in. In this way, he is sketched out on all sides, and this sketch is an object-sketch; at any moment, an object may arrive to fulfill it with its matter.[17] But it is still the case that the master of the house "is not there." He is elsewhere; he is absent.

382

16 TN: ...je connais autrui par les sens. I haven't been able to establish whether Sartre is quoting anyone in particular here, or simply invoking the empiricist idea that our knowledge is acquired through sense experience.

17 TN: Ainsi est-il esquissé de toutes parts ... The French word esquisse is often used (for example, by Ricoeur) to translate Husserl's Abschattung (usually translated into English as "adumbration"); Sartre's use of phenomenological vocabulary here (including remplir, "to fulfill") is not quite as clear in English.

But we have seen, precisely, that absence is a structure of *being-there*. To be absent is to-be-elsewhere-within-my-world; it is to be already given for me. The moment I receive a letter from my cousin in Africa, his being-elsewhere is concretely given to me through the letter's indications themselves, and this being-elsewhere is a being-somewhere: already, it is his body. There is no other way to explain how the beloved woman's very letter can sensually stir her lover: the body of the beloved one is present as an absence in these lines and on this paper. But as being-elsewhere is a *being-there* in relation to a concrete system of implement-things within a *concrete situation*, it is already facticity and contingency. It is not only the *encounter* that I have had today with Pierre that defines his contingency and mine but his absence yesterday defined in the same way our contingencies and our facticities. And this facticity of the absent person is given implicitly in the implement-things that indicate him; his sudden appearance adds nothing to it. Thus the Other's body is his *facticity*, as an implement and as the synthesis of sensory organs, insofar as it is revealed to my facticity. It is given to me the moment the Other exists for me within the world; the Other's presence or his absence makes no difference.

But now Pierre appears; he comes into my bedroom. This appearing changes nothing in the fundamental structure of my relation to him: it is contingent, but his absence was contingent. The objects indicate him to me: when it opens before him, the door he is pushing indicates a human presence, in the same way as the armchair in which he sits down, etc.; but the objects had not ceased to indicate him while he was absent. And, of course, I exist for him, and he is talking to me; but I existed in the same way yesterday, when he sent me this telegram, which is now on my table, to let me know he was coming. And yet, there is something new, which is that now he appears against the ground of the world as a *this* that I am able to look at, to grasp, and to make use of directly. What does this mean? In the first place, it means that the Other's facticity—i.e., the contingency of his being—is now *explicit*, rather than being implicitly contained within the implement-things' lateral indications. This facticity is precisely what *he exists* in and through his for-itself; it is what he constantly lives, through nausea, as a non-positional apprehension of a contingency that he is, as a pure apprehension of himself insofar as he is a *de facto* existence. In brief, it is his *coenesthesia*. The Other's appearance discloses the taste of his being as an immediate existence. Only I do not grasp this taste in the way that he grasps it. For him, the nausea is not knowledge; it is a non-thetic apprehension of the contingency that he *is*; it is a surpassing of this contingency toward the for-itself's own possibilities; it is a contingency that is existed, a contingency that is undergone and rejected. It is the very same contingency—and none other—that I am grasping now. Only I *am not* this contingency. I surpass it toward my own possibilities, but this surpassing is a transcending *of an other*. This contingency is given to me in its entirety, and without recourse; it is irremediable. The Other's for-itself separates itself from this contingency, and constantly surpasses it. But, insofar as I transcend the Other's transcendence, I freeze it: it is no longer a remedy against facticity; it emanates from it. In this way, nothing gets interposed between the Other's pure contingency as a *taste* that is *for itself* and my consciousness. What I grasp really is *this* taste, as it is existed. Only, by the mere fact of my alterity, this taste appears as a *this* which is known and given in the midst of the world. The Other's body is given to me as the pure in-itself of his being—an in-itself among in-itselfs, and that I surpass toward my possibilities. The Other's body is revealed therefore by two equally contingent characteristics: it is here, and could be elsewhere—which means the implement-things might be arranged differently in relation to him; he is like this, and could be otherwise—which means I grasp his original contingency in the form of an objective and contingent configuration. But in reality these two characters are one and the same. The second only presentifies, only explicates for me, the first. The Other's body is the pure fact of the Other's presence in my world as a being-there that is translated into a being-like-this. Thus, the Other's very existence as an Other-for-me implies that he is disclosed as a tool that possesses the property of knowing, and that this property of knowing is attached to some objective existence. That is what we will call the necessity of the Other's being contingent for me. As soon as there is an Other, we are obliged to conclude that he is an instrument furnished with some kind of sensory organs. But these points only record the abstract necessity of the Other's having a body. Insofar as I encounter it, the Other's body is the disclosure as an object-for-me of the contingent form assumed by the necessity of this contingency. Any Other must have sensory organs, but not necessarily *these* sensory organs, not *a face*, and, finally, not this *face*. But all this—the face, the sensory organs, and the presence—is nothing but the contingent form of the necessity that the Other should *exist himself* as belonging to a race, a class, a background, etc., insofar as this contingent form is surpassed by a transcendence *that does not have to exist it*. What, for the Other, is his *taste of himself* becomes the *other's flesh* for me. Flesh is the pure contingency of presence. Ordinarily it is masked by clothing, makeup, the haircut or beard, the expression, etc. But the moment always comes, in the course of prolonged interaction with a person, when all these masks are undone and I find myself in the presence of the pure contingency of his presence; in this case, through a face or other body parts, I have the pure intuition of flesh. This intuition is not only a knowing; it is an affective apprehension of an absolute contingency, and this apprehension is a particular type of *nausea*.

The Other's body is therefore the facticity of a transcended-transcendence insofar as that refers to my facticity. I can never grasp the Other as a body without grasping my body at the same time, inexplicitly, as the center of reference indicated by the Other. But, equally, we cannot perceive the Other's body as flesh in the form of an isolated object, related to other *thises* by pure relations of externality. That is true only of a *corpse*. The Other's body as flesh is given to me immediately, as the center of reference of a situation that is synthetically organized around it, and it is inseparable from this situation. We should not therefore ask how the Other's body can be first a body for me, and thereafter enter into situation. Rather, the Other is given to me from the outset as a *body in situation*. Therefore, we do not find, for example, that the body comes first and action comes afterward. Rather, the body is the objective contingency of the Other's action. In this way we rediscover, at another level, an ontological necessity that we noted in relation to my body's existence for me: we said on that occasion that the for-itself's contingency can be existed only in and through a transcendence; it is the seizing back of the for-itself— which is constantly surpassed, and constantly seizing back anew— by the in-itself, against the ground of an initial nihilation. Similarly, here, an Other's body as flesh cannot insert itself into a situation that is antecedently determined. Rather, it is precisely that on whose basis there is a situation. Here, too, it can exist only in and through a transcendence. Only this transcendence is from the start transcended; it is itself an object. Thus, Pierre's body is not, first, a hand able, subsequently, to pick up this glass: such a conception would have the effect of placing a corpse at the origin of the living body. Rather it is the hand-glass complex, insofar as the hand's flesh underscores the original contingency of this complex. Far from the body's relation to objects being a problem, we can never grasp the body outside this relation. In this way the Other's body is *signifying*. Its meaning is nothing other than a frozen movement of transcendence. A body is a body insofar as this mass of flesh that it is is defined by the table it looks at, the chair it selects, the sidewalk on which it walks, etc. But, to develop this further, there can be no question of exhausting the meanings that constitute the body by referring to its concerted actions, its rational use of equipment-structures. The body is the totality of signifying relations to the world: in this sense it is also defined by reference to the air it breathes, the water it drinks, the meat it eats. Indeed, the body cannot appear without maintaining signifying relations with the totality of what is. Like *action*, life is a transcended-transcendence, and it is meaningful.[18] There is no difference in kind between life, conceived as a totality, and action. Life represents the set of meanings that we transcend toward objects that are not posited as *thises* against the ground of the world. *Life* is the Other's *body-ground*, in opposition to his *body-figure*, insofar as this body-ground can be apprehended, no longer implicitly and non-positionally by the Other's for-itself but precisely by *me*, explicitly and objectively: in that case it appears as a signifying figure against the ground of the universe, but without ceasing to be a ground, and precisely *as a ground*, for the Other. But we need to make an important distinction here: the Other's body, in point of fact, appears "to my body." In consequence, there is a facticity to my point of view on the Other. In this respect, we must not confuse my possibility of grasping an organ (an arm, a hand) against the ground of a bodily totality with my explicit apprehension of the Other's body, or of particular structures of this body insofar as they are lived by the Other as the *body-ground*. It is only in the second case that we are apprehending the Other as life. Indeed, in the first case, it may happen that what we are apprehending as the ground is for him the figure. When I look at his hand, the rest of his body becomes unified as the ground. But it might be precisely his forehead or his thorax that exists

18 TN: Although Sartre does not explicitly mention Bergson in this passage, it seems likely that he has his philosophy in mind: "life" is a topic of much discussion in Bergson (along with the "vital impulse," etc.).

non-thetically as the figure, against a ground into which his arms and hands have been diluted.

The consequence, of course, is that the being of the Other's body is a synthetic totality for me. Therefore: (1) I can never apprehend the Other's body except on the basis of a total situation which indicates it; (2) I can never perceive any particular organ of the Other's body in isolation, and each specific organ is always indicated to me on the basis of the totality of flesh or of life. In this way, my perception of the Other's body is radically different from my perception of things.

(1) The Other moves between limits which appear in an immediate connection with his movements, and which are the terms within which the meaning of these movements is indicated to me. These limits are at the same time spatial and temporal. Spatially, it is the glass placed *at a distance* from Pierre that is the meaning of his current movement. Thus, within my perception itself, I go from the "table-glass-bottle, etc.," collection to the movement of his arm, in order to learn from it what it is. If the arm is visible and the glass is hidden, I perceive Pierre's movement purely on the basis of the idea of *situation* and on the basis of terms at which I aim emptily, beyond the objects that are hiding the glass from me, as the movement's meaning. Temporally, I always grasp Pierre's movement, as it is revealed to me in the present, on the basis of points in the future toward which it extends. In this way I am acquainted with the body's present by its future and, more generally still, by the world's future. We will never understand anything about the psychological problem of our perception of the Other's body if we have not first grasped this essential truth, that the Other's body is perceived quite differently from other bodies: because, in order to perceive it, we always move from what is outside it, in space and time, to it itself; we grasp its movement "back to front," through a kind of reversal of time and space. To perceive the Other is to be informed by the world of what he is.

(2) I never perceive an arm that rises alongside a motionless body: I perceive Pierre-who-is-raising-his-arm. And we should not take that to mean that, through a judgment, I relate the hand's movement to a "consciousness" that is thought to bring it about; rather, I can only grasp the movement of the hand or arm as a temporal structure of the entire body. Here it is the whole that determines the order and the movement of the parts. To be convinced that we really are talking about a primordial perception of the

386

Other's body here, one needs only to recall the horror that is aroused by the sight of a broken arm that "does not seem to belong to its body" or one of those rapid perceptions in which we see, for example, a hand (whose arm is hidden) climbing like a spider along the wing of a door. In these various cases, the body disintegrates, and this disintegration is grasped as exceptional. On the other hand we are familiar with the positive proofs for which the Gestalt theorists have often argued. It is striking, in fact, that a photograph records a huge magnification of Pierre's hands when he stretches them in front of him (because it grasps them in their true dimensions, and without any synthetic connection to the bodily totality), whereas we perceive these same hands without any apparent magnification when we observe them with the naked eye. In this sense, the body appears on the basis of the situation as the synthetic totality of *life* and of *action*.

After these various observations it goes without saying there is no difference at all between Pierre's body and Pierre-for-me. All that exists for me is the Other's body, with its different meanings; to-be-an-object-for-the-Other and to-be-a-body are two ontological modalities that are strictly equivalent translations of the for-itself's being-for-the-Other. In this way, the meanings do not refer to some mysterious psyche: they *are* this psyche, insofar as it is a transcended-transcendence. Doubtless there is a cryptology of the psyche; certain phenomena are "hidden." But that does not mean at all that the meanings refer to something "beyond the body." They refer to the world and to themselves. In particular, those manifestations of emotion or, more generally, those phenomena that are inaccurately called "*expressions*" in no way *indicate* to us a hidden affection, lived through by some psyche, which might form the immaterial object of the psychologist's research: these frowns, this blushing, this stammer, this slight trembling of the hands, these sly looks which seem to be at the same time timid and threatening, do *not* express anger; they *are* the anger. But we must understand this clearly: in itself, a clenched fist is nothing, and signifies nothing. But also, we never perceive *a clenched fist*: we perceive a man who, in a specific situation, clenches his fist. This meaningful act, considered in connection with the past and the possibles, and understood on the basis of the synthetic totality "body in situation," *is* the anger. It does not refer to anything apart from actions within the world (of hitting, insulting, etc.), i.e., to new signifying attitudes of the body. We cannot move outside this: the "psychological object" is delivered in its entirety to perception, and it is inconceivable apart from bodily structures. If this has not yet been appreciated, or if those—such as the behaviorists—who have maintained it have not themselves well understood what they wanted to say and have caused a scandal around them, that is because we readily believe that all our perceptions are of the same kind. In fact, perception must immediately deliver up to us the spatio-temporal object. Its fundamental structure is internal negation, and it delivers the object to me *as it is*, not as a hollow image of a reality that is out of reach. But, precisely because of that, to each type of reality there corresponds a new structure of perception. The body is the ultimate psychological object, *the only psychological object*. But if we consider that it is a transcended-transcendence, its perception cannot *by its nature* be of the same type as the perception of inanimate objects. And we should not take that to mean that it is progressively enriched but rather that, from the outset, it has another structure. Hence it is not necessary to resort to habit, or to the argument from analogy, in order to explain how we *understand* expressive behavior: such behavior is delivered to perception from the outset as comprehensible; its meaning forms part of its being, just as the color of a sheet of paper forms part of the paper. In order to understand it, therefore, it is no more necessary to refer to further behavior than to refer to the color of the table, of the foliage or of other sheets of paper in order to perceive the color of the page that is placed in front of me.

However, the Other's body is immediately given to us as what the other *is*. In this sense, we grasp it as that which is constantly surpassed toward a goal by each particular meaning. Take a man walking. From the beginning I understand his walking on the basis of a spatio-temporal whole (street-road-sidewalk-shops-cars, etc.), of which certain structures represent the forth-coming meaning of his walking. I perceive this walking by going from the future to the present, even though the future with which I am concerned belongs to universal time, and is a pure "now" which is not yet here. The walking itself, as a pure becoming, elusive and nihilating, is the *present*. But this present is the surpassing toward a future point of *something* that is walking: beyond the pure and elusive present of the movement of the arm, we try to grasp the substrate of the movement. This substrate, which—except in the case of a

388

corpse—we never grasp *as it is*, is nonetheless always there as surpassed, as *the past*.[19] When I talk about a moving-arm, I regard this arm, which *was at rest*, as the movement's substance. We noted, in Part Two, that this conception cannot be maintained: it cannot be the motionless arm that moves; movement is a sickness in being.[20] Still, it remains true that a psychological movement refers to two terms, the future term of its *accomplishment*, and the past term: the motionless organ that it alters and surpasses. And it is precisely as a constant and elusive reference toward a past-being that I perceive the movement-of-the-arm. I do not see this past-being (the arm, the leg, the body in its entirety at rest); I can only ever glimpse it through the movement that surpasses it, and to which I am present, as a pebble at the bottom of the river may be glimpsed, through the movement of the waters. Yet this immobility of being that is constantly *surpassed* and never *actualized*, to which I constantly refer in order to name that which is moving, is pure facticity, pure flesh, the pure in-itself as the constantly pastified past of the transcended-transcendence.

This pure in-itself that exists only as something *surpassed*, in and through this surpassing, descends to the level of a *corpse* if it ceases to be revealed and at the same time concealed by the transcended-transcendence. As a corpse (i.e., as *a life's pure past, the mere remains*), it still cannot really be understood, other than on the basis of the surpassing that no longer surpasses it: it is *what was surpassed toward constantly updated situations*. But on the other hand, insofar as it appears in the present as pure in-itself, it exists in relation to the other *thises* in the simple relation of indifferent externality: the corpse *is no longer in situation*. At the same time it collapses in itself into a multiplicity of beings, each of which maintains relations of pure externality with the others. *Anatomy* is the study of the external-ity that always subtends facticity, insofar as this externality is only ever perceptible on a corpse. *Physiology* is the synthetic reconstitution, on the basis of corpses, of the living organism. It is condemned from the start to understand nothing of life, since it conceives of it merely as a par-ticular modality of death, since it sees the corpse's infinite divisibility as primary, and is not aware of the synthetic unity of the "surpassing toward," for which the infinite divisibility is purely and simply the *past*. Not even the study of life in a living thing, or vivisection, or the study

389

---

19 TN: . . . *toujours là comme le dépassé*, le passé. Sartre repeats the pun here.
20 TN: Sartre is referring to the discussion of movement in Part Two, Chapter 3, section IV.

of the life of protoplasm, or embryology, or the study of an egg: none of these is able to rediscover life. The observed organ is living, but it is not immersed within the synthetic unity of *a* life; it is understood on the basis of anatomy, i.e., on the basis of death. It would therefore be a huge mistake to believe that the Other's body that is originally disclosed to us is the body of anatomo-physiology. The error is as serious as that of confusing our senses "for us" with our sensory organs for the Other. Rather, the Other's body is the facticity of transcended-transcendence, insofar as this facticity is constantly a *birth*, which is to say that it refers to the indifferent externality of a constantly surpassed in-itself.

These considerations allow us to explain what we refer to as "character." We must note, in fact, that a character has a distinct existence only as an object of knowledge for the Other. Consciousness does not know its character—unless it determines it reflectively, on the basis of the Other's point of view; it exists it in a pure lack of distinction, non-thematically and non-thetically, in its experience of its own contingency, and in the nihilation through which it recognizes and surpasses its facticity. That is why a pure introspective description of oneself does not deliver any character: Proust's hero "does not have" any character that can be directly grasped; insofar as he is conscious of himself, he is revealed to himself in the first place as a set of general reactions that are common to all men (the "mechanisms" of passion, of the emotions, the order of the appearance of memories, etc.), in which anyone can recognize himself: because these reactions belong to the psyche's general "nature." If we succeed (as Abraham tried to do in his book on Proust)[21] in determining the character of the Proustian hero (in relation, for example, to his weakness, his passivity, the singular association in him of love with money), that is because we are interpreting raw givens: we take up an external view on them; we compare them, and try to extract from them permanent and objective relations. But this requires us to step back: as long as the reader, in accordance with the general perspective of reading, identifies himself with the novel's hero, the character of "Marcel" will elude him; better still, he does not exist at this level. Only if I shatter the complicity that unites me to the writer will he appear, if I no longer consider the book as a confidant but as a confidence or, better still, as

21 TN: Sartre is referring to Abraham (1930), which is not available in English translation.

390   a *document*. Therefore this character exists only at the level of the for-the-Other, which is the reason why the maxims and descriptions of the "*moralistes*"—i.e., the French authors who embarked on an objective and social psychology—never overlap with the subject's lived experience. But if a character is essentially *for the Other*, it cannot be distinguished from the body, as we have described it. To suppose, for example, that *temperament* is the *cause* of character, that a "sanguine temperament" is the *cause* of irascibility,[22] is to posit character as a psychological entity which presents all the aspects of objectivity and yet is subjective and *undergone* by the subject. In fact, the Other's irascibility is known from the outside, and transcended from the outset by my transcendence. In this respect, it is no different from a "sanguine temperament," for example. In both cases we apprehend the same apoplectic flushing, the same aspects of the body, but we transcend these givens differently, according to our projects: we will be concerned with the *temperament* if we consider this flushing as a manifestation of the *body-ground*, which is to say by severing it from its links with the situation; if we tried even to understand it *on the basis of a corpse*, we would be able to begin a physiological and medical study of it; if, on the contrary, we consider it by coming to it from the global situation, it will be anger itself, or even the promise of anger or, better still, a pledge of anger—i.e., a permanent relation with implement-things, a potentiality. Therefore the distinction between temperament and character exists only in thought, and character is identical with the body. That is what justifies the attempts of numerous authors to establish a physiognomy as the basis for characterological research and, in particular, Kretschmer's excellent studies of the character and structure of the body.[23] The Other's character is, in effect, immediately given to intuition as a synthetic whole. That does not mean that we are able then and there to describe it. It takes time to bring different structures to light, to explicate specific givens that we have immediately grasped affectively,

22 TN: Sartre is not using "sanguine" here in the modern sense but in the sense in which it is used in the theory of the humors, i.e., to mean "relating to the blood, ruddy."

23 TN: Ernst Kretschmer (1888–1964) was a German psychiatrist who researched the human constitution and established a classification of body types. Sartre is using "physiognomy" in the archaic sense, where it means the art of judging character from appearance (especially facial appearance).

to transform that global indistinction which is the Other's body into an organized figure. We can make mistakes, and we may also appeal to general and discursive knowledge (laws that are empirically or statistically established in relation to other subjects) in order to *interpret* what we see. But, in any case, what we are doing is nothing more than explicating and organizing—with a view to prediction and to action—the content of our initial intuition. Doubtless that is what is meant by those people who repeat that "first impressions are never wrong." From the first encounter, the Other is indeed given in his entirety, and immediately, without any veil or mystery. To learn, in this case, is to understand, to develop, and to appraise.

Nonetheless, it is in what he *is* that the Other is in this way given. Character does not differ from facticity, i.e., from original contingency. Now, we grasp the Other as *free*; we noted earlier that freedom is an objective quality of the Other, as an unconditioned power to change situations. This power is indistinguishable from the power that originally constitutes the Other, and which makes it the case that a situation exists in general: to be able to change a situation is, in effect, precisely to make it the case that a situation exists. The Other's objective freedom is only a transcended-transcendence; as we have established, it is an object-freedom. In this sense, the Other appears as something that has to be understood on the basis of a situation that is constantly changed. That explains why the body is always the *past*. Hence the Other's character is revealed to us as what is *surpassed*. Even irascibility as a promise of anger is always a promise that has been surpassed. In this way, character is given as the Other's facticity, insofar as it is accessible to my intuition, but also insofar as it only *is* in order to be surpassed. In this sense, to "get angry" is already, by virtue of the very fact of consenting to it, to surpass one's irascibility, to give it a meaning: the anger will appear therefore as the object-freedom's reclamation of its irascibility. And that does not mean that we are thereby directed toward a subjectivity but merely that what we are transcending here is not just the Other's facticity but his transcendence, and not just his being—i.e., his past—but his present and his future. Although the Other's anger always appears to me as a free-anger (which is evident, by virtue of my *judging* it), I can always transcend it, i.e., I can inflame it or calm it; better still, it is by transcending it, and only by transcending it, that I can grasp it.

In this way, the body, as the facticity of the transcended-transcendence, is always a body-that-points-beyond-itself: both within space (i.e., the situation) and within time (i.e., the object-freedom). The body for the Other is the ultimate magical object. In this way the Other's body is always "a-body-that-is-more-than-a-body," because the Other is given to me wholly, and without intermediary, in the constant surpassing of his facticity. But this surpassing does not direct me to a subjectivity: it is the objective fact that the body—whether as an organism, as a character, or as a tool—never appears to me without *surroundings*, and must be determined on the basis of these surroundings. The Other's body must not be confused with his objectivity. The Other's objectivity is his transcendence, as transcended. The body is the facticity of this transcendence. But the Other's corporeality and his objectivity are completely inseparable.

392   III. THE THIRD ONTOLOGICAL DIMENSION OF THE BODY

I exist my body: that is its first dimension of being. My body is used and is known by the Other: that is its second dimension. But, insofar as I *am for the Other*, the Other is disclosed to me as the subject for whom I am an object. That is even my fundamental relation with the Other, as we have seen. I exist therefore for myself as known by the Other—and, in particular, in my very facticity. I exist for myself as known by the Other in the capacity of a body. That is the third ontological dimension of my body, which is what we are about to investigate: with that, we will have disposed of the question of the body's modes of being.

With the appearance of the Other's look, I have the revelation of my object-being, which is to say of my transcendence as transcended. An object-Me is revealed to me as the unknowable being, as the flight into the Other that I am, as fully responsible. But if I can neither know this "me" nor even conceive of it in its reality, at least I am not unable to grasp some of its formal structures. In particular, I feel that the Other reaches me in my *de facto* existence; what I am responsible for is my being-there-for-the-Other. This *being-there* is precisely the body. In this way, the encounter with the Other does not only reach me in my transcendence: in and through the transcendence that the Other surpasses, the facticity that my transcendence nihilates and transcends exists for the Other and, to the extent to which I am conscious of existing for the Other, I no longer apprehend my own facticity only in its non-thetic nihilation, no longer only by *existing* it, but in its flight toward a being-in-the-midst-of-the-world. The impact of the encounter with the Other is an empty revelation for me of my body's existence, out there, as an in-itself for another. Thus my body is not given merely as what I simply *live*: rather, in and through the contingent and absolute fact of the Other's existence, what I live is itself extended outside me, in a dimension of flight that escapes me. The depth of being of my body for myself is this constant "outside" to my innermost "inside." To the extent to which the Other's omnipresence is the fundamental fact, the objectivity of my being-there is a constant dimension of my facticity: I exist my contingency insofar as I surpass it toward my possibles and insofar as it covertly flees from me, toward the irremediable. My body is there not only as the point of view that I am but also as a point of view on which points of view are currently being taken, and that I can never take up; on all sides, it escapes me. That means, first, that this system of *senses*, which are unable to apprehend themselves, are given as being apprehended elsewhere and by others. This apprehension, which is therefore manifested emptily, does not have the character of a factual necessity. As my facticity is pure contingency, and is non-thetically revealed to me as a factual necessity, the being-for-the-Other of that facticity has the effect of multiplying that facticity's contingency: it gets lost, and flees from me into an infinity of contingency which escapes me. In this way, in the very moment in which I live my senses, as that intimate point of view on which I am unable to take up any point of view, their being-for-the-Other haunts me: they *are*. They are, for the other, in the way in which this table and this tree are for me: they are in the midst of *some world*; they are in and through the absolute flowing away of my world toward the Other. Thus the relativity of my senses, which I am unable to think in the abstract without destroying my world, is at the same time constantly presentified to me by the existence of the other; but this appresentation[24] is pure and elusive. In the same way, my body is for me the instrument that I am, and which cannot be used by any other instrument; but, to the extent to

393

24 TN: For *apprésenter*, see the section on Husserl vocabulary in Notes on the Translation.

which the Other, in the original encounter, transcends my being-there toward his possibilities, this instrument that I am is presentified to me as an instrument immersed within an infinite instrumental series, even though I am unable in any way to take up a point of view to survey this series from outside it. Insofar as it is alienated, my body escapes me toward a being-a-tool-among-tools, toward a being-a-sensory-organ-grasped-through-some-sensory-organs, and does so with an alienating destruction and a concrete collapse of my world, which flows toward the Other and which the Other will seize back within his world. When, for example, a doctor listens to my chest, I *perceive his ear* and, to the extent to which the objects of the world indicate me as the absolute center of reference, this perceived ear indicates certain structures as figures that I exist against my body-ground. These structures are precisely—and within the same arising of my being—something purely lived through; they are what I exist and what I nihilate. So we find here, in the first instance, the original connection between designation and what is lived: the things I perceive designate what "I exist" subjectively. But the moment I apprehend, with the collapse of the sensory organ that is the "ear," the doctor as listening to the sounds of my body, and feeling my body with his body, what was lived through and designated becomes designated as *a thing outside my subjectivity*, in the midst of a world which is not mine. My body is designated as alienated. The experience of my alienation comes about in and through affective structures, such as timidity. To "feel oneself blushing," to "feel oneself sweating," etc.: these are inaccurate phrases, which the timid person uses in order to explain his state: what he means by them is that he has a vivid and constant consciousness of his body, not as it is for him but as it is for the *other*. This constant unease, which is the apprehension of my body's alienation as irremediable, can determine psychoses such as erythrophobia;[25] these are nothing but the metaphysical and horrified apprehension of the existence of my body for the other. We often say that somebody timid is "embarrassed by his own body." Strictly speaking, this phrase is incorrect: I cannot be embar-

25　TN: ... *des psychoses comme l'éreutophobie* ... Sartre uses the specialist medical term, which refers to an irrational fear of blushing (often an element in social anxiety): I have used the corresponding medical term in English. This disorder would not today be accurately classified as a "psychosis," a word that Sartre is using loosely.

rassed by my body such as I exist it. It is my body as it is for another that ought to embarrass me. But here again, the phrase is still unhappy, because I can only be embarrassed by some tangible thing that is present within my universe, and which hampers me in my use of other tools. Here the embarrassment is more subtle, because the thing that hampers me is absent: I never encounter my body for the Other as an obstacle; on the contrary it is because it is never there, because it remains elusive, that it can hamper me. I try to reach it, to master it, to make use of it as an instrument—because it is also given as *an instrument in a world*—in order to give it the shape and the attitude it should have, but it is precisely, as a matter of principle, beyond my reach, and all the actions that I undertake to appropriate it escape me in their turn and become frozen at a distance from me as my body-for-the-other. Thus I am constantly obliged to act "blindly," to guess where to shoot, without ever knowing the results of my shot. That is why the timid person, after he has recognized the futility of these attempts, will endeavor to eliminate his body-for-the-other. When he wishes "not to have a body anymore," or to be "invisible," etc., it is not his body-for-himself that he wants to annihilate but this elusive dimension of the alienated-body.

   In effect, we attribute as much reality to the body-for-the-other as to the body-for-us. Better still, the body-for-the-other *is* the body-for-us, but alienated and elusive. It seems to us then that the other person performs a function for us of which we are incapable, and yet which it is incumbent on us to perform: *seeing us as we are.* Language, by revealing (emptily) to us the major structures of our body-for-the-Other (while our existed body is ineffable), encourages us to unload entirely our alleged task onto the Other. We resign ourselves to seeing ourselves through the other person's eyes, which means we try to learn what our being is through the revelations of language. In this way, a whole system of verbal correspondences appears, through which we come to designate our body as it is for the other, by using those designations to refer to our body as it is for us. It is at this level that the analogical assimilation of the Other's body with my body comes about. Indeed, in order for me to be able to think that "my body is for the Other as the Other's body is for me," it is necessary that I should have encountered the Other in his objectifying subjectivity, and then as an object; for me to judge the Other's body as an object that resembles my body, he must have been given to me as an object, and my body must have disclosed for its part an object-dimension. An analogy or resemblance can never be what first constitutes the Other's body-object and my body's objectivity; but, on the contrary, these two objecthoods must antecedently exist in order for any analogical principle to come into play. Here, therefore, it is through language that I learn of my body's structures for the Other. Nonetheless, we must take care to note that it cannot be at the unreflected level that language and its meanings can slide between my consciousness and the body that it exists. At that level, the body's alienation toward the Other and its third dimension of being can only be emptily experienced; they are only an extension of lived facticity. No concept or cognitive intuition can be attached to them. The objecthood of my body-for-the-Other is not an object for me, and cannot constitute my body as an object: it is experienced as the flight of the body that I exist. In order for the items of knowledge that the Other has of my body, and which he communicates to me through language, to be able to give to my body-for-me a structure of some particular type, they have to be applied to an object, and my body has to already be an object for me. It is therefore at the level of reflective consciousness that they can come into play: it is not facticity, insofar as it is the pure *existed* of non-thetic consciousness that they come to qualify, but instead the facticity that is apprehended by reflection as a quasi-object. It is this conceptual layer which, by inserting itself between the quasi-object and reflective consciousness, completes the objectification of the psychological quasi-body. Reflection, as we have seen, apprehends facticity and surpasses it toward an irreal entity, whose *esse* is a pure *percipi*, which we have called the *psyche*. This psyche is constituted. The items of conceptual knowledge that we acquire through our history—all of which arise from our interaction with the Other—come to produce a constitutive layer of the psychological body. In brief, insofar as we suffer our body reflectively, we constitute it through complicit reflection as a quasi-object—in this way, the observation comes from ourselves. But as soon as we know it—which is to say we apprehend it in a purely cognitive intuition—we constitute it, through this very intuition, with the Other's knowledge; i.e., we constitute it as something that it could never be for us by itself. The knowable structures of our psychological body, therefore, simply and emptily indicate its constant alienation. Instead of living this alienation, we emptily constitute it by surpassing our lived facticity toward the quasi-object that is the psychological-body, and by further surpassing this *suffered* quasi-object toward characteristics of being which necessarily cannot be given to me, and which are merely signified.

Let us return, for example, to our description of "physical" pain. We saw how reflection, by "suffering" it, constituted it into an ache. But we were obliged to stop our description there, because we lacked the means to go any further. Now we are able to pursue it: I can aim at the ache which I am suffering in its in-itself, which is to say, precisely, in its being-for-the-Other. At that moment I *know* it, which means that I aim at it in the dimension of its being that escapes me, and in the face that it turns toward others, and my aiming becomes suffused with the knowledge that language has brought to me. In other words, I use instrumental concepts that come to me from the Other, and which I could in no circumstance have formed on my own, or thought by myself of directing on to my body. It is by means of the Other's concepts that I *know* my body. But from this it follows that, even within my reflection, I am taking up the Other's point of view on my body; I try to grasp it as if I stood in relation to it as the Other. It is obvious that in this case the categories that I will apply to my ache constitute it emptily, i.e., in a dimension that escapes me. Why, then, do we talk about intuition? It is because, in spite of everything, the *suffered body* provides the core, the matter, for the alienating meanings that surpass it: it is this ache which escapes from me, toward new characteristics that I establish as its organizing limits and empty schemas. It is in this way, for example, that my ache—which I suffer as something psychological—will appear to me reflectively as a *stomachache*. We should be clear that the pain "in the stomach" is the stomach itself, insofar as it is painfully lived. As such, before the interposition of the layer of alienating cognition, it is not a local sign, not something identified. The gastralgia is the stomach, present to consciousness as a pure quality of pain. As such, we have seen, the ache is distinguished by itself—and without any intellectual operation of identification or discrimination—from any other pain or any other ache. Only the "stomach," at this level, is something ineffable, which cannot be named or thought: it is only this suffered figure, detached against the ground of the existed-body. The objectifying knowledge which now surpasses the suffered ache toward the denominated *stomach* is knowledge of a specific

396

objective nature of the stomach: I know that it is shaped like a set of bagpipes, that it is a pocket, that it produces juices and diastases, that it is wrapped in a muscular tunic with small fibers, etc. I may also know— because I have learned this from a doctor—that it is afflicted by an ulcer. And, further, I can represent this ulcer to myself, more or less clearly. I may envisage it as a gnawing animal, a mild internal rot; I may conceive it by analogy with abscesses, fever blisters, pus, cankers, etc. All of this necessarily stems either from knowledge that I have acquired from others, or from knowledge that others have of me. In any case, it cannot constitute my ache insofar as I *possess* it but rather insofar as it escapes me. The stomach and the ulcer become directions of flight, perspectives of alienation of the object I possess. It is at this point that a new layer of existence appears: we had surpassed the lived pain toward the suffered ache; we surpass the ache toward the *illness*. The illness, as something *psychological*, is of course quite different from the illness that the doctor knows and describes: it is a state. Here it is not a matter of microbes or lesions of the tissue but of a synthetic form of destruction. This form *necessarily escapes me*; from time to time it shows itself in "flashes" of pain, in my ache's "crises," but the rest of the time it remains out of reach, without disappearing. In that case it is objectively detectable *by others*: others made it known to me, and others can diagnose it; it is present for others when I am not even conscious of it. It is therefore in its innermost nature a pure and simple *being for the Other*. And when I am not suffering, I talk about it; I behave in relation to it as I would toward an object that is necessarily out of my reach, an object of which others are the custodians. If I have hepatic colic, I do not drink wine, in order not to arouse the pains in my liver. But my aim is precise: not arousing the pains in my liver cannot be distinguished in any way from this other aim, obeying the proscriptions of the doctor who revealed them to me. In this way, another person is responsible for *my illness*. And yet this object, which is brought to me through others, retains some characteristics of a degraded spontaneity, by virtue of the fact that I apprehend it through my ache. Our goal is not to describe this new object, or to emphasize its characteristics of magical spontaneity, destructive finality, harmful potency, or my familiarity with it and its concrete relations with my being (because it is, above all else, my illness). We merely wish to point out that, in the illness itself, the body is given; just as the body was what supported the

397

ache, it is now the substance of the illness, and what the illness destroys; it is through the body that this destructive form extends. In this way, the damaged stomach is present through the gastralgia as the very matter out of which this gastralgia is made. It is there, it is present to intuition, and I apprehend it, with its characteristics, through the suffered pain. I grasp it as "eaten away at," as "a pocket in the shape of bagpipes," etc. I do not see it, of course, but I know that it *is my pain*. That is the source of the phenomena falsely described by the term "endoscopy." In reality, and contrary to Sollier's claim, my pain itself does not teach me anything about my stomach.[26] Rather, through and in my pain, my knowledge constitutes a stomach-for-the-Other, which appears to me as a concrete and determinate absence, with just the number of objective characteristics that I have been able to know about it. But, necessarily, the object that is thus determined is like the pole of alienation of my pain; it is, necessarily, what I am without having it to be, and without being able to transcend it toward anything else. In this way, just as my being-for-the-Other haunts the facticity that I non-thetically live, so a being-an-object-for-the-Other haunts—like a dimension through which my psychological body escapes—the facticity that is constituted as a quasi-object for complicit reflection. Likewise, my pure nausea can be surpassed toward a dimension of alienation: in that case it will present me with my body-for-the-Other, in its "demeanor," its "bearing," its "physiognomy"; my nausea will then be given in the form of *disgust* with my face, disgust with my overly white flesh, with my overly rigid expression, etc. But we need to reverse these terms; it is not that I am disgusted with all of that. Rather, the nausea *is* all of that, as non-thetically existed. And my nausea is extended by my knowledge, toward what it is for the Other. For the Other is the one who apprehends my nausea as, precisely, flesh, and as having the nauseous character of all flesh.

398

The preceding observations have not exhausted our description of the appearances of my body. We still need to describe a type of appearance that we will designate as *abnormal*. In effect, I am able to see my hands, to

26 TN: Paul Sollier (1861–1933) was a French doctor and psychologist; his most famous patient was Proust. Sartre probably meant to use Sollier's term "*autoscopie*" rather than "*endoscopie*": the title of one of Sollier's works (1903) is Les Phénomènes d'Autoscopie. Sartre's text tells us what Sollier claimed.

touch my back, to smell the odor of my sweat. In this case, my hand, for example, appears to me as an object among other objects. It is no longer indicated as a center of reference by the surroundings; it is organized alongside them within the world and, with them, my hand indicates my body as a center of reference. It forms part of the world. Likewise, it is no longer the instrument that I am unable to handle with instruments; on the contrary, it forms part of the implements that I discover in the midst of the world; I can *make use of it*, for example, by means of my other hand, as when I strike my right hand onto my left fist, in which an almond or a walnut is clasped. My hand is then integrated within the infinite system of used-implements. Nothing in this new type of appearance should cause us concern or make us reconsider the preceding points. Nonetheless, it needed to be mentioned. It ought to be easily explained, on condition that we return it *to its place* in the order of the body's appearances, which is to say on condition that we examine it last, and as an "aberration" in our constitution. In effect, this appearance of my hand simply means that, in certain well-defined circumstances, we are able to take up the Other's point of view on our own body or, alternatively, that our own body can appear to us like the Other's body. The thinkers who started out from this appearance to produce a general theory of the body radically reversed the terms of the problem, and ran the risk of understanding nothing about the question. We must take care to note, in effect, that this possibility of *seeing* our body is a pure, absolutely contingent *de facto* given. It cannot be deduced, either from the necessity that the for-itself should "have" a body, or from the *de facto* structures of the body-for-the-Other. It is easy to conceive of bodies that are not able to take up any view on themselves; this even seems to be the case for certain insects who, although they have a differentiated nervous system and sensory organs, are not able to make use of this system and these organs to know themselves. We are dealing therefore with a structural peculiarity that we are obliged to mention, without attempting to deduce it. To have hands, or to have hands that are able to touch each other: these two facts are at the same level of contingency and, as such, belong either in pure anatomical description or in metaphysics. We cannot take them as our foundation for a study of embodiment.

399

In addition, we must note that this appearance of the body does not present us with the body insofar as it acts and perceives but insofar as it is acted and perceived. In brief, as we pointed out at the start of this chapter, it is possible to conceive of a system of visual organs in which one eye was able to see the other. But the eye that was seen would be seen as a thing, not as a being of reference.[27] Likewise, the hand that I take hold of is not apprehended as a hand that can take hold but as an object of apprehension. In this way, the nature of our body for ourselves—to the extent to which we are able to take up the Other's point of view on it— escapes us entirely. Moreover, we should note that, even if the arrangement of sensory organs allows us to see the body as it appears to the Other, the body's appearing in this way as an implement-thing is very delayed in infancy; in any case, it is subsequent to consciousness (of) the body in the strict sense, and of the world as a structure of equipment; and it is subsequent to the perception of the Other's body. A child has known for a long time how to take something, to pull it toward him, push it away and hold it, when he learns how to take his own hand, and to see it. Frequent observations have shown that a child of two months does not see his hand as his hand. He looks at it and, if he moves it further from his field of vision, he turns his head and looks for it, as if its return to its place in full sight did not depend on him. It is by means of a series of psychological operations and syntheses of identification and recognition that he will come to be able to establish systems of cross-references between the existed-body and the seen-body. And, even then, he must already have begun to learn about the Other's body. Thus, the perception of my body belongs, chronologically, after the perception of the Other's body.

If we consider it in its place and at its date, in its original contingency, there is no reason to think it will cause further problems. The body is the instrument that I am. It is the facticity of my being-in-the-world, insofar as I surpass it toward my being-in-the-midst-of-the-world. Of course, it is radically impossible for me to take up a global point of view on this facticity, or I would cease to be it. But why should we be surprised by the fact that certain structures of my body can, without ceasing to be centers of reference for objects in the world, become ordered from a radically

27 TN: I feel sure that Sartre has made a mistake here, and wrote *être de référence* where he should have put—as elsewhere, throughout—*centre de référence*. The former does not make much sense.

different point of view in relation to other objects, in order to indicate alongside them this or that sensory organ of mine as a partial center of reference, which detaches itself as a figure against the body-ground? It is in the nature of things impossible that my eye should see itself. But what is surprising about my hand being able to touch my eyes? If someone were to find this surprising, it would be because he had understood the necessity for the for-itself to arise as a concrete point of view on the world as if it were an ideal obligation, one that is strictly reducible to knowable relations between objects and mere rules for the development of my knowledge—instead of seeing it as the necessity of a concrete and contingent existence in the midst of the world.

Chapter 3

CONCRETE RELATIONS WITH THE OTHER

So far we have only described our fundamental relationship with the Other. This relation has allowed us to explicate the three dimensions of the being of our body. And although our original relation to the Other is primary (in comparison to the relation of my body to the Other's body, it has become clear to us that some knowledge of the nature of the body is indispensable for any study of the specific relations between my being and that of the Other. In fact these latter presuppose facticity, on both sides, i.e., our existence as a body in the midst of the world. It is not that the body is the instrument and cause of my relations with the Other. But it constitutes their meaning, and it marks out their limits: it is as a body-in-situation that I apprehend the Other's transcended-transcendence and it is as a body-in-situation that I experience myself, as alienated for the Other's benefit. Now that we know what our body is, we are able to examine these concrete relations. They are not mere specifications of the fundamental relation; although each of them includes the original relation to the Other within it, as its essential structure and foundation, they are entirely new modes of being of the for-itself. In fact they represent the various attitudes of the for-itself in a world in which there are others. Each of them, therefore, presents in its own way the bilateral relation:

for-itself-for-the-Other, in-itself. If, therefore, we succeed in explicating the structures of our most basic relations with the-other-in-the-world, we will have completed our task; in fact, our question at the beginning of this work concerned the for-itself's relations with the in-itself; but we have learned now that our task was more complex; the for-itself's relation with the in-itself is in the other's presence. When we have described that concrete fact, we will be in a position to draw conclusions about the fundamental relations between these three modes of being—and perhaps we can start to construct a metaphysical theory of being in general.

402   The for-itself as nihilation of the in-itself temporalizes itself as flight toward. In effect, it surpasses its facticity—or its being given, or its past, or its body—toward the in-itself that it would be if it were able to be its own foundation. This could be put into terms that are more psychological—and that are, for this reason, incorrect, even if they are perhaps clearer—by saying that the for-itself tries to escape its de facto existence, in other words its being-there, as an in-itself of which it is not in any way the foundation, and that this flight takes place toward an impossible and constantly pursued future where the for-itself might be in-itself-for-itself, i.e., an in-itself that would be its own foundation in relation to itself. Thus the for-itself is at the same time a flight and a pursuit; at the same time it flees the in-itself and it pursues it; the for-itself is a pursuing-pursued. But—to reduce the danger of a psychological interpretation of the preceding remarks—we should remember that the for-itself does not exist first, in order subsequently to try to attain to being: in short, we should not conceive of it as an existent that could be endowed with tendencies, as this glass is endowed with certain specific qualities. This flight in pursuit is not a given that is added on to the for-itself's being as an extra: rather, the for-itself is this very flight; it cannot be distinguished from the original nihilation; to say that the for-itself is pursuing-pursued, or that it is in the mode of having its being to be, or that it is not what it is and it is what it is not, amounts to one and the same thing. The for-itself is not, and cannot be, the in-itself, but it is the relation to the in-itself; it is even the only possible relation to the in-itself. Surrounded at all sides by the in-itself, the for-itself escapes it only because it is nothing, and separated from it by nothing. The for-itself is the foundation of all negativity and all relation: it is the relation.

This being so, the Other, in arising, reaches right to the heart of the for-itself. Through and for the other, the pursuing flight is frozen into in-itself. Already being constantly seized back by the in-itself, the for-itself was at the same time already a radical negation of fact, an absolute positing of value—and, at the same time, penetrated by facticity throughout. At least it escaped through its temporalization; at least its character as a detotalized totality conferred on it a perpetual "elsewhere." But it is this very totality that the Other summons up before him, and transcends toward his own "elsewhere." It is this totality that is totalized: for the Other, I am irremediably what I am, and my freedom itself is a property added to my being. Thus the in-itself seizes me back even into the future and freezes me entirely in my very flight—which becomes a foreseen and contemplated flight, a given flight. But this frozen flight is never the flight that I am for myself: it is frozen *out there*. I experience this objectivity of my flight as an alienation that I can neither transcend nor know. And yet, by the mere fact that I experience it, and that it bestows on my flight this in-itself that it is fleeing from, I am obliged to turn back toward it and take up an *attitude* in relation to it. Such is the origin of my concrete relations with the Other; they are governed entirely by the attitudes that I take up toward the object that I am for the Other. And as the Other's existence reveals to me the being that I am, without my being able either to appropriate this being or even to conceive of it, this existence motivates two opposing attitudes: the Other looks at me and, in so doing, he holds the secret of my being; he knows what I am. Thus the innermost meaning of my being is outside me, imprisoned in an absence; the Other has the advantage over me. I can try, therefore, insofar as I flee from the in-itself that I am without being its foundation, to negate this being that is bestowed on me from outside; in other words, I can turn back toward the Other to confer objecthood on him in my turn, since the Other's objecthood destroys my objectivity for the Other. But, on the other hand, and insofar as the Other in his freedom founds my being-in-itself, I can try to retrieve this freedom and to take hold of it without taking its character of freedom away from it: if I were able, in effect, to assimilate this freedom that founds my being-in-itself, I would be, in relation to myself, my own foundation. These are the two basic attitudes that I take up in relation to the Other: transcending the Other's transcendence or, on the contrary, swallowing up this transcendence within me without taking away its character of transcendence. And, here again, we should interpret these words with care: it is not at all true that, in the first place, I am, and that, thereafter, I "try" to objectify or to assimilate the Other; rather, to the extent that my being arises in the Other's presence, to the extent that I am a pursuing flight and a pursuing-pursued, I am, in the very root of my being, a pro-ject of objectification or assimilation of the Other. I undergo the Other: that is the original fact. But this undergoing of the Other is in itself an attitude toward the Other, which is to say that I can be in the presence of the Other without this "in the presence of" taking the form of having it to be. Thus we are still describing structures of the for-itself's being, even though the Other's presence in the world is an absolute fact, evidenced by itself, but contingent, i.e., something that is impossible to deduce from the ontological structures of the for-itself.

Each of these two attempts that I am is opposed to the other. Each one of them is the other's death, which means the failure of one of them motivates the adoption of the other. In this way my relations toward the Other are not dialectical but circular—even though each attempt is enriched by the other's failure. So we will study each of them in turn. But we should take note that, in the depths of each one, the other always remains present, precisely because neither of them can be maintained without contradiction. Better still, each attempt lies within the other, and gives rise to the death of the other; thus we can never get out of the circle. We should not lose sight of the present observations as we set about studying these fundamental attitudes toward the Other. As these attitudes produce and destroy each other in a circle, it is equally arbitrary whether we begin with one or begin with the other. However, as we are obliged to choose, we will consider first the behavior by which the for-itself attempts to assimilate the Other's freedom.

404

I. OUR FIRST ATTITUDE TOWARD THE OTHER: LOVE, LANGUAGE, MASOCHISM

Everything that is true of me is true of the Other. While I attempt to free myself from the Other's hold, the Other tries to free himself from mine; while I try to enslave the Other, the Other tries to enslave me.

The relations we are concerned with here are not at all unilateral relations to an object-in-itself but reciprocal and shifting relationships. The following descriptions should therefore be envisaged within the perspective of *conflict*. Conflict is the original meaning of being-for-the-Other.

If we set out from the Other's initial revelation as the *look*, we are obliged to acknowledge that we experience our elusive being-for-the-Other in the form of a *possession*. I am possessed by the Other; the Other's look models my body in its nudity, gives birth to it, sculpts it, produces it as it is, sees it as I will never see it. The Other holds a secret: the secret of what I am. He makes me be and, in so doing, he possesses me—and this possession is nothing other than his consciousness of possessing me. As for me, in recognizing my objecthood, I feel that he has this consciousness. As a consciousness, the Other is for me at the same time someone who has stolen my being, and someone who brings it about that "there is" a being that is my being. Thus I have some understanding of this ontological structure; I am responsible for my being-for-the-Other but I am not its foundation; it appears to me, therefore, in the form of a contingent datum for which I am nonetheless responsible, and the Other founds my being insofar as this being takes the form of the "there is"; but even though he founds it in the entirety of his freedom—in and through his free transcendence—he is not responsible for it. Thus, to the extent that I am disclosed to myself as responsible for my being, I claim this being that I am; i.e., I want to retrieve it or, in more precise terms, I am the project to retrieve my being. I want to stretch out my hand to lay hold of this being that is appresented to me as *my being*, but at a distance, like Tantalus's meal, and to found it by my particular freedom. That is because if—in one sense—my object-being is intolerably contingent and a pure "possession" of me by another, this being is—in another sense—like an indication of what I have to retrieve and to found, in order to be the foundation of myself. But this is conceivable only if I can assimilate the Other's freedom. In this way, my project to reclaim myself is fundamentally a project to reabsorb the other. However, my project must leave intact the other's nature. This means: (1) In order to do this, I do not stop affirming the Other, i.e., denying, in relation to myself, that I am the other: as the foundation of my being, the other cannot become diluted in me without my being-for-the-Other vanishing. If therefore I am planning to actualize my

405

unity with the Other, that means I plan to assimilate the other's alterity as such, as my own possibility. My aim, in effect, is to make myself be by acquiring the possibility of taking up the other's point of view on myself. But this, however, is not a matter of acquiring a pure abstract faculty of knowledge. My project is not to appropriate the pure *category* of the other: that category is neither conceived of, nor even able to be conceived. But, in the circumstance of the concrete experience—suffered and felt—of the other, it is this concrete other as an absolute reality whom I want to incorporate in his alterity. (2) The other whom I want to assimilate is not at all the object-other. Or—alternatively—my project to incorporate the other does not in the least correspond to a seizing back of my for-itself as myself, and a surpassing of the Other's transcendence toward my own possibilities. My concern is not to erase my objectivity by objectifying the other—which would amount to my *delivering myself from* my being-for-the-Other—but, quite to the contrary, it is as an other-who-looks that I wish to assimilate the other, and this project of assimilation involves an increased recognition of my being-looked-at. In brief, I identify myself completely with my being-looked-at in order to maintain before me the other's looking freedom and, as my object-being is the only possible relation between me and the other, this object-being is the only instrument I can use to bring about the assimilation of the *other freedom* with myself. Thus, in reaction to the failure of the third *ecstasis*, the for-itself wants to identify itself with the Other's freedom, in its founding of its being-in-itself. To be an Other to oneself—the ideal that is always concretely aimed at in the form of being *this Other* to oneself—is the primary value in our relations with the Other; my being-for-the-Other, therefore, is haunted by the indication of an absolute-being, able to be itself insofar as it is other, and to be other insofar as it is itself, and which, in freely giving itself its self-being as other and its other-being as self, might instantiate the very being of the ontological proof, i.e., God. This ideal can be achieved only if I overcome the original contingency of my relations to the Other, i.e., the fact of there being no relationship of internal negativity between the negation through which the Other establishes himself as other from me and the negation through which I establish myself as other from the other. We have seen that this contingency is insurmountable: it is the *fact* of my relations with the Other, just as my body is the *fact* of my being-in-the-world. Unity with the Other is therefore unrealizable in fact. And it is also unrealizable *de jure*, because the assimilation of the for-itself and the Other within a single act of transcendence would lead necessarily to the disappearance of the Other's character of alterity. Thus, the condition of my planning to identify myself with the Other is that I persist in denying, in relation to myself, that I am the other. In short, this project of unification is a source of *conflict*, since, while I experience myself as an object for the Other and plan to assimilate him in and through this experience, the Other apprehends me as an object in the midst of the world and does not remotely plan to assimilate me to himself. What would be required therefore—since my being for the Other involves a double internal negation—would be to act on the internal negation through which the Other transcends my transcendence and makes me exist for the other, i.e., *to act on the Other's freedom*.

This unrealizable ideal, insofar as it haunts my project for myself in the presence of the Other, cannot be equated with love, insofar as love is an enterprise, i.e., an organic set of projects concerning my own possibilities. But it is love's ideal, its motivation and its goal, the value that belongs to it. Love as a basic relation to the Other is the set of projects through which I aim to realize this value.[1]

These projects place me in a direct relation with the Other's freedom. It is in this sense that love is conflict. We have noted that the Other's freedom is, in effect, the foundation of my being. But, precisely because I exist through the Other's freedom, I lack all security, and I am in danger in that freedom; it molds my being and *makes me be*; it confers values upon me and withdraws them; and, from that freedom, my being receives a constant, passive escaping from itself. Irresponsible and out of reach, this protean freedom in which I have become committed can commit me in its turn in a thousand different ways of being. My project to reclaim my being can be fulfilled only if I take hold of that freedom and reduce it to being a freedom that submits to my freedom. At the same time, it is the only way in which I can act upon the free internal negation through which the other constitutes me as another, i.e., through which I can pre-

---

1 TN: From this point on (i.e., when Sartre begins his discussion of love), I will frequently characterize the Other as "she" (even if Sartre has used *il*). See my note on the difficulties presented by gender pronouns in Notes on the Translation for an explanation of my policy in this part of the text.

pare the ground for the other's future identification with me. This will perhaps become clearer if we reflect on this problem, which is apparently purely psychological: Why does the lover want to be *loved*? If in fact love were merely the desire for physical possession, it could, in many cases, be easily satisfied. For example, Proust's hero, who installs his mistress in his home, who can see and possess her at every hour of the day, and has managed to make her totally dependent materially, ought to be free of trouble. However, we know that he is, on the contrary, eaten up by worry. It is through her consciousness that Albertine escapes from Marcel, even when he is at her side, and that is why the only respite he can have is when he contemplates her while she sleeps. It is certain therefore that love wants to captivate "consciousness." But why does it want this? And how?

The concept of "property," which is used so often to explain love, cannot in fact be central. Why should I want to appropriate the Other, if not precisely because the Other makes me be? But that implies, precisely, a specific mode of appropriation: it is the other's freedom as such that we want to seize. Not through will to power: the tyrant does not care about love; he is content with fear. If he seeks the love of his subjects it is for political reasons and, if he can find a more economic way of subjugating them, he will adopt it at once. Contrary to this, the person who wants to be loved does not desire to subjugate the being he loves. He does not want to become the object of a boundless, mechanical passion. He does not want to possess an automatism, and if you want to humiliate him, you need only portray for him his loved one's passion as the outcome of psychological determinism: the lover will feel devalued in his love and his being. If Tristan and Isolde are driven wild by a love potion, they become less interesting—and it can happen that the total subjugation of the being he loves kills the lover's love. His goal has been overshot: if the loved one is transformed into an automaton, the lover finds himself on his own. Thus the lover does not desire to possess his loved one in the way we can possess a thing: he demands a special type of appropriation. He wants to possess a freedom as freedom.

But, on the other hand, he could not be satisfied by that preeminent form of freedom that consists in a free and voluntary commitment. Who could be happy with a love that presented itself purely as a loyalty to a sworn faith? Who, then, would accept someone's saying "I love you because I have freely committed myself to love you, and I do not want to go back on my word: I love you out of fidelity to myself?" Thus the lover demands an oath, and is irritated by the oath. He wants to be loved by a freedom, and demands that this freedom, as freedom, should no longer be free. He wants the other's freedom to determine itself by itself to become love—and not only at the start of the adventure but at every instant—and he wants, at the same time, this freedom to be captivated by itself; he wants it to turn back on itself—as in madness, or a dream—in order to will its own captivity. And this captivity must be an act of resignation that is at the same time both free and shackled between our hands. What we desire from the Other in love is neither a determinism of the passions nor a freedom beyond reach but a freedom that plays at being determined by passion, and that gets caught in its own game.[2] And, for himself, the lover does not demand to be the cause of this radical modification of freedom but to be its unique and favored occasion. Indeed, he could not want to be its cause without immediately plunging the loved one into the midst of the world, like a tool that can be transcended. That is not the essence of love. In love, on the contrary, the lover wants to be "everything in the world" for his beloved, which is to say that he places himself alongside the world. He will sum up and symbolize the world: he is a this that includes all other thises; he is, and agrees to be, an object. But, on the other hand, he wants to be the object in which the Other's freedom agrees to lose itself, the object in which the Other agrees to find something like a second facticity, her being and her raison d'être: the object that limits transcendence, the object toward which the Other's transcendence transcends all other objects—but that cannot be transcended in any way. And, throughout, he desires the circle of the Other's freedom; in other words he desires, at every moment, in the acceptance, by the Other's freedom of this limit to her transcendence, that this acceptance should already be present, as the motive of the acceptance in question. It is as an end that has already been chosen that he wants to be chosen as an end. This allows us to grasp what it is that

408

2 TN: . . . le déterminisme passionnel . . . The French adjective passionnel has an old-fashioned feel; it is often used to describe personal relationships. Sartre may well be influenced by Charles Fourier's concept attraction passionnelle. Fourier (1772–1837) was a French socialist philosopher who argued, among other things, for a liberation of man's passions.

the lover fundamentally demands of the loved one: he does not want to act on the other's freedom but to exist *a priori* as this freedom's objective limit, i.e., to be given in a single stroke alongside it, even as it arises, as the limit that freedom must accept in order to be free. In virtue of this, what the lover demands of the Other's freedom is that it should become thickened, and become bogged down: this structural limit is in effect a *given*, and the mere appearance of the given as the limit of freedom means that the freedom *makes itself exist* within that given, while prohibiting itself from surpassing it. And the lover regards this prohibition *at the same time* as something lived through, i.e., as something undergone (in a word, as facticity) and, at the same time, as freely consented to. It must be capable of being freely consented to, since it has to belong to the arising of a freedom that chooses itself as freedom. But it must be merely lived through, since it has to be an ever present impossibility, a facticity that flows back right into the heart of the Other's freedom; and this is psychologically expressed in the demand that the free decision to love me, which the loved one has previously taken, should slide like a spellbinding motive *inside* her present free commitment.

We can now grasp the meaning of this demand: that facticity, which must—in my demand to be loved—be a *de facto* limit for the Other, and which must end up by being *her own* facticity, is *my* facticity. It is insofar as I am the object which the Other brings into being that I must be the inherent limit of her transcendence itself, so that the Other, as she arises to being, makes me exist as the absolute, the unsurpassable—not as a nihilating for-itself but as being-for-the-Other-in-the-midst-of-the-world. In this way, to want to be loved is to infect the Other with one's own facticity, to want to force her constantly to re-create you, as the condition of a freedom that submits and commits itself; it is to want freedom to be the foundation of fact and, at the same time, that fact should reign over freedom. If this result could be achieved, the first consequence would be that I was *safe* within the other's consciousness. That is because, in the first place, the reason for my worry and my shame is that I apprehend and experience myself in my being-for-the-Other as something that can always be surpassed toward something else, purely as the object of a value judgment, purely a means, purely a tool. My worry arises from the fact that I necessarily and freely accept this being that an Other, in absolute freedom, makes me be: "God knows what I am for her! God knows how she thinks of me." That means: "God knows how she makes me be," and I am haunted by this being, whom I am afraid of meeting one day at a bend in the road, who is such a stranger to me and who is nonetheless my *being*, and about whom I also know that, in spite of my efforts, I will never meet him. But if the Other loves me, I become *unsurpassable*, which means that I must be the absolute end; in this sense I am saved from *equipmentality*; my existence in the midst of the world becomes exactly correlative to my transcendence-for-myself, since my independence is absolutely protected. The object that the Other has to make me be is an object-transcendence, an absolute center of reference around which all the implement-things in the world are arranged as pure *means*. At the same time, as freedom's absolute limit—i.e., as the limit of the absolute source of all values—I am protected against any eventual devaluation; I am the absolute value. And, to the extent that I accept my being-for-the-Other, I accept myself *qua* value. Thus, to want to be loved is to want to place oneself beyond the entire system of values posited by the Other, as the condition of all valuation and as the objective foundation of all values. This demand is a standard theme in the conversations of lovers, whether—as in *La Porte Étroite*[3]—the person who wants to be loved identifies herself with an ascetic morality of self-overcoming and wants to embody the ideal limit of this overcoming, or whether, more commonly, the lover demands that his loved one should in her actions sacrifice traditional morality, and is concerned to know if the loved one would betray her friends for him, "would steal for him," "would kill for him," etc. From this point of view, my being must escape the loved one's *look*; or, rather, it must be the object of a look with another structure; I must no longer be seen against the ground of the world as a *this* among other *thises* but I must be the starting point for the revelation of the world. Indeed, to the extent that freedom, in its arising, is what makes a world exist, I must actually be—as the condition-limit of this arising—the condition of the arising of a world. I must be the one whose function is to make the trees and the water exist, the towns and the fields and other men, in order then to give them to the Other who arranges them into a world—just as the mother, in matronymic societies, receives the deeds and the family name, not in order to keep them but in order immediately to pass them on to her children. In one sense, if I am

3 TN: *La Porte Étroite* (1909) is a novel by the French author André Gide. It is translated into English as Gide (2007).

410 to be loved, I am the object through whose procurement the world will exist for the other; in another sense, I am the world. Instead of being a "this," carved out against the ground of the world, I am the object-ground against which the world stands out. Thus I am reassured: the Other's look no longer penetrates me with finitude; it no longer freezes me into merely being what I am; I cannot be seen as ugly, or small, or cowardly, since these characteristics necessarily represent a factual limitation of my being and an apprehension of my finitude as finitude. Of course, my possibles remain transcended possibilities, dead-possibilities; but all the possibles are mine; I am all the dead-possibilities in the world; I thereby cease to be a being who understands himself in terms of other beings, or his actions; rather, in the loving intuition that I demand, I must be given as an absolute totality, on whose basis all beings, and all its own actions, are to be understood. One might say, adapting slightly a famous Stoic phrase, that "the loved one can turn three somersaults."[4] Indeed, the ideal of the sage and the ideal of the person who wants to be loved coincide, in that both of them wish to be an object-totality accessible to a global intuition, which would apprehend actions in the world of the loved one and of the sage as partial structures, to be interpreted on the basis of the totality. And just as the sage's wisdom is presented as a state to be attained through an absolute metamorphosis, in the same way the Other's freedom must undergo an absolute metamorphosis for me to achieve the condition of the loved one.

So far this description fits Hegel's famous description of the relations between master and slave quite well. What Hegel's master is for the slave is what the lover wants to be for his loved one. But the analogy ends here, because the master, in Hegel's account, only demands the slave's freedom laterally and, so to speak, implicitly, whereas the lover demands the beloved's freedom first. In this sense, if I am to be loved by the other, I must be freely chosen as loved. We know that, in the common terminology of love, the loved one is referred to as the chosen. But this choice must not be relative and contingent: the lover is irritated and feels himself devalued by the thought that the loved one chose him among others. "So, if I had not come to this town, if I had not visited X's house, you would not have known me, and you would not have loved me?" This thought distresses the lover: his

4 TN: Chrysippus reportedly remarked that "a wise man will turn three somersaults for an adequate fee."

love becomes one love among others, limited by the loved one's facticity and by his own facticity, at the same time as by the contingency of their meetings: it becomes a *love within the world*, an object that presupposes the world and that can in turn exist for others. To express what he demands, he uses clumsy words, sullied by "thinghood"; he says: "We were made for each other," or even uses the phrase "kindred spirit." But this requires interpretation: he knows full well that the idea of "being made for each other" refers to an original choice. This choice might be God's, as the being who is absolute choice: but here God only represents the demand for the absolute pushed to its limit. In fact, what the lover demands is that the loved one should have made an absolute choice of him. That means his loved one's being-in-the-world must be a loving-being. This loved one's arising must be a free choice of her lover. And, as the other is the foundation of my object-being, I demand of her that her freely arising being should have as its sole and absolute end her choice of *me*—i.e., that she should have chosen to be in order to found my objecthood and my facticity. In this way my facticity is "saved." It is no longer that unthinkable and insurmountable given from which I flee: it is that for which the other freely makes herself exist; it exists as the end that she sets herself. I have infected her with my facticity, but, as it is insofar as she is a freedom that she has been infected by it, she returns it to me as a facticity that has been reclaimed and consented to; she is its foundation so that it can be her end. On the basis of this love, then, I apprehend my alienation and my own facticity differently. It is—insofar as it is for-the-Other—no longer a fact but a right. My existence occurs because it is *called for*. This existence, insofar as I accept it, becomes pure generosity. I am because I bestow myself. It is through my goodness that these beloved veins on my hands exist. How good I am to have eyes, hair, eyebrows, and to lavish them tirelessly in a flood of generosity on that tireless desire that the other freely makes herself be. Where, before we were loved, we were troubled by this unjustified and unjustifiable protuberance that was our existence, where we felt ourselves "*de trop*," now we feel that this existence has been reclaimed and willed, right down to the last detail, by an absolute freedom that is conditioned by it at the same time—and that, along with our own freedom, we are willing ourselves. That is the basis of love's joy, when it exists: to feel ourselves justified in existing.

By the same token, if the loved one is able to love us, she is quite prepared to be assimilated by our freedom, because this being-loved that we wish for is already the ontological proof, applied to our being-for-the-Other. Our objective essence implies the Other's existence and, reciprocally, the other's freedom founds our essence. If we were able to internalize the whole system, we would be the foundation of ourselves.

Such is, therefore, the lover's true aim, insofar as his love is an enterprise, i.e., a pro-ject for himself. This project must give rise to a conflict. The loved one, indeed, apprehends the lover as an object-other among others, which means she perceives him against the ground of the world, transcends him and utilizes him. The loved one is the one who *looks*. She cannot then make use of her transcendence to establish an ultimate limit to her surpassing, or make use of her freedom to captivate itself. The loved one cannot wish to love. The lover must therefore seduce the loved one, and his love cannot be distinguished from this enterprise of seduction. In seducing the Other, my aim is not at all to reveal my subjectivity to her: in any case, I would not be able to do this except by *looking at* the Other; but through that look I would cause the Other's subjectivity to disappear—which is what I want to assimilate. To seduce is to accept—entirely, and as a risk to be run—my objecthood for the Other, to place myself before her look and make myself looked at by her, and to incur the danger of *being-seen* in order to make a new start and to appropriate the other in and through my objecthood. I refuse to leave the territory where my objecthood is experienced; this is the ground on which I want to take up the struggle, by making myself into a *fascinating object*. In Part Two we defined fascination as a state: we said that it is a non-thetic consciousness of being *nothing* in the presence of being. Seduction aims to bring about in the Other the consciousness of her nothingness as she faces the seductive object. Through seduction I aim to constitute myself as a fullness of being and to make myself *recognized as such*. To that end, I constitute myself as a signifying object. My actions must *indicate* in two directions. On the one hand, they point toward a depth of objective, hidden being, which we refer to incorrectly as "subjectivity"; the action is not merely done for its own sake but indicates an infinite and undifferentiated series of other real and possible actions that I offer as constituting my objective and unperceived being. In this way I try to guide the transcendence that is transcending me, to refer it toward the infinity of my dead-possibilities, precisely in order to be unsurpassable—and to the extent to which the only thing that cannot be surpassed is, precisely, the infinite. On the other hand, each one of my actions attempts to indicate the world in the greatest possible breadth, and to present me as being linked to the world's vastest regions—whether I present the world to my loved one and try to constitute myself as the necessary intermediary between her and the world, or whether I simply demonstrate, through my actions, my endlessly varied powers over the world (money, power, connections, etc.). In the first case, I try to constitute myself as infinite in depth; in the second case, I try to identify myself with the world. Through these various methods I propose myself as unsurpassable. This proposition is not sufficient on its own: it is only an investment in the Other, and it cannot acquire the value of a fact without the consent of the Other's freedom, which has to captivate itself as it recognizes itself as nothingness, in the face of my absolute plenitude of being.

It might be said that these different attempts at expression presuppose language. We will not disagree, and we will even say: they are language or, alternatively, a fundamental mode of language. For, if there are psychological and historical problems concerning the existence, learning, and use of some particular language, there is no particular problem in relation to the so-called invention of language. Language is not a phenomenon that is added on to our being-for-the-Other: it is being-for-the-Other from the outset, i.e., the fact that a subjectivity experiences itself as an object for the other. In a universe of pure objects, there would be no circumstance in which language could be "invented," since it presupposes at its origin a relation to another subject; and within the intersubjectivity of our for-Others it is not necessary to invent it, because it is already given in our recognition of the other. By virtue solely of the fact that, no matter what I do, my freely conceived and executed actions, and my pro-jects toward my possibilities, have an external meaning that eludes me and that I undergo, I am language. It is in this sense—and only in this sense— that Heidegger is right in asserting that: I am what I say.[5] This language is not, indeed, an instinct belonging to the constituted human creature,

413

---

5 Sartre's note: The phrase comes from A. De Waehlens, *La Philosophie de Martin Heidegger*, p. 99 (Louvain, 1942). Cf. also the text from Heidegger which he quotes: *"Diese Bezeugung meint hier nicht einen nachträglichen und beiherlaufenden Ausdruck des Menschseins, sondern sie macht das Dasein des Menschen mit aus"* (*Hölderlin und das Wesen der Dichtung*, p. 6). TN: The corresponding passage from the published English translation of this text is "This attestation does not mean a subsequent and additional expression of man's being; rather, it forms a part of man's existence" (Heidegger 2000: 54).

nor is it an invention of our subjectivity—but nor must it be reduced purely to *Dasein*'s "being-outside-itself." It is part of the *human condition*; it is from the outset the experience that a for-itself can have of his being-for-the-Other and, thereafter, the surpassing of this experience, and the making use of it toward possibilities that are my possibilities—i.e., my possibilities of being this or that for the Other. It is not therefore distinct from our recognition of the Other's existence. The other's arising as a look that confronts me makes language arise with it, as the condition of my being. This primitive language is not necessarily seduction, and we will see other forms of it; moreover, we have observed that no attitude is basic in relation to the Other and that they succeed each other in a circle, each one implying the other. But, conversely, seduction does not presuppose any earlier form of language: it is in its entirety a realization of language, which means that seduction can reveal language entirely, and in one stroke, as the basic mode of expression. It goes without saying that by "language" we mean all expressive phenomena and not the spoken word, which is a derivative and secondary mode, whose appearance may become an object of historical study. In particular, in the case of seduction, the aim of language is not to put forward something *to be known* but to make something experienced.

But in this first attempt to find a fascinating language, I am groping blindly, as all I have to guide me is the abstract and empty form of my objecthood for the other. I cannot even conceive of the effect that my movements or my attitude will have, since they are always reclaimed and founded by a freedom that will surpass them, and since they can have meaning only if this freedom confers it on them. In this way the "meaning" of my expressions always escapes me: I never know exactly if I am signifying what I want to signify or even if I *am* signifying; I would need to be able to read inside the other, which is, as a matter of principle, inconceivable. And, lacking any knowledge of what in fact I am expressing for the Other, I constitute my language as an incomplete phenomenon of flight outside me. From the moment I express myself, I can only guess at the meaning of what I express (which is to say, in short, the meaning of what I am), since—from this perspective—to express and to be are one and the same. The Other is always there, present and experienced as that which gives language its meaning. Each expression, each gesture, each word is—on my side—a particular trial of the Other's alienating reality. The psychiatric patient is not alone in being able to say—as, for example, in psychotic delusions of control—"Someone is stealing my thoughts."[6] Rather, the very fact of expression is a theft of one's thought, since the thought needs the help of an alienating freedom in order to constitute itself as an object. That is why this first dimension of language—insofar as I make use of it for the other—is *sacred*. A sacred object is, in effect, an object in the world that points to a transcendence beyond the world. Language reveals to me the freedom of the person silently listening to me, i.e., his transcendence.

But in that same moment I remain, for the other, a signifying object—as I always have been. There is no route which, beginning from my objecthood, can indicate my transcendence to the other. Attitudes, expressions, and words can only ever point, for him, to other attitudes, other expressions, and other words. In this way language remains for the Other just a property of a magical object, and a magical object itself: it is an action at a distance whose effect the Other knows exactly. Thus the word is *sacred* when I am the one using it, and *magical* when heard by the other. So I do not know my language any better than I know my body for the other. I cannot hear myself speaking or see myself smiling. The problem of language is exactly parallel to the problem of bodies, and the descriptions that were applicable in one case also apply in the other.

However, even if the activity of fascination were to bring about in the Other a being-fascinated, it would not succeed on its own in bringing about love. We can be fascinated by an orator, an actor, a tightrope walker: that does not mean that we love him. Admittedly, we cannot take our eyes off him; but he still stands out against the ground of the world, and the attitude of fascination does not present the fascinating object as the ultimate limit of transcendence: quite on the contrary, it is an attitude of transcendence. When therefore does the loved one become a lover in her turn?

6 TN: I have made two decisions in relation to this sentence: (a) Sartre starts by referring to *le psychopathe*, which was at one time used in French to mean "psychiatric patient." I have not used the English term "psychopath," because it would be misleading. (b) He refers to *des psychoses d'influence*, which does not map onto any phrase in English psychiatric vocabulary. (Sartre may have come across it through Alfred Lévy's book, published in France in 1914, *La Psychose d'Influence*.) The best translation seems to me to be "psychotic delusions of control."

The answer is simple: when she forms the project to be loved. In itself, an Other-object is never sufficiently strong to occasion love. If the ideal of love is the appropriation of the Other as the Other—i.e., as a looking subjectivity—this ideal can be projected only on the basis of my encounter with the Other-subject, not with the Other-object. Seduction can only adorn the Other-object who tries to seduce me with the character of a *precious* object, "to be possessed"; it may lead me to take great risks to conquer her; but we should not confuse this desire to appropriate an object in the midst of the world with love. Love can only arise within the loved one out of the experience she undergoes of her alienation, and of the flight of her being away toward an other. But, once again, if this is the case, the loved one will only transform herself into a lover if she plans to be loved—in other words if what she seeks to conquer is not a body but the other's subjectivity as such. Indeed, the only means that she can conceive of by which to actualize this appropriation is to make herself loved. Thus we can see that to love is, in essence, the project to make oneself loved. In consequence, this new contradiction and this new conflict arise: each of the lovers is entirely captive to the other, insofar as each wants to be loved by the other to the exclusion of anyone else; but at the same time each of them demands from the other a love that cannot be reduced to the "project-to-be-loved." What the lover demands, in fact, is that the other, without seeking from the outset to be loved, should have an intuition that is simultaneously contemplative and affective of her loved one as the objective limit to her freedom, as the inescapable and chosen foundation of her transcendence, as the totality of being and the supreme value. The love that is hereby demanded from the other cannot *ask for* anything: it is a pure commitment, without reciprocity. But such a love, precisely, could exist only as a demand on the part of the lover, and the lover is made captive in a wholly different way: in his demand itself, he is held captive; to the extent that love is indeed a demand to be loved, he is a freedom that wants to be a body, and demands an "outside"; he is a freedom, therefore, that acts out its flight away toward the other, a freedom that, as a freedom, lays claim to its alienation. The lover's freedom, in its very effort to make itself loved as an object by the other, alienates itself as it flows into his body-for-the-other; in other words, it produces in its existence a dimension of flight away toward the other; this freedom is a constant refusal to posit itself as pure ipseity, because this affirmation of itself as itself would lead to the collapse of the Other as look, and to the arising of the object-other—and therefore to a state of affairs where the very possibility of being loved disappears, since the other is reduced to her dimension of objectivity. This refusal therefore constitutes freedom as dependent on the other, and the other as a subjectivity becomes the insurmountable limit of the for-itself's freedom: its goal and its supreme end, insofar as she holds the key to the for-itself's being. Again, we encounter here the ideal of love's enterprise: alienated freedom. But it is the person who wants to be loved who, insofar as he wants to be loved, alienates his freedom. My freedom alienates itself in the presence of the pure subjectivity of the other who founds my objectivity; it could not become alienated before an other-object. In that form, indeed, the loved one's alienation—which the lover dreams of—would be contradictory, since, necessarily, the loved one could found the lover's being only by transcending it toward other worldly objects: this movement of transcendence therefore cannot constitute the object it surpasses as a transcended object and, at the same time, as the object-limit of any transcendence. Thus each person, in the loving couple, wants to be the object for whom the other's freedom alienates itself in an original intuition; but this intuition—which would be love in the true sense of the word—is only a contradictory ideal of the for-itself: in consequence, each lover is alienated only to the precise degree to which he or she demands the Other's alienation. Each one wants to be loved by the other, without taking into account that to love is to want to be loved—and thus that, in wanting to be loved by the other, each one only wants the other to want to be loved by them. In this way, the relations in love form an unending system of referrals, analogous to the pure reflection-reflected structure of consciousness, with the *value* "love" as the presiding ideal, i.e., a fusion of consciousnesses in which each one would preserve its alterity in order to found the other. That is because each consciousness is separated from the other by a nothingness that is insurmountable, since it is—at the same time—an internal negation by one of the other, and a *de facto* nothingness between the two internal negations. Love is a contradictory attempt to overcome the *de facto* negation while at the same time maintaining the internal negation. I demand the other to love me and I do all that I can to fulfill my project, but if the other loves me, she radically disappoints me even in her love: I required her to found my being

416

as a favored object by maintaining herself in her pure subjectivity before me; and, the moment she loves me, she experiences me as a subject and is ruined by her objectivity in relation to my subjectivity. The problem of my being-for-the-Other remains therefore without a solution, and each lover remains, for himself or for herself, as a total subjectivity; nothing occurs to relieve either of the duty that each of them has to make himself or herself exist for itself; nothing removes their contingency or saves them from facticity. At least each of them has gained by no longer being in danger from the other's freedom—but not at all in the way they believe: it is not because the Other makes the lover's being into an object-limit of her transcendence but because the other experiences him as a subjectivity and wishes to experience him only as such. Even so, the gain is constantly compromised: in the first place, each consciousness is able to free itself suddenly from its chains and to contemplate the Other as an *object*. Then the bewitchment comes to an end, and the other becomes a means among other means; he is still an object for the Other, as he desires to be, but an object-tool, an object that is constantly transcended; the illusion, the play of mirrors that forms love's concrete reality, suddenly ends. And then, in love, each consciousness seeks to house its being-for-the-Other *in a sheltered place* within the other's freedom. The assumption here is that the other is beyond the world as a pure subjectivity, as the absolute through which the world comes to being. But it suffices for the lovers to be *looked at* together by some third party for each of them to experience the objectification, not just of his or her self but of the other. At the same time the other becomes for me no longer the absolute transcendence who founds me in my being but a transcendence that is transcended—not by me but by someone else—and my original relationship to her—i.e., my relation to my lover of being loved—becomes frozen into a dead-possibility. It is no longer the experienced relation between an object that sets a limit to any transcendence and the freedom that founds it; rather it is an object-love, alienating itself in its entirety toward the third person. That is the real reason why lovers seek solitude. It is because the appearance of a third person—whoever he is—means the destruction of their love. But a *de facto* solitude (we are alone in my bedroom) is not at all a *de jure* solitude. In fact, even if nobody sees us, we exist for *every* consciousness and we are conscious of existing for all of them: it follows that love, as a fundamental mode of being-for-the-Other, contains in its being-for-the-Other the seeds of its own destruction. We have just defined the threefold destructibility of love: in the first place it is, in essence, an illusion and an infinite referral, because to love is to want to be loved, and therefore to want the other to want me to love her. And a preontological understanding of this trickery is given within love's very impulse: hence the lover's constant dissatisfaction. This is not caused, as it is too frequently said, by the loved one's unworthiness but by an implicit understanding of the fact that the intuition that belongs to love is, as a foundation-intuition, unattainable. The more someone loves me, the more I lose my *being*, and the more I am returned to my own responsibilities and my own possible way of being. In the second place, it is always possible that the other will wake up: she can at any moment summon me before her as an object: hence the lover's constant insecurity. In the third place, love is an absolute that is constantly being *relativized* by others. One would have to be alone in the world with one's loved one for love to retain its character as an absolute axis of reference: hence the lover's constant shame (or pride—which in this case comes to the same thing).

Thus I will have tried in vain to lose myself in objectivity: my passion will have been of no use; the other has returned me—either by herself or through others—to my unjustifiable subjectivity. This observation may provoke total despair and a new attempt to bring about the assimilation of the Other and myself. Its ideal will be the opposite of the one we have just described: instead of planning to absorb the other while retaining her alterity, I will plan to make the other absorb me, and to lose myself in her subjectivity in order to rid myself of my own. This enterprise is translated in concrete terms into the attitude of *masochism*: since the Other is the foundation of my being-for-the-Other, if I could be relieved by the Other of the trouble of making myself exist, I would no longer be anything other than a being-in-itself, founded in its being by a freedom. In this case it is my own subjectivity that I regard as the obstacle to the primordial act through which the Other might found me in my being; it is that, above all, that I need to negate with *my own freedom*. I try therefore to commit myself entirely within my object-being, to refuse to be anything more than an object, to lie restfully within the other; and, as I experience this object-being in shame, I want and I love my shame as a profound sign of my objectivity; and, as the Other apprehends me as an object through *sexual desire*,[7] I want to be desired, and I make myself in shame an object of desire. This attitude would be quite similar to that of love if, rather than seeking to exist for the other as the object that sets a limit to her transcendence, I tried desperately, on the contrary, to make myself be treated as an object among others, as an instrument to be used: here it is a matter of negating my transcendence, and not hers. My project this time will not be that of capturing her freedom but, on the contrary, I wish this freedom to be, and to want itself, radically free. In this way, the more I feel myself surpassed toward other ends, the more I will exult in the abdication of my transcendence. Ultimately, I plan to be nothing more than an *object*, that is, radically an *in-itself*. But insofar as this in-itself will be founded by a freedom that has absorbed my own, my being will become once again its own foundation. Masochism, like sadism, involves an assumption of guilt.[8] I am guilty, in effect, simply by virtue of being an object. I am guilty in relation to myself, since I consent to my absolute alienation, and guilty in relation to the Other, because I provide her with the opportunity to be guilty, i.e., to radically fail my freedom as such. Masochism is an attempt not to fascinate the other through my objectivity but to become fascinated myself by my objectivity-for-the-Other, i.e., to make the Other constitute me as an object in such a way that I grasp my subjectivity non-thetically as a *nothing*, in the presence of the in-itself that I represent in the eyes of the Other. It is characterized by a sort of vertigo: vertigo, not in the face of a precipice made out of rock or earth but in the face of the abyss of the Other's subjectivity.

But masochism in itself is and must be a failure: in order to become fascinated by my me-object, in fact, I would have to be able to actualize an intuitive apprehension of this object as it is *for the other*—which is necessarily impossible. Thus my alienated me, far from allowing me to begin to be fascinated by it, remains necessarily elusive. Well might the masochist crawl on his knees, display himself in ridiculous postures, offer himself to be used as a mere inanimate instrument: it is *for the other* that he will be obscene or merely passive, for the other that he will *submit* to these postures; as far as he is concerned, he is condemned forever to *set them for himself*. It is in and through his transcendence that he positions

---

7 Sartre's note: Cf. the following section.
8 Sartre's note: Ibid.

himself as a being to be transcended; and the more he tries to taste his objectivity, the more he becomes submerged, to the point of anguish, by the consciousness of his. In particular the masochist who pays a woman to whip him is treating her as an instrument and thereby places himself in a relation of transcendence to her. Thus the masochist ends up by treating the other as an object and transcending her toward her own objectivity. Recall, for example, the tribulations of Sacher-Masoch, who, in order to make himself scorned, insulted, reduced to a humiliating position, was constrained to make use of the great love that women felt for him, i.e., to act upon them insofar as they experienced themselves as an object for him. Thus, one way or another, the masochist's objectivity escapes him; and it can even happen—it happens most often—that in seeking to grasp his objectivity he finds the objectivity of the other, thereby liberating his subjectivity, in spite of himself. Masochism is necessarily, therefore, a failure. Nothing in that should surprise us, if we consider that masochism is a "vice" and that vice is, essentially, a love of failure. But this is not the place to describe the distinctive structures of vice. It is enough to point out that masochism is a subject's constant effort to annihilate his subjectivity by getting the other to reassimilate it, and that this endeavor is accompanied by the exhausting and delicious consciousness of failure, to the point where failure itself becomes the subject's main aim.[9]

II. THE SECOND ATTITUDE TOWARD THE OTHER: INDIFFERENCE, DESIRE, HATRED, SADISM

The failure of the first attitude toward the other may provide my opportunity to take up the second. But, in actual fact, neither of these two really comes first: each of them is a fundamental reaction to the original situation of being-for-the-Other. I may be led, therefore, by just that impossibility of my assimilating the other's consciousness via my objecthood   420

9 Sartre's note: At the end of this description, we must categorize at least one form of exhibitionism among the masochistic attitudes—for example, when Rousseau shows the washerwomen "not the obscene object but the ridiculous object." See *Confessions*, Book III. TN: Sartre is referring to a famous incident in Rousseau's *Confessions* (published in France in 1782 and translated into English as Rousseau 2008) in which he displays his backside to some washerwomen.

for her, to turn deliberately toward the other and to *look at* her. In this case, to look at the Other's look is to posit myself in my own freedom and to attempt, from the depths of that freedom, to confront the other's freedom. In this way, the meaning of the conflict I am seeking is to bring to light the struggle of two freedoms confronting each other as freedoms. But this intention is bound to be immediately disappointed because, by the mere fact of affirming myself in my freedom as I confront the Other, I make the other into a transcended-transcendence, i.e., an object. The history of this failure is what we are going to try to retrace now. We know its basic outline: toward the Other who looks at me, I direct in turn my look. But a looking cannot be looked at: as soon as I look toward it, it vanishes, and I can no longer see anything but the eyes. At this moment, the Other becomes a being whom I possess and who recognizes my freedom. It seems that I have achieved my aim, since I possess the being who has the key to my objecthood and I am able to make her experience my freedom in a thousand ways. But in reality everything has collapsed, because the being that remains between my hands is an object-Other. As such, she has lost the key to my object-being, and all she possesses of me is a pure and simple image, which is nothing more than one of the ways she is objectively affected, and which can no longer touch me; and if she experiences the effects of my freedom, if I can act on her being in a thousand ways and transcend her possibilities with all of my possibilities, that is insofar as she is an object in the world and, as such, not in any position to recognize my freedom. My disappointment is entire, since I am trying to appropriate the Other's freedom and I suddenly perceive that I can act on the other only insofar as this freedom has collapsed beneath my gaze. This disappointment will give rise to my subsequent attempts to seek the Other's freedom *through* the object that she is for me, and to find the special strategies through which I might appropriate this freedom, through a total appropriation of the Other's body. We can anticipate that these attempts are necessarily doomed to failure.

But it may also happen that my first reaction to my being-for-the-Other is to "return her gaze."[10] In other words, I can choose myself, as

---

10 TN: ... *"regarder le regard"* ... "Gaze" sounds better in this sentence, which is supposed to be idiomatic. I revert to cognates of "to look" in the following sentence to maintain the centrality of this verb for Sartre.

I arise in the world, as looking back at the looking other, and build my own subjectivity upon the collapse of the other's subjectivity. Let us call this attitude *indifference toward the Other*. We are dealing in this case with *blindness* in relation to others. But the term "blindness" should not lead us astray: I do not submit to this blindness as a state; I am my own blindness in relation to others, and this blindness includes an implicit understanding of my being-for-the-Other, i.e., of the Other's transcendence in her looking. Only this understanding is what I myself decide to conceal. I practice therefore a sort of *de facto* solipsism; other people are figures that pass in the street, those magical objects that are liable to act across a distance, and on which I can act by behaving in particular ways. I scarcely pay attention to them, and I act as if I were alone in the world: I skirt "those people" as I skirt the walls; I avoid them just as I avoid obstacles, so that their object-freedom means no more to me than their "coefficient of adversity"; I do not even imagine that they might look at me. Of course, they have some knowledge of me, but this knowledge does not touch me: it consists merely in modifications in their being that are not passed on from them to me, and that are tainted by what we might call a "suffered subjectivity" or an "object-subjectivity:" in other words, these modifications are the effect of my action on these people; they do not communicate what they are but what I am. These "people" are functions; the ticket inspector is no more than the function of punching tickets; the café waiter is no more than the function of serving customers. On that basis I can make use of them to maximize my interests, if I know their *keys*, and the "watchwords" that can activate their mechanisms: hence the "*moraliste*" psychology we received from seventeenth-century France; hence the treatises of the eighteenth century, Béroalde de Verville's *Le Moyen de Parvenir*, Laclos's *Les Liaisons Dangereuses*, Hérault de Séchelles's *Traité de l'Ambition*, which provide us with a practical knowledge of the other and the art of acting upon him.[11] In this state of blindness, I am unaware of the other's absolute subjectivity, as the foundation of my being-in-itself and, concurrently, of my being-for-the-other—and especially my "body

421

---

11 TN: The titles of the books Sartre lists here are translated into English as follows: *The Way to Succeed*; *Dangerous Liaisons*; *Theory of Ambition*. Sartre gets the last title slightly wrong in French: it should be *Théorie d'Ambition*. Although only Laclos's book (translated into English as Laclos 1995) is still well-known today, all of these eighteenth-century works were influential in France.

for the other." In one sense, I am reassured: I "have a nerve" or, in other words, I am not remotely conscious of the fact that the other's look might freeze my possibilities and my body; the state that I am in is the opposite of the state we know as "timidity." I am at ease, and not an embarrassment to myself, because I am not *outside*, and I do not feel myself to be alienated. This state of blindness can continue for a long time, if it suits my fundamental bad faith; it can extend, with interruptions, over several years, over a whole lifetime: some men die without—apart from some brief and terrifying moments of illumination—ever suspecting what the *other* is. But even someone completely immersed in this state would not cease to feel its insufficiency. And, as with all bad faith, that insufficiency provides a motivation to come out of it, because my blindness in relation to the other obliterates at the same time any lived apprehension of my *objectivity*. However, the other as freedom and my objectivity as an alienated-me are *there*, unnoticed—not in any thematic form but given in my very understanding of the world and of my being in the world. The ticket inspector, even if he is seen as a mere function, directs me in his very function toward my being-outside, even though this being-outside is neither grasped nor able to be grasped. This explains my constant feeling of unease, of something missing. The fact is that my fundamental project in relation to the Other—whichever attitude I take up—is two-fold: on the one hand I protect myself against the danger to which I am exposed by my being-outside-in-the-Other's-freedom, and on the other hand I make use of the Other in order at last to totalize the detotalized totality that I am, to close the incomplete circle, and finally to make of myself my own foundation. Now, on the one hand I am thrown back, by the disappearance of the Other as a look, upon my unjustifiable subjectivity, and my being is reduced to that constant pursued-pursuit of an elusive being in-itself-for-itself; without the other I am able to grasp, laid bare, the terrible necessity allotted to me of being free, i.e., the fact that I cannot hand over to anyone else the task of making myself be, even though I did not choose to be or to be *born*. But, on the other hand, although my *blindness* in relation to the other seems to relieve me of the fear of being in danger from the other's freedom, it nonetheless incorporates an implicit understanding of that freedom. Therefore, in that very moment in which I can believe myself to be an absolute and unique subjectivity, it positions me at the highest level of objectivity,

422

since I am seen without even being able to experience my being seen or able, through this ordeal, to protect myself against my "being-seen." I am possessed without being able to confront my possessor. In the direct experience of the Other who looks, I can defend myself as I experience the other, and it remains possible for me to transform the other into an object. But if the other is an object for me *while she looks at me*, then I am in danger without knowing it. In this way my *blindness* is disquieting because it is accompanied by my consciousness of an elusive "roving eye" that threatens to alienate me without my knowing it. This uneasiness will induce a new attempt on my part to seize the Other's freedom. But that will mean that I turn back on the Other-object that shadows me, and try to use it as an instrument to reach its freedom. Only, just because I approach the "Other" as an *object*, I cannot require her to account for her transcendence, and furthermore, as I myself am adopting the perspective of the Other's objectification, I cannot even conceive of what it is that I wish to appropriate. Thus my attitude toward this object I am considering is irritating and contradictory: not only can I not get what I want from it but, in addition, this quest makes the very knowledge of what I want evaporate. I undertake a desperate search for the other's freedom and, along my way, I *find myself committed* in a search whose meaning has been lost; all my efforts to restore to the search its meaning only deprive me of more of it and arouse my shock and unease—just as when I try to recover the memory of a dream and the memory melts between my fingers, leaving me with a vague and irritating impression of a state of absolute knowledge without any object, or just as when I try to spell out the content of an incorrect recollection, and this explication itself makes it collapse into translucency.

My original attempt to take hold of the other's free subjectivity through her objectivity-for-me is *sexual desire*. It might seem surprising to see, cited   423
in the context of the primary attitudes that merely demonstrate our basic way of accomplishing our being-for-the-Other, a phenomenon that is usually classified as a "psycho-physiological reaction." In fact, for most psychologists, desire, as a conscious datum, is closely correlated with the nature of our sexual organs, and it is only in conjunction with a thorough study of these that we will be able to understand it. But as the details of the differentiated bodily structures (mammalian, viviparous, etc.) and, thereafter, the specific structure of the sex (uterus, tubes, ovaries, etc.)

are absolutely contingent, and have no place whatsoever in an ontology of "consciousness" or "*Dasein*," the same seems to apply to sexual desire. Just as our sexual organs are a contingent and particular datum about our body, so the desire that corresponds to them should be seen as a contingent modality of our psychological life, which means that the only way to describe it will be within an empirical psychology founded on biology. This shows up in the name—"*sexual instinct*"—that we use to refer to desire and all the psychological structures to do with it. This term—"instinct"— is in fact always used to describe contingent formations of psychological life that have the twofold character of being coextensive with the entire duration of that life (or which, in any case, are not owed to our "history") and of not being able to be deduced from the psyche's essence itself. That is why the existentialist philosophies have not felt obliged to concern themselves with sexuality. Heidegger, especially, doesn't make the slightest reference to it in his existential analytic, with the result that his "*Dasein*" strikes us as sexless. And of course it is possible to take the view that the specification of "human reality" as "masculine" or "feminine" is a contingent matter; of course we can say that the problem of sexual differentiation has nothing to do with that of Existence (Existenz), since a man "exists" no more and no less than a woman.

These points are not absolutely convincing. We can agree, if need be, that sexual difference belongs in the domain of facticity. But must that imply that the "for-itself" is sexual "by accident," simply through the contingency of its having *that* kind of body? Can we suppose that the vast business of sexual life is surplus to the human condition? Yet at first sight it seems that desire and its opposite—sexual horror—are fundamental structures of our being-for-the-Other. Obviously, if sexuality originates in being *sexed* as a physiological and contingent determination of man, it will not be crucial to the being of our for-the-Other. But are we not entitled to ask whether this problem might be of the same kind as the one we encountered in connection with sensation and the sensory organs? We are told that man is a sexual being because he possesses a sexual organ. And what if the opposite were true? What if the sexual organ were merely the instrument, and more like an *image*, of a fundamental sexuality? And what if man only possesses a sexual organ because he is originally and fundamentally a sexual being, as a being who exists in the world in relationship to other men? Infantile sexuality precedes the physiological maturation of the sexual organs; eunuchs do not, as such, cease to feel desire. Nor do many old people. The state of being able to *make use* of a sexual organ, apt to fertilize and to provide pleasure, only represents one phase and aspect of our sexual life. There is a mode of sexuality that is capable of "satisfaction," and the fully formed sexual organ represents and concretizes this possibility. But there are other modes of sexuality that are not satisfied in this way and, if we take these modalities into account, we must acknowledge that sexuality, which appears at birth, only disappears at the moment of death. Moreover, neither penile turgescence nor any other physiological phenomenon (or the mere fact of being conscious of these physiological modifications) will ever be able to explain or to provoke sexual desire—no more than vasoconstriction or pupillary dilation can explain or provoke fear. In both these cases, although the body plays an important role, we will have to consult our being-in-the-world and our being-for-the-Other to gain a sound understanding: what I desire is a human being, not an insect or a mollusk, and I desire her on the basis of her and of my being in situation in the world, and of her being an other for me and my being an *other* for her. The fundamental problem of sexuality can therefore be put like this: is sexuality a contingent accident bound up with our physiological nature, or is it a necessary structure of being-for-itself-for-the-Other? It follows, simply from the fact that the question can be raised in these terms, that it is for ontology to decide. That will be possible only if, precisely, it takes on the task of determining and establishing the meaning of our sexual existence for the other. To be sexed, in effect, means—at the conclusion of our description of the body, undertaken in the last chapter—to exist sexually for an Other who exists sexually for me—with the understanding, of course, that this Other is not necessarily or in the first instance for me—and neither am I for her—a *heterosexual* existent, but only a sexed being in general. Considered from the point of view of the for-itself, this apprehension of the Other's sexuality cannot be seen as a pure disinterested contemplation of his primary or secondary sexual characteristics. The Other is not in the first place sexed for me because I conclude—from the distribution of his hair, the roughness of his hands, the sound of his voice, his strength—that he is of the masculine sex. Those are derivative conclusions that point toward a primary state. The first apprehension of the Other's sexuality, as it is lived and undergone, can only be *desire*: it is

425   in desiring the other (or in discovering that I am incapable of desiring her), or in apprehending her desire for me, that I encounter her sexed-being; and desire reveals my sexed-being and her sexed-being *at the same time*, my body as sex and *her* body. In order to decide the nature and the ontological place of sex, therefore, a study of desire is required. What, then, is desire?

And, in the first place, *what* do we desire?

We should abandon immediately the idea that desire is always a desire for sensual pleasure or a desire to bring some painful state to an end. If we start from this condition of immanence, we cannot explain how a subject might proceed from it to "attach" his desire to an object. No subjectivist, immanence-based theory will be able to explain the fact that it is not merely a state of satisfaction that we desire but *a* woman. So we should define desire in terms of its transcendent object. Still, it would be quite wrong to say that what is desired, in desiring, is our "physical possession" of the desired object, if what we mean by "possessing" the object is making love with it. Of course the sexual act relieves us for a moment from our desire, and it is possible in some cases that it is explicitly stipulated as the outcome that desire wishes to achieve— when, for example, the desire is painful and tiring. But in these cases the desire itself must be conceived of as the object to be "eliminated," and that can happen only by means of a reflective [act of] consciousness. But, by itself, desire is unreflective; as such, it cannot posit itself to itself as an object to be eliminated. Only a rake represents his desire to himself, treats it as an object, stimulates it, dims it down, postpones its satisfaction, etc. But then, we should take note, what has become desirable is the desire. The mistake here arises from our having learned that the sexual act removes desire. In consequence we combine an item of knowledge with the desire itself and, for reasons quite external to the essence of the desire (procreation, the sanctity of motherhood, the exceptional strength of the pleasure caused by ejaculation, the symbolic value of the sexual act), we attach sensual pleasure to it from outside as its normal mode of satisfaction. Thus the average man is unable, by virtue of his conformism and his lazy thinking, to conceive of any end to his desire other than ejaculation. This has enabled us to conceive of desire as an instinct, whose origin and goal are strictly physiological, since—in the case of the man, for example—its cause is erection and its endpoint is ejaculation. But desire on its own does not remotely entail the sexual act; it does not present it as a theme; it does not even make a start on it, as we can see in the case of the desire manifested by very young children, or by adults who do not know the "technical" side of love. Similarly, desire does not desire any particular amorous practice; the diversity of such practices, which vary according to social group, is sufficient proof of this. In general terms, desire is not a desire to do something. "Doing" enters the scene, from elsewhere, later: it combines with desire and requires an apprenticeship; there is a technique to love, with its own ends and means. As desire, therefore, does not posit as its supreme goal its own elimination, or select a particular action as its ultimate end, it is straightforwardly a desire for some transcendent object. We return here to that affective intentionality, discussed in earlier chapters, that Scheler and Husserl have described. But what is the object of desire? Should we say that what is desired, in desire, is a *body*? In one sense this cannot be denied. But we need to be clear. Of course it is the body that troubles us: a glimpsed arm, or a breast, or perhaps a foot. But we have to see that in the first instance we desire an arm, or a breast, only insofar as they are encountered against the ground of the entire body, which is present as an organic totality. As a totality, the body itself may be concealed; it may be that all I see is a naked arm. But it is there, as the basis on which I apprehend the arm as an arm; it is just as present, and just as connected to the arm I can see, as the arabesques in the carpet that are hidden by the legs of the table are present and connected to the arabesques I can see. And my desire does not get this wrong: it is not directed to a collection of physiological elements but to a complete figure or, better still, to a figure in *situation*. Someone's posture, as we will note later, plays an important role in provoking desire. But, along with someone's posture, the immediate surroundings are given and— eventually—the world. But this shows us how far we have traveled from a mere physiological itch: desire posits the world, and the body is desired on the basis of the world, and the beautiful arm on the basis of the body. The procedure here is exactly the same as the one we described in the last chapter, by means of which we apprehend the Other's body on the basis of her situation in the world. And this should not surprise us in the least, since desire is nothing but one of the major ways in which the Other's body can be revealed. But by the same token we do not desire a

426

body as a purely material object: a purely material object is precisely not *in situation*. In this way, the organic totality that is immediately present in desire is desirable only insofar as it reveals not only a life but, in addition, an adapted consciousness. Nonetheless, as we will see, this being-in-situation of the Other disclosed by desire is of an entirely new type. Moreover, the consciousness that we have in view is still only a *property* of the desired object, which means it is no more than the direction in which the objects in the world are flowing away, insofar as this flowing away remains contained and localized within my world, of which it forms a part. Of course it is possible to desire a woman sleeping, but only to the extent that her sleeping appears against the ground of her consciousness. Consciousness always remains, therefore, at the horizon of the desired body: it provides its meaning and its unity. A living body as an organic totality in situation, with consciousness at its horizon: such is the object to which desire is *addressed*. And what does desire want from this object? We cannot establish this until we have answered a preliminary question: *Who* is the one who desires?

427   Without doubt, I *am* the one who desires, and desire is a distinctive mode of my subjectivity. Since its only way of being is as a non-positional consciousness of itself, desire is a mode of consciousness. Nonetheless, we should not think that the only difference between a desiring consciousness and, for example, a cognitive consciousness lies in the nature of its object. When the for-itself chooses itself as desire, it does not indifferently produce a state of desire while remaining itself unaltered—in the way that a cause, in Stoic philosophy, produces its effect. It transports itself to a specific level of existence, which is not the same, for example, as that of a for-itself choosing itself as a metaphysical being. In all cases, as we have seen, consciousness maintains some relationship with its own facticity. But this relationship can vary from one mode of consciousness to another. The facticity of a painful consciousness, for example, is a facticity revealed in the course of a constant flight from it. The facticity of desire is not the same. A man who desires *exists* his body in a particular way and, in so doing, places himself at a particular level of existence. Indeed, everyone can agree that to desire is not simply *to want* something; it is not a clear and translucent *wanting* which aims, through our body, at some specific object. Desire defines itself as a kind of *trouble*. And this expression—"trouble"—can help us to specify its nature: we oppose

troubled water to transparent water, a troubled look to a clear gaze.[12] In its essential characteristics, troubled water remains water; it retains the fluidity of water, but its translucency is "troubled" by an elusive presence within it—everywhere and nowhere—that makes the water appear by itself to become thickened. This can of course be explained in terms of the presence of solid fine particles, suspended within the liquid, but that is the explanation of an *expert*. We first grasp troubled water as altered by the presence of an invisible *something* that fails to make itself distinct and takes the form of pure *de facto* resistance. If we say that a desiring consciousness is *troubled*, it is by analogy with troubled water. To clarify the analogy, we may compare sexual desire with another form of desire, for example with hunger. Hunger, like sexual desire, presupposes a particular bodily state, defined in this case by impoverished blood, increased salivary secretion, contractions of the digestive tract, etc. These various phenomena are described and classified from the Other's perspective. For the for-itself, they take the form of pure facticity. But this facticity *does not compromise* the very nature of the for-itself, because the for-itself immediately flees from it, toward its possibles, i.e., toward a specific state of satisfied-hunger which, as we noted in Part Two, is hunger's in-itself-for-itself. In this way hunger is a pure surpassing of bodily facticity and, to the extent that the for-itself is non-thetically conscious of this facticity, it is immediately conscious of it as a state of facticity it has surpassed. The body is in this case fully *past*, and has been *sur-passed*.[13] Of course, sexual desire exhibits the structure common to all appetites: a bodily state. Another person may notice various physiological modifications (the erection of the penis, swelling of the nipples, modifications in the circulatory system, rise in body temperature, etc.). And this facticity is existed by the desiring consciousness; it is *on its basis*—or, as we might put it, *through it*—that the desired body appears as desirable. Nonetheless, if we

428

---

12 TN: Sartre's exploration of desire through the idea of *trouble* (a relatively literary word in French) cannot be translated here completely successfully. Sartre contrasts "troubled" consciousness with its (normal) translucent state; the analogy with water works in French but not in English because the French phrase *eau trouble* means "cloudy water" or "muddy water," whereas its literal English translation as "troubled water(s)" means "moving water(s)" or "turbulent water(s)." The reader should bear the intended connotation of "trouble" in mind.

13 TN: Sartre's French sentence uses a similar pun: *Le corps est bien ici le passé, le dé-passé.*

limit our description to this, sexual desire will appear to be *crisp* and *clear*, as if it were comparable to the desire to eat and drink. It will be a pure flight from facticity toward other possibles. Now, everyone knows that a huge gulf separates sexual desire from our other appetites. We all know the infamous expression "Making love with a pretty woman when you feel like it is like drinking a glass of iced water when you're thirsty," and we also know that it strikes us as an unsatisfactory, and even scandalous, comparison. The fact is that, when I desire a woman, I am not situated outside that desire: desire *compromises* me; I am complicit with my desire. Or, rather, desire can be summed up in its entirety as a lapse into complicity with the body. We need only consult our own experience: we know that in sexual desire consciousness seems to become "thicker," that we feel as if we are allowing ourselves to be invaded by facticity, that we cease to flee from it and we slide, instead, into a *passive* consent to the desire. At other times it can seem as if consciousness is invaded by facticity even as it seeks to flee it, and becomes opaque to itself. It is like a pasty upheaval of *fact*. The phrases that we use to refer to desire also record this particularity. We say that it *overcomes* you, that it *submerges* you, that it *numbs* you. Can we imagine using the same words to refer to hunger? Do we think of hunger as *submerging* us? With the possible exception of a description of the impact of starvation, that would make no sense. But, on the contrary, even the weakest desire can already submerge us. Unlike hunger, we are not able to hold it at a distance and "think about something else" while we maintain our desire as an indistinct tone, like a sign coming from the body-ground. Rather, *to desire is to consent to desire*. Our weighed-down consciousness swoons, and slides into a state of languor comparable to sleep. Each of us has observed, moreover, the terrifying effects of desire in someone else: a man in a state of desire will suddenly become heavily tranquilized; his staring eyes will appear to be half-shut, and his movements bear the stamp of a heavy and pasty contentment; often he will seem to have fallen asleep. And when we "fight against desire" the object of our resistance is precisely this torpor. If we succeed in our resistance, our desire will, before it disappears, become crisp and clear like hunger, and then we will "wake up" and find ourselves lucid, but with a heavy head and a pounding heart. All these descriptions, of course, miss their mark: what they really show is our way of interpreting desire. They do, however, point to desire's central fact: in desiring, conscious-

429

ness chooses to exist its facticity at another level. It no longer flees its facticity but it attempts to submit to its own contingency, insofar as it apprehends another body—in other words, another contingency—as desirable. In this sense, desire does not merely disclose the Other's body; it reveals my own body as well. And the body is revealed not as an *instrument* or as *a point of view* but in its pure facticity, i.e., as the simple, contingent form of the necessity of my contingency. I *feel* my skin and my muscles and my breath, but I do not feel them in order to transcend them *toward* something—as in the case of emotion or appetite—but as a living and inert *datum*; I do not feel them simply as the supple and unobtrusive instrument of my action on the world but as a *passion* through which I am committed, and in danger, within the world. The for-itself *is not* this contingency, it continues to exist it, but it undergoes the vertigo of its own body or, as we may prefer to say, this vertigo is precisely its way of existing its body. Non-thetic consciousness gives itself up to the body; it *wants to be* its body and to be nothing but body. In desire, the body—instead of being no more than the contingency from which the for-itself flees toward its own possibles—simultaneously becomes the for-itself's most immediate possible: desire is not only a desire for the Other's body; it is, within the unity of a single act, the non-thetically lived pro-ject of sinking into one's body. In this way, the act of fainting may constitute the utmost degree of desire, as the utmost degree of one's consent to one's body. It is in this sense that desire can be said to be one body's desire for another body. It is indeed an appetite *toward* the Other's body, which is lived as the for-itself's vertigo in relation to its own body; and the being who desires is a consciousness *making itself body*.

But if it is true that desire is a consciousness that makes itself body in order to appropriate the Other's body, which is apprehended as an organic totality in situation, with consciousness at its horizon, what does desire mean? In other words: Why does consciousness make itself—or try in vain to make itself—body, and what does it expect from the object of its desire? It will be easy to answer this if we reflect on the fact that, in desire, I make myself flesh *in the presence of the Other in order to appropriate the Other's flesh.* That implies that it is not sufficient merely to take hold of someone's shoulders, or of her side, or to draw her body alongside me: these parts must in addition be grasped by means of that specific instrument, my body, insofar as it thickens my consciousness. In this sense, one might say that it is not just that, in taking hold of these shoulders, my body is a means for touching the shoulders but rather that the Other's shoulders are a means for me to disclose my body as a fascinating revelation of my facticity, i.e., as flesh. Desire, therefore, is the desire to appropriate a body insofar as this appropriation reveals my body to me in the form of flesh. But what I want, when I want to appropriate this body, is to appropriate it *as flesh*. Now, that is not what it is for me in the first instance: the Other's body appears as a synthetic form in actuality; as we have seen, we cannot perceive the Other's body as pure flesh, i.e., as an isolated object whose relations to the other "*thises*" are external. The Other's body is from the outset a body in situation; flesh, on the contrary, appears as *the pure contingency of presence*. Ordinarily it is covered by scarves and clothes, etc.; above all, a person's *movements* cover it from view; nothing presents itself "in its flesh" less than a dancer, even a naked one. Desire is an attempt to strip the body of its movements along with its clothes, and to make it exist as pure flesh; it is an attempt *to incarnate* the Other's body. It is in this sense that a caress is an appropriation of the Other's body: it is obvious that, if a caress is supposed only to skim or to skirt the surface of the body, it can bear no relation to the powerful desire it is supposed to fulfill. A caress, like a glance, remains at the surface; it is not able to *appropriate* someone else. We are familiar with the anticlimax of that well-known phrase "the contact of two epidermises."[14] A caress does not merely want to make *contact*; it appears that only man can reduce it to that, and in doing so he misses its true meaning. In fact a caress is not merely a skimming of the surface: it is an act of *modeling*. In caressing the Other I give birth to her flesh, through my caress, beneath my fingers. A caress is the set of rituals that *incarnates* the Other. But, it might be asked, was she not incarnated already? No: that is my point. The Other's flesh did not exist for me explicitly, since I apprehended the Other's body in situation; neither did it exist for her, since she transcended it toward her possibilities, and toward the object. Out of my caress the Other is born as flesh—for me and for herself. And by "flesh"

14 TN: Sartre is quoting Nicolas Chamfort (1741–1794), one of the eighteenth-century *moralistes*. In his *Maximes et Pensées*, Chamfort famously says: "*Love . . . is nothing but the exchange of two fantasies and the contact of two epidermises.*" A selection of Chamfort's aphorisms is available in translation as Chamfort (1969).

we do not mean a *part* of the body, such as the dermis, the connective tissue or, indeed, the epidermis; nor is it important that the body be "at rest," or drowsy—although its flesh often shows up better that way. But it is in stripping the body of its actions that the caress reveals the flesh, in severing it from the possibilities that surround it: a caress is designed to uncover, beneath the action, the backdrop of inertia—i.e., the pure "being-there"—that supports it. For example, in *taking* and *caressing* another's hand I encounter, beneath the *prehension* that *at first* defines the hand, an expanse of flesh and bone that I can hold; in the same way, my act of looking is a caress when it uncovers—beneath the jump that first presents the dancer's legs—the lunar expanse of her thighs. Thus the caress is not distinct from desire: to caress someone with one's eyes and to desire her are one and the same; *the caress expresses desire, as language expresses thought.* And indeed the caress reveals the Other's flesh as flesh to me *and to the Other.* But it reveals this flesh in a quite specific way: we might reveal someone's inertia to her, and her passivity as a transcended-transcendence,   431 by grabbing hold of her—but that is not how a caress works. In caressing the Other, my body is not a synthetic form in actuality, caressing her; rather, it is my fleshed body that gives birth to the Other's flesh. The point of the caress is to give rise, through the pleasure it occasions, to the Other's body; she is born, to herself and to me, as a passivity that has been *touched,* to the extent that my body makes itself flesh in order to touch her with its own passivity, i.e., by letting itself be caressed alongside her, rather than by caressing her. That is why the movements of love have a languor that appears almost studied: rather than *taking hold* of a part of the other's body, one *carries* one's own body to place it against the other's body; rather than pushing or touching in any active sense, one *sets alongside.* It seems as if I *carry* my own arm like an inanimate object and I *set it down* by the side of the woman I desire, and as if the fingers that I run across her arm are inert at the end of my hand. Thus the revelation of the Other's flesh takes place through my own flesh; in my desire and in the caress that expresses it, I incarnate myself in order to actualize the Other's incarnation, and my caress, in *actualizing* the Other's incarnation, discloses my own incarnation to me; in other words I make myself flesh in order to lead the other to actualize her own flesh *for herself* and for me, and my caresses give birth to my flesh for me insofar as it is, for the Other, *flesh that gives birth to her as flesh;* I get her to taste my flesh with her flesh, in order to oblige her to feel herself to be flesh. And, in this way, possession appears in its true form as a *twofold reciprocal incarnation*. Thus desire involves an attempt to incarnate consciousness (which is what we referred to earlier as a "thickening" of consciousness, a *troubled* consciousness, etc.), in order to actualize the other's incarnation.

We still have to determine desire's *motive* or, alternatively, its meaning. That is because (as anyone who has followed the descriptions we have offered so far will long since have understood) to be, for the for-itself, is to choose its way of being, against the ground of the absolute contingency of its being-there. Desire does not therefore *happen* to consciousness, in the way that heat *happens* to the piece of iron that I bring closer to the flame. Consciousness chooses itself as desire. Of course, for that to happen there will normally be a motive: I do not desire just anyone, at any time. But we have shown, in Part One of this book, that a motive arises on the basis of the past, and that consciousness, by *turning back* toward it, bestows on it its weight and value. There is no difference, therefore, between our choice of the motive for our desire and the meaning of a consciousness that—arising in the three ecstatic dimensions of duration—makes itself desirous. Desire, like emotion, or the attitude of imagination or—quite generally—all the for-itself's attitudes, has a meaning that constitutes it and surpasses it. The description that we have just undertaken would lack all interest if it did not lead us next to ask the question: *Why does consciousness nihilate itself in the form of desire?*

432   A couple of preliminary observations will help us to answer this question. In the first place, we should note that the desiring consciousness does not desire its object against the ground of an unchanged world. In other words, the aim here is not to bring the desirable object into view as a particular *this*, against the ground of a world whose instrumental relations with us and whose organization in terms of structures of equipment remain the same. Desire works like emotion: we have observed elsewhere[15] that emotion does not apprehend the object by which it is moved in an unchanged world but rather that it corresponds to a global modification of consciousness and of its relations with the world, and

---

15 Sartre's note: See my *Esquisse d'une Théorie Phénoménologique des Émotions*. TN: This text (whose French title Sartre gets slightly wrong here) is translated into English as Sartre (1994).

manifests itself therefore as a radical alteration of the world. Similarly, desire is a radical modification of the for-itself, since the for-itself moves to a new plane of being to make itself be, and sets itself to exist its body in a different way, to become thickened with its own facticity. For the for-itself, correlatively, the world must also come to being in a new way: desire has its own world. Indeed, if my body is no longer felt as the instrument of which no other instrument can make use—i.e., as the synthetic organization of my actions in the world—if it is lived as flesh, I will apprehend the objects in the world as references back to my flesh. In other words, I make myself passive in relation to them, and they are revealed within that perspective, through this passivity and in it (as the passivity is the body, and the body does not cease to be a point of view). In this case it is the transcendent collection of objects that reveals my incarnation to me. A contact is a *caress*, which means my perception of the object does not *use* it, and surpass the present in pursuit of an end; rather, within the attitude of desire, to perceive an object is to let myself be caressed by it. I hereby become more sensitive to the object's matter (lumpy, smooth, warm, greasy, rough, etc.) than to its form and to its instrumentality and, in my desiring perception, I uncover something like the objects' *flesh*. My shirt rubs against my skin and I feel it: this shirt, which is ordinarily the most distant of objects, becomes immediately sensible to me; the warmth of the air, the blowing of the wind, the rays of the sun, etc.—everything is in some way present to me, as if placed right up against me, and revealing my flesh through its flesh. From this point of view desire is not only the thickening of a consciousness with its own facticity: it is, correlatively, the body's coming to be bogged down in the world, and the world becoming bog-like; consciousness becomes stuck in a body that becomes stuck in the world.[16] Here, therefore, the proposed ideal is that of being-in-the-midst-of-the-world; the for-itself tries to actualize its being-in-the-midst-of-the-world as the ultimate project of its being-in-the-world; that is why sexual bliss is so frequently associated with death—which is also a metamorphosis, a state of

433

16 Sartre's note: Of course, here, as elsewhere, we need to allow for things' coefficient of adversity. Objects do not only "caress" us. But, within the general perspective of the caress, they can also strike us as an "anti-caress," i.e., with a quality of harshness, cacophony, or hardness that—just because we are in a state of desire—we experience as intolerable.

"being-in-the-midst-of the-world." We are familiar, for example, with the theme of the "false death" so thoroughly explored in all literatures.[17]

But desire is not first and foremost a relation to the world. The world is only the ground against which my relations with the other explicitly appear. Usually it is the occasion of the other's *presence* that discloses the world as a world of desire. Derivatively, it may take on that appearance when some *particular* other is absent—or even when there is a *complete* absence of *any* other person. But we have already noted that absence is a concrete existential relationship between the other and myself that appears against the original ground of my being-for-the-Other. It is of course possible that, encountering my body when I am on my own, I suddenly feel myself to be flesh, to be "suffocated" by desire, and to apprehend the world as "suffocating." But this solitary desire is a call for someone else, or for the presence of an undifferentiated other. I desire to reveal myself as flesh through and for another flesh. I try to cast a spell over the other, and to make him appear; and the world of desire points, in the empty space that is left for him, to the *other* I am calling for. Thus desire is in no way a physiological accident, a pruritus in the flesh that makes us fix randomly on the other's flesh. Rather, and quite to the contrary, in order for *there to be* my flesh and the other's flesh, my consciousness must antecedently have flowed into the mold of desire. This desire is a primitive mode of my relations with the Other, constituting the other as desirable flesh against the ground of a world of desire.

We are now in a position to elucidate desire's innermost meaning. My primary reaction to the Other's look is, in effect, to constitute myself as looking. But if I look at her look, in order to defend myself against the Other's freedom and to transcend it as a freedom, the Other's freedom and her look will both collapse: I see her *eyes*; I see a being-in-the-midst-of-the-world. Henceforth, the other will escape me: I wanted to act upon her freedom, to appropriate it, or, at the least, to make this freedom recognize mine, but

---

17 TN: ... *le thème de la "fausse morte"* ... The phrase *la fausse morte* means "false (or "fake") death," but, as *morte* is in the feminine, the reference here is to a falsely dead *female*. Sartre probably has in mind the poem by Paul Valéry whose title is that very phrase: "La Fausse Morte." The phrase *petite mort* is also used in French as a euphemism for "orgasm," and indeed Valéry's poem describes a woman who appears dead but is actually in a state of postcoital stupor. An English translation is included in Valéry (1950).

now it has died, and it has absolutely ceased to be in the world where I meet the other-object, for it is characterized by its transcending of the world. Of course I can take hold of the other, grab her, or push her; I can—if I have the power—force her to perform certain acts or to utter certain words, but it is as if I were trying to take hold of a man who is running away, leaving me with his coat in my hands. What I possess is the man's coat, his remains; I will only ever take hold of a body, a psychological object in the midst of the world, and, although all of this body's actions can be interpreted in terms of freedom, I have entirely lost the key to this interpretation: I can act only on a facticity. If I retain my *knowledge* of the Other's transcendent freedom, 434 this knowledge is a useless annoyance, pointing to a reality that is necessarily beyond my reach, and revealing that at every moment I am *missing* it, that in everything I do I am "blindfolded," and that my action acquires its meaning elsewhere—in a sphere of existence from which I am necessarily excluded. I can make someone cry for mercy or beg forgiveness, but I will remain forever ignorant of the meaning of this submission for, and in, the other's freedom. At the same time, moreover, my *knowledge* deteriorates: I lose a clear understanding of the state of *being-looked-at* which is, as we know, the only way in which I can experience the other's freedom. Thus I have forgotten even the meaning of the enterprise in which I am committed. Confronted with this other—whom I see and can touch—I am lost, and I no longer know what to do with her. I may just about retain a vague memory of a certain *beyond* in relation to the thing I can see and touch, a "beyond" that is—I know—exactly what I want to appropriate. At this point, I *make myself desire*. Desire is an action whose aim is to cast a spell. Its point, since I am able to grasp the other only in her objective facticity, is to mire her freedom within that facticity: it must be made to "set" within it—as we might say of a custard that it has "set"—so that the Other's for-itself reaches to the surface of her body, so that it extends throughout her body and so that, in touching this body, I can at last touch the other's free subjectivity. That is the true meaning of the word "possession." Of course, I want to *possess* the other's body, but I want to possess it insofar as it has itself become "possessed," i.e., insofar as the other's consciousness has become identified with it. Such is desire's impossible ideal: to possess the other's transcendence purely as a transcendence and yet *as a body*; to reduce the other to her mere facticity, because then she exists in the midst of my world, but to make it happen that this facticity constantly appresents her nihilating transcendence.

But the truth is that it is not possible for the other's facticity (her pure being-there) to be given to my intuition without a thoroughgoing modification of my own-being. As long as I surpass my personal facticity toward my own possibilities, as long as I exist my facticity through a movement of flight, I also surpass the other's facticity—just as, moreover, I surpass the pure *existence of things*. In my very arising, I make them emerge in their instrumental existence; their pure and simple being is concealed by the complexity of the referential relations by which their *workability* and their equipmentality are constituted. In picking up a penholder, I already surpass my being-there toward the possibility of writing, but I am also surpassing the penholder as a mere existent toward its potential and, again, I surpass that potential toward the existence of various items in the future, i.e., the "words to be written down" and, eventually, the "book to be written." That is why the being of existents is usually concealed by their function. The same goes for the being of the other: if the other appears to me as a servant, an employee, a bureaucrat, or merely as the passerby whom I must avoid, or as that voice speaking in the neighboring room that I am trying to *understand* (or, on the contrary, that I want to forget about, because it is "stopping me from sleeping"), it is not only her extraworldly transcendence that escapes me but also her "being-there" as a pure contingent existence in the midst of the world. That is because, precisely insofar as I treat her as a servant or an office worker, I surpass her toward her potentialities (a transcended-transcendence, dead-possibilities), through the very project through which I surpass and nihilate my own facticity. If I want to get back to her simple presence and to taste it *as presence*, I will have to try to reduce myself to my own presence. Any surpassing of my being-there is, in effect, a surpassing of the other's being-there. And if the world surrounds me as the situation that I surpass toward myself, I will apprehend the other on the basis of *her situation*, i.e., already as a center of reference. And of course the desired other must also be apprehended in situation: what I desire is a woman *in the world*, standing *near a table*, naked on a bed, or seated *at my side*. But if desire flows back from the situation toward the being who is in situation, it does so in order to dissolve the situation and to erode the Other's relations within the world: the movement of desire that goes from the "surroundings" to the desired person isolates her; it destroys those surroundings and encircles the person in question, in order to make her pure facticity stand out. But for that to be possible, each of the objects that refers back to the person must, precisely, and at the same time as it points her out to me, become frozen in its pure contingency; and in consequence this movement back toward the Other's being is a movement back toward myself, as a pure being-there. I destroy my possibilities in order to destroy the world's possibilities, and to constitute the world as the "world of desire"—i.e., as a world that has lost its structure, having lost its meaning, and in which things stick out like fragments of pure matter, like brute qualities. And as the for-itself is choice, that is possible only if I pro-ject myself toward a new possibility: that of being "sucked into my body like ink into blotting paper," of being summed up in my pure being-there. This project, insofar as it is not merely conceived and presented thematically but lived—i.e., insofar as its actualization cannot be distinguished from its conception—is my being troubled.[18] In point of fact, it would be a mistake to take the preceding descriptions to imply that I deliberately put myself into a state of trouble, with the intention of rediscovering the other's pure "being-there." Desire is a lived pro-ject that does not require any preliminary deliberation; rather, it carries its meaning and its interpretation within itself. The moment I throw myself in the direction of another's facticity, the moment I want to set aside her actions and her duties in order to reach her in her flesh, I incarnate myself, because I can neither want nor conceive of the other's incarnation other than through and in my own incarnation; and even an empty sketch of desire (as when we absent-mindedly "undress a woman with our eyes") is an outline of my troubled state—for I can desire only with my arousal; it is only by undressing myself that I can undress the other, and I can sketch and outline the other only by sketching my own flesh.

But my incarnation is not only the precondition for the other's appearance as flesh *before my eyes*. My aim is to incarnate her *in her own eyes* as flesh, so I must drag her on to the terrain of pure facticity; she must be summed up for herself as being no more than flesh. Thus might I be reassured

436

18 TN: As before, the term *trouble* that Sartre uses for the state of sexual arousal does not always translate well as "trouble" in English but, as Sartre clearly intends to be describing the same phenomenon throughout, I am sticking to the term as a reminder (and only occasionally using or adding "arousal" to keep the sexual meaning in view).

about the constant possibilities of a transcendence able at any instant to transcend me entirely: *it will be no more than this*; it will remain contained within the limits of an object; by virtue of this very fact, moreover, I will be able to touch this transcendence, to feel it, to possess it. The other meaning therefore of my incarnation—i.e., of my troubled state—is that it speaks a spellbinding language. I make myself flesh in order to fascinate the Other through my nudity and to provoke in her the desire for my flesh, just because this desire will be—in the other—nothing but an incarnation that resembles my own. In this way desire is an invitation to desire. The only way to the Other's flesh is through my flesh, and I place my flesh against her flesh in order to awaken it to the meaning of flesh. In fact, when I caress the other, when I slowly slide my inert hand against her side, I make her feel my flesh and she can only do that, herself, by becoming inert; the tingle of pleasure that runs through her in that moment is, precisely, the awakening of her consciousness of flesh. If I stretch out my hand, move it away, or clench it, I return to my body in actuality—but at the same time I make my hand as flesh vanish. In allowing my hand gradually to flow down her body, turning it into a gentle brushing movement, almost without meaning—a pure existence, a pure instance of matter, something a bit like silk, a bit like satin, slightly gritty—I give up being the person who determines landmarks and unfolds distances, and I become pure mucus. At this moment, the communion of desire is achieved: each consciousness, by becoming incarnate, has brought about the other's incarnation; each arousal has given birth to the other's arousal and thereby increased its own. In each caress I can feel my own flesh, and the other's flesh through my own flesh, and I am conscious that this flesh that I feel and appropriate through my flesh is flesh that is felt-by-the-other. And it is no coincidence that desire—even though it aims at an entire body—succeeds especially in making contact with it through the areas of flesh that are the least differentiated, the most crudely supplied with nerves, the least capable of spontaneous movement: through the breasts, buttocks, thighs, and belly, which are like an image of pure facticity. It is for that reason, also, that the truest caress consists in the contact made by the most carnal parts of the two bodies, the contact of stomachs and chests: after all, a caressing hand is an agile thing, too close to being a honed tool, but the opening up of one flesh against the other, of one flesh through the other, is desire's true aim.

Nevertheless, desire is itself doomed to failure. We have seen that the act of coitus, which usually brings desire to an end, is not in fact its distinctive aim. There are of course several elements within our sexual structure, and especially the erections of the penis and the clitoris, which necessarily give expression to the nature of desire. Indeed an erection is nothing but an affirmation of flesh through flesh. It is therefore absolutely necessary that it should not be *voluntary*, in other words, such that we could employ it as an instrument—but rather that it is, on the contrary, an instance of a biological and autonomous phenomenon whose autonomous and involuntary expansion accompanies and signifies the movement through which consciousness becomes bogged down within the body. What needs to be understood is that no organ that is agile, prehensile, and connected to striated muscles could ever be a sexual organ, or someone's *sex*;[19] if sex were to appear in the form of an organ, it could not be anything more than a manifestation of vegetative life. But contingency comes back in once we consider that, indeed, *there are* sexes—and sexes such as *these*. In particular, the male's penetration of the female—even though it is consistent with the radical incarnation that desire wishes to be (and we should take note, indeed, of the organic passivity of the sexual organ in coitus: it is the entire body that comes forward and moves back, which *carries* the sexual organ forward or withdraws it; it is our hands that help with the intromission of the penis; the penis itself appears as an instrument to be handled, an instrument that one pushes forward, pulls back, and uses, and in the same way the opening up and lubrication of the vagina cannot be voluntarily brought about)—remains a perfectly contingent modality of our sexual life. And another purely contingent element is sexual pleasure, in the proper sense of the term. The fact is that the state in which consciousness becomes bogged down within the body normally reaches its conclusion—i.e., a particular kind of ecstasy, in which consciousness is no longer anything but consciousness (of the) body—and, in consequence, becomes a reflective consciousness

---

19 TN: ... *un organe sexuel, un sexe* ... Sartre may intend to exploit different meanings of the French term *le sexe* here, showing how it can be used as a synonym for "sexual organ" as well as to mean the characteristic of being sexed (i.e., as male or female). His argument in the text is that we ought not to regard the possession of sexual organs as fundamental to our sexuality.

BEING-FOR-THE-OTHER

of embodiment.[20] Indeed our pleasure—like a pain that is too intense—motivates the appearance of reflective consciousness, which pays "*attention to the pleasure.*" Only the pleasure is the death of desire, and its failure. It is the death of desire because it is not only its completion but its limit and its end. Moreover, this is only an organic contingency: it *so happens* that our incarnation is manifested in an erection, and that the erection ends with ejaculation. But, in addition, pleasure opens the floodgate to desire because it motivates the appearance of a reflective consciousness of pleasure, whose object becomes the orgasm, i.e., an attention to the incarnation of the for-itself that is now reflected on and, by the same token, a forgetting of the other's incarnation. This no longer belongs in the domain of contingency. Of course, the fact that the move into fascinated reflection is occasioned by pleasure, by that specific mode of incarnation, remains contingent—and there are many cases where the transition into reflection occurs without the intervention of desire—but in desire, insofar as it is an attempt at incarnation, there is the constant danger that consciousness, in becoming incarnate, will lose sight of the other's incarnation, and that its own incarnation will absorb it to the extent of becoming its ultimate aim. In this case, the pleasure of caressing is transformed into the pleasure at being caressed, and what the for-itself demands is to feel its body opening out within it, even to the point of nausea. With that, the contact is broken and desire fails in its aim. It may even happen quite often that this failure on the part of desire motivates a move to masochism, which is to say that consciousness, apprehending itself in its facticity, demands to be apprehended and transcended by the other's consciousness as a body-for-the-Other through the other. In this case the object-other collapses and the other-look appears, and my consciousness becomes a consciousness swooning in its flesh, before the other's gaze.

But, conversely, desire lies at the origin of its own failure insofar as it is the desire *to take* and *to appropriate*. It is not enough, it turns out, that my own troubled state should give rise to the other's incarnation: desire is the desire to appropriate that incarnate consciousness. It is naturally

---

20 TN: Sartre's brackets around "of the" is meant to have the same effect as his earlier bracketing in "consciousness (of) self." As before, the idea is that ordinarily the body, in our consciousness (of the) body, is not an object for consciousness; with the climax of sexual pleasure, Sartre is claiming, the body *does* become an object of reflection.

prolonged, therefore, not by means of *caresses* but by prehensile and penetrative acts. The caress had as its only aim to impregnate the other's body with consciousness and freedom. But now that the body is saturated, I must take it, grab hold of it, enter inside it. But simply by virtue of my present attempts to grasp, to drag, to take hold, and to bite, my body ceases to be flesh; it returns to being the synthetic instrument that I am; and, with that, the *other* ceases to be an incarnation: she goes back to being an instrument in the midst of the world that I apprehend on the basis of her situation. Her consciousness—which had risen to the surface of her flesh, and which I was trying to *taste*[21] with my flesh—vanishes as I look at her: it remains no more than an *object*, containing object-images inside it. At the same time my troubled state disappears: this does not mean I have stopped desiring but that the desire has lost its materiality, and has become *abstract*; it is a desire to handle and to take, and I persist in taking—but my very persistence makes my incarnation disappear. Now I am surpassing, once again, my body toward my own possibilities (the possibility, here, of taking) and, in the same way, the Other's body, surpassed toward its potentialities, descends from the level of flesh to that of a pure object. It is implicit in this situation that the reciprocal incarnation—which was, precisely, desire's distinctive goal—will be broken. The other may remain troubled; she may remain as flesh *for herself*; and that I can understand; but it is a flesh that I can no longer apprehend through my own flesh, a flesh that is no longer anything but a *property* of the object-other, and not the incarnation of an other-consciousness. Thus I am a *body* (a synthetic totality in situation), confronting a *flesh*. I find myself more or less in just the situation that I was trying, through my desire, to leave, i.e., I am trying to make use of the Other-object to make her account for her transcendence and, precisely because she is *entirely* an object, her transcendence eludes me *entirely*. I have even, once again, lost any clear understanding of what I was seeking, and yet I am committed to seeking it. I take, and I encounter myself in the act of taking, but what I have in my hands is *other* than the thing I wanted to take; I feel this and I suffer through it, but I am incapable of saying what it was that I wanted

439

---

21 Sartre's note: Doña Prouhèze, *Le Soulier de Satin*, 2nd day: "He will not know the taste that I have." TN: This play (written by Paul Claudel in 1929) is translated into English as *The Satin Slipper* (Claudel 1931).

to take because, along with my troubled arousal, even my understanding of my desire escapes me; I am like someone who, waking from his sleep, finds himself clenching his hands on the edge of his bed—without being able to remember the nightmare that induced his action. This is the situation that lies at the origin of *sadism*.

Sadism implies passion, aridity, and persistence. It is persistent because it is a state of a for-itself that grasps itself as committed to something without understanding *what* it is committed to, and which persists in its commitment without having either any clear awareness of the goal it has adopted, or any precise recollection of the value placed on this commitment. It is arid because it appears when desire has been emptied of its trouble. The sadist has rediscovered his body as a synthetic totality, and a center of action; he has returned to the constant flight from his own facticity; confronted with the other, he experiences himself as a pure transcendence, and is horrified *for his sake* by his troubled state, which he considers to be humiliating; it is also possible that he is quite simply unable to *actualize* it in himself. To the extent that he coldly persists, that he is persistent and arid at the same time, the sadist is impassioned. His goal, like that of desire, is to apprehend and enslave the other not only as an object-other but as a pure transcendence made incarnate. But, with sadism, the emphasis is placed on the instrumental appropriation of the incarnate-other. In fact the sadistic "moment," within sexuality, is when the for-itself that has become incarnate surpasses its incarnation in order to appropriate the other's incarnation. Sadism is, therefore, both a refusal to become incarnate, and the flight from any kind of facticity—and at the same time an attempt to take hold of the other's facticity. But, as the sadist cannot, and does not want to, actualize the other's incarnation through his own incarnation and as, by virtue of this very fact, his only recourse is that of treating the other as an implement-object, he tries to use the other's body as a tool to actualize the other's incarnate existence. Sadism is an endeavor to make the Other incarnate through violence, and this "forced" incarnation must already involve the appropriation and the use of the other. The sadist seeks—as in desire—to strip the other of the actions that conceal her. He tries to uncover the flesh beneath the action. But whereas, in desire, the for-itself loses itself in its own flesh in order to disclose to the Other that she is flesh, the sadist rejects his own flesh, while at the same time arranging his instruments in order to force the

other to reveal her flesh. The object of sadism is immediate appropria-   440
tion. But the sadist's position is precarious, for he does not take pleasure
only in the other's flesh but, in his direct contact with that flesh, also
in his own non-incarnation. He *wants* the non-reciprocity of the sexual
relations; he takes pleasure in being an appropriative and free power
confronted with a freedom made captive by flesh. That is why the sadist
wants to presentify flesh *in another way* to the Other's consciousness: he
wants to presentify it by treating the Other as an instrument; he presentifies it through pain. In pain, facticity effectively takes consciousness
over and eventually reflective consciousness becomes fascinated by the
facticity of unreflected consciousness. So incarnation is indeed possible
through pain. But at the same time the pain is obtained *through instruments*;
the body of the supplicant for-itself has become no more than an instrument for producing pain. In this way the for-itself can from the outset
be under the illusion of having taken instrumental hold of the other's
freedom—that is, of having decanted that freedom into flesh without
ceasing to be the one who *provokes*, who grabs hold, who grasps, etc.

As for the type of incarnation that sadism would like to actualize, it
corresponds exactly to what we describe as "*obscenity*." The obscene is
a *species* of being-for-the-Other that belongs to the *genus* of the ungraceful. But not all ungraceful things are obscene. When a body appears
with *grace*, it shows itself as a psyche in situation. Above all, it reveals its
transcendence, as a transcended-transcendence; it is in actuality, and it
is to be understood on the basis of the situation and the pursued end.
Each movement, therefore, is grasped within a perceptual process that
moves from the future to the present. Accordingly, a graceful action
has on the one hand the precision of a well-adapted machine and, on
the other, the supreme unpredictability of the psyche, since—as we
have seen—the psyche is, for the Other, the *unpredictable object*. A graceful action is therefore perfectly comprehensible insofar as we consider
the element within it that has *flowed*.[22] Better still, this flowing part of
the action is underpinned by a sort of aesthetic necessity implied by its

22 TN: ... *ce qui, en lui, est* écoulé. Sartre's italicized use of *écouler* in this context suggests
Bergson's philosophy. This connection is made explicit a few lines later by Sartre, in
the reference to Bergson's account of gracefulness. The idea of the mechanical, later in
the paragraph, is also influenced by Bergson.

perfect adaptation. At the same time, the future goal illuminates the act in its totality; but the whole of the future dimension of the act remains unpredictable, even though one has the sense—from the body itself as it is in actuality—that as soon as it has flowed by it will appear as necessary and well adapted. This moving image of necessity and freedom (as a property of the object-other) is what constitutes, in the true sense of the word, grace. Bergson gave us a good description of it. The graceful body is an instrument that manifests freedom. The graceful action, insofar as it reveals the body as a precision tool, provides it at each moment with its justification for existing: the hand is for taking hold and exhibits in the first instance its being-in-order-to-take-hold. Insofar as it is apprehended on the basis of a situation that requires prehension, it appears itself to be required in its being, to be called for. And insofar as it manifests its freedom through the unpredictability of its movement, its being appears to originate within it: it is as if it produces itself in response to the justifying call made by the situation. Grace figures therefore as the objective image of a being that could be its own foundation in order to . . . Grace, therefore, clothes and conceals facticity: the nakedness of the flesh is present in its entirety, but it cannot be seen. It follows that the most extreme act of teasing, and grace's hardest challenge, is to exhibit one's body unveiled, without clothing, veiled by nothing other than grace itself. The most gracious body is the naked body, whose acts surround it with an invisible garment while robbing it of its flesh, even though its flesh is wholly present to the spectators' view. The moment when the ungracious appears, on the contrary, is when an element of grace is hindered in its movement. The movement may become mechanical. In this case, the body remains part of a whole that justifies it, but in the capacity of a mere instrument; its transcended-transcendence disappears, and with it the situation (as it laterally over-determines the implement-objects of my universe) also vanishes. The actions may also be jerky and violent; in this case, what collapses is the adaptation to the situation. The situation remains, but it is as if a gap, a hiatus, has slipped between it and the other in situation. In this case, the other remains free, but this freedom is grasped only in the form of pure unpredictability and it resembles the clinamen of Epicurean atoms[23] or—in a

441

23 TN: Clinamen is the Latin word coined by Lucretius in his defense of the Epicurean doctrine of atomism. It refers to the allegedly unpredictable "swerve" of atoms, by which free will is secured.

word—indeterminism. At the same time, the action's end continues to be posited, and we continue to perceive the other's movement on the basis of the future. But the consequence of the maladaptation is that the perceptual interpretation in terms of the future is always either too wide or too narrow: it is a *more or less* interpretation. In consequence, the justification of the other's movement and being is imperfectly achieved: in the end, a clumsy person is unjustifiable; all his facticity—which was committed within, and absorbed by, the situation—turns back on him. A clumsy person liberates his facticity inopportunely and suddenly places it before our eyes: just when we were expecting to grasp a key to the situation, emanating spontaneously from the situation itself, we suddenly encounter the unjustifiable contingency of a maladapted presence; we are confronted with the existence of an existent. Nonetheless, while the body remains entirely in action, its facticity does not yet amount to flesh. *Obscenity* appears when the body adopts postures that unclothe it entirely of its actions and reveal the inertia of its flesh. The sight of a naked body, from behind, is not obscene. But some kinds of involuntary waddling movements of the rump are obscene. For here it is the walker's legs alone that are active, and the rump they are carrying seems like an isolated cushion, whose swinging movement merely obeys the laws of gravity. This rump cannot be justified by the situation; on the contrary, it is wholly destructive of any situation, since it has the passivity of a thing and is carried like a thing by the legs. All at once it presents itself as unjustifiable facticity; like all contingent beings, it is "*de trop.*" It is isolated within this body whose present meaning is walking; even if some fabric veils it, it is naked, for it no longer participates in the transcended-transcendence of the body in actuality; its pendulum movement, rather than being interpreted on the basis of something forth-coming,[24] is interpreted and known on the basis of the past, like a physical fact. Naturally these observations may also apply to cases where it is the whole body that becomes flesh, whether this be through some limpness in its movements that cannot be interpreted by means of the situation, or through a deformation of its structure (for example, a proliferation of fat cells) that exhibits an overabundant facticity in relation to the effective presence required by the situation. And this revealed flesh is especially

442

24 TN: ... *à partir de l'à-venir* ... Sartre's pun, used earlier in the text, is repeated here.

obscene when the person who encounters it is not in a state of desire and *whose desire is not excited*. A particular maladaptation, destroying the situation at the very moment in which I grasp it—and which delivers up to me the flesh's inert expansion beneath the thin clothing of the movements in which it is dressed—and at a time when I am not, in relation to this flesh, in a state of desire: that is what I call "obscene."

Now we can see the meaning of the sadist's demand: grace reveals freedom as the property of an object-other and obscurely refers—like the contradictions within the sensible world in a case of Platonic recollection—to a transcendent *beyond* of which we retain only a vague memory, and that we can reach only by means of a radical modification of our being, i.e., by resolutely taking on our being-for-the-Other. At the same time, it unveils and veils the other's flesh or, alternatively, it unveils it in order immediately to veil it again: where the flesh is graceful, the other is inaccessible. The sadist aims to destroy the state of grace in order to constitute—*in reality*—another synthesis of the other: he wants to make the Other's flesh appear; in its very act of appearing, the flesh will destroy grace, and facticity will absorb the other's object-freedom. This absorption is not an annihilation: for the sadist, the other-as-free is manifested as flesh; the identity of the *other-object* is not destroyed in the course of these metamorphoses, but the relations between flesh and freedom are reversed. In the state of grace, facticity was contained and veiled by freedom; in the new synthesis to be performed, it is facticity that contains and conceals freedom. The sadist aims, therefore, to make the flesh appear brusquely, and by means of force, i.e., without the help of his own flesh, but by using his body as an instrument. He aims to make the other adopt postures and positions such that her body takes on the aspect of the *obscene*; in this way he remains at the level of instrumental appropriation, since he engenders the flesh by acting on the other with force, and the other becomes an instrument between his hands—the sadist *handles* the other's body, leans on her shoulders to bend her toward the ground, to make her back stick out, etc. And, on the other hand, the goal of this instrumental use is immanent within the use itself: the sadist treats the other as an instrument in order to make the other's flesh appear; the sadist is the being who apprehends the other as an instrument whose function is her own incarnation. The sadist's ideal is therefore to reach the

443

point where the other has already become flesh without ceasing to be an instrument—a flesh giving birth to flesh—where, for example, the thighs are already offered up in an obscene and expansive passivity and are still instruments to be handled, which can be pulled apart and bent, in order to make the buttocks stick out further and to make them incarnate in their turn. But we should not get this wrong: what the sadist is seeking with such persistence, what he wants to shape with his hands and to bend beneath his fist, is the other's freedom: it is there, within this flesh and, since there is a facticity to the other, it is this flesh; what the sadist is trying to appropriate, therefore, is freedom. In this way the sadist's endeavor is, through violence and through pain, to bog down the other in her flesh while he appropriates the other's body by virtue of treating it as flesh that will engender flesh; but this appropriation surpasses the body it appropriates, because it wants to possess it only to the extent that it has the other's freedom mired within it. That is why the sadist wants visible proof of this enslavement, through flesh, of the other's freedom: he will aim to make the other beg forgiveness; by means of torture and threats he will compel her to humiliate herself, to renounce what she holds most dear. This, it has been claimed, is because of his taste for domination, the will to power. But this explanation is vague or absurd. What ought to be explained first is the taste for domination. And, precisely, this taste cannot precede sadism as its foundation, for it exists at the same level and it is born—like sadism—out of anxiety in the face of the other. Indeed, if the sadist takes pleasure in extracting a renunciation through torture, the reason is analogous to the one that allows us to interpret *love's* meaning. Indeed, we saw that love does not require the other's freedom to be abolished but to be enslaved insofar as it is free, i.e., freedom's enslavement by itself. In the same way, sadism does not seek to eliminate the freedom of the tortured person but to force that freedom to freely identify itself with her tortured flesh. That is why the moment of pleasure, for the torturer, is when the victim retracts, or is humiliated. In effect, whatever pressure is brought to bear on the victim, her abjuration remains *free*: it is a spontaneous production, a response to the situation; it manifests human-reality. Whatever the victim's resistance and no matter how long she has waited before begging for mercy, she could have waited, in spite of everything, ten minutes, or one minute, or one second,

longer. She *decided* on the moment when pain became unbearable. And
the proof of this is that later she will relive this abjuration in remorse
and shame. Thus she is wholly accountable for it. But, on the other
hand, the sadist considers himself at the same time to be the cause. If
the victim resists and refuses to beg for mercy, the game only becomes
more enjoyable: one more turn of the screw, an additional twist, and
eventually every resistance will give way. The sadist presents himself as
having "all the time in the world." He is calm, and does not rush; he
lays out his instruments like a technician, trying them out one after the
other, like a locksmith trying various keys in a lock, and he takes pleasure in this ambiguous and contradictory situation: on the one hand he
plays the role of someone patiently making use of means, in the midst
of a universal determinism, in pursuit of an end that will come about
automatically—like the lock that automatically opens when the locksmith
finds the "right" key—and, on the other hand, this determinate end
can be actualized only by the other's free and entire adherence to it.
Therefore it remains both predictable and unpredictable at the same
time, and throughout. And for the sadist, the object achieved is ambiguous, contradictory and unsteady, since it is the strict outcome of a
technical use of determinism and—at the same time—the manifestation of an unconditioned freedom. And the spectacle offered to the
sadist is that of a freedom struggling against the expansion of flesh and,
eventually, freely choosing to be submerged within the flesh. In the
moment of abjuration, the result that was sought is achieved: the body
is completely flesh, breathless and obscene; it remains in the position
in which the torturers have put it, not the one it would have adopted
by itself; the ropes that bind it support it like an inert thing and, in
consequence, it has ceased to be a spontaneously moving object. And
it is with that very body that a freedom chooses, in its abjuration, to
identify; this deformed and panting body really is the image of a freedom broken and enslaved.

These notes do not aim to exhaust the problem of sadism. We merely
wish to show that its seed is contained within desire itself, as the failure
of desire: indeed, the moment I seek to *take* the Other's body, whose
incarnation I have induced by making myself incarnate, I break the reciprocity of the incarnation, I surpass my body toward its own possibilities
and I move in the direction of sadism. In this way sadism and masochism

are the two reefs of desire, whether I surpass my troubled arousal toward an appropriation of the other's flesh, or whether—intoxicated by my own trouble—I attend only to my own flesh, and cease to demand anything from the other, apart from that she should look at me, which will help me to actualize my flesh. It is because of this flimsiness in desire, and its constant oscillation between these two reefs, that we habitually refer to "normal" sexuality as "sado-masochistic."

Nonetheless, sadism itself—like blind indifference and like desire—contains the principle of its own failure. In the first place, the apprehension of the body as flesh is profoundly incompatible with its instrumental 445 use. If I make flesh into an instrument, it refers me to other instruments and to potentialities, in short, to a future: its *being-there* is justified in part by the situation that I create around me—as the presence of nails and the matting to be nailed to the wall justify the existence of the hammer. Suddenly its nature as flesh (i.e., as unusable facticity) gives way to that of an implement-thing. The "implement-flesh" structure that the sadist tried to create falls to pieces. This profound disintegration may be masked, as long as the flesh is an instrument for revealing flesh, because I have thereby constituted an implement whose goal is immanent. But when the incarnation is complete, when I actually have before me a breathless body, I no longer know how to *make use* of this flesh: I can no longer assign any goal to it, precisely because I have made its absolute contingency apparent. It "is there" and its purpose in being there is "nothing." In consequence, I cannot take hold of it insofar as it is flesh, and I am unable to integrate it within a system of instruments without its materiality as flesh—its "carnation"—immediately escaping me. I can only remain speechless before it, in a state of contemplative astonishment, or otherwise make myself incarnate in turn, and allow the state of trouble to take me over, in order at least to resituate myself in the territory where flesh discloses itself to flesh in its entire carnation.[25] In this way sadism, in the very moment when its goal is about to be reached, gives way to desire. Sadism is the failure of desire and desire is the failure

25 TN: *Carnation* in French is a rarely used term, which refers to the color of skin – it is sometimes translated as "skin-tone." The same word exists in English, although it has fallen into disuse. I use it here because Sartre clearly wants to make a connection with the idea of "incarnation."

of sadism. The only way out of the circle is through satisfaction,[26] and the so-called physical possession. This, in fact, offers a new synthesis of sadism and desire: the turgescence of the sexual organ manifests incarnation; the fact of "entering into" or of being "penetrated" symbolically achieves the sadistic and masochistic attempt at appropriation. But if pleasure allows the circle to be broken, it is because it kills both desire and sadistic passion at the same time, without satisfying them.

At the same time, and on another level entirely, sadism contains a different reason for failure. In effect, what it seeks to appropriate is the victim's transcendent freedom. But it is just this freedom that remains necessarily out of reach. And the more the sadist insists on treating the other as an instrument, the more this freedom escapes him. He can act on freedom only as an objective property of the object-other, i.e., freedom in the midst of the world, with its dead-possibilities. But insofar as his goal is that of recuperating his being-for-the-Other, he will necessarily miss it, because the only Other he comes across is the other within the world, who has nothing but "images in her head" of the sadist who relentlessly persists with her.

The sadist discovers his mistake when the victim *looks at* him, i.e., when he experiences the absolute alienation of his being in the other's freedom: at that moment he realizes not only that he has failed to retrieve his "being-outside" but, further, that the activity through which he is trying to retrieve it has itself been transcended and become frozen into "sadism," as a *habitus*[27] and as a property, with its cortege of dead-possibilities, and that this transformation has taken place through and for the other whom he wishes to enslave. He discovers at that moment that he cannot act on the other's freedom, even by forcing the other to humiliate herself and to beg for mercy, because it is precisely in and through the other's absolute freedom that a world comes to exist in which there is a sadist, and torture instruments, and a thousand pretexts for humiliating and disavowing himself. Nobody has given a better account of the power of the victim's act of looking back at his executioners than Faulkner in the

---

26 TN: I assume that Sartre's term *assouvissement* (satisfaction) is being used euphemistically to mean "orgasm."

27 TN: Sartre probably borrows the Latin term *habitus* from the well-known French sociologist Marcel Mauss (1872–1950). In Mauss's work *habitus* refers to someone's socially acquired dispositions and, in particular, their bodily techniques.

final pages of *Light in August*. Some "good people" have just gone after the Negro Christmas and castrated him. Christmas is dying:

> But the man on the floor had not moved. He just lay there, with his eyes open and empty of everything save consciousness, and with something, a shadow, about his mouth. For a long moment he looked up at them with peaceful and unfathomable and unbearable eyes. Then his face, body, all, seemed to collapse, to fall in upon itself, and from out the slashed garments about his hips and loins the pent black blood seemed to rush like a released breath . . . upon that black blast the man seemed to rise soaring into their memories forever and ever. They are not to lose it, in whatever peaceful valleys, beside whatever placid and reassuring streams of old age, in the mirroring faces of whatever children they will contemplate old disasters and newer hopes. *It will be there, musing, quiet, steadfast, not fading and not particularly threatful, but of itself alone serene, of itself alone triumphant.*[28] Again from the town, deadened a little by the walls, the scream of the siren mounted toward its unbelievable crescendo, passing out of the realm of hearing.[29]

Hence this explosion of the Other's gaze within the sadist's world makes the meaning and the goal of sadism collapse. At the same time the sadist discovers that it was this freedom-here that he wanted to enslave and, simultaneously, he understands the futility of his efforts. Once again we are directed from looking-being to being-looked-at; we have not stepped out of this circle.

In making these observations we have not aimed to exhaust the sexual question, still less that of our attitudes toward the Other. We merely wanted to note that the sexual attitude is a basic type of behavior in relation to the Other. It goes without saying that this behavior necessarily includes within it the original contingency of being-for-the-Other, and of our own facticity. But what we will not accept is that it is governed from the outset by our physiological and empirical constitution. From the moment that "there is" a body and "there is" the other, our reaction   447

28 Sartre's note: My emphasis.
29 Sartre's note: *Lumière d'Août*, p. 385 (NRF, 1935). TN: Sartre quotes from the French translation. The English original is William Faulkner, *Light in August*, first published in 1932. The cited passage is from Faulkner (2005: 349–350).

is one of *desire*, of *love*—and the derivative attitudes that we have cited. Our physiological structure only expresses symbolically, and in a sphere of absolute contingency, the possibility that is constantly available to us of taking up one or other of these attitudes. Thus we can say that the for-itself is sexual even as it arises before the Other and that, through it, sexuality enters the world.

We are not of course claiming that the attitudes we can take up toward the Other can be reduced to those sexual attitudes that we have just described. If we have enlarged on them at length, it is for two purposes: first, because they are fundamental, and because all of men's complex ways of behaving toward each other are, in the end, only elaborations of these two primary attitudes (and of a third attitude—hatred—soon to be described). Without doubt the concrete instances of behavior (collaboration, struggle, rivalry, emulation, commitment, obedience,[30] etc.) are infinitely more delicate to describe, because they depend on the historical situation and the concrete particularities of each for-itself's relation with the other; but they all contain within themselves, as their skeleton, the relations of sexuality. And that is not because of the existence of some "*libido*" that we can see creeping into everything but simply because the attitudes we have described are the fundamental projects through which the for-itself *actualizes* its being-for-the-Other and attempts to transcend this *de facto* situation. This is not the place to demonstrate how pity, admiration, disgust, envy, gratitude, etc., can contain love and desire. But each person may ascertain it by referring to his own experience, and also to the eidetic intuition of these various essences. This does not imply, of course, that these different attitudes are simply disguised forms of sexuality. But we must see that sexuality is integrated within them as their foundation, and that they include and surpass it—just as the notion of a circle includes and surpasses that of a segment rotated around one of its fixed endpoints. These foundation-attitudes may remain concealed, as a skeleton is concealed by the flesh that surrounds it. That is even what ordinarily happens: the bodies' contingency, the structure of the original project that I am, the history that I historialize, may make it the case that ordinarily the sexual attitude remains implicit within more complex modes of behavior; in particular, we do not often explicitly desire other

---

30 Sartre's note: Compare also maternal love, pity, goodness, etc.

people "of the same sex." But, beneath the prohibitions of morality and social taboos, the primary structure of desire remains—at the least in that particular form of trouble known as sexual disgust. And we must not interpret this permanence of the sexual project as if it remained "in us" as an unconscious state. A project of the for-itself can exist only in a conscious form. Only it exists integrated within, and blending into, some particular structure. This was what the psychoanalysts sensed when they made sexual affectivity into a "*tabula rasa*," to be determined entirely by each individual history. Only we should not believe that sexuality is in its origin *undetermined*: in fact, all of its determining characteristics accompany it from the moment the for-itself arises in a world where "there are" others. What remains undetermined, and must be fixed by each person's history, is the type of relation with the other, in which the sexual attitude (desire-love, masochism-sadism) will be manifested explicitly in its pure form.

It is precisely because these attitudes are primary that we have chosen them to point out the *circle* of our relations with the Other. Indeed, as they are an integral part of *all* our attitudes toward others, their circularity comes to encompass the entirety of all our behavior in relation to the Other. Just as love encounters its failure within itself, and desire arises from love's death—to collapse in its turn, and give way to love— each of our ways of behaving in relation to the other-object contains within it an implicit and concealed reference to an other-subject, and in this reference lies their death: with the death of one way of behaving in relation to the other-object a new attitude arises, whose aim is to take hold of the other-subject—and this latter reveals in its turn its own fragility, and collapses to make way for the opposite behavior. Thus we are indefinitely sent back from the other-object to the other-subject, and *vice versa*; we never stop running, and this pursuit, with its sudden reversals of direction, is what constitutes our relation to the Other. At whichever point we consider it we are in one or the other of these attitudes, as dissatisfied by the one as by the other; we may stay in the attitude we have adopted for a longer or shorter period of time—according to our bad faith, or our particular historical circumstances—but the attitude is never sufficient in itself; it always obscurely points us toward the other one. The fact is that we could take up a consistent attitude toward the Other only if she were revealed to us *at the same time* as subject and as object, as a transcending-transcendence and as a transcended-transcendence, which is by definition impossible. In this way, endlessly thrown from our look-being to our being-looked-at, falling back from each one to the other in alternating upheavals, we are always—whichever attitude we have adopted—in a state of instability in relation to the Other. We pursue the impossible ideal of simultaneously apprehending her freedom and her objectivity; to put it in Jean Wahl's terms, we are, in relation to the other, in the state of "trans-descendence" at one moment (when we apprehend her as an object and integrate her within the world) and in a state of "trans-ascendence" at another (when we experience her as a transcendence that transcends us);[31] but neither of these two states is sufficient in itself; and we can never concretely take up a position of equality, i.e., a position in which the recognition of the Other's freedom might lead to the Other's recognition of our freedom. The Other eludes me as a matter of principle: when I seek her, she runs away from me and, when I run away from her, she possesses me. Even if I wished to act—in accordance with Kantian morality—by taking the Other's freedom as an unconditioned end, this freedom would become a transcended-transcendence by the very fact of my making it my goal; and on the other hand, I cannot act for her own good unless I make use of the other-object as an instrument in order to actualize this freedom. I am obliged in fact to grasp the other as an object-instrument in situation; and thus the only power I have will be to modify the situation in relation to the other, and the other in relation to the situation. Thus I am led to the paradox that is the downfall of all liberal politics and which Rousseau's phrase sums up: I must "force" the other to be free.[32] This use of force, even if it does not always—or even most often—take the form of violence, is nonetheless what governs men's relations with each other. If I console, if I reassure, it is in order to clear away the fears or sorrows that obscure the Other's freedom; but the consolation, or the reassuring argument, organizes a

31 TN: The philosopher Jean Wahl (to whom Sartre has already referred earlier in the text) coined the terms "trans-ascendence" and "trans-descendence" to distinguish between two kinds of transcendence; the first moves toward a "higher" being, the second toward something "lower."

32 TN: Rousseau says this in his *Social Contract*: "Whoever refuses to obey the general will shall be constrained to do so by the whole body; which means . . . he shall be forced to be free" (Rousseau 2002: 166).

system of means with the aim of *acting* on the other and consequently integrating her in turn within the system as an implement-thing. And, in addition, the person who seeks to console imposes an arbitrary distinction between freedom, which he assimilates to the use of Reason and pursuit of the Good, and affliction, which appears to him to be the result of psychological determinism. The consoling person acts, therefore, to separate the freedom from the affliction, as one might separate two components of some chemical product from each other. By the mere fact that he views freedom as something that can be separated out, he transcends it and does violence to it and he is unable, from his standpoint, to grasp this truth: that it is freedom itself which *makes itself* afflicted and, in consequence, to act in order to liberate freedom from affliction is to act against freedom.

However, it would be wrong to think that a tolerant and "*laissez-faire*" morality would be more respectful of the Other's freedom: from the moment I exist I place a *de facto* limit on the Other's freedom; I *am* that limit, and each one of my projects draws this limit around the other: charity, *laissez-faire*, tolerance, or any attitude of abstention; each of these is a project of myself that commits me and commits the Other without her consent. To exercise tolerance in the Other's surroundings amounts to forcibly throwing the Other into a tolerant world. It is necessarily to deprive her of the free possibilities for courageous resistance, perseverance, and self-affirmation that she would have had the opportunity to develop in a world of intolerance. This becomes clearer still if we consider the problem of education: a strict education treats the child as an instrument, since it attempts to bend him forcibly to submit to values he has not accepted; but a liberal education, despite its use of other methods, chooses *a priori*, to just the same extent, the principles and values that will be honored in the ways the child is treated. To treat the child with persuasion and gentleness is no less a way of coercing him. "Respect for the Other's freedom" is therefore an empty phrase: even if we were able to form the project of respecting this freedom, every attitude that we took up in relation to the other would violate this freedom that we were claiming to respect. Nor is the extreme attitude of affecting complete indifference toward the other a solution: we are already thrown into the world alongside the other; our arising is a free limitation of her freedom and nothing—not even suicide—can alter this original situation; whichever acts we perform, in effect, are

450

accomplished in a world in which the other is already there, and in which I am, in relation to the other, *de trop*.

This singular situation appears to lie at the origin of the notion of guilt and sin. In the face of the other, I am guilty. I am guilty, in the first instance, when, exposed to the other's look, I experience my alienation and nudity as a state of degradation I am obliged to accept; that is the meaning of the well-known "and they knew that they were naked" in the Scriptures.[33] I am guilty, in addition, when I look in my turn at the Other, because, in the very act of affirming myself, I constitute her as an object and an instrument, and confer upon her this alienation that she will have to accept. In this way, the original sin is my arising within a world where there is an other and, no matter what my subsequent relations with the other are, they can only be variations on the original theme of my guilt.

But this guilt is accompanied by powerlessness—although this powerlessness fails to absolve me of my guilt. As we have seen, no matter what I do for the other's freedom, my efforts amount to treating the other as an instrument and positing her freedom as a transcended-transcendence: but, on the other hand, no matter how much power I may have at my disposal to coerce the Other, I will only ever reach her in her object-being. I can only ever provide her freedom with opportunities to show itself, without ever managing to increase or to decrease it, to direct it or to take hold of it. Thus I am guilty in relation to the Other in my very being, because as my being arises it endows her, in spite of herself, with a new dimension of being, and yet I lack the power either to take advantage of my misdeed or to make amends for it.

It may happen that the for-itself, having experienced these various avatars in the course of its historialization, decides—in full knowledge of the futility of his previous attempts—to pursue the other's death. This free determination is known as "hatred." A fundamental act of resignation is implicit within it: the for-itself abandons his ambition to actualize his union with the other; he relinquishes any use of the other as an instrument to retrieve his being-in-itself. He wants only to return to a freedom without any *de facto* limits, i.e., to get rid of his elusive being-an-object-for-the-other and to abolish its dimension of alienation. That

---

33 TN: Sartre is quoting from Genesis, chap. 3, verse 7.

is equivalent to the project of actualizing a world in which the other does not exist. A for-itself who hates accepts that he is nothing more than a for-itself; taught by his various experiences that it is impossible to make use of his being-for-the-Other, he prefers instead to be only a free nihilation of his being, a detotalized totality, a pursuit whose own ends are set by himself. The project of the person who hates is not to be an object at all—and hatred presents itself as an absolute positing of the for-itself's freedom in the face of the other. That is why, in the first place, hatred does not degrade the hated object. In fact, it places the debate on its true ground: what I hate in the other is not this appearance, or that shortcoming, or this particular act. It is her existence in general, as a transcended-transcendence. That is why hatred implies a recognition of the other's freedom. Only this recognition is abstract and negative: hatred knows only the other-object, and attaches itself to this object. This is the object it wants to destroy, in order to eliminate at the same time the transcendence which haunts it. The for-itself who hates only glimpses this transcendence, as an inaccessible "beyond," as the constant possibility of his alienation. The Other's transcendence is not, therefore, ever apprehended in its own right; moreover, it could not be, without becoming an object. I experience it, rather, as a constantly escaping characteristic of the Other-object, as an aspect of her most accessible empirical qualities that is "not supplied" or "still owing," as a kind of constant monition which advises me that "the real question lies elsewhere." That is why hatred goes through the revealed psyche; one does not hate the psyche itself. It is also the reason why it makes no difference whether we hate the other's transcendence through what we empirically refer to as her "vices" or her "virtues." What I hate is the psychological-totality in its entirety, insofar as it directs me to the other's transcendence: I do not stoop so low as to hate some particular objective detail. That is what distinguishes "hating" from "detesting." And hatred does not necessarily appear on account of some harm that I have just undergone. On the contrary, it can arise just where we might have reason to expect gratitude, i.e., in the case of a good deed: what provokes hatred is merely an act of the Other through which I have been made to undergo her freedom. This act is humiliating by itself: it is humiliating insofar as it concretely reveals my instrumental objecthood in the face of the Other's freedom. This revelation becomes immediately obfuscated, subsides into the past, and becomes opaque. But it allows me to feel, precisely, that "something" is there for me to destroy in order to become free. It is for this reason, moreover, that gratitude is so close to hatred: to be grateful for a good deed is to recognize that the other was entirely free in acting as she did. No constraint, not even that of duty, determined her to do it. She bears the entire responsibility for her action, and for the values presiding over its execution. I myself was no more than a pretext, the material on which her action worked. On the basis of this recognition, the for-itself can make his project either love or hate, as he pleases: he can no longer ignore the other.

A second consequence of these observations is that, in hating one person, I hate everyone else. The goal that I wish symbolically to achieve, in pursuing the death of some other person, is the general principle of the Other's existence. The other whom I hate actually represents the *others*. And my project to eliminate her is a project to eliminate the Other in general, i.e., to win back my for-itself's non-substantial freedom. Hatred includes an understanding of the fact that my dimension of being-alienated, which I acquire from others, *really* enslaves me. It is the abolition of this slavery that becomes my project. That is why hatred is a *dark* feeling, i.e., a feeling that aims to eliminate another and which, as a project, is knowingly projected in defiance of others' disapproval. The hatred that another person bears toward someone else worries me; I disapprove of it and try to prevent it because—even though it is not explicitly aimed at me—I know that it concerns me and is opposed to me. And, indeed, it aims to destroy me, not because it seeks to eliminate me but by virtue of the fact that what it primarily demands is my disapproval—in order to override it. Hatred demands to be hated, to the extent to which hating someone's hatred amounts to an anxious recognition of the freedom of the person who hates.

But hatred, in its turn, is a failure. Its initial project is, indeed, to abolish other consciousnesses. But even if it were to succeed in that—if hatred were able, in other words, to abolish the other person in the present moment—it would not be able to make it the case that the other had not been. Moreover, the other's abolition, even if it is felt to be the triumph of hatred, implies an explicit recognition that the Other *did exist*. From then on, my being-for-the-Other, in sliding into the past, becomes an irremediable dimension of myself. It is what I have to be, in the form of having-been-it. I cannot therefore get rid of it. "Well," I may be told, "at least

you are escaping it in the present, and you will escape it in the future."
But no. Someone who has, on one occasion, been for the Other remains
contaminated in his being for the rest of his days, even were the Other to
be entirely eliminated: he will continue to apprehend his dimension of
being-for-the-Other as a permanent possibility of his being. He will not
be able to win back what he has lost; he has lost all hope, even, of acting
upon this alienation and turning it to his profit, since the destroyed other
has taken the key to this alienation with her into her grave. That which I   453
was for the other becomes frozen by the other's death, and I will continue
to be it, irremediably, in the past; I will also be it—and in the same way—
in the present, if I persevere in the attitude, the projects and the way of life
that the other has judged. The other's death constitutes me as an irremediable object, exactly as my own death does. Thus hatred's triumph, even as
it arises, becomes transformed into failure. Hatred does not enable us to
get out of the circle. It merely represents the final attempt, the attempt of
despair. After the failure of this attempt, the for-itself can only reenter the
circle and submit to being endlessly tossed between one and the other of
the two fundamental attitudes.[34]

III. "BEING-WITH" (*MITSEIN*)[35] AND THE "WE"

It will be brought to our attention, of course, that our description is
incomplete because it makes no place for certain concrete experiences
in which we find ourselves not in conflict with the Other but in community with him.[36] And it is true that we often say "*we*." The very existence and the use of this grammatical category necessarily direct us to a
real experience of *Mitsein*. "We" can be a subject and, in this form, it can

---

34 Sartre's note: These considerations do not rule out the possibility of a morality of deliverance and salvation. But this can be achieved only after a radical conversion, which we
   cannot discuss here.
35 TN: To remind the reader, *Mitsein* is a reference to Heidegger's concept in *Being and Time*,
   usually translated as "Being-with." Heidegger uses it to emphasize his point that, for the
   most part, we experience ourselves not as an isolated "I" but *with others*. See Heidegger
   (1980: chap. IV).
36 TN: As the collective groupings discussed in this section do not involve love, sex, etc., I
   have reverted at this point to using the pronoun "he" for the Other. See my discussion
   in Notes on the Translation.

be assimilated to the plural of "I." And of course the parallelism between grammar and thought is, in many cases, dubious: perhaps we are even required to revise this question entirely, and to study the relation between language and thought in a completely new form. Still, it remains true that it seems impossible to conceive of a "we" subject without it referring at least to the idea of a plurality of subjects, simultaneously apprehending each other as subjectivities, i.e., as transcending-transcendences and not as transcended-transcendences. If it is to be more than a mere *flatus vocis*,[37] the word "we" must denote a concept that subsumes an infinite variety of possible experiences. And these experiences appear *a priori* to contradict the experience of my object-being for the Other, or the experience of the Other's object-being for me. In the "we" subject, nobody is an object. The *we* encompasses a plurality of subjectivities, each of whom 454 recognizes the others as subjectivities. However, this recognition is not the object of any explicit thesis: what is explicitly posited is a common action, or the object of a common perception. "We" resist; "we" mount an attack; "we" sentence the culprit; "we" watch such and such a performance. In this way, our recognition of subjectivities is analogous to non-thetic consciousness's recognition of itself: or, better still, it must be *laterally* performed, by a non-thetic consciousness whose explicit object is such and such a performance in the world. The *we* is best illustrated for us by the spectator of a theatrical performance, whose consciousness expends itself in grasping the imaginary spectacle, in making use of its patterns to predict what will happen next, in positing imaginary beings like the hero, the traitor, the prisoner, etc.—and yet which, in that very movement in which it arises as a consciousness of the show, constitutes itself non-thetically as a consciousness (of) being a *co-spectator* of the show. Indeed, all of us know that unconfessed unease that grips us in a half-empty auditorium or—on the contrary—the enthusiasm that is unleashed and strengthened when the auditorium is full and enthusiastic. It is clear, moreover, that the experience of the we-subject can manifest itself in any circumstance whatsoever. I am sitting outside a café: I observe the other customers and I know that I am observed. This remains a wholly banal instance of conflict with the Other (the other's object-being for me, my object-being for the other). But now, all at once, some incident in the

---

37 TN: This Latin phrase means a name or a sound without a corresponding referent. The phrase is used in philosophy by nominalists, to deny the existence of universals.

street occurs: a minor collision, for example, between a delivery-tricycle and a taxi. Immediately, in the very instant at which I become a spectator of the incident, I experience myself non-thetically as committed within a we. The earlier rivalries and minor conflicts have disappeared, and it is precisely the consciousnesses of all the customers which provide the we with its substance: we watch the event; we take sides. This is the "unanimism" that Romains set out to describe in La Vie Unanime or in Le Vin Blanc de La Villette.[38] Here we find ourselves back with Heidegger's Mitsein. Were we wasting our time, then, in criticizing it earlier?[39]

Here we will point out only that we have not wished to cast doubt on the *experience* of the we. We have limited our demonstration to showing that this experience cannot be the foundation of our consciousness of the Other. Indeed, it is clear that it could not constitute an ontological structure of human-reality: we have proved that the existence of the for-itself in the midst of others is, in its origin, a metaphysical and contingent fact. It is clear, furthermore, that the we is not an intersubjective consciousness, or a new type of being that extends beyond and encompasses its parts in a synthetic whole, like the sociological notion of the collective consciousness. The we is experienced by a particular consciousness: it is not necessary for *all* the customers outside the café to be conscious of being we for me to feel myself to be committed with them within a we. The following everyday dialogue is familiar: "We are very dissatisfied." "Not at all, my dear: speak for yourself." It follows that some ways of being conscious of the we are deviant—without this implying that such a consciousness is, as such, in any way abnormal. If this is the case, then, for a consciousness to become conscious of being committed within a we, it must be necessary first for the other consciousnesses entering into this community to be given to it in some other way, i.e., as a transcending-transcendence or a transcended-transcendence. The we is a certain kind of specific experience that is produced, in special cases, on

455

38 TN: Jules Romains (1885–1972) was a French writer and a founding member of Unanisme, a literary movement concerned with the experience of group consciousness and collective life. Romains's collection of poems La Vie Unanime ("Unanimous Life") appeared in 1908, and the novel Le Vin Blanc de La Villette ("The White Wine of La Villette") in 1923. The street scene that Sartre describes in the text evokes the situations Romains writes about in his poems.

39 Sartre's note: Part Three, Chapter 1.

the foundation of our being-for-the-Other in general. Our being-for-the-Other precedes and founds our being-with-the-other.

In addition, any philosopher who wants to study the we must be cautious and must know what he is talking about. In fact there is not only a we-subject: grammar teaches us that there is also a we-complement, i.e., a we-object. Now, in accordance with everything we have said so far, it will be easily understood that the we in "We are looking at them" cannot be on the same ontological level as the we in "We are being looked at."[40] We are not dealing here with subjectivities qua subjectivities. In the sentence "They are looking at me," I want to indicate that I am experiencing myself as an object for the Other, as an alienated Me, as a transcended-transcendence. If the sentence "We are being looked at" is to refer to a real experience, it is necessary that in this experience I should feel myself to be committed with others in a community of transcended-transcendences of alienated "Mes." Here the we refers us to an experience of being-objects in common. Thus there are two radically different forms of the experience of the we, and the two forms correspond exactly to the looking-being and the being-looked-at which constitute the for-itself's fundamental relations with the other. It is these two forms of the we that we should examine now.

(A) The "we"-object

We will begin by examining the second of these experiences: it happens to be easier to grasp its meaning, and we may be able to make use of it as a route through which to study the other. We should note in the first place that the we-object throws us into the world; we experience it through shame, as a communal alienation. This is illustrated by that significant episode in which the galley slaves are choked by anger and shame because a beautiful woman dressed in finery comes to visit their ship and sees their rags, their labor, and their wretchedness. This is

40 TN: ... que le nous de "ils nous regardent." Sartre's example sentence would normally translate into English as "they are looking at us" but, because the French (in which nous is used for both subject and object) allows Sartre to use the same word (i.e., nous) in both the sentences he gives as examples, I have rephrased this second sentence using the passive form, which allows the word we to be retained. An alternative would have been to talk about the us-object.

clearly a case of collective shame and collective alienation. How then is it possible to experience oneself as an object alongside others, collectively? In order to find out, we must return to the fundamental characteristics of our being-for-the-Other.

So far we have considered the simple case in which I, alone, am facing the other—who is also alone. In this case, I look at him or he looks at me, I try to transcend his transcendence or I experience mine as transcended, and I feel my possibilities as dead-possibilities. We form a *couple* and we are each in *situation* in relation to the other. But this situation exists objectively only for one or the other of us. In effect, there is no *reverse side* to our reciprocal relation. Only our description has not taken account of the fact that my relation with the other appears against the infinite ground of my relation and *his* relation to *everyone else*, i.e., to the quasi-totality of consciousnesses. From this fact alone it follows that my relation with *this* other (which I experienced just now as the foundation of my being-for-the-Other), or the other's relation with me, can at any moment—depending on the intervening reasons—be experienced as objects for others. This can clearly be seen in the case where some *third person* appears. Let us suppose, for example, that the other is looking at me. At that moment, I experience myself as wholly *alienated*, and I accept myself as such. Along comes the third person. If he looks at me, I experience Them collectively, through my alienation, as "Them" (them-subjects).[41] This "them," as we know, tends toward the "they."[42] It makes no difference to the fact that I am looked at; it does not reinforce—or hardly—my original alienation. But if the third person looks at the other who is looking at me, the problem becomes more complex. I may in fact be able to apprehend the third person, *not directly* but in relation to the other, who becomes an other who is looked at (by the third person). In this way the third transcendence transcends the transcendence which is transcending me, and thereby helps to disarm it. A metastable state is established here,

---

41 TN: *S'il me regarde, je Les éprouve . . . comme "Eux" (eux-sujets) . . . Eux* is more commonly equivalent to English "them" than to "they," although in some contexts the latter will be more correct. And it might seem more appropriate as a means to refer (as Sartre is referring here) to *subjects*; however, because I am using "they" (following Heidegger's translators) to translate *l'on*, I have stuck to "them" for *Eux* here.

42 TN: *Cet "eux" tend, nous le savons, vers l'on.* Again, my policy for *l'on* has required me to modify this sentence in English.

which will soon decompose, either because I ally myself to the third person, in order to look at the other, who is transformed at that point into our object (and here I have an experience of the we-subject to be discussed later), or because I look at the third person and, in so doing, I transcend this third transcendence which is transcending the other. In this case the third person becomes an object in my universe, and his possibilities are dead-possibilities; he cannot free me from the other. Yet he is looking at the other who is looking at me. We can regard the resultant situation as indeterminate and inconclusive, since I am an object for the other, who is an object for the third person, who is an object for me. Only freedom, by leaning on one or other of these relationships, is able to give this situation a structure.

But it may also happen that the third person looks at the other *whom I am looking at*. In this case, I may look at both of them and, in this way, disarm the third person's gaze. The third person and the other will then appear to me as Them-objects. I may also apprehend that the third person is looking at the other, insofar as—without seeing the third person—I can pick up from the other's behavior that he knows that he is looked at. In this case I experience *from the other and in relation to the other* the third person's transcending-transcendence. I experience it as a radical and absolute alienation of the other. He escapes from my world, and no longer belongs to me; he is an object for another transcendence. He does not therefore lose the character of an object but he becomes ambiguous: he does not escape me through his own transcendence but through the third person's transcendence. Now, whatever I may be able to apprehend on him and of him, he is always *other*; he is as many times other as there are others to perceive him and to think of him. In order to reappropriate the other, I must look at the third person and confer objecthood upon him. But, on the one hand, that is not always possible; and, on the other hand, the third person may himself be looked at by other third parties—which means he may be indefinitely other to the way I see him. The result is a basic inconsistency in the other-object, and an infinite journey for the for-itself who tries to reappropriate this objecthood. That is the reason, as we have seen, why lovers isolate themselves. I can experience myself as looked at by the third person while I am looking at the other. In this case I experience my alienation non-positionally at the very same time as I posit the other's alienation. I experience my possibilities for

457

making use of the other as an instrument as dead-possibilities, and my transcendence—which is on the point of transcending the other toward my own ends—falls back into a transcended-transcendence. I let go. The other does not thereby become a subject, but I no longer feel that I myself am characterized as an object. The other becomes something *neutral* that is purely and simply there, and with which I do nothing. This will be the case, for example, if I am surprised in the act of beating and humiliating someone weak. The appearance of the third person "detaches" me: the weakling is no longer "to be beaten" or "to be humiliated"; now he is nothing but pure existence, no longer anything, not even "a weakling"—or, if he does become one again, it will be through the third person's intervention. *I will learn from the third person that this man was a weakling* ("You have no shame; you attack a weakling," etc.): the quality of being weak will be bestowed on him in my eyes by the third person; it will no longer form part of my world but of a universe where I exist, along with the weakling, for the third person.

This brings us finally to the case that concerns us: I am engaged in a conflict with the other. The third person comes along and looks at us, encompassing both of us within his gaze. Correlatively, I experience my alienation and my objecthood. I am out there, for the Other, as an object in the midst of a world that is not "mine." But the other, whom I was looking at or who was looking at me, undergoes the same modification, and I encounter this modification of the other simultaneously with the one that I experience. The other is an object in the midst of the third person's world. Moreover, this objecthood is not a mere modification of his being, in *parallel* to the one I undergo; rather, the two objecthoods impinge on me and on the other within a global modification of the *situation* I am in, and in which the other finds himself. Before the third person looked at us, there was a situation circumscribed by the other's possibilities, and in which my status was that of an instrument— and an inverse situation, circumscribed by my own possibilities, which included the other. Each of these situations was the death of the other, and we could only grasp either one of them by objectifying the other. With the appearance of the third person I feel, all at once, that my possibilities are alienated and, in the same moment, I discover that the other's possibilities are dead-possibilities. Nonetheless, the situation does not disappear, but it flees from my world and from the other's world, and becomes constituted as an objective form in the midst of a third world. In this third world, the situation is seen, judged, transcended, and used, but suddenly a leveling of the two opposite situations occurs, and there is no longer any structure of priority which places me ahead of the other or, inversely, him ahead of me, since *for the third person* our possibilities are, equally, dead-possibilities. Therefore, I suddenly experience the existence, in the third person's world, of an objective situation-form in which we—the other and myself—figure as *equivalent* and *joint* structures. Within this objective situation, conflict does not arise from the free arising of our transcendences; rather, it is registered and transcended by the third person as a *de facto* given, which defines us and detains us, each with the other. Far from it being the case that the other's possibility of hitting me and my possibility of defending myself exclude each other, each of these—for the third person—complements, involves, and implies the other as dead-possibilities—and that is precisely what I experience, in a non-thetic form, and without any *knowledge* of it. Thus, what I experience is a being-outside in which I am organized with the other within an indissoluble and objective whole, a whole in which I am *no longer distinguished* from the other but to whose constitution I contribute, jointly, with the other. And to the extent that I accept, as a matter of principle, my being-outside for the third person, I must in the same way accept the other's being-outside; what I accept is the commonality of equivalence through which I exist as committed within a form to whose constitution I, like the other, contribute. In brief, I accept myself as committed *outside* in the other and I accept the other as committed *outside* in me. And the experience of the *we*-object is this fundamental acceptance of this commitment—which, without apprehending it, I carry before me— and this free recognition of my responsibility as including the other's responsibility. Thus the we-object is never *known*, in the sense in which, for example, knowledge of our Self may be delivered by reflection; it is never *felt*, in the sense in which a feeling can disclose a concrete object to us, such as something disagreeable, hateful, disturbing, etc. Nor is it merely *experienced*, for what is experienced is the pure situation of solidarity with the other. The we-object is revealed only through my acceptance of this situation, i.e., through the necessity of my having, within my free accepting, to accept the other *as well*, because of the situation's internal reciprocity. Thus, in the absence of the third person, I am able to say "I

459

am fighting the other." But as soon as he appears, with the leveling of the other's possibilities and my own into dead-possibilities, the relationship becomes reciprocal and I am obliged to feel that "we are fighting each other." Indeed, the phrase "I am fighting him *and* he is fighting me" would clearly be inadequate: in fact I am fighting him because he is fighting me, and reciprocally: the project of fighting germinated in his mind as it did in mine and, for the third person, it is united in *a single project*, common to this *them-object* which he encompasses within his gaze and which even constitutes the unifying synthesis of this "them." I must therefore accept myself as I am apprehended by the third person, as an integral part of the "them." And this "them," which is accepted by a subjectivity as his meaning-for-the-Other, becomes the *we*. This *we* cannot be captured by reflective consciousness. On the contrary, the appearance of reflection coincides with the collapse of the *we*; the for-itself disengages and posits its ipseity against *the others*. Indeed, we need to understand that from the outset the for-itself feels its belonging to the we-object as an even more radical alienation, since he is no longer obliged merely to take up what he is for the Other but, in addition, a totality that he is not—even though he forms an integral part of it. In this sense, the *we* is a sudden experience of the human condition as being committed among others, insofar as that is an objectively registered *fact*. The we-object—although it is experienced in the context of a particular solidarity, and is centered on this solidarity (I will feel shame precisely because *we* were surprised while *we* were fighting)—has a meaning that extends beyond the specific circumstance in which it is experienced, which seeks to subsume my belonging as an object within the human totality (minus the third person's pure consciousness) that is grasped, equally, as an object. It corresponds therefore to an experience of humiliation and powerlessness: the person who feels himself to be constituting a *we* with other men feels stuck within an infinity of foreign existences; he is radically alienated, and helpless.

Some situations seem more suited than others to trigger the experience of the *we*. Common work is a case in point: when several people experience themselves as apprehended by a third person while they jointly work on the same object, the very meaning of the manufactured object refers us to the laboring collectivity, in the form of a *we*. The movement that I make—which the item to be assembled demands—has meaning only if it is preceded by such and such a movement by my neighbor, and followed by some other movement, made by some other worker. From this a more easily accessible form of "we" ensues, since it is the demand of the object itself and its potentialities—as well as its coefficient of adversity—which point toward the workers' we-object. We experience ourselves, then, as apprehended in the capacity of a "we" through a material object "to be created." The materiality sets its seal on the solidarity of our community and we appear to ourselves as an instrumental and technical arrangement of means, each of which has its place assigned by an end. But if, empirically, some situations appear in this way to favor the arising of a we, we should not lose sight of the fact that any human situation, insofar as it commits us in the midst of others, is experienced as a we the moment a third person appears. I am walking in the street, following some man whom I only see from behind; I have the minimum technical and practical relatedness to him that is conceivable. However, it only needs a third person to look at me, to look at the road, or to look at him to make it the case that I am bound to him through the solidarity of the we: we are striding down the rue Blomet,[43] one behind the other, on a morning in July. There is always a point of view from which someone looking at various for-itselfs is able to unite them within a we. Conversely, just as the look only manifests in material terms the original fact of my existence for the other, and just as I can, therefore, experience myself as existing for the other in the absence of any particular episode of being looked at, it is not necessary, either, for any particular act of looking to freeze and to penetrate us in order for us to be able to experience ourselves outside, and as integrated within a we. All it takes is the existence of the detotalized-totality "humanity" for any particular group of individuals to be able to feel itself as a we in relation to all, or some part of, other men, whether these men are present "in flesh and blood" or whether they are real but absent. In this way I can always grasp myself—in the presence or absence of a third person—as a pure ipseity, or as integrated in a we. This leads us to various special cases of the "we" and, in particular, to the so-called class consciousness. Class consciousness is, obviously, an acceptance of a particular we in the context of a collective situation that is

---

43 TN: Out of interest, the rue Blomet is quite a long street in the 15th arrondissement of Paris.

more clearly structured than usual. It is not important to define this situation here; our concern is only with the nature of the *we* that is taken up. If a society, by virtue of its economic or political structure, is divided into the oppressed classes and the oppressor classes, the situation of the oppressor classes provides the oppressed classes with the image of an ever-present third person, scrutinizing them and transcending them through his freedom. It is not their hard work, the low standard of living, or the sufferings that they endure which constitute the oppressed community into a class; in fact their common work could—as we will see in the next section—constitute the laboring community into a "we-subject," insofar as it experiences itself—regardless of the coefficient of adversity of *things*—as transcending objects within the world toward its own end. The standard of living is something entirely relative, and will be assessed in different ways according to circumstances (it might be *undergone*, or *accepted*, or demanded in the name of a shared ideal); the sufferings endured, considered in themselves, tend rather to isolate the suffering people than to unite them; in general they are sources of conflict. In any case, the mere comparison that the members of the oppressed commu- 461
nity are able to make between the harshness of their condition and the privileges enjoyed by the oppressor classes is never sufficient to constitute a class consciousness; at the most it will arouse individual jealousies or specific feelings of despair; it is not possible for it to unify the people and cause each person to accept that unification. But, insofar as it constitutes the *condition* of the oppressed class, this set of characteristics is neither simply undergone nor simply accepted. It would be equally mistaken, however, to say that it is grasped from the outset by the oppressed class as something *imposed* by the oppressor class; on the contrary, it takes a long time to construct and to spread a *theory* of oppression. And the value of that theory would only be *explanatory*. The fundamental fact is that a member of the oppressed community—who is, merely as a person, engaged in fundamental conflicts with other members of this community (love, hate, competing interests, etc.)—must grasp his condition, and that of the other members of this community, as one in which he is looked at and thought about by other consciousnesses that escape him. The "master," the "feudal lord," the "bourgeois," and the "capitalist" do not appear merely as powerful people who give orders but further, and above all else, as *third* persons, i.e., as those who are outside the oppressed

community and *for whom* this community exists. It is therefore *for them* and *in their freedom* that the reality of the oppressed class comes to exist. They bring it into being by looking at it. It is to them, and through them, that the identity between my condition and that of the other oppressed people is revealed; it is for them that I exist within an organized situation with others, and that my possibles as dead-possibilities are strictly equivalent to others' possibles; it is for them that I am *one* worker, and it is through and within their revelation as a looking-Other that I experience myself as one among others. In consequence, I encounter the *we* in which I am integrated—or "the class"—*outside*, in the third person's gaze, and it is this collective alienation that I accept, in saying "we." From this standpoint, the impact of the third person's privileges and "our" burdens, of "our" poverty, is in the first instance only that of their *meaning*; they signify the third person's independence in relation to us; they present our alienation to us more clearly. As they are not, for all that, any the less *endured* and as, in particular, our labor and our fatigue are no less *suffered*, it is through my subjection to this suffering that I experience my being-looked-at-as-a-thing-committed-within-a-totality-of-things. It is on the basis of my suffering, of my poverty, that I am grasped by the third person, collectively with others—i.e., on the basis of the world's adversity, on the basis of the facticity of my condition. Without the third person, however great the world's adversity, I would grasp myself as a triumphant transcendence; with the third person's appearance, I experience *us* as we are grasped in terms of things, and as things that the world has defeated. Thus the oppressed class finds its unity as a class in the knowledge that the oppressor class gains of it, and the arrival of class consciousness in an oppressed person corresponds to his accepting, in shame, a we-object. We will see in the next section what "class consciousness" might involve for a member of the oppressor class. The important point here, in any case—as the example we have just chosen adequately demonstrates—is that the experience of the we-object presupposes that of being-for-the-Other, of which it is only a more complex modality. It belongs therefore, as a particular case, within the framework of our previous descriptions so far. Moreover, it contains within it a potentiality for disintegration, since it is experienced through shame and since the *we* collapses the moment the for-itself, faced with the third person, lays claim to his ipseity and looks, in turn, at him. This individual assertion of ipseity is moreover only one of the possible ways of eliminating the we-object. In some highly structured situations—such as, for example, class consciousness—the project revealed by the acceptance of the *we* is no longer that of escaping the *we* through an individual reclamation of ipseity but of liberating the *we* in its entirety from objecthood by transforming it into a we-subject.[44] This is basically a variation of the project we have already described, of transforming the person who is looking into someone who is looked at; it is the everyday transition from one of these two major fundamental attitudes of our for-the-Other to the other. Indeed, the oppressed class can only affirm itself as a we-subject in relation to the oppressor class, and at its expense—i.e., by transforming it into "them-objects" in its turn. Only the particular *person*, who is objectively committed within the class, aims to bring the class in its entirety with him, in and through his project to turn things round. In this sense, the experience of the we-object invokes that of the we-subject, as the experience of my being-an-object-for-the-other invokes my experience of the Other's-object-being-for-me. Similarly, in so-called crowd psychology, we encounter collective infatuations (*Boulangisme*, etc.)[45] that are a specific form of love: in this case the person saying "we" recovers—in the midst of the crowd—love's original project, but it is no longer on his own account: he demands the third person to save the entire community in its very objecthood, by sacrificing his freedom to it. Here, as before, disappointed love leads to masochism. We can see this in the case in which the community throws itself into a state of servitude, and demands to be treated as an object. In that case too, the crowd contains a multiplicity of individual men's projects: the crowd has been constituted as a crowd by the leader or the speaker who looks at it; its unity is an object-unity that each of its members can read in the gaze of the third person

44 TN: ...*de délivrer le nous ... par l'objectité en le transformant en nous-sujet.* I think Sartre has made a mistake in this sentence and that, instead of *par*, he meant to write *de*. Translating the French text as it is (i.e., without correcting the mistake) would give: "liberating the we ... *through* objecthood."

45 TN: *Boulangisme* was a nationalist political movement in France: the politician and general Georges Boulanger (1837–1891) was its figurehead. It remains a matter of dispute whether it should be understood as primarily a right-wing proto-fascist current or as one which united people on the left. The context suggests that Sartre has in mind its appeal for left-wing sympathizers.

dominating it, and thus each person forms the project of losing himself within this objecthood, of giving up his ipseity entirely, in order to be nothing more than an instrument in the leader's hands. But this instru-

463   ment, into which he wishes to merge, is no longer purely and simply his personal for-the-Other; it is the crowd-as-objective-totality. The crowd's monstrous materiality and its innermost reality (even though these are only experienced) are fascinating for each of its members; each person demands to be drowned within the crowd-instrument through its leader's look.[46]

Throughout these various cases we have seen the we-object constituting itself on the basis of a concrete situation in which one part of the detotalized-totality of "humanity" is immersed to the exclusion of the other. We are only *we* in the eyes of the others, and it is on the basis of our being looked at by others that we can affirm ourselves as *we*. But this implies that an abstract and unrealizable project of the for-itself might exist, aiming at an absolute totalization of himself and *all* others. This attempt to recuperate the human totality cannot take place without the existence of a third party—distinct, by definition, from humanity—in whose eyes humanity is in its entirety an object. This third person is unrealizable and is merely the object of the limiting concept of alterity. He occupies the position of "third person" in relation to all possible groupings and is unable, in any case, to enter into community with any particular human grouping; he is a third person in relation to whom nobody else can be constituted as a third person. This concept is none other than that of the looking-being who can never be looked at, i.e., the idea of God. But, as God is characterized as a radical absence, the attempt to realize a humanity that is *ours* is endlessly renewed and leads endlessly to failure. In this way, the humanist "we"—as a we-object—suggests itself to each individual consciousness as an ideal that is impossible to achieve, even while each person retains the illusion of being able to reach it by progressively expanding the circle of communities to which he belongs: this humanist "we" remains an empty concept, the mere sign of a possible extension of "we" in its everyday usage. Whenever we use the term *we* in this sense (to refer to a suffering humanity, a trans-

---

46 Sartre's note: Cf. the numerous cases where ipseity is rejected. The for-itself *refuses to emerge, in anguish, out of the* "we."

gressing humanity, or to establish an objective meaning of History, by envisaging man as an object developing his potential), we are confined to pointing toward a certain particular experience to be undergone in the presence of the absolute third person, i.e., God. In this way the limiting concept of humanity (as the totality of the we-object) and the limiting concept of God each imply and are correlative to the other.

(B) The we-subject

It is the world that acquaints us with our belonging to a subject-community, and especially the existence in the world of manufactured objects. These objects have been worked on by men for them-subjects, i.e., for a transcendence that is not individualized or numbered, and which coincides with the undifferentiated gaze that we referred to earlier as the "they," because the worker—whether or not he is enslaved—works in the presence of an undifferentiated and absent transcendence, whose free possibilities the worker confines himself to sketching out—in their absence—in the object he works on. In this sense the worker, whoever he is, experiences in his work his instrument-being for the other; work, unless it is strictly in the service of the worker's own ends, is a mode of alienation. Here the alienating transcendence is the consumer, which is to say the "they," whose projects the worker can only anticipate. When therefore I use a manufactured object I encounter within it a sketch of my own transcendence; it tells me which action I should perform, that I must turn, or push, or pull, or press. Moreover a hypothetical imperative is involved, which directs me to an end that belongs equally to the world: if I wish to sit down, if I wish to open the tin, etc. And this end has itself been anticipated in the object's constitution as an end posited by some arbitrary transcendence.[47] It belongs now to the object as its most fitting potentiality. In this way it is true that a manufactured object introduces me to myself in the form of "they," i.e., it reflects back to me the

---

47 TN: ... comme fin posée par une transcendance quelconque. Sartre uses quelconque repeatedly in this passage. It has the meaning of "any old person" or "some arbitrary person," "whoever," etc., and it is related to the concept l'on (which I continue to translate as the Heideggerean "they"). For stylistic reasons I have opted to express this idea using slightly different phrases in different sentences; later in the passage, where there is more emphasis on the word itself, I translate quelconque as "everyman."

image of my transcendence as that of "some or other" arbitrary transcendence. And if I allow my possibilities to be channeled by the implement constituted in this way, I experience myself as any arbitrary transcendence: if someone travels from the metro stop "Trocadéro" to "Sèvres-Babylone," "they" change at "La Motte-Picquet." This change is foreseen, indicated on the maps, etc.; if I change line at La Motte-Picquet, I am the "they" who changes there. Of course, I am differentiated from each metro user, as much by the individual arising of my being as by the remote ends I am pursuing. But these latter ends are only at the horizon of my action. My immediate ends are "their" ends, and I apprehend myself as being interchangeable with any of my neighbors. In this sense we lose our real individuality, because the project that we are is precisely the project that others are. In this metro corridor there is only a single, identical project, inscribed into its matter a long time ago, into which a living and undifferentiated transcendence flows. To the extent that I am actualized, when I am alone, as any arbitrary transcendence, I only experience a being-undifferentiated (if, alone in my bedroom, I open a tin with the right tin-opener). But if this undifferentiated transcendence plans whatever projects it has alongside other transcendences, experienced as real presences, similarly absorbed in projects which are identical to my projects, in that case I actualize my project as one among a thousand identical projects, planned by the same undifferentiated transcendence, and my experience is of a common transcendence aiming at a single goal, of which I am only an ephemeral particular instance; I insert myself within the great human current that, unremittingly, and ever since the metro has existed, streams through the corridors of "La Motte-Picquet-Grenelle" station.[48] But we must note: (1) This experience is psychological in kind, and not ontological. It in no way corresponds to a real unification of the for-itselfs in question. Nor is it based in any immediate acquaintance with their transcendence as such (as in the case of being-looked-at); what motivates it, instead, is the objectifying twofold apprehension of the object which is transcended in common, and of the bodies which surround my own. In particular, the fact that I am committed with others in a shared rhythm that I contribute to bringing into being is an

465

---

48 TN: "La Motte-Picquet-Grenelle" is the full name of the metro station. Sartre abridges its name in his earlier mention of it.

element that is especially conducive to my perceiving myself as committed within a we-subject. That is the meaning of the soldiers' march, and
it is also the meaning of the rhythmical work that is done in teams. We
must note that in this case, in fact, the rhythm issues freely from me; it is
a project which I accomplish through my transcendence; it synthesizes a
future with a present and a past, within a perspective of regular repetition; this rhythm is produced by me. But at the same time it blends into
the general rhythm of work or of marching done by the concrete community that surrounds me; it only acquires its meaning through it—as I
may appreciate, for example, when the rhythm I adopt is "not in time."
However, the inclusion of my rhythm within the others' rhythm is apprehended "laterally"; I do not use the collective rhythm as an instrument,
nor do I contemplate it in the sense in which I might contemplate, for
example, some dancers on a stage; it surrounds me and carries me along
without being an *object* for me; I do not transcend it toward my own possibilities but I run my transcendence into its transcendence and my own
aim—to perform this work, to arrive at this place—is an end which
belongs to a "they," and which cannot be distinguished from the group's
own collective goal. Thus the rhythm that I generate comes into being
jointly with me and laterally, as a collective rhythm; it is *my* rhythm to the
extent that it is their rhythm, and *vice versa*. That is precisely the basis of the
experience of the we-subject: in the end, it is *our rhythm*. But, as we can
see, that can happen only if, by antecedently accepting a shared end and
shared instruments, I constitute myself as an undifferentiated transcendence by discarding any personal ends that go beyond the shared ends that
are currently being pursued. Thus, while it is a condition of the very
experience of undergoing my being-for-the-Other that a real and con-   466
crete dimension of being should arise, the experience of the we-subject is
purely a psychological and subjective event in a particular consciousness
which corresponds to an internal modification of the structure of this
consciousness but which does not appear on the foundation of a concrete
ontological relation with others and does not actualize any "*Mitsein*." It is
just one way of being aware of myself in the midst of others. And of
course this experience may be sought out as the symbol of an absolute
and metaphysical unity of all transcendences; indeed, it seems to eliminate the original conflict between transcendences by making them converge upon the world. In this sense, the ideal we-subject will be the *we* of

a humanity that has made itself mistress of the earth. But the experience of the *we* belongs in the domain of individual psychology and remains a mere symbol of the desirable unity of transcendences; in fact it is in no way a lateral and real apprehension, by a particular subjectivity, of subjectivities as such; the subjectivities remain out of reach and radically separated. But it is things and bodies, it is the ways my transcendence is materially channeled, that lead me to apprehend it as being extended and supported by other transcendences, without it being the case either that I come out of my self or that others come out of theirs; I learn through the world that I am part of a *we*. That is why my experience of the we-subject does not remotely imply a similar and correlative experience in others; that is also why it is so unstable, because it requires specific arrangements in the midst of the world and disappears along with those arrangements. In truth, a multiplicity of structures within the world designate me as *everyman*; first, there are all the implements, ranging from "tools" in the strict sense to buildings with their lifts, their water or gas pipes, and their electricity, and taking in along the way the modes of transport, the shops, etc. Each shopfront, each window, reflects back my image as an undifferentiated transcendence. Furthermore, my professional and technical relations with others also announce me as everyman: for the café waiter I am *the* customer; for the ticket inspector I am *the* user of the metro. Finally, the incident in the street that suddenly occurs in front of the café terrace where I am seated designates me, again, as an anonymous spectator and as a pure "gaze which *makes this* incident *exist* from the outside."[49] The play whose performance I attend at the theater and the exhibition of paintings that I visit equally designate the spectator's anonymity. And, of course, I turn myself into everyman when I try on some shoes or uncork a bottle, or enter a lift, or laugh at the theater. But the experience of this undifferentiated transcendence is a contingent, inner event that concerns only me. Certain specific circumstances supplied by the world may add to it the impression of being *we*. But it cannot amount in any case to anything more than a purely subjective impression which commits nobody apart from me.

467

(2) The experience of the we-subject cannot be first, and it can-

---

49 TN: ..."*regard qui fait exister cet incident comme un dehors.*" I do not know why Sartre puts part of the sentence within quotation marks, or why he emphasizes the subpart.

not constitute a primordial attitude toward others, since its fulfillment requires, on the contrary, a prior and twofold recognition of the Other's existence. In the first place, in point of fact, any manufactured object must—in order to qualify as such—invoke the producers who made it and the rules for using it which other people have determined. Faced with an inanimate and uncrafted object, whose operation I myself determine, and to which I myself assign a new use (if, for example, I use a stone as a hammer), I have a non-thetic consciousness of my *person*, i.e., of my ipseity, of my own ends and my free inventiveness. As a matter of their essential structure, the rules for use, the "instructions" for manufactured objects—which, in their simultaneous rigidity and ideality, resemble *taboos*—place me in the other's presence; and it is because the other treats me as an undifferentiated transcendence that I am able to actualize myself as one. It only takes, for example, those large signs placed above the doors of the station or waiting room, on which someone has written the words "exit" and "entrance"—or those pointing fingers on posters which designate a building or a direction. Here, again, we are dealing with hypothetical imperatives. But here the way the imperative is formulated allows the other who is speaking, and directly addressing me, to be clearly visible. Clearly, the printed sentence is addressed *to me*, and represents an immediate communication from the other to me: I am *targeted*. But if the other is aiming at me, he aims at me as an undifferentiated transcendence. Accordingly, if in order to leave I make use of the way out designated as the "exit," my use of it does not in any way draw on the absolute freedom of my *personal* projects: no tool is constituted by my *invention*, and I do not surpass the pure materiality of a thing toward my possibles. Rather, a human transcendence, guiding my own transcendence, has already slipped in between the object and myself; the object is already *humanized*, and signifies "the human kingdom." Considered merely as an opening on to the street, the "exit" is strictly equivalent to the entrance; neither its coefficient of adversity nor its visible utility mark it out as an exit. I do not comply with the object itself when I use it as an "exit"; I adapt to the human order, *recognizing* the other's existence through my act itself, and I establish a dialogue with the other. Heidegger said all this, and he was right to say it. But the conclusion which he forgets to draw is that, for an object to appear as manufactured, it is necessary for the other to already be given in some other way. A person who had not already experienced the other could have no way of distinguishing a manufactured object from the pure materiality of an uncrafted thing. Even were he to use it in accordance with the manufacturer's directions, he would be reinventing this way of using it and thereby effecting a free appropriation of a natural thing. To take the way out that is labeled "exit" without having read the sign or knowing the language is to be like the Stoic's madman who says "It's daytime" in the daytime, not as a result of an objective observation but in accordance with the inner workings of his madness. If, then, a manufactured object makes reference to others and—through that—to my undifferentiated transcendence, it is because I am already acquainted with others. Thus the experience of the we-subject is constructed on the original experience of the Other and can only be secondary and subordinate to it.

But in addition, as we have seen, to apprehend oneself as an undifferentiated transcendence—which is, in essence, as a pure instantiation of the "human species"—is not yet to grasp oneself as a structural part of a we-subject. For that to happen, one must encounter oneself as *everyman* within an arbitrary human current. It is necessary therefore to be surrounded by others. We have also seen that, in this experience, the others are not felt in any way to be subjects, nor are they grasped as objects. They are not posited *at all*. Of course, my starting point is their *de facto* existence in the world, and my perception of their actions, but I do not apprehend their facticity or their movements *positionally*: I have a lateral and non-positional consciousness of their bodies as correlative to my body, of their actions as unfolding in conjunction with my actions, in such a way that I am unable to tell whether it is my actions that are generating their actions or their actions that are generating mine. These few remarks suffice to make it clear that, in the experience of the *we*, the others who form part of the *we* cannot originally be given to me to be known as others. On the contrary, for an experience of my relations with the Other to take the form of "*Mitsein*," there must first be some knowledge of what the Other is. On its own, without a prior recognition of what the other is, the *Mitsein* would be *impossible*. I "am with . . .": fine, but *who* are you with? In addition, even if this experience was ontologically primary, it is not possible to see, without a radical modification of this experience, how to make the transition from a completely undifferentiated transcendence to an experience of any particular people. Furthermore, if the other was not given, the experience of the *we*, as it broke up, would only give rise to the apprehension of pure instrument-objects within the world delimited by my transcendence.

We do not claim that these few observations have exhausted the question of the *we*. They aim only to point out that the experience of the we-subject is in no way a metaphysical revelation; it depends closely on various forms of being-for-the-Other and is no more than an empirical amplification of some of these. That accounts, evidently, for the extreme instability of this experience. It comes and goes erratically, and we are left either confronting some object-others or being looked at by an anonymous "they." It does not appear as a definitive solution to the conflict but as a temporary cooling down, established in the conflict's very midst. It would be futile to wish for a human *we* in which the intersubjective totality could become conscious of itself as a unified subjectivity. Such an ideal could only be a daydream, produced by taking to their limit—and making absolute—experiences that are fragmentary and strictly psychological. Moreover, this ideal itself implies a recognition of the conflict of transcendences as the original state of being-for-the-Other. This is the key to explaining an apparent paradox: as the unity of the oppressed class stems from its experiencing itself as a we-object in the face of the undifferentiated "they" of the third person or the oppressor class, it is tempting to think that, symmetrically, the oppressor class grasps itself as a we-subject facing the oppressed class. But the oppressor class's weakness is that, although it has at its disposal a precise and strict apparatus for coercion, it is in itself profoundly anarchic. The "bourgeois" is not to be defined merely as some *Homo economicus*, possessed of power and particular privileges within a society of a certain kind: he can be described from the inside as a consciousness who does not recognize that he belongs to a class. Indeed, his situation does not allow him to grasp himself as being committed, in common with the other members of the bourgeois class, within a we-object. On the other hand, however, it follows from the very nature of the we-subject that his experiences of it will only be fleeting, and without metaphysical significance. It is common for the "bourgeois" to deny that classes exist: he attributes the existence of a proletariat to the action of agitators, to unfortunate incidents, to injustices that could be remedied by minor adjustments; he asserts that the interests of capital

469

and labor are held in common; against a solidarity based on class, he pits a wider solidarity, a national solidarity integrating worker and boss within a Mitsein that eliminates their conflict. This is not a case, as it is all too often said to be, of a maneuver, nor is it an imbecilic refusal to see the situation in its true light. But the member of the oppressor class can see before him the totality of the oppressed class, as an objective grouping of "they-subjects," without correlatively actualizing his commonality of being with the other members of the oppressor class: the two experiences are in no way complementary. In fact, one only needs to face an oppressed community on one's own, in order to grasp it as an object-instrument, and to grasp oneself as the internal-negation of this community, i.e., merely as the impartial third party. It is only when the oppressed class sets itself—by means of revolt or a sudden increase in its

470   powers—to confront the oppressor class as a "they-are-looking," only at that moment, that the oppressors will experience themselves as we. But it will be in fear and shame, and as a we-object.

Thus the ordeal of the we-object and the experience of the we-subject are not at all symmetrical.[50] The first reveals a dimension of real existence and corresponds to the original ordeal of the for-the-Other, only enriched. The other is a psychological experience actualized in a historical man, immersed in a worked universe and in a society of a particular economic type; it reveals nothing in particular, and it is a purely subjective "Erlebnis."

It seems therefore that the experience of the we, although it is real, is not such as to change the results of our earlier investigations. We are dealing in all cases with either a we-object or a we-subject. The we-object depends directly on the third person, which is to say on my being-for-the-Other, and it is constituted on the foundation of my being-out-there-for-the-other. The we-subject is a psychological experience which presupposes that the existence of the other as such has been revealed to us, in some way or other. It is therefore futile for human-reality to try to escape this dilemma: one either transcends the other or allows oneself to be transcended by him. The essence of relations between consciousnesses is not Mitsein; it is conflict.

---

50 TN: ...entre l'épreuve ...et l'expérience ... See my note on épreuve in the section on vocabulary relating to the mind in Notes on the Translation.

At the end of this long description of the for-itself's relations with the other we have therefore acquired this certainty: the for-itself is not only a being which arises as the nihilation of the in-itself that it is, and the internal negation of the in-itself that it is not. The moment the other appears, that nihilating flight is entirely seized back by the in-itself, and frozen into the in-itself. On its own, the for-itself is transcendent in relation to the world; it is the nothing through which *there are* things. The other, as he arises, confers on the for-itself a being-in-itself-in-the-midst-of-the-world as a thing among things. This petrifaction of the in-itself[51] through the other's look is the innermost meaning of the Medusa myth. We have therefore advanced in our investigation: we wanted, in effect, to ascertain the for-itself's original relation to the in-itself. First we learned that the for-itself was a nihilation and a radical negation of the in-itself; now we are observing that it is also, and without contradiction, wholly in-itself, and present in the midst of the in-itself, in virtue solely of the other's participation. But this second aspect of the for-itself represents its *outside*: the for-itself is by its nature a being that cannot coincide with its being-in-itself.

These remarks might provide the basis for a general theory of being, which is the very goal we are pursuing. However, it is still too early to make a start on it: the description of the for-itself as merely projecting its possibilities beyond being-in-itself will not in fact suffice. The projection of these possibilities does not statically configure the world: in every moment the world is changed by it. If, for example, we read Heidegger with this point in view, we will be struck by the deficiency of his hermeneutic descriptions. Adapting his terminology, we might say that he describes *Dasein* as the existent who surpasses existents toward their being. And here "being" signifies the existent's meaning, or its way of being. And it is true that the for-itself is the being through whom existents reveal their way of being. But Heidegger says nothing about the fact that the for-itself is not only the being who constitutes an ontology of existents but, in addition, the being through whom ontic modifications arise within existents, in their capacity as existents. Obviously, we should consider this permanent possibility of *acting*—i.e., of modifying

471

---

51 TN: Sartre has probably made a mistake here, and intended to write *pour-soi*, which would make more sense.

the in-itself in its ontic materiality, in its "flesh"—as an essential characteristic of the for-itself; as such, its foundation needs to be located in an original relation between the for-itself and the in-itself that we have not yet elucidated. What is it *to act*? Why does the for-itself act? How *can* it act? These are the questions that we must answer now. We have all the elements for an answer: nihilation, facticity and the body, being-for-the-Other, and the distinctive nature of the in-itself. We must examine them anew.

Part Four

To have, to do, and to be[1]

Having, doing, and being are the fundamental categories of human reality. Every type of human behavior can be subsumed within them. Knowing, for example, is a mode of having. These categories are not unconnected, and several writers have emphasized these relationships. Denis de Rougemont brings a relation of this type to light when he writes, in his article about Don Juan, "He *was* not enough to *have*."[2] And, again, we point to a similar connection when we show a moral agent doing (faire)

---

1 TN: *Avoir, faire*, and *être* are often grouped together linguistically as the three most important French verbs, all of them irregular. *Faire* can mean both "to make" and "to do," and, as Sartre uses the verb in both senses, this can create difficulty for translation. In the present chapter, where Sartre is discussing action, "to do" works well; later, when he is talking about our desire to produce things, "to make" is clearly better. My policy will be that, for the most part, I will use "to do" or "to make, or to do"; where neither of these works, I will use "to make." Sometimes I remind the reader that it is the same French verb by putting *faire* in brackets within the sentence where it occurs.

2 TN: Denis de Rougemont (1906–1985) was a Swiss cultural theorist who wrote in French and moved to Paris in 1930. Sartre may have read Rougemont's best-known work on its publication in 1939. It is available in translation as Rougemont (1983).

something in order to make (*faire*) himself, and making himself in order to be.

However, since the anti-substantialist tendency has won out in modern philosophy, most thinkers have tried, in the domain of human behavior, to imitate those of their predecessors who replaced substance in physics by mere movement. For a long time, morality aimed to provide man with a means of *being*. That was the meaning of Stoic morality or of Spinoza's *Ethics*. But if man's being is to become absorbed into the succession of his actions, the aim of morality will no longer be to raise man to a higher ontological dignity. In this sense, Kantian morality is the first great ethical system to substitute doing for being as action's supreme value. The heroes of *L'Espoir* occupy for the most part the territory of *doing*, and Malraux shows us the conflict between the old Spanish democrats, who are still attempting to be, and the communists, whose morality resolves into a series of precise and circumstantial obligations, in which each of which targets a particular *doing*.[3] Who is right? Is the supreme value of human action *to do* or *to be*? And, whichever solution we adopt, what becomes of *having*? Ontology ought to be able to advise us in relation to this problem; it is moreover one of its essential tasks, if the for-itself is the being that defines itself through *action*. We should not therefore finish this work without sketching out, in broad outline, an examination of action in general and the essential relations between *doing*, *being*, and *having*.

---

3 TN: Sartre has already referred to this novel, based on Malraux's experiences of the Spanish Civil War, at EN 147 and EN 150.

Chapter 1

BEING AND DOING

Freedom

I. THE FIRST CONDITION OF ACTION IS FREEDOM

It is strange that the arguments about determinism and free will have endlessly continued, with examples being cited in favor of one or the other claim, without any preliminary attempt being made to explicate the structures contained within the very idea of *action*. In fact, the concept of an act contains numerous subordinate notions, which we need to organize and place within a hierarchy: to act is to modify the way the world is *figured*, to arrange the means in view of an end; it is to produce an organized, instrumental structure such that, through a series of sequences and connections, the modification brought about in one of the links brings in its wake modifications in the entire series and, in the end, produces some foreseen result. Still, that is not the most important point. The point we should note at the outset is that an action is, by definition, *intentional*. The clumsy smoker who inadvertently blows up a powder keg has not *acted*. In contrast, the worker charged with dynamiting a quarry, and who has obeyed the orders he was given, has acted when he has set off the anticipated explosion: he knew, in effect, what he was doing or—alternatively—he was intentionally actualizing a conscious project. That does not imply, of course, that we must foresee every consequence of our acts: the emperor Constantine did not foresee, when he established himself in Byzantium, that he was creating a city of Greek language and culture whose appearance would ultimately provoke a schism within the Christian Church and would contribute to the decline of the Roman Empire. Yet, to the extent that he fulfilled his project of creating a new residence for the emperors in the Orient, he performed an act. Here the adequation of the result to the intention is sufficient to allow us to talk of action. But, if that is correct, we may observe that an action necessarily implies, as its condition, some recognized "desidera-tum," i.e., an objective lack or even a negatity. The intention to create a rival to Rome can come to Constantine only through his apprehension of an objective lack: Rome lacks a counterweight; to this town, still deeply pagan, it is necessary to oppose a Christian city that, for now, *is missing*. The creation of Constantinople can be understood as *an act* only if, first, the conception of a new town preceded the action itself or if, at the least, this conception functions as the organizing theme of all the subsequent steps. But this conception cannot just be a representation of the town as *possible*. It grasps the town in its essential characteristic, as a possible that is desirable and not achieved. In other words, from the moment the act is conceived, consciousness has been able to withdraw from the full world of which it is conscious and to leave the terrain of being, in order openly to approach that of non-being. As long as consciousness is con-sidering what is, and considering that exclusively in its being, it will be constantly referred from being to being, and it will be unable to find any ground within being to motivate a discovery of non-being. The imperial system, insofar as Rome is its capital, works positively and in some spe-cific real manner that can easily be disclosed. Might it be said that tax returns are low, that Rome is not sheltered from invasions, that it doesn't have the right geographical situation for the capital of a Mediterranean empire under threat from barbarians, that the corrupted moral attitudes there make it difficult for the Christian religion to spread? How can we fail to see that all these considerations are *negative*, i.e., that their target is what is not, and not what is? To say that 60 percent of the anticipated taxes have been collected might pass, at a stretch, for a positive apprecia-tion of the situation *as it is*. To say that the returns are *low* is to consider the situation through a situation that is posited as an absolute end and which, precisely, *is not*. To say that the corrupted moral attitudes there hinder the spread of Christianity is not to consider that expansion for

478

what it is, as a process of propagation whose rate we are able to determine by means of the ecclesiastics' reports: it is to posit it as being insufficient in itself, i.e., as suffering a secret nothingness. But of course it appears like that only if we surpass it toward a limit-situation that is posited *a priori* as valuable—for example, toward a specific rate of religious conversions, a specific popular morality—and this limit-situation cannot be conceived merely on the basis of a consideration of the real state of things, because the most beautiful girl in the world can only give us what she *has* and, likewise, the most wretched situation can only, by itself, be designated as what it *is*, without any reference to an ideal nothingness. Insofar as man is immersed within his historical situation, he may not even conceive of the defects and lacks within a particular political or economic organization, not because (as people foolishly say) he "is used to it," but because he grasps it in its plenitude of being and he cannot even imagine that it might be otherwise. We must reverse common opinion here, and accept that it is not the harshness of a situation, or the sufferings it imposes, which provide the grounds for conceiving of another state of things in which everyone would do better; on the contrary, it is on the day when we become able to conceive of another state of things that a new light is thrown on our hardships and our sufferings, and we *decide* that they are intolerable. The worker in 1830 is capable of revolt if salaries are reduced, because he can easily conceive of a situation in which his wretched standard of living would nonetheless be higher than the one which others intend to impose on him. But he does not represent his sufferings as intolerable; he puts up with them, not through resignation but because he lacks the culture and reflection necessary for him to conceive of a social condition in which these sufferings would not exist. Thus he *does not act*. Having taken command of Lyon after a riot, the workers of the Croix-Rousse do not know what to do with their victory; disoriented, they go back home, and the regular army finds them without difficulty.[1] Their misfortunes do not seem to them "habitual" but *natural*: they *are*, that is all, and they constitute the worker's condition; they do not stand out, they are not seen in clear light, and, in consequence, the worker integrates them within his being; he suffers

479

1 TN: La Croix-Rousse is the name of a hill and a district in Lyon. It was an area where silk workers lived, working in very poor conditions, and in which a number of workers' uprisings occurred.

without considering his suffering and without bestowing value on it. For the worker, to suffer and to be amount to the same thing; his suffering is the pure affective content of his non-positional consciousness, but he does not contemplate it. It cannot therefore be, on its own, a motive for his actions. Rather, quite to the contrary, it will appear to him as intolerable when he has formed the project to change it. That means he will have had to take a distance, or step back, from it and to have performed a twofold nihilation: on the one hand, he will have to posit an ideal state of things as a pure nothingness in the present; on the other hand, he will have to posit the current situation as a nothingness in relation to this state of things. He will have to conceive of a state of happiness associated with his class as a pure possible, i.e., as a certain nothingness at present; on the other hand, he will return to the present situation in order to see it in the light of this nothingness, and to nihilate it in its turn, by asserting: "I am not happy." From this, two important consequences follow: (1) No factual state, whatever it is (a political or economic structure of society, a psychological "state," etc.), is capable of motivating any action by itself. That is because an action is a projection of the for-itself toward what is not, and nothing that is can ever determine by itself what is not. (2) No factual state can determine consciousness to apprehend it as a negativity or a lack. Better still, no factual state can determine consciousness to define it and delimit it, since, as we saw, Spinoza's phrase "Omnis determinatio est negatio" remains profoundly true.[2] Now, it is an explicit condition of every action not only that a state of things be disclosed as "a lack of . . ." (i.e., as a negativity) but in addition—and antecedently—that the state of things under consideration should be constituted into an isolated system. There is no factual state—satisfactory or not—other than through the for-itself's nihilating power. But this nihilating power cannot be limited to a mere withdrawal in relation to the world. Indeed, insofar as consciousness is "invested" by being, insofar as it simply suffers what is, it must be subsumed within being: it is necessary to surmount and negate the organized figure "worker-who-finds-his-suffering-natural" for it to be able to become the object of a revelatory contemplation. This means, of course, that it is purely by means of his separating from himself—and

480

---

2 TN: Sartre first quotes this phrase at EN 49.

from the world—that the worker is able to posit his suffering as an intolerable suffering and in consequence *to make it the motive* of his revolutionary action. That implies, therefore, the permanent possibility for consciousness of making a break with its own past, of separating itself from it, in order to be able to consider it in the light of a non-being and to be able to confer on it the meaning that it *has* on the basis of a projected meaning that it *has not*. There is no circumstance or way in which the past on its own can give rise to *an act*, i.e., the positing of an end, in whose light, thrown back on it, it is seen. This is what Hegel glimpsed when he wrote that "the spirit is the negative," even though he seems not to have remembered it when he came to set out his own theory of action and of freedom.[3] In fact, once we attribute to consciousness this negative power in relation to the world and itself, once nihilation becomes an integral part of the *positing* of an end, we have to acknowledge—as the indispensable and fundamental condition of any action—the freedom of the being who acts.

Thus we are able to grasp from the outset what is missing from those tedious arguments between determinists and the partisans of the freedom of indifference.[4] The latter are concerned to find instances of decision where no previous reason exists, or deliberations in relation to two opposed actions that are equally possible and for which the grounds (and the motives) have exactly the same weight. In response, it is easy for the determinists to say that there is no action without a reason, and that the most insignificant movement (raising one's right hand rather than one's left hand, etc.) refers us to reasons and motives that confer its meaning on it. It could not be otherwise, since any action must be *intentional*: in effect, it must have an end, and the end, in its turn, will refer to a reason. Indeed, that is the character of the unity of the three temporal ecstases: the end, or the temporalization of my future, implies a reason (or a motive), i.e., it points toward my past, and the present is the arising of my act. To talk of an act without a reason is to talk of an act that lacks the intentional structure of all action, and the partisans of

481

---

3 TN: Sartre has quoted the same phrase from Hegel earlier, at EN 53.
4 TN: In the philosophical tradition, the "freedom of indifference" is our power to select between alternative actions. Descartes comments on this conception of freedom in his *Meditations*.

freedom, by seeking it at the level of the act's very performance, only manage to make freedom seem absurd. But the determinists in their turn let themselves off the hook by stopping their investigation at the mere labeling of "reason" and "motive." The essential question, in effect, lies beyond the complex organization of "reason-intention-act-end": in fact, we ought to ask how a reason (or a motive) can be constituted as such. Now, we have just seen that, if no act occurs without a reason, that is not at all in the sense in which we might say that no phenomenon occurs without a cause. Indeed, in order to be a reason, the reason must be *experienced* as such. Of course, that does not mean that it must be thematically conceived of and explicated in any way, as in the case of deliberation. But it does at least mean that the for-itself has to confer on it the value of a motive or reason. And, as we have just seen, this constitution of the reason as such cannot refer back to another real and positive existent, i.e., to an earlier reason. Otherwise the very nature of the act, as intentionally engaged within non-being, would vanish. The motive can be understood only through the end, i.e., something nonexistent; the motive is therefore in itself *a negativity*. If I agree to be paid a pittance, it is probably out of fear—and fear is a motive. But it is *fear of dying of hunger*, and so the only meaning to this fear lies outside it, in an ideally posited end: the preservation of a life that I grasp as "endangered." And this fear in its turn can be understood only in relation to the *value* that I implicitly place on this life, i.e., it refers to that hierarchical system of ideal objects in which values consist. In this way, the motive comes to learn what it is through the set of beings that "are not," through ideal existences and through the future. In the same way as the future returns to the present and the past to illuminate it, so my projects as a whole turn back to confer on the motive its structure as a motive. It is only because I escape the in-itself by nihilating myself in the direction of my possibilities that this in-itself is able to acquire the value of a reason or a motive. Reasons and motives have meaning only within a pro-jected set that is precisely a set of nonexistents. And, in the end, this set is myself as a transcendence; it is me insofar as I have myself to be, outside myself. If we recall the principle we recently established—namely, that it is the apprehension of a revolution as possible that confers on the worker's suffering the value of a motive—we are obliged to conclude from it that it is by fleeing a situation in the direction of our possibility of modifying it that we organize that situation into a structure of reasons and motives. The nihilation through which we take a step back in relation to the situation, and the ecstasis through which we pro-ject ourselves toward a modification of this situation are one and the same. The result is that it is indeed impossible to find an act without a motive, but we should not conclude that the motive is the cause of the act: it is an integral part of it. Indeed, and as we cannot distinguish the project that has resolved on a change from the act, the motive, the act, and the end are constituted in one single arising. The meaning of each of these three structures calls for the other two. But the organized totality of the three cannot further be explained by any particular structure, and its arising as a pure temporalizing nihilation of the in-itself is one and the same as freedom. It is the act that determines its ends and its motives, and the act is the expression of freedom.

However, we cannot stop at these superficial considerations: if freedom is the fundamental condition of any act, we must attempt to describe freedom more precisely. But we will encounter a great difficulty at the start: description, usually, is an activity of explication, focusing on the structures of a particular essence. But freedom has no essence. It is not subject to any logical necessity; we should say in relation to it what Heidegger says of *Dasein* in general: "In it, existence precedes and commands essence."[5] Freedom is made into action, and we usually make contact with it through the act that it organizes, with the reasons, motives, and ends that it implies. But precisely because this act has an essence, it appears to us as *constituted*; if we want to get back to the constitutive power, we will have to abandon all hope of finding any essence for it. Such an essence would require, in fact, a new constitutive power, and so on, up to infinity. How, then, are we to describe an existence that is constantly making itself and which refuses to be contained within a definition? Even the designation "freedom" is dangerous if that suggests that the word refers to a concept, as words usually do. Indefinable and unnameable, will freedom not be indescribable?

We encountered similar difficulties when we wanted to describe the

---

5 TN: Although Sartre gives no reference for this citation, Heidegger makes similarly worded claims in *Being and Time* and elsewhere. Heidegger writes, for example, that "*Dasein*'s 'Essence' is grounded in its existence" (Heidegger 1980: §25).

being of the phenomenon, and nothingness. These difficulties did not stop us, since there can be descriptions that do not aim at the essence but at the existent itself, in its particularity. Of course I am not able to describe a freedom that is common to myself and the other; I am not able therefore to envisage an essence of freedom. On the contrary, it is freedom that is the foundation of all essences, since it is by surpassing the world toward his own possibilities that man discloses intraworldly essences. But what we are dealing with is my freedom. Similarly, when I described consciousness, it was not a matter of some nature that certain individuals have in common but rather of my particular consciousness,

483   which, like my freedom, is beyond any essence or—as we have shown several times—for which *to be* is to have been. To reach this consciousness in its very existence, I was able to avail myself precisely of a particular experience: the *cogito*. As Gaston Berger has shown,[6] Husserl and Descartes ask the *cogito* to deliver up a truth *about essence*: in the one case we will reach the connection between two simple natures, while, in the other, we will grasp the eidetic structure of consciousness. But if consciousness must in its existence precede its essence, both of them have made a mistake. All we can ask of the *cogito* is that it acquaint us with a factual necessity. We will also turn to the cogito in *order* to determine freedom as a freedom that is *ours*, as a pure factual necessity, i.e., as an existent that is contingent but that I *cannot* fail to experience. I am indeed an existent who *learns* of his freedom through his acts—but I am also an existent whose individual and unique existence temporalizes itself as freedom. As such I am necessarily a consciousness (of) freedom, since nothing exists in consciousness except as a non-thetic consciousness of existing. In this way my freedom is constantly in question in my being: it is not a quality that is added on, or a *property* of my nature; it is, to be exact, the fabric of my being; and as my being is in question in my being, I must necessarily possess a certain understanding of freedom. It is this understanding that it is our intention, now, to explicate.

To reach the core of freedom, we may be helped by the various obser-

---

6 Sartre's note: Gaston Berger, *Le Cogito chez Husserl et chez Descartes* (1940). TN: Sartre has got the title and date of publication wrong. He must have intended to refer to Gaston Berger's *Le Cogito dans la Philosophie de Husserl*, published in 1941 and translated into English as Berger (1972). Gaston Berger (1896–1960) was a French philosopher.

vations that we ought at this point to summarize. We established in our first chapter that, if negation comes to the world through human-reality, this latter must be a being that is able to actualize a nihilating break with the world and with itself; and we had established that the permanent possibility of this break and freedom are just one and the same. But, on the other hand, we had noted that this permanent possibility of nihilating what I am—in the form of "having-been" it—implies that man has a particular type of existence. We were able then to determine, on the basis of analyses such as that of bad faith, that human-reality was its own nothingness. To be, for the for-itself, is to nihilate the in-itself that it is. In these conditions, freedom can be nothing other than this nihilation. Through it, the for-itself escapes from its being, as from its essence; through it, the for-itself is always something other than what we can say about it, because it is at the least that which escapes this very naming, which is always beyond the name we give to it, beyond the property we acknowledge it to have. To say that the for-itself has to be what it is, to say that it is what it is not by not being what it is, and to say that exis- 484 tence precedes and conditions its essence, or vice versa, and according to Hegel's formula, that in its case "*Wesen ist was gewesen ist*,"[7] is to say one and the same thing: namely, that man is free. By the mere fact, indeed, that I am conscious of the reasons that solicit my action, these reasons are already transcendent objects for my consciousness; they are outside. I may try in vain to cling on to them; by my very existence I escape them. I am condemned to exist forever beyond my essence, beyond the motives and reasons for my action: I am condemned to be free. In other words, we cannot find any limits to my freedom other than itself or, alternatively, that we are not free to cease to be free. To the extent that the for-itself wants to conceal its own nothingness from itself and to incorporate the in-itself as its true mode of being, it attempts at the same time to conceal its freedom from itself. The innermost meaning of determinism is to establish within us an unfailing continuity of existence in itself. In the determinist outlook, the motive, conceived as a psychological fact— i.e., as a full, given reality—is articulated, without any break in continuity, with the decision and the act, which are conceived, equally, as

---

7 TN: Sartre repeats this quotation a few times in the text. The first instance is at EN 70.

psychological givens. The in-itself has taken hold of all of these "data": the motive provokes the act as a cause provokes its effect; everything is real; everything is full. Thus, the rejection of freedom can be conceived only as an attempt to apprehend oneself as being-in-itself; these go hand in hand with each other; human-reality is a being whose freedom is at stake in its being, because it tries constantly to refuse to recognize it. Psychologically, in each one of us, that amounts to trying to take motives and reasons as things. We try to lend them permanence; we do not face up to the fact that at each moment their nature and weight depend on the meaning I give to them, and we regard them as constants. In other words, I consider the meaning that I gave them just now or yesterday—a meaning which, because it is past, is irremediable—and I generalize from its frozen character right into the present. I try to persuade myself that my reason *is* as it *was*. As such, my reason could pass, in its entirety, from my past consciousness into my present consciousness: it would inhabit it. In other words, I attempt to give the for-itself an essence. Similarly, we may posit our ends as if they were transcendences, which is not a mistake. But rather than seeing them as transcendences that are posited and maintained in their being by my own transcendence, we suppose that I encounter them as I arise in the world: they come from God, from nature, from "my" nature, from society. These ready-made and pre-human ends will therefore define the meaning of my act even before I conceive of it, just as my reasons—as pure psychological givens—will give rise to my act without my even noticing. Reason, act, and end constitute a "continuum," something full. These abortive attempts to stifle freedom beneath the weight of freedom—they collapse when anguish in the face of freedom suddenly arises—are sufficient to show that, basically, freedom coincides with the nothingness that lies at man's heart. It is because human-reality *is not enough* that it is free, because it is constantly separated from itself, and because a nothingness separates what it has been from what it is, and from what it will be. In short, it is because its present being is itself a nihilation in the form of a "reflection-reflecting." Man is free because he is not an itself but self-presence.[8] A being that is

485

---

8 TN: *L'homme . . . n'est pas soi mais présence à soi*. Because I am translating the first *soi* as "itself" (see my note on pronouns in Notes on the Translation), the elegance of the French sentence is lost in English.

what it is cannot be free. Freedom is precisely the nothingness that is *been* at the heart of man and which obliges human-reality *to make itself*, rather than *to be*. As we have seen, for human-reality to be is *to choose itself*: nothing comes along from outside—or from inside, either—for it to *receive* or *accept*. Human-reality is entirely abandoned, without help of any kind, to the unbearable necessity of making itself be, right down to the last detail. In this way freedom is not *a* being: it is man's being, i.e., his nothingness of being. If we conceived man in the first instance as a fullness, it would be absurd to seek afterward within him for moments or psychological regions where he might be free: we might as well look for a gap inside a container that we have previously filled right up to the rim. Man cannot be sometimes free and sometimes a slave: he is free in his entirety and always, or he is not.

These remarks can lead us, if we know how to make use of them, to new discoveries. They will enable us in the first place to clarify freedom's relations with what we refer to as the "will." A fairly widespread tendency aims in fact to equate free actions with voluntary actions, and to reserve determinist explanation for the world of passions. That is basically Descartes's point of view. The Cartesian will is free, but there are "passions of the soul."[9] In addition, Descartes attempts to interpret these passions in physiological terms. Later, an attempt will be made to establish a purely psychological determinism. The intellectualist analyses that someone like Proust, for example, tried to provide for jealousy or for snobbery may serve to illustrate this conception of a "mechanism" of the passions. We are required then to conceive of man as free and at the same time determined; and the essential problem would be the relations between this unconditioned freedom and the determined processes of psychological life: How will freedom dominate the passions? How can it use them to its advantage? A wisdom from afar—Stoic wisdom—teaches us that to dominate the passions we should compromise with them; in short, we are advised to behave in relation to affectivity as man acts in relation to nature in general, when he obeys it in order better to command it. Human-reality appears therefore as a free power that is besieged by a collection of determined processes. We can distinguish between

9 TN: *Les Passions de l'Âme* is the title of Descartes's last-published treatise.

486   acts that are entirely free, determined processes over which the free will
has power, and processes that necessarily escape the human-will.

We can see that such a conception is wholly unacceptable. But let us try to understand our reasons for rejecting it better. There is one objection that goes without saying and which we will not waste time expanding: that a clear-cut duality of this kind is inconceivable within the unity of the psyche. How indeed are we to conceive of a being that is *one* and yet which, on the one hand, is constituted as a series of facts, each of which determines the others and which are, in consequence, existents in externality and, on the other hand, as a spontaneity determining itself to be and falling only under its own jurisdiction? *A priori*, this spontaneity would not be capable of any action over a determinism that was already *constituted*: On what could it act? On the object itself (the present psychological fact)? But how could it modify an in-itself that, by definition, is only and can only be what it is? On the law that itself governs the process? But whether we act on the present psychological fact in order to modify it in itself, or we act on it in order to modify its consequences, it amounts to the same. And, in both cases, we encounter the same impossibility that we pointed out earlier. Moreover, what instrument would be available to this spontaneity? If a hand is able to take something, it is because it can be taken. Since spontaneity is by definition *out of reach*, it cannot in its turn *reach* anything: it can only produce itself. And if it were to make use of some special instrument, we would have to conceive of its nature as intermediate between the free will and the determined passions, which is not acceptable. Conversely, of course, the passions cannot have any hold over the will. It is in fact impossible for a determined process to act on a spontaneity, in just the way that it is impossible for objects to act on consciousness. Thus any synthesis of the two types of existents is impossible: they are not homogeneous, and they will each remain in their incommunicable solitude. The only connection that a nihilating spontaneity could have with mechanical processes is to produce itself, by itself, through *an internal negation on the basis of these existents*. But then, precisely, it will only *be* insofar as it denies, in relation to itself, that it is these passions. Thenceforth, spontaneity will necessarily grasp the determinate πάθος in its entirety as a pure transcendent, i.e., as something that is necessarily *outside*, as something that it *is not*. The only effect therefore of this internal negation would be to found the πάθος within the world and it would exist—like any object in the midst of the world—for a free spontaneity that is at the same time both consciousness and will.[10] This discussion shows that two solutions, and only two, are possible: either man is entirely determined (which is inadmissible, especially because a consciousness that is determined—i.e., motivated externally—becomes a pure externality itself, and ceases to be a consciousness) or, indeed, man is entirely free.

487

But these remarks are not yet what, for us, is especially important. Their impact is only negative. The examination of the will must enable us, on the contrary, to move forward in our understanding of freedom. And that is why what strikes us in the first instance is that, if the will is to be autonomous, it is impossible to regard it as a psychological fact that is *given*, i.e., in-itself. It cannot belong to the category of "states of consciousness" defined by the psychologist. Here, as everywhere else, we hold that the state of consciousness is simply an idol of positivist psychology. The will, if it is to be a freedom, is necessarily a negativity and a power of nihilation. But in that case we can no longer see why we should reserve autonomy for it. In fact we have trouble in conceiving of these holes of nihilation that volitions are supposed to be, which are thought to arise within the fabric—a fabric that is dense and full—of passions and of πάθος in general. If the will is nihilation, the whole of the psyche must likewise be nihilation. Besides—and we will shortly return to this—where do we get the idea that a passionate "event" and a pure and simple desire are not nihilations? Is passion not in the first place a project and an enterprise, does it not precisely posit a state of things as being intolerable, and is it not thereby obliged to withdraw from that and to nihilate it by isolating it and considering it in the light of an end, i.e., of a non-being? And doesn't passion have its own ends, which are recognized precisely in the very moment in which it posits them as nonexistent? And if nihilation is precisely freedom's being, how can we deny autonomy to the passions, in order to grant it to the will?

But there is more to be said: far from it being the case that the will is the unique or, at least, the supreme manifestation of freedom, it requires on the contrary—like any event of the for-itself—the foundation of an

---

10 TN: The Greek word here is *pathos*.

original freedom in order to constitute itself as the will. In effect, the will posits itself as a reflective decision in relation to certain ends. But it does not create these ends. Rather, it is a way of being in relation to these ends: it decrees that the pursuit of these ends will be reflective and deliberative. Passion may posit the same ends. In the face of a threat, for example, I may take to my heels, fearful of dying. In this passionate event, the value of life is not any the less implicitly posited as a supreme end. Someone else may understand, on the contrary, that he should stay where he is, even if resistance seems to him at first to be more dangerous than flight; he "holds out." But his aim, even though it is better understood and explicitly posited, remains the same as in the case of the emotional reaction. Only the means of attaining it are more clearly conceived; some of them are rejected as doubtful or inefficacious, while others are organized more solidly. Here the difference turns on the choice of means and on the degree of reflection and explication, and not on the end. Yet the runaway is said to be "impassioned," and we reserve the term "self-willed" for the man who resists.[11] What we have here therefore is a difference in the subjective attitude in relation to a transcendent end. But if we do not want to fall into the error that we were denouncing earlier, and to regard these transcendent ends as pre-human and as an *a priori* limit to our transcendence, we are wholly obliged to acknowledge them to be the temporalizing projection of our freedom. As we have seen, human-reality cannot receive its ends, either from outside or from a supposed inner "nature." It chooses them and, through this very choice, confers upon them a transcendent existence as the external limit of its projects. From this point of view—and if we fully grasp that *Dasein*'s existence precedes and commands its essence—human-reality, in and through its very arising, decides to define its own being through its ends. My being is therefore characterized by my positing of my ultimate ends, which can be identified with the initial bursting forth of the freedom that is mine. And it is an *existence* that bursts forth; it is nothing like an essence or a property of a being, i.e., something engendered in conjunction with an

11 TN: . . . *le fuyard est dit 'passionel' et nous réservons l'épithète de 'volontaire' à l'homme qui résiste.* It is difficult to translate this sentence in a way that both sounds colloquial and retains the echo, in Sartre's French, of the philosophical distinction between the passions and the will.

idea. In this way freedom, being equivalent to existence, is the foundation of the ends that I will try to accomplish either through my will or through my impassioned efforts. We cannot therefore limit it to voluntary acts. On the contrary, volitions are, like passions, specific subjective attitudes through which we try to accomplish the ends that our original freedom posits. We should not, of course, construe "original freedom" as a freedom that might exist *before* the voluntary or impassioned action but rather as a foundation that is strictly contemporary with the will or the passion and that each of these latter *manifests* in its own way. Nor should we oppose freedom to the will or to passion in the way in which Bergson's "deep-seated self" is opposed to the superficial self: the for-itself is entirely ipseity and cannot have any "deep-seated self"—unless we understand by that certain transcendent structures of the psyche. Freedom is nothing other than the *existence* of our will and our passions, insofar as this existence is a nihilation of facticity, i.e., the existence of a being that is its being in the mode of having to be it. We will return to this. Let us remember in any case that the will determines itself within the framework of motives and ends that the for-itself has already posited in a transcendent project of itself toward its possibles. If this were not the case, how could we understand deliberation, which involves an assessment of means in relation to ends that already exist?

If these ends are already established, what remains to be decided at every instant is the way that I will behave in relation to them—in other words, the attitude I will take up. Will I act in accordance with my will or my passions? Who can decide this, other than me? If in fact we were to allow that circumstances make the decision for me (for example, I might exercise my will where the danger is small, but if the risk grows I topple into passion), we thereby remove freedom altogether: indeed, it would be absurd to assert that the will is autonomous when it appears, but that external circumstances strictly determine the moment of its appearing. But on the other hand how can we defend the idea that a will which is not yet in existence could suddenly decide to break the chain of passions and suddenly arise on the ruins of that chain? Such an account would lead us to regard the will as a *power* that is sometimes manifest to consciousness and sometimes remains hidden, but which in any case possesses the "in-itself" existence and permanence of a property. That is exactly what we cannot allow: however, it is certain that ordinary opin-

489

ion does conceive of the moral life as a struggle between a will-thing and some passions-substances. What we see there is a kind of psychological Manichaeism that is utterly indefensible. In fact, it is not enough to will something: one must will to will it. Take for example a given situation: I may react to it emotionally. We have shown elsewhere that emotion is not a physiological thunderstorm:[12] it is a response adapted to the situation; it is a mode of behavior whose meaning and form are the object of an intention belonging to consciousness which aims to accomplish a particular end by some particular means. In a state of fear, fainting and cataplexy aim to eliminate the danger by eliminating our consciousness of the danger. There is an intention to lose consciousness in order to abolish the fearsome world in which consciousness is committed, and through which it comes to being. We are dealing therefore with magical ways of behaving which induce symbolic fulfillments of our desires and which reveal, at the same time, a magical stratum of the world. In opposition to these ways of behaving, behavior of the voluntary and rational type envisages the situation in technical terms, rejects magic, and concentrates on grasping the determined series and instrumental structures by which the problems may be resolved. It will organize a structure of means, taking instrumental determinism as its basis. As a result, it will uncover a technical world, i.e., a world in which each equipment-structure refers to another wider structure, and so on. But who will decide whether I choose the magical or the technical aspect of the world? It cannot be the world itself—which, in order to become manifest, waits upon its discovery. The for-itself must therefore, in its project, choose to be the one through whom the world is disclosed as magical or rational, which is to say that it must give itself, as a free project of itself, a magical existence or a rational existence. It is *responsible* for the one as for the other, for only if it has chosen itself can it be. It appears therefore as the free foundation of its emotions, as of its volitions. My fear is free and manifests my freedom: I have placed all my freedom into my fear and I choose myself as fearful in this circumstance or that; in some other circumstance I will exist as self-willed and courageous and I will have placed all my freedom

490

---

12 Sartre's note: J.-P. Sartre, *Esquisse d'une Théorie Phénoménologique des Émotions* (Hermann, 1939). TN: This text is translated into English as *Sketch for a Theory of the Emotions* (Sartre 1994).

into my courage. In relation to freedom, no psychological phenomenon is favored. All my "ways of being" manifest it equally, since they are all ways of being my own nothingness.

This will show up even better in a description of what we know as the "reasons and motives" of action. We have sketched this description in the preceding pages: now is the time to return to it and resume it with more precision. Do we not say, in effect, that the passion is the *motive* for the act—or even that the act of passion is the one that has passion as its motive? And doesn't the will appear to be the decision that follows a deliberation about our motives and our reasons? What, then, is a reason? What is a motive?

We normally take "reason" to mean the reason for an act,[13] i.e., the set of rational considerations that justify it. If the government decides to convert its securities, it will give its *reasons*: to reduce public debt, to stabilize the Treasury. Equally, it is in terms of *reasons* that historians habitually explain the actions of ministers or monarchs. For a declaration of war, reasons will be sought: the moment is right; the country being attacked is broken apart by internal disturbances; it is time to put an end to an economic conflict that is in danger of dragging on. If Clovis converts to Catholicism when so many barbarian kings are Arians, it is because he sees in it an opportunity to win favor with the episcopate, which is all-powerful in Gaul, etc. We may note that a reason is hereby characterized as an objective assessment of the situation. The reason for Clovis's conversion is the political and religious state of Gaul, the balance of power between the episcopate, the major landowners and the common people; the state of the public debt is the motive for the conversion of securities. However, this objective assessment can be made only in the light of a presupposed end and within the limits of a for-itself's project toward this end. For the power of the episcopate to be revealed to Clovis as a reason for conversion—i.e., for him to be able to consider the objective consequences that this conversion might have—he must already have posited the conquest of Gaul as an end. If we suppose that Clovis has other ends, he might find reasons in the situation of the episcopate for becoming an

---

13 TN: *On entend ordinairement par motif la raison d'un acte* . . . For a reminder of why I have to use the word "reason" twice here, see my note on the *mobile* and *motif* vocabulary in Notes on the Translation.

Arian or remaining a pagan. He might even find that his examination of the state of the Church provides no reason for acting in any particular way: then, in relation to this subject, there is nothing for him to discover; he will leave the situation of the episcopate "not-disclosed," in complete obscurity. What we will call a "reason," therefore, is the objective grasp of a determinate situation insofar as this situation is revealed in the light of a specific end as being able to be used as a means to achieve this end.

491

The motive, on the contrary, is usually regarded as a subjective fact. It is the collection of desires, emotions, and passions that drive me to perform a certain act. The historian does not look for motives, and only reports them out of despair when the act in question cannot adequately be explained by reasons. When Ferdinand Lot writes, for example, having shown that the reasons which are usually given for Constantine's conversion are inadequate or mistaken: "It being proved that Constantine had everything to lose and apparently nothing to gain by embracing Christianity, there is only one possible conclusion, namely that he yielded to a sudden impulse, which we may call one of a pathological or supernatural order as we prefer,"[14] he abandons any explanation in terms of reasons—which strike him as irrelevant—and prefers an explanation that appeals to motives. The explanation must therefore be sought in the historical agent's psychological state—or even in his "mental" state. Naturally, the result is that the event becomes entirely contingent, since another individual—with other passions and other desires—would have acted differently. The psychologist, unlike the historian, prefers to look for motives: indeed he usually supposes these to be "contained within" the state of consciousness that provoked the action. The ideal rational action will, therefore, be the one whose motives are practically non-existent and whose sole inspiration is an objective assessment of the situation. An irrational or impassioned action will be characterized by the inverse proportion. The relation between the reasons and the motives, in the everyday case in which they both exist, remains to be explained. For example, I may join the socialist party because I believe this party serves

14 Sartre's note: Ferdinand Lot, *La Fin du Monde Antique et le Début du Moyen Âge*, p. 35 (Renaissance du Livre, 1927). TN: Ferdinand Lot (1866–1952) was a French historian. The book to which Sartre refers was translated into English as Lot (1931); the quoted passage is at p. 32.

the interests of justice and humanity or because I think it will become the major historical force in the years to follow my joining it: these are reasons. And at the same time I may have some motives: a feeling of pity or charity for certain categories of oppressed people, shame at being "on the right side of the barricade," as Gide says, or, again, a complex of inferiority, a desire to scandalize those close to me, etc. What might we be trying to say when we state that I joined the socialist party because of these reasons *and* these motives? Obviously we are dealing here with two radically distinct layers of meaning. How are we to compare them? How can we determine the share that each of them has in the decision we are considering? This difficulty, which is certainly the greatest difficulty among those raised by the everyday distinction between reasons and motives, has never been resolved; indeed, very few people have even glimpsed it. The fact is that it amounts to positing the existence, in another form, of a conflict between the will and the passions. But if classical theory shows itself to be incapable of assigning their distinctive influence to reasons and to motives in the simple case where they both contribute to reaching the same decision, it will be completely impossible for it to explain and even to *conceive of* a conflict between reasons and motives in which each group demands a particular decision. We need therefore to start the whole discussion again, from the beginning.

492

Certainly, a reason is objective: it is the contemporary state of things, as it is disclosed to consciousness. It is *objective* that the Roman aristocracy and the masses are corrupt in Constantine's time or that the Catholic Church is willing to favor a monarch who will, in Clovis's time, help it to defeat Arianism. Nonetheless, this state of affairs can be revealed only to a for-itself, since the for-itself is, in general, the being through whom "there is" a world. Better still, it can be revealed only to a for-itself who chooses itself in some way or other, i.e., a for-itself who has made for itself its own individuality. In order to discover the instrumental implications of implement-things, we must have projected ourselves in some way or other. Objectively, a knife is an instrument made of a blade and a handle. I may apprehend it objectively as an instrument for slicing, for cutting; but, for want of a hammer, I may apprehend it the other way round as an instrument for hammering: I can make use of its handle to drive in a nail, and this apprehension is no less *objective*. When Clovis weighs up the assistance that the Church may provide him with, it is not clear whether a group of prelates or even an individual bishop has made any overtures to him, or even that a member of the clergy has clearly thought about an alliance with a Catholic monarch. The only facts that are strictly objective—those facts that any for-itself at all might observe—are the Church's great power over the populations of Gaul, and the Church's anxiety concerning Arian heresy. For these observations to become organized as a reason for conversion, they must be separated from the whole—and for that they must be nihilated—and transcended toward their own potentiality: the Church's potentiality, objectively apprehended by Clovis, will be to lend its support to a converted king. But this potentiality can be revealed only if the situation is surpassed toward a state of affairs that does not yet exist—surpassed, in short, toward a nothingness. In a nutshell, the world can only give its advice if we interrogate it, and we can only interrogate it in relation to a clearly defined end. Far from determining the action, therefore, a reason only appears in and through the project of an action. It is in and through the project of establishing his domination over the whole of Gaul that the state of the Western Church appears objectively to Clovis as

493   a reason for converting. In other words, the consciousness that makes a reason salient within the world as a whole already has its own structure, it has set its own ends, it has projected itself toward its possibles, and it has its own distinctive way of depending on these possibilities: in this case, the distinctive way of relating to one's possibles is affective. And this internal organization that consciousness has adopted—in the form of a non-positional consciousness (of) self—is strictly correlative to its carving out of reasons within the world. Now, if we think about it, we have to admit that the for-itself's internal structure—through which the for-itself's reasons for acting are made to arise within the world—is an "irrational" fact, in the historical sense of the term. We can in fact understand the technical utility of Clovis's conversion quite rationally, in terms of the hypothesis in which his project was to conquer Gaul. But in relation to his project of conquest, we cannot do the same. It cannot "be explained." Should we interpret it as an effect of Clovis's ambition? But what precisely is the ambition, other than the intention to conquer? How should we distinguish Clovis's ambition from the precise project to conquer Gaul? It would therefore be pointless to conceive of this original project of conquest as "driven" by some preexisting motive, i.e., ambi-

tion. It is quite true that ambition is a motive, since it belongs entirely to subjectivity. But, as it cannot be distinguished from the project to conquer, we will say that this first project of his possibilities, in the light of which Clovis discovers a reason for converting, is precisely the *motive*. Then everything is clarified and we are able to conceive of the relations between these three terms: reasons, motives, ends. What we have here is a particular case of being-in-the-world: just as it is the for-itself that makes it happen, in its arising, that there is a world, so in this case it is the for-itself's very being—insofar as its being is a pure project toward an end—that makes it happen that *there is* a specific objective structure of the world that, in the light of this end, deserves to be called a "reason." The for-itself is therefore conscious of this reason. But this positional consciousness of the reason is as a matter of principle a non-thetic consciousness of itself as a project toward an end. In this sense it is a motive, which means it experiences itself non-thetically as a project—more or less harsh, more or less passionate—toward an end, in the very moment in which it constitutes itself as a consciousness revealing the world's organization in terms of reasons.

Thus, reason and motive are correlatives, exactly as any non-thetic consciousness (of) self is the ontological correlative of a thetic consciousness of the object. Just as any consciousness of something is a consciousness (of) self, the motive is in the same way nothing but the apprehension of the reason, insofar as this apprehension is conscious (of) self. But, obviously, it follows that the reason, the motive, and the end are the three indissoluble terms in the bursting forth of a living and free consciousness, projecting itself toward its possibilities and defining itself through these possibilities.

How, therefore, does the motive come to appear to the psychologist 494 as the affective content of an act of consciousness, insofar as this content determines another act or a decision? It is because the motive—which is not distinct from our non-thetic consciousness of self—slides into the past with that very consciousness, and stops being alive at the same time as it does. As soon as a consciousness is pastified, it is what I have to be in the form of "was." Thereafter, when I return to yesterday's consciousness, it retains its intentional meaning and its meaning as a subjectivity but, as we saw, it is frozen and lies outside like a thing, since the past is in itself. The motive, then, becomes what I am conscious of. It may appear to me in the form of "knowledge" (as we saw earlier, the dead past haunts the present in the guise of knowledge); it may also happen that I turn back toward the motive in order to explicate and to formulate it, guided by the knowledge that it has now become, for me. In this case the motive is an object of consciousness; it is this very consciousness of which I am conscious. It appears therefore—like my memories in general—as mine and, at the same time, as transcendent. We are usually surrounded by these motives that no longer "grip" us because the decisions we make are not only to perform this or that action but also to accomplish actions we have decided on the night before, or to pursue enterprises to which we are committed; in general, whatever the moment in which consciousness grasps itself, consciousness apprehends itself as committed, and this very apprehension implies a knowledge of our motives for the commitment, or even a thematic and positional explication of these reasons. It goes without saying that our grasp of our motive immediately refers us to the correlative reason, since the motive—even when it has been pastified and frozen into in-itself—retains, at least in its meaning, that it was conscious of a reason, i.e., the discovery of an objective structure of the world. But as the motive is in-itself and the reason is objective, they are presented as a pair without ontological difference; indeed, we saw that our past gets lost in the midst of the world. That is why we put them on an equal footing and why we can talk about an action's reasons and its motives as if each of these could come into conflict or compete with the others, in some determinate ratio, in order to reach the decision.

Only, if the motive is transcendent, if it is only the irremediable being that we have to be in the mode of "was"—if, like all of our past, it is separated from us by a breadth of nothingness—it can act only if we reclaim it; on its own, it has no power. It is, therefore, through the bursting forth of the committed consciousness itself that a value and a weight come to be conferred on its earlier motives and reasons. That they have been and that its mission is to maintain their existence in the past: these matters do not depend on consciousness. That I wanted this, or that, remains irremediable and even constitutes my essence, since my essence is what I was. But as to the meaning that this desire, this fear, these objective considerations about the world, have for me now, when I project myself toward my futures, only I can decide that. And I only decide this, precisely, through the very act by which I pro-ject myself toward my ends. My recovery of my earlier motives—or their rejection, or their new appraisal—is not distinct from the project through which I assign new ends to myself and through which, in the light of these ends, I apprehend myself as discovering a supporting reason in the world. Past motives, past reasons, present reasons and motives, future ends: all these are organized into an indissoluble unity by the very arising of a freedom that is beyond reasons, motives, and ends.

From this it follows that the will's deliberation is always rigged. How in fact can I evaluate reasons and motives whose value, precisely, has been conferred on them before any deliberation and through the choice that I make of myself? The illusion here is caused by the attempt to regard reasons and motives as entirely transcendent things that I might weigh as if they were weights, and which could possess a weight as a permanent property even while, on the other hand, we want to regard them as contents of consciousness—which is contradictory. In fact, reasons and motives only have the weight that my project—i.e., the free production of the end, and of the act as having to be actualized—confers on them. When I deliberate, the die is already cast. And if I must come to deliberate, it is simply because it is part of my original project to take account of my motives *by means of deliberation* rather than through this or that other mode of discovery (through passion, for example, or quite simply by action, which reveals the organized collection of my reasons and ends in the way in which my speech informs me of my thought). There is therefore a choice of deliberation as a procedure that will tell me what I am projecting and, in consequence, what I am. And the free spontaneity organizes the *choice* of deliberation alongside the collection of motives-reasons and the end. When the will intervenes, the decision is taken and it has no value apart from that of an announcement.

The voluntary act is distinguished from nonvoluntary spontaneity by the fact that the latter is a purely unreflected consciousness of its reasons, through the pure and simple project of its act. As for the motive, it is not an object for itself in unreflected action but a mere non-positional consciousness (of) self. The structure of a voluntary act, on the contrary, requires the appearance of a reflective consciousness that grasps its motive as a quasi-object, or even intends it—through the reflected consciousness—as a psychological object.[15] In this case, since the motive is grasped through the intermediary of the reflected consciousness, it is somewhat separate: to take up Husserl's famous formulation, the mere act of voluntary reflection, through its reflective structure, operates the ἐποχή in relation to the reason; it suspends it, placing it between brackets. In this way a semblance of evaluative deliberation can be introduced, owing to the fact that a deeper nihilation separates the reflective consciousness from the unreflected consciousness (or motive), and owing to the suspension of the motive. Nonetheless, as we know, if the reflection's result is to widen the fissure that separates the for-itself from itself, that does not yet make it its goal. The goal of the reflective scissiparity is, as we saw, to retrieve the reflected so as to constitute the unrealizable "in-itself-for-itself" totality that is the fundamental value posited by the for-itself even as it arises in its being. If therefore the will is essentially reflective, its goal is not so much to decide which end is to be achieved, because it has in any case placed its bets; instead, the will's deep intention bears on the way to achieve this already posited end. Insofar as he decides and acts, the for-itself who exists in the voluntary mode wills to retrieve himself. The for-itself does not will only that he should be carried toward an end, or that he should choose himself as the one carried toward such an end: he also wills to retrieve himself as a spontaneous project toward this end or that. The will's ideal is to be an "in-itself-for-itself," in the form of a project toward a specific end: that is obviously a reflective ideal, and it is the meaning of the satisfaction that may accompany a judgment such as "I did what I wanted." But it is clear that reflective scissiparity in general has its foundation in a project that is deeper than itself which, in Part Two, Chapter 3, for want of a better term, we called its "motivation."[16] Now that we have defined "motive" and "reason," we should call this project that underlies reflection an "intention." To the extent therefore that the will is an instance of reflection, the fact of placing oneself at the level of the will in order to act requires as its foundation a more basic intention. It is not enough for the psychologist to describe such and such a subject as bringing about his project in the

---

15 TN: . . . *ou même qui l'intentionne* . . . The verb "to intend" is not used here in the ordinary sense of "intending to do something" but in the technical phenomenological sense, where it means to take something as the intentional object of consciousness.

16 TN: I think Sartre has made a mistake here; the discussion of "motivations" comes earlier in Part Two.

mode of voluntary reflection; he must in addition be able to provide us with the *deep intention* that makes it happen that the subject actualizes his project in this mode of volition, rather than in any other mode—it being understood, moreover, that just any mode of consciousness would have led to the same actualization, once the ends had been posited by an original project. Thus we have reached a freedom that is deeper than the will, merely by showing ourselves to be more *demanding* than the psychologists, i.e., by asking the question *why*, at the point where they confine themselves to noting that the mode of consciousness is volitional.

This brief examination does not aim to exhaust the question of the will: on the contrary, we should attempt a phenomenological description of the will for its own sake. That is not our aim: we hope simply to have shown that the will is not a preeminent manifestation of freedom but a psychological event with a distinctive structure, constituted at the same level as the others, and which is, no more or less than the others,   497 supported by an original and ontological freedom.

By the same token, freedom appears as an unanalyzable totality: the reasons, motives, and ends, just as much as the way in which the reasons, motives, and ends are grasped, are organized as a unity within the framework of this freedom, and must be understood on its basis. Does that amount to saying that we must represent freedom as a series of unpredictable upheavals, comparable to the Epicurean *clinamen*? Am I free to will just anything, at just any moment? And when I want to explain such and such a project, must I, at every instant, encounter the irrationality of a free and contingent choice? For as long as it seemed that the acknowledgment of freedom would have as its consequence these dangerous conceptions in complete contradiction to experience, many good minds turned away from the belief in freedom. It has even been possible to claim that determinism—if one avoids confusing it with fatalism—is "more human" than the theory of free will. If indeed it highlights the strict conditioning of our actions, it does at least give the *reason*[17] for each of them, and if it is strictly limited to the psychological domain—if it gives up looking for any further conditioning in the structure of the universe—it shows that the connection in our actions is in ourselves: we act as we are and our acts contribute to making us.

---

17 TN: ... *au moins donne-t-il la raison de chacun* ... The word translated as "reason" here is *raison*, rather than *motif*.

Let us examine more closely, however, the small number of certain results that our analysis has enabled us to acquire. We have shown that freedom and the for-itself's being are just one and the same: human-reality is free precisely to the extent to which it has its own nothingness to be. It has this nothingness to be, as we saw, in many dimensions: first, by temporalizing itself, i.e., by being always at a distance from itself, which implies that it can never let itself be determined by its past to do this action or that; next, by arising as a consciousness of something and (of) itself, i.e., by being self-presence and not merely self, which implies that nothing can exist in consciousness that is not a consciousness of existing and that, in consequence, nothing external to consciousness can motivate it; and, last, by being a transcendence, which is to say not something that exists first in order to place itself *afterward* in relation to such and such an end but, on the contrary, a being that is from the outset a pro-ject, i.e., which defines itself through its end.

Thus it is no part of our intention here to invoke something arbitrary or capricious: an existent that, as consciousness, is necessarily separated from all other existents, because they only have any connection with it to the extent that they are for it, and which decides on its past (in the form of tradition) in the light of its future rather than allowing it purely and simply to determine its present, and which is acquainted with what

498   it is by *something other than itself*, i.e., by an end that it is not and that it projects from the other side of the world; this is what we mean by a "free existent." That does not mean at all that I am free to stand up or sit down, to come in or go out, to run away or to confront the danger, if we mean by "freedom" a capricious pure contingency, unlawful, gratuitous, and incomprehensible. Of course, each of my acts, even the smallest, is wholly free in the sense we have just clarified; but that does not mean that it can be *anyhow*, or even that it is unpredictable. Yet—it will be said—if we cannot understand it either on the basis of the state of the world or on the basis of the totality of my past, taken as something irremediable, how could it be possible for it not to be gratuitous? Let us take a closer look.

According to the view that is generally accepted today, to be free does not only mean to choose oneself. A choice is said to be free if it is such that it could have been other than it is. I have gone on an excursion with some friends. After several hours of walking, I am growing tired, and eventually my fatigue becomes oppressive. At first I resist and then suddenly I let myself go: I give in; I throw my bag down on the side of the road, and I drop down beside it. I will be reproached for my action, with the implication that I was free, which means not only that nothing and nobody determined my action but also that I could have resisted my fatigue, done as my fellow travelers did, and waited for my rest until we reached our stop. I will defend myself by saying that I was *too* tired. Who is right? Or, instead, hasn't the debate been established on the wrong grounds? There is no doubt that I could have done otherwise, but that is not the problem. We should instead formulate it like this: could I have done otherwise without markedly changing the organic totality of projects that I am, or would the fact of resisting my fatigue, rather than remaining a mere local and accidental modification of my behavior, be possible only with a radical transformation of my being-in-the-world— a transformation that is, moreover, *possible*. In other words, I could have done otherwise, agreed: but *at what cost?*

We will reply to this question first with a *theoretical* description that will allow us to grasp our central claim. Then we can see whether concrete reality shows itself to be more complicated and if, without contradicting the results of our theoretical investigation, it might not lead us to enrich these results and make them more flexible.

We should note first that fatigue, in itself, cannot induce my decision. It is only—as we saw in relation to physical pain—the way in which I exist my body. In the first instance, it is not the object of a positional consciousness but my consciousness's very facticity. If therefore I am walking through the countryside, it is the surrounding world that reveals itself to me, that is the object of my consciousness; that is what I transcend toward the possibilities that are mine—for example, to arrive this evening at the place that I settled on earlier. Only, to the extent that I 499 grasp this landscape with my eyes, which unfold the distances, with my legs, which climb the slopes and thereby cause new scenes and new obstacles to appear and to disappear, with my back, which carries the bag, I have a non-positional consciousness (of) this body—which regulates my relations with the world and signifies my engagement in the world—in the form of fatigue. Objectively, and correlated with this non-thetic consciousness, the roads are revealed as interminable, the inclines as *more difficult*, the sun as more intense, etc. But I am still not thinking my fatigue; I do not grasp it as a quasi-object of my reflection. There comes a moment, however, when I try to consider it and to retrieve it, and this intention itself ought to be interpreted. Let us, however, take it for what it is. It is not a contemplative apprehension of my fatigue; rather—as we saw in relation to pain—I *suffer* my fatigue. In other words, a reflective consciousness is directed on my fatigue in order to live it and to confer upon it a value and a practical relation to myself. It is only at this level that my fatigue can appear to me as bearable or as intolerable. In itself, it will never be anything like that; rather, it is the reflective for-itself who, as he arises, suffers his fatigue as intolerable. The essential question arises here: my fellow travelers are in good health like me; they are more or less as fit as I am, so, even though it is not possible to *compare* psychological events that unfold in different subjectivities, I will ordinarily conclude—and witnesses will conclude on the basis of an objective consideration of our bodies-for-the-Other—that they are more or less "as tired as I am." How therefore does it happen that they suffer from their fatigue in a different way? It will be said that the difference is because "I am soft" and they are not. But, even though this assessment has an undeniable practical bearing and can be counted on when it is a matter of deciding whether or not to invite me on another excursion, it cannot satisfy us here. As we have seen, in fact, to be ambitious is to have the project of conquering a throne or honors; it is not a *given*, something that might push one toward conquest, but the conquest itself. Similarly "being soft" cannot be a factual given, and it is only a name that is given to the way in which I suffer my fatigue. If therefore I want to understand the conditions in which I may suffer my fatigue as intolerable, we should not appeal to givens that are alleged to be factual, which reveal themselves to be only a choice; we should try to examine this choice itself and to see whether it might be explained within the perspective of a wider choice, in which it is integrated as a secondary structure. If in fact I question one of these companions, he will explain that of course he is tired, but he *likes* his fatigue: he surrenders to it as if to a bath; it seems to him in some way to be the favored instrument for discovering the world around him, adapting to the stony harshness of the paths, discovering the "mountainous" import of the slopes; similarly, it is this slight insolation on his neck and this slight humming in his ears that enable him to achieve direct contact with

500

the sun. In the end, the feeling of effort for him is that of conquered fatigue. But as his fatigue is nothing other than the passion that he endures in order that the dust on the paths, the burning of the sun, the harshness of the roads, should maximally exist, his effort—which is to say this gentle familiarity with a fatigue that he loves, to which he surrenders, and which, however, he directs—presents itself as a way of appropriating the mountain, of suffering it right to the end and triumphing over it. In our next chapter, in fact, we will see what the words "to have" mean, and the extent to which "*doing*" or "*making*" something is a means of *appropriation*. Thus my companion lives his fatigue within a larger project that is a trusting surrender to nature, a passion consented to in order for it to exist at its peak, and at the same time a gentle domination and appropriation. It is only in and through this project that his fatigue can be understood and can have a meaning for him. But this meaning and this larger project are still, by themselves, "*unselbstständig.*" They are not enough because they presuppose, precisely, my companion's particular relationship to his body, on the one hand, and, on the other hand, his relationship to things. Indeed, it may easily be understood that there are as many ways of existing one's body as there are for-itselfs, even though, naturally, certain original structures are invariable and constitute human-reality in each instance: we will deal elsewhere with the relation of the individual to the species (as it has been incorrectly described) and with the conditions of universal truth. For now, we are able to conceive, on the basis of a thousand significant events, that there is, for example, a specific type of flight from facticity that consists precisely in surrendering oneself to this facticity, which is to say, in short, in trustingly taking it up and loving it, in order to try to retrieve it. This original project of retrieval is therefore a specific choice made by the for-itself of itself in the presence of the problem of being. Its project remains a nihilation, but this nihilation turns back to the in-itself it nihilates, and is expressed by a particular valorization of facticity. This is expressed notably in the thousand ways of behaving that we describe as *surrender*. To surrender to fatigue, to heat, to hunger, and to thirst, to collapse with relish onto a chair, a bed, to relax, to try to be absorbed into one's own body, no longer beneath the eyes of another (as in the case of masochism) but in the for-itself's original solitude: none of these modes of behavior may ever be limited to itself, and we feel this keenly, since, in another person, they irritate or attract us; their con-

501 dition is an initial project to reclaim the body, i.e., an attempt to solve the problem of the absolute (the in-itself-for-itself). This initial form may itself be limited to a profound tolerance of facticity: in that case the project to "make oneself body" will mean the happy surrender to a thousand passing little indulgences, a thousand little desires, a thousand weaknesses. Recall Mr. Bloom in Joyce's *Ulysses* inhaling with satisfaction, while he responds to the needs of nature, "the intimate smell rising from under him."[18] But it may also happen—and this is the case with my companion—that, through the body and by deferring to the body, the for-itself tries to reclaim the totality of the non-conscious, i.e., the whole universe insofar as it is a set of material things. In this case the synthesis of the in-itself with the for-itself that is aimed at will be the quasi-pantheist synthesis of the totality of the in-itself with the for-itself who reclaims it. Here the body is an instrument of the synthesis: it loses itself in its fatigue, for example, in order that this in-itself should maximally exist. And as it is the body which the for-itself exists as *its own*, this passion of the body coincides for the for-itself with the project of "making the in-itself exist." In its entirety this attitude—which belongs to one of my fellow travelers—may express itself through the obscure feeling of a kind of mission: he goes on this excursion because the mountain he is going to climb and the forests he is going to pass through *exist*, and it is his mission to be the person through whom their meaning will be made manifest. And he thereby attempts to be the person who founds them in their very existence. We will come back in our next chapter to this appropriative relation of the for-itself to the world, but we do not yet have at our disposal the necessary materials to elucidate it in full. In any case, what appears obvious after our analysis is that, in order to understand the way in which my companion *suffers* his fatigue, a regressive analysis is necessarily required, which will lead us right up to an initial project. Is the project that we have outlined "*selbstständig*" now? Certainly—and we may easily be convinced: in fact, by repeated regression, we have reached the original relationship that the for-itself chooses with its facticity and with the world. But is this original relationship anything other than the for-itself's being-in-the-world itself, insofar as this being-in-the-world is a choice—i.e., have we reached the

18 TN: Sartre is alluding to a moment in the "Calypso" episode of *Ulysses*. Joyce's English differs slightly: Bloom is "seated calm above his rising smell" (Joyce 1960: 84).

original type of nihilation through which the for-itself has its own noth-ingness to be? From this point on no interpretation may be attempted, because it would implicitly presuppose the for-itself's being-in-the-world, just as all the demonstrations that have been attempted of Euclid's postulate implicitly presuppose the adoption of this postulate.

In consequence, if I apply the same method to interpret the way in which I suffer my fatigue, I will in the first place grasp in myself, for example, a mistrust of my body, a manner of not wanting to "put up with it," of counting it for nothing, which is merely one of the many 502 possible modes for me of *existing my body*. I will discover without diffi-culty an analogous mistrust in relation to the in-itself and, for example, an original project to reclaim the in-itself that I am nihilating *through the intermediary of others*—which returns me to one of the initial projects that we listed in the previous part. In consequence, rather than managing my fatigue "easily," I will apprehend it "awkwardly," as an unwelcome phenomenon that I wish to be rid of—simply because it incarnates my body and my brute contingency in the midst of the world, whereas my project is to rescue my body and my presence to the world through the other's acts of looking. I am also returned to my original project, i.e., to my being-in-the-world, insofar as this being is choice.

We are not concealing from ourselves how much the method of this analysis leaves to be desired. The fact is that everything remains to be done in this domain: it is a matter, in fact, of drawing out the mean-ings implied by an act—by *every* act—and of moving from there to meanings that are richer and deeper, until we come across the meaning which no longer implies any other meaning and which points only to itself. Most people practice this retracing dialectic spontaneously; we can even observe that, given within one's knowledge of oneself or the Other, there is a spontaneous understanding of the hierarchy of interpretations. A gesture indicates a "*Weltanschauung*," and we *sense* it. But nobody has tried to systematically draw out the meanings implied by an act. Only one school of thought has set out from the same initial evidence as we have, and that is the Freudian school. For Freud, as for us, an act cannot be limited to itself: it immediately refers to deeper structures. And psychoanalysis is the method that enables us to expli-cate these structures. Freud wonders, as we do: Under which condi-tions is it possible for this person to have accomplished this particular action? And, like us, he refuses to interpret the action by means of the antecedent moment, i.e., to conceive of a horizontal psychological determinism. The act appears to him as *symbolic*, which is to say that it seems to express a deeper desire that cannot itself be interpreted on the basis of an initial determination of the subject's libido. Only Freud is aiming in this way to constitute a vertical determinism. In addition, with this approach his conception will necessarily refer to the subject's past. For him, affectivity is at the root of the action, in the form of psychophysiological drives. But this affectivity is from the outset a blank slate in each of us; it is external circumstances and, in the end, the subject's *history* that will decide whether such and such a tendency will fix on such and such an object. It is the child's situation within his family that will determine the birth of the Oedipus complex in him: in other societies, made up of families of another type—and as has been noted, for example, among the primitive peoples of the Pacific coral islands—this complex cannot be formed. In addition, it is external circumstances, again, that will decide whether, at the age of puberty, the complex will "be liquidated" or, on the contrary, will remain the pole of sexual life. In that way, and through the mediation of history, Freud's vertical determinism is still based on a horizontal determinism. Of course, some symbolic action expresses an underlying and contemporary desire, just as this desire manifests a deeper complex, and all this within a single psychological process; but it is no less true that the complex preexists its symbolic manifestation, and it is the past that has constituted it as it is, in accordance with the classic connections— transference, condensation, etc.—that we find mentioned not only in psychoanalysis but in every attempt at a deterministic reconstruction of psychological life. In consequence, the dimension of the future does not exist for psychoanalysis. Human-reality loses one of its ecstases and has to be interpreted only by means of a regression, setting out from the present, toward the past. At the same time, the subject's fundamental structures, which are signified in his acts, are not signified for him but for an objective witness who makes use of discursive methods to explicate these meanings. No preontological understanding of the meaning of his acts is accorded to the subject. And that can be easily conceived, since, in spite of everything, these acts are only an effect of the past—which by definition is out of reach—rather than seeking to inscribe their goal within the future.

503

We must limit ourselves therefore to taking as our inspiration the psychoanalytic *method*, which is to say that we must try to draw out the meanings of an act on the basis of the principle that every action, however insignificant it may be, is not simply the effect of the previous psychological state and does not depend on a linear determinism but is included, on the contrary, as a secondary structure within global structures and, finally, within the totality that I am. Otherwise, indeed, I would have to understand myself either as a horizontal flux of phenomena, each of which is conditioned from outside by the preceding one, or as a substance that supports the senseless flowing of its modes. Both of these outlooks would result in our mixing up the for-itself and the in-itself. But if we accept the method of psychoanalysis—and we will return to this at length in the following chapter—we need to apply it *in the opposite direction*. We conceive of each act, in fact, as a phenomenon that can be understood, and we do not allow for a determinism by "chance," any more than Freud. But, rather than understanding the phenomenon in question on the basis of the past, we conceive of the act of understanding as a return from the future toward the present. The way in which I suffer my fatigue does not depend at all on the accident of the slope I am climbing or the more or less restless night that I have spent: these factors may contribute to constituting my fatigue itself, but not the way I suffer it. But we refuse to see in it—as a disciple of Adler would—an expression of the inferiority complex, for example, in the sense in which this complex would be an earlier formation. We do not deny that a certain raging and stiffened way of fighting against fatigue may express a so-called inferiority complex. But the inferiority complex itself is a project of my own for-itself in the world, in the presence of the other. As such, it is always transcendence; further, as such, it is a way of choosing oneself. This inferiority, which I struggle against and yet recognize, was *chosen* by me at the outset; without doubt, it is the meaning of my various forms of "failure behavior," but it is precisely nothing other than the organized totality of my failure behavior as a projected template, as the general specification for my being, and each failure behavior is itself a transcendence, since each time I surpass the real toward my possibilities. To give in to fatigue, for example, is to transcend the path still to be covered by constituting it with the meaning "path that is too difficult to follow." It is impossible to consider the feeling of inferiority seriously

504

without determining it on the basis of the future and my possibilities. Even observations such as "I am ugly," "I am stupid," etc., are in essence anticipations. It is not a matter purely of observing my ugliness but of grasping the coefficient of adversity presented by women, or society, to my undertakings. And that can be discovered only by and in the choice of these undertakings. Thus the inferiority complex is a free and global project of myself, as inferior next to another; it is the way in which I choose to take on my being-for-the-Other, the free solution that I find for the insurmountable scandal of the other's existence. Thus we must understand my inferiority reactions and my failure behavior on the basis of the free sketch of my inferiority as the choice of myself in the world. We grant to the psychoanalysts that every human reaction can *a priori* be understood. But we reproach them with having failed to recognize just this initial "understandability" by trying to explain the reaction in question by means of an earlier reaction, which reintroduces the mechanism of causality: we must define the understanding in other terms. We can understand any action as a project of oneself toward a possible. In the first place it can be understood insofar as it offers a rational content that may immediately be grasped—I put my bag on the ground *in order to* rest for a moment—which is to say insofar as we immediately grasp the possible that it projects and the end at which it aims. Next, it can be understood because the possible we are considering refers to other possibles, and these to others, and so on right up to the ultimate possibility that I am. And the understanding goes in two opposite directions: through a regressive psychoanalysis, we move back from the act in question right up to my ultimate possible; through a synthetic progression, we come back down to the envisaged act and we grasp its integration within the total figure.

505

This figure, which we designate as our ultimate possibility, is not *one* possible among others—not even, as Heidegger would have it, the possibility of dying or of "no longer realizing a presence in the world."[19] Each particular possibility, in fact, is articulated within an ensemble. This ultimate possibility must on the contrary be conceived as the unitary synthesis of all our current possibles: each of these possibles dwelling in an

---

19 TN: ... "*ne plus réaliser de presence* ..." Sartre is quoting here from Corbin's translation of Heidegger (Heidegger 1938c: 140). The passage appears in §50 of *Being and Time*.

undifferentiated state within the ultimate possibility until some particular circumstance comes to throw it into relief, without, however, eliminating its membership of the totality. Indeed we noted in Part Two[20] that the perceptual apprehension of any object comes about against the *ground of the world*. By that, we meant that what psychologists are in the habit of calling "perception" could not be limited to the objects that are strictly "seen" or "heard," etc., at a specific instant but rather that the objects in question refer by means of various implications and meanings to the totality of the existent in itself *on whose basis* they are apprehended. Thus it is not true that I move, step by step, from this table to the bedroom where I am, and then, leaving it, from there to the hallway, the staircase and the street—in order eventually, by reaching the limit, to conceive of the world as the sum of all these existents. But, quite to the contrary, I cannot perceive any implement-thing, other than on the basis of the absolute totality of all existents, because my initial being is being-in-the-world. Thus we find in things, insofar *"as there are" things* for man, a constant call toward their integration, which means that in order to grasp them we move down from the total and immediately actualized integration to reach this particular structure which can be interpreted only in relation to this totality. But if on the other hand *there is* a world, it is because we arise in the world all at once and in totality. We noted in fact, in that same chapter devoted to transcendence, that the in-itself was not capable on its own of any worldly unity at all. But our arising is a Passion, in the sense that we lose ourselves in nihilation in order for the world to exist. Thus the first phenomenon of being-in-the-world is the original relation between the totality of the in-itself or world and my own detotalized totality: I choose myself in my entirety in the world in its entirety. And just as I come from the world to a particular *this*, I come from myself as a detotalized totality to the sketch of one of my particular possibilities, since I can only grasp a particular *this* against the ground of the world in the circumstance of a particular project of myself. But in that case, just as I can only grasp some *this* against the ground of the world by surpassing it toward this or that possibility, so too can I only project myself beyond the *this* toward this or that possibility against the ground of my ultimate and total possibility. In this way my ultimate and total

506

---

20 Sartre's note: Ibid., Part Two, Chapter 3.

possibility—as the original integration of all my particular possibles—and the world—as the totality that is bestowed on existents through my arising to being—are two strictly correlative notions. I can perceive the hammer (in other words, make a start on my "hammering") only against the ground of the world but, conversely, I can begin this act of "hammering" only against the ground of the totality of myself, and on its basis.

Thus we have found the fundamental act of freedom, the act that gives its meaning to any particular action I may be led to consider: this constantly renewed act cannot be distinguished from my being; it is the choice of myself within the world and, by the same token, my discovery of the world. This allows us to avoid the pitfall of the unconscious which psychoanalysis comes up against from the outset. Indeed, it might be objected, if there is nothing in consciousness which is not the consciousness of being, this fundamental choice must be a *conscious* choice; but can you strictly claim that you are conscious, when you give in to fatigue, of all the implications presupposed by this act? Our answer will be that we are perfectly conscious of them. Only this consciousness itself must be limited by the structure of consciousness in general, and of the choice that we make.

As far as the latter is concerned, we must emphasize the fact that we are not at all dealing here with a deliberate choice. And that is not because it is *less* conscious or *less* explicit than a process of deliberation but on the contrary because it is the foundation of any deliberation and because, as we have seen, any deliberation requires an interpretation on the basis of an original choice. We must therefore protect ourselves against the illusion that turns original freedom into a *positing* of reasons and motives as *objects*, and then a *decision* on the basis of these reasons and motives. On the contrary, once we have a reason and motive, which is to say an evaluation of the things and structures in the world, we already have a positing of ends and, in consequence, choice. But that does not mean that the underlying choice is thereby unconscious. It is one and the same as the consciousness that we have of ourselves. This consciousness, as we know, can only be non-positional: it is we-consciousness because it cannot be distinguished from our being. And as our being is precisely our original choice, our consciousness (of) choice is identical to the consciousness that we have (of) ourselves.

To choose, one has to be conscious and, to be conscious, one has to choose. Choice and consciousness are one and the same thing. This is what many psychologists have sensed when they asserted that consciousness "is selection."[21] But by failing to trace this "selection" back to its ontological foundation, they continued to occupy a perspective from which selection appears as a gratuitous function of a consciousness that is moreover substantial. We might in particular reproach Bergson for this. But if it has been fully established that consciousness is nihilation, we can conceive that to have consciousness of ourselves and to choose ourselves are but one and the same. This is what explains the difficulties encountered by moralists such as Gide when they wanted to define the purity of feelings. What is the difference, Gide asked,[22] between a feeling that we want to have and a feeling that is *felt*? The truth is that there is none: "to want to love" and to love are one and the same, since to love is to choose oneself as loving by becoming conscious of loving. If the πάθος is free, it is choice. We have sufficiently stressed— in particular in the chapter about Temporality—that Descartes's *cogito* must be extended. In fact, as we saw, to become conscious (of) oneself never means to become conscious of an instant, because the instant is only a mental creation and—even if it existed—a consciousness that grasped itself in the instant would grasp *nothing*. I can become conscious of myself only as *this* man engaged in this or that undertaking, counting on this or that success, fearing this or that outcome, and, through the collection of these anticipations, sketching out his *figure* in its entirety. And that is just how I grasp myself, in this moment while I am writing; I am not the mere perceptual consciousness of my hand tracing signs on the paper, for I am far ahead of this hand, reaching right out to the book's completion and the meaning of this book—and of philosophical

---

21 TN: Sartre is clearly thinking here of Bergson (who is mentioned a couple of sentences later), although the term "psychologist" also suggests William James, whose work Sartre also knew. Both Bergson and James claim "selection" to be a crucial function of consciousness.

22 Sartre's note: *Journal des Faux-Monnayeurs*. TN: The book referred to in Sartre's note is the *Journal* (published in France in 1926), in which André Gide recorded the composition of his famous 1925 novel *Les Faux-Monnayeurs*. The novel is translated into English as *The Counterfeiters* (Gide 1990).

activity in general—in my life; and it is within the framework of this project, which is to say the framework of what I am, that specific projects toward more limited possibilities are inserted, such as expounding this idea in such and such a way, or ceasing to write for a moment, or flicking through a work in which I am looking for such and such a reference, etc. Only the mistake would be to think that, corresponding to this global choice, there is an analytic and differentiated consciousness. My ultimate and initial project—because it is both of these at once—is, as we will see, always the sketch of a solution to the problem of being. But this solution is not first conceived and then actualized: we *are* this solution, we make it exist through our very commitment and therefore we can grasp it only by living it. In this way we are always entirely present to ourselves but, precisely because we are entirely present, we cannot hope to have an analytic and detailed consciousness of what we are. This consciousness, moreover, can only be non-thetic.

But, on the other hand, the world sends back to us, through its very articulation, the image of what we are. This does not mean (as, moreover, we have seen) that we are able to decipher this image—i.e., to examine it in detail and subject it to analysis—but rather that the world necessarily appears to us as we are; indeed, it is by surpassing it toward ourselves that we make the world appear the way it is. We choose the world—not in its in-itself construction but in its meaning—by choosing ourselves. For the internal negation through which we make the world appear (by denying, in relation to ourselves, that we are the world) can exist only if it is at the same time a projection toward a possible. It is the very way in which I entrust myself to the inanimate, in which I surrender myself to my body—or, on the contrary, in which I stiffen myself against both of these—that makes my body and the inanimate world, with their distinctive value, appear. There too, in consequence, I have full consciousness of myself and my fundamental projects and, this time, this consciousness is positional. Only, precisely because it is positional, what it delivers to me is the transcendent image of what I am. The value of things, their instrumental role, their real proximity and distance (which bear no relation to their spatial proximity and distance), do nothing other than sketch out my image, which is to say my choice. My clothing (uniform or suit, soft or starched shirt), untidy or neat, sophisticated or vulgar, my furniture, my street, the town where I live, the books with which I surround myself,

508

my ways of entertaining myself, everything that is mine, which is in the end the world of which I am constantly conscious—at least as the meaning implied by the object I am looking at or using—everything teaches me, myself, about my choice, i.e., about my being. But the structure of positional consciousness is such that I cannot reduce this knowledge to a subjective apprehension of myself, and it directs me to other objects that I am producing or arranging in relation to the order of the preceding objects, without being able to notice that I am hereby sculpting in more and more detail my figure within the world. In this way we are fully conscious of the choice that we are. And if it is objected that, according to these remarks, one would have to be conscious not of *having chosen* ourselves but of *choosing* ourselves, our answer will be that this consciousness is expressed through the twofold "feeling" of anguish and responsibility. Anguish, abandonment, responsibility, either muted or at full strength, constitute in fact the *quality* of our consciousness insofar as this latter is purely and simply freedom.

Earlier we raised a question: I gave in to fatigue, we said, and probably *I could have* done otherwise, but *at what cost?* We are now in a position to answer it. Our analysis has just shown us, in effect, that this act was not *gratuitous*. Of course, it could not be explained by a motive or a reason conceived as the content of an earlier "state" of consciousness; but it needed to be interpreted on the basis of an original project of which it formed an integral part. In consequence it becomes clear that we cannot suppose the action could have been modified without at the same time supposing a fundamental modification in my original choice of myself. This way of giving in to my fatigue and dropping down onto the edge of the road expresses a certain initial stiffening against my body and the inanimate in-itself. It belongs in the category of a certain vision of the world in which difficulties may appear as "not worth putting up with" and in which, precisely, the motive—being pure non-thetic consciousness and in consequence an initial project of oneself toward an absolute end (a specific aspect of the in-itself-for-itself)—is the apprehension of the world (the heat, the distance from the town, the futility of one's efforts, etc.) as a *reason* to stop walking. Thus this *possible*—to stop—only gains its meaning *in theory* in and through the hierarchy of possibilities that I am, on the basis of this ultimate and initial possible. That does not imply that *I must necessarily* stop but merely that I can refuse to stop only through a

509

radical conversion of my being-in-the-world, which is to say by a sudden metamorphosis of my initial project, which is to say by a different choice of myself and of my ends. Moreover, this modification is always possible. The anguish which, when it is disclosed, manifests our freedom to our consciousness testifies to this constant alterability of our initial project. In anguish we do not simply grasp the fact that the possibles we are projecting are constantly eaten into by the freedom still to come; in addition, we apprehend our choice—which is to say ourselves—as being *unjustifiable*, which means we grasp our choice as something that does not derive from any earlier reality and as having, on the contrary, to serve as the foundation of the set of meanings which constitute reality. The unjustifiability is not only the subjective acknowledgment of the absolute contingency of our being but also that of the internalization of this contingency, and my taking it on for myself. For the choice, as we will see, which is born out of the contingency of the in-itself which it nihilates, transports that contingency to the level of the for-itself's own gratuitous determination by itself. In this way we are constantly engaged in our choice, and constantly conscious of the fact that we ourselves can suddenly reverse this choice and change course, because we project the future through our very being, and we constantly eat away at it through our own existential freedom, declaring to ourselves by means of the future what we are, and lacking any grip on this future, which remains always *possible* without ever passing into the ranks of the *real*. Thus we are constantly *threatened* with the nihilation of our current choice, constantly threatened with choosing ourselves—and in consequence with becoming—other than we are. Just because our choice is absolute, it is *fragile*, which is to say that, by positing our freedom through it, we posit at the same time the constant possibility of its becoming something that is "on this side," and pastified, in relation to an "over on that side" that I will be.

510   We should be clear nonetheless that our current choice is not such as to provide us with any *reason* for making it past through a subsequent choice. In fact, our choice originally creates all the reasons and all the motives that might lead us to partial actions, and it arranges the world with its meanings, its equipment-structures and its coefficient of adversity. This absolute change by which we are threatened from our birth to our death remains constantly unpredictable and incomprehensible. If we even envisage other fundamental attitudes as *possible*, we only ever

consider them from outside, as the behavior of the other. And if we try to conform our actions to it, they do not for all that lose their character of externality and of transcended-transcendence. Indeed, to "understand them" would be to have already chosen them. We will return to this.

In addition, we should not represent the original choice as "producing itself from one instant to the other"; that would return us to the "instantaneist"[23] conception of consciousness which Husserl, for example, could not leave behind. Since, on the contrary, it is consciousness that temporalizes itself, we must conceive of the original choice as unfolding time and as participating in the unity of the three ecstases. To choose ourselves is to nihilate ourselves, i.e., to make it the case that a future arrives to acquaint us with what we are by conferring a meaning on our past. Thus there is not, as in Descartes, a succession of instants, separated by nothingnesses, such that my choice at instant t is unable to act on my choice at instant t_1. To choose is to make it the case that, along with my commitment, a certain finite extension of concrete and continuous duration arises, which is precisely what separates me from the actualization of my original possibles. Thus freedom, choice, nihilation, and temporalization are just one and the same thing.

However, the instant is not an empty philosophers' invention. Of course, when I am engaged in my task there is no subjective instant: for me at this moment, for example, in which I am writing, trying to grasp my thoughts and to put them in order, there is no instant but only my constant pursued-pursuit toward the ends that define me (the explication of the ideas that will be the basis of this work); and yet we are constantly threatened by the instant. In other words, we are such that, through the very choice of our freedom, we can always make the instant appear as a break in our ecstatic unity. What, then, is an instant? The instant cannot be carved out within the process of temporalization of a concrete project: we have just shown this. But neither can it be assimilated to the first term or the final term (if it has to exist) of this process. That is because both these terms are incorporated from inside within the totality of the process and form an integral part of it. Each of them therefore has only one

---

23 TN: . . . la conception instantanéiste . . . As it is not really an English word, I have put this adjective in scare quotes. It is extremely rare, also, to find it in French.

511   of the characteristics of the instant: the first term, in fact, is incorporated in the process whose first term it is, insofar as it is *its* beginning. But, on the other hand, it is limited by a nothingness before it, insofar as it is *a* beginning. The final term is incorporated in the process that it terminates, insofar as it is *its* end: the last note belongs to the melody. But it is followed by a nothingness that limits it, insofar as it is *an* end. The instant, if it is to be capable of existing, must be bounded by a double nothingness. That is wholly inconceivable, as we have shown, if the instant must be given prior to all the processes of temporalization. But within the temporalization's very development, we are able to produce instants if certain processes arise on the collapse of earlier processes. In that case the instant will be a beginning *and* an end. In brief, if the end of a project coincides with the beginning of another project, an ambiguous temporal reality will arise that will be limited by an earlier nothingness insofar as it is a beginning, and by a later nothingness, insofar as it is an end. But this temporal structure will only be concrete if the commencement is itself given as the end of the process that it pastifies. A beginning that is given as the end of an earlier project: that is what an instant must be. It will only exist therefore if we are, in relation to ourselves, a beginning and an end within the unity of a single act. Now, this is precisely what occurs in the case of a radical modification of our fundamental project. Through the free choice of this modification, indeed, we temporalize a project that we are and we become acquainted with our chosen being through a future; in this way the pure present belongs to the new temporalization as a beginning, and it receives its own nature as a beginning from the future that has just arisen. It is only the future, in fact, which can return to the pure present to characterize it as a beginning; otherwise this present would be just any old present. In this way the choice's present already belongs, as an integrated structure, to the new totality which has begun. But, on the other hand, it is not possible for this choice not to determine itself in *connection* with the past which it has to be. It is even, as a matter of principle, a decision to grasp as past the choice whose place it is taking. A converted atheist is not merely a believer: he is a believer who has denied atheism in relation to himself, who has rendered as past in himself his project of being atheist. In this way the new choice presents itself as a beginning insofar as it is an end and as an end insofar as it is a beginning; it is bounded by a double nothingness and, as such, it has brought about

a fracture in the ecstatic unity of our being. However, the instant is itself only a nothingness because, wherever we direct our view, we will grasp only a continuous temporalization which—depending on the direction in which we look—will be either the completed and closed series which has just passed, carrying its final term with it, or else the living temporalization that is beginning, and whose first term is caught up and carried along by the future possibility.

Thus each fundamental choice defines the direction of the pursued-pursuit at the same time as it temporalizes itself. That does not mean that it *provides an initial impulse*,[24] or that there is anything already acquired, of which I might take advantage as long as I stay within the limits of this choice. On the contrary, the nihilation is pursued continuously and, in consequence, my free and continuous reclamation of this choice is indispensable. Only this reclaiming does not happen *from instant to instant*, as I freely take up my choice again: because in this case there is no instant, the reclamation is so tightly incorporated in the whole of the process that it has none of the meaning of an instant, nor can it have. But precisely because it is free, and constantly taken up by freedom again, my choice has freedom itself as its limit, which means it is haunted by the specter of the instant. As long as I continue to *reclaim* my choice, the pastification of the process will come about in perfect ontological continuity with the present. The pastified process is still organized with the present nihilation, in the form of *knowledge*—i.e., as a lived and internalized meaning—without ever being an *object* for the consciousness which projects itself toward its own ends. But, precisely because I am free, I always have the possibility of positing my immediate past as an object. In other words, while my previous consciousness was a pure non-positional consciousness (of) the past (insofar as it constituted itself as an internal negation of the co-present real, and became acquainted with its meaning by ends that it posited as *reclaimed*) with its new choice, consciousness posits its own past as an object, which means it *assesses* it and orients itself in relation to it. This act of objectification of the immediate past is one and the same thing as the new choice of other ends: it plays a part in making the instant spring up as a nihilating break in the process of temporalization.

24 TN: ... un *élan initial* ... Sartre is almost certainly alluding here to Bergson's ideas.

It will be easier for the reader to understand the results we have obtained through this analysis if we compare them to another theory of freedom—for example, that of Leibniz. When Adam takes the apple, for Leibniz as for us, it would have been *possible* for him not to take it.[25] But for him, as for us, the implications of this move are so numerous and so ramified that, in the end, to assert that it would have been possible for Adam not to take the apple amounts to saying that another Adam would have been possible. Thus Adam's contingency is one and the same as his freedom, since this contingency means that this *real* Adam is surrounded by an infinite number of possible Adams, each of which is character-ized, in relation to the real Adam, by a slight or deep alteration in all his attributes, which is in the end an alteration in his substance. For Leibniz, therefore, the freedom called for by human-reality is like an organization of three different notions. Someone is free if he (1) rationally determines himself to perform an act; (2) is such that this act can be fully under-stood in terms of the very nature of the person who committed it; (3) is contingent, which is to say exists in such a way that other individuals committing other acts in relation to the same situation would have been possible. But, owing to the necessary connection between possibles, another act by Adam would only have been possible for and by another Adam, and the existence of another Adam implied that of another world. We acknowledge with Leibniz that Adam's act commits Adam's person in his entirety, and that another act would have been understood in the light of, and in the framework of, another Adam person. But Leibniz falls back into a necessitarianism that is completely opposed to the idea of freedom when he places the very formula of Adam's substance at the start, like a premise from which Adam's act will follow as one of its partial conclusions, i.e., when he reduces the chronological order to being only a symbolic expression of the logical order. One result of this, indeed, is that the act is strictly necessitated by Adam's very essence, so that the contingency which, according to Leibniz, makes freedom possible is entirely contained within Adam's essence. And this essence is not chosen by Adam himself but by God. Therefore it is true that

---

25 TN: Leibniz discusses the question of whether Adam could not have taken the apple in his correspondence with Arnauld, translated as Leibniz (1967).

the act committed by Adam follows necessarily from Adam's essence and hence that it depends on Adam himself and on nobody else, which is certainly one condition of freedom. But, for Adam himself, Adam's essence itself is a *given*: Adam did not choose it; he could not have chosen to be Adam. In consequence, he does not in any way bear responsibility for his being. After that, the fact that it is possible to attribute to him—once it is given—a relative responsibility for his act does not make much difference. For us, on the contrary, Adam is not defined by his essence, because essence, for human-reality, comes after existence. He is defined through the choice of his ends, i.e., through the arising of an ecstatic temporalization that has nothing in common with the order of logic. In this way, Adam's contingency expresses the finite choice he has made of himself. But now it is the future, not the past, that acquaints him with his *person*: he chooses to learn what he is through the ends toward which he projects himself—i.e., through the totality of his tastes, his inclinations, his hates, etc., insofar as there is a thematic organization and an inherent *meaning* to this totality. We will not therefore fall prey to the objection that we made against Leibniz when we said: "Of course, Adam chose to take the apple, but he did not choose to be Adam." For us, in fact, the problem of freedom is located at the level of Adam's own choice of himself, i.e., the determination of essence by existence. In addition, we acknowledge with Leibniz that another movement by Adam, implying another Adam, implies another world, but by "other world" we do not mean an organization of compossible things within which the other possible Adam might find his place: simply another aspect of the world will be revealed, corresponding to Adam's other being-in-the-world. Finally, for Leibniz, the possible movement of the other Adam, being organized ⁵¹⁴ within another possible world, preexists for all eternity—insofar as it is possible—the actualization of the contingent and real Adam. Here too, for Leibniz, essence precedes existence, and the chronological order depends on the eternal order of logic. For us, on the contrary, the possible is only a pure and formless possibility of being other, as long as it is not *existed* as possible by a new project of Adam's, toward new possibilities. Thus Leibniz's possible eternally remains an abstract possible, whereas, in our view, a possible can appear only by possibilizing itself, i.e., by coming to tell Adam what he is. In consequence, the order of psychological explanation in Leibniz goes from the past to the present, to just the extent to which this succession expresses the eternal order of essences; finally everything is frozen within logical eternity, and the only contingency is that of the principle which means that Adam is a postulate of the divine understanding. For us, on the contrary, the order of interpretation is strictly *chronological*; it does not seek in any way to *reduce* time to a succession that is purely logical (*reason*) or logico-chronological (*cause, determinism*). Interpretation is, therefore, on the basis of the future.

But what is especially worthy of emphasis is that the whole of our preceding analysis is purely *theoretical*. It is only *in theory* that another movement by Adam is possible only within the limits of a total upheaval in the ends through which Adam chooses himself as Adam. We have presented things in this way—and we may in so doing have appeared to be Leibnizian—in order to expound our view with the maximum of simplicity. In fact the reality is far more complex. The fact is that the order of interpretation is purely chronological and not logical: the *understanding* of an act on the basis of the original ends posited by the for-itself's freedom is not an *intellection*. And the descending hierarchy of possibles, from the ultimate and initial possible right down to the derived possible that we are trying to understand, has nothing in common with a deductive series that moves from a principle to its consequence. In the first place, the connection between the derived possible (to stiffen oneself against one's fatigue or to surrender to it) and the fundamental possible is not a connection of *deducibility*. It is a connection between a totality and a partial structure. The view of the total project enables us "to understand" the particular structure in question. But the Gestaltists showed us that the stability of complete figures does not rule out the variability of certain secondary structures. I am able to add or subtract various lines from a given figure without altering its specific character. There are other lines, on the contrary, whose addition would immediately cause the figure to disappear, and another figure to appear. The same thing holds with respect to the relation of secondary possibles to my fundamental possible, or to the formal totality of my possibles. Of course, the meaning of any secondary possible that we examine always refers back to the total meaning that I am. But other possibles might have replaced this one without the total meaning changing, which means they could still—and just as effectively—have referred to this totality as the figure that allows them to be understood—or, in the ontological order of their actualization, they might just as well have been projected as means to achieve the totality, and within the light of this totality. In brief, to understand is to interpret a *de facto* connection, not to grasp a necessity. In this way, the psychological interpretation of our acts will frequently recall the Stoic notion of "indifferents."[26] To relieve my fatigue, it is indifferent whether I sit down at the side of the road or take a hundred steps further, in order to stop at the inn that I can see in the distance. Therefore the apprehension of the complex and global figure that I have chosen as my ultimate possible is *not sufficient* to account for the choice of one of these possibles rather than the other. What we have here is not an act without any motives or reasons but a spontaneous invention of motives and reasons which, even as it fits within the framework of my fundamental choice, thereby enriches it. In the same way, each *this* must appear on the ground of the world and in the perspective of my facticity, but neither my facticity nor the world allows us to understand why I apprehend this glass now, rather than this inkwell, as a figure detaching itself against the ground. In relation to these indifferents, our freedom is entire and unconditioned. Moreover, this way of choosing one possible indifferent, and then abandoning it for another, will not make an *instant* arise as a break in duration: on the contrary, these free choices are all integrated—even if they are successive and contradictory—within the unity of my fundamental project. This does not mean we should regard them as gratuitous: indeed, whatever they are, they will always be interpretable on the basis of the original choice and, to the extent that they enrich and concretize it, they will always bring their motive with them—i.e., the consciousness of their reason or, alternatively, the apprehension of the situation as being articulated in this or that way.

In addition, an accurate assessment of the connection between a secondary possible and the fundamental possible is made especially delicate by the fact that no *a priori* scale exists to which we might appeal to determine this connection. Rather, and on the contrary, it is the for-itself himself who chooses to regard the secondary possible as signifying the fundamental possible. Often, when we have the impression that the free subject is turning away from his fundamental goal, we are introducing an observer's coefficient of error; in other words, we are making use of our own scales in order to assess the relation of the examined act to

26 TN: In Stoic philosophy "things indifferent" are indifferent from the moral point of view—for example, actions that are neither morally required nor morally prohibited.

its ultimate ends. But the for-itself, in its freedom, does not only invent its primary and secondary ends—it invents at the same time the entire system of interpretation that allows some of these to be connected with others. In no circumstance, therefore, can there be any question of establishing a universal system for understanding secondary possibles on the basis of primary possibles; rather, in each case, the subject must provide his personal touchstones and his personal criteria.

Finally, the for-itself is able to take voluntary decisions that are opposed to its chosen fundamental ends. These decisions can only be voluntary, i.e., reflective. Effectively, they can result only from an error—committed in good or bad faith—about the ends I am pursuing, and this error can be made only if reflective consciousness encounters the set of motives that I am in the form of an object. Unreflected consciousness, as the spontaneous projection of itself toward its possibilities, can never be wrong about itself: indeed, we need to be careful not to describe the errors we make in our assessment of the objective situation as "mistakes about ourselves"—errors which may lead to consequences within the world that are entirely opposed to those we wanted to achieve, even without any misrecognition of the proposed ends. The reflective attitude, on the contrary, brings with it a thousand possibilities of error, not to the extent that it apprehends the pure motive—i.e., the reflected consciousness—as a quasi-object but insofar as it aims, through this reflected consciousness, to constitute real psychological objects which (as we saw in Chapter 3 of Part Two) are themselves merely probable objects, and which can even be false objects. It is therefore possible, because of errors I have made about myself, for me to reflectively—i.e., voluntarily—impose on myself projects that contradict my initial project, without however fundamentally modifying my initial project. This is how, for example, if my initial project aims to choose myself as inferior in the midst of others (the so-called inferiority complex) and if stammering, for example, is a behavior to be understood and interpreted on the basis of the first project, I may, for social reasons and through a failure to recognize my own choice of inferiority, decide to correct my stammer. I may even *manage* it—without having ceased, however, to feel myself, and to want to be, inferior. To obtain a result, I need only make use of technical means. This is what we ordinarily call a voluntary reform of oneself. But these results will only *displace* the disability from which I suffer: another will arise in its place, to express in its own way the total end I am pursuing. As this profound inefficacy of a voluntary act directed on oneself may seem surprising, we should analyze our chosen example more closely.

We should note in the first place that, even though it is totally free, the choice of total ends is not necessarily, or even often, a joyful operation. We should not confuse the necessity of our having to choose ourselves with the will to power. Our choice may be made with resignation or unease; it may be a form of escape, or accomplished in bad faith. We are able to choose ourselves as fleeing, evasive, hesitant, etc.: we may even choose not to choose ourselves; in these various cases, we posit our ends beyond a factual situation, and the responsibility for these ends falls on us; whatever our being is, it is a choice, and it depends on us to choose ourselves as "great" or "noble" or "low" and "humiliated." But, precisely, if we have chosen humiliation as the very fabric of our being, we will actualize ourselves as humiliated, embittered, inferior, etc. We are not dealing here with *givens* that lack any meaning. But someone who actualizes himself as humiliated thereby constitutes himself as a *means* of attaining certain ends: the chosen humiliation may, for example, be equivalent—like masochism— to an instrument whose purpose is to rid us of our for-itself existence; it may be a project to renounce, in favor of others, our anguished freedom; our project may be to get our being-for-the-Other to absorb entirely our being-for-itself. In any case, an "inferiority complex" can arise only if it is founded upon a free apprehension of our being-for-the-Other. As a *situation*, this being-for-others will act like a *reason*, but for that to happen it must be revealed by a *motive*, which is nothing other than our free project. Thus the inferiority which we feel and live out is the instrument we have chosen in order to make us resemble a *thing*, i.e., to make ourselves exist purely as an "outside" in the midst of the world. But it goes without saying that it has to be lived in conformity with the *nature* that we confer on it through this choice, which is to say in shame, anger, and bitterness. Thus *to choose* inferiority does not mean that we quietly settle for an *aurea mediocritas*;[27] it is to produce and to accept the revolt and the despair constitutive of the revelation of this inferiority. I may persist, for example, in exhibiting myself in a specific type of work and output *because* I am inferior at it, while in some other domain I might be able to reach the average without difficulty. This

---

27 TN: This is the Latin term for "golden mean." The concept is best known for its role in Aristotle's philosophy, where it represents the desirable middle way between two excessive extremes.

is the unsuccessful endeavor I have chosen because it is unsuccessful: either because I prefer to come last—rather than to get lost in the crowd—or because I have chosen discouragement and shame as the best way to attain *being*. But it goes without saying that I can only *choose*, as my field of action, the domain in which I am inferior if this choice implies a reflective will to be superior at it. To choose to be an inferior artist is necessarily to choose *to want* to be a great artist; otherwise the inferiority would be neither undergone nor acknowledged: indeed, to choose to be a modest artisan does not imply the pursuit of inferiority at all; it is simply one example of the choice of finitude. The choice of inferiority, on the contrary, implies the constant actualization of a *gap* between the end pursued by the will and the end that is obtained. The artist who wishes to be great and who chooses himself as inferior intentionally maintains this gap; he is like Penelope, and destroys at night what he does during the day. In this sense he constantly remains, in his artistic productions, at the level of *the will* and accordingly manifests a desperate energy. But his will is itself in *bad faith*, which is to say that it flees the acknowledgment of the true ends chosen by spontaneous consciousness and constitutes false psychological objects in the form of *motives* in order to be able to deliberate about these motives and to decide on their basis (the love of glory, the love of the beautiful, etc.). Here the will is not at all opposed to the fundamental choice but, quite to the contrary, it can only be understood in its goals and in the principle of its bad faith, within the perspective of the fundamental choice of inferiority. Better still, if—in its capacity as reflective consciousness—it constitutes in bad faith false psychological objects in the form of motives, in its capacity as an unreflected and non-thetic consciousness (of) self, it is on the contrary a consciousness (of) being in bad faith and therefore a consciousness (of) the fundamental project pursued by the for-itself. In this way the divorce between the spontaneous consciousness and the will is not a factual given which is merely observed. But, on the contrary, this duality is initially projected and brought about by our fundamental freedom; it can be conceived only in and through the deep unity of our fundamental project, which is to choose ourselves as inferior. But this divorce, precisely, implies that the voluntary deliberation decides with bad faith to compensate for or to conceal our inferiority by means of tasks whose basic goal is to enable us on the contrary *to measure* this inferiority. Thus, as we see, our analysis allows us to accept the two levels at which Adler situates the inferiority complex:

518

like him, we accept a fundamental acknowledgment of this inferiority and, like him, we accept a dense and ill-balanced development of acts, works, and affirmations whose purpose is to compensate for or conceal this deep feeling. But: (1) We refuse to conceive of the fundamental acknowledgment as unconscious: so far from being unconscious is it that it even constitutes the bad faith of the will. We do not on this account place, between the two levels we are envisaging, the difference between the unconscious and the conscious but rather the difference which separates the unreflected and fundamental consciousness from the reflective consciousness which depends on it. (2) It seems to us that the concept of bad faith—as we established in Part One—ought to replace the concepts of censure, repression and unconscious which Adler uses. (3) The unity of consciousness, as it is revealed to the *cogito*, is too deep for us to accept this split into two levels unless it is taken up by a deeper synthetic intention which leads back one level to the other and unifies them. So we grasp an additional meaning in the inferiority complex: not only is the inferiority complex acknowledged but this acknowledgment is a *choice*; the will does not only try to conceal this inferiority by means of weak and unstable affirmations but a deeper intention runs through it which *chooses* precisely the weakness and instability of these affirmations, with the intention of making this inferiority— which we aspire to flee and which we will experience in shame and with the feeling of failure—more visible. In this way the person who suffers from "*Mindwertigkeit*"[28] has *chosen* to be his own executioner. He has chosen shame and suffering, which does not mean (it is quite the opposite) that he is obliged to feel joy when they come into being with the utmost violence.   519

But, for all that they are chosen in bad faith by a will that produces itself within the limits of our initial project, it is no less true that these new possibles are actualized, to a certain extent, *against* the initial project. To the extent that we want to conceal our inferiority from ourselves, precisely in order *to create* it, we may want to eliminate our timidity and our stammering, which manifest at the level of spontaneity our initial inferiority project. In that case we will make a systematic and reflective effort to make these manifestations disappear. We make this attempt in the state of mind that is characteristic of the patients who come to seek

---

28 TN: *Mindwertigkeit* is the German word, used in Adler's psychology, for "inferiority."

psychoanalysis. In other words we try, on the one hand, to actualize something which, on the other hand, we refuse: in this way the patient voluntarily decides to seek out the psychoanalyst in order to be cured of certain disturbances that he is no longer able to hide from himself—and, merely on account of placing himself within the doctor's hands, he runs the risk of being cured. But on the other hand, if he runs this risk, it is in order to persuade himself that he has done everything to be cured to no avail and, therefore, that he is incurable. He approaches the psychoanalytic treatment therefore with bad faith and a bad will. The goal of all his efforts will be to make him fail, even while he continues voluntarily to participate. Similarly, the psychaesthenics studied by Janet *suffer* from an obsession they intentionally maintain, and *want* to be cured of it. But their will to be cured of it has precisely as its goal to affirm these obsessions as *sufferings* and in consequence to actualize them in all their violence. We know the rest: the patient is unable to own up to his obsessions; he rolls on the ground, and he sobs, but he does not decide to make the required confession. It would be pointless here to talk about a struggle of the will against the illness: these processes take place within the ecstatic unity of bad faith, in a being who is what he is not and who is not what he is. Similarly, when the psychoanalyst is close to grasping the patient's initial project, the latter gives up treatment or begins to lie. It will be fruitless to explain these resistances by an unconscious rebellion or anxiety: How in that case could the unconscious be informed of the progress of the psychoanalytic inquiry, unless it were precisely a consciousness? But if the patient plays the game right to the end, he will have to undergo a partial cure, which is to say that he will have to cause the disappearance within him of the morbid phenomena which led him to request the doctor's help. In this way he will have chosen the lesser evil: having come in order to persuade himself that he is incurable, he is obliged—in order to avoid bringing his project to light and, in consequence, nihilating it and freely becoming other—to start anew by playing at the cure. Similarly, the methods that I use to cure myself of stammering and timidity may have been tried in bad faith. It remains no less the case that I may be obliged to acknowledge their efficacy. In this case the timidity and stammering will disappear: this is the lesser evil. An artificial and voluble self-confidence will come to replace them. But these cures are like the cure for hysteria by electric treatment. We know that this medication may lead a hysterical spasm in the leg to disappear but that, sometime later, we see the spasm reappearing in the arm. The fact is that the cure for hysteria can only come about in its totality, because hysteria is a totalizing project of the for-itself. Partial medications will only displace its manifestations. In this way the cure for timidity or stammering is consented to and chosen within a project which leads to the occurrence of other disturbances—for example, precisely, to the occurrence of an empty and similarly unbalanced self-confidence. As in fact the motive through which a *voluntary* decision arises is found within the free fundamental choice of my ends, this decision can attack these very ends only in appearance; it is therefore only within the framework of my fundamental project that the will can be efficacious; and I can only "get rid of" my "inferiority complex" through a radical modification of my project, for which the reasons and motives can in no way be found in the previous project, not even in the sufferings and shame that I experience, because these latter have as their explicit purpose to *actualize* my inferiority project. Thus, for as long as I remain "in" the inferiority complex, I cannot even conceive that I might get out of it, because, even if I dream of getting out of it, this dream has its precise function, which is to allow me to experience still further the abjection of my state; it can therefore only be interpreted in, and through, the intention to be inferior. And yet, at each moment, I apprehend this initial choice as contingent and unjustifiable; at each moment, therefore, I am well placed to suddenly envisage it *objectively* and, in consequence, to surpass it and to pastify it by making the liberating *instant* appear. This explains my anguish, the fear that I have of suddenly being exorcised, i.e., of becoming radically other; but it also explains the frequent occurrence of "conversions" that lead me to transform totally my original project. These conversions, which philosophers have not studied, have often, on the contrary, inspired literary writers. Let us recall the instant in which Gide's Philoctetes[29] even gives up his hatred, his fundamental project, his *raison d'être*, and his being; recall the *instant* in which Raskolnikov decides to give himself up.[30] These extraordinary and marvelous instants, in which the earlier project collapses into the past in the light of a new project which arises on its ruins and which is still only being sketched out, in

521

29 TN: Philoctetes is the main character in Gide's play *Philoctète* (1899), based on Sophocles' *Philoctetes*.
30 TN: Raskolnikov is the main character in Dostoyevsky's novel *Crime and Punishment* (translated as Dostoyevsky 1992).

which humiliation, anguish, joy, and hope are tightly blended, in which we let go in order to take hold and take hold in order to let go, have often seemed to provide the clearest and most moving image of our freedom. But they are just one of its manifestations among others.

Presented like this, the "paradox" of the inefficacy of voluntary decisions will seem less offensive. It amounts to saying that, through our will, we are able to *construct* ourselves entirely, but that the meaning of the will that governs this construction is itself to be found in the original project that it may appear to negate and, consequently, that this structure has a function that is quite different from the one it makes public and, finally, that it can never modify the original project from which it derives, any more than the consequences of a theorem can be turned back against it and change it.

At the end of this long discussion, we appear to have succeeded in making our ontological understanding of freedom a little clearer. We should now gather up the various results we have obtained into a single overview.

(1) A first look at human-reality informs us that, in its case, being can be reduced to doing. The nineteenth-century psychologists who pointed out the motor structures of tendencies, attention, perception, etc., were right. Only movement itself is an act. Thus we do not find anything *given* in human-reality, in the sense in which temperament, character, the passions, and the principles of reason could be acquired or innate *data*, existing in the manner of things. On its own, an empirical examination of human-being shows it to be an organized unity of modes of behavior or "comportments."[31] To be ambitious, cowardly, or irascible is simply to behave in some particular way, in some particular circumstances. The behaviorists were right to hold that positive psychology should consist only in the study of modes of behavior in strictly defined situations. Just as the works of Janet and the Gestaltists have equipped us to uncover emotional behavior, so we should talk in the same way about perceptual behavior, since we can never conceive of perception apart from an attitude in relation to the world. Even the scholar's disinterested attitude, as Heidegger showed, takes up a disinterested position in relation to the

31 TN: Sartre may intend the reader to associate the term *comportement* with Merleau-Ponty's *La Structure du Comportement*, published in France in 1942, and translated into English as Merleau-Ponty (1963).

world and is, in consequence, one mode of behavior among others. Thus human-reality does not exist first in order to act, but being, in its case, is acting, and to cease to act is to cease to be.

(2) But if human-reality is action, it evidently follows that the determining of its action is itself an action. If we reject this principle, and if we accept an earlier state of the world or of itself can determine it to act, that amounts to placing something *given* at the origin of the series. In that case these *acts* disappear as acts, to make way for a series of *movements*. That is how the notion of behavior in Janet and the behaviorists destroys itself. The existence of an act implies its autonomy.

(3) Moreover, if an act is not just *movement*, it must be defined by means of an *intention*. This intention, however we regard it, can only be something that surpasses the given toward a result to be obtained. This given, indeed, being pure presence, is unable to move out of itself. Precisely because it is, it is what it is, fully and uniquely. It cannot therefore do justice to a phenomenon which gets all its meaning from a result to be attained, i.e., a nonexistent. For example, when psychologists make a tendency into a factual state, they fail to see that they are removing all its character as an *appetite* (*ad-petitio*) from it. If in fact the sexual tendency may be differentiated from sleep, for example, it can only be by means of its end, and this end, precisely, is not. The psychologists ought to have asked themselves what sort of ontological structure could belong to a phenomenon that is acquainted with what it is by something that has not yet come to be. Intention, which is the fundamental structure of human-reality, cannot therefore in any case be explained by a given, even if we claim that it emanates from it. But if we want to interpret it through its end, we must take care not to confer on this end the existence of a *given*. If we were able to accept, indeed, that the end is given prior to the effort to attain it, we would have to grant a sort of being-in-itself to this end, at the heart of its nothingness, and a power to attract of a distinctively magical type. Besides, we would have no more success in understanding the connection of a given human-reality with an end given separately than the connection, in realist theories, between the consciousness-substance and the reality-substance. If the tendency or the act must be interpreted by its end, it is because the structure of intention is to posit its end outside it. In this way the intention, by choosing the end that announces it, makes itself be.

(4) Since the intention is a choice of the end and the world is revealed through our behavior, it is the intentional choice of the end which reveals the world, and the world reveals itself this way or that (in this order or that) according to the chosen end. The end, which lights up the world, is a state of the world to be obtained, and not already in existence. The intention is a thetic consciousness of the end. But it can be that only by becoming a non-thetic consciousness of its own possibility. Thus my *end* may be a good meal, if I am hungry. But this meal, projected, beyond the dusty road along which I am making my way, as this road's *meaning*[32] (it goes *toward* a hotel where the table is laid, the dishes are ready, they are waiting for me, etc.), can only be grasped as the correlative of my non-thetic project toward my own possibility of eating this meal. In this way, through its twofold but unitary arising, the intention lights up the world on the basis of an end that does not yet exist and which defines itself through the choice of its possible. My end is a specific objective state of the world, and my possible is a specific structure of my subjectivity; the first of these is revealed to thetic consciousness, while the other flows back on to non-thetic consciousness in order to characterize it.

523

(5) If intention cannot be explained by the given, it must—simply by arising—actualize a break with what is given, no matter what that is. It could not be otherwise, or we would have a present plenitude following, with no break in continuity, a present plenitude, and we would not be able to prefigure the future. For that matter, this break is necessary for the given to be *assessed*. If it were not assessed, the given could never in fact be a reason for action. But this assessment can only be achieved by our withdrawing from the given, by a bracketing of the given, which presupposes just such a break in continuity. Furthermore, the assessment, if it is not to be gratuitous, must be made in the light of something. And this something which is used to assess the given can only be the end. Thus the intention, in a single unitary arising, posits the end, chooses itself, and assesses the given on the basis of the end. In these conditions the given is assessed relatively to something which does not yet exist; being-in-itself is lit up by the light of non-being. The result is the coloring of the given in a double nihilation: on the one hand the given is nihilated insofar as,

32 TN: ... *comme le sens de cette route* ... Sartre's French makes a pun out of two meanings of the French word *sens*: "meaning" and "direction."

through the break that is made with it, it loses all efficacy in relation to the intention; on the other hand it undergoes a new nihilation by virtue of the efficacy that is returned to it on the basis of a nothingness, its assessment. As human-reality is an act, we can conceive of it only as a break in its being with the given. It is the being that makes it the case that *there is* any given, by breaking with it and illuminating it in the light of the not-yet-existing.

(6) This necessity—that the given can appear only within the framework of a nihilation which reveals it—is one and the same as the *internal negation* that we described in Part Two. It would be pointless to imagine that consciousness might exist without any given: in that case it would be conscious (of) itself as a consciousness of nothing, i.e., absolute nothingness. But if consciousness exists on the basis of the given, that does not at all mean that it is conditioned by the given: it is purely and simply a negation of the given; it exists as disengaged from a specific existing given and committed toward a specific end that does not yet exist. But, in addition, this internal negation can only belong to a being that constantly withdraws from itself. If it were not its own negation it would be what it is, i.e., a pure and simple given. It would not thereby have any connection with any other *datum*, since the given, in essence, is only what it is. Any possibility of a world appearing would, therefore, be ruled out.   524 In order not *to be* a given, the for-itself must constantly constitute itself as stepping back from itself, i.e., as leaving itself behind, as a *datum* that it no longer is. From this characteristic, it follows that the for-itself is the being for whom there is *no rescue*, and *no support*, in what it *was*. But, on the contrary, the for-itself is free, and it can make it the case that there is a world, because it is *the being that has to be what it was in the light of what it will be*. The for-itself's freedom appears therefore as its *being*. But as this freedom is not a given, or a property, it can be only by choosing itself. The for-itself's freedom is always *committed*: the freedom in question here bears no relation to some undetermined power, able to preexist its choice. We only ever apprehend ourselves as a choice in its making. But freedom is simply the fact that this choice is always unconditioned.

(7) A choice like this, made in the absence of any support, and which dictates its motives to itself, may appear *absurd*—and indeed it is. The fact is that freedom is the *choice* of its being, but not the *foundation* of its being. We will return to this relation between freedom and facticity in the present chapter. For now, it is enough to say that human-reality can

choose itself as it wishes but it cannot not choose itself; it cannot even refuse to be; indeed suicide is a choice, and an affirmation of being. Through this being that is *given* to it, human-reality participates in the universal contingency of being and, thereby, in what we have called "absurdity." This choice is absurd, not because it lacks any reason but because there was no possibility of not choosing. Whatever it is, the choice is founded and repossessed by being, because it is a choice that is. But we must note here that this choice is not absurd in the sense in which, in a rational universe, a phenomenon might arise that was not connected to other phenomena by any *reasons*. The sense in which choice is absurd is that it is the means through which any foundation and any reasons arrive in being, and through which the very notion of absurdity acquires its meaning. It is absurd insofar as it lies beyond all reasons. Freedom, therefore, is not purely and simply contingent, insofar as it turns back toward its being, to illuminate it in the light of its end: freedom constantly escapes contingency; it internalizes, nihilates, and subjectivizes its contingency, which, thus modified, passes over entirely into gratuitous choice.

(8) The free project is fundamental, because it is my being. We cannot regard ambition, or a yearning to be loved, or an inferiority complex, as fundamental projects. On the contrary, these need to be understood on the basis of a first and total project—which can be identified by our inability to interpret it any further on the basis of any other project. To explicate this initial project, a special phenomenological method will be necessary, that we will call "existential psychoanalysis." We will discuss it in the next chapter. For now, we can say that the fundamental project that I am does not concern my relations with this or that particular object in the world but my being-in-the-world as a whole, and—since the world itself is revealed only in the light of an end—this project posits as its end a specific kind of relation to being, which the for-itself wants to maintain. This project is not instantaneous, because it cannot be "in" time. Neither is it timeless, in order afterward to "allow some time for itself."[33] That is why we reject Kant's "choice of intelligible

525

33 TN: ...*se "donner du temps"*... Sartre writes playfully here: the French phrase between his quotation marks is used in contexts where English speakers might say "spend time on it" or "give it some time."

character."³⁴ The structure of the choice necessarily implies that it is a choice in the world. A choice that was a choice *on the basis of nothing*, a choice *against nothing*, would not be a choice of anything, and would be annihilated as a choice. Choice can only be phenomenal—so long, however, as we understand this to mean that the phenomenon, here, is the absolute. But the choice temporalizes itself even as it arises, since it makes it the case that a future approaches, to illuminate the present and to constitute it as the present by assigning the meaning of *pastness* to the in-itself "data." However, we should not understand this to mean that the fundamental project is coextensive with the for-itself's entire "life." Since freedom is a being-without-a-support and without-a-springboard, the project must constantly renew itself in order to be. I am perpetually choosing myself and I can never be described as having-been-chosen, or I would collapse back into the pure and simple existence of the in-itself. The necessity of my constantly choosing myself is one and the same thing as the pursued-pursuit that I am. But precisely because it is a matter of a *choice*, this choice, insofar as it takes place, designates other choices in general as possibles. The possibility of these other choices is not explicated or posited but it is lived through with a feeling of unjustifiability, which is expressed by the *absurdity* of my choice and, in consequence, of my being. Thus my freedom eats into my freedom. In being free, in fact, I project my total possible, but I thereby posit that I am free and that I can always nihilate this first project and make it past.³⁵ Thus, in the moment when the for-itself thinks it is grasping itself and becoming acquainted—through a pro-jected nothingness—with what it *is*, it is escaping itself, because it thereby posits that it can be other than it is. It needs only to explicate its unjustifiability for the *instant* to arise, i.e., the appearance of a new project as the former project collapses. However, since an explicit condition of this new project's arising is the nihilation of the former project, the for-itself is not able to confer upon itself a new existence: the moment it pushes its discontinued project back into the past, it has this project—in the form of "was"—to be. In other words, this discontinued project belongs henceforth to its

34 TN: Kant discusses our choice of "intelligible character" in his *Critique of Pure Reason* (Kant 1998: 536–545).
35 TN: Here again Sartre uses the verb *passéifier*.

situation. No law of being can assign a number, *a priori*, to the various projects that I am: in point of fact, the for-itself's existence conditions its essence. But we must consult each for-itself's history in order to form, in relation to each particular for-itself, a particular idea. Our particular projects concerning the actualization within the world of some particular end are integrated within the global project that we are. But, precisely because we are entirely choice and act, our global project does not determine these partial projects: they must themselves be choices, and a certain margin of contingency, unpredictability, and absurdity characterizes each of them, even while each project, insofar as it projects itself, is always to be understood in relation to my being-in-the-world in its totality, insofar as it is a specification of the global project in the circumstance of particular elements of my situation.

With these observations, we believe we have described the for-itself's freedom in its original existence. But the reader will have noted that this freedom requires a given—not as its condition but on a number of counts: first of all, freedom can be conceived of only as the nihilation of a given (5) and, to the extent that it is an internal negation and consciousness, freedom falls under (6) the necessity that requires consciousness to be conscious of something. In addition, freedom is the freedom to choose—but not the freedom not to choose. Not to choose is, in fact, to choose not to choose. It follows that choice provides the foundation of chosen-being but not the foundation of the choosing. This gives rise to the absurdity (7) of freedom. Here, again, we are directed to something given, which is nothing but the for-itself's very facticity. Finally, the global project, even though it lights up the world in its totality, may become specified in the context of this or that element of the situation and, in consequence, of the world's contingency. All these remarks, therefore, refer us to a difficult problem: the problem of the relations between freedom and facticity. And, furthermore, they bring into view the material objections that we are sure to be challenged with: Can I choose to be tall if I am short? To have two arms if I am maimed? etc.—objections that are concerned, precisely, with the "limits" that my factual situation might be thought to place on my free choice of myself. We ought therefore to examine freedom's other aspect, its "reverse side": its relation with facticity.

II. FREEDOM AND FACTICITY: THE SITUATION

The decisive argument brought by "good sense" against freedom is a reminder of our powerlessness. Far from being able to change our situation at will, it seems that we are unable to change ourselves. I am not "free" to escape the destiny of my class, my nation, my family, or even to build up my power or my wealth, or to overcome my most trivial appetites or habits. I am born a worker, French, with inherited syphilis or tuberculosis. Whatever it may be, the history of a life is a history of a failure. The coefficient of adversity of things is such that it takes years of patience to obtain the tiniest result. And still it will be necessary to "obey nature in order to command it,"[36] i.e., to insert my action within the mesh of determinism. Man seems far less to "make himself" than "to be made," by climate and soil, race and class, language, the history of the community to which he belongs, heredity, the individual circumstances of his childhood, the habits he acquires, the major and minor events of his life.

This argument has never seriously troubled the advocates of human freedom: Descartes was the first to acknowledge that the will is infinite and at the same time that we have to "endeavor to conquer ourselves rather than fortune."[37] The point is that we need to draw some distinctions here; many of the facts pronounced by the determinists cannot be taken into account. In particular, the coefficient of adversity of things cannot be an argument against our freedom, because it is through us, which is to say by means of an end that we have posited beforehand, that this coefficient of adversity arises. This rock, which manifests a profound resistance if I want to move it, will on the contrary become a valuable aid if I want to climb up it in order to contemplate the landscape. In itself—if it is even possible to consider how it might be in itself—it is neutral, which is to say that, before it can show itself to be an adversary or a help, it awaits the illumination of an end. And further, it can show itself in one

36 TN: Sartre is paraphrasing the British philosopher Francis Bacon (1561–1626): "Nature, to be commanded, must be obeyed."

37 TN: Sartre is quoting from Descartes's 1637 *Discourse on Method*: "My third maxim was to endeavor always to conquer myself rather than fortune, and change my desires rather than the order of the world." Translated into English as Descartes (1911).

or the other way only within an equipment-structure that has already been established. Without the pickaxes and ice axes, the paths that have already been traced, the climbing technique, the rock will be neither easy nor difficult to climb; the question would not arise, and would not sustain a relation of any kind with the technique of mountaineering. Thus, although brute things (what Heidegger calls "brute existents") may limit our freedom of action from the outset, it is our freedom itself which must previously have constituted the framework, the technique, and the ends, in relation to which these things will show themselves to be limits. If the rock even reveals itself to be "too difficult to climb" and if we have to give up the ascent, we should note that it has only revealed itself as such by virtue of having been originally apprehended as "climb-able"; it is our freedom therefore which constitutes the limits it will thereafter encounter. Of course, after these remarks, an unnameable and unthinkable *residuum* remains, which belongs to the in-itself in question and which makes it the case that, within a world that is lit up by our freedom, this rock will be conducive to climbing, and this other one will not. But this *residue* is far from being an original limit to freedom; rather, it is thanks to it—i.e., thanks to the brute in-itself, as such—that our freedom can arise as freedom. Common sense agrees with us, indeed, that a being who can be said to be *free* is one whose projects can be *actualized*. But for the act to be able to involve an actualization we need to be able to distinguish, *a priori*, the mere projection of a possible end from the actualization of that end. If it is sufficient to conceive of something for it to be actualized, I will find myself suddenly plunged into a world resembling the dream-world, where the possible is no longer in any way distinct from the real. I am condemned, then, to see the world changing in accordance with the changes of my consciousness; I cannot exercise, in relation to my conception, the "bracketing" and the suspension of judgment that would distinguish a mere fiction from a real choice. An object that appears the minute it is merely conceived will no longer be either chosen or only wished for. With the abolition of the distinction between a mere *wish*, a *representation* that I might be able to choose, and *the choice*, freedom will disappear too. We are free when the ultimate term, by which we are acquainted with what we are, is an *end*—which is to say not a real existent which, like the one in the hypothesis we have just entertained, appears in order to fulfill our wish but an object which does not yet exist. But on this basis, this *end* can be transcendent only if it is separated from us at the same time as it is accessible. We can be separated from this end only by a set of real existents—just as this end can be conceived only as a forth-coming state of the real existents separating me from it. It is nothing more than the outline of an order of existents, which is to say of a series of positions into which the existents will be placed, on the basis of their current relations. Through its internal-negation, in fact, the for-itself lights up the existents in their mutual relationships through the end that it posits, and projects this end on the basis of the specifications it apprehends in the existents. As we have seen, this is not circular, because the for-itself arises all at once. But if that is so, the order of the existents is itself indispensable for freedom itself: they are what separate it from, and reunite it with, its pursued end, by which it is acquainted with what it is. In consequence, the resistances disclosed by freedom in the existent, far from being a danger to freedom, only allow it to arise as freedom. There can only be a free for-itself if it is committed within a resisting world. Outside this commitment, the notions of freedom, determinism, and necessity lose all of their meaning.

In addition, we must make it quite clear, against common sense, that the phrase "to be free" does not mean "to obtain what one wanted" but "to be determined in one's wanting (in the broad sense of "choosing") by oneself." In other words, success makes no difference to freedom. The argument which opposes common sense to the philosophers stems here from a misunderstanding: the popular and empirical concept of "freedom," produced by historical, political, and moral circumstances, is equivalent to the "ability to obtain the ends one has chosen." The technical and philosophical concept of freedom, which is the only one we are considering here, only means: the autonomy of choice. We must note, however, that, since any choice is identical to some *doing*, it pre-supposes, in order for it to be distinct from a dream or a wish, that its actualization has begun. Thus we are not saying that a prisoner is always free to get out of prison, which would be absurd, nor that he is always free to wish for his release, which would be a statement of the obvious that lacked any impact, but that he is always free to seek an escape (or to be freed)—i.e., that, whatever his condition, he can pro-ject his escape and learn for himself about his project's value by beginning to act. Our description of freedom, which does not distinguish between choosing

529

and doing, obliges us for that reason to give up any distinction between the intention and the action. The intention can no more be separated from the action than thought from the language that expresses it and, as it can happen that we can learn our thoughts from our words, so our actions can teach us our intentions, which is to say they can enable us to extricate them, schematize them, and make objects out of them, rather than limiting ourselves to living them, i.e., to being non-thetically conscious of them. This essential distinction between the freedom of choice and the freedom to obtain was certainly seen by Descartes, following the Stoics. It puts an end to all the debates about "willing" something and "being able to do" it, in which the advocates of freedom remain opposed to its adversaries today.

It remains no less true that freedom encounters, or seems to encounter, limits by virtue of the *given* that it surpasses or nihilates. To show that a thing's coefficient of adversity, and its character as an *obstacle* (together with its character as an *implement*), is indispensable to the existence of a freedom is to make use of an argument that cuts two ways, because, if it enables us to establish that freedom is not curtailed by the given, it points on the other hand to something like an ontological conditioning of freedom. Might we not have grounds for saying, along with some contemporary philosophers: there is no freedom without an obstacle? And as we cannot allow that freedom creates its obstacle by itself—which will strike anyone who has understood what a spontaneity is as absurd—we seem to have here something like an ontological primacy of the in-itself over the for-itself. We must therefore regard our earlier remarks as simply an attempt to clear the ground, and take up the question of facticity again, from the beginning.

We established that the for-itself was free.[38] But that does not mean that it is its own foundation. If to be free meant to be its own foundation, freedom would have to decide its being's *existence*. And this necessity can be understood in two ways. First, freedom would have to decide its being-free, i.e., it would not only have to be the choice

---

38 TN: ...*que le pour-soi était libre.* Perhaps Sartre uses the past tense here by mistake; he obviously does not mean to imply that the for-itself was free only in the past, and not also in the present.

of some end but to choose itself as freedom. This would presuppose, 530
therefore, that the possibility of being free and the possibility of not
being free existed equally before any free choice of one of them—
i.e., before any free choice of freedom. But as that would require an
antecedent freedom choosing to be free, we would be in an infinite
regress, because that freedom would require another earlier freedom in
order to choose, and so on. In fact, we are a freedom that chooses, but
we do not choose to be free: we are condemned to freedom, as we said
earlier, thrown into freedom or—as Heidegger says—"abandoned."[39]
And, as we can see, this abandonment has no other origin than the
very existence of freedom. If therefore we define freedom as the escape
from the given, from fact, there is a fact about the escape from fact. It
is the facticity of freedom.

But the fact that freedom is not its foundation may be understood in
another way, which will lead to identical conclusions. If in fact freedom
could decide the existence of its being, not only would being as not-free
have to be possible but, further, my absolute nonexistence would also
have to be possible. In other words, we saw that the end, in freedom's
initial project, turns back toward its reasons in order to constitute them;
but, if freedom was obliged to be its foundation, the end would in addition have to turn back toward existence itself, in order to make it arise.
We can see what the result would be: the for-itself would be drawn out
of nothingness in order to attain its self-proposed end. This would be a
de jure existence, legitimized by its end, not an existence de facto. And it
is true that there is one way—among the thousand ways in which the
for-itself tries to separate itself from its original contingency—which
consists in trying to make oneself recognized by the Other as a de jure
existence. We are only concerned with our individual rights within the
framework of a vast project whose goal is to confer our existence on us
on the basis of the work that we do. It is for that reason that men so often
try to identify themselves with their work, and try to see themselves as
nothing but "the President of the Court of Appeal," "the Paymaster,"
etc. The existence of each of these jobs is justified by its end. To be

39 TN: *délaissés*. . . Sartre seems to be using the French word *délaissement* (and cognates) to trans-
    late Heidegger's German term *Geworfenheit* (which translates most literally into English as
    "thrownness").

identified with one of them is to hold one's own existence as rescued from contingency. But these efforts to escape from original contingency only establish its existence more strongly. Freedom cannot decide its existence through the end it posits. Of course, it only exists through the choice that it makes of an end, but it does not govern the fact that *there is* a freedom, whose end acquaints it with what it is. A freedom that was able to produce itself in its existence would have lost just what freedom means. In fact freedom is not a simple, undetermined power. If it were so, it would be a nothingness or in-itself—and it is a deviant synthesis of the in-itself with nothingness that has made it possible to conceive it

531   as a bare power, preexisting its choices. It determines itself, simply by arising, as a "doing" [*faire*]. But, as we saw, *doing* something requires the nihilation of a given. We make something *out of* something. In this way freedom is a lack of being in relation to a given being—not the arising of some full being. And if it is this hole in being, this nothingness of being as we have just said, it requires *all of being* in order to arise as a hole in the heart of being. It cannot therefore determine itself in existence on the basis of nothingness, because anything produced on the basis of nothingness could only be being-in-itself. We have proved moreover, in Part One of this work, that nothingness could not appear anywhere unless it was at the heart of being. At this point we meet the requirements of common sense: empirically, we can be free only in relation to a state of affairs, and in spite of this state of affairs. We say that I am free in relation to this state of affairs when it does not constrain me. In this way, the empirical and practical conception of freedom is wholly negative; it starts by considering a situation and noting that this situation *leaves me free* to pursue this or that end. We might even say that this situation conditions my freedom, in the sense in which it *is there in order not to constrain me*. Remove the prohibition on walking the streets after the curfew, and what could my freedom to walk about at night (which a permit, for example, has conferred on me) mean?

Thus freedom is a lesser being, which presupposes being, in order to subtract itself from it. It is free neither to not exist nor to not be free. We can grasp the connection between these two structures immediately; in effect, because freedom is an escape from being, it cannot occur *beside* being, as if it approached being laterally with the aim of surveying it: one cannot escape from a jail in which one is not locked

up. A projection of the self at the margin of being can in no way constitute itself as a nihilation of this being. Freedom is an escape from an
engagement within being; it is the nihilation of a being that it is. That
does not mean that human-reality exists first, in order to be free *afterward*. "Afterward" and "first" are terms created by freedom itself. The
movement through which freedom arises is made simply through the
twofold nihilation of the *being that it is*, and the being in whose midst it
is. Naturally, it is not this being in the sense of being-in-itself. But it
makes it happen that *there is*, behind it, this being which it is, by illuminating it in its deficiencies, in the light of the end it chooses. Freedom
has to be this being, behind it, which it has not chosen and, to precisely
the extent to which it turns back toward it to illuminate it, it makes it
happen that this being which belongs to it appears in relation with the
plenum of being, which is to say that it exists in the midst of the world.
We said that freedom is not free to not be free and that it is not free to
not exist. The point is indeed that the fact of not being able to not be
free is freedom's *facticity*, and the fact of not being able not to exist is
its *contingency*. Contingency and facticity are one and the same: there is a
being which freedom has to be in the form of *not being* (which is to say
nihilating) it. To exist—as the *fact* of freedom—or to have, in the midst
of the world, a being to be is one and the same thing, which means that
freedom is from the outset a *relation to the given*.

But what is this relation to the given? And should we take that to
mean that the given (the in-itself) conditions freedom? Let us take a
closer look: the given is not the *cause* of freedom (since it can only produce more given), nor its *reason* (since any "reason" comes into the
world through freedom). Neither is it a *necessary condition* of freedom,
since we are in the domain of pure contingency. Neither is it an *indispensable matter*, to which freedom has to apply itself, because that would
presuppose that freedom exists ready-made, as an Aristotelian form or
a Stoic *pneuma*, and seeks a matter to work on. The given plays no role
in constituting freedom, since freedom internalizes itself as an internal
negation of the given. It is simply the pure contingency which freedom
applies itself to negating as it makes itself a choice; it is the plenitude of
being that freedom colors with insufficiency and negativity, as it illuminates it in the light of an end that does not exist; it is *freedom itself* insofar
as it *exists*—and insofar as, whatever it does, it cannot escape its exis-

532

tence. The reader will have understood that this given is nothing but the in-itself nihilated by the for-itself which has it to be, or the body as the point of view on the world, or the past as the *essence* which the for-itself was: three ways of referring to the same reality. Through the nihilating step it takes back, freedom establishes a system of relations, from the point of view of its end, between the in-itselfs (in the "plural"), which is to say between the *plenum* of being which is here revealed as *world* and the being that it has to be in the midst of this *plenum*, and which is revealed as *a* being, as *a* "this" which it has to be. Thus, through its very projection toward an end, freedom constitutes a particular *datum* that it has to be as a being, in the midst of the world. It does not choose it, for that would be to choose its own existence; rather, through the choice it makes of its end, it makes it happen that it reveals itself in this or that way, in this or that light, in connection with the discovery of the world itself. Thus, freedom's very contingency, and the world which surrounds that contingency with its own contingency, will appear to it only in the light of the end it has chosen, which is to say not as brute existents but in the unity of the light thrown by the same nihilation. And freedom can never grasp this whole as a pure *datum*, because that would require it to be outside all choice and, therefore, to cease to be freedom. Let us say that the "*situation*" is freedom's contingency within the world's *plenum* of being, insofar as this *datum*, which is there only *in order not to constrain freedom*, is revealed to that freedom only as *already lit up* by the end that it chooses. In this way the *datum* never appears to the for-itself as a brute and in-itself existent; it is always encountered *as a reason*, since it is revealed only in the light of an end which illuminates it. Situation and motivation are one and the same. The for-itself discovers itself as engaged within being, invested with being, threatened by being; it discovers the state of affairs surrounding it as a reason for reacting defensively, or by an attack. But it can make this discovery only because it freely posits the end in relation to which the state of affairs is threatening or advantageous. We should learn from these remarks that the *situation*—a joint project of the contingency of the in-itself and of freedom—is an ambiguous phenomenon within which it is impossible for the for-itself to discern the contributions of freedom and the brute existent. Indeed, just as freedom is an escape from a contingency which it has to be, in order to escape from

533

it, so is the situation a free coordination and free qualification of a brute given which cannot be qualified in just any way. There I am at the foot of this rock, which seems to me to be "not climbable." Therefore the rock appears to me in the light of a projected rock-climbing—a secondary project whose meaning is given on the basis of an initial project which is my being-in-the-world. In this way the rock is outlined against the ground of the world as a result of the initial choice of my freedom. But, on the other hand, what my freedom is unable to decide is whether or not the rock "to be climbed" will lend itself to my climbing. That forms part of the rock's brute being. However, the rock can only manifest its resistance to the climbing if it is included by freedom within a "situation" whose general theme is rock-climbing. For the walker who is simply passing by on the road, and whose free project is purely the aesthetic ordering of the landscape, the rock is encountered neither as climbable nor as not-climbable: it only manifests itself as beautiful or ugly. Thus it is impossible to determine in each particular case what is due to freedom and what is due to the brute being of the for-itself.[40] The given in itself in the form of *resistance* or *aid* is revealed only in the light of the pro-jecting freedom. But the illumination organized by the pro-jecting freedom is such that in its light the in-itself is encountered *as it is*, i.e., as resistant or favorable—it being clear that the given's resistance is not accepted directly as an in-itself quality of the given but only as pointing, through a free illumination and a free refraction, toward an elusive *quid*. Therefore it is only in and through freedom's free arising that the world can develop and reveal the resistances that may make the projected end impossible to achieve. A man can encounter an obstacle only within the field of his freedom. Better still, it is impossible to decree *a priori* what, in the character that some particular existent has as an obstacle, is due to the brute existent and what is due to freedom. Something that is an obstacle for me, indeed, may not be one for someone else. No absolute obstacle exists; rather, the obstacle reveals its coefficient of adversity through the techniques that are freely invented, freely acquired; it also reveals it as a function   534

---

40 TN: …*l'être brut du pour-soi.* I think this must be a mistake in the French text. We should assume that Sartre meant "the brute being of *the in-itself.*"

of the value of the end that freedom posits. This rock will not be an obstacle if I want, at any cost, to reach the top of the mountain; it will on the contrary discourage me if I have freely set some limits to my desire to do the projected ascent. Thus the world, through the coefficients of adversity, reveals to me the way I care about the ends I assign to myself, in such a way that I can never know if the information it gives me is about me or about it. In addition, the given's coefficient of adversity is never a simple relation to my freedom, as a pure nihilating bursting forth: it is a relation, illuminated by freedom, between the *datum* that is the rock and the *datum* that my freedom has to be, i.e., between the contingency that it is not and its pure facticity. Where the desire to climb is equal, the rock will be easy to get up for this athletic ascensionist, difficult for this other person, a novice, poorly trained and with a puny body. But, in turn, the body only reveals itself as well trained or badly trained in relation to a free choice. It is because I am there, and I have made of myself what I am, that the rock develops a coefficient of adversity in relation to my body. For the lawyer who has stayed in town and pleads his case, his body hidden beneath his lawyer's robe, the rock is neither difficult nor easy to climb: it is merged within the totality of "the world" without sticking out from it any way. And, in a sense, it is I who choose my body as puny, as I pit it against the difficulties I generate (mountain-climbing, cycling, sport). If I have not chosen to do sport, if I stay in the towns and concern myself exclusively with business or with intellectual work, my body will not be characterized from that point of view at all. Thus we can begin to see the paradox of freedom: there is freedom only *in a situation*, and there is a situation only through freedom. Human-reality meets resistances and obstacles that it has not created everywhere, but these resistances and obstacles only have meaning in and through the free choice that human-reality *is*. But to grasp the meaning of these remarks more clearly, and to reap their benefit, we should now analyze some specific examples in their light. What we have called freedom's "facticity" is the given that it *has to be*, and which it lights up with its project. This given manifests itself in several ways, although within the absolute unity of a single illumination. It is *my place, my body, my past, my position*—insofar as that is already determined by what the others indicate—and, finally, my fundamental relation to the Other. We will examine these different structures of the situation in turn, and with specific examples. But we must never lose sight of the fact that none of them is given on its own and that, in considering one in isolation, we are confined to making it show up against the synthetic ground of the others.

(A) My place

My place is defined by the spatial order, and the particular nature of the "*thises*" which are revealed to me against the ground of the world. Naturally, it is the place "I inhabit" (my "country" with its soil, its climate, its riches, its hydrographic and orographic configuration), but also, more simply, it is the arrangement and the order of the objects appearing to me now (a table, on the other side of the table a window, the street, and the sea) and which point to me as the very principle of their order. It is not possible for me not to have a place, or my relation to the world would be as if from outside, and the world would no longer manifest itself any way at all, as we saw earlier. Moreover, even though my current place may have been assigned to me by my freedom (I "came" here), I was only able to occupy it by virtue of the one I occupied before and by following paths that are traced by the objects themselves. And this earlier place refers me to another, and this latter to another, and so on right up *to the pure contingency of my place*, which is to say the place which no longer refers to anything owing to me: the place assigned to me by birth. It will really not help to explain this last place as the one that was occupied by my mother when she brought me into the world: the chain is broken; the places that my parents freely chose cannot count for anything in an explanation of my places. And if we consider one of these in relation to my place of origin—as for example one might say "I was born in Bordeaux because my father, who was a civil servant, was given a post there" or "I was born in Tours because my grandparents owned property there and my mother took refuge close by to them when she learned, during her pregnancy, of my father's death"—it is in order to bring out more clearly the degree to which, *for me*, my birth and the place it assigns to me are contingent things. In this way to be born is, among other features, to *take one's place* or rather, in accordance with what we have just said, to *receive* it. And as this original place will be the basis on which I will occupy new places, according to determinate rules, this seems to present a major restriction of my freedom. Moreover, as soon as we reflect on it, the question becomes more complicated. The advocates of free will point out that, actually, from the standpoint of any place I occupy now, I am offered an infinite number of other places to choose from; the opponents of freedom emphasize the fact that an infinite number of places are hereby denied to me and in addition that objects present me with an aspect which I have not chosen and which excludes all the others—and they add that my place is too closely tied up with the other conditions of my existence (the diet, the climate, etc.) for it not to contribute to making me. Between the partisans and the opponents of freedom, it seems impossible to decide. That is because the debate has focused on the wrong questions.

536

In fact, if we want to raise the question correctly, we need to start out from this antinomy: human-reality initially receives its place in the midst of things—it is through human-reality that things can come to have something like a place. Without human-reality, there would be neither space nor place—and yet this human-reality, through whom things are placed, receives its own place among things, without in any way dictating it. To tell the truth, there is no mystery about this: but our description must start out from the antinomy, which will provide us with the exact relation between freedom and facticity.

Geometrical space, which is to say a pure reciprocity in spatial relations, is, as we saw, a pure nothingness. The only concrete location it is possible for me to encounter is absolute extension, which is to say just that type of extension that is defined in terms of my place as the center and in which distances are measured absolutely and without reciprocity from the object to myself. And the only absolute extension is one that unfolds from a place where I am absolutely. No other point can be chosen as the absolute center of reference without dragging us immediately into universal relativity. If there is an extension, within whose limits I can apprehend myself as free or not-free, which presents itself to me as a help or as a (separating) hindrance, it can only be because, before anything else, I exist my place, without choice and without necessity either, as the pure absolute fact of my being-there. I am there: not here but there. That is the absolute and incomprehensible fact at the origin of extension and, in consequence, of my original relations with things (with these things, rather than those ones). It is a purely contingent fact, an absurd fact.

Only, on the other hand, this place *that I am* is a relation. It is a univocal relation, of course, but it is a relation all the same. If I am confined to *existing* my place, I cannot at the same time be elsewhere in order to establish this fundamental relation; I cannot even have an obscure understanding of the object in relation to which my place is determined. I am able only to exist the internal determinations that may be called forth in me by the elusive and unthinkable objects that, unbeknownst to me, surround me. By the same token, the very reality of absolute extension will disappear, and I lose anything resembling a place. Moreover, I am neither free nor not-free: a pure existent, without any constraint, but without any means either of negating any constraint. In order for something like an extension which is originally defined as my place to come into the world, and at the same time to strictly define me, it is not only necessary for me to exist my place—i.e., for me *to have to be there*—but it must also be possible for me not to be fully there, in order to be able to be over there, next to the object that I locate ten meters away from me and on whose basis I become acquainted with my place. In effect, the univocal relation that defines my place is expressed as a relation between something that I am and something that I am not. For this relation to be revealed, it must be established. It requires therefore that I am able to perform the following operations: (1) *To escape what I am and to nihilate* it so that, even while I am still *existed*, what I am can nonetheless be revealed as the term of a relation. This relation is immediately given, not through the pure contemplation of objects (it might be objected, if we tried to derive space from pure contemplation, that objects are given with absolute *dimensions*, not with absolute *distances*) but in our immediate action ("he is coming over to us," "let's steer clear of him," "I am running after him," etc.), and as such it implies an understanding of what I am as being-there. But at the same time, what I am really needs to be defined on the basis of the being-there of other *thises*. As being-there, I am the person to whom someone comes running, the person who still has an hour of climbing before reaching the mountain summit, etc. What is involved therefore when, for example, I look at the mountain summit is a movement of escape out from me accompanied by a return movement back that I perform from the standpoint of the mountain's summit, in the direction of my being-there, in order to *situate* myself. Thus I am obliged to be "what I have to be" through the very fact of escaping from it. To define myself

537

by my place, I need first to escape from myself, in order to posit the coordinates on whose basis I will be able to define myself more narrowly as the center of the world. We should note that my *being-there* cannot determine the surpassing that establishes and situates things, since it is a *pure given*, unable to project, and since, moreover, in order to define one-self narrowly as this or as that *being-there*, the surpassing followed by the movement back must already have determined it. (2) *To escape by an internal negation the thises-in-the-midst-of-the-world that I am not, and through which I become acquainted with what I am.* As we have seen, the discovery of these and the escape from them are the outcome of one same negation. Here, too, the internal negation is first and spontaneous in relation to the *datum* as what is un-covered. We cannot allow that it *induces* our apprehension; but, on the contrary, for there *to be* any *this*, which acquaints the being-there that I *am* with its distances, what is required is precisely that I should, through pure negation, escape from it. Nihilation, internal negation, a determin-ing movement of return to the being-there that I am: these three opera-tions are just one and the same. They are only the moments of an original transcendence throwing itself toward an end by nihilating me, in order to acquaint me through the future with what I am. Thus it is my freedom that comes to confer on me my place and to define it as such by situating me; I can only be strictly *limited* to *this* being-there that I am because my ontological structure is to not be what I am and to be what I am not.

538   Moreover, this determining of my location, which presupposes tran-scendence in its entirety, can take place only in relation to an end. It is in the light of the end that my place acquires its meaning. For I can never be *simply there*. Rather, my place is apprehended precisely as an *exile* or—on the contrary—as the natural, reassuring, and favorite place that Mauriac called the *querencia*, in comparison with the place in the arena to which the wounded bull always returns.[41] It is in relation to what I am project-ing to do—in relation to the world in its totality and, therefore, to all of my being-in-the-world—that my place can appear to me as an aid or an impediment. To be at a place is in the first place to be far from . . . or

---

41 TN: François Mauriac (1885–1970) was a famous French novelist. He took the word *querencia* from his reading of Ernest Hemingway's 1932 non-fiction book about bull-fighting, *Death in the Afternoon* (Hemingway 2003).

near to . . . , which is to say that the place is endowed with a meaning in relation to a specific being that does not yet exist, and that one wishes to attain. The place is defined by the accessibility or inaccessibility of this end. It is therefore in the light of non-being and the future that my position can currently be understood: being-there is to be able to reach the teapot by taking just one step, to be able to dip my pen into the ink by stretching out my arm, to need to turn my back to the window if I want to read without tiring my eyes, to be obliged to mount my bicycle and put up with the exhaustion of a sweltering afternoon for two hours if I want to see my friend Pierre, to take the train and have a sleepless night if I want to see Anny. For a colonial, being-there is to be twenty days away from France—better still, if he is a government official and waiting for his paid trip, it is to be six months and seven days away from Bordeaux or Étaples. For a soldier, being-there is to be a hundred and ten, or a hundred and twenty, days away from his basic training. Everywhere, the future—a pro-jected future—intervenes: it is my future life in Bordeaux, in Étaples, the soldier's future discharge, the word "future" that I will inscribe with my ink-soaked pen; all of this signifies my place to me and makes me exist it with irritation, impatience, or nostalgia. If on the contrary I am running away from a group of men or from public opinion, then my place is defined by the time it will take for these people to discover me at the far end of the village where I am lodging, or for them to reach this village, etc. In this case, what presents my place to me as favorable is my isolation. Here, to be in a place is to be sheltered.

This choice of my end slides even into relations that are purely spatial (high and low, right and left, etc.), to give them an existential meaning. The mountain is "overwhelming" if I am still at its foot; if I am at its summit, on the contrary, it is taken up in the very project of my pride, and symbolizes the superiority I attribute to myself in relation to other men. The position of the rivers, the distance from the sea, etc., come into play and are endowed with symbolic meaning: my place, constituted in the light of my end, reminds me symbolically in all its details, and in the connections between its parts, of this end. We will return to this when we come to define the object and the methods of existential psychoanalysis more closely. We can never grasp the brute relation of *distance* to objects outside the meanings and the symbols that make up our particular way of constituting it, especially as the brute relation itself only has meaning in relation to

539

the choice of techniques that allow us to measure and traverse the distances. This town, situated twenty kilometers away from my village and connected to it by a tram line, is a great deal closer to me than a rocky summit situated four kilometers away, but at an altitude of two thousand eight hundred meters. Heidegger showed us how the places assigned to our implements by our everyday concerns have nothing in common with pure, geometric distance. Once my spectacles are on my nose, he tells us, they are much farther away from me than the object I can see through them.[42]

Thus we are obliged to say that the facticity of my place is revealed to me only in and through the free choice that I make of my end. Freedom is indispensable to the discovery of my facticity. Every point in the future I am pro-jecting teaches me about this facticity; it is on the basis of this chosen future that it appears to me, with its character of powerlessness, contingency, weakness, and absurdity. It is in relation to my dream of seeing New York that the fact that I live in Mont-de-Marsan is absurd and distressing. But, inversely, facticity is the only reality that freedom is able to encounter, the only reality it can nihilate by positing an end, the only reality on whose basis it makes any sense to posit an end. For, if the end is able to illuminate the situation, that is because it is constituted as a projected change in that situation. My place appears on the basis of the changes that I plan. But *to change* something implies precisely that there is something to be changed—which is of course my place. Thus *freedom is the apprehension of my facticity*. It would be absolutely futile to try to define or to describe this facticity's *quid* "before" freedom has turned back toward it to grasp it as a specific deficiency. Before freedom has delimited my location as a lack of some particular kind, my place "is not," strictly speaking, anything at all, since extension itself—on whose basis every place has to be understood—does not exist. On the other hand, the question itself is unintelligible, because it introduces a "before" that has no meaning: it is freedom itself, in fact, which temporalizes itself, in accordance with the directions of "before" and "after." It remains no less the case that, without this brute and unthinkable *quid*, freedom could not be freedom. It is the very facticity of my freedom.

It is only in the act through which freedom has discovered facticity and

---

42 TN: Heidegger gives this example in *Being and Time* (Heidegger 1980: §23).

apprehended it as its *place* that this place, thus defined, manifests itself as a *hindrance* to my desires, an *obstacle*, etc. How otherwise would it be possible for it to be an obstacle? An obstacle *to what*? A constraint *on doing what*? An emigrant who, after the failure of his political party, was going to leave France to go to Argentina is said to have given this answer when someone pointed out to him that Argentina was "quite far": "Far from what?" he asked. And it is quite clear that, if Argentina seems "far" to those who remain in France, that is in relation to an implicit national project that valorizes their position as Frenchmen. For the internationalist revolutionary, Argentina is a center of the world like any other country. But if we have from the outset constituted French soil, through a first project, precisely as our absolute place—and if some catastrophe forces us into exile—it is in relation to this initial project that Argentina will appear to be "quite far," or a "land of exile," and that we will feel ourselves to be expatriates. In this way freedom itself creates the obstacles that make us suffer. It is freedom itself which in positing its end—and in choosing that end either as "inaccessible" or as "only accessible with difficulty"—makes our location appear as a resistance to our projects that is insurmountable or that can be overcome only with difficulty. Again, it is freedom which, by establishing the spatial connections between objects—as a first type of equipmental relation—and deciding on the techniques that enable the distances to be measured and covered, constitutes its own *restriction*. But precisely there can be no freedom without *restraint*, since freedom is choice. Every choice, as we will see, presupposes some elimination and selection; every choice is a choice of finitude. In this way freedom can be truly free only by constituting facticity as its own restriction. There would therefore be no point in saying "I am not free" to go to New York, on account of my being a minor civil servant in Mont-de-Marsan. On the contrary, it is in relation to my project to go to New York that I will *situate* myself in Mont-de-Marsan. My location in the world, Mont-de-Marsan's relationship to New York and to China, would be quite different were my project to become, for example, a wealthy farmer in Mont-de-Marsan. In the first case Mont-de-Marsan appears against the ground of the world in an arrangement that connects it with New York, Melbourne, and Shanghai; in the second case, it emerges against an undifferentiated ground of world. As for the *real* importance of my project to go to New York, I alone can decide that. It may just be a way of choosing to be dissatisfied by Mont-de-Marsan, and in this case everything is centered

540

around Mont-de-Marsan; I simply feel a need to constantly nihilate my place, to live in a constant state of withdrawal in relation to the city where I live—it may also be a project to which I commit myself entirely. In the first case I will apprehend my place as an insurmountable obstacle, and I will simply have made use of a particular perspective to define it indirectly within the world; in the second case, on the contrary, the obstacles no longer exist and my place will no longer be a point of attachment but a point of departure: for, in order *to go* to New York, some point of departure—whichever it is—is obviously required. Thus, at any moment whatsoever, I will apprehend myself as committed within the world, in my contingent place. But this commitment is precisely what gives my contingent place its meaning, and what my freedom is. Of course, in being born, I *take up my place*, but I am responsible for the place I take up. Here we can see more clearly the inextricable connection between freedom and facticity within the situation, since without facticity freedom would not exist—as a power to nihilate and to choose—and, without freedom, facticity would not be uncovered and would not even have any meaning.

541

(B) My past

We have a past. Of course we have been able to establish that this past does not determine our acts in the way that an earlier phenomenon determines the consequent phenomenon, and of course we have shown that the past has no power to constitute the present and to sketch out the future in advance. It remains no less the case that the freedom that escapes toward the future cannot give itself a past at whim, nor, *a fortiori*, can it produce itself without a past. It has its own past to be, and this past is irremediable. It even looks, at first sight, as if freedom is unable to change it in any way: the past is something out of reach that haunts us from a distance, without our being able even to turn back to it, to confront it and consider it. If the past does not determine our actions, it is at least such as to make it impossible for us to make any new decision except *on its basis*. If I have studied to go to the Naval College[43] and become a naval officer, whatever the moment

---

43 TN: The institution Sartre refers to here is the École Navale, which trains naval officers. The US counterpart would be the Naval Academy; the British equivalent would be the (Royal) Naval College.

in which I review and weigh things up for myself, I am committed; at the very instant in which I apprehend myself I am on watch, on the deck of the boat of which I am second-in-command. Of course, I may suddenly rebel against this fact, hand in my resignation, or decide to commit suicide: these extreme measures are taken in the context of the past that is mine; if they aim to destroy it, that is because it exists and my most radical decisions cannot reach any further than my adoption of a negative position in relation to my past. But that is, essentially, to acknowledge its immense importance as a platform and as a point of view: any action that aims to separate me from my past must in the first place be conceived on the basis of *this past here*, which means it must recognize, first and foremost, that it arises *on the basis of* this particular past that it wishes to destroy; as the proverb says, our actions follow us.[44] The past is present and merges imperceptibly into the present: it is the suit I chose six months ago, the house that was built for me, the book that I began last winter, my wife, the promises made by me to her, my children. Everything that I *am* is what I have to be, in the mode of having-been-it. Thus the importance of the past cannot be exaggerated, since for me "*Wesen ist was gewesen ist*," to be is to have been.[45] But here we find, once again, the paradox that we pointed to earlier: I cannot conceive of myself without a past; better, I could not even *think* anything about myself, since I think about what I *am* and since I am in the past; but, on the other hand, I am the being through whom the past comes to itself, and comes into the world.

542

Let us examine this paradox more closely: freedom, being a choice, is a change. It is defined by the end that it pro-jects, i.e., by the future that it has to be. But precisely because the future is the state-that-has-not-yet-come-to-be-of-what-is, it can be conceived of only in close connection with what is. And it cannot be *what is* that illuminates what has not yet come to be, because *what is* is a *lack* and in consequence can only be known as such on the basis of what is missing from it. It is the end that illuminates what is. But in order to seek the forth-coming end, to be acquainted by it with what one is, it is necessary to already be beyond what is, to have taken a nihilating step back that brings it clearly into view as an isolated system.[46] What is, therefore, acquires its meaning

44 TN: This is a version of "As you sow, so shall you reap."
45 TN: Sartre has already quoted this phrase (from Hegel) earlier in the text, e.g., at EN 70.
46 TN: ...*à l'état de système isolé*. The concept of an "isolated system" comes from physics; in fact, in the natural world, it is impossible for a truly isolated system to exist.

only when it is *surpassed* toward the future. What is, therefore, is the past. We can see how the past, in its capacity of "what must be changed," is indispensable to the choice of the future—and, at the same time how, in consequence, it is impossible for any free surpassing to occur except on the basis of a past—and that, on the other hand, this very *nature* of being past comes to the past from the original choice of a future. In particular, the past owes its irremediable character to my distinct choice of the future: if the past is the basis on which I conceive and project a new state of affairs in the future, it is itself what is *left in place*;[47] in consequence, the past itself lies outside any perspective of change. Thus, for it to be possible for the future to be actualized, the past must be irremediable.

I might easily not exist: but, if I exist, I cannot fail to have a past. That is the form taken in this case by the "necessity of my contingency." But on the other hand, as we have seen, two characteristics above all qualify the for-itself:

(1) nothing is in consciousness without being consciousness of being;
(2) my being is in question in my being—which means that nothing happens to me that has *not been chosen*.

We saw, indeed, that a past that was only *past* would collapse into an honorary existence in which it would lose any link with the present. For us to "have" a past, we must maintain it in existence, through our very project toward the future. We do not receive our past, but the necessity of our contingency implies that we are not able to not choose it. That is what it means "to have one's own past to be": we can see that, considered from a purely temporal point of view, this necessity is fundamentally indistinguishable from the primary structure of freedom, which has to be a nihilation of the being that it is and which, through this very nihilation, makes it the case that *there is* a being that it is.

But if freedom is the choice of an end in accordance with the past, the
543 past, conversely, is what it is only in relation to the chosen end. There is an immutable element in the past: I had whooping cough when I

---

47 TN: Sartre writes "*le futur ... est ... ce qui est* laissé sur place." Strictly, one would translate this as "the future is what is *left behind*," but, because Sartre may intend us to dwell on the term "place," I have slightly varied the translation.

was five—and an element that is as variable as it can be: the brute fact's meaning, in relation to the totality of my being. But as, on the other hand, the past fact is penetrated throughout by its meaning (I cannot "remember" my childhood whooping cough apart from some precise project which defines its meaning), it is in the end impossible for me to distinguish the brute immutable existence from the variable meaning that comes with it. When I say "I had whooping cough when I was five," a thousand pro-jects are presupposed, in particular the use of the calendar as a frame of reference for my individual existence (and therefore the taking up of an initial stance in relation to the social), a resolute belief in the stories that others tell me about my childhood (which clearly goes with a respect or affection for my parents, which constitutes its meaning), etc. The brute fact itself *is*: but, apart from the testimonies of others, its date, the technical name for the illness—a set of meanings that depend on my projects—what exactly might it *be*? Therefore this brute existence, *even though it necessarily exists and is immutable*, represents something like the ideal and unattainable goal of a systematic explication of all the meanings that a memory includes. There is, no doubt, a "pure" matter to the memory, in the sense in which Bergson talks about pure memory,[48] but when it manifests itself it is only ever in and through a project that involves the appearance of this matter in its purity.

Now the meaning of the past depends closely on my present project. That does not mean at all that I may vary the meaning of my previous actions according to whim but, quite to the contrary, that the fundamental project that I am decides absolutely on the meaning that the past which I have to be may have, for me and for others. I alone, in fact, am able to decide at each moment on the *impact* of the past, not by debating, deliberating, and evaluating in each case the importance of such and such an earlier event but, by pro-jecting myself toward my goals, I rescue the past as well as myself and I *decide* on its meaning through my action. Who will decide whether that mystical crisis at the age of fifteen "was" a pure accident of puberty or, on the contrary, the first sign of a future conversion? Me, according to the decision I may make—aged twenty, or

---

48 TN: Sartre is presumably alluding to the theory presented in Bergson (1911b).

thirty—to convert. At one stroke, the project of conversion confers on an adolescent crisis the value of a premonition that I did not take seriously. Who will decide whether the time I spent in prison, after a theft, was productive or regrettable? Me, according to whether I give up stealing or become hardened. Who will decide on the educational value of a trip, or the sincerity of a vow of love, the purity of a past intention, etc.? It will be me, always according to the ends through which I light up these things.

544   Thus the whole of my past is there, insistent, urgent, and imperious, but I choose its meaning and the orders that it gives me through the very project of my end. Without doubt, these commitments weigh on me, and without doubt the conjugal bond that I accepted in the past, the house that I bought and furnished last year, limit my possibilities and dictate my behavior; but this is precisely because my projects are such that I reaccept the conjugal bond, because I do not make of it a "conjugal bond that is in the past, moved on from, dead." On the contrary, my projects—which imply my faithfulness to the commitments I have made, or the decision to lead an "honorable life" as a husband and father, etc.—necessarily illuminate my past conjugal vow and endow it with its still-present value. Thus the urgency of the past comes from the future. If I were suddenly—like Schlumberger's[49] hero—to change radically my fundamental project—were I, for example, to seek to free myself from the continuity of my happiness—my earlier commitments would lose all their urgency. They would only remain there in the way that those towers and ramparts from the Middle Ages remain, as something that nobody would deny but whose only meaning is to recall (as a stage that was passed through earlier) a civilization and a phase of political and economic existence that we have gone beyond and which are, today, perfectly dead. It is the future that decides whether the past is living or dead. The past is, indeed, originally a project, like my currently arising being. And, to just the extent to which it is a project, it is an anticipation; its meaning comes from the future which it outlines in advance. When the past slides entirely into the past, its absolute value depends on the confirmation or invalidation of the anticipations which it was. But,

---

49 Sartre's note: Schlumberger, Un Homme Heureux (NRF). TN: Jean Schlumberger (1877–1968) was a French writer. His novel Un Homme Heureux (which translates as A Happy Man) was published in France in 1920. It is not available in English translation.

precisely, it is entirely up to my current freedom whether to confirm the meaning of these anticipations by reaffirming them, which is to say by anticipating, after them, the future that they were anticipating or by invalidating them simply by anticipating another future. In this case the past collapses like an expectation that has been disarmed and tricked; it has "no strength." The fact is that the past gets its only strength from the future: whatever my way of living or evaluating my past, I can only do so in the light of a pro-ject of myself in the future. Thus it is the order of my choices for the future that will determine an order in my past, and this order is not remotely chronological. In the first place there will be the past that is *still living* and still confirmed: my love commitment, those business contracts, this image of myself, to which I am faithful. Then the ambiguous past which no longer pleases me, and which I retain indirectly: for example, this suit that I am wearing—which I bought at a particular time, when I enjoyed being fashionable—displeases me now intensely and, on this account, the past in which I "chose" it is truly dead. But, on the other hand, my current project to make savings is such that I have to go on wearing this suit, rather than acquire a different one. In consequence it belongs to a past which is dead and alive at the same time, like those social institutions which were created for a particular purpose and have survived the regime that established them, because they have been put to purposes which are quite different, and sometimes even opposed. The living past, the half-dead past, throwbacks, ambiguities, antinomies: the set of these layers of being-past is organized by the unity of my project. It is through this project that the complex cross-referring system is set up, by which any fragment of my past is placed within a ranked and multifaceted structure in which, as in a work of art, each partial structure indicates, in various ways, various other partial structures and the total structure.

545

   Furthermore, this decision in relation to the value, order, and nature of our past is, quite simply, *historical choice* in general. If human societies are historical, that is not due merely to the fact that they have a past but because they *take it up*, as a *monument*. When American capitalism decides to enter the 1914–1918 European war because it sees there an opportunity for profitable operations, it is not *historical*: it is merely utilitarian. But when, in the light of its utilitarian projects, it resumes the former relations between the United States and France, and gives to these the *meaning* of a debt of honor owed to France by the Americans, it becomes historical and, in particular, it historializes itself through the famous phrase "Lafayette, we are here!" Needless to say, if a different vision of their interests at the time had led the United States to side with Germany, there would have been no shortage of elements from the past which could have been taken up as monumental: for example, it is possible to imagine propaganda based on the idea of "a brotherhood of blood," which would essentially take account of the proportion of Germans who emigrated to America in the nineteenth century. There is no point in regarding these references to the past as mere exercises in publicity: the essential point, in fact, is that they are *necessary* in order to command the support of the masses and, therefore, that the masses demand a political pro-ject that illuminates and justifies their past. In addition, it goes without saying that the past is hereby *created: there was* the constitution of a common French-American past which *signified,* on the one hand, the Americans' major economic interests and, on the other hand, the *current* affinities between two democratic capitalist systems. Similarly, in around 1938, we saw younger generations, who were worried about the events that were taking shape internationally, suddenly came to view the 1918–1938 period in a new light and described it, even before the 1939 war had broken out, as the "interwar years." Immediately, the period in question was constituted as a limited figure, surpassed and disavowed, while those who had lived through it, pro-jecting themselves toward a future in continuity with their present and immediate past, had experienced it as the beginning of an unlimited and continuous progression. The current project, therefore, decides whether some fixed period of the past is continuous with the present or if it is a discontinuous fragment from which we are emerging, and which is moving further away. Thus we would need a human history that had *ended* in order for some event— for example the storming of the Bastille—to acquire a definitive meaning. Nobody denies, indeed, that the Bastille was stormed in 1789: that is the immutable fact. But should we see, in this event, an inconsequential riot, a popular outburst against a half-demolished fortress which the Convention—anxious to create a past it could advertise—was able to transform into a remarkable achievement? Or should we regard it as the first demonstration of the power of the people, through which the popular force became stronger, gained in confidence, and was in a position to carry out the "October March" on Versailles? To think that we could decide on this today would be to forget that the historian is himself *historical*, i.e., that, in illuminating "History" in the light of his projects and those of his society, he historializes himself. What we must say therefore is that the meaning of the social past is constantly "pending."[50]

Now, just like societies, the human person has a past that is *monumental* and *pending*. At an early stage, the sages sensed this constant putting into question of the past, and the Greek tragedians, for example, expressed it by means of this proverb, which recurs in all their plays: "Call no man happy until he is dead."[51] And the for-itself's constant historialization is a constant affirmation of its freedom.

That said, we should not suppose that the past's character as "pending" appears to the for-itself as a vague or unfinished aspect of its previous history. On the contrary, in the same way as the for-itself's choice—which it expresses in its own way—the past is apprehended at each moment by the for-itself as being strictly determined. Similarly, and however their meaning may in other respects have evolved, the Arch of Titus and Trajan's Column appear to the Roman or the tourist who looks at them as fully individualized realities. And, in the light of the project which illuminates it, it is revealed as being wholly constraining. Indeed, the past's character as "pending" is not in any way miraculous; it only expresses, at the level of the pastified and the in-itself, the pro-jective and "waiting" aspect that human-reality *had* before it turned into the past. It is because that human-reality was a free pro-ject, eaten into by an unpredictable freedom, that it can become "in the past" hostage to the for-itself's subsequent projects. The homologous character that human-reality was waiting to be given by a future freedom becomes something that it is condemned, as it pastifies itself, constantly to await. In this way the past is indefinitely suspended because human-reality "was" and "will be" in a constant state of waiting. And this waiting and the state of suspension only affirm freedom still more clearly as what originally constitutes them. To say that the for-

50 TN: ... *perpétuellement "en sursis."* See my note about the phrase *en sursis*, which derives I think from Heidegger, in Notes on the Translation.
51 TN: This phrase is in Aeschylus's *Agamemnon*. As Sartre says, it is also attributed to other Greek writers.

547   itself's past is pending, or that its present is one of waiting, or that its future is a free project, or that it cannot be anything without having it to be, or that it is a detotalized totality, is one and the same thing. But this precisely does not imply that there is anything undetermined about my past as it is revealed to me in the present: it merely puts into question the status of my current encounter with my past as definitive. But just as my present awaits a confirmation or an invalidation that nothing allows us to predict, in the same way my past, which is carried along in this waiting, is *precise* exactly in proportion to the *precision* of my waiting. But its meaning, although it is strictly individualized, depends completely on this waiting which itself depends on an absolute nothingness, i.e., a free project that does not yet exist. My past is therefore a concrete and precise proposition which, *as such*, awaits ratification. That is certainly one of the meanings that Kafka's *The Trial*[52] is trying to expose, this constantly *processual* character of human-reality. To be free is to be constantly *in the course of freedom's proceedings*.[53] It remains the case that the past—if we stay with my current free choice—is, once this choice has determined it, an integral part and a necessary condition of my project. An example will help us to understand. For a soldier on "half-pay"[54] during the Restoration, his past is that of having been a hero in the retreat from Russia. And our analysis so far allows us to understand that this past itself is a free choice of the future. It is by choosing not to rally around Louis XVIII's government and the new customs, by choosing to hope right to the end for the Emperor's triumphal return, by choosing even to conspire in order to hasten this return, and to prefer half-pay to a full wage, that Napoleon's old soldier chooses for himself the past of a hero of the Battle of Berezina. Someone who had formed the pro-ject of rallying to the new government would certainly not have chosen the same past. But, conversely, if he is only on half-pay, if he lives in a barely decent state of destitution, if he becomes embittered and wishes for the return of the Emperor, that is because he

---

52 TN: Sartre has mentioned Kafka's novel, *The Trial*, at EN 305. Its French title, *Le Procès*, retains the intended connection with Sartre's emphasis in this passage on *process* and *proceedings*.

53 TN: ... *en instance de liberté*. *En instance* is a legal phrase, used for ongoing actions such as divorce proceedings.

54 TN: ... *un "demi-solde"* ... This phrase, which literally means "someone on half-pay," is often used in French to refer to retired or inactive soldiers receiving a pension for their earlier service.

was a hero in the retreat from Russia. Let us be clear: this past does not act before it is taken up and constituted, and no determinism at all is involved; but once the past of "a soldier of the Empire" is *chosen*, the for-itself behaves in a way that *actualizes* this past. There is not even any difference between choosing this past and bringing it about through one's behavior. In this way, the for-itself, by trying to make his glorious past into an intersubjective reality, constitutes it in the eyes of others as an objectivity-for-the-Other (the prefects' reports, for example, about the danger posed by these old soldiers). Treated by others as such, he acts thenceforth to make himself worthy of a past that he has chosen in compensation for his current destitution and decline. He is uncompromising, and loses any chance of a pension: the reason is that he "cannot" show himself unworthy of his past. In this way, we choose our past in the light of a specific end, but thereafter it imposes itself on us and consumes us. This is not because it has an existence *by itself* that is different from the existence that we have to be but simply because: (1) it is the materialization, as it is currently revealed, of the end that we are; (2) it appears in the midst of the world, for us and for the Other; it is never alone but immerses itself in the universal past and, in consequence, offers itself up to be evaluated by others. Just as a geometer is free to generate any figure he likes but is unable to conceive of one that does not immediately maintain an infinite number of relations with other possible figures, so our free choice of ourselves, by giving rise to a specific evaluative ordering of our past, makes an infinite number of relations appear, connecting this past to the world, and to the Other. And this infinite number of relations is presented to us as *an infinite number of ways in which to act*, since our past itself is appraised by us in the future. And, to the extent that our past appears within the framework of our essential project, we are *constrained* to act in these ways. To will this project is, in fact, to will this past, and to will this past is to will to bring it about by means of a thousand secondary actions. In logical terms, the requirements of the past are hypothetical imperatives: "If you want to have such a past, act in such and such a way." But as the first term is a concrete and categorical choice, the imperative is also itself transformed into a categorical imperative.

548

But since my past's constraining power is borrowed from my free and reflective choice, and has just that amount of strength conferred by that choice on itself, it is impossible to determine *a priori* the constraining power of a past. My free choice does not decide only on its content and the ordering of this content but also how closely this past adheres to where I am now. If, within a fundamental perspective which we do not yet need to determine, one of my principal projects is to *make progress*, i.e., to be always, and at any cost, *further along* a certain path than I was the evening, or the hour, before, this progressive project will imply a series of *detachments* in relation to my past. In that case the past will be something I look down at, from the height of my progress, with a kind of slightly scornful pity; it is an object of moral evaluation and judgment that is strictly *passive*, that exists only in order for me to be able to break away from it: "What a fool I was, then!" or "How nasty I was!" I am no longer part of it, and I no longer want to be part of it. It is not, of course, that it has ceased to exist, but it exists only as *this me that I am no longer*, i.e., as *this being that I have to be, as a me that I am no longer*. Its function is to be what I have chosen of myself, in order to oppose myself to that, which enables me to take my measure. A for-itself like this will therefore choose itself without any solidarity with itself, which does not mean it abolishes its past but that it posits it in order to lack any solidarity with it, precisely in order to assert its complete freedom (what is past is a specific type of commitment in relation to the past, and a specific kind of tradition). There are, on the contrary, some for-itselfs whose project involves a refusal of time and a close solidarity with the past. In their desire to find some solid ground these people have, on the contrary, chosen the past as what they *are*, so that everything else is merely an indefinite flight, unworthy of tradition.[55] They have chosen *in the first place* to refuse that flight, i.e., *to refuse to refuse*; in consequence, the role of the past is to demand their fidelity. In this way we can see that the first group can confess disdainfully and easily to a mistake they have made, whereas for the others the same confession will be impossible unless they deliberately change their fundamental project; they will deploy all the bad faith in the world, and every loophole they can find, in order to avoid any dent in this faith in what is, which constitutes an essential structure of their project.

549

Thus, like the for-itself's location, the past becomes integrated into the for-itself's situation when, through its choice of the future, it confers

---

55 TN: ... *fuite indéfinie* ... It is difficult to translate this sentence clearly. I think the "flight" here refers to the "flight" (or passing) of time.

on its past facticity a value, a hierarchical ordering, and an urgency on the basis of which it motivates its actions and its behavior.

(C) My surroundings

My "surroundings" should not be confused with the place that I occupy, which we discussed earlier. My surroundings are the implement-things that surround me, with their own coefficients of adversity and their equipmentality. Of course, by occupying my place I am founding my discovery of my surroundings, and by changing place—an operation that, as we saw, I may freely perform—I am founding the appearance of new surroundings. But, conversely, the surroundings can change, or be changed by others, without my having anything to do with their change. Of course, as Bergson accurately observed in *Matière et Mémoire*,[56] a change in my place implies a complete change in my surroundings, whereas we would have to envisage a total and simultaneous change in my surroundings in order to talk of a change in my place—but such a global change in my surroundings is inconceivable. But it remains no less true that my field of action is constantly traversed by objects that appear and disappear, where these events have nothing to do with me. In general terms, the coefficient of adversity and equipmentality of a structure does not depend only on my place but on the implements' own potentiality. Thus I am thrown, from the moment I exist, in the midst of existences that differ from me, and whose potentialities are unfolding, for and against me. I want to reach, by bicycle, the neighboring town as quickly as possible. This project involves my personal ends, an assessment of my place and the town's distance from my place, and the free adaptation of means (my *efforts*) to the end I am pursuing. But a tire bursts, the sun is too intense, the wind is blowing head-on, etc., all of which are phenomena I had not foreseen: these are my surroundings. Of course, they manifest themselves in and through my principal project: through it, the wind can appear as a headwind or as a "good" wind; through it, the sun can reveal itself as a favorable or an incon-

550

56 TN: This work by Bergson, published in France in 1896, is translated into English as *Matter and Memory* (Bergson 1911b).

venient heat. The synthetic organization of these constant "accidents" constitutes the unity of what the Germans refer to as my "Umwelt,"[57] and this "Umwelt" can be discovered only within the limits of a free project, which is to say the choice of the ends that I am. However, it would be far too simple to allow our description to stop there. If it is true that each object around me introduces itself within a situation that is already revealed, and that the sum of these objects cannot constitute a situation on its own, and if it is true that each implement detaches itself against the ground of a situation in the world, it remains no less the case that the sudden transformation or sudden appearance of an implement may contribute to a radical change in the situation: let my tire burst, and my distance from the neighboring town suddenly changes; now it is a distance to be counted in steps, and not in turns of the wheel. In consequence, I may become certain that the person I want to see will already have caught their train when I get to their house, and this certainty may bring with it other decisions of mine (to return to my point of departure, to send a telegram, etc.). I may even, if I am sure for example that I will not be able to make the deal that I had planned with this person, fall back on someone else and sign another contract. And what if I should even abandon my attempt entirely, and be obliged to record a total failure of my project? In that case I will say that I *was not able* to inform Pierre in time, to reach an understanding with him, etc. Isn't this explicit recognition of my *powerlessness* the clearest acknowledgment of my freedom's limits? No doubt, as we have seen, we should not confuse my freedom *to choose* with my *freedom to obtain* anything. But isn't it my choice itself which is at stake here, since the adversity of my surroundings is precisely, in many cases, what brings about the change in my project?

We ought, before we get to the heart of this debate, to clarify and delimit it. If it is possible for changes that occur in my surroundings to give rise to modifications in my projects, this can happen only with two provisos. The first is that these changes cannot bring me to abandon my original project, which provides, on the contrary, the measure of their

---

57 TN: *Umwelt* is German for "environment" or "surroundings." The term features in Heidegger's *Being and Time*.

importance. If in fact they are apprehended as *reasons* for abandoning this or that project, it can be only in the light of a more fundamental project; otherwise they could not be reasons at all, since a reason is apprehended by a motive-consciousness which is itself the free-choice of an end. If the clouds which cover the sky can prompt me to give up my project to go on an excursion, it is because they are apprehended within a free projection, in which the excursion's value is linked to a certain state of the sky, which takes us, step by step, to the value of an excursion in general, to my relation to nature and to the place of this relation within the set of relations that I maintain with the world. In the second place, the object that has appeared or disappeared cannot in any case *induce* me to give up my project, even in part. This object would need in fact to be apprehended as a *lack* within the original situation; it would be necessary therefore for the *given* of its appearance or its disappearance to be nihilated, for me to step back "in relation to it" and, in consequence, for me to decide on myself in its presence. As we have already shown, even the executioner's grip does not exempt us from being free. That does not mean that it is always possible to get around the difficulty, to make good the damage, but simply that the *impossibility itself* of continuing in a certain direction must be freely constituted. It enters into things through our free renunciation, rather than our renunciation being induced by the impossibility of the actions that were to be performed.

That said, we must acknowledge that, here too, the presence of the given, far from being an obstacle to our freedom, is called for by its very existence. This freedom is a specific freedom that I am. But who am I, if not a certain internal negation of the in-itself? Without this in-itself which I negate, I would vanish into nothingness. We have pointed out, in our Introduction, that consciousness can be used as an "ontological proof" of the existence of an in-itself. If indeed there is consciousness of something, this "something" must from the outset have a being that is *real*, which is to say *not relative to consciousness*. But we can see now that this proof has a wider scope: if I must be able to *do* something in general, I must act on beings whose existence is *independent* of my existence in general, and particularly of my action. My action may *reveal* this existence to me, but it does not condition it. To be free is to-be-free-to-change. Freedom therefore implies the existence of the surroundings to be changed: obstacles to be overcome, tools to be used. Of course, it is freedom that reveals

551

them as obstacles, but through its free choice it can only interpret the *meaning* of their being. It is necessary for them to quite simply be there, wholly brute, for there to be freedom. To be free is *to-be-free-to-do* and it is *to-be-free-in-the-world*. But if that is the case, freedom, by recognizing itself as a freedom to change, recognizes and implicitly foresees in its original project the independent existence of the given on which it acts. It is internal negation which reveals the in-itself as independence, and it is this independence which constitutes the in-itself in its character as a *thing*. But henceforth, what freedom posits, simply through arising in its being, is that its way of being is *to deal with something other than itself*. To do something is precisely to change something that has no need of anything but itself to exist; it is to act on something that is necessarily indifferent to one's action, and able to pursue its existence or its evolution without it. Without this indifferent externality of the in-itself, the very notion of *doing* something would lose its meaning (as we showed earlier, in relation to the wish and the decision) and, in consequence, freedom itself would collapse. Thus the very project of a freedom in general is a choice which involves the expectation and acceptance of resistances that are in any case quite commonplace. Not only does freedom constitute the framework in which in-itselfs which are in other respects indifferent will be revealed as resistances but, further, its very project, in general, is the project *to do* something in a resisting world, by triumphing over these resistances. Any free project foresees, as it pro-jects itself, the margin of unpredictability due to the independence of things, precisely because it is on the basis of this independence that a freedom is constituted. The moment I plan to go to the neighboring village to find Pierre, punctures, a headwind, a thousand predictable and unpredictable accidents, are given in my proj-ect itself and constitute its meaning. So the unexpected puncture that interferes with my projects comes *to take its place* in a world that is sketched out in advance by my choice, because I have never stopped, if I can put it like this, *expecting it to be unexpected*. And even if my journey was inter-rupted by something I had not thought of even in my wildest dreams, like a flood or a rockslide, this unpredictable event was, in a certain way, predicted: within my pro-ject a certain margin of indeterminacy was left "for the unpredictable," just as the Romans reserved, in their temple, a place for the unknown gods—and that is not because of any experience of "bad shocks" or empirical prudence but because of the very nature of my project. Thus we can say that, in one way, nothing surprises human-reality. These observations allow us to bring to light a new characteristic of free choice: every one of freedom's projects is an *open project*, and not a closed project. Although it is entirely individualized, it contains within it the possibility of further modifications. Any project involves, in its structure, an understanding of the "*Selbstständigkeit*" of the things in the world. It is this constant prediction of the unpredictable, as the margin of indeterminacy in the project that I am, that enables me to understand that, rather than surprising me with its novelty or extraordinariness, an accident or catastrophe will always burden me with a certain "seen-this-before—expected-this" aspect, with its very obviousness and a kind of fatalistic necessity that we express with the words "that was bound to happen." Nothing ever astonishes in the world, and nothing surprises us, unless we ourselves have determined ourselves to be astonished. And the primary content to astonishment is not that such and such a particular thing exists within the limits of the world but rather that there is a world in general, which is to say that I am thrown among a totality of existents which are profoundly indifferent to me. The fact is that, by choosing an end, I am choosing to have relations with these existents, and that these   553 existents should have relations with each other; I choose that they will combine with each other in order to acquaint me with what I am. Thus the adversity to which things bear witness is sketched out in advance by my freedom as one of its conditions, and it is on a freely projected meaning of adversity in general that this or that structure is able to manifest its individual coefficient of adversity.

But, as on every occasion where the situation is in question, we must emphasize the fact that there is a reverse side to the described state of affairs: if freedom sketches out in advance adversity in general, it does so in a way that confirms the in-itself's indifferent externality. No doubt adversity arrives in things through freedom, but it does so to the degree to which freedom illuminates its facticity as "being-in-the-midst-of-an-indifferent-in-itself." Freedom presents things to itself as adverse, i.e., it confers a meaning on them which makes them into things; but it is by accepting the given itself that the given will be meaningful, i.e., by accepting one's exile, in order to surpass it, in the midst of an indifferent in-itself. In addition, and conversely, the contingent given that is accepted can support this primary meaning, which supports all the other meanings—"exile in the midst of indifference"—only in and through a free acceptance of the for-itself. That indeed is the situation's basic structure, appearing here with the utmost clarity: it is through its very surpassing of the given toward its ends that freedom makes the given exist as *this* given *here*—before it there was no "this," no "that," and no "here"—and the given that is thereby *designated* does not take just any form but is a brute existent that is accepted in order to be surpassed. But at the same time as freedom surpasses *this given here*, it chooses itself as *this* surpassing *here* of the given. Freedom is not just any surpassing of any old given but, by taking on the brute given and conferring its meaning on it, it has by the same token chosen itself: its end is precisely *to change this given here*, even while the given appears as this given here in the light of the chosen end. In this way freedom arises as the crystallization of an end *through a given*, and as the discovery of a given *in the light* of an end: these two structures are simultaneous and inseparable. Later on, in fact, we will see that the universal values of the chosen ends can be brought out only through analysis; every choice is the choice of a concrete change to be made to a concrete given. Every situation is concrete.

Thus the adversity of things and their potentialities are in general illuminated by the chosen end. But an end can exist only for a for-itself who accepts himself as abandoned in the midst of indifference. Through this acceptance, he adds *nothing* new to this contingent and brute abandonment, apart from a *meaning*: he makes it the case that from now on *there is* a state of abandonment; he makes it the case that this abandonment is disclosed as a situation.

554　In Part Two, Chapter 4, we saw that the for-itself, by arising, brings the in-itself to the world;[58] in a still more general way, the for-itself was the nothingness through which "there was" any in-itself, i.e., things. We saw, too, that in-itself reality lies there, close at hand, with its *qualities*, without distortion or addition. Only, we are separated from it by the various categories of nihilation that we establish by our very arising: the world, space and time, potentialities. We saw, in particular, that although we are surrounded by presences (this glass, this inkwell, this table, etc.), it is not possible to grasp these presences as such, because they can only deliver up anything of themselves from the other side of

58 TN: There is obviously a mistake in the French text here, as there is no Chapter 4 in Part Two. What Sartre goes on to say suggests he is indeed referring to material within Part Two, but I cannot be sure which precise section he had in mind.

a movement or an action that is pro-jected by us, i.e., in the future. We are now able to understand the meaning of this state of affairs: nothing separates us from things *except our freedom*. It is because of freedom that there can be things—with all their indifference, unpredictability, and adversity—and that we are inescapably separated from them, because it is against the ground of nihilation that these things appear and are revealed as being connected with each other. Thus my freedom's project adds nothing to things: it makes it the case that *there are* things (which is to say, precisely, realities that are characterized by a coefficient of adversity and usability); it makes it the case that things are encountered *in experience* (which is to say that they successively detach themselves against the ground of the world, in the course of a process of temporalization); finally, it makes it the case that things manifest themselves as being out of reach, independent, separated from me by the very nothingness that I am secreting and that I am. It is because freedom is condemned to be free—i.e., because it can choose itself [only] as freedom[59]—that there are things, i.e., a plenitude of contingency, at the heart of which freedom is itself contingent. It is through my accepting and surpassing of this contingency that it is possible for there to be a *choice* and at the same time for things to be organized in a *situation*. And it is the contingency of freedom and the contingency of the in-itself that are expressed *in situation* through the unpredictability and adversity of my surroundings. Thus I am absolutely free, and responsible for my situation. But in addition I am only ever free *in situation*.

(D) My fellow man

To live in a world haunted by my fellow man is not only to be able to encounter the other at every turn of the road but also to find myself committed within a world whose structures of equipment may have a meaning that does not come in the first place from my free project. And it is also, in the midst of this world that is *already* endowed with a meaning, to have to deal with a meaning that is *mine* and that I did not give to myself

59 TN: The French text says "*ne peut se choisir comme liberté*": I think the word *que* has been accidentally omitted. The square brackets around "only" indicate that this is my addition, made in the interest of sense.

either, a meaning that I discover myself "already to possess." When therefore we ask what is implied for our "situation" by the original and contingent fact of our existing in a world in which "there are" also others, this
way of formulating the problem requires us to study in turn three layers
of reality which enter into the constitution of my concrete situation: the
implements that are *already* meaningful (the station, the railway timetable,
the artwork, the poster that mobilizes the army); the meaning that I discover as *already mine* (my nationality, my race, my physical appearance);
and, last, the other as the center of reference indicated by these meanings.

Indeed, everything would be quite simple if I belonged to a world
whose meanings were uncovered only in the light of my own ends. I really
would be able to position things as implements or structures of equipment within the limits of my own choice of myself; that choice would
make of the mountain a difficult obstacle to overcome, or a point of view
over the countryside, etc.; the problem of knowing the mountain's meaning *in itself* would not arise, since I am the one who brings meanings to
reality in itself. The problem would also be far simpler if I were a monad
without doors or windows and if I merely knew, in some way or other,
that other monads existed or were possible, each of which was conferring
new meanings on the things I can see. In that case (which is the one to
whose examination philosophers have too often confined themselves), it
would suffice for me to regard other meanings as *possible*; and in the end,
since the plurality of meanings corresponds to the plurality of consciousnesses, this would be equivalent to the possibility, constantly open to me,
of making *another choice* of myself. But we saw that this monadic conception
harbors a hidden solipsism, precisely because it tends to conflate the plurality of meanings that I can attach to reality with the plurality of signifying systems, each of which refers back to a consciousness that I am not.
And besides, this monadic description shows itself to be inadequate for
the domain of concrete experience; there is, in fact, something to "my"
experience other than a plurality of possible experiences; objective meanings exist that present themselves to me as not having been brought to
light by myself. I, through whom meanings arrive in things, find myself
committed within a world that is *already meaningful* and which reflects back
to me meanings that I did not put there. Consider, for example, the countless meanings, independent of my choice, that I encounter if I live in a
town: streets, houses, shops, trams and buses, signposts, the sounds of car

horns, wireless music, etc. If I were alone, of course, I would encounter the existent as brute and unpredictable—*this* rock, for example—and I would confine myself, in short, to making it the case that *there was* a rock, which is to say *this* existent *here* and nothing outside it. But I would at the least be conferring on it the meaning of something "to climb," "to avoid," "to contemplate," etc. When I encounter a house at a bend in the road I do not reveal only a brute existent within the world; I do not make it the case only that *there is* a "this," characterized in such and such a way. Rather, the meaning of the object revealed to me here resists and remains independent of me: I discover that the building is an apartment building or the offices of the Compagnie du Gaz, or a prison, etc. Here the meaning is contingent, and independent of my choice, and it is presented with the same indifference as the in-itself's reality: it has become a *thing* and cannot be distinguished from the in-itself's *quality*. In the same way, I encounter things' coefficient of adversity before I experience it; a host of notices warn me: "Slow down, dangerous bend," "Attention! School," "Danger of death," "100m to Cassis," etc. But the fact that these meanings are deeply inscribed in things and share their indifferent externality—at least in appearance—does not make them any less indicative of a mode of behavior to be adopted that concerns me directly. I will use the pedestrian crossing, I will go into *this* shop to buy *this* implement, for which the instructions are very precisely laid out in a leaflet that is given to the customer, and then I will use this implement—a fountain pen, for example—to fill in such and such a form, in a particular set of conditions. Do I not discover here some narrow limits to my freedom? If I do not follow, step by step, the directions that others give me, I will no longer be able to find my way; I will take the wrong street, miss my train, etc. Moreover, these directions are for the most part imperatives: "Enter that way," "Leave that way"; that is what the words "Entrance" and "Exit," painted above the doors, signify. I submit to these directions: to the coefficient of adversity in things that is engendered by me, they add a coefficient of adversity that is strictly human. In addition, if I submit to this structure, I depend on it: the benefits it provides me with may dry up; it only takes some civil unrest, or a war, and suddenly the most essential products become scarce, whether I like it or not. I am dispossessed, halted in my plans, deprived of what is necessary to achieve my ends. And, in particular, we noted that instructions, labels, orders, prohibitions, and

556

nameplates are addressed to me insofar as I am just *anybody*; to the extent that I obey, that I place myself within the network, I submit to the goals of *any* old human-reality and I bring them about by *any* old technique. I am therefore changed in my own being, since I *am* the ends I have chosen and the techniques by which they are actualized: any old ends, any old techniques, any old human-reality. At the same time, since the world only ever appears to me through the techniques that I use, the world is also changed. This world, seen through the use that I make of the bicycle, the car, or the train to travel through it, shows me a face that is strictly correlative to the means I am using—the face, therefore, *that it offers to everyone.* It must obviously follow—it might be said—that my freedom escapes me from all sides: there is no longer a *situation*, in the shape of a meaningful world that is structured around the free choice of my spontaneity; there is a *state* that is imposed on me. This is what we ought to examine now.

557

It is beyond doubt that my membership of an inhabited world has the status of a *fact*. It is connected, indeed, to the original fact of the Other's presence in the world, a fact that, as we saw, cannot be deduced from the for-itself's ontological structure. And although this fact only drives deeper the roots of our facticity, it does not derive from our facticity either, insofar as this latter translates the necessity of the for-itself's contingency. What we should say, instead, is that the for-itself exists *de facto*, i.e., that its existence cannot be equated either to a reality that is generated in accordance with a law, or to a free choice, and that among the *de facto* characteristics of this "facticity"—i.e., among those characteristics that can be neither deduced nor proved but that can simply "be seen"—there is one that we call existence-in-the-world-in-the-presence-of-others. Whether or not my freedom has to take up this *de facto* characteristic in order for it to be effective in any way is something that we will discuss a little later. It remains no less the case that, with respect to the techniques for appropriating the world, the fact of the collective ownership of the techniques is the consequence of the very *fact* of the other's existence. At this level, therefore, facticity shows itself through the fact of my appearing in a world that is revealed to me only through techniques that are collective and already constituted, which aim to make me grasp it in a way whose meaning has been defined outside me. These techniques will determine my membership of communities: of *the human species*, the national community, the professional and familial group. But as we must emphasize, apart from my being-for-the-Other (to be discussed later), the only positive way in which I can *exist my de facto membership* of these communities is the use that I constantly make of the techniques associated with them. Indeed, membership of the human species is defined by the use of some very elementary and very general techniques: to know how to walk, how to pick something up, how to judge the relief and the relative size of perceived objects, how to talk, how to distinguish, in general, between the true and the false, etc. But we do not possess these techniques in this abstract and universal form: to know how to speak is not to know how to say and to understand words in general; it is to know how to speak a specific language and thereby to manifest one's membership of humankind *at the level* of the national community. Besides, to know how to speak a language is not to have an abstract and pure knowledge of the language, as it is defined by dictionaries and academic grammars: it is to make it one's own through the distortions and selections of one's province, profession, and family. In this way we can say that the *reality* of our membership among humans is our *nationality* and that the reality of our nationality is our membership of our family, region, profession, etc.—in the sense in which the *reality* of language is some particular language and the reality of that language is its dialect, slang, patois, etc. And, conversely, the truth of a dialect is the particular language, and the truth of that language is language in general: this means that we are referred by the concrete techniques through which our membership of a family or a locality is manifested to more abstract and general structures that constitute something like their meaning and their essence, and these refer to others, still more general, until we get to the universal and perfectly simple essence of *any old* technique, through which *any old* being appropriates the world.

558

Thus, to be French, for example, is only the truth of being a Savoyard. But to be a Savoyard is not simply to live in the high valleys of Savoy: it is, among a thousand other things, to ski in the winter, and to use skiing as a mode of transport. And, more precisely, it is to ski according to the French method, not the method that is used in the Arlberg region, or by Norwegians.[60]

---

60 Sartre's note: We are simplifying here: there are influences and interferences between techniques, and the Arlberg method has for a long time been dominant in our country. The reader will easily be able to restore to these matters their complexity.

But, since the mountain and the snowy slopes can be grasped only through a technique, that is precisely to discover the *French* meaning of ski slopes. Indeed, depending on whether one uses the Norwegian method, which is more suitable for gentle slopes, or the French method, which is more suitable for hard slopes, the same slope will seem to be gentler or harder in exactly the way that a hill will seem more or less hard to the cyclist depending on whether he has "used a low or a medium gear."[61] In this way the French skier makes use of a French "gear" to go down the skiing area and, wherever he is, this gear discloses a particular type of slope to him—which is to say that the Swiss or Bavarian Alps, the regions of Telemark or the Jura, will always offer him a meaning, difficulties, a structure of equipmentality or of adversity that is purely French. Similarly, it would be easy to show that most attempts at defining the working class take as their criterion either production, consumption, or a certain kind of "*Weltanschauung*" associated with the inferiority complex (Marx, Halbwachs, de Man),[62] i.e., in every case, certain techniques for elaborating or appropriating the world, through which it offers what we might call its "proletarian face," with its violent contradictions, its massive uniform areas of desert, its zones of darkness and its areas of light, the simple and urgent ends that illuminate it.

559   Now, it is evident—even though my membership of such and such a class or such and such a nation does not derive from my facticity, as the ontological structure of my for-itself—that my *de facto* existence, i.e., my birth and my place, brings in its wake my way of apprehending the world and myself through certain techniques. Now, these techniques, which I have not chosen, are what give the world its meanings. I am no longer the one, it seems, who decides on the basis of my ends whether the world will appear to me with the simple and clear-cut oppositions of the "proletarian" universe or with the innumerable and complicated nuances of the "bourgeois" world. I am not only thrown in the face of the brute existent; I am thrown into a world that is working-class, French, with the character of Lorraine or of the South, and which offers me its meanings when I have done nothing to reveal them.

Let us take a closer look. We showed just now that my nationality was only the truth of my membership of a province, a family, a professional

61 TN: . . . "*sera mis en moyenne ou en petite vitesse.*" I do not know why Sartre places this phrase within quotation marks.

62 TN: Hendrik de Man (1885–1953) was a Belgian socialist and politician.

grouping. But should we stop there? If the language is only the truth of the dialect, is the dialect the reality which is absolutely concrete? Is the jargon of a profession, in the way in which "one" speaks it, or the Alsatian patois—whose rules it has been possible to determine by a linguistic and statistical study—the primary phenomenon, the one that is founded in pure fact, in original contingency? Linguists' investigations can mislead us here: their statistics bring to light the constants, the phonetic or semantic distortions of a given type; they allow us to reconstitute the evolution of a phoneme or a morpheme within a given period in such a way as to make it seem that the word or the syntactic rule has an individual reality, with its own meaning and history. And in fact individuals appear to have little influence on the evolution of language. Social facts such as invasions, the main lines of communication, and commercial relations seem to be the essential causes of linguistic changes. But that is because we have not taken up a genuinely concrete standpoint, and so we are given no more than what we sought. For a long time psychologists have been pointing out that the material element in language is not the word, not even the word in a dialect, or the word used in a family, with its particular distortions; the elementary structure of language is the sentence. Indeed it is from within the sentence that the word can acquire a real referential function; outside it, when it is not quite simply an inscription whose aim is to group together meanings that are wholly disparate, it is merely a propositional function. Where it appears on its own in speech, it has a "holophrastic" quality that has often been emphasized; this does not mean that, by itself, we can limit it to one precise meaning, but that it is integrated within a context, as a secondary figure within a principal figure. Outside the complex and active structures in which it is included, therefore, the word has only a purely virtual existence. It cannot therefore exist "in" a consciousness or an unconscious before the use that is made of it: the sentence is not made of words. We should not stop at that: Paulhan showed in Les Fleurs de Tarbes that there are entire sentences, "commonplaces," which, just like words, do not preexist the use that is made of them.[63] These sentences that are commonplace expressions when they are considered from the outside by the reader—who reconstructs the meaning as he moves from one sentence

560

---

63 TN: Jean Paulhan (1884–1968) was a French writer and literary critic, whose most famous work is Les Fleurs de Tarbes, first published in 1936 (and translated into English as Paulhan 2006).

to the next—lose their banal and conventional character if we take up the point of view of the author, who, for his part, was able to see *the thing to be expressed* and was pursuing what was most urgent, producing an act of reference or recreation without lingering over the actual elements of this act. If that is how things are, neither words, nor syntax, nor "ready-made sentences" preexist the use that is made of them. Taking the verbal unit to be the meaningful sentence, we should see this as a constructive act that can be conceived only by a transcendence that surpasses and nihilates the given toward an end. To understand a word in the light of the sentence is *very exactly* to understand any given whatsoever on the basis of the situation, and to understand the situation in the light of original ends. To understand one of my interlocutor's sentences is indeed to understand what he "*wants to say*,"[64] which is to say to embrace his movement of transcendence, to throw myself alongside him toward possibles, toward ends, and then to return to the set of organized means in order to understand them through their function and their goal. Besides, spoken language is always deciphered on the basis of the situation. References to the weather, the time, the place, the surroundings, the situation of the town, the province, and the country are given before speaking begins. It is enough for me to have read the newspapers and to *see* that Pierre looks well[65] and has a worried manner for me to understand the "Things are not going well" with which he approaches me this morning. It is not his health that is "not going well," since he has a good color, nor is it his finances, nor his household: it is the situation in our town or our country. I *already knew that*: in asking "How are you?" I was already drafting my interpretation of his answer; I was already heading toward the four corners of the earth, ready *to come back* from them to Pierre in order to understand him. In listening to someone speaking, we are "speaking to" him, not simply because we mime in order to decipher but because we project ourselves from the outset toward possibles, and our understanding has to be *on the basis of the world*.

But if the sentence preexists the word, we are directed to the *speaker*

---

64 TN: ... *comprendre ce qu'il "veut dire"* ... There is a familiar translation difficulty here: the French phrase *vouloir dire* translates quite simply as "to mean" (in the sense of what one intends one's words to mean), but Sartre's pun on the phrase's literal meaning (i.e., "to want to say") gets lost in English.

65 TN: ... *que je voie la bonne mine et l'air soucieux* ... It seems likely there is a mistake in the French text here, and that Sartre's intention was to describe Pierre as *not* looking well.

as the concrete foundation of speech. If we fish a word out of sentences from various periods, it may really seem as if it is "living" by itself; this borrowed life resembles that of the knife in fantasy films that can plant itself into the pear; it is made out of the juxtaposition of instants; it is cinematic, and constituted within universal time. But if the words seem to be living when we project our semantic or the morphological film, they do not go so far as to constitute sentences; they are only traces of the passing sentences, just as roads are only traces of the passage of pilgrims or processions. The sentence is a project that can be interpreted only on the basis of the nihilation of something given (the very given that is *designated*) and on the basis of a posited end (its *designation*, which itself presupposes other ends in relation to which it is only a means). If the sentence cannot be determined by the given, any more than by the word, but, on the contrary, the sentence is necessary in order to light up the given and to understand the word, the sentence is a moment of the free choice of myself, and it is as such that my interlocutor understands it. If a particular language is the reality of language in general, if the dialect or slang is the reality of the particular language, the reality of the dialect is the *free act* of designation through which I choose myself as *designating*. And this free act cannot be an *assemblage* of words. Of course, if it were purely an assemblage of words conforming to technical formulas (the laws of grammar), we could talk about factual limits that are imposed on the speaker's freedom; these limits would show up in the material and phonetic nature of the words, the vocabulary of the language that is being used, the speaker's personal vocabulary (the n words at his disposal), the "individual character of the language," etc. But we have just shown that it is not like that. It has been claimed, recently,[66] that something like a living order of words exists, dynamic laws of language, an impersonal life of the *logos* or, in short, that language is a *nature* and that, in order to be able to make use of it in certain respects, man needs to serve it, as he does with Nature. But that is because language is being considered *once it is dead*, which is to say once it *has been spoken*—by breathing into it an impersonal life and a force, affinities, and aversions, that have in fact been borrowed from the personal freedom of the speaking for-itself.

561

---

66 Sartre's note: Brice Parain, *Essai sur le Logos Platonicien*. TN: Brice Parain (1897–1971) was a French philosopher and essayist. The book to which Sartre refers was published in 1942, and has not been translated into English.

Language has been made into *a language that speaks itself on its own*. That is just the mistake that we should not make, with respect to language as with *all other techniques*. If we make man arise in the midst of techniques that can be applied on their own, of a language that can speak itself, a science that can make itself, a town that can build itself according to its own laws—if we freeze meanings into in-itself, even while retaining for them a human transcendence—we will reduce man's role to that of a pilot, making use of the determined forces of the wind, the waves, the tides, in order to steer a ship. But step by step each technique, in order to be directed toward human ends, will require another technique: for example, to manage a boat, one must speak. By this means we will perhaps arrive at the technique of techniques—which, in its turn will apply itself on its own—but we have lost forever any possibility of meeting the technician.

If, completely to the contrary, it is by speaking that we make it the case that there are words, we are not thereby abolishing the *necessary and technical* connections or the *de facto* connections that are organized within the sentence. Better still, we give this necessity a *foundation*. But, precisely in order for it to appear, in order for the words to maintain relations between themselves, for each of them to attract—or to push away—the others, they must be united within a synthesis that is not owed to them. Eliminate that synthetic unity, and the block of "language" will crumble; each word will return to its solitude, and at the same time lose its unity, by becoming torn between various incommunicable meanings. Thus it is within the free project of the sentence that the laws of the language are organized; grammar is made as I speak; freedom is the only possible foundation of the laws of the language. Besides, for *whom* do the laws of grammar exist? Paulhan gave us the materials for an answer: it is not for the person who speaks but for the person who listens. The person speaking is only the choice of a *meaning*, and he grasps the order of his words only insofar as he *makes* it.[67] The only relationships that he will be able to grasp within this structured whole are specifically the ones that he has established. If, later on, we discover that two—or several—words maintain not *one* but several precise relations with each other and that

---

67 Sartre's note: I am simplifying: we can also learn what we think from our sentence. But that is because it is possible, to a certain extent, to adopt the point of view of an Other in relation to it—exactly as we can in relation to our body.

the result is a multiplicity of meanings for a single sentence that can be ranked or opposed to each other—if, in short, we discover "the Devil's share"[68]—it can only be under the following two conditions: (1) the words must have been gathered and presented by a free and meaningful act of bringing them together; (2) this synthesis must be viewed from outside, i.e., by the Other and in the course of a hypothetical deciphering of the possible meanings of this combination. In that case, indeed, each word that is apprehended first as an intersection of meanings is linked to another word that is, equally, apprehended in that way. And the combination will be multivocal. The grasp of the true meaning—i.e., the meaning deliberately intended by the speaker—may throw the other meanings into the shadows or subordinate them to it; it will not eliminate them. In this way, language, a free project for me, has specific laws for the other. And these laws themselves can only operate within an original synthesis. We can appreciate therefore all the difference that separates the event of a "sentence" from a natural event. A fact of nature comes about in conformity with a law that it manifests, but this law is a pure, external rule of production, of which the fact we are considering is just one example. The "sentence" as an event contains the law of its organization within itself, and it is within the free project of designating that it is possible for lawful relations between the words to arise. Indeed, there cannot be any laws governing speech before someone speaks. And every word is a free project of designation, flowing from the personal for-itself's choice, and needing to be interpreted on the basis of this for-itself's global situation. What comes first is the situation, on the basis of which I understand the meaning of this sentence, where this meaning is in itself not to be regarded as a given but as an end that is chosen in a free surpassing of the means. That is the only reality that the linguist's work can encounter. On the basis of this reality, the application of regressive analysis may bring certain

563

---

68 TN: ... si l'on découvre la "part du diable" ... This expression (which translates literally as "the devil's share") refers to the unforeseen effects of human fallibility in our undertakings. In this case, Sartre is thinking of the way our sentences may have unintended meanings. Sartre may be associating this expression with the work of Denis de Rougemont (explicitly referred to earlier in Part Four), whose book La Part du Diable was published in France in 1942 and translated into English as The Devil's Share (Rougemont 1944). Alternatively, Sartre may be alluding to Gide, whose use of the same phrase is mentioned at EN 305.

more general, simpler structures to light which are something like lawful schemata. But these schemata, which may, for example, be equivalent to the dialect's laws, are in themselves abstract. Far from presiding over the constitution of the sentence, and being the mold into which it is poured, they exist only in and through this sentence. In this sense, the sentence appears to be like a free invention of its laws. What we rediscover here, quite simply, is the original characteristic of every situation: it is specifically through its free surpassing of the given as such (the linguistic apparatus) that the free project of the sentence can make the given appear as *this* given (with these laws of the arrangement and pronunciation of the dialect). But the free project of the sentence is precisely the intention to take up *this given here*; it does not take up just any old thing but targets an end that does not yet exist, through existing means on which it confers precisely their meaning as means. In this way the sentence is an arrangement of words that become *these words* only through that arrangement itself. This is exactly what the linguists and psychologists sensed, and we can use their confusion here as something against which to check our view: in fact they believed they had found a circle in the elaboration of speech because, in order to speak, one must know one's thought. But how can we know this thought, as a reality that is explicated and set down in concepts, if not precisely by speaking it? Thus language refers us to thought, and thought to language. But we are able now to understand that there is no circle or, rather, that this circle—from which, it was thought, we could get out by inventing pure psychological idols, such as the verbal image, or the wordless and imageless thought—is not peculiar to language: it characterizes the situation in general. It does not mean anything other than the ecstatic connection of the present, the future, and the past, i.e., the free determination of the existent by the not-yet-existing and of the not-yet-existing by the existent. Thereafter we may discover abstract operative schemata which represent something like the lawful truth of the sentence: the dialectical schema, the schema of the national language, the schema for language in general. But these schemata, far from preexisting the concrete sentence, are themselves affected by *Unselbstständigkeit* and only ever exist as they are embodied and maintained in their very embodiment by a freedom. Here, of course, language is only the example of a social and universal technique. The same would hold for every other technique: it is the chop of the axe that reveals the

axe, the hammering that reveals the hammer. We will be able to detect,   564
in a particular excursion, the French method of skiing and within this
method the general art of skiing as a human possibility. But this human
art is never anything by itself: it exists only in *potentiality*; it is embodied
and manifested in the *actual* and particular art of the skier. This enables
us to sketch out a solution to the individual's relation to the species.
Without the human species there would be no truth, that is clear; all that
would be left would be an irrational and contingent abundance of individual choices, to which no law could be assigned. If something like a
truth exists, and is capable of unifying individual choices, it is the human
species that can provide us with it. But if the species is the truth of the
individual, it cannot be a *given* within the individual without a deep contradiction. Just as the laws of language are upheld and embodied through
the free concrete project of the sentence, so the human species—as the
set of techniques by which men's activity can be defined—far from
preexisting the individual, who would then demonstrate it, in the way
that some particular fall exemplifies the law of falling bodies, is the set
of abstract relations that the free individual choice upholds. In order to
choose itself as a person, the for-itself makes it the case that an internal
organization exists, which he surpasses toward himself, and this internal
technical organization is the national or the human in him.[69]

Very well, we will be told. But you have evaded the problem, because
the for-itself has not created these linguistic or technical structures to
communicate with itself: the for-itself took them up from others. I agree:
the rule for the agreement of participles does not exist outside anyone's
free combining together of some specific participles for the purpose of
some particular designation. But when I make use of this rule that I have
learned from others, it is because others are making it exist in their personal projects that I use it myself. My language is therefore subordinate to
the Other's language and, in the end, to the national language.

We do not mean to deny this. Neither is it our concern to show the
for-itself to be the free foundation of its being: the for-itself is free, but

---

69 TN: *Le pour-soi, pour se choisir comme personne* . . . This is one of those passages where, because
Sartre is talking about the for-itself qua *person*, I have had to shift pronoun from "itself"
to "himself." I continue to switch between "itself" and "himself" in the following
pages. See my note on pronouns in Notes on the Translation.

in a condition, and it is this relation between its condition and its freedom that we are trying to clarify as the "situation." What we have just established is in fact only a part of the reality. We have shown that the existence of meanings that do not emanate from the for-itself cannot constitute an external limit to its freedom. The for-itself is not in the first place a man, in order subsequently to be "himself," and does not constitute himself as himself on the basis of an essence of man that is given *a priori*. Rather, and completely to the contrary, it is in order to choose himself as a personal self that the for-itself maintains particular social and abstract characteristics in existence, which make him into a *man*; and the necessary connections that accord with the elements of man's essence appear only on the foundation of a free choice. In this sense, each for-itself is responsible in his being for the existence of a human species. But we still need to elucidate the undeniable fact that the for-itself can only choose himself from a point beyond specific meanings of which he is not the origin. Each for-itself, in effect, can be for-itself only by choosing himself beyond his nationality and species—just as the for-itself can speak only by choosing what he will designate beyond syntax and morphemes. This "beyond" is enough to assure the for-itself's complete independence in relation to the structures that he surpasses, but it remains no less true that the for-itself constitutes himself as a "beyond" in relation to *these* structures *here*. What does that mean? That the world in which the for-itself arises is a world for other for-itselfs. That is what is *given*. And through that very fact, as we saw, the meaning of the world is *alienated* from him. This means that the for-itself finds himself in the presence of meanings that do not enter the world through him. The for-itself arises within a world that is given to him as having been *already looked at*, traversed, explored, and worked on from all sides, and whose very texture has already been defined by these investigations. And in the very act through which the for-itself unfolds his time, he temporalizes himself within a world whose temporal meaning is already defined by other temporalizations: that is the fact of simultaneity. There is no question here of a limit to freedom but, rather, it is in *that world there* that the for-itself must be free; it is in taking account of these circumstances—and not *ad libitum*—that the for-itself must choose himself. But on the other hand, in arising, the for-itself does not *undergo* the other's existence; he is obliged to demonstrate it to himself, in the form of a choice. For it is

565

through a choice that he will grasp the other as a subject-other or object-other.[70] For as long as the other is for him a looking-other, there can be no question of foreign *techniques* or meanings; the for-itself experiences himself as an object in the Universe, beneath the other's look. But the moment the for-itself, by surpassing the other toward his ends, makes the other into a transcended-transcendence, what was a free surpassing of the given comes to appear as a meaningful mode of behavior, given within the world (frozen into in-itself). The object-other becomes an *indicator of ends* and, through its free project, the for-itself throws himself into a world where object-undertakings refer to ends. In this way the other's presence as a transcended transcendence reveals structures of means to ends that are *given*. And, as the end decides on the means, and the means decide on the end, the for-itself, in arising before the object-Other, finds himself pointed toward ends within the world; he enters a world that is populated by ends. But if techniques and their ends arise in this way before the for-itself's gaze, we must be clear that it is through the for-itself's free taking up of his position in the face of the other that they become *some techniques*. On his own, the other cannot make his projects reveal themselves to the for-itself as techniques and, consequently, *for the other*, insofar as the for-itself transcends himself toward his possibles, *no technique exists* but rather a concrete *doing* that is determined on the basis of its individual end. The cobbler who resoles a shoe does not feel himself to be "in the process of applying a technique"; he grasps the situation as requiring such and such an action, this piece of leather there as calling for a nail, etc. The for-itself *makes techniques arise* within the world *as ways in which the other behaves insofar as he is a transcended-transcendence*, the moment he takes up a position in relation to the other. It is at that moment and only then that the bourgeois and the workers, the French and Germans and, finally, men appear within the world. In this way the for-itself is responsible for the fact that the other's behavior is revealed within the world in the form of techniques. The for-itself cannot make the world in which he arises be traversed by this or that technique (he cannot make the world in which he appears be "capitalist" or "ruled by a natural economy," or in a "parasitic civilization"), but he makes it the

566

---

70 Sartre's note: We will see further on that the problem is more complex. But these remarks suffice for now.

case that what the other lives as a free project has an existence *outside* as a technique, precisely by being the one through whom the other comes to have an outside. In this way, it is in choosing and historializing himself that the for-itself historializes the world itself, and makes it *dated* by his techniques. Thereafter, precisely because the techniques appear as objects, the for-itself is able to choose to appropriate them. In arising within a world in which Pierre and Paul speak in a particular way, and drive or cycle on the right, etc., and by constituting these free modes of behavior into meaningful objects, the for-itself makes it the case that there is a world where *one* shakes with one's right hand, *one* speaks French, etc.;[71] it makes it the case that the internal laws of the other's act, which were founded and maintained by a freedom committed within a project, become the objective rules of the behavior-object and that these rules become universally applicable for any analogous behavior, and for that matter become the support of *any old* behavior or agent-object. This historialization, the effect of its free choice, does not in any way restrict its freedom but, quite the opposite, it is *in that world there* and in no other that its freedom comes into play; it is in relation to its existence in that world there that it puts itself into question. That is because to be free is not to choose the historical world in which one arises—which would make no sense—but to choose oneself within the world, whichever it is. In this sense, it would be absurd to suppose that a specific technical *state* might restrict human possibilities. Of course, a contemporary of Duns Scotus will not know about the use of automobiles or airplanes, but he only appears as not knowing this from the point of view that is *ours*, from which we apprehend it privatively, on the basis of a world in which the automobile and airplane exist. For him, as someone with no relation of any kind to these objects and the techniques that refer to them, there is at this point something like an absolute nothingness, unthinkable and undetectable. A nothingness like this could *in no way* limit the for-itself who chooses himself: however one looks at it, it cannot be grasped as a lack. Therefore a for-itself who historializes himself in Duns Scotus's time nihilates itself at the heart of a plenum of being, i.e., within a world that is, like ours, *all that it can be*. It would be absurd to assert that the

567

---

71 TN: ... *un monde où on prend sa droite* ... I use "one" here, as there is no explicit dialogue with Heidegger and in this instance it sounds better than "they."

Albigensians lacked any heavy artillery with which to resist Simon de Montfort, because the Trencavel noble and the Count of Toulouse chose themselves to be as they were within a world where artillery had no place: it was in that world there that they considered their strategy, and they planned their military resistance in that world; they chose themselves as supporters of the Cathars in that world. And as they were only what they chose to be, they *were absolutely* within a world that was just as absolutely full as the world of the *Panzerdivisionen*[72] or the RAF. What is true for techniques which are as material as these ones also holds true of subtler techniques: the fact of existing as a minor feudal lord in Languedoc in the time of Raymond VI is not a *determinant* if we place ourselves within the feudal world in which this lord exists and chooses himself. It only appears as privative if we make the mistake of looking at this division between *Francia* and the Midi from the current viewpoint of the unity of France. The feudal world offered the lord who was Raymond VI's vassal an infinite number of possibilities to choose; we do not possess a greater number. A question as absurd as this is often asked in a kind of utopian dream: what would Descartes have been if he had known about contemporary physics? That supposes that Descartes has an *a priori* nature which is more or less delimited and altered by the state of science in his time, and that we can transport this brute nature into the contemporary age, in which it would react to a wider and more precise body of knowledge. But that is to forget that Descartes is who he chose to be, that he is an absolute choice of himself on the basis of a world with knowledge and techniques that this choice takes up and illuminates at the same time. Descartes is an absolute, in possession of an absolute date, and is wholly unthinkable at another date, because he made his date in making himself. He is the one, and not someone else, who determined the exact state of mathematical knowledge immediately before him, not through an empty inventory that might have been done from any point of view and in relation to any axes of coordinates but by establishing the principles of analytical geometry, i.e., by inventing precisely the axes of coordinates that enabled the state of this knowledge to be defined. Here again,

---

72 TN: *Panzerdivisionen* (German) is the name of the armored divisions used by the Germans in the Second World War.

it is free discovery and the future that allow us to throw light on the present; the perfecting of the technique, with a view to an end, is what allows us to assess the state of the technique.

In this way, when the for-itself asserts itself in the face of the object-other, it discovers *techniques* at the same time. From that moment it can appropriate them, i.e., it can *internalize* them. But it follows that: (1) by using a technique, the for-itself surpasses it toward its end, and is always beyond the technique that it uses; (2) by virtue of being internalized, the

568   technique, which was purely the signifying and frozen behavior of any old object-other, loses its character as a technique, and becomes straight-forwardly included within the free surpassing of the given toward the ends; it is taken up and maintained by the freedom that founds it, in just the way in which a dialect or language is maintained by the free project of a sentence. The feudal system, as a technical relation between men, does not exist; it is only a pure abstraction, maintained and surpassed through the thousand projects of some liege man in relation to his lord. By this, we do not mean at all to arrive at a kind of historical nominalism. We do not want to say that the feudal system is the sum of relations between the vassals and liege lords. On the contrary, we believe that it is the abstract structure of these relations; for a man of this time, any project must be actualized as the surpassing toward the concrete of this abstract moment. It is not therefore necessary to generalize on the basis of innumerable individual experiences in order to establish the principles of feudal tech-nique: this technique exists necessarily and completely within each indi-vidual behavior, and it can in each case be brought to light. But it is there only in order to be surpassed. In the same way, the for-itself cannot be a person—which is to say to choose the ends which it is—without being a man, the member of a national community, a class, a family, etc. But these are abstract structures that are maintained and surpassed through its project. The for-itself makes itself French, from the South, in order to be *himself* at the horizon of these determinations. And, likewise, the world that is revealed to him appears as possessing certain meanings that are correlative to the adopted techniques. It appears as a world-for-the Frenchman, a world-for-the-worker, etc., with all the characteristics that we can expect. But these characteristics have no "*Selbstständigkeit*"; it is above all his world, i.e., the world illuminated by his ends, that allows itself to be discovered as French, proletarian, etc.

However, the other's existence brings about a *de facto* limit to my freedom. The fact is that, through the arising of the other, certain determinations that I *am*—without having chosen them—appear. Here I am, indeed, a Jew or an Aryan, handsome or ugly, one-armed, etc. I am all of that *for the other*, without any hope of grasping this meaning that I have *outside*, or, even less, of changing it. Through language alone will I learn what I am; and even then it will only ever be as the object of an empty intention; any intuition of it is forever denied to me. If my race or my physical appearance were only an image in the Other or the Other's opinion of me, we would soon be done with it: but, as we have seen, we are concerned here with objective characteristics which define me in my being-for-the-Other. As soon as a freedom other than my own arises to confront me, I begin to exist in a new dimension of being and, this time, it is not a matter of my conferring a meaning on brute existents, or of taking up on my own account the meaning that others have conferred on certain objects: it is myself whom I can see conferred with a meaning, and I do not have what I need to take up this meaning on my own account, since it cannot be given to me except in the form of an empty intention. Thus, something about me—according to this new dimension—exists in the manner of the *given*, at least for me, since this being that I am is *undergone*: it is, without *being existed*. I learn of it and I undergo it in and through the relations that I maintain with others, in and through their behavior in relation to me; I encounter this being at the origin of a thousand prohibitions and a thousand resistances that I come up against at every moment. Because I am a *minor*, I do not have this or that right; because I *am a Jew*, in certain societies, I will be deprived of certain possibilities, etc. Yet I cannot *in any way* feel myself to be Jewish, or feel myself to be a minor or a pariah, to such an extent that I may react against these interdictions by declaring that race, for example, lies purely and simply in the collective imagination, and only individuals exist. Thus I suddenly encounter here the total alienation of my person: I am something that I did not choose to be. What are the consequences of this with respect to the situation?

569

We must recognize that we have just encountered a *real* limit to our freedom, i.e., a way of being that is forced on us, without being founded in our freedom. But still, we need to be clear: the limit that is imposed does not come from the *action* of others. We noted, in an earlier chapter, that we are not dispossessed of our freedom even by torture: we give in to it *freely*. More generally, my encounter with a prohibition on my path—"Jews are prohibited from entering here," "Jewish restaurant, no entry for Aryans," etc.—refers us to the case we considered earlier (collective techniques), and this prohibition can have meaning only on and through the foundation of my free choice. So, according to the free possibilities that I have chosen, I may contravene the prohibition, count it as nothing, or on the contrary confer upon it a coercive power which it can hold only by virtue of the weight I accord to it. Of course it will entirely preserve its character as "emanating from an alien will," and of course it will have the specific structure of *taking me as an object* and of thereby manifesting a transcendence which transcends me. It remains no less true that it takes shape only within my universe and derives its own power of constraint only within the limits of my own choice, and according to whether I prefer life to death in any circumstance or, on the contrary, I regard death, in certain particular cases, as preferable to some types of life, etc. The true limit to my freedom lies purely and simply in the very fact that another apprehends me as an object-other and in this other, consequent fact that my situation ceases to be a situation for the other and becomes an objective figure, within which I exist as an objective structure. It is this alienating objectification of my situation that is my situation's permanent and specific limit, just as the objectification of my being-for-itself into being-for-the-other is the limit of my being. And it is precisely these two characteristic limits which represent the boundaries of my freedom. In brief, by virtue of the Other's existence, I exist in a situation which *has an outside* and which, by this very fact, has an alienating dimension that I can in no way remove from it, no more than I can directly act upon it. This limit to my freedom is, we can see, posited by the Other's pure and simple existence, which is to say by *the fact* that my transcendence exists for a transcendence. Thus we may grasp a truth of great importance: we saw just now, while we were remaining within the category of existence-for-itself, that only my freedom could limit my freedom; now we can see, by bringing the other into consideration, that at this new level my freedom also meets its limits in the existence of the Other's freedom. Thus, at whichever level we position ourselves, the only limits that a freedom meets will be found by it within freedom. Just as thought, for Spinoza, can be limited only by thought, in the same way freedom can be limited only by freedom, and its limitation comes about, as an internal finitude, from the *fact* that it cannot not be freedom, which is to say that it is condemned to be free and, as an external finitude, from the *fact* that, being freedom, it is for other freedoms which freely apprehend it, in the light of their own ends.

Having said this, we ought first to note that this alienation of the situation does not represent an internal break, nor the introduction of something given as a brute resistance within the situation, such as I live it. Quite to the contrary, the alienation is neither an internal modification nor a partial change in the situation; it does not appear in the course of temporalization; I only ever encounter it *within* the situation and it is not, in consequence, ever given to my intuition. But, as a matter of principle, it escapes me; it is the situation's very externality, which is to say its being-outside-for-the-other. We are dealing therefore with an essential characteristic of any situation in general; this characteristic cannot act upon its content but is accepted and taken up by the very person who *puts himself in situation.* In this way, the very meaning of our free choice is to make a situation arise which expresses it and of which an essential characteristic is to be *alienated,* i.e., to exist for the other as a figure in itself. We cannot escape from this alienation, since it would be absurd to think even of existing otherwise than in situation. This characteristic does not manifest itself through an internal resistance but, on the contrary, it is felt in and through its very elusiveness. It is therefore, in the end, not an obstacle which freedom encounters head-on but a sort of centrifugal force within its very nature, a weakness in its mix which means that everything it undertakes will always have a side that it has not chosen, which escapes it and which, for the other, will be pure existence. A freedom that willed itself as freedom could only will this characteristic at the same time. However, this does not belong to freedom's *nature,* because here there is no nature; besides, even if there were one, we would not be able to infer this from it, since the existence of others is an entirely contingent fact; rather, to enter the world as a freedom confronting others is to enter the world as alienable. If to will oneself as free is to choose to be in this world here, confronting others, someone who wills this will also will his freedom's *Passion.*

571

The alienated situation, on the other hand, and my own alienated-being are not objectively discovered and noted by me. In the first place, in fact, we have just seen that anything that is alienated necessarily exists only *for the other*. But, in addition, a pure observation, even if it were possible, would not be sufficient. In fact I cannot *experience* this alienation without at the same time *recognizing* the other as a transcendence. And, as we have seen, this recognition would be meaningless if it were not a *free* recognition of the Other's freedom. Through this free recognition of the Other—through the alienation that I undergo—I *accept* my being-for-the-Other, whatever it may be, and I accept it precisely because it is my bridge to the Other. Thus I can apprehend the Other as a freedom only in the free project of apprehending him as such (indeed, it remains always possible for me to freely apprehend the Other as an object), and there is no difference between the free project of *recognition* of the Other and the free acceptance of my being-for-the-Other. It is here therefore that my freedom somehow retrieves its own limits, because I can apprehend myself as limited by the Other only insofar as the Other exists for me, and I can make the Other exist for me as a recognized subjectivity only by accepting my being-for-the-Other. There is no circle here: rather, through my free acceptance of this alienated-being that I undergo, I suddenly make the Other's transcendence exist for me as such. It is only by recognizing the anti-Semites' *freedom* (whatever use they make of it) and by accepting this *being-Jewish* that I am for them, it is only in this way that *being-Jewish* will appear as the situation's external objective limit; if I prefer, on the contrary, to consider them as pure *objects*, my being-Jewish will immediately disappear to give way to the simple consciousness (of) being a free transcendence that cannot be qualified. To recognize others and, if I am Jewish, to accept my being-Jewish are one and the same thing. Thus, the other's freedom confers limits on my situation, but I can *experience* these limits only if I reclaim this being for the other that I am, and give it a meaning in the light of the ends I have chosen. And, certainly, this acceptance itself is *alienated*, it has its "outside," but it is through it that I can experience my being-outside as an "outside."

How, in consequence, will I experience the objective limits of my being—Jew, Aryan, ugly, handsome, a king, a civil servant, an untouchable, etc.—when language has informed me about those limits that are mine? It cannot be in the way in which I intuitively *apprehend* the beauty, ugliness, or race of the other, any more than it can be in the way in which I have a non-thetic consciousness (of) projecting myself toward this or that possibility. It is not that these objective characteristics must necessarily be *abstract*: some of them are abstract, others not. My beauty, my ugliness and the insignificance of my features are grasped by the other in their fully concrete state, and his language will indicate this concretion to me; that is what I will reach toward, emptily. It is not at all therefore a matter of abstraction but of a collection of structures of which some are abstract, but whose totality is an absolute concretion; only it is a collection that is indicated to me as necessarily escaping me. In effect, it is what I *am*. Now, as we noted at the start of Part Two, the for-itself cannot *be* anything. For-me, I am no more a teacher or a café waiter than I am handsome or ugly, Jewish or Aryan, witty, vulgar or distinguished. We will call these characteristics "*unrealizables*." We must be careful not to confuse them with "*imaginaries*." We are dealing here with existences that are perfectly real, but the people to whom these characteristics are really *given are* not these characteristics; and I, who *am* them, am unable to realize them. For example, if someone tells me that I am *vulgar*, I have often apprehended, through intuition, the nature of vulgarity in others; thus I am able to apply the word "vulgar" to my own person. But I cannot connect the meaning of this word to my person. All that is there is only the indication of a connection to be made (but that can be made only by internalizing and subjectivizing the vulgarity, or by objectifying the *person*—two operations that will give rise to the immediate collapse of the reality being discussed). Thus we are surrounded to infinity by *unrealizables*. Some of these *unrealizables* are keenly felt by us as irritating absences. Who has not felt a profound disappointment at not being able after a long exile to *realize* that he "is in Paris"? The objects are there, and familiarly presented, but I myself am only an absence, only the pure nothingness that is necessary in order for Paris *to be there*. My friends or my relatives offer me the image of a promised land when they say: "At last, you're here! You have come back to Paris!" But access to this promised land is completely denied to me. And if most people deserve to be reproached for using a "double standard," depending on whether they apply it to others or to themselves, and if they are inclined to reply, when they feel guilty of a fault for which they had blamed someone else, the night before, "That is not the same thing," that is because, indeed, "it is not the same thing." One of the actions is in fact a *given object* of moral assessment, while the other is a pure transcendence whose justification is carried by its very existence, since its being is choice. By comparing the *results*, we may be able to convince its author that the "outside" of the two acts is strictly identical, but even with a boundless good will he will not be able to *realize* this identity. That is the source of a good many struggles of the moral conscience, especially the despair at not being able *truly* to despise oneself, at not being able to realize oneself as guilty, at constantly feeling a gap between the meanings one expresses—"I *am* guilty," "I have sinned," etc.—and one's real apprehension of the situation. That is the source, in short, of all the anguishes of "bad conscience," which is to say the bad faith consciousness whose ideal is to judge itself, i.e., to take up the viewpoint of another in relation to oneself.

573

But if some particular kinds of *unrealizable* impress us more than others, if they have been the object of psychological descriptions, they should not blind us to the fact that an infinite number of unrealizables exist, since they represent the reverse side of the situation.

However, these unrealizables are not only appresented as unrealizables: indeed, for them to have the character of unrealizables, they must be disclosed in the light of some project that aims to realize them. And indeed that is just what we recently noted, when we showed the for-itself *accepting* its being-for-the-other in and through the very act that *recognizes* the other's existence. Correlatively to this project of acceptance, therefore, the unrealizables disclose themselves as "*to be realized*." In the first place, my acceptance effectively takes place within the perspective of my fundamental project: I do not restrict myself to passively receiving the meaning of "ugliness," "handicap," "race," etc., but on the contrary I can apprehend these characteristics—merely as meanings—only in the light of my own ends. That is what we are expressing—but by completely reversing the terms—when we say that the fact of being of a particular race may *determine* a reaction of pride or an inferiority complex. In fact, race, disability, or ugliness can *appear* only within the limits of my own choice of inferiority or pride;[73] in other words, they can appear only with a meaning that my freedom confers on them. That means, once again, that they *are* for the other but that they can be for me only if I *choose* them. The law of my freedom, which means that I am not able to be without choosing myself, even applies here: I do not choose to be

73 Sartre's note: Or of any other choice of my ends.

what I am for the other, but I can only try to be for myself what I am for the other by choosing myself such as I appear to the other, i.e., by an elective act of acceptance. A Jew is not first a Jew, in order *afterward* to be ashamed or proud; but it is his pride at being a Jew, his shame, or his indifference that will reveal his being-Jewish to him, and this being-Jewish is nothing without the free way of taking it up. Simply put, although I have at my disposal an infinite number of ways of accepting my being-for-the-Other, I cannot not accept it: here we encounter again that condemnation to freedom that we defined earlier as *facticity*. I cannot abstain completely in relation to what I am (for the other)—since *to reject* is not to abstain but is still a way of accepting—but neither can I undergo it passively (which, in one sense, amounts to the same); in rage, hatred, pride, shame, disgusted rejection, or joyful assertion, I have to choose to be what I am.

574

In this way, the for-itself encounters its unrealizables as "unrealizables to be realized." This does not take away their character as *limits*; quite to the contrary, they are presented to the for-itself as objective and external limits *to be internalized*. They have therefore a distinctly *compulsory* character. We do not encounter them like an instrument "to be used" within the movement of the free project that I am. Rather, the unrealizable appears *at the same time* both as *a priori* given limit to my situation (since I have this being for the other) and, in consequence, as existing without waiting for me to give it existence and also as being able to exist only within and through the free project through which I will accept it—with this act of acceptance, obviously, being identical to the synthetic organization of all the actions that aim at *realizing* the unrealizable *for myself*. At the same time, as it is given as an unrealizable, it shows itself as being beyond any attempt that I might make to realize it. An *a priori* which, in order to be, requires my commitment even while it depends only on that commitment and places itself from the outset beyond any attempt to realize it: What is this, therefore, if not precisely an *imperative*? It is indeed something *to be internalized*, which is to say that it comes from outside as *ready-made*; but an *order*, no matter what it is, is defined precisely always as an externality that is taken up internally. For an order to be an order—and not a mere sound, or a pure factual given which someone is merely trying to turn round—it is necessary for me to take it up with my freedom, for me to make of it a structure of my free projects. But for it to be an order, and not a free movement toward my own ends, it must retain, even at the heart of my free choice, the character of *externality*. It is an externality that persists in its externality even in and through the for-itself's attempt to internalize it. That is precisely the definition of the *unrealizable to be realized*, and that is why it is given as an imperative. But we take the description of this unrealizable further: it is in fact *my* limit. But, precisely because it is *my* limit, it cannot exist as the limit of some given being but as my freedom's limit. Therefore my freedom, in choosing freely, chooses its limits; in other words, the free choice of my ends—i.e., of what I am for myself—requires me to accept the limits of this choice, whatever they may be. Here again the choice is a choice of finitude, as we noted earlier, but rather than the chosen finitude being an internal finitude—i.e., a determination of freedom by itself—the finitude that I accept in taking up the unrealizables is an external finitude. I choose to have a being at a distance, which limits all my choices and constitutes their reverse choices, which is to say that I choose that my choice should be bounded by something other than itself. Should I become annoyed by this, and try, by using every means, to reclaim these limits—as we saw in the previous part of this work—it will be necessary, even for the most vigorous of these attempts at recuperation, to found it in the free act of taking up, as *limits*, the limits that one wishes to internalize. In this way freedom takes up the unrealizable limits on its own account and places them within the situation, by choosing to be a freedom that is limited by the other's freedom. The result is that the situation's external limits become the *situation-limit*, i.e., that they are incorporated into the situation *from inside* with the characteristic of being "unrealizable," in the form of "unrealizables to be realized," as the chosen and fugitive reverse side of my choice. They become one meaning of my desperate endeavor *to be*, even though they are situated *a priori* beyond this endeavor, exactly as death—another type of unrealizable that we do not need to consider right now—becomes a situation-limit, on condition that it is taken as an *event in life*, even though it points toward a world where my presence and my life are no longer realized, i.e., toward life's "beyond." The fact that *there* is a beyond to life, insofar as it gains its meaning only through and in my life and yet remains for me unrealizable, and the fact that there is a freedom beyond my freedom, a situation beyond my situation, and for which what I live as situation is given as an objective figure in the midst of the world: both

575

of these are types of situation-limit whose paradoxical character is to limit my freedom from every side and yet to have no meaning other than that which my freedom confers on them. With respect to class, race, the body, the other, one's job, etc., there is a "being-free-for . . ." Through this, the for-itself projects itself toward one of its possibles, which is always its ultimate possible: because the possibility in question is the possibility of *seeing oneself*, which is to say of being someone other than oneself, to see oneself from outside. In the one case as in the other there is a projection of the self toward an "ultimate," which, internalized by that very act, becomes the thematic and unreachable meaning of the ranked possibles. One can "be-in-order-to-be-French," "be-in-order-to-be-a-worker"; the son of a king can "be-in-order-to-reign." What we have here are limits and *states* that negate our being, which we have to accept—in the sense in which, for example, a Zionist Jew resolutely accepts himself within his race, i.e., he concretely accepts, once and for all, the permanent *alienation* of his being, just as the revolutionary worker, through his revolutionary project itself, accepts a "being-in-order-to-be-a-worker." And, like Heidegger (even though the expressions that he uses—"authentic" and "inauthentic"—are, because of their implicit moral content, questionable and lacking in sincerity), we may point out that the attitude of rejection and flight that always remains possible is, in spite of itself, a free acceptance of what it flees. Thus, the bourgeois makes himself bourgeois   576 by denying that there are classes, as the worker makes himself a worker by asserting that they exist and by actualizing his "being-in-the-class" through his revolutionary activity. But, precisely because they are external and can be internalized only as unrealizables, these external limits to freedom will never be a *real* obstacle to it, nor a limit that is undergone. Freedom is total and infinite, which does not mean that it *has no* limits but that it never *encounters* them. The only limits that freedom comes up against in every instant are those which it imposes on itself, and which we have discussed in relation to the past, my surroundings and techniques.

(E) My death

After death had come to seem the quintessential example of the inhuman—since it lay on the other side of "the wall"—it was suddenly thought better to consider it from an entirely different point of view, i.e., as an event in human life. This change is easily explicable: death is a *term*, and every term (whether it be the final or the first) is a *Janus bifrons*,[74] whether we regard it as adhering to the nothingness of being that limits the process in question or whether, on the contrary, we encounter it as pressed into the series that it terminates, as a being that belongs to an existing process and is, in one way, constitutive of its meaning. In this way, one side of a melody's final chord turns, in its entirety, toward silence, i.e., toward the nothingness of sound that will follow the melody; in one sense it is made out of silence, since the silence that will follow is already present in the resolution chord as its meaning. But, by another side entirely, it adheres to that *plenum* of being in which the melody in question consists: without it, this melody would remain in midair, and this final indecision would reach back upstream, note by note, to confer on each one of them an unfinished character. Rightly or wrongly—as we are not yet able to determine—death has always been regarded as the final term of human life. As such, it was natural that a philosophy concerned first and foremost to clarify the position of humanity in relation to the absolute inhuman surrounding it should consider death in the first place as a door opening on to the nothingness of human-reality—whether this nothingness was, furthermore, an absolute cessation of being, or existence in a non-human form. Thus we might say that there has been—in correlation with the major realist theories—a realist conception of death, to the extent that this latter appeared as an immediate contact with the nonhuman; death thereby escaped man, at the same time as molding him to the nonhuman absolute. Of course, it was out of the question for any idealist and humanist conception of reality to tolerate any encounter of man with the inhuman, even as his limit. Were that the case, all that would be required to show man in a nonhuman light would be to take up the perspective of that limit.[75] The idealist attempt to *reclaim* death has not primarily been the

577

---

74 TN: *Janus bifrons* refers to the image of the two faces of the Roman god Janus, who is often depicted with two faces, one looking toward the past, the other toward the future.

75 Sartre's note: Compare, for example, Morgan's Platonism in *Sparkenbroke*. TN: Charles Langbridge Morgan (1894–1958) was an English-born playwright and novelist. Death is a major theme in his novel *Sparkenbroke*, first published in 1936, and translated into French in 1937.

work of philosophers but of poets like Rilke[76] or novelists like Malraux. It sufficed to envisage death as the final term belonging to the series. If in this way the series retrieves its *"terminus ad quem,"*[77] precisely because of this *"ad,"* which marks its interiority, death becomes humanized and internalized as the end of life: man is no longer able to meet anything other than the human; there is no longer any *other side* to life, and death is a human phenomenon; it is the ultimate phenomenon of life, and remains life. As such, it influences, against the current, the entire life: life is limited by life, and becomes, like Einstein's world, "finite but unlimited"; death becomes the meaning of life, just as the resolution chord is the meaning of the melody. There is nothing miraculous about this: it is a term in the series in question and—as we know—each term in a series is always present to all the terms of the series. But the death that is hereby retrieved does not remain merely human; it becomes *mine*. By becoming internalized, it is individualized; it is no longer the great unknowable by which a human is limited but the phenomenon of my personal life which makes this life into a unique life, i.e., a life that does not recommence, at which we can never have another shot. I thereby become responsible for *my death*, as for my life—not for the empirical and contingent phenomenon of my demise but for this character of finitude by virtue of which my life, like my death, is my life. It is in this sense that Rilke endeavors to show that each man's end resembles his life, since the entire individual life has been a preparation for this end; it is in this sense that Malraux, in *Les Conquérants*, shows how European culture, by giving some Asians a sense of their death, suddenly imbued them with the despairing and intoxicating truth that "life is unique."[78] It was left to Heidegger to give a philosophical form to this humanization of death: if indeed *Dasein* does not *undergo* anything, precisely because it is a project and anticipation, it

---

76 TN: Rainer Maria Rilke (1875–1926) was an Austrian poet and novelist who published poems in French as well as German. As Rilke's themes include man's loneliness, despair, etc., he is sometimes described as an "existentialist."

77 TN: The Latin phrase translates literally as "the end to which," and is used within English to mean "a final limiting point in time"—for example, to refer to the latest possible date for something.

78 TN: Malraux's novel *Les Conquérants* (translated as Malraux 1991) was published in France in 1928 and describes the revolutionary struggle in China.

must be the anticipation and project of its own death as the possibility of no longer actualizing a presence in the world. Thus death became *Dasein*'s ownmost possibility; the being of human-reality is defined as "Being-toward-death."[79] Insofar as *Dasein* decides on his project toward death, he realizes his freedom toward death and constitutes himself as a totality through his free choice of finitude.

At first sight, such a theory can only seduce us: by internalizing death, it serves our own purposes; by being internalized, freedom retrieves this apparent limit to our freedom. However, we should not allow either the convenience of these views or the incontestable amount of truth that they contain to lead us astray. We must take up our investigation of this question by going back to the beginning.

It is clear that human-reality, through whom worldhood enters reality, cannot encounter the inhuman; the concept of the "inhuman" is itself a concept belonging to man. We must therefore abandon any hope, even if death was in *itself* a transition to a nonhuman absolute, of regarding it as a window on to this absolute. Death reveals nothing other than our-selves, and from a human point of view. Does that mean that it belongs *a priori* to human-reality?

What we should note right at the start is death's absurd character. In this sense, any temptation to regard it as a resolution chord at the end of a melody must be strictly pushed away. It has often been said that we are in the situation of a condemned prisoner, among other condemned prisoners, who does not know the date of his execution but who sees his fellow prisoners being executed every day. That is not quite cor-rect: we ought rather to compare ourselves to someone sentenced to death who is bravely preparing himself for his execution, who is put-ting all his efforts into cutting a good figure on the scaffold and who, meanwhile, is carried away by an epidemic of Spanish flu. This was understood by Christian wisdom, which recommends that we prepare for death as if it might arrive *at any moment*. In this way we have hoped to reclaim death by metamorphosing it into a "death that is awaited." If in fact the meaning of our life becomes a waiting for death, the latter can

79 TN: Heidegger outlines Being-toward-death in Heidegger (1980: Division Two, chap. 1).

only, in arriving, fix its seal on life. That is basically the most positive aspect of Heidegger's "resoluteness" (*Entschlossenheit*). Unfortunately, this advice is much easier to give than to follow, not because of a natural weakness of human-reality or an original pro-ject of inauthenticity but because of death itself. We can, indeed, wait for *one* particular death, but we cannot simply wait for *death*. The sleight of hand that Heidegger performs is easy enough to detect: he begins by individualizing the death of each one of us, by pointing out that it is the death of a *person*, an individual, and the "only thing that nobody can do for me," and then he exploits this incomparable individuality which has been—on the basis of *Dasein*—conferred on death, in order to individualize *Dasein* itself. It is by freely projecting itself toward its ultimate possibility that *Dasein* will accede to authentic existence, and tear itself away from everyday banality to attain the irreplaceable uniqueness of a person. But here there is a circle: How in fact can we prove that death has this individuality and the power to confer it? Certainly, if we describe death as my death, I am able to await it: it is a distinct and defined possibility. But is the death that will strike me my death? First of all, to say that "dying is the only thing that nobody can do for me" is entirely gratuitous. Or rather, there is an obvious bad faith in the reasoning: if in fact we consider death as the ultimate subjective possibility, an event which concerns only the for-itself, it is evident that nobody can die for me. But in that case it follows that none of my possibilities, seen from that point of view—which is that of the *cogito*—whether it is taken up within an authentic or an inauthentic existence, may be projected by someone else. Nobody can love for me, if by that we mean making those vows that are my vows, feeling those emotions (however banal they may be) that are my emotions. And here the "my" has nothing to do with a personality that I have won from everyday banality (which would allow Heidegger to retort that, for a love that I experience to be my love, and not the way "they" love, within me,[80] it is precisely necessary that I should be "free toward death") but, quite simply, with the ipseity that Heidegger explicitly accords to each

579

---

80 TN: ... *non l'amour en moi de "On"* ... My decision to translate Heidegger's *das Man* (to which Sartre's *on* corresponds) as "the *they*" has meant I have had to slightly modify this sentence.

Dasein—whether it exists in an authentic or inauthentic mode—when he asserts that "*Dasein* is in each case mine." Thus, from this point of view, the most everyday love is—like death—irreplaceable and unique: nobody can love for me. If, on the contrary, we consider my acts within the world from the point of view of their function, their efficiency, and their result, it is clear that another can always do what I am doing. If it is a matter of making this woman happy, or protecting her life or her freedom, of giving her the means of finding salvation or merely of making a home with her, of "giving her children"—if *that* is what we call loving someone—then someone else could love in my place, and he could even love someone for me: that is even the meaning of those sacrifices, recounted a thousand times in sentimental novels, which show us the loving hero, wishing for the happiness of the woman whom he loves and stepping aside for his rival because the latter "will know how to love her better than he can." Here the rival is nominally given the task of "*loving for*" the hero, because loving someone is defined simply as "making them happy through the love that one brings them." And the same will go for all my actions. Only my death will *also* belong in this category: if to die is to die in order to edify, to bear witness, for one's country, etc., anyone can die in my place—as in the song, in which the person to be eaten is the one who draws the short straw.[81] In brief, there is no kind of personalizing power that belongs especially to my death. Quite on the contrary, it becomes my death only if I have already taken up the standpoint of subjectivity; it is my subjectivity, defined through the prereflective *cogito*, which makes my death into something subjective which is irreplaceable, and not death which gives my for-itself an irreplaceable ipseity. In this case, death cannot be characterized as my death *because it is death* and, in consequence, its essential structure as death is not sufficient to make it into the kind of personalized and qualified event that we might *await*.

580   But, in addition, death cannot be in any way awaited, unless it is designated very precisely as my death sentence (the execution that will take place in a week, the outcome of my illness, which I know to be imminent and brutal, etc.), because what it reveals is nothing but the

---

81 TN: Sartre refers to a well-known French nursery rhyme, "*Il était un petit navire*," in which the starving sailors draw straws to decide which of them will be fed to the others.

absurdity of any waiting, even if the waiting is exactly for it. In the first place, in fact, we need to carefully distinguish here between two meanings of the verb "to await" that we have continued to conflate: to expect death is not to await death.[82] We can only await a determined event that some equally determined processes are about to actualize. I can await the arrival of the train from Chartres because I know that it has left the station at Chartres and that each turn of the wheel is bringing it closer to the station in Paris. Of course, it may be delayed; it is even possible that an accident will happen. But it remains no less the case that the process itself through which its arrival at the station will be actualized is "under way," and here the phenomena that may delay or eliminate this arrival at the station only mean that the process is merely a relatively closed system, which is relatively isolated and that it is in fact—as Meyerson says— immersed within a universe with a "fibrous structure."[83] Thus I can say that I am awaiting Pierre, and that "I expect his train will be late." But, precisely, the possibility of my death only means that, biologically, I am only a relatively closed and relatively isolated system; it only shows that my body belongs within the totality of existents. Its type is that of the probable lateness of trains, not that of Pierre's arrival. It belongs with the unforeseen, unexpected hitch, of which we must always take account, by preserving its specific character of being unexpected—but that we cannot await, because by nature it is lost in indeterminacy. If we concede, in fact, that the factors strictly condition each other—which is not even proved, and would involve a metaphysical choice—they are infinite in number, and their implications are infinitely infinite. As a collection, they do not constitute a system; the effect we are envisaging—my death—at least from the point of view we are considering, cannot be expected at any date, nor in consequence awaited. Perhaps, while I am peacefully writing in this bedroom, the state of the universe is such that my death has

82 TN: Sartre's pun on attendre ("to wait for") and s'attendre à ("to expect") cannot be reproduced in English. In fact the verb attendre can, by itself, mean both "to await something" and "to expect something"; Sartre exploits this ambiguity, which gets lost in translation, later in the same paragraph.

83 TN: Sartre makes an earlier reference to Meyerson at EN 172. Meyerson uses the phrase "fibrous structure," which he borrows from Arthur Balfour in his De l'Explication dans les Sciences (published in 1921, and translated as Meyerson 1991). The idea is that the scientist draws out and investigates one "fiber" at a time from the complicated and tangled weave of the whole fabric of reality.

become considerably closer; but perhaps, on the contrary, it has just moved considerably further away. If, for example, I am waiting for a mobilization order, I may believe that my death is close, which is to say the probability of a death in the near future has significantly increased; but in point of fact it is possible that at the same time an international conference has met in secret and that it has found the way to prolong peace. Thus I cannot say that the passing minute has brought me closer to death. It is true that it brings me closer if I consider the fact that my life is limited, but, within these very elastic limits (I may die a centenarian or, tomorrow, at the age of thirty-seven), I cannot know if in fact it is bringing me closer or taking me further away from this term. And there is a considerable *qualitative* difference between a death at the limit of old age and a sudden death that annihilates us in our maturity or youth. To await the first of these is to accept that life is a *limited* undertaking; it is one way among others of choosing finitude, and of selecting our ends on finitude's foundation. To await the second would mean I was waiting for my life to be a *failed* undertaking. If the only deaths that existed were the deaths brought about by old age (or by an explicit death sentence), I might be able to *await* my death. But the distinctive feature of death is that, precisely before it is due, it can always surprise those who are waiting for it at such and such a date. And if a death in old age may merge into the finitude of our choice and thereby be lived as our life's resolution chord (we are given a task and *given time* in order to fulfill it), a sudden death, on the contrary, is something that cannot in any way be expected, because it is indeterminate and, by definition, we cannot expect it at any date. With such a death it is always possible for us to die, taken by surprise, before the expected date and, in consequence, that our waiting for it is—*as an act of waiting*—an imposture, or for us to *survive* beyond that date and, as we amounted to no more than our waiting for it, that we survive beyond ourselves. Moreover, as a sudden death is only qualitatively different from the other kind insofar as we *live* one or the other, and as, biologically—i.e., from the point of view of the universe— they do not differ in any way with respect to their causes and determining factors, the lack of determinacy in the one extends in fact to the other; thus it is not possible, other than through blindness or bad faith, to *await* a death in old age. We have in fact every chance of dying before we have fulfilled our task or, on the contrary, of surviving beyond it. The probability therefore of our death presenting itself—like Sophocles's death, for example—in the manner of a resolution chord is very weak. But if it is only *chance* that decides the character of our death (and, therefore, of our life), then even the kind of death which most closely resembles the end of a melody cannot be awaited as such; chance, in deciding it, wholly deprives it of the character of a harmonious end. Indeed, in order to confer its meaning on a melody, the end of the melody must emanate from the melody itself. A death like that of Sophocles will therefore *resemble* a resolution chord, but it will not *be* one—just as the group of letters formed by throwing several blocks may perhaps resemble a word, but is not one. This constant appearance of chance at the heart of my projects cannot therefore be grasped as my possibility but, on the contrary, as the nihilation of all my possibilities, a nihilation that *itself no longer forms part of my possibilities*. Thus death is not my possibility of no longer actualizing a presence within the world but *a nihilation that is always possible of my possibles, and which lies outside my possibilities*.

Moreover, if we start out from a consideration of meanings, this can 582 be expressed in a slightly different way. As we know, human-reality is *signifying*. Therefore it becomes acquainted with what it is by what it is not or—alternatively—that it is still forth-coming.[84] If therefore it is constantly committed within its own future, we are prompted to say that it is waiting for this future to be confirmed. Indeed, insofar as it is in the future, our future[85] sketches out in advance a present that *will be*; we place ourselves in the hands of this present which, by itself, in the capacity of the present, must be able to confirm or to disconfirm the meaning, sketched out in advance, that I am. As this present will itself freely reclaim the past in the light of a new future, we are not able to *determine* it but only to project and to wait for it. The meaning of my current behavior is the reprimand that I wish this person, who has seriously offended me, to receive. But how can I know that this reprimand will not become transformed into an irritated and timid stuttering, and that the meaning of my present behavior will not be transformed in *the past*? Freedom limits freedom, and the past draws its meaning from the present. As we have shown, this

---

84 TN: *... qu'elle est à venir à soi-même*. Once again, Sartre makes use of this pun.

85 TN: *En tant que futur ... l'avenir est ...* Here Sartre switches between two different French words for "future": *avenir* and *futur*. I do not think anything turns on this.

explains the paradox that our current behavior is *both* wholly translucent to us (the prereflective *cogito*) and *at the same time* wholly concealed by a free determination that we are obliged to await: the adolescent is both fully conscious of the mystical meaning of his behavior and, at the same time, obliged to defer to the entirety of his future in order to decide whether he is in the process of "going through a crisis of puberty" or committing himself for good to the path of devotion. In this way our subsequent freedom, insofar as it is not our current possibility but the foundation of possibilities that we are not yet, constitutes something like an opacity in full translucency, something akin to what Barrès called a "mystery in full light."[86] That explains why, necessarily, we have *to wait for ourselves*. Our life is only one long waiting: waiting, first, for the actualization of our ends (to be committed to an undertaking is to be waiting for its outcome), waiting above all for ourselves (even if this undertaking is achieved, even if I have been able to make myself loved, to obtain this distinction or that honor, the place, the meaning, and the value of this undertaking within my life remain to be determined). That does not stem from a contingent defect in human "nature," from an agitation that prevents us from confining ourselves to the present and which might be corrected by exercise, but from the very nature of the for-itself, which "is" to the extent to which it temporalizes itself. Thus we must regard our life as being made up not only of periods of waiting but of waitings for waitings, which are themselves waiting for waitings. That is the very structure of ipseity: to be a self is to come toward oneself. All of these waitings obviously make reference to a final term that could be *awaited* without any longer waiting for anything, a state of rest that would be *being*, and no longer a waiting to be. The whole series is suspended from this final term that is by definition never *given*, and which is the value of our being, i.e., obviously a plenitude of the "in-itself, for-itself" type.[87] Through this final term, our reclamation of our past would be achieved once and for all; we would know *forever* whether this ordeal of our youth was productive or harmful, whether

583

86 TN: Maurice Barrès (1862–1923) was a French novelist, journalist, and politician. His collection of writings, *Le Mystère en Pleine Lumière*, was published in France in 1926. I have not been able to find any English translation.
87 TN: ... *du type "en-soi, pour-soi."* I think there is an error in the French text here, and that the comma ought to be replaced by a hyphen.

this crisis of puberty was a whim or really prefigured my subsequent commitments; the curve of our life would be fixed forever. In short, the account would be settled. The Christians have tried to present death as this final term. The Reverend P. Boisselot, in a private conversation with me, led me to understand that the "Last Judgment" was precisely this settling of accounts, which means we can no longer have another shot and that we *are*, at last, what we *have been*, irremediably.

But here there is a mistake, analogous to the one we pointed out earlier in Leibniz, even though it is located at the other end of existence. For Leibniz we are free, since all our acts unfold from our essence. However, the fact that our essence was not chosen by us is enough to make all this freedom, in matters of detail, conceal a total servitude: God chose Adam's essence. Conversely, if it is the drawing up of the account which gives our life its meaning and its value, it hardly matters that all the acts from which the weave of our life is made are free: its very meaning escapes us if we do not ourselves choose the moment when the account is to be drawn up. That is what was keenly sensed by the libertine author of an anecdote echoed by Diderot. Two brothers appear before the divine tribunal, on the Day of Judgment. The first says to God: "Why did you make me die so young?" and God replies: "To save you. If you had lived longer, you would have committed a crime, like your brother." So the brother asks, in turn: "Why did you make me die so old?" If death is not a free determination of our being, it cannot terminate our life: one minute more or less, and perhaps everything will change; if this minute is added to, or taken away from, my account, even if we allow that I am using it freely, the meaning of my life escapes me. Now, for Christians, death comes from God: he chooses our hour and, in general, I clearly understand that, even if I am the one who makes it the case in general, by temporalizing myself, that there are minutes and hours, I am not the one who establishes the minute of my death: the sequences of the universe decide that.

If that is so, we cannot even say any longer that death confers from outside a meaning on life: a meaning can come only from subjectivity itself. Since death does not appear on the foundation of our freedom, it can only *deprive life of all meaning*. If I await acts of waiting for waiting, and if, all at once, the object of my final act of waiting and the person who is waiting are eliminated, the waiting retrospectively acquires a character of *absurdity*. For thirty years of his life this young man has been

584   waiting to be a great writer; but this waiting itself was not sufficient: it
will be a conceited and foolish stubbornness, or a deep understanding
of his value, depending on the books that he will write. His first book
has appeared but, taken in isolation, what does it mean? It is the book of
someone starting out. Let us grant that is good: it will receive its meaning only through the future. If it is the only book, it is an inauguration
and, at the same time, a testament. There was only one book for him
to write, so he is limited and encircled by his work; he will not be "a
great writer." If the novel takes its place within a mediocre series, it
is an "accident." If it is followed by other, better books, it may place
its author in the first rank. But now it is death, indeed, that strikes the
writer, at the very moment when he was anxiously testing himself to
find out if he is "cut out" to write another work, at the moment when
he is waiting for himself. That is sufficient to make everything fall into
indeterminacy: I cannot say that the dead writer is the author of a *single*
book (in the sense in which he might have had only one book to be
written), nor that he has written several (since, in fact, only one has
appeared). I cannot say anything: if we suppose that Balzac died before
Les Chouans,[88] he would remain as the author of a few execrable novels
of adventure. But all of a sudden, this very waiting that this young dead
man *was*—this waiting to be a great man—loses any kind of meaning;
it is neither an obstinate and conceited blindness nor the true meaning
of his own value, since nothing will ever decide this. It would be pointless, in fact, to attempt to decide it by considering the sacrifices which
he accepted for his art, the obscure and harsh life which he agreed to
lead: so many mediocre people have had the strength to make similar sacrifices. On the contrary, the final value of this behavior remains
in suspense or, alternatively, all of it together—particular instances of
behavior, of waiting, values—falls all at once into absurdity. Thus, death
is never what gives life its meaning: it is, on the contrary, that which
eliminates all meaning from it. If we are to die, our life has no meaning,
because its problems never receive any solution and because even the
meaning of its problems remains indeterminate.

88 TN: *Les Chouans* is an 1829 novel by French novelist and playwright Honoré de Balzac
(1799–1850), translated as *Balzac* (1972).

To escape this necessity, any recourse to suicide would be futile. Suicide cannot be regarded as an end to life of which I am the distinctive foundation. Indeed, as an act in my life, it requires a meaning itself, which the future alone can give it; but as it is the *last* act of my life, this future is denied it; thus it remains wholly indeterminate. If in fact I escape death, or "fail myself," will I not judge my suicide, later, to be an act of cowardice? Might the course of events now show me that other solutions were possible? But as these solutions can only be my own projects, they can appear only if I am living. Suicide is an absurdity that plunges my life into absurdity.

We should note that these remarks are drawn from a consideration not of death but, on the contrary, of life. It is because the for-itself is the being for whom being is in question in its being, and because the for-itself is the being who always lays claim to an "after," that there is no place for death within the being that it is for-itself. What could it mean to await death, therefore, apart from a waiting for an indeterminate event that reduces to absurdity any waiting activity, including even that of waiting for death? The activity of waiting for death will destroy itself, because it will be the negation of all waiting. My pro-ject toward *a* death is comprehensible (suicide, martyrdom, heroism), but not the project toward my death as the indeterminate possibility of no longer actualizing a presence within the world, because this project would be the destruction of all projects. Thus death cannot be my ownmost possibility;[89] it cannot even be one of my possibilities.

Besides, to the extent that it can be revealed to me, death is not only the ever possible nihilation of all of my possibles—a nihilation that lies outside my possibilities—and it is not only the project that destroys all projects and destroys itself, the impossible destruction of all my waiting and my expectations:[90] it is the triumph of the Other's viewpoint over the viewpoint on myself *that I am*. That is probably what Malraux means when, in *L'Espoir*, he says of death that it "transforms life into

585

---

89 TN: . . . *ne saurait être ma possibilité propre* . . . I translate *propre* as "ownmost" in order to echo the language used by Heidegger, whose characterization of death Sartre is opposing.

90 TN: . . . *de mes attentes* . . . A pun on the two meanings of the French word *attente* ("waiting" and "expectation") is probably intended here: as the pun cannot be reproduced, I have added the second word to the sentence.

destiny."[91] Indeed death is only the nihilation of my possibilities in its negative aspect; as, in point of fact, I am only my possibilities through the nihilation of the being-in-itself that I have to be, death—as the nihilation of a nihilation—posits my being as in-itself in the sense in which, for Hegel, the negation of a negation is an affirmation. As long as the for-itself is "living," it surpasses its past toward its future, and the past is what the for-itself has to be. When the for-itself "ceases to be living" this does not entail the abolition of its past: the disappearance of the nihilating being does not affect the past in its being, whose type is in-itself; it sinks into the in-itself. My life in its entirety is; that does not mean that it is a harmonious totality but that it has ceased to be pending in relation to itself, and that it can no longer change itself merely through its consciousness of itself. But, on the contrary, the meaning of any particular phenomenon in this life is fixed from that point on, not by itself but by that open totality in which the arrested life consists. As we have seen, this meaning in its primary and fundamental aspect is an *absence of meaning*. But in its secondary and derivative aspect, a thousand scintillations, a thousand iridescences of relative meanings may play over this fundamental absurdity of a "dead" life. For example, whatever its ultimate pointlessness may have been, it remains the case that Sophocles's life was happy, that Balzac's life was prodigiously hard-working, etc. Naturally, these general qualifications can be further narrowed down; we may risk a description or an analysis at the same time as a narration of this life. We will obtain some more distinct characteristics; for example we may be able to say about this dead woman, as Mauriac says of one of his heroines, that she lived in "cautious despair"; we may apprehend the meaning of Pascal's "soul" (i.e., of his inner "life") as "superb and bitter," as Nietzsche wrote. We can go so far as to qualify such and such an episode as "cowardly" or "tactless" without losing sight of the fact, however, that the contingent stop that was put to that "being-constantly-pending" of the living for-itself allows us to confer (on the foundation of a radical absurdity) only a relative meaning to the episode in question, and that this meaning is an *essentially provisional* meaning, whose provisional quality has *accidentally become* defin-

591 TN: Sartre has already referred to this novel at EN 147, EN 150 and EN 475.

itive. But these various explanations of the meaning of Pierre's life had the effect, when it was Pierre himself who was applying them to his own life, of changing its meaning and orientation, because every description of one's own life, when it is hazarded by the for-itself, is a project of the self beyond that life and, as the project which alters it is thereby aggregated within the life that it alters, it is Pierre's own life whose meaning was being metamorphosed as it continuously temporalized itself. But, now that his life is dead, only the *other's memory* can prevent it from shriveling up in its in itself plenitude and cutting all its ties to the present. The characteristic of a dead life is that it is a life of which the other becomes the guardian. That does not mean merely that the other keeps hold of the life of "the deceased" by carrying out an explicit and cognitive reconstitution of it. Quite to the contrary, such a reconstitution is just one of the possible attitudes that the other may take up in relation to the dead life and, in consequence, the shape of a "reconstituted life" (within the family environment by means of the memories of close relatives, within the historical environment) is a particular destiny that comes to characterize some lives, to the exclusion of others. The necessary result is that the opposite quality—"a life that has fallen into oblivion"—also represents a specific destiny that we can describe, which comes to certain lives from the other.[92] To be forgotten is to be the object of an attitude of another, and of an implicit decision by the Other. To be forgotten, in fact, is to be resolutely apprehended for eternity as an element that has merged within a mass (the "feudal lords of the thirteenth century," the "bourgeois whigs" of the eighteenth century, the "Soviet bureaucrats," etc.); it is in no way *to be annihilated* but it is to lose one's personal existence in order to be constituted alongside others in a collective existence. This is a good demonstration of what we wished to prove, which is that the other cannot *at first* be without contact with the dead, in order to decide (or in order for circumstances to decide) *afterward* that he will have such and such a relation with certain particular dead people (those he knew while they were alive, the "great dead men," etc.). In reality, the relation to the dead—

---

92 TN: ...*à partir de l'autre.* Here "other" must be understood as "other person"; otherwise the sentence seems ungrammatical.

to *all* of the dead—is an essential structure of the fundamental relation that we have called "being-for-the-Other." In arising into being, the for-itself has to take up a position in relation to the dead; its initial project organizes them into large anonymous masses or distinct individuals, and it determines the separation or the absolute proximity of these collective masses, as of these individuals: he unfolds the temporal distances from them to him, in temporalizing himself, just as he unfolds spatial distances on the basis of his surroundings. By becoming acquainted, through his end, with what he is, he decides on the *importance* of each of the deceased communities or individuals; this group, which for Pierre will be utterly anonymous and amorphous, will be particularized and structured for me; that other one, which is thoroughly uniform for me, will manifest, for Jean, its individual components. Byzantium, Rome, Athens, the last Crusade, the Convention[93]—so many immense necropolises which I can see from far off or close up, in a cavalier or detailed fashion, according to the position that I take up, that I "am," to the point at which it is not impossible, so long as one understands this the right way, to define a "person" in terms of his dead, which is to say in terms of the sectors of individualization or collectivization he has determined within his necropolis, by the roads and paths he has traced, the lessons he has decided to be taught, the "roots" he has put down. Of course, the dead choose us, but it is necessary in the first place for us to have chosen them. Here we encounter again the original relation which joins facticity to freedom; we choose our attitude toward the dead, but it is not possible for us not to choose one. An attitude of indifference toward the dead is quite possible (we can find examples of it in the "*Heimatlos*,"[94] in certain revolutionaries, or individualists). But this indifference—which consists in making the dead "die again"—is, in relation to them, one behavior among others. Thus, through its very facticity, the for-itself is thrown into a complete "responsibility" in relation to the dead; he is obliged to freely decide on their fate. In particular, when it is a matter of the dead who sur-

93 TN: The text only says *la Convention*, but the reference here is to the French National Convention (1792–1795).

94 TN: The German word *Heimatlos* literally means "homeless," but is often used to refer to stateless people, such as some refugees.

round us, it is not possible for us not to decide—explicitly or implicitly—
on the fate of their undertakings. This is manifest when we are talking
about a son who takes up his father's business, or a disciple who takes
up the school and doctrines of his teacher. But, even though the connection is less clearly visible in a good many circumstances, it is also
true in all cases in which the dead person and the living person in question belong to the same historical and concrete community. It is I, and
the men of my generation, who decide the meaning of the efforts
and the undertakings of the previous generation, whether they reclaim
and continue their social and political endeavors, or whether they effect
a decisive break and send back the dead into impotence. As we have
seen, the worth and the meaning of Lafayette's undertaking are determined by America, in 1917. Thus, from this point of view, the difference between life and death appears clearly: life decides on its own
meaning, because it is always "suspended"; in its essence it has a power   588
of self-critique and self-metamorphosis which means it defines itself as
a "not-yet" or, alternatively, that its way of being is to change what it
is. A dead life does not for all that cease to change, and yet it is *done*; its
die is cast, therefore, and henceforth it will undergo its changes without being in any way responsible for them. What happens to the life
here is not just an arbitrary and definitive totalization but, in addition,
a radical transformation: nothing can any longer *happen* to the life from
within it; it is entirely closed, and nothing more can enter into it; but,
from outside, its meaning does not stop changing. Right up to the death
of this apostle of peace, the meaning of his undertakings (madness, or
a profound sense of reality, success, or failure) was within his hands;
"as long as I am here, there will be no war." But to the extent to which
this meaning exceeds the limits of a single individuality, to the extent
to which the person is acquainted with what he is by an objective situation to be brought about (peace in Europe), death represents a complete *dispossession*: it is the other who *dispossesses* the apostle of peace of the
very meaning of his efforts—and, therefore, of his being—by taking up
the task, despite himself and merely through his arising, of transforming into a failure or a success, into madness or the intuition of a genius,
the very undertaking through which the person was becoming
acquainted with what he was in his being. Thus the very existence of
death alienates us entirely, in our own life, to the advantage of the

Other. To be dead is to become prey to the living. That means therefore that a person who tries to grasp the meaning of his future death is obliged to discover himself to be the future prey of others. There is therefore a case of alienation that we did not consider, in the section of this work that we devoted to the For-the-Other: the alienations that we examined, in fact, were of the type that we could nihilate by transforming the other into a transcended-transcendence, just as we could nihilate our *outside* by an absolute and subjective positing of our freedom. As long as I am living, I can escape what I *am* for the other by showing myself, through the ends that I freely posit, that I *am* nothing and that I make myself be what I am; as long as I am living, I can belie what the other uncovers in me by already pro-jecting myself toward other ends and, in any case, by discovering that my dimension of being-for-myself is incommensurable with my dimension of being-for-the-other. In this way I was incessantly escaping my outside, and incessantly grasped back by it, without a definitive victory belonging, "in this dubious battle," [95] to one or the other of these modes of being. But, without becoming exactly allied with either of these adversaries in this battle itself, *the fact of death* bestows the final victory on the viewpoint of the other, by taking the battle and what is at stake to new territory, which is to say by suddenly eliminating one of the combatants. In this sense, to die is to be condemned, whatever ephemeral victory one may have won against the other, and even if one has made use of the other to "sculpt one's own statue," [96] to no longer exist other than through the other, and to receive from him one's meaning and the very meaning of one's victory. Indeed, if one shares the realist opinions that we expounded in Part Three, one is obliged to acknowledge that my *existence after death* is not the mere spectral survival, "in the other's consciousness," of mere representations (images, memories, etc.) that concerned me. My being-for-the-Other is a real being and if, after my demise, it remains between the

589

95 TN: ..."*en ce combat douteux*"... Sartre probably places this phrase in quotation marks to allude to the American writer John Steinbeck's novel *In Dubious Battle*. The novel, first published in 1936, appeared in French translation in 1940 with the title *En un Combat Douteux*. Sartre took an interest in Steinbeck's work, and more widely in contemporary American fiction.

96 TN: Sartre is quoting the Neo-Platonist philosopher Plotinus (204/5–270 CE).

Other's hands, like a coat that I have left him with, it is in the form of a real dimension of my being—a dimension that has become my only dimension—and not a flimsy ghost. Richelieu, Louis XV, my grandfather, are in no way the sum of my memories, not even the sum of the memories or the pieces of knowledge of all those people who have heard of them; they are beings that are objective and opaque but which have simply been reduced to the single dimension of externality. In this capacity, they will continue their history in the human world, but they will no longer ever be anything but transcended-transcendences in the midst of the world. In this way, my death does not only disarm my acts of waiting by definitively removing any *waiting*, and by leaving indeterminate my actualization of the ends by which I am acquainted with what I am—but, in addition, it confers a meaning from outside on everything that I lived as a subjectivity; it seizes back all this subjective domain, which was able to protect itself, as long as it "was living," against externalization, and it deprives it of all subjective meaning, in order to hand it over, on the contrary, to any *objective* meaning that the other cares to give it. Nonetheless, we should point out that this "destiny" which is in this way conferred on my life also remains, for its part, in suspense, or pending, because the answer to this question: "What will be the definitive historical destiny of Robespierre?" depends on the answer to this prior question: "Does History have a meaning?"—which is to say, "Must it become complete, or does it merely *end*?" This question has not been resolved—perhaps it is insoluble, since all the answers given to it (including the answer given by idealism: "The history of Egypt is the history of Egyptology") are themselves historical.

Thus, in allowing that I can encounter my death within my life, we are able to see that it cannot be a pure halt in my subjectivity, which, as an internal event within it, would in the end concern this subjectivity alone. If it is true that dogmatic realism was wrong to see in death the *state of being dead*—which is to say as a transcendent in relation to life—it remains no less true that the death that I can encounter as *mine* necessarily involves something other than me. Indeed, insofar as it is a nihilation of my possibles that is always possible, it is outside my possibilities and I cannot therefore await it, which is to say throw myself toward it as I do toward my possibilities. It cannot therefore belong to the for-itself's ontological structure. Insofar as it is the triumph of the other person over

590

me, it refers us to a fact that is, of course, fundamental—but, as we have seen, wholly contingent—which is the other's existence. We would not know this death if the other did not exist: it could not be revealed to us, nor in particular could it be constituted as the metamorphosis of our being into destiny; it would be, in point of fact, the simultaneous disappearance of the for-itself and the world, the subjective and the objective, of the signifier and of every meaning. If death can, to a certain extent, be revealed to us as the metamorphosis of those particular meanings that are my meanings, it is in consequence of the fact of the existence of a signifying other, who ensures that the meanings and the signs are taken up. It is because of the other that my death is my falling out of the world as a subjectivity, rather than being the annihilation of consciousness and of the world. There is therefore an undeniable and fundamental character of fact—which is to say a radical contingency—about death, as about the Other's existence. This contingency removes it in advance from any ontological conjectures. And to meditate on my life by considering it on the basis of death would be to meditate on my subjectivity by taking up the other's viewpoint on it; we have seen that this is not possible.

Thus, against Heidegger, we should conclude that death, far from being my own possibility, is *a contingent fact* which, as such, escapes me on principle and which originates in my facticity. I cannot discover my death, nor can I await it or take up an attitude in relation to it, because it is that which reveals itself to be undiscoverable, which disarms every act of waiting, which slides into all our attitudes—and especially into those one might take up in relation to it—in order to transform them into externalized and frozen modes of behavior, whose meaning is handed over forever to people other than ourselves. Death, like birth, is a pure fact; it comes to us from outside and transforms us into an "outside." At bottom it is indistinguishable from birth, and what we are calling "facticity" is the identity of birth and of death.

Does that mean that death traces out the limits of our freedom? By abandoning Heidegger's Being-toward-death, have we abandoned forever the possibility of freely giving our being a meaning for which we are responsible?

Quite on the contrary, it seems to us that death, by revealing itself to us as it does, frees us entirely from its alleged constraint. A little reflection will make this clearer.

But we need first of all to radically separate the two ideas that are ordinarily joined, of death and of finitude. We usually seem to think that it is death that constitutes our finitude and reveals it to us. The result of this contamination is that death assumes the shape of an ontological necessity, and finitude, on the contrary, borrows from death its character of contingency. Heidegger, in particular, seems to have constructed his entire theory of *"Sein-zum-Tode"*[97] on a complete identification of death with finitude; in the same way, when Malraux tells us that death reveals life's uniqueness to us, he seems to think that the reason we are unable to have another shot and are, therefore, finite is just because we are going to die. But if we examine this matter more closely, we will see their mistake: death is a contingent fact that has to do with our facticity; finitude is an ontological structure of the for-itself who determines its freedom, and exists only in and through the free project of the end that acquaints me with my being. In other words, even if it were immortal, human-reality would remain finite because in choosing itself as human it *makes* itself finite. To be finite is, in fact, to choose oneself, i.e., to become acquainted with what one is by projecting oneself toward one possible, in a way that excludes others. The very act of freedom is therefore the acceptance and creation of finitude. If I make myself, I make myself finite and, in consequence, my life is unique. From that point on, even if I am immortal, I am prohibited from "having another shot"; the irreversibility of temporality prohibits this, and this irreversibility is nothing but the distinctive characteristic of a freedom that temporalizes itself. Of course, if I am immortal and I have had to set aside possible B in order to actualize possible A, the opportunity to actualize that rejected possible will be offered to me again. But, by virtue merely of the fact that this opportunity will be presented *after* the opportunity that was rejected, it will not be the same and thenceforth, by irremediably setting aside the first opportunity, I will have made myself finite for eternity. From this point of view, an immortal, just like a mortal, is born several people and makes himself just one. For all that it is temporally indefinite, which is to say without limits, its "life" will be no less finite in its very

591

---

97 TN: Heidegger's phrase from *Being and Time*, *Sein-zum-Tode*, translates into English as "Being-toward-death."

being because it makes itself unique. Death has nothing to do with it—it arrives "in the meantime"—and human-reality's revelation of its own finitude does not amount to a discovery of its mortality.

Thus death is in no way an ontological structure of my being, at least not insofar as it is for-itself; it is the other who is mortal in his being. There is no place for death in being-for-itself; it can neither await it, nor actualize it, nor project itself toward it. It is in no way the foundation of its finitude and, in general terms, the for-itself can neither found it from within, as the pro-ject of original freedom, nor receive it from outside as a quality. What is it, then? Nothing but a specific aspect of facticity and being-for-the-other, which is to say nothing but something given. It is absurd that we are born, and it is absurd that we die; moreover, this absurdity is presented as the permanent alienation of my being—a possibility that is no longer my possibility but that of the other. It is therefore an external and de facto limit of my subjectivity. But can we not recognize here the description that we gave in the preceding paragraph? This de facto limit that we are obliged, in one sense, to endorse—since nothing can penetrate us from outside, and in some sense we have to feel death if we are to be able even to name it—but which, on the other hand, is never encountered by the for-itself, since this limit is nothing to do with it apart from the indefinite permanence of its being-for-the-other: What could this limit be other than, precisely, one of the unrealizables? What is it, other than a synthetic aspect of our reverse side? Mortal represents the present being that I am for-the-Other; dead represents the future meaning of my current for-itself for the other. It is really a matter, therefore, of a permanent limit to my plans; and, as such, this limit is to be accepted. It is therefore an externality that remains as externality even in and through the for-itself's attempt to realize it: what we defined earlier as the unrealizable to be realized. There is no fundamental difference between the choice through which freedom accepts its death as its subjectivity's elusive and inconceivable limit, and the one through which it chooses to be a freedom limited by the fact of the other's freedom. Thus death is not my possibility, in the sense defined previously; it is a limit-situation, as the chosen and fugitive reverse side to my choice. It is not my possible, in the sense of my own end, informing me of my being; but by virtue of being the ineluctable necessity of existing elsewhere as an outside and an in-itself, it is internalized as what is "ultimate," i.e., as the thematic

592

meaning, out of reach, of the hierarchy of possibles. In this way it haunts me in the very heart of each of my projects, as their ineluctable reverse side. But, precisely as this "reverse side" is not to be accepted as my possibility but as the possibility of there no longer being any possibilities for me, it does not *make a dent* in me.[98] The freedom that is *my freedom* remains total and infinite, not because death does not limit it but because freedom never encounters this limit; death is in no way an obstacle to my projects but only a destiny, *somewhere else*, of these projects. I am not "free to die,"[99] but I am a free mortal. As death escapes from my projects because it is unrealizable, so I myself escape from death in my very project. As something which is always beyond my subjectivity, there is no place for it within my subjectivity. And this subjectivity does not assert itself *against* it but independently of it, even though this assertion is immediately alienated. We cannot therefore think about death, nor can we await it, nor can we take arms against it; but at the same time our projects are, as projects—as a matter of principle, and not, as Christians say, because of our blindness—independent of it. And, although there are countless possible attitudes in the face of this unrealizable that is to be realized "in addition to the bargain," there is no reason to classify them as authentic or inauthentic, since, in fact, our death will always be "more than we bargained for."[100]

These various descriptions, bearing on my place, my past, my surroundings, my death, and my fellow man, do not claim to be exhaustive, or even detailed. Their aim is simply to enable us to form a clearer conception of what a "situation" is. Thanks to them, it will be possible for us to define more precisely this "being-in-situation" which characterizes the for-itself insofar as it is responsible for its way of being without being the foundation of its being.

(1) I am an existent *in the midst of* other existents. But I can only "actualize" this existence in the midst of others, grasp the existents surrounding

593

---

98 TN: ...*elle ne m'entame pas.* The verb *entamer* can mean "to start," as well as "to dent" or "to make inroads into." The point here is that my freedom is not limited by my death.

99 TN: ... "*libre pour mourir*" ... I am not sure why Sartre puts this phrase in quotation marks: probably he is alluding to (and repudiating) Heidegger's notion of "freedom-toward-death" in Heidegger (1980).

100 TN: ...*par-dessus le marché.* I use "bargain" to match Sartre's idiomatic French expression.

me as *objects*, and grasp myself as a *surrounded* existent, if I choose myself not in my being but in my way of being; only then can I even give a meaning to this notion of "*in the midst of.*" The choice of this end is the choice of a *not-yet-existing.* My position in the midst of the world, defined through the relation of the equipmentality or adversity of the things surrounding me to my own facticity—which is to say the discovery of the dangers I am risking within the world, the obstacles that I may meet with there, the assistance I may be offered—in the light of a radical nihilation of myself, and a radical and internal negation of the in-itself, brought about from the point of view of an end that I freely posit: that is what we are calling the *situation.*

(2) The situation exists only correlatively to a surpassing of the given toward an end. It is the way in which the given that I am and the given that I am not are encountered by the for-itself that I am, in the mode of not-being it. To talk about the *situation* is therefore to talk about "the position apprehended by the for-itself who is in situation." It is impossible to consider a situation from the outside; it becomes frozen into an *in itself* figure. In consequence, we can describe the situation neither as objective nor as subjective, even though the partial structures of this situation (the cup I am using, the table on which I am leaning, etc.) may and must be strictly objective.

The situation cannot be *subjective,* because it is neither the sum nor the unity of the *impressions* that things make on us: it is *the things themselves,* and myself among things, because the only effect of my arising within the world as the pure nihilation of being is to make it the case that *there are* things, and it adds *nothing.* In this respect, the situation makes visible my facticity, which is to say the fact that things *are there,* simply as they are, without either the necessity or the possibility of being otherwise, and that I *am there,* among them.

But it cannot be *objective* either, in the sense of a pure given which the subject could observe without being in any way committed within the system thereby constituted. In fact, by virtue of the given's very meaning (a meaning without which there *would not even be* any given), the situation reflects the for-itself's freedom to it. If the situation is neither subjective nor objective, it is because it does not constitute an item of *knowledge,* or even an affective understanding of the state of the world through a subject; rather, it is a *relation of being* between a for-itself and the in-itself that it nihilates. The situation is the subject in his entirety (it is nothing other than his situation) and it is also the "thing" in its entirety (there is never anything more than the things). It is, if you like, the subject lighting things up through his very surpassing—or it is things sending back to the subject his image. It is the complete facticity, the absolute contingency of the world, of my place, my past, my surroundings, of the fact of my fellow man—and it is my freedom without limits, as that which makes it the case that there is a facticity for me. It is this dusty, ascending path, this raging thirst of mine, this refusal of people to give me anything to drink because I do not have money, or am not from their country, or their race; it is my state of abandonment in the midst of these hostile populations, with this fatigue in my body that will perhaps prevent me from reaching the goal I had fixed for myself. But it is also, precisely, this goal, not insofar as I formulate it clearly and explicitly but insofar as it is there, everywhere around me, as that which unifies and explains all the facts, and organizes them into a totality that can be described, rather than making of them a disordered nightmare.

(3) If the for-itself is nothing other than its situation, it follows that being-in-situation defines human-reality, by accounting at the same time for its being-there and its being-beyond. Human-reality is, in effect, the being that is always beyond its being-there. And the situation is the organized totality of being-there, as interpreted and lived in and through the being-beyond. No situation, therefore, is privileged; by this we mean that there is no situation in which the given stifles beneath its weight the freedom that constitutes it as such—nor, conversely, is there any situation in which the for-itself is more free than in others. This should not be understood in the sense of that "internal freedom" of Bergson's, which Politzer mocked in La Fin d'une Parade Philosophique,[101] and which led simply to allowing the slave the independence of his inner life, and of his heart in chains. When we assert that the slave is just as free in

101 TN: Georges Politzer (1903–1942) was a French Marxist philosopher, of Hungarian origin, executed in 1942 by the Nazis. The 1929 publication to which Sartre refers (not translated into English but whose title translates as The End of a Philosophical Parade), was a polemical pamphlet, directed especially against Bergson, in which Politzer attacked the dominant French academic philosophy of the time for its abstraction and lack of engagement with contemporary historical and political circumstances.

TO HAVE, TO DO, AND TO BE

his chains as his master, we do not mean to talk about a freedom that remains indeterminate. The slave in chains is free *in order to break them*; in other words, the very meaning of his chains will appear to him in the light of the end he has chosen: to remain a slave, or to risk the worst in order to emancipate himself from slavery. Of course, the slave will not be able to obtain the master's wealth and standard of living; but it is also true that those are not the objects of his *projects*; he can only dream of possessing those treasures. His *facticity* is such that the world presents to him another face, and the problems he has to posit and to resolve are different; in particular, it is fundamentally on the ground of *slavery* that he is obliged to choose himself and, through that very act, to give a meaning to this obscure constraint. If for example he chooses rebellion, then his slavery, far from being *in the first place* an obstacle to that rebellion, only gains its meaning and its coefficient of adversity through it. Precisely because the life of the slave who rebels and dies in the course of his rebellion is a free life, precisely because the situation illuminated by a free project is full and concrete, precisely because this life's urgent and crucial question is "Will I achieve my goal?"— precisely because of all that, the slave's situation is incomparable with the master's. The meaning of each of them, in fact, is obtained only for a for-itself in situation, and on the basis of the free choice of its end. A comparison could be made only by a third party and, in consequence, it could take place only between two objective figures in the midst of the world. It would be established, moreover, in the light of the third person's freely chosen pro-ject: there is no absolute point of view in which one could position oneself in order to compare situations that are different; each person actualizes just one situation: his *own*.

(4) As it is illuminated by ends which are themselves pro-jected only on the basis of the *being-there* that they illuminate, the situation presents itself as eminently *concrete*. Of course, it contains and supports some abstract and universal structures, but it has to be understood as the *particular face* that the world turns toward us as our unique and personal opportunity. We may recall Kafka's allegory: a shopkeeper comes to the castle to plead his case; a fearsome guard blocks his entrance. He does not dare to go further, waits there, and dies while he is waiting. At the hour of his death, he asks the guardian: "How is it that I was the only one waiting?" And the guardian replies: "This door was made only for

you." [102] That is just how it is for the for-itself, if we are willing to add, moreover, that *each person makes his own door.* The concrete aspect of the situation is shown in particular by the fact that the for-itself *never aims* at fundamental ends that are abstract and universal. Doubtless we will see in the next chapter that the choice's deep meaning is universal, and that the for-itself thereby makes it the case that a human-reality exists as a species. It will still be necessary to *extricate* the meaning, which is *implicit;* and for that we will make use of existential psychoanalysis. And, once it has been extricated, the for-itself's final and initial meaning will appear as an *"unselbstständig"* that, in order to be manifested, needs a particular concretion. [103] But the for-itself's end, as it is lived and pursued within the project through which it surpasses and founds reality, is revealed to the for-itself in its concretion as a particular change in the situation it is living (to break one's chains, to be king of the Franks, to liberate Poland, to fight for the proletariat). And, further, it will not even be for the proletariat in general that, in the first place, one pro-jects to fight; instead, the proletariat will be aimed at through some concrete grouping of workers to which the *person* belongs. The fact is that the end illumi-nates the given only because it is chosen as the surpassing of this given. The for-itself does not arise with an end that is *wholly given.* But, by "mak-ing" the situation, it "makes itself," and *vice versa.*   596

(5) Just as the situation is neither objective nor subjective, it cannot be regarded either as the free outcome of a freedom or as the set of con-straints that I undergo; it is a product of the constraint's illumination by the freedom that gives the constraint its meaning. Between brute exis-tents, there can be no connection; the connections are founded by free-dom, which groups them into structures of equipment, and it is freedom which projects the *reason* for the connections, i.e., its end. But, precisely because I thereby come to project myself toward an end through a world of *connections,* I am able now to encounter sequences, connected series, structures, and I must determine myself to action in accordance with

---

102 TN: Sartre is referring to Franz Kafka's parable "Before the Law" ("Vor dem Gesetz" in German). This was published in self-standing form in Kafka's lifetime, and subse-quently formed part of his novel *The Trial,* which was published posthumously in 1925 (translated as Kafka 1994).

103 Sartre's note: Cf. the following chapter.

laws. These laws, and the way I use them, determine the failure or the success of my endeavors. But it is through freedom that the relations prescribed by law come into the world. Thus freedom shackles itself within the world as a free project toward its ends.

(6) The for-itself is temporalization: therefore it is *not*; it "makes itself." It is the *situation* that must account for *that substantial permanence* which we are apt to recognize in people ("he hasn't changed," "he is still the same") and which the person, in many cases, experiences empirically as his. In fact my free perseverance in the same project does not imply any permanence, as we have seen; quite to the contrary, it is a constant renewal of my commitment. However, the realities that are included within and illuminated by the project as it develops and is confirmed, present, on the contrary, the permanence of the in-itself and, to the extent that they transmit back to us our image, their perennial quality steadies us; frequently, we even take their permanence for our own. In particular, the permanence of our place and surroundings, of our fellow man's judgments about us, and of our past, figure a degraded image of our *perseverance*. For the duration of my self-temporalizing, I am always French, a civil servant or a proletarian for the Other. This unrealizable has the character of an invariable limit of my situation. Similarly, what we refer to as a person's temperament or character, and which is nothing but his free project insofar as it is-for-the-Other, also appears, to the for-itself, as an invariant unrealizable. Alain saw quite clearly that character is a *pledge*. The person who says "I am awkward" is making a free commitment to the anger to which he consents and, by the same token, a free interpretation of certain ambiguous details of his past. In this sense, there is no character—there is only a pro-ject of oneself. However, we should not fail to recognize the aspect of character that is "*given*." It is true that for the other, who apprehends me as an object-other, I *am* irritable, hypocritical or frank, cowardly or brave. This aspect is transmitted back to me by the Other's look: in undergoing this look, my character, which was a free lived project, conscious (of) itself, becomes something unrealizable to be accepted "*ne varietur*."[104] So it depends not only on the other but on the position I have taken up in relation to the other, and on my perseverance in maintaining this position: for as long as I allow the Other's gaze to fascinate me, my character will

597

104 TN: This Latin phrase is often used in legal contexts; for example, in documents it means "must not be changed."

represent to my own eyes the substantial permanence of my being as an unrealizable, "*ne varietur*"—as suggested by some banal sentences, uttered daily, such as: "I am forty-five years old, and I am not going to start changing today." Often, the for-itself's character is even what it attempts to retrieve, in order to become the in-itself-for-itself that it projects to be. We ought nonetheless to note that this permanence of the past, of one's surroundings, and of one's character are not qualities that are *given*; they show up on things only in correlation with the continuity of my project. It would, for example, be pointless to hope that one might return after a war, after a long exile, to find some mountainous landscape unchanged and to found, on the inertia and apparent permanence of these rocks, one's hope for a renaissance of the past. This landscape will disclose its permanence only through a project of perseverance: these mountains have a *meaning* within my situation; they depict, in one way or another, my belonging to a nation at peace, and under its own control, which has a specific standing within the international hierarchy. If I return to them after a defeat and during the occupation of part of the territory, they cannot present the same face to me at all: the fact is that I myself have other pro-jects and have committed myself in a different way within the world.

Finally, we have seen that internal upheavals of the situation, through autonomous changes in the surroundings, are always to be foreseen. These changes can never *induce* a change in my project but, on the foundation of my freedom, they may bring about a simplification or a complication in the situation. In consequence, my initial project will be revealed to me with more or less simplicity. For a person is never either simple or complex: it is his situation that can be one of these or the other. I am, in fact, nothing but my project of myself beyond a determinate situation, and this project sketches me out in advance, on the basis of the concrete situation just as, moreover, it illuminates the situation on the basis of my choice. If therefore the situation as a whole is simplified—if rockslides, collapses, and instances of erosion have impressed on it a distinct appearance, with crude features and violent oppositions—I myself will be simple, because, as my choice—the choice that I am—is the apprehension of *that* situation *there*, it can only be simple. New complications will have the effect, as they are reintroduced, of presenting me with a complicated situation, beyond which I will rediscover myself as complicated. Anyone who was in a position to notice the almost animal degree of simplicity with which the prisoners

598

of war returned, in consequence of the extreme simplification of their situation, will have observed this. This simplification could not modify their project itself, in its meaning, but, on the foundation of freedom itself, it led to a condensation and uniformity of the surroundings which were constituted in and through a more distinct, more brutal, and more condensed apprehension of the captive's fundamental ends. In short, we are dealing with an internal metabolism, and not a global metamorphosis which would also affect the situation's figure. Yet these are changes that I encounter as changes "in my life," i.e., as changes within the unitary framework of a single project.

III. FREEDOM AND RESPONSIBILITY

Although the following considerations are of more concern to a moralist, we have judged that it may be profitable to return, after these descriptions and arguments, to the for-itself's freedom, and to try to understand what the fact of this freedom represents for the destiny of humanity.

The essential consequence of our previous remarks is that man, being condemned to be free, carries the weight of the whole world on his shoulders: he is responsible for the world and for himself, as a way of being. We are using the word "responsibility" in its ordinary sense of a "consciousness (of) being the incontestable author of an event or an object." In this sense, the for-itself's responsibility is overwhelming, since he is the one who makes it the case that *there is* a world, and since it is he, too, who *makes himself be*; whatever the situation in which he finds himself, the for-itself has to accept this situation in its entirety, with its own coefficient of adversity, even if it is unsustainable. He has to accept it with the proud consciousness of being its author because the worst disadvantages, or the worst threats from which my person is in danger, can have meaning only through my project, and they appear against the ground of the commitment that I am. It is therefore foolish to think of complaining, since nothing alien has decided what we will feel, what we will live, and what we are. Moreover, this absolute responsibility is not an acceptance: it is merely what the consequences of our freedom logically demand. What happens to me happens to me through me, and I am unable either to assign it to myself, or to rebel against it, or to resign myself to it. Besides, everything that happens to me is *mine*; we must take this to mean in the first place that, as a man, I am always equal to what happens to me, because what happens to one man, through other men and through himself, can only be human. The most atrocious war situations, the worst tortures, do not create an inhuman state of affairs. There is no inhuman situation: it is only that, through fear, flight, and the recourse to magical modes of behavior, I can *decide* on the inhuman; but this decision is human and I will bear the entire responsibility for it. But, in addition, the situation is mine because it is the image of my free choice of myself, and everything it presents me with is *mine*, as that represents and symbolizes me. Am I not the one who decides on the coefficient of adversity of things, and even on their unpredictability, by deciding on myself? Thus there are no *accidents* in a life; an event in society that suddenly breaks out and drags me with it does not come from outside; if I am mobilized in a war, this war is my war, it is in my image and I deserve it. I deserve it in the first place because I could always avoid it, through suicide or desertion: these ultimate possibles are those which must always be present to us when we envisage a situation. Since I did not avoid it, I *chose* it; it might be through spinelessness, through cowardice in the face of public opinion, because I prefer certain values to that of actually refusing to make war (the esteem of those close to me, the honor of my family, etc.). In any case, it is a question of choice. This choice will be continually reiterated thereafter, right up to the end of the war; we must therefore concur with J. Romains's saying: "In war, there are no innocent victims." [105] If, therefore, I have preferred war to death or to dishonor, it is just as if I bear the entire responsibility for this war. Doubtless, other people declared it and we may be tempted, perhaps, to regard me simply as an accomplice. But this notion of complicity has only a juridical meaning; it does not apply here, because it depended only *on me* that this war should not exist for me and through me, and it was I who decided that it would exist. There was no constraint, because constraint can have no purchase on freedom;

---

105 Sartre's note: J. Romains, *Les Hommes de Bonne Volonté*: "Prélude à Verdun." TN: *Les Hommes de Bonne Volonté* is the title of a series of novels by Jules Romains, including *Prélude à Verdun* (1937), which were published between 1932 and 1947 in France, and are translated into English as Romains (1933–1947).

I had no excuse because (as we have said and repeated in this book) what distinguishes human-reality is that it has no excuse. The only thing left for me to do, therefore, is to lay claim to this war. But, in addition, the war is *mine* because, by the mere fact that it arises within a situation that I bring into being, and that I can encounter it there only by committing myself for or against it, I am no longer able now to distinguish the choice I make of myself from the choice I make of the war: to live this war is to choose myself through it and to choose it through my choice of myself. There can be no question of regarding it as "four years of holiday" or as a "suspension," or as an "adjournment of the session," while my most important responsibilities lie elsewhere, in my conjugal, or familial, or professional life. But in this war that I have chosen, I choose myself from one day to the next, and I make it mine as I make myself. If it is to be four empty years, I am the one who bears the responsibility for that. Finally, as we pointed out in the previous paragraph, each person is an absolute choice of himself on the basis of a world of knowledge and techniques which this choice accepts and illuminates at the same time; each person is an absolute, who possesses an absolute date and is unthinkable at any other date. It is therefore irrelevant to wonder what I would have been if this war had not broken out, because I chose myself as one of the possible meanings of the period that was, imperceptibly, leading to war; I cannot be distinguished from that very period, and I could not be transported into any other period without contradiction. Thus I *am* this war, which bounds and limits the period preceding it, and allows it to be understood. In this sense, to define the for-itself's responsibility more clearly, we need to add to the phrase that we quoted just now—"There are no innocent victims"—this one: "We get the war that we deserve." In this way, wholly free, indiscernible from the period whose meaning I have chosen to be, and as profoundly responsible for the war as if I myself had declared it, unable to live anything without integrating it within my situation, committing myself to it entirely, and leaving my mark on it, I must exist without remorse or regret, just as I lack any excuse because, from the moment I arise in being, I carry the weight of the world that is mine on my own, without it being possible for anything or any person to alleviate it.

However, this responsibility is of a very particular type. Indeed, someone might respond to me by saying "I didn't ask to be born"—which

600

is a naïve way of emphasizing our facticity. I am indeed responsible for everything except my responsibility itself, because I am not the foundation of my being. It is therefore just as if I were forced to be responsible. I am *abandoned* in the world; this does not mean that I linger, passive and forsaken, within a hostile universe, like a plank floating on water, but, on the contrary, that I find myself suddenly alone and without aid, committed within a world for which I bear the entire responsibility, without being able—whatever I do, and not even for an instant—to separate myself from this responsibility, because I am responsible even for my desire to flee my responsibilities. To make myself passive within the world, to refuse to act on things and on others, is still to choose myself, and suicide is one way among others of being-in-the-world. However, I rediscover my responsibility as absolute, by virtue of the fact that my facticity—which is to say, in this case, the fact of my birth—eludes a direct grasp and is even inconceivable, because my birth never appears to me as brute fact but always through a pro-jective reconstruction of my for-itself: I am ashamed of being born or astonished by it, or I rejoice in it, or, by trying to take my life, I assert that I am living and I accept life in its badness. Thus, in a certain sense, I *choose* to be born. This choice itself is thoroughly affected by facticity, since I am not able not to choose; but this facticity, in turn, will appear only insofar as I surpass it toward my ends. Thus facticity is everywhere, but it eludes me; I never encounter anything but my responsibility, which is why I cannot ask "*Why* was I born?" or curse the day of my birth or assert that I did not ask to be born, because these different attitudes toward my birth— i.e., toward the *fact* that I actualize a presence within the world—are precisely nothing other than ways of accepting this birth, in full responsibility, and making it *mine*. Here, too, I never encounter anything but myself and my projects, so that in the end my abandonment, which is to say my facticity, consists merely in my being condemned to be fully responsible for myself. I am the being who is, as a being whose being is in question in his being. And this "is" of my being is like something present and elusive.

601

In these conditions, since any event in the world can be disclosed to me only as an *opportunity* (an opportunity that can be *put to use, missed, neglected,* etc.) or, better still, since we can regard everything that happens to us as a *chance*—which is to say it can appear to us only as a means of actualizing this being that is in question in our being—and since others, as transcended-transcendences, are, in their case too, only *opportunities* and *chances*, the for-itself's responsibility extends to the world in its entirety as a peopled-world. That is precisely how the for-itself apprehends itself in anguish, i.e., as a being who is the foundation neither of its being nor of the other's being, nor of the in-itselfs that form the world, but who is forced to decide on the meaning of being, within him, and everywhere outside of him. Someone who actualizes, in his anguish, his condition of *being* thrown into a responsibility that stretches back even to his abandonment no longer has any remorse, or regret, or excuse; he is no longer anything but a freedom which is absolutely disclosed to itself, and whose being resides in this very disclosure. But most of the time, as we pointed out at the beginning of this book, we flee from anguish in bad faith.

Chapter 2

TO DO AND TO HAVE

I. EXISTENTIAL PSYCHOANALYSIS

If, as we have tried to establish, it is true that human-reality becomes acquainted with itself and defines itself through the ends it pursues, an investigation and a classification of these ends becomes indispensable. In fact, in our last chapter, we examined the for-itself only in relation to its free project, which is to say the impulse through which it throws itself toward its end. We ought now to ask about this end itself, because it *forms part* of absolute subjectivity, as its transcendent and objective limit. This was glimpsed by empirical psychology, which allows that a particular man is defined by his desires. But here we should guard against two mistakes: first of all, by defining man in terms of his desires, the empirical psychologist remains a victim of the substantialist illusion. He sees desire as being in the man, as the "content" of his consciousness, and he believes that the desire's meaning lies inherent within the desire itself. In this way he avoids anything that might evoke the idea of transcendence. But if I desire a house, a glass of water, a woman's body, how can this body, this glass, or this building reside within my desire, and how can my desire be anything other than a consciousness of these objects as desirable? We must therefore be careful not to conceive of desires as little psychological entities inhabiting consciousness: they are consciousness itself, in its original pro-jective and transcending structure, insofar as it is necessarily conscious of something.

603   The other mistake is closely connected to the first; it consists in taking psychological investigation to be finished once we have reached the concrete set of empirical desires. In this way, a man can be said to be defined by the bundle of tendencies that empirical observation has been able to establish. Naturally the psychologist will not confine himself always to finding the sum of these tendencies: he will enjoy bringing to light their similarities, affinities, and harmonies; he will aim to present the set of desires as a synthetic organization, in which each desire acts upon and influences the others. A critic, for example, wishing to undertake Flaubert's "psychology," writes that he

> seems in his early youth to have felt as his normal state a continual exaltation, made up of the twofold feeling of his grandiose ambition and his invincible strength. . . . *Therefore* the exhilaration in his young blood turned into a passion for literature, as often happens to precocious souls when they approach the age of eighteen and discover in the energy of style, or the intensities of fiction, how to deceive the need for plenty of action, or an excess of feeling, which torments them.[1]

There is an attempt, in this passage, to reduce an adolescent's complex personality to a few primary desires, in the way in which a chemist reduces compound substances to being only a combination of pure elements. These primary data will be the grandiose ambition, and the need for plenty of action and an excess of feeling; these elements, when they are combined, produce a permanent state of exaltation. This latter, being nourished—as Bourget observes in some sentences that we did not quote—by much reading of well-chosen texts, will attempt to deceive itself, by expressing itself in fictions that will channel it and symbolically satisfy it. And here we have, in outline, the genesis of a literary "temperament."

1 Sartre's note: Paul Bourget, *Essais de Psychologie Contemporaine: G. Flaubert.* TN: This work was published in 1883, and has not been translated into English. Paul Bourget (1852–1935) was an influential French novelist and cultural critic.

But, in the first place, this kind of psychological *analysis* starts from the premise that an individual fact is produced by the intersection of abstract and universal laws. The fact to be explained—which in this case is the young Flaubert's literary dispositions—is resolved into a combination of *typical* and abstract desires, as we might encounter them in "the adolescent in general." Here, what is concrete is only their combination; in themselves they are only schemata. By hypothesis, therefore, the abstract is prior to the concrete and the concrete is only an organization of abstract qualities; the individual is only the intersection of universal schemata. But—in addition to the logical absurdity of such a premise—we can clearly see, in the example we have chosen, that it fails to explain precisely what gives the pro-ject we are considering its individuality. The fact that "the need to feel excessively"—a universal schema—deceives itself and becomes channeled through the need to write is not an *explanation* of Flaubert's "vocation"; on the contrary, it is what needs to be explained. Of course we may invoke a thousand slender circumstances, unknown to us, which have shaped this need to feel into a need to act. But, in the first place, this abandons any explanation and falls back precisely on something undetectable.[2] Furthermore, it displaces what is purely individual—which is banished from Flaubert's subjectivity—into the external circumstances of his life. Finally, Flaubert's correspondence proves that from his earliest childhood, long before his "adolescent crisis," Flaubert was tormented by the need to write.

604

At each stage of the aforementioned description we encounter a gap. Why do ambition and the feeling of his strength produce in Flaubert a state of *exaltation* rather than calm expectation or gloomy impatience? Why does this exaltation become particularized into a need to act too much and to feel too much? Or, rather, what is this need doing here, at the end of the paragraph, where—through a process of spontaneous generation—it has suddenly appeared? And why precisely does it choose to be symbolically satisfied, rather than seeking fulfillment in acts of violence, love affairs, debauchery, or by running away? And why is this symbolic satisfaction, which does not moreover have to be artistic (for example, there is also

---

2 Sartre's note: As Flaubert's adolescence in fact does not show, as far as we know, anything particular in this respect, we have to suppose the influence of an unknown quantity of facts which, by definition, escape the critic.

mysticism), found in *writing*, rather than in painting or music? "I could have been," Flaubert writes somewhere, "a great actor." Why didn't he try to be one? In brief, we have understood nothing; we have seen a succession of accidents, of desires, each of which emerges fully armed against the others, without any possibility of grasping their genesis. The *transitions*, becomings, and transformations have been carefully hidden, and the task of bringing order into this succession has been limited to an appeal to sequences that have been empirically observed (the need to act preceding, in the case of the adolescent, the need to write) but which, taken literally, are unintelligible. And yet that is what we call "psychology." Open a biography at random and that is the kind of description you will find in it, more or less mixed up with accounts of external events and allusions to the great explanatory idols of our age: heredity, education, social background, physiological constitution. Sometimes, however—in the better books—the connection established between the antecedent and consequent, or between two concurrent and interacting desires, is not conceived merely in terms of the regularity of a sequence; sometimes it lends itself to "understanding," in the sense intended by Jaspers in his general treatise of psychopathology.[3] But this understanding remains a series of *general* connections. For example, the connection between chastity and mysticism, weakness and hypocrisy, might be perceived. But we still do not know the concrete relation between *this* chastity (*this* abstinence in relation to such and such a woman, *this* struggle against this precise temptation), and the individual content of the mysticism; moreover, this is exactly how psychiatry contents itself with bringing to light the general structures of delusions, and does not try to understand the individual and concrete content of psychoses (why this man believes that he is this historical character rather than any other, why his compensatory delusion[4] is satisfied by these notions of grandeur rather than by those others, etc.).

605

3 TN: ... *elle est "compréhensible"* ... Sartre is alluding to Jaspers's work *Allgemeine Psychopathologie*, translated into English as *General Psychopathology* (Jaspers 1963). The German term for the capacity emphasized by Jaspers is *Verstehen*, which is normally translated into English as "understanding."

4 TN: Sartre may have come across the notion of "compensatory delusion" through the work of the French psychiatrist Marcel Montassut (1897–1975), whose paper "Un Délire de Compensation" was published in 1924.

But, above all, these "psychological" explanations ultimately refer us to inexplicable basic givens. These are psychology's pure elements. We are told, for example, that Flaubert had a "grandiose ambition," and the aforementioned description rests entirely on this original ambition. So be it. But this ambition is an irreducible fact, and wholly unable to satisfy the intellect, since in this case the only reason for this irreducibility is a refusal to push the analysis any further. At the point where the psychologist stops, the fact under consideration is presented as basic. This is what explains the troubled state of resignation and dissatisfaction we are left with, when we read these psychological essays. "There we are," we say to ourselves, "Flaubert was ambitious. He was like that." To wonder why he was like that would be just as pointless as to try to find out why he was tall and blond: we have to stop somewhere; that is precisely the contingency of all real existence. This rock is covered with moss, and the rock beside it is not. Gustave Flaubert had literary ambitions and his brother Achille lacked them. That is how it is. In the same way, we wish to know the properties of phosphorus and attempt to reduce them to the structure of its component chemical molecules. But why are there molecules of this type? That is how it is, and that's all. Flaubert's psychology will consist in summing up, if it is possible, the complexity of his behavior, his feelings, and his tastes in terms of some properties, somewhat comparable to those of chemical substances, and beyond which it would be foolish to wish to go further. And yet we have the obscure sense that Flaubert did not "receive" his ambition. It is meaningful; therefore it is free. It cannot be accounted for by heredity, or a bourgeois background, or education, still less by the physiological considerations about the "nervous temperament" that were fashionable for some time: a nerve is not significant; it is a colloidal substance that has to be described in its own right, and which does not transcend itself in order to become acquainted, through other realities, with what it is. In one sense Flaubert's ambition is a fact with all its contingency—and it is true that it is impossible to reach further back, beyond the fact—but, in another, it makes itself, and our dissatisfaction serves us as a guarantee that we will be able to apprehend, beyond this ambition, something more, something like a radical decision which, 606 without ceasing to be contingent, would be the truly irreducible psychological element. What we require, therefore—and what nobody ever tries to give us—is a genuine irreducible, i.e., something irreducible whose irreducibility would be *evident* for us, which would be presented not as the psychologist's premise and the result of his refusal or incapacity to go further but which we could note with a feeling of satisfaction. And this requirement is not due, in our case, to that incessant pursuit of a cause, to that infinite regress which is often said to constitute rational investigation and which, in consequence, far from being specific to psychological inquiry, will be found in all disciplines and all problems. It is not the childish search for a "because" that would not give way to a "why?"— but, on the contrary, it is a requirement founded in a preontological understanding of human-reality and in a related refusal to consider man as something that can be analyzed and reduced to basic givens, to determinate desires (or "tendencies"), supported by the subject in the way that an object supports its properties. If in fact we are obliged to consider him in that way, we will have to choose: *Flaubert* the man, whom we may love or hate, blame or praise, who is for us the *other*, who directly attacks our own being merely by virtue of having existed, will be from the outset the unqualified substrate of these desires, i.e., a kind of indeterminate clay that passively receives them—or, alternatively, he will be reduced to the mere bundle of these irreducible tendencies. In both cases the *man* disappears; we no longer meet "him," *to whom* such and such an adventure *happened*: either, in seeking the *person*, we encounter a metaphysical substance, useless and contradictory, or, alternatively, the being we are looking for vanishes into a dust made up of phenomena interconnected by external relations. Now, what each of us requires, in our very effort to understand the Other, is in the first place that we should never have to resort to this idea of substance, which is inhuman because it stays this side of the human. And, next, it is that the being under consideration should, nonetheless, not crumble into dust, and that we should be able to find within it a unity (of which substance was only a caricature), that must be a unity of responsibility, a unity that we can love or hate, blame or praise—in brief, the unity of a *person*. This unity, the being of the man under consideration, is a *free unification*. And the unification cannot come *after* some diversity which it unifies. Rather, for Flaubert, as for any subject of a "biography," *to be* is to unify oneself within the world. The irreducible unification that we need to encounter, which is Flaubert, and which we are asking the biographers to reveal to us, is therefore the unification of an *original project*, a unification that must be revealed to us in the form of a

non-substantial absolute. And so we must abjure any irreducible items and, by   607
using as our criterion the evidence itself, continue our investigation until
it is evident that we cannot and should not go any further. In particular,
we should not try to reconstitute a person out of his inclinations, any
more than we should attempt, according to Spinoza, to reconstitute a
substance or its attributes by adding together its modes. Any desire that is
presented as irreducible is absurdly contingent, and drags into absurdity
human-reality taken as a whole. If for example I declare that one of my
friends "likes boating," I deliberately propose to bring the investigation
to an end there. But, on the other hand, in doing this I constitute a contingent *fact* that nothing can explain and which, even if it has the gratuitous quality of a free decision, has none of its autonomy. For I cannot
regard this inclination toward boating as Pierre's fundamental project; in
itself it has a secondary and derivative quality. Those who describe a personality in this way, by successive strokes, almost imply that each one of
these strokes—each of the desires considered—is connected to the others
by relations that are purely contingent and external. Those who, on the
contrary, attempt to explain this affective condition end up taking the
path of what Comte called *materialism*, i.e., the explanation of the higher in
terms of the lower. It might be said, for example, that the subject being
considered is "sporty," that he enjoys exerting himself and, in addition,
that he is a countryman who especially likes outdoor sports. Thus, beneath
the desire to be explained, we locate more general and less differentiated
tendencies, which relate to it uniformly, in the way in which a zoological
genus relates to the species. In this way, psychological explanation (when
it does not suddenly decide to come to a halt) sometimes places an emphasis on relations that consist purely of concurrence or constant succession
and, at other times, offers a mere classification. To explain Pierre's inclination for boating is to regard it as a member of the family of inclinations
for outdoor sports, and to connect this family with the family of tendencies toward sport in general. Moreover, we can find categories which are
even more general and impoverished, if we classify the taste for sport as
one aspect of the love of risk—which can itself be presented as a particu-
larization of the fundamental tendency toward games. It is obvious that
this so-called explanatory classification has no more value or interest than
the classifications used in ancient botany: it rests on the assumption, as in
those classifications, that the abstract has a priority of being in relation to

the concrete: as if the tendency to play games existed first in a general form, and became particularized later—according to the circumstances—into the love of sport, this latter into an inclination toward boating and this last, finally, into the desire to row on this particular river, in these conditions and in this season—and, as with those classifications, it fails to explain the concrete enrichment, at every stage, of the abstract drive under consideration. And yet how can we believe in a desire to row that is only a desire to row? Can we really accept that it should be reduced to being merely what it is? The most discerning of the moralists have illustrated the way in which desire surpasses itself; Pascal, for example, believed he had uncovered the need for diversion in hunting, in the *jeu de paume*[5] and in a hundred other pastimes—so that, within an activity that would, reduced to itself, be absurd, he revealed a meaning that transcends it, i.e., a reference to the reality of man in general, and his condition.[6] Similarly, have we not learned from Stendhal—in spite of his connection with the ideologues—and from Proust—in spite of his intellectualist and analytical tendencies—that love and jealousy cannot be reduced strictly to the desire to possess one woman but that they aim to take hold, through the woman, of the entire world? That is the meaning of Stendhal's "crystallization," and it is precisely for this reason that love, as Stendhal describes it, appears as a mode of being-in-the-world, i.e., as a fundamental relation of the for-itself to the world and to itself (ipseity), through some particular woman: the woman represents only a conducting element placed within the circuit.[7] These analyses may be inaccurate or incompletely true: nonetheless, they allow us to glimpse a method that differs from pure analytic description. The same may be said about the observations of the Catholic novelists who immediately see, in carnal love, its surpassing toward God or, in Don Juan, "a man who is never satisfied" or, in sin, "a place empty of God."[8] The task here is not to find

---

5 TN: This game (whose title is not usually translated into English) was a game played with a ball on a court, and a precursor of (indoor) tennis.

6 TN: Sartre is referring to Pascal's observations, in his *Pensées* (Pascal 1995), of man's need for "diversion" (as *divertissement* is usually translated into English).

7 TN: Sartre is referring to Stendhal's famous 1822 essay *De l'Amour*, translated as *On Love* (Stendhal 2009).

8 TN: I have not been able to find sources for these quotations; in relation to the last phrase, Sartre may well have in mind the playwright Paul Claudel (who writes of Christ's "filling an emptiness").

something abstract behind the concrete: an impulse toward God is not *less concrete* than the impulse toward such and such a particular woman. On the contrary, it is a matter of finding, beneath some partial and incomplete aspects of the subject, the genuine concretion—which can only be the totality of his impulse toward being, his original relation to himself, to the world and to the other, within the unity of *internal* relations and a fundamental project. This impulse can only be purely individual and unique: rather than taking us away from the *person* (as in Bourget's analysis, for example, which constitutes the individual by adding together general maxims), it will not lead us to find, underlying the need to write—and to write *these* books—a need for activity in general but, on the contrary, in rejecting with equal force both the theory of compliant clay and the theory of the bundle of tendencies, we will encounter the person in his constitutive initial project. That is why the irreducibility of the result we arrive at will be disclosed as evident: not because it is the poorest and most abstract result but because it is the richest; here, what we grasp in intuition will be an individual plenitude.

The question that arises may, therefore, be put in roughly these terms: if we admit that the person is a totality, we cannot hope to recompose him through an addition or organization of the various tendencies that we have empirically uncovered in him. Rather, and on the contrary, he is expressed in his entirety—although from a different angle—in each inclination, each tendency—rather as Spinoza's substance is entirely expressed in each of its attributes. If that is the case, we should be able to discover in each tendency of the subject, and each of his ways of behaving, a meaning that transcends it. This particular jealousy, *at its date*, in which the subject is historialized in relation to a specific woman, signifies, in the eyes of somebody able to read it, the global relation to the world through which the subject is constituted as a "himself." In other words, this *empirical* attitude is by itself the expression of the "choice of an intelligible character."[9] And if that is the case, there is no mystery, and neither is there any intelligible plane that is merely able to be thought, while we can grasp and conceptualize only the plane of the subject's empirical existence: if the empirical attitude *signifies* the choice of intelligible character, that is because it is *itself* this choice. In fact the distinctive character of the

609

9 TN: Sartre is referring again (as earlier in the text) to Kant's doctrine here.

intelligible choice—and we will return to this—is that it can exist only as the transcendent meaning of each concrete and empirical choice: it is not made in the first instance in some unconscious, or at the noumenal level, in order *afterward* to be expressed in this or that observable attitude; it does not even have *ontological* primacy in relation to the empirical choice but it is, as a matter of principle, something that must always be extricated from the empirical choice as its "beyond," and as the infinity of its transcendence. Thus if I am rowing on the river I am—either here or in any other world—nothing but my concrete boating pro-ject. But this project itself, as the totality of my being, expresses my original choice in some particular circumstances; it is nothing but the choice of myself as a totality in these circumstances. That is why a special method is needed in order to extricate this fundamental meaning attached to my choice, which can only be the individual secret of its being-in-the-world. It is therefore by means of a *comparison* of a subject's various empirical tendencies that we may attempt to discover and to isolate the fundamental project that they have in common, rather than merely by adding or reconstructing these tendencies: in each one of them, the person exists in his entirety.

Naturally, there are an infinite number of possible projects, just as there are an infinite number of possible men. If we must nonetheless acknowledge certain characteristics that they hold in common and try to classify these within broader categories, we should first establish some individual investigations into the cases that lend themselves most easily to study. In these investigations we will be guided by this principle: to stop only when we encounter something whose irreducibility is evident, i.e., never to believe that we have reached the initial project unless the projected end appears as the *very being* of the subject we are considering. That is why we are unable to stop at classifications such as "authentic project" and "inauthentic project of oneself," like the one Heidegger wants to establish.[10] Apart from the fact that such a classification is, despite its author, and even in its terminology, marred by an ethical concern, it is ultimately based on the subject's attitude toward his own death. But if death is a source of anguish—and if, in consequence, we can flee from anguish or throw ourselves resolutely into it—it is a truism

610

10 TN: Sartre is referring to Heidegger's discussion of authenticity in Heidegger (1980).

to say that is because we are attached to life. It follows that we cannot regard our anguish in the face of death, a resolute decision, and a flight into inauthenticity as fundamental projects of our being. On the contrary, they can be understood only on the foundation of an initial project *to live*, i.e., on the basis of an original choice of our being. In each case we ought, therefore, to reach beyond the results of Heidegger's hermeneutic, toward a project that is still more fundamental. And this fundamental project should not make reference to any other, and must be conceived on its own. It cannot therefore be concerned with death, or life, or any particular characteristic of the human condition: a for-itself's original project *can aim only at its being*; indeed, the project of being, or desire to be, or tendency toward being, does not derive from some difference in physiology or empirical contingency; it cannot be distinguished, in fact, from the for-itself's being. That is because the for-itself is a being whose being is in question in its being in the form of a project of being. *To be* for-itself is to become acquainted with what one is through a possible and in terms of a value. The possible and the value belong to the for-itself's being. That is because the for-itself is described ontologically as a *lack of being*, and the possible belongs to the for-itself as *what is missing from* it, just as value haunts the for-itself as its *missed* totality of being. What we expressed, in Part Two, in terms of a lack can be equally well expressed in terms of *freedom*. The for-itself chooses because it is a lack: freedom is one and the same as the lack; it is the concrete mode of being of the lack of being. Ontologically, therefore, it makes no difference whether we say that value and the possible exist as the internal limits of a lack of being that can exist only as a lack of being, or that freedom, in arising, determines its possible and thereby circumscribes *its* value. Thus the point at which we can reach back no further, and where we meet something evidently irreducible, is the point when we reach the *project of being*: for evidently one can go no further back than *being*, and, between the project of being, the possible, value, and, on the other hand, *being*, there is no difference. Man is fundamentally the *desire to be*, and the existence of this desire is not to be established through empirical induction; it comes out of an *a priori* description of the for-itself's being, since desire is a lack and the for-itself is the being that is, in relation to itself, its own lack of being. The original project that is expressed in each of our empirically observable tendencies is therefore the *project of being*; or, alternatively, each empirical tendency relates to the original project of being as its expression and symbolic fulfillment—as conscious drives, in Freud's view, relate to the complexes and the original libido. Moreover the desire to be does not in any sense exist first, in order to become expressed *afterward* by the *a posteriori* desires; instead, it is nothing other than the symbolic expression it discovers within the particular desires. There is not first *one* desire to be, and then a thousand particular feelings; rather, the desire to be only exists, and is only manifested, in and through our jealousy, avarice, love of art, cowardice, or courage, and the thousand empirical and contingent expressions in consequence of which human-reality only ever appears to us as *manifested by such and such a man*, by a particular person.

As for the being that is the object of this desire, we know *a priori* what it is. The for-itself is the being that is, in relation to itself, its own lack of being. And the being that is missing from the for-itself is the in-itself. The for-itself arises as the nihilation of the in-itself, and this nihilation is defined as a pro-ject toward the in-itself: between the nihilated in-itself and the projected in-itself, the for-itself is a nothingness. Thus the goal and the end of the nihilation that I am is the *in-itself*. Thus human-reality is the desire to-be-in-itself. But the in-itself that it desires cannot be pure in-itself, contingent and absurd, and comparable in every respect to the in-itself that it encounters and nihilates. In fact, as we have seen, we can understand nihilation in terms of a rebellion on the part of the in-itself, which nihilates itself in opposition to its contingency. To say that the for-itself exists its facticity—as we saw in the chapter about the body—is equivalent to saying that nihilation is a being's futile endeavor to found its own being and that its withdrawal, in order to found it, is the source of the infinitesimal gap through which nothingness enters within being. The being that is the object of the for-itself's desire is, therefore, an in-itself that might relate to itself as its own foundation, i.e., an in-itself whose relation to its facticity would be like the for-itself's relation to its motivations. In addition, the for-itself—being the negation of the in-itself—cannot simply desire to return to the in-itself. Here, as with Hegel, the negation's negation cannot return us to our point of departure. But, quite to the contrary, the reason why the for-itself lays claim to the in-itself is precisely the detotalized totality "in-itself nihilated into for-itself"; in other words, the for-itself's project is *to be as for-itself* a being that is what it is; it is as a being that is what it is not and that is not what it is that the for-itself has the project to be what it is; it is as a consciousness that it wants to have the in-itself's impermeability and infinite density; it is as the nihilation of the in-itself, and the constant escape from contingency and facticity, that it wants to be its own foundation. That is why the possible is generally pro-jected as what is missing from the for-itself in order for it to become in-itself-for-itself; and the fundamental value presiding over this project is, precisely, the in-itself-for-itself, i.e., the ideal of a consciousness that could be the foundation of its own being-in-itself purely by means of its own being conscious of itself. To this ideal, we can give the name "God." So we can say that the best way to conceive of human-reality's fundamental project is to regard man as the being whose project is to be God. Whatever the myths and rites of any religion we may consider, God is in the first instance "felt by the heart" of man, heralding and defining him in his ultimate and fundamental project.[11] And if man possesses a preontological understanding of God's being, it is not bestowed on him by nature's grand spectacles or the power of society: but God, as the value and supreme goal of transcendence, represents the permanent limit in terms of which man becomes acquainted with what he is. To be a man is to aim to be God; or, alternatively, man is fundamentally the desire to be God.

"But," someone might say, "if that is the case, if man even as he arises points toward God as his limit, if he can choose only to be God, what becomes of freedom?" For freedom is nothing but a choice that creates its own possibilities for itself, whereas this initial project to be God by which man is "defined" seems here to verge on a human "nature" or "essence." To this, our reply will be, precisely, that if desire's *meaning* is in the last resort the project to be God, desire is never *constituted* by that meaning but represents on the contrary a *particular discovery* of its ends. And the starting point for the pursuit of these ends is a particular empirical situation; indeed it is through this pursuit itself that the environment is constituted into a *situation*. The desire to be is always actualized as the desire for a way of being. And this desire for a way of being is, in turn, expressed as the meaning of the myriad concrete desires which consti-

11 TN: ... *"sensible au coeur"* ... Sartre is quoting from Pascal's *Pensées*, where Pascal says that God is felt "by the heart," and not through reason (Pascal 1995: §278).

tute the fabric of our conscious life. Thus we find ourselves confronted with symbolic architectures that are extremely complex and which have *at least* three levels. Within empirical desire I may discern the symbolization of a fundamental and concrete desire which is *the person*, and which represents the way in which he has decided that being will be in question in his being; and, within the world, this fundamental desire in turn concretely expresses, in the particular situation in which the person is invested, an abstract and meaningful structure which is the desire to be in general, and which we must take to be *human-reality in the person*, which makes up his commonality with the others and allows us to claim that there is a truth about man, and not merely a set of incomparable individuals. A state of absolute concreteness and wholeness, therefore, an existence in the form of a totality, belongs to the free and fundamental desire, or the *person*. Empirical desire is only its symbolization. It refers to it, and draws its meaning from it—while remaining at the same time something partial and reducible, because empirical desire is unable to be

613   conceived by itself. On the other hand, the desire to be, in its abstract purity, is the *truth* of the fundamental concrete desire, but it does not belong to the domain of the real. Thus the fundamental project, or the person, or the free actualization of the truth of humanity, is omnipresent, and in every desire (with the restrictions mentioned in the previous chapter concerning, for example, "indifferents"):[12] we only ever grasp it through our desires—just as, even though space is a particular reality and not a concept, we are only able to grasp space through the bodies that inform it—or, alternatively, it is like Husserl's *object*, which is only delivered to us through its "*Abschattungen*" and which, however, cannot be contained within any one *Abschattung*. In the light of these remarks, we are able to see that, although the abstract and ontological structure instantiated by the "desire to be" may well represent the fundamental and *human* structure of the person, it cannot fetter his freedom. Freedom—as we showed in the previous chapter—is equivalent in every respect to nihilation: the only being that we can describe as free is the being that nihilates its being. Moreover, we know that nihilation is a *lack of being* and could not be otherwise. Freedom is, precisely, the being that makes itself as a

---

12 TN: Sartre refers to the Stoic doctrine of "indifferents" at EN 515.

lack of being. But as desire, as we have established, is identical to the lack of being, freedom can arise only as a being that makes itself the desire to be, i.e., as the project-for-itself of being in-*itself-for-itself*. We arrive here at an abstract structure that cannot in any way be regarded as freedom's nature or essence, because freedom is existence and existence, in it, precedes essence; freedom arises immediately as concrete and cannot be distinguished from its choice, i.e., from the *person*. But the structure we are considering may be said to be freedom's truth, which is to say that it is freedom's human meaning.

It must be possible to establish the human truth of the person, as we have tried to do, by means of an ontological phenomenology—the nomenclature of empirical desires must be the object of a distinctively psychological investigation; we may use observation and induction and—if required—experimentation to draw up this list and to point out to the philosopher relations that can be understood, which may connect together various desires and actions, and to highlight certain concrete connections between "situations" that are defined in experimental terms (and which are only generated, basically, by restrictions that have been placed, for the sake of positivism, on the subject's fundamental situation in the world) and the experimental subject. But to establish and classify fundamental desires, or *persons*, neither of these two methods is suitable. There can be no question in point of fact of our ascertaining *a priori* and ontologically something that appears with all the unpredictability of a free act. And that is why we will restrict ourselves here to pointing out in very rough terms the possibilities of such an inquiry and its outlook: 614
that it is possible to submit any man to an inquiry of this kind is a feature of human-reality in general or, alternatively, something that an ontology can establish. But the inquiry itself and its results stand, by definition, completely outside the possibilities of an ontology.

On the other hand, a straightforward empirical description will only be able to give us lists of names and bring us into the presence of pseudo-irreducibles (the desire to write, to swim, a taste for risk, jealousy, etc.). In point of fact we ought not only to draw up a list of actions, drives, and inclinations; we must go further and *decipher* them, which is to say we need to know how to *interrogate* them. This inquiry can only be undertaken in accordance with the rules of a specific method. We will call this method "existential psychoanalysis."

The *principle* of this psychoanalysis is that man is a totality and not a collection. In consequence, he is expressed in his entirety by his most insignificant and most superficial demeanors; in other words, there is no taste, tic, or human act that does not reveal something.

The *goal* of psychoanalysis is to *decipher* man's empirical behavior, i.e., to place in full daylight the revelations each behavior contains, and to determine them conceptually.

Its *point of departure* is *experience*; its *reference point* is the preontological and fundamental understanding of the human person possessed by man. Even though most people may in fact neglect the clues that are contained in a movement, a word, or a facial expression, and be mistaken about the revelation they provide, each person is no less possessed of the *a priori sense* of the revelatory value of these manifestations, and no less capable of deciphering them, at least if someone helps him and takes his hand. Here, as elsewhere, we do not hit upon the truth by accident: it does not belong in a domain where we are required to seek it out without ever having any antecedent sense of it, in the way in which we can go looking for the sources of the Nile or the Niger. It belongs *a priori* to human understanding, and the essential work is a hermeneutic, i.e., the work of deciphering, establishing, and conceptualizing it.

Its *method* is comparative: since in fact each instance of human behavior symbolizes in its way the fundamental choice that needs to be uncovered and since, at the same time, this choice is concealed in each instance by accidental characteristics and its historical juncture, it is by comparing these ways of behaving that we will be able to make the unique revelation, differently expressed in each one of them, come forth. We are provided with a first sketch of this method by Freud and his disciples. It is appropriate, therefore, to point out here more precisely the ways in which existential psychoanalysis takes its inspiration from psychoanalysis in the strict sense, and the ways in which it differs from it radically.

615

Both of them consider all the discernible objective manifestations of "psychological life" to maintain the relation of symbolization to symbol with the fundamental and global structures which strictly constitute the *person*. Both of them hold that there are no primary data—inherited inclinations, character, etc. Existential psychoanalysis knows of nothing *before* the original arising of human freedom; empirical psychoanalysis presents the individual's initial affectivity as a virgin wax *before* its history.

The libido is nothing outside its concrete fixations, apart from a permanent possibility of becoming fixed in any way on any object. Both consider the human being as a constant historialization and seek to discern the meaning, orientation, and incarnations of this history, rather than static and permanent givens. Both of them, on account of this, consider man within the world and do not conceive that we might interrogate a man about what he is without taking account above everything of his situation. Psychoanalytical modes of inquiry aim to reconstitute the subject's life from his birth to the moment of his treatment; they make use of all the objective documents that they are able to find: letters, testimonies, diaries, "social" information of all kinds. And what they are aiming to recover is not so much a pure psychological event as a dyad: the crucial event of childhood and the psychological crystallization around this event. What we have here is again a *situation*. Each "historical" fact, from this point of view, will be regarded at the same time as a *factor* in psychological evolution and as a *symbol* of this evolution. Because in itself it is nothing, it can act only in accordance with the way in which it is taken up, and this very manner of taking it up symbolically translates the individual's inner disposition.

Empirical and existential psychoanalysis both look for a fundamental attitude in situation, which cannot be expressed through simple and logical definitions, because it is prior to any logic, and which demands to be reconstructed in terms of the laws of specific syntheses. Empirical psychoanalysis seeks to determine the *complex*, whose very name points to the multifaceted character of all the meanings that relate to it. Existential psychoanalysis seeks to determine the *original choice*. This original choice, which is made in the face of the world and is the choice of a position within the world, is totalizing. Like the complex, the original choice is prior to logic; it *chooses* the person's attitude in relation to logic and principles. In interrogating it, therefore, there can be no question of conforming to logic. The original choice gathers together the totality of the existent, within a pre-logical synthesis and, as such, it is the center of reference for an infinite number of multifaceted meanings. In neither 616 of our two types of psychoanalysis is the subject regarded as being in a privileged position from which to proceed to these inquiries into himself. Each of them aims to be a strictly objective method, which treats the findings of reflection, just as much as the testimony of others, as documents. Of course, the subject *can* carry out a psychoanalytical inquiry into himself. But he will have to give up all at once the advantage of his particular position and interrogate himself exactly as if he were someone else. Empirical psychoanalysis sets out, in fact, by postulating the existence of an unconscious psyche which evades the subject's intuition as a matter of principle. Existential psychoanalysis rejects the premise of the unconscious: for it, psychological facts are coextensive with consciousness. But if the fundamental project is fully *lived* by the subject and, as such, fully conscious, that does not at all mean that it must by the same token be *known* by him but quite the contrary; the reader will recall perhaps how careful we were in our Introduction to distinguish between consciousness and knowledge. Admittedly, as we also saw, reflection may be regarded as a quasi-knowledge. But what it grasps at each instant is not the for-itself's pure project as it is symbolically expressed—and often in many ways at once—through the concrete behavior that it apprehends: it is the concrete behavior itself, which is to say the particular desire at its date, densely tangled in its characteristics. It grasps symbol and symbolization at the same time; it is, certainly, entirely constituted by a preontological understanding of the fundamental project; better still, insofar as reflection is *also* a non-thetic consciousness of the self in the form of reflection, it *is* this very project, as well as the nonreflective consciousness. But it does not follow from this that it has the instruments and techniques necessary to isolate the symbolized choice, to determine it in concepts and to place it on its own in the full light of day. It is penetrated by a great light without being able to express what the light illuminates. It is not at all a matter of an unsolved puzzle, as the Freudians believe: everything is there, illuminated; reflection takes possession of all of it, grasps all of it. But, rather, this "mystery in full light" comes about because this possession lacks the means which ordinarily allow for *analysis* and *conceptualization*.[13] It grasps everything, all at once, without shadows, without salience, without proportion—not because these shadows, these values, these points of salience, exist somewhere and are hidden from it but rather because it is the role of a different human attitude to establish

---

13 TN: Sartre's earlier use of the phrase in quotation marks (at EN 582) makes it clear that he is alluding to Maurice Barrès.

them, and they can only exist *through and for* knowledge. Reflection, which is unable to serve as the basis for existential psychoanalysis, merely provides it with the raw materials in relation to which the psychoanalyst is obliged to take up an objective attitude. Only in this way will he be able *to know* what he *already understands.* The outcome is that the complexes 617 that are uprooted from the unconscious depths, like the projects that are uncovered by existential psychoanalysis, are apprehended from *the Other's point of view.* Accordingly the *object* that is hereby brought to light will be articulated in terms of the structures of a transcended-transcendence, i.e., its being will be being-for-the-Other even if, moreover, the psychoanalyst and the subject of the psychoanalysis are identical. Thus the project that both types of psychoanalysis bring to light can only be the person's totality, the irreducible fact of transcendence, as they are in their *being-for-the-other.* What escapes forever from these investigative methods is the project as it is for itself, the complex in its own being. This project-for-itself can only be *enjoyed;*[14] there is an incompatibility between existence for itself and objective existence. But the object of the psychoanalyses does not have any less of the *reality of a being;* furthermore, the subject's knowledge of it can help to *illuminate* reflection, and the latter can thereby become something to be enjoyed as a quasi-knowledge.

There the resemblances between the two types of psychoanalysis come to an end. They differ to the extent that empirical psychoanalysis has decided what is irreducible, rather than allowing it to make itself known in an evident intuition. Indeed the libido, or the will to power,[15] constitutes a psychobiological residue that is not clear in itself and which does not strike us as *needing to be* the irreducible term of research. In the end it is experience which establishes that the foundation of the complexes is this libido or this will to power, and the results of empirical inquiry are utterly contingent and unconvincing; nothing prevents us from being able to conceive *a priori* of a "human-reality" which does not express itself

14 TN: ... *joui* ... This is the first of two uses of *jouir* in the paragraph: in translating it as "to enjoy," I have in mind the sense in which that verb can mean "to have," as, for example, when we say someone "enjoys" good health. As before, the reader should also bear in mind the sexual connotations of the French verb and noun.

15 TN: The French phrase *volonté de puissance* is used to translate Nietzsche's concept *Der Wille zur Macht*, which is usually translated into English as "the will to power."

through the will to power, whose libido does not constitute the original and undifferentiated project. The choice, on the contrary, to which existential psychoanalysis leads us back, accounts for its original contingency, precisely because it is a choice, because the contingency of the choice is the reverse side of its freedom. In addition, insofar as it is founded on the *lack of being*, conceived of as a fundamental character of being, it is legitimized *as a choice*, and we know that we do not have to push back any further. Each result will be therefore fully contingent and at the same time legitimately irreducible. Moreover, it will always remain *particular*, which is to say that we will not reach, as the ultimate goal of our research and the foundation of all behavior, an abstract and general term—the libido, for example—which becomes differentiated and concretized into complexes and then into individual instances of behavior by the action of external facts and the subject's history but, on the contrary, a choice that remains unique and which is, from its origin, absolutely concrete; individual ways of behaving may express or *particularize* this choice, but they cannot make it any more concrete than it is already. For this choice is nothing other than the *being* of each human-reality, and whether one says that some partial behavior *is*, or that it expresses, the original choice of this human-reality comes to the same thing, since there is no difference for human-reality between existing and choosing itself. We can understand, in consequence, that existential psychoanalysis does not need to go beyond the fundamental "complex," which is precisely a choice of being, in order to reach some abstraction like the libido, which supposedly explains it. The complex is the ultimate choice; it is a choice of being and it *makes itself such*. Each time it is brought to light it reveals itself to be an irreducible event. From this it necessarily follows that the libido and the will to power do not belong to existential psychoanalysis—either as general characteristics which all men have in common, or as irreducible terms. At the most we might observe, after investigation, that for some subjects these express, in the form of particular configurations, a fundamental choice that we cannot reduce to either of them. We have seen, in fact, that desire and sexuality in general express the for-itself's original attempt to retrieve its being that has been alienated by the Other. The will to power also presupposes, at its origin, being-for-the-Other, an understanding of the other and the choice to gain one's salvation through the other. The foundation of this attitude must be in an initial choice that

618

enables us to understand how being-in-itself-for-itself may become radically assimilated with being-for-the-Other.

The fact that the final term in this existential inquiry must be a *choice* distinguishes more clearly still the psychoanalysis whose method and principal features we are outlining: through that claim, it abandons the assumption that the environment acts mechanically on the subject under consideration. The environment can only act on the subject to the precise extent to which he understands it, which is to say transforms it into his situation. No objective description of this environment could therefore be of use to us. From the outset, the environment conceived as a situation refers us back to the for-itself which chooses, exactly as the for-itself refers to his environment through his being in the world. In abandoning any type of mechanical causation, we also abandon any *general* interpretations of the symbolism we have in view. As our aim cannot be that of establishing empirical laws of succession, we will not be able to construct a universal symbolism. Instead, the psychoanalyst will have to reinvent a symbolism each time, according to the particular case he is considering. If being is a totality, it is not in fact conceivable that basic links of symbolization might exist (feces = gold, pincushion = breast, etc.), retaining a constant meaning in each case, which is to say remaining unaltered when one moves on from one signifying structure to another structure. In addition, the psychoanalyst will never lose sight of the fact that the choice is a living one and that, in consequence, it may always be *revoked* by the subject he is studying. We demonstrated, in the previous chapter, the importance of the *instant*, which represents the sudden changes in orientation and the taking up of a new position in relation to an unchanging past. Henceforth we must always be ready to consider that symbols can change in meaning, and to abandon the system of symbols used so far. Thus existential psychoanalysis has a duty to be entirely flexible and to be guided by the slightest observable changes in the subject: the task here is to understand the *individual*, and often even an instant. Because of this, the method that was used for one subject may not be employed for another subject, or for the same subject in a later period.

And precisely because the aim of the inquiry must be to discover a *choice*, and not a *state*, this inquiry will be obliged to remember on each occasion that its object is not some given, buried in the shadows of the unconscious, but a free and conscious determination—which is not

619

even an inhabitant of consciousness but is as one with that consciousness itself. Empirical psychoanalysis, to the extent to which its method is more valuable than its principles, often heads in the direction of an existential discovery, even though it always stops on the way. When it gets nearer in this way to the fundamental choice, the subject's resistances suddenly collapse, and all at once he *recognizes* the image of himself with which he is presented, as if he were seeing himself in a mirror. This involuntary testimony on the part of the subject is precious to the psychoanalyst; in it he sees a sign that he has reached his goal; he is able to move on from his investigations, in the strict sense, to the treatment. But nothing in his principles or his initial premises allows him to understand or to make use of this testimony. What would entitle him to do this? If the complex really is unconscious, which is to say if the sign is separated from its meaning by a barrier, how could the subject recognize it? Is it the unconscious complex which recognizes itself? But doesn't it lack *understanding*? And if we had to concede to it a faculty of understanding signs, would we not have to turn it at the same time into an unconscious which is conscious? What indeed is it to understand if it is not to be conscious that one has understood? Should we say, on the contrary, that it is the subject insofar as he is conscious who recognizes the image put forward? But how would he be able to compare it to what truly affects him, since that is out of reach and he has never had knowledge of it? At most he will be able to judge that the psychoanalytic explanation of his case is a *probable* hypothesis, which derives its probability from the amount of behavior it explains. He will therefore find himself, in relation to this interpretation, in the position of a third party, of the psychoanalyst himself: he has no privileged position. And if he *believes* in the probability of the psychoanalytical hypotheses, will this mere belief, which remains within the limits of his consciousness, also be able to burst through the barriers that form a dike against his unconscious drives? Doubtless the psychoanalyst has a vague image of a sudden coincidence of the conscious with the unconscious. But he has deprived himself of the means to conceive of this coincidence in positive terms.

620   However, the subject's illumination is a fact. There is indeed an intuition there, accompanied by evidence. The subject, guided by the psychoanalyst, does something more, and better, than assenting to a hypothesis: he touches and he sees what he is. That can only really be understood

if the subject has never stopped being conscious of his deep drives or, better, if these drives are not to be distinguished from his consciousness itself. In this case, as we saw earlier, psychoanalytic interpretation does not bring him to *gain consciousness* of what he is: it makes him *gain knowledge* of it. It is therefore the task of existential psychoanalysis to claim that the subject's final intuition is final.

This comparison provides us with a better understanding of what existential psychoanalysis must be if it is to be able to exist. It is a method that aims to bring to light, in a strictly objective form, the subjective choice through which each person makes himself a person, i.e., acquaints himself with what he is. As what it looks for is a *choice of being* at the same time as a *being*, it must reduce individual modes of behavior to the fundamental relations of *being*—not of sexuality or will to power—that are expressed in this behavior. It is therefore guided from the beginning toward an understanding of being and must not take on any goal other than that of finding being, and the being's way of being as it confronts that being. Before it has reached that goal, it is not allowed to stop. It will make use of the understanding of being that is a characteristic of the inquirer insofar as he is himself human-reality; and, as it seeks to disengage being from its symbolic expressions, it will have to reinvent each time, on the basis of a comparative study of types of behavior, a system of symbols with the intention of deciphering them. Its criterion of success will be the number of facts that its hypothesis allows it to explain and to unify, along with an evident intuition of the irreducibility of the final term at which it arrives. In addition to this criterion there will be, in all cases where this is possible, the subject's decisive testimony. The results that are thereby achieved—i.e., the individual's ultimate ends—may at that point become the object of a classification, and it is on a comparison of these results that we will be able to base some general considerations about human-reality as an empirical choice of its own ends. The actions studied by this psychoanalysis will not only be dreams, parapraxes,[16] obsessions, and neuroses but also, and especially, the person's thoughts from the night before, his well-adapted and successful actions, his style, etc. This psychoanalysis has not yet found its Freud: at the most we may

16 TN: ... *les actes manqués* ... This French expression is normally used to translate Freud's term "parapraxis" (or, in other English translations, "bungled acts").

be able to get a sense of it from some especially accomplished biographies. We hope moreover to be able to attempt to provide two examples of it, in relation to Flaubert and Dostoyevsky. But it does not greatly matter to us here whether this method exists: the important thing for us is that it should be possible.

621   II. TO DO AND TO HAVE: POSSESSION

The findings about behavior and desire that can be obtained through ontology should serve as the principles of existential psychoanalysis. That does not mean that there are abstract desires that exist, common to all men, prior to any specification but that there are structures to concrete desires which fall under the study of ontology because every desire expresses all of human-reality, and this applies no less to the desire to eat or to sleep than to the desire to create a work of art. As we have shown elsewhere,[17] indeed, our knowledge of man must be totalizing; in this area, empirical and partial items of knowledge are devoid of meaning. We will therefore have finished our task if we use the knowledge that we have acquired so far to lay down the bases for existential psychoanalysis. It is there, in fact, that ontology should come to a stop: its final discoveries are the first principles of psychoanalysis. From that point on, another method will be necessary, since the object is different. What therefore does ontology teach us about desire, insofar as desire is the being of human-reality?

Desire is a lack in being, as we have seen. As such, it is immediately *directed on* the being that it lacks. This being, as we have seen, is in-itself-for-itself, a consciousness that has become substance, a substance that has become its own cause, a Man-God. In this way the being of human-reality is not originally a substance but a lived relation: the terms of this relation are the original in-itself, frozen in its contingency and facticity, and whose essential characteristic is that it *is*, that it *exists*, and, on the other hand, the in-itself-for-itself or value, which corresponds to

---

17 Sartre's note: *Esquisse d'une Théorie Phénoménologique des Émotions* (Hermann, Paris, 1939). TN: This text (whose French title Sartre gets slightly wrong here) is translated into English as Sartre (1994).

the contingent in-itself's ideal, and is characterized as being beyond all contingency and all existence. Man is neither one nor the other of these beings, because he is not: he is what he is not, and he is not what he is; he is the nihilation of the contingent in-itself insofar as the "itself" involved in this nihilation is its forward flight toward the in-itself that is its own cause. Human-reality is purely the endeavor to become God, an endeavor that is without any given substratum, and in which there is nothing to make this effort. Desire expresses this endeavor.

Nonetheless, desire is not defined only in relation to the in-itself-that-is-its-own-cause. It is also relative to a brute and concrete existent, commonly known as the desire's object. This object will sometimes be 622 a piece of bread, sometimes a car, sometimes a woman, sometimes an object that has not yet been produced and which is nonetheless determinate, as when an artist desires to create a work of art. In this way desire expresses in its very structure man's relation with one or several objects in the world; it is one of the aspects of being-in-the-world. From this point of view, it seems at first that this relation does not belong to just one type. We talk of the "desire for something" only as an abbreviation. In fact a thousand empirical examples show that we desire to possess this object or to make [faire] that thing or to be someone. If I desire this painting, it means that I desire to buy it, in order to appropriate it. If I desire to write a book, or to go for a walk, it means I desire to do that book, or to do that walk.[18] If I adorn myself, it is because I desire to be beautiful; I educate myself in order to be learned, etc. Thus, right from the outset, the three great categories of concrete human existence make their appearance in their original relationship: to do, to have, and to be.

It is easy to see, however, that the desire to do or to make something is not irreducible. One makes an object in order to maintain a certain relationship with it. This new relationship may be immediately reducible to "having" it. For example, I chisel a walking stick out of the branch of a tree (I "make" a stick with a branch) in order to have this stick. The "making" [faire] can be reduced to a means of having. That is most often the case. But it may also happen that my activity does not immediately

18 TN: ... faire ce livre, faire cette promenade ... Although "to do that book" sounds a little odd, I translate that way to signal Sartre's repetition of the verb faire.

appear to be reducible. It may seem to be gratuitous, as in the case of scientific research, sport, and aesthetic creation. Yet the *doing*, in these various cases, is not irreducible either. If I create a painting, a play, a melody, it is in order to be at the origin of some particular existence. And this existence is of interest to me only to the extent to which the creative relation that I establish between it and myself gives me a particular property right over it. It is not only that this painting, for which I have had the idea, should exist: it must, further, exist *through me*. The ideal would obviously be, in one sense, that I would sustain it in being through a kind of continuous creation and that, by so doing, it would be *mine* in the form of a constantly renewed emanation. But, in another sense, it is necessary for it to be radically distinct from myself, in order for it to be *mine* and not *me*; the danger here would be, as in Descartes's theory of substances, that through a lack of independence and objectivity its being would become reabsorbed into my being; and so it is also necessary that it should exist *in itself*, i.e., that it should constantly renew its existence *by itself*. Thereafter my work will appear as a creation that is continuous but frozen into the in-itself; it forever bears my "mark," which means it is forever "my" idea. Every work of art is a thought, an "idea"; to the extent that it is nothing but a meaning, its traits are clearly spiritual. But, on the other hand, this meaning, this thought which is, in one sense, constantly in actuality, as if I were perpetually forming it, as if some mind were tirelessly conceiving it—a mind that is *my* mind—this thought maintains itself on its own in being, and does not in any way cease to be active when I am not currently thinking it. I am therefore in the twofold relationship with it of a consciousness that *conceives* it and a consciousness that *encounters* it. It is precisely this twofold relationship that I express when I say that it is *mine*. We will be able to see its meaning when we have clarified the meaning of the category "to have." And it is in order to maintain this twofold relationship within the synthesis of appropriation that I create my work. This synthesis of the me and the not-me (intimacy, the translucency of thought; opacity, the indifference of the in-itself) is what I am aiming it, and is precisely what will make this work into my property. In this sense, I am able to appropriate to myself not only those works that are artistic in the strict sense, but this stick, which I have chiseled from a branch, will also belong to me twice over: in the first place, as an everyday object that is available for my use

623

and which I own, just as I own my clothes or my books, and, in the second place, as my work. Those people, therefore, who prefer to surround themselves with everyday objects that they have made themselves are refining the art of appropriation. They are combining with a single object, and in a single syncretic act, an appropriation by means of use and an appropriation by means of creation. We find the unity of a single project, from the case of artistic creation to that of the cigarette which "is better when you have rolled it yourself." In a short while we will return to this project, in relation to a special type of property, akin to a degraded version of it, which goes by the name of luxury, because—as we will see—"luxury" does not refer to a quality of the possessed object but to a quality of the possession.

Knowing—as we showed in the prelude to this fourth part—is still another form of appropriation. And that is why scientific investigation is no more than an attempt at appropriation. The truth that is discovered, like the work of art, is my knowledge; it is the noema of a thought that is only revealed when I form the thought, and which consequently appears to be in some way maintained by me in its existence. It is through me that an aspect of the world is revealed, and it is revealed to me. In this sense I am the creator and the possessor. And this is not because I regard the aspect of being that I uncover as a mere representation but, quite to the contrary, because this aspect that is uncovered only through me really and profoundly *is*. I am able to say that I *manifest* it, in the sense in which Gide tells us that "we must always make manifest." [19] But I encounter an independence analogous to that of the work of art in my thought's truth, i.e., in its objectivity. This thought that I am forming, and whose existence derives from me, is at the same time pursuing its existence by itself, to the extent to which it is at the same time *everyone's thought*. It is me twice over, since it is the world revealing itself to me, and me in the company of others, as I form my thought with another's mind—and it is closed off from me twice over, since it is the being that I am not (insofar as it is revealed to me) and since it is everyone's thought, from the moment it appears, a

624

---

19 TN: ... *"nous devons toujours manifester"* ... I have not been able to trace this quotation (*verbatim*) to its alleged source in Gide's writing. However, in his diaries, Gide does characterize the purpose of a literary work as being "to manifest," and he says the same about the role of the hero. See for example Gide (2000: 8).

thought that is destined to anonymity. Here again we can express this synthesis of the me and the not-me with the term "mine." But in addition, within the very idea of discovery, of revelation, an idea of the appropriation involved in using something is included. Sight is an enjoyment[20] of something; to see something is to *deflower* it. If we examine the comparisons that are usually made in order to express the relation between the knower and the known, we will see that many of them are presented in terms of a certain *rape by being seen*. The unknown object is presented as being immaculate, virgin, and is comparable to a *whiteness*. It has not yet "given up" its secret; man has not yet "*wrested*" it from it. All the images emphasize the object's ignorance of the investigations and instruments targeted at it: unaware that it is known, it goes about its business without noticing the spying eyes, like a woman surprised by a passerby as she is washing. Various darker and more precise images, such as nature's "inviolate depths," evoke the act of coitus more clearly. We tear nature's veils away, and we unveil it (cf. Schiller's "Veiled Statue at Sais");[21] all investigation always includes the idea of a nudity that is exposed to the elements by moving the obstacles that cover it, as Actaeon moves aside the branches in order better to see Diana at her toilet. And, besides, knowledge is a hunt. Bacon calls it "Pan's hunt."[22] The scholar is a hunter who surprises a naked white figure, and violates her through his gaze. The set of these images, therefore, shows us something that we may call the *Actaeon complex*. In following up this idea of hunting, moreover, we will come across another symbol of appropriation, which is perhaps still more primitive: for we hunt in order to eat. Curiosity in an animal is always sexual or to do with food. To know something is to eat it with one's eyes.[23] In fact we can observe here, in relation to the knowledge that we gain through the senses, a process that reverses the one revealed by the case of the artwork. In this latter case, we noted the relation of frozen emanation in

20 TN: *La vue est jouissance* ... The term *jouissance* is often used to refer to *sexual* enjoyment (and orgasm in particular), and the rest of the sentence shows Sartre's intention to exploit this connotation here. As the English "enjoyment" lacks this connotation, the reader should bear the possible additional meaning in mind.

21 TN: The German title of Friedrich Schiller's poem (1795) is *"Das verschleierte Bild zu Sais."*

22 TN: Sartre is referring to the English seventeenth-century philosopher Francis Bacon (1561–1626), who discusses the myth of Pan in his "On the Wisdom of the Ancients" (Bacon 1985).

23 Sartre's note: For a child, to know is effectively to eat. He wants to *taste* what he can see.

which it stands to the mind. The mind continually produces it, and yet it stands alone, as if in a state of indifference in relation to this production. This relation exists, in this form, in an act of knowledge. But it does not exclude its opposite: in knowing, consciousness pulls its object toward it and incorporates it; knowledge is assimilation; the works of French epistemology are teeming with metaphors about food (absorption, diges-tion, assimilation). Thus there is a movement of dissolution between the object and the knowing subject. The known is transformed into me; it becomes my thought and thereby consents to receive its existence from me alone. But this movement of dissolution becomes frozen, owing to the fact that the known remains in the same place, endlessly absorbed and eaten, and endlessly intact, entirely digested, and yet entirely out-side and undigested, like a pebble. We can note the importance, in naïve imaginations, of the symbol of the "undigested digested": the stone in the ostrich's stomach; Jonah in the whale's stomach. It stands for a dream of non-destructive assimilation. Unhappily however, as Hegel noted, desire destroys its object.[24] (In this sense, he said, desire is the desire to eat.) In reaction against this dialectic necessity, the for-itself dreams of an object that I might assimilate entirely, that would be me—without dissolving in me—while retaining its in-itself structure, because what I desire is exactly this object and, if I eat it, I no longer have it, and I no longer encounter anything but myself. This impossible synthesis of assimilation and the preserved integrity of what is assimilated converges, in its deepest roots, with sexuality's fundamental drives. Indeed, carnal "possession" provides us with the irritating and seductive image of a body that is constantly pos-sessed and constantly new, on which our possession leaves no trace. This is the deep symbolic meaning of the quality of "smooth," or "polished." Something smooth can be picked up and felt; it remains no less impene-trable, and escapes no less, like water, from our appropriative caress. That is why there is so much emphasis, in erotic descriptions, on the smooth whiteness of the woman's body. It is smooth: it re-forms itself beneath the caress, as water re-forms itself after the stone, in passing through it, pierced it with a hole. And at the same time, as we have seen, the lover's dream is really to be identified with his beloved object while at the same

24 TN: Hegel talks about desire destroying its object at Hegel (1977: §174). I have not been able to find a source in Hegel for the equation between desire and eating men-tioned by Sartre in the next sentence.

time preserving her individuality: the other should be me, without ceasing to be other. That is exactly what we encounter in scientific inquiry: the known object, like the stone in the ostrich's stomach, is entirely inside me, assimilated, transformed into myself, and it is entirely me; but at the same time it is impenetrable, unable to be transformed, entirely smooth, in a state of indifferent nudity like a body that is loved and caressed in vain. It remains outside; to know is to eat on the outside, without consuming. We see the sexual and the alimentary currents merge and interpenetrate, in order to constitute the Actaeon complex and the Jonah complex; we see the digestive and sensual roots joining together to give birth to the desire to know. Knowledge is at the same time *penetration* and a caress *on the surface*, digestion and a contemplation from a distance of an object that cannot be deformed, the production of a thought by means of a continuous creation and the observation of that thought's total objective independence. The known object is my *thought as a thing*. And that is precisely what I profoundly desire when I set out on my research: to grasp my thought as a thing, and the thing as my thought. The syncretic relation that blends together such diverse drives can only be a relation of *appropriation*. That is why the desire to know, however disinterested it may appear, is a relation of appropriation. One of the forms that *having* may take is *knowing*.

There remains a type of activity that we are inclined to present as entirely gratuitous: the activity of *play* and the "drives" related to it. Can we discern any appropriative drive in sport? Certainly, we must note from the outset that play, in opposing itself to the spirit of seriousness, seems to be the least possessive attitude; it strips the real of its reality. Seriousness is present when we start out from the world and attribute more reality to the world than to ourselves, at the very least when someone endows himself with reality to the extent that he belongs to the world. It is not an accident that materialism is serious, nor is it an accident either that we find it everywhere and always as the revolutionary's doctrine of choice. Revolutionaries are serious. They know themselves from the outset on the basis of the world that crushes them, and they want to change this world that is crushing them. In that respect they find themselves in agreement with their old enemies, the property owners, who also know themselves and assess themselves on the basis of their position in the world. Thus all serious thinking is thickened by the world, and coagulates; it is an abdication on the part of human-reality in favor of the world. The serious man is "of the world" and no longer seeks help from himself; he no longer even imagines the possibility of leaving the world, because he has given himself the type of existence of a rock, the consistency, the inertia, the opacity of being-in-the-midst-of-the-world. It goes without saying that the serious man buries in his depths any consciousness of his freedom, he is in *bad faith* and his bad faith aims to present him to his own eyes as a consequence: everything is a consequence for him, and there is never any principle; that is why he is so attentive to the consequences of his acts. Marx put forward the first dogma of seriousness when he affirmed the object's priority over the subject, and man is serious when he takes himself for an object.

Indeed, like Kierkegaard's irony, play liberates subjectivity. What is play, in fact, if not an activity of which man is the first origin, whose principles are posited by man, and whose consequences can only be in accordance with the principles he has posited? The moment a man apprehends himself as free and wishes to make use of his freedom, and no matter how much anguish he feels, his activity is one of play: he is, in effect, its first principle, and escapes from "natured nature";[25] he posits the value and rules of his acts himself and agrees to play only according to the rules that he himself has posited and determined. This explains why, in one sense, the world is "less real." It seems therefore that the man who plays, who applies himself to discovering himself as free in his action itself, could not in any way be concerned *to possess* a worldly being. His goal, whether he aims at it through sport, mime, or games that he plays[26] in the strict sense of the term, is to make contact with himself as a certain kind of being, precisely the being that is in question in its being. Nonetheless, the effect of these observations is not to show us that the desire *to do* is, in the case of play, irreducible. They teach us, on the con-

627

25 TN: I have added the quotation marks round this phrase, as it is rarely quoted in English. Sartre is probably alluding to Spinoza (1632–1677), who uses the Latin distinction in his *Ethics* between *natura naturans* and *natura naturata*. The former denotes nature's self-causing activity, while the latter—"nature natured"—refers to nature understood as the passive effect of a causal chain.

26 TN: ... *les jeux proprement dits* ... *Jeux*, the French word for "games," is the plural of *jeu* (the word for "play") and related to the verb *jouer* ("to play"). In order to approximate to Sartre's point about the "strict sense of the word," I have inserted the verb "to play" in the sentence.

trary, that the desire to do may here be reduced to a certain desire to be. The action is not in itself its own goal; nor does its explicit purpose represent its goal and its innermost meaning; rather the function of the action is to manifest and presentify to itself the absolute freedom that is the person's very being. This particular type of project, which has freedom for its foundation and its aim, deserves special study. Indeed, it differs radically from all the others in aiming at a radically different type of being. We ought to explain in detail its relations with the project to-be-God that we have taken to be the deep structure of human-reality. But we cannot pursue this study here: in fact it belongs to an *ethics* and it requires us first to have determined the nature and role of purifying reflection (the object of our descriptions so far has only been "complicit" reflection); in addition, the position that it requires us to take up, in relation to the values that haunt the for-itself, can only be *moral*. It remains no less true that the desire to play is fundamentally a desire to be. In this way the three categories "to be," "to do," and "to have" can be reduced, here as everywhere else, to two: the "to do" is purely transitive. A desire can only be, at bottom, a desire *to be* or a desire *to have*. On the other hand it is rare to find play in the absence of any appropriative drive. I leave to one side the desire to perform, to beat a record, which may act as a stimulus on the sportsman; I am not even talking about the desire "to have" a beautiful body or harmonious muscles, which is connected with the desire to appropriate objectively one's own being-for-the-other. These desires do not always intervene and, moreover, they are not fundamental. Rather, there is an appropriative component in the sporting action itself. Sport is in fact the free transformation of an environment within the world into an element of support for an action. This makes it, like art, something creative. Take a field of snow, a mountain pasture. To see it is already to possess it. In itself, it is already grasped in vision as a symbol of being.[27] It represents pure externality, radical spatiality; its lack of differentiation, its monotony, and its whiteness manifest the absolute nudity of substance; it is the in-itself that is nothing but in-itself, the being of the phenomenon which suddenly manifests itself outside any phenomenon. At the same time, its solid immobility expresses the in-itself's objective permanence

---

27 Sartre's note: See §3. TN: I think Sartre is referring here to the next section of this chapter (section III).

and resistance, its opacity and its impenetrability. Yet this initial enjoy-ment of it in intuition will not suffice for me. This pure in-itself, which resembles the absolute and intelligible plenum of Descartes's extension, fascinates me as the pure appearing of the not-self; what I want, then, is precisely that this in-itself should relate to me by means of the relation of emanation—while at the same time remaining in itself. That is already the meaning of the snowmen and snowballs made by youngsters: the goal is to "do something with this snow," i.e., to impose a form on it which adheres to the matter so thoroughly that the latter seems to exist for the sake of the former. But if I come closer, if I want to establish appropriative contact with the field of snow, everything changes: its scale of being is modified, so it exists inch by inch rather than existing across large spaces; and spots, twigs, and cracks have the effect of individualiz-ing each square centimeter. At the same time, its solidity melts into water. I sink into the snow right up to my knees, and if I pick up some snow in my hands, it turns into liquid between my fingers and flows away, leav-ing nothing behind; the in-itself is transformed into nothingness. At the same time, my dream of appropriating the snow vanishes. Besides, I do not know what to do with this snow that I have approached in order to look more closely at it: I cannot take hold of the field, or even reconstitute it as the substantial totality that offered itself up to my gaze, and which has suddenly and doubly collapsed. The meaning of skiing is not only that it enables me to move about quickly and to acquire a technical skill, and neither is it play (as I increase my speed, or the difficulty of my route, according to whim); it is also that it enables me to possess this field of snow. Now I am doing something with it. In other words, through my very activity as someone skiing, I modify its matter and its meaning. By virtue of appear-ing to me now, in my trajectory itself, as a slope to go down, it recovers a continuity and a unity that it had lost. Now the snow is connective tis-sue. It is contained between two terms, joining the point of departure with the point of arrival and as, in my descent, I do not consider it in itself, an inch at a time, but focus always on a point to be reached beyond the position I am presently occupying, it does not collapse into an infinity of individual details but is traveled across toward the point I assign to myself. This journey is not only an activity of displacement but also, and espe-cially, a synthetic activity of organization and combination: I extend the ski field before me in the same way as the geometer who, according to

Kant, can apprehend a straight line only by drawing it. In other respects this organization is marginal, and not focal: the field of snow is not unified for its own sake and in itself; the goal I have posited and clearly grasped, the object of my attention, is the endpoint at which I will arrive. The snowy space becomes a mass from below, implicitly; its cohesion is that of the white space contained within a circumference, for example, when I look at the circle's black line without explicitly paying heed to its surface. And, precisely because I maintain it marginally, implicitly, and unspoken, it adapts to me; I have it firmly in hand, and I surpass it toward its end as the upholsterer surpasses the hammer he is using toward its end, which is to nail a hanging to the wall. There can be no more complete appropriation than this instrumental appropriation; here the synthetic activity of appropriation is a technical activity of utilization. The snow arises as my act's matter, in the way in which the hammer arises as the pure fulfillment of the act of hammering. At the same time, I have chosen a certain point of view in order to apprehend this snowy slope: this point of view is a determinate *speed*, emanating from me, that I am able to increase or decrease at will, and which constitutes the field I am crossing into a determinate object, entirely distinct from what it would be at another speed. The speed organizes the structures according to its will; an object does or does not form part of a particular group, according to whether I have or have not adopted such and such a speed (we may think, for example, of Provence as it is seen "on foot," "by car," "by rail," "by bicycle": it presents as many different countenances, according to whether Béziers is an hour, a morning, or two days away from Narbonne, which is to say whether Narbonne is isolated and posited for itself with its surroundings, or whether it constitutes a coherent group, along with Béziers and Sète, for example. In this latter case, Narbonne's *relation to the sea* is directly accessible to intuition; in the other, it is *denied*, and can be an object only for a pure concept). I am therefore the one who *informs* the field of snow through the free speed that I allot to myself. But, at the same time, I am acting on my *matter*. The speed does not only impose a form upon a matter that is already in some way given; it *creates a* matter too. The snow, which subsided beneath my weight when I walked, which melted into water when I tried to take hold of it, suddenly solidifies as it is acted on by my speed; it carries me. It is not that I have lost sight of its lightness, its insubstantiality, its perpetual evanescence. Quite the contrary: it is precisely this lightness, this evanescence, this secret liquidity, which carry me, which means they condense and merge into each other in order to carry me. The fact is that I have a special relation of appropriation with the snow: that of gliding. We will study this relation in detail later. For now, we may grasp its meaning. By gliding I remain, as we say, superficial. That is not correct: of course, I am only skimming the surface, and this skimming deserves by itself a full investigation. But I do not for all that actualize any less of a synthesis of depth; I feel the layer of snow becoming organized even in its deepest parts in order to support me; my gliding is an action *at a distance*, which ensures that I master the matter without needing to dig myself into, or to get stuck within, this matter in order to control it. Gliding is the opposite of taking root. A root is already half-assimilated to the earth that feeds it, as a living concretion of the earth; it can make use of the earth only by becoming earth itself, i.e., by submitting itself, in a sense, to the matter of which it wants to make use. Gliding, on the contrary, actualizes a material unity in the dimension of depth without penetrating any further than the surface: it is like a feared master who has no need to insist or raise his voice to be obeyed. What an admirable image of power! This explains the well-known advice "Thus lightly touch and quickly go,"[28] which does not mean "Remain superficial; do not go deeper" but, on the contrary, "Actualize some syntheses of depth, but without compromising yourself." And gliding is an appropriation precisely because the synthesis of a supporting structure that is actualized through speed applies only to the person gliding, and only for the time in which he is gliding. The snow's solidity applies only to me, and only I am aware of it; it is a secret that it delivers to me alone, and that is already no longer true *behind me*. This glid-

630

---

28 TN: The "well-known" French phrase quoted by Sartre—*"Glissez, mortels, n'appuyez pas"*—is not well-known in English. Sartre (2000) tells us in his autobiography *Les Mots* that his grandmother used to say this to him. It comes from Pierre Charles Roy (1683–1764), who wrote:

>   *Sur un mince cristal l'hiver conduit leurs pas:*
>   *Le précipice est sous la glace;*
>   *Telle est de vos plaisirs la légère surface.*
>   *Glissez, mortels, n'appuyez pas.*

I have borrowed Samuel Johnson's English translation of the final line: "Thus lightly touch and quickly go."

ing, therefore, actualizes a strictly individual relation with matter, a historical relation; it gathers itself together and solidifies in order to carry me and it falls back, swooning, in its fragmentation, behind me. In this way, by means of my movement, I have achieved for myself something unique. The ideal of gliding is therefore to glide without a trace: it is gliding across water (by rowboat, motorboat, and above all by water-skiing, which, although it came late, represents something like the limit toward which, from this point of view, all water sports were tending). Gliding across snow is already less perfect; there is a trace behind me, and I have—however slightly—compromised myself. Gliding across ice, which scratches the ice and encounters a matter that is already wholly organized, is very inferior in quality and, if despite everything it comes off, that is for other reasons. This explains our mild disappointment when we see the imprints on the snow left behind by our skis: how much better it would be if it re-formed itself as we passed! Moreover, when we let ourselves glide down the slope, we entertain the illusion that we are making no mark on it; we ask the snow to behave like this water that it secretly is. In this way, gliding seems to resemble a continuous creation: our speed, which is comparable to consciousness and, in this case, symbolizes consciousness,[29] engenders in the matter, as long as it lasts, a deep quality which remains only as long as the speed exists, a kind of gathering together that overcomes its indifferent externality and which is undone— like a bundle—behind the gliding movement. A form-giving unification, and a synthetic condensation of the field of snow that gathers itself into an instrumental structure, which is used, in the way we use a hammer or an anvil, and adapts itself compliantly to the action, which is implicit within it and its fulfillment, a continuous and creative action on the snow's very matter, a solidification of the snowy mass by means of the gliding across it, an assimilation of the snow to water that can bear weight, docile and without memory, to a woman's naked body, left intact by the caress, and troubled to its core: such is the skier's action on reality. But at the same time the snow remains impenetrable and out of reach; in a sense, the skier's action only develops its potential. It makes it yield what it is

631

---

29 Sartre's note: We looked at the relationship of movement to the for-itself in Part Three.

able to render; it is only through the sporting action that the homogeneous and solid matter delivers up to it its solidity and homogeneity, but this solidity and this homogeneity remain properties that are hatched within the matter. This synthesis of the me with the not-me, which is brought about in this case by the action of the sport, is expressed—as in the case of speculative knowledge and the work of art—by the affirmation of the skier's right over the snow. It is my field of snow: I have crossed it a hundred times and, through my speed, I have a hundred times engendered this condensing and supporting force; it is *mine*.

To this aspect of appropriation through sport, we must add this other one: the overcoming of difficulty. It is more widely understood, and we will barely dwell on it. Before I can descend this snowy slope, I was obliged to climb up it. And this ascent presented me with another side of the snow: its resistance. I felt this resistance with my fatigue, and I was able to gauge at each moment the progress of my victory. Here the snow is assimilated to *an other*, and the everyday expressions "taming," "overcoming," "dominating," etc., show clearly that it is a matter of establishing the relation, between me and the snow, of master and slave. We can also find this aspect of appropriation in *climbing*, in *swimming*, in obstacle races, etc. The peak on which we have planted a flag is a peak we have *appropriated*. In this way, a crucial aspect of sporting activity—and especially open-air sports—is the conquest of these enormous masses of water, earth, and air which seem *a priori* to be impossible to tame and to utilize; and in each case it is not a matter of possessing the element for itself but, instead, the type of in-itself existence that is expressed through the medium of this element; it is the substance's homogeneity that we want to possess, in the form of the snow; it is the in-itself's impenetrability and its timeless permanence that we want to appropriate in the form of the earth or the rock, etc. Art, science, and our playful activities are, either totally or in part, activities of appropriation, and what they wish to appropriate, beyond the concrete object of their quest, is being itself, the absolute being of the in itself.

Thus ontology teaches us that desire is originally the desire *to be*, and that it is characterized as a free lack of being. But it also teaches us that desire is a relation with a concrete existent in the midst of the world, and that this existent is conceived in terms of the in-itself; it teaches us that the for-itself's relation to this desired in-itself is appropriation. We

632   find ourselves, therefore, in the presence of a twofold determination of desire: on the one hand, desire is defined as the desire to be a certain being which is the in-itself-for-itself, and whose existence is ideal; on the other hand, desire is defined, in the vast majority of cases,[30] as a relation with a contingent and concrete in-itself, whose appropriation is projected. Is this a case of overdetermination? Are these two characteristics compatible? Existential psychoanalysis can be secure in its principles only if ontology has antecedently determined the relation between these two beings: the concrete and contingent in-itself (or the desire's object) and the in-itself-for-itself (or the desire's ideal), and only if it has explicated the relation that connects appropriation, as a type of relation to the in-itself, to being itself, as a type of relation to the in-itself-for-itself. This is what we will attempt to do now.

What is *appropriation* or, alternatively, what do we mean in general by possessing an object? We have seen the reducibility of the category of "*making*" or "*doing*" (*faire*), in which we can at some times discern being, and at other times having; does this also apply to the category of *having*?

I see that to possess an object is, in a great many cases, to be able *to use* it. However, this definition does not satisfy me: in this café I am using this saucer and this glass; however, they are not mine; I cannot "use" this painting hanging from my wall, and yet it is *mine*. And nor is it important that, in some cases, I have the right to destroy what I possess; a definition of property in terms of that right would be highly abstract and, moreover, in a society where the economy is "managed," a boss may own his factory without having the right to close it; in the Roman Empire, the master owned his slave and did not have the right to put him to death. Besides, what does the *right* to destroy, or the right to use, mean here? I can see that this right points to something social, and that property seems to be defined within the framework of life in a society. But I can also see that a right is purely negative, and limited to preventing others from destroying or using what belongs to me. Of course, one can try to define property as a social function. But, first, if society does indeed

30 Sartre's note: Apart from in the precise case where it simply is the *desire to be*: the desire to be happy, to be strong, etc.

confer the *right* to ownership, according to certain principles, it does not follow that it creates the relation of appropriation. The most that can be said is that it *legitimizes* it. Quite to the contrary, in order for property to be able to be raised to the level of the *sacred*, it is necessary for it to exist in the first place as a spontaneously established relation between the for-itself and the concrete in-itself. And if we are able to imagine a more just collective organization in the future, where individual possession would cease—at least within certain limits—to be protected and sanctified, that still does not mean that the appropriative connection will cease to exist; it might be that it remains, in fact, at least as a *private* relation, between man and thing. Similarly, in primitive societies where the conjugal relation has not yet been legitimized and where the transmission of status is still matronymic, this sexual relation still exists, at least as a kind of common-law marriage. We must therefore distinguish between possession and the right to possess. For the same reason, I must reject any definition of the Proudhonian type—"Property is theft"—for it is beside the point. It may be, in fact, that private property is the *product* of theft, and that maintaining this property has *the effect* of despoiling an Other. But whatever its origins and its effects, it remains no less possible to describe and define property in itself. The thief regards himself as the owner of the money he has stolen. What we are concerned with, therefore, is the description of the precise relation of the thief to the goods he has stolen, just as much as the relation of the lawful owner to the property he has "honestly acquired."

633

If I consider an object that I possess, I can see that the quality of "being possessed" does not refer to it as a purely external appellation, marking its relation of externality with me: quite to the contrary, this quality defines it deeply; it appears to me and it appears to others as forming part of its being. This can be taken to such an extent that some men, in primitive societies, may be defined by saying that they are *possessed*; these men are given, in themselves, as *belonging to* . . . This can also be seen in primitive funeral ceremonies where the dead are buried with the objects that belong to them. The rational explanation—"so that they can use them"—has obviously come later. Instead, it seems that, at the time when this sort of custom spontaneously appeared, it did not seem necessary to question it. The objects had this unusual property of *belonging to* the dead.[31] They formed a totality with him; there could no more be a question of burying the deceased without his everyday objects than of burying him, for example, without one of his legs. The corpse, the cup he drank from, the knife he used, *add up to just one dead person*. The principle underlying the custom of burning widows in Malabar is easily understood:[32] the woman has been *possessed*; the dead man therefore drags her into his death, and in legal terms she is dead; the only remaining task is to help her to pass from this legal death to her *de facto* death. Those objects that cannot be buried are haunted. A ghost is nothing but the concrete materialization of the "*possessed-being*," of the house and furniture. To say that a house is haunted is to say that neither money nor effort can wipe out the absolute and metaphysical fact of *its possession* by an earlier occupant. It is true that the ghosts who haunt manors are degraded Lares deities. But what are the Lares deities themselves if not layers of possession that have been deposited, one after the other, on the house's walls and furniture?[33] Even the phrase that we use, in referring to the relation of an object and its owner, highlights the deep penetration of appropriation: to be possessed is to be *somebody's own* . . .[34] In other words, the possessed object has

634   been reached *in its being*. Moreover, as we have seen, the destruction of the possessor implies the *de jure* destruction of his possessed object and, conversely, the survival of a possessed object implies the *de jure* survival of its possessor. The bond of possession is an internal bond *of being*. I encounter the possessor in and through the object he possesses. That obviously explains the importance of *relics*, by which we do not mean only religious relics but also, and especially, the entire set of a famous man's belongings (the Museum Victor Hugo, the "objects that belonged to" Balzac, or Flaubert, etc.) in which we try to rediscover them, or our "souvenirs" of a dead loved one which seem to "perpetuate" his memory.

---

31 TN: Sartre uses the French expression *être à* ("to belong to") to convey the idea that the belongings are part of (the being of) their owners: I have had to approximate to this.

32 TN: Sartre is referring to the Malabar coast in southwest India, where *sati* was practiced. The title of an eighteenth-century tragedy by the French playwright Antoine-Marin Lemierre (1733–1793), *La Veuve du Malabar*, may well have reminded Sartre of this location in particular.

33 TN: Sartre has referred to the Lares earlier in the text, at EN 145.

34 TN: . . . *c'est être à* . . . Again Sartre is exploiting the structure of this French phrase, used to attribute ownership.

This internal and ontological link between the possessed and the possessor (which customs such as branding with a hot iron have often attempted to materialize) cannot be explained by any "realist" theory of appropriation. If it is true that realism can be defined as a doctrine that makes subject and object into two independent substances, each possessing an existence for itself and through itself, we will no more be able to conceive of appropriation than of knowledge, which is one of its forms; in the one case, as in the other, these will remain external relations that join, for a time, the subject to the object. But, as we have seen, it is necessary to attribute substantial existence to any object of knowledge. The same goes for property in general: it is a possessed object that exists in itself, and which is defined by permanence, a general atemporality, and a sufficiency of being—in short, by substantiality. The *Unselbstständigkeit* must, therefore, be placed on the side of the possessing subject. It is not possible for one substance to appropriate another substance, and, if we apprehend in things a certain quality of *"being possessed,"* it is because at its origin the for-itself's internal relation to the in-itself that is its property originates in the for-itself's insufficiency of being. It goes without saying that the possessed object is not *really* affected by the act of appropriation, any more than a known object is affected by knowledge: it remains untouched (apart from the case in which the possessed thing is a human being, a slave, a prostitute, etc.). But this quality of being possessed does not affect it any less *ideally*, in its signification: its meaning, in brief, is to reflect this possession to the for-itself.

If the possessor and the possessed are joined by an internal relation based on the for-itself's insufficiency of being, the question that arises is how to determine the nature and meaning of the *couple* that they form. As the internal relation is in fact synthetic, it brings about a unification of the possessor and the possessed. In other words, the possessor and the possessed constitute, ideally, a single reality. To possess something is to be joined with a possessed object in the way of appropriation; to want to possess something is to want to be joined to an object through this relation. Thus the desire for a particular object is not simply the desire for this object; it is the desire to be joined to this object through an internal relation, in such a way as to constitute with it the unity of the "possessor-possessed." The desire *to have* is basically reducible to the desire to be related to a specific object in a specific *relation of being*.

635

To determine this relation, our preceding remarks about the scholar's, the artist's, and the sportsman's behavior will be most useful. In each of these forms of behavior, we discerned a certain appropriative attitude. And, in each case, a feature of the appropriation was that the object appeared to us both as a subjective emanation of ourselves and, at one and the same time, in a relation of indifferent externality with us. The *mine* therefore appeared to us as a relation of being that is intermediate between the absolute internality of the *me* and the absolute externality of the *not-me*. In the same syncretic movement, it is the me becoming not-me and the not-me becoming me. But we must give a better description of this relation. In the project of possession, we encounter an "*unselbstständig*" for-itself, separated by a nothingness from the possibility that it is. This possibility is the possibility of appropriating the *object*. In addition we encounter a *value* that haunts the for-itself and which is like an ideal indication of the total being that would be actualized through the union in identity of the possible and the for-itself which is its possible, i.e., in this case the being that would be actualized if I were in the indissoluble unity of the identical, myself and my property. In this way appropriation would be a relation of being between a for-itself and a concrete in-itself, and this relation would be haunted by the ideal indication of an identification between this for-itself and the possessed in-itself.

To possess something is for it to *belong to me*,[35] i.e., for me to be the true purpose of the object's existence. Where the possession is given concretely and completely, the possessor is the possessed object's *raison d'être*. I possess this pen; in other words, this pen exists *for me*, and it was made *for me*. In the beginning, moreover, I am the one who makes the object that I want to possess for myself. My bow and my arrows: these signify objects that I have made for myself. The division of labor causes this initial relationship to fade but not to disappear. Luxury is a degraded version of it; in luxury's primitive form, I possess an object that I have *had made* for me, by people who are *mine* (slaves, servants born in the house). Luxury is therefore the form of property that comes closest to primitive property and which throws the next best light, after it, on the relation of *creation* by which appropriation is originally constituted.

---

35 TN: *Posséder, c'est avoir à moi* ... Sartre continues to exploit this construction.

This relation, in a society where the division of labor is pushed to the limit, is masked but not eliminated: the object that I possess was *bought* by me. Money represents my strength; it is less a possession in itself than an instrument for possessing. That is why, apart from the very particular case of greed, money becomes effaced by its *buying* power: it is evanescent, made in order to disclose the object, the concrete thing; it has only a transitive being. But *to me* it appears as a creative force: to buy an object is a symbolic action equivalent to creating the object. That is why money is a synonym of power: not only because it is in fact capable of getting us what we desire but, and especially, because it represents the efficacy of my desire as such. Precisely because it is transcended toward the thing, surpassed, and merely *implicated*, it represents my magical bond with the object. Money eliminates the *technical* connection between the subject and the object and renders the desire immediately operative, like the wishes of legends. Stop at a shop window with money in your pocket: the objects displayed are already more than halfway to being yours. In this way money establishes a connection of appropriation between the for-itself and the total collection of objects in the world. Through it desire is already, as such, informative and creative. In this way, through a process of continuous degradation, the creative link is maintained between the subject and the object. To have is in the first place *to create*. And the property connection that is thereby established is a connection of continuous creation: the possessed object is inserted by me into the figure of my surroundings; its existence is determined by my situation and by its integration within this very situation. My lamp is not only this electrical bulb, this lampshade, this wrought-iron base: it is a certain power to illuminate this office, these books, this table; it is a certain luminous shade of my nocturnal work, alongside my habits of reading or writing when it is late; it is animated, colored, defined by the way I use it; it is this use and only exists through it. Isolated from my office and my work, placed within a lot of objects on the salesroom floor, it has been radically "extinguished": it is no longer my lamp, not even a lamp in general; it has returned to its original materiality. Thus I am responsible for the existence of my possessions within the human order. Through my ownership, I raise them to a specific type of functional being, and my very life appears to me to be creative just because it perpetuates,

636

through its continuity, the quality of *being possessed* in each of the objects in my possession: I draw into being, along with me, the collection that surrounds me. If they are torn away from me, they die, just as my arm would die if someone tore it from me.

But the original and radical creative relation is a relation of emanation. To teach us about this relation, we have at hand the difficulties encountered by the Cartesian theory of substance. What I create—if, by "create," I mean "bring matter and form into existence"—is myself. The drama for the absolute creator—if he existed—would be the impossibility of leaving himself behind, because his creature could only be himself: from where in fact could its objectivity and its independence be drawn, since its form and its matter are *mine*? Only some kind of inertia could make it resume its shape in front of me, but, in order even for that inertia to apply, I am required to support it in existence through an act of continuous creation. Thus, to the extent to which I appear to myself as *creating* objects through the mere relation of *appropriation*, these objects are me. The pen and the pipe, the garment, the office or the house: *it is me*. The totality of my possessions reflects the totality of my being. I *am* what I *have*. It is *me* that I touch on this cup, on this ornament. This mountain that I climb *is me* to the extent to which I conquer it; and when I am at its summit—when I have "won," for the price of my effort, this wide perspective over the valley and surrounding peaks—I *am* the point of view; the panorama is me, expanded right up to the horizon, because it exists only through me, only for me.

But creation is an evanescent concept, capable of existing only through its movement. Bring it to a halt, and it disappears. At the extreme limits of its meaning, it is annihilated; either I am unable to find anything in it other than my pure subjectivity, or I encounter a naked and indifferent materiality that no longer bears any relation to me. *Creation* can only be conceived and maintained as a continuous transition from one term to the other. It must be the case that the object, in one single event of arising, is totally myself and totally independent of me. And that is just what we believe possession achieves. The possessed object—insofar as it is possessed—is a continuous creation, but it remains there nonetheless: it exists through itself, and it is in-itself; if I turn away from it, it does not thereby cease to exist; if I go away, it *represents* me in my office, in my bedroom, at this place in the world.

From the outset, it is impenetrable. This pen is entirely me, even to the extent that I no longer even distinguish it from the act of writing, which is my act. And yet, on the other hand, it is intact, and my ownership does not modify it; the relation between me and it is only an ideal relation. In one sense, I enjoy the possession of my property if I surpass it toward its use, but, if I want to contemplate it, the relation of possession fades away, and I no longer understand what possessing something means. The pipe is there, on the table, independent, indifferent. I pick it up with my hands, I finger it, I contemplate it, in order to actualize this appropriation, but, just because these movements have the purpose of allowing me to enjoy this appropriation, they miss their goal; between my fingers I have only a piece of inert wood. It is only when I surpass my objects toward a goal, when I make use of them, that I can enjoy their possession. In this way, the relation of continuous creation encompasses within it, as its implicit contradiction, the independence—absolute and in itself—of created objects. Possession is a magical relation; I am these objects that I possess, but outside and in confrontation with myself: I create them as independent of me; what I possess is myself, outside of myself, outside any subjectivity, like an in-itself that escapes me in every instant and whose creation I perpetuate in every instant. But, precisely because I am always outside of myself elsewhere, like some unfinished thing who becomes acquainted with its being through what it is not, when I possess something, I alienate myself for the sole benefit of the possessed object. The possessed thing is the strong term in the relation of possession: outside that, I am nothing but a possessing nothingness, nothing but the simple fact of possession, something incomplete, insufficient, whose sufficiency and completeness lie in that object over there. In possession, I am my own foundation insofar as I exist in itself: indeed, insofar as possession is a continuous creation, I apprehend the possessed object as being founded by me in its being. However, and on the one hand, to the extent that creation is an emanation, this object is reabsorbed within me, and is nothing but me while, on the other hand, to the extent that it is from the outset in-itself, it is not-me myself as I confront myself, objective, in itself, permanent, and impenetrable, existing in relation to myself in a relation of externality and indifference. Thus I am the foundation of myself insofar as I exist indifferently, and as in-itself, in

638

relation to myself. Now, that is precisely what the project of being in-itself-for-itself consists in. Because this ideal being is defined as an in-itself that might, as for-itself, be its own foundation, or as a for-itself whose original project would be not a way of being but a being—precisely the being-in-itself that it is. We can see that appropriation is nothing other than the *symbol* of the for-itself's ideal, or value. The dyad of the possessing for-itself and the possessed in-itself is equivalent to the being who exists in order to possess itself, and whose possession is its own creation, i.e., God. In this way, the possessor aims to enjoy the possession of his being in-itself, his being-outside. By means of possession I retrieve an object-being that I can identify with my being-for-the-Other. Through that very fact, the Other cannot surprise me; I already possess and enjoy the being that he wants to activate, i.e., myself-for-the-other. Thus possession is, in addition, *a defense against the other*. What is mine is myself as something nonsubjective, insofar as I am its free foundation.

Nonetheless, the *symbolic* and *ideal* nature of this relation cannot be overemphasized. I can no more fulfill my original desire to be my own foundation of myself by means of appropriation than Freud's patient can fulfill his Oedipus complex when he dreams that a soldier is killing the Tsar (i.e., his father). That is why *property* appears to its owner to be given in eternity and, at the same time, as requiring an infinite time to materialize. No act of *utilization* can truly actualize our appropriative enjoyment; instead, it refers to other appropriative acts, whose value is in each case merely incantatory. To possess a bicycle is to be able, in the first instance, to look at it, and then to touch it. But the action of touching it reveals itself to be insufficient; what is required is to be able to get on it and to go for a ride. But this *gratuitous* ride is itself insufficient; the bicycle would need to be used to do some shopping. And that refers us to uses that are longer, fuller—to long trips across France. But these trips themselves fragment into a thousand appropriative undertakings, each of which refers to others. In the end, as we might have predicted, it was enough to hold out a banknote for the bicycle to belong to me, but it will take my entire life to actualize this possession. In acquiring an object, this is just what I sense: possession is an undertaking that death will leave always unfinished. We are now able to grasp its meaning, which is that the relation symbolized by appropriation is impossible to achieve. In itself, there is nothing concrete about appropriation. It is not some real activity (like eating, drinking, sleeping, etc.) that can serve, in addition, as the symbol of a particular desire. On the contrary, it exists only in the capacity of a symbol; its symbolism is what gives it its meaning, its cohesion, its existence. We cannot, therefore, find any positive enjoyment in it outside its symbolic value; it is only an indication of a supreme enjoyment (that of the being that might be its own foundation), which always lies beyond all the appropriative undertakings which aim to achieve it. It is precisely the for-itself's recognition of the impossibility of *possessing* an object that brings in its wake a violent wish, on his part, to *destroy* it. To destroy something is to absorb it into me, and to maintain a relation with the destroyed object's being-in-itself as profound as that of creation. The flames that burn the farm to which I have set fire gradually actualize the fusion of the farm with myself: in becoming annihilated, it changes into *me*. Here I rediscover the relation of being that characterizes creation, but in reverse: I *am* the foundation of the burning barn; I *am* this barn, since I am destroying its being. Destruction—more subtly, perhaps, than creation—actualizes our appropriation, because the destroyed object is no longer there to present itself as impenetrable. It has the impenetrability and sufficiency of being of the in-itself that *it has been*; but, at the same time, it has the invisibility and translucency of the nothingness that I am, since *it is no longer*. This glass that I have broken, and which "was" on this table, is still there, but like an absolute transparency: all the beings that I can see are seen through it; this is what filmmakers have tried to convey by means of double exposure; it resembles a consciousness, even though it has the irreparability of the in-itself. At the same time, it is positively mine because it is only the fact that I have to be what I was that keeps the destroyed object from becoming annihilated: I re-create it by re-creating myself. In this way, to destroy something is to re-create it by assuming sole responsibility for the being of that which had existed for *everyone*. Destruction should, therefore, be classified as an appropriative form of behavior. Moreover, many appropriative undertakings have a structure that is, among other things, destructive: to utilize something is to use it up. In *using* my bicycle, I *use it up*, which means that the appropriative continuous creation is marked by a partial destruction. This process of becoming used up may, for strictly utilitarian reasons, be distressing, but, in the majority of cases, it causes a secret pleasure, almost enjoyment: that is because it *comes from us*; we are *consuming*.[36] We may observe that this expression "consumption" can refer to an appropriative destruction and at the same time to our enjoyment of food. To consume something is to annihilate it and to eat it; it is to destroy it by incorporating it. If I ride my bicycle I may be vexed that I am using up the tires, because it is difficult to get others; but the image of enjoyment that I enact with my body is that of a destructive appropriation, a "creation-destruction." The bicycle, by gliding along, and carrying me, and in its very movement, is created and made my own; but this creation impresses itself deeply into the object through the light and continuous wearing away of it that is imparted to it, and which is like the mark branded on a slave. The object belongs to me because I am the one who used it; the using up of what is *mine* is the reverse side of my life.[37]

These observations enable us to better understand the meaning of certain feelings or modes of behavior that are usually regarded as irreducible—for example, *generosity*. Indeed, the *gift* is a primitive form of destruction. We know that the potlatch, for example, involves the destruction of enormous quantities of commodities. These acts of destruction challenge the other, and bind him in chains. At this level it makes no difference whether the object is destroyed or given to the other: in one way or the other, the potlatch is an act of destruction and an enchaining of the other. In giving it away, I destroy the object just as much as by annihilating it: I eliminate the quality of being *mine* that profoundly constituted it in its being, and I remove it from my sight; I constitute it—in relation to my table, my bedroom—as *absent*; I alone will preserve for it the spectral and transparent being of *past* objects, because I am the one through whom these beings pursue an honorary existence after their annihilation. Thus the function of generosity is, above all else, destructive. The zeal for giving things by which some people are sometimes overcome is, above all else, a zeal for destruction, and *equivalent to*

36 TN: Again, Sartre probably intends to connote sexual enjoyment here; note too that the verb *consommer* (which I translate as "to consume") can also mean "to consummate."

37 Sartre's note: Brummell's elegance consisted in only wearing clothes that were already quite worn-out. He could not stand anything new: new things are like "clothes for Sunday," because they belong to nobody.

the attitude of a maniac, a "love" that keeps company with the smashing of objects. But this zeal for destruction that lies at the bottom of generosity is nothing other than a zeal to possess. Everything I give up, everything I give away, can be enjoyed in a superior way through the gift that I make of it: the gift is a bitter and brief enjoyment, almost sexual; to give something is to possessively enjoy the object that is given, to make a destructive-appropriative contact. But at the same time the gift casts a spell over the person to whom it is given: it obliges him to re-create, to sustain in being through a continuous creation, this "me" that I no longer want, and that has just—until its annihilation—been my possession, and of which nothing finally remains but an image. To give is to enslave. This aspect of the gift is not what interests us here, because it concerns above all our relations with the other. What we have aimed to point out is that generosity is not irreducible: to give is to appropriate by means   641 of destruction, by making use of this destruction to enslave the other. Generosity is, therefore, a feeling that is structured by the Other's existence and which indicates a preference for *appropriation through destruction*. It thereby leads us even more in the direction of *nothingness* than toward the in-itself (what is involved is a nothingness of the in-itself that is itself, obviously, in-itself but which, insofar as it is nothingness, can stand in a symbolic relation to the being that is its own nothingness). If, therefore, existential psychoanalysis comes across evidence of a subject's *generosity*, it must search further for his original project, and ask why the subject has chosen to appropriate by means of destruction rather than by creation. The answer to this question will disclose the original relation to being by which the *person* being studied is constituted.

These observations aimed only to bring to light the *ideal* character of the appropriative bond and the symbolic function of all appropriative behavior. We must add that the symbol is not deciphered by the subject himself. That is not because the symbol is prepared within some unconscious but because of the very structure of being-in-the-world. Indeed we saw, in the chapter about transcendence, that the ordering of equipment in the world was the image, projected into the in-itself, of my possibilities—i.e., the image of what I am—but that I would never be able to decipher this worldly image because it would take nothing less than the scissiparity of reflection for me to become, in relation to myself, something like the first draft of an object. Thus, as the circuit of ipseity is non-thetic—and, in consequence, my acquaintance with what I am remains non-thematic—this "being-in-itself" of myself that is sent back to me by the world can only be concealed from my *knowledge*. I can only adapt myself to it in and through the proximate action through which it is born. So to possess something does not mean at all that one knows oneself to be identified with the possessed object in a relation of creation-destruction but precisely that one *is in this relation* or, better still, that one *is this relation*. And the possessed object has an immediately apprehensible quality for us which transforms it entirely—the quality of being *mine*—but this quality is in itself quite indecipherable, it is revealed in and through action, it makes manifest that it has a specific meaning, but the moment we want to withdraw in relation to the object and to contemplate it, it vanishes without revealing its innermost structure and meaning. Indeed, this withdrawal is in itself destructive of the appropriative bond: in the previous instant I was committed within the ideal totality and, precisely because I was committed in my being, I was unable to know it; in the next instant the totality has broken and I am unable to discover its meaning from the disconnected pieces that composed it, as we can see in that contemplative experience—known as "depersonalization"—that some patients undergo in spite of themselves. We are therefore obliged to turn to existential psychoanalysis to disclose to us the meaning, in each particular case, of this appropriative synthesis whose general and abstract sense we have just defined by means of ontology.

642

What remains to be defined in general is the signification of the possessed object. This inquiry should complete our knowledge of the appropriative project. What, therefore, are we seeking to appropriate?

We can easily see, on the one hand and in abstract terms, that what we primarily aim to possess is not so much the object's way of being as the object's being itself. (Indeed, it is in its capacity as a concrete representative of being-in-itself that we desire to appropriate the object or, in other words, to apprehend ourself as the foundation of its being insofar as it is, ideally, ourself.) On the other hand, and in empirical terms, we can see that the appropriate object never counts *for itself alone*, or for its particular use. No particular act of appropriation has meaning outside its indefinite extensions; the pen I possess is equivalent to all pens; what I possess, in person in the pen, is the class of pens. But, in addition, what I possess in it is the possibility of writing, of drawing strokes with a certain shape and color (because I contaminate the instrument itself, and the ink that I am using): these strokes, their color, their meaning, are condensed within it just as much as the paper, its special resistance, its smell, etc. The crystallizing synthesis that Stendhal described in the case of love alone occurs in relation to *all* possession.[38] Every possessed object, detached against the ground of the world, manifests the entire world—as a beloved woman manifests the sky, the beach, the sea that surrounded her when she appeared. To appropriate this object is, therefore, symbolically to appropriate the world. Anyone can recognize this, by referring to their experience; for myself, I will cite a personal example, not by way of proof but to guide the reader's inquiry.

Some years ago, I came to the decision that I would no longer smoke. The beginning was tough and, really, I was less concerned by the *taste* of tobacco that I was going to lose than by the *meaning* of the act of smoking. An entire crystallization had occurred: I would smoke at the theater, in the morning while I worked, in the evening after dinner, and it seemed to me that by ceasing to smoke I would remove the interest of the play, the flavor of the evening meal, the fresh brightness of the morning's work. No matter how the unexpected event which struck my eyes was meant to be, it seemed to me that it was fundamentally impoverished once I could no longer be smoking as I greeted it. To-be-capable-of-being-encountered-by-me-as-I-smoked: such was the concrete quality that had become universally spread across things. It seemed to me that I was going to seize this quality from them and that, in the midst of this universal impoverishment, life was a bit less worth living. Now, smoking is an appropriative destructive reaction. The tobacco is a symbol of "appropriated" being, since it is destroyed to the rhythm of my breath by a manner of "continuous destruction," and passes into me, and since   643
its becoming me is symbolically manifested by the transformation into smoke of the solid substance that I consume. The connection of the landscape that is seen as one smokes with this little crematory sacrifice was, we have just seen, such as to make the latter appear as the symbol of the former. That means therefore that the reaction of destructive appropriation of the tobacco was symbolically equivalent to an appropriative

38 TN: Again Sartre is alluding here to Stendhal's account in *On Love* (2009).

destruction of the entire world. Through the tobacco I was smoking, it was the world that was burning, smoking itself, disappearing into smoke in order to enter into me. To keep to my decision I had to accomplish a kind of decrystallization, which is to say that, without paying undue attention to this, I reduced the tobacco to being no longer anything but itself: a burning herb. I cut its symbolic links to the world, and persuaded myself that I would remove nothing from the theatrical performance, from the landscape, from the book I was reading, if I considered them without my pipe; in other words, I made do with ways of possessing these objects other than this sacrificial ceremony. As soon as I was persuaded by this, my regret was reduced to a small thing: I lamented the fact that I would no longer sense the smell of the smoke, the heat of the bowl between my fingers, etc. But the result was that my regret was disarmed and became easy to bear.

Thus what we desire to appropriate in an object is fundamentally its being, and the world. These two appropriative ends amount in reality to just one. I seek to possess, behind the phenomenon, the being of the phenomenon. But this being, which, as we saw, is quite different from the phenomenon of being, is being-in-itself and not only the being of some particular thing. It is not that there is a transition to the universal here but rather the being, considered in its concrete nudity, thereby becomes the being of the totality. In this way we can see the relation of possession appear clearly: to possess is to want to possess the world through a particular object. And as possession is defined as an attempt to take hold of a being, in the capacity of a foundation, insofar as it is, ideally, ourself, any possessive project aims to constitute the for-itself as the foundation of the world or the concrete totality of the in-itself, insofar as this totality is, as a totality, the for-itself itself, existing in the mode of the in-itself. Being-in-the-world is the project of possessing the world, i.e., of taking hold of the whole world as that which is missing from the for-itself in order for it to become in-itself-for-itself; it is to be committed within a totality, which is precisely the ideal, or value, or the totalized totality and which would be ideally constituted through the fusion of the for-itself, as a detotalized totality that has to be what it is, with the world, as the totality of the in-itself that is what it is. Indeed, as we must fully understand, the for-itself's project is not to found a being in reason, i.e., a being that it conceives first—in form and in matter—in order thereafter to give it existence: such a being would, in effect, be purely abstract, a universal; its conception cannot come before its being-in-the-world but, on the contrary, presupposes it, as it 644 presupposes the preontological understanding of a [type of] being that is eminently concrete and present from the outset, which is the "there" of the for-itself's initial being-there, i.e., the being of the world. The for-itself does not exist first in order to think the universal, and to determine itself according to concepts: it is its choice and its choice cannot be abstract; otherwise the for-itself's very being would be abstract. The for-itself's being is an individual adventure, and its choice must be the individual choice of a concrete being. That is true, as we have seen, for the *situation* in general. The for-itself's choice is always the choice of a concrete situation in its incomparable singularity. But that is also true of the ontological meaning of that choice. When we say that the for-itself is a project *to be*, it does not conceive of the being-in-itself that it projects to be as a structure shared by all existents of a certain type; as we saw, its project is in no way a conception.[39] What the for-itself projects to be appears to it as an eminently concrete totality: it is *this* being. And of course we can foresee in this project the possibilities of a universalizing development, but in the way in which we may say of some lover that he loves all women, or all of woman, in one woman. As this concrete being whose foundation he projects to be cannot be *conceived*, as we have just seen, because it is concrete, it cannot be *imagined* either, because the imaginary is a nothingness and this being is eminently being. It must *exist*, which is to say it must *be encountered*, but its encounter amounts to no more than the choice that the for-itself makes. The for-itself is a choice-encounter, i.e., it determines itself as the choice to found the being that it encounters. That means the for-itself, as an individual undertaking, is the choice of *this world*, as the individual totality of being; it does not surpass it toward a logical universality but toward a new concrete "state" of the same world, in which being would be in-itself founded by the for-itself—which is to say that it surpasses it toward a concrete-being-beyond-the-existing-concrete-being. In this way being-in-the-world is

---

39 TN: I am faithful to Sartre in reproducing the inept grammatical structure of this sentence.

a project to possess this world, and the value that haunts the for-itself is the concrete indication of an individual being constituted through the synthetic function of this for-itself here and this world here. In effect being, wherever it is, wherever it comes from and from whatever standpoint we consider it—whether in-itself or for-itself or the impossible ideal of the in-itself-for-itself—is, in its primary contingency, an individual adventure.

Thus we are able to determine the relations that unite the categories of being and having. We have seen that desire may at the outset be the desire to be or the desire to have. But the desire to have is not irreducible. While the desire to be bears directly on the for-itself, and projects to confer upon it without intermediary the dignity of in-itself-for-itself, the desire to have targets the for-itself upon, within, and through the world. It is through the appropriation of the world that the project to have aims to actualize the same value as the desire to be. That is why these desires, which we can distinguish analytically, are in reality inseparable: we can find no desire to be that is not coupled with a desire to have, and *vice versa*; basically, it is a matter of two directions of attention in relation to a single goal or, alternatively, of two interpretations of the same fundamental situation, of which one aspires to confer being on the for-itself directly, and the other to establish the circuit of ipseity, which is to say by inserting the world between the for-itself and its being. As for the original situation, it is the lack in being that I am, which is to say that I make myself be. But precisely that being, which I make into my own lack, is absolutely individual and concrete: it is being that already exists and in the midst of which I arise as missing it. Thus the very nothingness that I am is individual and concrete, as being this nihilation and not another.

Every for-itself is a free choice; each of its actions, the most insignificant and the most important, translates this choice and emanates from it; it is to this that we have given the name freedom. Now we have grasped the *meaning* of this choice: it is a choice of being, either directly or through the appropriation of the world or, rather, both at once. In this way my freedom is the choice to be God, and all my actions and all my projects translate this choice and reflect it in a thousand different ways, for there are an infinite number of ways of being and ways of having. The aim of existential psychoanalysis is to find, through these empirical and concrete projects, the original way in which each person chooses his being. But, it might be said, we still need to explain why

I choose to possess the world through this particular thing or that. We can reply that this is precisely what is distinctive of freedom. However, the object itself is not irreducible. In it, we aim at its *being*, through its way of being or quality. And, as a way of being, quality—in particular material quality, the fluidity of water, the density of stone, etc.—only presentifies being in a specific way. What we choose therefore is a specific way in which being is disclosed and comes to be possessed. For us, yellow and red, the taste of tomato or of split peas, the rough and the soft, are not at all irreducible givens: we see them as symbolic expressions of a specific way in which being can offer itself, and we react with disgust or desire according to the way in which we see being show up in them. Existential psychoanalysis has to draw out the *ontological meaning* of qualities. It is only in this way—and not by means of sexual considerations—that we can explain, for example, certain constants in the "imaginations" of poets (the "geological" in Rimbaud, the fluidity of water in Poe) or, quite simply, each person's *tastes*, those famous tastes about which we say we should not argue, without realizing that they symbolize in their way an entire "*Weltanschauung*," an entire choice of being, and that this explains why they appear *obvious* to the person who has made them his. We should, therefore, sketch out this particular task of existential psychoanalysis here, as a suggestion for further research. For the irreducibility of free choice does not lie at the level of a person's taste for the sweet, or the bitter, etc., but at the level of his choice of the aspect of being to be revealed *through and by means of* the sweet, the bitter, etc.

646

III. THE REVELATION OF BEING THROUGH QUALITIES

It is quite simply a matter of attempting a psychoanalysis of *things*. This is what M. Bachelard has tried to do, with great talent, in his latest book, *Water and Dreams*.[40] This work holds great promise; in particular, the discovery of the "material imagination" is a genuine advance. In truth,

---

40 TN: Gaston Bachelard (1884–1962) was a French philosopher, and a professor at the Sorbonne from 1940. (Sartre's reference to Bachelard's lectures, some lines later, suggests that he had either attended these himself or knew someone who had.) *L'Eau et les Rêves* (translated as Bachelard 1983) was published in 1942.

the term "imagination" is not appropriate, and nor is this aspiration to seek, behind things and their gelatinous, solid, or fluid matter, the "images" that we project into them. As we have demonstrated elsewhere,[41] perception has nothing in common with the imagination: on the contrary, it strictly excludes it, and vice versa. To perceive is not in any way to assemble images out of sensations: we should abandon these claims of associationist origin entirely and, in consequence, the task of psychoanalysis will not be to look for images but rather to explicate the meanings that really belong to things. Doubtless, the "human" meaning of stickiness, of viscosity, etc., does not belong to the in-itself. But, as we have seen, potentialities do not belong to it either, and yet the world is constituted by them. Material meanings—the human meaning of icicles, of the granular, the compressed, the fatty, etc.—are just as real as the world, no more and no less, and to come into the world is to arise in the midst of these meanings. But no doubt this is merely a difference of terminology; and M. Bachelard seems less fearful, and to communicate the nub of his thinking when he talks in his lectures about psychoanalysing plants or entitles one of his works The Psychoanalysis of Fire. In fact, the method of objective deciphering is not to be applied to the subject but to things, and it does not presuppose any antecedent reference to the subject. When, for example, I want to determine the objective meaning of snow, I see, for example, that at certain temperatures it melts and that the melting of the snow is its death. There we have merely an objective statement of fact. And when I want to determine the meaning of this melting, I am obliged to compare it to other objects, situated in other regions of existence but equally objective, and equally transcendent, such as ideas, friendships, or people, of whom I can also say that they melt (money melts in my hands; I am dripping with sweat; I melt into water; some ideas—in the sense of objective social meanings—will "snowball," while others melt away;[42] he has become so much thinner, so melted down). In this way, no doubt, I will arrive at

647

---

41 Sartre's note: Cf. L'Imaginaire (NRF, 1940). TN: Translated into English as Sartre (2004b).

42 Sartre's note: We can also recall Daladier's "melting currency." TN: The French Radical politician Édouard Daladier (1884–1970) had championed a fiscal policy in the 1930s known as la monnaie fondante (usually translated as "softened currency"), according to which the value of unspent currency would diminish over time.

a specific relation, linking certain forms of being to certain others. The comparison of melting snow to certain other, more mysterious forms of melting (for example, in the content of various old myths: the tailor in Grimms' tales picks up a cheese in his hands, pretends that it is a stone, squeezes it so hard that the whey drips out of it; the witnesses believe that he has squeezed drops out of a stone, that he has expressed the liquid out of it) may inform us of a secret liquidity of things, in the sense in which Audiberti, with true inspiration, spoke of the secret blackness of milk.[43] This liquidity, which should itself be compared to the juice of fruit and to man's blood—which is in addition something like our secret and vital liquidity—refers us to a specific permanent possibility: the metamorphosis of something *compact and granular* (designating a certain quality of being of the *pure in-itself*) into a *homogeneous and undifferentiated fluidity* (another quality of being of the pure in-itself). And here we grasp, at its origin and in all its ontological meaning, the antinomy of the continuous and the discontinuous, the feminine and masculine poles of the world, whose later dialectical development we will see, right up to quantum theory and wave mechanics. Thus, we will succeed in deciphering snow's secret meaning, which is an ontological meaning. But where, in all that, is there any relation to subjectivity? To the imagination? We have only compared some wholly objective structures and formulated the hypothesis which may unify and group these structures together. That is why psychoanalysis applies, in this case, to the things themselves, and not to the men. It is also why I would be more cautious than M. Bachelard about any recourse at this level to the material imaginations of poets, even such poets as Lautréamont, Rimbaud, or Poe. Of course, it is fascinating to investigate "Lautréamont's Bestiary." But if in this investigation we have indeed returned to subjectivity, we will only obtain any truly significant results if we regard Lautréamont as an original and pure preference for animality[44] and if we have first determined animality's objective meaning.[45] If in fact Lautréamont *is what he prefers*, we must in the first place know the nature of what he prefers.

648

43 TN: Jacques Audiberti (1899–1965) was a French poet, playwright, and novelist.
44 Sartre's note: A preference for a particular kind of animality; this is precisely what Scheler means by *vital values*.
45 TN: Sartre's points here are in implicit disagreement with Bachelard, whose study of Lautréamont, focusing on the animal imagery in his poetry, was published in 1939.

And, of course, we know quite well that his "input" into animality will be different and greater than mine. But these subjective enrichments which tell us about Lautréamont are polarized by the basic structure of animality. That is why the existential psychoanalysis of Lautréamont presupposes in the first place that the objective sense of *animal* has been deciphered. Similarly, I have dreamt for a long time of establishing a *lapidary* for Rimbaud. But what sense would that have if we had not antecedently established the meaning of the geological in general? But, one might object, a meaning presupposes man. We do not disagree. Only man, being a transcendence, establishes significance even as he arises, and any signifier, by virtue of the very structure of a transcendence, involves a reference to other transcendent items that can be deciphered without any recourse to the subjectivity that established it. A body's potential energy is an objective quality of that body which must be able to be objectively calculated, by taking account uniquely of objective circumstances. And yet this energy can come to inhabit a body only in a world whose appearing is correlative to that of a for-itself. Similarly we can discover, by means of a strictly objective psychoanalysis, other potentialities that are more deeply engaged in the matter of things and which remain wholly transcendent, even though they correspond to a still more fundamental choice of human-reality, a choice of *being*.

This leads us to clarify the second point on which we differ from M. Bachelard. Certainly, any psychoanalysis must indeed have its *a priori* principles. It must know, in particular, *what it is looking for*; otherwise how could it find it? But as the goal of his research cannot itself be established by the psychoanalyst without incurring a vicious circle, it must be the object of a postulate—either sought from experience, or established through some other discipline. Freud's libido is obviously a straightforward postulate: Adler's will to power seems to be a generalization without method from empirical data—and in fact it must lack a method, since it is what allows the basis of psychoanalytic method to be laid down. M. Bachelard seems to rely on these precursors; the postulate of sexuality seems to dominate his research; at other times he refers us to *death*, to the trauma of birth, to the will to power; in short, his psychoanalysis seems to be surer of its method than of its principles and no doubt it counts on its results to throw light on the exact goal of its research. But this puts the cart before the horse; consequences will never enable a principle to be established, any more than the sum of its finite

modes will enable us to grasp the substance. It seems to us therefore that
we need to abandon these empirical principles or these postulates which
make man, *a priori*, a sexuality or a will to power and that we should   649
establish the goal of psychoanalysis rigorously, on the basis of ontology.
This is what we tried to do in the preceding paragraph. We saw that,
long before it can be described as *libido* or will to power, human-reality is
a *choice of being*, either directly or through the appropriation of the world.
And we saw that—when the choice is directed on appropriation—each
thing is chosen, in the last analysis, not for its sexual potential but according to the way in which it *renders* being, the way in which being shows
on its surface. A psychoanalysis of *things* and their *matter* must therefore
be concerned above all to establish the way in which each thing is the
objective symbol of being and human-reality's relation to this being. We
do not deny the need, after that, to uncover in nature an entire sexual
symbolism, but this is a secondary and reducible layer whose precondition is a psychoanalysis of the pre-sexual structures. Thus we regard
M. Bachelard's study of water, which teems with ingenious and profound insights, as an assembly of suggestions, like a precious collection
of materials which we ought now to make use of, in a psychoanalysis
that is conscious of its principles.

What ontology can in fact teach psychoanalysis is first of all the true
origin of the meanings of things and their true relation to human-reality.
Indeed, only ontology is capable of situating itself at the level of transcendence, and grasping being-in-the-world with its two terms, because it
alone takes up from the outset the perspective of the *cogito*. Again it is the
idea of facticity and of situation which will enable us to understand the
existential symbolism of things. We have seen, indeed, that it is possible
theoretically—and impossible practically—to distinguish facticity from
the project that constitutes it into the situation. We must make use of this
observation here: in fact, as we have seen, it would be wrong to believe
that a *this*, in the indifferent externality of its being and independently of
the for-itself's arising, could have any meaning whatever. Of course, its
quality, as we have seen, is nothing other than its being. The lemon's yellow, we said, is not a subjective mode of apprehension of the lemon: it
is *the lemon*. We have also shown[46] that the entire lemon extends through
its qualities and that each of these qualities extends throughout the oth-

46 Sartre's note: Part Two, Chapter 3, section III.

ers; that is exactly what we are calling a this. Every quality of a being is the being as a whole; it is the presence of its absolute contingency, its irreducible indifference. However, we have been emphasizing since Part Two the inseparability, even within a quality, of project and facticity. In fact we wrote: "In order for there to be a quality, it is necessary that there

650   is being for a nothingness that, by its nature, is not being . . . quality is a disclosure of being in its entirety, within the limits of the there is."[47] Thus, from the outset, we cannot accredit quality's meaning to being in itself, since the "there is"—i.e., the nihilating mediation of the for-itself—is already required for there to be any qualities. But on the basis of these remarks we will easily understand that the meaning of quality registers in its turn something akin to a strengthening of the "there is," since it is exactly where we find the foothold in order to surpass the "there is" toward being as it is absolutely and in itself. In each apprehension of quality there is, in this sense, a metaphysical attempt to escape our condition, to pierce the casing of nothingness of the "there is" and to penetrate right through to the pure in-itself. But obviously we can only apprehend quality as the symbol of a being which escapes us totally, even though it is there totally, in front of us, which is to say, in short, to make revealed being function as a symbol of being in itself. That means precisely that a new structure of the "there is" is constituted, which is the signifying layer, even though this layer is revealed within the absolute unity of the same fundamental project. We will call that the metaphysical tenor of each intuitive revelation of being; and that is exactly what we should arrive at and disclose by means of psychoanalysis. What is the metaphysical tenor of yellow, of red, of the smooth and the coarse? What is—a question we will raise after these elementary questions—the metaphysical coefficient of a lemon, of water, of oil, etc.? There are so many problems here, which psychoanalysis is obliged to resolve if it wants one day to understand why Pierre loves oranges and hates water, why he will happily eat tomato but refuses to eat broad beans, why he vomits if he is forced to swallow oysters or raw eggs.

Only we have also shown what a mistake it would be, for example, to think that we "project" our affective dispositions onto the thing, to illuminate or color it. First, we saw in fact a long time ago that a feel-

47 TN: Sartre is quoting his own words almost verbatim from EN 223.

ing is not at all an inner disposition but a transcendent and objectifying relation, which learns from its object what it is. But that is not all: an example will show us that the explanation in terms of *projection* (which is the sense of the all-too-familiar "a landscape is a state of mind")[48] begs the question. Let us take, for example, the particular quality known as the *viscous*. It is certain that for a European adult it signifies a host of *human* and *moral* characteristics that are easily reducible to relations of being. A handshake is [sticky or] viscous; a smile is [unctuous or] viscous; a thought, a feeling, can be viscous.[49] The received view is that in the first instance I have experienced certain displeasing modes of behavior and moral attitudes which I condemn and that, on the other hand, I have a sensory intuition of something viscous. Thereafter I come to establish a connection between these feelings and viscosity, and the viscous comes to function as a symbol for an entire class of human feelings and attitudes. I will therefore have enriched the viscous, by projecting onto it my knowledge concerning this human category of behavior. But how can we accept this explanation in terms of projection? If we suppose that we have in the first instance grasped our feelings as pure psychological qualities, how could we grasp their relation to viscosity? The feeling, grasped in its qualitative purity, could only be revealed as a specific, wholly non-extended disposition that is, in relation to particular values and particular consequences, blameworthy; in any case, it will not appear "as an image" if the image is not given first. And, on the other hand, if the viscous does not originally carry any affective meaning, if it is given only as a specific material quality, we are unable to see how it could ever be chosen as the symbolic representative of some specific psychological units. In brief, in order to establish a symbolic relation consciously and clearly between viscosity and the tacky low behavior of certain individuals, we would need to have already grasped the lowness in the viscosity, and the viscosity in certain kinds of lowness. It follows therefore that the

651

---

48 TN: ... "*un paysage est un état de l'âme*" ... Sartre probably takes this phrase from Henri Frédéric Amiel's *Journal Intime*, translated into English as Amiel (1921), to which he refers elsewhere. Amiel (1821–1881) was a Swiss philosopher, poet, and critic.

49 TN: *Une poignée de main est visqueuse, un sourire ... une pensée, un sentiment peuvent être visqueux.* It is odd even in French to describe these phenomena as "viscous." The additional English adjectives (in square brackets) show what I think Sartre meant. See my note on *la viscosité* in Notes on the Translation.

explanation by projection explains nothing, since it presupposes what was supposed to be explained. Moreover, even if it escaped that objection of principle, it would only meet another one, which is drawn from experience and is no less serious: the explanation by projection implies in fact that the projecting subject has attained, through experience and analysis, a certain knowledge of the structure and effects of the attitudes that he comes to describe as "viscous." According to this view, indeed, the recourse to viscosity does not enrich our experience of human lowness in the manner of *knowledge*; at the most, it offers a thematic unity, an image used to classify items of knowledge we have already acquired. On the other hand, if we consider it in isolation, viscosity in the strict sense may appear to us to be harmful in practical terms (because viscous substances stick to our hands, our clothes, because they stain), but not *repugnant*. We cannot in fact explain the disgust they inspire in us by means of the contamination of this physical quality with certain moral qualities. There must therefore exist some kind of process through which we learn the symbolic meaning of viscosity. But observation teaches us that the youngest children show signs of repulsion, in the presence of anything viscous, as if it were *already* contaminated by the mind; it also teaches us that they *understand*, as soon as they can speak, the value of words like "soft," "low," etc. when these are used to describe feelings. It is as if, in the universe in which we first arise, feelings and actions are laden with materiality, and composed like a substance: they are *really* soft, flat, viscous, low, high, etc.; and material substances have a psychological
652   meaning from the outset that makes them repugnant, horrifying, attractive, etc. No explanation in terms of projection or analogy is adequate here. And, to sum up, it is just as impossible for us to derive the value of a psychological symbol of the viscous from the brute quality of a *this* as it is for us to project this meaning onto the *this* on the basis of a knowledge of the psychological attitudes in question. How therefore should we conceive of this immense universal symbolism which is expressed in our hatreds, our likings, our attractions, for objects whose materiality ought in principle to remain meaningless? To make any progress in this study, we are required to give up a certain number of assumptions. In particular, we must no longer postulate *a priori* that the attribution of viscosity to such and such a feeling is only an image, and not an item of knowledge—and we should also refuse to allow, before we have fur-

ther information, that it is our psychology that allows physical matter to become symbolically informed, and that our experience of human lowness is prior to our apprehension of the "viscous" as meaningful.

Let us return to the original project. It is a project of appropriation. It obliges therefore the *viscous* to reveal its being; as the mode in which the for-itself arises in being is appropriative, the viscous is perceived as something "viscous to possess," which is to say that the original bond between me and the viscous is that I have the project to be the foundation of its being, insofar as, ideally, it is myself. From the outset, therefore, it appears as a possible myself to be founded; from the origin it is *psychologized*. That does not mean at all that I endow it either with a soul, as in primitive animism, or with metaphysical powers but only that its materiality itself is revealed to me as having a psychological meaning— this psychological meaning, moreover, being one and the same as its symbolic value in relation to being-in-itself. We may regard this appropriative way of making the viscous *render* all its meanings as something *a priori* and formal, even though it is a free project and identified with the for-itself's own being, since it does not depend primarily on the way of being that belongs to the viscous but only on its brute being-there, its pure, encountered existence. Any other appropriative encounter will be the same, insofar as it is a mere project of appropriation, and not in any way distinct from the pure "there is," and insofar as it is, depending on our way of seeing it, a pure freedom or a pure nothingness. But it is precisely within the scope of this appropriative project that the viscous discloses and develops its viscosity. This viscosity is therefore *already*—from the first appearance of anything viscous—an answer to a question, already a *gift of itself*: the viscous appears already as a first draft of the world's fusion with me; and what I learn about it, its character as a *ventouse that sucks me in*,[50] is already a reply to a concrete question; it answers with its very being, with its way of being, with its entire matter. And the answer that is given is fully fitted to the question, and at the same time opaque and indecipherable because it is rich with all its indescribable materiality. It is clear insofar as it exactly fits the question: the viscous

653

---

50 TN: *... son caractère de ventouse qui m'aspire ...* In the old-fashioned medicine that Sartre has in mind, a *ventouse* (now mostly used to assist delivery in childbirth) has several uses, e.g., to extract poison, etc.

allows itself to be apprehended as what is missing from me; it allows itself to be palpated in an appropriative inquiry; to this first sketch of an appropriation, it uncovers its viscosity. It is opaque precisely because, if the for-itself is what awakens a meaningful figure within the viscous, it is with all of its viscosity that the latter comes to fill it. It sends back therefore a full and dense meaning, and this meaning surrenders *being-in-itself* to us, insofar as the world is, at present, being manifested by the viscous and also *a first sketch of ourselves*, insofar as the act of appropriation sketches out something like a founding of the viscous. What approaches us then, like an objective quality, is a new *nature* which is neither material (and physical) nor psychological but which transcends the opposition between the physical and the psychological by disclosing itself to us as the ontological expression of the world in its entirety, i.e., it offers itself as a category for classifying all the *thises* in the world, whether they are material structures or transcended transcendences. Therefore, and by the same token, our apprehension of the viscous as such has created a particular way for the world's in-itself to present itself; it symbolizes being in its own way, which means that, for as long as our contact with the viscous lasts, it is for us as if viscosity were the meaning of the entire world, i.e., being-in-itself's sole mode of being, just as, for the primitive people of the lizard clan, all objects *are* lizards.[51] What, in the example we have chosen, might be the mode of being symbolized by the viscous? In the first place I can see that it is the homogeneity and imitation of liquidity. A viscous substance, like pitch, is an aberrant fluid. First, it seems to us to manifest a being which runs away in all directions, and everywhere resembles itself, a being which escapes from all sides and on which, however, we are able to float, a being without danger and without memory, changing eternally into itself, on which we make no mark, and which makes no mark on us, a being which glides, and on which we can glide, and which we can possess by gliding (a rowboat, a motorboat, water-skiing, etc.), and which—because it rolls over you—never possesses anything, a being that consists in eternity and infinite temporality, because it is a constant process of change in which nothing changes and which—through this synthesis of eternity and temporality—provides

---

51 TN: Sartre probably knew about this primitive system of totem-based clans through Durkheim's and Mauss's research. It is described in Durkheim and Mauss (2010).

the best symbol of a possible fusion of the for-itself, as pure temporality, with the in-itself, as pure eternity. But immediately the viscous is revealed as essentially suspect, because its fluidity exists in slow motion; it is a thickening of liquidity, which by itself represents solidity's rising triumph over the liquid or—in other words—a tendency of the indifferent in-itself (represented by the pure solid) to freeze liquidity, i.e., to absorb the for-itself that ought to be founding it. The viscous is water in the throes of death: it presents itself as a phenomenon of becoming; it does not have water's permanence in change but represents, on the contrary, something like a cross-section made through a changing state. This frozen instability of the viscous discourages possession. Water flows faster, but it can be possessed even as it escapes, as running water. The viscous escapes in a thick flow, which no more resembles that of water than the heavy low-level flight of a chicken resembles that of a sparrowhawk. And this flight itself cannot be possessed, because it negates itself as flight. It is almost, already, a solid permanence. Nothing testifies better to this suspect character of a "substance between two states" than the slowness with which the viscous merges into itself: a drop of water touching the surface of a stretch of water is instantaneously transmuted into the stretch of water; we do not apprehend the operation as the absorption of the drop, mouth-like, by the expanse but rather as a spiritualization and disindividuation of a particular being, which dissolves by itself into the greater whole from which it came. The symbol of an expanse of water seems to play a very important role in the constitution of pantheistic systems; it reveals a particular type of being's relation with being. But if we examine the viscous, we observe (even though it has mysteriously retained *all* its fluidity, in slow motion; we should not confuse it with a purée, where the incipient fluidity sustains sudden breaks, sudden blockages, and where the substance, after beginning *to pour*, suddenly rolls over into a ball) that, in the phenomenon of its transmutation into itself, it shows a constant hysteresis: the honey that runs off my spoon onto the honey in the pot begins by sculpting its surface, it stands out in relief, and its fusion into the whole takes on the aspect of a collapse, a diminution which resembles a *deflation* (think of the impact, on a child's sensibility, of the inflatable man who is "blown" like a glass, and lets out a frightful wailing as he deflates) and, at the same time, the spreading and flattening of the rather mature breasts of a woman lying stretched out on

654

her back. In this viscous substance melting into itself there is in fact, at the same time, a visible resistance, like the refusal of an individual who does not want to be annihilated in being as a whole and, at the same time, a softness taken to its furthest extreme: because something *soft* is nothing but an annihilation that is stopped midway; the soft provides us with the best image of our own destructive power and its limits. The slowness with which the viscous drop disappears into the whole is taken at first for *softness*, since it is like an annihilation that has been held back, which seems to be playing for time: but this softness is taken to its conclusion; the drop sinks into the viscous expanse. Several features of the viscous emerge from this phenomenon: first, that its contact is *soft*. Throw some water on to the ground: it *flows*. Throw a viscous substance: it stretches out and flattens, and it is *soft*; touch something viscous, and it does not move away but it yields. There is a pitiless hardness to water's very elusiveness which gives it a secret metallic meaning; in the end it is impossible to compress, like steel. The viscous may be compressed. At first, therefore, it gives the impression of a being that can be *possessed*. It does this in two ways: its viscosity and its adherence to itself prevent it from escaping, so I can pick it up in my hands, separate a certain amount of honey or pitch from the rest of the pot, and thereby *create* an individual object by means of continuous creation; but, at the same time, the softness of this substance, mashed in my hands, gives the impression of constantly *destroying*. The image we have here is indeed a destruction-creation. The viscous is *docile*. Only, just at the moment when I believe I possess it, by means of a curious reversal I am possessed by it. This is where its essential characteristic makes its appearance: its softness acts like suction. If an object that I hold in my hand is solid, I can put it down whenever I please; for me, its inertia symbolizes all my power; I am its foundation, but it does not found me; it is the for-itself that is gathering up the in-itself and, without compromising itself, raising it to the dignity of in-itself, while still remaining an assimilative and creative power; the for-itself absorbs the in-itself. In other words, within the synthetic, "In-itself-For-itself" being, possession affirms the for-itself's primacy. But now the viscous reverses the terms: suddenly the for-itself is *compromised*. I separate my hands, and I want to let go of the viscous, but it sticks to me, drinking me up and sucking me in; its mode of being is neither the reassuring inertia of a solid nor a dynamism, like the dynamism that drives water as it rushes away. It is a soft, drooling, and feminine activity, sucking me in; it lives obscurely under my fingers and makes me feel almost dizzy; it draws me into it, as the foot of a cliff might draw me toward it. The viscous has a tactile fascination. I am no longer in control of halting the process of appropriation. It continues. In one way, it is like the supreme docility of something possessed, a canine loyalty that is offered even when we no longer want it and, in another way, it is, beneath that docility, an appropriation of the possessor by the possessed. We can see the symbol that is abruptly disclosed here: some forms of possession are malignant; it is possible for the in-itself to absorb the for-itself, i.e., for a being that is the opposite of the "In-itself-For-itself" to be constituted, in which the in-itself would draw the for-itself into its contingency, its indifferent externality, its unfounded existence. At that moment I suddenly grasp the trap of the viscous: it is a fluidity that holds me back and compromises me; I cannot glide across the viscous, as all its suction pads hold me back, and it cannot glide over me; it clings to me, like a leech. However, my gliding is not simply denied, as it is denied by a solid, but degraded. The viscous seems to invite me, and to lend itself to gliding (for a viscous expanse at rest is not markedly distinct from an expanse of very dense liquid); only it is a trap; my gliding is sucked in by the slippery substance, and leaves its trace on me. The viscous resembles a liquid seen in a nightmare, in which all its properties become animated by a kind of life and turn against me. The viscous is the in-itself's revenge: a sickly-sweet and feminine revenge, which might be symbolized on another level by the quality of the sugary. That is why the sugary in the form of a tasted sweetness—an indelible sweetness that remains indelibly in one's mouth and survives the act of swallowing—perfectly complements the essence of the viscous. A sugary viscosity is the ideal of the viscous; it symbolizes the for-itself's sugary death (the wasp that sinks into the jam and drowns there). But at the same time the viscous is me, just by virtue of my having started to appropriate the viscous substance. This suction by the viscous that I can feel on my hands is the beginning of a continuity between the viscous substance and myself. These long and soft columns of substance, which fall away from me and reach right down to the viscous expanse (when, for example, having plunged my hand into it, I pull it back), symbolize something akin to a flowing of myself into the viscous. And the hysteresis that I notice, in the fusion of the base of these

656

columns with the expanse, symbolizes something like my being's resistance to its absorption within the in-itself. If I sink down into some water, if I dive in, if I allow myself to go with its flow, I am not at all disturbed, because I do not have the slightest fear of becoming diluted within it: I remain a solid within its fluidity. If I sink down into something viscous, I feel that I will lose myself in it, i.e., become diluted into the viscous, precisely because the viscous is in the process of becoming solid. From this point of view, the *pasty* presents the same aspect, but it does not fascinate or compromise us, because it is inert. In the very act of apprehending the viscous, a substance that is sticky, compromising, and lacks equilibrium, there is an element of anxiety about *metamorphosis*. To touch the viscous is to risk becoming diluted into viscosity.

Now this dilution is, taken alone, already terrifying, because it is the for-itself's absorption by the in-itself, like ink by blotting paper. But it is *additionally* terrifying, if one is to be metamorphosed into a thing, that this precise metamorphosis should be *into* something viscous. If I could even conceive of a liquefaction of myself, i.e., of my being's transformation into water, I would not be unduly affected by it, because water is the symbol of consciousness: its movement, its fluidity, that solidarity without solidarity with its being, its perpetual flight, etc., everything about it reminds me of the for-itself and, indeed, the first psychologists to point out the *duration* that is a characteristic of consciousness (James, Bergson) frequently compared it to a river. A river is the best way to conjure up an image of the constant interpenetration of the parts of a whole and their continual capacity to dissociate, and become available. But the viscous presents a horrible image: for any consciousness it is horrible in itself *to become viscous*. That is because the being of something viscous is a soft adherence and, through the suction action of all of its parts, each part is in cunning solidarity and complicity with all the others; each of these parts makes a vague and soft attempt to individuate itself, an attempt that is followed by the individual's collapse back, its emptied flattening, as it is sucked from all sides by the substance. A consciousness that *became viscous* would therefore be transformed by the thickening-out of its ideas. From the moment we arise in the world, such a consciousness haunts us, wanting to launch itself into the future, toward a project of itself and finding itself, in the very moment at which it is aware of achieving this, cunningly and invisibly held back by the suction of the past and forced to witness its slow dilution into that past from which it is running, and the invasion of its project by a thousand parasites, until at last it loses itself completely. The "stolen thoughts" involved in psychotic delusions of control provide us with the best image of this horrible condition.[52] But how is this fear expressed, at the ontological level, other than precisely through the for-itself's flight in the face of facticity's in-itself, i.e., precisely through its temporalization? The horror of the viscous is a horror of time's becoming viscous, of facticity's continual and imperceptible progression, and that it might suck up the for-itself which "exists" it. It is the fear neither of death, nor of the pure in-itself, nor of nothingness but of a particular type of being, which has no more existence than the in-itself-for-itself and which the viscous merely *represents*. This ideal being, which I condemn with all my strength, haunts me in the way that *value* haunts me in my being. In it, the unfounded in-itself has priority over the for-itself; we may refer to this ideal being as an *anti-value*.

In this way, in the project to appropriate the viscous, viscosity suddenly shows itself as the symbol of an anti-value, which is to say of a type of being that is not actual but threatened, which will continually haunt consciousness as the constant danger it flees, and in so doing suddenly transforms the project of appropriation into a project of flight. Something has appeared which is not the result of any earlier experience but only of the preontological understanding of the in-itself and the for-itself and which is properly the *meaning* of the viscous. In one way, it is an experience, since viscosity is an intuitive discovery; and, in another way, it is like the invention of an adventure of being. On this basis a specific new danger appears for the for-itself, a threatening mode of being that is to be avoided, a concrete category which it will reencounter everywhere. The viscous does not symbolize any psychological attitude *a priori*: it manifests a certain relation of being with itself, and this relation is from the outset *made psychological* because I came across it in the first stages of an appropriation and because the viscosity sent back to me my image. Thus, from my first contact with the viscous, I am enriched by an ontological scheme that may be used, beyond the distinction between the psychological and

658

---

52 TN: Sartre has referred earlier to these psychoses (*psychoses d'influence*) at EN 414.

the nonpsychological, to interpret the meaning of being of all existents of a certain category, a category which, moreover, arises as an empty frame *before* the experience of the various types of the viscous. I have cast it into the world through my original project in relation to the viscous; it is an anti-value and, at the same time, an objective structure of the world, defining a sector within which viscous objects come to be organized. Henceforth, whenever an object manifests this relation of being to me—whether it is a matter of a handshake, a smile, or a thought—it will by definition be apprehended as viscous; in other words, it will appear to me, beyond its phenomenal texture, to constitute—along with every kind of pitch, glue, honey, etc.—the large ontological sector of viscosity. And reciprocally, to the extent that the *this* which I want to appropriate represents the entire world, the viscous, from my first intuitive contact with it, appears to me to be replete with obscure meanings and references beyond itself. The viscous discloses itself as being "much more than the viscous"; from the moment it appears it transcends every distinction between the psychological and the physical, between the brute existent and the worldly meanings; it is a possible meaning of being. The first experience that a child may have of the viscous therefore enriches him psychologically and morally: he will not need to reach adulthood in order to discover the kind of agglutinative lowness which we call, figuratively, "viscous": it is there, alongside it, in the very viscosity of the honey or the glue. What we say in relation to the viscous holds for all the objects which surround the child: the mere revelation of their matter stretches his horizon out to the furthest limits of being and confers on him, at the same time, a collection of *keys* for deciphering the being of all human facts. That does not mean that he *knows* from the start the "ugly" aspects of life, its "characteristics" or, on the contrary, the "beauties" of existence. Only he has in his possession all the *meanings of being*, of which ugliness and beauty, modes of behavior, psychological traits, sexual relations, etc., will never be more than particular exemplars. The sticky, the pasty, the vaporous, etc., the holes in sand and soil, caves, the light, the dark, etc., reveal pre-psychological and pre-sexual modes of being to him, which he will spend his life, thereafter, in explicating. No "innocent" child exists. In particular, we will acknowledge, with the Freudians, the innumerable relations to sexuality maintained by certain matters and certain forms in the child's surroundings. But by that we do not mean that an already constituted sexual instinct has charged them with a sexual meaning. It seems to us, on the contrary, that these matters and forms are grasped in their own right and that they reveal to the child modes of being and relations to the for-itself's being that will elucidate and mold his sexuality. To give just one example, many psychoanalysts have been struck by the attraction by which the child is drawn to all kinds of *holes* (holes in sand, in soil, grottoes, caves, crevices), and they have explained this attraction either by the anal character of infantile sexuality, or by a prenatal shock, or even by a premonition of the sexual act in its strict sense. We will not accept any of these explanations: the one about "birth trauma" is extremely fanciful. The one that equates the hole to the female sexual organ presupposes an experience on the part of the child that he cannot have or a premonition that cannot be justified. As for the child's "anal" sexuality, we do not wish to deny it, but for it to illuminate the holes which he encounters in the field of perception, and to give them a symbolic charge, the child would need to apprehend his anus as a hole; better still, his apprehension of the essence of the hole, or the orifice, would have to correspond to the sensation he has of his anus. But we have shown the subjective character of the "body-for-me" enough to make it understood that it is impossible for the child to grasp any part of his body as an objective structure of the universe. It is for the Other that the anus appears as an orifice. It cannot be lived that way; it could not be disclosed in that aspect even by the intimate care which the mother gives to the child, since the anus, which is an erogenous zone and susceptible to pain, does not have any tactile nerve endings. It is on the contrary through the Other—through the words the mother uses to refer to the child's body—that he learns that his anus is a *hole*. For him, therefore, the objective nature of the hole perceived in the world is what will illuminate the objective structure and the meaning of the anal zone, and will give a transcendent *meaning* to the erogenous sensations that he was confined hitherto only to "exist." Now, as itself, the *hole* is the symbol for a mode of being that existential psychoanalysis needs to clarify. We cannot develop this here. However, we can see immediately that it presents itself from the outset as a nothingness "to be filled" with my own flesh: the child cannot restrain himself from putting his finger or his entire arm into a hole. It offers me therefore an empty image of myself; to make myself exist within the world which awaits me, I need only to flow into it. The hole's ideal is therefore that of an excavation which can be molded carefully to my flesh, so that, if I take the trouble and narrowly adjust myself to it, I will contribute to bringing into existence the plenum of being in the world. Thus, in plugging a hole I am in the first place making a sacrifice of my body in order that a plenitude of being should exist, which is to say I suffer the for-itself's Passion in order to shape, to perfect, and to save the in-itself's totality.[53] We may grasp in this, at its origin, one of the most fundamental tendencies of human-reality: the tendency *to fill*. We come across this tendency in the adolescent and the adult; a good part of our lives is spent in plugging holes, in filling gaps, in bringing about and symbolically founding fullness. The child recognizes, on the basis of his earliest experiences, that he himself is holed. When he puts his finger in his mouth, he is trying to wall up the holes in his face; he waits for his finger to merge into his lips and palate and *to plug* the buccal orifice, in the way in which one uses cement to plug a crack in the wall. He seeks the density, the uniform and spherical plenitude, of Parmenidean being and, if he sucks his finger, it is precisely in order to dilute it, to transform it into a sticky paste to close up the hole of his mouth. Among the tendencies which underlie the act of eating, this one is certainly one of the most fundamental: the food is the "mastic" that will close up the mouth; to eat is, among other things, to plug oneself. It is only from there that we can pass on to sexuality: the obscenity of the female sex organ is that of all *gaping* things; it is a *call for being*, as all holes are, moreover; in herself the woman is calling for a foreign flesh which, penetrating and diluting her, must transform her into a plenitude of being. And conversely the woman feels her condition to be like an appeal, precisely because she is "holed." That is the true origin of Adler's complex. Doubtless the sex organ is a mouth, and a voracious mouth which swallows the penis—which may well bring in the idea of castration: the act of love castrates the man—but that is because, before anything else, the sex organ is a hole. What we have here therefore is a *pre-sexual* contribution which becomes a component of sexuality as an empirical and complex human outlook, but whose origin in no way derives from being-sexed, and has nothing in common with the fundamental sexuality

660

---

53 Sartre's note: We should note the importance of the opposite tendency, the tendency to bore holes, which would require on its own an existential analysis.

whose nature we explicated in book III.[54] It remains no less true that the experience of the hole, when the child sees reality, includes an ontological premonition of sexual experience in general; it is with his flesh that the child plugs the hole and, before any sexual specification, the hole is an obscene expectation, a call for flesh.

We can appreciate how important it will be, for existential psychoanalysis, to elucidate these immediate and concrete existential categories. On that basis we can grasp some extremely general projects of human-reality. But the psychoanalyst's interest lies, first and foremost, in determining the free project of the particular person, on the basis of the individual relation which connects him with these different symbols of being. I might like to have contact with the viscous, and have a horror of holes, etc. That does not mean that the viscous, the greasy, the hole, etc., have lost their general ontological meaning for me but, on the contrary, that *because* of this meaning I determine myself in such and such a way in relation to them. If the viscous is indeed the symbol of a being in which the for-itself is drunk up by the in-itself, what does that say about me as someone who, unlike others, likes the viscous? Which fundamental project of myself shall I be referred to if I wish to explicate this love for a murky in-itself which bogs me down? Thus people's *tastes* do not remain as irreducible givens; if we know the right questions to ask, they will reveal to us the person's fundamental projects. Even in people's food preferences, there is a meaning. We will see this if we fully reflect on the fact that every taste presents itself not as an absurd *datum* for us to excuse but as an evident value. If I like the taste of garlic it will seem irrational to me that others can fail to like it. To eat is, in fact, to appropriate by means of destruction and at the same time to plug oneself with a certain being. And this being is given as a synthesis of temperature, density, and flavor in the strict sense. In brief, this synthesis signifies *a certain being* and when we eat we do not confine ourselves to *knowing*, by means of taste, certain qualities of this being; in tasting them, we are appropriating them. Taste is an assimilation; the tooth reveals, through its very grinding action, the density of the substance that it transforms into a bolus. In addition, the synthetic intuition of the food is in itself an assimilative destruction. It reveals to me the being from which I will make my flesh.

661

54 TN: Although Sartre writes "book (*livre*) III" in this sentence, he must mean Part Three.

In consequence, what I accept or reject with disgust is the very being of this existent—or, alternatively, the totality of the foodstuff proposes, for being, a certain mode of being that I will accept or refuse. This totality is organized as a figure, in which the qualities of density and temperature are fainter, and come behind the flavor proper, which *expresses* them. The "sugary," for example, *expresses* the viscous when we eat a spoonful of honey or molasses, in the way that an analytic function expresses a geometric curve. In other words, all the qualities that are not in the strict sense the flavor—but which are collected together, melted, and sunk within the flavor—represent something akin to the flavor's *matter*. (This chocolate biscuit which at first resists my tooth, and then suddenly yields to it and crumbles: its resistance and then its crumbling *are* chocolate.) They are linked, besides, to certain temporal characteristics of the flavor, i.e., to its mode of temporalization. Some tastes are given all at once, others are like time-delayed rockets, others disclose themselves in stages, some slowly taper off until they disappear and others vanish at just the moment when we thought we had taken hold of them. These qualities are structured alongside the density and temperature; in addition, they express at another level the foodstuff's visual appearance. If I eat a pink cake, its taste is pink; the faint sugary smell and the buttercream's smoothness are its pink. Thus I can eat pink, just as I can see sugar. We can appreciate that the flavor, in consequence, acquires a complex architecture and a differentiated matter; it is this structured matter—in which a particular type of being is appresented—that we may assimilate or reject with nausea, according to our original project. It is not at all, therefore, a matter of indifference if we like oysters or clams, snails or shrimps, so long as we know how to disentangle the existential meaning of these foods. On a more general level, no taste or inclination is irreducible. They all represent a certain appropriative choice of being. It is the task of existential psychoanalysis to compare and to classify them. At this point ontology abandons us: it has enabled us simply to determine human-reality's ultimate ends, its fundamental possibles, and the value by which it is haunted. Each human-reality is at the same time the direct project to metamorphose its own for-itself into the in-itself-for-itself, and the project to appropriate the world as the totality of being-in-itself, in the form of a fundamental quality. Every human-reality is a Passion, in that its project is to lose itself in order to found being and at the same time to constitute the in-itself as escaping contingency by being its own foundation, the *Ens causa sui* that the religions know as God. In this way man's Passion is the opposite of Christ's, because man loses himself as man in order that God should be born. But the idea of God is contradictory and we lose ourselves in vain; man is a useless Passion.

663

CONCLUSION

664

665

I. IN-ITSELF AND FOR-ITSELF: SOME METAPHYSICAL OBSERVATIONS

Now we may conclude. In our Introduction, we discovered that consciousness is a call for being, and we showed that the *cogito* immediately refers us to a being-in-itself as the *object* of consciousness. But after describing the in-itself and the for-itself it seemed difficult to establish a connection between them, and we were afraid of falling into an insurmountable dualism. This dualism also threatened us in another way: to the extent that we were able to say, in effect, that the for-itself is, we found ourselves faced with two radically distinct modes of being, the being of the for-itself, that has what it is to be (i.e., it is what it is not and is not what it is), and the being of the in-itself, that is what it is. We wondered then whether the discovery of these two types of being might not lead us to establish a hiatus, splitting Being (as a general category belonging to all existents) into two incommunicable regions, in each of which the notion of Being would have to be taken in an original and particular sense.

Our investigations have enabled us to answer the first of these questions: the for-itself and the in-itself are joined by a synthetic bond that is nothing more than the for-itself itself. Indeed, the for-itself is nothing but the pure nihilation of the in-itself; it is like a hole within being. We are familiar with the amusing story often used in popular science to illustrate the principle of the conservation of energy: if just one of the atoms constituting the universe were annihilated, they say, the result would be a catastrophe that extended across the entire world and which would mark the end, in particular, of the Earth and the stellar system. We can make use of this image here: the for-itself appears as a tiny nihilation that originates within being; and this nihilation suffices to make a complete upheaval *happen* to the in-itself. This upheaval is the world. The for-itself's only reality is to be the nihilation of being. It becomes qualified only by virtue of its nihilating some individual and particular in-itself, not a being in general. The for-itself is not nothingness in general but a particular privation; it is constituted as the privation of *this being-here*. It is not therefore relevant to ask ourselves how the for-itself is able to unite with the in-itself, since the for-itself is in no way an autonomous substance. Insofar as it is nihilation, *it is been* by the in-itself; insofar as it is an internal negation, it becomes acquainted through the in-itself with what it is not and, consequently, with what it has to be. If the *cogito* leads necessarily outside itself, if consciousness is a slippery slope on which it is impossible to settle without being immediately thrown outside onto being-in-itself, that is because by itself, as absolute subjectivity, consciousness lacks any sufficiency of being; it directs us from the outset to the thing. Consciousness has no being apart from this precise obligation to be a revealing intuition of something. What does this mean, if not that consciousness is Plato's *Other*? We know the Stranger's wonderful descriptions, in *The Sophist*, of this other that we can grasp only as a "sort of dream," whose only being is its being-other—so that it can enjoy only a borrowed being—and which vanishes if we consider it in itself, to resume a marginal existence only if we direct our gaze on being, and which consumes itself in being other than itself, and other than being.[1] It even seems that Plato saw the dynamic characteristic presented by the other's alterity in relation to itself, since—in some texts— he sees in it the origin of movement. But he could have pressed on even further: he would then have seen that it was only in the capacity of consciousness that the other, or relative non-being, could have a sem-

---

1 TN: Sartre is referring to the passage in Plato's *Sophist* at 266b16 (Plato 2015: 174). NB: In some English translations "the Stranger" is called "the Visitor."

blance of existence. To be other than being is to be a consciousness (of) self in the unity of the temporalizing ecstases. And, indeed, what else could alterity be other than the to-and-fro of reflected and reflecting that we have described at the heart of the for-itself, since the only way in which the other can exist as other is by being conscious (of) being other? Alterity is, in effect, internal negation, and only a consciousness can constitute itself as internal negation. Any other conception of alterity would amount to positing it as in-itself, i.e., to establishing an external relation between it and being, which would require the presence of a witness in order to observe the other to be other than the in-itself. And, on the other hand, the other could not be other without emanating from being; in that respect it is relative to the in-itself, but it also could not be other without *making itself other*; otherwise its alterity would become a given, and therefore a *being* that may be viewed as in-itself. Insofar as it is relative to the in-itself, the other is affected with facticity; insofar as it makes itself, it is an absolute. That is what we noted in saying that the for-itself is not the foundation of its being-as-a-nothingness-of-being but that it constantly founds its nothingness-of-being. In this way the for-itself is an absolute that is "*unselbstständig*"—or what we called a "non-substantial absolute." Its reality is purely *interrogative*. If it is able to ask questions, it is because it is always *in question* itself; its being is never *given* but *questioned*, since it is always separated from itself by the nothingness of alterity; the for-itself is always in suspense because its being is constantly pending. If it were able ever to join up with its being, alterity would disappear at the same time and, along with it, all possibles, knowledge, and the world. Thus the *ontological* problem of knowledge is resolved by our affirmation of the in-itself's ontological primacy in relation to the for-itself. But that immediately generates a *metaphysical* questioning. In fact we cannot compare the way in which the for-itself arises on the basis of the in-itself to the *dialectical* genesis of Plato's Other on the basis of being. For Plato, being and other are in fact *genera*.[2] But we have seen on the contrary that being is an individual adventure. And, similarly, the for-itself's appearing is the absolute event that visits being.

667

---

2 TN: Here I follow Sartre's inconsistent vacillation, in his discussion of Plato's "Other," between the upper and lower case for the first letter, and the definite article and its absence. The term "other" in this discussion of Plato refers to "otherness" and is not to be confused with the Other, where Sartre uses this to refer to another *person*.

There is space therefore for a metaphysical problem here, which we can formulate like this: Why does the for-itself arise on the basis of being? Indeed, we can refer to the investigation of the individual processes by which this world here—as a concrete and particular totality—is born, as "metaphysics." In this sense, the relation of metaphysics to ontology is like that of history to sociology. We saw that it would be absurd to ask why being is and, in addition, that the question can have meaning only within the limits of a for-itself, and even requires that nothingness should be ontologically prior to being, whereas we have demonstrated the primacy of being over nothingness. The question could be raised only as a consequence of contamination with a question that is externally analogous but nonetheless quite different: Why is it that there is being? But we know now that these two questions must be carefully distinguished. The first is meaningless: all "why?" questions are in fact subsequent to being, and presuppose it. Being is, without reason, without cause, and without necessity; the very definition of being presents us with its original contingency. To the second question, we have already replied, because the domain in which it arises is not metaphysics but ontology: "there is" being because the for-itself is such that there is being. Through the for-itself, being receives the character of a *phenomenon*. But if questions about the origin of being or the origin of the world lack meaning, or receive their answer precisely within the field of ontology, the same does not hold for the origin of the for-itself. The for-itself is such that, in fact, it does have the right to turn back to its own origin. The being through which the "why" arrives in being has the right to ask 668 its own "why," since it is itself an interrogation, a "why?" To this question, ontology cannot reply, because here we are trying to explain an event, and not to describe the structures of a being. At the most, ontology can point out to us that the nothingness that is *been* by the in-itself is not a mere void without meaning. The meaning of the nothingness in nihilation[3] is to be been, in order to found being. Ontology supplies us with two pieces of information that may provide a basis for metaphysics: first, that every process of self-foundation is a breach in the being-identical of the in-itself, a withdrawal of being in relation to itself, and

---

3 TN: *Le sens du néant de la néantisation* ... The repetition in the French here gets lost in translation.

the appearing of self-presence, or consciousness. It is only by making itself for-itself that being might aspire to be its own cause. Consciousness as the nihilation of being appears therefore as a stage in the progression toward an immanent causality, i.e., toward the being that is its own cause. Only the progression stops there, owing to the for-itself's insufficiency of being. The temporalization of consciousness is not a progress leading up toward the dignity of the "*causa sui*" but a surface flow whose origin is, on the contrary, the impossibility of being its own cause. In this way the *ens causa sui* remains as something *missed*, the sign of an impossible surpassing *upward* that conditions, through its very nonexistence, the flat movement of consciousness—just as the effect of the attraction exercised vertically on the ocean by the moon is the horizontal displacement of the tide. The other clue that metaphysics may draw from ontology is that the for-itself is *effectively* the constant project to found itself as being, and the constant failure of this project. Self-presence, with the various directions of its nihilation (the ecstatic nihilation of the three temporal dimensions, the twinned nihilation of the reflected-reflecting dyad), represents this project as it first arises; reflection represents the project's duplication as it turns back on itself to found itself at least as a project and—through the failure of this project itself—an amplification of the nihilating hiatus; the cardinal categories of human-reality— "doing" and "having"—are reduced immediately or mediately to the project of being; finally, the plurality of "each and every one"[4] may be interpreted as a last attempt at self-foundation, which leads to the radical separation between being and the consciousness of being.

Thus ontology teaches us: (1) that, if the in-itself were to found itself, it could not even attempt to do so except by making itself consciousness, which is to say that the concept of "*causa sui*" carries within it that of self-presence, i.e., the nihilating decompression of being; (2) that consciousness is *in fact* the project to found itself, i.e., to attain the dignity of the in-itself-for-itself, or the in-itself-that-is-its-own-cause. But we cannot get any more from it. Nothing allows us to claim, at the level of ontology, that the nihilation of the in-itself into for-itself has as its meaning, from its origin and right at the heart of the in-itself, the project of being

669

---

4 TN: ... *des uns et des autres* ... This French phrase is used to refer to a group of people. As there is no exactly corresponding phrase in English, I have added the scare quotes.

its own cause. Quite to the contrary, ontology comes up against a deep contradiction here, since it is through the for-itself that the possibility of any foundation enters the world. To be the project of founding *itself*, the in-itself would have in the first place to be self-presence, i.e., already to be consciousness. Ontology must confine itself therefore to asserting that *everything happens as* if the in-itself, in a project to found itself by itself, modified itself into the for-itself. The role of metaphysics is to form *hypotheses* that enable us to conceive of this process as the absolute event that comes to crown the individual adventure that is being's existence. It goes without saying that these hypotheses will remain hypotheses, since we can expect no further confirmation or disconfirmation. Their *validity* will be determined simply by whether or not they enable us to unify the findings of ontology. Naturally, this unification should not be consti- tuted within the perspective of a historical becoming, since it is through the for-itself that temporality enters being. It would therefore make no sense to ask what being was *before* the for-itself appeared. But that does not make metaphysics any less obliged to try to determine the nature and the meaning of this process, which antedates history and is the source of all history, articulating the individual adventure (or the existence of the in-itself) with the absolute event (or the for-itself's arising). In par- ticular, it will be for the metaphysician to decide whether or not move- ment is a first "attempt" on the part of the in-itself to found itself, and how movement as "being's sickness" relates to the for-itself, as a more intense sickness, extending right up to nihilation.

The second problem, which we formulated as early as the Introduction, remains to be considered: if the in-itself and for-itself are two modali- ties of *being*, isn't there a hiatus even within the idea of being, and isn't our understanding of it split into two incommunicable parts, because its extension is constituted out of two radically heterogeneous classes? What is there in common, in fact, between the being who is what it is and the being who is what it is not and is not what it is? However, the conclu- sion to our preceding investigations can help us here; in fact we have just shown that the in-itself and the for-itself are not juxtaposed. Quite to the contrary, the for-itself without the in-itself is something like an abstrac- tion: it can no more exist than a color without a shape, or a sound without a pitch and a timbre; a consciousness that was conscious of nothing would be an absolute nothing. But if an *internal* relation connects consciousness to the in-itself, doesn't it follow that it becomes articulated with it to constitute a totality and that the title of *being*, or reality, belongs to that totality? Certainly, the for-itself is a nihilation but, in its capacity as nihilation, it

670   is; and it is *a priori* united with the in-itself. In this way the Greeks used to distinguish cosmic reality, which they called τὸ πᾶν, from the totality constituted out of this and the infinite void that surrounded it—a totality which they called τὸ ὅλον.[5] Of course, we were able to call the for-itself a nothing and to declare that there is nothing "outside"[6] the in-itself, other than a reflection[7] of this nothing, which is itself polarized and determined by the in-itself insofar as it is precisely the nothingness of *this in-itself*. But here, as in Greek philosophy, a question arises: What are we going to say is *real*, and to what will we attribute *being*? To the cosmos or to what was called τὸ ὅλον above? To the pure in-itself or to the in-itself surrounded by that sleeve of nothingness that we designated by the name "for-itself"?

But if we were to consider the total being to be constituted through the synthetic organization of the in-itself and the for-itself, would we not return to the difficulty we wanted to avoid? Won't we encounter, this time within the existent itself, the hiatus that we detected in the concept of being? What definition should we in fact provide for an existent which, as in-itself, is what it is and, as for-itself, is what it is not?

If we want to resolve these difficulties, we need to take note of what we demand of an existent in order to view it as a totality: its various structures must be held within a unitary synthesis, such that each one of them, considered separately, is only an abstraction. And of course consciousness, considered separately, is only an abstraction, but the in-itself does not need, on its own account, any for-itself in order to be: the for-itself's "Passion" only makes it the case that *there is* some in-itself. Without consciousness, the *phenomenon* of in-itself is an abstraction but not its *being*.

If we were to conceive of a synthetic organization in which the for-itself was inseparable from the in-itself and, conversely, the in-itself was indissolubly linked to the for-itself, we would need to conceive of the in-itself as receiving its existence from the nihilation that makes us con-

---

5 TN: The two Greek expressions in this sentence mean "the all" (*to pan*) and "the whole" (*to holon*); these philosophical ideas derive from Parmenides.

6 TN: ... "*en dehors*" *de l'en-soi*, rien ... The scare quotes here are Sartre's.

7 TN: ... *un reflet de ce rien* ... Sartre is referring here to the first-order reflection-reflecting structure, not to "reflection" as a cognitive act.

scious of it. What does this tell us, if not that the indissoluble totality of in-itself and for-itself is only conceivable in the form of the being that is "its own cause"?[8] This being, and no other, could have the value, absolutely, of the ὅλον we were just talking about. And if we are able to raise the question of the being of the for-itself articulated to the in-itself, this is because we define ourselves *a priori* in terms of a preontological understanding of the *ens causa sui*. Doubtless this *ens causa sui* is *impossible* and, as we saw, its concept contains a contradiction. It remains no less true that, since we raise the question of the being of the ὅλον by taking up the viewpoint of the *ens causa sui*, it is this viewpoint that we should adopt in order to investigate the credentials of this ὅλον. Indeed, doesn't it owe its appearance entirely to the fact of the for-itself's arising, and isn't the for-itself originally the project of being its own cause? In this way we can begin to grasp the nature of reality in total. Total being, whose concept would not be split apart by a hiatus and which, more-over, would not exclude the nihilating-nihilated being of the for-itself, and whose existence would be the unitary synthesis of the in-itself and consciousness—this ideal being would be the in-itself as founded by the for-itself, and identical to the for-itself who founds it; in other words, it would be the *ens causa sui*. But precisely because we are taking up the view-point of this ideal being in order to judge the *real* being which we call the ὅλον, we are obliged to acknowledge that the real is an abortive effort to attain the dignity of the self-caused. Everything happens as if the world, man, and man-within-the-world managed only to actualize a missing God. Everything happens therefore as if the in-itself and the for-itself pre-sented themselves in a *disintegrated* state, in relation to an ideal synthesis. This is not because an integration has ever *taken place* but, on the contrary, precisely because it is always indicated and always impossible. It is the constant failure that explains at the same time the in-itself's indissolubil-ity from the for-itself, and their relative independence. Similarly, when the unity of the functions of the brain is disrupted, the resultant phenom-ena may present a relative autonomy and yet—at the same time—they can manifest themselves only against the ground of the disintegration of a totality. It is this failure that explains the hiatus we encounter at

671

---

8 TN: ... "*cause de soi*" ... As the rest of the paragraph clarifies, Sartre translates from the Latin *ens causa sui*.

the same time in the concept of being and in the existent. If it is impossible to move from the notion of being-in-itself to that of being-for-itself and to reunite them within a common type, it is because the *de facto passage* from one to the other and their reunion are operations that cannot be performed. We know for example that, for Spinoza and for Hegel, a synthesis that is arrested before the synthesization is complete—whose terms are frozen within a relative dependence and at the same time a relative independence—is constituted immediately into an error. For example, the justification and the meaning of a semicircle's rotation around its diameter are to be found, in Spinoza's view, in the notion of the sphere.[9] But if we imagine that the notion of the sphere is by definition beyond our reach, the phenomenon of the semicircle's rotation becomes *false*: we have decapitated it. The idea of the rotation and the idea of the circle each remain, but without being able to unite within a synthesis that surpasses them and justifies them: each of them remains irreducible to the other. That is exactly what is happening here. We can say therefore that the "ὅλον" we are considering is—like a decapitated notion—in a state of constant disintegration. And it is in its capacity as a disintegrated structure that we are presented with it in its ambiguity, so that we may emphasize the dependence of the beings in question, or their independence, as we please. Here we have a passage that is not achieved, a short circuit. We rediscover, at this level, that notion of the detotalized totality that we have already encountered in relation to the for-itself itself, and in relation to the consciousnesses of others. But it is a third kind of detotalization. In the case of reflection where the totality is simply detotalized, the reflective *had* the reflected *to be* and the reflected had the reflective to be.[10] The twofold negation remained evanescent. In the case of the for-the-Other the (reflection-reflecting) that was reflected on was distinguished from the (reflection-reflecting) reflecting insofar as each of them *had not to be* the other.[11] In this way the for-itself and the

672

---

9 TN: Spinoza discusses this example at para 72 in his *Treatise on the Emendation of the Intellect*, first published in 1677 and available in English translation in Spinoza (1985).

10 TN: ... *le réflexif avait à être le réfléchi et le réfléchi avait à être le réflexif*. I quote to identify the French verbs of reflection used in this very complicated passage.

11 TN: ... *le (reflet-reflétant) reflété se distinguait du (reflet-reflétant) reflétant* ... See my preceding note and the note on "reflection" vocabulary in Notes on the Translation.

other-for-itself constitute a being in which each of them confers being-other to the other by making itself other. As for the totality of the for-itself and the in-itself, that is characterized by the for-itself making itself other in relation to the in-itself, but the in-itself is not at all, in its being, other than the for-itself: it is, purely and simply. If the relation of the in-itself to the for-itself were the inverse of the relation of the for-itself to the in-itself, this case would collapse into that of being-for-the-other. But it is precisely not so, and it is this lack of reciprocity that characterizes the "ὅλον" we were just talking about. To this extent, it is not absurd to raise the question of totality. When we studied the for-the-Other we noted in fact a "myself-Other" being that had the for-the-Other's reflective scissiparity to be. But at the same time, this "myself-Other" being appeared to us as being able to exist only if it brought with it an elusive external non-being. We wondered at that point if the antinomic character of totality was in itself irreducible and whether we should postulate spirit as the being that is and that is not. But it appeared to us that the question of the synthetic unity of consciousnesses lacked any meaning, because it presupposed that we were able to take up a point of view on the totality; yet we exist on the foundation of that totality, and are committed within it.

But if we cannot "take up a point of view on the totality," that is because the other himself, as a matter of principle, denies his being me as I deny my being him. It is the relation's reciprocity that prevents me from ever grasping it in its integrity. In the case of the for-itself-in-itself internal negation, on the contrary, the relation is not reciprocal and I am at the same time one of the terms in the relation and the relation itself. I apprehend being, and I *am* an apprehension of being; I am only an apprehension of being. And the being that I apprehend does not posit itself *against* me, in order to apprehend me in my turn; it is what I apprehend. Only its *being* does not at all coincide with its being-apprehended. In a sense, therefore, I can raise the question of the totality. Of course, I exist here as committed within this totality, but I can have an *exhaustive consciousness* of it since I am at the same time a consciousness of being and conscious (of) myself. Only, this question of the totality does not belong to the domain of ontology. From the standpoint of ontology, the only regions of being it is possible to elucidate are those of the in-itself, the for-itself and the ideal region of the "self-caused." For ontology, it is a matter of indifference whether we consider the for-itself in its articulation with the in-itself as a clear-cut *duality* or as a disintegrated being. It is for metaphysics to decide whether it is more profitable for knowledge (in particular for phenomenological psychology, anthropology, etc.) to deal with a being that we can call the *phenomenon*, and which is endowed with two dimensions of being, the in-itself dimension and the for-itself dimension (from this point of view, there will be *only one* phenomenon: the world), as, in Einstein's physics, it has been helpful to talk in terms of an *event* conceived as having spatial dimensions and a temporal dimension and determining its place in a space-time, or whether, despite everything, it remains preferable to preserve the old "consciousness-being" duality. The only observation that ontology will risk here is that, should it appear useful to use the new notion of the phenomenon as a disintegrated totality, we would need to talk *at the same time* in terms of immanence and transcendence. The pitfall, indeed, would be to fall into pure immanentism (Husserlian idealism) or into a pure transcendentism where the *phenomenon* is envisaged as a new type of *object*. Rather, immanentism will always be limited by the in-itself dimension of the phenomenon and transcendence by its for-itself dimension.

After it has decided on the question of the for-itself's origin and the nature of the phenomenon of the world, metaphysics will be able to approach various problems of the first importance, in particular that of action. Action, in fact, needs to be considered *at the same time* at the level of the for-itself and at the level of the in-itself, because it concerns a project whose origin is immanent, and which determines a modification in the transcendent's being. There would be no point, indeed, to asserting that action modifies only the thing's phenomenal appearance: if the phenomenal appearance of a cup can be modified to the point where the cup is annihilated as a cup, and if the cup's being is not other than its *quality*, the action in question must be capable of modifying the cup's very being. The problem of action requires therefore the elucidation of the transcendent efficacy of consciousness and sets us on the path of its true relation of being with being. It also reveals to us, in consequence of the act's repercussions in the world, a relation between being and being which, even though the physicist apprehends it externally, is neither pure externality nor immanence but which refers us to the Gestaltist notion of *figure*. From this point of departure, therefore, we may attempt a metaphysics of nature.

II. MORAL PERSPECTIVES

Ontology itself is unable to formulate moral prescriptions. It is concerned solely with what is, and no imperatives can be derived from its indicatives. However, it allows us to glimpse what an ethics that took up its responsibilities by confronting a *human-reality in situation* might be. Indeed, it has revealed to us the origin and nature of *value*; we saw that it is a *lack*, in relation to which the for-itself determines itself in its being as a *lack*. By virtue of the for-itself's *existing*, as we have seen, value arises to haunt its being-for-itself. It follows that the for-itself's various tasks may become the object of an existential psychoanalysis, since all of these aim to produce consciousness's missed synthesis with being, in the guise of value or the being that is its own cause. In this way existential psychoanalysis is a *moral description* because it conveys to us the ethical meaning of the various human projects; it points us to the necessity of abandoning a psychology based on interest, along with any utilitarian interpretation of human behavior, by showing us the *ideal* meaning of all of man's attitudes. These meanings lie beyond egoism and altruism, and also beyond those modes of behavior that we describe as *disinterested*. Man makes himself man in order to be God, we may say: and, considered from this point of view, ipseity might seem to be a kind of egoism; but precisely because there is no common measure between human-reality and the cause of itself that it wants to be, we might just as well say that man loses himself in order for the self-caused to exist. In which case all human existence may be regarded as a passion, and the all-too-familiar "self-love" will be only one means, freely chosen among others, of actualizing this passion. But the foremost result of existential psychoanalysis must be to make us abandon the *spirit of seriousness*. The spirit of seriousness has this dual characteristic: it regards values as transcendent givens that are independent of human subjectivity, and it transfers the character of being "desirable" from the ontological structure of things to their simple material constitution. So for the spirit of seriousness, for example, *bread* is desirable because we must live (a value written in the intelligible sky)[12] and because it is nourishing. The result of the spirit of seriousness (which, as we know) reigns over the world,

674

---

12 TN: Sartre also uses the phrase *ciel intelligible* in EH (Sartre 1973), where he associates it with Plato. He may have in mind Plato's famous allegory of the Cave (in *Republic*), from which the intelligible (eternal, etc.) can be seen only by looking outside and beyond the cave.

is to make things soak up—like blotting paper—their symbolic values, through their empirical idiosyncrasy; it foregrounds the desired object's opacity and posits it, in itself, as irreducibly desirable. Therefore we are already within the domain of morality—but at the same time within the domain of bad faith, for it is a morality that is ashamed of itself and dares not speak its name; it has obfuscated all its goals, in order to escape from anguish. Man seeks being blindly, hiding from himself the free project in which this search consists; he makes himself such that the tasks placed along his path *await* him. Objects are silent demands, and in himself he is nothing but a passive obedience to these demands.

675   Existential psychoanalysis will acquaint him with the real aim of his search, which is being as the in-itself's synthetic fusion with the for-itself; it will make him aware of his passion. In truth, many men have practiced this psychoanalysis on themselves, and have not waited until they know its principles in order to use it as a means of deliverance and salvation. Many men know, indeed, that the goal they are seeking is being and, to the extent that they possess this knowledge, they do not care about appropriating things for themselves, and try to actualize a symbolic appropriation of their being-in-itself. But to the extent that this attempt is still bound up with the spirit of seriousness, and they continue to believe that their mission to make the in-itself-for-itself exist is writ-ten into things, they are condemned to despair, because they discover at the same time that all human activities are equivalent—for they all aim to sacrifice man in order that the self-caused may arise—and that all of them are doomed, by definition, to failure. Thus, whether one gets drunk on one's own or leads the people, it comes down to the same thing. If either of these activities wins out over the other, it will not be because of its real goal but because of its degree of consciousness of its ideal goal; and in this case it may happen that the quietism of the solitary drunkard wins out over the pointless agitation of the leader of nations.

But ontology and existential psychoanalysis (or the spontaneous and empirical application that men have always made of these disciplines) must show the moral agent that he is *the being through whom values exist*. At that point his freedom will become conscious of itself and discover itself in anguish as the unique source of value, and the nothingness through which the *world* exists. As soon as the quest for being and the appropria-tion of the in-itself become disclosed as *its possibles*, freedom will apprehend, through and in anguish, that these are possible only against the ground of the possibility of other possibles. But hitherto, even though possibles could be chosen and revoked *ad libitum*, the theme that unified all choices of possibles was the value or ideal presence of the *ens causa sui*. What will freedom become if it turns back to face this value?[13] Will it carry it with it, whatever it does? Will the value it is trying to contemplate seize it back again, from behind, even in its turning back toward the in-itself-for-itself? Or will freedom instead, by the mere fact of grasping itself as a freedom in relation to itself, be able to bring to an end the reign of this value? Is it possible, in particular, for freedom to take itself as a value, insofar as it is the source of all value, or must it necessarily be defined in relation to a transcendent value that haunts it? And how should we understand the circumstance in which it is possible for freedom to will itself[14] as its own possible, and as its determining value? A freedom that wills itself as freedom is effectively a being-that-is-not-what-it-is and that-is-what-it-is-not which chooses, as being's ideal, to be-what-it-is-not and to not-be-what-it-is. It does not therefore choose to *reclaim* itself but to flee from itself, not to coincide with itself but always to be at a distance from itself. How should we understand this being, whose wish is to stay at arm's length, to be at a distance from itself? Is this a case of bad faith, or of some other fundamental attitude? And can this new aspect of being be *lived*? In particular, will freedom, by taking itself as its end, escape from every *situation*? Or will it, on the contrary, remain situated? Or will it become situated all the more precisely and individually by virtue of projecting itself more fully into anguish, as freedom's condition, and by laying greater claim to responsibility, as the existent through whom the world comes to being? All of these questions refer us to pure, and not complicit, reflection. They can be answered only within the domain of morality, to which we will devote a future work.

676

13 TN: ... *si elle se retourne sur cette valeur?* In this context, *se retourner* implies a "review" or "revisiting" of something, as the following sentences make clear.

14 TN: ... *elle pourrait se vouloir elle-même* ... Although *vouloir* often means "to want" or "to wish," it can also mean "to will." I have chosen the latter here in order to echo Kant's moral philosophy, with which Sartre is implicitly in dialogue here.

BIBLIOGRAPHY

Abraham, Pierre (1930), *Proust: Recherches sur la Création Intellectuelle* (Paris: Rieder).

Amiel, Henri Frédéric (1921), *Amiel's Journal*, trans. Mary Ward (London: Macmillan).

Bachelard, Gaston (1983), *Water and Dreams: An Essay on the Imagination of Matter*, trans. Edith Farrell (Dallas: Dallas Institute of Humanities and Culture).

Bacon, Francis (1985), *The Essays*, ed. John Pitcher (Harmondsworth: Penguin).

Balzac, Honoré de (1972), *The Chouans*, trans. Marion Ayton Crawford (Harmondsworth: Penguin).

Berger, Gaston (1972), *The Cogito in Husserl's Philosophy*, trans. Kathleen McLaughlin (Evanston, Ill.: Northwestern University Press).

Bergson, Henri (1911a), *Creative Evolution*, trans. Arthur Mitchell (New York: Henry Holt).

Bergson, Henri (1911b), *Matter and Memory*, trans. Nancy Margaret Paul and W. Scott Palmer (London: George Allen & Unwin).

Bergson, Henri (1960), *Time and Free Will*, trans. F. L. Pogson (New York: Harper & Row).

Chamfort, Nicolas (1969), *Products of the Perfected Civilisation: Selected Writings of Chamfort*, trans. W. S. Merwin (New York: Macmillan).

Claudel, Paul (1931), *The Satin Slipper*, trans. John O'Connor (London: Sheed & Ward).

Corneille, Pierre (2012), *Le Cid*, trans. John C. Lapp (Wheeling, Ill.: Harlan Davidson, Crofts Classics).

Descartes, René (1911), *Discourse on Method*, trans. S. Haldane and G. R. T. Ross (Cambridge: Cambridge University Press).

Descartes, René (1983), *Principles of Philosophy*, trans. V. R. Miller and R. P. Miller (Dordrecht: Kluwer).

Descartes, René (1989), *The Passions of the Soul*, trans. S. Voss (Indianapolis: Hackett).

Descartes, René (1996), *Meditations on First Philosophy: With Selections from the Objections and Replies*, ed. John Cottingham and Bernard Williams (New York: Cambridge University Press).

Dostoyevsky, Fyodor (1992), *Crime and Punishment*, trans. R. Pevear and L. Volokhonsky (London: Vintage Classics).

Durkheim, Émile, and Mauss, Marcel (2010), *Primitive Classification*, trans. Rodney Needham (Abingdon: Routledge).

Faulkner, William (2005), *Light in August* (London: Vintage).

Gide, André (1949), *Fruits of the Earth*, trans. D. Bussy (New York: Knopf).

Gide, André (1990), *The Counterfeiters*, trans. D. Bussy (London: Penguin).

Gide, André (2000), *Journals 1889–1913*, trans. J. O'Brien (Urbana: University of Illinois Press).

Gide, André (2007), *Strait Is the Gate*, trans. D. Bussy (New York: Mondial).

Hegel, G. W. F. (1977), *Phenomenology of Spirit*, trans. A. V. Miller (Oxford: Oxford University Press).

Hegel, G. W. F. (1986), *The Philosophical Propaedeutic*, trans. A. V. Miller, ed. M. George and A. Vincent (Oxford: Blackwell).

Hegel, G. W. F. (1991), *The Encyclopaedia Logic*, trans. and ed. T. F. Geraets, W. A. Suchtung and H. S. Harris (Indianapolis: Hackett).

Hegel, G. W. F. (1995), *Morceaux Choisis*, trans. H. Lefebvre and N. Guterman (Paris: Gallimard Folio).

Hegel, G. W. F. (2010), *The Science of Logic*, trans. and ed. George di Giovanni (Cambridge: Cambridge University Press).

Heidegger, Martin (1938), *Qu'est-ce que la Métaphysique? Suivi d'Extraits sur l'Être et le Temps et d'une Conference sur Hölderlin*, trans. Henry Corbin (Paris: Gallimard).

Heidegger, Martin (1938a), "Qu'est-ce que la Métaphysique?," in Heidegger (1938).

Heidegger, Martin (1938b), "Ce qui Fait l'Être-Essentiel d'un Fondement ou 'Raison,' " in Heidegger (1938).

Heidegger, Martin (1938c), "Extraits du Livre sur l'Être et le Temps," in Heidegger (1938).

Heidegger, Martin (1969), *The Essence of Reasons*, trans. Terrence Malick (Evanston, Ill.: Northwestern University Press).

Heidegger, Martin (1978a), *Basic Writings*, trans. David Krell (London: Routledge & Kegan Paul).

Heidegger, Martin (1978b), "Letter on Humanism," trans. David Krell, in Heidegger (1978a): 193–242.

Heidegger, Martin (1978c), "What Is Metaphysics?," trans. David Krell, in Heidegger (1978a): 95–112.

Heidegger, Martin (1980), *Being and Time*, trans. J. Macquarrie and E. Robinson (Oxford: Blackwell).

Heidegger, Martin (2000), *Elucidations of Hölderlin's Poetry*, trans. Keith Hoeller (New York: Humanity Books).

Heidegger, Martin (2010), *Being and Time*, trans. J. Stambaugh (revised edition) (New York: SUNY Press).

Hemingway, Ernest (2003), *Death in the Afternoon* (New York: Charles Scribner).

Husserl, Edmund (1960), *Cartesian Meditations: An Introduction to Phenomenology*, trans. Dorion Cairns (The Hague: Martinus Nijhoff).

Husserl, Edmund (1983), *Ideas Pertaining to a Pure Phenomenology and to a Phenomenological Philosophy*, First Book, trans. F. Kersten (The Hague: Martinus Nijhoff).

Husserl, Edmund (1991), *On the Phenomenology of the Consciousness of Internal Time*, trans. J. B. Brough (Dordrecht: Kluwer).

Husserl, Edmund (2001), *Logical Investigations*, trans. J. Findlay (Abingdon: Routledge).

Jaspers, Karl (1963), *General Psychopathology*, trans. J. Hoenig and M. W. Hamilton (Chicago: University of Chicago Press).

Joyce, James (1960), *Ulysses* (London: Bodley Head).

Kafka, Franz (1994), *The Trial*, trans. Idris Parry (London: Penguin).

Kafka, Franz (2009), *The Castle*, trans. Anthea Bell (Oxford: Oxford University Press).

Kant, Immanuel (1998), *Critique of Pure Reason*, trans. and ed. P. Guyer and A. Wood (Cambridge: Cambridge University Press).

Kierkegaard, Søren (2013), *Fear and Trembling, and The Sickness unto Death*, trans. Walter Lowrie (Princeton, N.J.: Princeton University Press).

Laclos, Pierre Choderlos de (1995), *Les Liaisons Dangereuses*, trans. Douglas Parmée (Oxford: Oxford University Press).

Leibniz, Gottfried Wilhelm (1967), *The Leibniz-Arnauld Correspondence*, trans. and ed. H.T. Mason (Manchester: Manchester University Press).

Leibniz, Gottfried Wilhelm (2014), *Leibniz's Monadology: A New Translation and Guide*, trans. Lloyd Strickland (Edinburgh: Edinburgh University Press).

Lot, Ferdinand (1931), *The End of the Ancient World*, trans. Philip and Mariette Leon (London: Routledge & Kegan Paul).

Malebranche, Nicolas (1997), *The Search after Truth, and Elucidations of The Search after Truth*, trans. and ed. Thomas M. Lennon and Paul J. Olscamp (Cambridge: Cambridge University Press).

Mallarmé, Stéphane (1996), *Collected Poems: A Bilingual Edition*, trans. Henry Weinfeld (Berkeley: University of California Press).

Malraux, André (1970), *Days of Hope*, trans. Stuart Gilbert and Alastair Macdonald (Harmondsworth: Penguin).

Malraux, André (1990), *Man's Fate*, trans. Haakon Chevalier (New York: Vintage).

Malraux, André (1991), *The Conquerors*, trans. Stephen Becker (Chicago: University of Chicago Press).

Merleau-Ponty, Maurice (1942), *La Structure du Comportement* (Paris: PUF).

Merleau-Ponty, Maurice (1963), *The Structure of Behavior*, trans. Alden Fisher (Boston: Beacon Press).

Meyerson, Emile (1991), *The Explanation of the Sciences*, trans. Mary-Alice and David A. Sipfle (Dordrecht: Kluwer).

Mill, John Stuart (1963–91), *The Collected Works of John Stuart Mill*, ed. John M. Robson (Toronto: University of Toronto Press).

Nietzsche, Friedrich (2009), *Ecce Homo: How One Becomes What One Is*, trans. Duncan Large (Oxford: Oxford University Press).

Pascal, Blaise (1995), *Pensées*, trans. A. J. Krailsheimer (Harmondsworth: Penguin).

Paulhan, Jean (2006), *The Flowers of Tarbes, or Terror in Literature*, trans. Michael Syrotinski (Champaign: University of Illinois Press).

Plato (1997), *Complete Works*, ed. John M. Cooper and D. S. Hutchinson (Indianapolis: Hackett).

Plato (2015), *Theaetetus and Sophist*, ed. and trans. Christopher Rowe (Cambridge: Cambridge University Press).

Proust, Marcel (2005), *Swann's Way*, trans. C. K. Scott Moncrieff and Terence Kilmartin, with revisions by D. J. Enright (London: Vintage).

Romains, Jules (1933–1947), *Men of Good Will* (14 vols), trans. W. Wells and G. Hopkins (New York: Knopf).

Rougemont, Denis de (1944), *The Devil's Share*, trans. Haakon Chevalier (New York: Pantheon Books).

Rougemont, Denis de (1983), *Love in the Western World*, trans. Montgomery Belgion (Princeton, N.J.: Princeton University Press).

Rousseau, Jean-Jacques (2002), *The Social Contract, and The First and Second Discourses*, ed. Susan Dunn (New Haven, Conn.: Yale University Press).

Rousseau, Jean-Jacques (2008), *Confessions*, trans. Angela Scholar (Oxford: Oxford University Press).

Sartre, Jean-Paul (1943), *L'Être et le Néant* (Paris: Gallimard).

Sartre, Jean-Paul (1965), *Being and Nothingness*, trans. and introduced by Hazel Barnes (New York: Washington Square Press).

Sartre, Jean-Paul (1970), "Intentionality: A Fundamental Idea of Husserl's Philosophy," trans. Joseph Fell, *Journal of the British Society for Phenomenology*, 1 (2): 4–5.

Sartre, Jean-Paul (1973), *Existentialism and Humanism*, trans. Philip Mairet (London: Methuen).

Sartre, Jean-Paul (1992), *Being and Nothingness*, trans. and introduced by Hazel E. Barnes (New York: Washington Square Press).

Sartre, Jean-Paul (1994), *Sketch for a Theory of the Emotions*, trans. Philip Mairet (London: Routledge).

Sartre, Jean-Paul (2000), *Words*, trans. Irene Clephane (Harmondsworth: Penguin).

Sartre, Jean-Paul (2004a), *The Transcendence of the Ego*, trans. Andrew Brown (Abingdon: Routledge).

Sartre, Jean-Paul (2004b), *The Imaginary: A Phenomenological Psychology of the Imagination*, trans. J. Webber (London: Routledge).

Sartre, Jean-Paul (2012), *Imagination*, trans. Kenneth Williford and David Rudrauf (Abingdon: Routledge).

Scheler, Max (1973), *Formalism in Ethics and Non-Formal Ethics of Values*, trans. and ed. M. S. Frings and R. L. Funk (Evanston, Ill.: Northwestern University Press).

Scheler, Max (2003), *Ressentiment*, trans. Lewis Coser and William Holdheim (Milwaukee: Marquette University Press).

Schopenhauer, Arthur (2008), *The World as Will and Presentation*, Vol. 1, trans. Richard E. Aquila and David Carus (New York: Pearson Longman).

Sophocles (2008), *Electra and Other Plays*, trans. David Raeburn (London: Penguin).

Spinoza, Baruch (1985), *The Collected Writings of Spinoza*, Vol. 1, trans. Edwin Curley (Princeton, N.J.: Princeton University Press).

Stekel, Wilhelm (1953), *Frigidity in Woman* (2 vols), trans. James Van Teslaar (London: Vision).

Stendhal (2009), *On Love*, trans. Sophie Lewis (London: Hesperus).

Valéry, Paul (1950), *Selected Writings* (New York: New Directions).

Valéry, Paul (2007), *Charms, and Other Pieces*, trans. Peter Dale (London: Anvil Press Poetry).

INDEX

Page numbers followed by "n" refer to notes, with the note number following "n."